THE JEWISH ALMANAC

THE JEWISH ALMANAC

Compiled and
Edited by
RICHARD SIEGEL
and
CARL RHEINS

"Nothing Jewish is alien to me."
Franz Rosenzweig

BANTAM BOOKS
TORONTO · NEW YORK · LONDON

THE JEWISH ALMANAC
A Bantam Book / October 1980

Picture Editors: Cheryl Moch and Vincent Virga

ACKNOWLEDGMENTS

"A Brief Account of the Persecution of the Jews," from *The Old Farmer's Almanac*, 1793. By permission of the *Old Farmer's Almanac*, Dublin, New Hampshire. "The Fade-Out of the Great Jewish Family Stores," (revised and expanded for the *Jewish Almanac*, 1980) by Isadore Barmash. Originally appeared as "The Fade-Out of the Great Jewish Family Stores," in the *National Jewish Monthly*, December, 1971, copyright © 1971. By permission of the author and publisher. "Names of God," and "*Mitzvot* on the Moon," from *Contemporary Halakhic Problems* by J. David Bleich; copyright © 1977. By permission of Ktav Publishing House Inc., New York. "Lenny Bruce: on Jewish and Goyish" from *How to Talk Dirty and Influence People: An Autobiography* by Lenny Bruce; copyright © 1972. Chicago: Playboy Press. By permission of the Estate of Lenny Bruce; Kitty Bruce, executrix. "Chicken Soup Rebound and Relapse of Pneumonia: Report of a Case," by Nancy L. Caroline, M.D. and Harold Schwartz, M.D., copyright © 1975. By permission of *Chest: Official Journal of the American College of Chest Physicians*, Vol. LXVII, 1975. "Yale's Hebrew Coat of Arms," by Arthur A. Chiel. Originally appeared as "Yale's Hebrew Seal," in the *Connecticut Jewish Ledger*, September 28, 1972; copyright © 1972. By permission of the publisher. Biographical information on 31 American and Canadian Jewish volunteers who died in Israel's war of independence from *American Volunteers and Israel's War of Independence* by A. Joseph Heckelman. New York: Ktav Publishing House, 1974; copyright © 1974. By permission of the publisher. "Jewish losses during World War II" reprinted from *Balance Sheet of Extermination* by Jacob Lestchinsky. New York: American Jewish Congress, 1946. By permission of the American Jewish Congress. "The Ten Wealthiest Jewish Families in America," by Dan Rottenberg. Originally appeared as "Supergelt," *Jewish Living*, Vol. II, No. 3, September/October 1979. Copyright © 1979. By permission of Adar Communications Company and the author. "More Jews on the Map: A Parody" by Sheldon Miller—Marder. Originally appeared as "A Purim Bicentennial Tour," *Sh'ma, A Journal of Jewish Responsibility*, Vol. VI, No. 110 (March 19, 1976). Copyright © 1976. By permission of the publisher. 11 lines from "The Book of Judith," (poem) by David Rosenberg in *A Blazing Fountain: A Book for Hanukkah*; copyright © 1978. By permission of Schocken Books Inc., New York. 1978 Nobel Lecture by Isaac Bashevis Singer. Copyright © 1978. By permission of the Nobel Foundation, 1978. Stockholm, Sweden. Tau Epsilon Phi, XI Chapter (MIT), Report of XI Chapter in "Chapter News," *The Plume of Tau Epsilon Phi*, Vol. LXXII, No. 4, October/December 1979. By permission of Tau Epsilon Phi Fraternity. "Selzer Boy," a parody by Allen Sherman of "Water Boy," a song by Avery Robinson, 1932. Copyright by Boosey and Hawkes, Inc. Renewed 1959. By permission of Boosey and Hawkes, Inc. "Big Wheel on Campus," by Eli N. Evans, by permission of Atheneum Publishers from *The Provincials: A Personal History of Jews in the South* by Eli N. Evans; copyright © 1973, by Eli N. Evans. Excerpts from "My Double Life and Excommunication," by Uriel da Costa from *Memoirs of My People*, Leo W. Schwarz, ed. Copyright 1943. By permission of the Jewish Publication Society of America, Philadelphia. List of "Jewish Free Loan Societies." Reprinted from *The Second Jewish Catalog* by Sharon and Michael Strassfeld; copyright © 1976. By permission of the authors and the Jewish Publication Society of America, Philadelphia. "Jewish Population in the United States, 1978," "World Jewish Population, and statistical data on U.S. cities and counties with Jewish populations of over 10,000." Reprinted from the *American Jewish Yearbook 1979*, Morris Fine and Milton Himmelfarb, eds.; copyright © 1978. By permission of the American Jewish Committee. The historical maps "Expulsions 1000–1500," "The Return of Jews to Zion 1948–1964," and "False Messiahs 400–1816" are used with permission of Macmillan Publishing Co., Inc. and Weidenfeld Ltd. from *Jewish History Atlas* (2nd ed.) by Martin Gilbert. Cartography by Arthur Banks. Copyright © 1969, 1976 by Martin Gilbert. Calendars for the Jewish Year, 1980–2000 C.E.; "The 613 Commandments," "Table of Scriptural Readings on Sabbaths," "Orders and Tractates of the Mishnah and Talmud," from the *Encyclopaedia Judaica*; copyright © 1972, Jerusalem. By permission of Keter Publishing House Jerusalem Ltd. "Table of Alphabets," reprinted from *Gesensius' Hebrew Grammar*, 2nd ed. (rev.), 1910. E. Kautzch, ed.; copyright © 1974. By permission of the Oxford University Press. Selected excerpts for "10 Hasidic Masters," reprinted from *Tales of the Hasidim: Early Masters* by Martin Buber; copyright, 1947, by Schocken Books, Inc.. By permission of the publisher. Biblical translations included in the following essays are reprinted from *The Holy Scriptures According to the Masorectic Text*. Jewish Publication Society of America, Philadelphia; copyright 1917, © 1962. By permission of the publisher: "30 Biblical Names Commonly Used in English," "The Comings and Goings of the Jewish Year," "Feminine Imagery in Judaism," "Deeds of Righteousness and Lovingkindness," and "Tzedekah." Selected excerpts from Solomon Simon, *My Jewish Roots*. Translated by Shlomo Katz. Copyright © 1956. Philadelphia: Jewish Publication Society of America. Reprinted with the permission of the publisher. Selected excerpts from Theodore H. Gaster's *The Holy and the Profane: Evolution of Jewish Folkways*, revised edition. Copyright © 1980. New York: William Morrow and Company. With the permission of the author and the publisher. The names and addresses of synagogues still in use in Eastern Europe are reprinted from *The Jewish Travel Guide 1979*, editedby Sidney Lightman. Copyright © 1979. London: Jewish Chronicle Publications. By permission of the publisher. The "Plan of the Warsaw Ghetto, 1940–1943" is reprinted with permission of Yad Vashem, Martyrs' and Heroes' Remembrance Authority, Jerusalem, Israel. Selected excerpts from Benzion C. Kaganoff, *A Dictionary of Jewish Names and Their History*. Copyright © 1977. New York: Schocken Books, Inc. Reprinted with the permission of the publisher.

(Note: Every effort has been made to locate the copyright owners of material reproduced in this book. Omissions brought to our attention will be corrected in subsequent editions.)

ISBN 0-553-01265-7

Published simultaneously in the United States and Canada

Bantam Books are published by Bantam Books, Inc. Its trademark, consisting of the words "Bantam Books" and the portrayal of a bantam, is Registered in U.S. Patent and Trademark Office and in other countries. Marca Registrada. Bantam Books, Inc., 666 Fifth Avenue, New York, New York 10103.

PRINTED IN THE UNITED STATES OF AMERICA

0 9 8 7 6 5 4 3 2 1

ACKNOWLEDGMENTS

This book was touched by the hands of many people. It is impossible to adequately recognize each one with full and proper appreciation. A few acknowledgments, however, cannot be resisted.

First, to all of our friends and contributors who listened to our ideas and fed us better ones, we offer a *l'chaim* (a toast "To Life") for their responsiveness, imagination, and enthusiasm.

To those whose contributions are not listed on the credits page—James Arnoff for his counsel and advice; Robert Milch, Cindy Cass, and Susan Grossman for their editorial assistance; and our photographic researchers Vincent Virga and Cheryl Moch—we offer blessings for their having eased our way and having saved us from mental collapse.

A special debt is owed to the editors at Bantam who helped us through the labor pains—Marilyn Abraham, Joelle Delbourgo, Cecilia Hunt, Beverly Susswein, Barbara Sanborn, and Nessa Rapoport. Their encouragement, insight, aid, and ruthless schedules gave us the strength to endure the rough goings.

To Marc Jaffe, former president and publisher of Bantam Books, we owe the very opportunity to explore these waters. From the first time when we discussed this idea Marc has not only expressed absolute faith in this project but has also helped shape the vision. His openness to new perspectives on Jewish life is refreshing and inspiring.

Near the beginning of our work on the book, and purely coincidentally, Carl married Brenda Gevertz, and Richard married Jeanne Bakst Maman and her then eight-year-old son Andrew. This book has been our constant, but often unwelcome, chaperone during this first year of our marriages. There is no way that this work could have been completed without the understanding, love, and support that these new families have provided during these often difficult months. They deserve a lot more than we were able to give them. Hopefully, we will now be able to show them the love, appreciation, and attention that we have been waiting for so long to give.

CONTRIBUTORS OF ORIGINAL MATERIAL*

Eds.	Material written by the editors of *The Jewish Almanac*
A.A.	Arlene Agus
A.C.	Aviva Cantor
A.J.G.	Arnold J. Goldman
A.K.	Arthur Kurzweil
A.M.	Allan Mintz
B.D.G.	Brenda Dale Gevertz
B.P.	Bernard Postal
B.W.H.	Barry W. Holtz
C.J.R.	Carl J. Rheins
C.W.	Chava Weissler
D.A.	Donald Altschiller
D.H.W.	Diane H. Winston
D.M.S.	David M. Szonyi
D.R.S.	Daniel R. Shevitz
D.S.	Danny Siegel
E.A.G.	Eric A. Goldman
E.E.G.	Everett E. Gendler
G.S.R.	Gita Segal Rotenberg
H.H.S.	Henry H. Sapoznik
H.L.G.	Howard L. Gevertz
H.N.K.	Howard N. Katz
I.C.S.	Ida Cohen Selavan
J.A.G.	Jacqueline A. Gutwirth
J.B.	Jane Blanksteen
J.B.S.	Jeanne B. Siegel
J.D.P.	Jonathan D. Porath
J.H.S.	Jesse H. Silver
J.J.G.	J.J. Goldberg
J.M.K.	Jack M. Kugelmass
J.R.	Joel Rosenberg
L.B.G.	Leonard B. Glick
M.A.G.	Marc A. Gellman
M.C.	Mitchell Cohen,
M.G.A.	Misha G. Avramoff
M.J.B.	Marc Joel Bregman
M.M.F.	Morris M. Faierstein
M.N.	Mordecai Newman
M.S.	Mark Stern
M.S.R.	Martin S. Rosen
N.H.	Nat Hentoff
P.C.	Paul Cowan
R.A.	Rachel Adler
R.A.R.	Robert A. Rockaway
R.A.S.	Richard A. Siegel
R.J.S.	Roy J. Silver
S.B.	Stephen Birmingham
V.P.	Velvel Pasternak
W.A.N.	William A. Novak
W.N.K.	William N. Kavesh
Z.M.S.	Zalman M. Schachter
Z.S.	Zev Shanken

*See page 597 for
biographies of the contributors.

CONTRIBUTORS OF REPRINTED MATERIAL

The following authors have been reprinted by permission of their publishers.

A.A.C. Arthur A. Chiel. "Yale's Hebrew Seal." In *Connecticut Jewish Ledger*, September 28, 1972.

D.R. Dan Rottenberg. "Supergelt." In *Jewish Living*, Vol. II, No. 3, September/October 1979.

E.N.E. Eli N. Evans. "Big Wheel on Campus." In *The Provincials: A Personal History of Jews in the South*. New York: Atheneum Publishers, 1973.

I.B. Isadore Barmash. "The Fade Out of the Great Jewish Family Stores." In *National Jewish Monthly*, December 1971.

I.B.S. Isaac Bashevis Singer. "1978 Nobel Lecture." Nobel Foundation: Stockholm, Sweden, 1978.

J.D.B. J. David Bleich. "Names of God," and "Mitzvot on the Moon." In *Contemporary Halakhic Problems*. New York: Ktav Publishing House, 1977.

L.B. Lenny Bruce. "On Jewish and Goyish." From *How to Talk Dirty and Influence People: An Autobiography*. Chicago: Playboy Press, 1972. By permission of Kitty Bruce, Executrix.

N.L.C. and H.S. Nancy L. Caroline and Harold Schwartz. "Chicken Soup Rebound and Relapse of Pneumonia: Report of a Case." In *Chest: Official Journal of the American College of Chest Physicians*, Vol. LXVII, 1975.

S.M-M. Sheldon Miller-Marder. "A Purim Bicentennial Tour." In *Sh'ma, A Journal of Jewish Responsibility*, Vol. VI, No. 110, March 19, 1976.

CONTENTS

INTRODUCTION

The Jewish Almanac is a book of observations—contemporary reflections on Jewish life, culture, and history. It is an attempt to rethink the contours of Jewish reality from the perspectives of 1980s America. *The Jewish Almanac* is but one reflection of a new attitude towards being Jewish: serious, but not deadly; light, but not self-deprecating; popular, but not trivial. It embraces the totality of Jewish experience from the most sacred to the most profane—without embarrassment and without apologetics. It affirms the commitment that the German Jewish philosopher/theologian/humanist Franz Rosenzweig (1886–1929) asked of the Jews in his generation, "Nothing Jewish is alien to me."

The scope of the book can be easily discerned by a quick perusal of its table of contents. A random sampling of the entries will clarify its tone. However, so that there will be no ambiguity as to its intentions, a few words about the orientation of the editors is, perhaps, appropriate.

1. We do not adhere to any particular Jewish ideology except that which embraces the legitimacy of all forms of Jewish expression. While it is true that the Jewish community has never been monolithic, the acceptance of pluralism is a relatively modern phenomenon—necessary and healthy.

2. We are not mere survivalists. The purpose of Jewish life is not simply self-perpetuation. What point is there in crying "*Gevalt*" all the time? It may be "hard to be a Jew," but it must also be worth the effort. We would like to focus more attention on its joys than on its "*oys.*"

3. We are optimistic about the future of the Jewish community and Jewish culture. We Jews are both a tenacious and a highly adaptable people—and Judaism still has more to offer that the world desperately needs. It may look as different from the *shtetl* (village) of Poland as the *shtetl* looked relative to the streets of rabbinic Babylonia, but we are betting that a new Jewish community will emerge from the no-longer-scattered remnants of the now global family.

4. We live in a bipolar Jewish world. Israel and North America have a symbiotic relationship—each feeding the needs of the other both physically and Jewishly, each depending on the other for its life both physically and Jewishly. Standing with one foot in Israel and the other in North America, one experiences a fullness of the Jewish body that is exhilarating. The interaction between these two family members—often fierce, but surprisingly equal—creates the environment for even more than a synthesis. It is in recognizing the necessity and desirability for these dual centers that the next stage in the evolution of the Jewish people will be set.

5. We are confident enough about being Jews that we can take the liberty to play a little. Gangster Jake "Greasy Thumb" Guzik, swimmer Mark Spitz, and Rabbi Nachman of Bratslav projected quite different images of the Jew, but they each have their place in the book. We do not equate them, but present them as elements of what constitutes Jewish life. In the pages of *The Jewish Almanac*, articles on kosher wines, Jewish political leaders, and Jewish best-sellers can be found alongside discussions of the Jewish calendar, the 613 commandments, and portraits of the Hasidic masters. It is in the curious interplay of these rather incongruous elements that the full flavor of Jewish experience is expressed.

Although many people have contributed to this book in time and energy, they do not necessarily share these observations. It is perhaps indicative of the emerging Jewish community, however, that the contributors' ranks include Orthodox, Conservative, Reform, Reconstructionist, Alternative, and Secular Jews; rabbis, reporters, professors, students, communal workers, artists, lawyers, and doctors—providing an example of both the diversity and the broad diffusion of intellectual wealth in the Jewish community. It should be clear, however, that we take full responsibility for any errors or inaccuracies that may appear in the book.

We encourage our readers to react to this material—to correct us where we are wrong, to disagree where we are controversial, and to suggest new ideas or categories of information. Who knows, there might be a sequel—and the readers will become the contributors. Correspondence can be addressed to us: c/o Bantam Books, Inc., 666 Fifth Avenue, New York, N.Y. 10103.

Welcome to the world of *The Jewish Almanac*!

Richard A. Siegel
Carl J. Rheins
New York City, April 1980

"My soul is not by the side of my people; my people *is* my soul. And by the same process, every one of us will then become aware of the future of Judaism and feel: I want to go on living; I want my future—a new, total life, a life for my own self, for my people within me, for myself within my people. For Judaism has not only a past; despite all it has already created, it has, above all, not a past but a future. Judaism has, in truth, not yet done its work, and the great forces active in this most tragic and incomprehensible of people have not yet written their very own word into the history of the world."

—Martin Buber, 1911

PART ONE
THE JEWS—IMAGES AND REALITY

IDENTITY CRISIS

A BRIEF HISTORY OF THE TERMS FOR "JEW"

Strictly speaking, it is incorrect to call an ancient Israelite a "Jew" or to call a contemporary Jew an "Israelite" or a "Hebrew." The first Hebrews may not have been Jews at all, and contemporary Palestinians, by their own definition of the term "Palestinian," have to include Jews among their own people—although in choosing the name "Palestine" for their homeland, they have picked a name that originally signified the opposite: an enclave of foreigners. A "Zionist" in the strict sense is not an expansionist: the original "Zion" was only a single hill in Jerusalem, not a whole land, much less "from the Nile to the Euphrates," as the maximalists maintain.

How these curiosities of terminology evolved is a complicated and interesting bit of history. In a general sense all of these terms—"Hebrew," "Israelite," "Jew," "Palestinian," and "Zionist"—are essential ingredients in both Jewish and world history, and understanding their knotty interrelation can shed much light on contemporary events in the Middle East. But let the definer beware: original meanings of these loaded words are no guide to subsequent meanings. How people misconstrue a word is as much a part of its meaning as the "correct" meaning, and the history of these five terms has included a number of creative—and sometimes tragic—misconstruals.

HEBREW:

The word "Hebrew" (*'Ivri*) occurs in the early narratives of the Pentateuch to refer to an Israelite, but only in those narratives, such as the Joseph story (Gen. 39–48) and the Exodus story (Exod. 3–10), that are set in Egypt, where Israelites are regarded as foreigners. There "Hebrew" is either used by Egyptians to refer to Israelites or by Israelites to refer to themselves in the presence of Egyptians—among themselves, the preferred term is *bene Yisrael*, "children of Israel," or "Israelites." A similar usage of "Hebrew" is found in the stories of the interaction between Israelites and Philistines in I Samuel and the interaction of Abram (Abraham) with Canaanites and other non-Israelites in Gen. 14 (see Gen. 14:13, where the Greek translator renders the term *'Ivri* by a word meaning "man of the yonder region"). Jonah, likewise, at sea with a crew of non-Israelites, refers to himself in their presence as a "Hebrew."

Since the term *'Ivri* is possibly based on the common preposition *éver*, meaning "across, beyond, yonder" (the suffix *i* is an adjectival ending called a gentilic, with the sense of "-ite"), the meaning of the term could have the general sense of "yonder-ite," i. e., "foreigner." But since a number of regions in the Middle East are designated by the term *Éver* (e. g., *Éver ha-Yarden*, "Transjordan," *Éver ha-Nahar*, "Trans-riverine," i. e., Trans-Euphrates), the term *'Ivri* could just as well designate a dweller of one of these familiar neighboring "Trans-" regions, with no connotation of foreignness—merely regional particularity. Confusion on the matter is compounded by the additional ambiguity in the frame of reference in which the designation "Hebrew" originated: were the "Hebrews" thought of as "those out yonder" from the standpoint of Mesopotamians or "those *from* out yonder" from the standpoint of Canaanites?

To complicate the matter further, a word similar in sound and meaning, *apiru*, *habiru*, or *khapiru*, occurs in extrabiblical ancient Near Eastern sources, where it may or may not designate an Israelite. The kings of the Canaanite city-states, in the land that was to become Israel, wrote many letters to the Egyptian Pharaohs, in the era just preceding the Israelite exodus from Egypt, complaining about "those upstart *apiru*," who seem to be either bandits or guerrilla revolutionaries (ones judgment depending on one's socio-economic affinities), who, one way or the other, wrought havoc with the local garrisons of Egyptian and Canaanite armies. These kings also used the term indiscriminately to refer to *one another* in their territorial rivalries and skirmishes (much in the same way that "communist" and "Marxist" are bandied about today), so the meaning of *apiru* is still less certain. Probably, the Canaanite kings believed it would legitimate their cause with the Pharaoh to denounce their enemies as *apiru* rabble, but after the Pharaohs became preoccupied with their own slave uprisings back home, they washed their hands of the whole lot of squabbling petty princes in Canaan.

It seems likely that *apiru* did not designate a specific ethnic group, even though the cuneiform symbol for "people" often appears alongside the word. More likely, it referred to slaves, fugitives, mercenary soldiers, itinerant artisans, foreigners in general, or anyone without the normal rights of citizens or property holders. In these senses, a worthy translation of *apiru* might be "transient" or "immigrant," a sense which fits well with the Biblical term *'Ivri* (the Hebrew word *'avar* means "to cross, pass, ford a river"). But alternative meanings have been suggested for *apiru*, including "dusty ones" (related to the Hebrew *aphar*, dust), suggesting a bedouin or desert dweller; "confederates" (from a word related to the Hebrew *haver*, "friend" or "colleague"—compare the name of the town Hebron, which probably means "place of confederation"); and "riverbank dwellers" (from an Arabic cognate).

The Bible also implicitly makes "Hebrew" into an ethnic term by making Eber an ancestor of the Israelites (Gen. 10:21, 24). In general, however, biblical usage seems to support the nonethnic sense of "foreigner, immigrant, wayfarer," which, during the early period of Israelite history, when migrations of nationalities back and forth across the Near East were quite common, was very likely applied to many ethnic groups, sometimes by people who themselves had at some point incurred the same designation. Compare the attitudes in our own time of "older" immigrants toward immigrants more recent than they.

Because of a usage occurring for the first time in the writings of the second century B.C.E. Palestinian Jewish writer Ben-Sira, "Hebrew" came to be the designation of the language of the Bible, and so in general for the postbiblical Hebrew language. The Hebrew language had begun as a northwest Semitic dialect, influenced by the immigration of Aramaic-speaking ancestors of the Jewish people. It is as a term for the classic and universal Jewish language that "Hebrew" is most Jewish. The Hebrew alphabet was first disseminated by the Canaanite people known as the Phoenicians, a group closely related to Israelites linguistically, though not culturally or religiously. The particular form of the Hebrew alphabet used today is actually Syrian (or Aramaic) in origin.

Because of the occasional biblical references to Israelites as "Hebrews," the term became a normal alternative for "Jew" throughout the Middle Ages and in modern times. It has occasionally been preferred by Jews themselves as a euphemistic term for "Jew," when the latter term was felt to be embarrassing (the Reform movement in America called its synagogue organization the "Union of American *Hebrew* Congregations," and its seminary "*Hebrew* Union College"). But because of the emergence of the slang pejorative "Hebe," the advantages of the adaptation are now dubious.

ISRAELITE:

Jews are principally called "Israelites" in the Bible (*bene Yisrael*, "children of Israel") because of their descent from Jacob who, at a major turning point in his career, was renamed by God *Yisra'el* ("He who fights God"). The story that accounts for the meaning of this renaming (Gen. 32:22ff.) is by no means a clear explanation of the name: Jacob, having spent twenty-one years in hiding from his brother Esau, whose birthright he had stolen, returns to his homeland with his wives, children, and servants. Crossing the river Jabbok (a Transjordanian tributary of the river Jordan), he meets a mysterious stranger who accosts him after he has sent his entourage on ahead and stands alone in the river. The two men wrestle through the night, and Jacob refuses to let the stranger go until the latter blesses him (at its most literal level, the blessing is simply a pledge to renounce hostilities—an important ingredient in Middle Eastern diplomacy to the present day). As the sun comes up, the stranger sees he cannot prevail against Jacob, even after wounding him in the inner thigh, and he finally offers his blessing: "No longer shall your name be called Jacob, but rather 'Israel,' for you have fought with gods (or God) and men, and have prevailed." Jacob's subsequent reunion with his brother Esau is surprisingly benign.

There are several ways to explain this enigmatic story: (1) The stranger is Esau himself, who concealed his identity in the darkness, and the word "God" should be understood in some figurative or symbolic way. (2) The stranger is a guardian angel of Esau, and the word "God" should be translated "angels." (3) The stranger is God Himself, or an angelic representative, who seeks to put Jacob through a final trial—indeed, his first real experience of direct combat—before reconciling him with his brother.

One way or another, this story is a folk etymology, and not a reliable guide to the original meaning of the name "Israel," which, depending on how its components are construed could mean "He-who-fights-God," "He-who-fights-*for*-God," "God fights," "God rules," or even, via corruption in pronunciation, "upright-one-of-God" (*yashar-El*) or "God is upright."

The name "children of Israel" is interchangeable throughout the Bible with "children of Jacob" or "House of Jacob" (*Bet Yaakov*); also synonymous with the poetic name *Bene Yeshurun*, "children of Yeshurun." The Jewish homeland is called *Eretz Yisrael* ("the Land of Israel"), which is sometimes also called *Eretz Canaan* ("the land of Canaan"). (The name "Canaan" has been variously explained as meaning "lowland," "merchant," or "purple dye," the last term referring to a key industry of the Canaanites, which is also the source of the name "Phoenician.")

The land and people "Israel" became a kingdom under the rules of Saul, David, and Solomon during the years 1100–900 B.C.E.. When King Solomon died, the kingdom split into a northern and a southern region, "Israel" and "Judah," respectively. The capital of the northern kingdom ceased to be Jerusalem (founded as a capital by David) and became Samaria (near the present-day Arab town of Nablus, the biblical city Shechem). Though the southern kingdom eventually became the bearer of Jewish identity in world history, the northern kingdom was closer in tribal composition to the old confederate league that had originally conquered the land. The kingdom of Israel was defeated by the Assyrians in 722 B.C.E., and the inhabitants were deported to the East—the start of the legends of the "Ten Lost Tribes of Israel." (Judah, the southern kingdom, survived until defeat by the Babylonians and the Babylonian exile in 586 B.C.E.) A few northern Israelites remained around Samaria, intermarrying with Assyrians, and preserving a form of the Israelite religion based on the Pentateuch. These were the people later called "Samaritans," whose rejection of post-Pentateuchal Jewish tradition led them into frequent conflicts with latter-day Jews. The Samaritans survive today as an Arabic-speaking minority in Israel and the West Bank, not fully integrated into either Jewish or Arab society.

"Israelite," like "Hebrew," became a common synonym for "Jew" throughout post-biblical history down to modern times, with perhaps less adaptability to pejorative usage than the other terms. Since the founding of the state of Israel in 1948 the term has come to jostle against the newer term "Israeli," which is not synonymous; in general, "Israelite" means a biblical follower of the religion of Moses and descendant of Jacob; "Israeli" means a citizen of the state of Israel, whether Jewish in religion or not, though, of course, most Israelis are Jewish. "Israel," "children of Israel," "Assembly of Israel" (*Kenesset Yisrael*) and "People Israel" (*Am Yisrael*) have always been the terms preferred by Jews for their own peoplehood. In fact, early Christianity paid its respects to the attractiveness of these names by thinking of Christendom as a new "Israel."

JEW:

The term "Jew" is originally derived from the tribal name "Judah," the name of the fourth son of Jacob. Judahites, that is, descendants of Judah, were organized (along with some neighboring tribes) by their kinsman King David into a mini-kingdom centered in Hebron before David became the first truly pan-Israelite monarch. Prior to this time the Judahites were cut off from their northern brethren by encampments of Philistines. When David captured the city of Jerusalem from the Jebusites (a Canaanite people), he opened up a vital corridor connecting the northern and the southern tribes, thus permitting unification of the nation Israel. David was then made king over all Israel, in preference to the surviving sons of Saul. The tenuous union of northern and southern tribes worked well during the reigns of David and his son Solomon, but when Solomon died the two regions again split off from one another. It is likely that the social and religious character of Judah, the southern kingdom, was different from that of the north—more cosmopolitan, less rooted in tribal territorial claims, more suited for survival as a culture during exile; in short, more "Jewish" in the pre-1948 understanding of the term.

The exile of Judah came in 586 B.C.E., when large numbers of the inhabitants were deported to Babylon. From then on, "Judean" came to be the principle term for a follower of the Mosaic religion, and it has remained so to the present day. In the book of Esther, set in Persia, the Benjaminite Mordecai (technically a member of the "Ten Lost Tribes") is called "yehudi," Judean or Jew; the book even introduces the verb *mityahed* "becoming Jewish, converting to Judaism." Both factors suggest that the term, though still rooted in ethnic considerations, had broadened its scope from tribal, territorial, and national terms to religious in a more universalistic sense. From the Hebrew *yehudi,* via Aramaic *yehudai,* Greek *ioudaios,* and Latin *iudaeus,* the term "Jew" passed into European languages.

The Second Jewish Commonwealth (440 B.C.E.–70 C.E.), founded under the Persian Empire, and ruled successively by the Greeks and the Romans, was called by the Romans "Judea." The Romans, in destroying the Temple in 70 C.E., sought for a time to abolish the Judean character of the Holy Land, and so renamed it "Philistia," after the Philistines who had inhabited the southwestern coastal plain. Titus and Vespasian, after their victories over Judea, were not given the title "Judaicus," which would have signified that Judea was a subjugated *land*—instead, "Judean" came to designate solely a religion, and in this restricted sense Jews came under the Roman Empire's protection as a "permitted religion."

Christians, in usurping the term "Israelite," began using the term "Jew" in a pejorative way. The Jews were "Judases," named after the man who betrayed Jesus, Judas Iscariot, and when the Church took over the Roman Empire, it withdrew Judaism from the category of "permitted religion." Jews were allowed to remain Jews, but non-Jews were forbidden, under strict penalties, to become Jews, and marriage of a non-Jew with a Jew was outlawed. Jews, moreover, were forbidden to seek converts to their religion.

Meanwhile, Jews themselves developed stricter standards for defining their religion. Originally, Judaism was somewhat loosely defined. The book of Ruth portrays Ruth the Moabite converting to Judaism by a simple statement of allegiance: "Your people shall be my people; your God, my God." Hillel the Elder is reported to have accepted a convert with the simple instruction "What is hateful to you, don't do to another—that is Torah; the rest is commentary; go and study." Eventually, however, several more specific criteria for Jewishness evolved. A person was Jewish by birth if born of a Jewish mother, regardless of the father's identity. A child of a Jewish father and gentile mother was not considered a Jew. A person was Jewish by conversion if he accepted the 613 commandments and became circumcized and baptized (the latter, a seemingly Christian practice, began as a Jewish purification ritual—it was required of converts on the assumption that non-Jews were ritually impure). Why converts should have to obey the commandments to be considered Jewish, while a born Jew could be a backslider or even an atheist, is one of the knotty problems that even today govern the debate over who is a Jew. Jewish law is less stringent on this matter toward female converts (who are, for now at least, held responsible for fewer commandments) than toward male converts.

Jews in the days of the Second Commonwealth also made a distinction, according to some Hellenistic sources, between Jews living in the land of Israel (who were called Judeans) and those outside the land (who were called Hebrews). This terminological distinction passed out of use after the Temple was destroyed, but the conceptual distinction was preserved in Jewish law, reflected, among other things, in the development of both a Palestinian and a Diaspora (Babylonian) Talmud.

As the Christian churches gradually invested the designation "Jew" with demonic connotations, it came to be used by Christians even in denouncing each other. Church heresies were branded as attempts to "judaize" the faith, even when the heretics themselves were intensely anti-Jewish. During the Middle Ages, the term "Jew" also took on socio-economic connotations. "Jew" came to signify "merchant," at first without any negative implication; later, it came to signify a practitioner of usury, an exploiter, a swindler. In English there is even a verb "to Jew," meaning to bargain mercilessly.

The word "Jew" first appeared in written English texts around the year 1000 C.E., although it was probably in common use much before that. It is found spelled in a variety of ways—Ieu, Ieuu, Iwe, Iow, Iue, Ive, Iewe, etc.—before it came to have its present spelling. Many of the uses of the word are pejorative in connotation. The Oxford English Dictionary lists among its historical examples of usage the following: "I am a Jew; hath not a Jew eyes?" (Shakespeare's Shylock, 1596); "She shall have skin like a mummy and the beard of a Jew" (Sheridan, 1775): and "You forget, Lady Lilac's as rich as a Jew" (Byron, 1820). The Book of Common Prayer, in a slightly more charitable vein, includes a prayer: "Haue mercy upon all Iewes, Turkes, Infidels and heretikes" (1548–9). The word also spawned a long, colorful list of compound words (some of which seem to have no apparent connection with Jews), such as: Jew's eye (a highly valued thing); Jew-bail (insufficient bail); jewbush (the milk plant); Jew carts (transports for stolen objects); Jew lizard (an Australian reptile); jewfish (fish of the family *Serranidae*), jew's mallow (a jute plant); Jew's myrtle (a species of myrtle); Jew's apple (an eggplant); Jew's ears (a Purim pastry); Jew's houses (smelting furnaces); Jew's tin (the metal smelted there); Jew's money (Roman coins found in Britain); Jew's pitch (bitumen from the Dead Sea); and of course, Jew's harp (a twanging instrument popular in peasant culture).

PALESTINIAN:

As noted earlier, "Palestine" originated as a Roman designation, in the form "Philistia," for the whole land of Israel. The Philistines themselves were most likely a Greek-speaking people who invaded the land of Canaan about the year 1100 B.C.E., not long after (indeed, possibly simultaneously with) the Israelite conquests. They were part of a general migration of "Sea Peoples" that spread across the eastern Mediterranean and Asia Minor at the end of the Bronze Age. The Homeric epics, the *Iliad* and *Odyssey*, recount some of the political and social instability that led to these migrations, as does the Bible itself in the legends of the Israelite exodus from Egypt (the Egyptians, having their hands full with the invasions of the "Sea Peoples," were a pushover for a slave rebellion). The name "Palestine" occurs in the Bible as *Pileshet*, and the Philistines are called *Pelishtim*—possibly a corruption of the Greek word *pelasgoi*, "Sea Peoples," that is, inhabitants of the Aegean islands, from whence the Philistine invaders originated. King David hired himself out to the Philistines for a while, and once he became more powerful than they, hired some of them for his own mercenary army. In that situation they are called *keretim u-feletim*, suggesting possibly an origin in the island of Crete. The Philistines were harsh conquerors of the Israelites, who, for a time, maintained a rigid monopoly on the manufacture of iron weapons. Eventually the threat of their power galvanized the twelve Israelite tribes into uniting against them, and they were driven out or absorbed.

Their name survived, however, and the Greek historian Herodotus called the land of Israel "the Philistine Syria," which came to be shortened to *Palaistinei*. In Roman and talmudic literature this name designated a province of the land of Israel, and the term was taken over temporarily by the Arabs after the Islamic conquest in the seventh century C.E. It fell into disuse for a time, was revived by the Crusaders, then fell into disuse again under Saracen and Ottoman rule.

In 1922 the British revived the term to designate at least part of the area specified by the League of Nations Mandate; the original area included both sides of the Jordan river, but in practice, the land west of the Jordan came to be designated as "Palestine" par excellence. Legally "Palestine" includes the area both of the present state of Israel and of the kingdom of Jordan. But present-day Palestinian Arabs refer only to the cisjordanian area as their homeland. The war fought in 1948 did not solve the question of Palestinian identity—the West Bank area and the Gaza Strip (the latter actually the original Philistine territory) were made part of Jordan and Egypt, respectively, while the rest of Cisjordan became Israel—and the 1967 war further jumbled up the respective claims of Jews and Arabs over the land. Palestinian Arabs of the P.L.O. persuasion claim that "Palestine" should include only children of the land's inhabitants—including Christians and Jews—prior to 1918. Jewish nationalists of the *Herut* persuasion (Menachem Begin's political party) likewise appeal to the status quo of the Mandate days but speak of "Palestinian Arabs" and "Palestinian Jews," the latter including Jews who have immigrated since that time, the former probably meaning Jordanians. Jordan itself is split ethnically: Palestinians comprise a majority of the population and dominate business, civil service, and intellectual life; the army and ruling royal family are Arabian bedouins.

ZIONIST:

The word "Zion" probably originally meant something like "promontory"; it is related to a Hebrew word *tziyyah*, meaning "dry place," or to the Hebrew adjective *metzuyyan*, "standing out, distinguished." The hill of Zion is one of the highest places in the city of Jerusalem. King David, in capturing this area, insured Israelite control over the vital central region of the land of Canaan and so made possible the union of the twelve tribes into a nation. King David himself is buried on Mt. Zion, and the locale eventually became a prophetic and poetic designation for the whole land of Israel or for the Temple Mount that in turn signified the Holy Land. It was natural for this term to signify the movement that led to the creation of a Jewish homeland and a Jewish state, but strictly speaking, the name "Zion" refers to a focal point rather than to an expanse of territory, and a "Zionist" is not one who wants to take over the whole land of Israel, let alone the whole Eastern Mediterranean area, but one who champions the unity of the Jewish people and Jerusalem as the capital of the Jewish nation. In a way this conception fits with the whole tangled history of the terms for "Jew." While Judaism has intermittently been a nation, territory, and ethnic entity and has never strayed very far from that concept, it has always been a religion and a culture. This means that when political power failed, linguistic and spiritual faculties took over and helped to maintain continuity in Jewish identity. If we assume that the very first Jews were those who wrenched themselves out of slavery in Mesopotamia and Egypt, then we must recognize that at least part of the Jewish community was a community of converts—people who voluntarily counted themselves in among the people Israel and accepted the contract of the Jewish covenant. That bond is a spiritual bond, and it has always transcended the vicissitudes of political power; that is why Jews can define the center of their existence as the hill of Zion but must see the periphery as an ever-changing (and often creatively changing) boundary. As such, Jews will always have a claim on the land of Israel, whatever troubled battles rage around King David's citadel and however the sharing of power in this war-torn land comes to be defined.

—J.R.

LENNY BRUCE: ON JEWISH AND GOYISH

Perhaps at this point I ought to say a little something about my vocabulary. My conversation, spoken and written, is usually flavored with the jargon of the hipster, the argot of the underworld, and Yiddish.

In the literate sense—as literate as Yiddish can be since it is not a formal language—"goyish" means "gentile." But that's not the way I mean to use it.

To me, if you live in New York or any other big city, you are Jewish. It doesn't matter even if you're Catholic; if you live in New York you're Jewish. If you live in Butte, Montana, you're going to be goyish even if you're Jewish.

Evaporated milk is goyish even if the Jews invented it. Chocolate is Jewish and fudge is goyish. Spam is goyish and rye bread is Jewish.

Negroes are all Jews. Italians are all Jews. Irishmen who have rejected their religion are Jews. Mouths are very Jewish. And bosoms. Baton-twirling is very goyish. Georgie Jessel and Danny Thomas are Christians, because if you look closely on their bodies you'll find a boil somewhere.

To trap an old Jewish woman—they're crafty and they will lie—just seize one and you will find a handkerchief balled-up in one of her hands.

I can understand why we can't have a Jewish President. It would be embarrassing to hear the President's mother screaming love at the grandchildren: "Who's Grandma's baby! Who's Grandma's baby!"

". . . And this is Chet Huntley in New York. The First Lady's mother opened the Macy's Day Parade screaming, *'Oy zeishint mine lieber'* and furiously pinching young Stanley's cheeks . . ."

Actually, she bit his ass, going "Oom, yum yum, is this a tush, whose tushy is that?" The Jews are notorious children's-ass-kissers. Gentiles neither bite their children's asses nor do they *hahhh* their soup.

Gentiles love their children as much as Jews love theirs; they just don't wear their hearts on their sleeves. On the other hand, Jewish mothers don't hang gold stars in their windows. They're not proud of their boys' going into the service. They're always worried about their being killed.

Celebrate is a goyish word. Observe is a Jewish word. Mr. and Mrs. Walsh are *celebrating* Christmas with Major Thomas Moreland, USAF (Ret.), while Mr. and Mrs. Bromberg *observed* Hanukkah with Goldie and Arthur Schindier from Kiamesha, New York.

—L. B. rep.

THE NAME GAME

30 BIBLICAL NAMES COMMONLY USED IN ENGLISH

Aaron
Meaning: (possibly) Messenger, mountain, to shine, singing, teaching.
Who: Brother of Moses and Miriam, founder of the Israelite priestly dynasty, direct ancestor to King David. Aaron served as the spokesman for Moses (described as a stutterer) before Pharoah and as the leader of the cultic activities during the desert wanderings; however, left in charge when Moses went up to Mt. Sinai to receive the Ten Commandments, Aaron succumbed to the people's impatient urgings and assisted them in constructing the Golden Calf.
Source: First reference in Exodus 4 ff. and throughout the following four books of the Torah.
When: c. 1280 B.C.E.

Abigail
Variants: Abby, Gail
Meaning: My father's joy.
Who: An early follower of David before he became king, she undermined her cruel husband Naval's orders by aiding David and his guerrillas. After Naval's death, David married her. She was known for her beauty, wisdom and power of prophecy.
Source: 1 Samuel, 25:14–42
When: c.1004–965 B.C.E.

Abraham
Meaning: Exalted-father or father-of-a-mighty-nation.
Who: First patriarch of the Hebrews; husband of Sarah and Hagar; father of Isaac and Ishmael. Abraham is described as being on intimate terms with God; at God's command, he left his father's home to wander towards "the land that I will show you," and at God's command he was ready to sacrifice his son, Isaac; however, he was also able to successfully challenge God to be just with regard to Sodom and Gomorrah, "Shall not the Judge of all the earth deal justly?"
Source: Genesis 11:26–25:10
When: During the early part of the Patriarchal Period, c. 1990–1570 B.C.E.

Adam
Meaning: Man, red, earth.
Who: The first and therefore the archetypal human being. Created by God on the sixth day of Creation, Adam was placed in charge of the Garden of Eden. After violating God's command by eating from the forbidden Tree of Knowledge of Good and Evil, Adam (and Eve) was expelled from the Garden and cursed: "By the sweat of your brow shall you get bread to eat."
Source: Genesis 1–3
When: c. 3760 B.C.E.

Amos
Meaning: Burdened or troubled.
Who: Originally an orchard tender and shepherd, Amos became one of the classical prophets who prophesied a period of suffering to be followed by a religious revival and the redemption of the people.
Source: The prophetic Book of Amos.
When: During the eighth century B.C.E. in the time of Uzziah, king of Judea and Jeroboam, king of Israel.

Benjamin
Meaning: Son-of-my-right-hand or son-of-the-south.
Who: The youngest of Jacob's twelve sons by Rachel (her second), who died in birthing him; Joseph's only full brother; patriarch of the Tribe of Benjamin. Since Benjamin was the only brother who did not participate in the sale of Joseph into slavery, he was honored by having the Holy Temple built on the territory alloted to his tribe.
Source: Genesis 35:16–50:16
When: During the latter part of the Patriarchal Period, c. 1990–1570 B.C.E.

Dan
Meaning: He judged.
Who: Fifth son of Jacob by Bilhah, Rachel's handmaiden; scion of the Tribe of Dan. Legend has it that his descendants were all idol worshippers.
Source: Genesis 30:6–50:16
When: During the latter part of the Patriarchal Period, c. 1990–1570 B.C.E.

Daniel
Meaning: God-is-my-judge or God-had-vindicated.
Who: An Israelite prophet who, as a youth, was taken to the Babylonian King Nebuchadnezzar's court in order to be taught Chaldean culture in preparation for Babylonian government service. Daniel maintained his faith, however, and, as a visionary, was able to divine writings on walls and survive a den of hungry lions.
Source: The hagiographic Book of Daniel
When: c. 545–535 B.C.E.

David
Meaning: Beloved.
Who: Second king of Israel, poet, shepherd, giant-slayer, military genius, David is traditionally considered to be the author of the Book of Psalms and scion of the dynasty from which the Messiah will come.
Source: 1 Samuel 16–2 Samuel; 1 Kings 1–2:12.
When: c. 1004–965 B.C.E.

Deborah
Meaning: A swarm of bees or to speak kind words.
Who: A judge of Israel, Deborah was also described as a prophetess, composer of poems, and counselor for the people. A military leader, as well, she commanded the northern tribes in their victorious battle against Sisera.
Source: Judges 4–5
When: c. 1125 B.C.E.

Dinah
Meaning: Judgement.
Who: The only recorded daughter of Jacob, by his wife Leah, Dinah was raped by Shechem, son of Hamor, while she was out visiting with "the daughters of the land." Her brothers, Simeon and Levi, avenged this offense by murdering all of the Shechemites.
Source: Genesis 30:21 and Genesis 34
When: During the later part of the Patriarchal Period, c. 1990–1570 B.C.E.

Elijah
Variant: Eliot
Meaning: The Lord-is-my-God.
Who: A prophet and miracle-worker, who, according to tradition, did not die and under various disguises, continues to accompany Israel in her exile. He visits the child at his circumcision and every family at the Passover *seder*; at some future date Elijah will herald the coming of the Messiah.
Source: 1 Kings 17:1–2 Kings 2:11.
When: c. 800 B.C.E.

Elisheva
Variant: Elizabeth
Meaning: The Oath-of-God or My-God is-Fullness.
Who: Wife of Aaron, the first high priest of Israel, and therefore the matriarch of the Israelite priestly class.
Source: Exodus 6:23
When: c. 1280 B.C.E.

Emanuel
Meaning: God-is-with-us.
Who: A child, prophesied by Isaiah to be born to Ahaz and his young wife, who will embody the reunification of the divided Israelite kingdoms of Ephraim and Judea; interpreted by Christians as a forecast of Jesus.
Source: Isaiah 7:14–17
When: In the indefinite future.

Esther
Variants: Hester, Estelle
Meaning: A star (also known as Hadassah, which means a myrtle tree).
Who: A Persian-Jewish woman who, as a result of her extraordinary beauty, won the contest for queen to King Ahasuarus. Through her wit and courage, plus some coaching from her uncle Mordechai, she managed to alter a royal decree to kill all of Persia's Jewry. The day upon which the Jews were thus saved is celebrated as the holiday of Purim.
Source: The hagiographic Book of Esther.
When: Possibly between the first and fifth century B.C.E.; however, most likely Esther was only a literary figure and not a real person.

Ezra
Meaning: Help or God-helps.
Who: A scribe who chronicled and supervised the Jews' return from the Babylonian Exile and their reestablishment of the cult, considered by some modern biblical scholars as the major redactor (editor) of the Bible as it is now known.
Source: The hagiographic Book of Ezra
When: c. 450 B.C.E.

Hannah
Variants: Ann, Anita, Nancy
Meaning: Merciful, gracious.
Who: Despairing because she was barren, Hannah went to pray at the temple of Shiloh. Her desire to be a mother was so great that she pledged that if granted a male child, she would give him over to God's service. She

subsequently bore a child and named him Samuel ("God Listened"), who became the last of the judges of Israel.
Source: 1 Samuel 1–2
When: c. 1000 B.C.E.

Isaac
Variant: Ike
Meaning: He-will-laugh.
Who: Second patriarch of the Israelites, husband of Rebekah, Isaac has been described as the son of a great father (Abraham) and the father of a great son (Jacob). Little is recorded about his life other than his almost being sacrificed by Abraham and his being deceived by Jacob into giving the patriarchal blessing to him instead of to Esau, the elder.
Source: Genesis 21:1–35:29
When: During the early part of the Patriarchal Period, c. 1990–1570 B.C.E.

Jacob
Variants: James, Jack
Meaning: Held-by-the-heel; supplanter.
Who: Son of Isaac and Rebekah; twin but younger brother of Esau (whom he supplanted); husband of Rachel and Leah. Through many severe trials, this patriarch ultimately earned the name Israel ("one who wrestles with God") and his place as father of the Twelve Tribes.
Source: Genesis 25:23–49:33.
When: During the later part of the Patriarchal Period, c. 1990–1570 B.C.E.

Jonathan
Meaning: God-has-given or gift-of-God.
Who: First son of Saul, the first king of Israel; loyal friend of David, the second king of Israel; brother to David's first wife, Michal. A brave fighter and excellent archer, Jonathan died with his father fighting the Philistines on Mt. Gilboa.
Source: 1 Samuel 14 ff. (especially chapters 18–20, 23 and 31)–2 Samuel 1:27.
When: c. 1004–965 B.C.E.

Joel
Meaning: God-is-willing.
Who: A prophet who preached in Judea, Joel forecast that the plagues besetting Jerusalem would end once the people returned to God with penetence, fasting, and prayer.
Source: The prophetic Book of Joel.
When: Either before 800 B.C.E. or after 500 B.C.E. depending on which scholarly reckoning one follows.

Joseph
Meaning: He will increase.
Who: The favored son of Jacob, by his favorite wife Rachel, Joseph was sold into slavery by his ten jealous brothers. Through various intrigues and manuevers, he emerged in Egypt as a minister second only to Pharoah. From this position he was able to spare his then reconciled brothers and father from the ravages of famine by bringing them to Egypt.
Source: Genesis 37:1–50:26
When: c. 1500 B.C.E.

Judith
Meaning: Praise.
Who: Heroine of the Jerusalem siege, she pretended to defect to Nebuchadnezzar's general Holoferns only to decapitate him when he was asleep.
Source: In the apocryphal Book of Judith.
When: 400 B.C.E.

Michael
Variants: Mitchel, Miles
Meaning: Who-is-like-God?
Who: One of the four archangels who enjoys a particularly close proximity to God, Michael is regarded as the patron angel of Israel. He stands to the right of God's throne and among other things, serves as the high priest of the heavens.
Source: The hagiographic Book of Daniel 10:13–21
When: Ageless and eternal.

Miriam
Variants: Mary, Marian, Maria, Maureen, Polly, Molly, Minnie, and May
Meaning: Bitter sea.
Who: A prophetess who was sister to Moses and Aaron. Upon seeing Pharoah's daughter discover the infant Moses in the Nile bullrushes, she recommended that the daughter hire a Hebrew wet nurse to take care of the baby. The wet nurse who Miriam "found" was Tziporah, Moses' real mother. After crossing the Red Sea, she led the women in celebratory song and dance.
Source: Exodus 2:4, Exodus 15:1–19, Numbers 12:10–15, Numbers 20:1
When: c. 1280 B.C.E.

Rachel
Meaning: From the Hebrew word for "ewe."
Who: Daughter of Rebekah's brother, Laban; younger sister of Leah; mother of Joseph and Benjamin; and favorite wife of Jacob. Rachel is described as "shapely and beautiful" (Gen. 29:17). She was, however, barren for many years and jealous of her sister's fecundity.
Source: Genesis 29–35
When: During the latter part of the Patriarchal Period, c. 1990–1570 B.C.E.

Rebekah
Meaning: To tie or to bind.
Who: Wife of Isaac; mother of the twins Esau and Jacob. Favoring Jacob, "a mild man, who stayed in the camp" over Esau who was "a skillful hunter, a man of the outdoors," Rebekah masterminded Jacob's

deception of Isaac in order to gain the patriarchal blessing.
Source: Genesis 24–28
When: Patriarchal Period, c. 1990–1570 B.C.E.

Ruth
Meaning: Friendship.
Who: Daughter-in-law to Naomi to whom Ruth, a Moabite woman, remained loyal after both of Naomi's sons died; great-grandmother to King David and therefore a direct ancestor to the Messiah through her second husband Boaz and their son, Obed.
Source: The hagiographic Book of Ruth
When: c. 1000 B.C.E.

Samuel
Meaning: God-has-heard.
Who: Dedicated as a Nazarite (forbidden from cutting their hair and drinking wine) by his mother, Hannah, Samuel was the last judge of Israel. Although concerned that the people's request for a king would leave them susceptible to subjugation at the hands of a despot, he nevertheless, after receiving assurances from God, oversaw the anointing of Saul as the first king of Israel.
Source: The prophetic books of First and Second Samuel
When: c. 1000 B.C.E.

Sarah
Variants: Sally, Sadie
Meaning: Princess.
Who: First matriarch of the Hebrews, wife and half-sister of Abraham, mother of Isaac, whom she bore at the age of ninety. Sarah was known for her great beauty, generous hospitality to strangers, and direct communication with God (rarely described of women in the Bible).
Source: Genesis 11:29–23:1
When: During early part of Patriarchal Period, 1990–1570 B.C.E.

—Z.S. and J.B.S.

JEWISH SURNAMES: WHAT THEY MEAN

When Jewish families adopted surnames, they took them from a variety of sources—occupations, geographical locations, physical or personal characteristics, nicknames, abbreviations, or first names of a father or mother (like Davidson, from David). Sometimes Jews were given last names against their will. The following is a sampling of Jewish surnames and their meanings in categories like those mentioned. The lists are based on *A Dictionary of Jewish Names and Their History* by Benzion C. Kaganoff (New York, 1977).

Occupational Names

Abzug	proofsheet (printer)
Ackerman	plowman
Becker	baker
Berger	shepherd
Bodner	cooper or barrelmaker
Braverman	brewer
Brenner	distiller
Feder	scribe (with quill pen)
Glass	glass trade
Korff	basket maker
Kramer	merchant
Lederer	tanner
Meltsner	malt dealer
Metzger	butcher
Pomerantz	orange (fruit) dealer
Portnoy	tailor
Schecter	slaughterer
Singer	cantor
Weber	weaver
Weiner	wine seller

Physical Characteristics

Bleich	pale
Borodaty	bearded
Dick	stout
Gelbart	yellow-bearded
Geller	yellow
Gross	large
Jung	young
Klein	small
Kraus	curly
Krumbein	bowlegged
Kurtz	short
Mankuta	left-handed
Roth	red
Rothbart	red-bearded
Schnell	fast
Schwartz	black
Schwartzbart	black-bearded
Stark	strong
Steinhart	hard as stone
Weisbart	white-bearded

Personal Characteristics or Nicknames

Bogatch	rich
Dienstag	Tuesday
Dunkelman	deeply religious
Ehmann	husband
Ehrlich	honest
Friedman	free man
Frohlich	happy
Gottlieb	God-loving
Gottschalk	God's servant
Kluger	wise
Langsam	easygoing

Lustig	happy
Scholem	peace
Sommer	summer
Springer	vivacious

Geographical names

Bachrach	town in Germany
Bamberg	town in Germany
Bellow	from Belev, Russia
Calisch	from Kalisz, Poland
Ettinger	from Oettinger, Germany
Guggenheim	town in Germany
Karlin	from a suburb of Pinsk, Russia
Kutover	from Kuty, Poland
Luria	town in Italy
Mintz	from Mainz, Germany

Names from Abbreviations

Brock	*ben* Rabbi Akiva (son of Rabbi Akiva)
Katz	*Kohen Zedek* (priest of righteousness)
Rabad	*Rosh av beth din* (head of court)
Schatz	*Sheliah tzibbur* (minister of congregation)
Siegel	*Segan Leviah* (assistant to Levites)

Patronymics and Matronymics

Abramsohn
Abromovitch
Isaacson
Malkov

The *-sohn* ending is German; *-vitch* is Slavic; *-ov* is also Slavic. The latter can be *-off*, *-ev*, *-eff*, or *-kin*; e.g., Rivkin are matronymics from Malka and Rivka.

Tribal Surnames

Genealogically Jews are divided into three categories: (1) the priests (*cohanim*) from Temple times who were descended from Aaron, the high priests; (2) the assistants to the priests, being the rest of the tribe of Levi; and (3) all of the others, called *Yisroel*. For descendants of the first two categories, surnames indicating tribal membership have developed, each with various forms:

Cohen

Cohen
Hohen
Kogan
Cogan
Kahane
Cohn
Kahn
Barkan ("son of Kahn")
Kaplan ("descended from priests")
Katz (abbreviation: "priest of righteousness")

Levites

Levy
Levin
Levine
Levinsky
Levitan
Levitt
Levitansky
Levinthal
Segal (abbreviation of *Segan Leviah*, member or assistant to Levites)
Chagall (variant of Segal or Siegal)

—A.K.

12 ISRAELI JEWS WHO HAVE CHANGED THEIR NAMES

Before Israel became an independent state, Zionist leaders encouraged Jews with European surnames to adopt new names to give Palestine more of a "Hebrew" flavor. With the arrival of independence, name changing became quite common, first among members of the Israeli army, and then among the general population. In fact, during the first year of Israeli's existence 17,000 people changed their names.

Considerable pressure was exerted officially and unofficially on Israelis to change their names. Perhaps the best known and most vociferous advocate was David Ben-Gurion, a.k.a. David Gruen. After an Israeli ship sailed to South Africa headed by a man named Vishnievsky, Ben-Gurion announced that "no officer will be sent abroad in a representative capacity unless he bears a Hebrew family name."

Significant objection has been voiced against changing European Jewish names to Hebrew names, and against the pressures exerted to this end. "Changing one's name is like cutting off the past," cry some of those who object. Ironically, those who are in favor of changing European names to Hebrew ones in Israel use the same argument! To change one's name, according to Jewish tradition, is to change one's fate. In the Torah, Abram became Abraham, Jacob became Israel, and Sarai became Sarah. Likewise, when a child is ill, his or her name is changed to "fool the angel of death." The following are a dozen Israelis who have changed their names:

1. Shmuel Yosef Agnon, Hebrew writer, from Samuel Joseph Czaczkes

2. Gershon Agron, former Mayor of Jerusalem, from Gershon Agrovsky

3. David Ben-Gurion, 1st Prime Minister of Israel, from David Gruen

4. Eliezer Ben-Yehuda, father of modern Hebrew, from Eliezer Yizhak Perelman

5. Izhak Ben-Zvi, 2nd President of Israel, from Izhak Shimshelevich

6. Levi Eshkol, 3rd Prime Minister of Israel, from Levi Shkolnik

7. Abraham Granott, head of Jewish National Fund, from Abraham Granovsky

8. Golda Meir, former Prime Minister of Israel, from Golda Myerson

9. Shimon Peres, Israeli politician, from Shimon Persky

10. Pinhas Sapir, Israeli labor leader, from Pinhas Koslowsky

11. Moshe Sharett, Israeli statesman and Zionist leader, from Moshe Shertok

12. Shneur Zalman Shazar, 3rd President of Israel, from Shneur Zalman Rubashov

—A.K.

75 AMERICAN JEWS WHO HAVE CHANGED THEIR NAMES

Former Name

Joey Adams (Joseph Abramowitz)
Mel Allen (Melvin Israel)
Woody Allen (Allen Konigsberg)
Lauren Bacall (Betty Joan Perske)
Theda Bara (Theodosia Goodman)
Rona Barrett (Rona Burstein)
Jack Benny (Benjamin Kubelsky)
Milton Berle (Milton Berlinger)
Joey Bishop (Joey Gottlieb)
Fanny Brice (Fanny Borach)
Mel Brooks (Melvin Kaminsky)
Dr. Joyce Brothers (Joyce Bauer)
Lenny Bruce (Leonard Alfred Schneider)
George Burns (Nathan Birnbaum)
Dyan Cannon (Samile Diane Friesen)
Eddie Cantor (Isidor Iskowitch)
Al Capp (Alfred Gerald Caplin)
Kitty Carlisle (Catherine Holzman)
Jeff Chandler (Ira Grossel)
Howard Cosell (Howard Cohen)
Tony Curtis (Bernard Schwartz)
Howard Da Silva (Howard Silverblatt)
Kirk Douglas (Issur Danilovich Demsky)

Theodosia Goodman

Benjamin Kubelsky

Catherine Holzman

Julius Garfinkle

Issur Danilovich Demsky

Bob Dylan (Robert Zimmerman)
Werner Erhard (John Paul Rosenberg)
John Garfield (Julius Garfinkle)
Jack Gilford (Jack Gellman)
Paulette Goddard (Pauline Levee)
Samuel Goldwyn (Samuel Goldfish)
Elliott Gould (Elliot Goldstein)
Lee Grant (Lyova Rosenthal)
Buddy Hackett (Leonard Hacker)
Herblock (Herbert Lawrence Block)
Judy Holliday (Judith Tuvim)
Harry Houdini (Ehrich Weiss)
Lou Jacobi (Louis Jacobovitch)
Al Jolson (Asa Yoelson)
Danny Kaye (Daniel Kaminsky)

Sonia Kalish

Shirley Schrift

Muni Weisenfreund

Alan King (Irwin Kniberg)
Bert Lahr (Irving Lahrheim)
Pinky Lee (Pinchus Leff)
Battling Levinsky (Barney Lebrowitz)
Jerry Lewis (Joseph Levitch)
Peter Lorre (Laszlo Loewenstein)
Jay Lovestone (Jacov Liebstein)
Tony Martin (Alvin Morris)
Paul Muni (Muni Weisenfreund)
Arthur Murray (Arthur Teichman)
Mike Nichols (Michael Igor Peschlowsky)
Jan Peerce (Jacob Pincus Perelmuth)
Tony Randall (Leonard Rosenberg)
Harry Reems (Herbert Streicher)
Joan Rivers (Joan Molinsky)
Harold Robbins (Harold Rubin)
Edward G. Robinson (Emmanuel Goldberg)
Billy Rose (William Rosenberg)
Barney Ross (Barney Rasovsky)
Mort Sahl (Morton Sahl Lyon)
Jill St. John (Jill Oppenheim)
Soupy Sales (Milton Hines)
Artie Shaw (Arthur Arshansky)
Dick Shawn (Richard Schulef)
Dinah Shore (Francis Rose Shore)
Beverly Sills (Belle Silverman)
Phil Silvers (Philip Silversmith)
I. F. Stone (Isadore Feinstein)
Irving Stone (Irving Tennenbaum)
Mike Todd (Avrom Girsch Goldbogen)
Sophie Tucker (Sonia Kalish)
Mike Wallace (Mike Wallach)
David Wallechinsky (David Wallace)
Nathaniel West (Nathan Weinstein)
Gene Wilder (Eugene Silverstein)
Shelly Winters (Shirley Schrift)
Ed Wynn (Isaiah Edwin Leopold)

—A.K., the Eds.

A RABBINIC PORTRAIT GALLERY

For he shall never be moved;
The righteous shall be held in
everlasting remembrance.
Psalms 112:6

THE MEMORY OF THE RIGHTEOUS IS FOR A BLESSING

1. **Rabbi Isaac Aboab I** (end of fourteenth century), originally from Spain, was the author of *Menorat ha-Meor* ("Candlestick of Light"), one of the most popular books on Judaism, having over 70 editions.

2. **Rabbi Jacob Ben Asher** (c. 1270–1340), a major halakhic authority, was known as the Baal ha-Turim after his influential magnum opus, the *Arab'ah Turim* ("Four Columns"), which is one of the earliest systematic compilations of Jewish law and custom.

3. **Rabbi Asher Ben Yehiel** (c. 1250–1327), also known as Asheri and the Rosh, was one of the foremost talmudic commentators and served as leader of German Jewry until 1303, when he immigrated to Spain.

4. **Rabbi Moses Ben Nahman** (1194–1270), also known as Nahmanides and Ramban, was an outstanding medieval Spanish author of talmudic literature, also a philosopher, kabbalist, biblical exegete, poet, and physician.

5. **Rabbi Moses Ben Maimon** (1135–1204), also known as Maimonides and Rambam, was one of the most influential figures in Jewish history; his *Mishneh Torah* and *Guide to the Perplexed* are seminal, though highly controversial, works in the areas of Jewish law and philosophy respectively; he was also a physician, astronomer, linguist, and talmudist.

6. **Rabbi Jacob Ben Meir** (c. 1100–1171), also known as Rabbenu Tam, was a grandson of Rashi and considered the greatest Talmud scholar of his generation; pupils came from all over the world to study with him at his *Bet Midrash* ("House of Study") in France.

7. **Rabbi Jonathan Eybeschutz** (c. 1690–1764) was head of the Yeshiva of Prague and renowned both as a talmudist (with 30 published works) and a kabbalist. Although a signer of the ban of excommunication on Shabbatai Zevi (a false Messiah), he was accused of being a secret Shabbatean himself.

8. **Rabbi Tzvi Ashkenazi** (1660–1718), also known as the Hakham Tzvi, was the head of the Ashkenazi community in Amsterdam for many years; he also adopted many Sephardic manners and customs from his studies in Salonika.

9. **Rabbi Abraham Gombiner** (c. 1637–1683) is known as the Magen Avraham (Shield of Abraham), the title of his terse and highly esteemed commentary to the *Shulhan Arukh* (the Code of Jewish Law).

10. **Rabbi Shabbetai Ben Meir Ha-Kohen** (1621–1662), a Lithuanian rabbi, is also known as the Shakh, an acronym of *Siftei Kohen*, the title of his commentary to the *Shulhan Arukh* (Code of Jewish Law).

11. **Rabbi David Ben Samuel Ha-Levi** (1586–1667) is also known as the Taz, an acronym for *Turei Zahav,* the title of his widely read and influential commentary on the *Shulhan Arukh.*

12. **Rabbi Moses Isserles** (c. 1525–1572), known by the acronym Rema, was a Polish rabbi, scholar, and halakhic (legal) authority who was beloved by the people and likened to Maimonides by his contemporaries.

13. **Rabbi Joseph Ben Ephraim Caro** (1488–1575), best known as author of the Shulhan Arukh (Code of Jewish Law), which quickly became and still remains the definitive compilation of Jewish law, also authored several other (and some say, more significant) works and was a kabbalist who received visitations from a heavenly mentor.

14. **Rabbi Meir Ben Gedaliah of Lublin** (1558–1616), also known as the Maharam, was an outstanding teacher, serving as head of the Yeshiva of Lublin and establishing several other yeshivot throughout Poland.

15. **Rabbi Yeshayahu Karelitz** (1878–1953), also known as the Hazon Ish, the title of his impressive and profound commentary on the *Shulhan Arukh* (Code of Jewish Law), was well versed in secular studies as well as Torah, a teacher of thousands, *the* halakhic authority of his generation, and a leader in attempts to apply Jewish law to the practical problems of modern Israel.

16. **Rabbi Ezekiel Ben Judah Landau** (1717–1793), also known as the Noda Bi-Yehuda, the title of his collection of over 860 rabbinic responsa, was rabbi of Prague and Bohemia.

17. **Rabbi Moses Sofer** (1762–1839), also known as the Hatam Sofer, was a rabbi in Pressburg, Hungary, where the famous yeshiva that he founded became the center of Orthodox opposition to the emerging Reform movement.

18. **Rabbi Akiva Ben Moses Guens Eger** (1761–1837), known for his modesty and humanity, was appointed chief rabbi of the Posen district in Germany, where he founded a prominent yeshiva; although a lifelong opponent of the Reform movement, he attempted to introduce modest changes into Orthodox Jewish life.

19. **Rabbi Elijah Ben Solomon Zalman** (1720–1797), popularly known as Elijah Gaon or the Vilna Gaon, is considered to be the most influential scholar in modern Jewish history; fearing the innovations and challenge to traditional values wrought by the emerging Hasidic movement, he fought to have it banned and suppressed.

20. **Rabbi Isaac Ben Judah Abrabanel** (1437–1508), virtually a Jewish renaissance man, wrote a major commentary on the Bible and served as the treasurer to King Alfonso V of Portugal.

21. **Rabbi Isaac Alfasi** (1013–1103), also known as the Rif, was an outstanding talmudist, whose code of laws was considered the most important legal compilation prior to Maimonides's *Mishneh Torah*.

22. **Rabbi Judah Ben Solomon Hai Alkalai** (1798–1878), a precursor of the religious Zionists, advocated the revolutionary concept of the return to Eretz Yisrael (the Land of Israel) as the first step in bringing the redemption of the world.

23. **Rabbi Israel Ben Eliezer** (c. 1700–1760), also known as the Baal Shem Tov (the Master of the Good Name) or the Besht, was the founder of modern Hasidism in Eastern Europe (see "10 Hasidic Masters").

24. **Rabbi Shlomo Ben Isaac** (1040–1105), known as Rashi, composed a monumental, detailed commentary on both the entire Bible and the entire Babylonian Talmud; concerned with the literal interpretation of the text, his commentaries are so universally studied that they have become almost integral to the text.

—J.B.S. and R.A.S.

10 HASIDIC MASTERS

"Hasidism" (Hebrew, *hasidut*) means devout piety, service to God and one's fellow human beings beyond the required norm. Although the term has applied to various religious revival movements in Judaism (the followers of the Maccabees, as well as the medieval German Jewish mystics were called *hasidim*), it is most often associated with the pietistic communities of Jews that arose in Poland, Russia, and Austria-Hungary in the eighteenth and nineteenth centuries, under the leadership of Hasidic masters called *tzaddikim* ("righteous" or "proven" men).

The late seventeenth century witnessed great spiritual and political turmoil for Eastern European Jews. Events such as the massacres of Jewry in the Ukraine in 1648, the abortive messianic movement of the deranged Turkish Jewish mystic Shabbatai Zevi in 1666, and the end of monarchy in Poland resulted in confusion, despair and considerable political and economic dislocation. As rabbinic authority began to crumble and the spiritual crisis among the people deepened these Jews found themselves badly in need of leadership.

The first *tzaddik,* and founder of Hasidism, was Israel ben Eliezer, known as the Baal Shem Tov (or "Besht" for short), a charismatic healer and preacher, who stressed to his followers the importance of serving God in joy and of "uplifting the sparks" of holiness found everywhere in one's daily life. This style represented on alternative both to the more somber, ascetic piety of the mystics of the time, and to the path of scholarly pedantry valued in the rabbinical courts.

The Besht's successor was Dov Baer, the Maggid ("Preacher") of Mezritch, who had come to Hasidism from a learned rabbinical career. Dov Baer was both a profound thinker and a capable organizer. He raised a generation of distinguished disciples, who spread out through Eastern Europe and preached so successfully that by 1814, when the last of these disciples died, the majority of Eastern European Jewry could be counted as adherents to Hasidism.

Hasidism began to decline, however, in the early nineteenth century, for two main reasons: (1) The Hasidim made peace with their opponents among the rabbinical and scholarly elite, tempering their more daring theological ideas, and accepting fuller communal and political responsibilities. (What had begun as an alternative now found itself part of the establishment.) (2) The Hasidim established dynasties in which the mantle of leadership passed in succession not to the Hasidic master's most capable disciple but to an elder son or a close relative, whose qualifications were not always the best available. Even so, Hasidism continued to be a significant force in Eastern European Jewish life until the destruction of European Jewry by the Nazis. Following the era of the Holocaust, only a few Hasidic dynasties were able to reestablish themselves as viable groups, resettling chiefly in the United States and Israel.

Some interpreters of Hasidism believe that the best approach to its world is through stories about the Hasidic masters. These stories convey something of the impact each master had on his followers and something of the experience of Hasidism as a way of life. Others insist that the stories are merely hagiographic embellishments rooted in common folklore, and that the best introduction to the world of the Hasidim is through their theoretical writings. Unfortunately, it is hard to determine how much even of this written material can be authentically attributed to a Hasidic master and how much was randomly associated with his name. Both stories and writings must be allowed to illuminate one another. Through careful reflection on each master's teachings and reported deeds, it is possible to eke out a sense of that *tzaddik*'s personality. The man and what one calls "his Torah" merge: Each *tzaddik* represents a particular embodiment of Torah; each is a unique system of thought and behavior that is capable of unified formulation as a "teaching," a spiritual way, a model to internalize. Some stressed joy; others, anguish. Some argued with God; others serenely surrendered to God. Some enjoyed human company; others became hermits. Some rooted for Napoleon; others for the Tsar. They have provided a precious set of punctuation marks for reality.

Israel ben Eliezer, the Baal Shem Tov, or "Besht" (1700–1760)

Born to poor and elderly parents in Okop, Podolia (south eastern Poland), Israel was orphaned as a child. In his youth he made a meager living as a *heder* (elementary religious school) teacher and synagogue caretaker. He married at eighteen, and for the next eighteen years he worked in a variety of trades, including school assistant and kosher slaughterer. His disciples, however, tell of how Israel surreptitiously wrought and encountered miracles during this phase of his life. He used to take the children in his care into the woods, entertaining them with songs and stories, and one day in those woods he saved them from Satan. Another time, a group of thieves offered to take him through an underground tunnel to the Holy Land, and a wall of fire rose up and separated him from them.

In his twenties, Israel withdrew into the Carpathian mountains, accompanied only by his wife, for seven years of solitary study and meditation. On his thirty-sixth birthday he determined to reveal his mystical powers. Prior to this time he had masqueraded as a simpleton and turned away those who had sought him out as a healer (rumors of his powers flowed from those who had managed to witness his bathing in the icy ritual bath on winter mornings or his fervent and meditative prayer). The day before his birthday a madman had been brought to him for cure. The next day, Israel agreed to attend to the ailing man.

He soon earned a reputation as "the Baal Shem Tov," the *good* theurgist, one not only adept at healing by incantations and the writing of amulets but also one possessed of outstanding spiritual attainment and wisdom. He taught a spiritual path radically different from the conventional piety of his time. In contrast to the morbid asceticism and esoteric kabbalistic practices current among the mystical elite, the Besht taught a method of joy and integration of one's worldly pursuits. For times of prayer he imparted meditations and homilies, accessible to the unlearned, about the power of prayer and the importance of each individual letter. Above all, he outlined methods of *deveykut,* "attachment" or communion with God, a notion articulated as far back as the Middle Ages, but one which received special emphasis in Hasidism.

Deveykut was not to be practiced only in prayer; it could infuse one's daily activities: eating, drinking, bargaining in the marketplace. An early Hasidic leader, Nachman of Kosov, is said to have rented his *deveykut*: He hired an assistant to follow him around and whisper an admonition to place God before him always, whenever he was out in the marketplace buying and selling grain. The Besht, on the other hand, tried to cultivate it as an *internal* faculty.

The Besht's talents were not poured into writing. Collections of his sayings were assembled by his followers, but he himself wrote nothing longer than a letter. His impact was primarily in the domain of teaching and personal example. Disciples told of his unconventional (for a pious Jew) behavior: telling stories in the marketplace during the hour of morning prayer, smoking his pipe and chatting with peasants at the time of evening prayer. Out of his life came a specific set of Hasidic doctrines that bear his personal stamp. He urged his followers to treat each word of prayer as a complete living being, to be prepared to surrender one's soul upon each letter. He showed how each action of one's daily business could be illuminated by a particular biblical verse or mystical intention.

Above all, he imparted an attitude of faith not dependent on a messianic redeemer: Instead of preaching an impending era of ecstasy, he spoke of cycles of ecstasy and ordinary vision that were a normal part of the human soul's life. In a famous letter to his brother-in-law, the Besht claimed that he had been addressed by the Messiah in a dream, who told him that he would arrive in the world "only when all Israel is capable of uniting the lower and upper worlds through prayer and meditation." In this manner he steadied the fires of religious fantasy then smoldering among the Jews of his time, and encouraged an involvement with the practical life.

Perhaps it is in the light of the foregoing that the following legendary incident must be understood: It is said that once, in a dream, the Besht met Shabbatai Zevi, the failed Messiah, who requested he heal him. At first, they established some connection, but then the Besht grew aware that Shabbatai was tempting him, and they wrestled. Shabbatai was forcefully cast into the underworld. Later, the Besht would say: "He had a spark of holiness in him, but his pride destroyed him."

The Besht was deeply attached to his wife. When she died, he claimed, "I had hoped to rise to heaven like Elijah in a storm of fire; but now I'm only half a body and cannot."

On the Psalm verse, "The Torah of the LORD is perfect," the Besht said, "It is still perfect; no one has touched it yet."

Jacob Joseph of Polnoye (d. 1782)

Rabbi Jacob Joseph was one of the closest and most gifted of the Besht's disciples, but for various reasons he did not succeed him as the leader of the Hasidic movement. According to Hasidic tradition, the Besht actively recruited Jacob Joseph by sending a disciple named Aryeh Leib to Jacob Joseph's town of Shargorod, to preach a Sabbath sermon. The sermon aroused Jacob Joseph's interest in the Besht and his teachings, and he sought out the Besht in the nearby town of Mohilev, where the latter was then visiting. Arriving on a Friday morning before prayer time, he found the Besht smoking his famous pipe, rather than studying or meditating—the typically "improbable" introduction frequently found in stories about the Besht. Jacob Joseph, in any case, was so moved by the prayers that, as he later reported, "I wept as I'd never wept in my whole life." And so, he became a disciple, raising hackles back home in Shargorod, where the Besht's style was not appreciated.

As a result of his conversion to Hasidism, Jacob Joseph was expelled from his rabbinical post in Shargorod (second largest city in Podolia) and was forced to serve in a number of smaller towns, ending with Polnoye, the town usually affixed to his name. Jacob Joseph's congregational troubles may also have flowed from clashes of personality: He was known for a bad temper, a factor which may also account for his inability (or unwillingness) to succeed the Besht, even though some believed he was the latter's truest disciple.

But unlike the Besht, Jacob Joseph did leave behind some important writings. A large volume of his sermons, the *Toldot Yaakov Yosef* is not only a key work for the theoretical understanding of Hasidism, it is a sensitive and incisive critique of the Jewish community of that era. It offered a panoramic view of the abuses then prevalent in synagogue and communal life: the gap between rich and poor, the idolatries of honor and status, the cupidity, materialism, and opportunism of rabbis, cantors, and slaughterers, the pretentiousness and irrelevance of legal erudition, the loose, immoral life-style of the well-to-do. Jacob Joseph's concerns seem strongly sociological and political, and his work is a valuable source for historians. Yet there is a sound and consistent religious doctrine at the heart of his critique, rooted in the symbolism of the Kabbalah.

Where the Besht had focused on the *deveykut* ("attachment") of the ordinary believer, Jacob Joseph posed as his particular subject the *tzaddik*, the Hasidic leader: his inner resources, his public image, his institutional importance, his cosmic function. Jacob Joseph's work is a virtual manual of spiritual leadership, as Machiavelli's *Prince* had been a manual of secular leadership. Exploring the models represented by Noah, Abraham, Jacob, Joseph, and Moses, the *Toldot* anatomized the role of the *tzaddik*, as recipient of a spiritual calling, as a source of holiness, as a bridge and channel between upper and lower worlds, as an embodiment of *deveykut*, as an institution, as the shaping form for inarticulate human spiritual yearnings, as a self-critical public servant, as a heavenly emissary on a mission of "descent" to redeem lost souls.

This was a vivid theoretical formulation of a new image of spiritual leadership, translating, in effect, the Besht's impact upon a loyal disciple into a programmatic model. At the same time there was, perhaps, the hidden personal signature of Jacob Joseph. In a manner that was a kabbalistic and Hasidic convention, his work played his name into a biblical quotation (Gen. 37:2), which, in context, seems to bridge two separate stories, that of Jacob and that of Joseph (". . . these were *the life-events of Jacob./Joseph* [meanwhile, was tending his brothers' sheepflocks, etc.] . . ."). Now, kabbalistically, "Jacob" was a symbolic name of the sixth emanation of God, called *Tiferet* ("Beauty"), the normal transcendent appearance of God in Scripture and prayer. "Joseph" was a name for the ninth emanation, called *Yesod* ("Foundation") or *Tzaddik* ("Righteous"), as in the biblical saying (Prov. 10:25): "The *tzaddik* is the foundation of the world."

This latter emanation is often associated with phallic and sexual symbolism ("Joseph" symbolizes both sexual restraint and sexual fulfillment, according to kabbalistic doctrine), as well as the sign of circumcision and Covenant. It characterizes the point in kabbalistic mythology where the masculine emanations of God unite with the feminine (the Shekhinah), the upper worlds with the lower, and the Holy One, Blessed be He, with Israel. This symbolic level underlies Rabbi Jacob Joseph's doctrine of the "descent" of the *tzaddik* (like Joseph into Egypt), i. e., the involvement of the Hasidic leader in the complicated give-and-take of the everyday world, and his care of those in need.

Dov Baer, the Maggid ("Preacher") of Mezritch (d. 1772)

Dov Baer had two careers: first as a scholar and kabbalist in the pre-Hasidic mold; then, as a Hasidic disciple and master. A frail man, weakened and diseased by ascetic practices, he first sought out the Besht for a cure. On his initial meeting with the Besht he found the latter (as the folktales delight in recounting) inexplicably mundane and foolish sounding. Later, the story goes, the Besht unexpectedly sent for him and asked him if he could expound a passage in the kabbalistic work *Etz Hayyim* ("Tree of Life") that dealt with angels. When the sage expounded the passage, the Besht said: "You have no true knowledge. Get up!" The Besht then expounded the same passage, and the room became engulfed in flames, and angels swirled about. The Besht then said to Dov Baer: "Your interpretations are correct, but there is no soul in what you say." Dov Baer became a disciple.

Actually, Dov Baer is said to have made only two visits to the Besht. The second time, he stayed for six months and absorbed most of the Besht's teachings. From thence, he became a *tzaddik* himself, and surrounded himself with disciples of exceptional intellectual and spiritual backgrounds. Unlike the itinerant Besht, the Maggid was a sedentary *tzaddik*, who gave discourses from his study table to a select inner circle. In a sense, the Maggid helped make Hasidism a two-tiered movement: an elite discipline of study, prayer, and meditation; a periodic "audience" of the *tzaddik* to the sick and the needy. This more magisterial conception of the *tzaddik* (or "*rebbe*," as the Hasidic leader also came to be called) changed the character of Hasidism to something quite different from that conceived by either the Besht or Rabbi Jacob Joseph.

It was the *torot*, the table teachings of the Maggid, for which he is most renowned. He never gave up the contemplative mysticism in which he had been trained: a type of piety going back to the mystics of Safed in the sixteenth century, which stressed the ascent of the soul and its gradual discarding of the garments of the material and animal world. Earlier mystics had usually portrayed this state as the goal of a mission to redeem Israel or specific Jewish communities or as the performance of *tikkun ha-olam* ("repair of the world"), the mystical regeneration of holiness and divine unity. Dov Baer, probably influenced by the Besht's emphasis on joyful service of God, stressed the importance of the ecstatic state as a spiritual joy in its own right, a transcendence of self-preoccupation and petty needs in ascent to the most profound degrees of divine self-unfolding.

In such a state, claimed the Maggid, the soul of the worshipper becomes like an empty tree through which the wind blows, a flute or harp played by God, a well or riverbed through which life flows. The Maggid himself must have conveyed some of this conception through the manner of his preaching, for a *maggid* (literally, "teller"), technically speaking, was someone who preached ecstatically, a kind of sybilline figure through whom emerged mystical speech like a voice from God. This style of self-surrender in some respects resembles practices of spiritualism and quietism prevalent in the left-wing Protestant world, such as those of the Ranters, Shakers, and Quakers, and in other respects resembles certain doctrines of Buddhism and Zen. The Maggid formulated his distinctive doctrine with imagery of "nothingness": "Nothing in the world can change from one reality to another unless it first turns into nothing, that is, into the reality of the between-stage. In that stage it is nothing and no one can grasp it, for it has reached the rung of nothingness, just as before creation. And then it is made into a new creature, from the egg to the chick. The moment when the egg is no more and the chick is not yet, is nothingness. And philosophy terms this the primal state which no one can grasp because it is a force which precedes creation; it is called chaos. It is the same with the sprouting seed. It does not begin to sprout until the seed disintegrates in the earth. . . ."

There was at least enough of the Besht lingering in the Maggid to allow him to speak on the lighter side about this same elusive translucency of spirit: "Said the Maggid to Reb Zusya, his disciple: 'I cannot teach you the ten principles of service. But a little child and a thief can show you what they are. From the child you learn three things: He is merry for no particular reason; Never for a moment is he idle; When he needs something, he demands it vigorously. The thief can instruct you in seven things: He does his service by night; If he does not finish what he has set out to do, in one night, he devotes the next night to it; He and those who work with him love one another; He risks his life for slight gains; What he takes has so little value for him that he gives it up for a very small coin; He endures blows and hardship, and it matters nothing to him; He likes his trade and would not exchange it for any other.' "

Elimelech of Lyzhansk (1717–1787)

A disciple of the Maggid, Elimelech lived principally in Galicia (southwestern Poland). He is the brother of the famous Rabbi Zusya ("When I get to heaven, they will not ask me 'Why were you not Moses?' they will ask me 'Why were you not Zusya?' "). Like Rabbi Jacob Joseph of Polnoye, Rabbi Elimelech wrote a considerable amount about the *tzaddik*, helping to fashion a well-articulated doctrine of "tzaddikism" that has been influential in Hasidism to the present day. Like Dov Baer, he exercised the *tzaddik*'s role, helping to shape it into a major institution in Jewish life: Following the Maggid's death, he headed a court financed by *pidyonot* ("ransoms"), tax payments accompanied by requests to the rabbis for prayers and remedies. These petitions, called *kvitlakh*, play a major role in Hasidic life today.

Elimelech himself followed an ascetic practice, like the pre-Hasidic mystics, although he acknowledged that such practice was not for everyone: "Some serve by eating; others by fasting," he would say. In his earlier years, he wandered with his brother Zusya from village to village, in symbolic identification with the wanderings of the Shekhinah (divine Presence). In his maturity, he spoke forcefully of the prerogatives of the *tzaddik*: "Each utterance of his creates an angel; the *tzaddik* decrees and God fulfills." And though he had insisted that a *tzaddik* must be a leader in all spheres of life besides the spiritual, in his old age he retreated to a regime of hermitage and contemplation.

One thinks of Rabbi Elimelech as shy, retiring, slightly built, laconic, decidedly melancholy, but with the corner of a smile and an understated wry wit. When struck hard by devotional fervor during the hour of prayer, he would check his watch and make sure he was really there.

Elimelech had a way of conveying more by silence than by speech. At the feast of Shavuot, he asked his disciples, "Could anything be lacking?" When a foolish youth amid his entourage cried out, "The wine of life that's drunk in Paradise!" Elimelech ordered him to fetch wine with two pails on a pole and not to talk to anyone outside. The young man managed to accomplish most of his mission, but upon reaching the house, he yelled out to the darkness, "Bogeyman! *Now* you can't do anything to me!" Instantly, the pole broke, the pails fell and cracked, and the young man felt himself struck in both cheeks. As he staggered into the house, Elimelech said, "Klutz! Sit down at the table."

Levi Yitzhak of Berditchev (1740–1810)

Next to the Besht, Rabbi Levi Yitzhak is one of the most beloved of Hasidic leaders, and the one who appears most frequently in fictional treatments of Hasidism: dozens of plays, stories, and poems exist that feature Levi Yitzhak as their hero. His most characteristic posture in popular memory is that of attorney at the heavenly bar—disputer, bargainer, and pleader with God in the tradition of Abraham, Moses, and Job. He is remembered for his compassion and gentleness, and for his willingness always to judge a person according to the scale of merit. Finding a young Jew standing and smoking in the street one Sabbath, Levi Yitzhak first asked him if he had forgotten that such an act was forbidden. The young man replied that he hadn't forgotten. Levi Yitzhak then asked if there was some mitigating circumstance that caused him to sin. The young man replied that he was sinning knowingly and voluntarily. The *tzaddik* then looked up to heaven and said, "Lord of the Universe, see the holiness of your people—they'd rather declare themselves sinners than utter a falsehood!"

Levi Yitzhak was born into a distinguished rabbinical family, his father a rabbi in Hoshakov, Galicia. Levi Yitzhak married into a wealthy family and had settled down to a life of scholarship, when he made the acquaintance of the *hasid* Schmelke of Nickolsburg, who won him over to the camp of the Hasidim. Levi Yitzhak then became a disciple of the Maggid of Mezritch, sitting as a member of his inner circle. Around this time differences between the Hasidim and their Orthodox opponents, the Mitnagdim, were becoming acute, and during the first thirteen years of his career as a Hasidic leader, Levi Yitzhak was driven from one pulpit to the next under attack by the Mitnagdim. In one case he had his house broken into, had his belongings stolen, was evicted, and was fired from his job in breach of contract: Fortunately, his next post, in Berditchev, went much better for him, and he served there without opposition for the last twenty-five years of his life.

Levi Yitzhak's rabbinical learning was considerable, although his opponents (strangely enough, from a present-day perspective) criticized his lack of kabbalistic knowledge. At times his style of conversation with God strikes one as talmudically disputateous, for example, the following: "Lord of the world, you must forgive Israel their sins. If you do this—good. But if not, I'll tell all the world that the phylacteries (*tefillin*) you wear are

A contemporary Hasidic* farbrangen *(gathering).
(Claudio Edinger)

invalid. What's the verse enclosed in your *tefillin*? A verse of David, your anointed king: 'Who is like thy people Israel, a unique nation on earth?' If you don't forgive Israel . . . [this] verse is untrue, and the *tefillin* are invalid."

Levi Yitzhak, in any case, did not need kabbalistic learning to attain the states of religious ecstasy for which he was also famous. Key words in the prayer services caused him to fly into such a frenzy of devotional fervor that often he would collapse into a catatonic state for hours. One visitor to his synagogue is alleged to have been driven into thirty days of uncontrollable laughter by watching Levi Yitzhak's bodily contortions in prayer. Levi Yitzhak is rumored to have put his hand through glass, held his fingers in a candle flame, danced atop a desk (and almost on a *megillah* scroll), fallen into a well, and upset a *seder* table, all without knowing what he was doing, during various acts of prayer. Of the various *tzaddikim,* he was probably the biggest insurance risk, next to Reb Nachman (see "Nachman of Bratslav" entry).

Levi Yitzhak talked, at various times during prayer, to the devil, one time telling him, "So if you're a *hasid,* too, and well-versed in the prayers, speak the prayers yourself."

Though gentle in his criticism, he never hesitated to rebuke those who fell away in their devotion. One time, he surprised two congregants, who had been talking for hours, by suddenly welcoming them to *shul* (synogogue). When they asked why just then he chose to welcome them, he replied "You've been far away, no? You in a marketplace, and you on a ship with a cargo of grain; when it grew quiet here, you came back. Welcome back!" Another time, he congratulated an influential evildoer on the street, saying, "Sir, I envy you! When you turn to God, each of your flaws will become a ray of light . . . I envy your flood of radiance!" Another time, he shouted to a busy marketplace from a rooftop, "You people are forgetting to fear God!"

He once espoused what today would be a feminist cause. Discovering that the women who kneaded the dough in the bakeries and matzah factories worked at terrible drudgery from early morning to late at night; he addressed a rebuke on the subject to his congregation: "The enemies of Israel accuse us of baking unleavened bread with the blood of Christians. But no, we bake them with the blood of Jews!"

Disputation with God finally killed him. On his last New Year observance, they were unable to blow the *shofar.* Levi Yitzhak cried, "Lord of the world, if we are denied the opportunity to fulfill your command, let Ivan the Gentile blow the ram's horn for you!" Whereupon, applying his own lips to the *shofar,* he blew a flawless sound. Afterward, he said, "I vanquished Satan, but it will cost me my life; I am a sin-offering for Israel." Shortly thereafter, he died.

Levi Yitzhak to God, ". . . You! You! You! Sky is you! Earth is you! You above! You below! Only You, You again, always You! You! You! You!"

Shneur Zalman, ("The Rav") of Liadi (1745–1813)

Rabbi Shneur Zalman is the founder of the Lubavitcher movement in Hasidism, one of the most militant and energetic present-day Hasidic communities. The Lubavitcher Hasidim maintain outposts on college campuses and in Jewish communities as remote as North Africa, and tirelessly campaign to encourage assimilated Jews to perform at least token rituals of prayer and Jewish practice. They are regarded as the most tolerant of Hasidim toward non-Hasidic practice, but they frequently couple this easygoing outlook with persistent pressures upon the non-Hasidic Jew to adopt a more Hasidic practice. "If you're not moving up the ladder," one Lubavitch teacher said recently, "you're moving down." A member of a rival school of Hasidism characterized a Lubavitcher as follows: "If he sees you drowning, he'll jump in to save you, even at the risk of his own life."

Shneur Zalman was a disciple of the Maggid of Mezritch and a close companion and pupil of the Maggid's son, the ascetic Rabbi Abraham "the Angel." The year of the Maggid's death (1772) began the period of open war between the Hasidim and the Mitnagdim. The Hasidim came under sharp attack for their alleged disdain of study, their disparagement of the scholars, their contortions in prayer, their formation of separate prayer rooms (*shtiblach*), their introduction of new customs in the prayerbook, their rival standards of kosher slaughtering. Shneur Zalman participated in a delegation to the Gaon of Vilna to seek a reconciliation. The attempt failed, and the controversy dragged on for another thirty years.

By choice or by assignment, Shneur Zalman brought Hasidism to White Russia, a region adjacent to Lithuania, the center of rabbinical scholarship and of opposition to Hasidism. One of the most intellectually gifted of the Maggid's disciples, Shneur Zalman developed an intellectual school of Hasidism known as "Habad" (an abbreviation, "HBD," for *Hokhmah, Binah, Da'at,* "Wisdom, Understanding, Knowledge," three upper emanations of God), a system blending the teachings of the Maggid with the kabbalistic doctrines of Isaac Luria. A basic compendium of Habad thought is Shneur Zalman's work the *Tanya* ("It is taught . . ."), published in 1797.

This work's emergence provoked one more bitter attack from the Mitnagdim, who denounced him to the tsarist authorities as one supporting a war effort of Turkey against Russia. He was consequently held in prison for several months but was finally released on the 19th of Kislev, 1798, a day still celebrated by Lubavitch Hasidim as a major holiday. Despite his unhappy experience, he later supported the Tsar against Napoleon, claiming, "If Bonaparte wins, the economic and political status of the Jews will improve, and the hearts of Israel will be drawn away from their father in heaven."

From the *Tanya*: "This is the meaning of the statement in the Zohar that 'The Torah, the Holy One, blessed be He, [and Israel] are one': The commandments are the innermost Supreme Will and God's true desire, which are clothed in the upper and nether worlds. . . . It follows that the performance of the commandments and their fulfillment is the innermost garment of the innermost Supreme Will, since it is this performance that induces the light and life of the Supreme Will to be clothed in the worlds."

To his interrogator in prison, who asked him to explain the biblical verse: "God said to Adam: 'Where art thou?' " Shneur Zalman replied, "In every era, God calls to every person: 'Where are you in your world? Thus many years and days allotted to you have passed, and how far along are *you*?' "

Yaakov Yitzhak ("The Seer") of Lublin (1745–1815)

Rabbi Yaakov Yitzhak was best described by another *hasid* as "everyone's master." He has had, according to one reckoning, over 188 disciples who became Hasidic leaders, including many founders of dynasties that have lasted into the present century. He was called "the Seer" after his death, because of his reputed ability to discern a person's entire history by looking at the piece of paper on which that person's petition (problem or question) was written. He also had a right eye larger than the left, which gave his vision an uncanny gaze and may have contributed to the impression of him as a "seer."

The "Seer" apparently preferred to devote

his energies more to the practical care of his followers and petitioners than to their education in spritual matters. The *tzaddik's* first task, according to him, was to provide for the livelihood of his flock—material well-being was a prerequisite to spiritual development. Some stayed away from his court, believing it was too immersed in worldly affairs. Nonetheless, he continued to be deluged with petitions.

Napoleon's invasion of Russia was thought by the Seer and many of his contemporaries to be the beginning of the war between Gog and Magog, the final battle before the era of the Messiah, foretold in Ezekiel 38. On two occasions the Seer is said to have tried to bring on the Messiah more directly. On the first he chose four important disciples, representing four major regions of Eastern Europe, and engaged with them in prayer and mystical meditation to hasten redemption. This attempt, on the first Passover *seder* of 1813, turned out disastrously: ritual objects were lost, disputes broke out, and their respective ceremonies were thoroughly disrupted. One disciple did manage to conduct his *seder* without trouble, but because he did so in Hungarian, rather than Hebrew, it was believed to have been unheard in Heaven. Hasidic tradition ascribes these mishaps to the work of Satan.

The Seer's second attempt was Simhat Torah of the following year. During the festivities the Seer went into his study, intending to stay there only briefly. When he failed to come out, his disciples began to wonder what had happened. When they opened the door, he was not there. Two hours later a *hasid* out for a walk discovered him lying outside badly hurt. He told his followers that Satan had thrown him out the window of his study for trying to hasten the messianic redemption. The Seer never fully recovered and died ten months later on the 9th of Ab, the anniversary of the Temple's destruction and the alleged birthday of the future Messiah.

One thinks of the Seer, however, engaged in more prosaic acts of redemption. He attended to hospitality with great devotion, encouraged followers not to succumb to depression, and maintained a liberal position about the paths of service: "It's impossible to tell people the way they should take. One way is through learning, another through prayer, another through fasting, and still another through eating and drinking. One should carefully observe which way his heart is drawn, then choose his way with all his strength."

One day, on his way to a ritual bathing with Rabbi Barukh of Medzhibozh, the Besht's grandson, the Seer was asked by Rabbi Barukh, "What do you see?" He answered, "The fields of the Holy Land." "What do you smell?" he was asked. "The air of the Temple Mount." And when they dipped in the stream, Rabbi Barukh asked, "What do you feel?" The Seer replied, "The healing stream of Paradise."

Yaakov Yitzhak of Przysucha, "The Holy Jew" (1766–1814)

A disciple of his namesake, Yaakov Yitzhak "The Seer" of Lublin, the younger Yaakov Yitzhak began as a close adherent and trusted pupil of his master and was appointed as spiritual advisor to a number of the younger students in the Seer's circle. Gradually the apprentice master and his young followers grew disenchanted with the Seer's practical style and complained that the primary duty of a Hasid was self-perfection through study and prayer, and that of a *tzaddik*, the spiritual care and training of his disciples. They broke away from the Seer and formed their own circle, which was the nucleus of what came to be called "Polish Hasidism," one of several attempts to revitalize Hasidism and return it to its former high spiritual goals.

The new circle manifested a renewed interest in study of Talmud, probably more for intellectual and spiritual rather than legalistic matters, and in the tradition of the Safed mystics of the sixteenth century, placed emphasis on spiritual preparation for individual rituals and religious commandments. Correct practice as prescribed in the legal codes was considered less important than taking ample time to develop a proper frame of mind for one's action. Forty years earlier the rabbis had attacked the Hasidim for their long delays in prayer; now, the practice was taken up again, self-consciously and in great seriousness.

The younger Yaakov Yitzhak earned the nickname "The Jew," according to Hasidic legend, on one of his periodic peregrinations to find the prophet Elijah, who was widely believed to be wandering the world in the guise of a peasant. On this occasion, he met a villager leading a mare by the rein, and said to his companion, "There he is!" The man exclaimed, "Jew! If you know, why let your tongue wag?" From then on, Yaakov Yitzhak was called "the Jew," and later "the holy Jew."

The Jew was said to have been a man of serene temperament, acknowledged by his teacher the Seer as a man who could not grow angry. One disciple of his claimed that the main thing he had learned from the Jew was how to sleep: "When I get into bed, I fall asleep instantly." The spiritual basis for this serenity is best described by the Jew himself in the following, one of his most striking recorded sayings: "One day, it dawned on me that one can't attain perfection by one's learning alone. I understood what is told of our father Abraham: that he explored the sun, moon and stars, and did not find God, and in this very not-finding, the presence of God was revealed to him. For three months, I mulled over his realization; then I explored until I, too, reached the truth of not-finding."

Nachman of Bratslav (1772–1811)

Rabbi Nachman was the great-grandson of the founder of Hasidism, the Besht. He possessed a richly mythopoetic sensibility, embodied most of all in his highly original interpretations of the Torah and in the strange, dreamlike tales—allegories of the journey of the soul in this world—for which he is most famous. These tales express rich psychological insights and comprise a highly suggestive body of mythical material, which students of myth, symbol, and analytic psychology have found worthy of close study.

Rabbi Nachman's version of Hasidism is idiosyncratic, centered in the unigue, complex personality of Nachman himself. The main body of Hasidic doctrine, promulgated by the Maggid and his disciples, had stressed a serenely contemplative devotional state, a pantheistic confidence in the unity of the world and God. Rabbi Nachman, by contrast, was preoccupied with the gap separating God from a part of Himself, the immanent aspect of divinity in the world from the transcendant God who is addressed in prayer. He thus made frequent use of the teachings of Isaac Luria, who had been preoccupied with the origins of evil and division in the world.

Rabbi Nachman's teachings were by no means serene. They reflected a turbulent sense of the chaos of the created world and of the paradoxes of faith that the Jew must embody in his own person. To Nachman, the world appeared as a topsy-turvy cauldron of constant, chaotic motion, through which the hero of faith must move, armed only with the paradoxical conviction that God is one, despite appearances. One scholar of Hasidism has called Nachman's system of belief "existential Hasidism."

Nachman himself led a turbulent life: an almost violently ascetic youth, a succession of congregational posts, painful quarrels with his fellow Hasidim, an eventful and adventurous journey to Constantinople and Palestine, and even, according to one legend of his life, a meeting with Napoleon. Toward the end of his life, he devoted himself to converting the *maskilim*, the "enlighteners," (modernized, assimilated Jews) back to a more traditional Jewish faith and practice.

Nachman's restless desire to bridge all worlds eventually exhausted his strength, and he died at the age of thirty-eight. Toward the end of his life, believing his theoretical teachings to be but "dry bones," he began telling his beautiful symbolic tales, designed to transform the complex world that the Jewish mystics had described in highly technical kabbalistic terms into childlike fables, accessible to common people. But the tales, as contemporary Jewish writer Elie Wiesel has suggested, often resemble those of that latter-day Jewish maker of parables, Franz Kafka. If they are childlike, they are also complex and cryptic. His followers believe they contain many profound mysteries.

It is sometimes said that a *tzaddik*'s greatest teaching is also his greatest hangup. Rabbi Nachman, who so often wrestled with melancholy, and who believed his anguish to be a primary means of devotional service, frequently counseled his followers to remain joyful and to fight depression. A book called *Meshivat Nafesh* ("Restorer of the Soul") consists of gleanings of his teachings on melancholy, to be used as a kind of spiritual smelling salts as the need provoked. In the Bratslaver synagogue that once stood in the Warsaw Ghetto was posted the motto: *Gevalt, Yidn, zayt zhe nisht meyaesh*! ("Jews! For heaven's sake, don't despair!")

From Rabbi Nachman's *Collected Sayings*: "When God decided to create, there was no place in which to create a world; everything was endless God! So He withdrew His light . . . thus creating an empty space. Within the 'empty space,' He brought forth all that exists in time and space. This 'empty space' can't be understood or grasped until the final revelation in the future. For two contradictory statements apply to it, an 'is' and an 'is not.' . . . There is, as it were, no God there . . . But in the truth of truth, God *must* be there, as well. The philosophers try to raise and answer questions that come from the 'empty space,' and get stuck there. . . . But Israel, through faith, transcends all such false 'wisdom' . . . Jews are believers in God without any philosophical investigation, just by wholeness of faith . . . in Him who both surrounds all worlds and fills all worlds—and thus do they transcend the 'empty space.' "

Rabbi Nachman recorded his dreams, as well, and reported them to his followers. In one such dream, he relates, "I was in a boundless forest. I wanted to return. . . . And one of you showed me a way to a garden . . . and said: *Without you, the letters inscribed in every scroll inside every Ark would be separated from the spirit that animates them . . . and the words would be as meaningless as the languages of the Tower of Babel . . .*"

Bratslaver Hasidism flourishes today, but these Hasidim are unique in acknowledging no living leader as their *rebbe*, but only Reb Nachman himself. For this reason they are sometimes called "the Dead Hasidim," but in fact their master is alive and well in his writings and in the zeal of his disciples.

Menachem Mendel of Kotzk (1787–1859)

The Kotzker Rebbe, as he is commonly known, was one of the most original and controversial figures in the history of Hasidism. He began as a disciple of "the Jew" of Przysucha and his so-called "Polish school" of Hasidism. Taking their teachings in an extreme direction, the Kotzker sought to form a small spiritual elite of Hasidim who could live with a radical and uncompromising demand for "truth" in the service of God. He is quoted as saying, "If I only had fifty disciples who could stand on the rooftops with me and acknowledge with absolute sincerity that God is the Lord of the Universe—for then, the Messiah would come!"

The Kotzker's search for capable disciples, however, apparently was not successful, and in 1839 he withdrew into his study and remained there for the last twenty years of his life. The reasons for this seclusion are unclear and surrounded by legend. Either prior to his withdrawal or on his deathbed, he is reputed to have said, "There is no Judgment and no Judge."

The Kotzker wrote no books, but there are innumerable short anecdotes and aphorisms purporting to represent his teachings. These statements are pithy and eminently quotable: "Killing of the ego is the truest sacrifice." "Everything in the world can be imitated except truth; truth that is imitated is no longer truth." "When one puts on a reverent face before One who has no face—this is idol worship." "What's all this talk about praying 'earnestly?' . . . Is there anything at all one shouldn't do earnestly?" "God dwells wherever a person lets Him in." "The Castle is burning, but it has a Lord." "Everything that people experience as puzzling and confused is called God's 'back.' But no one can see God's face, where everything is in harmony." "A wonder-worker can make a *golem*; but can he make a *hasid*?" And finally, perhaps his most characteristic teaching: "If I am I because I am I, and you are you because you are you, then I am I and you are you. But if I am I because you are you, and you are you because I am I, then I am not I and you are not you."

—M.M.F. and J.R.

JEWISH BANS OF EXCOMMUNICATION

While almost unknown in Jewish life today, excommunication (one of the meanings of *herem* in Hebrew) was once prevalent as the ultimate means of enforcing religious and communal authority. There are four distinct phases in the meaning and use of *herem*: the biblical era, the rabbinic period, the medieval and early-modern periods, and the modern period.

Biblical era (to 300 B.C.E.)

The Jewish Bible contains only one explicit reference to the use of excommunication against individuals (Ezra 10:8). Instead, the word *herem* almost always refers to the tribes that the Israelites tried to conquer on their way to or in Canaan (Palestine), as well as their cities, gods, and possessions. With the exception of children and virginal women, these tribes were to be annihilated, their cities and idols destroyed, and their cattle left untouched and unconfiscated. All were seen as carrying an active, *contagious* corruption; for that reason, even captured possessions were made "devoted" (*heherim*) to God.

In the prophetic books, disputes over *herem* twice initiated a military or political crisis. The first occurred following the Israelite conquest of Jericho, before which Joshua had ordered: "The city and everything in it are to be proscribed [*heherim*] for the Lord; only Rahab the harlot is to be spared, and all who are with her in the house, because she hid the messengers [i. e. spies] we sent. But you must beware of that which is proscribed, or else you will be proscribed: if you take anything from that which is proscribed, you will cause the camp of Israel to be proscribed; you will bring calamity upon it." (Josh. 6:17–18)

When a man named Achan of the tribe of Judah failed to follow this command—"I saw among the spoil a fine Shinar mantle, two hundred shekels of silver, and a wedge of gold weighing fifty shekels, and I coveted them and took them" (Josh. 7:20)—the Israelites were punished collectively by being defeated in their attempt to capture the encampment of Ai. A lot was taken to determine who was responsible for this defeat; when it indicated Achan, he confessed and, along with his family, was stoned.

A dispute over the application of *herem* also played an important part in the relationship between the prophet Samuel and Saul, the first king of Israel. Before entering the Land of Israel after leaving Egypt, the Israelites had been ordered to "blot out the memory of Amalek," the nation which "surprised you on the march, when you were famished and weary, and cut down all the stragglers in your rear." (Deut. 25:18–19; see Exod. 17:8–16 for the incident referred to)

The opportunity for doing so did not arrive until Saul's time. Through the mouth of Samuel, God ordered the king to "attack Amalek and proscribe all that belongs to him." After defeating the Amalekites, Saul "proscribed all the people, putting them to the sword; but Saul and the troops spared Agag [the Amalekite king] and the best of the sheep, the oxen, the second born, the lambs, and all else that was of value." (I Sam. 15:3, 8–9) God thereupon confessed to Samuel that "I regret that I made Saul king" (I Sam. 15:11). Samuel rebuked Saul, who insisted he had only taken the animals to sacrifice them to God. After being rebuked again by Samuel, the king admitted he had been wrong to disobey God and asked for forgiveness. The prophet responded by tearing Saul's robe (a symbol of majesty), leaving the king to plead for his honor. (I Sam. 15:14–30).

Only after Samuel had killed Agag did the two men leave each other's presence. They were not reconciled. This breach over *herem* was so serious that the incident concluded on this note: "Samuel never saw Saul again to the day of his death. But Samuel grieved over Saul, because the Lord regretted that

He had made Saul king over Israel" (I Sam. 15:35).

Two generations after the reign of Saul, the Israelites' practice of *herem* against their enemies fell into disuse. In fact, Solomon, ever the military pragmatist, impressed into his forces those Canaanites who had survived the wars of settlement. However, as biblical historian Yehezkel Kaufman has observed: "Terrible as it was, the *herem* had important social and religious consequences. [The people] Israel did not assimilate the indigenous population [of Canaan]. At the same time, it [*herem*] provided Israel's new religious idea with an environment in which to grow free of a popular pagan culture."

Rabbinic period (300 B.C.E.–500 C.E.)

During this period, when the Talmud was compiled and edited, the outstanding Jewish rabbis and scholars developed elaborate rules of personal conduct. Excommunication now referred to the "banning" or "anathema" of individuals within the Jewish community. It was imposed on three levels:

Nezifah ("severing")—the voluntary self-isolation for one to seven days of an individual who had insulted a scholar or communal leader and had been rebuked by him.

Niddui ("isolation")—banishment from communal life for seven to thirty days, imposed by a Jewish court (*Bet Din*) or by a prominent individual.

Herem ("banishment" or "anathema")—banishment from communal life for an indefinite period, which followed if the offender did not mend his ways while in *niddui*.

As catalogued by Maimonides in his twelfth-century *Mishneh Torah,* there are twenty-four reasons why a person can be placed in *niddui,* including (1) insulting a scholar, even after his death, (2) keeping dangerous dogs without properly guarding them, (3) the butcher's failure to have periodically inspected the sharpness of knives used for ritual slaughter, (4) causing *Hillul ha-Shem* ("desecration of the God's Name") through conduct that brings shame or embarassment to the community, (5) imposing *niddui* on someone without sufficient grounds for doing so. As the latter reason indicates, the power to excommunicate was sometimes abused by those seeking to mute their rivals, stifle dissent, or settle personal scores.

Niddui and *herem* did not involve a formal judicial process. While the offender had to be warned, the accuser was not required to bring formal evidence against him. While *niddui* was pronounced with a short formula, the pronouncement of *herem* was often accompanied by extensive imprecations.

The person in *niddui* (the *menuddeh*) or in *herem* (the *mehuram*) had to conduct himself as a mourner. He could only wash his face, hands, and feet, and could not cut his hair, wear fresh clothes or shoes indoors; nor could he be counted in the *minyan* (ten-man quorum for prayer) or *muzumin* (three-man quorum for the grace after meals). While the *menuddeh* was permitted to attend services or study with a rabbi, the *mehuram* was totally isolated: Even his family was required to sit three cubits from him during meals. A person who died while in *niddui* or *herem* also faced the posthumous humiliation of the "donkey's burial:" his casket was stoned, spat upon and otherwise reviled.

While *niddui* could be pronounced privately or in a *Bet Din, herem* involved a public ritual. The offender was first warned three times: on a Monday, Thursday, and the following Monday. If he did not mend his ways, the writ of excommunication was drawn up and read during synagogue services on a Monday, Thursday, or Saturday (the days on which the Torah is read). As witnesses holding wax candles watched, a rabbi or community leader, holding a Torah scroll, announced the offender's sins and his banishment from the community. Following the reading of the writ of excommunication, a *shofar* (ram's horn) was blown and the candles extinguished. Shortly thereafter, the Jewish authorities posted proclamations announcing the excommunication. Their intent was not only to publicly censure but to reassert their authority against a heretical or otherwise unruly individual.

Medieval and early-modern periods (500–1648)

During the medieval and early-modern periods, the pronouncement of *herem* (from this point on, the term *herem* will be used for both *niddui* and *herem*) became more the prerogative of the *kehilla* (Jewish communal governing body) and less that of rabbis and other religious figures. *Herem* was also imposed for a wider variety of reasons than in the past, including:

• *To enforce intellectual or religious conformity. Herem* was sometimes applied to books as well as to individuals. For example, in the early fourteenth century, the rabbis of Toledo and Castile, Spain, placed Maimonides's *Guide to the Perplexed* in *herem* for its attempt to find a rational basis for revelation.

• *To regulate economic and political affairs.* During the late Middle Ages the Jewish authorities in what is now Turkey prohibited price fixing under threat of *herem*. Numerous *kehillot* in Europe also banned additional Jews from entering a community (*herem ha-yishuv*), thereby reducing economic competition and curbing anti-Semitism.

- *To limit Jewish-Christian contact,* which was seen as leading to intermarriage, apostasy, and assimilation. In 1281 the Jewish authorities in Toledo proclaimed *herem* against all men having relationships with non-Jewish women.
- *To assert the Jewish community's authority against Christian or temporal rulers.* When in 1407 King Ruprecht of the Holy Roman Empire chose one Rabbi Israel of Krems as his *Hochmeister* (ruler of the Jews and collector of royal taxes), the majority of German rabbis excommunicated Rabbi Israel to protest the government appointment of a rabbinic authority. Ruprecht in turn declared this use of *herem* null and void, and fined those who recognized its legitimacy.
- *To raise funds.* In 1476 when rabbis meeting at the Frankfurt synod sought to raise substantial funds as a "gift" for Emperor Frederick III to secure his good will following a ritual murder charge, they asked Rabbi Joseph Colon of Mantua to issue an appeal on their behalf. In making his appeal to communal leaders throughout Europe, Rabbi Colon threatened to impose *herem* on those who did not gather funds.

In the generally small, united, "closed" (nonpluralist) communities of medieval and early-modern Jewry, the devastating effect of being placed in *herem* can hardly be exaggerated. A person who was excommunicated could not perform his basic religious obligations and was often economically ruined as well. In the words of the Israeli historian Jacob Katz, "The person excommunicated lost, in his own consciousness, the world in which he had existed—this world as well as the next."

Modern period (1648—)

Following the devastating Chmielnitski massacres of 1648, Jewish life became increasingly fragmented through new heretical, religious, and secular movements. Beginning with the false Messiahs Shabbatai Zevi and Jacob Frank (who ultimately converted to Islam and Catholicism, respectively) and continuing through the *Haskalah* (Jewish Enlightenment), Reform Judaism, and Zionism, all these movements were placed in *herem* by one or more "mainstream" Jewish leaders. In short, excommunication was used as part of a rearguard campaign to maintain the essential unity of *klal Yisrael* (the entirety of the Jewish people). It was an effort, however, that was doomed to fail, due to both Jewish and non-Jewish developments.

With the steady augmentation of centralized state power, many *kehillot* lost the ultimate power of excommunication. For example, as early as 1671 the *Cattaveri* (ecclesiastical authorities in Venice) took away from Jewish leaders the authority of imposing *herem*.

Also, the Enlightenment doctrine of freedom of conscience influenced Jewish thought as well, most notably in the writing of Moses Mendelssohn. In his introduction to Manesseh Ben Israel's *Vindiciae Judaeocum* (1782), this first major *Haskalah* philosopher opposed the institution of *herem*. An Orthodox Jew, as well as a friend of Lessing's (German dramatist and philosopher)—he was probably the model for "Nathan the Wise"—Mendelssohn insisted that religion, as opposed to statecraft, must be free of coercion.

Above all, the impact of *herem* was vitiated by the growing secularization of Jewish life. In the nineteenth and twentieth centuries Jews attempted, in a bewildering variety of ways, to synthesize "Jewish" modes of being. In this modern context, in which for many Jews a person's Jewishness is assumed voluntarily and doubt is intertwined with faith, *herem* would seem to be an anachronistic, inappropriate instrument for forcing obedience to commandments or to a belief system.

This is not to imply that excommunication has disappeared from modern Jewish life. When the American Reform rabbis who drafted the Pittsburgh Platform (1886) or Mordecai Kaplan, the founder of the new, twentieth-century movement known as Reconstructionism, proclaimed their belief in the God "idea" instead of the personal, conventional God of traditional Judaism, a number of Orthodox rabbis placed them in *herem*. Similarly, a number of squabbling Hasidic sects have excommunicated each other. What is striking, however, is how little all of this has seemed to matter. Perhaps not since the Vilna Gaon's *herem* against Hasidism (see below) has the excommunication of an individual or group captured the attention of a large number of Jews. Today, *herem* is rarely invoked, and even when it is, it does not constitute a "ban" so much as a form of strong protest or public censure.

FOUR EXAMPLES OF HEREM

Eliezer ben Hyrcanus (late first and early second centuries). A disciple of Jochanan ben Zakkai at the famous Palestinian academy of Yavneh and an outstanding scholar, Eliezer ben Hyrcanus was the only rabbi in the Talmud who was placed in *herem*. The story is told in tractate *Baba Metziah*: Eliezer was debating with other rabbis concerning the purity of an oven belonging to a man named Aknai. His arguments being of no avail, he resorted to supernatural "proof-texts." As the Talmud tells it: "He said to them: 'If the *halakhah* [Jewish law] agrees with me, let the carob tree prove it,' whereupon the carob tree was torn a hundred cubits out of its place. . . . He said to them [after they were still not convinced], 'If the *halakhah* agrees with me, let it be proved from heaven,' whereupon a *bat kol* [heavenly voice] cried out 'Why do you dispute with Eliezer, seeing that in all matters the *halakhah* agrees with him.' Rabbi Joshua arose and said, 'It [the deciding of *halakhic* disputes] is not in heaven; we pay no attention to a *bat kol*, for it is written in the Torah at Mount Sinai: One must follow the majority." (*Baba Metziah* 59b)

The passage goes on to inform us that on that same day, all objects that Rabbi Eliezer had declared pure were brought and burned, after which the colleagues proceeded to excommunicate Eliezer himself. After his death many regretted what they had done and declared him one of the greatest teachers of his age.

Uriel da Costa (1585–1640). Born into a Marrano family, Uriel da Costa became a minor church official in his adopted city of Amsterdam. After studying the Bible as a young man he decided to convert to Judaism.

From the time of his conversion, however, Uriel da Costa held heterodoxical views. For his 1624 work *Examen des Tradicoens Phariseas Conferidas con a Ley Escrita*, he was excommunicated by the elders of the Amsterdam Jewish community.

In 1633 he renounced his earlier views and rejoined the Jewish community. Yet da Costa soon openly espoused a deist philosophy, gave up Jewish rituals, and even tried to dissuade two Christian acquaintances from converting to Judaism. Denounced by his own nephew of violating *kashrut* (the Jewish dietary laws), he was placed in *herem* a second time.

Seven years later the ever-wavering da Costa again sought to join the Amsterdam Jewish community. To do so, he was forced to endure the humiliating ritual described in his autobiographical work *Exemplar Humanae Vitae*—an excerpt from which follows. Shortly after writing this work and presumably overcome by shame, he committed suicide.

"No sooner had I heard my sentence than I was fired with indignation and resentment. However, withholding my anger as well as I could, I answered only that I could not consent to undergo such a severe sentence. They consulted together and proceeded to excommunicate a second time. But not content with this, many of them spit upon me as they passed me in the streets and encouraged their children to do likewise. The only reason why they did not stone me was because they wanted power. This persecution lasted for a period of seven years, and should I relate all that I suffered it would seem incredible. For two parties violently persecuted me—the whole Jewish community and my family who sought their revenge in my disgrace. Nor would they be satisfied until they got me into their own power and jurisdiction, saying among themselves: 'He is stubborn. He will do nothing until he is forced to, and therefore ought to be compelled.' When I was sick nobody would attend me. If I suffered any other misfortune, it became a triumph and joy to them; if I proposed any one of them to act as judge between us the proposal was rejected. When I attempted to lay the whole case before a public magistrate, I found it very tedious and difficult, for judicial proceedings are at best both expensive and dilatory.

"During these troubles they would often exhort me to submit, saying, 'We are all your fathers and therefore you need not fear that we shall act unfairly or unkindly toward you. Only say that you are ready to perform whatever we ask of you, leave the rest to us and all shall be made easy.' This was the very point in dispute, and I understood how disgraceful it would be to surrender out of discretion and depend upon their mercy. Yet I wanted to put an end to this long affair and after much reluctance I prevailed upon myself to submit to their terms and to test their honor. For I argued with myself thus: If they deal dishonorably with me they will stand convicted by their own behavior and exhibit their implacable enmity toward me and how little they are to be trusted. At length this execrable and detested people did plainly show what their religion and principles are by treating men of honor and character as though they had been the vilest slaves. In a word, I said to them, 'I depend upon your mercy and I am ready to undergo whatsoever you are pleased to impose upon me.' Now let every man of truth and humanity observe my situation and judge the sentence which a particular set of people, under foreign jurisdiction, passed upon an innocent man.

"I entered the synagogue which was filled with curious spectators of both sexes. At the appointed time I walked up to the reading desk which was in the center and with a clear voice read aloud the form of confession which they had drawn up for me, namely, that I deserved to die a thousand deaths for the crimes I had committed such as the profanation of the Sabbath, the breach of my religious vows, etc., which I had carried so far as to dissuade others from being converts to Judaism. To atone for these violations I submitted to their sentence and was ready to undergo whatever they wished to lay upon me, promising not to be guilty of similar crimes in the future. When I had finished the reading I stepped down from the desk. The chief elder came up to me and, whispering in my ear, bid me go to a certain corner of the synagogue. When I had done this, the doorkeeper asked me to strip. Accordingly I stripped myself down to the waist, tied a kerchief about my head, pulled off my shoes and, holding up my arms above my head, clasped a kind of pillar in my hands, to which the doorkeeper tied them with a rope. Having thus prepared myself for my punishment, the verger stepped forward and with a scourge of leather thongs gave me nine and thirty stripes, according to the Jewish custom (it was a legal commandment that the number of stripes shall not exceed forty) for these very scrupulous and pious gentlemen take due care not to offend by overstepping their bounds. During the period of my whipping they sang a psalm. Then I was ordered to sit down on the ground whereupon an elder came forward and absolved me from my excommunication. So now the gates of heaven which were doubly locked and barred against me were suddenly flung wide open. O the ridiculous ideas and conceits of mortals! After this I dressed and went to the entrance of the synagogue where I prostrated myself. The doorkeeper held up my head while everyone, both young and old, passed over me, stepping with one foot on the lower part of my legs and making ridiculous gestures, more like monkeys than human beings. After they had all done this I got up and, being washed and made clean by a man who stood near me for that purpose, I went home."

Baruch de Spinoza (1632–1677). The founder of modern biblical criticism and the leading Jewish thinker of the seventeenth century, Spinoza endured what is almost certainly the best known excommunication in Jewish history. After a campaign against Spinoza's "evil opinions and acts" initiated by his brother-in-law, Samuel de Caceres, he was formally placed in *herem* in 1656 by the same Rabbi Monteira who had presided over the da Costa case. At the time, Spinoza was all of twenty-four. Among other things, the brilliant young philosopher had questioned the existence of angels, the immortality of the soul, and the divine origins of every word of the Bible. His elaborate writ of excommunication read in part: "Cursed shall he be in the daytime, and cursed when he riseth up! Curseth shall he be when he goeth out and curseth when he cometh in! May the Lord not forgive his sins. May the Lord's anger and wrath rage against this man, and cast upon him all the imprecations that are written in the Book of the Law! May the Lord wipe his name from under the Heavens; and may the Lord destroy him and cast him out from all the Tribes of Israel with all the maledictions that are written in the Book of the Law!"

Following the action of the Jewish community, the Amsterdam Municipal Council banished Spinoza from the city. He settled in a small town in the Dutch countryside, where in 1670 he published his *Tractatus Theologico-Politicus*, a clarion call for religious and intellectual freedom of expression.

The Vilna Gaon and Hasidism (1720–1797). Hasidism, the pietist, revivalist movement that was based on the teachings of the Baal Shem Tov (see "10 Hasidic Masters"), gained an immense following in eastern Europe during the second half of the eighteenth century. With its emphasis on spiritual fervor expressed in song and dance as well in enthusiastic prayer, its focus on the spiritual growth of the common man, and its elevating of the *rebbe* (the charismatic spiritual and personal leader) as opposed to the traditionally revered talmudic scholars and rabbis, Hasidism soon encountered the opposition of mainstream, rabbinic Judaism.

In 1772 the Gaon of Vilna (Elijah Ben Solomon Zalman), the most respected and scholarly Jewish religious authority in eastern Europe, inaugurated a kind of "counter-revolution" against them. Accused of adopting liturgical changes, altering the set times of services, and doing somersaults during prayer, the Hasidim were placed in *herem*: "They must leave our communities with their wives and children . . . and they should not be given a night's lodging; their *shehitah* [ritual slaughtering] is forbidden; it is forbidden to do business with them and intermarry them, or to assist them in their burial."

For five years two of the outstanding Hasidic *rebbes*, Shneur Zalman of Ladi and Menahem Mendel of Vitebsk, attempted to see the Vilna Gaon, hoping that the differences between the Hasidim and Mitnagdim (opponents of Hasidism) could be resolved. The Vilna Gaon refused to receive them and in 1781 issued a second writ of *herem* against the new movement. Thirteen years later he ordered that the *Tzavat ha-Ribash* ("Testament of Rabbi Israel Baal Shem Tov"), perhaps the most popular Hasidic work of its time, be publicly burned in the streets of Vilna.

The Gaon was too late. Although it soon split into many sects, Hasidism continued to flourish. In time, many Hasidim gave up some of what the Mitnagdim considered extreme and outrageous practices. For its part, normative rabbinic Judaism, or what is today called Orthodoxy, incorporated a number of Hasidic forms of expression.

With the failure of the Gaon of Vilna's two edicts of excommunication, a leaf was turned in the history of the institution of *herem*. In the future the leaders of normative Judaism knew that they would have to compete with other Jewish and secular belief systems without coercion for, among "the Jews of modernity," the "ban" could not be enforced.

—D.M.S.

WOMEN OF VALOR

THE FOREMOST JEWISH WOMEN OF AMERICA (As Selected by the Readers of The Jewish Tribune, September 26, 1924)

Top Row: Mrs. Mary Fels; Miss Henrietta Szold; Mrs. Nathan Straus
Bottom: Mrs. Rebekah Kohut; Miss Edna Ferber; Mme. Bertha Kalich.

THE JEWISH TRIBUNE'S contest to determine who, in the opinion of our readers, are the leading or most prominent Jewish women in America came to a close in our issue of last week. While it aroused much interest and brought many lists, the duration of the contest was too short to permit of the filing of a sufficient number of ballots, with the result that the names submitted were so varied that it would have been meaningless to attempt, on the basis of them, to select as many as twelve. But there was an unmistakable and almost unanimous consensus as to six women; their names were contained in almost every list turned in. Accordingly, it was deemed proper to announce only the names of the six whose portraits are shown above.

Altogether, a total of seventy-five names were submitted. Of these, almost one-third (twenty-one to be exact) are social and civic workers; adding to this number eleven philanthropists who contribute to movements for civic betterment, we see that thirty-two of the women placed in nomination are prominent in public affairs, either in the general body politic or in the more restricted Jewish community.

After the public workers, come the writers, fourteen in number. The musicians follow with eleven names; theatrical and "movie" folk with nine; then come three in the arts, one sculptor and two painters; six are miscellaneous.

The seventy-five nominated are the following:

Mary Antin, Theresa F. Bernstein, Sophie Braslau, Rose Brenner, Fannie Brice, Nessa Cohen, Irene Diner, Mrs. William Einstein.

Beatrice Fairfax (Lillian Lauferty), Mary Fels, Edna Ferber, Mrs. O. J. Freiman (Ottawa, Canada), Mrs. Felix Fuld, Alma Gluck, Miss Evelyn M. Goldsmith, Dr. Lura R. Goldsmith, Vera Gordon, Mrs. Richard Gottheil, Sidonia Matzner Gruenberg, Mrs. Daniel Guggenheim.

Mrs. Nathaniel Harris, Theresa Helburn, Dr. Anna W. Hochfelder, Mrs. Charles I. Hoffman, Fannie Hurst, Bertha Kalich, Rebekah Kohut, Isa Kremer, Mrs. Sarah Kussy.

Wanda Landowska, Mrs. Sam C. Lamport, Mrs. Irving Lehman, Sonia Levine, Mrs. Morris Lichtenstein, Sophia Irene Loeb.

Alice Menken, Caesar Misch, Erika Morini, Mrs. Henry Moskowitz, Alla Nazimova, Bertha Pearl, Mme. Belle Pevsner, Jessica Piexotto, Mrs. Joshua Piza.

Rosa Raisa, Marie Rappold, Mrs. Enoch Rauh, Bianca B. Robitscher, Mrs. Julius Rosenwald, Rose Rothenberg, Alma Reubens, Mrs. I. Rudie.

Mrs. Jacob H. Schiff, Rose Schneiderman, Mrs. Peter Schweitzer, Viola Brothers Shore, Mrs. Hannah Solomon, Mrs. William Sporborg, Estelle Sternberger, Rose P. Stokes, Mrs. Nathan Straus, Rose Strunsky, Henrietta Szold.

Mrs. Israel Unterberg, Lillian D. Wald, Bertha Wallerstein, Rita Weiman, Mrs. Stephen S. Wise, Anzie Yezierska, Fannie Bloomfield Zeisler, Manna Zucca.

10 AMERICAN JEWISH WOMEN REDISCOVERED

Among the most famous American Jewish women are the prominent names of Emma Lazarus, whose poetry graces the Statue of Liberty welcoming immigrants to America's golden shore, and Henrietta Szold, first president of Hadassah, the Women's Zionist Organization of America. Other equally successful and courageous American Jewish women have also served their community, although generally with less notoriety. These women are important not only for the work that they accomplished but also for the positive role models they provide young American Jewish women today. Presented here are sketches of ten such women.

Sarah Feyge Menkin Foner

First Woman Writer
of Modern Hebrew Literature

Born: 1856, Zagar, Lithuania

Died: 1937, Pittsburgh, Pennsylvania

For a woman to receive an intensive Jewish education in nineteenth century Lithuania was unusual. Even more unusual was that Sarah Feyge Menkin, a descendent of the Vilna Gaon, also learned Talmud, a study traditionally prohibited to women.

At twenty-five she published the first Hebrew novel written by a woman in modern times, *Ahavat Yesharim* (*The Love of the*

Righteous). She married Meyer Foner of Grodno, a scholar, teacher, and playwright. Her second book, *Derekh Yeladim o Sippur Mirushalayim* (*The Way of Children or a Story of Jerusalem*) was the first historical fiction for children written in modern Hebrew.

Her third book, *Beged Bogdim* (*The Cloak of Traitors*), appeared about the time her only child Newton was born, in 1891. After her fourth book, *Mizikhronot Yemey Yalduti* (*Memories of My Childhood*) was published, in 1903, she left her husband in Lodz, where they had been living, and came to the United States. There she became a Hebrew teacher and fund raiser for Hebrew schools. In 1919 she published a memoir in the journal *Shaharut*. She spent her last years with her son and his family in Pittsburgh.

QUOTES BY HER:
"And a girl can't become a Gaon?"—*Shaharut*, 1919

QUOTES ABOUT HER:
"Too bad she's a girl. If she were a boy she would probably become a Gaon in Israel."—Sarah Feyge's uncle quoted in *Shaharut*, 1919

Sophie Irene Simon Loeb
Child Rights Activist

Born: 1876, Russia

Died: 1929, New York

The comparative study of child care that she did while visiting Europe as a member of the Commission for the Relief of Widowed Mothers made Sophie Loeb one of the prime forces behind the passage of the 1914 Widows' Pension Law in New York.

One of the organizers of the Child Welfare Committee of New York, Loeb became its president for seven years and eventually rose to the position of the first president of the Child Welfare Committee of America. She participated in the First International Child Congress in 1926, and in 1927 she helped form an international code for the care of dependent and afflicted children. Her book, *Everyman's Child* (1920) contains a bill of rights of every child.

Monument in New York's Central Park to Sophie Irene Loeb

An ardent Zionist, Loeb toured Palestine in 1925 and wrote a book about her experiences, *Palestine Awake!* (1926).

Seven years after her death, the Alice In Wonderland fountain in New York's Central Park was dedicated to her memory. Engraved upon it: "In memory of Sophie Irene Loeb, Lover of Children. 'A Home for Every Child.' " Manhattan's Lower East Side, the first home of many Jewish immigrants settling in New York, also has a playground named in her honor.

Sophie Irene Loeb

QUOTES BY HER:
"As for me, I must say that what little I am today I owe to the orthodoxy and teachings of my mother. She it is who made me see the great hope that lies in Judaism."—"The Great Mistake of the Jew," *Jewish Tribune*, September 23, 1927

"The Palestine of the present day has been a mother to thousands of Jewish orphans . . . there is no land of greater promise than Palestine. It will have a renaissance unequalled by any other region of the world."—*Palestine Awake!* 1926.

QUOTES ABOUT HER:
"The woman who had done more than any other person to bring home to the general

public what child welfare really means."—Lionel Hill in *Jewish Tribune*, May 29, 1925

"America's greatest mother."—Senator W.H. Hodges of Florida, 1929

Adah Isaacs Menken

Actress and Poet

Born: 1835, New Orleans

Died: 1868, Paris

Her birth was shrouded in mystery, but Adah claimed Jewish descent. She started writing poetry at an early age, became an actress in a travelling show, and met Isaac Menken of Cincinnati in Texas, where her stagecoach broke down. The marriage lasted only a few years, during which time her hymns appeared regularly in *The Israelite*, founded by Rabbi Isaac Mayer Wise, one of her supporters. After her return to the stage, her most famous role was in *Mazeppa*, where, clad in a filmy garment over tights, she rode across the stage lashed to the back of a horse.

She travelled abroad and was reputed to be the mistress of Alexandre Dumas, père. Her collection of poems, *Infelicia*, was published after her death. Baron Lionel Nathan de Rothschild, whose right to take his seat in Parliament she had defended, erected a monument over her grave in Montparnasse.

QUOTES BY HER:

"*Infelicia*" will be my only monument."

The Sabbath

"It is the holy Sabbath day,
Let praise to God ascend.
In holiness thy soul array
And worldy thoughts suspend . . .
With rapture then behold the light
On this returning day;
Direct O God our steps aright
Nor from thee let us stray."

—*The Israelite*,
April 15, 1859

QUOTES ABOUT HER:

"Mrs. Isaacs Menken of New Orleans is considered a first class star on the stage all over the south west. The applause of the critics of New Orleans was re-echoed from all the theatres of the southern cities, where Mrs. I. Menken appeared in her matchless character." —*The Israelite*, April 16, 1858

"[There were] wild unfounded rumors that Adah was a *femme fatale*, a vampire bent on the destruction of as many men as she could attract. Her name became the butt of many a lewd remark, and among themselves, women gossiped about her in hushed whispers."—Allen Lesser, *Enchanting Rebel*, Philadelphia, 1947

Penina Moise

South Carolina Poet

Born: 1797, Charleston, South Carolina

Died: 1881, Charleston, South Carolina

A writer and school superintendent, Penina Moise had left school at twelve when her father died. She continued studying, began writing, and had her poems accepted for publication in various journals. In 1833 she published a small volume of her work, *Fanny's Sketch Book*.

As superintendent of the Beth Elohim Congregation Sunday School (the first Reform synagogue in America), she wrote hymns that are still found in the *Union Hymnal*. She gradually became blind in her sixties but continued writing. After the Civil War she taught, from memory, in a small private girls' school.

QUOTES BY HER:

"It is my peculiar felicity to be gifted with a sixth sense, that not only concentrates the powers of the other five, but expands its perceptions to sights and sounds invisible and inaudible to common organs."—*Charleston Courier*, quoted by Anita Libman Lebeson, *Recall to Life*

"Long past the allotted term
of mortal years,
My soul, a captive in the vale
of tears,
Flutters its wings to shake
the dust away,
Contracted in its narrow cage
of clay;
Conscious the hour of Freedom
is at hand,
When it will soar to Faith's
own fatherland.
Praise to my young associates
who delight
To be as 'twere to me a second
sight.
Through which alone I may
again behold,
Flowers and gems of
intellectual mold,
Whose gentle ministry, with
soothing power,
Brightens my spirit in its
cloudiest hour,
Till e'en through darkened
vision it perceives
The silver interlining Mercy
weaves."

—*Secular and Religious Works*, Charleston Council of Jewish Women, 1911

QUOTES ABOUT HER:

"Penina Moise was the literary pivot of Hebrew Charleston and her influence extended far beyond the circle of her co-religionists. Blind, poor, getting her living in her old age by keeping a little school, she yet created a literary salon, to which the best minds of Charleston flocked."—Charlotte Adams, *The Critic*

Belle Linder Israels Moskowitz

Political Advisor

Born: 1877, New York

Died: 1933, New York

When New York Governor Alfred E. Smith heard of her death from a heart attack, he rushed to New York City from Albany, where he was to attend the inauguration of Governor Herbert Lehman. Belle Moskowitz had been Smith's most important liberal advisor. She worked for him from 1918 until 1928, when she decided to leave politics after Smith lost the presidential campaign.

Born Belle Linder, she graduated Columbia University's Teachers College and began as a social worker at the Educational Alliance. She left work when she married Charles Israels, an architect. When Israels died in 1911, leaving her with three children to support, she returned to social work as head of the Committee on Amusement Resources for Working Girls. She later became field secretary of the Playground and Recreation Association, and was also on the staff of *The Survey*, published by the Russell Sage Foundation.

In 1914, she married Dr. Henry Moskowitz and with him, helped arbitrate strikes in the garment industry. At the time of her death she was secretary of the Educational Council of the Port of New York Authority.

QUOTES ABOUT HER:

"She is too well known to need any further comment."—Philip Cowen, *Memories of An American Jew*, New York, 1932

"Belle Moskowitz combined to a rare degree the qualities of statesmanship, executive ability and clear social thinking which made her an extremely valuable adviser and friend through many of my years of public life, particularly during the time in which I served as governor of New York."—Alfred E. Smith

Jessie Ethel Sampter

American Olah and Educator

Born: 1883, New York

Died: 1938, Kibbutz Givat Brenner, Pales.

Jessie E. Sampter was one of the first American-born women to make *aliyah*. Raised in a well-to-do assimilated home (her father was a follower of Dr. Felix Adler's Ethical Culture Movement), she became interested in Zionism through the writings of Josephine Lazarus and Henrietta Szold. She became part of the group around Rabbi Mordecai M. Kaplan, founder of Reconstructionism. Sampter's *Course in Zionism*, published in 1916 for Hadassah's School of Zionism, went through three editions and was read by an entire generation of young Americans.

Sampter arrived in Palestine after World War I. Moved by the plight of Yemenite Jews, she established evening classes for them and adopted a Yemenite orphan. With educator Alexander Dushkin, she brought the Boy Scout movement to Palestine, where it is named Tsofey Tsion, and translated the Boy Scout manuals into Hebrew.

Her house in Rehovot was used by Dr. Chaim Weizmann before he built his own home. The money realized from the subsequent sale of this house was given to Kibbutz Givat Brenner to build a rest house, called Beit Yesha in her memory. She spent her last years in Kibbutz Givat Brenner.

She wrote a number of books of prose and poetry, translated Chaim Nachman Bialik's poems for children, and wrote an autobiography (unpublished).

QUOTES BY HER:

"Since 1912, the appreciation of its own poetry by a group, the Jewish people, as an imminent experience, has drawn me away from the wider but colder fields of general American poetry. I preferred warmth to breadth, culture to cultivation."—*Brand Plucked from the Fire,* 1936

QUOTES ABOUT HER:

"She longed for religion and found it in the Jewish tradition . . . Spurning mere verbal expression of her interest in Zion, she settled in Israel and shared in the hardships of a pioneering life in a country that was still mostly desert."—Eugene Koh, Foreward to new edition of *White Fire,* 1977.

Rose Schneiderman

Union Organizer

Born: 1882, Savine, Poland

Died: 1972, New York City

In 1903 tiny, red-haired Rose Schneiderman helped organize the United Cloth, Hat, Cap and Millinery Workers Union. Thus began a lifelong career of union organizing and activism. A member of the Women's Trade Union

League from 1906, she became president of the New York Section in 1918 and was the national president of the WTUL from 1926 until she retired in 1949.

Schneiderman was a leader of the women's suffrage movement and a member of the Labor Advisory Board of the National Recovery Administration under Roosevelt.

QUOTES BY HER:

"After I had been working as a cap maker for three years it began to dawn on me that we girls needed an organization."

"To speak of peace and harmony now would be treason to the dead."—Speech after Triangle Shirtwaist Fire.

QUOTES ABOUT HER:

"[She was] a tiny red-haired bundle of social dynamite [and] did more to upgrade the dignity and living standards of working women than any other American."—*The New York Times,* August 14, 1972

Hannah Greenebaum Solomon

Founder of National Council of Jewish Women (NCJW)

Born: 1858, Chicago, Illinois

Died: 1942, Chicago, Illinois

By the time she was nineteen, Hannah Greenebaum was an accomplished musician and linguist and was active in Jewish affairs. Recognized by the mostly non-Jewish Chicago elite as an outstanding young woman, Greenebaum was invited to become one of the first two Jewish members (the other was her sister) of the prestigious Chicago Women's Club.

By 1890, married and a mother, Greenebaum—now Soloman—was appointed a member of the women's committee for the Parliament of Religions, to be held in conjunction with the Chicago Exposition of 1893. She won approval for a Jewish Women's Congress and gathered sixteen women to help her organize it. After a year of work, the Congress became a reality and on September 7, 1893, turned itself into the National Council of Jewish Women.

NCJW, the first national Jewish women's organization in the United States, sought to encourage women to work in religion, philanthropy, and education. Solomon travelled all over the United States to help set up daughter sections and was actively involved in the work of NCJW until her death.

QUOTES BY HER:

"Would [the Jewish Women's Congress] have permanence, or would it be a brief bright tale? In a flash, my thoughts crystallized to a decision: we *will* have a congress out of which must grow a permanent organization!"—*Fabric of My Life*

QUOTES ABOUT HER:

"Mrs. Hannah G. Solomon was the first woman in America to weld the Jewish women into a national body, with definite purposes that stirred them on to a new consciousness and new activities."—Philip P. Bregstone, *Chicago and its Jews.*

Rosa Fassel Sonneschein

Editor and Writer

Born: 1847, Prossnitz, Moravia

Died: 1932, St. Louis, Missouri

Sonneschein was born the youngest daughter of Rabbi Hirsch Baer Fassel. Married at seventeen to Rabbi Dr. Solomon H. Sonneschein, she followed her husband to America in 1869, where he became the first

Rosa Sonneschein

Reform rabbi in St. Louis. In 1878 she was one of the founders of The Pioneers, the first Jewish women's literary club in the United States. She wrote a history of the club in 1880.

After her marriage failed, Czech immigrant Rosa Fassel Sonneschein supported herself by writing journals in English and German. In 1895 she founded *The American Jewess,* the first Jewish women's periodical.

As a journalist for *The American Jewess,* Sonneschein attended the first Zionist Congress in Basle in 1897, one of only three Americans there. She continued to publish her magazine until 1899, when she sold it.

QUOTES BY HER:

"If the NCJW should adopt as an ideal the restoration of Jewish nationality, they would at once enlist the cooperation of their Jewish sisters in Europe."—*American Jewess*, October, 1896

QUOTES ABOUT HER:

"Mrs. Sonneschein of the *American Jewess* said to me at the time, 'they will crucify you yet—and I will be your Magdalene.' "—Theodore Herzl, *Diary*, September 3, 1897

Rachel Treelisky Vixman
Parliamentarian and Zionist Organizer

Born: 1887, Pittsburgh, Pennsylvania

Although she never attended high school, Rachel Treelisky passed the librarian examination at Pittsburgh's Carnegie Library. With no social work training, she became assistant to Charles I. Cooper, executive secretary of the United Hebrew Relief. She wrote for one local Jewish newspaper and sold subscriptions for another. In the evenings she organized hundreds of neighborhood children into Zionist clubs.

At the urging of Henrietta Szold, Vixman founded a Hadassah chapter in Pittsburgh and then expanded it to create the Western Pennsylvania regional Hadassah. During the Brandeis-Weizmann conflict over the direction of American Zionism, Vixman was instrumental in preventing a schism in Hadassah. A national vice president, she served as acting president when Irma Lindheim went abroad in the mid-1920's. In 1929 she was a delegate to the World Zionist Congress in Basle, and she visited Palestine at the time of the Hebron massacre.

Vixman was also a Certified Professional Parliamentarian. She wrote the introduction to a new edition of *Roberts Rules of Order* when she was eighty-five. At ninety, she served national conferences as Parliamentarian. The New York Culture Foundation, of which she was president, celebrated her ninetieth birthday in 1977.

QUOTES BY HER:

"I never went to high school but that didn't stop me."

"The Jewish woman must be the torchbearer in the spiritual regeneration of our people . . . this realization, together with the greater opportunities she has today of expressing herself and acquiring Jewish knowledge, is inspiring her to take an ever-increasing part in revitalizing Jewish life, both in the home and the community. Then we shall have the assurance of a greater appreciation of Jewish values; Jewish ceremonies and traditions will again play an important part in home life; the knowledge of Hebrew will add spiritual content; Palestine will infuse new courage to carry on. Our women must become the Deborahs to arouse the Baraks!"—*The Jewish Forum* symposium, "What is the Future of the Jewish Woman in America?"

—I.C.S.

WOMEN RABBIS: A SHORT LIST

Miriam the Prophetess, sister to Moses and Aaron, led the Children of Israel in dancing praise of God after the crossing of the Red Sea. Deborah the Judge led the Children of Israel in their war of liberation against Jabin, king of Canaan. She was a national leader, a counselor to the people, a "mother in Israel" (Judges 5:7). Miriam and Deborah, although not unique, are rare examples of women whom the tradition has deemed worthy of mention for their roles as communal leaders and religious teachers.

While previous generations may be excused as being premodern, the male monopolization of leadership and spiritual roles in the contemporary Jewish community can only be regarded as sexist. In recent years a few courageous women, by choosing to become rabbis, have challenged this male-dominated institution. Those branches of Judaism that recognize and attempt to integrate significant societal developments, Reform and Reconstructionism, were the first (and, to date, only) to open their seminary doors to women. The Conservative movement, although pushed to the brink in late 1979, managed to sidestep, shelve, and bury the issue for at least the next several years. For the Orthodox, the very idea of women rabbis is incompatible with what is understood as authentic Jewish life. It is clear that the Jewish woman still has a long way to go in relation to the Jewish religious institutions.

Those few women who have been ordained by the Reform and Reconstructionist movements are finding their reception by the Jewish community less than cordial. One of these women, Rabbi Laura Geller, has pointed out that the phenomenon of women's ordination to the rabbinate is confronting the community with a number of complex and critical questions that it is not yet capable of dealing with such as:

• What changes will this create in Jewish institutions, e.g. a transformation of the traditionally hierarchical relationship between rabbi and congregant?

• How will this affect the traditional images of God, i.e. is the image of God projected by women significantly different from that of men?

• What are the fears that this generates in the minds of both men and women regarding the changing patterns of sexuality?

Certainly the resolution to these and other questions are years in the future. However, as more and more women enter the field challenges to the institutional sexism of the Jewish religious structures will continue to be raised.

Beruriah
First Female Talmudist

Born: c. 100, Yavne (?) Eretz Yisrael

Died: c. 170, Tiberias, Eretz Yisrael

Daughter of Rabbi Hanina ben Teradyon, who was martyred in the Bar Kokhba uprising of 135 C.E., and wife of Rabbi Meir, Beruriah was the only woman whose opinion was accepted as *halakhah* (Jewish law). She was considered by her contemporaries to be a great scholar, teacher, and biblical exegete. There are a number of stories told about her in the Talmud and Midrash, the best known of which is about her keeping the news of the death of their two sons from Rabbi Meir in order not to grieve him on the Sabbath. Only after *havdalah* did she break the news, gently, in a parable: "Priceless jewels were left with me in trust. The original owner has come for them. Shall I return them to him?" Rabbi Meir answered yes, whereupon Beruriah showed him their dead sons. She comforted him with the words, "The Lord gave and the Lord has taken away." Her reputation is tarnished, however, by a Rashi commentary of unknown origin, which says she committed suicide after succumbing to a student, prompted by her husband to try to seduce her.

QUOTES ABOUT HER:

"Beruriah, wife of R. Meir and daughter of R. Hananya ben Teradyon . . . studied 300 laws from 300 teachers in one day. . . .—*Pesahim* 62b

"Beruriah's reputation rests as much upon her piety and devotion to her scholar husband as upon her scholarship . . .—Paula Hyman, *The Other Half: Women in the Jewish Tradition*

"Presumably she never received the *semichah* (ordination) to the rabbinate that promising young men normally received at the completion of their studies, which allowed the new rabbis to make religious and ritual judgments. During Beruriah's day there was apparently no legal reason why she could not have been ordained. . . ."—Leonard Swidler, "Beruriah: Her Word Became Law," *Lilith*, (Spring/Summer, 1977)

Regina Jonas
The First Woman Rabbi

Regina Jonas completed her theological studies at the Berlin Hochschule für die Wissenschaft des Judentums in the mid 1930's but was not ordained there. The Reverend Max Dieneman of Offenbach ordained her privately, and she practiced as a rabbi until 1940, when she was sent to the Theresienstadt Concentration Camp, where she died.

QUOTES ABOUT HER:

"The First Woman Rabbi"—Jacob R. Marcus, *The Israelite*, March 9, 1972

"Rabbi Sally (Priesand) is apparently antedated."—Martha Neumark Montor, *Cincinnati Horizons*, October, 1975

Irma Lindheim
"The Zionist Rabbi"

Born: 1886, New York

Died: 1978, Berkeley, California

Born into a wealthy German Jewish family, Irma Levy married at nineteen and raised a large family. Her Jewish awareness was aroused by a lecturer on "The Bible as Literature," at the Ethical Culture Society. Later she underwent an almost mystic conversion to Zionism after a train ride with Dr. Ben-Zion Mossensohn, principal of Herzliah in Tel Aviv. She met Henrietta Szold and became involved in work for Hadassah. Irma, also, established a Zionist meeting house in New York where, at the housewarming, she was called "The Zionist Rabbi."

In 1922, Lindheim became a special student of Rabbi Stephen S. Wise's Jewish Institute of Religion and two years later was accepted as a regular student, not without "a campaign waged with seriousness." In 1925 she visited Palestine and was so inspired that she left her rabbinical studies in order to devote her efforts to Zionism. She was elected second president of Hadassah in 1926, and was reelected for a second term. After her husband's death she decided to settle in Palestine. She resigned from the National Board of Hadassah and became a Socialist Zionist. At age forty-seven she joined

Kibbutz Mishmar Ha'Emek, where she is buried.

QUOTES BY HER:

"For a while I felt an acute regret that I was not a man and therefore could not become a Rabbi."—Irma Lindheim, *Parallel Quest*

"I decided I wanted to change my status. Having been voted best in scholarship in the Institute for two years, both by the faculty and the student body I decided I had earned acceptance as a regular student, instead of remaining labeled "special." This stirred up a hornet's nest. No woman ever had been permitted to become a candidate for the rabbinate, much less to become a rabbi! Henrietta Szold, studying for years at the Jewish Theological Seminar had attained a measure of learning I hardly dared hope to equal. . . . I was received by the faculty as a regular student, the faculty including the men most steeped in tradition, Rav Tzair [Tchernovitz] and David Yellin. It was not that I had any plan to function as a rabbi. I simply believed, in a time of women's gradual emergence as individuals in their own right, that if I prepared myself in accordance with the requirements of being a rabbi, the door would be opened for other women, should they wish and have the gift to minister to congregations. There was no intrinsic reason why they could not do well—perhaps in some cases better even than men."—*Parallel Quest*

QUOTES ABOUT HER:

"This is not everybody's handbook of Palestine, but a Jewish soul's book of Zion . . . the voice of one of her daughters crying to the Motherland, out of a heart of love and pity and, above all, out of faith which comes of understanding."—Rabbi Stephen S. Wise, Foreword to *Immortal Adventure*, Irma Lindheim

---

Ray Frank Litman

California Preacher

Born: 1865, California (?)

Died: , Champaign-Urbana, Illinois (?)

Descended from the Vilna Gaon, Ray Frank became known as an orator and is reputed to have preached before congregations in California. Rabbi Isaac Mayer Wise invited her in the pages of the *American Israelite*, in 1892, to become the first female student at Hebrew Union College. The item was picked up and misinterpreted by other periodicals to mean that she was the first woman rabbi in the world. The mistake inspired the story, "The Rabbi's Wife," which appeared in 1903 in *The New Era*, about a Rebbetzin Esther Frank who preached to her husband's congregation when he was ill.

Ray Frank was one of the founders of the National Council of Jewish Women and wrote for *The American Jewess*. She married Professor Simon Litman of the University of Illinois and "lived happily ever after."

QUOTES ABOUT HER:

"We can only encourage Miss Ray Frank or any other gifted lady who takes the theological course to assist the cause of emancipating women in the synagogue and congregation."—Rabbi Isaac Mayer Wise *The Israelite*, November 24, 1892

"To Miss Ray Frank, of California, is recorded the distinction of becoming the first woman rabbi in the world. She is the first woman student in the Hebrew College in Cincinnati and has been urged by Rabbi Moses, the most celebrated Jewish divine in Chicago, to accept a congregation as he says women are needed in the pulpit."—*The American Woman's Journal and the Business Woman's Journal*, 1893

"David it is time that I should realize the ideal you have always held before me. If Miriam the leader's sister led her women in song at a time of national danger thousands of years ago, why shall not the rabbi's wife lead her people in speech at a day when Judaism has reached a critical period and even women's aid may not be disdained.—Dr. A. S. Isaacs, "The Rabbi's Wife," *The New Era*, II, 6, May, 1903

The Honorable Lily H. Montagu

First Jewish Woman Lay Minister

Born: 1873, England

Died: 1963, England

By the time she was seventeen, Montagu, daughter of Orthodox Jewish banker, Samuel Montagu, was holding Sabbath services in English for children and had opened evening classes for working girls, which two years later became the West Central Jewish Club for Girls.

Under the influence of Dr. Claude G. Montefiore, she helped found the Liberal Jewish Movement (part of the Reform Movement) in England. She preached for the first time at the Liberal Jewish Synagogue on June 15, 1918, on "Kinship with God." In 1926 she was made a Lay Minister of the West Central Congregation. She preached frequently in England and in the United States and at the Reform Synagogue in Berlin.

She became a founder of the World Union for Progressive Judaism in 1926. In 1937 she received the Order of the British Empire for her club work. She was also one of the first women in England to be a Justice of the Peace.

QUOTES BY HER:

"Kinship with God is derived from the actual experience of prayer and from the effort after righteousness."—*Kinship with God,* 1918

"We have no power to explain God. If we could, we should be God ourselves."—*The Spiritual Possibilities of Judaism,* 1899

QUOTES ABOUT HER:

"She was the real founder of the Liberal Jewish Movement in England."—Dr. Claude G. Montefiore

"She holds a singular place which she has made her own through great perseverance and devotion, as well as through the revolution which allowed women to identify themselves in new ways."—Rabbi Leo Baeck

"By teaching others, she taught herself. By praying with others she was helped to formulate her own thoughts and to put into words the yearning for the Indefinable that was smouldering within her."—Eric Conrad, *Lily H. Montague: Prophet of a Living Judaism, 1953*

Martha Neumark Montor

Almost a Rabbi

Born: 1904, Berlin

At fourteen, Martha Neumark entered Hebrew Union College in Cincinnati with the intention of studying for the rabbinate. Nicknamed "Princess Pat" by her 99 male classmates (after her redheaded father Professor David Neumark, who brought the family to Cincinnati when Martha was three and continued to teach at HUC until his death in 1924), Martha successfully completed seven and a half years of the nine year rabbinical program.

Although both the faculty of HUC and the members of the Central Conference of American Rabbis agreed that "women cannot justly be denied the privilege of ordination," the six lay members of the Board of Governors of HUC voted down the two rabbinical members, denying her the possibility of becoming a rabbi.

In the summer of 1922, Martha Neumark received a Bachelor of Hebrew degree from HUC, and in the spring of 1924 she received a B.A. in philosophy and psychology from the University of Cincinnati. She worked as a volunteer assistant psychologist in Juvenile Court, and in 1925 she received the first Certificate of Sunday School Superintendent granted by the HUC School of Education in New York.

She married Henry Montor and moved to New York with him in 1925, where she spent many years as a writer and editor. She had two children with him before their divorce in 1956.

She did not remain professionally active in the Jewish world, retiring in 1975 from a position as Senior Rehabilitation Counsellor for the New York Department of Correction.

QUOTES BY HER:

"My work at the Hebrew Union College, my gradually enlarging acquaintance with Jewish lore, philosophy and history has made more firm my conviction that in no manner are women incapable of entering the ministry, either by reason of tradition, or because of their inherent incapacity. Women would add new blood to the ranks of the ministry, a thing much needed at present."—Martha Neumark, "The Woman Rabbi: An Autobiographical Sketch of the First Woman Rabbinical Candidate," *Jewish Tribune,* April 10, 1925

"I was, as far as I have been able to determine, the first woman, (more accurately girl!) ever actually to conduct a Friday night service for a Jewish congregation. For years during my childhood our family spent the summer months each year in the small village of Frankfort, Michigan. . . . For several summers . . . my father served as Rabbi for this summer resort Jewish congregation. . . . On this particular Friday night my father turned over the conduct of the entire service (except for the sermon, which he delivered) to me. . . . Comments by the congregants were both pro and con, but in the main they were kindly.—Personal communication from Mrs. Montor to Dr. Selavan, December 6, 1979

QUOTES ABOUT HER:

"During his first year in Berlin, on the third day of May, his second child was born—another daughter; he called her Martha. She too will be a rabbi like her famous father, as she is now in her sixth year a student at the Hebrew Union College, and is a senior at the University of Cincinnati; unless, within the next two years, she changes her mind and exhibits a preference to become a rebbitzen, instead."—*Hebrew Union College Monthly,* January, 1924

Pesha Chaya Poupko
Talmudist and Rebbitzen

Born: 1889, Kene, near Vilna

Died: 1976, Brooklyn, New York

The only woman mentioned in *Ohele-Shem* (Biographies of Rabbis), the daughter of the Chief Rabbi of Saratov, Pesha Chaya Poupko was the wife of the chief rabbi of Veliz, the mother of six rabbis, and the grandmother of nineteen rabbis. She received the same Jewish education as her brothers and passed the Saratov Gymnasium examination as an extern. The Chofetz Chayim, leading rabbi of his generation, cited her scholarly achievements when he supported the opening of Bais Yaakov schools for girls, founded by Sarah Schenirer. (Four decades later Rabbi Belkind, president of Yeshiva University, also referred to Poupko's piety and scholarship when he proposed the founding of Stern College for Women.)

Poupko was active in the underground Zionist movement both under the Tsars and under the Soviets. She personally initiated all her children in the study of Talmud and Hebrew grammar and taught Jewish girls Hebrew, Bible, and religion, all of which were forbidden by Stalin.

Upon arrival in the United States in 1932, a mother of eight, she went to evening high school and graduated. She believed in an intensive Torah education for girls, but rejected the inclusion of women in the *minyan* (religious quorum) and the ordination of women into the rabbinate.

QUOTES ABOUT HER:

"A wonderful matter should be mentioned: The wife of Rabbi Eliezer Poupko, when she was only thirteen years old, knew Talmud so well, that she taught it privately to a student, for a fee."—*Ohele-Shem*, Sch. N. Gottlieb, Pinsk, 1912

Henrietta Szold
First Woman admitted to the Jewish Theological Seminary of America

Born: 1860, Baltimore, Maryland

Died: 1945, Jerusalem, Israel

Best known for her Zionist activities, Henrietta Szold was probably the most erudite Jewish woman of her time. She received an excellent education from her father, Rabbi Benjamin Szold, who imbued her with confidence in her ability to master any discipline she chose. She believed in the primacy of the Jewish family and the importance of traditional education for women as the center of the family. But she also believed that women should be allowed to perform *mitzvot* not considered obligatory for them (such as saying Kaddish) when time or situation regularly allowed, as when a woman was not married or had grown children. Szold stuck to these ideas in letters, speeches, and articles, and in battles with both Reform and Orthodox Jews.

Szold taught Bible and Jewish history in her father's synagogue for many years. In 1903, after his death, she undertook the editing of his works. For this purpose, she received permission to enroll as the first woman in the Jewish Theological Seminary, the ordination arm of the Conservative Movement. She was accepted as a special student only on the understanding that she would not seek ordination. She later translated, edited, and wrote many works requiring great Jewish scholarship.

QUOTES BY HER:

"I believe that woman can best serve the interests of the synagogue by devoting herself to her home; by filling any administrative position for which her executive ability is greater than that of any available man . . . and by occupying the pulpit only when her knowledge of the law, history, and literature of Judaism is masterful, and her natural gift so extraordinary as to forbid hesitation, though even then it were the part of wisdom not to make a profession of public preaching and teaching, the old Jewish rule of not holding women responsible for religious duties performed at definite times having a deep-seated rational basis and wide applicability."—Irving Fineman, *Woman of Valor: The Life of Henrietta Szold*, 1961

QUOTES ABOUT HER:

"The woman who had more to contribute to American Jewish life than anyone else."—Israel Friedlander.

"The Jewish Theological Seminary was, of course, intended for male students only; but Henrietta's friend Cyrus Adler could vouch for her good intentions. . . . Early in 1903, after she had given her assurance that it was not her intention to become a rabbi—something even the most liberal Conservative, even Papa himself, could not have countenanced—Cyrus Adler wrote her that she would be admitted into the Seminary in the fall as a special student—in fact, as the only woman."—Irving Fineman, *Woman of Valor, Life of Henrietta Szold,* 1961

Hannah Rachel Werbermacher
The Maid of Ludomir

Born: 1805, Ludomir, Ukraine

Died: 1892, Israel

Hannah Rachel is one of the few women who could be considered a female Hasidic *rebbe*. People came from all over to receive her blessings. Her followers were called "The Hasidim of the Maid of Ludomir (*Di Ludmirer Moyd*)." They prayed in her synagogue and listened to her words of wisdom.

An only child, Hannah Rachel received a good basic Jewish education, which she continued on her own. After a miraculous recovery from an illness, she began performing many of the *mitzvot* traditionally reserved for men: wearing *tallit* and *tefillin*, spending her days in study and prayer. With money inherited after her father's death, she built a synagogue with a separate enclosure, from behind the closed doors of which she spoke to her Hasidim.

She was persuaded by the leading *tzaddik* of the day, R. Mottele of Tchernobil, to marry. She complied, at forty, and her influence dwindled. She separated (divorced?) from her husband and emigrated to Eretz Yisrael where she spent her last years endeavoring to hasten the coming of the Messiah.

QUOTES BY HER:
"Father, I have just been at the Higher Tribunal and have been given a new and sublime soul."—Samuel A. Horodezky, *Ha-Hasidut veha-Hasidim* (Hebrew), 1923

QUOTES ABOUT HER:
"Hasidism gave the Jewish woman permission to achieve the status of *tzaddik*, if she was worthy . . . while all of the women who achieved this status were daughters of Hasidic leaders, only one arose from the masses—the Maid of Ludomir."—Samuel A. Horodezky, *Ha-Hasidut veha-Hasidim*, (Hebrew), 1923

Women Who Have Been Ordained as Rabbis

The below list is arranged according to year of ordination and includes women rabbis ordained through June, 1979.

1972
Rabbi Sally Priesand was the first woman rabbi in the United States. She was ordained by Hebrew Union College—Jewish Institute of Religion (HUC-JIR) fifty years after the Reform movement's Central Conference of American Rabbis issued their statement, ". . . Woman cannot justly be denied the priviledge of ordination." She is now rabbi of Temple Beth El in Elizabeth, New Jersey. She holds an Honorary Doctorate of Humane Letters from Florida International University.

1974
Rabbi Sandy Sasso was the first woman to graduate the Reconstructionist Rabbinical College (RRC). She was also the first rabbi to share the pulpit with (her) husband, first on Long Island and now in Indianapolis, Indiana. Her present congregation is affiliated with both the Reconstructionist and Conservative movements, making Sasso the first woman rabbi to serve a Conservative congregation. She is married to Rabbi David Sasso and has two children.

1975
Rabbi Michal Bernstein, ordained by HUC-JIR, served Temple Beth Sholom in San Jose, California but left the pulpit because of a number of disappointments. She also resigned from the Central Conference of American Rabbis. She is now a mother, a lawyer, teaches religious studies, and serves as chaplain for two local hospitals and for the San Jose Fire Department.

***Rabbi Laura Geller* (Bill Aron)**

1976
Rabbi Dr. Rebecca Alpert is the only woman rabbi holding a doctorate, awarded by Temple University in 1978. Ordained by RRC, Alpert created the job she now holds with them, director of student affairs. As a high school student she thought it would be nice to be a rabbi, although there were no women rabbis at the time. "But you grow up in Brooklyn and you think anything is possible." She is married to Rabbi Joel Alpert, an RRC classmate.

Rabbi Laura Geller, ordained by HUC-JIR, is Hillel director at the University of Southern Callifornia in Los Angeles. "The people who have influenced me most have been Hillel directors who have a vision of a pluralistic Jewish community made up of people whose spiritual center radiates out toward a political commitment to be involved in *Tikun Olam* (setting the world right)."

Rabbi Ilene Schneider, ordained by the RRC, is principal of the Cyrus Adler High School of Beth Sholom Congregation in Elkins Park, Pennsylvania.

1978

Rabbi Karen L. Fox, ordained by HUC-JIR in New York, is the assistant director of the New York Federation of Reform Synagogues.

Rabbi Rosalind A. Gold, ordained by HUC-JIR, now serves at Temple B'rith Kodesh in Rochester, New York.

Rabbi Ruth Sandberg, ordained by RRC, serves Congregation Keneseth Israel, also in Elkins Park, Pennsylvania.

Rabbi Myra Soifer, ordained by HUC-JIR, is assistant rabbi of Temple Sinai in New Orleans, Louisiana.

1979

Rabbi Michal V. Bourne, ordained by HUC-JIR, serves with Congregation Emanu-El in San Francisco.

Rabbi Ellen W. Dreyfus, ordained by HUC-JIR, teaches in the New York City area.

Rabbi Vicki L. Hollander, ordained by HUC-JIR, is assistant rabbi and educational director of Larchmont Temple in Larchmont, a suburb of New York City.

Rabbi Linda Holtzman, ordained by the RRC, is rabbi of Beth Israel Congregation in Coatesville, Pennsylvania.

Rabbi Jan Kaufman, ordained by HUC-JIR, is assistant Hillel director at the University of Maryland in College Park.

Rabbi Beverly Jo Lerner, ordained by HUC-JIR, is assistant rabbi at the Hebrew Benevolent Congregation (The Temple) in Atlanta, Georgia.

Rabbi Beverly Weintraub Magidson, ordained by HUC-JIR, is associate Hillel director at Washington University in St. Louis, Missouri. She has taught biblical cantillation and syntax, and has served as cantor on the High Holidays.

Rabbi Janet Marder, ordained by HUC-JIR, teaches Hebrew at HUC. She plans to begin graduate work in the near future. She is married to Rabbi Sheldon Marder.

Rabbi Sheila C. Russian, ordained by HUC-JIR, is assistant rabbi with the Baltimore Hebrew Congregation in Maryland.

Rabbi Bonnie Steinberg, ordained by HUC-JIR, is Hillel director and Jewish chaplain at Hofstra University on Long Island, in Hempstead, New York. "The fact that I am a rabbi, and not a social worker, is a political statement and a model for women in our society."

Rabbi Gail Shuster-Bouskila, ordained by RRC, is the first woman rabbi to make *aliyah.* She is now teaching "Modern Jewish History" at the Young Judea Jerusalem Institute. She recently finished writing a children's book on the *midrash* woven into the Pesach *seder.*

Also of note:

Lynn Gottlieb—Rabbi to the Deaf, has studied at the Hebrew University, at Hebrew Union College, and at the Jewish Theological Seminary. She has also studied with individual teachers according to the ancient apprentice-teacher model, and is seeking private ordination. While serving as rabbi to the deaf community she has created a unique sign language for the liturgy. She is also a story-teller, weaving ancient tales in midrashic form, focusing particularly on biblical women.

Bonnie J. Koppell—First Jewish Woman Chaplain, a fourth-year student at the Reconstuctionist Rabbinical College in Philadelphia, was accepted as the first Jewish woman chaplain candidate by the United States Army and has the rank of second lieutenant in the Army Reserves.

Projections of the future:

In the Reform and Reconstructionist movements in the United States, approximately fifty women will be ordained in the next five years. The majority of these will be Reform rabbis, as over forty women are now enrolled at one of the three campuses of its seminary, Hebrew Union College. Although there are a number of women waiting to apply to the Conservative movement's rabbinical program at the Jewish Theological Seminary in New York, it is unlikely that its program will be open to women in the near future. Even if it were to accept women, however, the number of women to be ordained within the next five years would still remain the same, as the JTS rabbinical program requires five years of study.

—I.C.S.

AN INDIAN-FIGHTER, A DANCE-HALL GIRL, AND A SHARPSHOOTER:
3 JEWS IN THE OLD WEST

A Yiddish-speaking Indian chief? A rabbi named Belinsky who charms Indians with his devotion to the Torah? Unlikely personalities surely, but when portrayed several years ago by Mel Brooks in *Blazing Saddles* and Gene Wilder in *The Frisco Kid*, movie audiences roared. It was not only their comedic talents that evoked nationwide guffaws. Take the movie premise: traditional Jews living and working in the Wild West, in Frontier America. The idea itself sounds funny; the juxtaposition of such radically incongruent worlds creates the comedic absurd.

Yet life, as George Santayana should have remarked, is stranger than parody. Although there might not have been an Indian chief who spoke Yiddish, in the 1800's there was in fact a Westphalian-born Jew named Solomon Bibo who lived with the Acoma Pueblo tribe in New Mexico, spoke their language (Keres), and so incensed a Department of Interior official by this activity that he was labelled "a meddling Jew." There also was a nineteenth-century German-born Jewish travelling Shakespearean actor named Daniel Bandman who, while performing countless roles on tour throughout the West to critical acclaim (particularly in the mining camps of Montana), preached before the tiny, isolated Jewish communities dotting the vast territory. And a *meyseh* (legendary tale) is told about a Jew named "Navajo Sam" Dittenhoffer who outwitted the notorious outlaw Billy the Kid from staging a holdup.

Sigmund Shlesinger

Thus, Hollywood scripts aside, the real life stories of Jews in Frontier America—most of whom were traders, merchants, prospectors, and homesteaders—are often alive with the spirit that was the old Wild West. Three of these are recounted here.

Sigmund Shlesinger (1848–1928)
"The Little Jew" at the Battle of Beecher Island

The saga of Sigmund Shlesinger sounds like a humorous ditty composed by Allan Sherman. Yet, the story of this Hungarian-born Jewish itinerant peddler in Kansas, who became an acclaimed Indian fighter and later a *macher* (leader) in several Jewish organizations is stranger than fiction.

Arriving in New York in 1864 at the age of sixteen, Shlesinger took a job as a horsecar conductor but was too restless to remain there. A merchant from the West soon persuaded him to go to Kansas to make his fortune. However, Sigmund Shlesinger was no Jewish Horatio Alger. He worked at many different jobs that yielded financial rewards ranging from unprofitable to disastrous: he was a clerk in Leavenworth, Kansas, for one year, did odd jobs in Junction City, worked as a waiter, cook, and mule herder, and then met Abraham Hyman in Hays City, where they decided to open a cigar store. Since their entire stock was worth only about five dollars, they also sold newspapers to cavalrymen on the frontier. Among their more notable customers were General Custer, Buffalo Bill, and "Wild Bill" Hickok.

Not surprisingly, this enterprise was less than lucrative, and Shlesinger decided to go into his own business, which, as the expression goes, was "nothing to write home about." He did, however, write home about it: "I entered upon several ventures such as a bakery with a capital of a few dollars. I procured a piece of tent cloth and a couple of store boxes and fitted up a store room, about a dozen loaves of bread and as many pies represented my stock. A few of each were sold, the rest eaten. This wound up the business. I obtained a recipe to brew beer which I brewed in a wash boiler on a wood fire on the open prairie, the product proving a menace to the health of the . . . customers."

Shlesinger was at a crossroads in his life. Business was apparently not his forte and computer programming had not yet been invented. What was a nice Jewish boy to do?: what every other boy was doing then—joining the army.

In the 1860's railroads were under construction to transport the new settlers arriving in the West. The Indians, fearing the loss of their land, attacked the invaders. Soon many cavalry divisions were organized to protect the settlers and railroad workers.

Colonel George A. Forsyth accepted Shlesinger as a scout, although he "seemed to be inferior, and in all respects unfit for service; a Jew, small with narrow shoulders, sunken chest, quiet manner, and pipey voice, but little knowledge of fire-arms or horsemanship; he was indeed unpromising as a son of Mars." Why, then, was he accepted? Forsyth regretfully noted that "after forty-nine had been obtained . . . only [then] might [he] be counted on the rolls to make up the fifty and thus enable the expedition to start."

On August 28, 1868 the impoverished, sunken-chested Sigmund Shlesinger became a scout for the 9th Cavalry at $75 per month. In the annals of American military history his initial experiences as a uniformed soldier have rarely been repeated—except for Sergeant Bilko and Captain Yossarian: "I will never forget this first day's ride! I was not used to the saddle; my equipment, consisting of carbine, revolvers, saddle bags, roll of blankets, etc. were always where they should not have been. I could not adjust them so they would be comfortable . . . My bridle arm became stiff and lame in the effort to obey; every bone in my body began to ache; the ride and the day seemed never to end, and with every mile of travel my misery was bordering on torture."

Physical discomfiture was not Shlesinger's only problem. He occasionally became the butt of ridicule because of his religion. However—as if his early adventures were a prototype for a Western movie script—the opportunity finally arose for him to "prove himself a man."

In September 1868 the troop was searching for a band of Indians who had killed two men near Sheridan, Kansas. They soon spotted tracks near the Arickaree Fork of the Republican River, and then were attacked on a sandy island in the middle of a stream—later named Beecher Island for one of the scouts slain by a band of Indians under the leadership of Chief Roman Nose (sic!). The siege lasted almost a week, resulting in five dead and seventeen wounded among the scouts. Shlesinger, the small nineteen-year-old Jew with narrow shoulders, displayed such bravery in battle that Colonel Forsyth exulted, "—As for the little Jew! Well, the Indian that from dawn to dusk was incautious enough to expose any part of his person within the range of his rifle had no cause to complain of a want of marked attention on the part of that brave and active young Israelite. . . . He most worthily proved himself a gallant soldier among brave men."

Years later, the Battle of Beecher Island became legendary. Writing about the skirmish in the August 1893 issue of *The Army and Navy Magazine*. General James B. Fry recalled in verse,

When the foe charged on the
breastworks
With the madness of despair,
And the bravest of souls were
tested,
The little Jew was there.

When the weary dozed on duty,
Or the wounded needed care,
When another shot was called for,
The little Jew was there.

With the festering dead around
them,
Shedding poison in the air,
When the crippled chieftain
ordered,
The little Jew was there.

Sadly, Sigmund had a hard time convincing his friends that he was the little Jew that was there. When he returned to New York and mentioned the battle, people thought it was a *bubbe meyseh* (grandmother's tale). In exasperation, he showed his battlefield relics, only to be asked how much they had cost.

After a brief stint in New York Shlesinger moved to Cleveland, where he established a successful tobacco business and married Fannie Flesheim in 1874. Sigmund Shlesinger, who was described by an Army General as possessing "great courage, cool persistence, . . . a worthy descendant of King David," became a respected leader in Cleveland's Jewish community, holding the post of president both of the Knights of Pythias and of B'nai B'rith's Lodge no. 16.

As for the hero of the Battle at Beecher Island, the astute American Jewish historian, Jacob Rader Marcus, notes that Shlesinger's "leadership in Jewish social welfare societies required on occasion as much courage as rising above the breastworks to snap off a shot at Chief Roman Nose."

Josephine Sarah ("Sadie") Marcus

Wife of Wyatt Earp

"No one could convince me that Wyatt was a killer—he lived with Josie for fifty years!"

This remark reflected the feelings of many individuals who had known both the legendary Wyatt Earp and his Jewish wife—an adventuresome, strong-willed, and at times, rollicking person in her own right. Although Wyatt loved eating her Dutch-oven cornbread, Josie was not content with being a housewife. Her unusual experiences as the spouse of a Western lawman did not permit her to remain in the kitchen for long.

Josephine Earp, 1880

What motivated "a strictly raised girl not yet nineteen and from a prosperous German Jewish family," as she later wrote in her memoirs, to put her "dainty feet down from a train in a place like Benson [Arizona]"? At a young age Josie saw Gilbert and Sullivan's play, *H.M.S. Pinafore*, and immediately became stagestruck. She ran away from her parents home in San Francisco with a friend, Dora Hirsch, to perform with a road troupe, eventually ending up in Tombstone, Arizona in 1879. En route to Prescott they were almost ambushed by Indians but were assisted by a posse and a lawman named Johnny Behan, who later introduced her to his deputy sheriff, Wyatt Earp.

Though still a young man, Earp already had a colorful career as a lawman, saloonkeeper, gambler, and shotgun guard for Wells Fargo. He and his "crowd"—lawmen, outlaws, cowboys, and cattle rustlers—fascinated the young Jewish runaway. During their courtship Earp's reputation as a renowned lawman became enhanced at the Tombstone gunfight of October 26, 1881, popularly known as the gunfight at the O.K. Corral. Sadie, as Wyatt endearingly called her, witnessed this famous shootout, still a legend in the West.

Back home in San Francisco the Marcuses were appalled to read the headlines and worried about their daughter living in such a dangerous place. Little did they know that she was "keeping company" with its major protagonist.

Fearing reprisals from vengeful outlaws, Wyatt and Josie left Tombstone and were secretly married. Their travels took them to Denver, where they met the "happy-go-lucky" Bat Masterson, one of the deadliest gunslingers in the West. On the road Earp tried to teach his wife rifle shooting, but she dropped the gun and "ran for the tent." However, Josephine Marcus Earp was not a "dainty little lady." In the middle of winter she hiked up the Rocky Mountains with her husband, to the astonishment of local prospectors, who had never seen a woman make such a perilous climb.

Wanderlust soon propelled this Western lawman and his Jewish wife through Mexico, Colorado, Idaho, and Texas, continually encountering their friend Bat Masterson, who was always "on assignment." Seemingly unable to settle down, they caught gold fever at the turn of the century and hiked to Alaska to prospect, only to end up opening a saloon.

During the years in Alaska Josie became despondent. The fierce Arctic winters offered no relief. She was not able to bear children, having had two miscarriages. She loved the itinerant life of prospecting and gambling, and squandered large amounts of money. Fortunately, her family inheritance helped to sustain the Earps during the hard times.

The couple returned to California, and visited the Mojave Desert, which Josie found so awesome that it moved her, although she was not religious, to "informal prayer directed to [her] mother's *lieber Gott.*" In Los Angeles they built a house, where their lives were no different from that of the family of a "retired businessman or banker." Even in their golden years, though, they continued their lifelong pleasures of gambling and hiking.

The last time Wyatt Earp left their home was to vote in the 1928 election. Earp, who surprisingly enough was a teetotaler, voted for Al Smith, an opponent of Prohibition. He died in 1929 and his wife buried him in a Jewish cemetery, the Hills of Eternity, in Colma, California. His loving fellow adventurer and spouse, Josephine Sarah Marcus, passed away in 1944.

Philo Jacoby (1837–1922)

Editor and "Champion Rifle Shot of the World"

Philo Jacoby, a Polish-Jewish immigrant, had an unusual range of talents: Among other things, he was a top marksman and a journalist. Educated in a naval academy, he sailed with the merchant marine in England and Prussia, and arrived on the West Coast of the U.S. in 1859 as third mate of the clipper ship *Whirlwind.* A few years later he helped found a Jewish newspaper in San

Philo Jacoby

Francisco called *The Hebrew* and served as its editor.

The newspaper, a five-column broadsheet published in German and English, offered a fascinating potpourri of news and features for its immigrant readership. Besides carrying news items like the plight of Jews in lands such as Morocco and Italy, the journal published serialized essays on the history of Jews in Poland, a biography of the Dutch rabbi Manasseh ben Israel, and Biblical translations.

Like other newspapers of this era, *The Hebrew* carried quaint advertisements for potions, antidotes, and spirits. Unlike other newspapers, however, it also printed special notices for its "Israelite" readership. Among these ornately typeset ads was the following:

> *Matzoth!*
> The original pioneer
> *Matzoth Bakery*
> The undersigned, who are the Original Matzoth Bakers in this City and State, most respectfully announce to their Co-Religionists, that their arrangements for manufacturing Matzoth are most perfect. . . .

The notice assured the reader that the bakers were *shomer* and "Hebrew hands are only employed." The shop listed its specialties: "Cakes, confectionary and goose grease for the holy days."

Besides conveying the flavor of West Coast Jewish life, the paper also served as a forum for the iconoclastic views of its editor. In an editorial entitled, "Orthodox or Reform," Jacoby made the seemingly contradictory assertion: "We are both Orthodox and reform. We are Orthodox in maintaining the observance of the Sabbath and the ordinations of the Pentateuch in all their varied lessons. . . . We are reform in upholding the abolition of the selfish and debasing custom of the ages of tyranny, which separated the sexes in the synagogue . . . the fundamental principles of Judaism are immutable—no change can be effected with them without undermining the whole structure."

The editor proudly proclaimed that his views were expressed "in plain English and avoided the interlarding of Hebrew, Latin, Greek, Coptic, Chaldean, Arabic or even the more modern French and German . . . to prove our great learning."

Jacoby made no pretense to objective news reporting: "It has been noted with pleasure that the Prussian Commander-in-Chief of the Third Army Corps, Prince Frederick Charles, ordered that all Jewish soldiers should be permitted to celebrate the high festivals in September." Nor was he circumspect about voicing concern over anti-Semitism. When Memphis was rocked by a fraud scandal and Jewish involvement was widely publicized, the editor of *The Hebrew* wondered aloud why Jews were singled out: "Why stigmatize the religion of millions of people for the crime of a few individuals? Who ever heard of the arrest of a Protestant for larceny, or a Catholic . . . in the act of breaking into a dwelling?"

Like its successors, *The Hebrew* was not free from the backbiting and internal wrangling that afflicts many Anglo-Jewish newspapers. While contemporary papers may compete for Jewish Federation funding or ads, few have resorted to the tactics of Jacoby's journalistic arch-rival, Julius Eckmann, editor of *The Gleaner*. Eckmann went to the Catholic ministry, claiming that Jacoby was trying to convert the Gentile printer of *The Hebrew* to Judaism! Jacoby, incensed at such an inflammatory action, especially from a fellow Jew, contemplated a strong response. Eckmann was lucky though, his rival thought he was "too contemptible" to receive "just punishment."

In fact, Eckmann was very lucky. Philo Jacoby was known as the "Champion Rifle Shot of the World," a distinction he earned at the 1876 Philadelphia Centennial Exposition.

At a young age Jacoby had joined a local rifle club and, although a novice, startled the other members by making one hundred and one bulls-eyes at one hundred and fifty yards. After settling in the United States he became president of the California *Schuetzen* Club. Later he made three trips back to Europe, competed with top marksmen in Switzerland and Prussia and was crowned shooting champion of Austria and Germany.

Clearly Philo Jacoby did not make his mark only in the columns of *The Hebrew*. During his lifetime, this Polish immigrant, Anglo-Jewish journalist, received more than one hundred awards for marksmanship, including forty gold and silver goblets, a diamond badge, a champion belt, more than fifty medallions, and a gold medal won at the Vienna Exposition and presented to him by the Emperor Franz Joseph in 1890.

—D.A.

THE JEWISH UNDERWORLD: AMERICAN JEWISH GANGSTERS

They had names like Phil "The Stick" Kovalick, Charles "King" Solomon, Waxey Gordon, Louis "Shadows" Kravitz, Harry "Big Greenie" Greenberg, "Dandy Phil" Kastel, Jacob "Greasy Thumb" Guzik, Abe "Kid Twist" Reles, Jacob "Gurrah" Shapiro, Max "Boo Boo" Hoff, Abner "Longie" Zwillman, Arthur "Dutch Schultz" Flegenheimer, Jacob "Yasha" Katzenberg, Arnold "The Brain" Rothstein, Louis "Lepke" Buchalter, and Benjamin "Bugsy" Siegel. What they had in common was that they were all American gangsters and they were all Jews. It would not be an exaggeration to say that their influence on organized crime in the United States during the 1920's and 1930's rivaled, if not exceeded, that of their Italian counterparts.

Although there were Jewish criminals in the nineteenth century, it was the period between the World Wars—the eras of Prohibition and the Great Depression—that saw the rise of the American Jewish gangster as a force. In 1919 the United States government attempted to regulate morality by outlawing the manufacture and sale of alcoholic beverages. Prohibition offered an enormous opportunity for the mobster—to provide what society still wanted, namely booze. Another contributing factor to the rise of gangsterism was the morality of the age. At all levels of society this was a time when "anything goes," when an honest man was considered a "sucker," and when flaunting the rules was the norm. It has been said that if one were to compute the number of Americans who violated the Eighteenth Amendment, whether as producers, conveyers, or peddlers of intoxicants or as "protectors" of the trade, or as consumers, the total would probably be an overwhelming majority of the population.

It was in this milieu that the Jewish gangster rose to prominence. Contrary to the popular myth that Jewish criminals are involved mostly in white-collar crime, such as fraud or embezzelment, these men engaged in extortion, gambling, narcotics peddling, and murder. For a time they dominated the rackets in Boston, Cleveland, Detroit, Newark, Philadelphia, and New York. A composite portrait of the "typical" Jewish gangster of this period would show him to be a second generation American male of Eastern European parentage, city bred, and in his early twenties. His parents would be working class and traditional, rather than Orthodox, Jews; that is, they would observe a number of the Jewish traditions and holidays but would not comply with all the religious injunctions that an Orthodox Jew is required to perform. This typical Jewish gangster would not have finished high school and would remain strongly attached to his family throughout his life. Generally speaking, he was the only person in his immediate family to turn to a life of crime, his brothers and sisters following more respectable routes to economic advancement and social mobility.

He chose crime because it was the quickest way for him to achieve material success, power, recognition, and status—a means to become a somebody and move up and out of the ghetto. Legitimate work was hard, dull, and offered only slow economic and social mobility. Crime was exciting and provided a challenge for men of ability, aggressiveness, and daring. The ever-present element of danger—being caught by the police or killed by rivals—added to the excitement.

Jewish gangsters saw what they were doing in the same way that many of their non-Jewish colleagues saw themselves: They were providing a service. People wanted liquor, narcotics, gambling, and women; the gangster furnished them. Physical violence was accepted as a tool of the trade: it was a way to eliminate competition and protect one's interest.

The American Jewish community at large entertained ambivalent feelings about the Jewish gangster. The leaders were repelled by him because he epitomized the "bad

Jew": the evil man who provided ammunition for the anti-Semite and would bring onus and hatred upon the entire community. In the 1920's and 1930's these were not idle concerns; the American atmosphere was charged with the anti-Semitic fulminations and activities of Henry Ford, the Ku Klux Klan, Gerald L. K. Smith, Father Charles Coughlin and the German-American Bund. In addition, Jewish parents were in a perpetual state of anxiety lest their children be attracted to the lifestyle of the gangster and emulate him.

Nevertheless, many people in the community harbored a grudging admiration for the Jewish mobster because he competed physically with the non-Jew and gave as good as he got. The Jewish gangster had "made it" in America by beating the violent and physical Gentile at his own game. At a time when Jews in Europe were at the mercy of hostile governments and under constant threat of violence and pogroms, the gangster provided American Jews with secret vicarious satisfaction and pride.

A number of Jewish gangsters acquired respect because they assumed the role of protector and defender of their people. In Chicago the funeral of the Jewish gangster Samuel "Nails" Morton was attended by five thousand Jews who felt they owed him their thanks for protecting their neighborhood from Jew-baiters. Jewish mobsters in Detroit protected Jewish peddlers and grocery store owners from having to pay protection money to Polish and Italian hoodlums. And in the 1930's New York Jewish thugs broke up German-American Bund rallies in New York and New Jersey.

Despite their aversion to the gangster, even Jewish leaders were not above using his services on behalf of the community. Arnold Rothstein was asked to help end the New York garment district strike of 1926; and Jewish gangsters were asked to help secure arms during Israel's War of Independence.

In spite of their own success in crime, most Jewish gangsters kept their families separate and unimplicated in their criminal enterprises. West Coast mobster Mickey Cohen summarized this attitude when he said, "We had a code of ethics like the ones among bankers, other people in other walks of life, that one never involved his wife or family in his work." These men wanted their children to marry well and achieve respectability and acceptance in the legitimate world. Thus, they sent their children to the best schools and encouraged them to enter the professions, such as law and medicine. In this, they were very much like other Jewish parents of their generation.

The following are some of the more prominent Jewish figures in organized crime before World War II.

MOSES L. "MOE" ANNENBERG (1878–1942) was born in East Prussia and came to the United States in 1884. He was the circulation manager of all the Hearst newspapers and magazines in America when, in the 1920's, he conceived the idea of establishing a telegraphic news service for bookie joints that would carry fast and accurate information from race tracks across the country. According to the Internal Revenue Service, which collected evidence of his income tax evasion, Annenberg operated a racket that was a monopoly of the telegraph service from almost all the race tracks in the United States,

Moses L. "Moe" Annenberg

Canada, Mexico, and Cuba. His wire service was the American Telephone and Telegraph Company's fifth largest customer. So extensive was this operation that one insider equated it with the British Empire. During the Depression Annenberg's income from his racetrack wire service was conservatively estimated to be six million dollars a year. In 1939, while under investigation by the Justice Department, Annenberg divested himself of all his interest in the racing wire service. He did not attempt to sell it to anyone or to realize any salvage from it; he simply walked out. Nevertheless, he was convicted of income tax evasion, fined eight million dollars, and sentenced to three years in prison. Shortly after his release, he died.

LOUIS "LEPKE" BUCHALTER (1897–1944) was nicknamed "Lepkele" (little Louis) by his mother, and later, by J. Edgar Hoover, "the most dangerous criminal in the United States." Born on the Lower East Side of New York, where his family lived in a crowded flat over a small hardware store owned by his father, Louis was the only one of eleven children to embark on a life of crime. One brother became a rabbi, another a dentist, and a third a pharmacist. Little Louis got better-than-average marks in school and seems to have behaved himself, but he quit school at the age of fifteen, after completing the eighth grade, and went to work as a delivery boy. By the time Lepke was eighteen his family, except Louis, had moved out West. He turned down an older brother's offer to put him through high school and college and, instead, moved into a furnished room on the East Side.

Louis "Lepke" Buchalter

It was in this brawling neighborhood, that Buchalter embarked on his criminal career. He joined a group of local hoods, who rolled drunks, picked pockets, and robbed from pushcarts. His close associate at this time, and for the next thirty years, was Jacob "Gurrah" Shapiro, a surly, coarse young man. Just after his twenty-first birthday, Lepke was sent to jail for stealing a salesman's sample case. Paroled in 1917, he was back in prison the next year on a larceny charge, and was sent up again, for two years, in 1920.

Upon his release he turned his talent to labor racketeering. In his private life, a devoted family man who rarely drank or gambled, Lepke commanded an army of gangsters who extorted millions of dollars from his victims. Their weapons were destructive acids, bludgeons, blackjacks, knives, fire, icepicks, and guns. For a fee Lepke protected manufacturers from strikers and unionization of their shops by intimidating workers and using strong-arm tactics. He also forced unions to do his bidding by installing his own business agents or by creating rival unions. Lepke explained that the trick was a captive union and a captive trade association. "That way you got both management and labor in your pocket." Lucky Luciano once commented that "with the rest of us it was booze, gambling, whores, like that. But Lepke took the bread out of the workers' mouths."

Lepke's system worked and he became a legend. The few men who failed to heed the gang's orders or who dared to go to the police with their stories suffered "destruction, acid throwing, mayhem and murder." In the same way that he gained control over the unions through terror, Buchalter moved into legitimate business. Those who tried to fight him found their plants wrecked or their stocks ruined by a special Lepke task force, expert in the art of acid throwing. When a manufacturer surrendered, Lepke would place his men in the factory as managers, foremen, and bookkeepers. By 1932 Buchalter dominated a wide assortment of industries in New York, including the bakery and pastry drivers, the milliners, the garment workers, the shoe trade, the poultry market, the taxicab business, the motion picture operators, and the fur truckers.

At the pinnacle of his power Buchalter was the feudal lord of New York's underworld. His reputation through gangland was that he never lost his temper, but his own men feared him. They called him "The Judge," sometimes "Judge Louie." One associate, Sholem Bernstein, summed it up for all when he said, "I don't ask questions, I just obey. It would be more healthier."

In 1934 Buchalter helped to organize the Syndicate. Its creation converted the scattered, unconnected mobs in New York, Chicago, Kansas City, and other cities into a smooth-working, tightly-bound business. On the early board of directors of this confederation of crime bosses were Lepke, Johnny Torrio, Frank Costello, Lucky Luciano, Joe Adonis, "Bugsy" Siegel, and Abner Zwillman. They decided that this would be a loose working confederation, with each boss having his own territory and with the regional chiefs sitting together on a board of directors. The board would dictate policy and handle all negotiations on the inter-mob level.

It was Lepke who campaigned for a special enforcement group to keep the peace and insure that the Syndicate's decisions were carried out. Sometimes referred to as Murder Incorporated, this crack corps of killers was made up primarily of Jews from Brownsville, East New York, and Ocean Hill. They became the "official" execution squad for the Syndicate. When Dutch Schultz boasted that he would do things his way, he was killed. And it was Charley "The Bug" Workman and Mendy Weiss, two Murder Incorporated killers, who did the job on orders from Lepke.

In 1941 Lepke was indicted for the killing of Joseph Rosen, a garment trucker whom Lepke had driven out of business. Buchalter was the only top underworld figure of his generation to be tried, convicted, and executed for murder (at Sing Sing Prison on March 4, 1944).

JACOB "GREASY THUMB" GUZIK (1887–1956) is an exception to the generalization that Jewish gangsters were the only ones in their families to pursue a life of crime: Jake and his brothers all began their working careers in the rackets. Jake, however, rose to become the most famous of the Guzik brothers through his association with Al Capone. Jake became the Capone organization's treasurer and acquired the nickname "Greasy Thumb" from the green stain earned from counting Capone's money. Later in life Guzik brought numerous lawsuits against newspapers for portraying him as a gangster. He brushed aside queries as to the wisdom of this by saying, "I'm paying these judges, so why shouldn't I use them." At his death he received an Orthodox Jewish funeral and was eulogized as a man "who never lost faith in his God. Hundreds benefited by his kindness and generosity. His charities were performed quietly."

Jake "Greasy Thumb" Guzik

Meyer Lansky

ARTHUR "DUTCH SCHULTZ" FLEGENHEIMER (1900–1935). Although he was accepted into the Catholic Church on his deathbed, Arthur was born Jewish. His mother was a pious, patient woman whose great grief was that the son she adored turned out as he did. Arthur's playmates nicknamed him "Dutch Schultz" after an early twentieth century hoodlum. Starting out as a bootlegger, Flegenheimer moved into slot machines, the Harlem numbers racket, and the restaurant protection racket. By 1932 he was clearing two million dollars a year just from the restaurant racket. Dutch was killed in the men's room of a Newark chophouse by Charlie "The Bug" Workman and Mendy Weiss, when he defied a New York syndicate decision not to kill Thomas E. Dewey, then investigating organized crime in Manhattan.

MEYER LANSKY (SUCHOWLJANSKY) (1902–) is frequently mentioned by law enforcement officials as being one of the kingpins of organized crime in the United States. Since the 1920's he has been linked with names like Bugsy Siegel, Longie Zwillman, Lucky Luciano, Johnny Torrio, and Frank Costello. His alleged gambling empire was at one time said to encompass Florida, the Caribbean Islands, and Las Vegas. Although he has been indicted numerous times, Lansky was only convicted once, in 1953 on a gambling charge, and served three months in jail. In 1971 Lansky applied for Israeli citizenship. His application was rejected on the grounds that "he was a person with a criminal past, likely to endanger the public welfare." Lansky has long been associated with Jewish causes and despite this rebuff, he remained a strong supporter of Israel and of Jewish philanthropies.

ABE "KID TWIST" RELES (1907–1941) was a New York-born hoodlum and killer about whom it was said, "he committed just about every act of violence against which there is a law." Reles was one of Murder Incorporated's top gunmen, and it was his turning state's evidence, in 1940, that provided lawmen with their first inside look at the New York crime syndicate. His testimony assisted in the conviction and execution of seven major crime figures; Lepke Buchalter, was one of them. Reles died in 1941 when, while under police guard, he fell or was thrown from the Half Moon Hotel in Coney Island.

ARNOLD "THE BRAIN" ROTHSTEIN (1882–1928) was the pioneer big businessman of crime in the United States. Rothstein was born in New York City, the son of a respected, middle-class Jewish merchant. The elder Rothstein was versed in religious and Hebrew classical literature, was something of a philanthropist, and was chairman of the board of New York's Beth Israel Hospital. Arnold never achieved the kind of respectability his family hoped he would, but he did exceed their expectations in another area: By the time he died he had amassed a fortune estimated to be in the millions of dollars.

Rothstein understood the logic of coordination and the potential of organized crime. Though he is chiefly remembered as the man allegedly responsible for the "Black Sox" scandal—the attempt to fix the 1919 baseball World Series between the Chicago White Sox and the Cincinnati Reds—it was Rothstein who, during the 1920's, put together the largest gambling empire in the United States and controlled most of the gangs in New York, as well as that city's traffic in bootlegging, narcotics, and gambling. Rothstein attempted to bring order to the extreme competition prevailing in the bootlegging business. He supplied money, manpower, and protection; and if things went wrong, he was ready to provide bail and attorneys.

Rothstein moved freely in all circles, from politicians and statesmen to bankers and bums. On his payroll at one time or another were gangsters such as Waxey Gordon, Jack "Legs" Diamond, Lepke Buchalter, Albert Anastasia, and Frank Costello (who later rose to become a "boss" of the mob and the star attraction of the Kefauver Crime Committee Hearings), as well as a goodly number of public officials. So successful was Rothstein in organizing criminal enterprises and staying out of jail, that Damon Runyon dubbed him "The Brain." And his fame was such that he was immortalized during his lifetime by F. Scott Fitzgerald in *The Great Gatsby* as Meyer Wolfsheim. Despite this notoriety, Jewish community leaders in New York asked for (and received) his help in settling a strike in the garment district in 1926.

Rothstein's life of crime, for which he never spent a day in jail, ended when he was shot to death in New York's Park Central Hotel. True to his underworld creed, he refused to divulge the name of his assailant before he died. The final irony was that Arnold received an Orthodox Jewish funeral.

BENJAMIN "BUGSY" SIEGEL (1905–1947) was the archetypal movie mobster: handsome, hotheaded, ambitious, and ruthless—the petty thief and muscleman who rose to become a crime lord. He played an important role in New York City's underworld activities during the 1920's and 1930's and became a member of the East Coast crime syndicate's board of directors at the age of twenty-eight. Siegel established the beachhead of organized crime in California and opened Las Vegas for the mob. He recognized the tremendous opportunities for profit from legalized casino gambling in Nevada and with syndicate help built the Flamingo Hotel. After it was built, however, he tried to keep most of the profits for himself. This defiance of the Syndicate was to cost him his life. On a June evening in 1947 someone pointed a .30 caliber carbine at Siegel's face as he sat in the apartment of his girl friend, Virginia Hill, and pumped three bullets into his head. Siegel thus had the distinction of being the first member of the Syndicate's board of directors to be executed by his own.

ABNER "LONGIE" ZWILLMAN (1904–1959), called the "Al Capone of New Jersey," was one of the biggest bootleggers of the Prohibition era. By the 1930's he was the acknowledged leader of the New Jersey underworld and an associate of Dutch Schultz, Lepke Buchalter, Lucky Luciano, and Frank Costello. In 1934 Zwillman played an important role in the formation of the East Coast crime syndicate, and sat on its board

Benjamin "Bugsy" Siegel

of directors. Following the murder of Dutch Schultz in 1935, Zwillman was designated as "Public Enemy Number One of New Jersey." Despite his reputed criminal activities, Zwillman and his wife were respected by their neighbors and the Jewish community of Newark for their charitable work. Over a thousand people attended his funeral, with the service being conducted by Dr. Joachim Prinz, rabbi of Temple B'nai Abraham of Newark and president of the American Jewish Congress.

DETROIT'S PURPLE GANG. Not all Jewish gangsters were as nationally prominent or successful as the above. The "Purple Gang," which operated during the 1920's and 1930's, had its beginnings in the Jewish section of Detroit's East Side. Originally formed around Samuel "Sammie Purple" Cohen, the leadership of this group of petty criminals was initially assumed by the three Bernstein brothers—Abe, Isadore, and Ray—who had emigrated to Detroit from New York. Beginning with shoplifting and extortion, the gang moved up into the distilling and brewing business.

At the same time, another gang was also emerging on the East Side, known as the "Oakland Sugar House Gang." Several of this gang's members had gone to the same school and had begun associating together as adolescents. After school they would engage in petty crimes that often included stealing fruit, candy, and other small items from Jewish merchants. Later they graduated to rolling drunks and shaking down Jewish shopkeepers for money. Eventually the boys went into business for themselves, manufacturing alcohol for bootleg liquor out of their base of operation, the Oakland Sugar House located on Oakland St. The original members of this gang were Harry Fleisher, Henry Shore, Eddie Fletcher, Irving Milberg, Harry Altman, Harry Keywell, and Morris and Phil Raider.

In time, instead of competing, the two groups joined forces as "The Purple Gang" under the leadership of Abe Bernstein and branched out into the business of importing liquor across the Detroit River from Canada.

The Purple Gang was loosely organized, and instead of concentrating on a single racket, the individual members of the gang were generally for hire, going wherever the price was highest. As a result, they were often overextended. They were also careless in selecting jobs, slipshod in carrying out the work, and indiscreet in whom they double-crossed. This negligence, in the end, contributed to their demise. For several years, however, the Purples managed the prosperous business of supplying Canadian whisky—Old Log Cabin—to the Capone organization in Chicago. Despite its relatively high price, this brand could be sold easily because of its well-known quality. It was the hijacking of a shipment of Purple Gang Old Log Cabin whisky by the Bugs Moran gang of Chicago that led to the St. Valentine's Day Massacre of seven Moran gangsters in 1929.

Although their major source of income was bootlegging whisky, the Purples branched out into other fields in order to earn additional money. They hijacked prizefight films and forced movie theaters to show them for a high fee; they defrauded insurance companies by staging fake accidents; they kidnapped people; and they accepted contracts for killing the enemies of various hoods who did not want to do the job themselves.

Because they were flamboyant and well-known in the city's night spots, and because many of them liked to dress well, be seen in public, and live in fine houses, a romantic aura surrounded the Purples that distinguished them from other gangs in Detroit. The gang was destroyed from two directions: The police moved against them when gang members left behind too much evidence of their crimes, and a rival Sicilian gang, tired of competing with the Purples, decided to eliminate them. One by one, the Purples were murdered until most of them were either dead or afraid to remain in the Detroit area. So stealthy was the Sicilian move, that neither the Purples nor the public realized what was going on.

In July 1929 four members of the Purple Gang—Eddie Fletcher, Harry Sutton, Abe Axler, and Irving Milberg—were sentenced to twenty-two months in Leavenworth Penitentiary for conspiracy to violate the prohibition laws. In 1930 Morris Raider was sentenced to twelve-to-fifteen years in Jackson State Prison for shooting a boy he suspected of spying on members of the gang who were cutting whisky. And in 1931 Ray Bernstein, Irving Milberg, and Harry Keywell were found guilty of first degree murder and sentenced to life imprisonment for the ambush-slaying of three members of a rival gang.

Remaining leaders of the Purple Gang were systematically and mysteriously executed. In July 1929 Irving Shapiro was taken for a ride and slain. In November 1933 the bodies of Abe Axler and Eddie Fletcher were found in a car on an isolated country road. Each man had been shot numerous times in the face from close range. The murder of Harry Millman in November 1937 signalled the end of the Purple Gang in organized crime in Detroit.

The great Hebrew poet, Haim Nahman Bialik, once claimed that the Jewish people would achieve normality when there were Jewish prostitutes and thieves. A closer look at the Jewish experience in America shows that the Jews were perhaps, more "normal" than had been supposed.

—R.A.R.

THE JEWISH ATHLETE

THE JEWISH ALMANAC'S SPORTS HALL OF FAME

Auerbach, Arnold (Red) (1917—), member of the Basketball Hall of Fame. As coach, general manager, and president of the Boston Celtics, Auerbach created one of the most successful sports organizations in history. He played high school basketball in his native Brooklyn at a local junior college, and in 1937–40 at George Washington University. He served in the U.S. Navy in World War II, and in 1946 became the head coach of the Washington Capitals. After three successful years in Washington he moved to the Tri-City Blackhawks for the 1949–50 season, and then to Boston in 1950–51. The Boston Celtics had finished last in the Eastern Division the previous year with the third worst record in the seventeen-team National Basketball Association. Under Auerbach the team became a winner. Boston placed second in the Eastern Division four times in his first six seasons and in 1956–57, with the addition of Bill Russell, the Celtics won their first league championship. They lost the title to St. Louis the next season but with Russell, Bob Cousy, Bill Sharman, Frank Ramsey, Tom Heinsohn, John Havlicek, and the Jones boys—K. C. and Sam—the Celtics claimed the league championship an incredible eight straight times. Auerbach instilled pride and discipline in his players. They were a team, not just a collection of individual stars. When an opposing team played the Celtics they knew they were up against not only five great players but a sixth wild man on the bench. Auerbach was always in the game, berating referees, opposing players and coaches, spectators and officials, doing anything to motivate his team to win games. He was not a good loser. "Show me a good loser," he said, "and I'll show you a loser."

In 1950 he brought the first black player, Chuck Cooper, into the NBA and in 1966 he made Bill Russell the Boston coach. "I don't treat athletes by religion or by color," Auerbach explained. "To me a person is a person and I don't like it any other way." In 1965 he was named NBA Coach of the Year and awarded the Boston Medal of Achievement. In 1966, after twenty years as a head coach in the NBA, he retired with 1,037 regular season and playoff victories. With Auerbach as president and general manager between 1966 and 1979 the Celtics won four more NBA championships. In 1971 he was named the NBA's Silver Anniversary coach. He is a member of the Jewish Sports Hall of Fame, Wingate Institute, Israel.

Red Auerbach flanked by Bill Russell (l.) and Tommy Heinsohn (r.), 1964.

Brody, Talbert (Tal) (1943—), American Israeli basketball player. Brody went from a ten-year-old biddy leaguer at the Trenton, New Jersey, Jewish Community Center to an All-State selection in high school and All-America, All-Academic and All-Big Ten honors as a senior at the University of Illinois. A 6′ 1½″ guard, he was drafted by the Baltimore Bullets of the National Basketball Association in 1965. That summer he was in Israel for the Maccabiah Games and helped the United States win a gold medal in basketball. Asked to return to Israel to set up sports programs, he passed up pro ball, earned a Master's degree in educational psychology, and returned to Israel in 1966.

In Israel, Brody worked for the Ministry of Education and Culture, giving sports clinics and basketball instruction to physical education teachers. At the same time he performed with the Tel Aviv Maccabi basketball team. His playmaking, shooting, and aggressive defense made him an instant success. In 1967 he created a sensation when he almost led his team to the European Cup championship. Maccabi lost to an Italian team, but the impact on basketball in Israel was tremendous. From that time on Israel was a force to be reckoned with in European basketball. For that, Brody was named Israel's Athlete of the Year in 1967. The *Jerusalem Post* said that he had "revolutionized basketball in Israel," and "introduced the 'American Game' here, an entirely new approach to basketball . . . a much faster more open game than hitherto seen in Israel."

Brody played with the Maccabi club in 1967-68, and although he had decided to settle in Israel permanently, he returned to the United States to fulfill his military obligation. For the next two years he represented the U.S. Army and Armed Forces All-Star teams in national and international competition. He was back in Israel by late 1970 and became an instructor at Wingate Institute of Physical Education, established a sporting goods business, married an Israeli (Moshe Dayan was the guest of honor at the wedding), and rejoined the Tel Aviv Maccabi basketball team.

His hard work for basketball paid off in 1977 when Tel Aviv Maccabi won the European Cup in competition with twenty-three national champion club teams. To the surprise of everyone, Maccabi beat the Czechs and Red Army team, 91–79. Then on April, 7, 1977, Maccabi defeated a veteran team, Mobil Girgi of Varese, Italy, 78–77 in Belgrade for the European title.

Not long after the triumph Brody announced his retirement as a player. He said, however, that he would continue to coach and establish sports programs for the nation's youth. He once told a reporter, "I knew I could also have a good life in the United States, but I felt that in Israel I could do something special. I will always remain grateful to my home country for what it did for me and there is no better ambassador for the United States than I am."

Dreyfuss, Barney (1865–1932), baseball executive and innovator. Born in Germany, Dreyfuss entered baseball in 1888 as an official with the Louisville franchise of the American Association. In 1900 he aquired the Pittsburgh Pirates and served as owner and general manager of the team until his death. His Pirates won six National League championships and two World Series (1909, 1925) and produced numerous Hall of Famers. Dreyfuss did all of his own scouting and was considered the best judge of player talent in the game.

In 1903 Dreyfuss created the modern World Series when Boston, the American League champion, accepted his challenge to a post-season tournament. Boston won the Series but the Pirates earned more money than their rivals when the generous Pittsburgh owner turned over all of his proceeds to his players. In 1909 he built Forbes Field, the first modern baseball park. He served as vice-president of the National League in 1929–32. Dreyfuss was also a pioneer of professional football. He is a member of the Jewish Sports Hall of Fame, Wingate Institute, Israel.

Friedman, Benjamin (Benny) (1905—), charter member of the College Football Hall of Fame, Friedman was football's first great passer. In 1924 he was a bench warmer at the University of Michigan. "Fielding Yost had been the Michigan coach in my freshman season," Friedman recalled, "but he bowed to pressure and let George Little handle the team in 1924. Little could not see me as a quarterback because I did not have the characteristics he was looking for. He did not care for our people. I often wonder what would have happened had I stuck to a decision I made in my sophomore year and quit."

Persuaded to stick out the season by an assistant coach, Friedman received his first varsity experience in the third game of the season against Illinois. "From that time I started every game," said Friedman, "and played sixty minutes of most every game."

Friedman became Michigan's starting quarterback in 1925 when Yost returned as the head coach. It proved an inspired move. Michigan enjoyed a sensational year and Friedman became a first team All-American selection. He passed for eleven touchdowns and did all the place kicking. The Wolverines won seven games and lost one and were the Western Conference champions. The only defeat was by Northwestern, 3–2, in what Friedman called "the worst conditions on the worst weather day." His most satisfying game was against Wisconsin. He passed for a touchdown on the first play from scrimmage, and then ran a kickoff back eighty-five yards for another touchdown as Michigan trounced the Badgers, 21–0. The next week a Friedman field goal stopped Red Grange and Illinois, 3–0. In all, the Wolverines scored 227 points to 3 for the opposition. Yost, who coached Michigan for twenty-five years, said the 1925 team was his best.

With Friedman as captain in 1926 Michigan put together another 7–1 season. The only loss was to Navy, 10–0. Friedman played his most memorable college game against unbeaten Ohio State in Columbus. The Buckeyes led 10–0 after the first quarter. Friedman answered back with a touchdown pass to Michigan's great end Bennie Oosterbann, and then kicked the extra point. With twenty-seven seconds left before half time, he hit a forty-two-yard field goal from a difficult angle to tie the score, 10–10. In the second half he threw another touchdown pass, kicked the extra point, and Michigan outlasted Ohio State, 17–16. The man coach Yost called "the quarterback who never makes a mistake" was again a first team All-America choice and the Most Valuable Player in the Western Conference.

Friedman moved into the pro ranks in 1927 with the Cleveland Bulldogs of the National Football League. He proved a revelation. As George Halas, owner of the Chicago Bears, remembered it, "Benny Friedman . . . was the first pro quarterback to exploit the strategic possibilities of the pass. Until Friedman came along, the pass had been used as a desperation weapon in long yardage situations on third down—or when your team was hopelessly behind. Benny demonstrated that the pass could be mixed with the running plays as an integral part of the offense. Influenced by Benny's success, the rules committee moved to slenderize the . . . football . . . Streamlining the ball was the final step in the evolution of pro football from a running game into the passing and running game we know today."

Friedman quarterbacked Cleveland, Detroit, and the New York Giants in 1927–31. He wound up his pro career with the Brooklyn Dodgers football team in 1934.

He returned to collegiate football in 1934 as head coach at City College of New York. Friedman remained at CCNY until 1941, when he joined the U.S. Navy. Between 1949 and 1963 he served as head football coach and athletic director at Brandeis University. He is a member of the Jewish Sports Hall of Fame, Wingate Institute, Israel.

Greenberg, Henry (Hank) (1911—), member of the Baseball Hall of Fame. Greenberg was a first baseman-outfielder with the Detroit Tigers (1933–46) and the Pittsburgh Pirates (1947). While a Tiger, he led the American League in home runs and runs-batted-in (183 in 1937) four times each. He was chosen the American League's Most Valuable Player in 1935 (as a first baseman) and in 1940 (as an outfielder). At the height of the 1934 pennant race he had to decide whether he would play on Rosh Ha shanah and Yom Kippur. His decision to appear on Rosh Ha shanah and skip the Yom Kippur game was an important topic to baseball fans across the country. One Detroit fan complained that Jewish holidays came every year but the Tigers hadn't won a pennant since 1909. Detroit won the Rosh Ha shanah game as Greenberg hit two home runs, but lost on Yom Kippur.

Hank Greenberg hitting a home run against the White Sox.

All eyes were on Greenberg in 1938 when he challenged Babe Ruth's 60 home run record. His total of 58 fell short but did tie the record for a right-handed batter. Greenberg joined the U.S. Army Air Corps in 1941, served as a captain in the China-Burma-India theater, and returned in time to help the Tigers win the 1945 pennant and World Series. His career batting average was .313, with 331 home runs. He was an executive with the Cleveland Indians and Chicago White Sox between 1948 and 1963, and in 1975 became a stockholder in a new White Sox ownership. He helped raise money for the U.S. Maccabiah Games team in 1965, and in 1979 was made a member of the Jewish Sports Hall of Fame, Wingate Institute, Israel.

Holman, Nat (1896—), member of the Basketball Hall of Fame. "Mr. Basketball" learned to play the game in the parks, play-

Nat Holman and his City College basketball team celebrate their historic double NIT and NCAA victories, 1950.

grounds, and settlement houses of New York City's Lower East Side. An all-around athlete in high school, he decided on a career as a professional basketball player in 1916 while attending the Savage School of Physical Education. He served in the U.S. Navy in World War I, and in 1919 became the head basketball coach at the City College of New York. At the same time he continued to perform as a professional player. The 5′11″, 165-pounder was regarded as the finest ballhandler, play-maker, and set-shot artist of his day. He played for the New York Whirlwinds in 1920–21 and the Original Celtics in 1921–28. With Holman the Celtics rarely lost. They had a 193–11 won-lost record in 1922–23; 204–11 in 1923–24; and 134–6 in 1924–25. The Celtics joined the American Basketball League in 1926–27 and so dominated the opposition that the team was disbanded in 1928.

All during this period Holman was turning out winning teams at CCNY. "Unlike other coachs," Holman pointed out, "I had no scholarship players. They were all boys who entered CCNY because of their academic achievements. Yet they too found in basketball the things which spurred me on. They too brought to the game a dedication and skill that enabled CCNY to rise to basketball prominence during the years I was there."

He developed his greatest team in 1949–50. The 1950 CCNY team was the only college squad ever to win the National Collegiate Athletic Association championship and the National Invitation Tournament in the same year. Unfortunately, most of the players who won the "grand slam" were involved in a point-fixing scandal the following year. Suspended for a time, Holman was cleared of any responsibility and reinstated as coach. He ended his CCNY career in 1959 with a 423–190 won-lost record.

A proud Jew, Holman has always given his time and interest to the Jewish community. "Some of what I heard and learned sitting next to my father in the synagogue rubbed off on me," he said. "I have always been involved in and lent my name to Jewish communal activities. As early as 1922 I was the first national director of AZA, the B'nai B'rith youth organization. I was a member of the committee that helped send the first United States team to the World Maccabiah Games in Palestine in 1932, and the first American coach to go to Israel in 1949 to teach the Israelis to play basketball. I have been president of the United States Committee Sports for Israel. The greatest feeling in the world is to walk behind the athletes in the Maccabiah Games carrying the American flag."

In 1976 Holman received the Olympic Award from the Olympic Committee of Israel (he was only the third non-Israeli so honored) and was named the greatest New York City athlete in the sport of basketball by the Boys' Athletic League. In 1977 CCNY's new gym was named after him; the following year Israel's Wingate Institute dedicated the Nat Holman School for Coaches and Instructors. In 1979, sixty years after he became head coach at CCNY, Holman was made a member of the Jewish Sports Hall of Fame, Wingate Institute, Israel.

Holtzman, Kenneth (Ken) (1945—), a major league pitcher in 1966–79. He won All-America honors at the University of Illinois in 1965 and was signed to a bonus contract by the Chicago Cubs. The highlight of his rookie season was a victory over his boyhood idol Sandy Koufax. The two met for the first and only time as starting pitchers because of Yom Kippur. The great Dodger southpaw was scheduled to pitch on the holy day but skipped his turn to attend synagogue services. The Jewish lefthanders confronted each other the following day at Wrigley Field. Holtzman lost a no-hitter in the ninth inning but won the game, 2–1. With the Cubs in 1966–71 Holtzman pitched two no-hit games (1969 and 1971) and compiled a 74–69 won-lost record.

He asked to be traded after the 1971 season and Chicago sent him to Oakland where he became a major factor in the Athletics three straight World Series victories (1972–74). He won two American League playoff games and had four World Series wins. In 1973 he won 21 games and was chosen the American League's lefthand Pitcher of the Year. He left the Athletics after the 1975 season and was with Baltimore in 1976, the New York Yankees in 1976–78, and back with the Chicago Cubs in 1978–79. His career won-lost record through 1979 was 174–150.

"I am very proud of my heritage," Holtzman once told a reporter. "I believe in Jewish values and in my religion. I live as much of a Jewish life as possible, although it's a bit tough on the road. We've always had a kosher household. My record shows I never pitched on a Jewish holiday."

Ken Holtzman

Holzman, William (Red) (1920—), basketball player and coach. Holzman was an All-City guard in high school and an All-American at City College of New York in 1942. After a stint in the U.S. Navy in World War II, he joined the Rochester Royals of the National Basketball League in 1945. He became an All-League player in the NBL and helped the Royals win the National Basketball Association championship in 1950–51. In 1954 he became player-coach of the Milwaukee Hawks and led that struggling franchise (which had moved to St. Louis) for three seasons. The year after he left St. Louis, the players he had gathered together won the NBA title. One of those players was Bob Pettit, who remembered that "Red Holzman was my first coach. Immediately he moved me from center, where I had played in college, to a forward position. I think it was the biggest transition I made. It opened up a whole new world for me."

Red Holzman, 1978

Holzman became chief scout of the New York Knickerbockers from 1957 to December 1967 when he replaced Dick McGuire as the Knicks' head coach. He turned a team that was losing (15–22) into a winner (final record 43-39). In his first ten years as head coach of the Knicks they enjoyed seven winning seasons and in 1969–70 and 1972–73 won their first league championships. Holzman was named NBA Coach of the Year in 1970.

Senator Bill Bradley of New Jersey, who played for Holzman in New York, wrote about him in *Life on the Run* "Other men Holzman's age who became coaches in the NBA have difficulty communicating with black players . . . Holzman never makes racial mistakes. Everyone is subject to the same treatment. It seems natural that he senses the right course, for he grew up a Jew in a non-Jewish world, where discrimination was a very real part of his own life. He understands the dividing line between paranoia and reality."

In 1968 Holzman was elected to the CCNY Athletic Hall of Fame, and in 1970 was awarded the college's Townsend Harris Medal for "distinguished postgraduate achievement." He was the first recipient to be cited for athletic accomplishment.

Kirszenstein-Szewinska, Irena (1946—), Olympic champion who many consider the greatest woman track and field athlete of all time. She was born in Leningrad to Polish parents who had fled to Russia during World War II. The family later returned to Poland and settled in Warsaw. Kirszenstein's athletic ability became evident in school and her mother encouraged her to join a local sports club. She became a sprinter and long jumper, and by 1963 was included in the Association of Track and Field Statisticians world list in the 100- and 200-meter events. The following year she was in Tokyo for the Summer Olympic Games. The long-legged newcomer to international competition surprised everyone with silver medals in the 200-meter run and the long jump and a gold medal in the 400-meter relay.

If the economics student at Warsaw University wasn't a favorite with her countrymen before 1965, she became one afterward. In a dual meet with the United States in Warsaw she defeated two American Olympic champions in the 100- and 200-meter runs; ran a leg on the winning 400-meter relay team; and won the long jump competition. Her time in the 200 was 22.7 seconds, a new world record. Earlier in the season she tied the world record for 100 meters with an 11.1 clocking.

An Associated Press reporter who witnessed Kirszenstein's Warsaw triumph wrote: "In her native Poland . . . she is a national heroine. By the tens of thousands they stand and applaud her. They sing songs of her achievements. When Irena runs, all Poland goes into a tizzy . . . When she dressed and walked on Warsaw streets, traffic stopped. People stopped to look at her in awe . . . Many clamored for her autograph. [Some] anti-Semitic Poles found it convenient to forget she is Jewish."

For her 1965 successes she was named Poland's Athlete of the Year, and Tass, the official Russian news agency, voted her the Outstanding Woman Athlete in the World. In 1966, the British magazine *World Sport* picked her as Sportswoman of the Year after she won three gold medals (200, long jump, and 400 relay) and a silver medal (100) in the European Championships in Budapest.

Miss Kirszenstein married in 1967, and as Mrs. Szewinska won a gold medal in the 200 meters in 22.5, a new world record, and a bronze medal in the 100 meters at the 1968 Olympic Games.

Motherhood forced her to miss part of the 1969 season and all of the next year. She gave birth to a son in February 1970. She continued as an outstanding sprinter in 1971–73, but her place at the top was taken by the younger Renate Stecher of East Germany.

By 1974 Szewinska was ready to challenge the East German. As reported in *Track and Field News*, she "clipped a tenth from the 200-meter world mark with her 22-flat; showed where perhaps her talent truly lies by blasting the world 400 record by 1.1 seconds with a brilliant 49.9, the first sub-50 by a woman; dashed a 10.9 100 meters, second fastest ever; recorded an electric world best 200 meters with her 22.21; won the European 100 and 200, turning back double Olympic champion Stecher in both races and clocking 11.13 in the 100, the third fastest electric time ever . . . compiled an undefeated season at all distances and against the world's best sprinters; capped it all off with a stunning 48.6 anchor of Poland's 1,600 relay at Rome (European Championships)."

European sports editors voted her the UPI Sportswoman of 1974 and *Track and Field News* named her Woman Athlete of the Year. Her attempt at 400 meters had long been awaited in the track world. It was believed that with her long legs and poor start she was better suited to the longer distance. This proved correct. When she concentrated on the 400 at the Montreal Olympic Games in 1976 she easily won her race. Her time of 49.29 was a new world record.

In Montreal she was asked if motherhood had helped her running. "Oh, yes," she replied. "After 1968 I was very tired and was thinking about stopping. But after 1970 I began a second sports career after the birth of my son. I felt better, I trained better. I got more pleasure out of running. And I performed better." And why had she been so successful for so long? "Track is my passion," Mrs. Szewinska explained, "my hobby. I devote all of my free time outside my family to it. I never get tired from it or of it. That is why I'm still good enough to beat younger rivals."

Szewinska's record of success and durability is unmatched in the history of woman's track and field. Her total of seven Olympic (three gold) and ten European (five gold) medals may never be equalled.

Asked what her greatest joy had been, she answered, "The birth of my son. No title could give me as much pleasure."

Koufax, Sanford (Sandy) (1935—), member of the Baseball Hall of Fame. Koufax is considered by many to be the best left-handed pitcher of all time. He was a University of Cincinnati basketball player when he signed a Brooklyn Dodgers bonus contract in 1954. With limited baseball experience, he struggled to control his fast ball in Brooklyn, and then Los Angeles, in 1955–60. After six seasons he had a won-lost record of 36–40; but in 1959 he had equalled the major league record of eighteen strikeouts in a nine inning game.

In the next six years, after adding discipline and pinpoint control to his fast ball, he became the biggest attraction in the game. Despite injuries, he pitched in four World Series (1959, 1963, 1965–66), four All-Star games, and compiled a 129–47 record. He won 25 games in 1963; 26 in 1965, and 27 (a modern record for a National League left-hander) in 1966. He became the first man to pitch four no-hitters (1962–65), the last to pitch a perfect game, and was the National League earned-run champion five straight seasons (1962–66). His 382 strikeouts in 1965 was a major league record. He won the Cy Young Award as the best pitcher in baseball in 1963 and 1965–66, and was the National League's Most Valuable Player in 1963.

Koufax always observed the High Holy Days. When Yom Kippur occurred on the first day of the 1965 World Series with Minnesota he missed his starting assignment and attended services at Temple of Aaron, St. Paul, Minnesota. He came back and pitched shutouts in the fifth and seventh games and the Dodgers won the Series four games to three. Afterward he said, "I don't know why people insist on making something big out of that. A man is entitled to his belief and I believe I should not work on Yom Kippur. It's as simple as all that and I have never had any trouble on that account since I've been in baseball."

An arthritic elbow forced his retirement from baseball after the 1966 season. His career record was 165–87, with 2.76 ERA, 2,396 strikeouts, and 40 shutouts. In his twelve years with the Dodgers they won six National League pennants and four World Series. In 1970 he was named the Baseball Athlete of the Decade by the Associated Press, and in 1972 he became the youngest player voted into the Baseball Hall of Fame. He worked as a sports commentator in 1967–73. In 1965 he was elected an honorary member of the United States Maccabiah Games team after he helped raise money to send the team to Israel. He is a member of the Jewish Sports Hall of Fame, Wingate Institute, Israel.

Leonard, Benny (born Benjamin Leiner) (1896–1947), member of the Boxing Hall of Fame and the greatest lightweight of all time. Leonard lost his first fight and his last name when he began his ring career in 1911. The name change was necessary to keep his immigrant parents from discovering his "undesirable" occupation. His secret did not last long. As his victory total began to climb, most of New York's Lower East Side, including his mother and father, learned the truth. Except for being knocked out three times in his first three years, it was all good news for the ambitious youngster. His first big win came in 1915 when he defeated Joe Mandot, a seasoned veteran. The following year he fought lightweight champion Freddy Welsh in a no-decision contest in New Orleans. Disagreement remains about who won that match, but not about their second meeting in New York City, May 28, 1917. Leonard knocked out Welsh in the ninth round to become the new world title holder.

Benny Leonard

Leonard's most memorable ring encounters occurred between 1920 and 1923. In 1920 he knocked out Charlie White in the ninth round after being belted out of the ring by the hard hitting lefty. He lost on a foul to welterweight champion Jack Britton in 1922, and the next month was out on his feet after Lew Tendler landed a left to his jaw. Leonard had the presence of mind to engage his adversary in conversation and the startled Tendler hesitated long enough for the champion to pull himself together and gain the decision. They met again the following year in Yankee Stadium and it was no contest: Leonard gave the Jewish southpaw from Philadelphia a boxing lesson. Many ring experts insist that had Tendler come along at almost any other time he too would have been a world champion. Finally, in January 15, 1925, Leonard became the first lightweight champion to retire undefeated. "My mother was so happy," Leonard recalled. "I was twenty-nine, practically a millionaire, and without a scratch. The stock market crash in 1929 wiped me out. I was broke. In 1931, when I was thirty-five years old, I decided to make a comeback as a welterweight. In one year I had about twenty fights and was still undefeated . . . Then I met Jimmy McLarnin. He was ten years younger than I was, and he knocked me out in the sixth round. That was it. I retired for good." In 209 fights Leonard scored 68 knockouts and was defeated only five times.

How good was Leonard? Ray Arcel, a trainer for over fifty years, said, "Benny Leonard was the greatest fighter who ever lived. There was never a fighter I knew who could make you do things you didn't want to do like Leonard. He was one of the fastest thinkers in history."

Leonard served as a lieutenant commander in the U.S. Maritime Service in World War II, and was back in boxing in 1943 as a referee. In 1947, after he worked six bouts at New York's St. Nicholas Arena, he collapsed and died in the ring. Shortly after his death someone wrote that "when Leonard was accepted and admired by the fair-minded American community, the Jews of America felt that they themselves were being accepted." Leonard is a member of the Jewish Sports Hall of Fame, Wingate Institute, Israel.

Luckman, Sidney (Sid) (1916—), member of the College and Pro Football Halls of Fame and the first modern T formation quarterback. Luckman "was the only man in the country who was an All-America player beyond dispute," wrote *New York Herald-Tribune* sports editor Stanley Woodward about the Columbia halfback in 1938. Luckman had just concluded his collegiate career and Woodward reacted because only one major All-America selector had named Sid to the first team. It wasn't too surprising: the Lions had won only three games and lost six. Despite twenty touchdown passes, Luckman's three years at the Ivy League school produced a disappointing 10–14–1 record. "Unlike most great players, Luckman didn't have an outstanding cast of supporters when he played college ball," said Columbia coach Lou Little. "We would have had a very ordinary team, or less than that, without him."

Nevertheless, veteran coach Andy Kerr of Colgate made Luckman a first team All-East selection. "Luckman of Columbia," wrote Kerr, "is one of the best all-around backs in recent years. He is a splendid passer, kicks well, is a fine ball carrier and an excellent safety man." Luckman did have other boosters, because he placed third, behind Davey O'Brien of TCU and Pittsburgh's Marshall Goldberg, in the Heisman Trophy voting.

One of those most impressed by the six-foot, 195-pound halfback from Brooklyn was George Halas, owner of the Chicago Bears. Halas made Luckman his first draft choice in the player draft. In terms of football talent Luckman went from rags to riches. Halas was assembling a group of players that would soon become the greatest one-platoon football team of all time. He decided that Luckman, a single-wing halfback in high school and college, would be the perfect player to run his new T formation.

Sid Luckman, 1940

"He had a lot to learn about our man-in-motion T," Halas recalled in 1967. "We broke him in gradually during the 1939 season. When the 1940 season rolled around, he was ready to assume the role of 'Mr. Quarterback'—the finest in the history of the game, in my estimation." The *Official Encyclopedia of Football* says, "Halas added the man-in-motion to the ineffective T of older days and made it come alive. In 1939, he bet the future of his team on the ability of a . . . young halfback named Sidney Luckman to make it work. Luckman floundered for a few weeks, but suddenly, through unbeatable determination and endless hours of practice, he got it and a new era was born in football. Halas, Luckman, and the T grew to maturity together.

"Luckman went on to rank as the smartest field general of them all. His nickname 'Mr. Quarterback' was well earned . . . George Halas will testify under oath that Sid Luckman never called a wrong play during twelve years of action; that he was always thinking ahead of his opponents, his teammates, and everyone else, that he drove most of them crazy, including George Halas himself."

Any doubts about the T formation were dispelled in 1940. In the championship game, the underdog Chicago Bears demolished the Washington Redskins. Just three weeks before, the Redskins had beaten the Bears, 7–3. This time, in Washington, D.C., it was no contest. In the first half Luckman ran for a touchdown and passed for another; Chicago led 28–0 at half time. Luckman sat out the second half as the "Monsters of the Midway" thrashed the Eastern Division champions, 73–0. "Since then football hasn't been the same," said Halas thirty years later. "That made us major league. It showed the country the potential in professional ball."

Between 1940 and 1943 the Bears won four Western Division titles and three (1940–41, 1943) league championships. Luckman was named the NFL's Most Valuable Player in 1943 when he passed for a record seven touchdowns against the New York Giants in a regular season contest, and hurled five more in the title game with the Redskins. His 2,194 yards and 28 touchdown passes were new league records. Luckman was named All-NFL quarterback in 1941–44, 1947. In twelve years he passed for 14,683 yards and 139 touchdowns, and completed 51.8 percent of his attempted passes. Luckman retired as a player after 1950 but remained a coach into the 1970s.

When Luckman was enshrined in the pro Hall of Fame in 1965 Lou Little said, "He was a great passer, of course, and a great football brain, but people forget he was a great leader. That was some gang he had to handle, those Bears. But they responded to his leadership."

Luckman is a member of the Jewish Sports Hall of Fame, Wingate Institute, Israel.

Mendoza, Daniel (1764–1836), member of the Boxing Hall of Fame; considered the father of scientific boxing. Born in London's East End, Mendoza grew to manhood in a difficult period for England's Jews. He answered the insults against his people with his fists and by the age of fourteen was famous for victories over older and heavier men. In need of a champion, the Jewish community was quick to sing his praises, and when he fought Richard Humphries, the darling of the aristocracy, in 1788 they wagered large sums of money on him. His loss to Humphries left the Jews of London despondent. His subsequent victories over Humphries in 1789 and 1790 produced jubilation in Jewish circles, and he was acclaimed throughout the British Isles as the world's greatest fighter.

His boxing style was a revelation. He was a middleweight by modern standards (5′7″, 160 pounds in his prime) and almost always found himself matched against a larger man. To counteract this advantage he developed a system of defense and foot movements that had his opponent off balance and open for his punishing blows. These methods put an end to the brutal bare knuckle slugging matches of the past. "I think I have a right to call myself the father of the science," he said in an address in 1820, "for it is well known that prize fighting lay dormant for several years . . . It was myself and Humphries who revived it in our three contests for supremacy, and the science of pugilism has been patronized ever since . . ."

Always billed as "Mendoza the Jew," he traveled about the country giving sparring exhibitions and teaching the art of self defense. He was a great favorite in Ireland, where he defeated the Irish champion Squire Fitzgerald and introduced the science of boxing to the local gentry. In London he opened a boxing school that became a favorite with the rich and famous. He became the first boxer to appear on the stage, and the first Jew to speak to a King of England. One of Mendoza's patrons was the Prince of Wales.

Mendoza's social acceptance, and the rise of this two-fisted Jew, combined to ease the position of the Jewish community in England. Most of the virulent Jew-baiting came to an end. Nevertheless, a cry went up for a man to put an end to the dominance of the "foreigner." He was found in "Gentleman" John Jackson, a college champion, who challenged Mendoza in 1795 and defeated him by grabbing his shoulder length hair and battering him senseless. The Jackson fight and a few more ended Mendoza's ring career. He became a wealthy man, but his generosity soon had him deep in debt. For much of the rest of his life he was plagued by money problems and concern for his large family. Attesting to his great popularity, however, are the seven medals that were struck in his honor and the over twenty-five portraits painted of him and his fights.

Mix, Ronald (Ron) (1938—), member of the Pro Football Hall of Fame. "To some people I guess I represent a kind of racial hero," Mix once told a sportswriter. "Sure, it would be best if people would say, 'That's Ron Mix, a human being who made good.' But until that time in history comes around, I'm proud when they say, 'There's Ron Mix, a Jewish football player who made good.' "

Before he made good, Mix started out as an athlete of whom his high school football coach said, "This is a kid who was skinny and not very fast—but he made up for it by not being able to see." He improved enough by his senior year to earn an athletic scholarship to the University of Southern California as a 180-pound end. In his first two varsity seasons at USC he played on losing teams. His vision problems dictated a move to tackle and contact lenses. The Trojans were 8–2 in 1959 and Mix received All-America and All-Pacific Coast recognition. He was also co-captain of the team and was voted USC's outstanding lineman of the year.

In 1960 he entered professional football as a 6'4", 250-pound offensive tackle with the Los Angeles Chargers of the newly formed American Football League. The Baltimore Colts, champions of the rival National Football League, wanted to sign him but ". . . the Colts offered me only $8,500 to play in cold Baltimore," explained Mix, "and the Chargers offered me $12,000 to stay in Los Angeles, my home town. Since I was only going to play for two years and then quit to become a teacher, it was one of my easier decisions."

Mix did leave Los Angeles in his second pro year when the Chargers moved down the coast to San Diego. Under coach Sid Gillman the Chargers became one of the powers in the new league. With Mix winning All-AFL honors at tackle and guard, San Diego won the Western Division title five times in the first six years of the league's existence. They won only one league championship, however, a 51–10 victory over the Boston Patriots in 1963. During this period Mix attended law school at night and wrote articles on football for various publications.

In 1967 *Sport* magazine wrote about Mix: "His technique, desire, strength, and balance still impress. He's known as a 'pop-out' blocker, the kind who gets his man with a quick initial thrust . . . He can get to the outside linebacker or defensive end in a hurry." And an assistant coach who worked in both leagues said, "Ron Mix is the best offensive lineman in the AFL. I've seen films where he got pieces of three men on one play. Mix has tremendous balance. When he pulls and blocks the corner man, he often stays on his feet and gets the safety."

In 1969 when he announced his retirement, the Chargers made their final game of the season Ron Mix Day and retired his jersey, Number 74. In a decade with San Diego he was chosen All-AFL in 1960–68 and played in seven All-Star games. He was charged with just two holding penalties in ten seasons. In 1970, after the AFL merged with the NFL, Mix was unanimously selected to the All-Time American Football League team by the Pro Football Hall of Fame.

Mix finished law school in 1970 and passed the California state bar. In 1971 he played another season of football with the Oakland Raiders, and in 1973 rejoined the Chargers as executive counsel. After a year and a half he left San Diego and was named general manager of the Portland team in the short-lived World Football League.

In 1979 Mix became the second AFL player to enter the Pro Football Hall of Fame. When he learned about it he said, "As an offensive lineman it's nice to get some attention. You don't mind not getting attention while you're playing. All that running and lifting weights. It was a lot of hard work, this makes it all worth it."

Mix is a member of the Jewish Sports Hall of Fame, Wingate Institute, Israel.

Pike, Lipman (Lip) (1845–1893), baseball pioneer. In its obituary of October 21, 1893, the *Sporting Life of Philadelphia* said that Pike "could claim the unique distinction of being the first professional player, he having been paid a regular salary for playing ball in 1866, when he was engaged by the Athletic Club of Philadelphia." It went on to say, "He ranked high as a batsman during the sixteen successive seasons that he played professionally, being, like all left-handed men, a very hard hitter. It would require too much space to record all his batting feats, of which the most notable was the making of six home runs—five in succession—in a game played July 16, 1866, at Philadelphia. Pike was a sure catch and fast runner, played very well in the outfield, where he brought off many remarkable catches. Both as a batter and fielder he was singularly graceful in all his movements."

In 1870 Pike helped his home town Brooklyn Atlantics defeat the previously undefeated Cincinnati Reds in early baseball's most famous game. He played and managed in the first professional league, the National Association in 1871–75, and the National League in 1876–81. He batted .321 in the National Association and .304 in the National League. At the time of his death he was a member of Brooklyn's Temple Israel synagogue.

Rosen, Albert (Al) (1924—), Cleveland Indian third baseman, 1947–56. Rosen became a regular in 1950 and hit 37 home runs to lead the American League. He drove in over 100 runs in five successive years (1950–54), and led the league in runs-batted-in in 1952 and 1953. In 1953 he won the home run (43) and runs-batted-in (145) titles and just missed the batting championship with a .336 average. For that outstanding performance he was voted the league's Most Valuable Player, the first unanimous selection in the history of the award. He played in All-Star games in 1952–55, and Arch Ward, the originator of the mid-season classic, picked Rosen as the third baseman on his all-time All-Star team. In the 1954 contest Rosen tied two All-Star records with two home runs and five runs-batted-in, leading the American League to an 11–9 victory.

Al Rosen, 1953

"When Rosen was established and a star," wrote Roger Kahn in *The Passionate People*, "he was unhappy with his name once more. He wanted one even more Jewish than his own, perhaps Rosenthal or Rosenstein. He wanted to make sure that there was no mistake about what he was. 'When I was up there in the majors,' Al Rosen says, 'I always knew how I wanted it to be about me. I wanted it to be, "Here comes one Jewish kid that every Jew in the world can be proud of." '"

Between 1968 and 1977 Rosen was a member of the Cleveland Indians board of directors and a part-owner of the New York Yankees. In 1978–79 he was president of the Yankees. He is a member of the Jewish Sports Hall of Fame, Wingate Institute, Israel.

Ross, Barney (born Barnet Rosofsky) (1909–1967), member of the Boxing Hall of Fame and World War II hero. Ross was born in New York City and grew up in Chicago. His father, a grocer and former talmudic scholar, was killed in a holdup in 1924. When his mother suffered a nervous breakdown his two younger brothers and sister were placed in an orphanage. The grocery was lost, and plans for him to be a teacher of Hebrew were set aside. "Everything that happened to me afterward," he wrote later, "happened because of that senseless stupid murder."

Determined to bring his family together again, Ross turned to boxing as a means of earning quick money. He climaxed a successful amateur career in 1929 with victories in Chicago. Later that year he became a professional. From 1929 to 1932 he lost only twice.

He was outstanding in 1932 with wins over Ray Miller and Bat Battalino, two of the best men in his division. He was finally able to reunite his family shortly before he met lightweight champion Tony Canzoneri in Chicago, in June 1933. Ross won a ten-round decision over Canzoneri and three months later beat the former champion again, this time in New York City.

By 1934 Ross had gained weight and decided to take on the great welterweight champion Jimmy McLarnin. The two champions met in May 1934 in New York and Ross won a fifteen-round decision. The *Chicago Tribune* reported that "Barney's victory was clean cut, brilliant, and methodical. No other fighter has ever held both the lightweight and welterweight titles. Ross's skill and courage beat McLarnin . . . The defending champion was outfought, outboxed, and outmaneuvered." Chicago welcomed its hero home with a parade to City Hall and a meeting with the Governor of Illinois and the Mayor of Chicago.

McLarnin regained the welterweight title in September 1934; but in May 1935, a year after he won the welterweight title the first time, Ross recaptured it with a unanimous decision in New York's Polo Grounds. Just before the third McLarnin fight Ross relinquished the lightweight championship. He defeated Ceferino Garcia three times, and then in May 1938 he fought Henry Armstrong and that ended his ring career. Armstrong hit him with everything he had but Ross refused to go down. He was still on his feet after fifteen rounds. When the battered Ross was asked why he hadn't quit he said, "I wanted to go out like a champion."

His final ring record showed eighty-two pro bouts with only four losses. He was never knocked out. Boxing historian Nat Fleischer said, "He was one of the greatest lightweights and welterweights of all time. Barney was a very clever boy and a strong hitter."

Ross was back in the public eye in 1942. At the age of thirty-two he became a U.S. Marine. He enlisted in April, and by November was on Guadalcanal with the Second Marine Division. Americans and Japanese were locked in a fierce battle for control of the strategic Pacific island. On the night of November 19, 1942, he and four other Marines were cut off from the main body of U.S. troops by the advance of the Japanese. All except Ross were wounded in the first attack. He stopped the enemy with rifle fire and grenades. Ross remembered later, "After we ran out of ammunition, I kept the Japs at a distance with twenty-one grenades we had between us. When I tossed the twentieth, I fixed the bayonets and told the boys to pray. I did a little praying of my own too—in Hebrew." When the Marines were finally relieved the next morning twenty-two Japanese lay dead around Ross's defensive position. He had suffered shrapnel wounds in the hands and legs; he also contracted malaria. He was promoted to corporal and recommended for a medal. Ross went back into combat but was soon returned to the United States in poor physical condition. To ease his pain he was given drugs and became an addict. Before he was discharged from the Marines in 1944, he was awarded the Silver Star, America's third highest medal for valor.

In 1946, with his personal life a wreck because of drugs, Ross turned himself over to Federal narcotic authorities. After four months at the Public Health Service Hospital, Lexington, Kentucky, he was pronounced cured.

Ross waged his last fight against throat cancer. When he died at fifty-seven Rabbi William Gold said in his eulogy, "Barney Ross was his own worst enemy. He was so generous to others that the only person he neglected was himself. He left no funds, no estates named after himself. All he left to be remembered by is a world full of friends." Ross is a member of the Jewish Sports Hall of Fame, Wingate Institute, Israel.

Schayes, Adolph (Dolph) (1928—), member of the Basketball Hall of Fame. Schayes played his junior high school, high school, and college basketball in his native Bronx, New York. He entered New York University in 1945 as a sixteen-year-old freshman center, and three and a half years later graduated with All-America honors and the Haggerty Award as the number one player in the New York metropolitan area. He was anxious to play professional ball, but not everyone believed he was good enough. "I didn't think he was rugged or aggressive enough to survive in pro ball," said his NYU coach, Howard Cann. Schayes nevertheless signed with the Syracuse Nationals in 1948.

In need of a big man, Syracuse gave the 6'8" 220-pounder every opportunity to make good. To make better use of his speed and agility he was moved from center to a forward position and became basketball's first truly mobile big man, the prototype of the modern forward. He developed a long-range two-hand set-shot and a driving layup that was almost impossible to stop without fouling him. He was an excellent foul shooter, an outstanding rebounder, and an unselfish player who was often his team's assist leader. He was selected for the league All-Star Game twelve straight times and was voted to the All-NBA Team twelve times.

The Nationals abandoned Syracuse in 1963 and became the Philadelphia 76ers with Schayes as the new head coach. Philadelphia placed third in the Eastern Division in his first two seasons, then won the title in 1965–66. Schayes was named NBA Coach of the Year, but lost his job when Boston defeated the 76ers in the playoff semi-finals. He returned to coach in the NBA in 1970 with a new franchise, the Buffalo Braves. After one season and the first game of 1971–72 he was let go again. It was said by some that "he wasn't tough enough with his players, he was just too nice a guy." He was NBA Supervisor of Referees in 1966–70.

In 1977 Schayes was appointed head coach of the United States Maccabiah Games basketball team. When asked why he took the job he said, "I thought it would be exciting, an experience of a lifetime. I thought my son had a chance to make the team and I wanted to be there if he did." With the help of his son, 6'11" Dan Schayes, the United States upset Israel 92–91 in the championship final. Dolph Schayes is a member of the Jewish Sports Hall of Fame, Wingate Institute, Israel.

Scheckter, Jody (1950—), world driving champion. Son of a South African garage owner, Scheckter began racing go-karts at an early age. He graduated to stock cars in 1968–70 and enjoyed great success on local tracks. He continued to impress in Europe in 1971–72 and in the United States in 1973, where he won the American Formula 5000 championship. In the process he developed a reputation as a wild and aggressive driver with a road hogging style that aggravated many of his fellow competitors. At the time he said, "At this stage in my career I try as hard as I can. I suppose I'm aggressive. I think that anybody that really goes has got the fight in him to win. I know I've got it."

In 1972 he was named Motoring Sportsman of the Year in South Africa and awarded his Springbok colors, his nation's highest sports honor. In 1973 he was voted the Jewish South African Sportsman of the Year. With his flamboyant style of driving somewhat modified, he joined the Formula One circuit in 1974 and won the Swedish and British Grand Prix. He placed third in the world championship and was named Driver of the Year by the British Guild of Motoring Writers. He was less successful the following year but did win the South African Grand Prix before 110,000 delirious fans. In 1976 he again won the Swedish event and again placed third in the world competition. He was runnerup in the world championship the next year with victories in Argentina, Monaco, and Canada and was again chosen South African Maccabi Sportsman of the Year. In his acceptance speech he spoke of the dangers of his sport: "More dangerous than racing is being a South African racer, and even more dangerous than that is being a Jewish-South African racer." He experienced a poor year in 1978, but came back in 1979 to win in Belgium, Monaco, and Italy and become the first South African to win the world championship.

Mark Spitz holding his record seven Olympic Gold Medals, 1972.

Spitz, Mark (1950—), Olympic champion and member of the Swimming Hall of Fame. Spitz is considered the greatest swimmer in the history of the sport. When Arnold Spitz withdrew his son from Hebrew school, he told the Sacramento rabbi: "Even God likes a winner." Henceforth young Spitz would concentrate on swimming. Mark had learned to swim at six and competed in meets at age ten. "Mark has not always been a winner," *Swimming World* magazine reported. "He did well as a ten-year-old and held his own when twelve, but at thirteen and fourteen he began to show promise."

"When I was ten years old," Spitz remembered, "I had no idea where I was going when I started swimming. It was more or less like a social activity with my boyfriends and I had goals to be somebody like Johnny Unitas. I was introduced to a program that enabled me to see what swimming was really about when I went to Santa Clara [Swim Club] in 1964."

The Spitz family moved so Mark could attend coach George Haines' successful Santa Clara Swim Club. Mark's father was determined to give his son the best coaching available. As he told Mark, "Swimming isn't everything, winning is." When he was accused of pushing his son he said, "If I hadn't pushed my son, he would never have been at Santa Clara. If I pushed Mark, it was part of his development—and you know why I pushed him? Because he was so great, that's why. . . . If the parent isn't behind the child, there can be nothing outstanding—and it's not really a sacrifice. It's love."

In his first year at Santa Clara, Spitz qualified for the National Long Course championships in the 400- and 1,500-meter freestyle events. He was selected for the United States Maccabiah Games swimming team the following year and was a standout in Israel. He won four gold medals and set four new records. "Coming here [Israel] in 1965 was how it all began," he recalled. "I had finished fifth in the 1,500 at the Nationals. But getting all those firsts did something for me. Any kid of fifteen has to benefit."

Spitz became the third man in history to better 17 minutes in the 1,500 freestyle and won his first national title, the 100-meter butterfly, in 1966 as a high school sophomore. He had his first really outstanding year in 1967: two short course and two long course national titles; five American and seven world records in the butterfly strokes and the 400-meter freestyle. He also won five gold medals at the Pan-American Games in Winnipeg, Canada, a Sullivan Award nomination, and selection as World Swimmer of the Year by *Swimming World*.

After 1967 the experts were convinced Spitz was the best all-around swimmer in the world, and they said so. Descriptions of his personality, however, were less complimentary. Terms such as "temperamental," "arrogant," "brooding," "difficult," "aloof," and "spoiled brat" found their way into print, to which Spitz replied in 1967: "If I know I'm the best and feel it, and people then think I'm cocky, well, there's nothing I can do about it . . . I know everyone can't wait to see me knocked off . . . but I intend to swim through the 1972 Olympics—and I intend to go out a winner."

Many people, including George Haines, believed Spitz would win five or six gold medals in the 1968 Mexico City Olympic Games. It didn't happen. He won two gold medals in the relays: a silver in the 100 butterfly and a bronze in the 100 freestyle. It was a bitter disappointment. Even more bitter, perhaps, was the conduct of his teammates. Some of them shunned him and some rooted against him.

Looking back on it later Spitz said, "I didn't swim up to my potential. I had the worst meet of my life . . . maybe George Haines and I set too vigorous a program. Maybe my age and other circumstances were against us. I had my tonsils out a month after the Olympics but I'm not offering any alibis. I really don't know what happened."

"As for his troubles with his teammates," explained George Haines, "some of the older guys took his immaturity as conceit. He brought it on himself, but the older boys should have known better. I don't think it was as bad as has been indicated."

Sherm Chavoor, another coach, remembered it differently: "After the Olympic trials the swimmers went to train at Colorado Springs. Mark ran into a lot of anti-Semitism from his teammates. Some of the older guys really gave it to him. They tried to run him right off the team. It was 'Jew-boy' this and 'Jew-boy' that. It wasn't a kidding type of thing either. I heard it with my own ears. I remember one particularly brutal day on a golf course out there when it really got brutal.

"He didn't know how to handle it. He tried to get ready for a race and he'd get so wound up he'd come up with all sorts of imaginary sicknesses: sore throat, headache, like that. He was psyched."

In 1969 Spitz entered Indiana University. The Hoosiers, under the highly respected coach James (Doc) Counsilman, were the defending NCAA champions. Spitz' three victories as a freshman helped Indiana retain its collegiate championship. His problems with teammates did not surface again during his college career.

"He has shown what a great competitor he is," said Counsilman. "Here you have a boy who is the greatest swimmer in the world and he's swimming like he has to prove himself. A lot of people told me Mark was temperamental after I signed him. They told me that I'd have trouble with him. I've never seen any of that. He is easy to work with: really dedicated." In four years together Spitz and Indiana were always NCAA champions.

Spitz was back in Israel in the summer of 1969. The official report of the Eighth World Maccabiah Games said: "Olympian Mark Spitz, who carried the Stars and Stripes in the Opening Ceremonies, was named the outstanding athlete of the Games. He won six swimming gold medals . . . It was a homecoming for Spitz, who got his first taste of international competition in the Seventh Maccabiah . . . Joining him this time was his fifteen-year-old sister, Nancy, who matched his 1965 gold medal total . . ."

In 1971, after another sensational year of AAU and NCAA titles and world records, Spitz became the first Jewish recipient of the Amateur Athletic Union's James E. Sullivan Award. It is given to the amateur athlete "who best combines outstanding achievement with the qualities of character, sportsmanship, and leadership."

The Sullivan Award was fine but the big one was still the Olympic Games. Spitz was ready for Munich, West Germany, in 1972. He was outstanding in the Olympic trials in Chicago. He won the 100 and 200 freestyle and butterfly events, all with world records except the 200 butterfly. This set the stage for the greatest swimming exhibition ever given. In eight days at the Swimmhalle, Spitz won four individual (100 and 200 freestyle and 100 and 200 butterfly) and three relay gold medals, all in world record time. It was the most gold medals ever won by an individual in one Olympic meeting. His total of nine gold medals (two in 1968, seven in 1972) equalled the most gold medals won by any individual in Olympic history. Spitz had produced the greatest feat in competitive swimming history under the greatest possible pressure.

How did he accomplish it? He once explained, "Day in day out, swimming is ninety percent physical. You've got to do the physical work in training, and don't need much mental. But in a big meet like this, it's ninety percent mental and ten percent physical. Your body is ready, and now it becomes mind versus matter."

Spitz retired from competitive swimming after the 1972 Olympic Games. His record in 1965–72 shows nine Olympic gold medals, one silver, and one bronze; five Pan-American Games gold medals; ten Maccabiah Games gold medals; thirty-one National AAU titles; eight NCAA championships; and thirty-three world records. He was World Swimmer of the Year in 1967, 1971, and 1972.

In 1977 Spitz told a reporter for *Israel Today*: "I feel that being a Jewish athlete has helped our cause. We have shown that we are as good as the next guy. In mentality we have always been at the top of every field. I think the Jewish people have a more realistic way of looking at life. They make the most of what's happening at the present, while preparing for the future."

He is a member of the Jewish Sports Hall of Fame, Wingate Institute, Israel.

—J.H.S.

THE JEWISH ALMANAC'S ALL-TIME, ALL-STAR MAJOR LEAGUE BASEBALL TEAM

Starting Line-Up

First Base	Hank Greenberg
Second Base	Buddy Myer
Shortstop	Billy Nash
Third Base	Al Rosen
Outfield	Lipman (Lip) Pike
Outfield	Sid Gordon
Outfield	Benny Kauff
Catcher	Johnny Kling
Pitcher (R)	Ed Reulbach
Pitcher (L)	Sandy Koufax

Reserve

Outfield	George Stone
Catcher	Harry Danning
Pitcher (L)	Ken Holtzman
Pitcher (R)	Erskine Mayer
Pitcher (Relief)	Larry Sherry
Designated Hitter	Ron Blomberg
Designated Hitter	Mike Epstein

Starting Line Up

FIRST BASE

Hank Greenberg (see "Jewish Almanac's Sports Hall of Fame").

SECOND BASE

Charles Solomon (Buddy) Myer (1904–1974), lefthanded batter. Played seventeen years in the major leagues with Washington (A.L.), 1925–27, 1929–41; and Boston (A.L.), 1927–28. Washington won the American League championships in 1925 and 1933. Myer led the American League in stolen bases with 30 in 1928 and batting average with .349 in 1935. He hit .300 or better nine times. In 1,923 games he had 2,131 hits, 850 runs batted in, and a career batting average of .303. He stole 156 bases. In 1974 the Society of American Baseball Research named Myer the best major leaguer from Mississippi. He played football at Mississippi State.

SHORTSTOP

William (Billy) Nash (1865–1929), righthanded batter. Played fifteen years in the major leagues with Richmond (A.A.), 1884; Boston (N.L.), 1885–89, 1891–95; Boston (Players League), 1890; and Philadelphia (N.L.), 1896–98. Nash captained the Boston championship teams in 1890–93 and was Philadelphia manager in 1896. In 1,549 games he had 1,606 hits, 61 home runs, 977 runs batted in, and a career batting average of .275. In 1888 and 1891 he was National League runner-up in runs batted in. He stole 43 bases in 1887 and 249 in his career.

THIRD BASE

Al Rosen (see "Jewish Almanac's Sports Hall of Fame").

OUTFIELD

Lipman (Lip) Pike (see "Jewish Almanac's Sports Hall of Fame").

Sidney (Sid) Gordon (1917–1975), righthanded batter. Played thirteen years in the major leagues with New York (N.L.), 1941–43, 1946–49, 1955; Boston (N.L.), 1950–52; Milwaukee (N.L.), 1953; and Pittsburgh (N.L.), 1954–55. He hit 30 home runs in 1948, two home runs in one inning in 1949, and four home runs with the bases full in 1950. In 1,475 games Gordon had 1,415 hits, 202 home runs, 805 runs batted in, and a career batting average of .283. He did World War II service in 1944–45.

Benjamin (Benny) Kauff (1890–1961), lefthanded batter. Played eight years in the major leagues with New York (A.L.), 1912; Indianapolis (Federal League), 1914; Brooklyn (Federal League), 1915; and New York (N.L.), 1916–20. Indianapolis won the Federal League championship in 1914. Kauff led the Federal League in batting average (.370), hits (211), and stolen bases (75) in 1914, and in batting average (.342) and stolen bases (55) in 1915. The Giants won the National League pennant in 1917. In 859 games Kauff had 961 hits, 454 runs batted in, and a career batting average of .311. He did World War I service in 1918.

CATCHER

John (Johnny) Kling (1875–1947), righthanded batter. Played thirteen years in the major leagues with Chicago (N.L.), 1900–08, 1910–11; Boston (N.L.), 1911–12; and Cincinnati (N.L.), 1913. Chicago won the National League pennant in 1906–08, 1910, and the World Series in 1907 and 1908. The Cubs missed the pennant in 1909, when Kling held out all year for a bigger salary. He was manager of the Boston Braves in 1912. In 1,260 games he had 1,151 hits, 531 runs batted in, and a career batting average of .271. He stole 123 bases.

PITCHERS

Edward (Ed) Reulbach (1882–1961), righthander. Pitched thirteen years in the major leagues with Chicago (N.L), 1905–13; Brooklyn (N.L.), 1913–14; Newark (Federal League), 1915; and Boston (N.L.), 1916–17. His Chicago Cubs won the National League pennant in 1906–08, 1910, and the World Series in 1907 and 1908. He won 20 or more games in 1906 (20–4), 1908 (24–7), and 1915 (20–10); and World Series games in 1906 (a one-hitter) and 1907. In 1908 he pitched a double shutout against Brooklyn, winning the first game 5–0, and the second 3–0. His career won-lost record in 185–105, with 40 shutouts and a 2.28 ERA. In relief he was 18–7, with a 2.85 ERA.

Sandy Koufax (see "Jewish Almanac's Sports Hall of Fame").

Reserve

OUTFIELD

George Stone (1876–1945), lefthanded batter. Played seven years in the major leagues with Boston (A.L.), 1903; and St. Louis (A.L.), 1905–10. The twenty-nine-year-old rookie led the American League in hits with 187 in 1905. The next year he hit .358 to win the batting title and was runner-up in hits (208) and triples (20). He stole 35 bases. In 848 games Stone had 984 hits and a career batting average of .301.

CATCHER

Harry (The Horse) Danning (1911—), righthanded batter. Played ten years in the major leagues with New York (N.L.), 1933–42. The Giants won the National League pennant in 1933 and 1936–37, and the World Series in 1933. Danning played in 890 games, had 57 home runs, 397 runs batted in, and a career batting average of .285.

PITCHERS

Ken Holtzman (see "Jewish Almanac's Sports Hall of Fame").

Erskine Mayer (1891–1957), righthander. Pitched in the major leagues eight years with Philadelphia (N.L.), 1912–18; Pittsburgh (N.L.), 1918–19; and Chicago (A.L.), 1919. He was a 21-game winner in 1914 and 1915. The Phillies won the 1915 National League pennant but lost the World Series to Boston four games to one. Mayer dropped the second contest 2–1. He ended his baseball days with the scandal-ridden "Black Sox" in 1919. The incident so depressed him he gave up the game. His career won-lost record is 91–70, with a 2.96 ERA. In relief he was 14–5, with six saves and a 2.50 ERA.

Lawrence (Larry) Sherry (1935—), righthander. Pitched relief eleven years in the major leagues with Los Angeles (N.L.), 1958–63; Detroit (A.L.), 1964–67; and Houston (N.L.) and California (A.L.), 1968. He was the Los Angeles Dodgers pitching hero of 1959. He came up from the minor leagues during the season and compiled a 7–2 record, won a playoff contest, and won two World Series games and saved two others as the Dodgers defeated the Chicago White Sox four games to two. His career won-lost record is 53–44, with a 3.67 ERA. In relief he was 47–37, with 82 saves and a 3.56 ERA. His 13 relief victories led the National League in 1960.

DESIGNATED HITTERS

Ronald (Ron) Blomberg (1948—), lefthanded batter. Played eight years in the major leagues with New York (A.L.), 1969, 1971–76; and Chicago (A.L.), 1978. He was baseball's number one draft pick in 1967 and major league baseball's first designated hitter in 1973. He also played first base and the outfield. In 461 games Blomberg had 391 hits, 52 home runs, and a career batting average of .293.

Michael (Mike) Epstein (1943—), lefthanded batter. Played nine years in the major leagues with Baltimore (A.L.), 1966–67; Washington (A.L.), 1967–71; Oakland (A.L.), 1971–72; Texas (A.L.), 1973; and California (A.L.), 1973–74. He hit 30 home runs in 1969 and 26 in 1972 to help Oakland win the American League pennant and the World Series. In 1971 he tied a major league record with four home runs in four consecutive times at bat. He played in 907 games, had 130 home runs, 380 runs batted in, and a career batting average of .244. He played football at the University of California.

—J.H.S.

ALL-TIME, ALL-AMERICA JEWISH COLLEGE FOOTBALL PLAYERS

The first All-America Football team was chosen in 1889. The following Jewish players were first, second, or third team choices on at least one All-America team during their college careers. Two men who played college football before All-America selections began deserve mention: Moses Epstein of Columbia and Lucious Littauer of Harvard. Epstein played in intercollegiate football's third game against Rutgers in 1870; Littauer, who played for Harvard in 1875 and 1877, became college football's first coach in 1881.

1891	Phil King	Princeton	Quarterback	First Team
1892	Phil King	Princeton	Halfback	First Team
1893	Phil King	Princeton	Quarterback	First Team
1903	Sig Harris	Minnesota	Quarterback	First Team
1904	Sig Harris	Minnesota	Quarterback	Third Team
1905	Israel Levene	Pennsylvania	End	First Team
1906	Israel Levene	Pennsylvania	End	First Team
1909	Joe Magidsohn	Michigan	Halfback	Second Team
1910	Joe Magidsohn	Michigan	Halfback	First Team
1911	Arthur Bluethenthal	Princeton	Center	First Team
1911	Leonard Frank	Minnesota	Tackle	First Team
1911	Harry Kallet	Syracuse	End	First Team
1912	Arthur Bluethenthal	Princeton	Center	Third Team
1918	Joe Alexander	Syracuse	Guard	First Team
1918	Victor Frank	Pennsylvania	Guard	Second Team
1919	Joe Alexander	Syracuse	Guard	First Team
1920	Joe Alexander	Syracuse	Center	First Team
1920	Arnold Horween	Harvard	Fullback	First Team
1922	Max Kadesky	Iowa	End	Third Team
1924	George Abramson	Minnesota	Guard	Second Team
1925	Benny Friedman	Michigan	Quarterback	First Team
1925	Milton Levy	Tulane	Guard	Second Team
1926	Benny Friedman	Michigan	Quarterback	First Team
1927	Ray Baer	Michigan	Guard	Second Team
1927	Benny Lom	California	Halfback	First Team
1928	Benny Lom	California	Halfback	Second Team
1929	Benny Lom	California	Halfback	Second Team
1929	Louis Gordon	Illinois	Tackle	First Team
1929	Fred Sington	Alabama	Tackle	Third Team
1930	Fred Sington	Alabama	Tackle	First Team
1930	Gabe Bromberg	Dartmouth	Guard	Third Team
1932	Harry Newman	Michigan	Quarterback	First Team
1932	Franklin Meadow	Brown	End	Third Team
1932	Aaron Rosenberg	USC	Guard	First Team
1933	Aaron Rosenberg	USC	Guard	First Team
1934	Isadore Weinstock	Pittsburgh	Fullback	First Team
1934	Dave Smukler	Temple	Fullback	First Team
1937	Marshall Goldberg	Pittsburgh	Halfback	First Team
1937	Leroy Monsky	Alabama	Guard	First Team
1937	Sid Luckman	Columbia	Halfback	Third Team
1938	Sid Roth	Cornell	Guard	First Team
1938	Marshall Goldberg	Pittsburgh	Fullback	First Team
1938	Sid Luckman	Columbia	Halfback	First Team
1943	Mervin Pregulman	Michigan	Tackle and Guard	First Team
1943	William Stein	Georgia Tech	Quarterback	Third Team

1944	Maurice Furchgott	Georgia Tech	Guard	First Team
1946	Hyman Harris	Oregon	End	First Team
1947	Dan Dworsky	Michigan	Center and Linebacker	Third Team
1950	Bernard Lemonick	Pennsylvania	Defensive Guard	First Team
1952	Myron Berliner	UCLA	End	First Team
1958	Alan Goldstein	North Carolina	End	First Team
1959	Ron Mix	USC	Tackle	First Team
1967	Richard Stotter	Houston	Offensive Guard	First Team
1967	Bob Stein	Minnesota	Defensive End	First Team
1968	Bob Stein	Minnesota	Defensive End	First Team
1971	Gary Wichard	C. W. Post	Quarterback	First Team
1973	Randy Grossman	Temple	Tight End	Third Team
1978	Dave Jacobs	Syracuse	Placekicker	Third Team

—J.H.S.

ALL-TIME, ALL-AMERICA JEWISH COLLEGE BASKETBALL PLAYERS

1908	Ira Streusand	CCNY	First Team
1909	Samuel Melitzer	Columbia	Second Team
1916	Cyril Haas	Princeton	First Team
1917	Cyril Haas	Princeton	First Team
1918	Leon (Bob) Marcus	Syracuse	Second Team
1919	Leon (Bob) Marcus	Syracuse	First Team
1920	Maclyn (Mac) Baker	NYU	Second Team
1921	Maclyn (Mac) Baker	NYU	Third Team
1922	Louis Farer	CCNY	Third Team
1923	Samuel Pite	Yale	Third Team
1925	Emanuel (Menchy) Goldblatt	Pennsylvania	First Team
1925	Pincus (Pinky) Match	CCNY	Third Team
1926	Emanuel (Menchy) Goldblatt	Pennsylvania	First Team
1926	Carl Loeb	Princeton	First Team
1926	William (Red) Laub	Columbia	Second Team
1929	Edward Wineapple	Providence	First Team
1930	Max (Mac) Kinsbrunner	St. John's (N.Y.)	Third Team
1930	Louis Bender	Columbia	First Team
1931	Max (Mack) Posnack	St. John's (N.Y.)	First Team
1931	Louis Hayman	Syracuse	Third Team
1932	Louis Bender	Columbia	First Team
1932	Moe Spahn	CCNY	Second Team
1933	Jerry Nemer	Southern California	First Team
1933	Nathan Lazar	St. John's (N.Y.)	Second Team
1934	Moe Goldman	CCNY	Second Team
1936	Herbert Bonn	Duquesne	First Team
1936	Milton Schulman	NYU	First Team
1936	Ben Kramer	LIU	Second Team
1936	William Fleishman	Western Reserve	Third Team
1937	Jules Bender	Long Island	First Team
1937	Marvin Colen	Loyola (Ill.)	Second Team
1938	Meyer (Mike) Bloom	Temple	First Team
1938	Bernard Fliegel	CCNY	First Team
1938	Irving Torgoff	LIU	Third Team
1939	Irving Torgoff	LIU	First Team
1939	Bernard Opper	Kentucky	First Team
1939	Robert Lewis	NYU	Second Team
1939	John Bromberg	LIU	Third Team

1939	Daniel Kaplowitz	LIU	Third Team
1939	Jack (Dutch) Garfinkel	St. John's (N.Y.)	Third Team
1940	Louis Possner	De Paul	Second Team
1941	Oscar (Ossie) Schectman	LIU	First Team
1941	Moe Becker	Duquesne	First Team
1942	William (Red) Holzman	CCNY	Third Team
1943	Harry Boykoff	St. John's (N.Y.)	First Team
1943	Jerry Fleishman	NYU	Second Team
1944	Hyman (Hy) Gotkin	St. John's (N.Y.)	Third Team
1945	Hyman (Hy) Gotkin	St. John's (N.Y.)	Third Team
1946	Sid Tanenbaum	NYU	First Team
1946	Jackie Goldsmith	LIU	Second Team
1946	Harry Boykoff	St. John's (N.Y.)	Second Team
1947	Sid Tanenbaum	NYU	First Team
1948	Don Forman	NYU	Second Team
1948	Adolph Schayes	NYU	Third Team
1950	Irwin Dambrot	CCNY	First Team
1953	Irving Bemoras	Illinois	Second Team
1955	Leonard Rosenbluth	North Carolina	Third Team
1956	Leonard Rosenbluth	North Carolina	First Team
1957	Leonard Rosenbluth	North Carolina	First Team
1957	Larry Friend	California	First Team
1958	Alan Seiden	St. John's (N.Y.)	Second Team
1959	Alan Seiden	St. John's (N.Y.)	First Team
1959	Don Goldstein	Louisville	Second Team
1960	Jeff Cohen	William and Mary	Second Team
1961	Art Heyman	Duke	Second Team
1961	Howard Carl	De Paul	Second Team
1961	Jeff Cohen	William and Mary	Third Team
1962	Art Heyman	Duke	First Team
1963	Art Heyman	Duke	First Team
1963	Barry Kramer	NYU	First Team
1964	Barry Kramer	NYU	First Team
1964	Robert (Rick) Kaminsky	Yale	First Team
1965	Talbot (Tal) Brody	Illinois	Second Team
1966	Dave Newmark	Columbia	First Team
1968	Neal Walk	Florida	Second Team
1969	Neal Walk	Florida	First Team
1976	Ernest (Ernie) Grunfeld	Tennessee	Second Team
1977	Ernest (Ernie) Grunfeld	Tennessee	Second Team

—J.H.S.

JEWISH OLYMPIC MEDALISTS 1896–1980

The large number of Olympic medals won by the "People of the Book" is astounding. Consider these facts:

•Their victories are out of proportion to the world population of Jews during the last eighty years.

•Anti-Semitism kept many Jewish athletes off Olympic teams. Nazi Germany is the classic example.

•Many Jews boycotted the 1936 Berlin Games, thus losing an opportunity to win additional medals.

•The Holocaust wiped out the cream of Jewish athletes in Europe.

A landmark was reached in 1952 when the Soviet Union and Israel entered the Olympic movement, the Israelis over the strenuous objection of Arab nations.

Russian Jewish athletes have been particularly productive medalists. The best finish by an Israeli was a fifth by Soviet emigrant weightlifter in Montreal in 1976.

Listed below are Jewish medalists from 1896 to 1980, together with the cities in which the Games were staged. Beginning in 1924, the Winter Olympics site is listed first, followed by the location of the Summer Games in capital letters.

The list, because of name changes and the destruction of Jewish communities, must necessarily be regarded as incomplete.

1896 (ATHENS)
Gold
Alfred Hajos-Guttman, Hungary, 100-meter freestyle swimming
Alfred Hajos-Guttman, Hungary, 1,500-meter freestyle swimming
Paul Neumann, Austria, 400-meter freestyle swimming
Adolf Schmal, Austria, 12-hour cycling race
Alfred Flatow, Germany, gymnastics, parallel bars
Alfred Flatow, Germany, gymnastics, team parallel bars
Alfred Flatow, Germany, gymnastics, team horizontal bar
Gustav Felix Flatow, Germany, gymnastics, team parallel bars
Gustav Felix Flatow, Germany, gymnastics, team horizontal bar

Silver
Alfred Flatow, Germany, gymnastics, horizontal bar

Bronze
Adolf Schmal, Austria, 1,000-meter cycling time trial
Adolf Schmal, Austria, 10,000-meter cycling track race
Otto Herschmann, Austria, 100-meter freestyle swimming

1900 (PARIS)
Gold
Myer Prinstein, USA, athletics, triple jump

Silver
Myer Prinstein, USA, athletics, long jump
Otto Wahle, Austria, 1,500-meter freestyle swimming
Otto Wahle, Austria, 200-meter swimming obstacle race
Henri Cohen, Belgium, water polo
Jean Bloch, France, soccer

Bronze
Siegfried Flesch, Austria, fencing, individual saber

1904 (ST. LOUIS)
Gold
Myer Prinstein, USA, athletics, long jump
Myer Prinstein, USA, athletics, triple jump
Samuel Berger, USA, heavyweight boxing

Silver
Albert Lehman, USA, lacrosse
Philip Hess, USA, lacrosse
Daniel Frank, USA, athletics, long jump

Bronze
Otto Wahle, Austria, 400-meter freestyle swimming

1906 (ATHENS/unofficial)
Gold
Myer Prinstein, USA, athletics, long jump
Otto Scheff, Austria, 400-meter freestyle swimming
Henrik Hajos-Guttman, Hungary, 800-meter freestyle swimming relay
Dr. Jeno Fuchs, Hungary, fencing, individual saber
Charles Buchwald, Denmark, soccer

Silver
Edgar Seligman, Great Britain, fencing, team epee
Mihaly David, Hungary, athletics, shotput

Bronze
Hugo Friend, USA, athletics, long jump
Otto Scheff, Austria, 1,500-meter freestyle swimming

1908 (LONDON)
Gold
Richard Weisz, Hungary, Greco-Roman heavyweight wrestling
Jean Stern, France, fencing, team epee
Alexandre Lippmann, France, fencing, team epee
Dr. Jeno Fuchs, Hungary, fencing, individual saber
Dr. Jeno Fuchs, Hungary, fencing, team saber
Lajos Werkner, Hungary, fencing, team saber

Silver
Edwin "Barney" Solomon, Great Britain (Ireland), rugby
Bethel "Bert" Solomon, Great Britain (Ireland), rugby
Harry Simon, USA, free rifle
Charles Buchwald, Denmark, soccer
Harald Bohr, Denmark, soccer
Edgar Seligman, Great Britain, fencing, team epee
Alexandre Lippmann, France, fencing, individual epee

Bronze
Odon Bodor, Hungary, athletics, 1,600-meter relay
Charles "Clair" Jacobs, USA, athletics, pole vault
Otto Scheff, Austria, 400-meter freestyle swimming
Paul Anspach, Belgium, fencing, team epee
Karoly Levitzky, Hungary, rowing, single sculls

1912 (STOCKHOLM)
Gold
Paul Anspach, Belgium, fencing, individual epee
Paul Anspach, Belgium, fencing, team epee
Henri Anspach, Belgium, fencing, team epee
Jacques Ochs, Belgium, fencing, team epee
Gaston Salmon, Belgium, fencing, team epee
Dr. Jeno Fuchs, Hungary, fencing, team saber
Dr. Oszkar Gerde, Hungary, fencing, team saber

Zoltan Schenker, Hungary, fencing, team saber
Lajor Werkner, Hungary, fencing, team saber

Silver
Alvah T. Meyer, USA, athletics, 100-meter dash
Abel Kiviat, USA, athletics, 1,500-meter run
Charles Buchwald, Denmark, soccer
Imre Gellert, Hungary, gymnastics, team combined exercises
Ivan Osiier, Denmark, fencing, individual epee
Edgar Seligman, Great Britain, fencing, team epee
Dr. Otto Herschmann, Austria, fencing, team saber

Bronze
Margarete Adler, Austria, 400-meter swimming freestyle relay
Klara Milch, Austria, 400-meter swimming freestyle relay
Josephine Sticker, Austria, 400-meter swimming freestyle relay
Jean Hoffman, Belgium, water polo
Mor Kovacs-Koczan, Hungary, athletics, javelin throw

1920 (ANTWERP)
Gold
Samuel Mosberg, USA, lightweight boxing
Albert Schneider, Canada (USA citizen), welterweight boxing
Morris Fisher, USA, free rifle
Morris Fisher, USA, 300-meter team shooting
Morris Fisher, USA, prone team shooting

Silver
Albert Weil, France, 6.5-meter yachting
Gerard Blitz, Belgium, water polo
Maurice Blitz, Belgium, water polo
Samuel Gerson, USA, freestyle featherweight wrestling
Paul Anspach, Belgium, fencing, team epee
Alexandre Lippmann, France, fencing, individual epee

Bronze
Gerard Blitz, Belgium, 100-meter backstroke swimming
Frederick Meyer, USA, freestyle heavyweight wrestling
Montgomery "Moe" Herscovitch, Canada, middleweight boxing
Alexandre Lippmann, France, fencing, team epee

1924 (Chamonix/PARIS)
Gold
Harold Abrahams, Great Britain, athletics, 100-meter dash
Louis Clarke, USA, athletics, 400-meter relay
Elias Katz, Finland, athletics, 3,000-meter team cross-country
John "Jackie" Fields, USA, featherweight boxing
Alexandre Lippmann, France, fencing, team epee
Morris Fisher, USA, free rifle
Morris Fisher, USA, 300-meter team shooting

Silver
Elias Katz, Finland, athletics, 3,000-meter steeplechase
Harold Abrahams, Great Britain, athletics, 400-meter relay
Maurice Blitz, Belgium, water polo
Gerard Blitz, Belgium, water polo
Paul Anspach, Belgium, fencing, team epee
Janos Garay, Hungary, fencing, team saber
Zoltan Schenker, Hungary, fencing, team saber

Bronze
Baron Umberto Luigi de Morpurgo, Italy, tennis, singles
Zoltan Schenker, Hungary, fencing, team foil
Janos Garay, Hungary, fencing, individual saber
Sidney Jelinek, USA, rowing, coxed-fours

1928 (St. Moritz/AMSTERDAM)
Gold
Fanny Rosenfeld, Canada, athletics, 400-meter relay
Hans Haas, Austria, lightweight weightlifting
Dr. Sandor Gambos, Hungary, fencing, team saber
Attila Petschauer, Hungary, fencing, team saber
Janos Garay, Hungary, fencing, team saber

Silver
Fanny Rosenfeld, Canada, athletics, 100-meter dash
Lillian Copeland, USA, athletics, discus throw
Istvan Barta, Hungary, water polo
Attila Petschauer, Hungary, fencing, individual saber
Fritzie Burger, Austria, figure skating

Bronze
Ellis Smouha, Great Britain, athletics, 400-meter relay
Harry Isaacs, South Africa, bantamweight boxing
Harold Devine, USA, featherweight boxing
Samuel Rabin, Great Britain, freestyle middleweight wrestling
M. Jacob Michaelsen, Denmark, heavyweight boxing

1932 (Lake Placid/LOS ANGELES)
Gold
Lillian Copeland, USA, athletics, discus throw
Irving Jaffee, USA, 5,000-meter speed skating
Irving Jaffee, USA, 10,000-meter speed skating
George Gulack, USA, gymnastics, rings
Gyorgy Brody, Hungary, water polo
Istvan Barta, Hungary, water polo
Endre Kabos, Hungary, fencing, team saber
Attila Petschauer, Hungary, fencing, team saber

Silver
Hans Haas, Austria, lightweight weightlifting
Karoly Karpati, Hungary, freestyle lightweight wrestling
Abraham Kurland, Denmark, Greco-Roman lightweight wrestling
Peter Jaffe, Great Britain, Star class yachting
Phillip Erenberg, USA, gymnastics, club swinging
Fritzie Burger, Austria, figure skating

Bronze
Jadwiga Weiss-Wajsowna, Poland, athletics, discus throw
Albert Schwartz, USA, 100-meter freestyle swimming
Nickolaus Herschl, Austria, freestyle heavyweight wrestling
Nickolaus Herschl, Austria, Greco-Roman heavyweight wrestling
Nathan Bor, USA, lightweight boxing
Paul Winter, France, athletics, high jump
Endre Kabos, Hungary, fencing, individual saber
Rudolf Ball, Germany, ice hockey

1936 (Garmisch-Partenkirchen/BERLIN)
Gold
Samuel Balter, USA, basketball
Ibolya Csak, Hungary, athletics, high jump
Gyorgy Brody, Hungary, water polo
Karoly Karpati, Hungary, lightweight freestyle wrestling
Endre Kabos, Hungary, fencing, individual saber
Endre Kabos, Hungary, fencing, team saber
Ilona Elek, Hungary, fencing, individual foil

Silver
Jadwiga Weiss-Wajsowna, Poland, athletics, discus throw
Irving Maretzky, Canada, basketball

Bronze
Gerard Blitz, Belgium, water polo

1948 (St. Moritz/LONDON)
Gold
Frank Spellman, USA, middleweight weightlifting
Henry Wittenberg, USA, freestyle light-heavyweight wrestling
Ilona Elek, Hungary, fencing, individual foil

Silver
Steve Seymour, USA, athletics, javelin throw
Agnes Keleti, Hungary, gymnastics, team combined exercises

Bronze
James Fuchs, USA, athletics, shot put
Norman Armitage, USA, fencing, team saber

1952 (Oslo/HELSINKI)
Gold
Eva Szekely, Hungary, 200-meter breaststroke swimming
Judit Temes, Hungary, 400-meter freestyle swimming relay
Gyorgy Karpati, Hungary, water polo
Boris Gurewitsch, USSR, Greco-Roman flyweight wrestling
Claude Netter, France, fencing, team foil
Mikhail Perelman, USSR, gymnastics, team combined exercises
Agnes Keleti, Hungary, gymnastics, floor exercises
Sandor Geller, Hungary, soccer

Silver
Aleksandr Moiseyev, USSR, basketball
Grigoriy Novak, USSR, middle-heavyweight weightlifting
Henry Wittenberg, USA, light-heavyweight freestyle wrestling
Ilona Elek, Hungary, fencing, individual foil
Agnes Keleti, Hungary, gymnastics, team combined exercises

Bronze
James Fuchs, USA, athletics, shot put
Judit Temes, Hungary, 100-meter freestyle swimming
Lev Vainschtein, USSR, free rifle
Agnes Keleti, Hungary, gymnastics, team exercise with portable apparatus
Agnes Keleti, Hungary, gymnastics, asymmetrical bars

1956 (Cortina d'Ampezzo/MELBOURNE)
Gold
Leon Rotman, Rumania, canoe, 1,000-meter Canadian singles
Leon Rotman, Rumania, canoe, 10,000-meter Canadian singles
Laszlo Fabian, Hungary, kayak, 10,000-meter pairs
Mihaly Mayer, Hungary, water polo
Gyorgy Karpati, Hungary, water polo
Isaac Berger, USA, featherweight weightlifting
Agnes Keleti, Hungary, gymnastics, asymmetrical bars
Agnes Keleti, Hungary, gymnastics, floor exercises
Agnes Keleti, Hungary, gymnastics, balance beam
Agnes Keleti, Hungary, gymnastics, team exercise with portable apparatus
Aliz Kertesz, Hungary, gymnastics, team exercise with portable apparatus
Boris Rasinsky, USSR, soccer
Yevgeniy Babitsch, USSR, ice hockey

Silver
Eva Szekely, Hungary, 200-meter breaststroke swimming
Claude Netter, France, fencing, team foil
Allan Erdman, USSR, free rifle
Agnes Keleti, Hungary, gymnastics, individual combined exercises
Agnes Keleti, Hungary, gymnastics, team combined exercises
Aliz Kertesz, Hungary, gymnastics, team combined exercises
Rafael Gratsch, USSR, 500-meter speed skating

Bronze
Imre Farkas, Hungary, canoe, 10,000-meter Canadian pairs

Oscar Moglia, Uruguay, basketball
Boris Guikhman, USSR, water polo
Yves Dreyfus, France, fencing, team epee
Armand Mouyal, France, fencing, team epee
Yakov Rylsky, USSR, fencing, team saber
David Tyschler, USSR, fencing, team saber

1960 (Squaw Valley/ROME)
Gold
Leonid Geischtor, USSR, canoe, 1,000-meter Canadian pairs
Vyera Krepkina, USSR, athletics, long jump
Mark Midler, USSR, fencing, team foil

Silver
Boris Goikhman, USSR, water polo
Isaac Berger, USA, featherweight weightlifting
Allan Jay, Great Britain, fencing, individual epee
Allan Jay, Great Britain, fencing, team epee
Ildiko Rejto, Hungary, fencing, team foil
Guy Nosbaum, France, rowing, coxed-fours
Jean Klein, France, rowing, coxed-fours
Vladimir Portnoi, USSR, gymnastics, team combined exercises

Bronze
Leon Rotman, Rumania, canoe, 1,000-meter Canadian singles
Imre Farkas, Hungary, canoe, 1,000-meter Canadian pairs
Klara Fried-Banfalvi, Hungary, kayak, 500-meter pairs
Moyses Blas, Brazil, basketball
David Segal, Great Britain, athletics, 400-meter relay
Mihaly Mayer, Hungary, water polo
Gyorgy Karpati, Hungary, water polo
Albert Axelrod, USA, fencing, individual foil
Robert Halperin, USA, Star class yachting
Leonid Kolumbet, USSR, cycling, 4,000-meter team pursuit
Vladimir Portnoi, USSR, gymnastics, long horse vault
Rafael Gratsch, USSR, 500-meter speed skating

1964 (Innsbruck/TOKYO)
Gold
Lawrence Brown, USA, basketball
Gerald Ashworth, USA, athletics, 400-meter relay
Irena Kirszenstein, Poland, athletics, 400-meter relay
Gyorgy Karpati, Hungary, water polo
Mihaly Mayer, Hungary, water polo
Yuriy Vengerovskiy, USSR, volleyball
Rudolf Plukfelder, USSR, light-heavyweight weightlifting
Leonid Zhabotinskiy, USSR, heavyweight weightlifting
Mark Midler, USSR, fencing, team foil
Grigory Kriss, USSR, fencing, individual epee
Yakov Rylsky, USSR, fencing, team saber
Mark Rakita, USSR, fencing, team saber
Ildiko Ujlaki-Rejto, Hungary, fencing, individual foil
Ildiko Ujlaki-Rejto, Hungary, fencing, team foil
Boris Dubrovskiy, USSR, rowing, double sculls
Janos Farkas, Hungary, soccer
Arpad Orban, Hungary, soccer
Tamas Gabor, Hungary, team epee
Vitaliy Davidov, USSR, ice hockey

Silver
Mihaly Hesz, Hungary, kayak, 1,000-meter singles
Irena Kirszenstein, Poland, athletics, 200-meter dash
Irena Kirszenstein, Poland, athletics, long jump
Marilyn Ramenofsky, USA, 400-meter free-style swimming
Nelly Abramova, USSR, volleyball
Isaac Berger, USA, featherweight weightlifting

Bronze
Yves Dreyfus, France, fencing, team epee
James Bregman, USA, middleweight judo
Vivian and Ronald Joseph, USA, pairs figure skating

1968 (Grenoble/MEXICO CITY)
Gold
Mihaly Hesz, Hungary, kayak, 1,000-meter singles
Irena Szewinska-Kirszenstein, Poland, athletics, 200-meter dash
Mark Spitz, USA, 400-meter freestyle swimming relay
Mark Spitz, USA, 800-meter freestyle swimming relay
Yevgeniy Lapinskiy, USSR, volleyball
Valentina Vinogradova, USSR, volleyball
Leonid Zhabotinskiy, USSR, Heavyweight weightlifting
Boris Gurevitsch, USSR, freestyle middleweight wrestling
Eduard Vinokurov, USSR, fencing, team saber
Mark Rakita, USSR, fencing, team saber
Valentin Markin, USSR, Finn class yachting
Viktor Zinger, USSR, ice hockey
Vitaliy Davidov, USSR, ice hockey
Yevgeniy Zymin, USSR, ice hockey
Yuriy Moiseyev, USSR, ice hockey

Silver
Mark Spitz, USA, 100-meter butterfly swimming
Semyon Belitz-Geiman, USSR, 400-meter freestyle swimming relay
Grigory Kriss, USSR, fencing, individual epee
Grigory Kriss, USSR, fencing, team epee
Yosif Vitebskiy, USSR, fencing, team epee
Mark Rakita, USSR, fencing, individual saber
Ildiko Ujlaki-Rejto, Hungary, fencing, team foil
Anna Pfeffer, Hungary, kayak, 500-meter pairs
Alain Calmat, France, figure skating

Bronze
Naum Prokupets, USSR, canoe, 1,000-meter Canadian pairs
Irena Szewinska-Kirszenstein, Poland, athletics, 100-meter dash
Mark Spitz, USA, 100-meter freestyle swimming
Semyon Belitz-Geiman, USSR, 800-meter freestyle swimming relay
Mihaly Mayer, Hungary, water polo
Ildiko Ujlaki-Rejto, Hungary, fencing, individual foil

1972(Sapporo/MUNICH)
Gold
Mark Spitz, USA, 100-meter freestyle swimming
Mark Spitz, USA, 200-meter freestyle swimming
Mark Spitz, USA, 100-meter butterfly swimming
Mark Spitz, USA, 200-meter butterfly swimming
Mark Spitz, USA, 400-meter freestyle swimming relay
Mark Spitz, USA, 400-meter medley swimming relay
Mark Spitz, USA, 800-meter freestyle swimming relay
Faina Melnik, USSR, athletics, discus throw
Sandor Erdoes, Hungary, fencing, team epee
Valentin Mankin, USSR, Tempest class yachting
Vitaliy Davidov, USSR, ice hockey
Nikolai Melnikov, USSR, water polo

Silver
Andrea Gyarmati, Hungary, 100-meter backstroke swimming
Neal Shapiro, USA, equestrian team jumping
Eduard Vinokurov, USSR, fencing, team saber
Ildiko Sagine-Rejto, Hungary, fencing, team foil

Bronze
Irena Szewinska, Poland, athletics, 200-meter dash
Andrea Gyarmati, Hungary, 100-meter butterfly swimming
Peter Asch, USA, water polo
Vladimir Patkin, USSR, volleyball
Yevgeniy Lapinskiy, USSR, volleyball
Neal Shapiro, USA, equestrian individual jumping
Grigory Kriss, USSR, fencing, team epee
Anna Pfeffer, Hungary, kayak, 500-meter singles
Don Cohan, USA, Dragon class yachting

1976 (Innsbruck/MONTREAL)
Gold
Aleksandr Vinogradov, USSR, canoe, 500-meter Canadian pairs
Aleksandr Vinogradov, USSR, canoe, 1,000-meter Canadian pairs
Ernest Grunfeld, USA, basketball
Irena Szewinska, Poland, athletics, 400-meter run
Valeriy Schariy, USSR, light-heavyweight weightlifting
David Rigert, USSR, middle-heavyweight weightlifting
Eduard Vinokurov, USSR, fencing, team saber
Yuriy Liapkin, USSR, ice hockey

Silver
Nancy Lieberman, USA, basketball
Natalia Kushnir, USSR, volleyball
Larysa Bergen, USSR, volleyball
Anna Pfeffer, Hungary, kayak, 500-meter pairs
Valentin Mankin, USSR, Tempest class yachting

Bronze
Wendy Weinberg, USA, 800-meter freestyle swimming
Victor Zilbermann, Rumania, welterweight boxing
Edith Master, USA, equestrian team dressage
Ildiko Sagine-Rejto, Hungary, fencing, team foil

1980 (Lake Placid)
Silver
Vladimir Myshkin, USSR, ice hockey

—R.J.S.

MACCABIAH GAMES: THE MAKING OF A NEW JEW

"You bring home the bacon and I'll eat it," New York's wisecracking Mayor Jimmy Walker told the thirteen American athletes bound for the first Maccabiah Games at a City Hall reception in 1932.

The remark, addressed to the Jewish delegation enroute to Palestine, was no more inappropriate than that the Games, which celebrate athletic achievement, were named after Judah Maccabeus, a Hebrew religious zealot (second century B.C.E.) who fought against the encroaching Hellenization of Jewish life symbolized by the Greek Olympic-style games and the cult of the physical.

However Maccabeus, known as "the Hammer" because of his fighting skills, employed the physical for ultimately spiritual ends. His revolt against the occupying Syrian forces and their Hellenizing influence on the Jewish masses was the first recorded successful battle for religious freedom. The victory of Maccabeus and his band of zealots culminated in the recapture, cleansing and rededication of the Temple in Jerusalem on the 25th day of Kislev in 165 B.C.E., an event still commemorated in Jewish communities throughout the world on Hanukkah, the Festival of Lights.

In the late nineteenth century large numbers of Jews in Eastern Europe and the Middle East, suffering under religious oppression, turned to the development of their physical powers for their deliverance. Locked behind the walls of the ghetto, victimized by pogroms, humbled, ridiculed, and isolated from the outside world, they formed self-defense units and gymnastic clubs to rejuvenate the muscles of a people devoted for centuries to the study of the Talmud and Torah. They drew their model from the hero who had used his strength in the service of securing religious freedom; the Maccabi name was adopted by such athletic clubs in Constantinople by 1895–96. Austro-Hungary and Germany soon followed the Turkish example; supported by Zionist leaders Theodor Herzl and Max Nordau, the movement spread rapidly. Not all clubs took the Maccabi name. Some were called Bar Kochba, after another famed Hebrew warrior; others, Hakoah, the Hebrew word for "strength." On the eve of World War I more than 100 Maccabi-style clubs existed in Europe. Subsequent developments, however, were probably not what Judah Maccabeus would have envisioned or understood.

The World Maccabiah Games were the inspiration of Yosef Yekutieli, who wanted to build a bridge between Jewish youth in the Diaspora and in Palestine. Born in Russia in 1897, Yekutieli settled in Palestine in 1908 and served in the Turkish army in 1917–18. He was the only delegate from Palestine to the Maccabi World Congress in 1929, where he suggested a convocation of Jewish athletes in Palestine. The idea was unanimously accepted and dates for the games to be held in Tel Aviv, were set for March 29–April 16, 1932.

Twenty-two nations participated. The stadium was completed the night before the opening of the Maccabiah. The crude oval was built to seat 5,000 spectators but 25,000 jammed in and thousands more were turned away. Athletes were housed in private homes as close to the stadium as possible.

The American delegation competed under the aegis of the newly created United States Maccabi Association, founded in 1932 with Nathan L. Goldstein as president and Harvard long jumper David White as executive director. The thirteen American athletes (eleven men and two women), all of them doing double and triple duty, and many of them competing in events for the first time, "brought home the bacon." They captured thirteen gold and many silver and bronze medals. The USA, Austria, Czechoslovakia, Poland, Germany, Egypt, and Palestine swept all the first places on a program of men and women's track and field, men and women's swimming, men and women's gymnastics, water polo, field hockey, men's tennis, soccer football, European handball, boxing, and men and women's fencing. A woman fencer named Sherer gave Palestine its lone gold medal.

American gold medal winners included swimmer Harold Kramer (400-meter freestyle) and track and field athletes Gus Heymann (100-meter dash), Martin Feiden (high jump), Harry Werbin (5,000-meter run), Harry Schneider (discus, javelin, hammer, and triathlon), Leslie Flaksman (1,500-meter run), David White (long jump), and Sybil Koff (100-meter dash, high jump, and long jump). Other USA athletes were swimmers Eugene Sigel, Lou Abelson, and Eva Bein, and track and fielders Dave Adelman and Harold Ginsberg.

Not surprisingly the Maccabiah Games, which eventually gained International Olympic Committee recognition, have seen more

Opening ceremonies of the 10th Maccabiah Games

budding doctors, lawyers, engineers, and other professional people participants than any other athletic festival in the world.

American delegations to the Games also have been filled with Olympians and national, collegiate, and interscholastic champions and record holders. Olympic medalists include swimmers Mark Spitz, Marilyn Ramenofsky, and Wendy Weinberg; basketball players Larry Brown and Ernie Grunfeld; weightlifters Isaac Berger and Frank Spellman; track and field athletes Lillian Copeland and Gerald Ashworth; fencer Albert Axelrod; water polo player Peter Asch; and wrestler Henry Wittenberg.

The Maccabiah, sometimes called the "Jewish Olympics," gave Spitz (1965), Ramenofsky (1961), and Weinberg (1973) their first taste of international competition.

Several innovations of the Maccabiah have subsequently been copied by the Olympics. Basketball was a Maccabiah sport before it appeared in the 1936 Berlin Olympics. A woman, Debra Turner-Markus, was the final torch bearer in the 1965 Maccabiah, three years before a female had the same honor at the Mexico City Olympics in 1968.

Maccabiah athletes who reside in and compete for one nation may compete for another when they change their residence. (This is not true of the Olympics.) Thus Tal Brody, a member of the gold medal USA basketball team in 1965, led Israel to a 74-70 upset gold medal victory over America in the 1969 Maccabiah.

Track star Lorraine Lotzoff of South Africa, winner of the 100, 200, and 400 meters in 1965, met USA swimmer Richard Abramson at the Games that year. They were married and following motherhood she returned to Israel representing the USA in 1973. Mrs. Abramson captured a silver medal in the 200 and a bronze in the 100.

American David Berger, Maccabiah middleweight weightlifting gold medalist in 1969, made *aliyah* and, representing Israel in the 1972 Olympics, was one of the eleven Israeli sportsmen slaughtered by Arab terrorists in Munich.

The 1935 Maccabiah was known as the "Aliyah Games." With war clouds approaching in Europe, Germany sent an inflated delegation of 134 athletes plus several large bands to Palestine. Other European nations did likewise, the athletes and "musicians" settling in Palestine rather than returning to their native lands.

The 1935 American team again competed under the standard of the United States Maccabi Association. However, public support and financial aid was minimal and some athletes had to pay their own way. It was only through the last minute intervention of Manischewitz Matzos as well as a sizeable contribution from Mrs. Nathan L. Goldstein that steamship tickets for most of the athletes were procured.

The third Maccabiah was planned for 1938 but world events caused their cancellation. The Games were not resumed until 1950, this time in the newly created State of Israel, where they have since been staged.

The United States Committee Sports for Israel (130 East 59th Street, New York, NY 10022), in cooperation with the National Jewish Welfare Board, sponsored the 1950 American squad. The next Maccabiah was held in 1953 and USA representation became for the first time the sole responsibility of USCSFI, which has been the sponsor since.

Since 1957 the Games have been held on a four-year cycle the year after the Olympics. An International Maccabiah Games Committee, similar to the International Olympic Committee, was formed in 1963; it works closely with the Israel Organizing Committees for the Maccabiah.

Thirty-three nations and 2,276 athletes participated in the 1977 Games. The number of United States sportsmen and women was 289. The eleventh Maccabiah is scheduled for July 6–16, 1981.

Recalling the 1950 Games in which he was the USA's high point scorer, Roy Chernock, track and field coach at William and Mary, said: "Conditions, of course, were primitive, nothing like the modern facilities available in Israel today. But we loved it. We were housed in an abandoned British army rehabilitation center—where the Statler Hilton Hotel in Tel Aviv now stands. We were twenty-five in a room with no running water. There was one big outhouse for use by all. The food was sparse for athletes, but no one complained, because we were better fed than the Israelis who two years earlier had won their War of Independence.

"I remember being invited to dinner in an Israeli home," Chernock said. "Later I realized that the family had used their entire meat ration for a week just to entertain me."

Other moments that bear remembrance are:

In 1961, a memorial was held for nations that once had participated in the Maccabiah but whose Jewish communities had been wiped out in the Holocaust or were no longer able to compete. It was staged during Israel's bar mitzvah year and shortly after the traumatic experience of the Eichmann trial. The memorial, in English, French, and Spanish as well as Hebrew, was for Germany, Poland, Rumania, Czechoslovakia, Yugoslavia, Hungary, Bulgaria, Lithuania, Latvia, Egypt, Lebanon, Syria, Morocco, and Libya.

The last official appearance by a Turkish delegation was in 1961. After this, under pressure from Arab nations, only Turkish Jewish observers were sent to Israel, each of them kissing Israel's soil after deplaning at Lod (Ben-Gurion Airport) and the soil at each athletic site.

The first and last appearance of an Iranian delegation was in 1965. Sixty thousand Israelis in Ramat Gan Stadium booed the bewildered Iranians and drove them to tears because, unknowingly, their goose-stepping march touched the raw nerves of many Holocaust survivors.

The cold silence which greeted the first West German delegation as they paraded with their nation's flag brought tears to the eyes of the athletes during the 1969 opening ceremonies. However, once the competition began the Germans were cheered by the crowds.

The 1969 trip of the United States delegation to the Western Wall on *Tisha B'Av* was doubly emotional. Not only was this their first visit to reunited Jerusalem but also, when the American team returned to its quarters on the outskirts of Tel Aviv from Jerusalem, it learned that Israeli jets had been in an intense battle with Egyptian MIG fighters over Suez that morning.

The colorfully turbaned delegations from India were always an attraction at the Games. After 1969, however, they ceased attending the Maccabiah because of the exodus of Jews from India and because of the restrictive policies of Indira Gandhi, who bowed to Arab pressures.

Emotional memorial services were held for the eleven Munich martyrs during the 1973 opening ceremonials.

Proud one-member teams have come from Zaire, Japan, and the U.S. Virgin Islands.

Considerable *yiddishkeit* envelops the Maccabiah Games, for they are much more than an athletic carnival. Jewish young people from around the world quickly find the thread that binds them together. The athletic aspect of the Games becomes secondary. Barriers of language and culture quickly dissolve under the blazing blue Israeli sky. Lasting friendships are made. There is an understanding and appreciation of one another as well as of the modern Maccabees of Israel. And underlying it all is a spiritual and religious awakening. What eventually emerges from each two-week Maccabiah experience is something that Judah Maccabeus would probably have loved after all.

Maccabiah Records and Results (1932–1977)

Listed below are Maccabiah Games records (1932–1977) in those sports which are standard and measurable (time, distance, height, weight, and accuracy), followed by complete winning results of the 10th Maccabiah held in Israel July 12–21, 1977.

Abbreviations used are kg for kilograms and m for meters. One kilogram is equal to 2.2046 avoirdupois pounds, 1 meter equals 1.0936 yards. Since metric conversion tables vary, the one used for this volume is the official table of the worldwide Association of Track and Field Statisticians, adopted by that organization at its Rome Congress in 1960. The metric distance or height was the one measured.

Where possible first and last names are given as well as the complete composition of teams. Official results provided by the Maccabiah Games Organizing Committee do not, in many cases, contain them.

ATHLETICS (MEN)

100 m—Harold Bromberg, South Africa, 10.4 (1957)

200 m—Harold Bromberg, South Africa, 21.5 (1957)

400 m—William Shapiro, USA, 47.3 (1965)

800 m—Franklin Jankes, South Africa, 1:50.9 (1969)

1,500 m—Rayfel Roseman, Great Britain, 3:46.9 (1969)

5,000 m—William Morgan, USA, 14:23.6 (1965)

10,000 m—Gary Cohen, USA, 30:40.8 (1973)

110-m hurdles—Donald Slevin, USA, 14.4 (1973)

400-m hurdles—Milton Bresler, USA, 52.66 (1973)

400-m relay—USA (Douglas Finkel, David Lee, Emanuel Rosenberg, Leon Grundstein), 41.68 (1973)

1,600-m relay—USA (Russell Pearlman, Milton Bresler, Kerry Gold, Leon Grundstein), 3:16.6 (1973)

3,000-m walk—Shaul Ladani, Israel, 13:35.4 (1969)

20,000-m walk—Shaul Ladani, Israel, 1:37:54.0 (1973)

50,000-m walk—Shaul Ladani, Israel, 4:23:31.0 (1973)

High jump—Kerry Kring, USA (2.05 m) 6′ 8¾″ (1977)

Pole vault—Steven Greenberg, USA (4.50) 14′ 1¼″ (1977)

Long jump—Michael Herman, USA (7.27) 24′ 6″ (1961)

Triple jump—Jeffrey Gabel, USA (14.82) 48′ 7½″ (1969)

Shot put—Gary Grubner, USA (18.32) 60′ 1¼″ (1961)

Discus throw—Jay Pushkin, USA (52.78) 173′ 2″ (1977)

Hammer throw—Boris "Dov" Dkerassi, USA (66.56) 218′ 4½″ (1977)

Javelin throw—Joseph Gould, USA (71.36) 234′ 1½″ (1977)

Decathlon—Kenneth Kring, USA, 6,859 pts. (1977)

ATHLETICS (WOMEN)

100 m—Esther Roth, Israel, 11.75 (1973)

200 m—Esther Roth, Israel, 24.03 (1977)

400 m—A. Balas, Israel, 56.14 (1973)

800 m—Abigail Hoffman, Canada, 2:08.9 (1969)

1,500 m—Zehava Shmueli, Israel, 4:34.96 (1977)

100-m hurdles—Esther Roth, Israel, 13.50 (1977)

400-m relay—Israel, 47.88 (1977)

1,600-m relay—Israel, 3:53.78 (1977)

High jump—Ruth Zeloshenko, Israel (1.75 m) 5′ 9″ (1977)

Long jump—Esther Roth, Israel (5.81) 19′ ¾″ (1969)

Shot put—Mira Bulva, Israel (13.06) 42′ 10¼″ (1977)

Discus throw—Mira Bulva, Israel (43.78) 143′ 7½″ (1977)

Javelin throw—Carrie Piller, Holland (42.01) 137′ 10″ (1969)

Pentathlon—Ziva Rabinovitch, Israel, 3,385 pts. (1977)

SHOOTING

Free rifle (60 shots—prone)—Micha Kaufman, Israel, 595 pts. (1977)

Free pistol (60 shots)—Ronald Krelstein, USA, 537 pts. (1977)

Air rifle (40 shots)—Henry Hershkovitz, Israel, 371 pts. (1973)

Duel pistol (25 m)—Laurence Benater, South Africa, 576 pts. (1977)

Free rifle (3 positions)—Randolph Schwartz, USA, 1,117 pts. (1977)

Olympic air pistol (40 shots—standing)—Ronald Krelstein, USA (1973) and Laurence Benater, South Africa (1977), 373 pts.

Standing pistol—Laurence Benater, South Africa, 544 pts. (1977)

Olympic skeet—Melvin Swerdloff, USA, 183 pts. (1973)

Olympic trap—Maxim Kahan, Israel, 188 pts. (1977)

SWIMMING (MEN)

100-m freestyle—Mark Spitz, USA, 52.9 (1969)

200-m freestyle—Hilary Bergman, USA, 1:55.91 (1977)

400-m freestyle—Hilary Bergman, USA, 4:04.34 (1977)

1,500-m freestyle—Hilary Bergman, USA, 16:20.55 (1977)

100-m backstroke—Mark Heinrich, USA, 1:00.57 (1977)

200-m backstroke—Mark Gordin, USA, 2:09.59 (1977)

100-m breaststroke—Lance Michaelis, USA, 1:06.62 (1977)

200-m breaststroke—Lance Michaelis, USA, 2:25.16 (1977)

100-m butterfly—Samuel Franklin, USA, 56.70 (1977)

200-m butterfly—Michael Saphir, USA, 2:07.72 (1977)

200-m individual medley—Roy Abramowitz, USA, 2:17.9 (1973)

400-m individual medley—Hilary Bergman, USA, 4:39.31 (1977)

400-m freestyle relay—USA (Hilary Bergman, Steven Pomerantz, Samuel Franklin, Allan Fine), 3:34:36 (1977)

800-m freestyle relay—USA (Michael Saphir, Allan Fine, Mark Heinrich, Hilary Bergman), 7:59.07 (1977)

400-m medley relay—USA (Mark Heinrich, Lance Michaelis, Samuel Franklin, Allan Fine), 4:01.19 (1977)

SWIMMING (WOMEN)

100-m freestyle—Helen Plaschinski, Mexico, 1:01.45 (1977)

200-m freestyle—Wendy Weinberg, USA, 2:08.96 (1977)

400-m freestyle—Wendy Weinberg, USA, 4:26.14 (1977)

800-m freestyle—Wendy Weinberg, USA, 9:03.46 (1977)

100-m backstroke—Gillian Peters, Australia, 1:10.33 (1977)

200-m backstroke—Gillian Peters, Australia, 2:27.50 (1977)

100-m breaststroke—Shlomit Nir, Israel, 1:20.0 (1969)

200-m breaststroke—Anat Farkas, Israel, 2:52.33 (1977)

100-m butterfly—Borman Barton, USA, 1:04.39 (1977)

200-m butterfly—Wendy Weinberg, USA, 2:20.80 (1977)

200-m individual medley—Anita Zarnowiecki, Sweden, 2:32.6 (1973)

400-m individual medley—Elisa Denaburg, USA, 5:16.62 (1977)

400-m freestyle relay—USA (Donna Goldbloom, Sara Shuster, Norman Barton, Wendy Weinburg), 4:10.09 (1977)

400-m medley relay—USA (Elisa Denaburg, Bonnie Nathan, Norman Barton, Wendy Weinberg), 4:40.00 (1977)

WEIGHTLIFTING

Flyweight (up to 52 kg)

Snatch—Yaacov Gurevitz, Israel, 77.5 kg (1973)

Jerk—Yaacov Gurevitz, Israel, 92.5 kg (1973)

Total—Yaacov Gurevitz, Israel, 170 kg (1973)

Bantamweight (up to 56 kg)

Snatch—Willy Chemberlo, Israel, 82.5 kg (1973)

Jerk—Willy Chemberlo, Israel, 90.0 kg (1973)

Total—Willy Chemberlo, Israel, 172.5 kg (1973)

Featherweight (up to 60 kg)

Snatch—Ivan Katz, Australia, 100 kg (1973)

Jerk—Lennart Stahl, Sweden, 125 kg (1977)

Total—Ivan Katz, Australia, 222.5 kg (1973)

Lightweight (up to 67.5 kg)

Snatch—Aduard Wiez, Israel, 115 kg (1977)

Jerk—Aduard Wiez, Israel, 150 kg (1977)

Total—Aduard Wiez, Israel, 265 kg (1977)

Middleweight (up to 75 kg)

Snatch—Nils-Eric Sollevi, Sweden, 125 kg (1973)

Jerk—Michael Cohen, USA, 155 kg (1977)

Total—Michael Cohen, USA, 277.5 kg (1977)

Light-heavyweight (up to 82.5 kg)

Snatch—Shlomo Farid, Israel, 117.5 kg (1973)

Jerk—Teddy Kaplan, Israel, 152.5 kg (1973)

Total—Shlomo Farid, Israel, 267.5 kg (1973)

Middle-heavyweight (up to 90 kg)

Snatch—Shlomo Ben-Lulu, Israel, 127.5 kg (1973)

Jerk—Mark Miller, USA, 167.5 kg (1973)

Total—Shlomo Ben-Lulu, Israel, and Mark Miller, USA, 292.5 kg (1973)

Heavyweight (up to 100 kg)

Snatch—Adi Brana, Israel, 117.5 kg (1977)

Jerk—Adi Brana, Israel, and Barry Rubenstein, USA, 142.5 kg (1977)

Total—Adi Brana, Israel, 260 kg (1977)

Heavyweight (up to 110 kg)

Snatch—Matthew Guttman, USA, 127.5 kg (1977)

Jerk—Barry Senate, USA, 155 kg (1973)

Total—Matthew Guttman, USA, 277.5 kg (1977)

Super-heavyweight (over 110 kg)

Snatch—Terry Perdue, Great Britain, 142.5 kg (1973)

Snatch—Terry Perdue, Great Britain, 170 kg (1973)

Total—Terry Perdue, Great Britain, 312.5 kg (1973)

1977 Maccabiah Games Results

ATHLETICS (MEN)

100 m—Marc Davidovici, France, 10.76

200 m—Emanuel Rosenberg, USA, 21.83

400 m—Leonard Bogatin, Australia, 49.25

800 m—Steven Stern, Australia, 1:52.78

1,500 m—Richard Rothschild, USA, 3:52.41

5,000 m—Gary Cohen, USA, 14:26.66

10,000 m—Gary Cohen, USA, 31:19.23

110-m hurdles—John Citron, USA, 14.6

400-m hurdles—John Citron, USA, 54.68

3,000-m walk—Robert Rosencrantz, USA, 13:45.45

50,000-m walk—Shaul Ladani, Israel, 4:29: 18.4

400-m relay—USA, 41.95

1,600-m relay—Australia, 3:20.29

High jump—Kerry Kring, USA (2.05 m.) 6′ 8¾″

Long jump—Yehuda Levkovitch, Israel (6.88) 22′ 7″

Triple jump—Erez Ben-Ezra, Israel (14.07) 46′ 2″

Pole vault—Steven Greenberg, USA (4.50) 14′ 9¼″

Discus throw—Jay Pushkin, USA (52.78) 173′ 2″

Javelin throw—Joseph Gould, USA (71.00) 232′ 11¼″

Shot put—Joseph Gould, USA (17.00) 55′ 9¼″

Hammer throw—Boris "Dov" Djerassi, USA (66.56) 218′ 4½″

Decathlon—Kenneth Kring, USA, 6,859 pts.

ATHLETICS (WOMEN)

100 m—Esther Roth, Israel, 11.80

200 m—Esther Roth, Israel, 24.03

400 m—Dian Hupert, Israel, 57.18

800 m—Aazit Fabian, Israel, 2:14.68

1,500 m—Zehava Shmueli, Israel, 4:34.96

100-m hurdles—Esther Roth, Israel, 13.50

400-m relay—Israel, 47.88

1,600-m relay—Israel, 3:53.78

High jump—Ruth Zeloshenko, Israel (1.75 m) 5′ 9″

Long jump—Orna Uziel, Israel (5.80) 19′ ¼″

Discus throw—Mira Bulva, Israel (43.78) 42′ 10¼″

Javelin throw—Clara Flum, Israel (39.12) 128′ 4″

Shot put—Mira Bulva, Israel (13.06) 42′ 10¼″

Pentathlon—Ziva Rabinovitch, Israel, 3,385 pts.

BADMINTON

Men's singles—Epstein, Canada

Women's singles—Samson, Holland

Men's doubles—Epstein, Canada, and Samson, Holland

Women's doubles—Samson, Holland, and Unglik, Sweden

Mixed doubles—Samson and Samson, Holland

BASKETBALL

USA (Sheldon Bloom, Alan Bluman, Hal Cohen, Lewis Cohen, Leo Eisner, Stuart Klitenic, Joel Kramer, Howard Lassoff, Jay Lowenthal, Brian Magic, David Mosenson, Daniel Schayes, Eric Schlossberg, Willie Sims)

BOXING

Featherweight (up to 57 kg)—Shimon Grubman, Israel

Lightweight (up to 60 kg)—Barka Kasam, Israel

Light-welterweight (up to 63.5 kg)—William Shada, Israel

Welterweight (up to 67 kg)—Roman Smolansky, Israel

Light-middleweight (up to 71 kg)—Jean-Jacques Benchetrit, France

Middleweight (up to 75 kg)—Chaim Zilberschmidt, Israel

Light-heavyweight (up to 81 kg)—Roman Frankel, Israel

Heavyweight (over 81 kg)—Meir Drukman, Israel

BRIDGE

Israel (M. Hochzeit, Y. Levit, A. Stampf, A. Schwartz, D. Birman, Y. Kaufman; non-playing captain, R. Kunin) 193 pts.

CHESS

Israel "A" Team

CHESS, JUNIOR

Michael Rohde, USA

CRICKET

South Africa

DIVING (MEN)

3 m—Michael Tober, USA, 596.65 pts.

10 m—Michael Tober, USA, 488.15 pts.

DIVING (WOMEN)

3 m—Julie Bachman, USA, 473.70 pts.

10 m—Julie Bachman, USA, 371.90 pts.

FENCING (MEN)

Individual foil—Weinstein, Israel

Individual epee—Dreyfus, France

Individual saber—Edgar House, USA

Team foil—Israel

Team epee—France

Team saber—USA

FENCING (WOMEN)

Individual foil—Leonders, Holland

Team foil—Israel

FOOTBALL (SOCCER)

Israel

FOOTBALL, MINI-

Brazil

GOLF

Individual—Nathan Selwym, South Africa (73-75-74-75) 297

Team—Great Britain (Ronald Brass, Neville Chesses, Robert Davis, Martin Payne, Ian Stungo, Howard Taylor—best 4-score total), 1,210

GYMNASTICS (MEN)

Individual combined—Dov Loufi, Israel, 54.95

Floor exercise—Michael Silverstein, USA, 9.65

Side horse—Michael Moyal, Israel, 9.30

Rings—Michael Silverstein, USA, 9.20

Vault—Dov Loufi, Israel, 9.35

Parallel bars—Samuel Schuh, USA, 8.95

Horizontal Bar—Michael Silverstein, USA, 9.40

GYMNASTICS (WOMEN)

Individual combined—Sharon Shapiro, USA, 36.65

Vault—Karen Leighton, Great Britain, 9.20

Asymmetrical bars—Yael Kantor, South Africa, 9.55

Beam—Marcie Ravech, USA, 9.25

Floor exercise—Sharon Shapiro, USA, 9.65

HANDBALL, EUROPEAN

Israel

JUDO (MEN)

Up to 60 kg—Mauro Zyman, Brazil

60-65 kg—Zerach Hadad, Israel

65-71 kg—Yona Melnik, Israel

71-78 kg—Steven Cohen, USA

78-86 kg—Irwin Cohen, USA

86-95 kg—Patrice Levy, France

Over 95 kg—Bernard Lopkofker, USA

Open weight—Jean Zinniker, France

Team—USA

JUDO (WOMEN)

Up to 56 kg—Maria Matteman, Holland

56-61 kg—Susan Feingold, USA

61-66 kg—Liza Hahn, USA

66-72 kg—Kasmirah Liotard, Holland

KARATE

Under 65 kg—Anisten Patric, France

65-70 kg—Jack Serfati, France

70-75 kg—Malcolm Dorfman, South Africa

75-80 kg—Otto Rotehof, Holland

Over 80 kg—Shelton Millner, South Africa

Open—Otto Rotehof, Holland

Team—Holland

LAWN BOWLS (MEN)

Singles—Solly Hotz, South Africa

Pairs—South Africa

Triples—South Africa

Fours—South Africa

LAWN BOWLS (WOMEN)

Singles—Judy Armst, South Africa

Pairs—South Africa

Triples—South Africa

Fours—Israel

ROWING (MEN, 1,500-m course)

Single sculls—Jack Plackter, USA, 5:31.0

Double sculls—USA (Jack Plackter and Donald Rose), 5:33.5

Pairs-with-coxswain—USA (Hanley Bodek, Elliot Sussin, coxswain Murray Lukoff), 5:54.0

Pairs-without-coxswain—USA (Michael Bornstein and Scott Fisher), 5:54.0

Fours-with-coxswain—Argentina (Daniel Pilosof, Natalio Cotliar, Gabriel Rutemberg,

Julio Flanszbaum, coxswain Eduardo Glinsberg), 5:28.0

Fours-without-coxswain—USA (Michael Bornstein, Scott Fisher, Jack Plackter, Donald Rose), 5:05.0

ROWING (WOMEN, 1,000-m course)

Single sculls—Ineke Cohen, Holland, 4:23.30

Double sculls—Holland (Ineke Cohen and Lily Cockter), 4:05.0

SHOOTING

Individual free rifle (60 shots—prone)—Micha Kaufman, Israel, 595 pts.

Team free rifle—Israel (Micha Kaufman, Michael Gurevitz, Henry Hershkovitz, Shmuel Saporta), 2,355 pts.

Individual free pistol (60 shots)—Ronald Krelstein, USA, 537 pts.

Team free pistol—USA (Ronald Krelstein, Lester Baer, Herbert Rosenbaum, Stephen Nunberg), 2,091 pts.

Individual air rifle (40 shots)—Michael Gurevitz, Israel, 358 pts.

Team air rifle—Israel (Henry Hershkovitz, Hanan Kristal, Michael Gurevitz, Zelig Storch), 1,421 pts.

Individual duel pistol (25 m)—Laurence Benater, South Africa, 576 pts.

Team duel pistol—Israel (Shai Ben-Shalom, Doron Karmi, Aizik Rozin, Amos Kolman), 2,249 pts.

Individual free rifle (3 positions)—Randolph Schwartz, USA, 1,117 pts.

Team free rifle (3 positions)—Israel (Henry Hershkovitz, Zelig Storch, Michael Gurewitz, Hanan Kristal), 4,412 pts.

Individual Olympic air pistol (40 shots—standing)—Laurence Benater, South Africa, 373 pts.

Team Olympic air pistol—USA (Stephen Nunberg, Leonard Kaufner, Lester Baer, Herbert Rosenbaum), 1,474 pts.

Individual standard pistol—Laurence Benater, South Africa, 544 pts.

Team standard pistol—Israel (Shai Ben-Shalom, Amos Kolman, Michael Marton, Doron Karmi), 2,152 pts.

Individual Olympic trap—Maxim Kahan, Israel, 188 pts.

Team Olympic trap—Israel (Maxim Kahan, Ejud Shoshani, Oded Harel, Chananiah Yaacobi), 550 pts.

Individual Olympic skeet—Anselmo Zarfati, Italy, 177 pts.

Team Olympic skeet—Italy (Anselmo Zarfati, Vittorio Moscato, Renato Dinepi, Renato Efrati), 479 pts.

SQUASH

Individual—S. Machet, South Africa

Team—South Africa (E. Coll, I. Bacher, S. Machet, Kampel)

Veterans—N. Liberman, South Africa

Team Veterans—South Africa (W. Beder, N. Liberman, Kampel, P. Alter)

SWIMMING (MEN)

100-m freestyle—Steven Pomerantz, USA, 53.58

200-m freestyle—Hilary Bergman, USA, 1:55.91

400-m freestyle—Hilary Bergman, USA, 4:04.34

1,500-m freestyle—Hilary Bergman, USA, 16:20.55

100-m backstroke—Mark Heinrich, USA, 1:00.57

200-m backstroke—Mark Gordin, USA, 2:09.59

100-m butterfly—Samuel Franklin, USA, 56.70

200-m butterfly—Michael Saphir, USA, 2:07.72

100-m breaststroke—Lance Machaelis, USA, 1:06.62

200-m breaststroke—Lance Michaelis, USA, 2:25.16

400-m individual medley—Hilary Bergman, USA, 4:39.31

400-m freestyle relay—USA (Hilary Bergman, Steven Pomerantz, Samuel Franklin, Allan Fine), 3:34.36

800-m freestyle relay—USA (Michael Saphir, Allan Fine, Mark Heinrich, Hilary Bergman), 7:59.07

400-m medley relay—USA (Mark Heinrich, Lance Michaelis, Samuel Franklin, Allen Fine), 4:01.19

SWIMMING (WOMEN)

100-m freestyle—Helen Plaschinski, Mexico, 1:01.45

200-m freestyle—Wendy Weinberg, USA, 2:08.96

400-m freestyle—Wendy Weinberg, USA, 4:26.14

800-m freestyle—Wendy Weinberg, USA, 9:03.46

100-m backstroke—Gillian Peters, Australia, 1:10.33

200-m backstroke—Gillian Peters, Australia, 2:27.50

100-m breaststroke—Anat Farkas, Israel, 1:20.31

200-m breaststroke—Anat Farkas, Israel, 2:52.33

100-m butterfly—Norma Barton, USA, 1:04.39

200-m butterfly—Wendy Weinberg, USA, 2:20.80

400-m Individual medley—Elisa Denaburg, USA, 5:16.62

400-m freestyle relay—USA (Donna Goldbloom, Sara Shuster, Norma Barton, Wendy Weinberg), 4:10.09

400-m medley relay—USA (Elisa Denaburg, Bonnie Nathan, Norma Barton, Wendy Weinberg), 4:40.00

TABLE TENNIS

Men's singles—Rene Hatem, France

Women's singles—Blanka Rohan, West Germany

Men's doubles—D. Polak and M. Stein, Israel

Women's doubles—Blanka and Hana Rohan, West Germany

Mixed doubles—Hana Rohan, West Germany, and S. Mendelsohn, Israel

Men's team—Israel

Women's team—West Germany

TENNIS

Men's singles—Steven Krulevitz, USA

Men's doubles—Peter Rennert and Joel Ross, USA

Women's singles—Dana Gilbert, USA

Women's doubles—Ilana Kloss and Helen Weiner, South Africa

Mixed doubles—Stacy Margolin and Peter Rennert, USA

Men's seniors—Richard Goldstein and Marvin Gimprich, USA

VOLLEYBALL

Israel

WATER POLO

Israel "A" Team

WEIGHTLIFTING

Featherweight (up to 60 kg)—Lennart Stahl, Sweden, 90 kg snatch, 126 kg jerk, 215 kg total

Lightweight (up to 67.5 kg)—Aduard Wiez, Israel, 115, 150, 265

Middleweight (up to 75 kg)—Michael Cohen, USA, 122.5, 155, 277.5

Light-heavyweight (up to 82.5 kg)—Elie Adjoutie, France, 112.5, 142.5, 255.0

Middle-heavyweight (up to 90 kg)—Brian Romer, Australia, 100, 150, 250.0

Heavyweight (up to 100 kg)—Adi Brana, Israel, 117.5, 142.5, 260.0

Heavyweight (up to 110 kg)—Matthew Guttman, USA, 127.5, 150, 277.5

Super-heavyweight (over 110 kg)—Adnan Hodrog, Israel, 120, 145, 265.0

WRESTLING, GRECO-ROMAN

Light Flyweight (up to 48 kg)—Mark Ohriner, USA

Flyweight (up to 52 kg)—Russell Rainer, USA

Bantamweight (up to 57 kg)—William Pincus, USA

Featherweight (up to 62 kg)—Leonid Putichin, Israel

Lightweight (up to 68 kg)—Howard Stupp, Canada

Welterweight (up to 74 kg)—Zeev Zigelbaum, Israel

Middleweight (up to 82 kg)—David Strauss, USA

Light-heavyweight (up to 90 kg)—Emanuel Tzoya, Greece

Heavyweight (up to 100 kg)—Lazar Ostrinsky, Canada

Super-heavyweight (over 100 kg)—Avraham Ashuri, Israel

WRESTLING, FREESTYLE

Light flyweight—Leonard Gang, Canada

Flyweight—Russell Rainer, USA

Bantamweight—Richard Sorkin, USA

Featherweight—William Pincus, USA

Lightweight—Howard Stupp, Canada

Welterweight—Ethan Reeve, USA

Middleweight—Martin Schwartz, USA

Light-heavyweight—Garry Kallos, Canada

Heavyweight—Lazar Ostrinsky, Canada

Super-heavyweight—Michael Weitsman, USA

—R.J.S.

NO LONGER "GREENHORNS"

THE 10 WEALTHIEST JEWISH FAMILIES IN AMERICA

A bare 125 years ago, the wealthy American families portrayed below were not Americans at all, nor were they wealthy. All of them lived across the Atlantic, most of them in abject poverty. Yet in the short space of the past 60 years—in some cases, merely the past dozen years—their wealth has outstripped that of legendary American capitalists like Carnegie, Frick, Vanderbilt, Morgan, Harriman, Armour, Swift, and McCormick.

What follows is an attempt to determine the true aristocrats of American Jewish wealth today. Who are they? How did they make their money? How much are they really worth?The findings may smash some myths about Jewish wealth and reinforce others. For one thing, it is now clear that dozens of American Jews—including some whose names are barely known to the general public—have amassed colossal fortunes that rank near those of the wealthiest non-Jews. On the other hand, there is certainly no truth to the anti-Semitic canard that Jewish money dominates the country. The Pritzkers of Chicago, the wealthiest Jewish family in America, are worth perhaps $750 million. By comparison, the Mellons and du Ponts are each worth between $3 and $5 *billion*, the Gettys and Daniel Ludwig between $2 and $3 billion, and the Rockefellers between $1 and $2 billion.

Indeed, the Pritzkers ranked only tenth in the survey of the wealthiest Americans conducted in 1978 for *Town & Country* magazine. That survey turned up 74 American families or individuals worth $200 million or more: of those 74, ten were Jewish—a figure which, if disproportionately high (Jews amount to less than 3 percent of the total population), still suggests that Jews are of minimal importance among the nation's superrich.

It will also be apparent that Jews have been all but excluded from the traditional wellsprings of American wealth: oil, land, and banking. Of the ten superwealthy Jewish families, none made its money from banking, and the two who made fortunes in oil—Marvin Davis and the Blausteins—controlled only part of the total process; except for Leon Hess of Amerada Hess, no Jew has ever played a leading role in an integrated oil company. Some of the Jewish superrich have made money in urban real-estate development, but none has controlled the vast rural baronies that are the stuff of American legends.

Though a remarkably diverse lot, the Jewish superrich do share one characteristic aside from their wealth. From Samuel Rosenwald, who fled Germany in 1854 to avoid compulsory military service, to Max Stern, who left the same country in 1926 to escape the rising tide of German anti-Semitism, the family founders came to America not for wealth, but for survival. Survival was the instinct their families had cultivated through the centuries of persecution, and once they found themselves in a land where mere survival was no longer a pressing concern, it was only a matter of time before they applied their inherited resourcefulness to other challenges. In the process of creating their fortunes, they fueled countless enterprises and philanthropies that have benefited much of society. The Czar's loss—and the Kaiser's, and the Emperor's, and the Fuehrer's—has been America's gain.

The Pritzker Family, Chicago

The very private Pritzkers first caught the public eye in 1973 when they bought *McCall's* magazine from Norton Simon, Inc., for $8 million. Impressive as that price tag may have been, it was merely the tip of the iceberg for a family that in the 1970s had become the most spectacular example of new American wealth.

The Pritzker's holdings run from the Hyatt hotels to Hammond organs to Cerro-Marmon Corporation (mining and manufacturing) to W. F. Hall Printing to trucking concerns to a real-estate empire that by itself is said to be worth $500 million.

"They're the most remarkable bunch I've ever dealt with," an associate once told the *Wall Street Journal*. "They are highly talented individually, and they work together beautifully. This gives them the kind of flexibility that doesn't exist elsewhere at their level of operations. They've closed a lot of important deals because they were able to move faster than the competition." Adds Gaylord Freeman, retired chairman of Chicago's First National Bank: "They are aggressive acquirers, but they're also fine operating men. They've consistently done a good job of developing the properties they've taken over."

The family's founder, Nicholas J. Pritzker (1871–1957), came to Chicago from Kiev at age nine with the first wave of Russian-Jewish immigrants. He became a pharmacist, then studied law and opened a general practice in 1902. His sons A.N. (for Abram) and Jack became lawyers, too, and the law firm of Pritzker & Pritzker is still the only concern bearing the family's name. But the firm has not accepted an outside client in 40 years because of potential conflicts of interest with the far-flung family enterprises.

A.N., still a bundle of energy today at 83, steered the family into deal making, often transacting business in a corner of the Standard Club, Chicago's leading Jewish watering hole. A.N.'s brother Jack, also still active at 75, is the family's real-estate specialist. Of A.N.'s three sons, the ebullient Jay, 57, specializes in deal making. Associates marvel at his ability to size up and consummate a transaction quickly; his voice is said to be constantly hoarse from telephone conversations. Jay's quieter brother Robert, 53, is an engineer by training and specializes in managing the concerns that Jay acquires. A third son of A.N., Donald Pritzker, was head of the Hyatt hotel chain when he died of a heart attack in 1972 at age 39.

The Pritzkers still have not quite adjusted to their superwealthy image. "We really don't think of ourselves as great business tycoons," says Robert. "We're just guys who happen to have some success."

S. I. Newhouse,* New York

Samuel Irving Newhouse is a short, fiercely determined 84-year-old communications mogul who abhors personal publicity, scorns systematic planning, sneers at the organizational trappings of modern business, and maintains no corporate headquarters and no regular office—not even a set of files in his 12-room Park Avenue duplex apartment. He and his sons S.I. Jr., 52 and Donald, 50, are also the sole stockholders of an empire that embraces 21 daily newspapers (in cities like St. Louis, Cleveland, New Orleans, Portland, Newark, and Jersey City), five magazines (including *Vogue*, *Mademoiselle*, and *Glamour*), six television stations, four radio stations, and 20 cable-TV systems.

According to the best estimates, his empire ranks first in profits and third in revenues (behind Time, Inc., and Los Angeles' Times Mirror Company) among the nation's communications companies.

Newhouse was born on Manhattan's Lower East Side and raised in Bayonne, N.J., the eldest of eight children of immigrants from Russia and Austria. As a 17-year-old attending high school at night, he worked for a Bayonne lawyer who was given control of the floundering *Bayonne Times* in payment of a fee. Frustrated with the paper's management, he dispatched office-boy Newhouse to take charge, offering him half the paper's profits in lieu of a salary. Newhouse accepted the challenge, pulled the paper into the black through his aggressive selling of ads to local merchants, and was making $30,000 a year by the time he was 21.

The Newhouse operations are run by a close-knit cadre of blood relatives (at one time Newhouse had 64 brothers, cousins, sons, and in-laws on the payroll, but the number today is about one-fourth that). Newhouse is both praised and damned because he treats his media properties strictly as businesses—nothing more nor less. Unlike William Randolph Hearst or Walter Annenberg, Newhouse never imposes his opinions on his news executives. On the other hand, his papers are uniformly undistinguished, and the patriarch's own words help explain why.

"I'm not trying to save the world," he once told *Business Week*. "Number One in our operation is whether our editor produces a product that the reader continues to prefer. Once we have that kind of product and a good reaction from the reader, then there's no problem getting advertising."

*Now deceased.

Marvin Davis, Denver

"The more you drill," reasons 54-year-old Marvin Davis, "the more chance you have to come up with oil."

That straightforward philosophy has made Davis' wholly-owned Davis Oil Company one of the top wildcatters in the U.S. In 1976, for example, Davis Oil was Number One among the nation's 10,000 independent oil concerns, with 311 wells sunk, of which 75 struck oil. Only two major companies—Shell and Amoco Production—had more discoveries that year.

Davis Oil was founded by Marvin's father, a former British sailor who made his first fortune in Manhattan's garment industry and then went on to promote and invest in oil deals. Young Marvin studied engineering at Syracuse and New York Universities, then joined the family oil business in Houston and followed it to Denver in 1952. Today his oil holding is augmented by interests in banking and real-estate development. His son once told a friend that the family is worth $700 million. That estimate seems high as a net worth figure, but since Davis Oil is a private company, no one can say for sure.

Like most supermillionaires, Davis was rich before he was famous. He didn't enter the public spotlight until late 1977, when he agreed to buy the Oakland Athletics for $12 million and move the baseball team to Denver. "He has the near-billionaire status an independent requires to keep alive in pro sport today," Athletics owner Charles Finley commented at the time. The deal was aborted when Finley's nemesis, baseball commissioner Bowie Kuhn, refused to grant his approval.

The Bronfman Family, New York and Montreal

The late Samuel Bronfman (1891–1971) did more than parlay a small hotel and bar in Winnipeg into the world's largest liquor empire—the Seagram Company. He also made certain that his four children would retain tight control of the empire he left. Today those four—Edgar, 50, Charles, 48, Minda de Gunzburg, 54, and Phyllis Lambert, 52—control 34 percent of Seagram stock, a chunk worth some $350 million. In addition, their Cemp investment company (an acronym formed by their first initials) is the largest private landowner in Canada. And the family also has extensive interests in oil, computer services, and entertainment.

Samuel was the third son of Yechiel Bronfman, who owned a prospering grist mill and tobacco farm in Bessarabia before anti-Semitism forced him to flee to Canada in 1889. To guard his family's religious orthodoxy, Yechiel paid his local rabbi to accompany them.

On his deathbed, Yechiel entrusted the family business to Sam. It was 1919—the very year that Prohibition was enacted in the U.S. When the Bronfmans opened their first distillery in 1925, a thirsty market was waiting for them south of the Canadian border. Sam Bronfman never denied that Prohibition made him rich. "I never went on the other side of the border to count the empty Seagram's bottles," he once remarked.

The family still has its turreted, red-brick Victorian mansion in Montreal, where Sam's widow Saidye, 83, resides. But the new family patriarch and company chairman, Edgar, is an American citizen living in Westchester County, New York. Edgar is credited with the epigram, "To turn $100 to $110 is work. To turn $100 million into $110 million is inevitable." Brother Charles runs Seagram's Canadian operation from Montreal. Sister Minda is married to Baron Alain de Gunzburg of Paris, a distant relative of the Rothschilds, and sister Phyllis Lambert, a divorcée, is an architect.

Throughout his life, Sam Bronfman remained an Orthodox Jew as well as a major philanthropist. In 1941 he organized the Combined Jewish Appeal (the Canadian equivalent of the UJA). For Sam's 75th birthday in 1962, his four children gave $1 million to build a new wing onto the Israeli Museum in Jerusalem—a tribute to their father's fascination with what he once called "the timelessness of the Jew who regenerates himself despite all the handicaps, inhibitions, and assaults."

The Haas Family, San Francisco

Everyone knows Levi's blue jeans, one of the world's most popular brand names. One out of every three jeans sold in America carries the Levi's label: Levi Strauss & Company claims the widest distribution of all clothing makers. Yet few people outside San Francisco know of the modest Haas family that controls 49 percent of Levi Strauss stock (a holding worth some $400 million) and deserves most of the credit for the company's booming post-World War II success.

Walter Haas, Sr., now 90, came from an early Los Angeles family that had prospered as wholesale grocers and founders of a utility. On a cable car in San Francisco in 1913, he met his future wife, Elsie Stern, grandniece of Levi Strauss (1829–1902), the legendary founder whom the gold rush had lured to the San Francisco docks.

Haas eventually became president of Levi Strauss, and during his tenure, from 1928 to 1970, pulled the company out of the red to a position of unquestioned leadership. Equally important, Haas and his family became famous as pioneers in labor relations. Haas was one of the first employers in the garment business to provide jobs on a year-round basis; when production stopped, he paid his employees for re-laying factory floors. Long before minority hiring became fashionable, Haas set a policy of hiring and promoting members of ethnic minority groups and physically handicapped persons.

Although officially retired, Walter, Sr., still spends four days a week in the office. His sons Walter Haas, Jr., 63, and Peter Haas, 60, run the company today as chairman and president, respectively. Also, still active from the family's first generation is Daniel Koshland, 87, a first cousin as well as brother-in-law of Walter Haas Sr. And a third generation is waiting in the wings: Walter Jr.'s son Robert is senior vice-president of the company.

The Crown Family, Chicago

Henry Crown is a spare, inconspicuous octogenarian with a droll white mustache, a disarming grin, an awesome memory, fierce pride, and a sometimes ferocious temper. His family empire includes 15 percent of General Dynamics Corporation (a holding worth more than $100 million), 7 percent of Hilton Hotels, 4 percent of Esmark, 17 percent of the St. Louis & San Francisco Railway, and stock in some 300 other companies; vast real-estate holdings, from apartment buildings in Chicago and Newark to farm and coal lands in Illinois; and family ownership of a handful of operating companies, worth at least $50 million.

Although the Crown wealth has recently been surpassed by the newer Pritzker fortune, the similarities between the two families are astonishing. Both dynasties were founded by fugitives from Czarist persecution (Henry Crown's father Arie came from Lithuania) who arrived in Chicago in the early 1880s. Both Henry Crown and A. N. Pritzker, the founders of their respective fortunes, are men of dynamism and charm who are still active today; both are 83 years old; each had three sons who became the operating brains of the business: each had one son who died in his prime of a heart attack (Robert Crown died in 1969 at age 48).

Henry Crown and his six brothers and sisters grew up in near poverty after their father's suspenders shop in Chicago was destroyed by fire in 1900. At age 23, after jobs as clerk, office boy, and salesman, Henry teamed up with his older brother Sol to borrow $10,000 and start Material Service Corporation, a building-supply business. Two years later, in 1921, Sol died suddenly and Henry became president. At the time there were some 80 building supply companies in Chicago alone, but Crown pulled ahead of the crowd in the 1920s when he discovered that transportation costs could be cut dramatically if materials were shipped to Chicago by water instead of by rail. By 1959, when he sold it to General Dynamics, Material Service was the largest building supply firm in the world.

A friend says Henry Crown is "one of the most astute negotiators in the history of the world. When he goes into a deal, he knows the size of your underwear." And son Lester, 54, is said to be every bit as sharp as his father. (Lester also owns interests in the Chicago Bulls, the St. Louis Blues, and the New York Yankees.) Henry's youngest son, John, is a Chicago divorce court judge.

Henry Crown says he has given at least $100 million to charity in his life. He admits that he may retire some day, but says, "I'm enjoying life and wonder if I would if I retired."

Leonard Stern, New York

The founder of Hartz Mountain Industries may not be the wealthiest of America's superrich, but he is certainly the youngest and the hungriest. In 1951, when he was only 21, he took over a foundering pet-supply business from his father and proceeded to expand its sales tenfold through aggressive merchandising techniques. Then, in 1972, he took his company public—but not before spinning off its valuable real-estate holdings to his own personal company, so that public investors in effect paid $37 million for the equivalent of $4.5 million in assets plus goodwill.

The stock subsequently boomed until Stern's 70 percent share was worth some $400 million. It later settled back to the $130 million level, and now Stern has bought out his public shareholders—for $70 million cash—and merged the pet-supply company into his privately owned real-estate concern. That company owns, among other things, more than a thousand acres of prime northern New Jersey land, including a 700-acre Meadowlands plot just ten minutes from Manhattan where Stern is developing a giant $100 million shopping mall. Stern bought that land for about $10 million in 1969; after it's developed, it should be worth more than $350 million.

Leonard's father, Max Stern arrived in the U.S. from Germany in 1926. He had no money, but he did have 2,100 Hartz Mountain canaries, which he set about peddling to pet retailers even before he learned to speak English. In 1930 his company expanded into the more profitable pet-foods business. As his wealth grew, he became a major philanthropist.

Always in a hurry, Leonard peddled door to door as a boy, graduated *cum laude* from NYU in two and a half years, and earned his MBA degree at night while working as a $40-a-week clerk in a variety store by day—hardly the sort of behavior expected of a millionaire's son.

Today Leonard owns a New York co-op on Fifth Avenue (his office is in Harrison, New Jersey), a summer home on Long Island, and an apartment in the Virgin Islands. "When I think of my wealth," he told *Fortune* at the tender age of 35, "I find it unbelievable, ungraspable." Not so ungraspable, apparently, that he'd object to having more. "Leonard used to be driven to be the youngest of the richest," a former close associate recently told *Forbes*. "He now wants to be the richest of the richest."

Walter Annenberg, Philadelphia and Palm Springs

Walter Annenberg's father, Moses (1878-1942), made his fortune in the early years of the 20th century in Milwaukee and Chicago through newspaper promotion, real estate, and the *Morning Telegraph*, the national horse-racing daily. He moved east and bought the *Philadelphia Inquirer* in 1936, when son Walter was 28. Walter took over the family's Triangle Publications empire when his father died six years later, and expanded it to include *TV Guide*, *Seventeen* magazine, the *Philadelphia Daily News*, six television and nine radio stations, and 27 cable-TV franchises.

Although Triangle is privately held, the value of its properties is now becoming apparent as Annenberg, 71, liquidates his holdings for lack of an heir (his only son, Roger, killed himself in 1962 at age 24).

Annenberg's father, Moses, spent the last two years of his life in prison for tax evasion, and Walter's career since has been preoccupied with attempts to rehabilitate the family's image. He used the *Inquirer* as a personal tool to praise his friends and attack his enemies. He underwrote journalism schools named for his father at the University of Pennsylvania and Temple University, but was rebuffed when he tried to dictate staff and curriculum. Through his long and generous support of Richard Nixon (including a $250,000 donation to the 1972 reelection campaign) he became Ambassador to Great Britain, only to see the honor besmirched by Watergate.

Annenberg is not a practicing Jew, although he has made donations to some Jewish causes. He is the owner of Inwood, a sprawling white-stucco Georgian manor in a Philadelphia suburb. Today he spends most of his time in the $5 million home he built in the early 1970s on 400 acres near Palm Springs, California, the latest retreat of the nation's wealthy and famous.

The Rosenwald Family

Julius Rosenwald (1862–1932) was the organizational genius who bought a 25 percent share of Sears Roebuck in 1895 and went on to transform Sears from a small mail-order house to an international concern that today does more than $23 billion in annual sales—the world's largest retailer. As recently as 1968 his descendents still owned 12.5 percent of Sears stock, a block which, at today's market prices, would be worth about $750 million. Today their Sears holdings are somewhat smaller, but only because they have funneled their money into investment companies, radio stations, and art collections.

Julius' eldest son, Lessing, who died in June 1979 at 88, was a former Sears chairman and one of the world's leading collectors of artwork and prints; but he and his wife of 65 years lived a relatively simple and unostentatious life in a compact clapboard-and-stone home in Philadelphia. His youngest brother, William, 76, of New York, has been the controlling stockholder of Ametek, Inc., a conglomerate; American Securities Corporation, a family-owned investment banking firm; and Western Union International, formerly the overseas arm of Western Union. Their sister Edith Rosenwald Stern lives in New Orleans, where she and her late husband were active supporters of racial equality and outspoken opponents of the Huey and Earl Long political machine. Their son Edgar Stern, Jr., 57, operates radio stations, real estate, and other investments in New Orleans and St. Louis through his Royal Street Investment Corporation.

Of Julius Rosenwald it has been said that he was one man who was never corrupted by money or power. Before he died he gave away about $63 million to philanthropic causes, and in his public appearances he seldom lost an opportunity to stress the role that luck had played in advancing his career. He hated nepotism almost as much as extravagance and waste, and took special pains to see that his children received no special favors at Sears (Lessing joined the company in a menial capacity at age 20).

The fact that Julius Rosenwald was a Jew in the anti-Semitic power structure of turn-of-the-century Chicago may have had something to do with his humility. The Rosenwalds have long been ambivalent and self-conscious about their Jewishness. They have been outstanding figures in Jewish philanthropy, but Lessing Rosenwald was also one of the founders of the American Council for Judaism, which in the 1940s campaigned vigorously against the establishment of the State of Israel. Julius Rosenwald himself, upon his retirement, turned Sears' leadership over to Robert E. Wood, a brilliant executive who drove some very talented Jews away from the company. It has been said that Julius chose Wood as his successor precisely because he felt his own Jewishness had hampered Sears' effectiveness in a predominantly Christian business world.

The Blaustein Family, Baltimore

Unlike most oil tycoons, the Blausteins have never owned a major integrated oil company—that is, one that handles every step of the oil process, from drilling through refining to marketing. But what the Blausteins have lacked in power they have made up for in the innovations of the fortune's founder, Louis Blaustein (1869–1937), and his son Jacob Blaustein (1892–1970).

Louis, who came to America from Lithuania in his teens, began his career as a peddler. Among other things, he sold kerosene, which at the time was delivered in leaky wooden barrels. Louis devised the idea of delivering kerosene in a steel tank with a spigot placed on top of the wagon—the forerunner of the modern oil tank car.

Next Louis and Jacob created, in downtown Baltimore, the original American drive-in gas station—previously, autos had been serviced at the curb. Next the Blausteins invented a gas pump that let the motorist see just how much gas he was getting. But their greatest innovation was the development of the world's first high-test antiknock gas—a brand known then and now as Amoco.

Jacob Blaustein sold his company to Standard Oil of Indiana for stock that made the family the largest shareholders of Indiana Standard; they have some 5.25 million shares today, worth about $315 million. The family's total net worth probably approaches $400 million.

Jacob Blaustein's only son, Dr. Morton Blaustein, a geologist in his 60s, is the head of American Trading & Production Corporation, the nerve center of the family investments. His cousin (and Jacob's nephew), Henry Rosenberg, Jr., 49, is chairman of Crown Central Petroleum, a family-controlled oil-refining and -marketing (but not -producing) company that operates 250 service stations, besides wholesaling to other retailers.

In the course of amassing his fortune, Jacob Blaustein dabbled as a diplomat—with remarkable success. He persuaded Vyacheslav Molotov to accept the human rights provisions of the United Nations charter in 1945, convinced David Ben-Gurion to accept the partition of Palestine in 1947, and arranged with Konrad Adenauer for West Germany's payment to victims of Hitler's war crimes.

Had it not been for his mother's instincts, Jacob Blaustein himself might have fallen victim to the Holocaust. In 1910, when his father was working for Standard Oil of New Jersey, the company wanted to send him to Germany to organize an affiliate there. Louis Blaustein was amenable, but his wife Henrietta refused. "I had enough of the old country," she said. "I'm not going back. Our children were born in America and I want them reared in America, a free country."

—D.R. rep.

THE TOP TEN . . . AND SOME RUNNERS-UP

$700 Million to $1 Billion
The Pritzker Family, Chicago, Hyatt Hotels, Cerro-Marmon Corporation, real estate. Principal members: A. N. Pritzker, 83; Jack Pritzker, 75; Jay Pritzker, 57; Robert Pritzker, 53.

$600 Million to $700 Million
Samuel I. Newhouse, 84, New York. Newhouse Newspapers, Newhouse Broadcasting Corporation, Condé Nast Publications.

$400 Million to $600 Million
The Bronfman family. Descendants of Samuel Bronfman (1891–1971), patriarch of Seagram Company (liquor distilling), Principal members: Saidye Bronfman, 83, Montreal; Edgar Bronfman, 50, New York; Charles Bronfman, 48, Montreal; Minda de Gunzburg, 54, Paris; Phyllis Lambert, 52.

The Crown Family, Chicago. General Dynamics, real estate, numerous investments. Principal members: Henry Crown, 83; Lester Crown, 54.

Marvin Davis, 54, Denver. Davis Oil (nation's largest independent oil driller).

The Haas family, San Francisco. Levi Strauss & Company (blue jeans). Principal members: Walter Haas, Sr., 90; Daniel

Koshland, 87; Walter Haas, Jr., 63; Peter Haas, 60.

Leonard Stern, 41, New York. Hartz Mountain Industries (pet foods, real-estate development).

$300 Million to $400 Million

Walter Annenberg, 71, Philadelphia and Palm Springs. Triangle Publications (*TV Guide, Seventeen, Daily Racing Form*).

The Blaustein family, Baltimore. Descendants and relatives of Louis Blaustein (1869–1937) and his son Jacob Blaustein (1892–1970), founders of American Oil Company, now a subsidiary of Standard Oil of Indiana. Family also controls Crown Central Petroleum, real estate. Principal members: Dr. Morton Blaustein; Henry Rosenberg, Jr., 49.

The Rosenwald family. Children and grandchildren of Julius Rosenwald (1862–1932) of Sears Roebuck. Principal members: William Rosenwald, 76, New York; Edith Rosenwald Stern, 78, New Orleans; Edgar B. Stern, Jr., 57, New Orleans; Philip M. Stern, 53, Washington; Julius Rosenwald II, 65, Philadelphia.

$200 Million to $300 Million

Leon Hess, 65, New York. Amerada Hess (oil and chemicals).

Samuel Lefrak, 61. New York. Real estate.

Milton Petrie, 77, New York. Petrie Stores (women's clothing).

Laurence Tisch, 56, and brother **Preston Tisch**, 53, New York. Loew's Corporation (cigarettes, hotels, theaters).

$150 Million to $200 Million

The Guggenheim family. Mining and metallurgy; descendants of Meyer Guggenheim (1827–1904). Principal members: Peggy Guggenheim, 81, Venice, Italy; Peter Lawson-Johnston, 52, New York; Robert Guggenheim, Jr., 69, Newport Beach, California; Roger W. Strauss, Jr., 62, New York.

The Lauder family, New York. Estee Lauder cosmetics. Principal members: Estee Mentzer Lauder; Joseph Lauder; Leonard Lauder, 45.

Norton Simon, 62, Los Angeles. Founder of Norton Simon, Inc. (food processing and soft drinks); owns extensive art collection.

Jules Stein, 83, Los Angeles. Founder of MCA, Inc. (record and movie production).

$100 Million to $150 Million

Hyman Belzberg, 53, and brothers **Samuel Belzberg**, 50 and **William Belzberg**, 46, Vancouver, British Columbia. Far West Financial Corporation, First City Financial Corporation.

Raymond Epstein, 61, and brother **Sidney Epstein**, 56, Chicago. A. Epstein & Sons International (construction and engineering).

Sol Goldman, 61, New York. Real estate.

Katharine Graham, 62, Washington. Washington Post Company.

Joseph Hirshhorn, 80, Greenwich, Connecticut. Mining.

Meyer Lansky, 77, Miami Beach. Organized crime.

The Sulzberger family, New York. New York Times Company. Principal members: Iphigene Ochs Sulzberger, 86; Arthur O. Sulzberger, 53; Marian Sulzberger Heiskell, 60; Ruth Sulzberger Holmberg, 58, Chattanooga; Judith Sulzberger Levinson, 55.

$75 Million to $100 Million

Sam Israel, Jr., 69, New Orleans. Leon Israel & Brothers (coffee importers).

Lester Levy, 56, and brothers **Milton Levy**, 54, and **Irvin Levy**, 50, Dallas. NCH Corporation (industrial cleaners and paints).

The Meyerhoff family, Baltimore. Monumental Corporation (insurance, real-estate, investments). Principal members: Joseph Meyerhoff, 80; Harvey Meyerhoff, 51; Jack Pearlstone, Jr., 61.

William S. Paley, 78, New York. Head of CBS since 1928.

Victor Posner, 61, Miami Beach. Sharon Steel, NVF Industries, numerous other investments.

The Rosenbloom family, Los Angeles. Family of the late Carroll Rosenbloom (1907–1979), garment manufacturer and owner of Los Angeles Rams.

The Shapiro family, Maryland Cup Corporation (paper cups, straws, plates). Principal members: Merrill Bank, 64, Baltimore; Henry Shapiro, 64, Chicago; Dr. Albert Shapiro, 66, Baltimore.

Charles E. Smith, Washington. Charles E. Smith Companies (real estate).

Lew Wasserman, 66, Los Angeles. MCA, Inc. (motion picture and record production).

$50 Million to $75 Million

The Block family, New York. Block Drug Company (drug store chain). Principal members: Leonard Block, 67; James Block, 42; Thomas Block; Susan Block Stearns; Peggy Block Danziger; Adele Block.

Nathan Cummings, 83. New York. Founder of Consolidated Foods Corporation; major shareholder in General Dynamics Corporation.

Leonard Davis, 55, New York. Founder of Colonial Penn Group (insurance).

Harold Farb, Houston. Furniture and real estate.

Max Fisher, 71. Detroit. Aurora Gasoline Company.

The Gordon family, Houston. Gordon Jewelry (retail stores). Principal members: Harry Gordon, 70; Aaron Gordon, 68; I. L. Miller, Sr., 74; Daniel Gordon, 38; James Gordon, 33.

Maurice R. Greenberg, 54, New York. American International Group (insurance holding company).

Bud Grossman, 58, Minneapolis. Gelco Corporation (soft drink bottling, vehicle leasing, petroleum marketing).

Irving Harris, 69, Chicago. Toni home permanents, Pittway Corporation, Standard Shares.

Irwin Jacobs, 38, Minneapolis. Jacobs Industries (investments).

The Kempner family, Galveston, Texas. U.S. National Bank of Galveston, Imperial Sugar Company. Principal members: Harris Kempner, 76; Isaac H. Kempner III, 47; Harris Kempner, Jr., 39.

Helen Regenstein, Chicago. Widow of industrialist Joseph Regenstein (1889–1957), who controlled Arvey Corporation (now headed by son Joseph Regenstein, Jr.) and Velsicol Chemical Corporation (now a subsidiary of Northwest Industries).

Roy V. Titus, 70, New York. Son of Helena Rubinstein (1871–1965), cosmetics matriarch.

The Smith family, Houston. Big Three Industries. Principal members: A. K. Smith, 68; Harry K. Smith, 67; Russel K. Smith, 33; Jaclyn Smith (TV actress).

Ervin Wolf, 53, New York. Inexco Oil (offshore oil production).

The Zale family, Dallas. Zale Corporation (retail jewelry stores). Principal members: Morris B. Zale, 78; Ben Lipshy, 68; William Zale, 76; Donald Zale, 45; Bruce Lipshy, 38.

—D.R. rep.

STEPHEN BIRMINGHAM'S LIST OF THE 12 MOST FASHIONABLE JEWISH COUNTRY CLUBS IN THE UNITED STATES

NEW YORK: Century Country Club. The Old Guard German-Jewish banking crowd still rules the roost here in Westchester County, where members of the Loeb, Lehman, and Warburg families still maintain large estates. For years, Russians and retailers were equally frowned upon, and when the publisher Alfred A. Knopf (Russian) joined Century a few years back there was much huffing and puffing. Now times have changed. Still, a second Westchester club, Sunningdale, is said to be "for Jews waiting to get into Century," and a third, Old Oaks, is "for Jews waiting to get into Sunningdale."

LOS ANGELES: Hillcrest Country Club. Though not the powerhouse of the motion picture industry that it was in the days of the moguls—Mayer, Thalberg, Goldwyn, Zukor, et al.—it is still the club favored by film company and television executives, and the decor is purest Hollywood. Bridge and gin rummy are played here at high stakes, and oil discoveries under the club's grounds made some of the earlier stockholders very happy.

SAN FRANCISCO: Beresford Country Club. Here in the hills of the Peninsula, not far from its WASP counterpart, the Burlingame Country Club, gather members of California's fine old Jewish pioneering families: Schwabachers, Fleishhackers, Haases, Koshlands, and Hellmans, who came with the Gold Rush. The story goes that when the club asked Lord Beresford if they could use his name, Lord Beresford replied that he had no objection, but reminded the club of the Beresford family motto: *Christ Above All.*

CHICAGO: Lake Shore Club. Much of the membership of the opulent downtown Standard Club can be found here on weekends—lawyers, bankers, industrial types, and their families. There is an excellent dining room, and there are excellent bridge games. Chicago, a no-nonsense sort of city, cares less about what part of Europe one's ancestors came from than other places do.

CINCINNATI: Losantiville Country Club. In an old German City, the old German-Jewish families—the Iglauers, Fleischmanns, Freibergs, and Friedlanders take themselves very seriously. Socially, the Eastern European families occupy a world apart, and belong to the Crest Hills Country Club, where one wouldn't find lobster on the menu. One would at Losantiville.

ST. LOUIS: Westwood Country Club. More German-Jewish feelings of superiority are encountered here among the city's bankers, industrialists, and old-line retailing families such as the Baers and the Stixes (of Stix, Baer, & Fuller), who also have connections in Cincinnati.

WASHINGTON, D.C.: Woodmont Country Club. In a not very Jewish city, Woodmont still manages to claim the best (i.e., German) Jewish membership. To prove the point, there is a five-figure initiation fee. But one wouldn't find a Washington mover and shaker such as Senator Jacob Javits playing golf at Woodmont. He would be lunching with someone from the State Department at the Capitol Hill Club downtown.

ATLANTA: Standard Club. The Standard is said to have been formed in "reaction" to the WASP-y and super-exclusive Piedmont Driving Club, which Griffin Bell had to quit when he joined Jimmy Carter's Cabinet. But this is not possible, since the Standard was formed—originally as a club exclusively for German Jews—twenty years before the Piedmont. When Robert Lipshutz was named Carter's White House Counsel, he had to quit the Standard because of the club's restrictive membership policies.

PHILADELPHIA: Philmont Country Club. A few old German and Sephardic families—descendants of early Franks, Levys, and Gratzes—still can be found in this genteelly quiet club. But Philadelphia's richest (probably) and most powerful (certainly) Jew, Walter H. Annenberg, will have none of it. Instead, he belongs to the Century in New York and Hillcrest in Los Angeles.

DALLAS: Columbian Club. Stanley Marcus (of Neiman-Marcus), in his perpetual *Quest for the Best* (his autobiography), has given this club in his home town his dignified nod of approval. He admires the food here. The atmosphere is restrained and elegant, as befits Dallas, which likes to think of itself as less flamboyant than that "other" Texas city . . .

HOUSTON: Westwood Country Club. Watch the jewels flash and the minks swirl about the ladies who lunch here. Rolls-Royces and Mercedeses and an occasional paltry Cadillac fill the parking lot. With its customary fondness for superlatives, this has been called "the richest club in the world."

CLEVELAND: Standard Club. Atlanta's Standard Club thinks it is better than Cleveland's, but Cleveland prefers its own—though one member, reflecting Cleveland's poor self-image and increasing feelings of inferiority, says, "That is, if you have to live in Cleveland."

—S.B.

THE FADE-OUT OF THE GREAT JEWISH FAMILY STORES

In 1968 Andrew Goodman, the president of Bergdorf Goodman, solemnly called off plans to open the plush retail store's first branch in Chicago. His son Edwin, grandson and namesake of one of Bergdorf's founders, had just decided to resign as company vice-president and manager of the proposed Chicago store. The then twenty-eight-year-old scion threw himself instead into economic development activities in the racially troubled Bedford-Stuyvesant section of Brooklyn.

Mr. Goodman continued to hope that his only son, who had a demonstrated adeptness for the retail business, would return to Bergdorf's. But two years later, when Edwin became manager of a New York FM radio station, Andrew Goodman began to listen seriously to feelers from interested purchasers. He signed an agreement to sell Bergdorf Goodman to a large West Coast retail chain. Edwin has since said that he originally went into the business because he was "supposed to," the same way his father had followed in grandfather's footsteps. But Edwin decided that retailing was not as exciting as getting involved in the problems of the city.

In 1961 Jerome K. Ohrbach, heir apparent to the Ohrbach discount apparel chain—"a business in millions, a profit in pennies"—decided that he preferred Wall Street to retailing. His father Nathan Ohrbach, who had founded the store in 1924, then sold out to a Dutch mercantile firm.

The waning interest of heirs in family-owned businesses is one of the major reasons for the fading of Jewish entrepreneurship from the American retail scene. The famous old names remain—Ohrbach's, Bergdorf Goodman, Neiman-Marcus, Hecht's, Joseph Magnin, Abraham & Straus—but the families are mostly gone and ownerships have shifted to publicly-owned companies with stock traded on the exchange.

There are other reasons, too, for the transfer of family-owned department stores: the advancing age of the owner, the absence of heirs, a desire to protect one's family from the big bite of inheritance taxes, and, frequently, a need for expansion capital and a realization by the original family or its heirs that specialized know-how, facilities, and assets are needed to keep the business competitive and thriving.

What would those Jewish immigrants who crisscrossed the American countryside with horse and wagon and eventually opened tiny stores that grew to giant companies think of what has happened to the fruits of their labors? Chances are that they would shrug, and after a hurried glance at today's balance sheet, concede that time, progress, and change make it all necessary.

The store that was to become the world's largest—Macy's Herald Square, in Manhattan—was owned for a long time by an important Jewish family. Founded in 1858 by Rowland H. Macy, a Quaker from a seafaring family, it was sold at his death eighteen years later for $1.2 million to Isidor and Nathan Straus, brothers who leased china departments in stores, including one in Macy's. Not merely content with operating Macy's, in 1893 they bought an interest in Wechsler and Abraham, a Brooklyn store that they eventually renamed Abraham & Straus. Thus, the two biggest stores in New York were at one time owned by the same Jewish family.

What happened afterward is not uncommon in family businesses: dissension among their sons compelled the brothers to concentrate on the separate stores.

The descendants of Nathan Straus inherited Macy's, remaining among its top executives even after the store ultimately went the public ownership route.

After successful development by Abraham and Isidor Straus, the A. & S. descendants chose to sell out to Federated Department Stores of Cincinnati, protecting their businesses by pooling assets in a holding company. The chief architect of the project was Fred Lazarus, Jr., then president of F. & R. Lazarus, a large department store in Columbus, Ohio, founded in 1851 by his grandfather Simon Lazarus. The other participants in the sale were Simon Frank Rothschild of A. & S., grandson of Abraham Abraham, the store's founder, Louis Kirstein, general manager of Filene's of Boston, and Samuel Bloomingdale, president of Bloomingdale's in New York.

The "Lazari," as the Lazaruses of Federated are known in retailing, are among the industry's most respected families. The dynasty's founder was a Prussian immigrant, who not only started the Lazarus store in Columbus but also served as the first rabbi of Temple Israel, the oldest Jewish congregation in the city. His great grandson Ralph Lazarus is chairman of the board of Federated, while numerous other members of the family hold posts in the Cincinnati headquarters or in the store divisions.

Many of these great department stores were started by Jewish peddlers—immigrants from Germany, Austria, Russia, and Poland. First they walked, then they rode horseback, and as their fortunes improved they advanced to wagons, carriages, and automobiles. Among them was Adam Gimbel, a Bavarian immigrant, who started his first store in Vincinnes, Ind., and whose great grandson Bruce A. Gimbel until 1974 headed the vast chain that included Saks Fifth Avenue before it was sold to a British company. Younker's, Iowa's biggest store, was founded by three Polish immigrants, Lipman, Marcus, and Samuel Younker.

Bergdorf's, synonymous with luxury and aristocratic appeal, began as a partnership between Herman Bergdorf, a tailor from

Macy's then . . .

. . . and now

Alsace, and Edwin Goodman, a men's clothing designer and tailor from Rochester, N.Y. Neiman-Marcus, as renowned as Bergdorf for the same reasons, was started in 1907 by A. L. Neiman, a retail promotion man, his wife Carrie, and her brother Herman Marcus, a department store buyer.

David May took up mining in Colorado but abandoned it in 1879 for a clothing store that eventually became one of America's billion-dollar retailers. In many ways the story of the May Department Stores parallels the success and growth of Federated Department Stores. Today, a professional management team has succeeded the May family in heading the company of 170 stores, including Hecht's in Washington and Baltimore.

In the past ten to fifteen years particularly, the business of running retail stores has not only become more complex but more of a financial and real estate activity than it ever was before. Because of such spurs as proliferating competition—including the increasing market shares of such merchandising colossi as Sears Roebuck and J. C. Penney—and the astonishing success of the discounters, many a family-owned establishment has been forced to open additional stores just to stay alive. This, plus the need to obtain the money and service lifeline that big corporations can offer, has thrown many a community store into the arms of the large public company.

There are, of course, examples of continued family togetherness in the retailing industry. In 1966 Eugene Ferkauf, an instinctive merchant, who had built the Korvette discount stores in eighteen years to a $700 million business, merged his company into Spartans Industries, Inc., an apparel manufacturing and retailing concern. Charles C. Bassine, a leading Jewish philanthropist and founder of Spartans, assumed the top spot in the merged organization. Early in 1971 Bassine arranged another consolidation—the Spartans-Korvette complex and the Arlen Group of real estate companies, one of the country's most active builders of shopping centers.

Arlen was headed by Arthur G. Cohen, a brilliant administrator and real estate marketer who is married to a Bassine daughter. The merger was approved, but not without some not unwarranted questions of nepotism. An impassioned Bassine proclaimed, "I am proud to call him my son-in-law. I wish all of you such a son-in-law." Since then, Arlen has sold Korvette to a French company, which has made drastic changes in policy.

Two other major retailing establishments based in New York, Alexander's and Mays, continue in the hands of the founding families, although both companies offered some of their ownership in a public stock issue some years ago.

Founded in 1928 by George Farkas (d. 1980), a Bronx-born dynamo, who became head of his orphaned family at sixteen, Alexander's, Inc., a 15-store discount apparel chain, is run today by four Farkas sons. Alexander, Robin, Bruce, and Jonathan Farkas have varying degrees of their father's spark and have brought an additional measure of either graduate or business school training to their posts in the $330 million company.

Not long after his retirement in 1969 the elder Farkas confided, "You know, the toughest thing for a father who has been successful in business is to decide to leave his children alone to run the business the way they see it. The temptation is to butt in once in a while, or to offer suggestions, but you've got to restrain yourself. That's the way to keep them in it."

The other New York store where the family ties remain strong is J. W. Mays, a powerful discount chain founded by the late Joe Weinstein. His son-in-law, Max L. Shulman, who came from a legal background, has served as Mays' president for more than a decade. Shulman's own son has come into the business as well. Under the Shulman tenure the company has expanded rapidly and is today among the New York area's largest sellers of family apparel.

One distinction shared by both Alexander's and Mays is that they are among the few New York retailers who in recent years have opened new stores in that city's troubled midtown areas.

The celebrated Hess's in Allentown, Pa., is another of the exceptions that has resisted the trend to consolidation. Philip I. Berman, a self-made man who was born on a farm, is its president and a major stockholder. He was personally selected as the purchaser for Hess's by the late Max Hess, whose father founded the store, rather than have it go to an outside corporation. Then, in 1979 Mr. Berman, who found his own family reluctant to join the business, sold his control to a shopping center company, but he still remains Hess's chairman.

While Jewish family firms have declined in department store retailing, Jewish family entrepreneurship has risen dramatically in a newer field of merchandising—the discount store.

In the two decades since its beginnings in the deserted textile mills of New England, the discounting industry has grown to the extent that its sales volume in the United States now equals that of conventional department stores. Average annual growth for the discount stores has been about fifteen percent against seven percent for the conventional stores.

Among the discount chains created by Jewish founders and still operated by them or their children or proteges are Zayre Corporation of Newton, Mass.; Interstate Stores, Hartfield-Zodys in Los Angeles; Fedmart in Los Angeles; King's Department Stores of Springfield, Mass.; Caldor in Norwalk, Conn., and Unishops, headquartered in Jersey City, N.J.

Zayre's, incidentally, considered one of the best managed discount chains, is a phonetic translation of a Yiddish word. In a discussion of names for the store chain, an executive observed that some suggestions were "*zehr gut*." Someone then remarked that "*Zehr* wasn't bad either." So Zayre it became.

Generally, ownership by outside corporations has helped the onetime independent, family-owned department stores to thrive, even increase their share of the regional market. And their practice of philanthropy hasn't been adversely affected by the transfers in ownership, either. In fact, there is reason to believe that Jewish merchants, freed from the problems of ownership, have become even more generous in their charitable efforts. This was dramatically evident in June 1967 when so many of them rallied to the cause of Israel.

The present era of the conglomerate and its focus on diversification in investments will surely continue the trend toward mergers and consolidations. The Jewish family-ownership of independent department stores will probably continue to diminish, passing from the retail scene. But their names—just as R. H. Macy's—will live on. And the then new dimension in merchandising created by the Jewish founders of the great stores continues as a unique American institution.

—I.B. rep.

PART TWO
THE WANDERING PEOPLE

NOMADIC JUDAISM

I will bestow My blessing upon you and make your descendants as numerous as the stars of heaven and the sands on the seashore.
—Genesis 22:17

WORLD JEWISH POPULATION

North America	
United States	5,781,000
Canada	305,000
Caribbean and Central America	
Barbados	70
Costa Rica	2,500
Cuba	1,500
Curaçao	700
Dominican Republic	200
El Salvador	350
Guatemala	2,000
Haiti	150
Honduras	200
Jamaica	500
Mexico	37,500
Nicaragua	200
Panama	2,000
Trinidad	300
South America	
Argentina	300,000
Bolivia	2,000
Brazil	150,000
Chile	27,000
Colombia	12,000
Ecuador	1,000
Paraguay	1,200
Peru	5,200
Surinam	5,000
Uruguay	50,000
Venezuela	15,000
Europe	
Albania	300
Austria	13,000
Belgium	41,000
Bulgaria	7,000
Cyprus	30
Czechoslovakia	13,000
Denmark	7,500
Finland	1,320
France	650,000
Germany	34,000
Gibraltar	650
Great Britain	410,000
Greece	6,000
Hungary	80,000
Ireland	4,000
Italy	39,000
Luxembourg	1,000
Malta	50
Netherlands	30,000
Norway	950
Poland	6,000
Rumania	34,700
Spain	10,000
Sweden	16,000
Switzerland	21,000
Turkey	27,000
USSR	2,678,000
Yugoslavia	6,000
Africa	
Algeria	1,000
Egypt	400
Ethiopia	28,000
Kenya	400
Libya	20
Morocco	18,000
Rhodesia (Zimbabwe)	2,000
South Africa	118,000
Tunisia	7,000
Zaire	750
Zambia	400

Asia	
Afghanistan	200
Burma	200
China, People's Republic of	30
Hong Kong	250
India	8,000
Indonesia	100
Iran	60,000
Iraq	350
Israel	3,076,000
Japan	400
Lebanon	400
Pakistan	250
Philippines	200
Singapore	500
Syria	4,500
Yemen	1,000
Australia and New Zealand	
Australia	70,000
New Zealand	5,000

Sources: American Jewish Yearbook (1979); Wiener Library Bulletin; Jewish Week (New York).

MEMBER STATES OF THE UNITED NATIONS WITH 50 JEWS OR LESS*

Angola
Bahrain
Bangladesh
Benin
Bhutan
Botswana
Burundi
Cambodia (Kampuchea)
Cameroon
Cape Verde
Central African Republic
Chad
China
Comoros
Congo
Cyprus
Djibouti
Dominica
Equatorial Guinea
Fiji
Gabon
Gambia
Ghana
Grenada
Guinea
Guinea-Bissau
Guyana
Iceland
Ivory Coast
Jordan
Kuwait
Laos
Lesotho
Liberia
Libya
Madagascar
Malawi
Malaysia
Maldives
Mali
Malta
Mauritania
Mauritius
Mongolia
Mozambique
Nepal
Niger
Nigeria
Oman
Papua New Guinea
Qatar
Rwanda
São Tomé and Principe
Saudi Arabia
Senegal
Seychelles
Sierra Leone
Solomon Islands
Somalia
South Yemen
Sri Lanka
Sudan
Swaziland
Tanzania
Thailand
Togo
Uganda
United Arab Emirates
Upper Volta
Vietnam
Western Samoa

* Excluding foreign nationals (U.S. and Israeli diplomatic personnel, UN officials, U.S. military and Peace Corps volunteers, journalists, businessmen, and military and technical advisors).

—C.J.R.

CITIES OF THE WORLD WITH JEWISH POPULATIONS OVER 100,000

Metropolitan New York	1,998,000
Greater Los Angeles	455,000
Tel Aviv-Jaffa	394,000
Paris	300,000
Greater Philadelphia	295,000
Moscow	285,000
Greater London	280,000
Jerusalem	272,000
Metropolitan Chicago	253,000
Miami	225,000
Haifa	210,000
Kiev	170,000
Boston	170,000
Leningrad	165,000
Greater Washington, D.C.	160,000
Montreal	115,000
Toronto	115,000

—Eds.

U.S. JEWISH POPULATION

	Population (1977)	Estimated Jewish Population (1978)	Estimated Jewish %
Alabama	3,690,000	8,825	0.2
Alaska	407,000	720	0.2
Arizona	2,296,000	33,180	1.4
Arkansas	2,144,000	3,280	0.2
California	21,896,000	688,555	3.1
Colorado	2,619,000	31,830	1.2
Connecticut	3,108,000	99,615	3.2
Delaware	582,000	9,500	1.6
District of Columbia	690,000	40,000	5.8
Florida	8,452,000	391,280	4.6
Georgia	5,048,000	30,680	0.6
Hawaii	895,000	1,500	0.2
Idaho	857,000	500	0.1
Illinois	11,245,000	267,175	2.4
Indiana	5,330,000	24,345	0.5
Iowa	2,879,000	7,745	0.3
Kansas	2,326,000	10,325	0.4
Kentucky	3,458,000	11,385	0.3
Louisiana	3,921,000	16,040	0.4
Maine	1,085,000	7,600	0.7
Maryland	4,139,000	185,745	4.5
Massachusetts	5,782,000	253,400	4.4
Michigan	9,129,000	90,145	1.0
Minnesota	3,975,000	34,480	0.9
Mississippi	2,389,000	3,395	0.1
Missouri	4,801,000	72,770	1.5
Montana	761,000	495	0.1
Nebraska	1,561,000	8,155	0.5
Nevada	633,000	13,880	2.2
New Hampshire	849,000	4,690	0.6
New Jersey	7,329,000	442,480	6.0
New Mexico	1,190,000	5,155	0.4
New York	17,924,000	2,143,485	12.0
North Carolina	5,525,000	12,580	0.2
North Dakota	653,000	1,085	2.0
Ohio	10,701,000	158,500	1.5
Oklahoma	2,811,000	6,040	0.2
Oregon	2,376,000	10,800	0.5
Pennsylvania	11,785,000	418,440	3.6
Rhode Island	935,000	22,000	2.4
South Carolina	2,867,000	8,090	0.3
South Dakota	689,000	690	0.1
Tennessee	4,299,000	17,070	0.4
Texas	12,830,000	70,275	0.5
Utah	1,268,000	2,300	0.2
Vermont	483,000	2,465	0.5
Virginia	5,135,000	58,715	1.1
Washington	3,658,000	15,385	0.4
West Virginia	1,859,000	3,840	0.2
Wisconsin	4,651,000	30,020	0.6
Wyoming	406,000	310	0.1
Total	216,332,000	5,780,960	2.7

Source: *American Jewish Yearbook* (1979).

U. S. CITIES AND COUNTIES WITH JEWISH POPULATIONS OVER 10,000

Alameda-Contra Costa Counties, California	28,000
Albany, New York	13,500
Alexandria, Virginia (incl. Falls Church, Arlington County)	30,000
Atlanta, Georgia	22,000
Atlantic City, New Jersey	11,800
Baltimore, Maryland	92,000
Bergen County, New Jersey	100,000
Boston, Massachusetts	170,000
Bridgeport, Connecticut	14,500
Buffalo, New York	22,000
Camden, New Jersey	26,000
Chicago Metro Area	253,000
Cincinnati, Ohio	30,000
Cleveland, Ohio	75,000
Columbus, Ohio	13,000
Dallas, Texas	20,000
Denver, Colorado	30,000
Detroit, Michigan	75,000
Essex County, New Jersey	95,000
Fort Lauderdale, Florida	60,000
Framingham, Mass.	16,000
Hartford-New Britain, Conn.,	23,500
Hollywood, Florida	55,000
Houston, Texas	27,000
Indianapolis, Indiana	11,000
Kansas City, Missouri	19,000
Las Vegas, Nevada	13,500
Long Beach, California	12,500
Los Angeles Metro Area	455,000
Lower Bucks County, Pennsylvania	18,000
Lynn, Massachusetts	19,000
Miami, Florida	225,000
Milwaukee, Wisconsin	23,900
Minneapolis, Minnesota	22,090
Montgomery County, Maryland	70,000
Monmouth County, New Jersey	30,000
Morris-Sussex Counties, New Jersey	15,000
Nassau-Suffolk Counties, New York	605,000
New Haven, Connecticut	20,000
New Orleans, Louisiana	10,600
New York City	1,228,000
Norfolk and Virginia Beach Virginia	11,000
Northern Middlesex County, New Jersey	17,500
Ocean County, New Jersey	12,000
Orange County, California	35,000
Orlando, Florida	10,000
Palm Beach County, Florida	40,000
Philadelphia Metro Area	295,000
Phoenix, Arizona	25,000
Pittsburgh, Pennsylvania	51,000
Prince Georges County, Maryland	20,000
Providence, Rhode Island	22,000
Raritan Valley, New Jersey	18,000
Richmond, Virginia	10,000
Rochester, New York	21,500
Rockland County, New York	25,000
San Diego, California	23,000
San Francisco, California	75,000
San Jose, California	14,500
Seattle, Washington	13,000
Springfield, Massachusetts	11,000
Stamford, Connecticut	11,000
St. Louis, Missouri	60,000
St. Petersburg, Florida	10,000
Syracuse, New York	11,000
Union County, New Jersey	39,500
Washington, D.C. Metro Area	160,000
Westchester County, New York	165,000
Worcester, Massachusetts	10,000

Source: American Jewish Yearbook (1979). *Jewish Currents* (April 1980).

Laying the cornerstone of Tel Aviv, 1909

ISRAEL'S 25 LARGEST CITIES, 1977

	Population		Population
Tel Aviv	394,000	Ramla	37,400
Jerusalem	366,300	Lod	36,700
Haifa	227,900	Hadera	36,100
Beersheba	98,900	Acre	36,000
Netanya	85,700	Kfar Saba	33,800
Rishon Lezion	73,500	Dimona	27,600
Nazareth	56,900	Nahariya	27,300
Ashdod	54,600	Tiberias	26,300
Rehovot	54,000	Kiryat Gat	21,800
Shechem	50,200	Afula	18,600
Herzlia	49,700	Eilat	16,600
Ashkelon	48,700	Kiryat Shmona	15,500
Hebron	44,800		

Source: Israel Population Center, Jerusalem.

ENDANGERED JEWISH POPULATIONS

"There is a divine covenent in everyone's heart: To love his native soil—despite its climate." (Midrash: Genesis Rabbah 34:15)

	Jewish Population (1979)
USSR	2,678,000
Argentina	300,000
South Africa	118,000
Iran	60,000
Ethiopia	28,000
Poland	6,000
Syria	4,500
Rhodesia (Zimbabwe)	2,000
Cuba	1,500
Iraq	350
Libya	20

Sources: *American Jewish Yearbook* (1979); *Wiener Library Bulletin; Jewish Week* (New York).

—C.J.R.

JEWS ON THE MAP

American Geographical Places Named After Jews

Although a traveller through the United States will undoubtedly pass through hundreds of places with odd names in all of the 50 states—historic names, hard-to-pronounce names—he may never see or even never hear of places bearing such common Jewish surnames as Cohen, Levy, Goldman, Edelstein, Altman, Strauss, and Goldstein.

Such places are on the maps of American states. Most Jewish tourists are unaware of them, however, because so many of these 87 towns, villages, hamlets, counties, mountains, lakes, and forests are not along the main travelled highways.

These places are named after Jews in the same way that hundreds of thousands of other places got their names—from the men and women who helped build our country.

There are one or more places named after Jews in 35 states. More than a third of them are in the South. Texas and Louisiana each have seven places bearing the names of Jews. Alaska, the newest state, has three places, while California and Arkansas each have five.

JEWISH POPULATIONS

The combined population of the 88 places named for Jews is 230,000. Most of them have no Jewish residents. The largest towns having Jewish patronymics are Levittown, New York on Long Island, and Levittown, Pennsylvania. Both were founded by and named after the Levitt brothers, Jewish real estate developers, and both have substantial Jewish communities, including synagogues.

The only other town with a good-sized Jewish populace that was named after a Jew is Spivak, Colorado. Set in the mountains above Denver, this town consists essentially of the 36 buildings of the American Medical Center, a cancer hospital and research center founded in 1904 as the Jewish Consumptives Relief Society. The village is named after the late Dr. Charles L. Spivak, for many years director of the society, which was created to provide a mountain haven for tuberculosis sufferers from congested eastern cities.

OLDEST TOWN

The oldest place named after a Jew is Aaronsburg, Pennsylvania, population 350. It was founded in 1779 by Aaron Levy, a Revolutionary patriot. It is located on Route 45, a few miles from the geographic center of Pennsylvania. Levy, an Indian trader, soldier, and merchant who helped finance the American Revolution by buying large quantities of war bonds, acquired 334½ acres in the frontier area of Centre County and laid out his town. Purchasers of lots received deeds signed by Levy and his wife in Hebrew.

COUNTIES

Of the 3,068 counties in the United States only two are named after Jews. One is Castro County in the Panhandle section of Texas, south of Amarillo. The other is Levy County, on the Gulf Coast of Florida. Both are named after men who played leading parts in the early history of their states.

Castro County is named after Henry Castro, a French Jew. In 1838 he attempted to raise a large loan for the Republic of Texas. Four years later the president of the Republic of Texas, General Sam Houston, appointed him Texan consul-general in France, where he helped the cause of the new republic. In 1844 Castro settled in Texas, bringing with him 5,000 colonists in 27 ships. The town of Castroville, on the west bank of the Medina River, is also named after this man who spent $150,000 of his own money to help populate Texas.

Levy County in Florida was named after David Levy Yulee, who helped write the first constitution of Florida. In 1841 he was chosen to represent the Florida Territory in the U.S. House of Representatives. In 1845 he became the first Jew to win a seat in the U.S. Senate. The town of Yulee, on the northeast Georgia-Florida boundary, is named after him; Levy Lake, a popular resort in Florida's Alachua County, is named after Moses Levy, Yulee's father, who settled Florida when it was still a Spanish territory.

WELL-KNOWN JEWS

Only six places on the map of the United States are named after Jews whose role in U.S. history is well known. One of these is the relatively new settlement of Brandeis, California, known as Santa Susana until recently. Currently the site of Brandeis Camp Institute, which trains Jewish youth leaders, it bears the name of Justice Louis D. Brandeis, the first Jew to serve on the Supreme Court of the United States.

Seligman, Missouri, is named after Joseph Seligman, banker, synagogue leader, and friend of Presidents Lincoln and Grant, who from 1860 to 1880 was the most eminent Jew in America. The town was founded during the construction of the Missouri Pacific Railroad, which Seligman's firm financed. Seligman, Arizona, is named after Jesse Seligman, Joseph's brother, because he helped build the old Atlantic and Pacific Railroad, now part of the Atchison, Topeka, and Santa Fe, on whose route the town stands. Joseph Seligman turned down the office of Secretary of the Treasury under Grant.

There are two towns named after the famous Gratz family, whose trading ventures and land deals before, during and after the American Revolution helped pave the way for colonization between the Alleghenies and the Mississippi. Gratz, Pennsylvania, is named after Hyman Gratz, a brother of Rebecca Gratz, educator and social worker from Philadelphia. The once important river town of Gratz, Kentucky, is named after Hyman and his brother, Simon, who once envisioned the place as a major port of call.

The sixth place named for a prominent Jew is the tiny hamlet of Alexander, Idaho, which recalls Moses Alexander, the first Jew to be elected governor—of Idaho, in 1915.

PIONEER TOWNS

Quite a few place names of Jewish origin are memorials to forgotten pioneers who fought Indians, built roads and railroads, discovered new routes over mountains, and opened new areas to settlement. They include Mears Junction and Mears Park, Colorado, named after Otto Mears, an immigrant Jew who was a famous frontiersman, colonizer, negotiator with the Indians, and railroad builder; Solomon, Arizona, named after Isador Elkan Solomon, pioneer trader and Indian fighter; Brandenburg, Kentucky, named after Colonel Solomon Brandenburg, who fought in the War of 1812; the Gerstle River, in Alaska, named after Lewis Gerstle, the mercantile and fur shipping giant who helped build Alaska's first industries; Mount Ripinski, Alaska, named after Solomon Ripinski, an early teacher and government official; Heppner, Oregon, named after the first permanent settler in Oregon's Morrow County; Erlanger, Kentucky, a city of some 13,000 in Kenton County, named after

Baron Frederick D'Erlanger, a German-English Jewish financier who headed the banking syndicate that rescued the Cincinnati Southern (now the Southern) Railroad from bankruptcy in 1881. The latest place named after a Jew is the Shalowitz Seamount, a newly discovered underwater mountain in the northeast Pacific Ocean off the Oregon-Washington coast. Shalowitz is an expert on marine law.

The 87 names of Jews on the map of the United States follow. ALABAMA—Falkville; ALASKA—Mount Applebaum, Gerstle River, Mount Neuberger, Mount Ripinski; ARIZONA—Mayer, Seligman, Solomonsville; ARKANSAS—Altheimer, Felsenthal, Goldman, Levy, Weiner; CALIFORNIA—Bieber, Brandeis, Goldstein Peak, Reinstein Peak, Twain-Harte; COLORADO—Mears Junction, Mears Peak, Spivak; CONNECTICUT—Gilman; FLORIDA—Levy County, Levy Lake, Yulee; GEORGIA—Mendes; IDAHO—Alexander, Falks, Stein Mountain; ILLINOIS—Edelstein; IOWA—Solberg; KENTUCKY—Brandenburg, Erlanger, Gratz, Ottenheim, Levi; LOUISIANA—Bunkie, Geismar, Goldman, Kaplan, Marksville, Rosa; MINNESOTA— Greenberg Island, Sax; MISSISSIPPI—Kahnville, Marks, Meyersville; MISSOURI—Seligman; MONTANA—Philipsburg, Bob Marshall Wilderness; NEBRASKA—Wolbach; NEVADA—Lehman Caves National Monument, Sutro; NEW JERSEY—Brontmanville, Rosenhayn; NEW MEXICO—Ilfeld, Levy, Newman, Seligman, Strauss; NEW YORK—Belmont Lake State Park, Fleischmanns, Levittown; NORTH CAROLINA—Robbins; OKLAHOMA—Spiro; OREGON—Heppner, Mayer State Park; PENNSYLVANIA—Aaronsburg, Gratz, Levittown; SOUTH CAROLINA—Cohens Bluff, Levys; SOUTH DAKOTA—Strool; TEXAS—Castro County, Castroville, Kempner, Kopperl, Labatt, Sanger; VERMONT—Gilman; VIRGINIA—Manassas; WASHINGTON—Marcus, Marovitz Creek, Moses; WISCONSIN—Rothschild, Salinger; WYOMING—Hahn's Peak.

—B.P.

MORE JEWS ON THE MAP: A PARODY

The following is the game of Jewish geography with a new twist—mentally traversing unmapped territory.

The first stop is a lovely inn on the shores of Lake Afiko, Minn., for a Passover vacation. Or if one prefers the seashore, the quaint port of Tish, R.I., is perfect for *tashlikh*. Of course if a spa is more what one had in mind, Labree, Ut., is ideal. Tree planters will not want to miss the famous forest at Tubish, Vt. And when down in the bayou country, one owes oneself a visit to the twin Kehilot of Tevee, La., and Tefee, La. (When the Mississippi floods its banks the residents of these towns usually flee upstream to Noah's, Ark.)

Those with big appetites will find Tzim, Miss., to their tastes, but should probably avoid the sparsely populated Tzom, Cal. As the season of Form 1040's begins one might want to consider a move to the city of refuge, Patur-Mee, Mass. But if it's Torah that is sought, where else but Chu, Mich.? And for marriage, Chu, Pa., naturally. Having done a Teshu, Va., trip one must stop over at Gemar Hatimato, Va. But the favorite spot down that way is the Peter Pan town for perpetual adolescents (and their parents), Barmitz, Va.

And if there is time to get lost, there is the proverbial town so small it's not yet on the map: Eshet-Hai, Ill. (One can look and look, but who can find it?)

Other cit(i)ed sites of Jewish interest include:

Chutz, Pa.	Zay, De.
Tefill, In.	Oy, Va.
Mitz, Va.	Vayehi, Ore.
Yarmel, Ky.	Hida Hida Hididdy, Ida.
Phara, Oh.	
Ani Ma'ah, Minn.	Al Achat Kama Veka, Ma.
Gottin, U.	
Bracha Levat, Ala.	Zil, Pa.
Sah, N. Dak.	Bil, Ha.
Yekum Pur, Kan.	Binyan, Cal.
Bat, Col.	May, Del.
Gantze Megil, La.	Don't Be A, N.J.
Shula, Miss.	Kochle, Fl.
Hinei, N.Y.	Choch, Ma.
Yizk, Ore.	Abee Gezu, N.D.
Lehavd, Ill.	Farshtun, Kan.
Atzma, Ut.	Hamotzi Lechem Minha, Ariz.
Hallelu, Ia.	
Meshu, Ga.	Hoo, Ha.
Baruch, Utah	Mamzer, Ut.
Ga, Nev.	Ba, Al.
Rebbetz, In.	Knai, Del.
Chass, Id.	Emm, Miss.
Shep Nach, U.S.	Ksh Kabib, Ill.
Yaffa Yarko, N.Y.	Litv, Ak.
Kol Hatan Vekol, Colo.	
Sala, Mi.	

When journeying to Canada, one might similarly visit Tah, Que., Vilna Ga, Ont., Chevra, Man., and Lands, Man.

—S.M.-M. Rep.

WHATEVER HAPPENED TO THE TEN LOST TRIBES?

Where are the lost ten tribes of Israel? Will they ever be reunited with their brethren of Judah in a wholly reconstituted Hebrew nation? To most people these may not be especially compelling questions; but for some, the subject persists as a fundamental challenge, a mystery that literally must be solved if history is to achieve culmination.

The beginnings of the story are familiar. Late in the eleventh century B.C.E. the charismatic King David united into a single nation his own tribe of Judah and the northern tribes of Samaria, known collectively as Ephraim or Israel. Under his son Solomon this united Hebrew kingdon achieved a degree of power and splendor that is still celebrated. But the glory was short-lived: Solomon's successors were too weak to hold the kingdom together, and by the end of the tenth century B.C.E., Judah—now joined by the smaller tribe of Benjamin and some members of Levi—once again stood apart from Israel. In the eighth century B.C.E. the latter were overwhelmed by a catastrophe from which the Hebrew nation was never fully to recover: the Assyrians, the most invincible imperialists of their time, invaded and occupied Samaria, and deported most of the population of Israel to the distant reaches of their own empire. The event is recorded only briefly in Second Kings, where it is told that the tribes were carried off to Assyria and placed "in Halah, and in Habor, on the river of Gozan, and in the cities of the Medes"—that is, to a region in what is now northwestern Iran, southwest of the Caspian Sea.

The Judean tribes who escaped this onslaught endured their own deportation and exile at the hands of the Babylonians in the sixth century B.C.E.; but, of course, not long afterward many of them were returned to their homeland, where they rebuilt the Temple and restored their natural identity. From that time onward, their history alone became that of the Jewish people.

But what of the lost tribes? The only point on which there has been almost no disagreement is that, although some may have found their way to Babylonia and joined their Judean brethren, the majority never returned to their homeland. Most people have accepted the obvious explanations for what happened to them: nothing in particular; they simply melted into the host populations and disappeared from history. But for many Jews—and even more significantly for many Christians—such an answer is absolutely unacceptable. The ten tribes of Israel, they maintain, were a major segment of the people through whom the glorious promises of the Lord to the patriarchs were to be fulfilled. If they are irretrievably lost, how can history ever achieve consummation? To the orthodox, Jewish and Christian alike, the coming of the Messiah, be it for the first or second time, is to be attended by the restoration of the entire Hebrew nation to the Promised Land.

Thus, throughout the centuries there has been a steady conviction that lost Israel can and must be found, that they will be reunited with their wandering brethren of Judah, and that the reconstituted Hebrew people will once again dwell in their homeland in all the splendor of ancient times. But for Christians the significance of the search and the expectations for its denouement have taken an essential twist: Israel came to denote those Hebrews who had disappeared long before the Crucifixion; Judah—the Jews—were those who were present at that event and bore responsibility for it. The Millennium—that thousand year period of glory that would follow the Second Coming of the Messiah—would begin only after the ten tribes had been restored along with Judah, and, of course, only when all had acknowledged the Kingship of the Savior. Thus the discovery of the lost tribes was established, along with the conversion of the Jews, as an indispensable prerequisite for the fulfillment of history and the ultimate salvation of humanity—no small matter.

That the ten tribes still existed as such and that the day would come when they would be incorporated into the Jewish people, was the generally accepted view of most Jews until modern times. To have believed otherwise would have meant rejecting the words of the prophets, most especially Ezekiel, through whom the Lord had delivered an unmistakable promise: "Behold, I will take the children of Israel from among the nations, whither they are gone, and will gather them on every side, and bring them into their own land; and I will make them one nation in the land, . . . and they shall be no more two nations, neither shall they be divided into two kingdoms any more at all" (Ezek. 37:21–22). The continued existence of at least one tribe was confirmed by the apocryphal Book of Tobit (third century B.C.E.), the narrator of which identifies himself as an exiled member of the tribe of Naphtali; and if that was questionable authority, there was the renowned first century C.E. historian Flavius Josephus, who had declared himself committed to historical truth and who confidently reported in his *Jewish Antiquities* that "somewhere beyond the Euphrates" the ten tribes were still in existence: "an immense multitude," in fact, "not to be estimated in numbers." References to the tribes also appear repeatedly in the Talmud; and although it is apparent that the rabbis were uncertain where the lost brethren were living, most were certain of their existence. Only the great Rabbi Akiva (50–135 C.E.) declared that they were utterly lost and would never return, probably because he expected the Messiah too imminently for such preliminary events to take place.

Jewish history thereafter is dotted with reports by men who claimed to have visited some or all of the tribes and who were well prepared to satisfy the natural curiosity of the Jews about how their long-lost brethren were faring. Perhaps the most notorious was a ninth-century merchant-traveller, Eldad ha-Dani (the Danite), whom one authority (Adolphe Neubauer) characterizes as "a daring impostor crowned with an unexpected success." In his diary, which achieved widespread popularity for centuries and elicited much learned commentary, Eldad identified himself as a member of the lost tribe of Dan and declared that his own tribe, along with Gad, Asher, and Naphtali, were settled in "the land of Cush" (Ethiopia and vicinity), where they lived in impressive circumstances, their wealth regularly replenished by the spoils of phenomenally successful military exploits. (Incidentally, these four tribes were probably not grouped by accident; according to Genesis 30, their eponymous ancestors were Jacob's son by his concubines, Bilhah and Zilpah, the servants of Rachel and Leah.) Eldad also knew where the other six tribes were to be found; he had encountered each in his wanderings through Arabia and had discovered their men to be not only learned, pious, wealthy, and wise but also valorous warriors. He offered an eyewitness report on the river Sambatyon (the Sabbath river), beyond which, according to talmudic tradition, the ten tribes had been exiled. The river, it was generally believed, flowed only six days of the week and rested on the Sabbath, and that was indeed what Eldad found; moreover, on Friday evening it had been surrounded by fire (or thick clouds in some versions of the diary) so that no one could even approach it.

Another popular account of the lost tribes appeared in the diaries of the twelfth-century traveller Benjamin of Tudela, who visited and described Jewish communities throughout the Levant and Middle East. A more sober journalist than Eldad, Benjamin made no claim to have encountered the tribes himself, only to have heard that somewhere far to the east was the river Gozan and that there dwelt Dan, Asher, Zebulon, and Nephtali. They were a sturdy and independent people, he had been told, remarkable for their scholarly accomplishments (of course) but also mighty warriors; their allies, strange to report, were fierce barbarians who had only two small holes for a nose and who lived on raw meat from all sorts of animals—clean and unclean—but were friendly nonetheless to their presumably kosher and adequately nosed neighbors. Benjamin had also heard that descendants of the tribes of Reuben, Gad, and Manasseh, numbering in the hundreds of thousands, were living splendidly in Arabia near Yemen. They too fulfilled what seems to have been the imagined ideal for a nation of Israelites: they were both scholars and warriors, devoted to Torah and the terror of their enemies.

Over the centuries travellers continued the search for the lost tribes everywhere from India and Afghanistan to Arabia and Abyssinia. Benjamin of Tudela had an almost equally renowned successor in the person of Joseph Israel Benjamin (1818–64), better known as Benjamin II, who devoted a lifetime to a futile search for the tribes. He travelled throughout the Middle East and North America and also journeyed to America, but he was forced to conclude that the lost tribes, like their brethren of Judah, were wanderers who would never be found intact. He encountered one group, however, who did impress him as a genuine remnant;

these were the so-called Bene Israel, a people who survive to this day in Bombay and vicinity and who claim descent from a small band of Israelites who were shipwrecked off the west coast of India many centuries ago. (A contemporary Bene Israel historian, H.S. Kehimkar, offers another explanation for the name: it was adopted, he says, to avoid the "hatred which Mohamedans [sic] bear towards the name Yehudi [Jew].")

But perhaps the most determined of all searchers for the lost tribes were a small cohort of nineteenth-century "Hebrew Christian" missionaries: Jewish converts who dedicated themselves to the task of locating and redeeming their brethren wherever they might have wandered, so that they might be ready to answer the call when the Messiah returned. For some such men the Jews of London or Warsaw were challenge enough. But for a few hardy souls it was the wandering brethren in distant and exotic lands—most particularly the long lost descendants of the tribes of Israel—who offered the real challenge; and thus they set out to make their own special contribution toward hastening the Second Coming. The most memorable of these optimists was the indefatigable Joseph Wolff, a missionary for The London Society for Promoting Christianity Amongst the Jews (familiarly known as "The Jews' Society"). The son of a rabbi from Germany, Wolff was baptized into Catholicism as a teenager, intending to become a priest; but he eventually migrated to England, converted once again to Anglicanism, and embarked on a singular career as a missionary to Jews and Muslims. From 1821 to 1845 he travelled widely throughout the Middle East, North Africa, and western Asia, visiting Jewish communities everywhere, but always hoping especially to encounter descendants of the lost tribes. He styled himself "Apostle of our Lord Jesus Christ for Palestine, Persia, Bokhara and Balkh"—the latter two because he was certain that they were the Habor and Halah of Second Kings. Favorably impressed with the claims of the Jews of Bokhara and of Bombay to be descended from the lost tribes, he was also certain that still other remnants were to be found in China, if only he could reach them. He journeyed to Kabul to check reports that the Afghans were Israelites, but after encountering some of them in a series of bizarre adventures decided that they were not. Wolff's travels even took him to the United States, where he preached before Congress; but being no believer in the theory (to be discussed next) that the American Indians were descendants of the lost tribes, he made no attempt to carry his message in that direction.

The American Indians

The preceding has concerned people who assumed that the lost tribes would be found somewhere in or near the Middle East. But more creative researchers have sought and found them everywhere from Japan to Tanzania. One of the most durable fantasies has centered on American Indians, who were first proposed in the sixteenth century for the role of discovered lost tribesmen, when Spanish missionary friars concluded that such an identity would place their charges firmly within the biblical scheme for the genealogy of humankind and thereby resolve a problem of origins that might otherwise have presented grave difficulties. The problem, simply stated, was: from which of Noah's three sons, Shem, Ham, or Japheth, were these strange folk descended? Until the discovery of the Indians, everyone was seemingly accounted for; but since they appeared to be neither Hamites (black people), Semites, nor Japhetics (Europeans and Chinese!), the matter was indeed puzzling. Identifying them as Israelites established them comfortably in the second category, of course, and neatly solved the puzzle. The Dominican friar Diego Duran advanced the point by arguing that the Spanish conquest of America was, in fact, one of the afflictions ordained by the Lord for Israel as punishment. Then, too, if the Indians were indeed lost Israel, the wearisome task of converting them would take on heightened significance as redemption of the Lord's own chosen people.

One of the most noteworthy discoverers of Hebrews in the New World was a Portuguese named Antonio de Montezinos (also known as Aaron Levy), who arrived in Amsterdam in 1644 with a tale calculated to amaze: two years previously, he said, he had been led deep into the mountainous wilderness of Ecuador to a meeting with four Indians who had greeted him with *Shema Yisrael.* Conversation with them (in Hebrew) revealed that they were members of the tribe of Reuben and that remnants of the tribe of Levi also lived nearby. The leader of the Amsterdam Jewish community, a prominent rabbi named Manasseh ben Israel (1604–1657), was profoundly impressed by this revelation. Here were remnants of the Hebrews in one of the very last places on earth where they had not previously been discovered! And was it not generally accepted that the coming of the Messiah and the final redemption of the world would take place only when the Lord's own people had been dispersed "from one end of the earth even unto the other" (Deut. 28:64)? To Manasseh the message seemed unmistakable: the end of time was at hand. In 1650 he published his conclusions in a treatise entitled *The Hope of Israel*. The ten tribes, he had decided, must have wandered very far indeed from their homeland, leaving remnants not only in Media (the northwest part of modern Iran) but in locations as distant as Ethiopia and China. Some, he thought, must have made their way into Tartary (north-central Asia) and from there to Greenland and Labrador; others may well have moved into China, from where, according to the geography of his time, they could readily have reached the New World.

The notion that the Indians were lost tribesmen became even more popular in North America, and by the eighteenth century many Americans accepted the possibility, if not the proven fact, that the people whom they were overwhelming and displacing were degenerated descendants of the very nation with which they were so intimately identified through religious faith. One of the most widely circulated volumes on the subject was a *History of the American Indians* by a trader named James Adair. This appeared in London in 1775, with abundant documentation in the form of cognates and grammatical parallels relating Indian languages to Hebrew, observations on physical characteristics said to be shared by both peoples, and an assortment of supposedly shared cultural and psychological traits. The idea gained even more respectability with the publication in 1816 of a slim volume by Elias Boudinot, a distinguished public figure who had been president of the Continental Congress and director of the United States Mint. His book was entitled *A Star in the West; or, A Humble Attempt to Discover the Long Lost Ten Tribes of Israel, Preparatory to Their Return to Their Beloved City, Jerusalem*. He distinguishes carefully between Israel and Judah—the one being "outcasts," the other "dispersed"—and insists that prophecy will be fulfilled through the restoration of both: "For no believer in revelation . . . can admit that they are lost to the world." He concludes that white Americans would do well to treat American Indians more humanely—if not for the sake of simple decency, then for their own future well-being—for "all those who have oppressed and despised them, wherever they are, will become subjects of the anger and fury of Jehovah their God."

In 1827 a young man named Joseph Smith, living in the village of Manchester, New York, received divine revelations that led to his discovery of a set of gold plates on which were inscribed an account of the settlement of America by a family of Hebrews, along with the subsequent history of their descendants, among some of whom Jesus had appeared in person. Smith's translation of the plates became known as *The Book of Mormon* and, of course, became the bible of a new faith. Although it is commonly asserted that Mormons believe the American Indians to be descended from the lost tribes, that is not precisely the case. *The Book of Mormon* teaches that a Hebrew man named Lehi, a descendant of Joseph, left Jerusalem about 600 B.C.E. (more than one hundred years after the Assyrian exile) and sailed to America in a ship built in response to a divine message similar to the one received earlier by Noah. Two of Lehi's sons, Laman and Lemuel, rebelled against his paternal authority, for which they and their descendants, called Lamanites, were punished by becoming dark-skinned. The modern Lamanites, now erroneously called Indians, will become "white and delightsome" again when they repent and receive the Messiah.

The Falasha

Another group who have frequently been identified as lost tribesmen are the Falashas, an Ethiopian people who practice a distinctive version of pre-talmudic Judaism and call themselves *Beta Israel* (House of Israel); some writers have even suggested that they might be descended from the very people described by Eldad the Danite. Authorities on Ethiopian ethnic history reject this notion outright; the Falashas, they say, are descended from Ethiopian converts to Judaism and show no evidence of Hebrew ancestry. But their supposed identity has not gone unrecognized by black people in the United States. Over the years a number of religious sects have arisen that either identify American blacks with Falashas or claim other connections with the lost tribes. One of the better known was The Church of God and Saints of Christ, founded early in the century by William Crowdy, a railroad cook who received prophetic revelations informing him that black people were in reality descendants of the lost tribes and that in fact all Jews were originally black-skinned but changed color as a result of intermixture with whites. Another group are the Commandment Keepers, or "Black Jews," who claim to be Falashas who lost memory of their identity. They say that "all so-called Negroes are the lost sheep of the House of Israel" and practice their own version of Judaism; they maintain congregations in New York City and ordain their own rabbis. Finally may be mentioned the Hebrew Israelites, or "Black Hebrews," a sect originating in Chicago who claim to be directly descended from the original Hebrew nation. Some settled in Israel, where they attracted numbers of reporters who wanted to know about their relationship to the lost tribes.

The Anglo-Saxons

But of all the revelations connected with the lost tribes, surely the most surprising is that of a small but determined group of English people who are convinced that they and all their Anglo-Saxon brethren—in Great Britain, the Commonwealth nations, and America—are the lineal and literal (not just spiritual) descendants of the entire people of Israel. The story of this astonishing persuasion begins, according to some (generally nonsympathetic) historians with the declarations of one Richard Brothers (1757–1824), a naval officer who retired early into a delusional world from which he was never to emerge. Sometime around 1793 Brothers began receiving divine communications to the effect that he was descended from King David through James, brother of Jesus, and that he should therefore "inform the king of England that I call you my nephew." The Nephew of the Almighty, as he soon came to be called, published a number of volumes recording his revelations, beginning in 1794 with *A Revealed Knowledge of the Prophecies and Times. Book the First. Wrote under the direction of the Lord God, And Published by his Sacred Command; It Being the First Sign of Warning for the Benefit of All Nations. Containing, with Other Great and Remarkable Things Not Revealed to any Person on Earth, the Restoration of the Hebrews to Jerusalem, By the Year 1798: Under their Revealed Prince and Prophet* and culminating in 1822 with *A Correct Account of the Invasion and Conquest of this Island by the Saxons . . . Necessary to be Known by the English Nation, the Descendants of the Greater Part of the Ten Tribes.* The essence of the Lord's message to Brothers was that the British people were "of the Hebrews—descended from Israel," that "the visible Jews" were but few compared with "the great multitude professing Christianity, but all descended from the former Jews in the Land of Israel." The time for the Return was at hand, Brothers declared, and he had been appointed to lead the Israelite procession from England back to the Promised Land, where he would reign in glory.

Among the many who found this prospect irresistible was Nathanial Brassey Halhed, member of the Parliament and a respected philologist; his contribution to the cause was *A Calculation of the Millennium*, which presented mathematical proof that Brothers would begin his millennial reign in Jerusalem on November 19, 1795, just about at sunrise—to be precise, at 23¼ seconds after 6:40 A.M.

Brothers assured the termination of his career when he inserted in a new edition of *A Revealed Knowledge* a divinely inspired imperative addressed to the king himself: "The Lord God commands me to say to you, George III, King of England, that immediately on my being revealed in London to the Hebrews as their Prince and to all nations as their Governor, your crown must be delivered up to me, that all your power and authority may cease." This earned him commitment to an asylum; and although he was eventually released and continued issuing similar announcements, he was too obviously imbalanced to be taken seriously by any but a handful of loyal disciples.

Not long afterward, however, the question of Anglo-Saxon ancestry was re-examined by a far more sober writer. John Wilson (1799–1870) was a professional lecturer on theology and phrenology who appears to have developed, entirely on his own, the conviction that a correct reading of the Bible, combined with what was then becoming known about early European history, led inexorably to the conclusion that the Saxons, who were said to be descended from a people of Media called *Sakai*, or *Sakasuna* (Sons of Sakai), were none other than the exiled Israelite tribes; that they were, in fact, literally what their name suggested: Isaac's sons; and that the contemporary Anglo-Saxon people were therefore revealed as lineal descendants of the lost tribes. The exiled Israelites, announced Wilson, had lost all memory of their true identity but not their national unity. Over the centuries they had wandered northwestward, making their way across Europe, leaving behind unmistakable signs of their presence—the tribal name Dan, for instance, thinly disguised in the Danube, Don, and Dnieper rivers—and ultimately settled into their predestined homelands in northern Europe. They were, therefore, the indubitable ancestors of the very English men and women who sat listening to him in lecture halls.

In 1840 Wilson published a book on his discoveries; at first entitled *Lectures on Ancient Israel and the Israelitish Origins of the Modern Nations of Europe*, it evolved through several editions over the next few years into the more explicitly titled *Our Israelitish Origin*, by which time he had concluded that it was the British people above all who were the core descendants of the lost tribes. He continued with books and periodicals on the subject until his death in 1870—a respectable and respected man, but not of the sort to attract more than a handful of believers.

Among that handful, however, was one man who, though entirely unknown to Wilson, was so profoundly inspired by his revelation that he pondered over it for some thirty years, by which time he was ready to present to the world his own expanded version of Anglo-Saxon history and to inaugurate the movement that soon came to be known as British Israelism or Anglo-Israelism. Edward Hine (1825–1891) was a teenaged boy when he heard Wilson speak, but the message sustained him through the years of an indifferent career as a bank manager until 1870, when he embarked on his true vocation by publishing the first of several pamphlets that, for inventiveness and style, stand second to none in the history of literature on the lost tribes. *Seventeen Positive Identifications of the English Nation with the Lost House of Israel* appeared anonymously, but it sold so well that the identity of the author soon became public knowledge. Encouraged by the response, Hine presented in the following year an enlarged version with *twenty-seven* "identifications," and a few years later, *forty-seven*. (With characteristic optimism he promised seventy-seven to follow, but that pamphlet never materialized.)

Hine's publications generated widespread enthusiasm in a nation that, in the heyday of imperialism, found it not difficult to believe that they were true heirs to the Lord's promises to Israel. But there were also skeptics, of course; among them was the distinguished Oxford orientalist George Rawlinson, who responded with a scholarly article undermining the historical foundations of the new revelation and characterizing the publications of both Wilson and Hine as "idle and unprofitable exercitations." Delighted with the publicity, Hine counterattacked with another pamphlet, *Oxford Wrong in Objecting to the English Being Indentical with Israel*, consisting in the main of some fifty pages of point by point refutation of Rawlinson's arguments, interspersed with challenges to "the Professor" to descend from his ivory tower and debate the entire matter before impartial judges. Unfortunately for the history of lost tribes scholarship, Rawlinson ignored the challenge.

Hine launched two periodicals to spread the word and travelled back and forth across Great Britain, sometimes lecturing almost daily for weeks. His popularity was short-lived, however, for his flair for pamphleteering and public speaking was not matched by organizational talent, and by the next decade he had been displaced by men with equal dedication to the cause but more discipline. Their leader was Edward W. Bird (1823–1903), a retired judge from India, who wrote under the name "Philo-Israel." As he explained, he was a descendant of "Margaret, daughter of Phillip III, King of France, and wife of Edward I, King of England, 1298 A.D. I am, therefore, if Anglo-Israelites be correct, descended from Norman Benjamin, and I am an Israelite of the Israelites. I love my country, and therefore I am 'Philo-Israel,' a lover of Israel." Bird and his colleagues established a London Anglo-Israel Association, which in time evolved into the British Israel World Federation, an organization that survives to this day with affiliates in most Commonwealth countries.

The Anglo-Israel message reached the United States, almost from the time of its beginning, in the form of the revelation that, while the British people were primarily descended from Joseph's son Ephraim (the leader among the ten tribes), Americans were descended from his brother Manasseh. Hine himself toured the United States and Canada in the 1880's and lectured on this point everywhere from Brooklyn to Toronto. But the most notable American Anglo-Israelite was Charles A. L. Totten (1851–1908), a professor of military science at Yale and a passionate millennarian, who published voluminously on the subject in magazines and newspapers, and collected his writings in a series of altogether unique volumes with such titles as *The Hope of History, The Secret of History,* and *The Answer of History*. Totten died in 1908, but his writings were inspiration for the founding some twenty-five years later of the Anglo-Saxon Federation of America, an organization that accepted the identity with lost Israel as axiomatic and that also still exists, but with a very small membership.

The establishment of the state of Israel caused understandable anger and resentment among Anglo-Israelites, who could only conclude that their rightful name and inheritance had been usurped by a small remnant of Judahites whose credentials were, at the most generous estimate, only those of two of the twelve tribes. In 1946 the British Israel World Federation had submitted a memorandum to the Anglo-American Joint Commission on Palestine, arguing that "the birthright of Israel, which includes the possession of Palestine, was held by Joseph, the ancestor of the two tribes of Ephraim and Manasseh, neither of which is within modern Jewry . . . The Jews cannot, therefore, claim to hold the 'title deeds' to Palestine; and the only people who may justly claim possession of Palestine on behalf of all Israel are the tribes of Ephraim and Manasseh"—by whom they meant, of course, the people of Great Britain and the United States.

Although the Anglo-Israelite message currently attracts only a limited formal following, a number of prominent fundamentalist ministers in the United States accept it and incorporate it into their teaching. For example, Herbert W. Armstrong, founder of the Worldwide Church of God and publisher of *Plain Truth* magazine, which claims a circulation of millions, is a firm believer in the "Identity" and regularly writes articles on the subject—no doubt to the puzzlement of readers who have never heard of Anglo-Israelism. For those who believe, however, the message is powerful indeed. As one Anglo-Israelite writer (G. E. A. Coley) expressed it: "Then let us say it, deliberately, fearlessly, thats while we are thrilled through every fibre of our being at the sheer stupendous wonder of it, we are Israel, we are the Chosen Race."

The final word must be left to the late Allen Godbey, an erudite Old Testament scholar at Duke University, whose book entitled *The Lost Tribes a Myth*, first published in 1930, should have effectively demolished all hopes and expectations that the lost Israelites will ever be found. For one thing, Godbey pointed out, the Hebrews, like most people of their time, were subjected to endless raiding, plunder, and population dispersal by more powerful enemies; the Assyrian exile was simply one of many such catastrophes, and not necessarily the worst, that they endured throughout their history. For another—and this is the essential message of his book—over the centuries Judaism has been propagated as a faith among many who bore no genetic relation to the ancient Hebrews; and it is now an anthropological truism that the Jews are not a "race" with a single ancestry, but a people united by a sense of shared history and destiny. Dreamers may continue to declare that they have discovered the lost tribes of Israel; but for those who survive as Jews in today's world the search for a revitalized identity must proceed from more promising and immediate foundations.

—L.B.G.

THE JEWS AS OUTCASTS

34 TIMES WHEN JEWS WERE EXPELLED FROM THEIR HOMES

Jews have been a "wandering" people from the time of their beginnings. History is filled with dozens of peremptory edicts expelling Jews from where they had made their homes. At times the edicts were the result of trumped up charges against the Jews or Judaism, later determined to be false. At other times they were the consequence of an economic situation which the authorities believed would be improved if the Jews were removed. Almost always the bans were only temporary, as below. Their cumulative impact on the psyche of the Jewish people, however, has been traumatic and may very well be indelible. The following list is far from complete. Hardly a major Jewish community has not been expelled by its "host" country, only to be let back in again and later, expelled once more.

1012 C.E. MAINZ. Following the conversion to Judaism of a priest in Mainz, Emperor Henry II ordered all Jews expelled from this old Jewish community.

1182 C.E. FRANCE. King Philip Augustus was taught when he was six years old that Jews killed Christian children. In 1181 the king had all wealthy Jews thrown into prison. The next year he expelled all the Jews from France and confiscated their property; however, he allowed them to return in 1198.

1276 C.E. UPPER BAVARIA. The Jews were expelled from this region for the first of several times, returning a few years later. Before long, 180 Jews were burned at the stake following a blood libel in 1285.

1290 C.E. ENGLAND. King Edward I, on

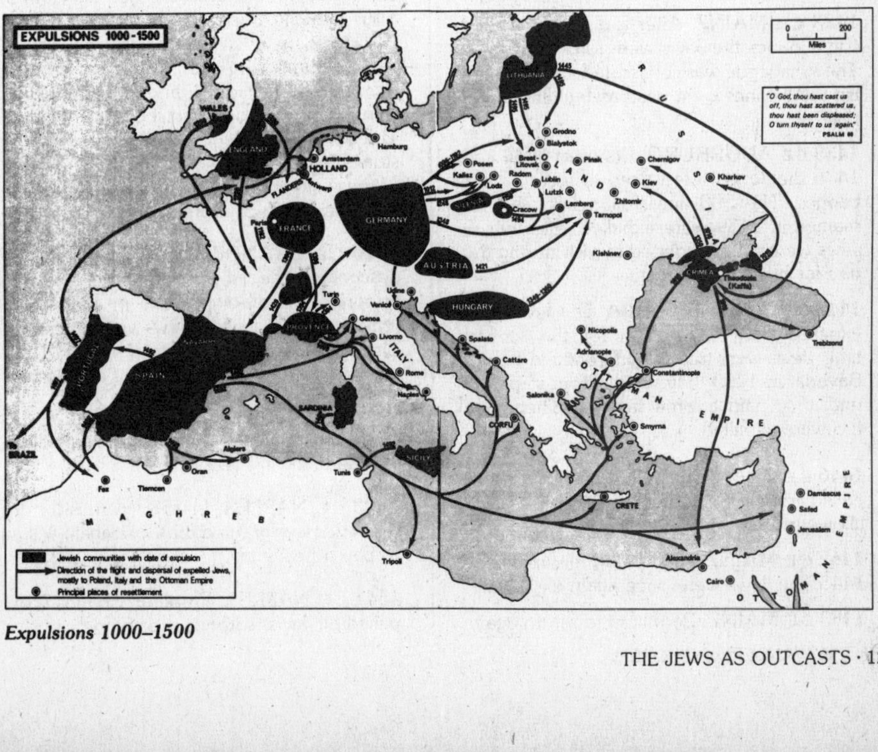

Expulsions 1000–1500

July 18, issued an edict banishing all Jews (approximately 16,000) by November 1, All-Saints' Day. Jews did not return to England in any significant numbers until the beginning of the seventeenth century.

1306 C.E. **FRANCE.** In 1291, Philip the Fair of France prohibited Jews who had been expelled from Gascony and England from settling in his country. Then, in 1306, he expelled the native Jews of France. By 1315 his son, Louis X the Quarreler, had allowed the Jews to return.

1322 C.E. **FRANCE.** Massacres of the Jews took place throughout the country during the reign of Philip V. In 1322 he expelled those who remained alive, but allowed them to return in 1359.

1394 C.E. **FRANCE.** On September 17, Charles VI expelled the Jews from his kingdom, claiming that there were "several grave complaints and outcries" concerning "the excesses and misdemeanors which the said Jews had committed and they continued to act in this manner every day against Christians."

1420 C.E. **LYONS.** Not part of the Kingdom of France, Jews were expelled from Lyons by a special edict.

1424 C.E. **COLOGNE.** While at various times the archbishop and city council had issued permission for Jews to live in Cologne, the last such edict expired in October and was not renewed. Without this protection the Jews were forced to leave.

1438 C.E. **MAINZ.** After a dispute with the City Council the Jews were forced to leave. The synagogue was confiscated and the Jewish tombstones were used as building material.

1439 C.E. **AUGSBURG.** Between 1434 and 1436 the Jews were forced to wear yellow badges. The 300 Jewish families who remained in 1439 were expelled, after which Jews were only permitted to visit during the day for business purposes.

1442 C.E. **UPPER BAVARIA.** The Jews were expelled from this region for the second time. Jews were treated differently in Lower Bavaria: in 1450 they were all put in prison until they paid a large ransom. Then they too were expelled.

1446 C.E. **BRANDENBURG.** Jews were expelled from this German region, but were allowed to return a year later.

1462 C.E. **MAINZ.** After being readmitted in 1445, the Jews were once again expelled.

1483 C.E. **MAINZ.** Permitted to return again in 1473, the Jews were expelled still another time.

1483 C.E. **WARSAW.** Although the Jews were officially expelled in 1483, by 1486 there was record of a new Jewish community in Warsaw.

1492 C.E. **SPAIN.** On March 31 an edict of expulsion was signed in Granada which essentially offered the Jews the option to convert or leave. So ended what is known in Jewish history as the Golden Age of Spain. Over 100,000 Jews left Spain following this edict, leaving the Iberian peninsula virtually empty of Jews until the present day.

1492 C.E. **ITALY.** Spain's Italian possessions also expelled the Jews (approximately 40,000). In Sicily alone, 6,300 homes were confiscated.

1496 C.E. **PORTUGAL.** Following the expulsion from Spain, some 150,000 Jews fled to Portugal, where they were required to pay a fee in order to remain. On December 4, 1496, however, Emanuel I the Fortunate ordered that by November of the following year no Jews would be allowed to remain.

1496 C.E. **NAPLES.** An edict of expulsion was issued in 1496, but was not implemented until 1510. Two hundred wealthy Jewish families were excluded from this edict but were required to pay a heavy annual tax in order to remain.

1498 C.E. **NUREMBERG.** In this Bavarian city eighteen Jews were burned to death in 1467, having been accused of killing four Christians. In 1479 Jews were required to recite a humiliating oath: when they refused, the situation worsened, and a formal expulsion edict was declared by Maximilian I. The Jewish cemetery was destroyed and its stones were used as building material. One of these stones can still be seen in the spiral staircase of the St. Lorenzkirche.

1510 C.E. **BRANDENBURG.** A charge of desecrating the Host caused the trial and burning of thirty-eight Jews in 1510. The remaining 400 to 500 Jews were expelled. The Jews were permitted to resettle in 1543 after it was determined that the accusations had been groundless.

1515 C.E. **GENOA.** The Jews were readmitted the following year.

1533 C.E. **NAPLES.** In 1535 permission for residence was granted for those again willing to pay a heavy tax.

1541 C.E. **NAPLES.** Emperor Charles V expelled all Jews, without exception.

Relatives waiting at New York's Battery Park for new arrivals.

1541 C.E. **PRAGUE.** King Ferdinand I, under pressure from the citizens of Prague, expelled the approximately 1,200 Jewish residents.

1550 C.E. **GENOA.** In 1567 the expulsion was extended outside the city of Genoa to include the entire republic.

1551 C.E. **BAVARIA.** Expelled for the third time, Jewish leaders bargained for the release of four Jews who were being held prisoner by promising, in exchange, to never again return to Upper or Lower Bavaria.

1557 C.E. **PRAGUE.** Allowed to return the year before, the Jews were re-expelled by King Ferdinand I, acting on his own this time. In 1562 they were again permitted to return.

1569 C.E. **PAPAL STATES.** A Papal Bull (official statement of the Catholic Church), released by Pope Pius V, was titled *Hebraeorum gens.* It accused Jews of various crimes, including the practise of magic. The Bull ordered the expulsion of Jews from all papal territories except Rome and Ancona.

1649 C.E. **HAMBURG.** Fleeing from persecution in the Ukraine and Poland, many Jews arrived in Hamburg in 1648. The following year however, Hamburg expelled all of its Jews. They were allowed to return by 1658.

1669 C.E. **VIENNA.** Emperor Leopold I influenced by his fanatic wife, decided to expel the poor Jews in 1669 and the others in 1670. All property was confiscated and the Great Synagogue of Vienna was made into a Catholic Church.

1744 C.E. **BOHEMIA AND MORAVIA.** Maria Theresa ordered the expulsion of all Jews; in Prague, Jews were banished from 1745 to 1748.

1891 C.E. **MOSCOW.** On the eve of Passover a law was issued abolishing the rights of Jewish craftsmen to residence in Moscow, thereby exiling thousands of families. In 1892 rewards were offered to those who discovered Jews in hiding. An estimated 30,000 Jews were expelled. The press in Moscow was forbidden to report on the expulsion.

—A.K.

THE FIRST HISTORY OF THE JEWS PUBLISHED IN THE UNITED STATES

A brief account of the Perſecution of the JEWS.

THE ſeventy years captivity of the Jews began 606, before Chriſt; they about Cyrene, headed by one Andreæ, murdered about 100,000 Greeks and Romans, they eat their entrails, and covered themſelves with the ſkins of thoſe they aſſaſſinated, 115 after Chriſt. Above 580,000 deſtroyed by the Romans 135. Firſt arrived in England, 1079. Thinking to invoke the divine clemency at the ſolemnization of the Paſſover, ſacrificed a young lad of twelve years old, the ſon of a rich tradeſman at Paris, by firſt whipping his fleſh from his bones, and then crucifying him; for which cruelty the criminals were executed, and the reſt baniſhed France, 1180; from this circumſtance the Jews have been ever ſince held in deteſtation. Maſſacred, Sept. 3, 1189. Seven were condemned to pay the King 20,000 marks, or ſuffer perpetual impriſonment, for circumciſing a Chriſtian child at Norwich, and attempting to crucify him, 1235. Two hundred and upwards were apprehended for crucifying a child at Lincoln, eighteen of whom were hanged, and the reſt heavily fined, 1255. Seven hundred were ſlain in London, becauſe a Jew would have forced a Chriſtian to pay him more than two ſhillings per week for the loan of 20, 1262. Every Jew, who lent money on uſury, was commanded to wear a plate upon his breaſt, ſignifying that he was an uſurer, or to quit the realm, 1274. Two hundred and ſixty-ſeven were hanged and quartered for clipping, 1277; the ſame year the Jews crucified a child at Northampton, for which fifty were drawn at horſes' tails, and hanged. All the ſynagogues were ordered to be deſtroyed, 1282. All the Jews in England were apprehended in one day, their goods and chattles confiſcated to the King, and they, to the number of 15660, baniſhed the realm, having only ſuſtenance money allowed, 1287; they remained baniſhed 364 years, till Oliver Cromwell reſtored them. A general maſſacre of them at Verdun, (France) by the Peaſants, who, from a pretended propheſy, conceived the Holy Land was to be recovered from the infidels by them; 500 of theſe Jews took ſhelter in a caſtle, and defended themſelves to the laſt extremity, when for want of weapons, they threw their children at the enemy, and then killed each other, 1317. Driven out of France, 1394. Driven out of Spain, to the number of one hundred and fifty thouſand. 1492; they retired to Africa, Portugal, and France. It was againſt them that the inquiſition was there firſt eſtabliſhed. There was not a Jew in England from 1610 to 1624. An act paſſed to naturalize, 1753; but was repealed on the petition of all the cities in England, 1754. Four were executed in London for murdering a ſervant, 1771.

From: The First Edition of THE FARMER'S ALMANAC (1793)

JEWISH HISTORY THROUGH JEWISH EYES

10 TIMES THE PEOPLE DANCED, 10 TIMES THE PEOPLE CRIED

All national histories have their moments of triumph and times of despair. Most Jews carry with them a sense that their people's history has been marked by more tragedies than joys. But not until one consults the chronology tables in the *Encyclopaedia Judaica* does one realize how historically accurate is this sense. The moments of celebration, of triumph, of dancing, almost get lost among the countless synonyms for persecution, expulsion, pogrom, auto-da-fé, massacre—for all those events that left Jews crying.

Still, happy moments exist in Jewish history and they deserve to be recalled along with the tragedies. In this article, ten joyous and ten tragic events (or series of events) have been highlighted. Care was taken to touch different points along the 4,000-year history of the Jews, and an attempt was made to select significant events beyond those of the moment.

THE PEOPLE DANCED . . .

1. Crossing of the Red Sea

The crossing of the Red Sea was the final stage of the Exodus of the Children of Israel from slavery in Pharaoh's Egypt, and while there remained forty years of emotional and spiritual reajdustments to freedom, the Children of Israel perceived this event as a triumphant and transcendent moment in history, and celebrated it accordingly.

Moses, their leader, sang a hymn of thanksgiving to God while "Miriam, the prophetess, the sister of Aaron, took a timbrel in her hand; and all the women went out after her with timbrels and with dances. And Miriam sang unto them:

Sing ye to the Lord, for He is highly exalted.
The horse and rider hath He thrown unto the sea." (Exod. 15:20–21)

Though the Bible records only two verses of Miriam's song, commentators believe the original version was much longer.

Without indulging in a Hollywood-like scenario of the crossing of the Red Sea, one can easily imagine that the event must have stirred the hearts and minds of a slave nation to the heights of joy, if not frenzy. The drama of the Exodus lay in the suddenness of freedom. One moment the Children of Israel were being pursued by the Egyptians; the next moment, the sea's waters had obliterated the enemy.

Narrow escapes from danger lend themselves to ecstatic celebrations of gratitude, and the revelry indulged in on that early spring morning on the banks of the Red Sea must have been as joyous as any in human history.

For the Jewish people, the enslavement of their ancestors in Egypt has been the model of all that is evil in human society. Accordingly, the Exodus from slavery is seen as the prototype of all that is noble and liberating and worthy of celebration.

2. King David's Dance

The settlement of the Jewish people in the Land of Israel took over two hundred years, marked by battles against the seven nations already living in the land. These battles were considered religious wars, i.e., they were expected of the Jewish people as part of a covenant made with God. With no separation of church and state, military and political milestones were viewed as religious experiences, hence worthy of religious celebration.

Under the leadership of prophets and kings the loosely amalgamated Jewish tribes de-

***Pharoah's army being drowned in the Red Sea, from Cecil B. De Mille's production of* The Ten Commandments.**

veloped into a united kingdom. It was during the forty-year reign of King David (1055–1015 B.C.E.) that Jerusalem became the seat of power and that the Ark of the Covenant was brought to the city of David. Amidst a procession of Levites, masses of people, trumpet blasts, and dancing, the Ark was transported to Jerusalem. It symbolized the spiritual and political unification of the people; King David participated fully in the joyful celebration: "And David danced before the Lord with all his might; and David was girded with a linen ephod. So David and all the house of Israel brought up the Ark of the Lord with shouting, and with the sound of the horn." (2 Sam. 6:14–15)

Traditional commentators explain that the linen ephod was part of the priestly garb, but it would seem from the sarcastic remarks of Michal, David's wife, that he had disgraced himself during his frenzied dancing by uncovering himself.

Although this eventually led to marital breakdown, David refused to apologize for his behavior, insisting: "Before the Lord will I make merry." (2 Sam. 6:21) The God who had protected David merited the king's total loyalty, and no limits could be placed on the King's expression of that loyalty.

3. Water Drawing Festival

During the Sukkot morning service at the Second Temple in Palestine (520 B.C.E.–70 C.E.), a special libation of water was made on the altar along with the customary wine libation. The evidence available does not make clear the reasons for the water libation, but since Sukkot coincides with the much-needed first winter rains in Palestine, there is reason to believe that the water libation symbolized the people's petition for rain. (Today the annual prayer for rain, *Geshem*, is offered on the final day of Sukkot.)

Whatever the rationale behind the water libation, it stirred the imagination of the people to create the most festive event on the Jewish calendar: *Simhat Beit ha-Sho'evah*, the Water Drawing Festival. At the end of the first day of Sukkot the people would gather in the outer court of the Temple. There they watched men of piety and renown dance through the night, bearing fiery torches in their hands. The Levites, men responsible for the workings of the Temple, would stand on the fifteen steps of the Gate of Nicanor and, to the accompaniment of flutes, harps, cymbals, and lyres, sing hymns of praise to God. Four golden candlesticks, each seventy-five feet long, were placed in the court and lit by four young priests. Their light was so brilliant that the Talmud records that "there was no courtyard in Jerusalem that was not lit up with the light of the water drawing festival."

Perhaps it was the joy and relaxation which follow the end of the harvest season; perhaps it was the last social affair before the rainy season, but the Water Drawing Festival was a time of unmitigated joy: "They said that anyone who had not witnessed the Water Drawing Festival had never seen rejoicing."

4. The Deliverance of Purim

The holiday of Purim celebrates the eleventh-hour deliverance of the Jews of Persia from annihilation. The Book of Esther, which chronicles the story behind the holiday, tells of a villain, Haman, who had convinced the king of Persia to eradicate all the Jews in his kingdom. Haman's hatred for the Jews had been kindled by one Jew named Mordecai who had refused to bow down before him, as was the custom in the Orient. Haman's anger did not stop at Mordecai, but broadened to include all the Jews in the land; his reasoning typified classic anti-Semitism: "There is a certain people scattered abroad and dispersed among the peoples in all the provinces of thy kingdom; and their laws are diverse from those of every people; neither keep they the king's laws; therefore it profiteth not the king to suffer them." (Esther 3:8)

Through the intervention of Queen Esther the Jewish people were saved; on the very gallows erected for Mordecai, Haman was hung. What followed was "feasting and gladness, and of sending gifts to one another, and presents to the poor." (Esther 9:22) This exuberance is re-enacted with such subsequent celebration of Purim by the Jewish people. Purim is the one holiday on which a Jew is required to get drunk, (so drunk that one cannot distinguish between Mordecai and Haman); the holiday's customary masquerading, noisemaking, and feasting heighten the carnival-like mood of the day.

The rejoicing of the Jews of Persia was that of any people suddenly spared death; their frenzied dancing, an essential ingredient in the celebration of Purim, is understandable in the light of the tragedies of Jewish history.

5. Persian Conquest of Jerusalem

Close to the end of the 570-year rule of the Roman-Byzantine Empire over Palestine the Jews experienced a brief period of hope and joy. In 603 C.E. the Persians attempted to assail the Roman Empire, making their way from Antioch and Damascus, and reaching Palestine in 614. As the Persian forces approached the Land of Israel, the Jews became increasingly filled with messianic dreams; viewing the Persians as their redeemers, they aided them in their conquest of the Galilee and later, Jerusalem. Benjamin of Tiberias, a wealthy and respected Jew, is reported to have contributed all his wealth to provide ammunition and provisions for the Jewish troops.

When the Persians captured Jerusalem in May 614 they handed the city over to the Jews, perhaps as a reward for the Jewish assistance in the conquest, perhaps out of respect for the Jews' attachment to the city. For three years Jerusalem was once again under Jewish rule. During this time the Jews began to remove the Christians and their churches and monasteries from Jerusalem. Part of this was that some Christians, among them a few priests, grew so fearful of the Jews that they converted to Judaism.

It is possible that in the messianic fervor which colored this period an attempt was made to re-introduce sacrifices at the site of the destroyed Temple in Jerusalem.

The Persians eventually retracted their promises to the Jews of Palestine, but for three unusual years the Jews were certain that the Messiah was on the way.

6. Balfour Declaration

In their long struggle for the establishment of a Jewish state, the Zionists achieved a major breakthrough with the Balfour Declaration. This declaration (actually a letter), dated November 2, 1917, from the British Secretary of State for Foreign Affairs, Lord Arthur James Balfour, to Lord Rothschild, stated in part:

> His Majesty's Government view with favour the establishment in Palestine of a national home for the Jewish people, and will use their best endeavours to facilitate the achievement of this object, it being clearly understood that nothing shall be done which may prejudice the civil and religious rights of existing non-Jewish communities in Palestine . . .

Continued British support for the idea of a Jewish homeland was implicit in establishment of the Palestine Mandate at San Remo in 1920. But even before this, the Balfour Declaration was looked upon by the Jews of the world as an event worth celebrating.

There were spontaneous displays of enthusiasm in many parts of the Jewish world. In the Allied countries, there were huge demonstrations and processions displaying the Union Jack alongside the Zionist flag. A Jew who had spent his adolescence in Russia recalls the huge parade in his hometown, where he was honored by leading the processions and bearing the Zionist flag: "We felt that all we had to do was to pack our bags and leave, and the Jewish state would be built."

The ambiguous wording of the Balfour Declaration was to create later problems, but the gratefulness of the Jews to Lord Balfour was demonstrated time and again in naming children and settlements after him, and in marking November 2 as a historic and joyous day for the Jewish people.

A celebration in Madison Square Garden for the creation of the State of Israel.
(Alexander Archer)

7. The U.N. Partition Plan (1947)

No one who lived through the United Nations vote to partition Palestine, thus creating a Jewish state, will ever forget the excruciating tension surrounding the debate. Great Britain, which had held a mandate over Palestine since the end of the First World War, could not seem to govern Palestine to anyone's satisfaction: neither the Jews, nor the Arabs, nor the British themselves. Great Britain finally asked the United Nations to recommend a solution to the problem. After investigation, the United Nations Special Committee on Palestine (UNSCOP) unanimously recommended that the Mandate over Palestine be terminated and Palestine be granted independence. The majority opinion of UNSCOP believed that partition of Palestine into a Jewish state and an Arab state, with Jerusalem as a separate entity, provided the best chance for peace. Though partitioning the Land of Israel did not seem equitable to the Jews of Palestine, it would legally assure a Jewish state with worldwide backing. This made the partition plan acceptable.

Everything hung on the vote of Saturday, November 29, 1947.* The Zionists had lobbied hard in order to secure the necessary two-thirds majority, but until the last moment victory was not sure, especially with regard to votes from some South American nations. The decisive vote was 33 countries for partition, 13 opposed, and 10 abstentions.

For the Jews of the world who were glued to the radio (and for those Sabbath observers who received the news second-hand), the vote at Lake Success drove them into the streets for spontaneous celebrations. As they danced they knew that the Arab nations would carry out their threat of invasion, but the knowledge that the world had cooperated in the creation of the Jewish state was reason enough for celebration.

8. Simhat Torah in Moscow

A sign on a Moscow bulletin board in 1966 read: "The 'symphony' of Simhat Torah will be performed on the night of October 6, as usual, at the usual time and place."

For the Jews of the Soviet Union the annual Simhat Torah (Rejoicing with the Torah) celebration outside the Great Synagogue in Moscow has become an act of solidarity with world Jewry as well as a religious experience. Once a year Jews of all ages and persuasions dance on Arkhipova Street to celebrate this festival, while reminding the world that "the people of Israel live." The often repeated "official" prediction that this public affirmation is a passing fad is disproved by the sea of over 30,000 youth who can be seen among the dancing Jews. The obvious presence of police and KGB agents does not seem to inhibit the multitudes who choose to defy a prohibition against public gatherings by singing and dancing throughout the night.

The Jews dancing in the streets of Moscow render more than just the police impotent. They testify to the failure of Soviet education to eradicate their collective will to survive as Jews. Neither schools nor youth movements nor the Communist Party have paralyzed the feet of these Russian Jews.

The Jews of the free world have chosen Simhat Torah as the time to demonstrate on behalf of their brethren in the Soviet

*The General Assembly resolution of November 29, 1947, to partition the Palestine mandate into two independent states, provided the British with a six-month transition period to dismantle their colonial administration. Official proclamation of Israel's independence, the fifth day of the Hebrew month of Iyar (corresponding to May 14, 1948), was in time to coincide with the withdrawal of the last British soldier from Palestinian soil. It is the fifth of Iyar which is celebrated every year.

Union. In an act of solidarity, they dance the *hora* in the street, ever hoping that their circle will be soon enlarged.

9. The Six-Day War

For eight years Arab saboteurs had been infiltrating into Israel. Israeli settlements in the north were constantly being shelled from Syrian positions on the Golan Heights. The immediate cause of the Six-Day War, however, lay to the south. On May 17, 1967, Egyptian President Gamal Abdel Nasser demanded the dismantling of the UN Emergency Force which had kept the peace between Israel and Egypt since the Sinai Campaign of 1956. And on May 20 Nasser closed the strategic Straits of Tiran to Israeli shipping.

While the rest of the world reacted but little to this act of aggression, Israel was gradually being encircled by 250,000 enemy troops, over 2,000 tanks, and 700 fighter planes and bombers. The Israelis were not alone in sensing imminent destruction, however; world Jewry feared for the survival of the Jewish state. Jews everywhere mobilized unprecedented financial support and volunteered their services, sharing with the Israelis the vivid memories of an earlier holocaust. As one Israeli soldier said: "In those days before the war we came closest to that Jewish fate from which we have run like haunted beings all these years."

On June 5, 1967, the Israeli air force undertook a pre-emptive strike against the air forces of Egypt, Jordan, and Syria, and successfully destroyed 391 planes on the ground and 60 more in air combat. The complete air superiority which Israel commanded from the start was to keep her losses to a minimum and ultimately lead to victory.

When Jordan's King Hussein, in spite of Israel's warnings, chose to enter the war, the possibility of reunifying Jerusalem presented itself. On June 7, when Israeli forces broke through the Lion's Gate and captured the Old City of Jerusalem, the Israeli flag was raised over all Jerusalem at 10:15 a.m. The Temple Mount and the Western Wall were again in Jewish hands. The event was overwhelming. Soldiers who fought for the capture of eastern Jerusalem openly wept at the Western Wall. Jerusalemites, denied entry to half of their city for nineteen years, crossed the previously barbed-wired streets to gaze at the ancient sites. The conquest of Jerusalem was transformed into a religious pilgrimage, and as the Jews celebrated their survival, symbolized in the reunification of their ancient and modern capital, they gave thanks and spoke of a messinaic redemption.

10. Entebbe Rescue

While the U.S. was celebrating its 200th year of independence, Israelis were celebrat-

Israeli troops rejoice after capturing the Golan Heights during the Six Day War, 1967.

ing a modern-day miracle. In spirit American Jews joined the huge crowds dancing at Ben-Gurion Airport, outside Tel Aviv, to welcome home the heroes of an almost unbelievable drama, one of the most spectacular military rescue operations in history.

Israelis rejoicing after the rescue at Entebbe.

The passengers on Air France Flight 139 from Tel Aviv to Paris had been taken hostage by four armed terrorists who boarded the aircraft during a stopover in Athens. The hijacked plane eventually landed at Entebbe Airport (Uganda) where the passengers became prisoners of one of Africa's most sadistic dictators, Idi Amin.

During the seven days that the Airbus sat on the tarmac at Entebbe, the eighty-three passengers with Jewish names or Israeli passports were separated from the others, an act starkly recalling the Nazi *selekzia*, the process of selecting who shall live and who shall die. (The non-Israeli hostages were released before the rescue.) The Government of Israel recognized that the time for verbal negotiations was over.

And so it happened that early on the morning of July 4, 1976, Israeli military operation Thunderbolt made its surprise landing at Entebbe. Flying between enemy Arab states while avoiding Russian-built radar stations, four Hercules transport planes and two Boeing 707s flew 2,500 miles undetected to airlift 103 hostages (including the Air France crew) to safety. Within ninety minutes, the Israeli raiding party had stormed the airport, killed the terrorists, gathered up the hostages, and was airborne again.

The reception accorded the commandos when the plane carrying the hostages touched down near Tel Aviv was of heroic proportions. People embraced and cried. Some shouted for joy. And many Jews danced in the realization that once again Jews could depend upon other Jews to rescue them.

. . . THE PEOPLE CRIED

1. Slavery in a Strange Land

As described in the book of Exodus the enslavement of the Children of Israel in Egypt is a particularly cruel part in ancient Jewish history. Fearing that the alien Israelites were becoming too numerous in the land, the Egyptians used them for forced labor. Despite the rigors of toil, the Children of Israel continued to multiply, however; Pharaoh, Egypt's ruler, felt compelled to ever more drastic measures, culminating in the drowning of all newborn baby boys: ". . . and the Children of Israel sighed because of their bondage, and they cried, and their cry came up unto God . . ." (Exod. 2:23)

Paradoxically, divine intervention, via Moses, only aggravated the conditions of slavery at first. The Israelites suffered increased hardships until the time of liberation.

Wishing to stress the inhumanity of Egyptian slavery, rabbis embroidered upon the biblical account in their commentaries. Taking the verse "And the Egyptians made the Children of Israel serve with rigor" (Exod. 1:13), Rabbi Simeon ben Zemach Duran interpreted "rigor" as the Egyptian decree that to save time the male slaves must sleep in the fields rather than return home to their wives; *Midrash ha-Gadol* interpreted it as work for which there was no purpose, such as building a storehouse which would be destroyed upon completion.

Even without such embellishments, the enslavement was clearly a time of unremitting agony, which was to shape the future direction of Judaism, and which was reflected in its concerns for the "stranger in a strange land."

2. Destruction of the Second Temple

Under the Roman Empire, Jerusalem was more than the administrative capital of the Jewish state. With its Holy Temple, Jerusalem was the very symbol of Jewish nationhood. Worship, study, and the administration of law were centered around the Temple, where Jewish pilgrims, as well as non-Jews, flocked, especially on the Festivals, to offer sacrifices and be absolved of their sins.

For many years Rome allowed the Jews of Palestine religious autonomy, but under Pontius Pilate (26–36 C.E.), systematic oppression began. A heavy burden of taxes, Roman interference in the Temple service, and the presence of a Roman army in Jerusalem physically and spiritually choked the Jewish people. Jewish community leaders became puppets to the Roman procurator in Jerusalem. When the humiliation suffered by the Jews rose to unbearable levels open rebellion erupted (66 C.E.).

A huge Roman army was dispatched to Palestine under the command of Vespasian. His armed troops crushed the Jewish opposition in the Galilee and Transjordan, and in the spring of 70 C.E. his son Titus laid siege to Jerusalem. Starvation and internal factions weakened the Jewish armies, and on the ninth of Av—coincidentally, the day the Babylonians destroyed the First Temple in 586 B.C.E.—Jerusalem fell, with the Temple in flames. According to the Roman historian Tacitus, 600,000 Jews were killed or died of starvation and disease during the year and a half of siege. Almost the same number were marched in chains to Rome. Jerusalem became a wasteland.

In commemoration of the disaster which initiated 2,000 years of Jewish exile, the ninth of Av is a solemn fast day in the Jewish calendar. On that day Jews read from the Book of Lamentations, which opens with the words:

How doth the city sit solitary,
that was full of people.
How is she become as a widow.
She that was great among the
nations, and princess among
the provinces,
How is she become a tributary.
She weepeth sore in the night,
and her tears are on her cheeks
She hath none to comfort her
among her lovers.

3. The Crusades

Despite the heroic, even romantic characteristics attributed to the Crusades of the eleventh and twelfth centuries, the military campaigns to redeem Palestine from the "infidel" Muslims were a period of mass slaughter, forced conversions, and suicides for the Jews of Western and Central Europe. For the first time Christians spoke of a Jewish plot against Christendom, and the blood libel found its origins in this period, the first such accusation being made in 1144, in Norwich, England.

As the Crusaders roamed through Europe en route to the Holy Land they murdered entire Jewish communities and pilaged the towns. Given the choice of conversion or death, *kiddush ha-Shem* (martyrdom for the sanctification of God's name) became a widespread response to Christian persecution. Because the Jewish communities of Europe had little hope of escaping the ravages of the Crusades, they found some solace in glorification of the martyred innocents.

During the First Crusade (1096-1099) the Jews of the Rhineland were slaughtered. Crusaders attacked the Jews of Speyer, Worm, Mainz, Cologne, Trier, Regensburg, Metz, and Prague. By the end of the Crusade more than 5,000 Jews were dead.

The casualties from the Second Crusade (1147–1149) were less extensive, owing in part to the "moderation" of the Crusade's spiritual leader, Bernard of Clairvaux. As victims of a blood libel, however, all members of the Jewish community of Blois, France, were burned at the stake in 1171.

The Third Crusade (1189–1192) was most violent in England, where Jews were massacred at Lynn, Norwich, Stamford, and Bury St. Edmunds. The worst carnage took place at York, where 150 Jews, under siege in a castle, chose to kill themselves rather than submit to baptism.

The Crusades marked a new and worsened relationship between the Jews and the Church, one that would not improve as long as anti-Semitic activities were sanctioned by Church officials.

4. Burning of the Talmud

In 1236 Pope Gregory IX was handed a list of thirty-five charges against the Talmud, the major code of Jewish law, including allegations that it attacked the Church and blasphemed its origins. The list had been compiled by a revengeful Jewish convert to Christianity, Nicholas Donin, who pointed out that as long as Jews equated the Talmud's authority with that of the Bible there was little chance of ever converting them to Christianity.

After investigation, Gregory sent a letter to all Church officials in France (and eventually to the kings of France, England, Spain, and Portugal) ordering the confiscation of Jewish books on the first Saturday of Lent when Jews were to be found in synagogue. Non-Jews refusing to part with their Hebrew texts were to be excommunicated. Books found to contain the alleged errors or obscenities were to be burned at the stake.

Gregory's letter led to the first case of public disputation between Jews and the Church when, on June 25–27, 1240, Rabbi Yehiel of Paris, the leading rabbi of his time, had to defend the merits of Judaism, i.e., the worth of the Talmud, against claims by the Church. Two years later, in June 1242, twenty-four wagons of books, equalling thousands of volumes, were publicly burned in Paris.

The tragedy of that conflagration—the first of many instigated by Church leaders—was so great that a contemporary scholar, Rabbi Meir of Rothenburg, described it as comparable to the burning of the Temple. His lament, *Sha'ali Serufah Ba'esh*, is included in the elegies recited to this day on the ninth of Av. It begins:

> *Inquire, O thou who art burned*
> *by fire,*
> *About the welfare of those who*
> *mourn for thee . . .*

5. The Spanish Inquisition

The Inquisition was a permanent court of the medieval Catholic Church, established to eradicate heresy from Central and Western Europe. Though originally created to counter Christian heretics, the Inquisition broadened its powers to interfere in the affairs of the Jewish communities. The Church justified this move by claiming that the Jews were responsible for certain forms of Christian heresy. (An earlier condemnation of Maimonides' books in 1232 may have provided the Church with its first chance at controlling internal Jewish life and set a precedent for future inquisitors.)

The first mass burning of Jews on the stake took place at Troyes, France (1288), but the cruel hand of the Inquisition was most severely felt in Spain. Whether the Spanish Inquisition was a political or theological phenomenon is still debated by historians, but everyone agrees that the Inquisition in Spain was created to deal with the phenomenon of Conversos, those who had abandoned their Jewish faith under duress but continued to maintain ties with their former brethren.

The Spanish Inquisition officially began in 1480, but it was in 1483, under Tomas de Torquemada, that it attained its greatest power. Conversos were condemned by the thousands, tortured, and burned at the stake. Dead Jews were exhumed from their graves and also burned at the stake. The property of those convicted was confiscated by the state and the Church.

Since the Spanish Inquisition used all means of torture to extract confessions of heresy, the hearings to determine the Jews' true beliefs were held in secrecy. The sentences, however, were announced at huge, pageant-filled public gatherings called autos-da-fé whose high point was marked by the burning of the sentenced Jews. Lighting the pyre was a religious duty and honor, often bestowed upon members of royalty.

The Spanish Inquisition claimed it uncovered some 13,000 Conversos who had stubbornly remained loyal to Judaism; in 1492, this convinced the authorities that the only way Spain could be unified in religion was to expel the Jews.

6. Shabbatai Zevi, the False Messiah

In one of the strangest episodes in Jewish history, a man's claim to be the Messiah convinced entire communities to restructure their life, their laws, and their beliefs. Shabbatai Zevi (1626–1676) was born and educated in Turkey, where his learning was acknowledged by all, as was his mental imbalance. During fits of depression he would withdraw to fight demonic powers that he felt were overcoming him. These moods alternated with periods of "illumination," during which he engaged in bizarre ritual practices and proclaimed himself the Messiah.

Shabbatai Zevi's claims won over the masses as well as leading rabbinic authorities. A combination of historical circumstances, such as the Chmielnicki massacre of 1648, the spread of kabbalistic ideas of sixteenth-century Safed, and an effective public relations man (Nathan of Gaza) made the normally conservative community surprisingly receptive to Shabbatai Zevi's radical pronouncements.

Shabbatai Zevi created mass hysteria among Jews all over the world when he charged them to expect the redemption in 1666. They undertook lengthy fasts, immersed themselves repeatedly in ritual baths, lay naked in the snow in self-mortification, sold their homes in order to raise money for the forthcoming trip to Palestine, pronounced the Ineffable Name (forbidden since the destruction of the Second Temple), went into trances, and paid homage to their new "Messiah."

Just as the world stood poised for redemption, however, the "Messiah" was arrested by Turkish authorities on September 5, 1666. Given the choice of death or conversion to Islam, he chose the latter, and took the name Mehmed Effendi.

This unanticipated reversal and apostasy sent shock waves throughout the Jewish world. Some Jews who had been totally convinced of Shabbatai Zevi's claims explained away his act, in mystical terminology, as a fulfillment or necessity of his mission. But for many other Jews, his conversion constituted a collapse of their universe. Prominent leaders prostrated themselves in shame; from within the Jewish community a cry of misery arose; from without there was jeering by Christians and Moslems. From the heights of utopia many Jews fell into despair.

7. Russian Pogroms

Between 1881 and 1921 Russian civilians attacked many different Jewish communities in Russia, destroying property, looting, murdering, and raping. There were three waves of attacks (1881–1884, 1903–1906, and 1917–1921), each surpassing the one before in scope and cruelty. Called pogroms, (from the Russian word for "devastation"), these rampages were carried out by the Russian masses while the government stood by idly or quietly aided the perpetrators.

Each wave corresponded to a political crisis within Russia. The pogroms of the 1880's broke out after the assassination of Czar Alexander II, whose murder was blamed on the Jews. After the pogroms the Russian government began to officially discriminate against Jews through restrictive laws, including quotas on Jews attending secondary schools and universities, and eventually, expulsion of Jews from Moscow. Now Jews began their mass migration to the United States and Argentina; other Jews laid the foundation for the Zionist movement in Palestine.

The second wave of pogroms corresponded to the Russian revolution of 1905. Eager to check rebellion, the government encouraged anti-Jewish sentiment in order to rechannel the revolutionary zeal of the masses. During Passover 1903, Kishinev was the scene of a particularly brutal pogrom. Forty-five Jews were left dead; hundreds were injured (both groups were savagely mutilated); approximately 1,500 Jewish homes and stores were looted. This wave reached 64 towns and 626 villages, with a total death toll estimated at over 800. In response Jewish nationalism increased, self-defense movements sprang up, and Jews emigrated to Palestine as part of the Second *Aliyah*.

The last wave of pogroms occurred during the Russian Revolution and the subsequent civil war. Soldiers of the White (anti-

The Wailing or Western Wall, Jerusalem

Bolshevik) armies were usually the perpetrators. According to the historian S. Dubnow, by the time this wave had subsided, 60,000 Jews had been killed and many more wounded.

The renowned Hebrew poet Chaim Nachman Bialik (1873–1934), deeply affected by the pogroms, traveled to Kishinev in 1903 to interview the survivors. While preparing his report on the atrocity, he wrote his famous poem "On the Slaughter," in which he cried out for either justice or the destruction of the world—mere vengeance being useless:

Cursed is he who says
"Revenge."
Vengeance for the blood of
a small child
Satan has not yet created.

8. The "Night of Broken Glass"

The horror of the Holocaust, which began with Hitler's appointment as German Chancellor on January 30, 1933, and ended on May 8, 1945, with the surrender of Nazi Germany to the Allies, is too enormous to be summarized adequately. The Nazi's barbaric destruction of 6 million Jews, including 2 million children, was not carried out in the heat of battle but as part of a methodical governmental program, using all the "advances" of modern science and industry to eliminate an entire people. Coupled with their assembly-line approach to murder, the Nazis waged a psychological campaign which denied the reality of the death camps and broke down Jewish resistance. While there were cases of organized revolt against the Nazis, circumstances were so overwhelming that resistance could rarely be a category of thought, let alone action.

The anti-Semitic program of the Nazis increased in stages. Many historians consider the night of November 9–10, 1938, as a major turning point, escalating toward what was to be a "final solution" for the Jews of Europe. On that Kristallnacht ("Night of Broken Glass"), Nazi attacks on Jews, Jewish-owned property, and synagogues were instigated throughout Germany and Austria. At least 30,000 Jewish men were arrested and sent to concentration camps. Nazi records report 815 shops destroyed, 29 warehouses and 171 dwellings burned or otherwise destroyed, 191 synagogues set on fire, and another 76 totally destroyed. Thirty-six Jews were killed and many more injured. Hitler's government punished the victims, levying an enormous fine against the Jewish community.

After Kristallnacht there was little place for the Jew in the German economy; with the subsequent dissolution of communal and cultural bodies, organized Jewish life was virtually impossible.

9. The "Illegal" Exodus 1947

Even as the fires of the Holocaust engulfed the Jews of Europe, the British government's policy poured salt on the wounds of those who had, somehow or other, escaped. Hiding out in forests and villages, Jewish refugees from Hitler's butchery slowly made their way to the one country committed to their survival—Palestine. However, Great Britain, which held the mandate over Palestine, had issued a White Paper in 1939 which restricted immigration of Jews to 10,000 per year. The only way the fleeing survivors could enter Palestine, therefore, was through "illegal" methods, which the mandatory government did everything in its power to stop. By 1940, radar stations were erected; airplanes searched the seas for immigrant vessels. Few of these over-laden vessels were seaworthy, and many were accidentally or intentionally sunk, including the *Patria* (250 dead) and *Struma* (768 dead). Even after the war and worldwide recognition of the Nazi butchery, when sixty-five boats stuffed with pathetic human cargo left for Palestine, most of them were intercepted by the British, who transferred the passengers to detention camps.

The struggle against this harsh British policy reached a climax during the summer of 1947 when on July 18, 1947, 4,515 refugees on board the *Exodus 1947* were denied permission to land in Palestine. Following a British decision to board and subdue the ship's crew and passengers, three were left dead and twenty-eight wounded. Later the passengers were transferred to three prison ships and taken to southern France. There the Jews refused to disembark. Through the heat of the summer, as they squatted in their hellish cages, the refugees resisted any offer short of entry into Palestine. Babies were born, refugees died, a hunger strike was held; however, the determination of the survivors continued.

After rejecting a British ultimatum, the imprisoned passengers were taken to Hamburg, Germany, where they were placed in a British internment camp.

While *Exodus 1947* waited in the French harbor, journalist Ruth Gruber spoke to the refugees. "Don't ask our names," insisted one leader. A woman began to nod and weep softly. "Yes," she said, "we have no names, only numbers."

10. Terrorism on Israel's Coast

Arab terrorists have conducted a campaign of horror against the unarmed civilians of Israel ever since 1948. Unlike the Arab massacres of 1920, 1921, 1929, and 1936–1939, these terrorist acts are proudly acknowledged by their perpetrators, who rush to take credit for their barbaric deeds.

The murder of schoolchildren in Ma'alot, the fatal attack on Israeli athletes at the Munich Olympics, and the explosion in Jerusalem's Zion Square are just a few of many Arab atrocities which have placed the country in mourning. On Saturday, March 11, 1978, one of the worst atrocities was committed.

A few hours before dark, terrorists entered the country from Lebanon by rubber dinghies and managed to hijack two buses on the coastal road, north of Tel Aviv. After a rampage of shooting at passing vehicles and at passengers on the buses, the terrorists gathered all the hostages in one bus and headed southward to Tel Aviv where they hoped to demand the release of jailed Arab terrorists. When the bus was stopped by a police road block a bloody battle ensued, during which the bus exploded in flames. Many hostages managed to flee the flames, but others, who had been strapped to their seats, could not.

Twenty-eight Israelis died that day, with an additional five later on, and seventy-two were wounded. Parents lost children, and children were orphaned. The death toll was the highest since statehood.

Eighteen months later, at the trial of the two surviving terrorists, their defense attorney stated that "the accused are not ashamed of their actions and are proud of their mission."

—G.S.R.

25 "MUST" PLACES TO VISIT FOR THE JEWISH TOURIST (outside of the United States and Israel)

Jews have been living all over the earth for thousands of years. There are few countries that have not contained a Jewish community, however small, at one time or another in their history.

The following section deals with places of Jewish interest to the traveller. In some of them, old synagogues, *mikvehs* (ritual baths), or cemeteries bear witness to a past forever stilled. In others, the communities continue to thrive alongside the vestiges of old monuments. All testify to the tenacity of Jewish existence.

In one's travels it is helpful to know that even in remote lands, far from home, there is a community of brethren. To visit with them is to affirm the tenet of "*Klal Yisrael*" (the oneness of Israel). The traveller can expect an enthusiastic welcome, help when needed, and an exchange of interesting stories over *Shabbat* dinner. The greatest of medieval Jewish travellers, Benjamin of Tudela, discovered this truth centuries ago.

Therefore, to the traveller, *derekh shalom* (May it be a journey of peace)!

Czechoslovakia

THE STATE JEWISH MUSEUM, PRAGUE

That so much of Jewish interest still exists in Prague today is due, in no small measure, to the demonic ironies of history. It was Adolf Eichmann's plan to set up a "Central Museum of the defunct Jewish race." As Europe's Jewish communities were systematically eliminated, religious articles were shipped to Prague to be catalogued for eventual display.

Today, these artifacts—over five thousand religious objects, twenty-four thousand and five hundred prayer books, six thousand items of historical value—are preserved in the State Jewish Museum, established and supported by the government of Czechoslovakia. The synagogues in Prague's "Old Town"—themselves miraculously preserved because they served as warehouses for confiscated Jewish goods—are the background for the extraordinary collection of ritual objects, embroidery, and silver. Most poignant is the Holocaust exhibit displaying the originals of the children's drawings from the Theresienstadt Concentration Camp, immortalized in the book, *I Never Saw Another Butterfly*.

Part of the museum complex, the **Alte-Neue Shul** at 2 Cervana Street, completed in 1270, is the oldest extant synagogue in the world. Although one must descend several steps to enter the synagogue, the building itself is Gothic in structure and feeling, with pointed vaults and arched ribs. It has been suggested that the somewhat unusual addition of a fifth rib to the vaulting was intended to ef-

The Alte Neue Shul, Prague

face the cross formed by the four diagonal ribs of the traditional Gothic vault. One should note, too, the flag presented to the Jews by Emperor Ferdinand III in 1648 in recognition of their heroic defense of the city against the invading Swedes. Its design, a Swedish cap in the center of the shield of David, became the official emblem of the Jewish community of Prague.

Next door to the Alte-Neue Shul is the **Jewish Town Hall.** Originally built in the sixteenth century and last reconstructed in the eighteenth century, it has a clock tower with two clocks. The main one, with Roman numerals, works in the conventional manner. The lower one, with Hebrew numerals, operates in counterclockwise fashion. Today, the Jewish Town Hall functions as the residence of the Prague Jewish community. Equipped with a kosher kitchen, it serves as the central meeting place for Czech Jews and foreign tourists. The community is always eager for warm Jewish contact.

Also of interest:

One should be sure to visit the nearby **Jewish cemetery.** During the war, it was the only area in which Jews were permitted to walk. Hence, children played and courtships flourished among centuries-old tombstones. An unusual feature of many of these tombstones is their representation of a man's name or profession. Thus, a man whose family name was Schneider or who worked as a tailor will have a pair of scissors carved above his name; a doctor, his physician's instruments. Of particular interest, is the tomb of Rabbi Judah Loew b. Bezalel (the "Maharal"), a sage so revered by Jew and non-Jew alike that in 1917 his statue was erected at the entrance of the Prague Town Hall.

Finally, one should take note of the **giant crucifix** mounted on the Charles Bridge. In 1609 a Prague Jew was accused of having blasphemed the image of Jesus. The punishment and fine imposed upon the Jewish community was the erection of this crucifix. It is emblazoned with the Hebrew words: "*Kadosh, Kadosh, Kadosh*" ("Holy, Holy, Holy is the Lord of Hosts," Isa. 6:3).

Denmark

MUSEUM OF THE DANISH RESISTANCE, COPENHAGEN

Of all the countries occuped by the Nazi forces in Europe, only Denmark was to emerge from the war with its Jewish community virtually unharmed. This was due to the active participation of the Danes themselves, who protected Jews and insisted that as full citizens, Jews were entitled to all attendant rights. When, in 1943, German pressure made this situation untenable, Danish citizens, led by captains and fishermen, rowed almost eight thousand Jews and their non-Jewish relatives to safety in Sweden. Working at night, at the risk of their lives, the operation took almost three weeks to complete. At the end of the war, most Jews returning to Denmark found their homes and property intact.

The museum, located on the Esplanadan, is dedicated to the history of the Resistance movement in Denmark and a special section is devoted to the Danish Jewish relationship. It is rare enough in Jewish history to have been so "adopted" and nurtured by another people. The Dane's part in helping one small segment of world Jewry survive should not be forgotten.

Also of interest:

The **main synagogue in Copenhagen** is at 12 Krystalgade, and Friday evening services in the summer are followed by a *Kiddush* to which all visitors are invited. Of particular interest is the adjoining **home for the aged.** The building is modern and cheerful, and the residents more than willing to share reminiscences of their war-time experience.

France

THE SYNAGOGUE AT CARPENTRAS

Carpentras, fourteen miles northeast of Avignon, houses France's oldest synagogue.

Originally built in 1367 and reconstructed in 1741–43, the synagogue in the Place de la Mairie has been classified a national monument. The interior is in the harmoniously proportioned style of the eighteenth century, with elegant wainscotting and finely-wrought iron railings, banisters, and chandeliers. One can still see the oven used by the community for the baking of *matzah*, as well as the ritual bath (*mikveh*), known locally as the *cabassadore*.

Those interested in further exploration should visit **Cavaillon,** fourteen miles southeast of Avignon. The synagogue, begun in 1772 and classified as a historical monument, is located in the Rue Hébraïque, seat of the former Jewish ghetto. Smaller than the synagogue at Carpentras, the interior, with its wood carving and wrought-iron work, surpasses it in detail. The bakery once used for the production of *matzah* adjoins the synagogue and forms part of the small **Museé Judēo-Comtadin.**

THE MARAIS, PARIS

One of the oldest sections of Paris, the Marais (marsh-lands) houses some of the most elegant of France's sixteenth, seventeenth, and eighteenth century hôtels (private town houses). It is also a workingman's quarter (though escalating property values are rapidly changing that) and the site of a large Jewish section. Much like the Lower East Side in New York, the Marais' crumbling narrow streets reveal vestiges of a once vibrant Jewish presence. Communal life centers around Rue des Rosiers, where shop signs in bakery windows, grocery stores, butcher shops, and bookstores are written in Yiddish and French. Although the Ashkenazic community is considerably diminished from its pre-World War II size, an influx of North African Jews has added a vitalizing presence to the neighborhood. Hence kosher restaurants specializing in *couscous* and pastry shops featuring honey-laden sweets abut their counterparts featuring gefilte fish and egg *kichel* (cake). Synagogues and *shtiblach* (small congregations) catering to both communities abound on the side streets.

A ten minute walk from the Marais section, towards the Seine river, at the corner of rue Geoffroy l'Asnier and rue Grenier sur l'Eau, is the **Memorial to the Unknown Jewish Martyr**. A bronze structure, shaped like a crematorium urn, stands as mute testimonial to the unsung murdered. The museum, with a library, reading room, and exhibition area, is dedicated to Jewish resistance to the Nazis throughout Europe. Too often bypassed, this museum should be on the Jewish tourist's itinerary.

Great Britain

BEVIS MARKS SYNAGOGUE, LONDON

The crown of British Jewry for over two hundred and eighty years, the Spanish and Portuguese Synagogue located on Bevis Marks is one of the finest examples of synagogue architecture of the eighteenth century. Modelled on the famous Sephardi Synagogue in Amsterdam, it is the oldest surviving synagogue of English Jewry. In it are benches from the earlier Creechurch Lane Synagogue built in 1657 upon the readmission of Jews to England under Cromwell. The main entrance is often locked, so call at the office around the corner at 4 Heneage Lane.

London has a flourishing and vibrant Jewish community with kosher restaurants, shopping areas, and synagogues serving the entire spectrum of Jewish ritual. The Sunday morning Petticoat Lane Market on London's East End abounds in Yiddish and Jewish folk culture and is reminiscent of New York's Lower East Side at the turn of the century. It is well worth a visit.

Hong Kong

OHEL LEAH SYNAGOGUE, HONG KONG

Immediately after Hong Kong was ceded to the British in 1842, the Sassoons, the Rothschilds of the Sephardic world, moved their offices from Canton to the new colony. Given the monopoly of the opium trade, then a legal enterprise, their already sizeable holdings burgeoned, together with the fortunes of this new commercial center of the Far East. Soon joined by the Kadoorie family, also of Iraqui origin, they made it their joint policy to employ only Jewish managers and clerks, primarily of Baghdadi stock.

Ohel Leah, the community's magnificent synagogue, was built by Sir Jacob Sassoon in memory of his mother and opened in 1900. Surrounded by a wide expanse of grass and trees, the structure seems set into the surrounding sky. The interior, constructed in Sephardic style, has the *bimah* (pulpit) placed in the center of the congregation. Today, the synagogue serves a mixed Sephardi and Ashkenazi population. The latter, composed originally of Russian Jews from Shanghai, now has a large group of transient Western businessmen.

The synagogue is adjacent to the **Jewish Recreation Club** at 70 Robinson Road. Despite the shrinking number of Jews, the one hundred and fifty or so who still remain are determined to keep the community going.

Hungary

DOHÀNY STREET SYNAGOGUE, BUDAPEST

Located at #2 Dohàny Utca (street) in the heart of Budapest, this is the largest synagogue in Europe. Constructed in 1859 and seating more than 3000, its four balconies bespeak of a flourishing Hapsburg past. It is said (though the story may be apocryphal) that it was here, in May 1873, that Theodore Herzl celebrated his bar mitzvah.

Synagogue services are of the "Neolog" variety—somewhere between traditional Conservative and Reform. (On *Shabbat* morning, a non-Jewish organist plays the organ for men and women sitting separately!).

Hungarian Jewish victims of the Nazis lie buried in the synagogue grounds, and there is a memorial dedicated to a daughter of Hungary, the poet and martyr, Hannah Senesh.

Of all the Eastern European countries, Hungary's Jewish life is the most active. Budapest has several kosher restaurants, a seminary for the training of rabbis, a wonderful **Jewish museum** (attached to the Dohàny Street synagogue), a vibrant Orthodox community, and most surprisingly, an active, visible Hasidic community!

India

THE BENE ISRAEL COMMUNITY, BOMBAY

The origins of the Bene Israel (who prefer this appellation to the term Jews), the manner and date of their arrival to India, is shrouded in legend. The community claims that its ancestors, persecuted by Antiochus Ephiphanes, fled the Galilee in 175 B.C.E. En route to India their ship was wrecked. Seven men and seven women survivors, bereft of all personal and religious belongings, were cast ashore on the Konkan coast, twenty-six miles south of Bombay, where they remained. Isolated from Jewish contact, they spoke Marathi, the language of their Hindu neighbors, and adopted much of Hindu custom and dress. At the same time, they clung fiercely to the fundamentals of Jewish life, as they remembered them. They refused to work on the Sabbath, observed circumcision, dietary laws, some fasts and festivals (although not Hanukkah, because they left Israel before that event could be known to them), and recited the *Shema* at every religious gathering. They were apparently unaware of the existence of other Jews in India until the mid-eighteenth century, when they came into contact with Cochin Jewry.

Today, the Bene Israel comprise the overwhelming majority of India's Jewish community of eight thousand. The bulk of the Bene Israel lives not far from the Bombay Central Station. The area is a poor tenement district, its narrow streets bearing the sounds of music and the smell of spices and incense. The group is remarkably cohesive, and even those who move away, return to pray in the prayer halls and synagogues of the Jewish communal neighborhood. To the Western eyes, the Bene Israel are physically indistinguishable from their Indian neighbors, and while men wear European clothing, most women prefer the sari.

The Bene Israel prayer halls are in the Jewish Colony, Kurla, 7 and 28b Elphinston Road, Parel 12. In addition, there are several synagogues in the Kolaba district. The well-known Bene Israel lawyer, Shellim Samuel (Kolaba Court, 3rd floor, Kolaba Causeway), who is acknowledged the unofficial spokesman of the community, is happy to meet with visitors.

JEWTOWN, COCHIN

Over four hundred years ago, the rajah of Cochin, on the Malabar coast in southwestern India (now part of the State of Kerala), alloted to newly arrived Jewish immigrants land to build their own community. That enclave still exists today and is known by the name and mailing address: "Jewtown, Cochin."

Historically, the Jewish community of Cochin has been divided into three distinct groups: "White Jews," "Black Jews," and *meshuhrarim* or "Freedmen" (Emancipated). The influence of the Indian caste system is patent in the decision of these groups not to intermarry.

The "White Jews," known as "*Paradesi*" (or foreigners) are descendants of Spanish, Dutch, Iraqui, and German Jews. They observe the Sephardi rites with some Ashkenazi modifications. The "Black Jews" (formerly ninety percent of Cochin Jewry) maintain their separate synagogues and observe the rituals of Oriental Jews. They physically resemble the surrounding Indian population. The *meshuhrarim*, as their name suggests, are descendants of manumitted slaves. Until a sitdown protest in 1932 integrated the Paradesi Synagogue of the White Jews, the *meshuhrarim* were only permitted to sit on the floor, not in the pews. Moreover, although they were considered Jews, they were not called up to the Torah except on Simhat Torah.

The Jewtown section is cut through by Jewtown Road. Its commercial center still bears traces of stores owned by Jews, most of whom have emigrated to Israel. The Kadavumbhagam Synagogue, once a center of worship of Black Jews, is now shuttered and closed. At the north end of the road, separated only by a fence from the former rajah's palace, is the Paradesi Synagogue. In 1978 the synagogue celebrated its four hundred and tenth anniversary. Of special note is the synagogue's clock tower, the dials of which face in three different directions. The one facing the rajah's palace has numerals in English letters, the side facing the harbor is inscribed in native Malayalam, and the face fronting on Jewtown has Hebrew numerals.

The synagogue is famed for its floor of Chinese tiles in a willow pattern, its crystal chandeliers and hanging silver lamps, and its Torah's golden crown, the gift of a rajah. Superseding these by far is the community's most revered possession: two copper tablets engraved in the ancient Tamil language. The tablets declare that the Hindu ruler of Malabar grants privileges to one, Joseph Rabban "so long as the world and the moon exist." Although the date of its issuance is fiercely disputed—the Cochin tradition dates it to the fourth century C.E., scholars to approximately one thousand C.E.—the tablets are cherished as the earliest historical evidence pertaining to settlements of Jews on Indian soil.

Iran

THE MAHALLEH OF TEHERAN

The Jewish presence in Persia dates back over two thousand years. Exiled to the city of the Medes by the Assyrians but restored to freedom by Cyrus the Great, Jewish fortunes in Persia remained fairly stable through centuries of successive dynasties and religious changes. With the advent of the Safavid dynasty in the sixteenth century, however, and their introduction of the Shiite conception of ritual uncleanness, Persian Jewry underwent a change so profound as to radically affect the very character and condition of their existence.

The Shiites maintained that anything touched by an infidel defiled the true believer. Jews were forbidden to shop in the markets, where they might contaminate food, or handle coins with Koranic inscriptions or walk in the rain lest drops from their clothes fall and pollute a pious passerby. Systematically excluded from all public life, forced to build homes and synagogues of humble elevation, forbidden to ride a horse for fear their head be above a Shiite's, required to wear clothes clearly distinguishable from those of the believer, confined to the *mahalleh* (Jewish quarter), Jews fell into lives of bitter squalor and degradation. Not until 1925, with the advent to power of Shah Reza Pahlevi (father of the deposed Shah), were these conditions lifted and the Jews permitted to leave the ghetto.

Despite this option, many Jews continue to live in the *mahallehs* of Teheran, as they do in Isfahan and Shiraz). Familiarity, attachment, and economic necessity dictate this choice. The *mahallehs* are poor, their streets narrow and unpaved. Behind thick walls are homes and modest synagogues of mud-dried bricks. Often there are no outward signs identifying synagogues, but among the myriads of children playing in the streets, there are always two or three who will be happy to escort the tourist.

The *mahalleh* is the closest one can come to conjuring up life as it was lived in the Middle Ages. Most who live there are peddlers, petty merchants, artisans, and small shopkeepers. All of life seems to be conducted out-of-doors. The shoemaker repairs boots on the street; the barber trims his customer's hair in the open air. Every where small, windowless shops display their wares to the passersby. At the kosher butcher, the remains of slaughtered animals hang on hooks, their hooves neatly piled in a corner. Down the street, live chickens in old-fashioned coops await purchase. The *shochet* (ritual slaughterer) obliges his customers on the spot. A walk through the back alleyways of the *mahalleh* is an experience in the mysteries, smells, and sounds of hundreds of years of perseverance.

TOMBS OF MORDECAI AND ESTHER, HAMADAN

The city of Hamadan (the biblical Ecbatana), in western Iran, has been identified with one of the most momentous events in ancient Jewish history. According to the Book of Ezra, the decree of Cyrus the Great in 536 B.C.E allowing the Jews to rebuild the Temple in Jerusalem, was found in the royal archives of Hamadan. In the Middle Ages Hamadan's Jewish population was said to have numbered over thirty thousand souls. Today, only a handful remain.

According to tradition, the ancient mausoleum in the central part of town contains the tombs of Mordecai and Queen Esther. Despite the skepticism of modern day scholars, the Jews in Iran believe the spot to be the real resting place of the heroes of Purim. The tomb is considered a holy place by the Moslems as well, and both groups can be found there praying together.

Italy

ARCH OF TITUS, ROME

Standing across from the Roman Forum, the Arch of Titus has been a major Jewish tourist site for centuries. It was constructed by the Emperor Domitian to commemorate Rome's victory over the Jews and the destruction of the Temple in the year 70 C.E. The famous image of the procession of Jewish captives, their Temple vessels carried as spoils, their sacred *menorah* borne triumphantly aloft by the victors, has seared Jewish memory and consciousness for centuries.

Traditionally Jews would not walk under the Arch preferring, instead, to pay a fee to be allowed to go through a neighboring house. Thus they refused to accept the victory claimed by the Romans and their descendants over the Jewish people. Only with the liberation of Rome from the Nazis in 1945 did the members of the Jewish Brigade march triumphantly under the Arch, symbolizing the revitalization of the Jewish nation.

Also of interest:

A short walk from the Forum along the shores of the Tiber River in the San Angelo district, is the **old Jewish ghetto.** The ghetto houses a large class of small shopkeepers and peddlers, and older residents may still be heard speaking the characteristic Judeo-Italian dialect among themselves. The neighborhood has kosher butchers and restaurants and many of the buildings are splashed with proudly pro-Israel graffitti. The **Great Synagogue of Rome** built in 1900–04 is situated here as well. Its monumental architecture well befits what is probably the world's oldest continuous Jewish community in existence today.

GHETTO OF VENICE

In 1516, the Venetian authorities decreed that Jews must live in a special and separate quarter, and thus established Europe's first ghetto. Indeed, the very word itself, most probably derives from its original location, known locally as the *getto nuovo* (lit. "new foundry"). Today, at the entrance of the ghetto, one can still see the original stone inscription declaring the premise a Jewish area whose portals were to be closed by nightfall.

Five of Italy's most extraordinary synagogues, their very names revealing the diverse origins of the Venetian Jewish community, are to be found in the old ghetto. They are the Great German Synagogue, Grande Scuola Tedesca, built in 1529, which also contains the Jewish Museum; the Spanish Synagogue, Scuola Spagnola, built in 1555; two Italian synagogues, the Scuola Canton, built in 1533, and the Scuola Italiana, built in 1575; and the Levantine Synagogue, Scuola Levantina, built in 1538.

Not to be overlooked is the community's old-age home, Casa Israelitica di Riposo. Each resident has his/her own room, furnished with possessions from home. The residents are most gracious and willingly answer tourist's questions. Kosher meals are available in the dining room, but must be ordered in advance.

The ghetto can be reached from the Grand Canal by disembarking at the San Marcuola stop, walking away from the canal until Rio Terra S. Leonardo, where yellow street signs in Hebrew and Italian indicate the direction.

Japan

JEWISH COMMUNITY CENTER OF TOKYO

The six hundred members of the Japanese Jewish community are represented by the Jewish Community Center of Japan at 8–8 Hiroo, 3–chome, Shibuya-Ku, in Tokyo. The Beth David Synagogue, a kosher dairy restaurant, and various cultural and educational activities all operate out of the Center.

Of immense interest to the traveller are the stories of how these Jews came to Japan. The melange of Russian Jews from Manchuria, Polish refugees from Hitler, Oriental Sephardic Jewish traders, and even an occasional Japanese convert, make the visit extremely worthwhile.

The Center's phone numbers are 400–2559 and 400–6866.

Netherlands

THE PORTUGUESE SYNAGOGUE, AMSTERDAM

The first appreciable Jewish community in Amsterdam was composed of Spanish and Portuguese Marranos who settled there at the turn of the seventeenth century. The newcomers, although not formally recognized as citizens, enjoyed religious freedom and protection of their life and property.

The most visible sign of this acceptance and of the community's growth and prosperity, is the magnificent Portuguese Synagogue at Mr. Visserplein 3. Erected in 1675, it became a model for Sephardi synagogues built elsewhere (*cf.* entry on Bevis Marks Synagogue in London). The synagogue is still used today. The sawdust on the floor, the pewter candelabra, the generous space divided by Ionic columns, and the central *bimah* (pulpet) still stand as in Bernard

Picart's eighteenth-century engraving of the synagogue's dedication. One should be sure to attend Friday evening services. The synagogue, seen by candlelight, seems suffused with the glow of a happier era.

The long, close relationship between the Dutch and Jewish peoples makes several other sites in this city worth a visit.

Although the Jewish quarter that so fascinated Rembrandt, who lived there, no longer exists, his house still remains. It includes Rembrandt's painting of his contemporary and friend, Rabbi Manasseh ben Israel. (The latter is buried in the old Portuguese cemetery, Ouderkerk-on-the-Amstel, a few miles southeast of Amsterdam). One should also visit **the monument outside the Meijerplein synagogue** (the synagogue itself is in disuse) dedicated to the dockers who, in 1941, struck in protest against the Nazi deportation of Jews.

Anne Frank's house, Amsterdam

Located at 263 Prinsengracht, the **house of Anne Frank,** where she hid with her family and four others, is now part of a **museum and an International Youth Center.** One passes behind the hidden bookcase entrance and ascends a frighteningly steep staircase to see the tiny rooms in which she lived from July 1942 until August 1944. The photographs on the walls—now yellowed and fading—are there just as she left them. It is here that Anne Frank wrote her diary, here that this fourteen-year-old spirit, undeterred by the bestiality closing in on her, could yet "look up into the heavens [and] think it will all come right."

Netherlands Antilles

MIKVE ISRAEL-EMANUEL SYNAGOGUE, CURACAO

Mikve-Israel, founded in 1651, is the oldest synagogue in the Western Hemisphere. The present structure, with its famed sand floor, dates from 1730–32. In 1864 a Reform congregation, Emanu-el, was organized and the two merged in 1963. Mikve Israel-Emanuel, located on the corner of Columbusstraat and Kerkstraat, is a member of the World Union for Progressive Judaism (Reform).

The synagogue houses the Jewish Museum's collection of ceremonial pieces, documents and other exhibits relating to the Jews of Curacao. One should be sure to visit the Jewish cemetery which, established in 1656, is among the oldest in the Western Hemisphere.

Poland

AUSCHWITZ DEATH CAMP, OŚWIĘCIM

The major portions of the infamous Auschwitz Death Camp have been preserved as a State Museum by the Polish Government. The first camp, Auschwitz I, was used as a "model camp" for visits by the Red Cross. The blocks have been turned into museums. Displayed there are the awful piles of suitcases, children's clothing, human hair, shoes, eyeglasses. Block 27 houses the Jewish Pavillion. It contains a powerful record of Jewish life and death at the camp, but is often kept locked. One should be certain to ask the guide to have it opened.

The gas chambers and ovens of Auschwitz I are intact.

Located some two miles down the road from the first camp is the death factory of Auschwitz, Birkenau/Brzezinka. One can see the entire expanse of the camp from the top of the railroad tower. Where the train tracks end, monuments with markers in Hebrew, Yiddish, and English can be seen. Memorial prayers, the reciting of psalms, the mourner's *Kaddish,* and private prayers and meditations are especially appropriate.

JEWISH WARSAW

There are two Jewish Warsaws, the first of the bitter past, the second of the unpromising present. There is no future.

In the heart of the ghetto district, at the corner of Anielewiz and Zamenhof Streets, is located the great monument to the ghetto fighters, executed by the Jewish sculptor Rapaport. Located a few minutes away, across from #1 Mila Street, is a marker in Polish, Yiddish, and Hebrew, at the site of the final bunker of the famous ghetto revolt.

The accompanying plan of the wartime Warsaw Ghetto allows for a comparison of the streets of today with those of forty years ago.

The Jewish Historical Institute, 79 Swierozewskiego Street, on Dzherzhinsky Square, features displays and exhibits of the Holocaust. The building, erected on the site directly across from the Institute, stands on the place of the most famous synagogue of all pre-War Poland, the Tlomacki Street Shul. For an interesting conversation, one should ask a Polish Jew of that generation which great *hazanim* (cantors) he heard in the Tlomacki Shul.

The sole synagogue in Warsaw, the "Nozhik Shul," is located at 6 Krajowej Rady Narodowej (now the extension of Emilli Plater Street, also known as 6 Twarda Street). The few remaining Jews, as well as those at the Offices of the Jewish Community, greet visitors warmly.

One should plan to visit the Gensia Street Jewish cemetery. Among the notable men buried there are S. Ansky, author of *The Dybbuk* and Y. L. Peretz, the famous Yiddish author.

Spain

THE JUDERÍAS OF SEVILLE AND CORDOBA

Virtually no physical monuments remain of the Jewish presence in Spain, yet folk memory has preserved the reality of that presence. In almost every city in which Jews once lived there is a street called Calle de la Judería (Street of the Jews). In some, as in Segovia, a distinction is made between Calle de la Judería Vieja, where the professing Jews once lived, and Calle de la Judería Nueva, inhabited by *conversos* (converts) who, although baptized, were still not con-

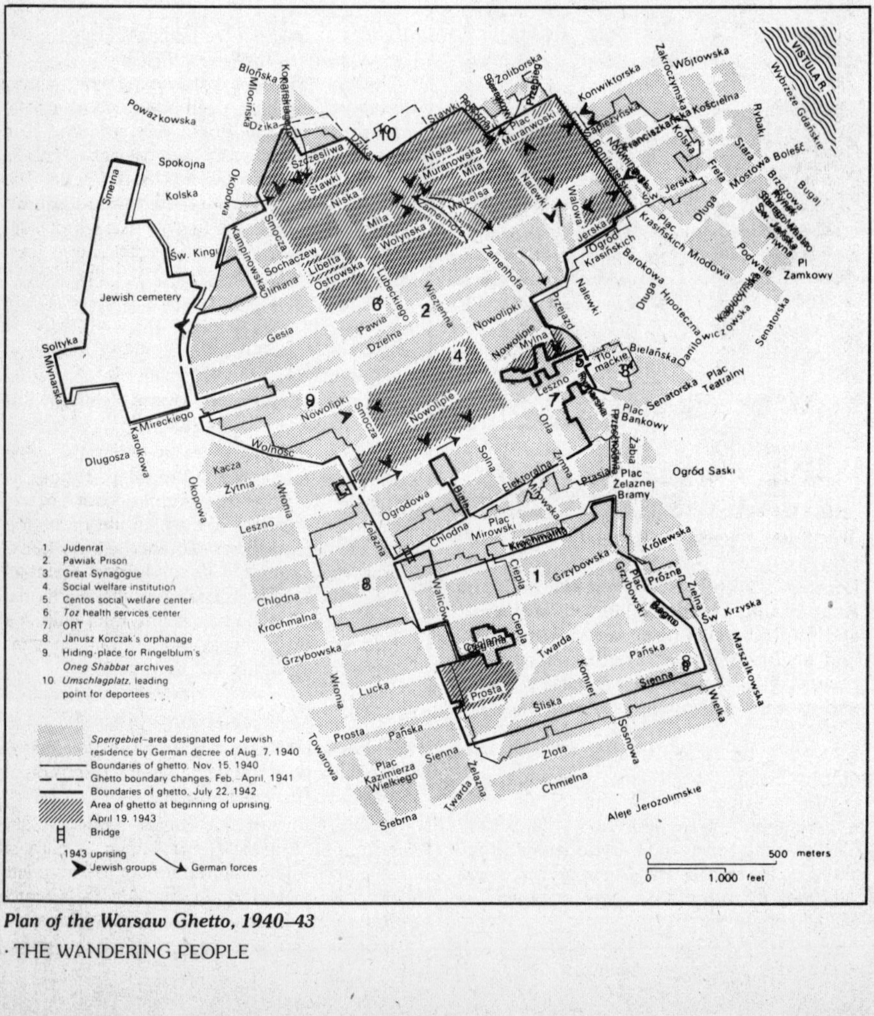

Plan of the Warsaw Ghetto, 1940–43

sidered true Christians by their neighbors. Sometimes, an entire section of a city bears the name La Judería (Jewish Quarter). The old Jewish quarters in Seville and Cordoba are especially evocative.

The former Jewish quarter in Seville is located in the Santa Cruz section of the city. The area is noted for the quiet elegance of its narrow streets; its aristocratic white-washed homes open onto flowered patios, and small squares are made more gracious by the fragrant smell of orange trees. Once there were twenty-three synagogues in the city; none exist today. One should walk in this area in the late evening and in the stillness of the night imagine the quarter as it was six hundred years ago.

Cordoba has preserved more tangible evidence of its Jewish community. Its most important monument, located at Judios 20, is the Rambam synagogue built in 1315. Delicate stucco tracery and quotations from the Psalms decorate the small square room. The adjacent room was probably used for teaching and the small assembly hall as a *Beth Din* (Court of Law). The nearby Plaza Maimonides has a statue erected in his honor. This most revered of scholar-philosophers was born in Cordoba in 1135 in a home (now a tenement) fronting on the square. Cordoba's Judería is smaller than Seville's, but its very compactness gives an immediacy to one's understanding of its former communal life. A walk through its narrow streets summons up images of a proud community in a resplendent age.

"EL TRANSITO" SYNAGOGUE, TOLEDO

Few monuments remain in Spain as symbolic of the efflorescence of Spanish Jewry as the synagogue of Don Samuel Halevi Abulafia. Built in 1357 with money he provided (Halevi was treasurer to King Peter the Cruel), the synagogue was renamed "El Transito" by the Jesuits who acquired it after the Expulsion. The synagogue's interior decoration is Moorish in idiom; the walls are adorned with carved foliage, alternating with verses from the Bible in exquisite Hebrew lettering. One should especially note the eastern wall, with its niche for the Torah. Inscriptions on either side record the erection of the building and bestow praises upon Peter the Great, Samuel Halevi and the God of Israel.

The rooms adjoining the synagogue are now part of the Museum of Sephardic Culture established by the Spanish government in 1971. Exhibits of tombstones, books, manuscripts, and ceremonial objects have all been donated by descendants of Spanish Jewry. The synagogue is located across the street from the house of El Greco. Few guide books remind the reader that the house originally belonged to Samuel Halevi.

Also of interest:
A five minute walk away is the **Church of Santa Maria La Blanca.** Originally Toledo's principal synagogue. It was founded by Joseph ibn Shushan in 1203 and confiscated by the Church authorities in 1411. Its modest facade belies a spacious interior, whose plan and structure, Moorish in execution, echoes the famous mosque of Cordova. Although the building is no longer used as a church, it remains a church property.

Tunisia

AL-GHARĪBA SYNAGOGUE, DJERBA

Situated off the coast of Tunisia, Djerba is an exquisite island of still unspoiled beaches. Local tradition has it that Jews arrived in the time of Solomon and founded the "Big Quarter" of the island. It is also said that in 70 C.E. a family of priests fleeing Jerusalem brought with them one of the Temple gates, now believed to be enclosed within the great synagogue of al-Gharība (the "extraordinary").

The Jewish population of Djerba consists primarily of *kohanim* (priests). No levites (priestly assistants) live there because it is believed they all perished when Ezra cursed them for not complying with his request to send Levites to Israel. So strong is this tradition, that a French consul surnamed Levy, who was working in Djerba, left the island, not trusting himself to remain there for more than the allotted year. He returned shortly thereafter, secure that having observed custom, he would safely complete his tour of duty.

Approximately one thousand Jews now live on the island. Most are small shop keepers and silversmiths. The community has its own printing press and is considered the "Vilna of North Africa." The day school is run entirely in Hebrew, and one can witness children learning mathematics in Hebrew and reading Agnon in the original.

The most impressive Jewish monument in Djerba is the magnificant al-Gharība synagogue located at the island's center. One enters, having removed one's shoes, to view the enormous interior, divided by rows of arches. The floor is covered with carpets of indeterminate age, and the walls, with tiles of an extraordinary blue. Amulets and prayers are everywhere displayed; the sense of sanctity is palpable. So revered is the synagogue, that each *Lag b'Omer* the entire Libyan

Jewish community came there on annual pilgrimage. Since Khaddafi's ascent to power, the adjoining dormitories, once filled to overflowing, lie empty and unused. Across the road from al-Gharîba is the cemetery. One may visit it during daylight hours.

Visitors should walk the streets of Houmt-Souk, the island's principal town, wearing a *Magen David* (Star of David) or carrying an El-Al bag. Jewish tourists are often invited for a meal of *couscous* or to share in *brikahs*, the island's specialty. (Every household is traditional and the food is, therefore, kosher.) Most people speak some Hebrew and, of course, French. The Tunisian government has been a "moderate" one in the Arab world, and Jewish life and tourism operate with little interference.

U.S.S.R.

BABI YAR, KIEV

Babi Yar, a ravine on the outskirts of Kiev, is the most important site of Soviet Jewish martyrdom. Beginning on the eve of Rosh Hashanah, 1941, until the end of Nazi rule, some 778 days later, over one hundred thousand men, women, and children were murdered. The overwhelming number of those killed were Jews.

***Monument at Babi Yar* (Richard Sobol)**

For many years the site remained abandoned and unrecognized. In 1963 the Soviet poet Yevgeni Yevtushenko challenged the authorities in his famous poem, the first line of which proclaimed, "No gravestone stands on Babi Yar." Recently the Soviet government has erected an impressive statue commemorating Babi Yar. Unforgiveably, it neglects to mention the rivers of Jewish blood spilled there.

Kiev Intourist usually includes Babi Yar on its standard itineraries. If not, any of the cab drivers should know the way.

ARCHIPOVA STREET, MOSCOW

Surely the most moving time to be at Moscow's Central Synagogue on Archipova Street is on the night of Simhat Torah. The occasion is unique in its fervent outpouring of emotion and its once-a-year abandon. Thousands of Jews dance in the street celebrating their past and proclaiming their hopes for the future. During the rest of the year, the synagogue, with its large librarylike columns in front, is the center for as much public Jewish activity as is tolerated in the Soviet capital.

Daily *minyanim* (prayer quorums) are held, attended mostly by the elderly, who can be seen approaching the synagogue with their *siddurim* (prayer books) cautiously secreted in newspapers or paper bags. Towards 11:00 A.M. on *Shabbat* morning, as well as later in the mid-afternoon, groups of Soviet Jewish activists and "refuseniks" gather to exchange information and to meet foreign tourists. While one must be careful not to endanger their fragile *modus vivendi*, contact is much sought after and warmly appreciated.

Archipova Street is a five minute walk from the Rossiya ("Russia") Hotel in Red Square, one block east of the "Ploshchad Nogina" Metro station.

THE COURTYARD OF THE GEORGIAN SYNAGOGUE, TBILISI

Various theories exist to account for the origin of the Jewish community in Georgia. One tradition asserts they are part of the ten lost tribes of Israel, citing as evidence the fact that there are no *kohanim* (priestly families) among Georgian Jews. Another maintains that Jews arrived as exiles from Judah after the expulsion by Nebuchadnezzar. In any event, Jewish settlement in Georgia is of long duration.

Today there are approximately twenty-eight thousand Jews in Georgia. About one-half live in Tbilisi, the Republic's capital. There are two synagogues in Tbilisi, a large one for Georgian Jews and a smaller one for the Ashkenazi population.

The Georgian Synagogue, located on 71 Leslidze Street, is full on weekdays, as well as on the Sabbath when hundreds of people, young and old, are in attendance. The synagogue's courtyard is the center for the most active and vocally Zionist Jewish community in Russia. At almost any hour, Jews can be found discussing the events of the day, plans for *aliyah* (emigration to Israel), or the latest government ordinances.

The community of Tbilisi is extremely traditional, within the limits permitted by the exigencies of Russian life. Holidays are celebrated, the *Shabbat* observed and kosher meat (mostly fowl) is available. The Tbilisi community maintains ties with all other communities in Georgia, offering help and financial resources when needed. No other Jewish community in the U.S.S.R. dares to maintain such close contact with its coreligionists.

The Jews of Tbilisi are extremely hospitable to travellers from abroad. They are eager to hear of Jewish life in Israel and America and unlike Jews in other parts of the U.S.S.R., often invite the tourist to their homes. It is important to meet a people whose fierce loyalty to their past and insistence on living a Jewish present has made them a model for Jews throughout the U.S.S.R.

Yugoslavia

SYNAGOGUE, ZUDIOSKA ULIÇA, DUBROVNIK

Dubrovnik, on the Dalmation coast of Yugoslavia, has had a Jewish community since the fourteenth century. The community expanded in the early sixteenth century, when Jews from Spain and Portugal sought refuge there on their way to various settlements in the Ottoman Empire. Under Venetian rule, a street was allocated to the Jews as a ghetto and its portals closed each evening. Located in a tiny courtway off the main street called the Stradoon (or Placa), Zudioska Uliça, or Street of the Jews, still bears its original name. The synagogue, built in 1532, is in a narrow ancient building on #3 of that street and occupies the second floor.

Dubrovnik's prewar community numbered two hundred fifty, but only seventeen Jews (fewer every year) still remain. The synagogue is administered by the elderly Tolentino brothers, who, together with their sister, act as anchor to the community. There are Friday evening services, especially during the summer, when tourists come by.

One should visit the synagogue (one of the oldest in Europe) and see the charming architecture of a small, typically Sephardic, layout. The Torahs, which the Tolentino brothers successfully hid from the Germans, were originally brought from Spain after the Expulsion. There is an old cemetery outside the city walls and the Tolentinos have the keys, as well as directions to the site.

Additional Sites in Brief

Argentina: Moisesville and Rivera. Founded by Baron Hirsch's Jewish Colonization Association in the nineteenth century, both these communities have considerable Jewish populations. The life of fifth-generation Jewish farmers is of special interest.

Austria: Vienna. Simon Wiesenthal, worldwide hunter of Nazi war criminals, directs the Documentation Center at Salztorgasse 6 (telephone: 93–98–05). It is worth the trip to talk with Wiesenthal about his life's work and about how others can be involved in assisting him.

Belgium: Antwerp. Antwerp houses the most ultra-Orthodox and Hasidic community of Europe. Beltz, Gur, Lubavitch, Satmar, Widznitz, and other Hasidic sects maintain active enclaves there. The flourishing Jewish life with its more than seven "Shomrei Shabbat" restaurants is unique.

Ethiopia: Abderaf. Abderaf, in the Humeira area northwest of Gondar, is an agricultural settlement of Falasha Jews. The entire community has been ravaged by civil war and unrest, and would welcome Jewish visitors and contact.

Rumania: Bucharest. Bucharest stands out among Eastern European and world Jewry for its strong centralized communal structure, headed by the only officially recognized chief rabbi of any Communist country, Dr. D.M. Rosen. The nearly two dozen synagogues (including the magnificent Choral Temple), the Talmud Torah, the Homes for the Aged, the Jewish newspaper, and the Jewish restaurant and soup kitchen, make it worthy of a special visit.

There are two necessary handbooks for the knowledgeable Jewish traveller. The *Traveller's Guide to Jewish Landmarks of Europe*, by Bernard Postal and Samuel Abramson (Fleet Press, New York, 1972) is invaluable. It gives historical background and details about Jewish communal life and sites for all of Europe. *The Jewish Travel Guide*, edited by Sidney Lightman (Jewish Chronicle, London, yearly editions) spans the entire world, listing synagogues, kosher restaurants, Jewish lodging facilities, and Jewish contacts throughout. For addresses and phone numbers, no better book exists. Also worthy of mention is Ida Cowen's *Jews in Remote Corners of the World* (Prentice Hall, Englewood Cliffs, N.J., 1971), a charming, personal and informative guide to the far-flung Jewish communities in, among other places, Tahiti, Fiji, Australia, the Far East, India, Afghanistan, Iran, and Turkey. It is especially useful for local customs and color.

—J.A.G., M.G.A., and J.D.P.

A WORLD LOST: EAST EUROPEAN JEWRY

YAHRZEITS (MEMORIAL DATES) OF 40 POLISH JEWISH COMMUNITIES

When one wants to observe the *yahrzeit* (anniversary of the death) of a person who was murdered without records during the Holocaust, there is often a problem of the proper date to observe. An exact date of death is usually not available. Jews who want to observe this Jewish tradition must, therefore, observe the date when the person who was killed was last known to be alive—usually the date on which the town where the Holocaust victim lived was liquidated. It is at least an appropriate date on which to remember the Holocaust victim in a special, personal way.

The following list of forty towns in Poland (as of the pre-September 1939 boundaries) and dates of liquidation by the Nazis is based on a book by Rabbi Israel Schepansky, *Holocaust Calendar of Polish Jewry*, which, in the words of the author, gives "the size of communities, dates and ways of liquidation of each community, and, where information is available, some other pertinent information."*

Similar information can be sought for locations outside Poland. Often the article about a town in the *Encyclopaedia Judaica* will offer this kind of data. In addition, Yad Vashem, Israel's official memorial to the Holocaust, gathers this type of information, as does the International Tracing Service (address: D-2548, Arolsen, West Germany), which will reply to inquiries regarding the *yahrzeit*.

1.	Baranowicze	12/17/42
2.	Bendin	8/1/43
3.	Bialystok	8/19–9/15/43
4.	Bilgoraj	11/2/42
5.	Boryslaw	2/1–5/30/43
6.	Busk	5/21/43
7.	Dobromil	7/29/42
8.	Dovinka	10/19/42
9.	Dubno	10/5/42
10.	Dubrava	7/26/43
11.	Frampol	11/2/42
12.	Jadowa	9/22/42
13.	Jaroslaw	9/28/39
14.	Jedlinsk	8/25/42
15.	Lemberg	6/21-27/43
16.	Lipsko	10/17/42
17.	Lomza	11/2/42
18.	Lublin	11/3/42
19.	Mielec	3/16/42
20.	Minsk	8/21/42
21.	Mir	8/15/42
22.	Myslowice	11/15/40
23.	Ostroleka	9/5/39
24.	Oszmiana	4/28/43
25.	Pinsk	10/29/42
26.	Plonsk	12/17/42
27.	Przemysl	9/3–10/30/43
28.	Radom	11/8/43
29.	Ropczyce	7/2/42
30.	Skalat	7/28/43
31.	Slonim	12/19/42
32.	Sokolow	9/22/42
33.	Sosnowica	8/16/43
34.	Stanislawow	2/22/43
35.	Tomaszow Lubelsk	2/25/42
36.	Wadowice	8/10/43
37.	Wlodawa	5/1/43
38.	Wolkowysk	11/2/42
39.	Wyszkow	9/11/39
40.	Wyszogrod	12/13/42

—A.K.

* Written in Hebrew, the *Calendar* is available for $3.50 from its author: Rabbi Israel Schepansky, 2220 Avenue L, Brooklyn N.Y. 11210.

JEWISH LOSSES DURING WORLD WAR II

	Jewish Population September 1939	Number of Jews Lost
Poland	3,250,000	2,850,000
U.S.S.R. (occupied area)	2,100,000	1,500,000
Rumania	850,000	425,000
Hungary	400,000	200,000
Czechoslovakia	315,000	240,000
France	300,000	90,000
Germany	193,000	110,000
Austria	90,000	45,000
Lithuania	150,000	130,000
Holland	150,000	105,000
Latvia	95,000	80,000
Belgium	90,000	40,000
Yugoslavia	75,000	55,000
Greece	75,000	60,000
Italy	57,000	15,000
Bulgaria	50,000	7,000
Denmark, Norway, Luxembourg, Estonia and Latvia	15,000	5,000
Total	8,255,000	5,957,000

Source: Jacob Lestchinsky, *Balance Sheet of Extermination* (New York: American Jewish Congress, 1946).

NAZI CONCENTRATION CAMPS AND EXTERMINATION CENTERS: A PARTIAL LIST

During the years 1933 to 1945, the Nazis built a system of camps to isolate "enemies of the regime." Most readers have heard or read about the major death camps, Auschwitz, Maidenek, and Treblinka, and a few others; but the systematic destruction of European Jewry was built upon a variety of Nazi camps. All camps were not "concentration camps," nor were all camps equipped with gas chambers and other means of mass murder.

The Nazis built transit camps, concentration camps, labor camps, and extermination centers. While the "official" functions of these categories of Nazi camps differed, the actual functions were similar or overlapped. In every kind of camp, the Jews were isolated from non-Jewish inmates.

Differences among camps were basically of degree. Extermination camps were designed to murder. Labor camps were designed to use Jews and other inmates as forced or slave labor. Of course Jews fell victim in every kind of camp, not just at death camps. It was only in the latter, however, where mass murders took place on a scale unknown before to humankind.

While many Jews may wish to protect themselves from the brutal memories of the Holocaust, the realities of that period are indelibly imbedded in Jewish historical consciousness.

The following is a list of twenty major camps—some concentration camps, others extermination centers. All contributed to the destruction of 6 million Jews and millions of non-Jews during the Holocaust.

Auschwitz

(south of Katowice, Poland; established April 27, 1940)

The largest concentration camp and extermination camp, Auschwitz was actually two camps (Auschwitz I and Auschwitz II, also known respectively as Auschwitz and Birkenau).

It is not known how many people were murdered at Auschwitz. No records exist of how many were gassed, tortured, shot, or

Yellow stars that Jews were required to wear during the Nazi period in (l. to r.) Holland, Germany, and France.

killed in some other way by the Nazis at this, the most infamous of the death camps; but it is estimated that between 1940 and 1945 nearly 4 million people died at this camp, and that among them 2½ million were Jews. Most of the killing took place at Auschwitz II (Birkenau).

When the camp was liberated on January 27, 1945, by the Russians, there were only 60,000 survivors.

Auschwitz entrance gate with sign reading "Work brings freedom."

Belzec

(eastern Poland; probably established March 1942)

Belzec was an extermination camp. It is not as familiar to most people as Auschwitz, but it was one of the most vicious Nazi camps. It was able to handle four or five transports of 1,000 people each, daily. Nearly 20,000 Jews from the Lublin, Poland, area alone were murdered at Belzec. Transports from east Galicia, Germany, Czechoslovakia, and Rumania also arrived at Belzec.

Of the 60,000 Jews who entered Belzec extermination camp, only one inmate survived the Holocaust.

Bergen-Belsen

(near Hanover, Germany; established July 1943)

Bergen-Belsen is a vivid example of a concentration camp, as opposed to an extermination camp. Although there was no technological system for mass murder, great numbers were murdered nonetheless. Originally Bergen-Belsen was used for Jews whom the Germans wished to exchange for Germans captured by the Allies; but its function changed when the Nazis no longer were willing to exchange Jews for prisoners.

Between July 1943 and the end of 1944 it is known that over 9,000 Jews from all over Europe were sent to Bergen-Belsen. Before the camp's liberation on April 15, 1945, over 30,000 Jews had died there. Conditions were so poor that 14,000 of the 60,000 inmates alive when the British liberated the camp died after liberation.

Anne Frank died in Bergen-Belsen.

Breendonck

(15 miles from Brussels, Belgium; established June 17, 1942)

Breendonck was an internment camp which housed 4,000 prisoners. It served as an assembly point for Jews who were later sent to Auschwitz.

It is the only Nazi camp which is still intact in Western Europe. It has been kept almost exactly as it looked during the war. The gallows and firing squad posts can be seen as they were, and the barbed wire fencing still stands as a symbol of events that took place there a generation ago.

Buchenwald

(near Weimar, Germany; established July 19, 1937)

Buchenwald was one of the most brutal camps in the Nazi system prior to the outbreak of World War II. Of the 238,380 prisoners sent to Buchenwald, 56,549 were killed or died there before April 11, 1945, when American troops liberated the camp. Most of the other prisoners were murdered elsewhere. On October 17, 1942, for example, all the Jews at Buchenwald were sent to Auschwitz with the exception of 200 building masons who stayed and were forced to continue the work assigned to them.

Besides outright murders, Buchenwald was one of the sites of pseudo-medical experiments committed by Nazis on the inmates. These experiments, as well as malnutrition and terribly unhygienic conditions, contributed to the death toll.

Chelmno

(37 miles from Lodz, Poland; established December 1941)

Chelmno was a Nazi extermination camp where 360,000 Jews were murdered, including 60,000 from Lodz and 11,000 Jews from Western Europe.

The Nazis used Chelmo as a "concentration camp" before it became an extermination center. Victims were often gassed in trucks, which then brought the bodies to nearby mass graves. Two crematoria were also constructed at Chelmno.

There were only two Jewish survivors of this death camp.

Dachau

(near Munich, Germany; established March 10, 1933)

Dachau was the first concentration camp established by the Nazis. From 1933 until April 29, 1945, when it was liberated by United States troops, Dachau functioned as a tool of Nazi evil.

Dachau exemplifies the large number of camps set up by the Nazis: there were actually about 150 branches of Concentration Camp Dachau in southern Germany. It is not known how many people passed through Dachau, but camp files registered 160,000 prisoners in the main site of Dachau and 90,000 more in the branches. It is known, however, that in the last days of the camp's activities, which were among the most active, there was no prisoner registration.

Dachau was the site of the first pseudomedical experiments by the Nazis.

Of the over 40,000 people killed at Dachau, between 80 and 90 percent were Jews.

Gen. Eisenhower at the liberation of Bergen-Belsen.

Drancy
(near Paris; established late 1940)

Drancy was the largest center for deportation of Jews in France. Deportations lasted from July 19, 1942, until August 17, 1944, when the camp was liberated. On the day of liberation, 1,500 inmates were found there.

Over 61,000 Jews were sent to death camps from Drancy.

Gurs
(near Pau, France; established 1941)

One of France's largest concentration camps, Gurs was notorious for its poor food supply and horrible sanitary conditions. Although it was not a death camp, eight hundred Jews died there in the winter of 1940.

It is known that in 1941, of the 15,000 internees at the camp, 7,200 were German Jews and 3,000 were Belgian Jews, most of whom were eventually sent to death camps.

Majdanek
(outside Lublin, Poland; established July 12, 1941)

It is estimated that 125,000 Jews were killed at Majdanek, either by gas or shooting. During 1942 to 1943, 130,000 Jews were sent to Majdanek from Slovakia, Bohemia, Moravia, Poland, Holland, and Greece. Many of these Jews were eventually sent to Auschwitz before July 24, 1944, when Majdanek was liberated.

On November 3, 1943, 18,000 Jews were machine-gunned to death in front of ditches that they had been forced to dig themselves.

Malines
(Belgium; established October 1941)

Malines, an internment camp, was used to gather Jews before they were sent to Eastern Europe and especially to Auschwitz. The first transport left Malines on August 4, 1942. Two days later, on August 6, the transport arrived at Auschwitz.

Between August 4, 1942, and July 1944 there were twenty-six transports, containing more than 25,000 Jews.

In September 1944 the camp was liberated by the Allies. A few hundred Jews remained as survivors.

Mauthausen
(12½ miles southeast of Linz, Austria; established 1938)

The commander of Mauthausen from February 1939 to May 1945, Franz Ziereis, is known to have given his son fifty Jews for target practice as a birthday present. In May 1945, when the U.S. troops liberated this camp, Ziereis was shot when he "tried to escape."

It is known that of the 335,000 prisoners who passed through this concentration camp (and its smaller satellite camps), 122,767 were murdered. Until 1944, Jews who arrived in Mauthausen never stayed alive for more than three days.

Today Mauthausen is a museum; much of the camp is intact. The museum is run by an international alliance of concentration camp survivors' committees. Samples of "death books" or registers of deaths kept by the Nazis at Mauthausen can be seen in the National Archives in Washington, D.C. Microfilm copies of these books are also at National Archives branches around the U.S.

Natzweiler-Struthof
(Alsace, France; established May 1941)

25,000 prisoners died in this concentration camp, which functioned until August 31, 1944. It provided the Reich University in Strasbourg with inmates to be used for pseudo-medical experiments.

In August 1943, 100 Jews were gassed after being sent from Auschwitz to supply the Reich University with specimens for their anthropological and skeleton collection.

Ravensbrueck
(Mecklenburg, Germany; constructed Spring 1939)

Ravensbrueck was a Nazi concentration camp for women only. Men were the high command of the camp, but the Nazi SS staff who actually ran the camp were mostly women, who became infamous because of their harsh cruelty.

Of the 132,000 women who passed through the camp. 92,000 perished. In 1942 all the Jewish women in the camp were sent to Auschwitz or Majdanek to make room for additional prisoners.

There was a gas chamber in the Camp. Many of the inmates were used for pseudo-medical experiments; survivors of these experiments often remained crippled for life.

Sachsenhausen-Oranienburg
(near Berlin;
established 1936)

After Kristallnacht on November 9–10, 1938, 10,000 Jews were sent to this Nazi concentration camp. The majority were later released when they were able to prove their ability to leave Germany. This was at the time when Nazi Germany was still allowing Jews to leave if they could obtain visas.

There was a Nazi counterfeiting operation at this camp, which forged British documents, false code books, and secret credentials; 140 Jewish inmates were forced to participate in this effort. In fact, in October 1942, when the Jewish inmates at this camp were sent to Auschwitz to be murdered, those who were part of the forging activities were allowed to stay.

It is known that of the 200,000 inmates at the camp, 100,000 perished.

Sobibor
(Lublin district, Poland;
established May 1942)

Sobibor was a Nazi extermination camp which collected Jews mostly from eastern Poland and occupied areas in the Soviet Union.

The victims arrived at the death camp by train. They were undressed and the women's hair cut off, after which the victims were put into gas chambers 500 at a time. The process of killing took fifteen minutes. The bodies were either buried in mass graves or burned. The victims' property was sorted and sent to Germany—along with the women's hair.

250,000 people were killed at Sobibor.

After the camp was shut down in October 1943, a grove of trees was planted on the site.

Stutthof
(22½ miles east of Danzig;
established September 2, 1939)

Of the approximately 52,000 Jews who passed through Stutthof, only 3,000 survived. Jews arrived at this camp as early as September 17, 1939. In 1943 several hundred Jews who were found in Bialystok after the ghetto uprising there were sent to Stutthof. In 1944 all Jewish prisoners were sent from Stutthof to Auschwitz. Between June and October of that year over 20,000 Jews, mostly women from Hungary and Lodz, Poland, had been sent to this camp. Most died from hunger or lack of water, or in the camp's gas chamber.

Theresienstadt
also known as Terezin
(40 miles from Prague;
established November-December 1941)

Theresienstadt was called a "model settlement" and used by the Nazis as a showcase when the International Red Cross visited. The inspectors saw a cafe, barber shop, bank, and other fake shops. From the outside it all looked fine.

***Crematorium at Theresienstadt* (Richard Sobol)**

33,539 Jews died at this "showcase," and 88,196 more were sent to other death camps. In September 1942 the camp was so crowded by the 53,000 inmates that there was a density of 1 person per 2.9 square yards.

Only 100 of the 15,000 child prisoners survived. The others were sent to Auschwitz to be killed.

The camp's most famous prisoner was Rabbi Leo Baeck, who survived along with 17,247 people who were in the camp when it was liberated by the Russians in May 1945.

Treblinka
(62 miles northeast of Warsaw;
established December 1941)

Treblinka was actually two camps. Treblinka I was used from December 1941 to July 1944; of 10,000 persons who went through Treblinka I, 7,000 were killed, 90 percent of those killed being Jews. The camp was led by S. S. Hauptsturmfuehrer von Eupen, a horseback riding enthusiast. His hobby gave him the opportunity to trample and kill prisoners.

After the war forty mass graves were uncovered in a nearby forest and over 6,500 bodies were found.

Treblinka II was established July 23, 1942, and was active until October 14, 1943. It was infamous for the efficient gas chambers and rail system which brought victims to the site. It is estimated that 731,500 people were killed at Treblinka II.

A model to scale of Treblinka, which was built by survivors of Treblinka II, is located at Kibbutz Lohamei ha-Getta'ot in Israel.

Westerbork
(northeast Holland;
established July 1942)

Westerbork was originally set up as a shelter for Jewish refugees fleeing from Germany who entered Dutch land illegally. However, on July 1, 1942, the Germans took command and it became the main transit camp for Dutch Jewry. Over 100,000 Jews arrested in the country were sent to Westerbork to work before being sent to the death camps.

—A.K.

SYNAGOGUES STILL IN SERVICE IN EASTERN EUROPE

A generation ago the Jewish population of Eastern Europe was nearly destroyed, yet today active Jewish communities exist in many of these countries. For example, it is estimated that there are approximately 80,000 Jews in Hungary, 34,700 in Rumania, and 6,000 in Poland.

The following is a guide to the synagogues regularly in use in the Eastern European countries, based on listings in *The Jewish Travel Guide* (published each year by the *Jewish Chronicle Publications*, 25 Furnival Street, Loncon EC4A 1JT, England), as well as on the list "Synagogues in the Soviet Union" (published by the National Conference on Soviet Jewry, 11 W. 42d St., New York, N.Y. 10036). These synagogues may or may not have a regular schedule of services. The *Jewish Travel Guide* and the *Traveler's Guide to Jewish Landmarks of Europe* by Bernard Postal and Samuel H. Abramson (New York, 1971) can lead interested people to Jewish institutions in Eastern Europe. The institutions themselves will be able to provide the most current information about functioning synagogues and their schedules.

These are not complete lists of synagogues in Eastern Europe. Such a complete list would probably be impossible to compile because (1) many small communities have small *shules* which are not registered with any agency; and (2) the number of synagogues which exist and function changes considerably from year to year. Many smaller communities and groups cannot meet on a regular basis due to lack of people. The following list of synagogues in Eastern Europe is the most complete one which exists, to our knowledge.

Czechoslovakia
Bratislava (Pressburg)
Synagogue, Heydukova 15
Brno
Synagogue, Skorepka 12
Galanta
(contact Rabbi I. Katz., tel. 2116)
Karlovy Vary (Karlsbad)
Synagogue, Vridelni 59
Kosice(Kaschau)
Synagogue, Puskinova ul. 3
Beth Hamidrash, Zvonarska ul. 5
Olomouc
Synagogue, Komenskeho 7
Ostrava
Synagogue, Zerotinova 8
Piestany
Synagogue, Hviezdoslavova 59
Plzen
Synagogue, Leninova ul.
Prague
Synagogue, Jerusalemska 7

Bulgaria
Sofia
Synagogue, 16 Exarch Lossif St.

East Germany
East Berlin
Synagogue, Rykestr. 53

Hungary
Budapest
Orthodox Central Synagogue, VII Kazincy utca 29
Dohany St. Synagogue, VII Dohany utca 4–6

In addition to these two main synagogues in Budapest, there are approximately 30 others throughout the city. The Central Board of Hungarian Jews, VII Sip utca 12, Budapest, maintains a list of these synagogues. Their phone number in Hungary is 226–478.

There are synagogues also in the following locations:

Debrecen

Gyor
Miskolc
Pecs
Sopron
Szeged

Local inquiry in these and other cities is necessary for more complete information.

Poland

Cracow
Remuh Synagogue, ul. Szeroka 40
Temple, ul. Miodowa 24

Lodz
Jewish Congregation, Zachodnia 78

Warsaw
Synagogue, ul. Krajowej Rady Narodowej 6

Synagogues are also known to be located in the following cities and towns:

Biala
Bielsko
Bytom
Czestochowa
Dzierzoniow
Gliwice
Katowice
Legnica
Lublin
Sosnowiec
Swidnica
Szczecin
Tarnow
Walbrzych
Wloclawek
Wroclaw
Zgorzelec

It is suggested that a traveller to these cities make an inquiry locally for complete details of location, times of services, and individual contacts.

Rumania

Arad
Neolog, str. Tribunal Dobra 10
Orthodox, str. Cozia 12

Bacau
Blank, str. N. Balcescu 55
Coreal Istilor, str. Stefan col mare 29
Kolier, str. Lernii 16
Veissman, str. Pielei 5

Botosani
Chohos, str. Zimbrului 7
Idis, str. Gh. Dimitrov 18
Mare, str. Muzicantilor 18
Mitteis, str. 7 Aprilie 27
Pescarilor, str. D. Voda 4
Scortari, Callea Nationala 177
Suliter Veig, str. D. Gherea 60
Terki, str. Marculescu 5

Brasov
Synagogue, str. Poarta Scheilor 27–29

Bucharest (principal synagogues)
Choral Temple, str. St. Vineri 13
Great Synagogue, str. Vasile Adamache 11
Joshua Tova, str. Nikos Beioania 9
Malbim, str. Bravilor 4
Sephardic-Spanish Synagogue, str. Banu Maracine 39

Cluj
Beth Hamidrash Ohel Moshe, str. David Francisc 16
Poale Tsedec, str. Baritiu 16
Sas Chevra, str. Croitorilor 13
Templul Deportatilor, str. Horea 21

Constanza
Synagogue, St. Sarmieagetuza 3
Templul Mare, str. C.A. Rosetti 2

Dorohoi
Beth Solomon, Piata Uniril 2
Clzmarilor, str. Spiru Haret 18
Cojocarilor, str. Trandafirilor
Cotiugarilor, str. Victoriei 12
Dobels, str. 30 Decembrie 45
Gaverona, str. Victoriei 1
Mare, Piata Uniril 4
Rabinson, str. Republicii 49
Rindarilor, Piata Unirii 6
Veisman, str. Vamil 7

Galati
Blintzer, str. Razboani 1
Meseriasolor, str. Dornei 11
Schenkman, str. Serei 13

Jassy
Kahane, str. Stefan cel mare 38
Katarski, str. Dimitrov 17
Mare, str. Sinagogilor 7

Oradea
Sas Hevra, str. Mihai Viteazu 4
Templul Mare Orthodox, str. Mihai Viteazu 4
Templul Neolog, str. Independedtei 22

Radauti
Chesed Sel Emeth, str. Toplita 2
Templul Mare, str. 1 Mai 1
Vijnitzer, str. Libertatii 49

Satu Mare
Mare Hatora, str. Decebal 4
Templul Coral, str. Decebai 4

Sibiu
Mare, str. Constitutiei 17

Sighet
Mare Sefarda, str. Viseului 10

Timisoara
Neologa, Splaiul Coloniel 2
Neologa, str. Marasestina 6

Tirgu Mures
Synagogue, str. Scolii 21

Vatra Dornei
Vijnitzer, str. 6 Martie 16
Templul Mare, str. 7 Noiembrie 54

USSR

Soviet spokesmen claim there are 92 synagogues in the country, but there have not been this many since the early 1960's. Below are 69 of all those that can be traced as surviving.

Akhaltsikh
(unknown)
Alma-ata
48 Tashkentskaya Ulltsa
Andizhan
7 Sovetskaya Ulltsa
Astrakhan
30 Babushkina Ulltsa
Baku
171 Pervomaiskaya Ulltsa
Bar (Vinnitskaya Oblast)
17 Marta Ulltsa

The Choral Synagogue, Leningrad (Richard Sobol)

Baranovichi (Brestskaya Oblast)
39 Svobodnaya Ulltsa
Batumi
6 Ninth March Ulltsa
Bendery
69 Kotovskogo Ulltsa
Berdichev
8 Sverdlov Ulltsa
Beregovo
17 Sverdlova Ulltsa
Birobidzhan
9 Chapayev Ulltsa
Bryansk
29 Uritsky Ulltsa
Bukhara
20 Tsentrainaya Ulltsa
Chernovtsy
53 Kobyiltsy Ulltsa
Chimkent
7 Svoboda Ulltsa
Daugavpils
(unknown)
Derbent
94 Tagi Zade Ulltsa
Dmepropetrovsk
Katsiubinsky Ulltsa
9 Kotsubinskogo Ulltsa
Dushanbe
26 Dekkanskaya Ulltsa
Gori
(unknown)
Irkutsk
17 Libknecht Ulltsa
Kaunas (formerly Kovno)
Krasnoarmelskaya Ulltsa
Kazan
Pravokabannaya Ulltsa
Kiev
29 Shchekovitskaya Ulltsa
Kishinev
8 Yakimovsky Pereulok
Klintsy
84 Lermontov Ulltsa
Kobi
(unknown)
Kokand
45 Marshala Govorov Ulltsa
Kuibyshev
84 Chapayev Ulltsa
Kulashi
(unknown)
Kutaisi
47 Shaumian Ulltsa
Leningrad
2 Lermontov Ulltsa
Makhachkala
103 Lenin Ulltsa
Malakhovka
20 Lermontov Ulltsa
Margelan
Ulltsa Shakirdzhanova 7, Tupik 4
Minsk
Tsianskaya Ulltsa
Moscow
3/5 Vyacheslavsky Pereulok
8 Arkipova Ulltsa
Nalchik
3 Osetinskaya Ulltsa
Namagan
Frunze Ulltsa
Novosibirsk
25 Rabochaya Ulltsa
Odessa
5 Lesnaya Ulltsa
Oni
(unknown)
Poti
(unknown)
Riga
8 Peltavas Ulltsa
Rostov
18 Gazetny Pereulok
Rybnitsa
Volkova Ulltsa
Samarkand
45 Khudzhumskaya Ulltsa
Slavuta
Shkoinaya Ulltsa
Sukhumi
48 Sovetskaya Ulltsa
Surami
Internatsionalnaya Ulltsa

Sverdlovsk
14 Kulbyshev Ulltsa
Tallin
9 Lasteaya Ulltsa
Tashkent
24 Sagban Ulltsa
9 Chekalova Ulltsa
15 Vtoraya Sapernaya
Tbilisi
47 Leselidze Ulltsa
65 Kozhevenny Pereulok
Tshakaya
(unknown)
Tskhinvali
(unknown)
Uzhgorod
47 Mukachevskaya Ulltsa
Vani
(unknown)
Vershad
Narodnaya Ulltsa
Vilnius (formerly Vilna)
39 Komyaunimo Ulltsa
Vinnitsa
59 Nekrasova Ulltsa
Zhitomir
78 Dobrovskaya Ulltsa

Where address is listed as unknown, the synagogues are reportedly in small villages not usually visited by tourists or may not be on the approved intourist list, and their addresses could not be verified.

Based on information gathered by the Soviet Jewry Research Bureau and *Insight Magazine* (London, England).

—A.K.

THE RETURN TO ZION

THE ZIONIST SPECTRUM FROM LEFT TO RIGHT

The Background

On a miserable January day in 1895 a high-ranking Jewish officer in the French army was publicly degraded at the Military Academy in Paris. Falsely convicted of betraying France to Germany, Captain Alfred Dreyfus was sentenced to life imprisonment at the notorious Devil's Island penal colony in French Guiana. In a chilling tone, a Viennese newspaper journalist reported the ceremony: " 'Alfred Dreyfus,' proclaimed the general in charge, 'you are unworthy to bear arms. In the name of the French Republic, I degrade you from your rank.' 'I declare and solemnly swear that you are degrading an innocent man,' cried Dreyfus, adding, '*Viva la France!*' As he was taken away, the crowd outside the Academy roared: '*A mort les juifs!*'—Death to the Jews!"

The event was traumatic and transforming for the young man reporting it, a Hungarian born, assimilated Jewish journalist and playwrite named Theodor Herzl. A little over a year later, a book appeared under his signature that was to have a major impact on the future course of Jewish history. It's title: *The Jewish State: An Attempt at a Modern Solution of the Jewish Question.* In it Herzl argued persuasively that the only way Jews would be able to escape from the dangers posed by modern anti-Semitism was to create their own state.

Herzl was not the first person to advocate such a solution to the so-called "Jewish

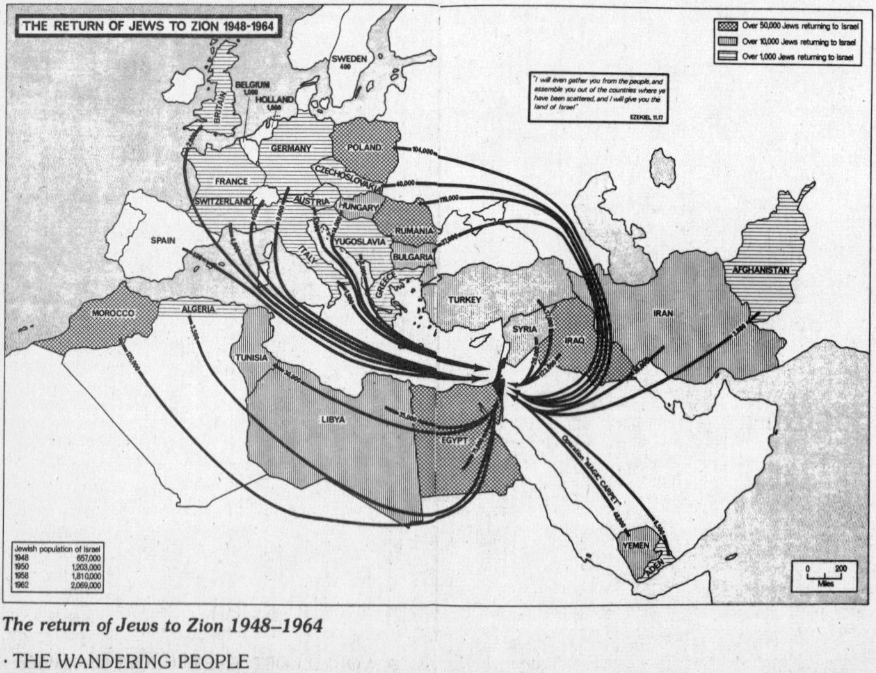

The return of Jews to Zion 1948–1964

Question." Several decades earlier two rabbis, Yehuda Alkalai and Zvi Hirsch Kalischer, had, quite separately, suggested a return of the Jews to their ancient homeland, the Land of Israel, as an effort towards self-redemption or forcing the messianic age. In 1862 a German-Jewish communist named Moses Hess had published a slim volume entitled

Dr. THEODORE HERZL GREETING Dr. MAX NORDAU.

ZIONIST CONGRESS AT BASLE.

Rome and Jerusalem, which called for the creation of a Jewish socialist commonwealth in Palestine as a statement of Jewish nationalism. Hess, the man responsible for the conversion of Friedrich Engels to communism, was apparently ahead of his time, for he was either ignored or viewed as an eccentric by most Jews when his book appeared. Yet, within it was an almost prophetic foreboding of the futility of assimilation and of the future destruction of European Jewry.

In 1881–82 Russian Jewry was rocked by pogroms in which hundreds of Jewish lives were taken, homes and places of work plundered, women raped and children beaten. These riots, which further exposed Jewish vulnerability, served as an impetus to the growth of Zionism. In the aftermath of these events many Jewish intellectuals, who had previously hoped to assimilate into their host cultures, began to despair of their futures. One of them, Leo Pinsker, shortly thereafter wrote a pamphlet entitled *Auto-Emancipation* arguing that the Jews would only be safe if they had political self-determination in a land of their own. For Pinsker, like Herzl, anti-Semitism was literally thrown into his face before he was shaken from his assimilationist complacency. Still other groups of pre-Herzlian Zionists, calling themselves *Hovevei Zion* ("Lovers of Zion"), began to emerge in Russia at this time. Although these groups propounded a political analysis similar to that of the other early Zionists, they were more practically oriented, actively promoting the emigration and settlement of Jews from Russia in Palestine.

It was Herzl's dynamism in the late 1890's that forged these disparate, emerging Zionist sentiments and groups into a movement. He accomplished this by convening the First Zionist Congress in Basle, Switzerland, in 1897 and there establishing the World Zionist Organization. He seems to have had an almost prophetic inkling of the future, for he wrote in his diaries that "In Basle, I created the Jewish State."

This state, however, was not to be created in the manner he prescribed. As head of the movement Herzl followed a policy of "grand diplomacy," pursuing potentates and prime ministers throughout the world, hoping to enlist their support by convincing them of his vision and, more importantly, that the creation of a Jewish state was in *their* interests. This endeavor ultimately failed. In fact, Herzl's strategy nearly ripped the Zionist movement asunder at one point when he was willing to accept a British offer for a Jewish homeland in *East Africa* ("The Uganda Plan")! His own movement rebuffed him, telling him that there was but one place where a Jewish state could be built, and that was in the Land of Israel.

Theodore Herzl

Herzl found himself opposed on many other issues as well, not the least of which was his often dictatorial methods for running the World Zionist Organization. Bitter disagreement came from those who were "practical Zionists" and believed that the movement had to focus its efforts on practical endeavors in Palestine, i.e. the physical building of a Jewish community. "Herzl has seen the

Sultan," complained a young chemist named Chaim Weizmann (later to become Israel's first president). "He had seen the Kaiser. He had seen the British Foreign Secretary. He was about to see this or that important man. And the practical effort was nothing." Weizmann, who ironically would be responsible for one of the most significant Zionist diplomatic victories—the 1917 Balfour Declaration in which Britain supported the creation of a Jewish home in Palestine—understood that the hard work had to be done on the land if a Jewish state was to be created. "Grand diplomacy," which even he would later have to pursue, would not succeed by itself.

Theordor Herzl died in 1904 at the young age of forty-four. By then, although a movement had been created, it was by no means a monolithic movement. Zionism, as a political phenomenon, was the product of and paralleled the many forces shaping European society in the late nineteenth and early twentieth centuries. It thus developed a pluralistic structure, with parties of varying shades of opinions operating in Palestine as well as in the Diaspora. This diversity, which still exists today, was rooted in the competing ideologies and nationalisms that swept Europe at the time of the birth of the Jewish national movement. In both its secular and religious manifestations Zionism reflected and coopted elements of these different *isms*. Just as the adherents of different world views confronted each other in Europe, so did their fellow spirits among the Zionists. There was, however, one major difference: Whereas German liberals, Russian monarchists, French socialists, and English conservatives had their own lands on which to wage their political, economic, or national struggles, the Jews had no such base and were a vulnerable minority everywhere.

All of the Zionist factions did agree that a new basis for Jewish life had to be created and that this would only be possible through the building of a Jewish state in Palestine. Unfortunately, however, this was often all that the varying Zionist factions could agree on. Their differences led to vigorous, often vicious, debates, to widely divergent trends within Zionism, and finally to the current spectrum of Israeli political parties.

"At the last municipal elections in Tel Aviv," wrote Arthur Koestler in *Thieves in the Night*, his novel about Palestine in the 1930's, "they had thirty-two competing party lists and each party was convinced of being the only true prophets of the kingdom of heaven." In a sense, each of the Zionist perspectives has presented itself as possessor of the keys to that kingdom. By looking at them in their broadest divisions, the varied aspects of this intensely ideological movement can be seen in greater relief.

The Left

LABOR/SOCIALIST ZIONISM:

In September 1906 a young man from the Polish village of Plonsk arrived in the port of Jaffa, on the coast of Palestine. David Gruen, a Socialist Zionist, would later describe his feelings in these words, "That night, my first night on Homeland soil, is engraved forever on my heart with its exultation of achievement. I lay awake—who could sleep through his first night in the Land? . . . I was in the Land of Israel, in a Jewish village there, and its name was Petah Tikvah—Gate of Hope!" Not long afterwards he changed his name to Ben-Gurion.

Ben-Gurion and his faction of the Zionist movement played by far the central role in creating the Jewish state. Their centrality was predicated on their outlook: They believed that the Jews in the Diaspora were in an essentially hopeless condition. In *galut* (exile) the Jews had been forced into marginal roles in the economies of their host countries, were vulnerable and visible because of their prevalence as middlemen in occupations, and were bound to face endemic anti-Semitism. Faced with this situation, the Jews had to recreate themselves, turn themselves into a working people in their own land. They would "rebuild the land and be rebuilt by it," as a popular song of the period proclaimed. The Jews in Europe, so they argued, led an "abnormal" economic existence because they did not participate in *all* of the vital industries and were totally divorced from the land. In the Land of Israel, however, these rebels believed that the Jews would at last become a "normal" nation, whose backbone would be the Jewish working class.

In their own country the Jews would not only build their own state but would also construct a model socialist society. The ultimate goal of these Socialist Zionist *halutzim* (pioneers) was a socialist Palestine in which the rich would not exploit the poor and all would live as equals in a democratic and egalitarian society.

From their perspective the way to accomplish these goals was through the day-to-day work of building a Jewish working class, a Jewish community, and a labor movement in Palestine. Rather than Herzl's "grand diplomacy," they came to advocate "revolutionary constructivism"—practical, concrete, creative endeavors to lay the foundations for the state-to-be. In addition, these socialist immigrants insisted on the principle of "Jewish labor," that is, that the Jews had to do their own physical work and not exploit the cheaper Arab labor. The kibbutz, probably the world's most successful example of agrarian socialism, and the *Histadrut*, one of the world's strongest trade union federations, are just two results and symbols of this effort.

Without this down-to-earth strategy it is possible that Israel might not have been created. Had a living Jewish community not been built, all of the (then) friendly U.N. resolutions and endorsements of the great powers would have meant little. "A homeland," wrote David Ben-Gurion in 1915, "is not given or got as a gift; it is not acquired by privilege or political contracts; it is not bought with gold or held by force. No, it is made with the sweat of the brow. It is the historic creation and collective enterprise of a people, the fruit of its labor, bodily, spiritual, and moral, over a span of generations."

It was the success of this vision that led the Labor/Socialist Zionist movement to become the major force in Jewish Palestine and in the Zionist movement by the 1930's. In 1948 it was Ben-Gurion (then head of *Mapai*, the Israel Workers party) who proclaimed the independence of the State of Israel, and until 1977 it was the *Mapai* party that dominated all Israeli governments.

In 1977, for the first time since the founding of the state, a right-wing coalition defeated the Labor alignment (composed of *Mapai's* successor—the Israeli Labor party—and the smaller *Mapam*-United Workers party) at the polls. This same right-wing coalition soon won supremacy in the World Zionist Organization as well, thus ending the more than fifty-year dominance of Labor in Zionist politics.

The Center

GENERAL ZIONISM:

General Zionism usually defined itself as a Zionism not committed to the varying ideologies of the right, the left, or the religious in the Zionist camp. Herzl was, no doubt, the first General Zionist, in that he focused primarily on the issue of creating a Jewish state and had a generally liberal, democratic outlook. Chaim Weizmann, despite his tactical differences with Herzl, would fit into this mold as well. The General Zionists, while maintaining a certain neutrality on many of the issues radically dividing left from right, represented primarily middle-class interests and elements within Zionism.

Though it may be generally categorized as occupying a centrist position, the General Zionists are by no means a unified body. There have been historical divisions within this group that have carried great political impact. Some General Zionists, for instance, were willing to work closely and reach compromises with the Labor Zionist movement when the latter had hegemony in Israeli politics. This faction of the General Zionists eventually formed Israel's Independent Liberal party. Other members, on the other hand, formed Israel's Liberal party and were part of the right-wing *Likud* coalition that defeated Labor in the 1977 elections. These Liberals always attacked the "socialism" of the Labor party and claimed that if the Liberal party gained power, they would institute a "free enterprise" system in Israel, which would supposedly solve the many woes of the Jewish state's economy. With the *Likud* victory they had the opportunity to prove their theories but instead seem to have created the conditions for the possible demise of their own party. After two and a half years in charge of Israel's Finance Ministry the Liberal's Simcha Ehrlich resigned, having brought the country to an annual inflation rate of one hundred percent.

THE RELIGIOUS ZIONISTS:

While Zionism was, above all, a secular and a political response to the crises confronting the Jews at the turn of the twentieth century, the idea of a return to Zion is an age-old Jewish religious/spiritual concept. According to the Bible the Jews first came to the Land of Israel at the command of and by the hand of God. It was there that the Davidic Kingdom flourished and it was there that the Holy Temple stood. The Temple symbolized the Jewish state and its destruction marked the beginning of exile. Daily, Jews pray for the return to Zion and the rebuilding of the Temple. Each Passover *seder* ends with the words "Next year in Jerusalem."

In spite of this constant yearning for spiritual return (or perhaps because of it), Jewish orthodoxy originally strongly opposed Zionism, viewing it as a blasphemous movement. From this perspective the Jews can only return to their ancient land when the Messiah comes to redeem them. Since the Messiah has not yet come, these efforts must be regarded as futile, at best, and possibly even evil, causing a delay in the real redemption.

Nevertheless, a religious Zionist movement, known as the *Mizrachi*, did emerge shortly after the turn of the century. The goal of the religious Zionists has been not only the creation of a Jewish state (for which they have worked alongside the secular Zionists) but a Jewish state governed by Jewish law as interpreted by the Orthodox or, in other words, a theocracy.

Although religious Zionism has always been

a minority movement within the Zionist world as a whole, its influence has substantially outweighed its numbers. In Israel the National Religious party (or *Mafdal*) usually garners enough seats in Israel's parliament to insure that it has a pivotal role to play in maintaining majority support in parliament for the prevailing government. In return for this critical political support, both Labor and *Likud* have had to make a variety of religious concessions to the *Mafdal*, usually resulting in a strengthening of the influence of orthodoxy in the country.

This process of bartering religious "favors" for political support actually predates the birth of Israel by almost half a century. In the early years of the Zionist movement Herzl's leadership was challenged by a faction led by Chaim Weizmann and a brilliant but haughty intellectual from Odessa named Ahad Ha'am (meaning "One of the People" in Hebrew—this was the pen name of Asher Ginsberg, a highly influential Zionist philosopher). Weizmann and Ahad Ha'am claimed that Herzl's strictly political efforts neglected, among other things, the dimension of cultural rejuvenation that was necessary for a Jewish national renaissance. However, as neither Ahad Ha'am nor Weizmann were Orthodox, the religious Zionists were suspicious of them and feared that these two might come to dominate Zionist cultural affairs to the neglect of religious concerns. Herzl, opposed to Ahad Ha'am and Weizmann for strictly political reasons, astutely promoted and courted the Orthodox as a critical counterforce.

The Right

REVISIONIST ZIONISM:

"In the beginning, God created politics." This remark has been attributed to Vladimir Jabotinsky, one of the most single-minded, brilliant, and fanatical leaders that the Zionist movement has produced. Few people have been neutral towards him—he is either loved (as in the case of his most famous pupil and advocate, Menachem Begin) or hated. A gifted orator and writer, Jabotinsky was one of the most vociferous foes of the Socialist Zionists and one of their most vocal critics after they became the dominant force in the Zionist movement.

Deriding the socialist pioneers who struggled to gain and work additional acres of land, Jabotinsky sought a political, diplomatic solution to the increasingly tense situation in Palestine, which pitted Jews and Arabs against each other and against the British. Wanting to return to Herzlian "grand diplomacy," he argued that Zionism needed to be "revised," hence his followers were called "Revisionists."

Jabotinsky and his followers were virulently opposed to the Jewish workers movement in Palestine, arguing that Zionism had to be "monistic," unidirectional, and free of "foreign" ideas such as socialism. This philosophy did not prevent them, however, from identifying with British capitalist ideals, despite these also being "foreign." Jabotinsky's view was that "in Zionism and in Palestine, you are but a puppet dangling on a wire and playing a prescribed part, and the hand that pulls the wire is called—The State-in-Building."

In the 1930's the Revisionists came more and more to resemble the extreme right in Europe. Ben-Gurion once called Jabotinsky "Vladimir Hitler." The Revisionist leader wrote in his *Ideology of Betar* (the Revisionist youth movement) that "it is the highest achievement of free men if they are capable of acting in unison with the absolute precision of a machine . . . When ten thousand Czech soldiers are stationed somewhere and at a sign from their commander they all make the same gesture at the very same moment, every onlooker feels that thus manifests itself the highest self-respect of a free and civilized nation." Indeed, Mussolini himself told the chief rabbi of Rome in 1935 that the only person who knew how to make Zionism succeed was "your fascist Jabotinsky." Furthermore, Jabotinsky and his followers were and continue to remain opposed to any compromise with Palestinian Arabs that might result in the yielding of any land that "historically" belonged to the Jews.

Ben-Gurion's response to Jabotinsky was that Zionism, like any national movement, could be good or bad depending on its social content, and that only through Jewish

Vladimir Jabotinsky

labor and concrete work, not through sloganeering, would a Jewish state be won. "The social content of Zionism," Ben-Gurion argued, "may be destructive, reactionary . . . and it may be positive, progressive, liberating, wrapped in freedom, social uplift, and moral beauty. A Zionism that is devoid of all social content, good or bad, such a Zionism is mere abstraction . . . All talk about 'pure' Zionism, in contradiction to 'mixed' Zionism is nothing but fraud and deception. The fascist Zionist who advocates 'blood, dirt, and slavery,' who wars on 'Marxists' and 'Leftists'; the middle-class Zionist who desires the rule of wealth and a class society; and the Socialist Zionist who strives for a free society of workers and for socialist Palestine—all mix their Zionism. The difference lies in the nature of the admixture."

After the creation of the State of Israel the Revisionists were organized into the *Herut* (Freedom) party and led by Menachem Begin (Jabotinsky having died in 1940). As part of the *Likud* (an electoral alliance bringing together *Herut*, the Liberals, and several other political factions), the Revisionists were finally victorious in the 1977 Israeli elections, leading to the premiership of Menachem Begin.

—M.C.

THE EARLY ZIONISTS: 10 PROFILES

Chaim Arlosoroff

Chaim (Victor) Arlosoroff (1899–1933)

A LIFE CUT SHORT

"My whole world went black and I fainted." Such was David Ben-Gurion's reaction to the murder of thirty-four-year-old Chaim Arlosoroff on the evening of June 16, 1933. Two men had approached Arlosoroff and his wife while they strolled on a Tel Aviv beach. In a matter of seconds the youthful political secretary of the Jewish Agency, who had just returned to Palestine from pressing Zionist business in Europe, was fatally shot. Arrested for the crime were Avraham Stavsky and Zvi Rosenblatt, both active in the extreme right wing of the Zionist movement, the "Revisionists." The latter group was violently opposed to the Socialist Zionist movement of which Arlosoroff was a leading light.

Arlosoroff was "a man of brilliant mind" according to Israel's first president, Chaim Weizmann. Born in the Ukraine in 1899, he was the grandson of a prominent rabbi. He moved with his parents to Germany after the 1905 Russian pogroms. The product of a strong traditional Jewish background, Chaim was also well educated at the University of Berlin in economics and sociology. While still in his teens he was influenced by the Labor Zionism of A. D. Gordon and the non-Marxist anarchist-socialism of Gustav Landauer (a German-Jewish revolutionary killed in the German revolution in 1919). He was also greatly inspired by Martin Buber, who was closely tied to the Palestinian *ha-Poel ha-Tzair* ("Young Worker") party, which stressed physical labor as a value and the need for Jews to return to Palestine as pioneers working the land and developing cooperative settlements. (The Kibbutz was partially a result of their efforts.)

By the time he was twenty Arlosoroff had written an important ideological statement of *ha-Poel ha-Tzair*: "Popular Socialism of the Jews." He argued that state building and society creating were intimately tied. For Arlosoroff there was a close spiritual tie between Judaism and socialism. In his view diaspora Jewry led an "abnormal" economic life because it was detached from the soil and over-represented in "middle-man" occupations. To be "normalized" they would have to return to their own land and become a "productive nation." He looked forward to a Socialist Jewish homeland in which a "new worker" would live in a society free of exploitation.

Shortly after arriving in Palestine in 1921 young Chaim found himself with gun in hand defending a Jewish settlement against Arab rioters. Nonetheless Jewish-Arab "mutual understanding" became a fundamental concern for him and he warned against "ostrich-like" attitudes towards Palestinian nationalism among the Zionists. About a decade later Arlosoroff, despairing that reactionaries had taken over the Palestinian Arab leadership, once suggested in a private letter a violent seizure of power from the British (who then controlled Palestine) and the formation of a "revolutionary" Zionist government.

Arlosoroff settled permanently in Palestine in 1924 but spent much of his time working and travelling for the Zionist movement. He played a crucial role in the formation of *Mapai* (the Israel Workers party, a forerunner of today's Israeli Labor party). He was thirty-two when he was elected to head the Jewish Agency's political department and thus became in essence Zionism's foreign minister. After his death his place was taken by Moshe Shertok, who later changed his name to Sharett and became Israel's first foreign minister and second prime minister.

A MURDER UNSOLVED

Arlosoroff's assassination led to an explosive trial. Palestine became a hothouse. The right wingers were viciously attacking the Labor Zionists and Arlosoroff was frequently the target of their nastiest epithets, as he was a very articulate foe of the Revisionist leader Vladimir Jabotinsky. Four decades later Golda Meir wrote that "Arlosoroff represented moderation, caution, a balanced approach to world problems and, of course, to our own, and his tragic death seemed the inevitable consequence of the kind of antisocialist right-wing militarism and violent chauvinism that was being advocated by the Revisionists."

The arrests of Rosenblatt and Stavsky were followed by that of the man who was accused of masterminding the killing: Abba Achimeir, a Revisionist leader who was known for his sympathies to Mussolini and was head of a group called "*Brit ha-Biryonim*" ("Union of Zealots"). It later came out that he wrote a brochure advocating terrorism and extolling the notion that the amount of blood spilled was the yardstick by which to judge revolutions. Arlosoroff's wife identified Stavsky and Rosenblatt, but the latter was eventually acquitted as was Achimeir. Stavsky, however, was found guilty and sentenced to hang. An ardent campaign was conducted by the Revisionists on his behalf. Claiming that Stavsky was condemned because he was a Revisionist, Jabotinsky called the case a "blood libel" and Rav Kook himself, chief Ashkenazi Rabbi of Palestine, spoke out for the convicted man, who was later freed because of lack of corroborative evidence.

Stavsky insisted that two Arabs killed the Jewish Agency leader while trying to molest his wife. One of the accused Arabs—an unsavory character in his own right who was already behind bars accused of another murder—confessed twice to the crime, withdrew the confessions and in the end accused Stavsky and Rosenblatt of bribing him to admit guilt for something he had not done. To this day the murder of Chaim Arlosoroff remains unresolved.

Ber Borochov (1881–1917)

"THE GENIUS OF POLTAVA"

For some reason the Czar decided that the Ukrainian town of Poltava was a good place to send political radicals for exile. Poltava was also an early center of Zionist activity and the home of a well organized, progressive Jewish community. It was in this atmosphere that Ber Borochov, the father of Marxist Zionism, grew up.

Borochov was an unusually talented youngster. By his late teens he was well versed in European thought and literature and also was fluent in numerous languages (his father was a noted Hebraist and Ber himself would later be a pioneer in the field of Yiddish philology). One Zionist writer who met him when he was about nineteen commented "he was educated far beyond his years. He had an excellent grounding in general philosophy, had advanced far in the higher mathematics and had studied with good results Marxian economics. He was, in addition, a man—or should I say boy—of unusual intellectual honesty." No wonder he was later called "the genius of Poltava."

In 1900 young "Borya" (as his family called him) moved to the city of Ekaterinoslav where he became active in the Russian Social Democratic party. He was soon expelled, no doubt in part because of his interest in nationalism and Zionism. He became an activist in the Zionist movement, having been taken under the wing of Menachem Mendel Ussishkin, the leading Russian Zionist, who then lived in Ekaterinoslav. Borochov returned to Poltava in 1902 and in 1904–1905 he fought arm in arm with Ussishkin for the defeat of "Territorialism." This was the view that a national solution to the Jewish problem did not have to take place in Palestine—the Jews could have their own land elsewhere.

Borochov's prominence, however, really began when he united the scattered Russian *Poalei Zion* ("Workers of Zion") groups into a united Socialist Zionist organization and gave that organization a unique ideological foundation.

BOROCHOVISM

"In the night of Purim 5666(1906), delegates from *Poalei Zion* groups from all the vast regions of Russia . . . assembled at Poltava in the Ukraine. At this conference all the existing little groups were fused into one party. It was a decisive step at a decisive moment . . . Borochov was its ideological center." So wrote one of the conferences participants, Borochov's childhood friend Yitzchak Shimshelevitz (who later moved to Palestine, changed his last name to Ben-Zvi and became the second president of Israel).

Borochov attempted to synthesize Zionism and Marxism. His "Our Platform" written for the *Poalei Zion*, became the best known presentation of his views. Marx had written that within all societies there are "relations of production," by which he essentially meant the system of property ownership. Further, one's place in the "relations of production" essentially defined one's class. To this analysis Borochov added the claim that there are also geographic, anthropological, and historical "conditions of production" that lead to the creation of groups and nations. But the Jews, no longer having their own land, had "abnormal" conditions of production. They thus lived among other nations and were always vulnerable. Borochov tried to show how this was particularly bad for the Jewish workers, whom he called a "chained Prometheus." In the end "The Jewish problem migrates with the Jews." Jews would only be normal when they had their own land and thus possess normal conditions of production. This accomplished, Jewish workers would engage in their own class struggle for socialism.

Borochov also tried to show that the Jews would come to Palestine out of historical necessity. This was his famous idea of a "stychic [elementary or spontaneous] process" of Jewish migration to their ancient land for economic, not emotional, reasons. Later Borochov discarded this notion.

In June 1906 Borochov was arrested by the Czarist police. After several months in prison his release was arranged and he left Russia for a ten-year exile. Until 1914 he was in Europe, where he helped found the World Union of *Poalei Zion* and continued to write on many topics. Shortly after World War I began he moved to New York where he spent three years doing party work, editing and writing, and helping in the struggle to create a democratic American Jewish Congress.

After the Czar was overthrown Borochov returned to Russia in the summer of 1917. However he found himself constantly at odds with the leaders of his own Russian *Poalei Zion*, in part because he had abandoned some of the more rigid aspects of "Borochovism." At one party meeting there were *Poalei Zionists* who spoke of "Saving Borochovism from Borochov." He was also very involved in the Ukrainian struggle for self-determination, His life was cut short at age thirty-six in December 1917, when he succumbed to pneumonia in Kiev.

Ahad Ha'am (1856–1927)

"ONE OF THE PEOPLE"

According to one memoirist, the Lubavitcher *Rebbe* once visited the Black Sea port of Odessa, where Ahad Ha'am lived, and, among other things, sent a message to his relative, Ahad Ha'am, requesting him to come for an audience. Ahad Ha'am turned him down saying that since they were equal in *yichus* (prominence of birth), equal in both Jewish and secular learning, and equal in number of followers, the *Rebbe* should come to him. The two men did not meet.

Ahad Ha'am—Asher Ginsberg

Asher Hirsch Ginsberg, best known by his pen name "Ahad Ha'am" ("One of the People"), was born in the province of Kiev to prosperous Hasidic parents. He moved to Odessa in 1884, having abandoned the Hasidic traditions and piety of his family. There he became active in the early Russian Zionist group, the *Hovevei Zion* ("Lovers of Zion") then led by Leo Pinsker. His first article, "The Wrong Way," was a critique of the *Hovevei Zion*'s attempts at creating settlements in Palestine. In a theme he would later develop further, he expressed his fears that Zionists would be so preoccupied in practical day-to-day endeavors and politics that they would neglect the crucial need for a spiritual and cultural Jewish national renaissance. Hence he became known as the father of "Spiritual Zionism" despite his own agnostic religious bent. "The heart of the people—that is the foundation on which the land will be regenerated," he argued.

A secret elite organization was formed called *Bnei Moshe* ("Sons of Moses") to promote the ideas of this haughty intellectual, ironically self-named "One of the People." In 1896 he became editor of *Ha-Shiloah*, an important Hebraist journal in which he published numerous essays in the next years.

SLAVERY IN FREEDOM

Ahad Ha'am's basic approach led him to be a severe critic both of Western European Jewry, as well as the Zionism of Herzl. As early as 1891 he chastised French Jewry who, in his view, debased their Jewishness while enjoying political emancipation and freedoms. To Ahad Ha'am this was "*spiritual slavery under the veil of outward freedom.*" He asked: "Do I envy these fellow Jews of mine their emancipation?—I answer, in all truth and sincerity: No! A thousand times No! The privileges are not worth the price! I may not be emancipated; but at least I have not sold my soul for emancipation. . . . I at least know 'why I remain a Jew'—or rather, I can find no meaning in such a question, any more than if I were asked why I remain my father's son."

He later chastised Herzl for viewing the world only through political eyes. The issue at stake, argued Ahad Ha'am in essays such as "The Jewish State and the Jewish Problem" (1897), was not only the future of Jews but the future of Judaism. It was highly unlikely, in his view, that most Jews would move to the Land of Israel even if a Jewish State was created. The goal, therefore, should be the establishment of a "fixed center for our national life in the land of its birth." This would be a spiritual center that would serve as an inspiration for the survival of Jewish culture throughout the world.

Shortly after the turn of the century Ahad Ha'am went to work for the Wissotzky tea firm and moved to London in 1907, where he continued his public activity. In 1922 he moved to Palestine, where he died five years later.

A.D. (Aharon David) Gordon (1856–1922)

COMRADE AND TEACHER

He was an improbable figure—a frail, forty-eight-year-old man, as middle class as he was middle aged, who made the seemingly preposterous decision to leave a fairly comfortable existence in the land of his birth to dedicate himself to a life of physical labor in a backwater, malaria-ridden province of the Ottoman Turkish Empire. Such a man was A.D. Gordon, who became a guru, practically a saint, for many in the young generation of Zionist pioneers toiling in Palestine just before the First World War. Shmuel Dayan, father of Moshe, called him "our great comrade and teacher."

Aharon David Gordon was born in 1856 to Orthodox, wealthy parents in Podolia, Russia. He grew up and spent most of his first fifty years on the estates (and in the employ) of the eminent Baron Gunzberg. In 1904, not long after Gunzberg sold the estate Gordon managed, he went off to Palestine (his family came later), where he created his own philosophy encapsulated in the words "Religion of Labor." Through physical labor in the Land of Israel, Gordon believed, both he and the Jewish people would be recreated.

"I commence all things anew," he wrote in ecstasy. "I begin at the beginning. The first thing that opens my heart is work. Not work for a livelihood, not work in obedience to a command, but work upon which a new light shines." The Jews were detached from nature and physical labor for too long. In his

A. D. Gordon

grand mystical vision Gordon saw his people returning to their ancient homeland, living in cooperative settlements, working the soil.

All forms of labor, Gordon stressed, were of equal worth. Thus he promoted the idea of the "dignity of labor." In his view "Work will heal us. Labor is a lofty human ideal, an ideal of the future. We are in need of fanatics in the cause of labor." These concepts were exactly suited to those young idealists who struggled to turn swamps into orchards in pre-World War I Palestine.

MAN AND NATURE

A new Jew, in tune with nature, would be born, as a long-exiled people rebuilt a land and was rebuilt by it. With this as his all-consuming passion, Gordon became a spiritual hero for the *ha-Poel ha-Tzair* ("Young Worker") Labor Zionist party. Gordon had a deep faith in communal living, and moved to Degania, famous today as the first kibbutz. For him a collective life fulfilled the individual by giving him or her an extended family. And a nation was the extension of such a family.

Gordon adamantly opposed the use of violence. Degania was the frequent victim of attacks and thievery by some of the local Arab population. Yet, when this older man took his turn on guard duty, he refused to carry a weapon to defend himself; he would only carry a whistle. Gordon urged "eternal vigilance" so that Jewish-Arab relations would be "just and worthy."

Most of his last years were spent on and off of Degania. By 1922 he was seriously ill and went to Safed, in the northern Galilee, for treatment. Suffering from cancer he was sent to Vienna for further care. Realizing the end was near, he returned to die at Degania. There he was buried near Lake Kinneret. The words "Man and Nature" were engraved on his tombstone.

Moses Hess (1812–1875)

THE COMMUNIST RABBI

"Everything we have tried is already in his book," wrote Theodor Herzl of Moses Hess's *Rome and Jerusalem* some forty years after that pioneering Zionist work was published. Martin Buber later commented that "However often one reads it, one is always surprised anew by the phenomenon of this man who goes along, as it were, with a divining-rod finding veins of gold."

Once called "the Communist Rabbi," Moses Hess was born in Bonn in 1812 and brought up by his Orthodox grandfather. As a young man he became a socialist and close friend of Karl Marx, whom he described as "the greatest—perhaps the only true philosopher actually alive." Hess has even been credited with the conversion of Friederich Engels, Marx's long-time collaborator, to communism. In the 1840's Hess shared Marx's antipathy to Judaism and advocated assimilation as the solution to the Jewish problem. He himself married a Christian prostitute.

While remaining a convinced socialist until the day he died, Hess eventually parted company with Marx. Their personalities were simply incompatible. Marx based his concepts on a careful and methodical analysis of political economy, while "the donkey Moses Hess," as Marx once called him, was an idealist with a propensity for devising grandiose visions for a new moral world order.

Hess played an active role when the European order was threatened by revolutionary events in 1848. With the defeat of the radicals, he was forced to flee Germany and in the following decade became intensely interested in anthropology and the national and racial differences among peoples. At the same time he was inspired by the struggle for unity and independence then taking place in Italy. In 1862 Hess surprised many of his friends by publishing *Rome and*

Moses Hess

Jerusalem, which advocated the creation of a Jewish socialist commonwealth in Palestine. The liberation of the "city on the Tiber" (Rome), he proclaimed, heralded the liberation of Jerusalem and the rebirth of the Jewish people.

NEW JERUSALEM

"After twenty years of estrangement," he began this Zionist classic, "I have returned to my people." Hess argued that the Jews would never achieve dignity and freedom as a dispersed minority in hostile lands. However, "that which Jews were not able to obtain as individuals the people can achieve as a nation."

Hess chastized assimilationists among the German Jews and some eighty years before the Holocaust spoke dire warnings as to their future. In contrast, he praised the spirit of Hasidism and claimed that Judaism was nationally, spiritually, and ethically socialist in its view of the world. "The Mosaic constitution," he wrote, "definitely guarantees equality for all the inhabitants of the land." Imbued with a deep sense of messianism, Hess suggested that the creation of a "New Jerusalem" in Palestine would be an important, exemplary step in the liberation of all humanity.

Few people took the book seriously. Western Jewry was not particularly interested in such radical ideas and Hess's socialist friends responded mostly with scorn or incredulity. In the last years of his life he maintained his interest in Jewish affairs and continued his activities on behalf of European socialism. Years after his death in 1875, workers inscribed "Father of German Social Democracy" on his tombstone.

"Since Spinoza," wrote Theodor Herzl, "Jewry has brought forth no greater spirit than the forgotten, faded, Moses Hess." After the birth of the Jewish State, Moses Hess's body was reintered in Israel in a cemetery by Lake Kinneret, next to a kibbutz.

Rabbi Abraham Isaac Kook (1865–1935)

ANTICIPATING THE MESSIAH

Religious Zionism probably never produced a man more powerful in character than Rabbi Abraham Isaac Kook, better known simply as "Rav Kook." A talmudic scholar, kabbalist, and religious nationalist, Kook sought dialogue with secular Zionists and fought the anti-Zionism that predominated traditional Judaism both in Palestine and Eastern Europe at the turn of the twentieth century.

Born in Greiva (now Griva), Latvia in 1865, Kook was destined to become the first Ashkenazi chief rabbi of modern Palestine. His upbringing was typical of many eastern European Orthodox Jews, and he attended the famous *Volozhin Yeshiva*. He served in rabbinical posts in several towns in Latvia before moving to Palestine in 1904. For an Orthodox rabbi to advocate a Jewish return to the Land of Israel, then under the Ottoman Turkish Empire, was a distinctly unpopular position, and Kook's position was especially unpopular because he saw such a return as presaging and hastening messianic redemption. For the Orthodox establishment of the time, this implied the heresy of trying to force God's hand.

In Palestine Kook became the rabbi of the port city of Jaffa, next to which the city of Tel Aviv would soon be built. Outside of his voluminous writings, he was involved in the Zionist effort in numerous practical ways. One of his important concerns was to build bridges to the young Socialist Zionist *halutzim* (pioneers) who were leading the constructive efforts to Palestinian Jewry and were generally hostile to orthodoxy and religion. Kook, a man fundamentally concerned with the clash between traditional Judaism and modern times and ideas, was both totally opposed to their secular nationalism and firmly convinced that these apparent heretics were acting within a divine plan by building the land.

***Rabbi Abraham Isaac Kook before* aliyah.**

Frequently the target of bitter criticism for his openness to these pioneers who threw away ritual, Kook supposedly responded to one of his detractors with the observation that when the Temple stood in Jerusalem no one, save the High Priest, dressed in vested garments on Yom Kippur, was permitted to enter Holy of Holies in the sanctuary. However, when the Temple was being built, any laborer, dressed in work clothes, could enter at any time. So, since Zionism presaged the Messianic Age, the pioneers should be viewed as part of the building process of the as yet uncompleted Temple. In Kook's view, "Jewish secular nationalism is a form of a self-delusion: the spirit of Israel is so closely tied to the spirit of God that a Jewish nationalist, no matter how secularist his intentions may be, must, despite himself, affirm the divine."

Having gone to Europe in 1914 to promote Zionism among the Orthodox, the outbreak of World War I forced him to remain there for several years. After returning he became Ashkenazi chief rabbi of Jerusalem and then of Palestine. He also founded a yeshiva in which the language of instruction was Hebrew (instead of the usual Yiddish) and the curriculum was much broader than the usual sole focus on Talmud.

KOOK'S ZIONISM, THE LAND, AND GUSH EMUNIM

In addition to his Messianic view of Zionism, Kook believed his religious nationalism contained both an "inner" element (the spiritual rebirth of the Jews) and an "outer" or more universal element (a rebuilt Jewry as a "Light unto the Nations"). Crucial to his Zionism, however, was the firm belief that the Land of Israel was as holy as the people of Israel. The land had a special, divine status in God's overall plan. "The Land of Israel," he wrote, "is not something apart from the soul of the Jewish people; it is no mere national possession . . . the Land of Israel is part of the very essence of our nationhood; it is bound organically to its very life and inner being." As such, "the hope for the redemption is the force that sustains Judaism in the Diaspora; the Judaism of the Land of Israel is the very redemption."

It is from these ideas that Kook's son, Rabbi Zvi Yehuda Kook, has forged an ideology for *Gush Emunim* ("Bloc of the Faithful"), the religious extremist group opposing Israeli withdrawal from any lands taken in the 1967 war that were Jewish according to the Bible. Whether or not the younger Kook correctly interprets his father's ideas within the larger framework of Rav Kook's worldview is widely disputed.

Bernard Lazare (1865–1903)

"ORTHODOX IN NOTHING"

In the fall of 1895 the newspaper owned by France's leading anti-Semite, Eduard Drumond, ran a contest. The question it posed to its readers was: What is the best way to eradicate the Jewish threat to France? The editor offered to place a knowledgeable Jew on the contest jury, provided that he or she was not a representative of what Jew-haters liked to call "Jewish Capitalism." Bernard Lazare, a young Jewish anarchist, volunteered and ended up in a duel with Drumond. Somehow neither combattant succeeded in killing his foe.

Not long afterwards Lazare, a Sephardic Jew born in Nîmes, France in 1865, became a Zionist. He had to go through his own purgatory first, however. He previously authored several tracts that were less than kind to Jews, to say the least. After his clash (one of many) with Drumond, Lazare became the leading advocate of Alfred Dreyfus, that unfortunate French Jewish officer whose fraudulent trial and conviction for treason led to a storm of anti-Semitism across France. It was through the efforts of Lazare that the great socialist Jean Jaures, the writer Emile Zola, and the future prime minister Georges Clemenceau, stood up for Dreyfus, who was eventually released.

In 1897 Theodor Herzl founded the World Zionist Organization (WZO) at the First World Zionist Congress in Basle, Switzerland. Lazare soon took an active role in the WZO but was a rather contrary figure. He was an anarchist and anarchists seek to abolish states, while the Zionists sought to create one. Once, referring to the WZO's "Basle Program," Chaim Weizmann (later Israel's first president) wrote in an exasperated letter that Bernard Lazare "does not recognize the Basle Program nor any other program."

While most radicals thought nationalism contradicted internationalism by definition, Lazare saw the nation as a bridge between the individual and the world at large. "I find nothing in nationalism," he wrote, "which would be contrary to socialist orthodoxy, and I, who am orthodox in nothing, do not hesitate for an instant in accepting nationalism alongside internationalism. . . . I believe that for internationalism to take root, it is necessary that human groups should previously have won their autonomy; it is necessary for them to be able to express themselves freely, it is necessary for them to be aware of who they are." In Lazare's view the Jewish response to anti-Semitism should be to recreate themselves as a nation.

JOB ON HIS DUNGHEAP

With such unorthodox views, it was perhaps inevitable that Lazare ended up in conflict not only with the leadership of French Jewry (whom he accused of cowering before anti-Semitism) but with Herzl as well. Lazare found Herzl's political style dictatorial and was furious when the head of the WZO negotiated with the Sultan while the Turks were persecuting the Armenians (whose cause Lazare also espoused). When Herzl began to stress the need to create a Zionist bank, the Zionist anarchist was angered to no end. He resigned from the WZO's Actions Committee (an important decision-making body) with these firey words, aimed at Herzl and his supporters: "You are bourgeois in thought, bourgeois in sentiment, bourgeois in ideas, bourgeois in social conception. . . . Before creating a people you institute a government . . . Like all governments you wish to disguise the truth . . . But I want to expose it so that all can see poor Job on his dungheap, scraping his ulcers." Job was, in this case, the suffering Jewish people.

Lazare continued to champion the Jewish cause despite his resignation. Wherever a Jewish community was in peril, he rushed to its aid. He once told his friend, the Catholic writer Charles Péguy, "I only feel at home when I arrive at a hotel." In his last years—he died in poverty in 1903 at the age of thirty-eight—he was particularly concerned with the fate of the Jews of Rumania, who were then subject to harsh persecutions.

Few people came to his funeral. Many Jews, Zionists among them, feared his proud, unflinching commitment to a new vision of his own people and the world. Péguy perhaps best captured Bernard Lazare's personality when he remarked that Rumanian Jewry remembered this passionate socialist-anarchist as "a flash of lightning, a rekindling of the truth which through all eternity will never be quenched." In Péguy's view, Lazare had "freedom in his skin."

Leo Pinsker (1821–1891)

"IT'S OUR COUNTRY"

In the midst of the pogrom, as Odessa's Jews were terrorized by violent, Jew-hating mobs, a drunken Russian woman pranced in one of the city's streets crying out, "It's our country!" That spring of 1881, shortly after Czar Alexander II was assasinated by populist radicals, Russian Jewry faced violence in some 160 cities. Leo Pinsker, an Odessa Jew, was so profoundly shaken by these events that it altered his entire view of life.

Born in 1821 in Tomaszōn, Russian Poland, he came to Odessa in his youth. It was in that rapidly developing Black Sea port that his father had helped found one of the earliest modern Jewish schools in the Czarist empire. Leo studied there and went on to obtain a law degree in 1844. However, it was virtually impossible for Russian Jews to practice law, so he turned to the study of medicine at the University of Moscow. He eventually returned to practice in Odessa, became an important intellectual figure there, and was an active advocate of the cultural assimilation of the Jews into Russian society.

In fact, Leo Pinsker became a leading member of the "Society for the Promotion of Enlightenment Among Jews." Russian, rather than Jewish, culture was promoted by this society and ardent Jewish particularism or separatism was abhorred by Pinsker, as well as by many of the intellectuals of the "Enlightenment" movement in Russian Jewry. And like many members of that intelligentsia, he found himself in 1881 faced with a challenge to his most cherished belief: that as the Czarist empire progressively emancipated itself from its own dark ages, a bright future might shine for its Jews.

As the pogromists rampaged in the streets that dream vanished from Pinsker. He concluded not only that Russian Jewry's future was dismal but that solely by taking their fate in their own hands would Jews be free of such terrors. Anti-Semitism was endemic and Jews could only rely on themselves to be emancipated; they again had to be a nation in their own right. The year after the pogroms, he published a brochure that was to have great impact: *Auto-Emancipation: An Appeal to his People by a Russian Jew.*

"WE MUST TAKE THE FIRST STEP. . ."

When Pinsker explained his new ideas to Vienna's prominent Rabbi Adolph Jellinek in 1882, he was told that anti-Semitism would "wither faster than you imagine since it has no roots in history." The Rabbi added, "We are at home here in Europe. . . . We are Germans, Frenchmen, Englishmen, Magyars, Italians and so on down to the marrow of our bones."

For Pinsker this was a delusion. He began *Auto-Emancipation* by arguing that "in the midst of the nations among whom the Jews reside, they form a distinctive element which cannot be assimilated, which cannot be readily digested by any nation." He analyzed the psychology of that incurable "aberration" known as anti-Semitism and claimed that having lost their homeland, non-Jews saw Jews as aliens, as walking ghosts of a people. "For the living," he said, "the Jew is a dead man; for the natives, an alien and a vagrant; for property holders, a begger; for the poor, an exploiter and a millionaire; for patriots, a man without a country; for all classes, a hated rival."

A political solution was required; the Jews had to emancipate themselves. "We must take the first step" he cried, urging the creation of a Jewish homeland. At first Pinsker felt that the homeland could be anywhere. Later, however, he was convinced by friends that the effort could only take place in the Land of Israel.

As a result of his pamphlet he became president of the early Russian Zionists, the *Hovevei Zion* ("Lovers of Zion"). Pinsker worked tirelessly on their behalf even though triumphs were few and rabbinical elements were constantly at odds with his secular approach. He seems to have despaired of the future of his ideas around the time of his death in 1891, six years before Theodor Herzl created the World Zionist Organization. Pinsker's remains were reburied in Jerusalem in 1934.

Henrietta Szold (1860–1945)

BALM FOR A BRUISED NATION

"Judaism does not canonize," writes historian Melvin I. Urofsky, "but if it did, nearly everyone would demand sainthood for Henrietta Szold." Born in 1860 in Baltimore to recently arrived Hungarian Jewish parents, Henrietta Szold led a life of self-sacrifice in the cause of Zionism and world Jewry.

She grew up in the town of her birth and became a teacher, as well as correspondent for the *New York Jewish Messenger* (signing her articles "Sulamith"). In the early 1880's she became concerned with the plight of Jewish refugees arriving in America to escape pogroms in Russia. Among the refugees were Zionists, intellectuals, and Hebraists who frequently came to meet at the home of Henrietta's father, a liberal and well-educated rabbi. She was a Zionist long before anyone had heard of Theodor Herzl or a World Zionist Organization. "I became converted to Zionism," she later said, "the very moment I realized that it supplied my bruised, torn and bloody nation, my distracted nation, with an ideal—an ideal that is balm to the self-inflicted wounds and the wounds inflicted by others."

In the 1890's Henrietta Szold worked for the newly formed Jewish Publication Society of America. Among other assignments, she helped translate and edit Heinrich Graetz's famous *History of the Jews*. She collaborated on the first *American Jewish Yearbook* and later became its editor. In 1902 she moved to New York City and became the first woman to take classes at the Jewish Theological Seminary. She studied Talmud and Hebrew, but in order to study them she had to promise not to try to obtain rabbinical ordination.

Szold left on a trip to Europe and Palestine in 1909 to recover from a physical breakdown, which had been the result of overwork and her unrequited love for the eminent scholar Louis Ginzberg. In Palestine she was particularly struck by the country's poor health conditions. Back in the U.S. in 1910, she became secretary of the young Federation of American Zionists.

HADASSAH

At the time of Purim, 1912, a chapter of the national "Daughters of Zion" organization was formed in New York, calling itself "Hadassah," the Hebrew name for Queen Esther. Not long afterwards the national organization took on the name Hadassah, and Henrietta Szold became its president. She sought a "definite project" for this women's Zionist organization, and she found it in 1916 when Hadassah became responsible for the American Zionist Medical Unit in Palestine. By 1930 Hadassah had created several hospitals, a nurses' training school, clinics, and numerous other health facilities throughout the country.

Henrietta Szold

Szold went to Palestine in 1920 and later served on the *Va'ad Leumi* (Jewish National Council) and on the executive of the World Zionist Organization. Jewish-Arab reconciliation became an important concern of hers and in the 1930's she became an advocate of a binational Palestine and opposed the Zionist rightists who wanted to respond to Arab terror with Jewish terror. She involved herself in groups advocating this perspective such as the League for Arab-Jewish Rapprochment and the *Ihud*, ("Union") which counted among its other leading members philosopher Martin Buber and the Hebrew University's first president, Judah Magnes.

When Henrietta Szold took charge of the Youth Aliya agency, she commented that although her new task "deals with children—it is not children's play." Her job was to take charge of the training and transfer to Palestine of Jewish youth trapped in the Nazi net in Europe. By the time of her death in 1945, this woman—who was herself never married and never a parent—became, in the words of American Zionist leader Louis Lipsky, "the beloved foster mother of thousands of orphaned children."

Menachem Mendel Ussishkin (1863–1941)

A MAN OF IRON

"Ussishkin was famous for his obstinancy," according to the memoirs of Zionist Shmarya Levin, "It is a curious circumstance that his house was at the corner of two streets, one called Iron Street, the other Obstinate Street . . . and his house was his symbol. 'I am not to be bargained with: I am iron on one side, and obstinancy on the other.' "

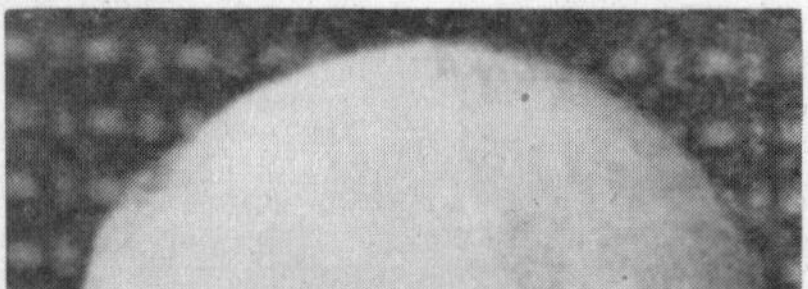

Menachem Ussishkin

The house was in the southern Russian city of Ekaterinoslav where Menachem Mendel Ussishkin, the central figure in the Russian Zionist movement at the turn of the century, then lived. Born near the town of Mogilev, an engineer by training, a man of strong likes and dislikes by disposition, Ussishkin's Zionist career began at the time of the 1881 Russian pogroms. After unsuccessfully trying to join a goup of pioneers bound for Palestine, he first became a leader of the early Russian Zionist group *Hovevei Zion* ("Lovers of Zion") and then of the World Zionist Organization which Theodor Herzl founded in 1897. Ussishkin, whom Levin called "an authentic leader by nature," had a keen eye for leadership qualities among the Russian Zionist youth and it is ironic that he enlisted as his lieutenants both Ber Borochov—later the leading ideologist of Marxist Zionism—and Vladimir Jabotinsky—later the leader of the Zionist right wing.

Ussishkin's stubbornness led him into numerous conflicts with Herzl. He strongly opposed the latter's stress on "grand diplomacy," that is, trying to create a Jewish state solely by obtaining the support of a European power. Ussishkin urged more concrete work in Palestine to build the Jewish community there. In a pamphlet entitled *Our Program* (1904) he wrote that "Long before a state is created the territory must actually belong in a political and economic sense to the people which desires to form a center in it." He suggested the formation of an organization of young Jewish men to do a national service for their people by going to work the soil of Palestine. He proposed that Jewish land in Palestine be nationally, not individually, owned and suggested also the formation of cooperative settlements there. Although a General Zionist and not a socialist, his ideas helped inspire radical Jewish youth going to Palestine to become pioneers.

THE "ZION ZIONIST"

When Herzl suggested to the World Zionist organization that a land other than Palestine might be a Jewish national home, Ussishkin proclaimed himself a "Zion Zionist" and fought the idea—successfully—with his full fury. In 1904 when Herzl (who died later that year) asked him, "Do you suppose that we shall get Palestine?" the Russian Zionist bellowed in reply, "Yes! And if you don't believe it, there is no place for you at the head of the Zionist movement!" The idea of a Zionism tied to anywhere but Palestine was buried at the 1905 World Zionist Congress, in no small measure due to Ussishkin's efforts.

His devotion to the Hebrew language and his singleminded personality led to a famous confrontation in 1918 when he addressed the Congress of Ukrainian Jews, which he chaired. Ussishkin insisted on making his speech in Hebrew and was met with cries of "Yiddish! Yiddish!" He stood on the platform for a full three hours and refused to be budged until finally permitted to speak in Hebrew. As it happens, languages were not his forte. American Zionist Louis Lipsky once wrote that "Ussishkin spoke Russian, Yiddish, and Hebrew, and a sort of German, but in none of them did he stick to syntax or to the use of words in their proper relations."

In 1919 Ussishkin was in the Zionist delegation to the Versailles peace talks and soon thereafter, believing that "any doctrine which is not accompanied by action must come to nothing," he moved to Palestine. There he continued his role in the World Zionist Organization and became chairman of the Jewish National Fund. In the late 1930's he was vociferously opposed to any plan to solve the Arab-Jewish conflict by partitioning Palestine. This man of iron died in 1941 and was buried in the city closest to his heart, Jerusalem.

—M.C.

DECLARATION OF INDEPENDENCE OF THE STATE OF ISRAEL

The Land of Israel was the birthplace of the Jewish people. Here their spiritual, religious and national identity was formed. Here they achieved independence and created a culture of national and universal significance. Here they wrote and gave the Bible to the world.

Exiled from the Land of Israel the Jewish people remained faithful to it in all the countries of their dispersion, never ceasing to pray and hope for their return and the restoration of their national freedom.

Impelled by this historic association, Jews strove throughout the centuries to go back to the land of their fathers and regain their statehood. In recent decades they returned in their masses. They reclaimed the wilderness, revived their language, built cities and villages, and established a vigorous and ever-growing community, with its own economic and cultural life. They sought peace, yet were prepared to defend themselves. They brought the blessings of progress to all inhabitants of the country and looked forward to sovereign independence.

In the year 1897 the First Zionist Congress, inspired by Theodor Herzl's vision of the Jewish State, proclaimed the right of the Jewish people to national revival in their own country.

This right was acknowledged by the Balfour Declaration of November 2, 1917, and reaffirmed by the Mandate of the League of Nations, which gave explicit international recognition to the historic connection of the Jewish people with Palestine and their right to reconstitute their National Home.

The recent holocaust, which engulfed millions of Jews in Europe, proved anew the need to solve the problem of the homelessness and lack of independence of the Jewish people by means of the re-establishment of the Jewish State, which would open the gates to all Jews and endow the Jewish people with equality of status among the family of nations.

Signatures affixed to the Declaration of Independence of the State of Israel

The survivors of the disastrous slaughter in Europe, and also Jews from other lands, have not desisted from their efforts to reach Eretz-Yisrael, in face of difficulties, obstacles and perils; and have not ceased to urge their right to a life of dignity, freedom and honest toil in their ancestral land.

In the second World War the Jewish people in Palestine made their full contribution to the struggle of the freedom-loving nations against the Nazi evil. The sacrifices of their soldiers and their war effort gained them the right to rank with the nations which founded the United Nations.

On November 29, 1947, the General Assembly of the United Nations adopted a Resolution requiring the establishment of a Jewish State in Palestine. The General Assembly called upon the inhabitants of the country to take all the necessary steps on their part to put the plan into effect. This recognition by the United Nations of the right of the Jewish people to establish their independent State is unassailable.

It is the natural right of the Jewish people to lead, as do all other nations, an independent existence in its sovereign State.

ACCORDINGLY WE, the members of the National Council representing the Jewish people in Palestine and the World Zionist Movement, are met together in solemn assembly today, the day of termination of the British Mandate for Palestine; and by virtue of the natural and historic right of the Jewish people and of the Resolution of the General Assembly of the United Nations.

WE HEREBY PROCLAIM the establishment of the Jewish State in Palestine, to be called Medinath Yisrael (The State of Israel).

WE HEREBY DECLARE that, as from the termination of the Mandate at midnight, the 14th–15th May, 1948, and pending the setting up of the duly elected bodies of the State in accordance with a Constitution, to be drawn up by the Constituent Assembly not later than the 1st October, 1948, the National Council shall act as the Provisional State Council, and that the National Administration shall constitute the Provisional Government of the Jewish State, which shall be known as Israel.

THE STATE OF ISRAEL will be open to the immigration of Jews from all countries of their dispersion; will promote the development of the country for the benefit of all its inhabitants; will be based on the principles of liberty, justice and peace as conceived by the Prophets of Israel; will uphold the full social and political equality of all its citizens, without distinction of religion, race, or sex; will guarantee freedom of religion, conscience, education and culture; will safeguard the Holy Places of all religions; and will loyally uphold the principles of the United Nations Charter.

THE STATE OF ISRAEL will be ready to co-operate with the organs and representatives of the United Nations in the implementation of the Resolution of the Assembly of November 29, 1947, and will take steps to bring about the Economic Union over the whole of Palestine.

We appeal to the United Nations to assist the Jewish people in the building of its State and to admit Israel into the family of nations.

In the midst of wanton aggression, we yet call upon the Arab inhabitants of the State of Israel to preserve the ways of peace and play their part in the development of the State, on the basis of full and equal citizenship and due representation in all its bodies and institutions—provisional and permanent.

We extend our hand in peace and neighbourliness to all the neighbouring states and their peoples, and invite them to co-operate with the independent Jewish nation for the common good of all. The State of Israel is prepared to make its contribution to the progress of the Middle East as a whole.

Our call goes out to the Jewish people all over the world to rally to our side in the task of immigration and development, and to stand by us in the great struggle for the fulfilment of the dream of generations for the redemption of Israel.

With trust in the Rock of Israel, we set our hand to this Declaration, at this Session of the Provisional State Council, on the soil of the Homeland, in the city of Tel-Aviv, on this Sabbath eve, the fifth of Iyar, 5708, the fourteenth of May, 1948.

PRESIDENTS AND PRIME MINISTERS OF ISRAEL

ISRAEL'S PRESIDENTS

The presidency of Israel is a ceremonial post, modelled after the figurehead role of the British monarchy. The president is elected by the Knesset for a five-year term; the term is designed to outlast, and thus transcend, the four-year life of the Knesset. Real political power, however, rests with the prime minister and the Cabinet.

"The symbolic institution of the presidency may be said to predate 1948. . . . The presidency of the World Zionist Organization had taken on a similar ceremonial character from the mid-1940's."

Chaim Weizmann (1874–1952)

President 1948–1952

VITAL STATISTICS:

Born in Motol, White Russia, to a middle-class, modernist family, and raised in nearby Pinsk. In 1892 he went to Germany to study chemistry and attended the Universities of Darmstadt in Berlin and Freiburg in Switzerland.

In 1906 he received a research appointment at Manchester University in England. There he married Vera Chatzman in 1906 (1882–1966), with whom he had conducted "a passionate five-year correspondence."

EARLY CAREER HIGHLIGHTS:

While still a student Weizmann became a follower of the "secular rabbi" Ahad Ha'am and was active in early Zionist groups in Switzerland. He missed the first Zionist Congress in 1897 because of his school schedule but attended the second in 1898 and every one thereafter until his death.

Weizmann made his first address to the Zionist Congress in 1908 and urged the synthesis of diplomacy and practical settlement work in Palestine, which came to be known as "Synthetic Zionism." Elected chairman of the movement's Standing Committee, he made his first visit to Palestine, which he found "depressing."

Weizmann's career changed irrevocably in 1916 when he discovered a laboratory process for synthesizing acetone, a solvent essential in munitions manufacture. Moving to London to work with the Defense Ministry, he used his many contacts to conduct a "private campaign" on behalf of Zionism. The result was the 1917 Balfour Declaration—official recognition by the British government.

The Balfour Declaration made Weizmann "the central figure in the public life of the Jewish people." In 1919 he led the Zionist delegation to the peace talks at Versailles and laid the cornerstone of the Hebrew University in Jerusalem—whose founding he had proposed in 1901.

Through the twenties Weizmann travelled widely as president of the World Zionist Organization (WZO) and was received by monarchs and prime ministers "as though he were already head of a state." Late in the decade, with tension growing between Jews, Arabs, and the mandatory administration in Palestine, his pro-British policies came under increasing attack within the Zionist movement. The Revisionists led the attack on Weizmann's brand of Zionism. In 1930 he resigned the presidency of the WZO in protest against new British mandatory restrictions on Jewish land purchase.

The 1935 Zionist Congress returned Weizmann to the presidency, the Revisionists having seceded from the WZO, and his prestige reached new heights with the 1937 Peel Commission Proposal to partition Palestine and create a Jewish state. However, the "infamous" British White Paper of May 1939 rescinded the partition plan and restricted Jewish immigration to Palestine on the very eve of the World War. Weizmann's faith in the British government was discredited. Even his own party, the General Zionists, split in 1940 into the anti-British General Zionists "A" (later the Liberal Party) and the smaller General Zionists "B," who continued to support him.

The war against Germany prevented a total break between the Zionists and Britain, and Weizmann remained as president. Decision making, however, passed entirely to the Jewish Agency Executive in Jerusalem, led by Ben-Gurion. By 1942 relations between Weizmann and Ben-Gurion had grown bitter, and in 1946 Weizmann, ailing and almost blind, stepped down as head of the WZO.

THE PRESIDENCY:

Weizmann was popularly proclaimed president of Israel at the moment of independence on May 14, 1948, almost an afterthought in his career. He was actually elected to the post in February 1949. Bitter over his exclusion from policy making, however, he restricted his activity to ceremonial appearances.

QUOTES BY HIM:

"England will . . . have mercy on us. . . . To Zion! Jews, to Zion let us go!" (1885)

"Palestine must be built without harming the legitimate interests of the Arabs. Not a hair on their head shall be touched. The Zionist Congress . . . has to learn the truth that Palestine is not Rhodesia." (1931)

QUOTES ABOUT HIM:

"Weizmann seemed like an eagle with folded wings . . . the King of the Poor . . . the King of the Jews that are still in Exile." (Rachel Yannait Ben Zvi)

"He was the first totally free Jew in the modern world." (Isaiah Berlin)

BALFOUR: "Are there many Jews like you?"
WEIZMANN: "Enough to pave the streets."

Yitzhak Ben Zvi (1884–1963)

President 1952–1963

VITAL STATISTICS:

Born Yitzhak Shimshelevitz in Poltava, Ukraine, Ben Zvi was raised in an intellectual, Zionist family environment. He received a traditional Jewish education and later attended a Russian gymnasium, enrolling briefly in the University of Kiev (1905).

After visiting Palestine in 1904 he returned to Russia and involved himself in socialist politics and Jewish self-defense. He was forced to flee in 1906, when a cache of arms was found in his father's house and his entire family was arrested (his father was sent to Siberia). He settled in Palestine in 1907.

Ben Zvi's celebrated affair with Rachel Yannait (1886–1979), a Poalei Zion leader in her own right, was immortalized in her memoir *Coming Home.* They were married in 1918 and had two sons.

He began using the name Ben Zvi (for his imprisoned father) after 1907.

EARLY CAREER HIGHLIGHTS:
Ben Zvi was one of the founders of *Poalei Zion,* along with his boyhood friend Ber Borochov. After his leadership role in the Jewish self-defense of 1905, he quickly established himself as one of the political leaders of the growing wave of socialist emigration, the *halutzim* (pioneers) of the Second Aliyah.

In 1909 he led in the establishment of Hashomer, the Jewish self-defense units in the Galilee, and later that same year, in the founding of the Hebrew Gymnasium of Jerusalem, in which he taught for several years.

In 1915, expelled by the Turks from Palestine along with the rest of the Hashomer leadership (another cache of arms was found in his house, ironically), Ben Zvi moved to New York. There he wrote a history in Yiddish of *Palestine, Past and Present* and was active in the founding of the American Jewish Congress.

In 1918 he crossed to Canada to enlist in Britain's Jewish Legion but was not posted to duty until after the war's end. Returning to Palestine in 1920, Ben Zvi was appointed to his first government post; he was named by the British high commissioner to the new Palestine Advisory Council. He angrily resigned a year later, protesting the weak British response to the Arab riots of 1921.

During the twenties he was elected to various government posts, including the Jerusalem City Council (which he also quit) and the National Council (Vaad Leumi) of the Jewish community. In 1931 he became chairman of the Council, and he represented Palestinian Jewry at the coronation of King George VI in 1937.

THE PRESIDENCY:
Ben Zvi was elected president in 1952, following Weizmann's death. The post was first offered to, and turned down by, Albert Einstein.

"Thanks to his simplicity and modesty, and his rapport with all elements of the people . . . the presidency became . . . a popular institution, close to the heart of every citizen in Israel" (Shazar). By sponsoring research, cultural events, and the arts, he made the office a focus and spotlight for the best in Israeli and Jewish life. He was an accessible figure, dedicating schools and appearing at festivals. At the same time he continued his scholarly pursuits and published volumes on ethnology and the history of Palestine.

He was reelected in 1957, following a brief controversy over the constitutionality of a second term. He died early in his third term.

QUOTES BY HIM:
"Our short-range goal is to achieve dominion in this country, economic and political. Our long-range goal—elimination of class oppression in our society, abolition of classes." (1907)

"The ingathering of the exiles is the central and loftiest idea of the State of Israel." (1952)

QUOTES ABOUT HIM:
"It's a pity that grandfather . . . didn't foresee the emergence of Palestinian socialism with such leaders at its head." (Marx's grandson, Jean Longuet)

Zalman Shazar (1889–1974)
President 1963–1973

VITAL STATISTICS:
Born Shneur Zalman Rubashov, in Mir, White Russia, to a devout Hasidic family (he was named for Shneur Zalman of Lyady, founder of Lubavitch Hasidism).

After a traditional education, leading to rabbinical ordination at sixteen, Rubashov broke with Orthodoxy and pursued history in various secular institutions, including the Academy of Jewish Studies in St. Petersburg and the Universities of Freiburg, Strasbourg, and Berlin (where he was interned as an enemy alien during World War I). He studied under, among others, historians Simon Dubnow and Friedrich Meinecke.

He married Rachel Katznelson, a labor activist, in 1912. They had one son. Zalman settled in Palestine in 1924 and took the name Shazar (acronym of his full name) in 1949.

EARLY CAREER HIGHLIGHTS:
Rubashov joined *Poalei Zion* in his teens, organizing the workers in his uncle's prayershawl factory, and taking an active role in Jewish self-defense during the 1905 pogroms. At Ben Zvi's invitation he moved to Vilna in 1907 to work for the party journal, *Der Anfang,* and was briefly arrested for subversion by Tsarist police.

The postwar years saw Rubashov's emergence as a leader of the anti-Bolshevik right wing of *Poalei Zion.* He was noted for his erudite, elegant writings in various Yiddish and Hebrew journals, and particularly for his synthesis of Zionism and socialism within traditional Jewish terms of reference.

Moving to Palestine in 1924, he was invited to serve as assistant editor of the new labor daily, *Davar,* under Berl Katznelson. After Katznelson's death in 1944 Rubashov succeeded him as editor-in-chief and as head of the labor publishing house Am Oved.

In 1947 he served in the Zionist delegation to the UN debate on partition. While in New York he visited the Lubavitcher rebbe, renewing his family connection to the Hasidic court. At Shazar's urging, the *rebbe* decided then to establish Kfar Habad, the Lubavitcher village outside Tel Aviv.

In 1949 he was named minister of education and culture in Ben-Gurion's first cabinet, and was responsible for enactment of the popular Compulsory Education Law of 1950.

THE PRESIDENCY:

During his two terms Shazar continued and furthered the tradition established by Ben Zvi, making the office a symbol and center of Jewish unity and Jewish culture. He sponsored studies and encouraged the arts—an invitation to his personal weekly study group was a status symbol among Jewish intellectuals all over the world.

His attachment to the Lubavitcher *rebbe,* whom he regularly visited on trips to the United States, aroused some accusations of "papism" among devoutly secularist circles, but was widely seen as a symbol of his attempts at rapprochement between religious and nonreligious Jews.

Shazar is credited by Gershom Scholem with the pioneering research into the Shabbatean heresy as precursor of Zionism. He published hundreds of monographs on history, mysticism, and socialism and was a highly regarded poet in both Yiddish and Hebrew.

QUOTES ABOUT HIM:

"His individual style is . . . an amalgam of lyricism, biblical influence, and their application to practical, contemporary problems." (Getzel Kressel)

". . . Then freedom will ring the land through,
In voices that tumble and frolic,
And among all the children in school
Will arise some little Bialik.
And he'll propose an amendment some day,
And he'll tell of that morning so clear
And of how he set out on his way
To the class of Reb Zalman Shazar."

(*The Compulsory Education Law,*
by Natan Alterman, 1950)

"Don't forget that you are president now, Zalman. You mustn't interfere." (Golda Meir)

Ephraim Katzir (1916—)

President 1973–1978

VITAL STATISTICS:

Born Ephraim Katchalski, in Kiev, Ukraine. His family moved to Palestine in 1925. He studied theoretical chemistry at the Hebrew University at Jerusalem, earning his Ph.D. in 1941.

He married Nina Gottlief in 1938. His brother Aharon Katzir (b. 1914), a world-renowned polymer chemist, was killed in the Lod airport massacre of 1972.

He took the name Katzir in 1973.

EARLY CAREER HIGHLIGHTS:

During the War of Independence, Katchalski participated in the establishment of the scientific research division of the Ministry of Defense. His scientific contributions to Israel's 1948 victory are still classified information.

In 1949 he became acting head of the Department of Biophysics at Weizmann Institute of Science in Rehovot, remaining as head of the department until 1966. Under his guidance the Weizmann Institute became a world leader in protein and enzyme research.

He served from 1966 to 1968 as chief scientist of the Defense Ministry, returning afterwards to Rehovot until his election as president.

THE PRESIDENCY:

Katzir was elected as Israel's youngest president and was the first candidate to run opposed. His nomination was widely seen as a move by Labor party leadership to block the popular candidacy of party maverick Yitzhak Navon. In the Knesset vote he defeated Ephraim Uhrbach, a leading talmudic scholar.

As president, Katzir often showed an unfortunate propensity for undiplomatic gaffes. His awkward attempts in his first months in office to project a more "Jewish" image offended both Jews and non-Jews. His most memorable slip was his unintended disclosure of Israel's still-secret nuclear capabilities, in a 1974 speech to a farmers' convention. This gave rise to a good deal of good-natured ribbing in the media, which remained a feature of his presidency.

In 1966 he became the first Israeli elected to the National Academy of Sciences (U.S.).

QUOTES BY HIM:

"There arose in Palestine and abroad men of action . . . but in the process we have largely ignored Jewish intellectuals and spiritual leaders." (1973)

"The ease and comfort that science has been able to bestow on mankind must be paid for . . . Israel has something to say in the matter of science and man." (1973)

Yitzhak Navon (1921—)

President 1978—

VITAL STATISTICS:

Born in Jerusalem, to an old-line Sephardic family that had been prominent in Jerusalem for centuries (the Navons settled in Turkey after leaving Spain in the expulsion of 1492). His maternal grandfather, a leading Moroccan rabbi, came to Palestine in 1900 when the prophet Elijah appeared to him in a dream.

Navon studied at the Hebrew University, receiving degrees in pedagogy, Hebrew literature, and Islamic culture.

In 1963 he married Ofira Erez. They have two children.

EARLY CAREER HIGHLIGHTS:

During his teens Navon briefly joined the right-wing Betar youth movement and its militia, the Irgun Zvai Leumi, for "social" reasons. He later enlisted in the Haganah, serving as director of its Arabic intelligence department between 1946 and 1949. After a two-year stint as a diplomat in Argentina, he became political secretary (bureau chief) to Israel's foreign minister, Sharett, in 1951.

Ben-Gurion "borrowed" Navon in 1952, in order to learn Spanish (he wanted to read *Don Quixote* in the original), and when the job was done, Navon stayed on as Ben-Gurion's aide until the latter's retirement in 1963.

Between 1963 and 1965, Navon served as deputy director-general of the Ministry of Education and Culture. He devoted his energies to eliminating illiteracy in Israel and was an active proponent of the rights of Israel's Arab minority.

In 1965 he left *Mapai,* along with Ben-Gurion, and was elected to the Knesset as a member of Rafi party. In the generally hawkish Rafi, Navon was the leading "dove." He became chairman of the Knesset's foreign affairs and defense committee in 1969.

THE PRESIDENCY:

Navon won the presidency in 1978, virtually unopposed, when Begin's ruling *Likud* party failed to present a candidate of sufficient stature. The election of a Labor party "dove" was seen as a personal defeat for Premier Begin. Navon moved quickly to develop a working relationship with Begin, however, and Begin's regard for the ceremonial importance of the presidency increased Navon's stature.

The presence of the popular young author and politician in the presidential mansion, with his beauty-queen wife and two small children, brought public affection for the post to new heights. As president, Navon has added new dimensions to his activities on behalf of Sephardic culture and Israeli Arab culture, appearing all over the country sponsoring pageants, contests, and projects of all kinds.

QUOTES ABOUT HIM:

"I'm glad you'll be president, but I suppose I'll lose a customer." (A Jerusalem sunflower-seed vendor, 1978)

QUOTES BY HIM:

"I hope the people won't mind a president who doesn't stay on the pedestal." (1978)

"I keep the [religious] laws between man and man. As for the laws between man and God, I'm sure I'll be forgiven when the time comes. It'll be all right, don't worry." (1973)

"Something has gone wrong . . . between the Jews and the Arabs of Israel." (1979)

ISRAEL'S PRIME MINISTERS

Israel is governed by a prime minister, but Israelis do not elect the individual directly. The electorate votes for a *party,* and the party with the most votes, rules—usually in coalition with other parties. The leader of the ruling party becomes the prime minister, who is accountable in theory to the president and in fact to the central committee of his party.

Party affiliation is a central fact of Israeli life. The parties are the oldest social institution in modern Israel: older than government, schools, rabbinate, kibbutzim, unions, and in many ways, creator of all these things. (For background on the parties and their ideologies, see "The Zionist Spectrum From Right to Left.")

David Ben-Gurion (1886–1973)

Prime Minister 1948–1953, 1955–1963

VITAL STATISTICS:

Born David Gruen (Green, Gryn) in Plonsk, White Russia, to a middle-class, Zionist, "Freethinking" family, Gruen emigrated to Palestine in 1906, working for several years as a laborer on the coast, later in the Galilee. Here he met Yitzhak Ben Zvi, his lifelong comrade and the second president of Israel.

He moved with Ben Zvi to Jerusalem in 1910 to enter politics and "journalism." In 1912 he followed Ben Zvi to Istanbul (then Constantinople) and back to Palestine in 1914, to New York in 1915, and then back to Palestine in a British uniform, as a member of the Jewish Legion.

In New York Ben-Gurion met and married (in 1917) Paula Munweiss (1892–1968), a Brooklyn nurse active in Poalei Zion. They had three children.

He adopted the pen name Ben-Gurion in 1910.

EARLY CAREER HIGHLIGHTS:

Ben-Gurion was fourteen when he founded his first Zionist movement, the Plonsk youth club, Ezra. Soon thereafter he joined *Poalei Zion.*

During his early political career, in Palestine and New York, Ben-Gurion was known for his opposition to the use of Yiddish and for his irascibility. He greeted the 1917 Bolshevik Revolution enthusiastically.

It was in 1921 that Ben-Gurion came into his own: he was elected secretary-general of the new Histradrut, the Federation of Hebrew Labor. Throughout the 1920's, he argued for "workers' unity" and oversaw the growth of the Histadrut's network of social institutions—the medical service (Kupat Holim), daily newspaper (*Davar*), sports league (Hapoel), school system, publishing house, marketing network, and more—and finally in 1930 the merger of the major Zionist labor parties into *Mapai,* which under his leadership dominated Palestinian politics. By 1929 Ben-Gurion was widely seen as leader of a "state within a state."

In 1933 he was elected to the Jewish Agency Executive, which had been established by the Zionist Organization under the terms of the League of Nations mandate, to represent Zionist interests in Palestine. As chairman of the Executive, Ben-Gurion became the virtual prime minister of the Palestinian Jewish community. Finally, with Weizmann's decline in the 1940's, he became the unchallenged leader of the Zionist movement, leading the 1937 acceptance of the Peel partition plan, the 1939 decision to cooperate with the British against Nazism "as if there were no White Paper," the 1942 Biltmore Program declaring statehood the immediate aim of Zionism (which cemented his ascendancy over Weizmann), the 1944 Operation Season against Begin's IZL (see "Begin"), and the illegal immigration of 1939–47.

Under Ben-Gurion's leadership the Histadrut and the Jewish Agency developed those "state-within-a-state" institutions that became in 1948 the infrastructure of independent Israel. The force of his personality and will commanded the loyalty of almost all Palestinian Jews. In his personal beliefs he combined socialism with a hard-boiled pragmatism and his own private blend of Oriental mysticism and Greek philosophy. Against Weizmann's moderate Zionism he championed the "activist" line against Britain and the Arabs.

He spent much of 1945–46 in Paris. There he met Ho Chi Minh; they discussed their common struggle against European imperialism, at opposite ends of Asia, and their common interest in socialism and Asian philosophy.

From 1947 he assumed personal command of the Haganah, and in 1948 he declared the State of Israel, with himself as prime minister and minister of defense of the provisional government.

PRIME MINISTER:

His control of the institutions of government was as stormy after statehood as it had been before.

The immediate priority after independence was to establish the state's sovereignty against invading Arab armies. Ben-Gurion personally ordered the declaration of Jerusalem as

Ben-Gurion addressing a workers meeting in Palestine.

Ben-Gurion inaugurating the road to Eilat, 1958.

capital (1948), the conquest of the Negev (1948), and the opening of Eilat (1949), the outlet to Asia.

His unification of the Israel Defense Forces under British-trained Haganah officers permanently alienated his party's left wing, which had advocated a Palmach-style "people's army," and led to open warfare with Begin's IZL.

His negotiations with West Germany over the issue of reparations in 1952–53 led to violent clashes with Begin, who called him a "hooligan." He, in turn, called Begin a "racist," "demagogue," and a "Hitler-type." During the time he was in office, Ben-Gurion was willing to join in a coalition with "all parties except Herut and the Communists."

In 1953, suddenly tired of politics, Ben-Gurion settled on Kibbutz Sde Boker in the Negev, hoping to serve as a model for the youth. He was assigned to sheep herding and pursued his study of yoga.

Ben-Gurion was recalled to Jerusalem in 1955 as defense minister, in the wake of the Lavon Affair (see "Sharett," below). His dissatisfaction with the findings of the investigatory committees on the matter became a passion that dominated the rest of his career. Throughout the decade he clashed with increasing frequency with Diaspora Jewish leadership, incensed over Diaspora Jewry's refusal to emigrate en masse to Israel.

He resigned as Premier in 1959, still seeking full airing of the Lavon Affair. Eshkol, as leader of the party's Gush machine (see below), engineered a compromise that returned Ben-Gurion to power; but he no longer commanded the party. Clashes became more frequent, and in 1963 he resigned for good, several weeks after the death of Ben Zvi.

In 1965 he led a small band of loyalists, including Yitzhak Navon (q.v.), Moshe Dayan, and Shimon Peres, out of *Mapai* to form Rafi—the Israel Workers' List. Rafi rejoined *Mapai* to form the Labor party in 1968, but Ben-Gurion stayed out and spent his declining years on the kibbutz, the "revered elder statesman" and "saint of Israeli statehood."

QUOTES BY HIM:

"The settlement of the land is the only true Zionism, all else being self-deception, empty verbiage and merely a pastime." (1965)

"What matters is not what the Gentiles say, but what the Jews do." (1935)

"We must assist the British in the war as if there were no White Paper, and we must resist the White Paper as if there were no war." (1939)

"Our future lies in Asia, even if our way of life is modelled on Europe . . . Israel stands at the gateway to Asia." (1965)

QUOTES ABOUT HIM:

"A combination of Danton and Beethoven in one." (A Swiss journalist)

"The most unapproachable man I ever knew." (Golda Meir)

Moshe Sharett (1884–1965)
Prime Minister 1954–1955

VITAL STATISTICS:
Born Moshe Shertok, in Kherson, Ukraine, he was brought to Palestine at age twelve by his parents, ardent members of the proto-Zionist Bilu. For two years they lived in an Arab village north of Jerusalem.

In 1908 the Shertoks moved to Jaffa and were among the pioneers of the new Jewish suburb of Ahuzat Bayit (Tel Aviv) in 1909. Moshe was enrolled in the first class of the new Gymnasium Herzliah.

In 1913 he went to Istanbul to study law and in 1915, enlisted in the Turkish army serving as a translator, and was later attached to the German army.

From 1920 to 1924 he studied at the London School of Economics. He married Zipporah Meirow in 1922. They had two children. He changed his name to Sharett in 1949.

EARLY CAREER HIGHLIGHTS:
Shertok first came in contact with the socialism of the *halutzim* while a student at the Gymnasium. He was influenced by the agrarian A.D. Gordon and helped found Legion ha-Tzofim (the Scouts Legion), the first Jewish youth group in Palestine.

In Istanbul, working with Ben-Gurion and Ben Zvi, he came under the influence of *Poalei Zion*, later joining it when in London. Berl Katznelson tapped him to be city editor of the new labor daily *Davar*—not, he would say, because he knew anything about journalism, as none of them did, but because he knew English. From 1931 to 1933 he edited an English-language edition of *Davar*, while serving as director-general of the Jewish Agency's Political Department—the "foreign ministry" of Palestinian Jewry.

In 1933 Shertok was named to head the department. He was responsible for day-to-day relations with the British mandatory government, and for Jewish community security in Palestine. It was largely his efforts that led to both the British decision to establish (1937) the paramilitary Jewish Settlement Police, which immediately became a front for Haganah activities, and the establishment of the British Army's Jewish Brigade in 1944.

Following statehood in 1948, Sharett became foreign minister and established Israel's diplomatic corps.

His political views were generally close to the moderate Weizmann position. He favored nonalignment in foreign policy but switched to a pro-America stance during the Korean conflict. "He remained convinced of eventual peace with the Arabs, and opposed reprisals except on a limited basis."

PRIME MINISTER:
In January 1954 Sharett succeeded Ben-Gurion as prime minister. Because he was functioning entirely in Ben-Gurion's shadow, this was an unhappy period for Sharett.

In 1954 a bungled Israeli bomb plot in Cairo, unauthorized by Sharett, led to public controversy over who had given the go-ahead. Defense Minister Pinchas Lavon denied responsibility but was forced to resign in 1955. The question of responsibility was never finally settled, though, and the "Lavon Affair" remained a central issue in Israeli politics through the 1970's.

In the elections of 1955 Ben-Gurion returned to the premiership. Sharett resigned the foreign ministry a short time later because of personal differences with Ben-Gurion.

The remainder of his career was devoted to Israel-Diaspora relations, and he was elected chairman of the Jewish Agency in 1960.

QUOTES BY HIM:
BEN-GURION: "Sharett and I have gone through 43 years of history together."
SHARETT: "Forty-four and a half, to be exact."

QUOTES ABOUT HIM:
"I have included Sharett in my cabinet not despite our differences but because of them." (Ben-Gurion, 1956)

"Our attitude toward BG is a mixture of faith and fear . . . Moshe we love and trust." (A *Mapai* official)

"I have learned how to say 'Your Excellency' in Hebrew. It's *'shma, Moshe'* [Listen, Moshe]." (A young British diplomat)

"He was the most beloved of Israel's leaders." (Zalman Shazar)

Levi Eshkol (1895–1969)
Prime Minister 1963–1969

VITAL STATISTICS:
Born Levi Shkolnik in Oratowo, Ukraine, to an affluent, deeply pious family, he was sent to secular gymnasium in Vilna at age sixteen in 1911. In 1914 he emigrated to Palestine in a Zeirei Zion settlement group.

During World War I he served as a private in the 39th Royal Fusiliers (the Jewish Legion), which he later described as a motley detachment of Palestinian pioneers and London Jewish tailors.

Following the war he joined Kvutzat Degania B, one of the first kibbutzim and remained connected to the kibbutz for the rest of his life.

His first marriage was unhappy, ending in divorce in 1927. In 1928 he married Elisheva Kaplan (1900–1959), a prominent labor activist. They had three daughters.

In 1964, while serving as prime minister, he married Miriam Zelikowitz (1927—).

He changed his name to Eshkol in 1949.

EARLY CAREER HIGHLIGHTS:

Shkolnik joined Zeirei Zion while still a student in Vilna. In Palestine he became a laborer but was quickly tapped as a union leader: he was called on to run the Workers' Communal Kitchen in Petah Tikva and was elected to the Agricultural Workers' Council. His capacity to drive himself and others was prodigious.

During the 1920's he taught himself accountancy and was regularly "borrowed" from the kibbutz by the party for sensitive missions: to Vienna to procure arms for the nascent Haganah underground; back to Vilna to organize Gordonian *aliyah* groups; to Germany in 1934 to negotiate the transfer of Jews and their funds to Palestine.

Through the 1930's and 1940's he held a succession of jobs and sat on numerous committees—usually simultaneously. He was in charge of finance and procurement for the clandestine Zionist army, Haganah; he conceived and organized Mekorot, the national water company. In 1944 he became general secretary of the Tel Aviv Labor Council, using the opportunity to reverse the fortunes of *Mapai* in that traditionally anti-Labor city and to organize the "Tel Aviv Gush"—the political "machine" that ran *Mapai* and the Labor party until 1974.

In the early years of statehood he held several posts in agriculture and land settlement, his first loves. During this period he directed the creation of the "development towns" for the absorption of the massive waves of immigrants flooding the country.

From 1952 he was minister of finance, which he called "prime minister for economic affairs" because of Ben-Gurion's near-total abdication from the internal arena. He remained in this post until becoming premier in 1963.

PRIME MINISTER:

His government marked, in a sense, the end of the honeymoon for the young Jewish republic. Ben-Gurion would have been a tough act to follow in any event; however, his noisy, controversial resignation left Eshkol, his handpicked successor, at the helm of a regime facing shaken public confidence.

Eshkol's style was private; though he was the leader, even boss, of the party, he had little public image as leader of the nation. The charismatic figures of the 1960's were others, often in the opposition: Dayan, Rabin, and of course Ben-Gurion himself.

It was Eshkol who engineered the shift to America-centered foreign and defense postures, in part through his personal relationship with President Lyndon Johnson, who admired his earthy sense of humor. Eshkol steered the country through the crises of recession, besiegement, and war (1967), through the disappointing diplomatic aftermath of 1967 and the war of attrition. When he died in office in 1969 he was still the unchallenged leader of a still unchallenged ruling party.

QUOTES BY HIM:

On development towns and state building: "We can patch the place up in a week and shove fifty families in. They can start growing stuff right away. We'll plan everything properly when they're in." (Early 1950's)

On Israel's military expertise, 1948:
ESHKOL: "Didn't you study chemistry in college?"
WEITZ: "It's three A.M. Don't you sleep?"
ESHKOL: "Nu, didn't you?"
WEITZ: "Well, yes."
ESHKOL: "Right. As of now you're in charge of chemical supplies for the rest of the war."

On government jobs:
"For over 10 years I was the most cursed and most discussed man in Israel, sitting in my office in the Treasury. Now I'm lucky enough to be just a plain Prime Minister, and yesterday's enemies have become today's best friends."

QUOTES ABOUT HIM:

"Here was a man who planned, worked, explained, and laughed a lot." (An anonymous friend)

Golda Meir (1898–1979)

Prime Minister 1969–1974

VITAL STATISTICS:

Born Goldie Mabovitch, in Kiev, Ukraine. Her father, a poor carpenter, brought the family in 1906 to Milwaukee, where she attended high school and Milwaukee Normal School (now the University of Wisconsin, Milwaukee) with a one-year interlude (1912) in which she ran away to Denver to live with her sister.

In Denver she met Morris Meyerson (1893–1951), and they were married in 1917. They moved to Palestine in 1921, at her insistence, and settled in Kibbutz Merhavya, leaving it (at his insistence) two years later. They had two children.

The Meyersons separated in 1928, Morris remaining in Jerusalem, while Golda moved to Tel Aviv, with the children, to pursue her political career. They were divorced in 1938. She changed her name to Meir in 1949.

EARLY CAREER HIGHLIGHTS:

Meir was introduced to *Poalei Zion* while living with her sister in Denver and joined in 1915, a year under the party's minimum age (eighteen).

On the kibbutz she developed her taste for political activism, and through the 1920's she struggled with her "conflict between my duty and my innermost desires." In 1928 she became secretary-general of the national Working Women's Council.

She spent 1932–34 in the U.S., as Histadrut representative to the Women's Labor Zionist organization, Pioneer Women. Among other achievements, she was instrumental in the opening of the first American Zionist summer camp, Habonim Camp Kvutza in Accord, New York, in 1932.

Prime Minister Golda Meir

Following her return to Palestine she was named to the Histadrut Executive Council, becoming head of its Political Department. In 1937 she represented Palestinian labor at the Socialist International, beginning a life-long involvement in that organization.

In 1946 she met secretly with King Abdullah of Transjordan, in an abortive attempt to keep him out of the impending war. A year later, she was appointed Israeli ambassador to Moscow. Her presence at High Holy day

Goldie Mabovitz Myerson—Golda Meir—playing the part of Liberty in a pageant of Jewish history, Milwaukee, 1919.

services in 1948 caused a massive demonstration by Soviet Jews.

She became foreign minister in 1956, after Sharett's resignation. As foreign minister she engineered the spread of Israeli missions and contacts through Africa, a cornerstone of Israeli foreign policy throughout the 1960's. She began the effort to recruit sabras (native-born Israelis) to the diplomatic ranks, to project the image of "the Israelis."

PRIME MINISTER:

Golda Meir opposed right-wing calls for annexation of the 1967 occupied territories, regarding them as a "bargaining chip for peace." At the same time she opposed left-wing calls to acknowledge national rights for the Palestinian Arabs, whom she did not view as a nation.

She was often called a "tough politician" and "gut-fighter," who brooked no opposition in her party, and often took criticism personally. Yet the very force of her personality made her a symbol of party and national unity.

Her personal ties with the leaders of the Socialist International, particularly Harold Wilson and Willy Brandt, were key in maintaining Western European support for Israel.

The 1973 war was seen in Israel as a failure of Israeli intelligence, and by many as a failure of Meir's foreign and defense policies. The 1974 findings of the Agranat Commission, investigating conduct of the war, led to her resignation early in her second term.

QUOTES BY HER:

"When peace comes we will perhaps in time be able to forgive the Arabs for killing our sons, but it will be harder for us to forgive them for having forced us to kill their sons." (1969)

"One of the great disappointments in myself has been that I never (was) able to return to . . . kibbutz." (1975)

"I am not a great admirer of the kind of feminism that gives rise to bra burning, hatred of men or a campaign against motherhood, but I have had a very great regard for those energetic, hard-working women . . ."

QUOTES ABOUT HER:

"She's the only man in my cabinet." (Ben-Gurion, apocryphal)

"I've wanted to meet you for a long time." (Anwar Sadat, 1977)

Yitzhak Rabin (1922—)

Prime Minister 1974–1977

VITAL STATISTICS:

Born in Jerusalem, to a family of *halutzim* (pioneers) active in *Poalei Zion*, he attended (1937) the prestigious Kadourie Agricultural High School in the Galilee, where his instructor in socialism and arms training was Yigal Paicovitch (Allon).

At Kadoorie he joined a kibbutz settlement group but left in 1939 to enlist in the Haganah and in 1941 was mobilized to the Haganah's full-time mobile strike-force, the left-wing Palmach.

He married Leah Schlossberg in 1948.

EARLY CAREER HIGHLIGHTS:

Rabin did not join a political party until he left the armed forces in 1967. But his early association with Allon, in school and in the Palmach, led to his identification in the public mind with the left-wing labor party Ahdut Ha-Avoda.

His first command assignment was an assault in 1945 on a British DP camp at Athlit. "It was an odd feeling to carry a terrified Jewish child—a child of the Holocaust . . . As my shoulders bore the hopes of the Jewish people, I suddenly felt a warm, damp sensation down my back. Under the circumstances, I could hardly halt."

In 1948, as commander of the Harel Brigade, he was responsible for opening the road to besieged Jerusalem and later led the assaults of Mt. Zion and the Old City.

At the end of the war he was deputy commander of the Palmach under Allon, and as commander of the key southern front he came to Ben-Gurion's attention. After the disbanding of the Palmach, he was one of the few Palmach officers to enter the newly unified Israel Defense Forces; but his attendance at a banned Palmach rally led to reprimand (1949) by a court-martial and harsh words from the prime minister.

Rabin held various posts on the General Staff throughout the 1950's, spending two years (1952–54) at the Royal Staff College in Camberley, England, becoming chief of operations (the number two man in IDF) in 1959, and chief of staff in 1964.

Rabin feuded with Moshe Dayan at various points in his career, beginning in 1949 when Dayan urged his removal from the southern command. In the early 1960's he opposed Dayan's protégé Shimon Peres, then deputy defense minister, in urging transfer of military acquisitions dependence from France to the U.S. As chief of staff (1964–67) he oversaw the Americanization of military supply, developing close ties with the hierarchy in Washington, and commanded the stunning Israeli victory of June 1967.

Leaving the army in 1967, he joined the unified Labor party and was appointed ambassador to Washington, where he served through the Nixon years, "the heyday of U.S.-Israel relations." He was accused in 1972 of endorsing Nixon for reelection—foreign interference in U.S. affairs.

He returned to Israel after the Yom Kippur War, and following the 1973 elections joined Golda Meir's cabinet as minister of labor.

PRIME MINISTER:

Rabin's administration was marked by controversy. Meir had resigned in early 1974, along with most of the veteran leadership, in the wake of public furor over conduct of the Yom Kippur War; Rabin was elevated by the party's central committee, winning in a dead heat over Shimon Peres, who became defense minister.

Except for a brief attempt to exclude the religious parties from the ruling coalition, Rabin continued all of the policies of the Meir administration, failing to calm the public debate over the Palestinians and the future of the occupied territories.

His partnership with Peres failed to become a working relationship, and during his tenure the Labor party often seemed leaderless. A common accusation was that Rabin was unaccustomed to political teamwork, having spent a lifetime in military command.

His regime was responsible for the 1975 Interim Agreements with Egypt and Syria, leading ultimately to the 1979 Israel-Egypt Peace Treaty after he left office.

In April 1977 Mrs. Rabin was revealed to have maintained a small private account in a Washington, D.C., bank, a violation of Israeli currency regulations. Rabin was forced to resign, one month before the Knesset elections.

QUOTES BY HIM:

"I know that many hearts were touched by the terrible price paid by the enemy. . . . Perhaps the Jewish people have never been trained for conquest . . . therefore, we conquer with mixed feelings." (1967)

"To share my deepest feelings with someone else . . . is just not in my character and has never been." (1979)

QUOTES ABOUT HIM:

"[UN Secretary-General Dag] Hammarskjold was shy and withdrawn, as only an aggressive and self-confident man can be. He reminds me of our own Yitzhak Rabin." (*Davar,* 1967)

"Well, have you learned to follow orders?" (Ben-Gurion, 1967)

Menachem Begin (1913—)

Prime Minister 1977—

VITAL STATISTICS:

Born in Brest-Litovsk, Poland, to a militantly nationalistic Zionist family, Begin received a "modern Orthodox" Jewish education and later studied law at Warsaw University. He has remained devoted to traditional Judaism throughout his life; while not Orthodox, he has felt such observances as Sabbath and dietary laws to be important symbols of national pride—the central element in his world view.

He fled Warsaw on the eve of the Nazi invasion in 1939, going first to Vilna, then, after brief internment in a Soviet prison camp, to Palestine in 1942.

He married Aliza Arnold in 1939. They have three children.

EARLY CAREER HIGHLIGHTS:

Begin joined *ha-Shomer ha-Tzair,* the left-wing Zionist youth group, in 1925 but was alienated by its pro-Soviet tendencies and quit after a year. He then joined Betar, the militant youth arm of the right-wing Zionists. During the 1930's he rose through the ranks of Polish Betar, becoming in 1939 Rosh Betar—the movement's head.

Fleeing eastward from the German advance, Begin was arrested in Vilna for unspecified "anti-Soviet activity," and imprisoned in 1941; he retained a lifelong bitterness toward Soviet communism. In 1942 he benefited from a general Soviet release of Polish citizens to serve in General Anders' Polish Army-in-Exile. His unit was posted to Palestine, where he was quickly demobilized and became commander of the Irgun.

The revolt ordered by Begin in 1944 against British mandatory rule in Palestine ran counter to official Zionist policy of cooperating with Britain against the Nazi enemy. After several unsuccessful attempts at rapprochement by Haganah leaders Moshe Sneh ("Begin made a pathetic impression . . .") and Eliahu Golomb ("We have to put an end to your operation at all costs . . .") the Haganah declared "Operation Season" against the IZL, and Begin went into hiding.

Menachem Begin, 1948

The end of the Second World War ended Operation Season as well, and the Haganah and IZL began coordinated actions against the British. This for Begin was "a very important landmark in his career." The pact nearly collapsed several times because of over-reaction by undisciplined IZL troops.

Begin's 1946 decision to dynamite British army headquarters in Jerusalem's King David Hotel, on the eve of the UN consideration of Palestine damaged IZL-Haganah cooperation. The ensuing British crackdown temporarily decimated IZL ranks, but they recovered sufficiently to play an active and controversial role in the early months of the War of Independence.

In June 1948 the month-old State of Israel accepted a UN ceasefire, including a thirty-day ban on arms importation. Several days later Begin attempted to land at Jaffa aboard the *Altalena,* an IZL arms ship. Negotiations for the ship's surrender were unsuccessful, and Ben-Gurion ordered the Haganah to shell and sink the *Altalena*; Begin "barely escaped with his life." Shortly thereafter the IZL was disbanded, and its members inducted into the new Israel Defense Forces. Begin went into politics, organizing the Herut party based on Revisionist principles. The party's symbol was a rifle superimposed over a map of pre-1922 Palestine; its slogan was "Only Thus."

As leader of the Parliamentary Opposition, Herut made a small showing in the 1949 Knesset elections, mainly among former IZL activists. Alone among the Zionist parties, Herut was ostracized from all government deliberations.

In 1955 Herut increased its standings in the Knesset elections, becoming the largest opposition party. Its strongest showings were among the disaffected new immigrants of Oriental extraction.

By 1965 Begin had gained increased "respectability," and his Herut joined with the procapitalist Liberal party to form Gahal.

In 1967 Gahal entered Eshkol's National Unity Government coalition, and Begin for the first time became minister (without portfolio) in an Israeli cabinet. He left the cabinet in 1970, rejecting government acceptance of the U.S. peace initiative to end the war of attrition with Egypt.

In 1973 Gahal joined with several smaller right-wing parties to form the *Likud*. In the Knesset elections of 1977 the *Likud* became the ruling party, and Begin became prime minister of Israel.

PRIME MINISTER:

Begin has supported attempts to establish more Israeli settlers in the occupied territories and to lift government economic controls. The latter led to runaway inflation, which has remained the burning issue on the national agenda.

The *Likud*'s slim plurality forced heavy dependence on coalition support from the small religious parties. The religious parties demanded antiabortion legislation, which Begin achieved in 1979 over the opposition of most of his party.

The central achievement of his administration and of his career was the signing in March 1979 of the peace treaty with Egypt. The peace process—begun in 1977 at Egyptian initiative with President Sadat's visit to Jerusalem—was carried out through the determined statesmanship of both leaders. In 1978 they were jointly awarded the Nobel Peace prize for their efforts. Begin's flexibility in reaching the compromise pact led to attacks from the irredentist right wing of his own Herut faction.

At the close of his third year in office, questions remained about Begin's ability to compromise in his lifelong goal of Jewish sovereignty in Judea and Samaria (the West Bank), which many regard as the key to further peace progress. In addition, his failing health led to doubts of his continued ability to rule. Nonetheless, the signing of the peace treaty seemed certain to guarantee his place in Israeli and world history.

QUOTES BY HIM:

"The State to which we aspired . . . still remains the objective of our generation. . . . A great deal more blood will be spilled for it." (1947)

"If an attempt is made to negotiate with the Germans, my people will go underground. There are some things dearer than life, some things worse than death." (1952)

"My party and I believed during all those years in opposition that we had a right to all of the Land of Israel, even when parts of it were not under our control. Do you really think that we can now agree to support the opposite of what we believe?" (1970)

"Mr. President [Sadat], I welcome you . . . we must see to it that no more of our sons are killed." (1977)

QUOTES ABOUT HIM:

"Menachem Begin (rhymes with Fagin) . . ." (*Time*, 1977)

"Mr. Begin, we are not anti-Semitic. We are anti-you." (*Al-Ahram*, 1978)

"The one-time master terrorist . . . the fiery orator in public, becomes a quiet person in private, a man who still kisses ladies' hands. . . ." (Bernard Postal, American Jewish newspaper editor)

—J.J.G. and H.N.K.

AMERICAN AND CANADIAN JEWS WHO DIED IN ISRAEL'S WAR OF INDEPENDENCE

During the desperate days of 1947, both the Haganah High Command and the Irgun actively sought to enlist overseas volunteers, Jewish and non-Jewish, to defend Israel's right to national independence. According to historian P. E. Lapide, "the *Yishuv* [Palestinian Jewish community] wanted experts—chief officers—to take command: fighter pilots, tank commanders, aircraft mechanics and radar technicians," especially those speaking English, the language which most Palestinian Jewish veterans of the British army understood. Of the over 1,700 American and Canadian Jewish volunteers who responded to this call, thirty-one fell in battle, including Colonel David "Mickey" Marcus, a 1924 graduate of the United States Military Academy and later a Brigadier General with the Israeli Defence Forces. In 1974 Rabbi A. Joseph Heckelman, himself an American volunteer of the War of Independence, compiled the definitive list of fallen American and Canadian Jewish volunteers as a tribute and memorial to his former comrades-in-arms.

1. **Stanley Andrews**—Born in New York City, April 23, 1923, Andrews died on October 20, 1948, when his Beaufighter was hit by ground fire during an attack on the Egyptian fortress at Iraq Sueidan.

2. **Philip "Phil" Balkin**—Born in Brooklyn, New York, February 7, 1929, Balkin died on December 27, 1948, when he fell in what proved to be the final campaign in Israel's War of Independence, the attack on Auju-el-Hafir.

3. **Louis Ball** (Ludwig Smargad)—Born in Vienna, Austria, March 10, 1922, Ball was killed in battle on July 9, 1948, during an attack on the Egyptian manned fortress at Iraq Sueidan. A naturalized American citizen, Ball was a veteran of the U.S. Army.

4. **William Bernstein**—Born in Passaic, New Jersey, January 27, 1923, Bernstein was a 1944 graduate of the U.S. Merchant Marine Academy and was later commissioned as a lieutenant (jg.) in the U.S. Navy, before serving as second mate aboard the *Exodus*. He was clubbed to death when the British boarded the *Exodus* on July 18, 1947.

5. **Wilfred "Zev" Cantor**—Born February 7, 1921, in Kiev, Russia, Cantor moved to Canada with his family, where at the age of eighteen he joined the RCAF. He died on October 24, 1948, when the DC-3 Dakota aircraft he was piloting exploded and crashed on takeoff from the Ekron airfield, killing all on board.

6. **William "Willy" Fisher**—Born in Padolia, Russia, August 28, 1923, Fisher, like Zev Cantor, moved with his family to Canada and later enlisted in the RCAF. He died with Cantor and Fred Stevenson when their DC-3 transport crashed at Ekron, October 24, 1948.

7. **Moshe Geberer**—Born in New York City, September 29, 1920, Moshe Geberer was killed by an Arab sniper's bullet, May 17, 1948, while on a scouting mission in southern Jerusalem. Before volunteering to serve in Palestine, Geberer had been active in *ha-Shomer ha-Tzair* and *Habonim* and had been a sergeant in the U.S. Army.

8. **William Gerson**—Died April 15, 1948, as his too heavily laden C-46 transport plane crashed on takeoff en route from Mexico City to Palestine.

9. **Aaron Hanovice**—Born in Houston, Texas, in 1922, Hanovice served with the U.S. Army in Palestine during World War II. He was killed in August 1947 when the truck convoy he was riding in was ambushed by Arabs.

10. **Joseph "Joe" Kahn**—Born in Philadelphia, Pennsylvania, on August 21, 1908, Kahn served as a staff sergeant in the Far East during World War II with the U.S. 26th Infantry Division. He was killed two hours before the truce was announced, during the *Irgun's* breakthrough into the Old City of Jerusalem.

11. **Jerome "Jerry" Kaplan**—Born in Bayonne, New Jersey, Kaplan fell in the Battle of Latrun, May 13, 1948, one day before the proclamation of the State of Israel.

12. **Jack Klein**—Born in New York City, June 2, 1916, Klein was killed in the course of setting land mines in the fields of Kfar Menahem, when a mine blew up in his hands. Before World War II Klein had been a leader of *ha-Shomer ha-Tzair* in the United States.

13. **Ari Lashner**—Born in New York City, April 8, 1915, Lashner was killed by a sniper from the east bank of the Jordan, March 15, 1948, after he climbed a pole to do some electrical repair work. During World

A rally in New York in support of a Jewish homeland in Palestine **(Alexander Archer)**

War II Lashner had served as a wireless officer with the U.S. Navy.

14. **Sidney Leizerowitz**—A native of Toronto, Canada, Leizerowitz was killed in the Galilee in October 1948 during Operation Hiram, which defeated the irregular forces of Fawzi Kaukji's Arab Liberation Army.

15. **Alvin Levine**—Born in Long Beach, New York, July 30, 1918, Levine, a veteran of the U.S. Army Air Corps, died with two other men aboard when their Israeli aircraft crashed into the Sea of Galilee in early December 1948.

16. **Baruch Linsky**—Born in Chicago, May 1, 1921, Linsky was active in *Aliya Bet* work before volunteering for the *Haganah* in 1948. A former University of California at Berkeley graduate student (M.A., 1945), Linksy was killed at Hulda, May 26, 1948.

17. **David "Mickey" Marcus**—Born in New York City, February 22, 1902, Marcus was the highest-ranking American volunteer to serve with the Israeli armed forces during the War of Independence. A 1924 graduate of the U.S. Military Academy at West Point, Marcus later participated in the Allied invasion of Normandy, leaving the U.S. Army at the end of the war with the rank of colonel. As commander of the Jerusalem front, Marcus was killed in error by one of his own sentries before dawn on June 11, 1948. He was later buried with full military honors at West Point.

18. **Mandel Math**—Born in Brooklyn, New

York, August 22, 1926, Math served with the U.S. Army during World War II, participating in the liberation of the Dachau and Buchenwald concentration camps. Math was killed in the Battle of Latrun on May 13, 1948.

19. **Harold "Zvi" Monash**—Born in Berlin, Germany, January 1, 1924, Monash was killed in fighting in the Jerusalem sector on April 25, 1948. A naturalized U.S. citizen, Monash was a combat veteran of the American army and had been wounded in the battle to liberate Rome.

20. **Ralph Moster**—Born in Hamilton, Ontario, August 24, 1924, Moster served in the RCAF during World War II. Commander of an Israeli airfield in the Negev, Moster was killed on December 2, 1948, when the aircraft he was flying went down over the Sea of Galilee.

21. **Moshe "Mosie" Perlstein**—Born in Jersey City, New Jersey, November 24, 1925, Perlstein was killed as part of a relief column attempting to resupply the Etzion settlements south of Jerusalem, January 16, 1948.

Colonel David "Mickey" Marcus

22. **Sam Pomerantz**—Born in New York City, September 23, 1910, Pomerantz died during a snow storm while attempting to fly a Spitfire fighter interceptor from Czechoslovakia to Palestine.

23. **Carmi Rabinowitz**—Born in New York City, August 11, 1924, Rabinowitz attended *Yeshivat Etz Chaim* in Borough Park, Brooklyn, and later served with the U.S. Army in North Africa. He was killed at Tel-a-rish by an Arab sniper on December 25, 1947.

24. **Moshe Aaron "Moe" Rosenbaum**—Born in Poland, March 30, 1920, Rosenbaum moved with his family to the United States, where he later enlisted in the U.S. Army Air Corps and was commissioned as a second lieutenant. Having survived a German POW camp during World War II, Rosenbaum was killed on May 21, 1948, attempting to land an American-built C-46 cargo transport plane on an Israeli airfield.

25. **Jacob Rothman**—Born in Brooklyn, New York, January 29, 1911, Rothman served as a chief radio officer with the U.S. Merchant Marine during World War II. He died on December 31, 1948, when the Israeli Air Force craft he was flying in crashed off the coast of Italy.

26. **Sidney Rubinoff**—Born in Toronto, Canada, February 20, 1926, Rubinoff served with the Canadian Army during World War II. A member of the Palmach, the striking arm of the *Haganah*, Rubinoff was killed in action on July 17, 1948.

27. **Reuben "Red" Schiff**—Born in Toronto, Canada in 1924, Schiff volunteered for service with the Canadian Army during World War II, and was wounded in Germany. Following the war, Schiff was active in *Aliya Bet* work. He died fighting in the Negev in 1948.

28. **Jack Shulman**—Born in Paris, France, January 14, 1928, Shulman went with his family to the United States, where he later served in the Army. Shulman fell on October 21, 1948, in the battle to capture Beersheba.

29. **Avraham David Stavsky**—Born in Brest Litovsk, Poland, in 1906, Stavsky immigrated to Palestine in 1932. A year later, Stavsky was convicted of the murder of Chaim Arlosoroff, a leading Labor party intellectual. Following his release from prison Stavsky went to the United States, where he became a citizen. He died on June 22, 1948, participating in the attempt by the *Irgun* to land illegal arms from the *Altalena*.

30. **Edward Leonard Troyen**—Born in New York City, October 22, 1926, Troyen served with the U.S. Army Air Corps in the European theater during World War II. Volunteering for an attack mission against an enemy target, Troyen was wounded by ground fire on July 18, 1948. He died the next day.

31. **Robert Lester Weeckman**—Born in Los Angeles, California, November 21, 1921, Weeckman served with the U.S. Army Air Corps during World War II and was a decorated aerial reconnaissance pilot, flying sixty-five missions. He was killed on July 9, 1948, when his German-built *Messerschmitt* was hit by enemy anti-aircraft fire in the vicinity of Gaza.

—The Eds.

PEACE AT LAST? THE CAMP DAVID ACCORDS AND THE ISRAEL-EGYPT PEACE TREATY

Text of Agreements Signed September 17, 1978

A FRAMEWORK FOR PEACE
IN THE MIDDLE EAST
AGREED AT CAMP DAVID

Muhamad Anwar el-Sadat, President of the Arab Republic of Egypt, and Menachem Begin, Prime Minister of Israel, met with Jimmy Carter, President of the United States of America, at Camp David from September 5 to September 17, 1978, and have agreed on the following Framework for peace in the Middle East. They invite other parties to the Arab-Israeli conflict to adhere to it.

PREAMBLE

The search for peace in the Middle East must be guided by the following.

—The agreed basis for a peaceful settlement of the conflict between Israel and its neighbors is United Nations Security Council Resolution 242, in all its parts.*

—After four wars during thirty years, despite intensive human efforts, the Middle East, which is the cradle of civilization and the birthplace of three great religions, does not yet enjoy the blessings of peace. The people of the Middle East yearn for peace so that the vast human and natural resources of the region can be turned to the pursuits of peace and so that this area can become a model for coexistence and cooperation among nations.

—The historic initiative of President Sadat in visiting Jerusalem and the reception accorded to him by the Parliament, government, and people of Israel, and the reciprocal visit of Prime Minister Begin to Ismailia, the peace proposals made by both leaders, as well as the warm reception of these missions by the peoples of both countries, have created an unprecedented opportunity for peace which must not be lost if this generation and future generations are to be spared the tragedies of war.

—The provisions of the Charter of the United Nations and the other accepted norms of international laws and legitimacy now provide accepted standards for the conduct of relations among all states.

—To achieve a relationship of peace, in the spirit of Article 2 of the United Nations Charter, future negotiations between Israel and any neighbor prepared to negotiate peace and security with it are necessary for the purpose of carrying out all the provisions and principles of Resolutions 242 and 338.

—Peace requires respect for the sovereignty, territorial integrity, and political independence of every state in the area and their right to live in peace within secure and recognized boundaries free from threats or acts of force. Progress toward that goal can ac-

*The texts of Resolutions 242 and 338 are annexed by this document.

The signing of the Israeli-Egyptian Peace Treaty at the White House, March 26, 1979.

celerate movement toward a new era of reconciliation in the Middle East marked by cooperation in promoting economic development, in maintaining stability, and in assuring security.

—Security is enhanced by a relationship of peace and by cooperation between nations which enjoy normal relations. In addition, under the terms of peace treaties, the parties can, on the basis of reciprocity, agree to special security arrangements such as demilitarized zones, limited armaments areas, early warning stations, the presence of international forces, liaison, agreed measures for monitoring, and other arrangements that they agree are useful.

FRAMEWORK

Taking these factors into account, the parties are determined to reach a just, comprehensive, and durable settlement of the Middle East conflict through the conclusion of peace treaties based on Security Council Resolutions 242 and 338 in all their parts. Their purpose is to achieve peace and good neighborly relations. They recognize that, for peace to endure, it must involve all those who have been most deeply affected by the conflict. They therefore agree that this Framework as appropriate is intended by them to constitute a basis for peace not only between Egypt and Israel, but also between Israel and each of its other neighbors which is prepared to negotiate peace with Israel on this basis. With that objective in mind, they have agreed to proceed as follows:

A. *West Bank and Gaza*

1. Egypt, Israel, Jordan and the representatives of the Palestinian people should participate in negotiations on the resolution of the Palestinian problem in all its aspects. To achieve that objective, negotiations relating to the West Bank and Gaza should proceed in three stages.

(a) Egypt and Israel agree that, in order to ensure a peaceful and orderly transfer of authority, and taking into account for security concerns of all the parties, there should be transitional arrangements for the West Bank and Gaza for a period not exceeding five years. In order to provide full autonomy to the inhabitants, under these arrangements the Israeli military government and its civilian administration will be withdrawn as soon as a self-governing authority has been freely elected by the inhabitants of these areas to replace the existing military government. To negotiate the details of a transitional agreement, the Government of Jordan will be invited to join the negotiations on the basis of this framework. These new arrangements should give due consideration both to the principle of self-government by the inhabitants of these territories and to the legitimate security concerns of the parties involved.

(b) Egypt, Israel, and Jordan will agree on the modalities for establishing the elected self-governing authority in the West Bank and Gaza. The delegations of Egypt and Jordan may include Palestinians from the West Bank and Gaza or other Palestinians as mutually agreed. The parties will negotiate an agreement which will define the powers and responsibilities of the self-governing authority to be exercised in the West Bank and Gaza. A withdrawal of Israeli armed forces will take place and there will be a redeployment of the remaining Israeli forces into specified security locations. The agreement will also include arrangements for assuring internal and external security and public order. A strong local police force will be established, which may include Jordanian citizens. In addition, Israeli and Jordanian forces will participate in joint patrols and in the manning of control posts to assure the security of the borders.

(c) When the self-governing authority (administrative council) of the West Bank and Gaza is established and inaugurated, the transitional period of five years will begin. As soon as possible, but not later than the third year after the beginning of the transitional period, negotiations will take place to determine the final status of the West Bank and Gaza and its relationship with its neighbors, and to conclude a peace treaty between Israel and Jordan by the end of the transitional period. These negotiations will be conducted among Egypt, Israel, Jordan, and the elected representatives of the inhabitants of the West Bank and Gaza. Two separate but related committees will be convened, one committee, consisting of representatives of the four parties which will negotiate and agree on the final status of the West Bank and Gaza, and its relationship with its neighbors, and the second committee, consisting of representatives of Israel and representatives of Jordan to be joined by the elected representatives of the inhabitants of the West Bank and Gaza, to negotiate the peace treaty between Israel and Jordan, taking into account the agreement reached on the final status of the West Bank and Gaza. The negotiations shall be based on all the provisions and principles of UN Security Council Resolution 242. The negotiations will resolve, among other matters, the location of the boundaries and the nature of the security arrangements. The solution from the negotiations must also recognize the legitimate rights of the Palestinian people and their just requirements. In this way, the Palestinians will participate in the determination of their own future through:

1) The negotiation among Egypt, Israel, Jordan, and the representatives of the inhabitants of the West Bank and Gaza to agree on the final status of the West Bank and Gaza and other outstanding issues by the end of the transitional period.

2) Submitting their agreement to a vote by the elected representatives of the inhabitants of the West Bank and Gaza.

3) Providing for the elected representatives of the inhabitants of the West Bank and Gaza to decide how they shall govern themselves consistent with the provisions of their agreement.

4) Participating as stated above in the work of the committee negotiating the peace treaty between Israel and Jordan.

2. All necessary measures will be taken and provisions made to assure the security of Israel and its neighbors during the transitional period and beyond. To assist in providing such security, a strong local police force will be constituted by the self-governing authority. It will be composed of inhabitants of the West Bank and Gaza. The police will maintain continuing liaison on internal security matters with the designated Israeli, Jordanian, and Egyptian officers.

3. During the transitional period, representatives of Egypt, Israel, Jordan, and the self-governing authority will constitute a continuing committee to decide by agreement on the modalities of admission of persons displaced from the West Bank and Gaza in 1967, together with necessary measures to prevent disruption and disorder. Other matters of common concern may also be dealt with by this committee.

4. Egypt and Israel will work with each other and with other interested parties to establish agreed procedures for a prompt, just, and permanent implementation of the resolution of the refugee problem.

B. *Egypt-Israel*

1. Egypt and Israel undertake not to resort to the threat or the use of force to settle disputes. Any disputes shall be settled by peaceful means in accordance with the provision of Article 33 of the Charter of the United Nations.

2. In order to achieve peace between them, the parties agree to negotiate in good faith with the goal of concluding within three months from the signing of this framework a peace treaty between them, while inviting the other parties to the conflict to proceed simultaneously to negotiate and conclude similar peace treaties with a view to achieving a comprehensive peace in the area. The Framework for the conclusion of a peace treaty between Egypt and Israel will govern the peace negotiations between them. The parties will agree on the modalities and the timetable for the implementation of their obligations under the treaty.

C. *Associated Principles*

1. Egypt and Israel state that the principles and provisions described below should apply to peace treaties between Israel and each of its neighbors—Egypt, Jordan, Syria, and Lebanon.

2. Signatories shall establish among themselves relationships normal to states at peace with one another. To this end, they should undertake to abide by all the provisions of

the Charter of the United Nations. Steps to be taken in this respect include:

(a) full recognition.

(b) abolishing economic boycotts.

(c) guaranteeing that under their jurisdiction the citizens of the other parties shall enjoy the protection of the due process of law.

3. Signatories should explore possibilities for economic development in the context of final peace treaties, with the objective of contributing to the atmosphere of peace, cooperation, and friendship which is their common goal.

4. Claims Commissions may be established for the mutual settlement of all financial claims.

5. The United States shall be invited to participate in the talks on matters related to the modalities of the implementation of the agreements and working out the timetable for the carrying out of the obligations of the parties.

6. The United Nations Security Council shall be requested to endorse the peace treaties and ensure that their provisions shall not be violated. The permanent members of the Security Council shall be requested to underwrite the peace treaties and ensure respect for their provisions. They shall also be requested to conform their policies and actions with the undertakings contained in this Framework.

For the Government of the Arab Republic of Egypt:	For the Government of Israel:
A. SADAT	M. BEGIN

Witnessed by:

JIMMY CARTER
Jimmy Carter, President
of the United States of America

ANNEX

Text of United Nations Security Council Resolution 242 of November 22, 1967

Adopted unanimously at the 1,382nd meeting
The Security Council

Expressing its continuing concern with the grave situation in the Middle East,

Emphasizing the inadmissibility of the acquisition of territory by war and the need to work for a just and lasting peace in which every State in the area can live in security.

Emphasizing further that all Member States in their acceptance of the Charter of the United Nations have undertaken a commitment to act in accordance with Article 2 of the Charter.

1. *Affirms* that the fulfillment of Charter principles requires the establishment of a just and lasting peace in the Middle East which should include the application of both the following principles:

(i) Withdrawal of Israeli armed forces from territories occupied in the recent conflict.

(ii) Termination of all claims or states of belligerency and respect for and acknowledgement of the sovereignty, territorial integrity, and political independence of every State in the area and their right to live in peace within secure and recognized boundaries free from threats or acts of force.

2. *Affirms further* the necessity

(a) For guaranteeing freedom of navigation through international waterways in the area.

(b) For achieving a just settlement of the refugee problem.

(c) For guaranteeing the territorial inviolability and political independence of every State in the area, through measures including the establishment of demilitarized zones.

3. *Requests* the Secretary-General to designate a Special Representative to proceed to the Middle East to establish and maintain contacts with the States concerned in order to promote agreement and assist efforts to achieve a peaceful and accepted settlement in accordance with the provisions and principles of this resolution.

4. *Requests* the Secretary-General to report to the Security Council on the progress of the efforts of the Special Representative as soon as possible.

Text of United Nations Security Council Resolution 338 of October 21/22, 1973

Adopted by the Security Council at its 1,747th meeting
The Security Council

1. *Calls upon* all parties to the present fighting to cease all firing and terminate all military activity immediately, no later than 12 hours after the moment of the adoption of this decision, in the positions they now occupy.

2. *Calls upon* the parties concerned to start immediately after the cease fire the implementation of Security Council Resolution 242 (1967) in all of its parts.

3. *Decides* that, immediately and concurrently with the cease-fire, negotiations start between the parties concerned under appropriate auspices aimed at establishing a just and durable peace in the Middle East.

FRAMEWORK FOR THE CONCLUSION OF A PEACE TREATY BETWEEN EGYPT AND ISRAEL

In order to achieve peace between them, Israel and Egypt agree to negotiate in good faith with a goal of concluding within three months of the signing of this framework a peace treaty between them.

It is agreed that:

The site of the negotiations will be under a United Nations flag at a location or locations to be mutually agreed.

All of the principles of UN Resolution 242 will apply in this resolution of the dispute between Israel and Egypt.

Unless otherwise mutually agreed, terms of the peace treaty will be implemented between two and three years after the peace treaty is signed.

The following matters are agreed between the parties.

(a) the full exercise of Egyptian sovereignty up to the internationally recognized border between Egypt and mandated Palestine;

(b) the withdrawal of Israeli armed forces from the Sinai;

(c) the use of airfields left by the Israelis near El Arish, Rafah, Ras en Naqb, and Sharm el Sheikh for civilian purposes only, including possible commercial use by all nations;

(d) the right of free passage by ships of Israel through the Gulf of Suez and the Suez Canal on the basis of the Constantinople Convention of 1888 applying to all nations; the Strait of Tiran and the Gulf of Aqaba are international waterways to be open to all nations for unimpeded and nonsuspendable freedom of navigation and overflight;

(e) the construction of a highway between the Sinai and Jordan near Elat with guaranteed free and peaceful passage by Egypt and Jordan, and

(f) the stationing of military forces listed below.

STATIONING OF FORCES

A. No more than one division (mechanized or infantry) of Egyptian armed forces will be stationed within an area lying approximately 50 kilometers (km) east of the Gulf of Suez and the Suez Canal.

B. Only United Nations forces and civil police equipped with light weapons to perform normal police functions will be stationed within an area lying west of the international border and the Gulf of Aqaba, varying in width from 20 km to 40 km.

C. In the area within 3 km east of the international border there will be Israeli limited military forces not to exceed four infantry battalions and United Nations observers.

D. Border patrol units, not to exceed three battalions, will supplement the civil police in maintaining order in the area not included above.

The exact demarcation of the above areas will be as decided during the peace negotiations.

Early warning stations may exist to insure compliance with the terms of the agreement.

United Nations forces will be stationed. (a) in part of the area in the Sinai lying within about 20 km of the Mediterranean Sea and adjacent to the international border, and (b) in the Sharem el Sheikh area to ensure freedom of passage through the Strait of Tiran; and these forces will not be removed unless such removal is approved by the Security Council of the United Nations with a unanimous vote of the five permanent members.

After a peace treaty is signed, and after the interim withdrawal is complete, normal relations will be established between Egypt and Israel, including full recognition, including diplomatic, economic and cultural relations, termination of economic boycotts and barriers to the free movement of goods and people, and mutual protection of citizens by the due process of law.

INTERIM WITHDRAWAL

Between three months and nine months after the signing of the peace treaty, all Israeli forces will withdraw east of a line extending from a point east to El Arish to Ras Muhammad, the exact location of this line to be determined by mutual agreement.

For the Government of the Arab Republic of Egypt:	For the Government of Israel:
A. SADAT	M. BEGIN

Witnessed by:

JIMMY CARTER
Jimmy Carter, President
of the United States of America

Text of Agreement Signed March 26, 1979

TREATY OF PEACE BETWEEN
THE ARAB REPUBLIC OF EGYPT
AND THE STATE OF ISRAEL

The Government of the Arab Republic of Egypt and the Government of the State of Israel:

PREAMBLE

Convinced of the urgent necessity of the establishment of a just, comprehensive, and lasting peace in the Middle East in accordance with Security Council Resolutions 242 and 338;

Reaffirming their adherence to the "Framework for Peace in the Middle East Agreed at Camp David," dated September 17, 1978;

Noting that the aforementioned Framework as appropriate is intended to constitute a basis for peace not only between Egypt and Israel but also between Israel and each of its other Arab neighbors which is prepared to negotiate peace with it on this basis;

Desiring to bring to an end the state of war between them and to establish a peace in which every state in the area can live in security;

Convinced that the conclusion of a Treaty of Peace between Egypt and Israel is an important step in the search for comprehensive peace in the area and for the attainment of the settlement of the Arab-Israeli conflict in all its aspects;

Inviting the other Arab parties to this dispute to join the peace process with Israel guided by and based on the principles of the aforementioned Framework;

Desiring as well to develop friendly relations and cooperation between themselves in accordance with the United Nations Charter and the principles of international law governing international relations in times of peace;

Agree to the following provisions in the free exercise of their sovereignty in order to implement the "Framework for the Conclusion of a Peace Treaty Between Egypt and Israel."

ARTICLE I

1. The state of war between the Parties will be terminated and peace will be established between them upon the exchange of instruments of ratification of this Treaty.

2. Israel will withdraw all its armed forces and civilians from the Sinai behind the international boundary between Egypt and mandated Palestine, as provided in the annexed protocol (Annex 1), and Egypt will resume the exercise of its full sovereignty over the Sinai.

3. Upon completion of the interim withdrawal provided for in Annex 1, the Parties will establish normal and friendly relations, in accordance with Article III (3).

ARTICLE II

The permanent boundary between Egypt and Israel is the recognized international boundary between Egypt and the former mandated territory of Palestine, as shown on the map of Annex II, without prejudice to the issue of the status of the Gaza Strip. The Parties recognize this boundary as inviolable. Each will respect the territorial integrity of the other, including their territorial waters and airspace.

ARTICLE III

1. The Parties will apply between them the provisions of the Charter of the United Nations and the principles of international law governing relations among states in times of peace. In particular:

a. They recognize and will respect each other's sovereignty, territorial integrity and political independence;

b. They recognize and will respect each other's right to live in peace within their secure and recognized boundaries;

c. They will refrain from the threat or use of force, directly or undirectly against each other and will settle all disputes between them by peaceful means.

2. Each Party undertakes to ensure that acts or threats of belligerency, hostility, or violence do not originate from and are not committed from within its territory, or by any forces subject to its control or by any other forces stationed on its territory, against the population, citizens, or property of the other Party. Each Party also undertakes to refrain from organizing, instigating, inciting, assisting, or participating in acts or threats of belligerency, hostility, subversion, or violence against the other Party, anywhere, and undertakes to ensure that perpetrators of such acts are brought to justice.

3. The Parties agree that the normal relationship established between them will include full recognition, diplomatic, economic, and cultural relations, termination of economic boycotts and discriminatory barriers to the free movement of people and goods, and will guarantee the mutual enjoyment by citizens of the due process of law. The process by which they undertake to achieve such a relationship parallel to the implementation of other provisions of this Treaty is set out in the annexed protocol (Annex III).

ARTICLE IV

1. In order to provide maximum security for both Parties on the basis of reciprocity, agreed security arrangements will be established including limited force zones in Egyptian and Israeli territory, and United Nations forces and observers, described in detail as to nature and timing in Annex I, and other security arrangements the Parties may agree upon.

2. The Parties agree to the stationing of United Nations personnel in areas described in Annex I. The Parties agree not to request withdrawal of the United Nations personnel and that these personnel will not be removed unless such removal is approved by the Security Council of the United Nations, with the affirmative vote of the five Permanent Members, unless the Parties otherwise agree.

3. A Joint Commission will be established to facilitate the implementation of the Treaty, as provided for in Annex I.

4. The security arrangements provided for in paragraphs 1 and 2 of this Article may at the request of either party be reviewed and amended by mutual agreement of the Parties.

ARTICLE V

1. Ships of Israel, and cargoes destined for or coming from Israel, shall enjoy the rights of free passage through the Suez Canal and its approaches through the Gulf of Suez and

the Mediterranean Sea on the basis of the Constantinople Convention of 1888, applying to all nations. Israeli nationals, vessels, and cargoes, as well as persons, vessels, and cargoes destined for or coming from Israel, shall be accorded non-discriminatory treatment in all matters connected with usage of the canal.

2. The Parties consider the Strait of Tiran and the Gulf of Aqaba to be international waterways open to all nations for unimpeded and non-suspendable freedom of navigation and overflight. The Parties will respect each other's right to navigation and overflight for access to either country through the Strait of Tiran and the Gulf of Aqaba.

ARTICLE VI

1. This Treaty does not affect and shall not be interpreted as affecting in any way the rights and obligations of the Parties under the Charter of the United Nations.

2. The Parties undertake to fulfill in good faith their obligations under this Treaty, without regard to action or inaction of any other party and independently or any instrument external to this Treaty.

3. They further undertake to take all the necessary measures for the application in their relations of the provisions of the multilateral conventions to which they are parties, including the submission of appropriate notification to the Secretary General of the United Nations and other depositaries of such conventions.

4. The Parties undertake not to enter into any obligation in conflict with this Treaty.

5. Subject to Article 103 of the United Nations Charter, in the event of a conflict between the obligations of the Parties under the present Treaty and any of their other obligations, the obligations under this Treaty will be binding and implemented.

ARTICLE VII

1. Disputes arising out of the application or interpretation of this Treaty shall be resolved by negotiations.

2. Any such disputes which cannot be settled by negotiations shall be resolved by conciliation or submitted to arbitration.

ARTICLE VIII

The Parties agree to establish a claims commission for the mutual settlement of all financial claims.

ARTICLE IX

1. This Treaty shall enter into force upon exchange of instruments of ratification.

2. This Treaty supersedes the Agreement between Egypt and Israel of September, 1975.

3. All protocols, annexes, and maps attached to this Treaty shall be regarded as an integral part hereof.

4. The Treaty shall be communicated to the Secretary General of the United Nations for registration in accordance with the provisions of Article 102 of the Charter of the United Nations.

For the Government of the Arab Republic of Egypt:	For the Government of Israel:
MOHAMED ANWAR EL-SADAT	MENACHEM BEGIN

Witnessed by:

JIMMY CARTER
Jimmy Carter, President
of the United States of America

THE POLITICAL FORTUNES OF THE DIASPORA JEW

10 JEWISH PRESIDENTS, PRIME MINISTERS, CHIEF MINISTERS, AND PREMIERS

Léon-André Blum
Premier of France
1936–1937, 1938, 1946–47

PERSONAL DATA:
The product of an old-line Alsatian Jewish family, Léon-André Blum, France's first Jewish and Socialist premier, was born in Paris on April 9, 1872. Although raised in a ritually observant home ("his mother observed Jewish dietary laws . . . and lit candles on the Sabbath"), Blum rejected all forms of Jewish ritual observance while still a teenager. A graduate of the Sorbonne (1894) with joint degrees in both literature and law, Blum was recognized from the outset as a brilliant writer, poet, and social critic. In 1907, for example, Blum published *Du Mariage*, a work which created "a sensation because of its advocacy of trial marriage." Blum's own private life, however, was more conventional. In 1896 he married Lise Bloch. The couple had one son, Robert, who later became president of Bugatti, the French automobile manufacturing firm. Following the death of his first wife in 1931, Blum married Therese Pereyra (d. 1938). In 1943 Blum married his third wife, Jeanne Levilliers Humbert, who survived him.

EARLY POLITICAL CAREER:
Like many other French intellectuals, Blum was first drawn to politics as a result of the Dreyfus Affair. In 1899 he joined the French Socialist party. It was not until 1919, however, that Blum was elected a member of the French Chamber of Deputies (National Assembly). Following a split in the Socialist party in 1920, in which the moderates lost control of both the party's official newspaper and treasury, Blum became a major force in helping the party rebuild itself.

MAJOR POLITICAL ACHIEVEMENTS:
Chosen to head France's left-of-center Popular Front government on June 4, 1936, Blum was unsuccessful during his first term in office (fifty-four weeks) in mobilizing public opinion to oppose the growing threat to peace posed by Hitler and Mussolini. As a pacifist, Blum resisted calls by General Charles de Gaulle and others that France develop an "elite force of professional soldiers poised for offensive action" against Germany. Instead, "he sought to retain Italy's friendship and as premier met with Nazi officials to discuss Germany's legitimate grievances."

Leon Blum

During his first two terms as premier, Blum also attempted to steer a neutral course with regard to the civil war raging in Spain. In 1936 he refused to sell French aircraft and other war materials to the Republican government in Madrid. With the defeat of that government Blum was severely criticized by many of his left-wing and liberal supporters. In domestic affairs Blum was able to introduce the five-day, forty-hour week, to nationalize the Bank of France, to institute a new system of paid vacations and collective bargaining, and to extend compulsory schooling to age fourteen.

JEWISH IDENTITY:

A strong supporter of plans to establish a Jewish homeland in Palestine, Blum had, as early as 1929, accepted an invitation from Chaim Weizmann to become a non-Zionist member of the Jewish Agency. Earlier, Blum had written: "I am a Jew. . . . One does not in any way insult me by recalling the race [sic] in which I was born, a race [sic] which I have never denied and towards which I retain only feelings of gratitude and pride."

IMPORTANT LITTLE KNOWN FACTS:

Following the collapse of the French armies in June 1940 and the subsequent emergence of the collaborationist regime at Vichy, Blum was arrested and tried at Riom in 1942 on the charge of having failed to guarantee the military security of the nation. As a result of international pressure the trial was suspended and Blum was returned to the Bourassol prison. In 1943 the Vichy government handed him over to the SS who, in turn, deported him to the *Buchenwald* concentration camp. Following his liberation in 1945, Blum returned to Paris and quickly reentered political life, serving briefly as premier from December 16, 1946 until January 17, 1947. While in *Buchenwald*, a new communal settlement, *Kfar* Blum, was erected in Palestine in his honor.

QUOTES ABOUT HIM:

"Your arrival in office, *M. le President du Conseil*, is incontestably a historic date. For the first time this old Gallic-Roman country will be governed by a Jew." —Xavier Vallat (1936)

"It is a Jew that one must see . . . hear, fight, and destroy. This Blum . . . this man is anything but French." —Charles Maurras (1936)

"Better Hitler than Blum." —French anti-Semitic slogan (c. 1936)

QUOTES BY HIM:

"We must create Europe. . . . We must do it with Germany and not for her. We must do it with Great Britain and not against her. . . . Nothing fruitful, nothing lasting is built on hatred and enslavement." —(1947)

Blum died March 30, 1950.

Kurt Eisner

Minister President and
Provisional Prime Minister
Bavarian "Socialist" Republic
1918–1919

PERSONAL DATA:

Described by his right-wing political opponents as that "hated Jewish ideologist," Kurt Eisner attempted to democratize South German society after World War I as the head of the short-lived Bavarian "Socialist" Republic. Born in Berlin on May 14, 1867, Eisner grew up in what one historian has described as "the center of the asphalt culture." His father, Emmanuel Eisner, was a less than brilliant Jewish businessman, who specialized in selling military decorations and accessories to Prussian officers, a fact that caused his son serious embarrassment. As a student the younger Eisner attended Berlin's "exclusive *Askanisches Gymnasium*" and the Friedrich Wilhelm University. Bored with the university, Eisner left before completing his doctoral thesis to begin a career as a journalist.

EARLY POLITICAL CAREER:

In 1898 Eisner was appointed political editor of *Vorwärts*, the official organ of the German Social Democratic party (SPD). Later he became political editor of the largest and most influential socialist paper in Bavaria, the *Münchener Post*. In 1917 Eisner broke with the SPD party leadership and a short time later helped found the Bavarian wing of the Independent Socialists (USPD), a new left-wing party committed to negotiating an immediate peace with the Allied powers.

MAJOR POLITICAL ACHIEVEMENTS:

With the final collapse of the German military effort in November 1918 Eisner's Independent Socialists seized power in Munich, and on November 8, 1918 Eisner declared Bavaria a "socialist republic." As minister president, Eisner was an immediate target of the German right-wing. On February 21, 1919, with less than three percent of the Bavarian electorate supporting him, Eisner chose to resign. While on his way to submit his letter of resignation, Eisner was assassinated by Count Anton auf Valley Arco, a half Jew and a member of the right-wing, anti-Semitic Thule *Kampfbund*.

JEWISH IDENTITY:

Eisner wrote in 1919 that although he had no connection with Judaism in a ritualistic sense, he was nevertheless proud to be a Jew.

QUOTES ABOUT HIM:

"He was one like Jesus, like Huss—oh *sancta simplicitas*—who were executed by stupidity and greed." —Gustav Landauer (1919)

"Both in a noble and pejorative sense Eisner was a naive man and this ought to remain as his historical epitaph." —Historian Allan Mitchell (1965)

QUOTES BY HIM:

"We . . . believe that not until after peace, when the united league of the world's democracies has been constituted, can the indispensable socialization be executed through the decisive influence of the newly resurrected power of the proletarian International [and] the cooperative effort of the peoples of the Earth." —(1919)

Sir Joshua Abraham Hassan

Q.C., C.B.E., M.V.O., J.P.
Chief Minister of Gibraltar
1964–1969, 1972—

PERSONAL DATA:

Born in Gibraltar on August 21, 1915 to an old-line Moroccan Jewish family, Hassan was educated at Line Wall College (Gibraltar) and later studied law in London. His first marriage, in 1945 to Rebecca Daniela Salazar, was later dissolved. In 1969 Hassan married Marcelle Bensimon. The president of the Gibraltar Labor party and the Association for the Advancement of Civil Rights, Hassan has four daughters.

EARLY POLITICAL CAREER:

As a young attorney, Hassan's political career began in 1945 when he was first elected mayor of the town of Gibraltar, a position that he held until 1950 and again from 1953 to 1959. In recognition of his many public contributions, including having served as chairman of the Gibraltar Central Planning Commission and as chairman of the Gibraltar Museum Management Committee, Hassan was knighted by Queen Elizabeth II in 1963.

MAJOR POLITICAL ACHIEVEMENT:

In 1964 Hassan successfully resisted pressure from the U.N. to force Britain to return the island colony to Spain.

JEWISH IDENTITY:

An observant and devoted Jew, Hassan has served as president of the managing board of the Gibraltar Jewish Community. He is also the current president of the local branch of *Keren Kayemet el-Israel* and has served as vice president of Gibraltar's *Nefusot Yehuda* Synagogue.

QUOTES ABOUT HIM:

"Gibraltar has evolved only two points of view on what is called the 'Spanish problem.' The majority view of Chief Minister Sir Joshua Hassan favors the status quo. A minority view wants total integration into Britain as a . . . parliamentary constituency." —*The New Republic* (1967)

"While holding the highest offices, Hassan continued to go from house to house collecting the contents of . . . JNF [Jewish National Fund] boxes." —*Encyclopaedia Judaica* (1971)

QUOTES BY HIM:

"If we had a plebiscite on whether Gibraltar was to remain British or become Spanish my only fear would be that we might get a 120 percent majority for the status quo." —(1964)

In response to *The Times* (London): "I am sorry you regard our determination to preserve our democratic freedoms, in the face of severe difficulties, as 'unconstructive stubbornness.' I do not think it should be assumed that the Spanish regime has been the only obstacle to a settlement; apart from political freedoms, centuries-old links between our people and Britain cannot be ignored." —(1976)

Bruno Kreisky

Chancellor of Austria 1970—

PERSONAL DATA:

Son of a Jewish woolen industry executive, Bruno Kreisky was born in Vienna on January 22, 1911. At age fifteen he rebelled against the bourgeois values that permeated his father's home and joined the Austrian Socialist party. He was active in its youth movement until the party was outlawed in 1934. A short time later Kreisky joined the Socialist underground movement and was arrested by the Austrian government for political subversion. Tried and convicted, he was sentenced to eighteen months in prison. Following the Nazi invasion of Austria in March 1938 Kreisky was again arrested, this time by the Gestapo. Escaping from the Germans in late 1938, Kreisky fled to Sweden, where he found asylum. In 1942, while in exile, Kreisky married Vera Fuerth. The couple has two children: Peter and Susi. Educated at the University of Vienna, Kreisky is the

Bruno Kreisky

author of *The Challenge: Politics on the Threshold of the Atomic Age*, *Aspects of Democratic Socialism*, and *Neutrality and Co-Existence*.

EARLY POLITICAL CAREER:
Following the Allied victory in 1945 Kreisky joined the Austrian Foreign Service and was appointed first secretary of the Austrian legation in Stockholm. Between 1959 and 1966 Kreisky served as Austria's minister of foreign affairs. In 1967 he replaced Bruno Pittermann, also a Jew, as chairman of the Austrian Socialist party.

MAJOR POLITICAL ACCOMPLISHMENTS:
On March 1, 1970 Kreisky became the first Jew and the first socialist ever elected chancellor of the post-war Austrian Republic. He was reelected to an unprecedented fourth term on May 6, 1979.

JEWISH IDENTITY:
Having described the Jewish people as "*ein misses Volk*" (a *nebach* or wretched people) and having labelled Zionism as a form of "Jewish racism," it is no surprise that Jewish writers have termed Kreisky an "auto anti-Semite." Although not unaware of these charges ("some people think I am a traitor"), Kreisky has had little use for either Judaism or Zionism, preferring instead to identify himself as a socialist and an agnostic—or as an Austrian patriot, as in October 1973, when on the eve of the Yom Kippur War Kreisky closed down Schonau Castle in Vienna as a refugee center for Jewish emigrants from the U.S.S.R., citing the potential threat to Austria posed by Arab terrorists.

IMPORTANT LITTLE KNOWN FACTS:
Kreisky has the distinction of being the first Jewish head-of-state to ever appoint an ex-Nazi to his cabinet, an honor that he acquired in 1970 when he appointed former Waffen SS man Hans Oellinger as Austria's minister of agriculture.

QUOTES ABOUT HIM:
"The Jews in the Socialist Party are reaching for power . . . Pittermann and Kreisky will you emigrate abroad again as you did once before." —Anonymous anti-Semitic election brochure (1964)

"He is a man who hates his father and mother." —Menachem Begin (1978)

QUOTES BY HIM:
"My goal is to turn Austria into a modern country and end all kinds of taboos that have dominated her life." —(1970)

"I am not for racism and I refuse also Jewish racism. My [fatherland] is Austria and no other country." —(1973)

On Menachem Begin:
A ". . . political grocer . . . a little Polish lawyer from Warsaw or whatever he was. They are so alienated, they think in such a warped way, these eastern Jews."

On Simon Wiesenthal: "A Jewish Fascist."

Luigi Luzzatti
Prime Minister of Italy
1910–1911

PERSONAL DATA:
Born in Venice on March 1, 1841, Luzzatti began at an early age "to devote himself to the study of literature, philosophy, and natural sciences and to search into the depths of religious systems." As a student Luzzatti attended both the *Gymnasium* and *Lycee* in Venice and later received a law degree from the University of Padua. Although nonobservant in Jewish ritual matters, Luzzatti had as a youth attended services in the Venetian Sephardic synagogue and later chose as his wife, Amalia Levi, the daughter of a prominent Italian Jewish family.

EARLY POLITICAL CAREER:
A champion of the lower classes, Luzzatti began his political career in the late 1850's when he attempted to found a mutual aid society for Venetian gondoliers. A short time later he was expelled from Venice as a revolutionary and "went to Milan where he became Professor of Economics at the *Instituto Tecnico*." Between 1863 and 1866 Luzzatti travelled from town to town preaching the

need for "people's banks and cooperative societies." Having attained great popularity as a result of his proposed reforms, Luzzatti was elected a member of the Italian parliament in 1871.

MAJOR POLITICAL ACHIEVEMENTS:
As the first Jew to become prime minister of Italy, Luzzatti sought during his brief term in office to improve Italy's system of elementary education, to eradicate malaria, and to extend the right to vote to all but "illiterates."

JEWISH IDENTITY:
A strong supporter of Jewish minority rights in Eastern Europe, Luzzatti interceded on several occasions prior to World War I on behalf of the Jewish communities in Rumania and Poland. Later, he became a strong supporter of Zionist agricultural work in Palestine arguing that, "the Jew should prefer tilling the soil to all other labor."

QUOTES ABOUT HIM:
"He was a wise and good man, closely bound up with Italian history of the last half century, having been the most striking representative figure of that period. Italy's high place among the nations in social legislation is due to Luzzatti's work. I frequently had cause during the last few years to appreciate the wisdom of Luzzatti's counsel in connection with measures which the Fascist government is carrying out through the cooperative [movement]. It is necessary, in order to reestablish the great political equilibrium of the people, that such men exist." —Benito Mussolini (1927)

QUOTES BY HIM:
"The Rumanian Jews are the last serfs still existing in Europe." —(1913)

"The bold experience of colonization undertaken by the Jews in Palestine has a value transcending that of the problems of race and Zionism. It proves that the Jews can, after twenty centuries be again unsurpassable cultivators, and it proves too that the Syrian land, for thousands of years a squalid, desolate, rocky desert, can become once more a smiling desert." —(1925)

Luzzatti died March 29, 1927.

David Saul Marshall

Chief Minister of Singapore
1955–1956

PERSONAL DATA:
Born in Singapore on March 12, 1910 to an old-line Iraqi-Persian Jewish family, Marshall studied at St. Joseph's Institution, St. Andrews, as well as at London University. After having been admitted to the English bar in 1937 Marshall returned home to begin an important career as a labor lawyer.

EARLY POLITICAL CAREER:
A staunch anti-Communist and opponent of British colonial rule, Marshall was first elected to public office in April 1955 when he won a seat in Singapore's Colonial Legislative Assembly. A short time later Marshall was chosen by the ruling left-of-center, multiracial United Labor Front to become Singapore's first chief minister, a position equivalent to that of premier.

MAJOR POLITICAL ACHIEVEMENTS:
As chief minister, Marshall in late 1955 led a mission to London for talks with the British Colonial Office, negotiations that resulted in establishing a tentative agenda for Singapore's eventual independence. In 1956, frustrated by the slow pace of decolonization and under increasing political pressure from his own party's left wing, Marshall was forced to resign.

JEWISH IDENTITY:
Marshall has served as president of the Singapore Jewish Welfare Board (1946–1953) and has been a trustee of Singapore's *Manasseh Meyer Talmud Torah* Fund. According to Mrs. Marshall (a non-Jew), however, their children are being "raised . . . as Christians."

IMPORTANT LITTLE KNOWN FACTS:
Having enlisted in the Singapore Volunteer Corps in 1938, Marshall was taken prisoner by the Japanese following their conquest of Malaya in 1942. After the war Marshall returned home from a Japanese POW camp and helped found the Singapore War Prisoners' Association.

QUOTES ABOUT HIM:
"The Clement Attlee of the Singapore Labor movement." —*The New York Times* (1955)

QUOTES BY HIM:
"There is no future for Jews in Singapore. . . . Singapore has gone over to the Moslems." —(1975).

René Joel Simon Mayer

Premier of France 1953

PERSONAL DATA:
The grandson of a rabbi, René Joel Simon Mayer was born in Paris on May 4, 1895.

His parents were Jacob Justin and Marthe Dupont Mayer, and he was a cousin by marriage of the Rothschild banking family. Shortly after graduating from the University of Paris Faculty of Law in 1914, Mayer volunteered for military service. As a lieutenant in the Field Artillery, Mayer saw extensive combat, and in 1918 received the *Croix de Guerre*, France's highest military honor. Later, Mayer became a Grand Officer of France's *Legion d'Honneur*. His only son, Antoine, a parachutist, was killed in World War II.

EARLY POLITICAL CAREER:

During the 1930's Mayer served as vice president of the *Compagnie des Chemins de Fer du Nord* and the *Compagnie Internationale des Wagons-Lits*. Stripped of these positions by the anti-Semitic Vichy regime in September 1940, Mayer joined the French resistance. In 1943 he became a member of the French Committee for National Liberation and later served as minister of transport in General Charles de Gaulle's first provisional government. Running as a Radical Socialist, Mayer was first elected to the French National Assembly in 1946 as a representative of the white settler minority in Constantine, Algeria.

MAJOR POLITICAL ACHIEVEMENT:

As the second Jewish premier of France (January 8, 1953–June 27, 1953) Mayer "based his policy on friendship with Great Britain" and the United States and sought a strong European Defense Community (EDC). Like other heads of the French Fourth Republic, his cabinet was weak and his term in office short.

JEWISH IDENTITY:

During his lifetime Mayer served as vice president of the *Alliance Israélite Universelle* and was a member of the Central *Consistoire* of French Jews.

IMPORTANT LITTLE KNOWN FACTS:

A strong supporter of civilian aviation, Mayer was a founder of Air France, the French national airline.

QUOTES ABOUT HIM:

"He belongs to that brilliant association of ex-premiers who have given France the EDC and Dien Bien Phu, and the Tunisian and Madagascar massacres." —*Le Canard Enchaîné* (1955)

QUOTES BY HIM:

"It is apparent . . . that in Indochina the major objective of the *Vietminh* . . . is not simply the Gulf of Tonkin but also the Gulf of Siam and the approaches to India. The battle being waged by French and Vietnamese troops in the rice paddies and on the plateaus are serving not merely to protect Indochina against subversion but to protect the whole of Southeast Asia." —(1953)

Mayer died December 13, 1972.

Pierre Mendès-France

Premier of France
1954–1955

PERSONAL DATA:

Born in Paris on January 11, 1907 to one of France's "oldest Jewish families," Mendès-France achieved a brilliant record as a student and at one time held the record as the youngest person to ever graduate from the prestigious *Ecole des Sciences Politiques*. The father of two children, Bernard and Michel, Mendès-France is also the author of no less than thirteen books.

Pierre Mendes France

EARLY POLITICAL CAREER:
Having joined the French Radical Socialist party at age sixteen, Mendès-France enjoyed a meteoric rise in politics. In 1932 he became the youngest member of the French National Assembly. Three years later he was elected mayor of Louviers and in 1938 served briefly as under secretary for finance in Léon Blum's second Popular Front government.

MAJOR POLITICAL ACHIEVEMENTS:
Chosen by the National Assembly to become premier on June 18, 1954, Mendès-France was responsible for ending France's military involvement in Vietnam, for securing French backing for West German rearmament, and for pacifying Tunisia, at least temporarily, by granting that country internal political autonomy.

JEWISH IDENTITY:
An outspoken supporter of Israel and Zionism, Mendès-France once quipped, "our family is a [Marrano] family, that is, of Jewish-Portuguese origin. . . . They left Portugal between 1500 and 1600 and have [been in] Bordeaux ever since."

IMPORTANT LITTLE KNOWN FACTS:
With the outbreak of World War II in September 1939 Mendès-France enlisted in the French Air Force, was commissioned as a junior officer, and served briefly in Syria as a navigator-observer before being transferred back to France. On June 9, 1940 Mendès-France was wounded defending Louviers from the advancing Germans. Later, tried and convicted as a "deserter" by the Vichy collaborationist regime, he was imprisoned. Escaping from his captors in 1941, Mendès-France travelled to London, where he joined the RAF's Free French Flying unit, the *Groupe* Lorraine, otherwise known as the "342." Mendès-France holds the *Croix de Guerre*, the *Rosette de la Resistance*, and is an officer of the *Legion d'Honneur*.

QUOTES ABOUT HIM:
A political target of both right-wing and left-wing anti-Semites, Mendès-France was once described by Jacques Duclos, the head of the French Communist party, as a "cold-footed little Jew." —(1954)

"Don't throw stones at him, he is a sincere and tortured man." —Guy Mollet (1956)

QUOTES BY HIM:
On Vietnam:
"I gave myself a month to make peace in Indo-China, and was accused by some of 'defeatism.' In reality, I can now reveal that the French Generals in Indo-China were desperate to have the cease-fire within a fortnight, i.e., on July 5, 1954; as they could not guarantee being able to hold out any longer." —(1955)

Sir Julius Vogel
K.C.M.G.
Prime Minister of New Zealand
1873–1875, 1876

PERSONAL DATA:
Born in London's East End on February 24, 1835, Vogel was educated at the University College School and began his career as a clerk in the offices of his maternal grandfather, Alexander Isaac, a West Indian merchant, who had taken Vogel in after the death of his parents in 1849. Like many other poor Englishmen, Vogel was attracted by the news of the Australian gold rush. In 1852 he left London for the Melbourne gold fields. During the next nine years, however, Vogel failed in his attempts to become an assayer, to become co-owner of a drug store, or to get elected to public office. Abandoning Australia in 1861, Vogel emigrated to New Zealand, where he soon became a partner and editor of the colony's first daily newspaper, the *Otago Daily Times*. Later, Vogel married the daughter of William Clayton, a government architect, and a non-Jew. The couple had four children: one daughter, and three sons, one of whom was later killed fighting in the Matabele War in South Africa.

EARLY POLITICAL CAREER:
In 1862 Vogel was elected a member of the Otago Provincial Council. A year later Julius ran and was elected a member of the New Zealand House of Representatives, "where his mastery of financial issues brought him to the fore."

MAJOR POLITICAL ACHIEVEMENT:
In 1870, as treasurer of the central government, Vogel put forth what has come to be known as the "Grand Go-Ahead" policy in New Zealand. Under Vogel's plan the New Zealand government borrowed £10,000,000 from Great Britain to finance the expansion of railroads, highways, and an inter-island communications and telegraph system, as well as to develop a vigorous immigration policy designed to insure New Zealand the manpower necessary for its internal development. As a result of Vogel's scheme, New Zealand was able to double its population within ten years. The colony also added over 1,100 miles of new railroads, new roads,

and a comprehensive telegraph system. These achievements did not come cheaply. Under Vogel's leadership the national debt also doubled and there was considerable waste and mismanagement of funds. One British colonial office administrator went so far as to describe Vogel as "the most audacious adventurer that . . . ever held power in a British colony." Others were less polite! One of his political enemies called him "Jew-lius Rex." Another described him as a "startling figure of a little Jew from Otago."

IMPORTANT LITTLE KNOWN FACTS:
"Dubbed the Disraeli of New Zealand," Vogel had advocated, as early as 1865, that Great Britain annex the Hawaiian Islands before the United States did so. Later in his *Anno Domini 2000*, an almanac for the year 2000 C.E., Vogel "propounded his dreams," including the prophecy that one day "an air cruiser travelling one hundred miles an hour would leave Melbourne in the morning and arrive at Dunedin [New Zealand] at night."

JEWISH IDENTITY:
While a member of the New Zealand House of Representatives, Vogel strongly opposed the introduction of compulsory religious education in state supported schools. Vogel, however, was a strong supporter of Jewish education as it existed in nineteenth-century New Zealand and established two prizes for the best pupils in Hebrew at an Auckland synagogue school.

QUOTES ABOUT HIM:
"The persistency with which he faced trouble and embarrassment, the hopefulness he showed under stress of ill fortune, the sympathy and pleasantness of manner which won him friends at all times were elements in his curious and interesting character no less remarkable than the fertility and imaginative power of his busy brain." —*Encyclopaedia Britannica* (1910)

"His public policies were extensions of that greedy and sanguine nature which was revealed in his inveterate gluttony and gambling. He suffered from gout as well as gold fever." —Historian Keith Sinclair (1961)

QUOTES BY HIM:
"I desire to see New Zealand become the headquarters of the British possessions in Polynesia. I think, from its geographic position, from its climate, and from the character of its people, it is not too much to expect that it will arrive at that position." —(1874)

Vogel died on March 13, 1899.

Sir Roy Welensky
K.C.M.G.
Prime Minister of the Federation of Rhodesia and Nyasaland 1956–1963

PERSONAL DATA:
Born on January 20, 1907 in Salisbury Rhodesia (Zimbabwe), Welensky's father, Michael, was a Lithuanian-born Jew, who had escaped service in the Czarist army by amputating a finger and had later attempted to earn a living in Germany and the United States by smuggling horses and running a saloon. His mother, Leah, a ninth generation Afrikaner, converted to Judaism after having met "Mike" in the South African gold fields. As one of thirteen children, Roy Welensky's childhood was marred by severe poverty. At age fourteen he was forced to leave school. Seven years later, while working as a fireman for the Rhodesian Railways, Roy married Elizabeth Henderson, a waitress in a Bulawayo cafe (d. 1969). Welensky has two surviving children from his first marriage, Joan and Michael, and one child from his second marriage to Valarie Scott.

EARLY POLITICAL CAREER:
Welensky first became active in electoral politics in 1938 when he was elected a member of the Northern Rhodesian Legislative Council. Three years later he founded the Rhodesian Labor party.

MAJOR POLITICAL ACHIEVEMENT:
Working under the direction of his political mentor, Sir Godfrey Huggins (Lord Malvern), Welensky succeeded in 1956 in forming the white dominated Federation of Rhodesia and Nyasaland, a political experiment that lasted until December 31, 1963, when by unilateral act of the British government, the Federation was dissolved.

JEWISH IDENTITY:
Taunted in his youth as a "fat Jew-boy," Welensky later successfully resisted attempts by anti-Semitic supporters of Sir Oswald Mosley to gain control of the Rhodesian Railwaymen's Union.

IMPORTANT LITTLE KNOWN FACTS:
In 1926 Welensky became the first Jew to ever win the Rhodesian professional heavyweight boxing title.

QUOTES ABOUT HIM:
"To liberals of all parties in Britain and to Africans in his own country. . . . Sir Roy is a

white supremacist all the more dangerous because he affects the enlightened disguise of 'partnership.' " —*Commentary Magazine* (1962)

"Your Honor, Nyasaland belongs to the Africans, not to you and your white men." —Mmbelwa II, Chief of the Angonis Tribe (1957)

"Roy Welensky stands as the biggest (6 ft. 2 in., 282 lbs.) and most powerful symbol of white supremacy in the largest and richest white colonial bastion still left in Africa." —*Time Magazine* (1962)

QUOTES BY HIM:

"I am a Jew and I have never forgotten being persecuted by Fascist elements in Rhodesia before the war."

"I know that the African National Congress is saying, 'Freedom at any Price!' This is an emotional appeal to a not-so-advanced people. I hope those who talk this way realize what would become of the ordinary black man in this country." —(1958)

"If the Federation were to go under you would see the lights go out in this part of Africa." —(1962)

—C.J.R.

JEWISH MEMBERS OF U.S. CABINETS

NAME	POST	PRESIDENT	YEARS
Oscar S. Straus	Commerce and Labor	T. Roosevelt	1908
Henry C. Morgenthau, Jr.	Treasury	F. D. Roosevelt; Truman	1933–1945
Abraham A. Ribicoff	Health, Education, and Welfare	Kennedy	1961–1962
Arthur J. Goldberg	Labor	Kennedy; Johnson	1961–1963
Wilbur J. Cohen	Health, Education, and Welfare	Johnson	1968–1969
Henry Kissinger	State	Nixon; Ford	1973–1977
Edward H. Levi	Attorney General	Ford	1975–1977
Harold Brown	Defense	Carter	1977–
Neil Goldschmidt	Transportation	Carter	1979–
Philip M. Klutznick	Commerce	Carter	1979–

Source: *Jewish Week* (New York)

JEWISH MEMBERS OF THE U.S. CONGRESS (1789–1980)

(R) Republican; (D) Democrat; (W) Whig; (ALP) American Labor Party; (S) Socialist; (A) American.

Senate

Alaska
Ernest H. Gruening (D), 1959–1969
Colorado
Simon Guggenheim (R), 1907–1913
Connecticut
Abraham A. Ribicoff (D), 1963–1980
Florida
David Levy Yulee (D), 1845–1851, 1855–1861
Richard Stone (D), 1974–
Louisiana
Judah P. Benjamin (W-D), 1853–1861
Benjamin Franklin Jonas (D), 1879–1885
Maryland
Isidor Rayner (D), 1905–1912
Michigan
Carl Levin (D), 1978–
Minnesota
Rudy Boschwitz (R), 1978–
Nebraska
Edward Zorinsky (D), 1976–
New York
Herbert H. Lehman (D), 1949–1957
Jacob K. Javits (R), 1957–
Ohio
Howard Metzenbaum (D), 1973–1974, 1976–
Oregon
Joseph Simon (R), 1898–1903
Richard Neuberger (D), 1955–1960

House of Representatives

Alabama
Philip Phillips (D), 1853–1855

Arizona
Sam Steiger (R), 1967–1977
California
Julius Kahn (R), 1899–1903, 1905–1924
Francis Kahn (R), 1925–1937
John Krebs (D), 1975–1979
Henry A. Waxman (D), 1975–
Anthony C. Beilenson (D), 1977–
Colorado
Ken Kramer (R), 1978–
Connecticut
Herman P. Koppelmann (D), 1933–1939, 1941–1943, 1945–1947
William M. Citron (D), 1935–1939
Abraham A. Ribicoff (D), 1949–1953
Florida
William Lehman (D), 1973
David Levy Yulee (D), 1841–1845 (represented Florida Territory)

Front page of* The Jewish Daily Forward, *November 5, 1914, announcing Meyer London's election to Congress.

Georgia
Elliot H. Levitas (D), 1975–
Illinois
Julius Goldzier (D), 1893–1895
Martin Emerich (D), 1903–1905
Adolph J. Sabath (D), 1907–1952
Sidney R. Yates (D), 1949–1963, 1965–
Abner J. Mikva (D), 1969–1973, 1975–1979
Indiana
Milton Kraus (R), 1917–1923
Iowa
Edward Mezvinsky (D), 1973–1975

Kansas
Daniel Glickman (D), 1977–
Louisiana
Adolph Meier (D), 1891–1908
Maryland
Isidor Rayner (D), 1887–1889, 1891–1895
Harry B. Wolf (D), 1907–1909
Daniel Ellison (R), 1943–1945
Samuel N. Friedel (D), 1953–1971
Gladys Noon Spellman (D), 1975–

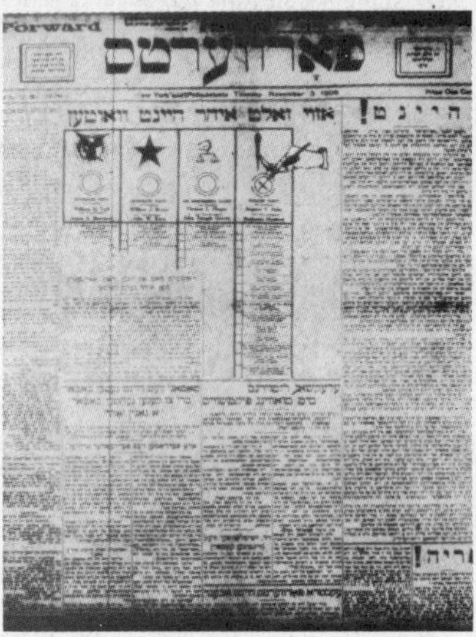

***"This is the way to vote today"—election day edition of* The Jewish Daily Forward.**

Massachusetts
Leopold Morse (D), 1877–1885, 1887–1889
Michigan
Julius Houseman (D), 1883–1885
Howard Wolpe (D), 1978–
Missouri
Nathan Frank (R), 1889–1891
New Jersey
Isaac Bachrach (R), 1915–1937
Charles S. Joelson (D), 1961–1969
New York
Emanuel R. Hart (D), 1841–1852
Edwin Einstein (R), 1879–1881
Isidor Strauss (D), 1894–1894
Israel F. Fischer (R), 1895–1899
Lucius N. Littauer (R), 1897–1907
Mitchell May (D), 1899–1901
Jefferson N. Levy (D), 1899–1901
Henry M. Goldfogle (D), 1901–1915, 1919–1921
Montague Lessler (R), 1902–1903
Jacob Cantor (D), 1913–1915
Meyer London (S), 1915–1919, 1921–1923
Issac Siegel (R), 1915–1923

Nathan D. Perlman (R), 1920–1927
Lester D. Volk (R), 1920–1923
Martin C. Ansorge (R), 1921–1923
Albert B. Rossdale (R), 1921–1923
Samuel Marx (D), 1922
Sol Bloom (D), 1923–1949
Emanuel Celler (D), 1923–1973
Samuel Dickstein (D), 1923–1945
Meyer Jacobstein (D), 1923–1929
William I. Sirovich (D), 1927–1939
William W. Cohen (D), 1927–1929
Theodore A. Peyser (D), 1933–1937
Morris M. Edelstein (D), 1940–1941
Arthur Klein (D), 1941–1945, 1946–1956
Leo Rayfiel (D), 1945–1947
Benjamin Rabin (D), 1945–1947
Abraham Multer (D) 1947–1967
Jacob K. Javits (R), 1947–1954
Leo Isacson (ALP), 1948–1949
Louis B. Heller (D), 1949–1954
Isidore Dollinger (D), 1949–1959
Sidney Fine (D), 1951–1956
Lester Holtzman (D), 1953–1961
Irwin Davidson (D), 1955–1956
Herbert Zelenko (D), 1955–1963
Ludwig Teller (D), 1957–1961
Leonard Farbstein (D), 1957–1971
Seymour Halpern (R), 1959–1973
Jacob H. Gilbert (D), 1960–1971
Benjamin Rosenthal (D), 1962–
Herbert Tenzer (D), 1965–1969
Joseph Resnick (D), 1965–1969
Richard L. Ottinger (D), 1965–1971, 1975–
James H. Scheuer (D), 1965–1973, 1975–
Lester Wolff (D), 1965–
Bertram L. Podell (D), 1968–1975
Allard K. Lowenstein (D), 1969–1971
Edward I. Koch (D), 1969–1977
Bella Abzug (D), 1971–1977
Benjamin A. Gilman (R), 1973–
Stephen J. Solarz (D), 1975–
Elizabeth Holtzman (D), 1975–1980
Frederick Richmond (D), 1975–
Theodore S. Weiss (D), 1977–
William Green (R), 1978–

Ohio

Willis Gradison, Jr. (R), 1975–

Pennsylvania

Lewis Levin (A), 1845–1851
Henry M. Phillips (D), 1857–1859
Myer Strouse (D), 1863–1867
Benjamin Golder (R), 1925–1933
Henry Ellenbogen (D), 1933–1938
Leon Sacks (D), 1937–1943
Samuel A. Weiss (D), 1941–1946
Earl Chudoff (D), 1949–1958
Herman Toll (D), 1959–1967
Joshua Eilberg (D), 1967–1978
Marc L. Marks (R), 1977–

Texas

Martin Frost (D), 1978–

West Virginia

Benjamin L. Rosenbloom (R), 1921–1925

Wisconsin

Victor Berger (S), 1911–1913, 1923–1929

Source: Martin H. Greenberg, *The Jewish Lists* (New York, 1979).

THE SEPARATION OF SYNAGOGUE AND STATE: SEVEN "LANDMARK" DECISIONS

Historically, American civil courts have tried to avoid becoming involved in Jewish ecclesiastical matters, not only because of Constitutional prohibitions, but because of the sensitive nature of the litigation. The courts have thus adopted a general rule that they will only hear cases involving religious matters where the primary legal question is one of a secular nature. They will decline to exercise jurisdiction over any matters that are primarily ecclesiastic in nature.

Jurisdiction of the *Bet Din:*

Observant Jews still refer civil matters, as well as religious questions, to rabbis for determination. The court, known as a *Bet Din,* consists of three rabbis versed in *halakhah* (Jewish law). The process is known as a *Din Torah* and the decision is final and binding. It is an arbitration process similar to that in use for civil proceedings throughout the United States. The question of course arises: what is the binding nature of such a proceeding on a civil court.

"The Case of the Unclear Decision": Kozlowsky v. Seville Syndicate, Inc.
314 N.Y.S. 2d 489
(New York, 1970)

The parties to this proceeding were three Orthodox Jews who owned all of the stock of a corporation whose chief asset was a New York City hotel. The parties quarreled and after numerous forays into the courts, sold the hotel and took back a rather large mortgage. No distribution of the mortgage payments was ever made, however, because of conflicting claims as to each recipient's proper share.

In the spring of 1968 the stockholders decided to settle their differences by means of a *Din Torah* and entered into an agreement submitting themselves to the jurisdiction of an Orthodox rabbi. After hearing the case the rabbi issued his decision regarding the respective rights of the three parties and forbade further court proceedings by any party.

Unfortunately, the *Din Torah* did not resolve all of the issues, and an interpretation of the rabbi's concluding document was requested. The parties went to a New York State court that was required to interpret a religious document in light of religious and civil law. In an important decision, Judge Matthew Levy discussed Jewish jurisprudence, using as some of his sources Kadushin, *Jewish Code of Jurisprudence,* and Kaplan's *Rabbinical Courts.* The gist of his decision was that the *Din Torah* was an arbitration proceeding complying with the requirements of New York law applicable to arbitrations in general and was, therefore, subject to interpretations based on New York law.

State Courts Look at Synagogue Policy

Another group of cases involves the religious policies and practices of synagogues. In most instances these cases emerged as a result of a dispute among members of a synagogue board of trustees about the religious orientation of the congregation. If appeals to reason fail, the next resort for the aggrieved party is usually the secular courts, whose judges find themselves in the unusually awkward position of being involved in what is essentially an internal Jewish dispute.

Those parties who go to court in these cases usually claim that the power of the state must be invoked to protect what are constitutionally protected religious rights. The courts have indicated, however, that they are willing to enter the arena of ecclesiastical disputes only when serious property rights are involved. The result is that those who want civil court review of religious disputes try to frame those disputes in terms of property, however tenuous the reasoning may be. The courts are not easily persuaded, as the record of decisions indicate, particularly where religious policies and practices of synagogues are involved. Take, for instance,

"The Case of the Judge Who Disapproved of Mixed Seating": Davis v. Scher 97 N.W. 2d 137 (Michigan 1969)

In this case Judge Kavanaugh of the Michigan Supreme Court had to determine the legality of an Orthodox congregation's change from separate to mixed seating. A member of the congregation tried to enjoin the trustees from having mixed seating, and the trustees claimed that the court was without jurisdiction because the question of seating was an ecclesiastical matter only.

Judge Kavanaugh agreed that the court could not hear the case unless property rights were involved; otherwise, according to the judge, the court would be entering into ecclesiastical matters involving freedom of religion. At the same time, he alluded to the fact that it is also a court's duty to preserve freedom of religion and to preserve the rights of minority groups. In a masterpiece of logic Judge Kavanaugh found that in this case property rights were involved in a very unique way. Kavanaugh's theory was that where a congregation is of a certain denomination or has certain practices, it cannot deviate from its original purposes and change its practices, even by majority vote, because in doing so, it would be depriving the minority of the use of the religious property itself. Once Judge Kavanaugh decided that the court did have jurisdiction, he had no difficulty in finding for the dissident members; they had presented the only testimony as to the original purpose of the congregation and the requirements of Orthodox Judaism as to seating.

Making Good on a Pledge

The decision to build a new sanctuary is often a momentous one. Most members who make pledges to such a building campaign fulfill their pledges and never consider the legal implications. Those who are more versed in the law know that a pledge to a building fund is as legally binding as any other contractual promise. Occasionally, there are those who believe that a pledge to a Jewish organization is a moral obligation but certainly not one that any civil court would enforce.

"The Case of the Unfulfilled Pledge": Congregation B'nai Shalom v. Martin. 160 N.W. 3d 784 (Michigan 1968)

This Conservative congregation in Michigan decided to build a new synagogue and named Martin, a member of the congregation, as chairman of the committee in charge of fund raising. A professional fund-raiser was also retained by the congregation to direct the overall effort. The professional fund-raiser suggested that a large pledge by Martin would be a significant inspiration to other members of the congregation. Martin and his family thereupon signed pledge cards to give $25,000 to the building fund. Unfortunately, there was a disagreement during the campaign and the Martin family withdrew its pledge.

The congregation brought action against the Martins to collect the pledge. The Martins raised two defenses: (1) the case was a religious and not a civil matter and therefore could only be decided by a *Bet Din,* and (2) under Jewish law, a pledge to a synagogue is a moral obligation only and not enforceable by a civil court.

There were a number of procedural problems that arose in the lower courts before the matter finally came before the Michigan Court of Appeals. Of significant interest is the affidavit filed by a rabbi acting as an expert witness. In testimony before the court the rabbi stated that the *Shulhan Arukh* (*Code of Jewish Law*) had a binding effect on both Orthodox and Conservative Jews.

The rabbi further pointed out that the *Shulhan Arukh* and long-standing Jewish tradition and custom prohibited a synagogue from bringing a suit against any of its members in a civil court and vice versa unless the case had first been brought before a *Bet Din.* The rabbi argued "that under Jewish law, matters of charity to the synagogue go to the heart of the Jewish religion; that a charitable contribution to a synagogue is considered a religious matter by and between the synagogue and the member; . . . that historically, pledges to a synagogue were always considered and are still considered as moral obligations and not the subject of a lawsuit. . . ."

The Michigan courts were certainly not going to decide whether the *Shulhan Arukh* was valid or binding on a Conservative congregation. To do so would have amounted to a civil determination of a religious principle. What the appellate court did instead was to concentrate solely on whether the religious principles involved—binding or not—were the *determinant* factors in this case. The court decided that they were not. As to the requirement that the case be tried before a *Bet Din,* the court held that there was no evidence showing that the parties ever used or knew about a *Bet Din* or were even familiar with this aspect of Jewish law. That being the case, it would be wrong to hold the parties to a custom about which they knew nothing.

The court also would not decide whether a pledge to a synagogue was solely a moral obligation or a legally binding one, as well. Instead, the court held that the determinant factor was whether the parties *intended* the pledge to be a moral obligation only. The court referred to the fact "that the pledge card, worded as are most pledge cards in any fund-raising campaign, demonstrate little tendency to create a 'moral' obligation rather than a legal obligation." The court went on to say that if there had been a desire to make the pledges a moral rather than a legal obligation, it would have been easy to do so by advising prospective donors of the fact and wording the pledge cards accordingly.

This complicated case was eventually sent back to the lower courts for a new trial because of procedural problems. There is nothing further in the court records about the case, and one can assume that it was settled out of court.

Firing a Rabbi

The dissatisfaction of a congregation with its spiritual leader usually results in a relatively peaceful parting of the ways at the end of a contractual term, accompanied by letters of thanks, a congregational dinner, and a small token of the congregation's esteem. On the other hand, the discharge of a rabbi mid term is a traumatic experience that not only evokes spiritual soul-searching but the appearance of legal documents as well.

"The Case of the Locked-Out Rabbi": Kupperman v. Congregation Nusach Sfard
240 N.Y.S. 2d
315 (New York 1963)

In this case a Bronx county court judge was faced with the problem of deciding under what circumstances a congregation could dismiss and remove its rabbi. The rabbi in this case had not only been discharged but the congregation had gone so far as to change the locks on the doors of the synagogue to make sure that the rabbi would be unable to officiate.

The rabbi sued for breach of contract, claiming that he had not been discharged properly according to the Religious Corporations Law of New York State and that all parties were bound by the decision of a *Bet Din* that had been convened to hear the matter.

The court, finding for the rabbi, held that in other denominations, the calling and firing of a spiritual leader is involved with a hierarchy with codified principles, policies, and customs, and therefore the pastoral relationship is one with which the courts will not interfere. In Judaism, however, there is no hierarchy and only a *minyan* (religious quorum) is required to conduct services. The contract between the rabbi and his congregation is but a "mundane contract of employment," not an ecclesiastical matter. As far as the *Bet Din* was concerned, the court held that while it respected the spiritual authority of a *Bet Din* and its ecclesiastical sanctions against individuals, the rabbi had sued the congregation as a religious corporation incorporated under the laws of New York State and the matter had to be determined by the court based on the statutory law of the State.

Kashrut

Several cases involve the question of *kashrut* observance and supervision. Various Jewish groups that are interested in preserving Judaism view *kashrut* as indispensable to that end, and rightly insist that there be controls over the sale and preparation of food offered as being kosher. The state also has an interest in preventing any sort of fraud, particularly where food is involved, and has enacted penal laws to prevent sale of food designated as kosher that in fact is not. Many of the cases in this area deal with violations of these laws and convictions based on such violations.

"The Case of the Suspect Chickens": Erlich v. Municipal Court of the Beverly Hills Judicial District, 360 P. 2d 337 (California 1965)

Erlich was charged by the Municipal Court of Beverly Hills with selling chickens to the Beverly Hills Hilton Hotel that were not kosher but that he had claimed were kosher.

The law under which Erlich was charged made it a misdemeanor to sell with intent to defraud, meat falsely represented to be kosher or having been prepared from products "sanctioned by the orthodox Hebrew religious requirements." The law went on to say that, "the word kosher is here defined to mean a strict compliance with every Jewish law and custom pertaining and relating to the killing of the animal or fowl from which the meat is taken or extracted . . ."

Erlich's defense was that the law was so vague that it was unenforceable, because no two rabbis could agree as to the full extent of the meaning of the word "kosher." If there was such disagreement, any deviation by a seller of kosher food would constitute a crime under the law.

This argument had been advanced before, and this court was as unimpressed with it as prior courts had been. Citing earlier court decisions, the Supreme Court of California held that the term "kosher" is to be defined in terms of its ordinary usage in the trade. Those in the trade, said the court, know what laws and customs are generally followed by kosher suppliers, and that all a supplier has to do is to exercise judgment in good faith—he does not have to follow every law and custom to be deemed in compliance with the law.

Marriage and Divorce

The difficulties involved in the interaction between civil law and Jewish religious law are most apparent in the area of matrimonial problems. As the divorce rate increases the civil courts find that they must often investigate religious law and render decisions based upon an interpretation of what is a complicated and extensive body of law. Most often these cases concern decisions about a separation agreement between husband and wife that contains a provision that requires the obtaining of a *get,* a religious divorce according to Jewish law.

The validity of an agreement or promise to obtain a *get* has been recognized in New York State. The problem is, how does a civil court enforce the right without running afoul of the First Amendment? Requiring someone to perform a religious duty would tend to be a violation of one's freedom of religion. The courts have come up with some unique ways to handle this problem. For example, consider:

"The Case of the Reluctant Spouse": Koeppel v. Koeppel, 138 N.Y.S. 2d 336 (New York, 1959)

Mr. and Mrs. Koeppel executed a separation agreement, one provision of which was a promise by the husband to obtain a *get.* When the husband refused to comply with the agreement, the wife went into court to force him to seek a *get.* The husband contended that forcing him to obtain a *get* would amount to compelling him to practice a religion. He also claimed that it was not fair that he should be subjected to a procedure that would take "from two to two and one-half hours."

The court disposed of his first argument by holding that enforcing his promise was not compelling him to profess his faith but merely enforcing what was a voluntary agreement on his part. As to the second agrument, the court, in referring to his claim that the rabbinical process was overly lengthy, held, "That is not much out of a lifetime, particularly if it will bring peace of mind and conscience to one whom the defendant must at one time have loved."

The ruling in the Koeppel case and other

cases of this type does not imply that courts have the absolute ability to insure that a *get* is obtained. They cannot imprison a reluctant spouse or force a rabbinical court to convene. Instead they have fined a reluctant spouse or made it uncomfortable for one by making the performance of other terms of a separation agreement dependant on the fulfillment of the promise to obtain the *get*. This has the effect of accomplishing compliance without running into constitutional objections.

Honoring God

Rabbi Joshua Sackett, a twenty-four-year-old teacher at the Hebrew Academy, Norfolk, Virginia, made the mistake of appearing for a traffic violation before Judge Vernon Hitchings, a judge alleged to have disposed of over one million traffic cases in a twenty-three year period. He compounded the error by wearing a *yarmulke* in court, where respect for the law is demonstrated by doffing one's hat.

When Rabbi Sackett appeared in Judge Hitching's court, he was asked to remove his *yarmulke*. When he said that he could not remove it because of his religious beliefs, the judge reportedly said, "I don't care what your religion is. You're going to take that hat off in my courtroom or you can take your religion out of my courtroom."

Rabbi Sackett did remove his *yarmulke* under protest and the judge then dismissed the violation. After a number of complaints, Judge Hitchings apologized to Rabbi Sackett for his "error in judgment." Said the judge, "When I insisted upon the removal of your headcover, I had no idea of the implications thereof or intended an affront to the Jewish religion." In a marvelous understatement, he added, "In fact, I did not know you are a rabbi or a Jew."

—A.J.G.

DISSIDENT VOICES

JEWISH RADICALS OF THE 60'S: WHERE ARE THEY NOW?

In the 1960's it was usually assumed that a substantial proportion of the New Left's leaders were Jewish. That was not exactly the case. There were many Jewish radicals, of course, but not as many of them held leadership roles as many writers at the time tended to suggest. For every Jew in the Southern civil rights movement there were several blacks; there were white divinity students; there were well-to-do Protestants, whose New England ancestors had been abolitionists. Catholic and Protestant students, like Tom Hayden, Robb Burlage, Rennie Davis, and Paul Potter, comprised much of the early leadership of the Students for a Democratic Society (SDS). Many anti-war leaders—like Fathers Daniel and Philip Berrigan, the Rev. William Sloan Coffin, and Dave Dellinger—had strong links to the church. By contrast, the New York-based Yippies—whose prankish radicalism was symbolized by Abbie Hoffman and Jerry Rubin—was mostly led by Jews.

In those years the Jews who did emerge as radical leaders in the movement were mostly men. Later on during the violent Weather Underground stage of the movement, Jewish women like Kathy Boudin and Bernadine Dorhn took on active leadership roles, but they are still underground and impossible to contact. That demographic reality is reflected in entries that follow.

Most Jews in the New Left led relatively assimilated lives. Of course, they did toss in a Yiddish expression here and there. They, more than any other group, were "red diaper babies"—children of people who had been Socialists or Communists in the 1930's. Many were post-Holocaust Jews who connected their work in the civil rights and the antiwar movements with a deep determination never to let fascism in any form go unchallenged. But even those Jews who retained a strong sense of their culture rarely engaged in religious practices—like observing *Shabbat* or keeping kosher—acts that would differentiate them from other American radicals. Except within some fringe groups, Israel was not an issue that divided progressives in the 1960's. Back then, there was barely any perceptible tension between Christians and Jews in what seemed like a unified, American left.

Nonetheless, something must have been simmering. At a 1977 SDS reunion there was an unscheduled Jewish workshop, which drew about fifty of the two hundred people there. Some talked, for the first time, about being red diaper babies. Others, bred in working-class families, described the smouldering resentments they felt in the midst of the mostly upper-middle-class New Left, where many people who were supposed to be their comrades never seemed aware of their financial struggles.

At that reunion, some people also expressed an interest in religion. Nevertheless, only a few of the 60's Jewish radical leaders have become religious. Most of those interviewed here still lead highly secular lives.

There are, however, two places where the radical impulses of the 1960's and the more recent revival of religious Judaism do connect. One is the *baal teshuvah* yeshivot (religious environments for those returning to Judaism) in Israel and the United States. For the most part, these institutions have not attracted the well-known radical leaders, but they have reached some Jews who floated between the counterculture and the antiwar movement in the 60's. They were foot soldiers of the New Left, who looked on many of the people mentioned below as their leaders.

The other point of contact is that in the 1960's the ideas of the New Left influenced Jews from more traditional backgrounds. For instance, the concept of "participatory democracy"—the New Left's slogan—certainly converged with the freewheeling, antiinstitutional sentiments that produced the Havurah movement (alternative communities). Breira (a now-defunct organization that sought alternative solutions to many problems of contemporary Judaism), concerned about justice for Palestinians as well as Israel's survival, was linked to the civil right's movement's concern for blacks and the antiwar movement's concern for Vietnamese. The Jewish Defense League, though its politics were reactionary, was pervaded by the spirit of defiance that one found in SDS. Right now, the women's daavening groups (groups that convene to pray together in an intimate environment) and Rosh Hodesh (celebration of the New Moon, a woman's holiday) groups, which are becoming a vital part of the Havurah movement and of modern Orthodoxy, have been deeply influenced by the woman's movement.

So the New Left was intertwined with traditional Judaism in more ways than the biographies below suggest. It is possible that the tensions and connections between a progressive political world and a changing Jewish religious one will produce fertile soil for innovations in the years to come.

Mickey Flacks

Activities in the 60's: Mickey's husband Dick, a University of Michigan graduate student in sociology, was one of the most influential early theorists of the New Left. But Mickey, equally radical, was working then and felt that she had no place in a student organization. So she stayed on the fringes of the Students for a Democratic Society (she was at the legendary conference where the Port Huron statement was drafted), but joined organizations like Women's Strike for Peace, which had members of all ages.

In 1964 she and Dick moved to Chicago, where she fed, housed, and advised radical students and looked after her own children. During the violent 1968 Democratic Convention she took demonstrators to hospitals and bailed them out of jail. During the entire decade she was the kind of reliable, rather self-effacing person who—more than most leaders or bursts of rhetorical eloquence—enable a movement to survive.

Jewish background: Mickey, New York born, comes from a Yiddish-speaking, Old Left immigrant family. As a child, she and her parents were loyal to the pro-Moscow *Daily Freiheit* and contemptuous of the socialist, anti-Communist *Daily Forward*. Her roots, she says, are in the European secular Jewish tradition—organizations like the Bund, writers like Sholom Aleichem. As a girl, she participated in an effort to transplant that culture to America. She attended a *schule,* a secular, Yiddish-language school, where she learned about religious Judaism, about Jewish history, and about radicalism. Though she broke with the old Left—hating its authoritarianism—she tried to make the culture she had inherited relevant to the 60's. She translated Sholom Aleichem's short stories. Once, while riding to Washington for an antiwar rally, she attempted to render into an English that would appeal to American radicals the works of a poetess who wrote in Yiddish about sweatshops. It did not work, she says wryly.

Aftermath: In 1970 Dick Flacks got a job as professor of sociology at the University of California in Santa Barbara. Mickey, a biologist, became a research fellow there. She got very involved in local politics—as an environmentalist, as a crusader for decent low-income housing, as a director of Tom Hayden's senatorial campaign.

She tried to set up a *schule,* in Santa Barbara. (Her brother runs one in Los Angeles, with about one hundred students.) But there were not enough interested families to sustain the school. She began to teach Yiddish at Santa Barbara's Hillel House. Her son, Charles, had a secular bar mitzvah in 1978, where instead of reading the *haftarah* (prophetic passage), he delivered a *drusha* (commentary) on Jewish resistance to the Holocaust. One of the moments Mickey has cherished most came when Charles received the shears her father had used as a garment worker, as a symbol of the family's tradition.

Mickey is not sure if the tradition she represents can work in an America where Yiddish is a dying language. California certainly is not fertile soil for it. But she has seen how well it has sustained her own family, and that gives her some hope.

Jerry Rubin

Activities in the 60's: As a teenager in Cincinnati, Rubin, the son of a truck driver, was the ambitious editor of his high school newspaper and an ardent supporter of Adlai Stevenson. Ironically, it did not occur to him to define himself as a radical until, at the age of twenty-four, he went to Israel in 1961 and met a young man who called himself a Communist. In 1965, when Rubin was a graduate student at Berkeley, he became involved with the antiwar movement and used his sense of theater to outrage people. Once, testifying in front of the House Un-American Activities Committee, he dressed up as Uncle Sam and reduced the hearing to a shambles. He taunted his elders with the notion—which he picked up in Israel—that he and his allies might be Communists.

In 1967 he and Abbie Hoffman founded the Youth International Party (Yippie) and organized demonstrations at the Chicago Democratic Convention. Some demonstrations were serious; others, like the one where they announced they would run Pigasus, a pig, for President, were deliberately outrageous. The next year they were indicted by the Nixon Administration and became the featured performers of the trial of the Chicago Seven. For a while, Rubin, with his slogan "do it," represented the most iconoclastic, unruly, defiant wing of the New Left.

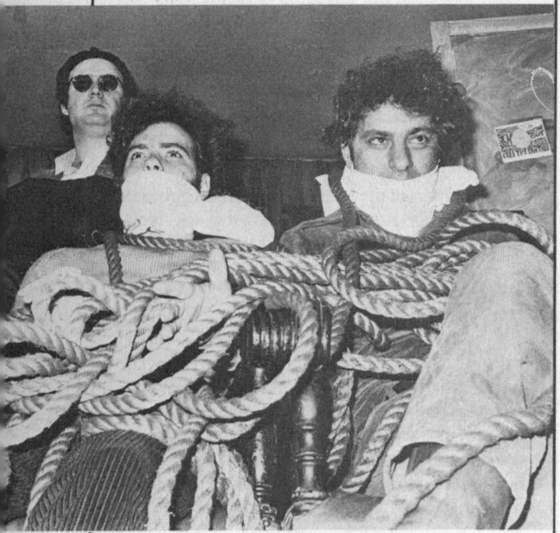

Jerry Rubin and Abbie Hoffman at a press conference in New York.

Jewish background: Jerry Rubin came from an old-world Eastern European Jewish family. To please his immigrant grandfather, his parents forced him to have a traditional Orthodox bar mitzvah, even though he did not know a word of Hebrew. He had been an early *heder* (Hebrew school) dropout. He regarded his grandfather's world as a dreary, repressive one; he hated the constant warnings about the *goyim*, the repeated admonitions not to marry a non-Jewish woman.

His stay in Israel left him feeling very ambivalent. He was comfortable in a land full of Jews, but he felt unforgivingly angry about Israel's treatment of Arabs. During his days as a radical leader that feeling sometimes led him to praise the PLO.

In spite of his grandfather's warnings, he married a non-Jew and has no plans to raise his children with any Jewish identity.

Aftermath: Rubin was bereft when the 1960's and his fame ended. He became involved in a series of therapies, from est to Yoga and described them, in 1976, in a book called *Growing (UP) at 37*. His next book, called *The War Between the Sheets* which took three years to write, was about the ambivalence that he contends men feel towards their penises in particular, and their sexuality in general, now that feminism has made women more sexually demanding.

He also has made the unexpected self-discovery that he is interested in business. He enjoys reading the *Wall Street Journal*, thinking about issues like cash-flow, and intends to launch his own full-fledged capitalist venture.

Abbie Hoffman

Activities in the 60's: Throughout the decade Hoffman was the radical prankster par excellence. After one stint in the southern civil rights movement and another trying to provide free services to hippies on New York's Lower East Side, he became a Robin Hoodlike stuntman, who could tear up money and drop it on the stock market one day, then write a book with the inviting title *Steal This Book* the next. Throughout the increasingly violent, polarized late 60's, he maintained his pool-hustler's wit and his clear sense of generosity.

Jewish background: Hoffman was born in Worcester, Mass., where he grew up in a Conservative Jewish family. He went to the predominantly Jewish Brandeis University. Unlike Jerry Rubin, who always seemed somewhat anxious to downplay his past, Hoffman revelled in his. During one of the most tumultuous moments of the Chicago Conspiracy trial he turned to Judge Julius Hoffman and told him "You're a *shanda* to the *goyim*"—a shame in front of the non-Jews.

Aftermath: In 1975 Hoffman was arrested for allegedly conspiring to sell cocaine. Instead of standing trial he went underground but continued to give interviews to newspaper and TV reporters in the same half-joking, half serious vein that had made him the Clown Prince of the 60's. He claims that he now lives in a small, rural town, that he has had plastic surgery and now looks like a non-Jew, that he is active in the antinuclear movement. While underground, he wrote an autobiography, *Soon to Be a Major Motion Picture.*

Arthur Waskow

Activities in the 60's: In the early part of the decade Waskow was one of a dozen bright young Washington liberals who worked for Senators and Congressmen, hoping to make the Democratic Party more responsive to progressive ideas. He wrote books on disarmament and civil rights, became a fellow at Washington's left-wing think tank, the Institute for Policy Studies, allied himself with the founders of SNCC, SDS, and the antiwar movement. In 1968, as part of the "dump Johnson" campaign, he was elected one of the District of Columbia's delegates to the Democratic Convention in Chicago. That year he told friends that his ambition was to be "Washington's Tom Hayden"—a political organizer, a symbol of the New Left.

Jewish background: Waskow was raised in an Orthodox section of Baltimore. Though his parents were not religiously observant, they bought chicken from a *shochet* (ritual slaughterer) and meat from a kosher butcher. While his cultural milieu was religious, his bar mitzvah, in an Orthodox *shul,* was a perfunctory affair: he remained relatively estranged from religious life until 1968.

He and his ex-wife Irene and their two children had always celebrated Passover *seders.* In 1968 the *seder* occurred the week Martin Luther King was assassinated. There were riots in Washington, D.C., which were only quelled by federal troops. With the city under military occupation, with the United States at war in Vietnam, with Lyndon Johnson in the White House, the symbolism of the feast of liberation seemed particularly vivid to him. That year he added a few lines to the Haggadah. The next year elaborating on these thoughts, he composed and published the *Freedom Seder,* which enraged traditionalists, but which made the holiday available to thousands of secular Jews who had never celebrated it before. The *Freedom Seder* was a modern rendition of the Haggadah, which incorporated statements on freedom from contemporary figures such as Martin Luther King and tied Passover to the civil rights and antiwar movements.

During the 1968 Democratic Convention, on Thursday night—the night after the bloodiest night of that awful week—Waskow found himself walking the streets of Chicago. Grant Park, ringed by the National Guard and full of tear gas, was so frightening that he decided to leave. He did not trust himself to take his seat as a delegate at the Democratic Convention; he felt so angry he thought he might become violent. He spent a little time at the fashionable Stockyard Inn, where some of his friends from the Institute for Policy Studies were talking about starting a new, radical third party. But the combination of lavish food and fantasy-ridden talk appalled him, particularly in contrast to what he had been seeing on the streets.

It was, he says, as if every bit of his carefully constructed American identity had been stripped away. He no longer felt comfortable with any of the groups he had always assumed he belonged to. He had been through a desert, and he had emerged a new person.

Aftermath: Waskow, deeply religious, defines himself as a *midrashist* (commentator or story teller). He has not abandoned his radical ideas, but he has tried to combine them with the Jewish tradition he has come to love. He has studied Hebrew two days a week for nearly a decade, and he studies Talmud once a week. He teaches two courses—"Sexuality and the Jewish Tradition" and "The First *Parsha* (Torah portion) of Exodus"—at the Jewish Study Center in Washington. He keeps kosher and observes the Sabbath.

In *Menorah,* a new Jewish journal which he edits, as well as in books and articles, Waskow deals with contemporary visions and approaches to Jewish life and experience. In addition to wrestling with conventional views of Jewish tradition, he seeks to apply the tradition to issues like civil rights, ecology, and disarmament that have always concerned him.

He wants to combine what he has learned from the 60's and what he has derived from Judaism, to help build a Jewish path through the modern world that neither bows down to tradition nor runs away from it.

Jack Newfield

Activities in the 60's: In the early 1960's Newfield, New York-bred, a graduate of Hunter College, wrote some pamphlets for the integrationist Student Non-Violent Coordinating Committee and was an early member of the Students for a Democratic Society. As a writer for the *Village Voice,* from 1964 on, he popularized New Left ideas, first through a series of widely read articles, then through his book on the New Left's rise, *A Prophetic Minority* (1966). An ardent Robert Kennedy supporter in 1968, Newfield was, perhaps, Kennedy's most important link to the New Left.

Jewish background: As a boy, Newfield was one of the last Jewish kids in the predominantly black Bedford Stuyvesant area of Brooklyn. He went to a small *heder* and had a bar mitzvah to please an immigrant grandfather, but the lessons bored him.

In the early 1960's Newfield became friendly with a woman who had survived Auschwitz. As he came to know her family the Holocaust became a deeply human experience for him. Invited in 1975 to participate in a tour of Israel, Newfield was ambivalent about accepting. After considerable reading, analysis, and discussion, he decided to go. The trip deepened and confirmed already existing sympathies for Israel. On his return he was committed to defending it, although he continued to disagree with Menachem Begin's annexationist policies.

Journalists make enemies, and they are the objects of canards that linger. In 1974 and 1975 Newfield wrote a series of articles in the *Voice* exposing the notorious nursing home owner Rabbi Bernard Bergman. He was labeled a "self-hating Jew" in publications like New York's *Jewish Press.* The accusation troubled him, and he carefully examined his values and motives. As he turned the issue over in his mind he became certain that he had exposed Bergman for the same reasons he exposed Assemblyman Sam Wright, a black, Congressman John Murphy, an Irishman, and Judge Dominic Rinaldi, an Italian: because of their corruption, not their backgrounds.

So, in the end, the charge that Newfield, radical turned muckraker, was a "self-hating Jew" actually made him more secure about his committment to Judaism.

Aftermath: Newfield is now one of the most respected journalists in America. Interestingly, his concern about many of the areas he has investigated—the courts, the prisons, organized crime—rose directly out of his background. Even in the New Left's glory days, he could not reconcile its rather sanguine view of crime with his own knowledge. Remembering the experiences of his relatives and other people he knew in Bedford Stuyvesant, he could not understand why so many leftists seemed to feel more compassion for criminals than they did for victims. The question was particularly troublesome because he was convinced that crime, more than any other issue, was pushing America to the right.

Nonetheless, he remained a steadfast egalitarian, committed to the ideal of social justice. He has spent much of the last decade drawing on his childhood experiences and the beliefs that the 60's nurtured, trying to discover a humane, progressive way of combating street violence and protecting the older people, who play such a lively role in his memory.

Heather Booth

Activities in the 60's: Heather, who entered the University of Chicago in 1963, describes herself as the kind of teenager "who kept waiting for the 60's to happen." As a high school student on Long Island she frequently went to Manhattan to participate in prodisarmament rallies. Nearer home, she picketed Woolworth's because the chain store discriminated against blacks in the South. In 1964, the summer of her freshman year, she worked as a volunteer in the Mississippi Summer Project—the two month long freedom summer, during which Andrew Goodman, Mickey Schwerner, and James Chaney were killled. During the next few years she was active in SDS and the antiwar movement. By 1970 she was also deeply committed to the woman's movement.

Jewish background: On her mother's side, Heather Booth comes from a long line of Hasidim. Her parents, Conservative Jews, used to show her pictures and films of her Orthodox relatives. When Heather was twelve, she met a rabbi at the Sand's Point, Long Island Synagogue whose ideas captured her imagination. She travelled to his synagogue several times a week for confirmation classes. She even toyed with the idea of becoming a rabbi herself until she learned that the job was off limits to women.

In the late 1950's the Sand's Point rabbi took a strong stand against the John Birch Society. He became so controversial his contract wasn't renewed. Heather, shocked by this injustice and disappointed that only men could be rabbis, lost some of her enthusiasm for formal Judaism. She went to Israel at the end of her senior year in high school. After spending a summer on a Mapam kibbutz near Beersheba, she visited Yad Vashem, the museum of the Holocaust. She emerged from the museum crying and shaking, and instead of rejoining her group, simply sat on a hill, staring into space for a time. She made a lifelong committment that day. She would devote all her powers, throughout all the days of her life, to seeing that nothing like that ever happened again to any group of human beings on earth.

Aftermath: Heather's desire to bring about social change never flagged. In the early 1970's she tried to define the lessons she had learned from the 60's—lessons about the movement's weaknesses and strengths—and incorporate them into a program that would help train a generation of organizers. The institution she developed, the Midwest Academy in Chicago, is still flourishing. It works with people from all sorts of groups—labor, feminist, consumer. Heather, married for fourteen years and the mother of two children, is still associated with it. With her incredible energy, she still has time to work as director of the Citizens'-Labor Energy Coalition, dedicated to creating an equitable energy pricing policy.

William Wimpisinger, head of the influential Machinists Union, harking back to the legendary woman who organized thousands of coal miners in the late nineteenth century, called her a "latter-day Mother Jones."

Heather says she still thinks of much of what she does as an extension of the committment she made that afternoon at Yad Vashem.

Lee Weiner

Activities in the 60's: In the early part of the decade Lee got involved in civil rights and disarmament work. After a year at the Hebrew University—where he got to know Jerry Rubin—he joined SDS. For three years he worked as a community organizer in a black ghetto on Chicago's Near North Side. He also became involved in antiwar activities.

Before the demonstrations at the 1968 Democratic Convention, Weiner found himself in a unique role. As an old friend of Jerry Rubin's and a political ally of Tom Hayden's, he could serve as a liaison between the prankish Yippies and the more conventionally political Mobilization Against the War in Vietnam. In addition he introduced people from both those groups to radicals from Chicago, whom he had known for years. Finally, since he had been working in the area where the demonstrations would take place, he was able to be somewhat of a buffer between the radicals and the police.

During that time he became prominent enough to be indicted as a defendant in the trial of the Chicago Seven. With Jerry Rubin, Abbie Hoffman, and himself as defendants, Leonard Weinglass and William Kunstler, both Jews, as their lawyers, and Judge Julius Hoffman, a Jew, on the bench, he began to see the affair as "an intergenerational Jewish morality play." That experience heightened his Jewish consciousness, which had waned during the years of the movement.

Weiner had a special reason for resenting the trial. He had always seen himself as a rather anonymous, low-level organizer, and now he had too much notoriety to do that sort of work. When the trial was over, he moved to New York, where he helped start a radical Jewish group called Brooklyn Bridge. Brooklyn Bridge sought to organize younger people who had not been reached by conventional Jewish organizations into a progressive force that saw no contradiction between supporting the right of the Black Panther Party to organize and the right of Soviet Jews to emigrate to Israel. The organization was quite effective, but Weiner soon found that his notoriety bred jealousy, and he drifted away from it after a year.

Jewish background: Weiner was raised on the South Side of Chicago. His parents were not religiously observant, but they did attend services at a Conservative synagogue, where he had his bar mitzvah. Some of his parents' friends were Jewish radicals who had belonged to the Communist party, and he loved to listen to them talk about organizing. Though his trip to Israel helped make his Judaism real to him, he half-forgot it during the 60's, when he regarded himself as a radical who happened to be Jewish.

Aftermath: For several years after Weiner left Brooklyn Bridge, he remained apolitical. First he worked as a psychiatric social worker, helping drug addicts and alcoholics. Then he set up his own practice. Then, in 1976, he worked for Jimmy Carter, organizing a congressional district in Ohio. When Carter won, Weiner was hired by ACTION as a program evaluator.

He left the agency in 1979 and joined an all-Jewish firm that specializes in direct mailing. At first he and his partners wanted to work with all the groups in the traditional liberal constituency—blacks, Hispanics, Jews, union members. They hoped to use mailing techniques that would help organizations build the kind of strong diversified membership base that enables coalition politics to work in communities, not just on paper.

Then, Andrew Young resigned as ambassador of the U.N., and the rift between blacks and Jews erupted. That was a kind of watershed for Weiner and his associates. They decided not to help any organizations or individuals who had contributed to anti-Semitism, even by remaining silent instead of denouncing people like Jesse Jackson. Weiner's firm began to focus more intensely on Jewish organizations like B'nai B'rith and the American Jewish Committee, seeking ways of providing a diversified, grassroots constituency for their leadership-heavy organizations.

In his own life Weiner has become somewhat more religiously observant. His son by a first marriage celebrated his bar mitzvah in Chicago in 1979. He and his current wife attend a Reform Temple but because they both miss the more formal services they knew as children, they are toying with the idea of joining a Conservative synagogue. They are also thinking of lighting Sabbath candles and beginning to observe *Shabbat* in some more conscious way.

Barbara Garson

Activities in the 60's: At the height of Lyndon Johnson's unpopularity, Barbara Garson was practically a household word because, in addition to being active in the antiwar movement at Berkeley, she wrote the play *MacBird* for a teach-in. The brilliant, witty spoof of Lyndon Johnson, and of the Kennedy's was fused with the plot of *Macbeth*. Soon, *MacBird* was a Broadway hit and the center of a critical controversy. Instead of taking advantage of her notoriety for further commercial success, Barbara decided to join activists who were organizing coffeehouses, near military bases, where G.I.'s could share their complaints about the army and the war. To her, that activity was as successful as her play.

Jewish background: Barbara was born in Brooklyn, on the outskirts of Flatbush. Neither her father, an office manager for an electronics company, nor her mother were particularly religious. They fasted on Yom Kippur but didn't celebrate Hanukkah or have a *seder*. Judaism was in their pores, nonetheless. Their neighborhood was "a completely enclosed environment," Barbara recalls. "It was so Jewish we didn't even have to think about being Jewish. You didn't have to fight Santa Claus or Easter. Those things just weren't part of our lives."

Ritualistic atavisms were part of the culture she grew up in. For example, if her parents saw meat cooked with cream, they wouldn't complain that it wasn't kosher; they'd say that the cream might curdle. They might eat boiled ham with salami or pastrami, but they'd never put a big, Southern-style ham in their oven and cook it with pineapples. They thought Spam might be poisonous.

Still, at Barbara's wedding, when she and her husband chose to read from the Song of Songs and to explain the reason they were breaking the glass, her parents felt a little uncomfortable with that degree of formal, explicit religion.

Aftermath: Shortly after Barbara's daughter Juliette was born, she and her husband separated. She was then living in places, like Greenwich Village, where Santa Claus and Easter were issues. So she decided to pass on the Jewish heritage she'd imbibed as a child by organizing Hanukkah celebrations and Passover *seders* for Juliette. She saw—and sees—those activities as a way of asserting the importance of family loyalty, of roots, at a time when those values are eroding.

As a writer, she misses the almost tactile sense of an audience that she had in the 1960's. She regained it once, when she wrote a children's play called *Dinosaur Door* for Juliette's class at P.S. 41 in the Village. She refuses to submit to the commercial demands of the literary marketplace. However, in the pieces she writes she often feels that she's lecturing to people she doesn't know instead of creating for her friends.

To her surprise her most recent play, *Leah*, draws on Jewish memories she barely knew she possessed. There's a scene, for example, where the characters sit *shiva* (seven days of mourning after a funeral). Yiddish words are sprinkled throughout the text. Part of *Leah* was produced at Actor's Studio, and Barbara was surprised when she saw very Jewish-looking actors showing up for the casting call. "I thought it was a play about all sorts of people. But it turned out to be a play about Jews." she says. That small bit of self-discovery surprised her.

Nick Egleson

Activities in the 60's: In 1966 SDS was becoming a national force to be reckoned with, and Egleson, who had just graduated from Swarthmore College, was its president. Before that, he had been a civil rights worker in Cambridge, Md., then a community organizer in the black ghettos of Philadelphia. That year, he became one of the first Americans to visit North Vietnam. In the spring of 1967, along with Martin Luther King and Stokely Carmichael, he addressed an antiwar rally of fifty thousand people in New York City.

Egleson is a very private, thoughtful person. He never wanted to use his status in SDS to make himself a celebrity. So, in the late 1960's and early 1970's, he returned to semiobscurity as an antidraft organizer and later as the coeditor of an underground newspaper in Cambridge, Mass.

He also studied the FBI's use of informers—people who infiltrated the New Left. He wanted to help radicals distinguish between realistic caution and the paralyzing paranoia that made many of them feel that there were spies wherever they went. Soon he became an authority on American intelligence agencies.

Jewish background: Egleson's father is a Protestant and his mother is a Jew.

For generations, his maternal family, the Cardozos, were among the most prominent in American Jewish life. Indeed, Egleson's ancestor, Benjamin Cardozo, was the second Jewish justice on the U.S. Supreme Court.

Egleson's parents had been sympathetic to

the left during the thirties (though they didn't discuss their beliefs much during the McCarthy years), and they sent Nick to City and Country, a freewheeling, left-wing private school in New York. But, unlike many Jews in or out of mixed marriages, no one in Egleson's family attempted to make a connection between Judaism and liberalism.

By Nick's generation, all traces of religion and ethnicity had vanished. For instance, he doesn't remember thinking about the fact that the Cardozos were Jewish until he was a teenager. At Taft, the prep school he attended, one of his closest friends, who had an obviously Jewish name, was frequently picked on. In retrospect, Egleson realizes that there was anti-Semitism in his classmates' attitudes, but he never felt personally threatened by it. When he had to state his religious affiliation—on government forms, for example—he always wrote "none."

"I don't think I was denying anything about Judaism," he says. "It simply wasn't an issue in my family. There must have been a denial some time, but I think it happened several generations earlier."

Aftermath: Now Egleson makes organizing materials, like slide shows, for trade unions and for groups that are concerned with social and political issues. He is married to a non-Jew and feels no impulse to get involved in anything Jewish or anything religious.

"Sometimes I wish that was different," he says. "I wish I was put together differently, that I wasn't so detached from the past. I think peoples' lives are enriched if they don't think that each generation is creating its culture anew. But I can't do anything about that in my life. I wish I had some connection to *a* past—but that wasn't how I was brought up."

—P.C.

IDENTITY ENDURES: JEWS AND JUDAISM IN THE U.S.S.R.

The issue of Soviet Jewry has emerged in the past two decades as a principal focus of Jewish communal concern, second only to Israel. Committees on Soviet Jewry have been formed in almost every Western country and literature on the subject can be found in more than thirteen languages.

As a cause, the plight of Soviet Jewry has stimulated the renewed awareness of Jewish values and motivated action on traditional ethical precepts: the saving of lives, the redemption of captives, and personal acts of charity. In addition, it has offered post-Holocaust Jewry an opportunity to prevent another national tragedy, perhaps to demonstrate that lessons of the past have been well learned.

As a movement, the campaign to aid Soviet Jewry has catapulted American Jewry into an unprecedented role as a political force in policy development of the world's two superpowers. The human rights aspect has attracted Jews never before affiliated with the organized community as well as a broad base of support among non-Jews. In so doing it has made possible more effective promotion of Jewish domestic interests.

As a priority issue on the Jewish agenda, Soviet Jewry has elicited major resources and active involvement from virtually the entire Jewish spectrum, from the religious to the secular, from the philanthropic to the political. Two vast networks gradually evolved to coordinate the two arms of the movement: advocacy, that is, the rights-and-rescue effort; and absorption.

Advocacy activities have been organized from the grassroots level up to the highest diplomatic circles with the aim of employing different strategies simultaneously. Efforts have included legislative action, private interventions by legal, academic and political figures, and professional action in spheres of U.S.-U.S.S.R. exchange: business, technology, science, and the arts.

Communal efforts have been aimed at gaining media attention as well as providing Soviet Jews with moral and material support. Rabbinic and lay leaders along with their constituents have mobilized for public demonstrations, lobbying and public education, letter-writing, travel to the Soviet Union, and more recently, transmission of much-sought-after cultural and religious materials needed to promote Jewish consciousness and sustain Jewish life within the Soviet Union.

Because of the scope of the issue, this article will deal only with the status of Soviet Jews and Western advocacy efforts. The information presented covers much ground but cannot by its nature, be comprehensive.

Russia's Believe it or Not

A renaissance of interest in Jewish life and learning, which began among a small but significant number of Soviet Jews during the last five years, has evolved into a far-reaching cultural/educational network and represents one of the most important recent developments in the Soviet community. The network calls itself Tarbut, after the Hebrew word for "culture," and has boldly declared its efforts to be legal rather than "underground."

It should be noted that the cultural and religious rights now being sought by "tarbutniks" (culture activists) are guaranteed them under Soviet and international law. Since providing for freedom of religion in the 1936 Constitution, the Soviets have signed seven international documents—in addition to their own revised constitution—which call for a broad spectrum of rights in this area, falling into three major spheres: culture and the arts, religion, and education and language. As the following analysis indicates, the difference between the *de jure* rights of Soviet Jews and their *de facto* rights is vast, and it is this injustice that the "tarbutniks" have begun to rectify.

CULTURE AND THE ARTS

(Numbers refer to either the Soviet Constitution or to international treaties and conventions to which the Soviet Union adheres, see reference notes below.)

THE PROMISE

Cultural development (2, 4, 5)
Participation in cultural life (1, 2, 4, 6)
Freedom of artistic work (1)
The rights of authors (1)
Development of literature and folk art (1)
Cultural exchange (1, 2, 5, 6)

A contemporary Russian newspaper cartoon entitled, "A Link in a Criminal Chain."

Access to cultural achievements (1, 2)
Conservation of cultures (4)

THE REALITY

In contrast to other ethnic and nationality groups, the Jewish community is prohibited from establishing schools, from publishing books, newspapers, and magazines and from forming their own troupes in the performing arts.

Editors of Jewish-interest journals are frequently subject to interrogations, threats of arrest, and confiscation of their material.

A Yiddish Chamber Theater was formed by Soviet officials and performs the works of Russian, rather than Jewish, playwrights to audiences that rarely include members of the Jewish community.

RELIGION

THE PROMISE

Freedom of thought, conscience and religion (1, 3)
Freedoms of speech and assembly (1)
Right to teach, practice, worship and observe (1, 3)
Right of faiths to interact and exchange information (2)
Individual and communal freedom to manifest religion (3)

THE REALITY

The city of Vilna, once called "Jerusalem of Lithuania," now has but one remaining synagogue. While precise statistics are difficult to obtain, it is estimated that fewer than ten rabbis and fifty synagogues remain to service 3 million Jews. No formal training or seminaries exist for rabbis, cantors, *mohels* (circumcisers), or *shochtim* (ritual slaughterers), except for the so-called "yeshiva" in Moscow.

No Hebrew Bible has been published since 1917; no prayer book since 1968. Manufacture of prayer shawls, phylacteries, and other ritual objects is forbidden. Although *matzah* baking is permitted, and a sufficient supply is available in large cities, distribution to small provincial cities remains unsatisfactory; no importation is allowed from the West. The Jewish community is denied active communication with or participation in international Jewish bodies. Kosher food is unavailable.

EDUCATION AND LANGUAGE

THE PROMISE

Right of parents to choose education for their children (4)
Liberty to choose religious and moral education (4)
Right to learn one's native language (1)
Freedom to manifest religion in teaching (3)
Linguistic rights of minorities (7)

THE REALITY

While the right to educate one's children in a school and language of one's choosing has been granted to many other Soviet ethnic groups, Jews remain bereft of educational facilities and materials necessary to perpetuate their heritage. The Soviet government maintains a Russified form of Yiddish. Hundreds of Jews have chosen to study Hebrew. The teaching of Hebrew has been outlawed by the Soviets even though the language is offered at six universities including Leningrad State University, Tbilisi State University, and Moscow State University.

Teachers of Hebrew and other Jewish classes currently being held informally in living rooms in fourteen Soviet cities have been restrained by sporadic legal charges—especially "parasitism"—a clear sign that expansion of these activities will not be tolerated.

REFERENCE NOTES

1. Constitution of the USSR
2. The Helsinki Agreement
3. Universal Declaration of Human Rights
4. International Covenant on Economic, Social, and Cultural Rights
5. UNESCO Principles of International Cultural Cooperation
6. UNESCO Constitution
   International Convention on the Elimination of All Forms of Racial Discrimination
7. UNESCO Covenant Against Discrimination in Education

—A.A.

Solidarity demonstration for Soviet Jewry. **(Isaac Berez)**

AN EXPERIENCE IN ESCAPE FROM THE SOVIET UNION

ROUTE TO

An imaginative board game conceived and designed by a 14-year-old Soviet Jewish girl and smuggled out of the USSR.

REEDOM

PUBLISHED BY THE
BOARD OF JEWISH EDUCATION OF GREATER NEW YORK
IN COOPERATION WITH THE
NEW YORK CONFERENCE FOR SOVIET JEWRY

Leaving Mother Russia

In the past twelve years, close to 600,000 Jews reached the decision that there was no future for them in the Soviet Union and took the first step toward leaving: requesting (and receiving) invitations from relatives in Israel. These affidavits, called *vyzovs*, serve to initiate the long and complex process of applying for permission to emigrate.

The *reunification of families* has become the operative international human rights principle underlying this process, and it is ostensibly to grant this right to its Jewish citizens that the Soviet government permitted 228, 701 of them to leave between October 1968 and December 1979. A secondary principle, that of *repatriation to homeland,* has also been exercised toward this end.

While a small percentage—less than 1 percent—of visa applications have been made directly to the United States, the procedure is viewed as risky and prospects for major breakthroughs are slim.

PROCEDURE

All applicants for exit visas must submit copies of the following to the local OVIR (visa office):

- *Vysov*—invitation from relatives in Israel;
- Document of employment status—including a *characteristika* (character reference);
- Proof of Residency—including validation of housing permit;
- Birth and marriage certificates;
- Photographs;
- University diplomas (where applicable);
- Statement of intent and autobiography;
- Parental or spousal permissions—if any are deceased, death certificates must be produced;
- Fee—total emigration cost for a family of four is approximately 4,175 rubles ($5,880), the equivalent of two years' salary for the average white collar worker. This figure includes payment for baggage, tickets, the visa itself, and a special fee for the renunciation of Soviet citizenship.

Failure to produce any of the above disqualifies the applicant, even if circumstances make it impossible to submit certain documents, as in the case of death certificates of parents lost or killed during wartime.

If, for any reason, an individual's documents are rejected by the OVIR office, he becomes, in effect, invisible. He has severed his ties with Soviet society; he is not yet linked to any other place; and worst of all, he is likely to be unknown in the West, and therefore isolated from all traditional systems of support. Thus he has virtually disappeared.

OBSTACLES

While none of the following rules has been applied universally, all are sufficiently widespread to constitute serious threats to emigration.

- *Denial of visa on the basis of "access to state secrets."* This classification has been applied even to dentists and elevator operators;
- *Five-year waiting period following military service;*
- *Inaccessibility of OVIR officials.* Some offices, serving thousands of applicants, are open only a few hours a day, two days a week;
- *Three-year employment requirement,* following completion of education;
- *Restriction of* vysovs *(invitations) to "first-degree relatives"* on the basis of "insufficient kinship." Since the nuclear families of many applicants reside outside of Israel, Israeli invitations often cannot be produced. With the increased migration to the United States, Canada, and Western Europe, a significant percentage of potential émigrés could thus be eliminated;
- *Personal and professional risks.* Applicants become vulnerable to job dismissals, school and university expulsion, conscription into the Red Army, withdrawal of residence permit, public denunciation, physical harassment, searches, and arrest.

The chart opposite details the emigration statistics in the years 1961–1979.

Bar variance distinguishes Israel-bound émigrés from those settling elsewhere as well as the unavailability of precise data on destination.

The dramatic rise in emigration in 1972 and 1973 appears to reflect the carrot-and-stick effect on the then-pending Jackson-Vanik Amendment. This bill was attached to the 1974 United States Trade Act as an attempt to link most favored nation status and other economic credits to emigration levels. The amendment was passed by Congress but the Trade Act was rejected by the Soviets.

The subsequent upsurge in the numbers leaving, in 1978–1979, is widely attributed to three pending areas of U.S.-U.S.S.R. interaction: the negotiation of SALT III (the Strategic Arms Limitation Treaty), the 1980 Moscow Olympics, and review of the Jackson-Vanik Amendment.

As is evident from the graph, the rise in emigration since 1976 has been accompanied by a gradual reversal in the proportion of Soviet Jews choosing Israel over other Western countries, a striking development which has engendered considerable discussion among world Jewry.

Those critical of this development fear that the Soviets will seize upon the supposed "fraudulent" use of Israeli visas as a pretext for stemming the emigration. Others feel that the West is ill-equipped to provide sufficient Jewish education to the immigrants to offset assimilation among this population which has minimal Jewish knowledge; the issue is a fundamental one of proper allocation of Jewish communal resources. Always in the background of the discussion is the concern that Israel is in desperate need of more immigrants.

Others in the Jewish community, however, welcome the opportunity to bring Jews to freedom regardless of destination, to integrate them religiously and culturally, and to grant Jews the choice of carving out their own destinies in much the same way as did the forebears of American and Canadian Jews. The trend toward emigrating to the West, they maintain, is largely due to the changing nature of the typical émigré, no longer the Zionist ideologue or religious Jew of past years. The preponderance of today's applicants seek professional opportunity and economic stability, the principal historical motives behind most major migrations.

Nevertheless, world-wide advocacy persists for the rights of Soviet Jews "to live as Jews or leave," in the hopes that the fortunes of that imperilled community will not be utterly dependent on the vicissitudes of history.

EMIGRATION STATISTICS 1961-1979

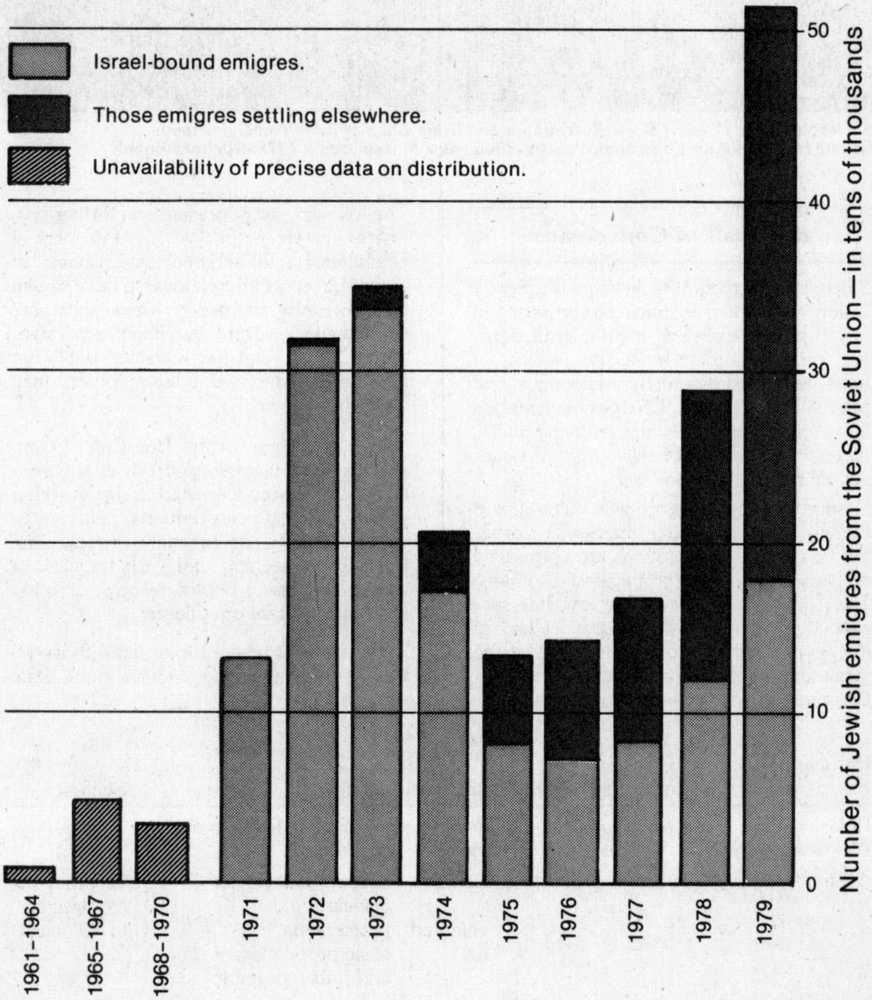

Soviet Refusniks (l. to r.) Boris Katz, Elana and Boris Chernobilsky, Isai Goldshtein, Genadi Hassin, Viktor Ellistratov, Yaacov Rakhlenko. Moscow, July 1978. **(Richard Sobol)**

Roll Call of Conscience

Since 1966, ninety-five Jews in the Soviet Union are known to have served terms in labor camps, exile, or mental institutions, and countless others have been victims of house and physical searches, detentions, and pre-trial investigations. Charges have ranged from "parasitism" (the crime of being unemployed) to "anti-Soviet activity," to the capital offense of "treason."

Despite a broad range of civil, cultural, and human rights encoded in the Soviet Constitution, criminal prosecutions are commonly employed as political tools against dissenters. This capricious abuse of the law has succeeded in temporarily silencing leaders of the Jewish activist movement, while at the same time containing emigration by the intimidation of potential visa applicants.

The following list of present and former prisoners, known in the West as Prisoners of Conscience and in Israel as Prisoners of Zion, represents those known to have served terms on false charges or whose sentences were unjustly severe by Soviet legal standards. Some were not identified until after their incarceration or release; others may never be known.

Those appearing on this Roll Call of Conscience have been singled out as a consequence of having identified as Jews—either publicly, through visa requests, petitions, or demonstrations, or privately, through the learning or teaching of Jewish subjects, or simply possessing books, records, or other material on Israel or Judaism.

Today, almost without exception, those on this list who have emigrated live in the State of Israel.

Prisoner of conscience	Born	Profession	Trial	Charges	Sentence
Ruta Aleksandrovich	1947	nurse	5/5/71 Riga Trial	anti-Soviet agitation and propaganda	1 year
Anatoly Altman	1942	Engraver	6/15/70 1st Leningrad Trial	treason, anti-Soviet agitation and propaganda, misappropriation of state and public property	12 years (commuted to 10 years)

Prisoner of conscience	Born	Profession	Trial	Charges	Sentence
Gennady Avramenko	—	—	—	—	—
Zinaida Avramenko	—	—	—	—	3½ years
Boris Azernikov	1946	dentist	10/71	anti-Soviet agitation and propaganda, anti-Soviet organization	3½ years
Iosif Begun	1932	radio engineer	3/3/77; 6/78	parasitism passport violations	2 years exile 2 years exile
Anna Berkovsky	1932	philologist	6/74	economic speculation	2 years
Yuri Berkovsky	1931	electrical engineer	6/74	possessing illegal weapon, economic speculation	2 years
Grigory Berman	1946	linguist	8/72	draft evasion	3 years
Mikhail (Mendel) Bodnya	1937	worker	12/15/70 1st Leningrad Trial	attempted theft of state property	4 years
Victor Boguslavski	1940	engineer	5/11/71 2nd Leningrad Trial	anti-Soviet organization and agitation	1 year
Igor Borisov	1942	—	12/23/70	hooliganism	3 years
Yuli Brind	1929	engraver/ mechanic	6/72	anti-Soviet slander	2½ years
Hillel Butman	1933	engineer	5/11/71 2nd Leningrad Trial	anti-Soviet propaganda, organization, treason	10 years
David Chernoglaz	1940	agronomist	6/21/71 Kishinev Trial	anti-Soviet propaganda and organization	5 years
Iosip Chornobilsky	—	locksmith/ tinsmith	3/66	slandering the state	—
Boris Davrashvilli	1929	—	6/72	hooliganism, assault and battery	2 years
Shlomo Dreizner	1932	engineer	5/5/71 2nd Leningrad Trial	anti-Soviet organization and agitation	3 years
Mark Dymshitz	1927	pilot	12/70 1st Leningrad Trial	treason, anti-Soviet agitation and propaganda, misappropriation of state and public property	death (commuted to 15 years)
Rostislav Eppelfeld	1942	musician	10/71	anti-Soviet agitation and propaganda	6 years
Yuri Federov	1943	student/ worker	12/70 1st Leningrad Trial	treason, anti-Soviet propaganda and organization, stealing state property	15 years strict regime
Aleksandr Feldman	1947	construction engineer	11/73	malicious hooliganism	3½ years

Prisoner of conscience	Born	Profession	Trial	Charges	Sentence
Oleg Frolov	1948	student	2/70 Riazan Trial	anti-Soviet propaganda and agitation/participation in anti-Soviet organization	5 years
Aleksandr Galperin	1946	engineer	6/21/71 Kishinev Trial	anti-Soviet propaganda and organization	2½ years
Ilya Glezer	1931	biologist	8/72	anti-Soviet activities	3 years prison, 3 years exile
Evgeny Glikhman	1936	—	none	—	strict regime mental hospital
Semyon Gluzman	1946	psychiatrist	10/72	anti-Soviet agitation and propaganda	7 years labor camp, 3 years exile
Pyotr Goldberg	—	manager of fruit and vegetable market	1974	—	6 years
Anatoly Goldfeld	1946	engineer	6/21/71 Kishinev Trial	anti-Soviet propaganda and organization	4 years
Grigory Goldshtein	1931	physicist	3/20/78	parasitism	1 year exile
Shiman Grilius	1945	engineer	2/70 Riazan Trial	anti-Soviet agitation and propaganda/ participation in anti-Soviet organization	5 years
Boris Kalendarov	1957	student	5/79	draft evasion	2 years
Lassal Kaminsky	1930	engineer	5/11/71 2nd Leningrad Trial	anti-Soviet agitation and organization	5 years
Yakov Kaufman	—	engineer and geologist	1/73	defaming the U.S.S.R.	3 years
Yakov Khantsis	1929	driver	8/70	malicious hooliganism	2½ years (released 5/71; resentenced 3/72 to 2 years)
Harry Kirzhner	1946	—	6/21/71 Kishinev Trial	anti-Soviet propaganda and organization	2 years
Leib Knokh	1944	technician	12/15/70 1st Leningrad Trial	treason, anti-Soviet agitation and propaganda, anti-Soviet activities, misappropriation of state property	13 years (reduced to 10 years)
Boris Kochubiyevsky	1936	engineer	6/69 Kiev Trial	slandering the Soviet state	3 years
Albert Koltunov	1921	manager, lottery administration	6/74	—	5½ years

Prisoner of conscience	Born	Profession	Trial	Charges	Sentence
Lev Kornblit	1922	mathematician	5/11/71 2nd Leningrad Trial	anti-Soviet agitation and organization	3 years
Mikhail Kornblit	1937	physician/ dentist	5/11/71 2nd Leningrad Trial	anti-Soviet activities	7 years
Valeri Kukui	1938	engineer	6/71	anti-Soviet slander	3 years
Eduard Kuznetsov	1939	interpreter/ translator	12/70 1st Leningrad Trial	treason, anti-Soviet propaganda, anti-Soviet	death (commuted to 15 years special regime)
Sender Levinson	1948	worker	5/75	violating trade laws	6 years
Semyon Levit	1943	physicist	6/21/71 Kishinev Trial	anti-Soviet propaganda and organization	2 years
Lazar Luibarsky	1926	engineer	1/73	slandering Soviet regime, revealing state secrets	4 years
Mark Lutsker	1949	student	8/73	draft evasion	2 years
Boris Maftsier	1947	—	5/24/71 Riga Trial	distributing slanderous information	1 year
Anatoly Malkin	1954	student	8/75	draft evasion	3 years
Vladimir Markman	1938	engineer	8/72	hooliganism, anti-Soviet slander	3 years
Iosif Mendelevich	1947	student	12/15/70 1st Leningrad Trial	treason, misappropriation of state and public property, anti-Soviet propaganda and organization	15 years (reduced to 12 years)
Ioif Mishener	1935	history teacher	7/70	spreading anti-Soviet literature	6 years
Vladimir Mogiliver	1940	engineer	5/5/71 2nd Leningrad Trial	anti-Soviet agitation and organization	4 years
Aleksei Murzhenko	1942	student/ worker	12/70	anti-Soviet propaganda and organization, treason, misappropriation of state property and funds	14 years strict regime
Mark Nashpitz	1948	dentist	3/31/75	disturbing public order	5 years exile
Ida Nudel	1931	economist	6/78	malicious hooliganism	4 years exile
Liliya Ontman	1937	—	1/8/70 Chernovits Trial	anti-Soviet calumnies and insults	2½ years
Reiza Palatnik	1936	librarian	6/6/71 Odessa Trial	anti-Soviet slander	2 years
Boris Penson	1946	artist	12/15/70 1st Leningrad Trial	treason, misappropriation of state and public property, anti-Soviet activities	10 years

Prisoner of conscience	Born	Profession	Trial	Charges	Sentence
Pinkhas Pinkhasov	1935	carpenter	11/73	deception of purchaser, slandering	5 years
Yuri Pokh	1950	student	6/72	draft evasion	3½ years
David Rabinovich	1947	technician	6/21/70 Kishinev Trial	theft of duplicating machine	1 year
Chaim Renert	1921	physician/ radiologist	1971	economic charges	5 years
Lev Roitburd	1936	engineer	8/75	resisting arrest	2 years
Mikhail Roiz	1948	radio engineer	8/78	draft evasion	1 year
Anatoly Shcharansky	1948	mathematician	7/10/78	treason, espionage	3 years imprisonment, 10 years special regime camp
Mikhail Shepshelovich	1943	worker	5/5/71 Riga Trial	—	2 years
Isaak Shkolnik	1936	mechanic	3/73	treason	7 years
Simon Shnirman	1957	technician	6/27/78	draft evasion	2½ years
Arkady Shpilberg	1938	engineer	5/27/71 Riga Trial	—	3 years
Mikhail Shtern	1918	endocrinologist	12/74	bribery	8 years
Hillel Shur	1936	engineer	6/21/71 Kishinev Trial	anti-Soviet propaganda and organization	2 years
Aleksandr Silnitsky	1952	student	11/75	draft evasion	2 years exile
Vladimir Slepak	1927	radio engineer	6/78	malicious hooliganism	5 years exile
Aleksandr Slinin	1955	student	7/74	draft evasion	3 years
Aleksandr Sokiriansky	1944	—	1/74	slander of Soviet regime	5 years
Kopel Spektor	1946	student	12/74	parasitism	2 years
Viktor Stilbans	1947	physician	5/11/70 2nd Leningrad Trial	anti-Soviet agitation and organization	1 year
Yakov Suslenski	1929	English teacher	10/70	spreading anti-Soviet literature with intent to undermine Soviet regime	7 years
Emilia Trachtenberg	1934	librarian	1971	disseminating slanderous material	3 years
Lazar Trachtenberg	1946	engineer	6/21/71 Kishinev Trial	anti-Soviet organization and agitation	2 years
Boris Tsitlionok	1944	technician	3/31/75	disturbing public order	5 years exile
Arkady Vainman	1952	student/ violinist	9/72	hooliganism	4 years
Leonid Vainman	1952	student/ violinist	9/72	hooliganism	4 years
Aleksandr Vilik	1956	student	2/79	draft evasion	1½ years

Prisoner of conscience	Born	Profession	Trial	Charges	Sentence
Yakov Vinarov	1954	—	8/75	draft evasion	3 years
Arkady Voloshin	1946	—	6/6/71 Kishinev Trial	anti-Soviet propaganda, organization	2 years
Valeri Vudka	1947	student	2/70 Riazan Trial	anti-Soviet propaganda and agitation/participation in anti-Soviet organizations	3 years
Yuri Vudka	1947	student	2/70 Riazan Trial	anti-Soviet propaganda and anti-Soviet organization	7 years
Lev Yagman	1940	engineer	5/11/70 2nd Leningrad Trial	anti-Soviet organization and agitation	5 years
Nikolai Yavor	—	mathematician	3/73	deliberate breach of peace/disrespecting society	1 year
Leonid Zabelishensky	1941	electrical engineer	12/73	—	6 months
Israel Zalmanson	1949	student	12/15/70 1st Leningrad Trial	treason, misappropriating state property, anti-Soviet propaganda and organization	8 years
Sylva Zalmanson	1944	engineer	12/15/70 1st Leningrad Trial	conspiring to steal a plane	8 years
Vulf Zalmanson	1939	engineer	12/70 1st Leningrad Trial	treason, anti-Soviet agitation and propaganda	10 years
Boris Zaturensky	1946	engineer	12/75	speculating in gold	3 years
Amner Zavurov	—	worker	1/12/77	passport violations, hooliganism	3 years

NAMES OF LABOR CAMPS

Berdyansk	Potma
Chistopol	Saransk
Krasnoyar	Sverdlovsk
Odessa	Valuiki
Omutninsk	Voroshilovgrad
Perm	

Jewish prisoners are often placed in special camps for political prisoners, and as a result have at times been subjected to anti-Semitic harassment by former Nazis or Nazi collaborators.

Moreover, those Jews attempting to observe *kashrut,* holidays or any Jewish rituals have had their prayer books confiscated, their *yarmulkes* beaten off their heads, or their beards shaven. Often they are punished with extended prison terms or repeated detention in isolation cells.

PRISON REGIMES

General Regime:
One visit and one food parcel every three months. Money allowance given to buy food in camp shop. No restriction on mail.

Strict Regime:
A food and clothing parcel and one letter allowed once a year. One visit every year, after half the sentence has been served.

Special Regime:
One letter every year, and one visit annually after half the sentence has been served. No food parcels allowed. Camp diet contains one-third of the calories vital to health.

—A.A.

PART THREE
THE NATURAL ORDER

JEWISH TIME

THE COMINGS AND GOINGS OF THE JEWISH YEAR

The Jewish calendar is calculated according to *both* the lunar and solar cycles. The months and dates for the festivals are determined by the phases of the moon, while the seasons are based on the revolution of the earth around the sun. This dual system is necessary because the lunar year (twelve months) is approximately eleven days shorter than the solar year. Left uncorrected over a number of years, the festivals would wander through the seasons. However, since many of the festivals are seasonally determined (Pesah at the spring harvest, Sukkot at the autumn harvest), the simple lunar calendar would be inadequate. To alleviate this difficulty, an extra month is periodically inserted into the calendar, thereby keeping the holidays in their proper season. Since in nineteen years the solar calendar would exceed the lunar by 209 days (or approximately seven lunar months), the Jewish calendar incorporates seven leap years in this span of time (known as the "small" or "lunar" cycle).

At one time the decision as to whether a year would be regular or expanded was based on observations of agricultural conditions; the cycle is now fixed so that the third, sixth, eighth, eleventh, fourteenth, seventeenth, and nineteenth years are intercalated. The extra month is added on after Adar and is known simply as Adar Sheni or Adar II (see below).

The use of the moon in the calculation of months was common and natural in ancient times because of its recurring cycles and observability. Given clear night skies, its phases are easily discernible waxing and waning. The moon rises forty-five minutes later each day. Thus, as the moon revolves around the earth it is in a constantly changing relationship to the sun. When directly between the earth and the sun, but on a different plane so that there is not an eclipse, none of the sun's light can be reflected off of it onto the earth, and at night the moon consequently looks dark. As the moon "rises" later and later parts of it will become visible for short periods immediately after sunset (during the day, the sun's brilliance obscures the moon). With each succeeding night more of the moon is visible for longer periods of time until the "full" moon is seen. This phase occurs when the moon "rises" as the sun "sets," or to put it another way, when the earth is between the sun and the moon, but on a different plane, so that the full face of the moon reflects the sun's light onto the nighttime earth. From this point the moon wanes until it again "rises" when the sun "rises" and is, therefore, once again "invisible."

In the past the new month was determined visually by the first appearance of a lunar crescent following its being "dark." As with other aspects of the calendar, the beginning of months has been fixed by astronomical calculations instead of observation since the middle of the fourth century C.E. The New Moon (Rosh Hodesh) is celebrated as a minor festival with special insertions in the prayer services and women being required to abstain from work. This latter custom, coupled with the strong parallels between lunar and feminine imagery, has led to this festival's being revived in recent years as a Jewish woman's celebration.

One lunar month is twenty-nine days, twelve hours, forty-four minutes and three and one-third seconds. In order to even this out, some Hebrew months are twenty-nine days, some are thirty days, and some are either twenty-nine or thirty days, depending on the year. When a month has thirty days, its last day is considered the first day of Rosh Hodesh, since part of it will fall in the new lunar month. The first day of the following month, therefore, is considered the second day of Rosh Hodesh.

In the determination of the calendar, some additional factors must be taken into con-

Aspects of the festivals as portrayed by an actor in 1879.

sideration. Most particularly, the date of Rosh Hashanah (New Year) must be set so that Yom Kippur (the Day of Atonement) will not fall on either a Friday or Sunday (which would cause complications and conflicts with the observance of Shabbat) and so that the festival of Hoshana Rabbah (the Great Hosanna) will not fall on Shabbat (which would make it impossible to carry and beat the willow branches, the central ritual in the celebration of the festival). Rosh Hashanah, therefore, never falls on Sunday, Wednesday, or Friday. As indicated below, these requirements also determine the days of the week on which the other months of the year can begin.

A curiosity of the Jewish year is that Rosh Hashanah falls in the seventh month. This is a consequence of there actually being several new year celebrations marked on the Jewish calendar. The New Year for the Trees (which determines the age of trees for various religious/agricultural purposes) is the fifteenth of Shevat. The new year for the months, for the festivals, and, therefore, for the religious cycle is the first of Nisan as already designated in the Torah. Although there was considerable rabbinic controversy as to whether Nisan should also mark the beginning of the civil year, it was ultimately determined that the years should be counted from the first of Tishri (Rosh Hashanah).

Originally months were simply designated by numbers. After the Babylonian Exile (586–536 B.C.E.) specific names for the months became more common and accepted. Given the Babylonian roots and direct parallels for the names of the Hebrew months, it is apparent that the names were simply brought back with the people.

As recorded in the Torah, two of the pilgrimage festivals, Pesah and Sukkot, although celebrated for seven days, had one-day special "holy convocations" at the beginning and end of the festivals. The third pilgrimage festival, Shavuot, was only celebrated for one day. After the destruction of the Temple it was decreed that in exile these holy convocations would be two days in duration, thus adding an extra day to the festivals. Since the founding of the State of Israel, these extra "Diaspora" days have been dropped in Israel and by the Reform movement and by many Conservative Jews. This accounts for the discrepancy in dates and scriptural readings for these festivals as found on different Jewish calendars.

In the following descriptions of the months, aside from the elements mentioned above (name, length, festivals), there are two other categories that may not be familiar—the Divine Name and the Tribe. Since there are twelve tribes of Israel and twelve permutations of the four-letter name of God (the Tetragrammaton, YHWH), one of each has become associated with the twelve months of the common year. Thus, the listing provides both the descriptive as well as symbolic resonances of the months of the Jewish year.

The Months:

TISHRE

Meaning: From Aramaic *shera* or *sherei*, "to begin."

Order: Seventh month in the religious or festival cycle; first in chronological or civil cycle.

Length: Always 30 days. The 1st never falls on Sunday, Wednesday, or Friday. In the twentieth century, its earliest beginning is September 6th and its latest beginning is October 5th.

Divine Name: VHYH

Tribe: Issachar

Astrological Sign: Libra, Balance (of sins and merits).

Special Days:

1st and 2nd: Rosh Hashanah (New Year), also known as Yom ha-Zikkaron (Day of Remembrance), Yom ha-Din (Day of Judgment), and Yom ha-Teruah (Day of Sounding the Shofar). Referred to in Numbers 29:1–6 as a "holy convocation," Rosh Hashanah is the first of the High Holy Days. It marks both the "birthday of the world," as counted from Creation, and also the beginning of the Ten Days of Repentance leading up to Yom Kippur. This mixture of both joyousness and solemnity gives the holiday an exhilarating but muted edge. Aside from special prayer services, which require a special prayer book (*mahzor*), other customs include the dipping of apples in honey (to symbolize a sweet year), the sending of wishes for a good and sweet year to friends, and the blowing of the *shofar* (ram's horn) to rouse the people to repentance.

Picart engraving of a Sukkot celebration

3rd: Tzom Gedaliah (the Fast of Gedaliah). Described in Zechariah 7:5 as the Fast of the Seventh Month, this fast day commemorates the assassination of Gedaliah, the governor of Judah appointed by Nebuchadnezzar of Babylonia, 586 B.C.E. (II Kings 25: 23–25; Jeremiah 41:1–3).

10th: Yom Kippur (the Day of Atonement). As commanded in Numbers 29:7–11, ". . . on the tenth day of the seventh month you shall have a holy convocation; and you shall afflict your souls, you shall do no manner of work . . ." Yom Kippur, also known as Shabbat Shabbatot (the Sabbath of Sabbaths), is generally considered to be the holiest day in the Jewish year. It is marked by a complete fast, abstinence from wearing leather, from washing, from wearing cosmetics or lotions, and from sexual intercourse. As the day on which humanity is judged, it is totally devoted to prayer and repentance. It is customary to give charity before the holiday in the spirit of atonement and repentance.

15th (and 16th): First day(s) of Sukkot (Tabernacles). "You shall dwell in booths seven days . . . in order that future generations may know that I made the Israelite people live in booths when I brought them

***A contemporary Sukkot celebration* (Marilyn L. Schrut)**

out of the land of Egypt, I the Lord your God" (Lev. 23:42, 43). Sukkot is the third of the three pilgrimage festivals. Historically it commemorates the wandering of the Israelites through the wilderness on their way to the Promised Land. Agriculturally it marks the final harvest before the onset of the winter rains. Aside from festival prayer services, it is celebrated by eating (and sleeping) in the *sukkah* (temporary booth) for the duration of the holiday and gathering and waving of the "Four Species" (*lulav*/ palm, *hadas*/myrtle, *aravot*/willows, and *etrog*/citron) symbolic of God's bounty and blessings. Sukkot is considered the most universal of the Jewish holidays, symbolized by the inviting of guests (both living and ancestral) to come together in the *sukkah,* and also in the scriptural readings, which speak of the ingathering of the nations to worship God in universal harmony (Zechariah 14).

17th through 21st: The Intermediate Days of Sukkot (Numbers 29:17–34).

21st: Hoshana Rabbah (the Great Hosanna). Although still a part of Sukkot, it has an air of solemnity owing to its being considered to be the day when the seal is placed on the verdict passed on Yom Kippur and also when the final judgment is passed concerning the amount of rainfall for the coming year. Hoshana Rabbah is celebrated with special rituals, including a procession of seven circuits around the synagogue while reciting supplications and petitionary prayers (*hoshanot*) and beating of willow branches.

22nd: Shemini Atzeret (the Eighth Day's Assembly). Although considered a separate holiday (Numbers 29:35–38), Shemini Atzeret functions as the conclusion to the Sukkot festival. The primary ritual observance is the introduction of the supplicatory "Prayer for Rain" *(Tefillat Geshem)* during the Additional Service.

23rd: Simhat Torah (Rejoicing of the Torah). Celebrated in Israel on the 22nd in conjunction with Shemini Atzeret, Simhat Torah marks the conclusion and new beginning of the yearly cycle of Torah readings. It is celebrated with seven processions around the synagogue carrying Torahs, dancing with the Torah, special ceremonies for the concluding and opening portions, and festive meals during the day. Because of the centrality of Torah to Judaism, this day is characterized by great joy and exuberance.

MARHESHVAN OR HESHVAN

Meaning: Related to the Assyrian *Arahsammu,* "eighth month."

Order: Eighth month in the religious or festival cycle; second in the chronological or civil cycle.

Length: It can have either 29 or 30 days in either common or leap years. The 1st never falls on Sunday, Tuesday, or Friday. In the twentieth century its earliest beginning is October 6th and its latest beginning is November 4th.

Divine Name: WHHY

Tribe: Dan

Astrological Sign: Scorpio.

Special Days:

Because there are no festivals or holidays in this month, it is considered "bitter" (*mar*), and some communities maintain the custom of not holding marriages during the month. The 17th is regarded as the date on which the biblical Flood began that destroyed the earth (Gen. 7:11).

KISLEV

Meaning: Unclear, perhaps related to *k'sil,* the biblical word for Orion, the Archer.

Order: Ninth month in the religious or festival cycle; third in the chronological or civil cycle.

Length: It can have either 29 or 30 days in

either common or leap years. The 1st never falls on Shabbat. In the twentieth century its earliest beginning is November 4th and its latest beginning is December 3rd.

Divine Name: WYHH

Tribe: Gad

Astrological Sign: Sagittarius, the Archer.

(Bill Aron)

Special Days:

25th through 2nd (3rd) of Tevet: Hanukkah (Dedication). In 165 B.C.E. the Syrian-Greek forces under the rule of Antiochus Epiphanes conquered Jerusalem, displacing the Jewish government and converting the Holy Temple into a place of pagan worship. With this invasion came a forced Hellenization to which many Jews capitulated. However, in an effort to preserve Jewish political autonomy and defend the principles of Jewish faith, a small group of religious zealots led by Judah Maccabee and his brothers waged war against both the foreign occupation and the Jewish assimilationists. Using basically guerilla tactics against overwhelming forces, this small band succeeded in frustrating the Syrians, recapturing the Temple, and purging the people. The postbiblical festival of Hanukkah commemorates this physical victory, but more significantly, it celebrates the rededication of the Temple and the hearts of the Jews to God's service.

On each night of the eight-day holiday, an additional candle is lit in a specially designed candleholder called a Hanukkiah or Hanukkah menorah. According to legend, when the Maccabees reentered the Temple, they found only enough undefiled oil to fuel the Temple's eternal light for one day. Miraculously, however, it lasted for eight days until fresh oil could be produced. From a folkloric perspective, these lightings are also associated with the winter solstice. Many folk traditions share the custom of lighting fires at the point in the year of greatest darkness and increasing them day after day as a form of symbolic participation in the "rekindling" of the sun. The intertwining of these two interpretations—juxtaposing history and myth, ritual and magic, miracle and nature—creates around Hanukkah candle-lighting an aura of wonder, mystery, and delight. Unlike the candles for any other celebration, these lights cannot be used for any functional purpose, but are placed as a symbol in the window. While the candles are burning it is customary to play *dreidel* (a spinning-top gambling game), exchange gifts, and eat potatoe *latkes* (pancakes).

TEVET

Meaning: Related to the Assyrian/Babylonian *tebetum* and Hebrew *tava,* it probably means "to drown" or "to be submerged" (in mud), because of its being the month of heaviest rainfall.

Order: Tenth month in the religious or festival cycle; fourth in the chronological or civil cycle.

Length: Always 29 days. The 1st never falls on Thursday or Shabbat. In the twentieth century its earliest beginning is December 4th and its latest beginning is January 2nd.

Divine Name: HYHW

Tribe: Asher

Astrological Sign: Capricorn.

Special Days:

Depending on whether Kislev is 29 or 30 days, either two or three days of Hanukkah fall in Tevet.

10th: The Fast of the Tenth Month (Zechariah 8:19). Commemorates the commencement of the siege of Jerusalem by Nebuchadnezzar in 586 B.C.E. (Jeremiah 42:4 ff.).

SHEVAT

Meaning: Perhaps related to words for beating or striking implements, a possible allusion to the beating rains of this month.

Order: Eleventh month in the religious or festival cycle; fifth in the chronological or civil cycle.

Length: Always 30 days. The 1st never falls on Sunday or Friday. In the twentieth century its earliest beginning is January 1st and its latest beginning is January 31st.

Divine Name: HYWH

Tribe: Naftal

Astrological Sign: Aquarius.

Special Days:

15th: Tu b'Shevat (New Year for the Trees). A minor holiday, Tu b'Shevat is the date from which to count the age of trees for the purpose of tithing and for determining maturation. Marking the season when the sap begins to rise in the trees and when the rains abate in Israel, it has been traditionally celebrated with the eating of fruits, often in ceremonies paralleling the Passover *seder.* Since the reclamation of the Land of Israel, it is celebrated with the planting of trees in Israel through the Jewish National Fund.

Children in Israel planting seedlings during a Tu b'Shevat celebration

ADAR

Meaning: Related to a Molochlike idol worshipped by ancestors of the Samaritans, or perhaps, "threshing floor" indicating the preparation of the granaries.

Order: Twelfth (and thirteenth) month in the religious or festival cycle; sixth (and seventh) in the chronological or civil cycle.

Length: In leap years, it is two months, Adar Rishon (Adar I) and Adar Sheni (Adar II). In regular years, it is always 29 days. In leap years, Adar I is 30 days and Adar II is 29 days. The first day of Adar (or Adar II in leap years) never falls on Sunday, Tuesday, or Thursday. In the twentieth century its earliest beginning as a regular month is February 12th and its latest beginning is March 2nd; as a double month, its earliest beginning is February 2nd and its latest beginning is February 11th.

Divine Name: HHYW

Tribe: Joseph

Astrological Sign: Pisces.

***A Purim masquerade* (Bill Aron)**

Special Days:

Most occasions celebrated in Adar during regular years are celebrated in Adar II during a leap year.

13th: Originally Nicanor Day, a feast celebrating the Hasmonean victory over the Syrian general Nicanor, it is now celebrated as the Fast of Esther prior to the Feast of Purim.

14th: Purim (The Feast of Lots). As recorded in the biblical Scroll of Esther (*Megillat Esther*), the Purim story is a classical melodrama depicting the unambiguous struggle between good and evil. Haman is the wicked anti-Semite, considered to be a descendant of Amalek (the ancient adversaries of Israel) and a prototype for all irrational, ill-willed, egocentric oppressors. As advisor to the rather dull-witted King Ahasuerus of Persia, described hyperbolically as ruler "from India to Ethiopia," Haman engineered the issuance of a decree that would have effectively destroyed the entire Jewish population. However, the courageous Jews Mordechai and his cousin/niece Esther undertook a daring and complex counteraction that eventually led to Haman's death and the salvation of the Persian Jews.

As a perennial remembrance of the triumph of good over evil, the Jews were enjoined to observe the 14th day of Adar "exactly like the days when the Jews had found relief from their enemies in the month which had been transformed from mourning to holiday, making them days of feasting and joy, the exchange of gifts among friends, and the giving of alms to the poor" (Esther 9:22). The holiday is joyously celebrated in the synagogue with a public reading of often elaborately and beautifully illuminated Scrolls of Esther. Children's masquerades and carnivals augment the festive spirit, as does an afternoon Purim feast accompanied with parodies, pranks, and plays. As mentioned in the *Megillah*, it is customary for friends to exchange little sweets, often triangular cookies known as *Hamantaschen* (Haman's Hat), and to give charity to the poor. Although a relatively minor holiday, Purim is considered to be the epitome of joyousness, marking an event, whether historical or fictional, of unmitigated joy for the Jewish people. "Rabah said: 'A person is obligated to feast on Purim until he/she can no longer distinguish between "Bless Mordechai" and "Curse Haman"'" (*Megillah* 7a).

15th: Shushan Purim. An extra day of Purim decreed for those who live in walled cities (like Jerusalem).

NISAN

Meaning: Related to the Babylonian first month *Nisannu*, "to start," or perhaps to Hebrew *nitzan*, "blossoms." Its pentateuchal name is *Aviv*, "spring."

Order: First month in the religious or festival cycle; seventh in the chronological or civil cycle.

Length: Always 30 days. The 1st never falls on Monday, Wednesday, or Friday. In the twentieth century its earliest beginning is March 13th and its latest beginning is April 11th.

Divine Name: YHWH

Tribe: Benjamin

Astrological Sign: Aries.

Special Days:

15th through 22nd (21st in Israel): Pesah (Passover), also known as Hag ha-Matzot (Festival of Matzah). Passover is the first of the three pilgrimage festivals. Historically it commemorates the exodus of the Israelites from Egyptian slavery to freedom. Agriculturally it marks the first barley harvest and the beginning of the spring calving. Aside from special prayer services on the first two days and last two days, Pesah is celebrated by the abstention from all leavened food products and by the eating of matzah (unleavened bread) for the duration of the festival. In addition, on the first two nights a special meal (*seder*) is held at home with the extended family and, often, other guests gathered together. The *seder* (lit. "order") is a ritual feast that parallels the original Passover meal eaten the night before leaving Egypt but also incorporates additional symbolic components adopted by tradition over the course of time. The "order" for this elaborate fifteen-stage ceremony, which has the telling of the Passover story at its center, is detailed in the *seder*'s "hand-

Passover seder for U.S. Armed Services, Paris 1919

book," the *Haggadah* ("Telling"). Although each household conducts its *seder* in its own characteristic fashion, generally everyone plays a role, whether in raising a question or suggesting an answer, reciting the story or singing the traditional songs. From the opening invitation, "Let all who are hungry come and eat," to the concluding messianic hope, "Next year in Jerusalem," the *Haggadah* weaves together diverse components of the Jewish people's history and self-identity, creating an atmosphere in which liberation can be viscerally reexperienced each year.

Mosaic floor from the Synagogue at Beit Alpha showing the signs of the Zodiac and solstices with their Hebrew names.

In leaving Egypt, the Jewish people were born. Passover is, thus, a festival both of redemption and creation. What had been separate tribes, without unified leadership, direction, or vision, emerged from the Red Sea bound together by a common transcendent experience. Although celebrated in families and addressed to each individual, Passover is ultimately the experience of the Jewish People, finally released from servitude to foreign rulers and beginning the journey to their Promised Land.

16th through Sivan 5: Omer. The Torah requires that the first sheaves (Heb. *omer*) of the barley crop be brought to the Temple in Jerusalem and presented as an offering to God. The Torah further instructs (Lev. 23:15, 16) that these sheaves be counted (*sefirat ha-omer*) for seven full weeks, beginning with the second night of Passover, which leads directly into the festival of Shavuot (Feast of Weeks) on the fiftieth day. In contemporary times, while the barley offering is not brought, the days are still counted as a transition from Passover to Shavuot—from the liberation from slavery to the receiving of God's law at Sinai. The omer is traditionally observed as a period of semi-mourning during which many people do not shave, do not hold parties with music, and do not marry.

27th: Yom ha-Shoah (Commemoration of the Holocaust). This is a recent addition to the calendar, which does not yet have standard ritual observances attached to it. It is most often marked by memorial services or special programs relating to the Holocaust.

IYYAR

Meaning: Related to the Hebrew *or*, "bright."

Order: Second month in the religious or festival cycle; eighth in the chronological or civil cycle.

Length: Always 29 days. The 1st never falls on Sunday, Wednesday, or Friday. In the twentieth century, its earliest beginning is April 12th and its latest beginning is May 11th.

Divine Name: YHHW

Tribe: Reuben

Astrological Sign: Taurus.

Special Days:

All of Iyyar is within the Omer period (see Nisan above).

5th: Yom ha-Atzmaut (Israel Independence Day). This is a recent addition to the calendar which does not yet have standard ritual observances attached to it except for the reciting of Hallel (Psalms of Praise) during the morning service.

18th: Lag ba-Omer (The Thirty-third Day of Omer). This is a semiholiday on which the restrictions of the Omer period are lifted. The historical reasons for this are unclear. Some consider it the day on which the plague that afflicted twenty-four thousand of Rabbi Akiva's disciples ceased (2nd century C.E.). Others celebrate it as the anniversary of the death of Rabbi Shimon ben Yohai, who was regarded as the author of the central kabbalistic book, the Zohar. It is generally celebrated as an outing day, with picnics, bonfires, games, and songs.

SIVAN

Meaning: Related to the Assyrian words for "to mark" or "to appoint."

Order: Third month in the religious or festival cycle; ninth in the chronological or civil cyle.

Length: Always 30 days. The 1st never falls on Monday, Thursday, or Shabbat. In the twentieth century its earliest beginning is May 11th and its latest beginning is June 9th.

Divine Name: YWHH

Tribe: Simeon

Astrological Sign: Gemini, Twins.

Special Days:

6th (and 7th): Shavuot (Feast of Weeks). This is the second of the three pilgrimage festivals mentioned in the Torah. Historically it commemorates the revelation at Mt. Sinai when God gave the Torah to the Israelites. Agriculturally it marks the first harvest of fruits and vegetables planted during that season. Aside from festival prayer services, the holiday is celebrated with an all-night study session (*tikun leil Shavuot*), which parallels the preparation for and anticipation of receiving the Torah at Sinai. It is customary to eat dairy products on Shavuot, particularly cheese blintzes (crepes).

TAMMUZ

Meaning: Named after the Babylonian god Dumuzi, parallel to the Greeks' Adonis, god of vegetation and plant life.

Order: Fourth month in the religious or festival cycle; tenth in the chronological or civil cycle.

Length: Always 29 days. The 1st never falls on Monday, Wednesday, or Shabbat. In the twentieth century its earliest beginning is June 10th and its latest beginning is July 9th.

Divine Name: HWHY

Tribe: Levi

Astrological Sign: Cancer, the Crab.

Special Days:

17th: Fast of the Fourth Month (Zechariah 8:19). This fast day commemorates several tragedies that befell the Jewish people, including the breaching of the walls of Jerusalem by Nebuchadnezzar (586 B.C.E.) and by Titus (70 C.E.), and the breaking of the Tablets of the Law by Moses because of the people's having sinned with the Golden Calf. This begins the three-week mourning period for the destruction of the Temple, which culminates with Tisha b'Av.

AV

Meaning: Named after the wood and reeds from which shelters were erected in Babylonia.

Order: Fifth month in the religious or festival cycle; eleventh in the chronological or civil cycle.

Length: Always 30 days. The 1st never falls on Sunday, Tuesday, or Thursday. In the twentieth century its earliest beginning is July 8th and its latest beginning is August 7th.

Divine Name: HWYH

Tribe: Judah

Astrological Sign: Leo, the Lion.

Special Days:

9th: Tisha b'Av (The Ninth of Av). The culmination of the three-week semimourning period beginning with Tammuz 17 and the more intensive nine-day semimourning period beginning with Av 1, this fast day commemorates the destruction of both the First (586 B.C.E.) and the Second (70 C.E.) Temples, as well as the expulsion of the Jews from Spain in 1492. It is the strictest of the four fasts related to the destruction and is commemorated with the reading of the Book of Lamentations and the singing of dirgelike melodies.

15th: Tu b'Av (The Fifteenth of Av). Formerly a joyous popular holiday, this day has been essentially nonobserved for centuries. Marking the beginning of the vintage season, women would dress in white and dance through the vineyards singing songs. It may have been a midsummer solstice festival, since the lighting of torches and bonfires seems to have accompanied these celebrations.

ELUL

Meaning: An onomatopoetic derivative from the Akkadian for "women singing."

Order: Sixth month in the religious or festival cycle; twelfth in the chronological or civil cycle.

Length: Always 29 days. The 1st never falls on Tuesday, Thursday, or Shabbat. In the twentieth century its earliest beginning is August 8th and its latest beginning is September 6th.

Divine Name: HHWY

Tribe: Zebulun

Astrological Sign: Virgo.

Special Days:

The entire month of Elul is devoted to beginning the process of repentance in anticipation of the High Holy Days/ the Ten Days of Repentance. Every day (except Shabbat) after the morning services, the *shofar* (ram's horn) is sounded to warn and rouse people to repentance. In the Sephardic traditions, Selichot (special supplicatory and penitential prayers) are recited during the entire month; while the Ashkenazic custom is to begin Selichot on the Saturday night preceding Rosh Hashanah or on the previous Saturday night if Rosh Hashanah falls on Monday or Tuesday. From the beginning of Elul it is proper and customary to extend New Year's blessings in conversation and correspondence.

—R.A.S.

SCRIPTURAL READINGS FOR SABBATHS AND HOLIDAYS

TABLE OF SCRIPTURAL READINGS ON SABBATHS

PENTATEUCH		PROPHETS
GENESIS		
Bereshit	1:1–6:8	Isa. 42:5–43:11 (42:5–21)[1]
Noah	6:9–11:32	Isa. 54:1–55:5 (54:1–10)
Lekh Lekha	12:1–17:27	Isa. 40:27–41:16
Va-Yera	18:1–22:24	II Kings 4:1–37 (4:1–23)
Hayyei Sarah	23:1–25:18	I Kings 1:1–31
Toledot	25:19–28:9	Mal. 1:1–2:7
Va-Yeze	28:10–32:3	Hos. 12:13–14:10 (11:7–12:12)
Va-Yishlah	32:4–36:43	Hos. 11:7–12:12 (Obad. 1:1–21)
Va-Yeshev	37:1–40:23	Amos 2:6–3:8
Mi-Ketz	41:1–44:17	I Kings 3:15–4:1
Va-Yiggash	44:18–47:27	Ezek. 37:15–28
Va-Yehi	47:28–50:26	I Kings 2:1–12
EXODUS		
Shemot	1:1–6:1	Isa. 27:6–28; 13; 29:22, 23 (Jer. 1:1–2:3)
Va-Era	6:2–9:35	Ezek. 28:25–29:21
Bo	10:1–13:16	Jer. 46:13–28
Be-Shallah	13:17–17:16	Judg. 4:4–5:31 (5:1–31)
Yitro	18:1–20:23	Isa. 6:1–7; 6; 9:5 (6:1–13)
Mishpatim	21:1–24:18	Jer. 34:8–22; 33:25, 26
{ Terumah	25:1–27:19	I Kings 5:26–6:13
{ Tetzavveh	27:20–30:10	Ezek. 43:10–27
Ki Tissa	30:11–34:35	I Kings 18:1–39 (18:20–39)
{ Va-Yakhel	35:1–38:20	I Kings 7:40–50 (7:13–26)
{ Pekudei	38:21–40:38	I Kings 7:51–8:21 (7:40–50)
LEVITICUS		
Va-Yikra	1:1–5:26	Isa. 43:21–44:23
Tzav	6:1–8:36	Jer. 7:21–8:3; 9:22, 23
Shemini	9:1–11:47	II Sam. 6:1–7:17 (6:1–19)
[2] { Tazri'a	12:1–13:59	II Kings 4:42–5:19
{ Metzora	14:1–15:33	II Kings 7:3–20
{ Aharei Mot	16:1–18:30	Ezek. 22:1–19 (22:1–16)
{ Kedoshim	19:1–20:27	Amos 9:7–15 (Ezek. 20:2–20)
Emor	21:1–24:23	Ezek. 44:15–31
{ Be-Har	25:1–26:2	Jer. 32:6–27
{ Be-Hukkotai	26:3–27:34	Jer. 16:19–17:14
NUMBERS		
Be-Midbar	1:1–4:20	Hos. 2:1–22
Naso	4:21–7:89	Judg. 13:2–25
Be-Ha'alotkha	8:1–12:16	Zech. 2:14–4:7
Shelah Lekha	13:1–15:41	Josh. 2:1–24
Korah	16:1–18:32	I Sam. 11:14–12:22
Hukkat	19:1–22:1	Judg. 11:1–33
Balak	22:2–25:9	Micah 5:6–6:8
Pinhas	25:10–30:1	I Kings 18:46–19:21
{ Mattot	30:2–32:42	Jer. 1:1–2:3
{ Masei	33:1–36:13	Jer. 2:4–28; 3:4 (2:4–28; 4:1, 2)
DEUTERONOMY		
Devarim	1:1–3:22	Isa. 1:1–27
Va-Ethannan	3:23–7:11	Isa. 40:1–26
Ekev	7:12–11:25	Isa. 49:14–51:3
Re'eh	11:26–16:17	Isa. 54:11–55:5
Shofetim	16:18–21:9	Isa. 51:12–52:12
Ki Tetze	21:10–25:19	Isa. 54:1–10

Ki Tavo	26:1–29:8	Isa. 60:1–22
{ Nitzavim	29:9–30:20	Isa. 61:10–63:9
{ Va-Yelekh	31:1–30	Isa. 55:6–56:8
Ha'azinu	32:1–52	II Sam. 22:1–51
Ve-Zot ha-Berakhah[3]	33:1–34:12	Josh. 1:1–18 (1:1–9)

[1]Parentheses indicate Sephardi ritual.
[2]Brackets indicate portions that are sometimes combined.
[3]This portion is not read on Sabbath but on Simhat Torah.

TABLE OF HOLIDAY SCRIPTURAL READINGS FOR THE DIASPORA AND FOR EREZ ISRAEL

	PENTATEUCH		PROPHETS
ROSH HA-SHANAH			
1st Day	Gen. 21:1–34; Num. 29:1–6		I Sam. 1:1–2:10
2nd Day	Gen. 22:1–24; Num. 29:1–6		Jer. 31:2–20
Shabbat Shuvah	Weekly portion		Hos. 14:2–10; Micah 7:18–20 or Hos. 14:2–10; Joel 2:15–17 (Hos. 14:2–10; Micah 7:18–20[1])
DAY OF ATONEMENT			
Morning	Lev. 16:1–34; Num. 29:7–11		Isa. 57:14–58:14
Afternoon	Lev. 18:1–30		The Book of Jonah; Micah 7:18–20
SUKKOT			
1st Day	Lev. 22:26–23:44; Num. 29:12–16		Zech. 14:1–21
2nd Day	Lev. 22:26–23:44; Num. 29:12–16 [Num. 29:17–19][2]	}	I Kings 8:2–21 [none]
3rd Day	Num. 29:17–22 [29:20–22]	Erez Israel	
4th Day	Num. 29:20–28 [29:23–25]	portion read	
5th Day	Num. 29:23–31 [29:26–28]	four times	
6th Day	Num. 29:26–34 [29:29–31]		
7th Day	Num. 29:26–34 [29:32–34]	}	
Shabbat during the Intermediate Days	Ex. 33:12–34:26; Daily portion from Num. 29		Ezek. 38:18–39:16
Shemini Azeret 8th Day	Deut. 14:22–16:17; Num. 29:35–30:1 [as for Simhat Torah]		I Kings 8:54–66 [as for Simhat Torah]
Simhat Torah 9th Day	Deut. 33:1–34:12; Gen. 1:1–2:3; Num. 29:35–30:1 [none]		Josh. 1:1–18 (1:1–9) [none]
HANUKKAH			
1st Day	Num. 7:1–17		
2nd Day	Num. 7:18–29 [7:18–23]	}	
3rd Day	Num. 7:24–35 [7:24–29]		
4th Day	Num. 7:30–41 [7:30–35]	Erez Israel	
5th Day	Num. 7:36–47 [7:36–41]	portion read	
6th Day	Num. 7:42–53 [7:42–47]	three times	
7th Day	Num. 7:48–59 [7:48–53]	}	
8th Day	Num. 7:54–8:4		
First Shabbat Hanukkah	Weekly and Hanukkah portions as for Erez Israel		Zech. 2:14–4:7
Second Shabbat Hanukkah	Weekly and Hanukkah portions as for Erez Israel		I Kings 7:40–50
Rosh Hodesh during Hanukkah	Weekly and Hanukkah portions as for Erez Israel and Num. 28. 1–15		
Rosh Hodesh and Shabbat Hanukkah	Weekly Rosh Hodesh, and Hanukkah portions as for Erez Israel		Isa. 66:1–24
Shekalim	Weekly portion; Ex. 30:11–16		II Kings 12:1–17
Zakhor	Weekly portion; Deut. 25:17–19		I Sam. 15:2–34 (15:1–34)
PURIM	Ex. 17:8–16		
Parah	Weekly portion; Num. 19:1–22		Ezek. 36:16–38 (36:16–36)

Ha-Hodesh	Weekly portion; Ex. 12:1–20	Ezek. 45:16–46:18 (45:18–46:5)
Shabbat Ha-Gadol	Weekly portion	Mal. 3:4–24
PASSOVER		
1st Day	Ex. 12:21–51; Num. 28:19–25	Josh. 5:2–6:1
2nd Day	Lev. 22:26–23:44; Num. 28:19–25	II Kings 23:1–9; 21–25 [none]
3rd Day	Ex. 13:1–16; Num. 28:19–25	
4th Day	Ex. 22:24–23:19; Num. 28:19–25	
5th Day	Ex. 33:12–34:26; Num. 28:19–25	
6th Day	Num. 9:1–14; 28:19–25	
Intermediate Shabbat	The order changes to allow for the reading as on the 5th day above	Ezek. 36:37–37:14 (37:1–14)
7th Day	Ex. 13:17–15:26; Num. 28:19–25	II Sam. 22:1–51
8th Day	Deut. 15:19–16:17[3]; Num. 28:19–25 [none]	Isa. 10:32–12:6 [none]
SHAVUOT		
1st Day	Ex. 19:1–20:23; Num. 28:26–31	Ezek. 1:1–28; 3:12
2nd Day	Deut. 15:19–16:17[3]; Num. 28:26–31 [none]	Num. 3:1–19 (2:20–3:19)
NINTH OF AV		
Morning	Deut. 4:25–40	Jer. 8:13–9:23
Afternoon	Ex. 32:11–14; 34:1–10	Isa. 55:6–56:8 (Hos. 14:2–10; Micah [7:18–20])
Other Fasts		
Morning and afternoon	Ex. 32:11–14; 34:1–10	Isa. 55:6–56:8
Rosh Hodesh	Num. 28:1–15	
Shabbat and Rosh Hodesh	Weekly portion; Num. 28:9–15	Isa. 66:1–24
Shabbat immediately preceding Rosh Hodesh	Weekly portion	I Sam. 20:18–12

[1]Parentheses indicate Sephardi custom
[2]Square brackets indicate Erez Israel custom
[3]On Shabbat, 14:22–16:17

Reprinted from: *The Encyclopædia Judaica*
(Jerusalem: Keter Publishing House), Vol. 15, pp. 1249–1252.

TWENTY-ONE-YEAR JEWISH CALENDARS

5740/41 — 1980

	January	February	March	April	May	June	July	August	September	October	November	December
1	12 Tevet	14	13 ↑ Tezavveh Zakhor	15 Pesah	15	17	17 Fast	19	20	21 Hoshana Rabba	22 Hayyei Sarah	23
2	13	15 Be-Shallah	14 Purim	16 Omer	16	18	18	20 Ekev	21	22 Shemini Azeret	23	24
3	14	16	15 Shushan Purim	17 Hol ha-Mo'ed	17 Emor	19	19	21	22	23 Simhat Torah Ve-Zot Ha-Berakhah	24	25 Hanukkah 1
4	15	17	16	18	18 Lag ba-Omer	20	20	22	23	24 Bereshit	25	26 2
5	16 Va-Yehi	18	17	19	19	21	21 Pinhas	23	24	25	26	27 3
6	17	19	18	20	20	22	22	24	25 Nizzavim Va-Yelekh	26	27	28 Mi-Kez 4
7	18	20	19	21 Pesah	21	23 Shelah	23	25	26	27	28	29 5
8	19	21	20 Ki Tissa Parah	22	22	24	24	26	27	28	29 Toledot	1 Tevet R.H. 6
9	20	22 Yitro	21	23	23	25	25	27 Re'eh	28	29	1 Kislev R.H.	2 7
10	21	23	22	24	24 Be-Har Be-Hukkotai	26	26	28	29	30 R.H.	2	3 8
11	22	24	23	25	25	27	27	29	1 Tishri Rosh Ha-Shanah	1 Heshvan R.H. No'ah	3	4
12	23 Shemot	25	24	26 Shemini	26	28	28 Mattot Masei	30 R.H.	2	2	4	5
13	24	26	25	27	27	29	29	1 Elul R.H.	3 Ha'azinu Shabbat Shuvah	3	5	6 Va-Yiggash
14	25	27	26	28	28	30 R.H. Korah	1 Av R.H.	2	4 ↓ Fast	4	6	7
15	26	28	27 Va-Yakhel Pekudei Ha-Hodesh	29	29	1 Tammuz R.H.	2	3	5	5	7 Va-Yeze	8
16	27	29 Mishpatim Shekalim	28	30 R.H.	1 Sivan R.H.	2	3	4 Shofetim	6	6	8	9
17	28	30 R.H.	29	1 Iyyar R.H.	2 Be-Midbar	3	4	5	7	7	9	10 Fast
18	29	1 Adar R.H.	1 Nisan R.H.	2	3	4	5	6	8	8 Lekh Lekha	10	11
19	1 Shevat R.H. Va-Era	2	2	3 Tazria Mezora	4	5	6 Devarim	7	9	9	11	12
20	2	3	3	4	5	6	7	8	10 Yom Kippur	10	12	13 Va-Yehi
21	3	4	4	5 Yom ha-Azma'ut	6 Shavout	7 Hukkat	8	9	11	11	13	14
22	4	5	5 Va-Yikra	6	7	8	9 Tishah be-Av	10	12	12	14 Va-Yishlah	15
23	5	6 Terumah	6	7	8	9	10	11 Ki Teze	13	13	15	16
24	6	7	7	8	9 Naso	10	11	12	14	14	16	17
25	7	8	8	9	10	11	12	13	15 Sukkot	15 Va-Yera	17	18
26	8 Bo	9	9	10 Aharei Mot Kedoshim	11	12	13 Va-Ethannan	14	16	16	18	19
27	9	10	10	11	12	13	14	15	17 Hol ha-Mo'ed	17	19	20 Shemot
28	10	11 ↑ Ta'anit Esther	11	12	13	14 Balak	15	16	18	18	20	21
29	11	12	12 Zav Shabbat ha-Gadol	13	14	15	16	17	19	19	21 Va-Yeshev	22
30	12		13	14	15	16	17	18 Ki Tavo	20	20	22	23
31	13		14		16 Be-Ha'alotkha		18	19		21		24

5741/42

1981

	January	February	March	April	May	June	July	August	September	October	November	December
1	25 **Tevet**	27	25	26	27	28	29	**1** **Av** R.H. *Masei*	2	3 Fast	4	5
2	26	28	26	27	**28** *Kedoshim*	29	30 R.H.	2	3	4	5	6
3	**27** *Va-Era*	29	27	28	29	1 **Sivan** R.H.	1 **Tammuz** R.H.	3	4	**5** *Va-Yelekh* Shabbat Shuvah	6	7
4	28	30 R.H.	28	**29** *Tazri'a* Ha-Hodesh	30 R.H.	2	**2** *Hukkat*	4	5	6	7	8
5	29	1 **Adar** R.H.	29	1 **Nisan** R.H.	1 **Iyyar** R.H.	3	3	5	**6** *Shofetim*	7	8	**9** *Va-Yeze*
6	1 **Shevat** R.H.	2	30 R.H.	2	2	**4** *Naso*	4	6	7	8	9	10
7	2	**3** *Terumah*	**1** **Adar II** R.H. Shekalim *Pekudei*	3	3 Yom ha-Azma'ut	5	5	7	8	9	**10** *Lekh Lekha*	11
8	3	4	2	4	4	6 Shavuot	6	**8** *Devarim*	9	10 Yom Kippur	11	12
9	4	5	3	5	**5** *Emor*	7	7	9 Tishah be-Av	10	11	12	13
10	**5** *Bo*	6	4	6	6	8	8	10	11	**12** *Ha'azinu*	13	14
11	6	7	5	**7** *Mezora*	7	9	**9** *Balak*	11	12	13	14	15
12	7	8	6	8	8	10	10	12	**13** *Ki Teze*	14	15	**16** *Va-Yishlah*
13	8	9	7	9	9	**11** *Be-Ha'alotkha*	11	13	14	15 Sukkot	16	17
14	9	**10** *Tezavveh*	**8** *Va-Yikra* Zakhor	10	10	12	12	14	15	16	**17** *Va-Yera*	18
15	10	11	9	11	11	13	13	**15** *Va-Ethannan*	16	17	18	19
16	11	12	10	12	**12** *Be-Har*	14	14	16	17	18 Hol ha-Mo'ed	19	20
17	**12** *Be-Shallah*	13	11	13	13	15	15	17	18	**19**	20	21
18	13	14	12	**14** *Aharei Mot* Shabbat ha-Gadol	14	16	**16** *Pinhas*	18	19	20	21	22
19	14	15	13 Ta'anit Esther	15 Pesah	15	17	17 Fast	19	**20** *Ki Tavo*	21 Hoshana Rabba	22	**23** *Va-Yeshev*
20	15	16	14 Purim	16 Omer	16	**18** *Shelah*	18	20	21	22 Shemini Azeret	23	24
21	16	**17** *Ki Tissa*	**15** *Zav* Shushan Purim	17	17	19	19	21	22	23 Simhat Torah *Ve-Zot Ha-Berakhah*	**24** *Hayyei Sarah*	25 Hanukkah 1
22	17	18	16	18	18 Lag ba-Omer	20	20	**22** *Ekev*	23	24	25	26 2
23	18	19	17	19 Hol ha-Mo'ed	**19** *Be-Hukkotai*	21	21	23	24	25	26	27 3
24	**19** *Yitro*	20	18	20	20	22	22	24	25	**26** *Bereshit*	27	28 4
25	20	21	19	**21** Pesah	21	23	**23** *Mattot*	25	26	27	28	29 5
26	21	22	20	22	22	24	24	26	**27** *Nizzavim*	28	29	**30** *Mi-Kez* R.H. 6
27	22	23	21	23	23	**25** *Korah*	25	27	28	29	1 **Kislev** R.H.	1 **Tevet** R.H. 7
28	23	**24** *Va-Yakhel*	**22** *Shemini* Parah	24	24	26	26	28	29	30 R.H.	**2** *Toledot*	2 8
29	24		23	25	25	27	27	**29** *Re'eh*	1 **Tishri** Rosh Ha-Shanah	1 **Heshvan** R.H.	3	3
30	25		24	26	**26** *Be-Midbar*	28	28	30 R.H.	2	2	4	4
31	**26** *Mishpatim*		25		27		29	1 **Elul** R.H.		**3** *No'ah*		5

5742/43

1982

	January	February	March	April	May	June	July	August	September	October	November	December
1	6 **Tevet**	8	6	8	8 *Aharei Mot Kedoshim*	10	10	12	13	14	15	15
2	7 *Va-Yiggash*	9	7	9	9	11	11	13	14	15 Sukkot	16	16
3	8	10	8	10 Shabbat ha-Gadol *Zav*	10	12	12 *Hukkat Balak*	14	15	16	17	17
4	9	11	9	11	11	13	13	15	16 *Ki Tavo*	17 Hol ha-Mo'ed	18	18 *Va-Yishlah*
5	10 Fast	12	10	12	12	14 *Naso*	14	16	17	18	19	19
6	11	13 *Be-Shallah*	11 *Tezavveh Zakhor*	13	13	15	15	17	18	19	20 *Va-Yera*	20
7	12	14	12	14	14	16	16	18 *Ekev*	19	20	21	21
8	13	15	13 Ta'anit Esther	15 Pesah	15 *Emor*	17	17 Fast	19	20	21 Hoshana Rabba	22	22
9	14 *Va-Yehi*	16	14 Purim	16 Omer	16	18	18	20	21	22 Shemini Azeret	23	23
10	15	17	15 Shushan Purim	17	17	19	19 *Pinhas*	21	22	23 Simhat Torah *Ve-Zot Ha-Berakhah*	24	24
11	16	18	16	18 Hol ha-Mo'ed	18 Lag ba-Omer	20	20	22	23 *Ve-Zot Nizzavim Va-Yelekh*	24	25	25 Hanukkah 1 *Va-Yashev*
12	17	19	17	19	19	21 *Be-Ha'alotkha*	21	23	24	25	26	26 2
13	18	20 *Yitro*	18 *Ki Tissa Parah*	20 4	20	22	22	24	25	26	27 *Hayyei Sarah*	27 3
14	19	21	19	21 Pesah	21	23	23	25 *Re'eh*	26	27	28	28 4
15	20	22	20	22	22 *Be-Har Be-Hukkotai*	24	24	26	27	28	29	29 5
16	21 *Shemot*	23	21	23	23	25	25	27	28	29 *Bereshit*	30 R.H.	30 R.H. 6
17	22	24	22	24 *Shemini*	24	26	26 *Mattot Masei*	28	29	30 R.H.	1 **Kislev** R.H.	1 **Tevet** R.H. 7
18	23	25	23	25	25	27	27	29	1 **Tishri** Rosh Ha Shanah	1 **Heshvan** R.H.	2	2 *Mi-Kez* 8
19	24	26	24	26	26	28 *Shelah*	28	30 R.H.	2	2	3	3
20	25	27 *Mishpatim Shekalim*	25 *Va-Yakhel Pekudei Ha-Hodesh*	27	27	29	29	1 **Elul** R.H.	3 Fast	3	4 *Toledot*	4
21	26	28	26	28	28	30 R.H.	1 **Av** R.H.	2 *Shofetim*	4	4	5	5
22	27	29	27	29	29 *Be-Midbar*	1 **Tammuz** R.H.	2	3	5	5	6	6
23	28 *Va-Era*	30 R.H.	28	30 R.H.	1 **Sivan** R.H.	2	3	4	6	6 *No'ah*	7	7
24	29	1 **Adar** R.H.	29	1 **Iyyar** R.H. *Tazri'a Mezora*	2	3	4 *Devarim*	5	7	7	8	8
25	1 **Shevat** R.H.	2	1 **Nisan** R.H.	2	3	4	5	6	8 *Ha'azinu* Shabbat Shuvah	8	9	9 *Va-Yiggash*
26	2	3	2	3	4	5 *Korah*	6	7	9	9	10	10 Fast
27	3	4 *Terumah*	3 *Va-Yikra*	4	5	6	7	8	10 *Yom Kippur*	10	11 *Va-Yeze*	11
28	4	5	4	5 Yom ha-Azma'ut	6 Shavuot	7	8	9 *Ki Teze*	11	11	12	12
29	5		5	6	7	8	9 Tishah be-Av	10	12	12	13	13
30	6 *Bo*		6	7	8	9	10	11	13	13 *Lekh Lekha*	14	14
31	7		7		9		11 *Va-Ethannan*	12		14		15

5743/44

1983

	January	February	March	April	May	June	July	August	September	October	November	December
1	**16** Tevet *Va-Yehi*	18	16	18 Hol ha-Mo'ed	18 Lag ba-Omer	20	20	22	23	**24** *Bereshit*	25	25 Hanukkah 1
2	17	19	17	**19**	19	21	**21** *Pinhas*	23	24	25	26	26 2
3	18	20	18	20	20	22	22	24	**25** *Nizzavim Va-Yelekh*	26	27	**27** *Mi-Kez* 3
4	19	21	19	21 Pesah	21	**23** *Shelah*	23	25	26	27	28	28 4
5	20	**22** *Yitro*	**20** *Ki Tissa Parah*	22	22	24	24	26	27	28	**29** *Toledot*	29 5
6	21	23	21	23	23	25	25	**27** *Re'eh*	28	29	30 R.H.	30 R.H. 6
7	22	24	22	24	**24** *Be Har Be Hukkotai*	26	26	28	29	30 R.H.	1 **Kislev** R.H.	1 **Tevet** R.H. 7
8	**23** *Shemot*	25	23	25	25	27	27	29	1 **Tishri** Rosh Ha-Shanah	1 **Heshvan** R.H. *No'ah*	2	2 8
9	24	26	24	**26** *Shemini*	26	28	**28** *Mattot Masei*	30 R.H.	2	2	3	3
10	25	27	25	27	27	29	29	1 **Elul** R.H.	**3** *Ha'azinu* Shabbat Shuvah	3	4	**4** *Va-Yiggash*
11	26	28	26	28	28	**30** R.H. *Korah*	1 **Av** R.H.	2	4 Fast	4	5	5
12	27	**29** *Mishpatim Shekalim*	**27** *Va-Yakhel Pekudei* Ha-Hodesh	29	29	1 **Tammuz** R.H.	2	3	5	5	**6** *Va-Yeze*	6
13	28	30 R.H.	28	30 R.H.	1 **Sivan** R.H.	2	3	**4** *Shofetim*	6	6	7	7
14	29	1 **Adar** R.H.	29	1 **Iyyar** R.H.	**2** *Be-Midbar*	3	4	5	7	7	8	8
15	**1** **Shevat** R.H. *Va-Era*	2	1 **Nisan** R.H.	2	3	4	5	6	8	**8** *Lekh Lekha*	9	9
16	2	3	2	**3** *Tazri'a Mezora*	4	5	**6** *Devarim*	7	9	9	10	10 Fast
17	3	4	3	4	5	6	7	8	**10** Yom Kippur	10	11	**11** *Va-Yehi*
18	4	5	4	5 Yom ha-Azma'ut	6 Shavuot	**7** *Hukkat*	8	9	11	11	12	12
19	5	**6** *Terumah*	**5** *Va-Yikra*	6	7	8	9 Tishah be-Av	10	12	12	**13** *Va-Yishlah*	*13*
20	6	7	6	7	8	9	10	**11** *Ki Teze*	13	13	14	14
21	7	8	7	8	**9** *Naso*	10	11	12	14	14	15	15
22	**8** *Bo*	9	8	9	10	11	12	13	15 Sukkot	**15** *Va-Yera*	16	16
23	9	10	9	**10** *Aharei Mot Kedoshim*	11	12	**13** *Va-Ethannan*	14	16	16	17	17
24	10	11 Ta'anit Esther	10	11	12	13	14	15	**17** Hol ha-Mo'ed	17	18	**18** *Shemot*
25	11	12	11	12	13	**14** *Balak*	15	16	18	18	19	19
26	12	**13** *Tezavveh Zakhor*	**12** *Zav* Shabbat ha-Gadol	13	14	15	16	17	19	19	**20** *Va-Yeshev*	20
27	13	14 Purim	13	14	15	16	17	**18** *Ki Tavo*	20	20	21	21
28	14	15 Shushan Purim	14	15	**16** *Be-Ha'alotkha*	17 Fast	18	19	21 Hoshana Rabba	21	22	22
29	**15** *Be-Shallah*		15 Pesah	16	17	18	19	20	22 Shemini Azeret	**22** *Hayyei Sarah*	23	23
30	16		16 Omer	**17** *Emor*	18	19	**20** *Ekev*	21	23 Simhat Torah *Ve-Zot Ha-Berakhah*	23	24	24
31	17		17		19		21	22		24		**25** *Va-Era*

5744/45

1984

	January	February	March	April	May	June	July	August	September	October	November	December
1	26 **Tevet**	28	27	28	28	1 **Sivan** R.H.	1 **Tammuz** R.H	3	**4** *Shofetim*	5	6	**7** *Va-Yeze*
2	27	29	28	29	30 R.H.	**2** *Naso*	2	4	5	6	7	8
3	28	30 R.H.	**29** *Pekudei Shekalim*	1 **Nisan** R.H.	1 **Iyyar** R.H.	3	3	5	6	7	**8** *Lekh Lekha*	9
4	29	**1 Adar I** R.H. *Terumah*	30 R.H.	2	2	4	4	**6** *Devarim*	7	8	9	10
5	1 **Shevat** R.H.	2	1 **Adar II** R.H.	3	**3** *Emor*	5	5	7	8	9	10	11
6	2	3	2	4	4	6 Shavuot	6	8	9	**10** Yom Kippur	11	12
7	**3** *Bo*	4	3	**5** *Mezora*	5 Yom ha-Azma'ut	7	**7** *Balak*	9 Tishah be-Av	10	11	12	13
8	4	5	4	6	6	8	8	10	**11** *Ki Teze*	12	13	**14** *Va-Yishlah*
9	5	6	5	7	7	**9** *Be-Ha'alotkha*	9	11	12	13	14	15
10	6	7	**6** *Va-Yikra*	8	8	10	10	12	13	14	**15** *Va-Yera*	16
11	7	**8** *Tezavveh*	7	9	9	11	11	**13** *Va-Ethannan*	14	15 Sukkot	16	17
12	8	9	8	10	**10** *Be-Har*	12	12	14	15	16	17	18
13	9	10	9	11	11	13	13	15	16	**17** Hol ha-Mo'ed	18	19
14	**10** *Be-Shallah*	11	10	**12** *Aharei Mot* Shabbat ha-Gadol	12	14	**14** *Pinhas*	16	17	18	19	20
15	11	12	11 Ta'anit Esther	13	13	15	15	17	**18** *Ki Tavo*	19	20	**21** *Va-Yeshev*
16	12	13	12	14	14	**16** *Shelah*	16	18	19	20	21	22
17	13	14	**13** *Zav* Zakhor	15 Pesah	15	17	17 Fast	19	20	21 Hoshana Rabba	**22** *Hayyei Sarah*	23
18	14	**15** *Ki Tissa*	14 Purim	16 Omer	16	18	18	**20** *Ekev*	21	22 Shemini Azeret	23	24
19	15	16	15 Shushan Purim	17 Hol ha-Mo'ed	**17** *Be-Hukkotai*	19	19	21	22	23 Simhat Torah *Ve-Zot Ha-Berakhah*	24	25 Hanukkah 1
20	16	17	16	18	18 Lag ba-Omer	20	20	22	23	**24** *Bereshit*	25	26 2
21	**17** *Yitro*	18	17	**19**	19	21	**21** *Mattot*	23	24	25	26	27 3
22	18	19	18	20	20	22	22	24	**25** *Nizzavim Va-Yelekh*	26	27	**28** *Mi-Kez* 4
23	19	20	19	21 Pesah	21	**23** *Korah*	23	25	26	27	28	29 5
24	20	21	**20** *Shemini* Parah	22	22	24	24	26	27	28	**29** *Toledot*	30 R.H. 6
25	21	**22** *Va-Yakhel*	21	23	23	25	25	**27** *Re'eh*	28	29	1 **Kislev** R.H.	1 **Tevet** R.H. 7
26	22	23	22	24	**24** *Be-Midbar*	26	26	28	29	30 R.H.	2	2 8
27	23	24	23	25	25	27	27	29	1 **Tishri** Rosh Ha-Shanah	**1 Heshvan** R.H. *No'ah*	3	3
28	**24** *Mishpatim*	25	24	**26** *Kedoshim*	26	28	**28** *Masei*	30 R.H.	2 *Ha'azinu* Shabbat Shuvah	2	4	4
29	25	26	25	27	27	29	29	1 **Elul** R.H.	**3**	3	5	**5** *Va-Yiggash*
30	26		26	28	28	**30** R.H. *Hukkat*	1 **Av** R.H.	2	4 Fast	4	6	6
31	27		**27** *Tazri'a* Ha-Hodesh		29		2	3		5		7

5745/46 — 1985

	January	February	March	April	May	June	July	August	September	October	November	December
1	8 **Tevet**	10	8	10	10	**12** *Naso*	12	14	15	16	17	18
2	9	**11** *Be-Shallah*	**9**	11	11	13	13	15	16	17	**18** *Va-Yera*	19
3	10 Fast	12	10 *Tezavveh Zakhor*	12	12	14	14	**16** *Va-Ethannan*	17	18 Hol ha-Mo'ed	19	20
4	11	13	11	13	**13** *Ahraei Mot Kedoshim*	15	15	17	18	19	20	21
5	**12** *Va-Yehi*	14	12	14	14	16	16	18	19	**20**	21	22
6	13	15	13 Ta'anit Esther	**15** Pesah	15	17	**17**↓ *Balak*	19	20	21 Hoshana Rabba	22	23
7	14	16	14 Purim	16 Omer	16	18	18 Fast	20	**21** *Ki Tavo*	22 Shemini Azeret	23	**24** *Va-Yeshev*
8	15	17	15 Shushan Purim	17 Hol ha-Mo'ed	17	**19** *Be-Ha'alotkha*	19	21	22	23 Simhat Torah *Ve-Zot Ha-Berakhah*	24	25 Hanukkah 1
9	16	**18** *Yitro*	**16** *Ki Tissa*	18	18 Lag ba-Omer	20	20	22	23	24	**25** *Hayyei Sarah*	26 2
10	17	19	17	19	19	21	21	**23** *Ekev*	24	25	26	27 3
11	18	20	18	20	**20** *Emor*	22	22	24	25	26	27	28 4
12	**19** *Shemot*	21	19	21 Pesah	21	23	23	25	26	**27** *Bereshit*	28	29 5
13	20	22	20	**22**	22	24	**24** *Pinhas*	26	27	28	29	1 **Tevet** R.H. 6
14	21	23	21	23	23	25	25	27	**28** *Nizzavim*	29	1 **Kislev** R.H.	**2** *Mi-Kez* 7
15	22	24	22	24	24	**26** *Shelah*	26	28	29	30 R.H.	2	3 8
16	23	**25** *Mishpatim Shekalim*	23 *Va-Yakhel Pekudei Parah*	25	25	27	27	29	1 **Tishri** Rosh Ha-Shanah	1 **Heshvan** R.H.	**3** *Toledot*	4
17	24	26	24	26	26	28	28	**30** R.H. *Re'eh*	2	2	4	5
18	25	27	25	27	**27** *Be-Har Be-Hukkotai*	29	29	1 **Elul** R.H.	3 Fast	3	5	6
19	**26** *Va-Era*	28	26	28	28	30 R.H.	1 **Av** R.H.	2	4	**4** *No'ah*	6	7
20	27	29	27	**29** *Shemini*	29	1 **Tammuz** R.H.	**2** *Mattot Masei*	3	5	5	7	8
21	28	30 R.H.	28	30 R.H.	1 **Sivan** R.H.	2	3	4	**6** *Va-Yelekh* Shabbat Shuvah	6	8	**9** *Va-Yiggash*
22	29	1 **Adar** R.H.	29	1 **Iyyar** R.H.	2	**3** *Korah*	4	5	7	7	9	10 Fast
23	1 **Shevat** R.H.	**2** *Terumah*	**1** **Nisan** R.H. *Va-Yikra* Ha-Hodesh	2	3	4	5	6	8	8	**10** *Va-Yeze*	11
24	2	3	2	3	4	5	6	**7** *Shofetim*	9	9	11	12
25	3	4	3	4	**5** *Be-Midbar*	6	7	8	10 Yom Kippur	10	12	13
26	**4** *Bo*	5	4	5	6 Shavuot	7	8	9	11	**11** *Lekh Lekha*	13	14
27	5	6	5	**6** *Tazri'a Mezora*	7	8	**9**↓ *Devarim* Tishah be-Av	10	12	12	14	15
28	6	7	6	7	8	9	10 Fast	11	**13** *Ha'azinu*	13	15	**16** *Va-Yehi*
29	7		7	8	9	**10** *Hukkat*	11	12	14	14	16	17
30	8		**8** *Zav* Shabbat ha-Gadol	9	10	11	12	13	15 Sukkot	15	**17** *Va-Yishlah*	18
31	9		9		11		13	**14** *Ki Teze*		16		19

5746/47

1986

	January	February	March	April	May	June	July	August	September	October	November	December
1	20 **Tevet**	**22** *Yitro*	**20** *Ki Tissa*	21	**22**	23	24	25	27	27	**29** *Bereshit*	29
2	21	23	21	22	23	24	25	**26** *Mattot Masei*	28	28	30 R.H.	30 R.H.
3	22	24	22	23	**24** *Aharei Mot*	25	26	27	29	29	1 **Heshvan** R.H.	1 **Kislev** R.H.
4	**23** *Shemot*	25	23	24	25	26	27	28	30 R.H.	**1** **Tishri** Rosh Ha-Shanah	2	2
5	24	26	24	**25** *Shemini Ha-Hodesh*	26	27	**28** *Shelah*	29	1 **Elul** R.H.	**2**	3	3
6	25	27	25	26	27	28	29	1 **Av** R.H.	**2** *Shofetim*	3 Fast	4	**4** *Toledot*
7	26	28	26	27	28	**29** *Be-Midbar*	30 R.H.	2	3	4	5	5
8	27	**29** *Mishpatim*	**27** *Va-Yakhel Shekalim*	28	29	1 **Sivan** R.H.	1 **Tammuz** R.H.	3	4	5	**6** *No'ah*	6
9	28	30 R.H.	28	29	30 R.H.	2	2	**4** *Devarim*	5	6	7	7
10	29	1 **Adar I** R.H.	29	1 **Nisan** R.H.	**1** **Iyyar** R.H. *Kedoshim*	3	3	5	6	7	8	8
11	**1** Shevat R.H. *Va-Era*	2	30 R.H.	2	2	4	4	6	7	**8** *Ha'azinu* Shabbat Shuvah	9	9
12	2	3	1 **Adar II** R.H.	**3** *Tazri'a*	3	5	**5** *Korah*	7	8	9	10	10
13	3	4	2	4	4	6 Shavuot	6	8	**9** *Ki Teze*	10 Yom Kippur	11	**11** *Va-Yeze*
14	4	5	3	5	5 Yom ha-Azma'ut	**7**	7	9 Tishah be-Av	10	11	12	12
15	5	**6** *Terumah*	**4** *Pekudei*	6	6	8	8	10	11	12	**13** *Lekh Lekha*	13
16	6	7	5	7	7	9	9	**11** *Va-Ethannan*	12	13	14	14
17	7	8	6	8	**8** *Emor*	10	10	12	13	14	15	15
18	**8** *Bo*	9	7	9	9	11	11	13	14	**15** Sukkot	16	16
19	9	10	8	**10** *Mezora* Shabbat ha-Gadol	10	12	**12** *Hukkat Balak*	14	15	16	17	17
20	10	11	9	11	11	13	13	15	**16** *Ki Tavo*	17	18	**18** *Va-Yishlah*
21	11	12	10	12	12	**14** *Naso*	14	16	17	18 Hol ha-Mo'ed	19	19
22	12	**13** *Tezavveh*	**11** *Va-Yikra Zakhor*	13	13	15	15	17	18	19	**20** *Va-Yera*	20
23	13	14	12	14	14	16	16	**18** *Ekev*	19	20	21	21
24	14	15	13 Ta'anit Esther	15 Pesah	**15** *Be-Har*	17	17 Fast	19	20	21 Hoshana Rabba	22	22
25	**15** *Be-Shallah*	16	14 Purim	16 Omer	16	18	18	20	21	**22** Shemini Azeret	23	23
26	16	17	15 Shushan Purim	**17**	17	19	**19** *Pinhas*	21	22	23 Simhat Torah *Ve-Zot Ha-Berakhah*	24	24
27	17	18	16	18 Hol ha-Mo'ed	18 Lag ba-Omer	20	20	22	**23** *Nizzavim Ya-Yelekh*	24	25	**25** *Va-Yeshev* Hanukkah 1
28	18	19	17	19	19	**21** *Be-Ha'alotkha*	21	23	24	25	26	26 2
29	19		**18** *Zav Parah*	20	20	22	22	24	25	26	**27** *Hayyei Sarah*	27 3
30	20		19	**21** Pesah	21	23	23	**25** *Re'eh*	26	27	28	28 4
31	21		20		**22** *Be-Hukkotai*		24	26		28		29 5

5747/48

1987

	January	February	March	April	May	June	July	August	September	October	November	December
1	30 **Kislev** Hanukkah R.H. 6	2	30 R.H.	2	2	4	4	**6** *Devarim*	7	8	9	10
2	1 **Tevet** R.H. 7	3	1 **Adar** R.H.	3	**3** *Tazri'a Mezora*	5	5	7	8	9	10	11
3	**2** *Mi-Kez* 8	4	2	4	4	6 Shavuot	6	8	9	**10** Yom Kippur	11	12
4	3	5	3	**5** *Va-Yikra*	5	7	**7** *Hukkat*	9 Tishah be-Av	10	11	12	13
5	4	6	4	6	6	8	8	10	**11** *Ki Teze*	12	13	**14** *Va-Yishlah*
6	5	7	5	7	7	**9** *Naso*	9	11	12	13	14	15
7	6	**8** *Bo*	**6** *Terumah*	8	8	10	10	12	13	14	**15** *Va-Yera*	16
8	7	9	7	9	9	11	11	**13** *Va-Ethannan*	14	15 Sukkot	16	17
9	8	10	8	10	**10** *Aharei Mot Kedoshim*	12	12	14	15	16	17	18
10	**9** *Va-Yiggash*	11	9	11	11	13	13	15	16	**17** Hol ha-Mo'ed	18	19
11	10 Fast	12	10	**12** *Zav* Shabbat ha-Gadol	12	14	**14** *Balak*	16	17	18	19	20
12	11	13	11 **Ta'anit Esther**	13	13	15	15	17	**18** *Ki Tavo*	19	20	**21** *Va-Yeshev*
13	12	14	12	14	14	**16** *Be-Ha'alotkha*	16	18	19	20	21	22
14	13	**15** *Be-Shallah*	**13** *Tezavveh Zakhor*	15 Pesah	15	17	17 Fast	19	20	21 Hoshana Rabba	**22** *Hayyei Sarah*	23
15	14	16	14 Purim	16 Omer	16	18	18	**20** *Ekev*	21	22 Shemini Azeret	23	24
16	15	17	15 Shushan Purim	17 Hol ha-Mo'ed	**17** *Emor*	19	19	21	22	23 Simhat Torah *Ve-Zot Ha-Berakhah*	24	25 Hanukkah 1
17	**16** *Va-Yehi*	18	16	18	18 Lag ba-Omer	20	20	22	23	**24** *Bereshit*	25	26 2
18	17	19	17	**19**	19	21	**21** *Pinhas*	23	24	25	26	27 3
19	18	20	18	20	20	22	22	24	**25** *Nizzavim Va-Yelekh*	26	27	**28** *Mi-Kez* 4
20	19	21	19	21 Pesah	21	**23** *Shelah*	23	25	26	27	28	29 5
21	20	**22** *Yitro*	**20** *Ki Tissa Parah*	22	22	24	24	26	27	28	**29** *Toledot*	30 R.H. 6
22	21	23	21	23	23	25	25	**27** *Re'eh*	28	29	1 **Kislev** R.H.	1 **Tevet** R.H. 7
23	22	24	22	24	**24** *Be-Har Be-Hukkotai*	26	26	28	29	30 R.H.	2	2 8
24	**23** *Shemot*	25	23	25	25	27	27	29	1 **Tishri** Rosh Ha-Shanah	1 **Heshvan** R.H. *No'ah*	3	3
25	24	26	24	**26** *Shemini*	26	28	**28** *Mattot Masei*	30 R.H.	2	2	4	4
26	25	27	25	27	27	29	29	1 **Elul** R.H.	**3** *Ha'azinu* Shabbat Shuvah	3	5	**5** *Va-Yiggash*
27	26	28	26	28	28	**30** R.H. *Korah*	1 **Av** R.H.	2	4 Fast	4	6	6
28	27	**29** *Mishpatim Shekalim*	**27** *Va-Yakhel Pekudei Ha-Hodesh*	29	29	1 **Tammuz** R.H.	2	3	5	5	**7** *Va-Yeze*	7
29	28		28	30 R.H.	1 **Sivan** R.H.	2	3	**4** *Shofetim*	6	6	8	8
30	29		29	1 **Iyyar** R.H.	**2** *Be-Midbar*	3	4	5	7	7	9	9
31	**1** **Shevat** R.H. *Va-Era*		1 **Nisan** R.H.		3		5	6		**8** *Lekh Lekha*		10 Fast

5748/49

1988

	January	February	March	April	May	June	July	August	September	October	November	December
1	11 **Tevet**	13	12	14	14	16	16	18	19	**20**	21	22
2	**12** *Va-Yehi*	14	13 Ta'anit Esther	**15** Pesah	15	17	**17** ↓ *Balak*	19	20	21 Hoshana Rabba	22	23
3	13	15	14 Purim	16 Omer	16	18	18 Fast	20	**21** *Ki Tavo*	22 Shemini Azeret	23	**24** *Va-Yeshev*
4	14	16	15 Shushan Purim	17	17	**19** *Be-Ha'alotkha*	19	21	22	23 Simhat Torah *Ve-Zot Ha-Berakhah*	24	25 Hanukkah 1
5	15	17	**16** *Ki Tissa*	18 Hol ha-Mo'ed	18 Lag ba-Omer	20	20	22	23	24	**25** *Hayyei Sarah*	26 2
6	16	**18** *Yitro*	17	19	19	21	21	**23** *Ekev*	24	25	26	27 3
7	17	19	18	20	**20** *Emor*	22	22	24	25	26	27	28 4
8	18	20	19	21 Pesah	21	23	23	25	26	**27** *Bereshit*	28	29 5
9	**19** *Shemot*	21	20	**22**	22	24	**24** *Pinhas*	26	27	28	29	1 **Tevet** R.H. 6
10	20	22	21	23	23	25	25	27	**28** *Nizzavim*	29	1 **Kislev** R.H.	**2** *Mi-Kez* 7
11	21	23	22	24	24	**26** *Shelah*	26	28	29	30 R.H.	2	3 8
12	22	24	**23** *Va-Yakhel Pekudei* Parah	25	25	27	27	29	1 **Tishri** Rosh Ha-Shanah	1 **Heshvan** R.H.	**3** *Toledot*	4
13	23	**25** *Mishpatim* Shekalim	24	26	26	28	28	**30** R.H. *Re'eh*	2	2	4	5
14	24	26	25	27	**27** *Be-Har Be-Hukkotai*	29	29	1 **Elul** R.H.	3 Fast	3	5	6
15	25	27	26	28	28	30 R.H.	1 **Av** R.H.	2	4	**4** *No'ah*	6	7
16	**26** *Va-Era*	28	27	**29** *Shemini*	29	1 **Tammuz** R.H.	**2** *Mattot Masei*	3	5	5	7	8
17	27	29	28	30 R.H.	1 **Sivan** R.H.	2	3	4	**6** *Va-Yelekh* Shabbat Shuvah	6	8	**9** *Va-Yiggash*
18	28	30 R.H.	29	1 **Iyyar** R.H.	**2**	**3** *Korah*	4	5	7	7	9	10 Fast
19	29	1 **Adar** R.H.	**1** **Nisan** *Va-Yikra* R.H. Ha-Hodesh	2	3	4	5	6	8	8	**10** *Va-Yeze*	11
20	1 **Shevat** R.H.	**2** *Terumah*	2	3	4	5	6	**7** *Shofetim*	9	9	11	12
21	2	3	3	4	**5** *Be-Midbar*	6	7	8	10 Yom Kippur	10	12	13
22	3	4	4	5	6 Shavuot	7	8	9	11	**11** *Lekh Lekha*	13	14
23	**4** *Bo*	5	5	**6** *Tazri'a Mezora*	7	8	**9** ↓ Tishah be-Av *Devarim*	10	12	12	14	15
24	5	6	6	7	8	9	10 Fast	11	**13** *Ha'azinu*	13	15	**16** *Va-Yehi*
25	6	7	7	8	9	**10** *Hukkat*	11	12	14	14	16	17
26	7	8	**8** *Zav* Shabbat ha-Gadol	9	10	11	12	13	15 Sukkot	15	**17** *Va-Yishlah*	18
27	8	9 *Tezavveh* Zakhor	9	10	11	12	13	**14** *Ki Teze*	16	16	18	19
28	9	10	10	11	**12** *Naso*	13	14	15	17	17	19	20
29	10	11	11	12	13	14	15	16	18 Hol ha-Mo'ed	**18** *Va-Yera*	20	21
30	**11** *Be-Shallah*		12	**13** *Aharei Mot Kedoshim*	14	15	**16** Va-Ethannan	17	19	19	21	22
31	12		13		15		17	18		20		**23** *Shemot*

5749/50

1989

	January	February	March	April	May	June	July	August	September	October	November	December
1	24 **Tevet**	26	24	**25** *Shemini* Ha-Hodesh	26	27	**28** *Shelah*	29	1 **Elul** R.H.	2 Rosh Ha-Shanah	3	3
2	25	27	25	26	27	28	29	1 **Av** R.H.	**2** Shofetim	3 Fast	4	**4** *Toledot*
3	26	28	26	27	28	**29** *Be-Midbar*	30 R.H.	2	3	4	5	5
4	27	**29** *Mishpatim*	**27** *Va-Yakhel* Shekalim	28	29	1 **Sivan** R.H.	1 **Tammuz** R.H.	3	4	5	**6** *No'ah*	6
5	28	30 R.H.	28	29	30 R.H.	2	2	**4** *Devarim*	5	6	7	7
6	29	1 **Adar I** R.H.	29	1 **Nisan** R.H.	1 **Iyyar** R.H. *Kedoshim*	3	3	5	6	7	8	8
7	**1** **Shevat** R.H. *Va-Era*	2	30 R.H.	2	2	4	4	6	7	**8** *Ha'azinu* Shabbat Shuvah	9	9
8	2	3	1 **Adar II** R.H.	**3** *Tazri'a*	3	5	**5** *Korah*	7	8	9	10	10
9	3	4	2	4	4	6 Shavuot	6	8	**9** *Ki Teze*	10 Yom Kippur	11	**11** *Va-Yeze*
10	4	5	3	5	5	**7**	7	9 Tishah be-Av	10	11	12	12
11	5	**6** *Terumah*	**4** *Pekudei*	6	6	8	8	10	11	12	**13** *Lekh Lekha*	13
12	6	7	5	7	7	9	9	**11** *Va-Ethannan*	12	13	14	14
13	7	8	6	8	**8** *Emor*	10	10	12	13	14	15	15
14	**8** *Bo*	9	7	9	9	11	11	13	14	**15** Sukkot	16	16
15	9	10	8	**10** *Mezora* Shabbat ha-Gadol	10	12	**12** *Hukkat Balak*	14	15	16	17	17
16	10	11	9	11	11	13	13	15	**16** *Ki Tavo*	17 Hol ha-Mo'ed	18	**18** *Va-Yishlah*
17	11	12	10	12	12	**14** *Naso*	14	16	17	18	19	19
18	12	**13** *Tezavveh*	**11** *Va-Yikra* Zakhor	13	13	15	15	17	18	19	**20** *Va-Yera*	20
19	13	14	12	14	14	16	16	**18** *Ekev*	19	20	21	21
20	14	15	13 Ta'anit Esther	15 Pesah	**15** *Be-Har*	17	17 Fast	19	20	21 Hoshana Rabba	22	22
21	**15** *Be-Shallah*	16	14 Purim	16 Omer	16	18	18	20	21	**22** Shemini Azeret	23	23
22	16	17	15 Shushan Purim	**17** Hol ha-Mo'ed	17	19	**19** *Pinhas*	21	22	23 Simhat Torah *Ve-Zot Ha-Berakhah*	24	24
23	17	18	16	18	18 Lag ba-Omer	20	20	22	**23** *Nizzavim Va-Yelekh*	24	25	**25** Hanukhah *Va-Yeshev* 1
24	18	19	17	19	19	**21** *Be-Ha'alotkha*	21	23	24	25	26	26 2
25	19	**20** *Ki Tissa*	**18** *Zav* Parah	20	20	22	22	24	25	26	**27** *Hayyei Sarah*	27 3
26	20	21	19	21 Pesah	21	23	23	**25** *Re'eh*	26	27	28	28 4
27	21	22	20	22	**22** *Be-Hukkotai*	24	24	26	27	28	29	29 5
28	**22** *Yitro*	23	21	23	23	25	25	27	28	**29** *Bereshit*	30 R.H.	30 R.H. 6
29	23		22	**24** *Aharei Mot*	24	26	**26** *Mattot Masei*	28	29	30 R.H.	1 **Kislev** R.H.	1 **Tevet** R.H. 7
30	24		23	25	25	27	27	29	**1** **Tishri** Rosh Ha-Shanah	1 **Heshvan** R.H.	2	**2** *Mi-Kez* 8
31	25		24		26		28	30 R.H.		2		3

5750/51

1990

	January	February	March	April	May	June	July	August	September	October	November	December
1	4 **Tevet**	6	4	6	6	8	8	10	**11** *Ki Teze*	12	13	**14** *Va-Yishlah*
2	5	7	5	7	7	**9** *Naso*	9	11	12	13	14	15
3	6	**8** *Bo*	**6** *Terumah*	8	8	10	10	12	13	14	**15** *Va-Yera*	16
4	7	9	7	9	9	11	11	**13** *Va-Ethannan*	14	15 Sukkot	16	17
5	8	10	8	10	**10** *Aharei Mot Kedoshim*	12	12	14	15	16	17	18
6	**9** *Va-Yiggash*	11	9	11	11	13	13	15	16	**17**	18	19
7	10 Fast	12	10	**12** *Zav* Shabbat ha-Gadol	12	14	**14** *Balak*	16	17	18	19	20
8	11	13	11 Ta'anit Esther	13	13	15	15	17	**18** *Ki Tavo*	19 Hol ha-Mo'ed	20	**21** *Va-Yeshev*
9	12	14	12	14	14	**16** *Be-Ha'alotkha*	16	18	19	20	21	22
10	13	**15** *Be-Shallab*	**13** *Tezavveh* Zakhor	15 Pesah	15	17	17 Fast	19	20	21 Hoshana Rabba	**22** *Hayyei Sarah*	23
11	14	16	14 Purim	16 Omer	16	18	18	**20** *Ekev*	21	22 Shemini Azeret	23	24
12	15	17	15 Shushan Purim	17	**17** *Emor*	19	19	21	22	23 Simhat Torah Ve-Zot Ha-Berakhah	24	25 Hanukkah 1
13	**16** *Va-Yehi*	18	16	18 Hol ha-Mo'ed	18 Lag ba-Omer	20	20	22	23	**24** *Bereshit*	25	26 2
14	17	19	17	**19**	19	21	**21** *Pinhas*	23	24	25	26	27 3
15	18	20	18	20	20	22	22	24	**25** *Nizzavim Va-Yelekh*	26	27	**28** *Mi-Kez* 4
16	19	21	19	21 Pesah	21	**23** *Shelah*	23	25	26	27	28	29 5
17	20	**22** *Yitro*	**20** *Ki Tissa* Parah	22	22	24	24	26	27	28	**29** *Toledot*	30 R.H. 6
18	21	23	21	23	23	25	25	**27** *Re'eh*	28	29	1 **Kislev** R.H.	1 **Tevet** R.H. 7
19	22	24	22	24	**24** *Be-Har Be-Hukkotai*	26	26	28	29	30 R.H.	2	2 8
20	**23** *Shemot*	25	23	25	25	27	27	29	1 **Tishri** Rosh Ha-Shanah	1 **Heshvan** R.H. *No'ah*	3	3
21	24	26	24	**26** *Shemini*	26	28	**28** *Mattot Masei*	30 R.H.	2	2	4	4
22	25	27	25	27	27	29	29	1 **Elul** R.H.	**3** *Ha'azinu* Shabbat Shuvah	3	5	5 *Va-Yiggash*
23	26	28	26	28	28	**30** R.H. *Korah*	1 **Av** R.H.	2	4 Fast	4	6	6
24	27	**29** *Mishpatim* Shekalim	**27** *Va-Yakhel Pekudei* Ha-Hodesh	29	29	1 **Tammuz** R.H.	2	3	5	5	**7** *Va-Yeze*	7
25	28	30 R.H.	28	30 R.H.	1 **Sivan** R.H.	2	3	**4** *Shofetim*	6	6	8	8
26	29	1 **Adar** R.H.	29	1 **Iyyar** R.H.	**2** *Be-Midbar*	3	4	5	7	7	9	9
27	**1** **Shevat** R.H. *Va-Era*	2	1 **Nisan** R.H.	2	3	4	5	6	8	**8** *Lekh Lekha*	10	10 Fast
28	2	3	2	**3** *Tazri'a Mezora*	4	5	**6** *Devarim*	7	9	9	11	11
29	3		3	4	5	6	7	8	**10** Yom Kippur	10	12	**12** *Va-Yehi*
30	4		4	5 Yom ha-Azma'ut	6 Shavuot	**7** *Hukkat*	8	9	11	11	13	13
31	5		**5** *Va-Yikra*		7		9 Tishah be-Av	10		12		14

5751/52

1991

	January	February	March	April	May	June	July	August	September	October	November	December
1	15 **Tevet**	17	15 Shushan Purim	17 Hol ha-Mo'ed	17	**19** *Be-Ha'alotkha*	19	21	22	23 Simhat Torah *Ve-Zot Ha-Berakhah*	24	24
2	16	**18** *Yitro*	**16** *Ki Tissa*	18	18 Lag ba-Omer	20	20	22	23	24	**25** *Hayyei Sarah*	25 Hanukkah 1
3	17	19	17	19	19	21	21	**23** *Ekev*	24	25	26	26 2
4	18	20	18	20	**20** *Emor*	22	22	24	25	26	27	27 3
5	**19** *Shemot*	21	19	21 Pesah	21	23	23	25	26	**27** *Bereshit*	28	28 4
6	20	22	20	**22**	22	24	**24** *Pinhas*	26	27	28	29	29 5
7	21	23	21	23	23	25	25	27	**28** *Nizzavim*	29	30 R.H.	**30** R.H. *Mi-Kez* 6
8	22	24	22	24	24	**26** *Shelah*	26	28	29	30 R.H.	1 **Kislev** R.H.	1 **Tevet** R.H. 7
9	23	**25** *Mishpatim* Shekalim	**23** *Va-Yakhel Pekudei* Parah	25	25	27	27	29	1 **Tishri** Rosh Ha-Shanah	1 **Heshvan** R.H.	**2** *Toledot*	2 8
10	24	26	24	26	26	28	28	**30** R.H. *Re'eh*	2	2	3	3
11	25	27	25	27	**27** *Be-Har Be-Hukkotai*	29	29	1 **Elul** R.H.	3 Fast	3	4	4
12	**26** *Va-Era*	28	26	28	28	30 R.H.	1 **Av** R.H.	2	4	**4** *No'ah*	5	5
13	27	29	27	**29** *Shemini*	29	1 **Tammuz** R.H.	**2** *Mattot Masei*	3	5	5	6	6
14	28	30 R.H.	28	30 R.H.	1 **Sivan** R.H.	2	3	4	**6** *Va Yelekh* Shabbat Shuvah	6	7	**7** *Va-Yiggash*
15	29	1 **Adar** R.H.	29	1 **Iyyar** R.H.	2	**3** *Korah*	4	5	7	7	8	8
16	1 **Shevat** R.H.	**2** *Terumah*	**1 Nisan** R.H. *Va-Yikra* Ha-Hodesh	2	3	4	5	6	8	8	**9** *Va-Yeze*	9
17	2	3	2	3	4	5	6	**7** *Shofetim*	9	9	10	10 Fast
18	3	4	3	4 Yom ha-Azma'ut	**5** *Be-Midbar*	6	7	8	10 Yom Kippur	10	11	11
19	**4** *Bo*	5	4	5	6 Shavuot	7	8	9	11	**11** *Lekh Lekha*	12	12
20	5	6	5	**6** *Tazri'a Mezora*	7	8	**9** *Devarim* Tishah be-Av	10	12	12	13	13
21	6	7	6	7	8	9	10 Fast	11	**13** *Ha'azinu*	13	14	**14** *Va-Yehi*
22	7	8	7	8	9	**10** *Hukkat*	11	12	14	14	15	15
23	8	**9** *Tezavveh* Zakhor	**8** *Zav* Shabbat ha-Gadol	9	10	11	12	13	15 Sukkot	15	**16** *Va-Yishlah*	16
24	9	10	9	10	11	12	13	**14** *Ki Teze*	16	16	17	17
25	10	11	10	11	**12** *Naso*	13	14	15	17	17	18	18
26	**11** *Be-Shallah*	12	11	12	13	14	15	16	18 Hol ha-Mo'ed	**18** *Va-Yera*	19	19
27	12	13 Ta'anit Esther	12	**13** *Ahrei Mot Kedoshim*	14	15	**16** *Va-Ethannan*	17	19	19	20	20
28	13	14 Purim	13	14	15	16	17	18	**20**	20	21	**21** *Shemot*
29	14		14	15	16	**17** *Balak*	18	19	21 Hoshana Rabba	21	22	22
30	15		**15** Pesah	16	17	18 Fast	19	20	22 Shemini Azeret	22	**23** *Va-Yeshev*	23
31	16		16 Omer		18		20	**21** *Ki Tavo*		23		24

5752/53

1992

	January	February	March	April	May	June	July	August	September	October	November	December
1	25 **Tevet**	**27** *Mishpatim*	26	27	28	29	30 R.H.	**2** *Mattot Masei*	3	4	5	6
2	26	28	27	28	**29** *Aharei Mot*	1 **Sivan** R.H.	1 **Tammuz** R.H.	3	4	5	6	7
3	27	29	28	29	30 R.H.	2	2	4	5	**6** *Va-Yelekh* Shabbat Shuvah	7	8
4	**28** *Va-Era*	30 R.H.	29	**1** **Nisan** R.H. *Tazri'a* Ha-Hodesh	1 **Iyyar** R.H.	3	**3** *Korah*	5	6	7	8	9
5	29	1 **Adar I** R.H.	30 R.H.	2	2	4	4	6	**7** *Shofetim*	8	9	**10** *Va-Yeze*
6	1 **Shevat** R.H.	2	1 **Adar II** R.H.	3	3	**5** *Be-Midbar*	5	7	8	9	10	11
7	2	3	**2** *Pekudei*	4	4	6 Shavuot	6	8	9	10 Yom Kippur	**11** *Lekh Lekha*	12
8	3	**4** *Terumah*	3	5	5	7	7	**9** *Devarim* Tishah be-Av	10	11	12	13
9	4	5	4	6	**6** *Kedoshim*	8	8	10 Fast	11	12	13	14
10	5	6	5	7	7	9	9	11	12	**13** *Ha'azinu*	14	15
11	**6** *Bo*	7	6	**8** *Mezora* Shabbat ha-Gadol	8	10	**10** *Hukkat*	12	13	14	15	16
12	7	8	7	9	9	11	11	13	**14** *Ki Teze*	15 Sukkot	16	**17** *Va-Yishlah*
13	8	9	8	10	10	**12** *Naso*	12	14	15	16	17	18
14	9	10	**9** *Va-Yikra Zakhor*	11	11	13	13	15	16	17	**18** *Va-Yera*	19
15	10	**11** *Tezavveh*	10	12	12	14	14	**16** *Va-Ethannan*	17	18 Hol ha-Mo'ed	19	20
16	11	12	11	13	**13** *Emor*	15	15	17	18	19	20	21
17	12	13	12	14	14	16	16	18	19	**20**	21	22
18	**13** *Be-Shallah*	14	13 Ta'anit Esther	**15** Pesah	15	17	**17** *Balak*	19	20	21 Hoshana Rabba	22	23
19	14	15	14 Purim	16 Omer	16	18	18 Fast	20	**21** *Ki Tavo*	22 Shemini Azeret	23	**24** *Va-Yeshev*
20	15	16	15 Shushan Purim	17	17	**19** *Be-Ha'alotkha*	19	21	22	23 Simhat Torah *Ve-Zot Ha-Berakhah*	24	25 Hanukkah 1
21	16	17	**16** *Zav*	18 Hol ha-Mo'ed	18 Lag ba-Omer	20	20	22	23	24	**25** *Hayyei Sarah*	26 2
22	17	**18** *Ki Tissa*	17	19	19	21	21	**23** *Ekev*	24	25	26	27 3
23	18	19	18	20	**20** *Be-Har*	22	22	24	25	26	27	28 4
24	19	20	19	21 Pesah	21	23	23	25	26	**27** *Bereshit*	28	29 5
25	**20** *Yitro*	21	20	**22**	22	24	**24** *Pinhas*	26	27	28	29	1 **Tevet** R.H. 6
26	21	22	21	23	23	25	25	27	**28** *Nizzavim*	29	1 **Kislev** R.H.	**2** *Mi-Kez* 7
27	22	23	22	24	24	**26** *Shelah*	26	28	29	30 R.H.	2	3 8
28	23	24	**23** *Shemini Parah*	25	25	27	27	29	1 **Tishri** Rosh Ha-Shanah	1 **Heshvan** R.H.	**3** *Toledot*	4
29	24	**25** *Va-Yakhel Shekalim*	24	26	26	28	28	**30** R.H. *Re'eh*	2	2	4	5
30	25		25	27	**27** *Be-Hukkotai*	29	29	1 **Elul** R.H.	3 Fast	3	5	6
31	26		26		28		1 **Av** R.H.	2		**4** *No'ah*		7

5753/54 — 1993

	January	February	March	April	May	June	July	August	September	October	November	December
1	**8 Tevet**	10	8	10	**10** *Aharei Mot Kedoshim*	12	12	14	15	16	17	17
2	**9** *Va-Yiggash*	11	9	11	11	13	13	15	16	**17**	18	18
3	10 Fast	12	10	**12** Shabbat ha-Gadol *Zav*	12	14	**14** *Balak*	16	17	18	19	19
4	11	13	11 Ta'anit Esther	13	13	15	15	17	**18** *Ki Tavo*	19 Hol ha-Mo'ed	20	**20** *Va-Yeshev*
5	12	14	12	14	14	**16** *Be-Ha'alotkha*	16	18	19	20	21	21
6	13	**15** *Be-Shallah*	**13** *Tezavveh Zakhor*	15 Pesah	15	17	17 Fast	19	20	21 Hoshana Rabba	**22** *Hayyei Sarah*	22
7	14	16	14 Purim	16 Omer	16	18	18	**20** *Ekev*	21	22 Shemini Azeret	23	23
8	15	17	15 Shushan Purim	17	**17** *Emor*	19	19	21	22	23 Simhat Torah *Ve-Zot Ha-Berakhah*	24	24
9	**16** *Va-Yehi*	18	16	18 Hol ha-Mo'ed	18 Lag ba-Omer	20	20	22	23	**24** *Bereshit*	25	25 Hanukkah 1
10	17	19	17	**19**	19	21	**21** *Pinhas*	23	24	25	26	26 2
11	18	20	18	20	20	22	22	24	**25** *Nizzavim Va-Yelekh*	26	27	**27** *Mi-Kez* 3
12	19	21	19	21 Pesah	21	**23** *Shelah*	23	25	26	27	28	28 4
13	20	**22** *Yitro*	**20** *Ki Tissa Parah*	22	22	24	24	26	27	28	**29** *Toledot*	29 5
14	21	23	21	23	23	25	25	**27** *Re'eh*	28	29	30 R.H.	30 R.H. 6
15	22	24	22	24	**24** *Be-Har Be-Hukkotai*	26	26	28	29	30 R.H.	1 **Kislev** R.H.	1 **Tevet** R.H. 7
16	**23** *Shemot*	25	23	25	25	27	27	29	1 **Tishri** Rosh Ha-Shanah	1 **Heshvan** R.H. *No'ah*	2	2 8
17	24	26	24	**26** *Shemini*	26	28	**28** *Mattot Masei*	30 R.H.	2	2	3	3
18	25	27	25	27	27	29	29	1 **Elul** R.H.	**3** Shabbat Shuvah *Ha'azinu*	3	4	**4** *Va-Yiggash*
19	26	28	26	28	28	**30** R.H. *Korah*	1 **Av** R.H.	2	4 Fast	4	5	5
20	27	**29** *Mishpatim Shekalim*	**27** *Va-Yakhel Pekudei Ha-Hodesh*	29	29	1 **Tammuz** R.H.	2	3	5	5	**6** *Va-Yeze*	6
21	28	30 R.H.	28	30 R.H.	1 **Sivan** R.H.	2	3	**4** *Shofetim*	6	6	7	7
22	29	1 **Adar** R.H.	29	1 **Iyyar** R.H.	**2** *Be-Midbar*	3	4	5	7	7	8	8
23	1 **Shevat** R.H. *Va-Era*	2	1 **Nisan** R.H.	2	3	4	5	6	8	**8** *Lekh Lekha*	9	9
24	2	3	2	**3** *Tazri'a Mezora*	4	5	**6** *Devarim*	7	9	9	10	10 Fast
25	3	4	3	4	5	6	7	8	**10** Yom Kippur	10	11	**11** *Va-Yehi*
26	4	5	4	5	6 Shavuot	**7** *Hukkat*	8	9	11	11	12	12
27	5	**6** *Terumah*	**5** *Va-Yikra*	6	7	8	9 Tishah be-Av	10	12	12	**13** *Va-Yishlah*	13
28	6	7	6	7	8	9	10	**11** *Ki Teze*	13	13	14	14
29	7		7	8	**9** *Naso*	10	11	12	14	14	15	15
30	**8** *Bo*		8	9	10	11	12	13	15 Sukkot	**15** *Va-Yera*	16	16
31	9		9		11		**13** *Va-Ethannan*	14		16		17

5754/55

1994

	January	February	March	April	May	June	July	August	September	October	November	December
1	18 Tevet *Shemot*	20	18	20	20	22	22	24	25	26 *Bereshit*	27	28 4
2	19	21	19	21 Pesah	21	23	23 *Pinhas*	25	26	27	28	29 5
3	20	22	20	22	22	24	24	26	27 *Nizzavim*	28	29	30 R.H. *Mi-kez* 6
4	21	23	21	23	23	25 *Shelah*	25	27	28	29	1 Kislev R.H.	1 Tevet R.H. 7
5	22	24 *Mishpatim*	22 *Va-Yakhel* Parah	24	24	26	26	28	29	30 R.H.	2 *Toledot*	2 8
6	23	25	23	25	25	27	27	29 *Re'eh*	1 Tishri Rosh Ha-Shanah	1 Heshvan R.H.	3	3
7	24	26	24	26	26 *Be-Har Be-Hukkotai*	28	28	30 R.H.	2	2	4	4
8	25 *Va-Era*	27	25	27	27	29	29	1 Elul R.H.	3 Fast	3 *No'ah*	5	5
9	26	28	26	28 *Shemini*	28	30 R.H.	1 Av R.H. *Mattot Masei*	2	4	4	6	6
10	27	29	27	29	29	1 Tammuz R.H.	2	3	5 *Va-Yelekh* Shabbat Shuvah	5	7	7 *Va-Yiggash*
11	28	30 R.H.	28	30 R.H.	1 Sivan R.H.	2 *Korah*	3	4	6	6	8	8
12	29	1 Adar R.H. *Terumah* Shekalim	29 *Pekudei* Ha-Hodesh	1 Iyyar R.H.	2	3	4	5	7	7	9 *Va-Yeze*	9
13	1 Shevat R.H.	2	1 Nisan R.H.	2	3	4	5	6 *Shofetim*	8	8	10	10 Fast
14	2	3	2	3	4 *Be-Midbar*	5	6	7	9	9	11	11
15	3 *Bo*	4	3	4	5	6	7	8	10 Yom Kippur	10 *Lekh Lekha*	12	12
16	4	5	4	5 *Tazri'a Mezora*	6 Shavuot	7	8 *Devarim*	9	11	11	13	13
17	5	6	5	6	7	8	9 Tishah be-Av	10	12 *Ha'azinu*	12	14	14 *Va-Yehi*
18	6	7	6	7	8	9 *Hukkat*	10	11	13	13	15	15
19	7	8 *Tezavveh* Zakhor	7 Va-Yikra	8	9	10	11	12	14	14	16 *Va-Yishlah*	16
20	8	9	8	9	10	11	12	13 Ki-Teze	15 Sukkot	15	17	17
21	9	10	9	10	11 *Naso*	12	13	14	16	16	18	18
22	10 *Be-Shallah*	11	10	11	12	13	14	15	17	17 *Va-Yera*	19	19
23	11	12	11	12 *Aharei Mot Kedoshim*	13	14	15 *Va-Ethannan*	16	18 Hol ha-Mo'ed	18	20	20
24	12	13 Ta'anit Esther	12	13	14	15	16	17	19	19	21	21 *Shemot*
25	13	14 Purim	13	14	15	16 *Balak*	17	18	20	20	22	22
26	14	15 *Ki Tissa* Shushan Purim	14 *Zav* Shabbat ha-Gadol	15	16	17 Fast	18	19	21 Hoshana Rabba	21	23 *Va-Yeshev*	23
27	15	16	15 Pesah	16	17	18	19	20 *Ki-Tavo*	22 Shemini Azerei	22	24	24
28	16	17	16 Omer	17	18 *Be-Ha'alotkha*	19	20	21	23 Simhat Torah *Ve-Zot Ha-Berakhah*	23	25 Hanukkah 1	25
29	17 *Yitro*		17	18 Lag ba-Omer	19	20	21	22	24	24 *Hayyei Sarah*	26 2	26
30	18		18 Hol ha-Mo'ed	19 *Emor*	20	21	22 *Ekev*	23	25	25	27 3	27
31	19		19		21		23	24		26		28 *Va-Era*

5755/56

1995

	January	February	March	April	May	June	July	August	September	October	November	December
1	**29 Tevet**	1 **Adar I** R.H.	29	1 R.H. **Nisan** *Tazri'a* Ha-Hodesh	1 **Iyyar** R.H.	3	**3** *Korah*	5	6	7	8	8
2	1 **Shevat** R.H.	2	30 R.H.	2	2	4	4	6	**7** *Shofetim*	8	9	**9** *Va-Yeze*
3	2	3	1 **Adar II** R.H.	3	3	**5** *Be-Midbar*	5	7	8	9	10	10
4	3	**4** *Terumah*	**2** *Pekudei*	4	4 Yom ha-Azma'ut	6 Shavuot	6	8	9	10 Yom Kippur	**11** *Lekh Lekha*	11
5	4	5	3	5	5	7	7	**9** ↓ *Devarim* Tishah be-Av	10	11	12	12
6	5	6	4	6	**6** *Kedoshim*	8	8	10 Fast	11	12	13	13
7	**6** *Bo*	7	5	7	7	9	9	11	12	**13** *Ha'azinu*	14	14
8	7	8	6	**8** *Mezora* Shabbat ha-Gadol	8	10	**10** *Hukkat*	12	13	14	15	15
9	8	9	7	9	9	11	11	13	**14** *Ki Teze*	15 Sukkot	16	**16** *Va-Yishlah*
10	9	10	8	10	10	**12** *Naso*	12	14	15	16	17	17
11	10	**11** *Tezavveh*	**9** *Va-Yikra* Zakhor	11	11	13	13	15	16	17	**18** *Va-Yera*	18
12	11	12	10	12	12	14	14	**16** *Va-Ethannan*	17	18 Hol ha-Mo'ed	19	19
13	12	13	11	13	**13** *Emor*	15	15	17	18	19	20	20
14	**13** *Be-Shallah*	14	12	14	14	16	16	18	19	**20**	21	21
15	14	15	13 Ta'anit Esther	**15** Pesah	15	17	**17** ↓ *Balak*	19	20	21 Hoshana Rabba	22	22
16	15	16	14 Purim	16 Omer	16	18	18 Fast	20	**21** *Ki Tavo*	22 Shemini Azeret	23	**23** *Va-Yashev*
17	16	17	15 Shushan Purim	17	17	**19** *Be-Ha'alotkha*	19	21	22	23 Simhat Torah *Ve-Zot Ha-Berakhah*	24	24
18	17	**18** *Ki Tissa*	**16** *Zav*	18 Hol ha-Mo'ed	18 Lag ba-Omer	20	20	22	23	24	**25** *Hayyei Sarah*	25 Hanukkah 1
19	18	19	17	19	19	21	21	**23** *Ekev*	24	25	26	26 2
20	19	20	18	20	**20** *Be-Har*	22	22	24	25	26	27	27 3
21	**20** *Yitro*	21	19	21 Pesah	21	23	23	25	26	**27** *Bereshit*	28	28 4
22	21	22	20	**22**	22	24	**24** *Pinhas*	26	27	28	29	29 5
23	22	23	21	23	23	25	25	27	**28** *Nizzavim*	29	30 R.H.	**30** R.H. *Mi-kez*
24	23	24	22	24	24	**26** *Shelah*	26	28	29	30 R.H.	1 **Kislev** R.H.	1 **Tevet** R.H. 7
25	24	**25** *Va-Yakhel* Shekalim	**23** *Shemini* Parah	25	25	27	27	29	1 **Tishri** Rosh Ha-Shanah	1 **Heshvan** R.H.	**2** *Toledot*	2 8
26	25	26	24	26	26	28	28	**30** R.H. *Re'eh*	2	2	3	3
27	26	27	25	27	**27** *Be-Hukkotai*	29	29	1 **Elul** R.H.	3 Fast	3	4	4
28	**27** *Mishpatim*	28	26	28	28	30 R.H.	1 **Av** R.H.	2	4	**4** *No'ah*	5	5
29	28		27	**29** *Aharei Mot*	29	1 **Tammuz** R.H.	**2** *Mattot Masei*	3	5	5	6	6
30	29		28	30 R.H.	1 **Sivan** R.H.	2	3	4	**6** *Va-Yelekh* Shabbat Shuvah	6	7	**7** *Va-Yiggash*
31	30 R.H.		29		2		4	5		7		8

5756/57

1996

	January	February	March	April	May	June	July	August	September	October	November	December
1	**9 Tevet**	11	10	12	12	**14** *Naso*	14	16	17	18 Hol ha-Mo'ed	19	20
2	10 Fast	12	**11** *Tezavveh Zakhor*	13	13	15	15	17	18	19	**20** *Va-Yera*	21
3	11	**13** *Be-Shallah*	12	14	14	16	16	**18** *Ekev*	19	20	21	22
4	12	14	13 Ta'anit Esther	15 Pesah	**15** *Emor*	17	17 Fast	19	20	21 Hoshana Rabba	22	23
5	13	15	14 Purim	16 Omer	16	18	18	20	21	**22** Shemini Azeret	23	24
6	**14** *Va-Yehi*	16	15 Shushan Purim	17 Hol ha-Mo'ed	17	19	**19** *Pinhas*	21	22	23 Simhat Torah *Ve-Zot Ha-Berakhah*	24	25 Hanukkah 1
7	15	**17**	16	18	18 Lag ba-Omer	20	20	22	**23** *Nizzavim Va-Yelekh*	24	25	**26** Va-Yeshev 2
8	16	18	17	19	19	**21** *Be-Ha'alotkha*	21	**23**	**24**	**25**	**26**	**27** 3
9	17	19	**18** *Ki Tissa Parah*	20	20	22	22	24	25	26	**27** *Hayyei Sarah*	28 4
10	18	**20** *Yitro*	19	21 Pesah	21	23	23	**25** *Re'eh*	26	27	28	29 5
11	19	21	20	22	**22** *Be-Har Be-Hukkotai*	24	24	26	27	28	29	1 **Tevet** R.H. 6
12	20	22	21	23	23	25	25	27	28	**29** *Bereshit*	1 **Kislev** R.H.	2 7
13	**21** *Shemot*	23	22	**24** *Shemini*	24	26	**26** *Mattot Masei*	28	29	30 R.H.	2	3 8
14	22	24	23	25	25	27	27	29	**1 Tishri** Rosh Ha-Shanah	1 **Heshvan** R.H.	3	**4** *Mi-Kez*
15	23	25	24	26	26	**28** *Shelah*	28	30 R.H.	2	2	4	5
16	24	26	**25** *Va-Yakhel Pekudei* Ha-Hodesh	27	27	29	29	1 **Elul** R.H.	3 Fast	3	**5** *Toledot*	6
17	25	**27** *Mishpatim* Shekalim	26	28	28	30 R.H.	1 **Av** R.H.	**2** *Shofetim*	4	4	6	7
18	26	28	27	29	**29** *Be-Midbar*	1 Tammuz R.H.	2	3	5	5	7	8
19	27	29	28	30 R.H.	1 **Sivan** R.H.	2	3	4	6	**6** *No'ah*	8	9
20	**28** *Va-Era*	30 R.H.	29	**1 Iyyar** R.H. *Tazri'a Mezora*	2	3	**4** *Devarim*	5	7	7	9	10 Fast
21	29	1 **Adar** R.H.	1 **Nisan** R.H.	2	3	4	5	6	**8** *Ha'azinu* Shabbat Shuvah	8	10	**11** *Va-Yiggash*
22	1 **Shevat** R.H.	2	2	3	4	**5** *Korah*	6	7	9	9	11	12
23	2	3	**3** *Va-Yikra*	4	5	6	7	8	10 Yom Kippur	10	**12** *Va-Yeze*	13
24	3	**4** *Terumah*	4	5 Yom ha-Azma'ut	6 Shavuot	7	8	**9** *Ki Teze*	11	11	13	14
25	4	5	5	6	**7**	8	9 Tishah be-Av	10	12	12	14	15
26	5	6	6	7	8	9	10	11	13	**13** *Lekh Lekha*	15	16
27	**6** *Bo*	7	7	**8** *Aharei Mot Kedoshim*	9	10	**11** *Va-Ethannan*	12	14	14	16	17
28	7	8	8	9	10	11	12	13	**15** Sukkot	15	17	**18** *Va-Yehi*
29	8	9	9	10	11	**12** *Hukkat Balak*	13	14	16	16	18	19
30	9		**10** *Zav* Shabbat ha-Gadol	11	12	13	14	15	17	17	**19** *Va-Yishlah*	20
31	10		11		13		15	**16** *Ki Tavo*		18		21

5757/58

1997

	January	February	March	April	May	June	July	August	September	October	November	December
1	22 **Tevet**	**24** *Yitro*	**22** *Ki Tissa*	23	24	25	26	27	29	29	1 R.H. **Heshvan** *No'ah*	2
2	23	25	23	24	25	26	27	**28** *Mattot Masei*	30 R.H.	1 **Tishri** Rosh Ha-Shanah	2	3
3	24	26	24	25	**26** *Aharei Mot*	27	28	29	1 **Elul** R.H.	2	3	4
4	**25** *Shemot*	27	25	26	27	28	29	1 **Av** R.H.	2	**3** *Ha'azinu* Shabbat Shuvah	4	5
5	26	28	26	**27** *Shemini* Ha-Hodesh	28	29	**30** R.H. *Korah*	2	3	4 Fast	5	6
6	27	29	27	28	29	1 **Sivan** R.H.	1 **Tammuz** R.H.	3	**4** *Shofetim*	5	6	**7** *Va-Yeze*
7	28	30 R.H.	28	29	30 R.H.	**2** *Be-Midbar*	2	4	5	6	7	8
8	29	1 **Adar I** R.H. *Mishpatim*	**29** *Va-Yakhel* Shekalim	1 **Nisan** R.H.	1 **Iyyar** R.H.	3	3	5	6	7	**8** *Lekh Lekha*	9
9	1 **Shevat** R.H.	2	30 R.H.	2	2	4	4	**6** *Devarim*	7	8	9	10
10	2	3	1 **Adar II** R.H.	3	**3** *Kedoshim*	5	5	7	8	9	10	11
11	**3** *Va-Era*	4	2	4	4	6 Shavuot	6	8	9	**10** Yom Kippur	11	12
12	4	5	3	**5** *Tazri'a*	5 Yom ha-Azma'ut	7	**7** *Hukkat*	9 Tishah be-Av	10	11	12	13
13	5	6	4	6	6	8	8	10	**11** *Ki Teze*	12	13	**14** *Va-Yishlah*
14	6	7	5	7	7	**9** *Naso*	9	11	12	13	14	15
15	7	**8** *Terumah*	**6** *Pekudei*	8	8	10	10	12	13	14	**15** *Va-Yera*	16
16	8	9	7	9	9	11	11	**13** *Va-Ethannan*	14	**15** *Sukkot*	16	17
17	9	10	8	10	**10** *Emor*	12	12	14	15	16	17	18
18	**10** *Bo*	11	9	11	11	13	13	15	16	**17**	18	19
19	11	12	10	**12** *Mezora* Shabbat ha-Gadol	12	14	**14** *Balak*	16	17	18 Hol ha-Mo'ed	19	20
20	12	13	11 Ta'anit Esther	13	13	15	15	17	**18** *Ki Tavo*	19	20	**21** *Va-Yeshev*
21	13	14	12	14	14	**16** *Be-Ha'alotkha*	16	18	19	20	21	22
22	14	**15** *Tezavveh*	**13** *Va-Yikra* Zakhor	15 Pesah	15	17	17 Fast	19	20	21 Hoshana Rabba	**22** *Hayyei Sarah*	23
23	15	16	14 Purim	16 Omer	16	18	18	**20** *Ekev*	21	22 Shemini Azeret	23	24
24	16	17	15 Shushan Purim	17	**17** *Be-Har*	19	19	21	22	23 Simhat Torah *Ve-Zot Ha-Berakhah*	24	25 Hanukkah 1
25	**17** *Be-Shallah*	18	16	18 Hol ha-Mo'ed	18 Lag ba-Omer	20	20	22	23	**24** *Bereshit*	25	26 2
26	18	19	17	**19**	19	21	**21** *Pinhas*	23	24	25	26	27 3
27	19	20	18	20	20	22	22	24	25 *Nizzavim Va-Yelekh*	26	27	**28** *Mi-Kez* 4
28	20	21	19	21 Pesah	21	**23** *Shelah*	23	25	26	27	28	29 5
29	21		**20** *Zav* Parah	22	22	24	24	26	27	28	**29** *Toledot*	30 R.H. 6
30	22		21	23	23	25	25	**27** *Re'eh*	28	29	1 **Kislev** R.H.	1 **Tevet** R.H. 7
31	23		22		**24** *Be-Hukkotai*		26	28		30 R.H.		2 8

5758/59

1998

	January	February	March	April	May	June	July	August	September	October	November	December
1	3 **Tevet**	5	3	5	5	7	7	**9** ↓ Tishah be-Av *Devarim*	10	11	12	12
2	4	6	4	6	**6** *Tazri'a Mezora*	8	8	10 Fast	11	12	13	13
3	**5** *Va-Yiggash*	7	5	7	7	9	9	11	12	**13** *Ha'azinu*	14	14
4	6	8	6	**8** *Zav* Shabbat ha-Gadol	8	10	**10** *Hukkat*	12	13	14	15	15
5	7	9	7	9	9	11	11	13	**14** *Ki Teze*	15 Sukkot	16	**16** *Va-Yishlah*
6	8	10	8	10	10	**12** *Naso*	12	14	15	16	17	17
7	9	**11** *Be-Shallah*	**9** *Tezavveh* Zakhor	11	11	13	13	15	16	17	**18** *Va-Yera*	18
8	10 Fast	12	10	12	12	14	14	**16** *Va-Ethannan*	17	18 Hol ha-Mo'ed	19	19
9	11	13	11	13	**13** *Aharei Mot Kedoshim*	15	15	17	18	19	20	20
10	**12** *Va-Yehi*	14	12	14	14	16	16	18	19	**20**	21	21
11	13	15	13 Ta'anit Esther	**15** Pesah	15	17	**17** ↓ *Balak*	19	20	21 HoshanaRabba	22	22
12	14	16	14 Purim	16 Omer	16	18	18 Fast	20	**21** *Ki Tavo*	22 Shemini Azeret	23	**23** *Va-Yeshev*
13	15	17	15 Shushan Purim	17	17	**19** *Be-Ha'alotkha*	19	21	22	23 Simhat Torah *Ve-Zot Ha-Berakhah*	24	24
14	16	**18** *Yitro*	**16** *Ki Tissa*	18 Hol ha-Mo'ed	18 Lag ba-Omer	20	20	22	23	24	**25** *Hayyei Sarah*	25 Hanukkah 1
15	17	19	17	19	19	21	21	**23** *Ekev*	24	25	26	26 2
16	18	20	18	20	**20** *Emor*	22	22	24	25	26	27	27 3
17	**19** *Shemot*	21	19	21 Pesah	21	23	23	25	26	**27** *Bereshit*	28	28 4
18	20	22	20	**22**	22	24	**24** *Pinhas*	26	27	28	29	29 5
19	21	23	21	23	23	25	25	27	**28** *Nizzavim*	29	30 R.H.	**30** R.H. *Mi-Kez* 6
20	22	24	22	24	24	**26** *Shelah*	26	28	29	30 R.H.	1 **Kislev** R.H.	1 **Tevet** R.H. 7
21	23	**25** *Mishpatim* Shekalim	**23** *Va-Yakhel Pekudei* Parah	25	25	27	27	29	1 **Tishri** Rosh Ha-Shanah	1 **Heshvan** R.H.	**2** *Toledot*	2 8
22	24	26	24	26	26	28	28	**30** R.H. *Re'eh*	2	2	3	3
23	25	27	25	27	**27** *Be-Har Be-Hukkotai*	29	29	1 **Elul** R.H.	3 Fast	3	4	4
24	**26** *Va-Era*	28	26	28	28	30 R.H.	1 **Av** R.H.	2	4	**4** *No'ah*	5	5
25	27	29	27	**29** *Shemini*	29	1 **Tammuz** R.H.	**2** *Mattot Masei*	3	5	5	6	6
26	28	30 R.H.	28	30 R.H.	1 **Sivan** R.H.	2	3	4	**6** *Va-Yelekh* Shabbat Shuvah	6	7	**7** *Va-Yiggash*
27	29	1 **Adar** R.H.	29	1 **Iyyar** R.H.	2	**3** *Korah*	4	5	7	7	8	8
28	1 **Shevat** R.H.	**2** *Terumah*	**1** **Nisan** R.H. *Va-Yikra* Ha-Hodesh	2	3	4	5	6	8	8	**9** *Va-Yeze*	9
29	2		2	3	4	5	6	**7** *Shofetim*	9	9	10	10 Fast
30	3		3	4 Yom ha-Azma'ut	**5** *Be-Midbar*	6	7	8	10 Yom Kippur	10	11	11
31	**4** *Bo*		4		6 Shavuot		8	9		**11** *Lekh Lekha*		12

5759/60

1999

	January	February	March	April	May	June	July	August	September	October	November	December
1	13 **Tevet**	15	13 Ta'anit Esther	15 Pesah	**15** *Emor*	17	17	19	20	21 Hoshana Rabba	22	22
2	**14** *Va-Yehi*	16	14 Purim	16 Omer	16	18	18	20	21	**22** Shemini Azeret	23	23
3	15	17	15 Shushan Purim	**17**	17	19	**19** *Pinhas*	21	22	23 Simhat Torah *Ve-Zot Ha-Berakhah*	24	24
4	16	18	16	18 Hol ha-Mo'ed	18 Lag ba-Omer	20	20	22	**23** *Nizzavim Va-Yelekh*	24	25	**25** *Va-Yeshev* Hanukkah 1
5	17	19	17	19	19	**21** *Be-Ha'alotkha*	21	23	24	25	26	26 2
6	18	**20** *Yitro*	**18** *Ki Tissa* *Parah*	20	20	22	22	24	25	26	**27** *Hayyei Sarah*	27 3
7	19	21	19	21 Pesah	21	23	23	**25** *Re'eh*	26	27	28	28 4
8	20	22	20	22	**22** *Be-Har Be-Hukkotai*	24	24	26	27	28	29	29 5
9	**21** *Shemot*	23	21	23	23	25	25	27	28	**29** *Bereshit*	30 R.H.	30 R.H. 6
10	22	24	22	**24** *Shemini*	24	26	**26** *Mattot Masei*	28	29	30 R.H.	1 **Kislev** R.H.	1 **Tevet** R.H. 7
11	23	25	23	25	25	27	27	29	**1** **Tishri** Rosh Ha-Shanah	1 **Heshvan** R.H.	2	**2** *Mi-Kez* 8
12	24	26	24	26	26	**28** *Shelah*	28	30 R.H.	2	2	3	3
13	25	**27** *Mishpatim Shekalim*	**25** *Va-Yakhel Pekudei* Ha-Hodesh	27	27	29	29	1 **Elul** R.H.	3 Fast	3	**4** *Toledot*	4
14	26	28	26	28	28	30 R.H.	1 **Av** R.H.	**2** *Shofetim*	4	4	5	5
15	27	29	27	29	**29** *Be-Midbar*	1 **Tammuz** R.H.	2	3	5	5	6	6
16	**28** *Va-Era*	30 R.H.	28	30 R.H.	1 **Sivan** R.H.	2	3	4	6	**6** *No'ah*	7	7
17	29	1 **Adar** R.H.	29	**1** R.H. **Iyyar** *Tazri'a Mezora*	2	3	**4** *Devarim*	5	7	7	8	8
18	1 **Shevat** R.H.	2	1 **Nisan** R.H.	2	3	4	5	6	**8** *Ha'azinu* Shabbat Shuvah	8	9	**9** *Va-Yiggash*
19	2	3	2	3	4	**5** *Korah*	6	7	9	9	10	10 Fast
20	3	**4** *Terumah*	**3** *Va-Yikra*	4	5	6	7	8	10 Yom Kippur	10	**11** *Va-Yeze*	11
21	4	5	4	5 Yom ha-Azma'ut	6 Shavuot	7	8	**9** *Ki Teze*	11	11	12	12
22	5	6	5	6	**7**	8	9 Tishah be-Av	10	12	12	13	13
23	**6** *Bo*	7	6	7	8	9	10	11	13	**13** *Lekh Lekha*	14	14
24	7	8	7	**8** *Aharei Mot Kedoshim*	9	10	11 *Va-Ethannan*	12	14	14	15	15
25	8	9	8	9	10	11	12	13	**15** Sukkot	15	16	**16** *Va-Yehi*
26	9	10	9	10	11	**12** *Hukkat Balak*	13	14	16	16	17	17
27	10	11 *Tezavveh Zakhor*	**10** Shabbat ha-Gadol *Zav*	11	12	13	14	15	17	17	**18** *Va-Yishlah*	18
28	11	12	11	12	13	14	15	**16** *Ki Tavo*	18 Hol ha-Mo'ed	18	19	19
29	12		12	13	**14** *Naso*	15	16	17	19	19	20	20
30	**13** *Be-Shallah*		13	14	15	16	17	18	20	**20** *Va-Yera*	21	21
31	14		14		16		**18** *Ekev*	19		21		22

5760/61

2000

	January	February	March	April	May	June	July	August	September	October	November	December
1	**23** **Tevet** *Shemot*	25	24	**25** *Shemini Ha-Hodesh*	26	27	**28** *Shelah*	29	1 **Elul** R.H.	2	3	4
2	24	26	25	26	27	28	29	1 **Av** R.H.	**2** *Shofetim*	3 Fast	4	**5** *Toledot*
3	25	27	26	27	28	**29** *Be-Midbar*	30 R.H.	2	3	4	5	6
4	26	28	**27** *Va-Yakhel Shekalim*	28	29	1 **Sivan** R.H.	1 **Tammuz** R.H.	3	4	5	**6** *No'ah*	7
5	27	**29** *Mishpatim*	28	29	30 R.H.	2	2	**4** *Devarim*	5	6	7	8
6	28	30 R.H.	29	1 **Nisan** R.H.	**1** **Iyyar** R.H. *Kedoshim*	3	3	5	6	7	8	9
7	29	1 **Adar I** R.H.	30 R.H.	2	2	4	4	6	7	**8** *Ha'azinu* Shabbat Shuvah	9	10
8	**1** **Shevat** R.H. *Va-Era*	2	1 **Adar II** R.H.	**3** *Tazri'a*	3	5	**5** *Korah*	7	8	9	10	11
9	2	3	2	4	4	6 Shavuot	6	8	**9** *Ki Teze*	10 Yom Kippur	11	**12** *Va-Yeze*
10	3	4	3	5	5 Yom ha-Azma'ut	**7**	7	9 Tishah be-Av	10	11	12	13
11	4	5	**4** *Pekudei*	6	6	8	8	10	11	12	**13** *Lekh Lekha*	14
12	5	**6** *Terumah*	5	7	7	9	9	**11** *Va-Ethannan*	12	13	14	15
13	6	7	6	8	**8** *Emor*	10	10	12	13	14	15	16
14	7	8	7	9	9	11	11	13	14	**15** Sukkot	16	17
15	**8** *Bo*	9	8	**10** *Mezora* Shabbat ha-Gadol	10	12	**12** *Hukkat Balak*	14	15	16	17	18
16	9	10	9	11	11	13	13	15	**16** *Ki Tavo*	17 Hol ha-Mo'ed	18	**19** *Va-Yishlah*
17	10	11	10	12	12	**14** *Naso*	14	16	17	18	19	20
18	11	12	**11** *Va-Yikra Zakhor*	13	13	15	15	17	18	19	**20** *Va-Yera*	21
19	12	**13** *Tezavveh*	12	14	14	16	16	**18** *Ekev*	19	20	21	22
20	13	14	13 Ta'anit Esther	15 Pesah	**15** *Be-Har*	17	17 Fast	19	20	21 HoshanaRabba	22	23
21	14	15	14 Purim	16 Omer	16	18	18	20	21	**22** Shemini Azeret	23	24
22	**15** *Be-Shallah*	16	15 Shushan Purim	**17**	17	19	**19** *Pinhas*	21	22	23 Simhat Torah *Ve-Zot Ha-Berakhah*	24	25 Hanukkah 1
23	16	17	16	18 Hol ha-Mo'ed	18 Lag ba-Omer	20	20	22	**23** *Nizzavim Va-Yelekh*	24	25	**26** *Va-Yeshev* 2
24	17	18	17	19	19	**21** Be-Ha'alotkha	21	23	24	25	26	27 3
25	18	19	**18** *Zav Parah*	20	20	22	22	24	25	26	**27** *Hayyei Sarah*	28 4
26	19	**20** *Ki Tissa*	19	21 Pesah	21	23	23	**25** *Re'eh*	26	27	28	29 5
27	20	21	20	22	**22** *Be-Hukkotai*	24	24	26	27	28	29	1 **Tevet** R.H. 6
28	21	22	21	23	23	25	25	27	28	**29** *Bereshit*	1 **Kislev** R.H.	2 7
29	**22** *Yitro*	23	22	**24** *Aharei Mot*	24	26	**26** *Mattot Masei*	28	29	30 R.H.	2	3 8
30	23		23	25	25	27	27	29	**1** **Tishri** Rosh Ha-Shanah	1 **Heshvan** R.H.	3	**4** *Mi-Kez*
31	24		24		26		28	30 R.H.		2		5

Reprinted from: *The Encyclopedia Judaica* (Jerusalem: Keter Publishing House), Vol. 1, pp. 139-149.

PERPETUAL CANDLE-LIGHTING CHARTS FOR MAJOR U.S. AND FOREIGN CITIES

The lighting of candles in the home is the universal Jewish ritual marking the inauguration of the Sabbath and Jewish holidays. Although technically it should be permissible to light the candles up until sunset (when the new day officially commences), in order to prevent inadvertent (and prohibited) late lightings, the time for lighting has been established as the onset of twilight. While this is to a certain extent dependent on local custom, the generally accepted time is eighteen minutes prior to sunset. Candles can, of course, be lit somewhat earlier if desired; however, once the candles are lit and the blessing over them recited, all of the proscriptions and conditions of the holiday take effect immediately.

The following charts list perpetual candle-lighting times for various cities around the world based on the eighteen minutes before sunset standard. Where local custom varies from this, proper adjustments should be made. (For instance, the custom in Jerusalem is forty minutes before sunset, and in Tel Aviv it is twenty-one minutes.) In daylight savings zones an additional hour should be added. For cities within the United States, every day is noted; for cities outside the United States, only every third day is listed, necessitating an averaging in order to determine the time for unmarked days. However, for all locations, these are *perpetual* charts, i.e. they do not vary from year to year.

—The Eds.

ATLANTA, GEORGIA

DAY	JAN.	FEB.	MAR.	APR.	MAY	JUNE	JULY	AUG.	SEPT.	OCT.	NOV.	DEC.
1	5:22 P.M.	5:51	6:16	6:40	7:03	7:25	7:34	7:20	6:46	6:04	5:28	5:11
2	5:23	5:52	6:17	6:41	7:03	7:25	7:34	7:19	6:44	6:03	5:27	5:11
3	5:24	5:53	6:18	6:42	7:04	7:26	7:34	7:18	6:43	6:02	5:26	5:11
4	5:25	5:54	6:19	6:42	7:05	7:26	7:34	7:17	6:42	6:00	5:25	5:11
5	5:25	5:55	6:19	6:43	7:06	7:27	7:34	7:16	6:40	5:59	5:24	5:11
6	5:26	5:55	6:20	6:44	7:06	7:27	7:33	7:16	6:39	5:58	5:23	5:11
7	5:27	5:56	6:21	6:44	7:07	7:28	7:33	7:15	6:38	5:56	5:23	5:11
8	5:28	5:57	6:22	6:45	7:08	7:28	7:33	7:14	6:36	5:55	5:22	5:11
9	5:29	5:58	6:23	6:46	7:09	7:29	7:33	7:13	6:35	5:54	5:21	5:11
10	5:30	5:59	6:23	6:47	7:09	7:29	7:32	7:12	6:33	5:53	5:20	5:12
11	5:31	6:00	6:24	6:47	7:10	7:30	7:32	7:11	6:32	5:51	5:20	5:12
12	5:31	6:01	6:25	6:48	7:11	7:30	7:32	7:10	6:31	5:50	5:19	5:12
13	5:32	6:02	6:26	6:49	7:12	7:31	7:32	7:08	6:29	5:49	5:18	5:12
14	5:33	6:03	6:27	6:50	7:12	7:31	7:31	7:07	6:28	5:48	5:18	5:13
15	5:34	6:04	6:27	6:50	7:13	7:31	7:31	7:06	6:27	5:46	5:17	5:13
16	5:35	6:05	6:28	6:51	7:14	7:32	7:30	7:05	6:25	5:45	5:16	5:13
17	5:36	6:06	6:29	6:52	7:15	7:32	7:30	7:04	6:24	5:44	5:16	5:14
18	5:37	6:07	6:30	6:53	7:15	7:32	7:29	7:03	6:22	5:43	5:15	5:14
19	5:38	6:08	6:30	6:53	7:16	7:33	7:29	7:02	6:21	5:42	5:15	5:14
20	5:39	6:08	6:31	6:54	7:17	7:33	7:28	7:01	6:20	5:40	5:14	5:15
21	5:40	6:09	6:32	6:55	7:17	7:33	7:28	6:59	6:18	5:39	5:14	5:15
22	5:41	6:10	6:33	6:56	7:18	7:33	7:27	6:58	6:17	5:38	5:14	5:16
23	5:42	6:11	6:33	6:56	7:19	7:33	7:27	6:57	6:15	5:37	5:13	5:16
24	5:43	6:12	6:34	6:57	7:20	7:34	7:26	6:56	6:14	5:36	5:13	5:17
25	5:44	6:13	6:35	6:58	7:20	7:34	7:25	6:54	6:13	5:35	5:13	5:17
26	5:45	6:14	6:36	6:59	7:21	7:34	7:25	6:53	6:11	5:34	5:12	5:18
27	5:46	6:14	6:36	7:00	7:22	7:34	7:24	6:52	6:10	5:33	5:12	5:19
28	5:47	6:15	6:37	7:00	7:22	7:34	7:23	6:51	6:09	5:32	5:12	5:19
29	5:48	6:16	6:38	7:01	7:23	7:34	7:22	6:49	6:07	5:31	5:12	5:20
30	5:49		6:39	7:02	7:23	7:34	7:22	6:48	6:06	5:30	5:11	5:21
31	5:50		6:39		7:24		7:21	6:47		5:29		5:21

BALTIMORE, MARYLAND

DAY	JAN.	FEB.	MAR.	APR.	MAY	JUNE	JULY	AUG.	SEPT.	OCT.	NOV.	DEC.
1	4:36 P.M.	5:09	5:41	6:12	6:41	7:09	7:19	7:01	6:20	5:32	4:48	4:26
2	4:37	5:10	5:42	6:13	6:42	7:09	7:19	7:00	6:18	5:30	4:47	4:26
3	4:38	5:12	5:43	6:14	6:43	7:10	7:19	6:59	6:17	5:29	4:46	4:26
4	4:39	5:13	5:44	6:15	6:44	7:11	7:18	6:58	6:15	5:27	4:45	4:26
5	4:40	5:14	5:45	6:16	6:45	7:11	7:18	6:56	6:14	5:25	4:44	4:26
6	4:41	5:15	5:46	6:17	6:46	7:12	7:18	6:55	6:12	5:24	4:43	4:26
7	4:42	5:16	5:47	6:18	6:47	7:13	7:18	6:54	6:10	5:22	4:42	4:26
8	4:43	5:17	5:48	6:19	6:48	7:13	7:17	6:53	6:09	5:21	4:41	4:26
9	4:44	5:19	5:49	6:20	6:49	7:14	7:17	6:52	6:07	5:19	4:40	4:26
10	4:45	5:20	5:50	6:21	6:50	7:14	7:17	6:51	6:06	5:18	4:39	4:26
11	4:46	5:21	5:51	6:22	6:51	7:15	7:16	6:49	6:04	5:16	4:38	4:26
12	4:47	5:22	5:52	6:23	6:52	7:15	7:16	6:48	6:02	5:15	4:37	4:26
13	4:48	5:23	5:53	6:24	6:53	7:16	7:15	6:47	6:01	5:13	4:36	4:26
14	4:49	5:24	5:54	6:25	6:54	7:16	7:15	6:46	5:59	5:12	4:35	4:26
15	4:50	5:26	5:55	6:26	6:55	7:16	7:14	6:44	5:58	5:10	4:34	4:27
16	4:51	5:27	5:56	6:27	6:56	7:17	7:14	6:43	5:56	5:09	4:34	4:27
17	4:52	5:28	5:57	6:28	6:57	7:17	7:13	6:42	5:54	5:07	4:33	4:27
18	4:53	5:29	5:58	6:29	6:57	7:17	7:12	6:40	5:53	5:06	4:32	4:28
19	4:54	5:30	5:59	6:30	6:58	7:18	7:12	6:39	5:51	5:05	4:32	4:28
20	4:55	5:31	6:00	6:31	6:59	7:18	7:11	6:37	5:49	5:03	4:31	4:29
21	4:57	5:32	6:01	6:32	7:00	7:18	7:10	6:36	5:48	5:02	4:30	4:29
22	4:58	5:33	6:02	6:33	7:01	7:18	7:10	6:35	5:46	5:01	4:30	4:30
23	4:59	5:34	6:03	6:34	7:02	7:19	7:09	6:33	5:45	4:59	4:29	5:30
24	5:00	5:36	6:04	6:35	7:03	7:19	7:08	6:32	5:43	4:58	4:29	4:31
25	5:01	5:37	6:05	6:36	7:03	7:19	7:07	6:30	5:41	4:57	4:28	4:31
26	5:02	5:38	6:06	6:37	7:04	7:19	7:06	6:29	5:40	4:55	4:28	4:32
27	5:03	5:39	6:07	6:38	7:05	7:19	7:06	6:27	5:38	4:54	4:28	4:33
28	5:05	5:40	6:08	6:39	7:06	7:19	7:05	6:26	5:37	4:53	4:27	4:33
29	5:06	5:41	6:09	6:40	7:07	7:19	7:04	6:24	5:35	4:52	4:27	4:34
30	5:07		6:10	6:40	7:07	7:19	7:03	6:23	5:33	4:50	4:27	4:35
31	5:08		6:11		7:08		7:02	6:21		4:49		4:35

BOSTON, MASSACHUSETTS

DAY	JAN.	FEB.	MAR.	APR.	MAY	JUNE	JULY	AUG.	SEPT.	OCT.	NOV.	DEC.
1	4:04 P.M.	4:40	5:16	5:52	6:26	6:56	7:07	6:46	6:01	5:08	4:20	3:55
2	4:05	4:41	5:17	5:53	6:27	6:57	7:07	6:45	5:59	5:07	4:19	3:55
3	4:06	4:43	5:18	5:54	6:28	6:58	7:06	6:44	5:57	5:05	4:17	3:54
4	4:07	4:44	5:20	5:55	6:29	6:58	7:06	6:42	5:56	5:03	4:16	3:54
5	4:08	4:45	5:21	5:56	6:30	6:59	7:06	6:41	5:54	5:01	4:15	3:54
6	4:09	4:47	5:22	5:57	6:31	7:00	7:06	6:40	5:52	5:00	4:14	3:54
7	4:10	4:48	5:23	5:59	6:32	7:00	7:05	6:39	5:50	4:58	4:13	3:54
8	4:11	4:49	5:24	6:00	6:33	7:01	7:05	6:37	5:49	4:56	4:12	3:54
9	4:12	4:51	5:25	6:01	6:34	7:02	7:05	6:36	5:47	4:55	4:10	3:54
10	4:13	4:52	5:27	6:02	6:35	7:02	7:04	6:35	5:45	4:53	4:09	3:54
11	4:14	4:53	5:28	6:03	6:36	7:03	7:04	6:33	5:43	4:51	4:08	3:54
12	4:15	4:54	5:29	6:04	6:37	7:03	7:03	6:32	5:42	4:50	4:07	3:54
13	4:16	4:56	5:30	6:05	6:39	7:04	7:03	6:31	5:40	4:48	4:06	3:54
14	4:18	4:57	5:31	6:06	6:40	7:04	7:02	6:29	5:38	4:46	4:05	3:54
15	4:19	4:58	5:32	6:08	6:41	7:05	7:01	6:28	5:36	4:45	4:05	3:54
16	4:20	5:00	5:34	6:09	6:42	7:05	7:01	6:26	5:35	4:43	4:04	3:55
17	4:21	5:01	5:35	6:10	6:43	7:05	7:00	6:25	5:33	4:42	4:03	3:55
18	4:22	5:02	5:36	6:11	6:44	7:06	6:59	6:23	5:31	4:40	4:02	3:55
19	4:24	5:03	5:37	6:12	6:45	7:06	6:59	6:22	5:29	4:38	4:01	3:56
20	4:25	5:05	5:38	6:13	6:46	7:06	6:58	6:20	5:28	4:37	4:01	3:56
21	4:26	5:06	5:39	6:14	6:47	7:06	6:57	6:19	5:26	4:35	4:00	3:57
22	4:27	5:07	5:41	6:15	6:48	7:07	6:56	6:17	5:24	4:34	3:59	3:57
23	4:29	5:08	5:42	6:17	6:49	7:07	6:55	6:15	5:22	4:32	3:59	3:58
24	4:30	5:10	5:43	6:18	6:49	7:07	6:54	6:14	5:21	4:31	3:58	3:58
25	4:31	5:11	5:44	6:19	6:50	7:07	6:53	6:12	5:19	4:30	3:57	3:59
26	4:32	5:12	5:45	6:20	6:51	7:07	6:52	6:11	5:17	4:28	3:57	4:00
27	4:34	5:13	5:46	6:21	6:52	7:07	6:51	6:09	5:15	4:27	3:56	4:00
28	4:35	5:15	5:47	6:22	6:53	7:07	6:50	6:07	5:13	4:25	3:56	4:01
29	4:36	5:16	5:48	6:23	6:54	7:07	6:49	6:06	5:12	4:24	3:56	4:02
30	4:38		5:50	6:24	6:55	7:07	6:48	6:04	5:10	4:23	3:55	4:02
31	4:39		5:51		6:55		6:47	6:02		4:21		4:03

BUFFALO, NEW YORK

DAY	JAN.	FEB.	MAR.	APR.	MAY	JUNE	JULY	AUG.	SEPT.	OCT.	NOV.	DEC.
1	4:33 P.M.	5:09	5:46	6:23	6:57	7:29	7:40	7:18	6:32	5:39	4:50	4:24
2	4:34	5:11	5:47	6:24	6:59	7:30	7:39	7:17	6:30	5:37	4:48	4:23
3	4:35	5:12	5:48	6:25	7:00	7:30	7:39	7:16	6:29	5:35	4:47	4:23
4	4:36	5:13	5:50	6:26	7:01	7:31	7:39	7:15	6:27	5:33	4:46	4:23
5	4:37	5:15	5:51	6:27	7:02	7:32	7:39	7:13	6:25	5:32	4:45	4:23
6	4:38	5:16	5:52	6:29	7:03	7:33	7:38	7:12	6:23	5:30	4:43	4:23
7	4:39	5:17	5:53	6:30	7:04	7:33	7:38	7:11	6:22	5:28	4:42	4:22
8	4:40	5:19	5:55	6:31	7:05	7:34	7:38	7:09	6:20	5:27	4:41	4:22
9	4:41	5:20	5:56	6:32	7:06	7:34	7:37	7:08	6:18	5:25	4:40	4:22
10	4:42	5:21	5:57	6:33	7:07	7:35	7:37	7:07	6:16	5:23	4:39	4:22
11	4:43	5:23	5:58	6:34	7:09	7:36	7:36	7:05	6:15	5:21	4:38	4:22
12	4:44	5:24	5:59	6:36	7:10	7:36	7:36	7:04	6:13	5:20	4:37	4:23
13	4:45	5:25	6:01	6:37	7:11	7:37	7:35	7:02	6:11	5:18	4:36	4:23
14	4:47	5:27	6:02	6:38	7:12	7:37	7:35	7:01	6:09	5:16	4:35	4:23
15	4:48	5:28	6:03	6:39	7:13	7:37	7:34	7:00	6:07	5:15	4:34	4:23
16	4:49	5:29	6:04	6:40	7:14	7:38	7:33	6:58	6:06	5:13	4:33	4:23
17	4:50	5:31	6:05	6:41	7:15	7:38	7:33	6:57	6:04	5:12	4:32	4:24
18	4:51	5:32	6:07	6:42	7:16	7:38	7:32	6:55	6:02	5:10	4:31	4:24
19	4:53	5:33	6:08	6:44	7:17	7:39	7:31	6:53	6:00	5:08	4:30	4:24
20	4:54	5:35	6:09	6:45	7:18	7:39	7:30	6:52	5:58	5:07	4:30	4:25
21	4:55	5:36	6:10	6:46	7:19	7:39	7:29	6:50	5:57	5:05	4:29	4:25
22	4:56	5:37	6:11	6:47	7:20	7:39	7:29	6:49	5:55	5:04	4:28	4:26
23	4:58	5:38	6:12	6:48	7:21	7:40	7:28	6:47	5:53	5:02	4:28	4:26
24	4:59	5:40	6:14	6:49	7:22	7:40	7:27	6:45	5:51	5:01	4:27	4:27
25	5:00	5:41	6:15	6:51	7:23	7:40	7:26	6:44	5:49	4:59	4:26	4:28
26	5:02	5:42	6:16	6:52	7:24	7:40	7:25	6:42	5:48	4:58	4:26	4:28
27	5:03	5:43	6:17	6:53	7:25	7:40	7:24	6:41	5:46	4:56	4:25	4:29
28	5:04	5:45	6:18	6:54	7:26	7:40	7:23	6:39	5:44	4:55	4:25	4:30
29	5:05	5:46	6:19	6:55	7:26	7:40	7:22	6:37	5:42	4:54	4:24	4:30
30	5:07		6:21	6:56	7:27	7:40	7:21	6:36	5:41	4:52	4:24	4:31
31	5:08		6:22		7:28		7:19	6:34		4:51		4:32

CHICAGO, ILLINOIS

DAY	JAN.	FEB.	MAR.	APR.	MAY	JUNE	JULY	AUG.	SEPT.	OCT.	NOV.	DEC.
1	4:13 P.M.	4:48	5:23	5:58	6:30	7:00	7:11	6:51	6:06	5:15	4:27	4:03
2	4:13	4:49	5:24	5:59	6:31	7:01	7:11	6:50	6:05	5:13	4:26	4:03
3	4:14	4:50	5:25	6:00	6:33	7:02	7:11	6:48	6:03	5:11	4:25	4:02
4	4:15	4:52	5:26	6:01	6:34	7:03	7:10	6:47	6:01	5:10	4:24	4:02
5	4:16	4:53	5:27	6:02	6:35	7:03	7:10	6:46	6:00	5:08	4:23	4:02
6	4:17	4:54	5:29	6:03	6:36	7:04	7:10	6:45	5:58	5:06	4:21	4:02
7	4:18	4:55	5:30	6:04	6:37	7:05	7:09	6:44	5:56	5:05	4:20	4:02
8	4:19	4:57	5:31	6:05	6:38	7:05	7:09	6:42	5:55	5:03	4:19	4:02
9	4:20	4:58	5:32	6:06	6:39	7:06	7:09	6:41	5:53	5:01	4:18	4:02
10	4:21	4:59	5:33	6:07	6:40	7:06	7:08	6:40	5:51	5:00	4:17	4:02
11	4:22	5:01	5:34	6:09	6:41	7:07	7:08	6:38	5:49	4:58	4:16	4:02
12	4:23	5:02	5:35	6:10	6:42	7:07	7:07	6:37	5:48	4:57	4:15	4:02
13	4:25	5:03	5:37	6:11	6:43	7:08	7:07	6:36	5:46	4:55	4:14	4:02
14	4:26	5:04	5:38	6:12	6:44	7:08	7:06	6:34	5:44	4:53	4:13	4:03
15	4:27	5:06	5:39	6:13	6:45	7:09	7:06	6:33	5:42	4:52	4:12	4:03
16	4:28	5:07	5:40	6:14	6:46	7:09	7:05	6:31	5:41	4:50	4:12	4:03
17	4:29	5:08	5:41	6:15	6:47	7:09	7:04	6:30	5:39	4:49	4:11	4:03
18	4:30	5:09	5:42	6:16	6:48	7:10	7:04	6:28	5:37	4:47	4:10	4:04
19	4:32	5:11	5:43	6:17	6:49	7:10	7:03	6:27	5:36	4:46	4:09	4:04
20	4:33	5:12	5:44	6:18	6:50	7:10	7:02	6:25	5:34	4:44	4:09	4:05
21	4:34	5:13	5:46	6:19	6:51	7:11	7:01	6:24	5:32	4:43	4:08	4:05
22	4:35	5:14	5:47	6:21	6:52	7:11	7:01	6:22	5:30	4:41	4:07	4:06
23	4:36	5:15	5:48	6:22	6:53	7:11	7:00	6:21	5:29	4:40	4:07	4:06
24	4:38	5:17	5:49	6:23	6:54	7:11	6:59	6:19	5:27	4:38	4:06	4:07
25	4:39	5:18	5:50	6:24	6:55	7:11	6:58	6:18	5:25	4:37	4:05	4:07
26	4:40	5:19	5:51	6:25	6:56	7:11	6:57	6:16	5:23	4:35	4:05	4:08
27	4:41	5:20	5:52	6:26	6:56	7:11	6:56	6:15	5:22	4:34	4:04	4:09
28	4:43	5:21	5:53	6:27	6:57	7:11	6:55	6:13	5:20	4:33	4:04	4:09
29	4:44	5:22	5:54	6:28	6:58	7:11	6:54	6:11	5:18	4:31	4:04	4:10
30	4:45		5:55	6:29	6:59	7:11	6:53	6:10	5:17	4:30	4:03	4:11
31	4:46		5:57		7:00		6:52	6:08		4:29		4:12

CINCINNATI, OHIO

DAY	JAN.	FEB.	MAR.	APR.	MAY	JUNE	JULY	AUG.	SEPT.	OCT.	NOV.	DEC.
1	5:08 P.M.	5:41	6:12	6:43	7:13	7:40	7:50	7:32	6:51	6:03	5:20	4:58
2	5:09	5:42	6:13	6:44	7:14	7:41	7:50	7:31	6:50	6:02	5:18	4:58
3	5:10	5:43	6:14	6:45	7:15	7:41	7:50	7:30	6:48	6:00	5:17	4:58
4	5:11	5:44	6:16	6:46	7:16	7:42	7:49	7:29	6:46	5:58	5:16	4:57
5	5:12	5:45	6:17	6:47	7:17	7:43	7:49	7:28	6:45	5:57	5:15	4:57
6	5:12	5:47	6:18	6:48	7:17	7:43	7:49	7:27	6:43	5:55	5:14	4:57
7	5:13	5:48	6:19	6:49	7:18	7:44	7:49	7:25	6:42	5:54	5:13	4:57
8	5:14	5:49	6:20	6:50	7:19	7:44	7:48	7:24	6:40	5:52	5:12	4:57
9	5:15	5:50	6:21	6:51	7:20	7:45	7:48	7:23	6:39	5:51	5:11	4:57
10	5:16	5:51	6:22	6:52	7:21	7:45	7:48	7:22	6:39	5:49	5:10	4:57
11	5:17	5:52	6:23	6:53	7:22	7:46	7:47	7:21	6:35	5:48	5:09	4:58
12	5:18	5:54	6:24	6:54	7:23	7:46	7:47	7:19	6:34	5:46	5:09	4:58
13	5:19	5:55	6:25	6:55	7:24	7:47	7:46	7:18	6:32	5:45	5:08	4:58
14	5:20	5:56	6:26	6:56	7:25	7:47	7:46	7:17	6:31	5:43	5:07	4:58
15	5:21	5:57	6:27	6:57	7:26	7:48	7:45	7:16	6:29	5:42	5:06	4:58
16	5:23	5:58	6:28	6:58	7:27	7:48	7:45	7:14	6:27	5:40	5:05	4:59
17	5:24	5:59	6:29	6:59	7:28	7:48	7:44	7:13	6:26	5:39	5:05	4:59
18	5:25	6:00	6:30	7:00	7:29	7:49	7:44	7:12	6:24	5:38	5:04	4:59
19	5:26	6:01	6:31	7:01	7:30	7:49	7:43	7:10	6:22	5:36	5:03	5:00
20	5:27	6:03	6:32	7:02	7:30	7:49	7:42	7:09	6:21	5:35	5:03	5:00
21	5:28	6:04	6:33	7:03	7:31	7:49	7:42	7:07	6:19	5:33	5:02	5:01
22	5:29	6:05	6:34	7:04	7:32	7:50	7:41	7:06	6:18	5:32	5:01	5:01
23	5:30	6:06	6:35	7:05	7:33	7:50	7:40	7:04	6:16	5:31	5:01	5:02
24	5:32	6:07	6:36	7:06	7:34	7:50	7:39	7:03	6:14	5:29	5:00	5:02
25	5:33	6:08	6:37	7:07	7:35	7:50	7:38	7:02	6:13	5:28	5:00	5:03
26	5:34	6:09	6:38	7:08	7:35	7:50	7:38	7:00	6:11	5:27	5:00	5:04
27	5:35	6:10	6:39	7:09	7:36	7:50	7:37	6:59	6:10	5:26	4:59	5:04
28	5:36	6:11	6:40	7:10	7:37	7:50	7:36	6:57	6:08	5:24	4:59	5:05
29	5:37	6:12	6:41	7:11	7:38	7:50	7:35	6:56	6:06	5:23	4:59	5:06
30	5:38		6:42	7:12	7:38	7:50	7:34	6:54	6:05	5:22	4:58	5:06
31	5:40		6:43		7:39		7:33	6:53		5:21		5:07

CLEVELAND, OHIO

DAY	JAN.	FEB.	MAR.	APR.	MAY	JUNE	JULY	AUG.	SEPT.	OCT.	NOV.	DEC.
1	4:50 P.M.	5:25	6:00	6:34	7:07	7:36	7:47	7:27	6:43	5:52	5:05	4:41
2	4:51	5:27	6:01	6:35	7:08	7:37	7:47	7:26	6:41	5:50	5:04	4:41
3	4:52	5:28	6:02	6:36	7:09	7:38	7:46	7:25	6:40	5:48	5:02	4:40
4	4:53	5:29	6:03	6:38	7:10	7:38	7:46	7:23	6:38	5:47	5:01	4:40
5	4:54	5:30	6:04	6:39	7:11	7:39	7:46	7:22	6:36	5:45	5:00	4:40
6	4:55	5:32	6:06	6:40	7:12	7:40	7:46	7:21	6:35	5:43	4:59	4:40
7	4:56	5:33	6:07	6:41	7:13	7:40	7:45	7:20	6:33	5:42	4:58	4:40
8	4:57	5:34	6:08	6:42	7:14	7:41	7:45	7:18	6:31	5:40	4:57	4:40
9	4:58	5:35	6:09	6:43	7:15	7:42	7:45	7:17	6:29	5:38	4:56	4:40
10	4:59	5:37	6:10	6:44	7:16	7:42	7:44	7:16	6:28	5:35	4:55	4:40
11	5:00	5:38	6:11	6:45	7:17	7:43	7:44	7:15	6:26	5:34	4:54	4:40
12	5:01	5:39	6:12	6:46	7:18	7:43	7:43	7:13	6:24	5:32	4:53	4:40
13	5:02	5:40	6:14	6:47	7:19	7:44	7:43	7:12	6:23	5:30	4:52	4:40
14	5:03	5:42	6:15	6:48	7:20	7:44	7:42	7:10	6:21	5:29	4:51	4:40
15	5:05	5:43	6:16	6:49	7:21	7:44	7:42	7:09	6:19	5:27	4:50	4:41
16	5:06	5:44	6:17	6:50	7:22	7:45	7:41	7:08	6:17	5:26	4:49	4:41
17	5:07	5:45	6:18	6:52	7:23	7:45	7:40	7:06	6:16	5:24	4:48	4:41
18	5:08	5:47	6:19	6:53	7:24	7:46	7:40	7:05	6:14	5:23	4:48	4:42
19	5:09	5:48	6:20	6:54	7:25	7:46	7:39	7:03	6:12	5:21	4:47	4:42
20	5:10	5:49	6:21	6:55	7:26	7:46	7:38	7:02	6:11	5:20	4:46	4:42
21	5:12	5:50	6:22	6:56	7:27	7:46	7:37	7:00	6:09	5:18	4:46	4:43
22	5:13	5:51	6:23	6:57	7:28	7:46	7:36	6:59	6:07	5:17	4:45	4:43
23	5:14	5:53	6:25	6:58	7:29	7:47	7:36	6:57	6:05	5:16	4:44	4:44
24	5:15	5:54	6:26	6:59	7:30	7:47	7:35	6:56	6:04	5:14	4:44	4:45
25	5:17	5:55	6:27	7:00	7:31	7:47	7:34	6:54	6:02	5:13	4:43	4:45
26	5:18	5:56	6:28	7:01	7:31	7:47	7:33	6:53	6:00	5:11	4:43	4:46
27	5:19	5:57	6:29	7:02	7:32	7:47	7:32	6:51	5:59	5:10	4:42	4:46
28	5:20	5:59	6:30	7:03	7:33	7:47	7:31	6:49	5:57	5:09	4:42	4:47
29	5:22	6:00	6:31	7:04	7:34	7:47	7:30	6:48	5:55	5:07	4:41	4:48
30	5:23		6:32	7:06	7:35	7:47	7:29	6:46	5:53	5:06	4:41	4:49
31	5:24		6:33		7:36		7:28	6:44				4:49

DENVER, COLORADO

DAY	JAN.	FEB.	MAR.	APR.	MAY	JUNE	JULY	AUG.	SEPT.	OCT.	NOV.	DEC.
1	4:28 P.M.	5:01	5:34	6:06	6:36	7:04	7:14	6:55	6:14	5:25	4:40	4:18
2	4:29	5:03	5:35	6:07	6:37	7:04	7:14	6:54	6:12	5:23	4:39	4:18
3	4:30	5:04	5:36	6:08	6:38	7:05	7:14	6:53	6:11	5:22	4:38	4:18
4	4:31	5:05	5:37	6:09	6:39	7:06	7:13	6:52	6:09	5:20	4:37	4:18
5	4:32	5:06	5:38	6:10	6:40	7:06	7:13	6:51	6:07	5:19	4:36	4:17
6	4:32	5:07	5:39	6:11	6:41	7:07	7:13	6:50	6:06	5:17	4:35	4:17
7	4:33	5:09	5:40	6:12	6:42	7:08	7:13	6:49	6:04	5:15	4:34	4:17
8	4:34	5:10	5:41	6:13	6:43	7:08	7:12	6:48	6:03	5:14	4:33	4:17
9	4:35	5:11	5:42	6:14	6:44	7:09	7:12	6:46	6:01	5:12	4:32	4:17
10	4:36	5:12	5:43	6:15	6:45	7:09	7:12	6:45	5:59	5:11	4:31	4:17
11	4:37	5:13	5:44	6:16	6:46	7:10	7:11	6:44	5:58	5:09	4:30	4:18
12	4:38	5:14	5:45	6:17	6:47	7:10	7:11	6:43	5:56	5:08	4:29	4:18
13	4:39	5:16	5:46	6:18	6:48	7:11	7:10	6:41	5:54	5:06	4:28	4:18
14	4:41	5:17	5:48	6:19	6:48	7:11	7:10	6:40	5:53	5:05	4:27	4:18
15	4:42	5:18	5:49	6:20	6:49	7:12	7:09	6:39	5:51	5:03	4:27	4:18
16	4:43	5:19	5:50	6:21	6:50	7:12	7:09	6:37	5:50	5:02	4:26	4:19
17	4:44	5:20	5:51	6:22	6:51	7:12	7:08	6:36	5:48	5:00	4:25	4:19
18	4:45	5:21	5:52	6:23	6:52	7:13	7:07	6:35	5:46	4:59	4:24	4:19
19	4:46	5:23	5:53	6:24	6:53	7:13	7:07	6:33	5:45	4:57	4:24	4:20
20	4:47	5:24	5:54	6:25	6:54	7:13	7:06	6:32	5:43	4:56	4:23	4:20
21	4:48	5:25	5:55	6:26	6:55	7:13	7:05	6:30	5:41	4:55	4:22	4:21
22	4:50	5:26	5:56	6:27	6:56	7:14	7:05	6:29	5:40	4:53	4:22	4:21
23	4:51	5:27	5:57	6:28	6:57	7:14	7:04	6:27	5:38	4:52	4:21	4:22
24	4:52	5:28	5:58	6:29	6:57	7:14	7:03	6:26	5:36	4:51	4:21	4:22
25	4:53	5:29	5:59	6:30	6:58	7:14	7:02	6:24	5:35	4:49	4:20	4:23
26	4:54	5:30	6:00	6:31	6:59	7:14	7:01	6:23	5:33	4:48	4:20	4:23
27	4:55	5:32	6:01	6:32	7:00	7:14	7:00	6:21	5:32	4:47	4:19	4:24
28	4:57	5:33	6:02	6:33	7:01	7:14	6:59	6:20	5:30	4:45	4:19	4:25
29	4:58	5:34	6:03	6:34	7:01	7:14	6:58	6:18	5:28	4:44	4:19	4:26
30	4:59		6:04	6:35	7:02	7:14	6:57	6:17	5:27	4:43	4:18	4:26
31	5:00		6:05		7:03		6:56	6:15		4:42		4:27

DETROIT, MICHIGAN

DAY	JAN.	FEB.	MAR.	APR.	MAY	JUNE	JULY	AUG.	SEPT.	OCT.	NOV.	DEC.
1	4:54 P.M.	5:30	6:05	6:41	7:14	7:45	7:56	7:35	6:50	5:57	5:09	4:44
2	4:55	5:31	6:06	6:42	7:15	7:46	7:55	7:34	6:48	5:56	5:08	4:44
3	4:56	5:32	6:07	6:43	7:17	7:46	7:55	7:33	6:46	5:54	5:07	4:44
4	4:57	5:33	6:09	6:44	7:18	7:47	7:55	7:31	6:45	5:52	5:06	4:44
5	4:58	5:35	6:10	6:45	7:19	7:48	7:55	7:30	6:43	5:51	5:04	4:43
6	4:59	5:36	6:11	6:46	7:20	7:48	7:54	7:29	6:41	5:49	5:03	4:43
7	5:00	5:37	6:12	6:48	7:21	7:49	7:54	7:28	6:40	5:47	5:02	4:43
8	5:01	5:39	6:13	6:49	7:22	7:50	7:54	7:26	6:38	5:46	5:01	4:43
9	5:02	5:40	6:15	6:50	7:23	7:50	7:53	7:25	6:36	5:44	5:00	4:43
10	5:03	5:41	6:16	6:51	7:24	7:51	7:53	7:24	6:34	5:42	4:59	4:43
11	5:04	5:43	6:17	6:52	7:25	7:51	7:52	7:22	6:33	5:41	4:58	4:43
12	5:05	5:44	6:18	6:53	7:26	7:52	7:52	7:21	6:31	5:39	4:57	4:43
13	5:05	5:45	6:19	6:54	7:27	7:52	7:51	7:19	6:29	5:37	4:56	4:44
14	5:07	5:46	6:20	6:55	7:28	7:53	7:51	7:18	6:27	5:36	4:55	4:44
15	5:08	5:48	6:22	6:56	7:29	7:53	7:50	7:17	6:26	5:34	4:54	4:44
16	5:09	5:49	6:23	6:58	7:30	7:54	7:49	7:15	6:24	5:32	4:53	4:44
17	5:11	5:50	6:24	6:59	7:31	7:54	7:49	7:14	6:22	5:31	4:52	4:45
18	5:12	5:51	6:25	7:00	7:32	7:54	7:48	7:12	6:20	5:29	4:52	4:45
19	5:13	5:53	6:26	7:01	7:33	7:55	7:47	7:11	6:19	5:28	4:51	4:45
20	5:14	5:54	6:27	7:02	7:34	7:55	7:47	7:09	6:17	5:26	4:50	4:46
21	5:15	5:55	6:28	7:03	7:35	7:55	7:46	7:08	6:15	5:25	4:49	4:46
22	5:17	5:56	6:30	7:04	7:36	7:55	7:45	7:06	6:13	5:23	4:49	4:47
23	5:18	5:58	6:31	7:05	7:37	7:55	7:44	7:04	6:11	5:22	4:48	4:47
24	5:19	5:59	6:32	7:07	7:38	7:56	7:43	7:03	6:10	5:20	4:47	4:48
25	5:21	6:00	6:33	7:08	7:39	7:56	7:42	7:01	6:08	5:19	4:47	4:48
26	5:22	6:01	6:34	7:09	7:40	7:56	7:41	7:00	6:06	5:17	4:46	4:49
27	5:23	6:03	6:35	7:10	7:41	7:56	7:40	6:58	6:04	5:16	4:46	4:50
28	5:24	6:04	6:36	7:11	7:42	7:56	7:39	6:56	6:03	5:15	4:45	4:51
29	5:26	6:05	6:37	7:12	7:43	7:56	7:38	6:55	6:01	5:13	4:45	4:51
30	5:27		6:39	7:13	7:43	7:56	7:37	6:53	5:59	5:12	4:45	4:52
31	5:28		6:40		7:44		7:36	6:51		5:11		4:53

HOUSTON, TEXAS

DAY	JAN.	FEB.	MAR.	APR.	MAY	JUNE	JULY	AUG.	SEPT.	OCT.	NOV.	DEC.
1	5:15 P.M.	5:41	6:03	6:22	6:40	6:59	7:08	6:56	6:26	5:49	5:17	5:04
2	5:16	5:42	6:03	6:23	6:41	7:00	7:08	6:56	6:25	5:48	5:16	5:04
3	5:17	5:43	6:04	6:23	6:42	7:00	7:08	6:55	6:24	5:47	5:15	5:04
4	5:18	5:43	6:05	6:24	6:42	7:01	7:08	6:54	6:23	5:46	5:15	5:04
5	5:18	5:44	6:05	6:24	6:43	7:01	7:08	6:53	6:21	5:45	5:14	5:04
6	5:19	5:45	6:06	6:25	6:43	7:02	7:08	6:53	6:20	5:43	5:13	5:04
7	5:20	5:46	6:07	6:25	6:44	7:02	7:08	6:52	6:19	5:42	5:13	5:04
8	5:21	5:47	6:07	6:26	6:45	7:03	7:07	6:51	6:18	5:41	5:12	5:04
9	5:21	5:48	6:08	6:27	6:45	7:03	7:07	6:50	6:16	5:40	5:11	5:04
10	5:22	5:48	6:09	6:27	6:46	7:03	7:07	6:49	6:15	5:39	5:11	5:05
11	5:23	5:49	6:09	6:28	6:47	7:04	7:07	6:48	6:14	5:38	5:10	5:05
12	5:24	5:50	6:10	6:28	6:47	7:04	7:07	6:47	6:13	5:36	5:09	5:05
13	5:25	5:51	6:10	6:29	6:48	7:05	7:06	6:46	6:12	5:35	5:09	5:05
14	5:25	5:52	6:11	6:30	6:49	7:05	7:06	6:45	6:10	5:34	5:08	5:06
15	5:26	5:52	6:12	6:30	6:49	7:05	7:06	6:44	6:09	5:33	5:08	5:06
16	5:27	5:53	6:12	6:31	6:50	7:06	7:05	6:44	6:08	5:32	5:07	5:06
17	5:28	5:54	6:13	6:32	6:50	7:06	7:05	6:43	6:07	5:31	5:07	5:07
18	5:29	5:55	6:14	6:32	6:51	7:06	7:04	6:42	6:05	5:30	5:07	5:07
19	5:30	5:55	6:14	6:33	6:52	7:06	7:04	6:40	6:04	5:29	5:06	5:08
20	5:31	5:56	6:15	6:33	6:52	7:07	7:04	6:39	6:03	5:28	5:06	5:08
21	5:31	5:57	6:15	6:34	6:53	7:07	7:03	6:38	6:02	5:27	5:06	5:09
22	5:32	5:58	6:16	6:35	6:54	7:07	7:03	6:37	6:00	5:26	5:05	5:09
23	5:33	5:58	6:17	6:35	6:54	7:07	7:02	6:36	5:59	5:25	5:05	5:10
24	5:34	5:59	6:17	6:36	6:55	7:07	7:02	6:35	5:58	5:24	5:05	5:10
25	5:35	6:00	6:18	6:36	6:55	7:08	7:01	6:34	5:57	5:23	5:05	5:11
26	5:36	6:00	6:18	6:37	6:56	7:08	7:00	6:33	5:55	5:22	5:04	5:11
27	5:37	6:01	6:19	6:38	6:56	7:08	7:00	6:32	5:54	5:21	5:04	5:12
28	5:38	6:02	6:20	6:38	6:57	7:08	6:59	6:31	5:53	5:20	5:04	5:12
29	5:38	6:03	6:20	6:39	6:58	7:08	6:59	6:30	5:52	5:19	5:04	5:13
30	5:39		6:21	6:40	6:58	7:08	6:58	6:28	5:51	5:19	5:04	5:14
31	5:40		6:21		6:59		6:57	6:27		5:18		5:14

LOS ANGELES, CALIFORNIA

DAY	JAN.	FEB.	MAR.	APR.	MAY	JUNE	JULY	AUG.	SEPT.	OCT.	NOV.	DEC.
1	4:37 P.M.	5:05	5:31	5:56	6:19	6:41	6:50	6:36	6:01	5:20	4:42	4:26
2	4:37	5:06	5:32	5:56	6:19	6:42	6:50	6:35	6:00	5:18	4:41	4:26
3	4:38	5:07	5:33	5:57	6:20	6:42	6:50	6:34	5:58	5:17	4:41	4:25
4	4:39	5:08	5:34	5:58	6:21	6:43	6:50	6:33	5:57	5:15	4:40	4:25
5	4:40	5:09	5:34	5:59	6:22	6:43	6:50	6:32	5:56	5:14	4:39	4:25
6	4:41	5:10	5:35	5:59	6:22	6:44	6:50	6:31	5:54	5:13	4:38	4:25
7	4:41	5:11	5:36	6:00	6:23	6:44	6:49	6:30	5:53	5:11	4:37	4:26
8	4:42	5:12	5:37	6:01	6:24	6:45	6:49	6:29	5:52	5:10	4:36	4:26
9	4:43	5:13	5:38	6:02	6:25	6:45	6:49	6:28	5:50	5:09	4:36	4:26
10	4:44	5:14	5:39	6:02	6:26	6:46	6:49	6:27	5:49	5:07	4:35	4:26
11	4:45	5:15	5:39	6:03	6:26	6:46	6:48	6:26	5:47	5:06	4:34	4:26
12	4:46	5:16	5:40	6:04	6:27	6:47	6:48	6:25	5:46	5:05	4:33	4:26
13	4:47	5:17	5:41	6:05	6:28	6:47	6:48	6:24	5:45	5:04	4:33	4:27
14	4:48	5:18	5:42	6:05	6:29	6:47	6:47	6:23	5:43	5:02	4:32	4:27
15	4:49	5:19	5:43	6:06	6:29	6:48	6:47	6:22	5:42	5:01	4:31	4:27
16	4:50	5:20	5:43	6:07	6:30	6:48	6:46	6:21	5:40	5:00	4:31	4:27
17	4:51	5:21	5:44	6:08	6:31	6:48	6:46	6:20	5:39	4:59	4:30	4:28
18	4:52	5:21	5:45	6:08	6:32	6:49	6:46	6:19	5:38	4:57	4:30	4:28
19	4:52	5:22	5:46	6:09	6:32	6:49	6:45	6:17	5:36	4:56	4:29	4:29
20	4:53	5:23	5:46	6:10	6:33	6:49	6:44	6:16	5:35	4:55	4:29	4:29
21	4:54	5:24	5:47	6:11	6:34	6:49	6:44	6:15	5:33	4:54	4:28	4:30
22	4:55	5:25	5:48	6:12	6:34	6:50	6:43	6:14	5:32	4:53	4:28	4:30
23	4:56	5:26	5:49	6:12	6:35	6:50	6:43	6:13	5:31	4:52	4:28	4:31
24	4:57	5:27	5:49	6:13	6:36	6:50	6:42	6:11	5:29	4:51	4:27	4:31
25	4:58	5:28	5:50	6:14	6:37	6:50	6:41	6:10	5:28	4:49	4:27	4:32
26	4:59	5:29	5:51	6:15	6:37	6:50	6:41	6:09	5:26	4:48	4:27	4:32
27	5:00	5:29	5:52	6:15	6:38	6:50	6:40	6:08	5:25	4:47	4:26	4:33
28	5:01	5:30	5:53	6:16	6:38	6:50	6:39	6:06	5:24	4:46	4:26	4:34
29	5:02	5:31	5:53	6:17	6:39	6:50	6:38	6:05	5:22	4:45	4:26	4:34
30	5:03		5:54	6:18	6:40	6:50	6:38	6:04	5:21	4:44	4:26	4:35
31	5:04		5:55		6:40		6:37	6:02		4:43		4:36

MIAMI, FLORIDA

DAY	JAN.	FEB.	MAR.	APR.	MAY	JUNE	JULY	AUG.	SEPT.	OCT.	NOV.	DEC.
1	5:23 P.M.	5:46	6:04	6:19	6:34	6:50	6:58	6:49	6:22	5:50	5:21	5:11
2	5:24	5:47	6:05	6:20	6:34	6:50	6:58	6:48	6:21	5:49	5:21	5:11
3	5:25	5:48	6:05	6:20	6:35	6:51	6:58	6:48	6:20	5:48	5:20	5:11
4	5:25	5:49	6:06	6:21	6:35	6:51	6:58	6:47	6:19	5:46	5:19	5:11
5	5:26	5:49	6:07	6:21	6:36	6:52	6:58	6:46	6:18	5:45	5:19	5:12
6	5:27	5:50	6:07	6:22	6:36	6:52	6:58	6:46	6:17	5:44	5:18	5:12
7	5:27	5:51	6:08	6:22	6:37	6:52	6:58	6:45	6:16	5:43	5:18	5:12
8	5:28	5:51	6:08	6:23	6:37	6:53	6:58	6:44	6:15	5:42	5:17	5:12
9	5:29	5:52	6:09	6:23	6:38	6:53	6:58	6:43	6:14	5:41	5:17	5:12
10	5:30	5:53	6:09	6:23	6:39	6:54	6:58	6:43	6:13	5:40	5:16	5:13
11	5:30	5:53	6:10	6:24	6:39	6:54	6:57	6:42	6:12	5:39	5:16	5:13
12	5:31	5:54	6:10	6:24	6:40	6:54	6:57	6:41	6:10	5:38	5:15	5:13
13	5:32	5:55	6:11	6:25	6:40	6:55	6:57	6:40	6:09	5:37	5:15	5:13
14	5:33	5:55	6:11	6:25	6:41	6:55	6:57	6:39	6:08	5:36	5:14	5:14
15	5:33	5:56	6:12	6:26	6:41	6:55	6:56	6:38	6:07	5:35	5:14	5:14
16	5:34	5:57	6:12	6:26	6:42	6:56	6:56	6:38	6:06	5:34	5:14	5:14
17	5:35	5:57	6:12	6:27	6:42	6:56	6:56	6:37	6:05	5:34	5:13	5:15
18	5:36	5:58	6:13	6:27	6:43	6:56	6:56	6:36	6:04	5:33	5:13	5:15
19	5:37	5:59	6:13	6:28	6:43	6:56	6:55	6:35	6:03	5:32	5:13	5:16
20	5:37	5:59	6:14	6:28	6:44	6:57	6:55	6:34	6:02	5:31	5:12	5:16
21	5:38	6:00	6:14	6:29	6:44	6:57	6:54	6:33	6:01	5:30	5:12	5:17
22	5:39	6:00	6:15	6:29	6:45	6:57	6:54	6:32	5:59	5:29	5:12	5:17
23	5:40	6:01	6:15	6:30	6:45	6:57	6:54	6:31	5:58	5:28	5:12	5:18
24	5:40	6:02	6:16	6:30	6:46	6:57	6:53	6:30	5:57	5:27	5:12	5:18
25	5:41	6:02	6:16	6:31	6:46	6:58	6:53	6:29	5:56	5:27	5:12	5:19
26	5:42	6:03	6:17	6:31	6:47	6:58	6:52	6:28	5:55	5:26	5:11	5:19
27	5:43	6:03	6:17	6:32	6:47	6:58	6:52	6:27	5:54	5:25	5:11	5:20
28	5:43	6:04	6:18	6:32	6:48	6:58	6:51	6:26	5:53	5:24	5:11	5:21
29	5:44	6:04	6:18	6:33	6:48	6:58	6:51	6:25	5:52	5:24	5:11	5:21
30	5:45		6:18	6:33	6:49	6:58	6:50	6:24	5:51	5:23	5:11	5:22
31	5:46		6:19		6:49		6:49	6:23		5:22		5:22

NEW YORK, NEW YORK

DAY	JAN.	FEB.	MAR.	APR.	MAY	JUNE	JULY	AUG.	SEPT.	OCT.	NOV.	DEC.
1	4:21 P.M.	4:56	5:29	6:03	6:34	7:03	7:13	6:54	6:11	5:21	4:35	4:11
2	4:22	4:57	5:30	6:04	6:35	7:03	7:13	6:53	6:09	5:19	4:34	4:11
3	4:23	4:58	5:31	6:05	6:36	7:04	7:13	6:51	6:07	5:17	4:32	4:11
4	4:24	4:59	5:32	6:06	6:37	7:05	7:13	6:50	6:06	5:16	4:31	4:11
5	4:25	5:00	5:34	6:07	6:38	7:06	7:12	6:49	6:04	5:14	4:30	4:11
6	4:26	5:02	5:35	6:08	6:39	7:06	7:12	6:48	6:03	5:12	4:29	4:11
7	4:27	5:03	5:36	6:09	6:40	7:07	7:12	6:47	6:01	5:11	4:28	4:11
8	4:28	5:04	5:37	6:10	6:41	7:07	7:11	6:46	5:59	5:09	4:27	4:11
9	4:29	5:05	5:38	6:11	6:42	7:08	7:11	6:44	5:58	5:08	4:26	4:11
10	4:30	5:07	5:39	6:12	6:43	7:08	7:11	6:43	5:56	5:06	4:25	4:11
11	4:31	5:08	5:40	6:13	6:44	7:09	7:10	6:42	5:54	5:04	4:24	4:11
12	4:32	5:09	5:41	6:14	6:45	7:09	7:10	6:40	5:53	5:03	4:23	4:11
13	4:33	5:10	5:42	6:15	6:46	7:10	7:09	6:39	5:51	5:01	4:22	4:11
14	4:34	5:11	5:43	6:16	6:47	7:10	7:09	6:38	5:49	5:00	4:21	4:11
15	4:35	5:13	5:45	6:17	6:48	7:11	7:08	6:36	5:48	4:58	4:20	4:12
16	4:36	5:14	5:46	6:18	6:49	7:11	7:07	6:35	5:46	4:57	4:20	4:12
17	4:37	5:15	5:47	6:19	6:50	7:11	7:07	6:34	5:44	4:55	4:19	4:12
18	4:39	5:16	5:48	6:20	6:51	7:12	7:06	6:32	5:42	4:54	4:18	4:13
19	4:40	5:17	5:49	6:21	6:52	7:12	7:05	6:31	5:41	4:52	4:17	4:13
20	4:41	5:19	5:50	6:22	6:53	7:12	7:05	6:29	5:39	4:51	4:17	4:13
21	4:42	5:20	5:51	6:23	6:54	7:13	7:04	6:28	5:37	4:49	4:16	4:14
22	4:43	5:21	5:52	6:24	6:55	7:13	7:03	6:26	5:36	4:48	4:15	4:14
23	4:45	5:22	5:53	6:26	6:55	7:13	7:02	6:25	5:34	4:47	4:15	4:15
24	4:46	5:23	5:54	6:27	6:56	7:13	7:01	6:23	5:32	4:45	4:14	4:15
25	4:47	5:25	5:55	6:28	6:57	7:13	7:01	6:22	5:31	4:44	4:14	4:16
26	4:48	5:26	5:56	6:29	6:58	7:13	7:00	6:20	5:29	4:42	4:13	4:17
27	4:49	5:27	5:57	6:30	6:59	7:13	6:59	6:19	5:27	4:41	4:13	4:17
28	4:51	5:28	5:58	6:31	7:00	7:13	6:58	6:17	5:26	4:40	4:12	4:18
29	4:52	5:29	6:59	6:32	7:00	7:13	6:57	6:16	5:24	4:39	4:12	4:19
30	4:53		6:00	6:33	7:01	7:13	6:56	6:14	5:22	4:37	4:12	4:20
31	4:54		6:01		7:02		6:55	6:12		4:36		4:20

ORLANDO, FLORIDA

DAY	JAN.	FEB.	MAR.	APR.	MAY	JUNE	JULY	AUG.	SEPT.	OCT.	NOV.	DEC.
1	5:22 P.M.	5:47	6:07	6:25	6:42	7:00	7:09	6:58	6:29	5:54	5:22	
2	5:23	5:48	6:08	6:26	6:43	7:01	7:09	6:57	6:28	5:52	5:22	
3	5:23	5:48	6:09	6:26	6:44	7:01	7:09	6:57	6:27	5:51	5:21	
4	5:24	5:49	6:09	6:27	6:44	7:02	7:09	6:56	6:26	5:50	5:20	
5	5:25	5:50	6:10	6:27	6:45	7:02	7:09	6:55	6:24	5:49	5:20	
6	5:26	5:51	6:10	6:28	6:45	7:03	7:09	6:54	6:23	5:48	5:19	
7	5:26	5:52	6:11	6:29	6:46	7:03	7:09	6:54	6:22	5:47	5:18	
8	5:27	5:52	6:12	6:29	6:47	7:04	7:08	6:53	6:21	5:46	5:18	
9	5:28	5:53	6:12	6:30	6:47	7:04	7:08	6:52	6:20	5:44	5:17	
10	5:29	5:54	6:13	6:30	6:48	7:04	7:08	6:51	6:19	5:43	5:16	
11	5:29	5:55	6:13	6:31	6:48	7:05	7:08	6:50	6:17	5:42	5:16	
12	5:30	5:55	6:14	6:31	6:49	7:05	7:08	6:49	6:16	5:41	5:15	
13	5:31	5:56	6:15	6:32	6:50	7:06	7:07	6:49	6:15	5:40	5:15	
14	5:32	5:57	6:15	6:32	6:50	7:06	7:07	6:48	6:14	5:39	5:14	
15	5:33	5:58	6:16	6:33	6:51	7:06	7:07	6:47	6:13	5:38	5:14	
16	5:33	5:58	6:16	6:34	6:51	7:07	7:06	6:46	6:11	5:37	5:14	
17	5:34	5:59	6:17	6:34	6:52	7:07	7:06	6:45	6:10	5:36	5:13	
18	5:35	6:00	6:17	6:35	6:53	7:07	7:06	6:44	6:09	5:35	5:13	
19	5:36	6:00	6:18	6:35	6:53	7:07	7:05	6:43	6:08	5:34	5:12	
20	5:37	6:01	6:19	6:36	6:54	7:08	7:05	6:42	6:07	5:33	5:12	
21	5:38	6:02	6:19	6:36	6:54	7:08	7:04	6:41	6:05	5:32	5:12	
22	5:38	6:03	6:20	6:37	6:55	7:08	7:04	6:40	6:04	5:31	5:11	
23	5:39	6:03	6:20	6:38	6:55	7:08	7:04	6:39	6:03	5:30	5:11	
24	5:40	6:04	6:21	6:38	6:56	7:08	7:03	6:38	6:02	5:29	5:11	
25	5:41	6:05	6:21	6:39	6:57	7:09	7:02	6:37	6:01	5:28	5:11	
26	5:42	6:05	6:22	6:39	6:57	7:09	7:02	6:36	5:59	5:27	5:11	
27	5:43	6:06	6:22	6:40	6:58	7:09	7:01	6:35	5:58	5:27	5:11	
28	5:43	6:07	6:23	6:41	6:58	7:09	7:01	6:33	5:57	5:26	5:10	
29	5:44	6:07	6:24	6:41	6:59	7:09	7:00	6:32	5:56	5:25	5:10	
30	5:45		6:24	6:42	6:59	7:09	7:00	6:31	5:55	5:24	5:10	
31	5:46		6:25		7:00		6:59	6:30		5:23		

PHILADELPHIA, PENNSYLVANIA

DAY	JAN.	FEB.	MAR.	APR.	MAY	JUNE	JULY	AUG.	SEPT.	OCT.	NOV.	DEC.
1	4:29 P.M.	5:02	5:35	6:07	6:37	7:05	7:15	6:57	6:15	5:26	4:41	4:19
2	4:30	5:03	5:36	6:08	6:38	7:06	7:15	6:56	6:13	5:24	4:40	4:19
3	4:30	5:04	5:37	6:09	6:39	7:06	7:15	6:55	6:12	5:23	4:39	4:18
4	4:31	5:06	5:38	6:10	6:40	7:07	7:15	6:54	6:10	5:21	4:38	4:18
5	4:32	5:07	5:39	6:11	6:41	7:08	7:15	6:52	6:09	5:20	4:37	4:18
6	4:33	5:08	5:40	6:12	6:42	7:08	7:14	6:51	6:07	5:18	4:36	4:18
7	4:34	5:09	5:41	6:13	6:43	7:09	7:14	6:50	6:05	5:16	4:35	4:18
8	4:35	5:10	5:42	6:14	6:44	7:10	7:14	6:49	6:04	5:15	4:34	4:18
9	4:36	5:12	5:43	6:15	6:45	7:10	7:13	6:48	6:02	5:13	4:33	4:18
10	4:37	5:13	5:44	6:16	6:46	7:11	7:13	6:46	6:00	5:12	4:32	4:18
11	4:38	5:14	5:45	6:17	6:47	7:11	7:13	6:45	5:59	5:10	4:31	4:18
12	4:39	5:15	5:46	6:18	6:48	7:12	7:12	6:44	5:57	5:09	4:30	4:18
13	4:40	5:16	5:47	6:19	6:49	7:12	7:12	6:43	5:56	5:07	4:29	4:18
14	4:41	5:18	5:49	6:20	6:50	7:13	7:11	6:41	5:54	5:06	4:28	4:19
15	4:42	5:19	5:50	6:21	6:51	7:13	7:11	6:40	5:52	5:04	4:27	4:19
16	4:43	5:20	5:51	6:22	6:52	7:13	7:10	6:39	5:51	5:03	4:26	4:19
17	4:44	5:21	5:52	6:23	6:53	7:14	7:09	6:37	5:49	5:01	4:26	4:20
18	4:46	5:22	5:53	6:24	6:54	7:14	7:09	6:36	5:47	5:00	4:25	4:20
19	4:47	5:23	5:54	6:25	6:54	7:14	7:08	6:34	5:46	4:58	4:24	4:20
20	4:48	5:25	5:55	6:26	6:55	7:15	7:07	6:33	5:44	4:57	4:24	4:21
21	4:49	5:26	5:56	6:27	6:56	7:15	7:07	6:32	5:42	4:55	4:23	4:21
22	4:50	5:27	5:57	6:28	6:57	7:15	7:06	6:30	5:41	4:54	4:22	4:22
23	4:51	5:28	5:58	6:29	6:58	7:15	7:05	6:29	5:39	4:53	4:22	4:22
24	4:53	5:29	5:59	6:30	6:59	7:15	7:04	6:27	5:37	4:51	4:21	4:23
25	4:54	5:30	6:00	6:31	7:00	7:15	7:03	6:26	5:36	4:50	4:21	4:23
26	4:55	5:31	6:01	6:32	7:00	7:15	7:03	6:24	5:34	4:49	4:20	4:24
27	4:56	5:32	6:02	6:33	7:01	7:15	7:02	6:33	5:32	4:47	4:20	4:25
28	4:57	5:34	6:03	6:34	7:02	7:15	7:01	6:21	5:31	4:46	4:20	4:25
29	4:58	5:35	6:04	6:35	7:03	7:15	7:00	6:20	5:29	4:45	4:19	4:26
30	5:00		6:05	6:36	7:04	7:15	6:59	6:18	5:28	4:44	4:19	4:27
31	5:01		6:06		7:04		6:58	6:16		4:42		4:28

PHOENIX, ARIZONA

DAY	JAN.	FEB.	MAR.	APR.	MAY	JUNE	JULY	AUG.	SEPT.	OCT.	NOV.	DEC.
1	5:13 P.M.	5:41	6:07	6:30	6:53	7:14	7:24	7:10	6:36	5:55	5:19	5:02
2	5:14	5:42	6:07	6:31	6:53	7:15	7:24	7:09	6:35	5:54	5:18	5:02
3	5:15	5:43	6:08	6:32	6:54	7:16	7:24	7:08	6:33	5:52	5:17	5:02
4	5:16	5:44	6:09	6:32	6:55	7:16	7:24	7:07	6:32	5:51	5:16	5:02
5	5:16	5:45	6:10	6:33	6:56	7:17	7:23	7:07	6:31	5:50	5:15	5:02
6	5:17	5:46	6:11	6:34	6:56	7:17	7:23	7:06	6:29	5:48	5:14	5:02
7	5:18	5:47	6:11	6:35	6:57	7:18	7:23	7:05	6:28	5:47	5:13	5:02
8	5:19	5:48	6:12	6:35	6:58	7:18	7:23	7:04	6:27	5:46	5:13	5:02
9	5:20	5:49	6:13	6:36	6:59	7:19	7:23	7:03	6:25	5:44	5:12	5:02
10	5:21	5:50	6:14	6:37	6:59	7:19	7:22	7:02	6:24	5:43	5:11	5:03
11	5:21	5:51	6:15	6:38	7:00	7:20	7:22	7:01	6:22	5:42	5:10	5:03
12	5:22	5:52	6:15	6:38	7:01	7:20	7:22	7:00	6:21	5:41	5:10	5:03
13	5:23	5:53	6:16	6:39	7:02	7:20	7:21	6:59	6:20	5:39	5:09	5:03
14	5:24	5:54	6:17	6:40	7:02	7:21	7:21	6:58	6:18	5:38	5:08	5:03
15	5:25	5:54	6:18	6:41	7:03	7:21	7:21	6:56	6:17	5:37	5:08	5:04
16	5:26	5:55	6:18	6:41	7:04	7:21	7:20	6:55	6:16	5:36	5:07	5:04
17	5:27	5:56	6:19	6:42	7:05	7:22	7:20	6:54	6:14	5:35	5:07	5:04
18	5:28	5:57	6:20	6:43	7:05	7:22	7:19	6:53	6:13	5:33	5:06	5:05
19	5:29	5:58	6:21	6:44	7:06	7:22	7:19	6:52	6:11	5:32	5:06	5:05
20	5:30	5:59	6:21	6:44	7:07	7:23	7:18	6:51	6:10	5:31	5:05	5:06
21	5:31	6:00	6:22	6:45	7:07	7:23	7:18	6:50	6:09	5:30	5:05	5:06
22	5:32	6:01	6:23	6:46	7:08	7:23	7:17	6:48	6:07	5:29	5:04	5:07
23	5:33	6:02	6:24	6:47	7:09	7:23	7:17	6:47	6:06	5:28	5:04	5:07
24	5:34	6:02	6:24	6:47	7:09	7:23	7:16	6:46	6:05	5:27	5:04	5:08
25	5:35	6:03	6:25	6:48	7:10	7:24	7:15	6:45	6:03	5:26	5:03	5:08
26	5:36	6:04	6:26	6:49	7:11	7:24	7:15	6:44	6:02	5:24	5:03	5:09
27	5:37	6:05	6:27	6:50	7:11	7:24	7:14	6:42	6:00	5:23	5:03	5:10
28	5:37	6:06	6:27	6:50	7:12	7:24	7:13	6:41	5:59	5:22	5:03	5:10
29	5:38	6:07	6:28	6:51	7:13	7:24	7:12	6:40	5:58	5:21	5:03	5:11
30	5:39		6:29	6:52	7:13	7:24	7:12	6:38	5:56	5:20	5:02	5:12
31	5:40		6:30		7:14		7:11	6:37		5:19		5:12

PITTSBURGH, PENNSYLVANIA

DAY	JAN.	FEB.	MAR.	APR.	MAY	JUNE	JULY	AUG.	SEPT.	OCT.	NOV.	DEC.
1	4:46 P.M.	5:20	5:53	6:26	6:57	7:26	7:36	7:17	6:34	5:45	4:59	4:36
2	4:47	5:21	5:54	6:27	6:58	7:27	7:36	7:16	6:33	5:43	4:58	4:36
3	4:48	5:22	5:55	6:28	6:59	7:27	7:36	7:15	6:31	5:41	4:57	4:36
4	4:49	5:24	5:57	6:29	7:00	7:28	7:36	7:14	6:30	5:40	4:56	4:36
5	4:50	5:25	5:58	6:30	7:01	7:29	7:35	7:13	6:28	5:38	4:55	4:35
6	4:50	5:26	5:59	6:31	7:02	7:29	7:35	7:11	6:26	5:37	4:53	4:35
7	4:51	5:27	6:00	6:32	7:03	7:30	7:35	7:10	6:25	5:35	4:52	4:35
8	4:52	5:29	6:01	6:34	7:04	7:30	7:35	7:09	6:23	5:33	4:51	4:35
9	4:53	5:30	6:02	6:35	7:05	7:31	7:34	7:08	6:21	5:32	4:50	4:35
10	4:54	5:31	6:03	6:36	7:06	7:32	7:34	7:06	6:20	5:30	4:49	4:35
11	4:56	5:32	6:04	6:37	7:07	7:32	7:33	7:05	6:18	5:29	4:48	4:35
12	4:57	5:33	6:05	6:38	7:08	7:33	7:33	7:04	6:16	5:27	4:48	4:36
13	4:58	5:35	6:06	6:39	7:09	7:33	7:32	7:03	6:15	5:26	4:47	4:36
14	4:59	5:36	6:07	6:40	7:10	7:33	7:32	7:01	6:13	5:24	4:46	4:36
15	5:00	5:37	6:09	6:41	7:11	7:34	7:31	7:00	6:11	5:22	4:45	4:36
16	5:01	5:38	6:10	6:42	7:12	7:34	7:31	6:58	6:10	5:21	4:44	4:37
17	5:02	5:39	6:11	6:43	7:13	7:35	7:30	6:57	6:08	5:19	4:43	4:37
18	5:03	5:41	6:12	6:44	7:14	7:35	7:29	6:56	6:06	5:18	4:43	4:37
19	5:04	5:42	6:13	6:45	7:15	7:35	7:29	6:54	6:05	5:17	4:42	4:38
20	5:06	5:43	6:14	6:46	7:16	7:35	7:28	6:53	6:03	5:15	4:41	4:38
21	5:07	5:44	6:15	6:47	7:17	7:36	7:27	6:51	6:01	5:14	4:41	4:39
22	5:08	5:45	6:16	6:48	7:18	7:36	7:26	6:50	6:00	5:12	4:40	4:39
23	5:09	5:46	6:17	6:49	7:19	7:36	7:26	6:48	5:58	5:11	4:39	4:40
24	5:10	5:48	6:18	6:50	7:19	7:36	7:25	6:47	5:56	5:09	4:39	4:40
25	5:11	5:49	6:19	6:51	7:20	7:36	7:24	6:45	5:55	5:08	4:38	4:41
26	5:13	5:50	6:20	6:52	7:21	7:36	7:23	6:44	5:53	5:07	4:38	4:41
27	5:14	5:51	6:21	6:53	7:22	7:36	7:22	6:42	5:51	5:05	4:37	4:42
28	5:15	5:52	6:22	6:54	7:23	7:36	7:21	6:41	5:50	5:04	4:37	4:43
29	5:16	5:53	6:23	6:55	7:24	7:36	7:20	6:39	5:48	5:03	4:37	4:43
30	5:18		6:24	6:56	7:24	7:36	7:19	6:38	5:46	5:02	4:36	4:44
31	5:19		6:25		7:25		7:18	6:36		5:00		4:45

ST. LOUIS, MISSOURI

DAY	JAN.	FEB.	MAR.	APR.	MAY	JUNE	JULY	AUG.	SEPT.	OCT.	NOV.	DEC.
1	4:32 P.M.	5:04	5:35	6:06	6:34	7:01	7:11	6:54	6:13	5:26	4:43	4:22
2	4:33	5:06	5:37	6:07	6:35	7:02	7:11	6:53	6:12	5:25	4:42	4:22
3	4:34	5:07	5:38	6:08	6:36	7:03	7:11	6:52	6:10	5:23	4:41	4:22
4	4:35	5:08	5:39	6:09	6:37	7:03	7:11	6:51	6:09	5:21	4:40	4:21
5	4:36	5:09	5:40	6:10	6:38	7:04	7:11	6:49	6:07	5:20	4:39	4:21
6	4:36	5:10	5:41	6:11	6:39	7:04	7:10	6:48	6:06	5:18	4:38	4:21
7	4:37	5:11	5:42	6:12	6:40	7:05	7:10	6:47	6:04	5:17	4:37	4:21
8	4:38	5:12	5:43	6:13	6:41	7:06	7:10	6:46	6:03	5:15	4:36	4:21
9	4:39	5:14	5:44	6:14	6:42	7:06	7:09	6:45	6:01	5:14	4:35	4:21
10	4:40	5:15	5:45	6:14	6:43	7:07	7:09	6:44	5:59	5:12	4:34	4:22
11	4:41	5:16	5:46	6:15	6:44	7:07	7:09	6:42	5:58	5:11	4:33	4:22
12	4:42	5:17	5:47	6:16	6:45	7:08	7:08	6:41	5:56	5:09	4:32	4:22
13	4:43	5:18	5:48	6:17	6:46	7:08	7:08	6:40	5:55	5:08	4:31	4:22
14	4:44	5:19	5:49	6:18	6:47	7:08	7:07	6:39	5:53	5:06	4:31	4:22
15	4:45	5:20	5:50	6:19	6:48	7:09	7:07	6:37	5:52	5:05	4:30	4:22
16	4:46	5:21	5:51	6:20	6:48	7:09	7:06	6:36	5:50	5:04	4:29	4:23
17	4:48	5:23	5:52	6:21	6:49	7:10	7:06	6:35	5:48	5:02	4:28	4:23
18	4:49	5:24	5:53	6:22	6:50	7:10	7:05	6:34	5:47	5:01	4:28	4:24
19	4:50	5:25	5:54	6:23	6:51	7:10	7:04	6:32	5:45	4:59	4:27	4:24
20	4:51	5:26	5:54	6:24	6:52	7:10	7:04	6:31	5:44	4:58	4:26	4:24
21	4:52	5:27	5:55	6:25	6:53	7:11	7:03	6:29	5:42	4:57	4:26	4:25
22	4:53	5:28	5:56	6:26	6:54	7:11	7:02	6:28	5:40	4:55	4:25	4:25
23	4:54	5:29	5:57	6:27	6:54	7:11	7:02	6:27	5:39	4:54	4:25	4:26
24	4:55	5:30	5:58	6:28	6:55	7:11	7:01	6:25	5:37	4:53	4:24	4:26
25	4:56	5:31	5:59	6:29	6:56	7:11	7:00	6:24	5:36	4:52	4:24	4:27
26	4:58	5:32	6:00	6:30	6:57	7:11	6:59	6:22	5:34	4:50	4:24	4:28
27	4:59	5:33	6:01	6:31	6:58	7:11	6:58	6:21	5:32	4:49	4:23	4:28
28	5:00	5:34	6:02	6:32	6:58	7:11	6:57	6:19	5:31	4:48	4:23	4:29
29	5:01	5:35	6:03	6:33	6:59	7:11	6:57	6:18	5:29	4:47	4:22	4:30
30	5:02		6:04	6:34	7:00	7:11	6:56	6:16	5:28	4:45	4:22	4:30
31	5:03		6:05		7:01		6:55	6:15		4:44		4:31

SAN FRANCISCO, CALIFORNIA

DAY	JAN.	FEB.	MAR.	APR.	MAY	JUNE	JULY	AUG.	SEPT.	OCT.	NOV.	DEC.
1	4:44 P.M.	5:15	5:45	6:14	6:42	7:08	7:17	7:01	6:21	5:35	4:53	4:33
2	4:44	5:16	5:46	6:15	6:43	7:08	7:17	7:00	6:20	5:34	4:52	4:33
3	4:45	5:17	5:47	6:16	6:44	7:09	7:17	6:59	6:18	5:32	4:51	4:33
4	4:46	5:18	5:48	6:17	6:45	7:10	7:17	6:57	6:17	5:31	4:50	4:33
5	4:47	5:20	5:49	6:18	6:46	7:10	7:17	6:56	6:15	5:29	4:49	4:33
6	4;48	5:21	5:50	6:19	6:46	7:11	7:17	6:55	6:14	5:28	4:48	4:33
7	4:49	5:22	5:51	6:20	6:47	7:11	7:16	6:54	6:12	5:26	4:47	4:33
8	4:50	5:23	5:52	6:21	6:48	7:12	7:16	6:53	6:11	5:25	4:46	4:33
9	4:51	5:24	5:53	6:22	6:49	7:12	7:16	6:52	6:09	5:23	4:45	4:33
10	4:52	5:25	5:54	6:23	6:50	7:13	7:15	6:51	6:08	5:22	4:44	4:33
11	4:52	5:26	5:55	6:23	6:51	7:13	7:15	6:50	6:06	5:20	4:44	4:33
12	4:53	5:27	5:56	6:24	6:52	7:14	7:15	6:48	6:05	5:19	4:43	4:33
13	4:54	5:28	5:57	6:25	6:53	7:14	7:14	6:47	6:03	5:17	4:42	4:33
14	4:55	5:29	5:58	6:26	6:54	7:15	7:14	6:46	6:01	5:16	4:41	4:34
15	4:57	5:31	5:59	6:27	6:54	7:15	7:13	6:45	6:00	5:15	4:41	4:34
16	4:58	5:32	6:00	6:28	6:55	7:15	7:13	6:43	5:58	5:13	4:40	4:34
17	4:59	5:33	6:01	6:29	6:56	7:16	7:12	6:42	5:57	5:12	4:39	4:34
18	5:00	5:34	6:02	6:30	6:57	7:16	7:12	6:41	5:55	5:10	4:38	4:35
19	5:01	5:35	6:02	6:31	6:58	7:16	7:11	6:40	5:54	5:09	4:38	4:35
20	5:02	5:36	6:03	6:32	6:59	7:17	7:10	6:38	5:52	5:08	4:37	4:36
21	5:03	5:37	6:04	6:33	6:59	7:17	7:10	6:37	5:51	5:06	4:37	4:36
22	5:04	5:38	6:05	6:34	7:00	7:17	7:09	6:36	5:49	5:05	4:36	4:37
23	5:05	5:39	6:06	6:34	7:01	7:17	7:08	6:34	5:47	5:04	4:36	4:37
24	5:06	5:40	6:07	6:35	7:02	7:17	7:07	6:33	5:46	5:03	4:35	4:38
25	5:07	5:41	6:08	6:36	7:03	7:17	7:07	6:31	5:44	5:01	4:35	4:38
26	5:08	5:42	6:09	6:37	7:03	7:18	7:06	6:30	5:43	5:00	4:34	4:39
27	5:10	5:43	6:10	6:38	7:04	7:18	7:05	6:29	5:41	4:59	4:34	4:40
28	5:11	5:44	6:11	6:39	7:05	7:18	7:04	6:27	5:40	4:58	4:34	4:40
29	5:12	5:45	6:12	6:40	7:06	7:18	7:03	6:26	5:38	4:57	4:34	4:41
30	5:13		6:13	6:41	7:06	7:18	7:02	6:24	5:37	4:56	4:33	4:42
31	5:14		6:13		7:07		7:01	6:23		4:54		4:43

WASHINGTON, DISTRICT OF COLUMBIA

DAY	JAN.	FEB.	MAR.	APR.	MAY	JUNE	JULY	AUG.	SEPT.	OCT.	NOV.	DEC.
1	4:39 P.M.	5:11	5:43	6:13	6:42	7:09	7:19	7:01	6:21	5:33	4:50	4:29
2	4:40	5:13	5:44	6:14	6:43	7:10	7:19	7:00	6:19	5:32	4:49	4:29
3	4:41	5:14	5:45	6:15	6:44	7:11	7:19	6:59	6:18	5:30	4:48	4:28
4	4:41	5:15	5:46	6:16	6:45	7:11	7:19	6:58	6:16	5:29	4:47	4:28
5	4:42	5:16	5:47	6:17	6:46	7:12	7:19	6:57	6:15	5:27	4:46	4:28
6	4:43	5:17	5:48	6:18	6:47	7:12	7:18	6:56	6:13	5:26	4:45	4:28
7	4:44	5:18	5:49	6:19	6:48	7:13	7:18	6:55	6:12	5:24	4:44	4:28
8	4:45	5:19	5:50	6:20	6:49	7:14	7:18	6:54	6:10	5:22	4:43	4:28
9	4:46	5:21	5:51	6:21	6:50	7:14	7:17	6:53	6:08	5:21	4:42	4:28
10	4:47	5:22	5:52	6:22	6:51	7:15	7:17	6:51	6:07	5:19	4:41	4:28
11	4:48	5:23	5:53	6:23	6:52	7:15	7:17	6:50	6:05	5:18	4:40	4:28
12	4:49	5:24	5:54	6:24	6:53	7:16	7:16	6:49	6:04	5:17	4:39	4:29
13	4:50	5:25	5:55	6:25	6:54	7:16	7:16	6:48	6:02	5:15	4:38	4:29
14	4:51	5:26	5:56	6:26	6:54	7:16	7:15	6:46	6:00	5:14	4:27	4:29
15	4:52	5:27	5:57	6:27	6:55	7:17	7:15	6:45	5:59	5:12	4:37	4:29
16	4:53	5:29	5:58	6:28	6:56	7:17	7:14	6:44	5:57	5:11	4:36	4:30
17	4:54	5:30	5:59	6:29	6:57	7:18	7:14	6:42	5:56	5:09	4:35	4:30
18	4:55	5:31	6:00	6:30	6:58	7:18	7:13	6:41	5:54	5:08	4:35	4:30
19	4:57	5:32	6:01	6:31	6:59	7:18	7:12	6:40	5:52	5:06	4:34	4:31
20	4:58	5:33	6:02	6:32	7:00	7:18	7:12	6:38	5:51	5:05	4:33	4:31
21	4:59	5:34	6:03	6:33	7:01	7:19	7:11	6:37	5:49	5:04	4:33	4:32
22	5:00	5:35	6:04	6:34	7:02	7:19	7:10	6:36	5:48	5:02	4:32	4:32
23	5:01	5:36	6:05	6:35	7:02	7:19	7:09	6:34	5:46	5:01	4:32	4:33
24	5:02	5:37	6:06	6:36	7:03	7:19	7:09	6:33	5:44	5:00	4:31	4:33
25	5:03	5:38	6:07	6:36	7:04	7:19	7:08	6:31	5:43	4:59	4:31	4:34
26	5:04	5:39	6:08	6:37	7:05	7:19	7:07	6:30	5:41	4:57	4:30	4:34
27	5:06	5:41	6:09	6:38	7:06	7:19	7:06	6:28	5:40	4:56	4:30	4:35
28	5:07	5:42	6:10	6:39	7:06	7:19	7:05	6:27	5:38	4:55	4:30	4:36
29	5:08	5:43	6:11	6:40	7:07	7:19	7:04	6:25	5:36	4:54	4:29	4:36
30	5:09		6:12	6:41	7:08	7:19	7:03	6:24	5:35	4:52	4:29	4:37
31	5:10		6:12		7:09		7:02	6:22		4:51		4:38

ARGENTINA, BUENOS AIRES

Jan.	1	6:52		17	5:52		31	4:33		14	5:04		28	6:01
	4	6:52		20	5:48	Jun.	3	4:32		17	5:06		31	6:03
	7	6:52		23	5:44		6	4:32		20	5:08	Nov.	3	6:06
	10	6:52		26	5:40		9	4:31		23	5:10		6	6:09
	13	6:52		29	5:35		12	4:31		26	5:12		9	6:12
	16	6:51	Apr.	1	5:31		15	4:31		29	5:14		12	6:15
	19	6:50		3	5:27		18	4:32	Sep.	1	5:17		15	6:18
	22	6:49		7	5:23		21	4:32		4	5:19		18	6:21
	25	6:47		10	5:19		24	4:33		7	5:21		21	6:24
	28	6:46		13	5:15		27	4:34		10	5:23		24	6:27
	31	6:43		16	5:12		30	4:35		13	5:25		27	6:29
Feb.	3	6:41		19	5:08	Jul.	3	4:36		16	5:27		30	6:32
	6	6:39		22	5:04		6	4:38		19	5:29	Dec.	3	6:35
	9	6:36		25	5:01		9	4:39		22	5:31		6	6:37
	12	6:33		28	4:57		12	4:41		25	5:34		9	6:40
	15	6:30	May	1	4:54		15	4:43		28	5:36		12	6:42
	18	6:27		4	4:51		18	4:45	Oct.	1	5:38		15	6:44
	21	6:23		7	4:49		21	4:47		4	5:40		18	6:46
	24	6:20		10	4:46		24	4:49		7	5:43		21	6:48
	27	6:16		13	4:43		27	4:51		10	5:45		24	6:49
Mar.	2	6:12		16	4:41		30	4:53		13	5:47		27	6:50
	5	6:08		19	4:39	Aug.	2	4:55		16	5:50		30	6:51
	8	6:04		22	4:37		5	4:57		19	5:53			
	11	6:00		25	4:36		8	4:59		22	5:55			
	14	5:56		28	4:34		11	5:01		25	5:58			

AUSTRALIA, MELBOURNE

Jan.	1	7:28		17	6:20		31	4:52		11	5:23		22	6:26
	4	7:28		20	6:15	Jun.	3	4:51		14	5:26		25	6:29
	7	7:28		23	6:11		6	4:50		17	5:28		28	6:32
	13	7:27		26	6:06		9	4:50		20	5:31		31	6:35
	16	7:26		29	6:02		12	4:50		23	5:33	Nov.	3	6:39
	19	7:25	Apr.	1	5:57		15	4:50		26	5:36		6	6:42
	22	7:23		4	5:52		18	4:50		29	5:38		9	6:45
	25	7:22		10	5:44		21	4:50	Sep.	1	5:41		12	6:48
	28	7:19		13	5:39		24	4:51		4	5:43		15	6:52
	31	7:17		16	5:35		27	4:52		7	5:46		18	6:55
Feb.	3	7:14		19	5:31		30	4:53		10	5:48		21	6:58
	6	7:12		22	5:27	Jul.	3	4:55		13	5:51		24	7:01
	9	7:08		25	5:23		6	4:56		16	5:53		27	7:05
	12	7:05		28	5:20		9	4:58		19	5:56		30	7:08
	15	7:02	May	1	5:16		12	5:00		22	5:58	Dec.	3	7:10
	18	6:58		4	5:13		15	5:02		25	6:00		6	7:13
	21	6:54		7	5:10		18	5:05		28	6:04		9	7:16
	24	6:50		10	5:07		21	5:06	Oct.	1	6:06		12	7:18
	27	6:46		13	5:04		24	5:08		4	6:09		15	7:20
Mar.	2	6:42		16	5:01		27	5:11		7	6:12		18	7:22
	5	6:38		19	4:59		30	5:13		10	6:14		21	7:24
	8	6:33		22	4:57	Aug.	2	5:16		13	6:17		24	7:26
	11	6:29		25	4:55		5	5:18		16	6:20		27	7:27
	14	6:24		28	4:54		8	5:21		19	6:23		30	7:28

BRAZIL, RIO DE JANEIRO

Jan.	1	6:26		17	5:52		31	5:00		14	5:20		28	5:47
	4	6:27		20	5:48	Jun.	3	4:59		17	5:22		31	5:48
	7	6:27		23	5:46		6	4:59		20	5:23	Nov.	3	5:50
	10	6:28		26	5:43		9	4:59		23	5:24		6	5:52
	13	6:28		29	5:40		12	4:59		25	5:25		9	5:53
	16	6:28	Apr.	1	5:37		15	5:00		29	5:26		12	5:56
	19	6:27		4	5:34		18	5:00	Sep.	1	5:26		15	5:58
	22	6:27		7	5:32		21	5:01		4	5:27		18	6:00
	25	6:27		10	5:29		24	5:02		7	5:28		21	6:01
	28	6:26		13	5:26		27	5:02		10	5:29		24	6:04
	31	6:25		16	5:24		30	5:03		13	5:31		27	6:05
Feb.	3	6:23		19	5:21	Jul.	3	5:04		16	5:31		30	6:08
	6	6:22		22	5:18		6	5:05		19	5:32	Dec.	3	6:10
	9	6:21		25	5:17		9	5:06		22	5:33		6	6:12
	12	6:19		28	5:14		12	5:07		25	5:33		9	6:14
	15	6:17	May	1	5:12		15	5:08		28	5:35		12	6:16
	18	6:15		4	5:10		18	5:10	Oct.	1	5:35		15	6:18
	21	6:13		7	5:08		21	5:11		4	5:37		18	6:19
	24	6:11		10	5:07		24	5:12		7	5:38		21	6:21
	27	6:07		13	5:05		27	5:14		10	5:39		24	6:22
Mar.	2	6:05		16	5:05		30	5:15		13	5:40		27	6:24
	5	6:02		19	5:02	Aug.	2	5:17		16	5:41		30	6:25
	8	6:00		22	5:02		5	5:17		19	5:43			
	11	5:57		25	5:01		8	5:19		22	5:44			
	14	5:55		28	5:01		11	5:20		25	5:46			

BRAZIL, SAO PAULO

Jan.	1	6:39		17	6:03		31	5:09		14	5:30		28	5:59
	4	6:40		20	5:59	Jun.	3	5:08		17	5:32		31	6:01
	7	6:40		23	5:57		6	5:08		20	5:33	Nov.	3	6:03
	10	6:41		26	5:54		9	5:08		23	5:34		6	6:05
	13	6:41		29	5:51		12	5:08		26	5:35		9	6:06
	16	6:41	Apr.	1	5:48		15	5:09		29	5:36		12	6:09
	19	6:40		4	5:45		18	5:09	Sep.	1	5:37		15	6:10
	22	6:40		7	5:42		21	5:10		4	5:38		18	6:13
	25	6:39		10	5:39		24	5:11		7	5:39		21	6:14
	28	6:39		13	5:36		27	5:11		10	5:40		24	6:17
	31	6:37		16	5:34		30	5:12		13	5:41		27	6:18
Feb.	3	6:36		19	5:31	Jul.	3	5:13		16	5:42		30	6:21
	6	6:35		22	5:28		6	5:14		19	5:43	Dec.	3	6:23
	9	6:33		25	5:26		9	5:15		22	5:44		6	6:25
	12	6:31		28	5:24		12	5:16		25	5:44		9	6:27
	15	6:29	May	1	5:22		15	5:18		28	5:46		12	6:29
	18	6:27		4	5:19		18	5:19	Oct.	1	5:46		15	6:31
	21	6:24		7	5:18		21	5:21		4	5:48		18	6:33
	24	6:23		10	5:16		24	5:22		7	5:49		21	6:34
	27	6:19		13	5:15		27	5:23		10	5:51		24	6:35
Mar.	2	6:17		16	5:14		30	5:24		13	5:52		27	6:37
	5	6:14		19	5:12	Aug.	2	5:26		16	5:53		30	6:39
	8	6:11		22	5:11		5	5:27		19	5:55			
	11	6:09		25	5:10		8	5:28		22	5:56			
	14	6:06		28	5:10		11	5:30		25	5:58			

CANADA, MONTREAL

Jan.	1	4:04		17	5:45		31	7:17		14	6:48		28	4:31
	4	4:07		20	5:49	Jun.	3	7:19		17	6:43		31	4:27
	7	4:10		23	5:52		6	7:22		20	6:38	Nov.	3	4:23
	10	4:13		26	5:56		9	7:24		23	6:33		6	4:18
	13	4:17		29	6:00		12	7:26		26	6:27		9	4:15
	16	4:21	Apr.	1	6:04		15	7:27		29	6:22		12	4:11
	19	4:24		4	6:08		18	7:28	Sep.	1	6:16		15	4:08
	22	4:29		7	6:12		21	7:29		4	6:11		18	4:05
	25	4:33		10	6:16		24	7:30		7	6:05		21	4:02
	28	4:37		13	6:20		27	7:30		10	6:00		24	4:00
	31	4:41		16	6:24		30	7:30		13	5:54		27	3:58
Feb.	3	4:46		19	6:27	Jul.	3	7:29		16	5:48		30	3:56
	6	4:50		22	6:31		6	7:28		19	5:42	Dec.	3	3:55
	9	4:54		25	6:35		9	7:27		22	5:36		6	3:54
	12	4:59		28	6:39		12	7:25		25	5:31		9	3:54
	15	5:03	May	1	6:43		15	7:23		28	5:25		12	3:54
	18	5:07		4	6:47		18	7:21	Oct.	1	5:19		15	3:54
	21	5:12		7	6:50		21	7:18		4	5:13		18	3:55
	24	5:16		10	6:54		24	7:16		7	5:08		21	3:56
	27	5:20		13	6:58		27	7:12		10	5:02		24	3:58
Mar.	2	5:24		16	7:01		30	7:09		13	4:57		27	4:00
	5	5:28		19	7:05	Aug.	2	7:05		16	4:51		30	4:02
	8	5:33		22	7:08		5	7:01		19	4:46			
	11	5:37		25	7:11		8	6:57		22	4:41			
	14	5:41		28	7:14		11	6:52		25	4:36			

CANADA, TORONTO

Jan.	1	4:34		17	6:08		31	7:33		14	7:06		28	4:58
	4	4:36		20	6:11	Jun.	3	7:35		17	7:02		31	4:54
	7	4:39		23	6:15		6	7:38		20	6:57	Nov.	3	4:50
	10	4:43		26	6:19		9	7:40		23	6:52		6	4:46
	13	4:46		29	6:22		12	7:41		26	6:47		9	4:42
	16	4:50	Apr.	1	6:26		15	7:43		29	6:42		12	4:39
	19	4:53		4	6:29		18	7:44	Sep.	1	6:37		15	4:36
	22	4:57		7	6:33		21	7:45		4	6:32		18	4:33
	25	5:01		10	6:37		24	7:45		7	6:26		21	4:31
	28	5:05		13	6:40		27	7:46		10	6:21		24	4:29
	31	5:09		16	6:44		30	7:45		13	6:16		27	4:27
Feb.	3	5:13		19	6:47	Jul.	3	7:45		16	6:10		30	4:25
	6	5:17		22	6:51		6	7:44		19	6:05	Dec.	3	4:24
	9	5:21		25	6:54		9	7:43		22	5:59		6	4:24
	12	5:25		28	6:58		12	7:42		25	5:54		9	4:23
	15	5:29	May	1	7:01		15	7:40		28	5:48		12	4:23
	18	5:33		4	7:05		18	7:38	Oct.	1	5:43		15	4:24
	21	5:37		7	7:08		21	7:35		4	5:37		18	4:25
	24	5:41		10	7:12		24	7:32		7	5:32		21	4:26
	27	5:45		13	7:15		27	7:30		10	5:27		24	4:28
Mar.	2	5:49		16	7:18		30	7:26		13	5:22		27	4:30
	5	5:53		19	7:22	Aug.	2	7:23		16	5:17		30	4:32
	8	5:57		22	7:25		5	7:19		19	5:12			
	11	6:00		25	7:28		8	7:15		22	5:07			
	14	6:04		28	7:30		11	7:11		25	5:02			

CANADA, VANCOUVER (B.C.)

Jan. 1	4:07	17	6:01	31	7:48	14	7:13	28	4:42
4	4:10	20	6:06	Jun. 3	7:51	17	7:08	31	4:36
7	4:13	23	6:10	6	7:54	20	7:02	Nov. 3	4:31
10	4:17	26	6:15	9	7:56	23	6:56	6	4:27
13	4:21	29	6:19	12	7:58	26	6:51	9	4:22
16	4:25	Apr. 1	6:24	15	8:00	29	6:44	12	4:18
19	4:30	4	6:28	18	8:01	Sep. 1	6:38	15	4:14
22	4:34	7	6:33	21	8:02	4	6:32	18	4:11
25	4:39	10	6:37	24	8:02	7	6:26	21	4:08
28	4:44	13	6:42	27	8:02	10	6:20	24	4:05
31	4:49	16	6:46	30	8:02	13	6:13	27	4:02
Feb. 3	4:54	19	6:51	Jul. 3	8:01	16	6:07	30	4:00
6	4:59	22	6:55	6	8:06	19	6:00	Dec. 3	3:59
9	5:04	25	7:00	9	7:59	22	5:54	6	3:58
12	5:08	28	7:04	12	7:57	25	5:47	9	3:57
15	5:13	May 1	7:09	15	7:54	28	5:41	12	3:57
18	5:18	4	7:13	18	7:52	Oct. 1	5:35	15	3:57
21	5:23	7	7:17	21	7:48	4	5:28	18	3:58
24	5:28	10	7:22	24	7:45	7	5:22	21	3:59
27	5:33	13	7:26	27	7:41	10	5:16	24	4:00
Mar. 2	5:38	16	7:30	30	7:37	13	5:10	27	4:02
5	5:43	19	7:23	Aug. 2	7:33	16	5:04	30	4:05
8	5:47	22	7:38	5	7:28	19	4:58		
11	5:52	25	7:41	8	7:24	22	4:52		
14	5:57	28	7:45	11	7:18	25	4:47		

CANADA, WINNIPEG, MANITOBA

Jan. 1	4:19	17	6:18	31	8:10	14	7:33	28	4:56
4	4:23	20	6:23	Jun. 3	8:13	17	7:27	31	4:51
7	4:26	23	6:28	6	8:15	20	7:21	Nov. 3	4:46
10	4:30	26	6:32	9	8:18	23	7:16	6	4:41
13	4:34	29	6:37	12	8:20	26	7:09	9	4:36
16	4:38	Apr. 1	6:42	15	8:22	29	7:03	12	4:32
19	4:43	4	6:46	18	8:23	Sep. 1	6:57	15	4:28
22	4:48	7	6:51	21	8:24	4	6:51	18	4:24
25	4:53	10	6:56	24	8:24	7	6:44	21	4:21
28	4:57	13	7:01	27	8:24	10	6:38	24	4:18
31	5:03	16	7:05	30	8:24	13	6:31	27	4:15
Feb. 3	5:08	19	7:10	Jul. 3	8:23	16	6:24	30	4:13
6	5:13	22	7:15	6	8:22	19	6:18	Dec. 3	4:12
9	5:18	25	7:19	9	8:20	22	6:11	6	4:10
12	5:23	28	7:24	12	8:18	25	6:04	9	4:10
15	5:28	May 1	7:29	15	8:16	28	5:58	12	4:09
18	5:33	4	7:33	18	8:13	Oct. 1	5:51	15	4:09
21	5:39	7	7:38	21	8:10	4	5:45	18	4:10
24	5:44	10	7:42	24	8:06	7	5:38	21	4:11
27	5:49	13	7:46	27	8:12	10	5:32	24	4:13
Mar. 2	5:53	16	7:51	30	7:58	13	5:26	27	4:15
5	5:59	19	7:55	Aug. 2	7:53	16	5:20	30	4:17
8	6:04	22	7:59	5	7:49	19	5:14		
11	6:08	25	8:03	8	7:44	22	5:08		
14	6:13	28	8:06	11	7:38	25	5:02		

ENGLAND, LONDON

Jan.	1	3:43		17	5:49		31	7:48		14	7:08		28	4:24
	4	3:47		20	5:54	Jun.	3	7:51		17	7:02		31	4:18
	7	3:50		23	5:59		6	7:54		20	6:56	Nov.	3	4:13
	10	3:54		26	6:04		9	7:57		23	6:50		6	4:08
	13	3:59		29	6:09		12	7:59		26	6:43		9	4:03
	16	4:03	Apr.	1	6:14		15	8:01		29	6:37		12	3:58
	19	4:08		4	6:19		18	8:02	Sep.	1	6:30		15	3:54
	22	4:13		7	6:24		21	8:03		4	6:24		18	3:50
	25	4:18		10	6:29		24	8:03		7	6:17		21	3:46
	28	4:23		13	6:34		27	8:03		10	6:10		24	3:43
	31	4:29		16	6:39		30	8:03		13	6:03		27	3:40
Feb.	3	4:34		19	6:44	Jul.	3	8:02		16	5:56		30	3:38
	6	4:40		22	6:49		6	8:01		19	5:49	Dec.	3	3:36
	9	4:45		25	6:54		9	7:59		22	5:42		6	3:35
	12	4:51		28	6:59		12	7:57		25	5:35		9	3:34
	15	4:56	May	1	7:04		15	7:54		28	5:29		12	3:33
	18	5:01		4	7:09		18	7:51	Oct.	1	5:22		15	3:33
	21	5:07		7	7:14		21	7:47		4	5:15		18	3:34
	24	5:12		10	7:18		24	7:43		7	5:08		21	3:35
	27	5:18		13	7:23		27	7:39		10	5:01		24	3:37
Mar.	2	5:23		16	7:28		30	7:35		13	4:55		27	3:39
	5	5:28		19	7:32	Aug.	2	7:30		16	4:48		30	3:41
	8	5:33		22	7:36		5	7:25		19	4:42			
	11	5:39		25	7:40		8	7:20		22	4:36			
	14	5:44		28	7:44		11	7:14		25	4:30			

FRANCE, PARIS

Jan.	1	4:47		17	6:40		31	8:26		14	7:52		28	5:21
	4	4:50		20	6:45	Jun.	3	8:29		17	7:46		31	5:16
	7	4:53		23	6:49		6	8:32		20	7:41	Nov.	3	5:11
	10	4:57		26	6:54		9	8:34		23	7:35		6	5:06
	13	5:01		29	6:58		12	8:36		26	7:29		9	5:02
	16	5:05	Apr.	1	7:03		15	8:38		29	7:23		12	4:58
	19	5:09		4	7:07		18	8:39	Sep.	1	7:17		15	4:54
	22	5:14		7	7:12		21	8:40		4	7:11		18	4:50
	25	5:19		10	7:16		24	8:40		7	7:05		21	4:47
	28	5:23		13	7:21		27	8:40		10	6:58		24	4:45
	31	5:28		16	7:25		30	8:40		13	6:52		27	4:42
Feb.	3	5:33		19	7:29	Jul.	3	8:39		16	6:46		30	4:40
	6	5:38		22	7:34		6	8:38		18	6:39	Dec.	3	4:39
	9	5:43		25	7:38		9	8:37		22	6:33		6	4:37
	12	5:48		28	7:43		12	8:35		25	6:26		9	4:37
	15	5:53	May	1	7:47		15	8:32		28	6:20		12	4:37
	18	5:58		4	7:51		18	8:30	Oct.	1	6:14		15	4:37
	21	6:03		7	7:56		21	8:27		4	6:08		18	4:38
	24	6:07		10	8:00		24	8:23		7	6:01		21	4:39
	27	6:12		13	8:04		27	8:20		10	5:55		24	4:40
Mar.	2	6:17		16	8:08		30	8:16		13	5:49		27	4:42
	5	6:22		19	8:12	Aug.	2	8:11		16	5:43		30	4:45
	8	6:26		22	8:16		5	8:07		19	5:37			
	11	6:31		25	8:20		8	8:02		22	5:32			
	14	6:36		28	8:23		11	7:57		25	5:26			

HOLLAND, AMSTERDAM

Jan. 1	4:19	17	6:29	31	8:33	14	7:51	28	5:02
4	4:23	20	6:35	Jun. 3	8:36	17	7:45	31	4:56
7	4:26	23	6:40	6	8:39	20	7:39	Nov. 3	4:51
10	4:31	26	6:45	9	8:42	23	7:33	6	4:45
13	4:35	29	6:50	12	8:44	26	7:26	9	4:40
16	4:40	Apr. 1	6:55	15	8:46	29	7:19	12	4:36
19	4:45	4	7:01	18	8:48	Sep. 1	7:12	15	4:31
22	4:50	7	7:06	21	8:49	4	7:05	18	4:27
25	4:55	10	7:11	24	8:49	7	6:59	21	4:23
28	5:01	13	7:16	27	8:49	10	6:51	24	4:20
31	5:06	16	7:21	30	8:49	13	6:44	27	4:17
Feb. 3	5:12	19	7:27	Jul. 3	8:48	16	6:37	30	4:14
6	5:17	22	7:32	6	8:46	19	6:30	Dec. 3	4:12
9	5:23	25	7:37	9	8:44	22	6:23	6	4:11
12	5:29	28	7:42	12	8:42	25	6:16	9	4:10
15	5:34	May 1	7:47	15	8:39	28	6:09	12	4:09
18	5:40	4	7:52	18	8:36	Oct. 1	6:02	15	4:09
21	5:46	7	7:57	21	8:32	4	5:55	18	4:10
24	5:51	10	8:02	24	8:28	7	5:48	21	4:11
27	5:57	13	8:07	27	8:24	10	5:41	24	4:12
Mar. 2	6:02	16	8:12	30	8:19	13	5:34	27	4:14
5	6:08	19	8:17	Aug. 2	8:14	16	5:28	30	4:17
8	6:13	22	8:21	5	8:09	19	5:21		
11	6:19	25	8:25	8	8:03	22	5:15		
14	6:24	28	8:29	11	7:57	25	5:08		

ISRAEL, BE'ER SHEVA'

Jan. 1	4:32	17	5:33	31	6:22	14	6:08	28	4:39
4	4:34	20	5:35	Jun. 3	6:24	17	6:05	31	4:36
7	4:36	23	5:37	6	6:25	20	6:02	Nov. 3	4:34
10	4:39	26	5:39	9	6:27	23	5:59	6	4:32
13	4:41	29	5:40	12	6:28	26	5:55	9	4:29
16	4:44	Apr. 1	5:42	15	6:29	29	5:52	12	4:29
19	4:46	4	5:44	18	6:30	Sep. 1	5:48	15	4:26
22	4:49	7	5:46	21	6:31	4	5:44	18	4:24
25	4:52	10	5:48	24	6:31	7	5:41	21	4:23
28	4:55	13	5:50	27	6:32	10	5:37	24	4:22
31	4:57	16	5:52	30	6:32	13	5:33	27	4:21
Feb. 3	5:00	19	5:54	Jul. 3	6:32	16	5:29	30	4:21
6	5:03	22	5:56	6	6:31	19	5:25	Dec. 3	4:21
9	5:05	25	5:58	9	6:31	22	5:21	6	4:21
12	5:08	28	6:00	12	6:30	25	5:17	9	4:21
15	5:10	May 1	6:02	15	6:29	28	5:14	12	4:22
18	5:13	4	6:04	18	6:28	Oct. 1	5:10	15	4:23
21	5:15	7	6:06	21	6:27	4	5:06	18	4:24
24	5:18	10	6:08	24	6:25	7	5:02	21	4:25
27	5:20	13	6:10	27	6:23	10	4:59	24	4:26
Mar. 2	5:22	16	6:13	30	6:21	13	4:55	27	4:28
5	5:24	19	6:14	Aug. 2	6:19	16	4:52	30	4:30
8	5:26	22	6:16	5	6:17	19	4:48		
11	5:28	25	6:18	8	6:14	22	4:45		
14	5:31	28	6:20	11	6:11	25	4:42		

ISRAEL, HAIFA

Jan.	1	4:27		17	5:31		31	6:24		14	6:09		28	4:36
	4	4:29		20	5:33	Jun.	3	6:26		17	6:06		31	4:33
	7	4:31		23	5:35		6	6:27		20	6:03	Nov.	3	4:30
	10	4:34		26	5:37		9	6:29		23	5:59		6	4:28
	13	4:36		29	5:40		12	6:30		26	5:55		9	4:25
	16	4:39	Apr.	1	5:42		15	6:31		29	5:52		12	4:23
	19	4:42		4	5:44		18	6:32	Sep.	1	5:48		15	4:21
	22	4:45		7	5:46		21	6:33		4	5:44		18	4:20
	25	4:47		10	5:48		24	6:34		7	5:40		21	4:18
	28	4:50		13	5:50		27	6:34		10	5:36		24	4:17
	31	4:53		16	5:52		30	6:34		13	5:32		27	4:16
Feb.	3	4:56		19	5:54	Jul.	3	6:34		16	5:28		30	4:16
	6	4:59		22	5:57		6	6:34		19	5:24	Dec.	3	4:16
	9	5:02		25	5:59		9	6:33		22	5:20		6	4:16
	12	5:04		28	6:01		12	6:32		25	5:16		9	4:16
	15	5:07	May	1	6:03		15	6:31		28	5:12		12	4:16
	18	5:10		4	6:05		18	6:30	Oct.	1	5:08		15	4:17
	21	5:12		7	6:08		21	6:29		4	5:04		18	4:18
	24	5:15		10	6:10		24	6:27		7	5:00		21	4:20
	27	5:17		13	6:12		27	6:25		10	4:56		24	4:21
Mar.	2	5:20		16	6:14		30	6:23		13	4:53		27	4:23
	5	5:22		19	6:16	Aug.	2	6:20		16	4:49		30	4:25
	8	5:24		22	6:18		5	6:18		19	4:45			
	11	5:26		25	6:20		8	6:15		22	4:42			
	14	5:29		28	6:22		11	6:12		24	4:39			

ISRAEL, JERUSALEM

Jan.	1	4:28		17	5:30		31	6:21		14	6:07		28	4:36
	4	4:30		20	5:32	Jun.	3	6:22		17	6:03		31	4:33
	7	4:32		23	5:34		6	6:24		20	6:00	Nov.	3	4:31
	10	4:35		26	5:36		9	6:25		23	5:57		6	4:28
	13	4:38		29	5:38		12	6:27		26	5:53		8	4:26
	16	4:40	Apr.	1	5:40		15	6:28		29	5:50		12	4:24
	19	4:43		4	5:42		18	6:29	Sep.	1	5:46		15	4:22
	22	4:46		7	5:44		21	6:30		4	5:42		18	4:21
	25	4:48		10	5:46		24	6:30		7	5:39		21	4:19
	28	4:51		13	5:48		27	6:30		10	5:35		24	4:18
	31	4:54		16	5:50		30	6:31		13	5:31		27	4:18
Feb.	3	4:57		19	5:52	Jul.	3	6:31		16	5:27		30	4:17
	6	4:59		22	5:54		6	6:30		19	5:23	Dec.	3	4:17
	9	5:02		25	5:56		9	6:30		22	5:19		6	4:17
	12	5:05		28	5:59		12	6:29		25	5:15		9	4:17
	15	5:07	May	1	6:01		15	6:28		28	5:11		12	4:18
	18	5:10		4	6:03		18	6:27	Oct.	1	5:07		15	4:19
	21	5:12		7	6:05		21	6:25		4	5:03		18	4:20
	24	5:15		10	6:07		24	6:24		7	5:00		21	4:21
	27	5:17		13	6:09		27	6:22		10	4:56		24	4:23
Mar.	2	5:19		15	6:11		30	6:20		13	4:52		27	4:24
	5	5:21		19	6:13	Aug.	2	6:18		16	4:49		30	4:26
	8	5:24		22	6:15		5	6:15		19	4:45			
	11	5:26		25	6:17		8	6:12		22	4:42			
	14	5:28		28	6:19		11	6:10		25	4:39			

ISRAEL, TEL AVIV

Jan.	1	4:29		17	5:32		31	6:23		14	6:09		28	4:38
	4	4:31		20	5:34	Jun.	3	6:25		17	6:06		31	4:35
	7	4:34		23	5:36		6	6:27		20	6:03	Nov.	3	4:32
	10	4:36		26	5:38		9	6:28		23	5:59		6	4:30
	13	4:39		29	5:40		12	6:29		26	5:56		9	4:27
	16	4:42	Apr.	1	5:42		15	6:31		29	5:52		12	4:25
	19	4:44		4	5:44		18	6:32	Sep.	1	5:48		15	4:24
	22	4:47		7	5:46		21	6:32		4	5:45		18	4:22
	25	4:50		10	5:48		24	6:33		7	5:41		21	4:21
	28	4:53		13	5:50		27	6:33		10	5:37		24	4:20
	31	4:55		16	5:53		30	6:33		13	5:33		27	4:19
Feb.	3	4:58		19	5:55	Jul.	3	6:33		16	5:29		30	4:18
	6	5:01		22	5:57		6	6:33		19	5:25	Dec.	3	4:18
	9	5:04		25	5:59		9	6:32		22	5:21		6	4:18
	12	5:06		28	6:01		12	6:32		25	5:17		9	4:19
	15	5:09	May	1	6:03		15	6:31		28	5:13		12	4:19
	18	5:11		4	6:05		18	6:29	Oct.	1	5:09		15	4:20
	21	5:14		7	6:07		21	6:28		4	5:05		18	4:21
	24	5:16		10	6:10		24	6:26		7	5:01		21	4:22
	27	5:19		13	6:12		27	6:24		10	4:58		24	4:24
Mar.	2	5:21		16	6:14		30	6:22		13	4:54		27	4:26
	5	5:23		19	6:16	Aug.	2	6:20		16	4:50		30	4:28
	8	5:26		22	6:18		5	6:18		19	4:47			
	11	5:28		25	6:20		8	6:15		22	4:44			
	14	5:30		28	6:22		11	6:12		25	4:41			

ITALY, ROME

Jan.	1	4:31		17	6:00		31	7:19		17	6:51		31	4:49
	4	4:34		20	6:03	Jun.	3	7:22		20	6:46	Nov.	3	4:45
	7	4:37		23	6:07		6	7:24		23	6:42		6	4:41
	10	4:40		26	6:10		9	7:26		26	6:37		9	4:38
	13	4:43		29	6:13		12	7:26		29	6:32		12	4:35
	16	4:47	Apr.	1	6:17		15	7:29	Sep.	1	6:27		15	4:32
	19	4:50		4	6:20		18	7:30		4	6:22		18	4:30
	22	4:54		7	6:23		21	7:31		7	6:17		21	4:27
	25	4:57		10	6:27		24	7:31		10	6:12		24	4:25
	28	5:01		13	6:30		30	7:31		13	6:07		27	4:24
	31	5:05		16	6:33	Jul.	3	7:31		16	6:01		30	4:23
Feb.	3	5:09		19	6:37		6	7:30		19	5:56	Dec.	3	4:22
	6	5:13		22	6:40		9	7:29		22	5:51		6	4:21
	9	5:17		25	6:43		12	7:28		25	5:46		9	4:21
	12	5:20		28	6:46		15	7:26		28	5:40		12	4:21
	15	5:24	May	1	6:50		18	7:24	Oct.	1	5:35		15	4:22
	18	5:28		4	6:53		21	7:21		4	5:30		18	4:23
	21	5:32		7	6:56		24	7:19		7	5:25		21	4:24
	24	5:35		10	6:59		27	7:17		10	5:20		24	4:25
	27	5:39		13	7:03		30	7:14		13	5:15		27	4:27
Mar.	2	5:43		16	7:06	Aug.	2	7:10		16	5:10		30	4:29
	5	5:46		19	7:09		5	7:07		19	5:06			
	8	5:50		22	7:11		8	7:03		22	5:01			
	11	5:53		25	7:14		11	6:59		25	4:57			
	14	5:57		28	7:17		14	6:55		28	4:53			

JAPAN, TOKYO

Jan. 1	4:20	17	5:32	31	6:32	14	6:15	28	4:33
4	4:23	20	5:34	Jun. 3	6:34	17	6:11	31	4:30
7	4:25	23	5:37	6	6:36	20	6:07	Nov. 3	4:27
10	4:28	26	5:39	9	6:37	23	6:04	6	4:24
13	4:31	29	5:42	12	6:39	25	6:00	9	4:21
16	4:34	Apr. 1	5:44	15	6:40	29	5:56	12	4:19
19	4:37	4	5:47	18	6:41	Sep. 1	5:52	15	4:17
22	4:40	7	5:49	21	6:42	4	5:47	18	4:15
25	4:43	10	5:51	24	6:42	7	5:43	21	4:13
28	4:46	13	5:54	27	6:43	10	5:39	24	4:12
31	4:49	16	5:56	30	6:43	13	5:34	27	4:11
Feb. 3	4:52	19	5:59	Jul. 3	6:43	16	5:30	30	4:10
6	4:55	22	6:01	6	6:42	19	5:26	Dec. 3	4:10
9	4:58	25	6:04	9	6:41	22	5:21	6	4:10
12	5:01	28	6:06	12	6:40	25	5:17	9	4:10
15	5:04	May 1	6:09	15	6:39	28	5:12	12	4:10
18	5:07	4	6:11	18	6:38	Oct. 1	5:08	15	4:11
21	5:10	7	6:14	21	6:36	4	5:04	18	4:12
24	5:13	10	6:16	24	6:34	7	5:00	21	4:13
27	5:16	13	6:19	27	6:32	10	4:55	24	4:15
Mar. 2	5:19	16	6:21	30	6:30	13	4:51	27	4:17
5	5:21	19	6:23	Aug. 2	6:27	16	4:47	30	4:19
8	5:24	22	6:26	5	6:24	19	4:44		
11	5:27	25	6:28	8	6:21	22	4:40		
14	5:29	28	6:30	11	6:18	25	4:36		

MEXICO, MEXICO CITY

Jan. 1	5:51	17	6:28	31	6:52	14	6:47	28	5:46
4	5:53	20	6:29	Jun. 3	6:53	17	6:45	31	5:45
7	5:55	23	6:30	6	6:54	20	6:43	Nov. 3	5:43
10	5:57	26	6:30	9	6:54	23	6:41	6	5:42
13	5:58	29	6:31	12	6:57	26	6:39	9	5:41
16	6:00	Apr. 1	6:32	15	6:58	29	6:36	12	5:41
19	6:02	4	6:33	18	6:58	Sep. 1	6:33	15	5:39
22	6:04	7	6:34	21	6:59	4	6:31	18	5:39
25	6:06	10	6:34	24	7:00	7	6:29	21	5:38
28	6:08	13	6:35	27	7:00	10	6:26	24	5:38
31	6:10	16	6:36	30	7:01	13	6:24	27	5:38
Feb. 3	6:11	19	6:37	Jul. 3	7:00	16	6:21	30	5:38
6	6:13	22	6:38	6	7:01	19	6:18	Dec. 3	5:39
9	6:15	25	6:39	9	7:01	22	6:15	6	5:39
12	6:16	28	6:40	12	7:00	25	6:12	9	5:40
15	6:18	May 1	6:41	15	7:00	28	6:10	12	5:41
18	6:19	4	6:41	18	7:00	Oct. 1	6:06	15	5:42
21	6:20	7	6:43	21	6:59	4	6:05	18	5:43
24	6:22	10	6:44	24	6:58	7	6:02	21	5:45
27	6:22	13	6:45	27	6:57	10	5:59	24	5:46
Mar. 2	6:24	16	6:47	30	6:56	13	5:57	27	5:48
5	6:24	19	6:47	Aug. 2	6:55	16	5:55	30	5:50
8	6:25	22	6:49	5	6:53	19	5:53		
11	6:27	25	6:50	8	6:51	22	5:51		
14	6:27	28	6:51	11	6:50	25	5:49		

SOUTH AFRICA, JOHANNESBURG

Jan.	1	6:46		17	6:05		31	5:06		14	5:30		28	6:04
	4	6:47		20	6:02	Jun.	4	5:06		17	5:31		31	6:06
	7	6:47		23	5:59		6	5:05		20	5:32	Nov.	3	6:08
	10	6:48		26	5:55		9	5:05		23	5:34		6	6:10
	13	6:48		29	5:52		12	5:05		26	5:35		9	6:12
	16	6:47	Apr.	1	5:49		15	5:06		29	5:36		12	6:14
	19	6:47		4	5:46		18	5:06	Sep.	1	5:37		15	6:16
	22	6:46		7	5:43		21	5:07		4	5:49		18	6:19
	25	6:45		10	5:40		24	5:07		7	5:40		21	6:21
	28	6:44		13	5:37		27	5:08		10	5:41		24	6:23
	31	6:43		16	5:34		30	5:09		13	5:42		27	6:25
Feb.	3	6:42		19	5:31	Jul.	3	5:10		16	5:43		30	6:28
	6	6:40		22	5:28		6	5:11		19	5:45	Dec.	3	6:30
	9	6:38		25	5:26		9	5:12		22	5:46		6	6:32
	12	6:36		28	5:23		12	5:14		25	5:47		9	6:34
	15	6:34	May	1	5:21		15	5:15		28	5:48		12	6:36
	18	6:31		4	5:19		18	5:17	Oct.	1	5:50		15	6:38
	21	6:29		7	5:16		21	5:18		4	5:51		18	6:40
	24	6:26		10	5:15		24	5:19		7	5:53		21	6:41
	27	6:23		13	5:13		27	5:21		10	5:54		24	6:43
Mar.	2	6:21		16	5:11		30	5:22		13	5:55		27	6:44
	5	6:18		19	5:10	Aug.	2	5:24		16	5:57		30	6:45
	8	6:15		22	5:09		5	5:25		19	5:59			
	11	6:11		25	5:08		8	5:27		22	6:00			
	14	6:08		28	5:07		11	5:28		25	6:02			

SWEDEN, STOCKHOLM

Jan.	1	2:40		17	5:35		31	8:27		14	7:25		28	3:49
	4	2:45		20	5:42	Jun.	3	8:32		17	7:17		31	3:41
	7	2:50		23	5:49		6	8:37		20	7:08	Nov.	3	3:34
	10	2:55		26	5:56		9	8:41		23	7:00		6	3:26
	13	3:01		29	6:03		12	8:44		26	6:51		9	3:19
	16	3:08	Apr.	1	6:11		15	8:47		29	6:43		12	3:12
	19	3:14		4	6:18		18	8:49	Sep.	1	6:34		15	3:06
	22	3:21		7	6:25		21	8:50		4	6:25		18	3:00
	25	3:29		10	6:32		24	8:50		7	6:16		21	2:54
	28	3:36		13	6:39		27	8:50		10	6:07		24	2:49
	31	3:43		16	6:46		30	8:48		13	5:59		27	2:44
Feb.	3	3:51		19	6:53	Jul.	3	8:47		16	5:50		30	2:40
	6	3:59		22	7:00		6	8:44		19	5:41	Dec.	3	2:37
	9	4:06		25	7:08		9	8:41		22	5:32		6	2:34
	12	4:14		28	7:15		12	8:37		25	5:23		9	2:32
	15	4:22	May	1	7:22		15	8:32		28	5:14		12	2:30
	18	4:29		4	7:29		18	8:27	Oct.	1	5:05		15	2:29
	21	4:37		7	7:36		21	8:21		4	4:56		18	2:29
	24	4:44		10	7:43		24	8:15		7	4:47		21	2:30
	27	4:52		13	7:50		27	8:09		10	4:39		24	2:32
Mar.	2	4:59		16	7:57		30	8:02		13	4:30		27	2:34
	5	5:05		19	8:03	Aug.	2	7:55		16	4:22		30	2:38
	8	5:14		22	8:10		5	7:48		19	4:13			
	11	5:21		25	8:16		8	7:40		22	4:05			
	14	5:28		28	8:22		11	7:33		25	3:57			

U.S.S.R., KIEV

Jan.	1	4:44		17	6:47		31	8:43		11	8:10		22	5:35
	4	4:47		20	6:52	Jun.	3	8:46		14	8:05		25	5:29
	10	4:55		23	6:57		6	8:49		17	7:59		28	5:23
	13	4:59		26	7:02		9	8:52		20	7:53		31	5:18
	16	5:03		29	7:07		12	8:54		23	7:47	Nov.	3	5:12
	19	5:08	Apr.	1	7:12		15	8:56		26	7:40		6	5:07
	22	5:13		4	7:17		18	8:57		29	7:34		9	5:02
	25	5:18		10	7:26		21	8:58	Sep.	1	7:28		12	4:58
	28	5:23		13	7:31		24	8:59		4	7:21		15	4:54
	31	5:28		16	7:36		27	8:59		7	7:14		18	4:50
Feb.	3	5:34		19	7:41		30	8:58		10	7:08		21	4:46
	6	5:39		22	7:46	Jul.	3	8:57		13	7:01		24	4:43
	9	5:44		25	7:51		6	8:56		16	6:54		27	4:40
	12	5:50		28	7:56		9	8:54		19	6:47		30	4:38
	15	5:55	May	1	8:00		12	8:52		22	6:40	Dec.	3	4:36
	18	6:01		4	8:05		15	8:49		25	6:33		6	4:35
	21	6:06		7	8:10		18	8:46		28	6:27		9	4:34
	24	6:11		10	8:15		21	8:43	Oct.	1	6:20		12	4:34
	27	6:16		13	8:19		24	8:39		4	6:13		15	4:34
Mar.	2	6:22		16	8:24		28	8:35		7	6:07		18	4:34
	5	6:27		19	8:28		30	8:31		10	6:00		21	4:35
	8	6:32		22	8:32	Aug.	2	8:26		13	5:53		24	4:37
	11	6:37		25	8:36		5	8:21		16	5:47		27	4:39
	14	6:42		28	8:40		8	8:16		19	5:41		30	4:42

U.S.S.R., LENINGRAD

Jan.	1	3:45		17	6:41		31	9:44		14	8:39		28	4:57
	4	3:49		20	6:53	Jun.	3	9:50		17	8:30		31	4:49
	7	3:54		23	7:00		6	9:54		20	8:22	Nov.	3	4:41
	10	4:00		26	7:07		9	9:59		23	8:13		6	4:33
	13	4:06		29	7:15		12	10:02		26	8:04		9	4:26
	16	4:13	Apr.	1	7:22		15	10:05		29	7:55		12	4:19
	19	4:20		4	7:29		18	10:08	Sep.	1	7:46		15	4:12
	22	4:27		7	7:37		21	10:08		4	7:32		18	4:06
	25	4:35		10	7:44		24	10:08		7	7:28		21	4:00
	28	4:42		13	7:51		27	10:08		10	7:19		24	3:55
	31	4:50		16	7:59		30	10:06		13	7:10		27	3:50
Feb.	3	4:58		19	8:06	Jul.	3	10:04		16	7:01		30	3:45
	6	5:06		22	8:14		6	10:02		19	6:52	Dec.	3	3:41
	9	5:14		25	8:21		9	9:58		22	6:42		6	3:38
	12	5:22		28	8:25		12	9:54		25	6:33		9	3:36
	15	5:30	May	1	8:36		15	9:49		28	6:29		12	3:34
	18	5:37		4	8:43		18	9:44	Oct.	1	6:15		15	3:33
	21	5:45		7	8:51		21	9:38		4	6:06		18	3:33
	24	5:53		10	8:58		24	9:31		7	5:46		21	3:34
	27	6:01		13	9:05		27	9:26		10	5:43		24	3:36
Mar.	2	6:08		16	9:12		30	9:18		13	5:39		27	3:38
	5	6:16		19	9:19	Aug.	2	9:10		16	5:31		30	3:42
	8	6:23		22	9:26		5	9:03		19	5:22			
	11	6:31		25	9:32		8	8:55		22	5:13			
	14	6:38		28	9:39		11	8:47		25	5:05			

U.S.S.R., MOSCOW

Jan.	1	3:48		17	6:23		31	8:49		11	8:02		22	5:01
	4	3:57		20	6:29	Jun.	3	8:53		14	7:58		25	4:54
	7	4:01		23	6:35		6	8:57		17	7:51		28	4:47
	10	4:06		26	6:42		9	9:00		20	7:44		31	4:40
	13	4:11		29	6:48		12	9:03		23	7:37	Nov.	3	4:34
	16	4:16	Apr.	1	6:55		15	9:05		26	7:29		6	4:28
	19	4:22		4	7:00		18	9:06		29	7:21		9	4:22
	22	4:28		7	7:06		21	9:07	Sep.	1	7:14		12	4:16
	25	4:34		10	7:12		24	9:08		4	7:06		15	4:10
	31	4:47		13	7:18		27	9:08		7	6:58		18	4:05
Feb.	3	4:53		16	7:24		30	9:07		10	6:50		21	4:01
	6	5:00		19	7:30	Jul.	3	9:06		13	6:42		24	3:57
	9	5:06		22	7:37		6	9:04		16	6:34		27	3:53
	12	5:13		25	7:43		9	9:01		19	6:26		30	3:50
	15	5:20	May	1	7:55		12	8:58		22	6:18	Dec.	3	3:47
	18	5:26		4	8:01		15	8:54		25	6:10		6	3:45
	21	5:33		7	8:07		18	8:50		28	6:02		9	3:43
	24	5:39		10	8:13		21	8:46	Oct.	1	5:54		12	3:42
	27	5:45		13	8:18		24	8:41		4	5:47		15	3:42
Mar.	2	5:52		16	8:24		27	8:36		7	5:39		18	3:43
	5	5:58		19	8:30		30	8:30		10	5:31		21	3:44
	8	6:05		22	8:35	Aug.	2	8:24		13	5:23		24	3:45
	11	6:11		25	8:40		5	8:18		16	5:16		27	3:47
	14	6:17		28	8:45		8	8:12		19	5:08		30	3:50

A TIME TO SOW AND A TIME TO REAP

The Jews, living in "exile" for two thousand years, are not usually identified as farmers. However, from the earliest biblical account of Adam in the Garden until the "blooming deserts" of modern Israel, the land has served as the basis of the Israelite economy and Jewish religious rituals. Each of the three major pilgrimage festivals—Passover, Shavuot, and Sukkot—is based on the agricultural cycles. So precious was the land that there is an obligation to rest it every seven years, an agricultural Sabbath parallel to the Sabbath day. The Land (of Israel) is, in fact, a central figure in Jewish history: promised to Abraham, conquered by Joshua; it was from the Land that the Jews were exiled in 586 B.C.E. and 70 C.E. and it was for the Land that the Jews yearned during their many years of wandering. To this day, Israel is referred to simply as *ha-Aretz* (the Land).

With such extensive connections, it is not surprising that an intimate knowledge of the ways of land has developed within the tradition. From observations about the moon to remedies for unsuccessful tree-grafts, the literature is replete with commentaries on virtually every aspect of agricultural life. Many of these, as may be expected, are long out-of-date; others have weathered the test of time. The following is a sampling of the wealth of agricultural knowledge amassed by the Jewish tradition. In it can be seen the intricate interconnections of sun, moon, wind, rain, seasons, cycles, human energy, and Divine blessing. (See "The Comings and Goings of the Jewish Year.")

Agricultural Time

His two months are olive harvest,
His two months are planting grain,
His two months are late planting;
His month is hoeing up of flax,
His month is harvest of barley,
His month is wheat harvest and feasting;
His two months are vine-tending,
His month is summer fruit (figs).

—Gezer Calendar,
tenth century B.C.E.

A momento of a vain attempt in the 1880s to establish a Jewish agricultural colony in the West before the Dakotas became States of the Union.

This school exercise tablet, written on soft limestone and found among the excavations at Gezer, is the earliest written record of a Jewish enumeration of time. The young student is learning the names of the months in relation to the agricultural tasks of the seasons. From the beginning, it would appear, Jewish calculations of time were intimately linked with the life-sustaining sequence of the seasonal cycle.

Biblical names of the months used before the Babylonian Exile (sixth century B.C.E.) reflect this. Aviv (Exod. 13:4, 23:15, 34:18; Deut. 16:1), usually translated as "Spring," seems related to the Canaanite designation for "month of ears of grain." Ziv (1 Kings 6:1, 37) means "month of blossoms." Etanim (1 Kings 8:2) means "month in which only permanent water courses flow." Finally, Bul (1 Kings 6:38) means "month of the great rains."

Equally significant are the post-Exilic, Babylonian-derived names of the Hebrew months, still in use today. A brief list shows connections with seasonal, astronomical, and agricultural phenomena:

Nisan	Month when early blossoms appear in the land (Hebrew *nitzan*)
Iyar	Month of brightness due to the proliferation of buds and flowers (Hebrew *or*)
Sivan	Perhaps connected with the time of ripening produce; in Babylonia dedicated to the moon god, Sin
Tammuz	Named after Dumuzu, the Akkadian analogue to Adonis, god of vegetation and plant life
Av	Named after the wood and reeds from which shelters were erected in Babylonia
Elul	Onomatopoetic derivative from the Akkadian for "women singing"—in celebration of Tammuz's return from the nether world and the consequent revival of vegetative growth after the burning heat of high summer
Tishri	"First" month of the year in Akkadian; dedicated to the sun god, supreme judge of the Babylonian pantheon, whose "balance" is re-established at autumnal equinox
Marheshvan	Literally "the eighth month"
Kislev	Uncertain in origin, but some would connect it with *k'sil*, the biblical word for Orion (Sagittarius, the Archer), so prominent in the night sky at this time of year
Tevet	"Drowned and submerged in mud," the rainiest of months in Babylonia (Hebrew: *tavua*)
Shevat	"Rod, staff, scepter," referring to the beating rains which descend so forcefully this month
Adar	"Cloudy," referring to the heavens which are still overcast during this last month of the rainy season; *or* "threshing floor," i.e., the month during which the granaries are readied for the new crop

The Seasons and the Solar-Lunar Calendar

With such seasonal awareness embedded in the very nomenclature of the months, it is not surprising to find widespread rabbinic interest in astronomy, the calendar, and the seasons.

> R. Simeon b. Pazzi said in the name of R. Joshua b. Levi on the authority of Bar Kappara:
> He who knows how to calculate the cycles of the seasons and the courses of the planets, but does not, of him Scripture says,
> "They regard not the work of the Lord, neither have they considered the operation of his hands" (Isa. 5:12)
>
> —Shabbat 75a

> Samuel said:
> I am as familiar with the paths of heaven as with the streets of Nehardea, with the exception of the comet, about which I am ignorant.
>
> —Berakhot 58b

Given this interest in astronomy, considerable attention is given to the complex relation of the solar to the lunar year.

> Samuel said:
> The lunar year consists of no fewer than 352, nor of more than 356 days.
>
> —Arakin 9b

> The sun is called great while the moon is called small; the sun is called great because it exceeds the moon by eleven days.
>
> —Exodus Rabbah XV, 22

God created 365 windows in the firmament, 183 in the east and 182 in the west; some of them were created to serve the sun and some for the moon, which comes up and travels after it, save for eleven windows into which the moon does not enter.

—Exodus Rabbah XV, 22

Said the Holy One, blessed be He . . .
Twelve constellations have I created in the firmament, and for each constellation I have created thirty hosts, and for each host I have created thirty legions, and for each legion I have created thirty cohorts, and for each cohort I have created thirty maniples, and for each maniple I have created thirty camps, and to each camp I have attached 365,000 myriads of stars, corresponding to the days of the solar year. . . .

—Berakhot 32b

A myriad being 10,000, this is a total of 1,064,340,000,000,000,000 stars.

The Seasons and the Soil

The succession of the seasons and their agricultural consequences are of more direct concern than astronomy. Awareness of human dependence on the soil was established from the earliest of times:

All the conversation of humankind concerns the earth:
"Has the earth produced, or has the earth not produced?"
And all humankind's prayers concern the earth:
"Lord! May the earth yield fruit!"
Or "Lord! May the earth be successful!"

—Genesis Rabbah XIII, 2

Not only commoners but kings are subject to this dependency, as is expressed in the following *Midrash*:

Even though he is a king and holds sway from one end of the world to the other, he is a "servant to the field"; if the earth yields produce, he can accomplish something; if the earth does not yield, he is of no use whatever.

—Leviticus Rabbah XXII, 1

Small wonder, then, that the rabbis tend to construe seasonally and very specifically such passages as this one from Genesis 8:22: "While the earth remaineth, seedtime and harvest, and cold and heat, and summer and winter, and day and night shall not cease."

"Seedtime"—this is autumn.
"Harvest"—this is spring.
"Cold"—this is winter.
"Heat"—this is summer.

—Pirkei d'Rabbi Eliezer 8

R. Simeon b. Gamaliel said on the authority of R. Meir, and R. Simeon b. Manasya said likewise:
[The second] half of Tishri, Marheshvan, and the first half of Kislev is seed-time; [the second] half of Kislev, Tevet, and half Shevat are the winter months; [the second] half of Shevat, Adar, and [the first] half of Sivan is the period of harvests; [the second] half of Sivan, Tammuz, and the first half of Av are summer; the second half of Av, Elul, and the first half of Tishri, hot months. R. Judah counted [these periods] from [the beginning of] Tishri; R. Simeon, from Marheshvan.

—Baba Metzia 106b; cf. also Genesis Rabbah XXXIV, 11

The qualities of the seasons are strikingly portrayed in a play on the four words used to designate the earth:

R. Simeon b. Gamaliel said:
It (the earth) has four names: *eretz*, *tevel*, *adamah*, *arka*. The name *eretz* corresponds to the vernal equinox which forces up (*me-altzah*) the crops; *tevel* to the summer solstice which lends savor to (*me-tabbelet*) the crops; *adamah* to the autumn, when the ground consists of clods of earth (due to autumn rains moistening the heat-parched summer ground); *arka* corresponds to the winter which causes the crops to wither (*moreket*).

—Genesis Rabbah XIII, 12

Their co-ordination with the path of the sun is also explicit:

R. Nathan said:
In summer the sun travels in the heights of the heaven, therefore the whole world is hot while the wells [springs] are cold; in winter the sun travels at the lower ends of the sky, therefore the whole world is cold while the wells are hot.
Our rabbis taught:
The sun travels over four courses: [during] Nisan, Iyar, and Sivan, it travels over the mountains, in order to melt the snows; [in] Tammuz, Av, and Elul, over the inhabited world, to ripen the fruits; [in] Tishri, Marheshvan, and Kislev, over seas, to dry up the rivers; in Tevet, Shevat, and Adar, through the wilderness, so as not to dry up the seeds [in the ground].

—Pesahim 94b

Exhibition of Jewish Farmers of America, 1909

The results are evident:

> At the winter solstice there are no grapes on the vine and no figs on the fig-trees. . . . But at the summer solstice there are grapes on the vine, figs on the fig-trees, and even the leaves are not withered.
>
> —Lamentations Rabbah I, 42

The tradition also records that there are those so attuned to the solar sequence that they can identify the months without the pages of a calendar. Two examples from the Talmud follow:

> Three cowherds were standing conversing, and were overheard by some rabbis. One of them said: "If the early and late sowing sprout together, the month is Adar; if not, it is not Adar." The second said: "If, in the morning, frost is severe enough to injure an ox, and at midday the ox lies in the shade of the fig-tree and scratches its hide, then it is Adar; if not, it is not Adar." And the third said: "When a strong east wind is blowing and your breath can prevail against it, the month is Adar; if not, it is not Adar."
>
> —Sanhedrin 18b

> "The rams have mounted the sheep and the valleys are covered with corn, they shout for joy, yea, they sing" (Psa. 65:14). R. Meir reasoned:
> "When do the rams mount the sheep? At the time when the valleys are covered over with corn. And when are the valleys covered over with corn? In Adar. The sheep conceive in Adar and bear in Av, and their New Year is in Elul.
> R. Eleazar and R. Simeon said:
> When do the rams mount the sheep? At the time when they [the ears of corn] shout for joy and sing. When do the ears of corn burst into song? In Nisan. They conceive in Nisan and bear in Elul, and their New Year is in Tishri.
>
> —Rosh Hashanah 8a

The Solstices: As the World Turns

The seasons' effect on the growth cycle figures explicitly in determining when a year is to be intercalated (with the addition of a leap month) so that solar and lunar years remain in seasonal harmony. Writing to the communities of the Diaspora, R. Simeon b. Gamaliel is quoted as saying:

> We beg to inform you that the doves are still tender and the lambs still young, and the grain has not yet ripened. I have considered the matter, and thought it advisable to add thirty days to the year.
>
> —Sanhedrin 11a

And the general rabbinic consensus?

> Our rabbis taught: A year may be intercalated on three grounds: on account of the premature state of the grain-crops; or that of the fruit-trees; or on account of the lateness of the *tekufah* (equinox). Any two of these reasons can justify intercalation, but not one alone. All, however, are glad when the state of the spring-crop is one of them.
>
> —Sanhedrin 11b

As is clear in the consideration of *tekufah*, the turning point of the sun in its course, it is critical that the movements of the sun and its seasonal shifts be plotted precisely:

> Samuel stated:
> The vernal equinox occurs only at the beginning of one of the four quarters of the day, viz. either at the beginning of the day or at the beginning of the night or at midday or at midnight. The summer solstice only occurs either at the end of one and a half, or at the end of seven and a half hours of the day or night. The autumnal equinox only occurs at the end of three, or nine hours of the day or the night, and the winter solstice only occurs at the end of four and a half, or ten and a half hours of the day or night. The duration of a season of the year is no longer than ninety-one days and seven and a half hours; and the beginning of one season is removed from that of the other by no more than one half of a planetary hour.
> Samuel further stated:
> The vernal equinox never begins under Jupiter but it breaks the trees, nor does the winter solstice begin under Jupiter but it dries up the seed. This, however, is the case only when the new moon occurred in the moon-hour or in the Jupiter-hour.
>
> —Erubin 56a

David Abudraham of Seville, a fourteenth-century Judeo-Spanish commentator on the Jewish liturgy, cites another tradition:

> As each season of the year begins, the hours of daylight and darkness vary. At spring the day and night are equal; at summer the day is one half again as long as the night; at autumn they once again are equal; at winter the dark is half again as great as the day.

The observation of significant points in the growth cycle could not fail to elicit ritual responses too:

> Our rabbis taught: One who sees the sun at its turning point (vernal equinox), the moon in its power, the planets in their orbits, and the signs of the Zodiac in their orderly progress, should say: "Blessed be He who has wrought the work of Creation."
>
> —Berakhot 59b

A curious custom of wearing clothing of particular colors at particular seasons is mentioned in one obscure apocryphal source, "The Throne and Hippodrome of Solomon the King":

Jewish agricultural workers in pre-war Czechoslovakia. **(Roman Vishniac)**

> His students asked R. Jose:
> Why the different-colored clothing which particular groups of people wear?
> He replied:
> They wear different colors in response to the four seasons. In autumn the seas are blue, hence the blue garments. In winter the snows descend, hence people wear white. In spring the sea is green and good for crossing, therefore people wear green. In summer the fruits are ripening red, and so the people dress in red.

Especially interesting, among customs observed at the change of the seasons, is that of not drinking water at the hour of solstice or equinox. David Abudraham, whose commentaries contain considerable folkloric material, transmitted the custom in these terms:

> I have found written that one should take care, at each of the four seasons, not to drink water at the hour of equinox or solstice, for at such times there is danger of swelling and illness from drinking the water.
> For it was at vernal equinox that the waters of Egypt were turned to blood (cf. Exod. 7:19–25).
> It was at summer solstice that Moses and Aaron struck rather than spoke to the rock, and blood gushed forth (cf. Num. 20:8).
> It was at the turn of autumn that Abraham, binding his son Isaac upon the altar (cf. Gen. 22), shed some drops of Isaac's blood, which spread through all the waters.
> And it was at winter solstice that Jeptha's daughter was sacrificed (cf. Judg. 11:29–

40), and all the world's waters were turned to blood.

And so annually, at the turning of the seasons, the ancient contaminations recur. . . . Some call these divinations or old wives' tales. But others say that for each season a guardian is appointed over the waters. At each change of seasons comes a changing of the guards, and at the precise moment of the exchange, the waters are without protection.

While this may be an unconscious memory of seasonal sacrifices offered in the dim past, whose bloody traces persist in folk tradition, it is clear that the change of the seasons was highly visible to the common people. Two further customs developed:

At these times [of seasonal changes] some place a piece of iron (*barzel*) upon well covers, storage tanks, or buckets containing water, confident that the Merits of the Mothers of *B*ilhah, *R*achel, *Z*ilpah, and *L*eah will protect us all from harm.

—*Taamei ha-Minhagim v'Otzar ha-Di'nim*

Still others, in lieu of drinking water, eat sweets at these times, that the season to come be a sweet one. But I say that for the person who worships the One God, trusting in Him alone, each season will be sweet in its turn.

—Abudraham

Ritualized responses to seasonal succession have their satisfactions—and their limitations. Agricultural uncertainties are a given, whatever rites humans may practice:

If a person sows, it is uncertain that he will reap the harvest; only when a person reaps is there certainty that he will eat.

—Sukkah 49b

Ancient Weather Forecasting

Weather is a perpetual preoccupation of those who live on the land. Thus the existence of wind was gratefully acknowledged:

R. Levi said:
Even assuming that you have ploughed, sown, hoed, removed the thorns, reaped, made sheaves, threshed, and laid up corn in the granaries, if the Holy One, blessed be He, did not bring out a little wind for you to winnow, what would you live from?

—Leviticus Rabbah XXVIII, 2

R. Phinehas said:
In the ordinary way, when a man washes his cloak during the rainy season, how much trouble he must go through until he can dry it! Yet people sleep in their beds and the Holy One, blessed be He, brings out a little wind and dries the earth!

—Leviticus Rabbah XXVIII, 2

Even more important was rain, whose timely arrival was devoutly prayed for, and whose characteristics were carefully noted:

When do we [begin to] make mention of the power of rain? R. Eliezer says:
On the first day of the Feast of Sukkot.
R. Joshua says:
On the last day of the Feast.

—Ta'anith 2a

The rabbis have taught: "And I will give you rains in their season." [This means that the soil shall be] neither soaked nor parched, but moderately rained upon. For whenever the rain is excessive it scours away the soil so that it yields no fruit.

—Ta'anith 22b

How much rain must descend that it may suffice for fructification? As much as would fill a vessel of three handbreadths. This is R. Meir's opinion. R. Judah said: In hard [soil], one handbreadth; in average [soil], two; in humid [soil], three.

—Genesis Rabbah XIII, 13

How much rain must fall for one to recite a blessing? R. Jose said in Rab Judah's name, and R. Jonah and Rab Judah said in Samuel's name:
At the beginning as much as will fructify [the earth]; at the end, even just a little.

—Genesis Rabbah XIII, 15

Rab Judah further said:
Wind after rain is as beneficial as rain, clouds after rain as beneficial as rain, sunshine after rain as beneficial as twofold rain. What does this exclude? —The glow after sunset and sunshine between the clouds.
Raba said:
Snow is beneficial to the mountains as fivefold rain to the earth.
Raba further said:
Snow is beneficial to the mountains, heavy rain to the trees, gentle rain to the fruits of the field, drizzling rain (*'urpila*) even to the seeds under a hard clod.

—Ta'anith 3b–4a

Naturally, there were attempts to predict the weather for the growing season:

R. Abba said to R. Ashi:
We rely upon [the weather information]

A Jewish farmer in Kansas, 1885

of R. Isaac b. Abdimi. For R. Isaac b. Abdimi said:
[At] the termination of the last day of Tabernacles, all watched the smoke of the wood pile. [If] it inclined towards the north, the poor rejoiced and landowners were distressed because [that was an indication] that the yearly rains would be heavy and the crops would decay. [If] it inclined towards the south, the poor were distressed and landowners rejoiced because [that was an indication] that the yearly rains would be scanty and the crops could be preserved. [If] it inclined towards the east, all were glad; towards the west, all were distressed.

—Baba Batra 147a

Abba Saul said: "Fine [weather at] the Festival of Pentecost is a good sign for all the year."
R. Zebid said: "If the first day of the New Year is warm, all the year will be warm; if cold, all the year will be cold."

—Baba Batra 147a

The directions on the compass had agricultural implications, as indicated in the following references:

The west is the region of the storehouses of snow and those of hail and cold and heat . . . The south is the source from which emanate the dews and rains that bring blessing to the world . . . The north is the region from whence the darkness goes forth to the world . . . The east is the source from which light goes forth into the world.

—Numbers Rabbah III, 12

The east [wind] is always beneficial; the west [wind] is always harmful; the north wind is beneficial for wheat that reached [the stage of] a third [of its maturity], and harmful for olives in blossom; and the south wind is injurious for wheat that reached [the stage of] a third [of maturity], and beneficial for olives in blossom.

—Baba Batra 147a

Our rabbis taught:
[If] the weather on the Festival of Pentecost is fine, sow wheat.
Mar Zutra stated:
It was said, "Cloudy."
The Nehardeans said in the name of R. Jacob:
"Fine" [does] not [mean] absolutely fine, nor does "cloudy" mean completely overcast, but even [when it is] "cloudy" and the north wind blows [the clouds], it is regarded as "fine."

—Baba Batra 147a

Farming Wisdom and Technique

There is no substitute for the accumulated wisdom of generations of farming practice, accompanied by a certain intuitive sense.

Already in biblical times the preferred hillside location for a vineyard was known, and due attention was paid to the need to clear stones:

> Let me sing of my well-beloved,
> A song of my beloved concerning his vineyard.
> My well-beloved had a vineyard
> In a very fruitful hill;
> And he digged it, and cleared it of stones,
> And planted it with the choicest vine,
> And built a watchtower in the midst of it,
> And also hewed out a vat therein;
> And he looked that it should bring forth grapes,
> And it brought forth wild grapes.
>
> —Isaiah 5:1–2

The Handelman family rides across the South Dakota Plains.

Another passage from Isaiah clearly distinguishes the operations of planting, sowing, and threshing for herbs from those for grains, along with some general rules for laying out plots:

> Does he who plows for sowing plow continually?
> Does he continually open and harrow his ground?
> When he has levelled its surface, does he not scatter dill, sow cummin, and put in wheat in rows
> and barley in its proper place,
> and spelt as the border?
> For He instructs him aright;
> His God teaches him.
> Dill is not threshed with a threshing sledge,
> nor is a cart wheel rolled over cummin;
> but dill is beaten out with a stick, and cummin with a rod.
> Does one crush bread grain?
> No, one does not thresh it for ever;
> Though the wheel of the wagon and its sharp edges move noisily,
> he does not crush it.
> This also comes from the Lord of hosts;
> Wonderful is His counsel, and great His wisdom.
>
> —Isaiah 28:24–29

Rabbinic tradition contains detailed instructions on planting, pruning, cutting, and grafting trees; a technique of grafting to increase the timber yield of the tree is mentioned.

> R. Joshua of Siknin said in the name of R. Levi:
> All other plants, if you cover their roots at the time of planting, do well, and if not, they do not do well; but a nut-tree, if its roots are covered at the time of planting, does not do well.
>
> —Song of Songs Rabbah VI, 11, 1

> When a nut-tree is pruned, it is for its benefit, since it renews its branches like hair which grows more quickly for being shorn and like the nails which soon grow again after being pared.
>
> —Song of Songs Rabbah VI, 11, 1

> R. Judah says: "Any grafting that has not taken root within three days will never do so."
>
> —Shebi'ith II, 6

> . . . are there fig-trees which do not produce fruit? Yes, as stated by Rahabah. For Rahabah said: "They bring white fig-trees and scrape them with a rope of date-tree bark on which seed is smeared, and they are then planted in alluvial soil, and they produce trunks but no fruit, and three branches of one will break down a bridge."
>
> —Tamid 29b–30a

> A person who comes to cut down a tree: a man who is not an expert lops off the branches, cutting down each branch separately and tiring himself out, but the clever man lays bare the roots and cuts down the tree.
>
> —Numbers Rabbah XX, 19

Hints of the psychic go beyond the purely physical:

> R. Tanhuma said:
> There was once a palm-tree in Hammethan which would not bear fruit. They grafted it and still it would bear no fruit. A palm-gardener said to them: "She sees a palm-tree at Jericho and longs for it." So

they brought a portion of the Jericho palm, grafted it, and forthwith the Hammethan palm bore fruit.

—Numbers Rabbah III, 1

The importance of a southern exposure for early ripening is noted, along with soil preparation:

They may bring the Omer-offering only from the fields in the south, and which had been broken up for the purpose, for upon these fields the sun rises and upon these the sun sets. How was [the field] prepared? In the first year it was broken up and in the second year it was ploughed twice, and it was sown seventy days before the Passover so that it might be close upon the [increasing strength of the] sun; thus it would bring forth stalks one span long and ears two spans long. It was then reaped, bound into sheaves, threshed, winnowed, cleansed, ground, and sifted, and then brought to the Temple-treasurer.

—Menahot 85a

The root systems of plants and their means of obtaining water are examined:

R. Eleazar b. Simeon said:
The earth drinks only as far as its upper layer. If so, what are the roots of the sycamore tree and the carob tree to do?
[Moreover,] R. Hanina b. Ikah and R. Berekiah in the name of R. Judah said:
The roots of wheat strike down fifty cubits into the earth; the soft roots of the fig-tree break through the rock.
Said R. Levi:
Once in thirty days the deep ascends and waters it.

—Genesis Rabbah XIII, 17

Interplanting was discussed in the Tractate Kilayim (Diverse Kinds), an early guide to permitted and prohibited "companion planting," and elsewhere. Some regard the prohibition of mixing species as an incomprehensible and irrational ancient taboo; others consider it to be ancient agricultural wisdom. An interesting episode involves the rabbinic sage Samuel:

Samuel's field laborer brought him some dates. As he partook of them he tasted wine in them. When he asked the laborer how that came about, he told him that the date trees were placed between the vines.
He said to him:
Since they are weakening the vines so much, bring me their roots tomorrow. When R. Hisda saw certain palms among the vines he said to his field laborers: "Remove them with their roots. Vines can easily buy palms but palms cannot buy vines."

—Baba Kamma 91b–92a

Along with secular procedures shared for ages with the other agriculturalists of the Mediterranean basin, there was a persistent awareness of special, biblically ordained agricultural practices:

R. Levi said:
In all their doings Israel are different from the other nations—in their plowing, in their sowing, in their planting, in their reaping, in their sheaf-gathering, in their threshing, in their garnering, in their wine-gathering . . . In their plowing, as it says, "Thou shalt not plough with an ox and an ass together." (Deut. 22:10) In their sowing, as it says, "Thou shalt not sow thy vineyard with two kinds of seed." (Deut. 22:9) In their planting, as it says, "Then ye shall count the fruit thereof as forbidden." (Lev. 19:23) In their reaping, as it says, "And when ye reap the harvest of your land, thou shalt not wholly reap the corner," etc. (Lev. 19:9) In their sheaf-gathering, as it says, "If thou forgettest a sheaf in the field," etc. (Deut. 24:19) In their corn-treading, as it says, "Thou shalt not muzzle the ox when he treadeth out the corn." (Deut. 25:4) In their garnering and wine-gathering, as it says, "Thou shalt not delay to offer of the fullness of thy harvest, and out of the outflow of thy presses." (Exod. 22:28) And it is also written, "As the corn of the threshing floor and as the fullness of the wine-press." (Num. 18:27) . . . [Further,] Israel reckons time by the moon and other nations by the sun.

—Song of Songs Rabbah V, 16, 5

In summary, Israelite agriculture was designed so that at no point in the cycle of the seasons could the farmer or shepherd forget that—

The earth is the Lord's,
and the fullness thereof;
The world,
and they that dwell therein.

—Psalm 24:1

Sowing Spiritual Seeds

There were those who worried about the burdens connected with soil and seasons. Bar Yohai, a radical mystic whose meditative practices removed him, for a time, from sympathetic involvement with the life-sustaining procedures of the earth, worriedly asked:

> If a man plows in the plowing season, sows in the sowing season, reaps in the reaping season, threshes in the threshing season, and winnows in the season of the wind, what is to become of the Torah?
>
> —Berakhot 35b

Others were confident that "for everything there is a season, and a time for every purpose under heaven." (Eccles. 3:1) For example, there is the discussion among the rabbis concerning the early Hasidim, the pietists, each of whose three hours of daily prayers was surrounded by an introductory and a concluding hour of meditative silence:

> But seeing that they spend nine hours a day over prayer, how is their knowledge of Torah preserved, and how is their work done? Because they are pious, their Torah is preserved, and their work is blessed [and so with little effort they accomplish much].
>
> —Berakhot 32b

Performed in the proper spirit, the life-sustaining tasks of the cycles of the seasons can connect the human being with *Hai ha-Olamim*, the Life of the universe and its Source. Thus the *avodah* which is "work" becomes simultaneously the *avodah* which is "worship." Pastures and hills, meadows and valleys truly "shout and sing together for joy." (Ps. 65:12–13) They join humankind in that spirit of celebration so beautifully expressed in a rabbinic "legalism," a catalog of prescribed blessings:

> R. Mesharsheya said:
> Over garden narcissus the blessing is "who createst fragrant woods"; over wild narcissus, "who createst fragrant herbs."
> R. Shesheth said:
> He who smells a citron or a quince should say, "Blessed be He who has given a sweet odor to fruits."
> Rab Judah says:
> If one goes walking in the days of Nisan [springtime] and sees the trees sprouting, he should say, "Blessed be He who has not left His world lacking in anything, and has created in it goodly creatures and goodly trees for the enjoyment of humankind."
>
> —Berakhot 43b

—E.E.G.

BY THE RIVERS OF BABYLON: SIGNIFICANT BODIES OF WATER IN JEWISH HISTORY

Water has played a major role throughout Jewish history and tradition. Symbolically, water was seen as cleansing, purifying, and rejuvenating. The ancient Temple service featured libations of water and cleansings of those coming to worship. In his eipc confrontation with the false prophets of Ba'al (1 Kings 18), Elijah doused his altar with water, which only served to heighten the wonder of the Lord's engulfing the sacrifice in flame.

The paradigm for the nearly mystical power of water is expressed best in the rituals associated with the *mikvah*, the ritual cleansing bath which became central to the devout married women's monthly religious and spiritual cycle, as well as for purification of men preparing themselves for spiritual roles.

In addition, water became the great symbol for Torah in Jewish life; water and Torah are life-sustaining, go from the haughty to the humble, and are available without limit to all of God's creatures. The rabbis gave a practical application to the verse in Exodus 15:22: ". . . and they travelled three days in the wilderness and found no water." Interpreted to mean that three days could not pass without the public study of Torah, this led to the determination that the Torah must be read on Mondays, Thursdays, and Saturdays.

Several religious ceremonies place particular emphasis on the use of water. The Sukkot holiday, in the time of the Temple, featured *Simhat Beit ha-Shoeivah* (the great and joyous Festival of the Water Carrier) and Rosh Hashanah afternoon became the occasion for the *Tashlikh* ceremony where one's sins are symbolically cast into the water.

In the mind of the ancients, the waters of the sea resembled contemporary visions of outer space: they were the great unknown where one travelled only by the grace of God. Prayers were composed to be recited prior to one's taking a sea journey, and a public ceremony the recitation of *Birkat ha-Gomel*, (the Blessing of Being Spared from Danger) was held upon safe return.

Specific bodies of water served also as major geographical determinates; hence a *get*, a writ of Jewish religious divorce, could only be written in a city located by a body of water, such as an ocean, river, or spring.

As a euphemism for God ("the well of living waters," Jer. 2:13), water became the symbol of the vital life force which propels man towards his Creator, and which permeates all of Jewish life in the symbolic, ritual, and spiritual dimensions.

The bodies of water listed below have gained significance for the Jewish people by their associations with Jewish history and folklore, biblical personalities, and modern events, in the spiritual and temporal realms. Keep in mind however, that in the Jewish religious view, ultimately *"ein mayim elah Torah,"* the real waters which nurture and sustain, revive and define, are only those symbolized by Torah.

Ancient Waters

THE EUPHRATES RIVER

The longest river in Western Asia, flowing for some 1,700 miles, the Euphrates has figured prominently in the life of the Jewish people since the beginnings of history. According to Genesis 2:14, the Euphrates was one of the four sources of the Garden of Eden, together with the Pishon, the Gichon, and the Tigris. On its banks were found some of the greatest cities of the ancient world, including Carchemish and Ur, the city of Abraham; and the river marked the northern boundary of the Promised Land (cf. Gen. 15:18).

The talmudic city of Pumbedita was situated on the banks of the Euphrates at the intersection of a number of canals. From the middle of the third century C.E. Pumbedita was one of the greatest religious and academic centers of world Jewry. Some of the luminaries of the talmudic world who lived and taught there include the sages Abbaye and Rava.

When the Psalmist wrote "By the waters of Babylon, there we sat down and wept, when we remembered Zion" (Ps. 137:1), he undoubtedly had in mind the waters of the Euphrates.

THE NILE RIVER

The lifeblood of Egypt, and of all the civilizations and cultures situated on its banks, the Nile was prominent in a Jewish context in the story of the biblical Exodus from Egypt. Moses was saved as a babe in a floating cradle by being protected in Nile bullrushes until he was discovered by Pharaoh's daughter. The first of the ten plagues was visited upon these same waters: they took on a blood-red appearance.

In the sixth century B.C.E. the small island of Elephantine in the Nile, near the modern city of Aswan, was inhabited by companies of Jewish mercenaries. Documents describing their previously unrecorded religious and cultural life were discovered only at the beginning of the twentieth century. These Jews maintained their own temple for worship, observed the Passover, and saw themselves as different from the surrounding cultures. However, with the expulsion of the Persians from Egypt at the end of the fifth century B.C.E. and the rise of the Egyptian kingdom, the position of the Jewish soldiers steadily declined; eventually, it became untenable.

Waters of Biblical Fame

THE RED SEA

The most famous misnamed body of water in Jewish history, *Yam Suf* literally means the "Reed Sea," not the "Red Sea"! The sea has two northern prongs, one leading to the port of Eilat, the other to the Gulf of Suez.

Besides being the site of the Exodus from Egypt, the Red Sea was considered one of the borders of the biblical Land of Israel (Exod. 23:31), and served as a vital naval and maritime center for King Solomon (1 Kings 9:26).

The drama of crossing the Red Sea captured the imagination of the talmudic rabbis. According to their *midrashim* (commentaries), the sea refused to part at the command of a mere mortal, Moses, and would only obey when God's Name was invoked. The children of Israel stood on the shore, fearful of entering the waters of the sea, until Nachshon from the tribe of Judah jumped in. As the waters reached his neck, they finally split and the rest of the people followed. In remembrance of this act of courage and faith the Israelis, during the 1948 War of Independence, named their April 6–15 campaign to break through Arab lines and send food convoys to the besieged city of Jerusalem, "Operation Nachshon."

THE JORDAN RIVER

Widely renowned in story and song, the Jordan is a disappointing body of water, narrow and only 127 miles long. Its small size belies its importance: many incidents in the Bible revolve around the Jordan. Jacob passed over it on his way to Haran (Gen. 32:10); Joshua led the Israelites across the river on their way to conquer the land of Canaan (Josh. 3); Na'aman came to be healed by its waters (2 Kings 5:10–14); and both Elijah and Elisha crossed the river under supernatural circumstances.

The Talmud calls the Jordan one of the four holy rivers of the Land of Israel (*Baba Batra* 74b); early Christian tradition ascribed sanctity to the river as the site of baptisms and miracles. American Negro spirituals have continued the tradition of viewing the river as possessing great healing and spiritual significance. More recently the Jordan has been of strategic importance in the wars between Israel and her Arab neighbors. Following the Six-Day War of 1967, the Jordan became the cease-fire line between Israel and Jordan; and so it remains today.

THE DEAD SEA

Known in Hebrew as *Yam ha-Melach* or the "Salt Sea," the Dead Sea is best known for being the lowest point on land of the earth, 1,305 feet below sea level. The cities of Sodom and Gomorrah were situated on its banks until their destruction, and Lot's wife perished nearby entombed as a pillar of salt. Israeli tourist guides will gladly point out a natural rock formation on the banks of the Dead Sea which suggests a woman's crusted form.

The caustic properties of the sea were recognized by the rabbis of the Talmud and inspired their requiring a final washing of the hands (*mayim ahronim*) at the end of a meal. They were apparently afraid that one might dip his fingers into the Dead Sea salts (which were used as a food spice) and then unintentionally rub the eyes, causing irritation and even damage.

The extreme salt content of the sea makes sinking a physical impossibility; tourists love to bob in its murky, chemical-laden slime to prove the point.

THE MEDITERRANEAN SEA

Known in Hebrew as *Yam ha-Gadol* or *Yam ha-Tihon*, this "Great Sea" forms the western border of the Land of Israel. Jonah set out to escape God by booking passage on a ship leaving for Tarshish (Spain), and ended

The Jordan River

up in its waters, spending the better part of three days in the belly of a great fish. After the fall of Judea and the destruction of the Temple in Jerusalem in 70 C.E., Roman galleys filled with Jewish slaves plied the Mediterranean ports.

In modern times, the terrorist threat "We will push you into the sea" has been taken to refer literally to the Mediterranean.

The rabbis stated that upon seeing the Mediterranean for the first time in thirty days, one should recite the following blessing: "Blessed are You, Lord our God, King of the universe, who created the Great Sea," reflecting its importance as the sea of the Land of Israel.

THE WELLS OF BEERSHEBA

An ancient well and oasis, Beersheba was the backdrop for many stories of biblical patriarchs. Abraham and Isaac dug wells there, and formed alliances with the neighboring tribes—critical acts for nomadic clans living in the desert. According to Genesis 21:32, Beersheba means "the well of the oath" or "the well of seven" because Abraham concluded a pact with Abimelech (a rival chieftain) by giving him seven ewes, whereupon they swore a mutual oath.

In the Biblical geography, Beersheba formed the southern-most boundary of Jewish settlement in Israel, and the Bible uses the phrase "from Dan until Beersheba" to connote the entire length of the country.

Until the twentieth century the site possessed little significance, but recently the town has developed into a thriving Israeli center for the entire Negev desert area and with the Israeli-Egyptian Peace Treaty, its importance will undoubtedly continue to grow.

THE JABBOK RIVER

A tributary of the Jordan whose name is perhaps an onomatopoetic expression of water flowing over rocks, the River Jabbok is associated with a critical event in the lives of the patriarchs. On his way home from more than a generation in exile, beset by self-doubt, guilt, and fearful expectation, Jacob was attacked by an angel at the crossing of the Jabbok. Wrestling with this figure (often associated with his brother Esau) throughout the night, Jacob was named Israel in the morning, or "one who strives with God and man and wins."

SHILOAH

The only natural spring and water source for Jerusalem, the Shiloah is also known as the Siloam or the Gichon Spring. During the reign of King Hezekiah it was expanded into an underground water tunnel, which can be explored today by the adventurous tourist.

LAKE KINNERET

Kinneret, in the northeast sector of Israel, is the only freshwater lake in the country. Its name comes from its harp-like shape (*kinor*, Hebrew for "harp"). Many ancient settlements bordered its shores, including Capernaum and Gennesar; it was the focal point for a number of the miracles recorded in the Christian scriptures.

The city of Tiberias, on its western shore, considered one of the four holy cities of Israel (together with Jerusalem, Hebron, and Safed), has been an area of settlement for Jews and non-Jews for two thousand years.

Waters of Early Modern and Modern Historical Significance

THE LOIRE RIVER

The Loire, in north-central France, runs through the town of Blois. In 1171 a Jewish trader, Isaac ben Elazar, was carrying animal skins by the river bank when one of them slipped loose and fell into the river. The commotion caught the attention of a Christian servant passing by, who reported to his master that he had seen a Jew disposing of the corpse of a Christian child in the waters. The entire Jewish community of Blois was arrested, charged with ritual murder of a child, and burned at the stake on May 26, 1171.

This first case on the European continent of the pernicious charge of "blood libel," that is, of using Christian blood for ritual purposes, was to be repeated with terrible consequences even up to the infamous 1913 trial of Mendel Beiless on a similar charge in a courtroom in Kiev, Russia.

The great French medieval rabbi Rabbeinu Tam established the twentieth day of Sivan as a fast day to commemorate the martyrdom of the thirty-one Jews of Blois.

THE SUEZ CANAL

This sea-level canal across the Isthmus of Suez connects the Mediterranean and the Red Sea. It was constructed under the direction of Ferdinand de Lesseps during 1859–1869. It has served as a major geopolitical and strategic objective for a century and has been a military objective in Israel's wars since 1956.

The 1956 Suez Campaign was precipitated by the Egyptian takeover of the Suez Canal Company and the ensuing British-French-Israeli attempt to reassert their rights in the area. The Six-Day War and the Yom Kippur War focused on the canal; Israeli capture of the waterway in 1967, and Egyptian success in crossing it in 1973, were the critical political factors of the conflicts.

In 1979, pursuant to the Israeli-Egyptian Peace Treaty, the canal was opened to Israel-flag shipping, symbolizing a new era in the history of the Suez Canal and of the region.

Non-bodies of Water

LAKE HULEH

Until the 1950's this was an area of swamp and a small (5-square-mile) lake just to the north of the Kinneret in northeastern Israel. Then the Jewish National Fund undertook the project of reclaiming the area to increase Jewish settlements in the eastern Galilee, and from 1951 through 1958 completely drained the malaria-infested lake, leaving behind the most fertile farmland and fish ponds in Israel.

SAMBATYON

A legendary river, said to have surrounded the Ten Lost Tribes of Israel deported by the Assyrians in 721 B.C.E., the Sambatyon flowed only six days a week and rested on the Shabbat. The rabbis of the Talmud still knew of such a body of water; when asked by the Roman Tinneus Rufus to prove the uniqueness of the Shabbat, Rabbi Akiva replied: "The Sambatyon River will prove it" (Sanhedrin 65b). He called it "the Sabbatyon."

The river was often mentioned in the later middle ages by kabbalists and those who indulged in intense messianic speculation. The false Messiah Shabbatai Zevi was said to have crossed the river in order to visit the Ten Lost Tribes and to marry the daughter of Moses (*mazel tov*)!

Undoubtedly when the Messiah comes, everyone will have the opportunity to see the river personally.

—J.D.P.

NOAH'S ARK: THE FIRST FLOATING WILDLIFE PRESERVE

Noah was a righteous man;
he was blameless in his age.
—Genesis 6:9

Noah is one of the few people whom the Torah honors as a "*tzaddik*," a righteous person (Gen. 6:9). The commentators, who regarded every word in the Torah as sacred and therefore employed for a precise reason, sought to explain why this name of distinction was bestowed upon Noah, whose character does not seem to be particularly saintly, exemplary, or distinguished.

As understood in some commentaries on the story of Noah's Ark, *tzaddik* is to be interpreted as "one who provides charity (*tzedakah*)" and sustains life, as Noah did for the many animals and few people in the ark. Because of his providing this life-sustaining charity, Noah and the other humans earned the "favor" of God and were allowed to emerge alive and well from the ark after the flood was over.

The high priority given to the care and feeding of the Ark-bound animals is not unique to this story but is consistent with the Jewish value of kindness to animals (*tzar baalei hayyim*). This value—officially codified as law in the Torah and elaborated upon in the Talmud, the medieval commentaries, and the responsa literature—permeates the many legends that grew up around the leading figures in the Torah and in Jewish history. Kindness to animals was so valued by Jewish tradition that it was considered an important measure of a person's piety and righteousness. From this derived the stories about how the shepherds Moses and David were elevated to national leadership because of their compassion for their lambs; as well as the many *maysehs* (moralistic folktales) about latter-day sages who rescued or fed stray cows and hungry chickens, watered thirsty horses, and freed caged birds.

Noah epitomized this value, serving as steward and preserver of God's creatures. Understandably, the nature of Noah's care came to be a focus of fascination and curiosity. His was the responsibility of managing, for an entire trying year, the first wildlife preserve in history. And the only one that floated.

The following are some of the many legends about Noah and his amphibious wildlife refuge.

STRUCTURE OF THE ARK

The ark built by Noah was rectangular, measuring 300 cubits in length, 50 in width, and 30 in height. Calculated by modern scholars, this amounts to 440 x 73 x 44 feet, yielding a displacement of 43,000 tons.

The building material was "gopher wood," a wood of the resinous type, probably cypress or cedar, coated inside and out with pitch. On top, one cubit from the roof, was a *tzohar*, interpreted variously as a skylight or a hatch. According to another opinion, however, this fixture was a hanging polished gem that enabled Noah to differentiate between night (when it shone) and day.

The ark had three stories. The second story was for Noah, his family, and the "pure" animals (those destined in the future to be kosher); the third story was for the "impure" animals; and the first story was for the garbage, shovelled there through a kind of diagonal trap door. There were an unspecified number of compartments, each species in a compartment.

On the second story the women had quarters on the west side and the men had quarters on the east, because sexual abstinence was required in the ark, both of people and animals. The animals, apparently more trusted than the humans, were not separated from their spouses.

HOW THE ANIMALS WERE ASSEMBLED

The gathering of the animals began one week before the rains descended. They came at God's command but of their own accord; although another view maintains that they were assembled by the angels. God made sure that no species was missing from the ark. One commentator, in fact, identifies 32 species of birds and 365 of reptiles.

Fish are not mentioned among the species taken aboard. According to one view the fish were not destroyed by the flood because they were the only creatures which did not sin by mating with other species. Another source says that Noah did bring fish aboard but many escaped into the water.

HOW MANY OF EACH SPECIES?

Until shortly before the flood started, God's instructions where that only one pair of each species was to be taken aboard. When the rain started, however, he decided that because the "impure" (nonkosher) animals outnumbered the "pure" ones, the number of the latter should be increased from two to seven, four males and three females. This was not so much a value judgement, as a recognition that these animals were needed for sacrifices and therefore had to constitute a larger pool.

An interesting question arises as to how Noah knew which were "pure" when the laws of *kashrut* were not yet given and were, in fact, hundreds of years in the future? One opinion maintains that God gave Noah a "sign,": The "pure" animals would crouch before trying to enter the ark, and the "impure" ones would stand; he should choose the crouchers. An alternative view, is that Noah, like all of the *tzaddikim* who lived prior to Sinai already knew Torah, and observed all of the *mitzvot* (commandments), either apprehending them instinctively or being specifically instructed by an angel of God.

HOW THE INDIVIDUAL ANIMALS WERE CHOSEN

While according to one opinion all the animals destined to be taken aboard the ark were born shortly before they entered, another maintains that Noah had to be selective because more animals appeared than were required.

God instructed Noah to take those animals which lay down as they reached the ark. In one case, a lioness appeared with two cubs, all three crouching. However, the cubs began to fight with their mother who then arose—thus disqualifying herself. Noah led the cubs into the ark.

An opposing view is that Noah ordered the animals to pass in front of the ark, but chose those who remained rooted in place.

Animals were, also, judged in terms of their previous behavior. Only those who had not "sinned" by mating with other species were admitted into the ark.

THOSE THAT DIDN'T MAKE IT

The fabulous *re'em*, a wild ox of enormous height, was simply too tall to get through the door. Noah tied it to the ark and it "plowed furrows" in the water. Its offspring, however, did come aboard.

The animals who were not accepted remained standing around the ark for seven days. When the rains began to descend, the sinful and doomed human population tried to storm the ark, promising to repent if taken in. However, lions and bears, themselves rejected, kept watch around the ark and attacked these people when they tried to overturn it. Most were slain; the rest escaped and died in the flood.

WHAT THEY ATE

Minority opinion among the commentators has it that Noah took aboard dried figs that served as food for both humans and beasts. The majority opinion, however, maintains that he took food appropriate for each species: chopped straw for the camel, barley for the donkey, vine tendrils for the elephants, *hazubah* (a shrubby plant) for the deer, and glass [sic] for the ostriches.

Part of the covenant that God made with Noah before he entered the ark was an assurance that all this produce would not decay while they were in the ark.

Noah did not know what to feed some of the animals—the little *zikit* (probably a chameleon), for example. Once, as Noah was cutting open a pomegranate a worm dropped out of the fruit, and the *zikit* devoured it. Noah took the cue. After that he kneaded bran and let it stand until it "bred" worms, which he could feed to the little animal.

WHO DID WHAT

In the division of responsibilities between Noah and his sons, Noah took care of the wild animals, Shem, the domesticated ones, Ham, the birds, and Japeth, the reptiles. The legends do not indicate what Noah's wife, Naamah, or her daughters-in-law did.

Noah and his sons needed God's "favor" to know which animals to feed at which times. Some ate once a day, others twice, still others three times. Some dined in the first hour of the day, some in the second or third, others in the first third of the night, or the middle, or at dawn.

Noah (and, some say, his sons as well), occupied with feeding animals around the clock, did not sleep for an entire year. This and the cold took a toll on Noah's health: he coughed and spit up blood.

Noah once found the *urshana* (probably a mythical bird) sleeping in a corner. When he asked whether it was hungry, the crea-

ture replied, "I saw you were very busy and I didn't want to add to your cares." Noah, impressed, blessed the creature with eternal life.

HOW THE ANIMALS BEHAVED

When the flood waters began to toss the ark from side to side, all those inside were "shaken up like lentils in a pot." The lions began to roar, the oxen lowed, the wolves howled, and all the other animals gave vent to their feelings, each through the sounds it had the power to utter. Eventually, as the ark began to float, they settled down. All the animals became tame in the ark. Noah walked on the snakes and scorpions without being injured.

Three incidents broke the peaceful atmosphere. The lion, who suffered with a fever all the time, did not annoy the other animals. However, once Noah fed the lion late and the beast struck him with its paw, laming him for life.

Then there were the three inhabitants of the ark who broke the rule of celibacy: Ham, the dog, and the raven. The raven openly called upon all the other animals to violate the prohibition but apparently they did not.

The third peace breaker was a cat. A pair of mice had been sitting placidly next to one of the cats. Suddenly remembering that her father [sic] had been in the habit of devouring mice, the cat jumped at the mouse. A hole miraculously materialized and the mouse escaped into it. The cat inserted her paw, and trying to pull the rodent out, clawed the mouse's cheeks and widened her mouth. The mouse escaped further injury, and after things quieted down, went to Noah and asked him to sew up her cheek.

Noah got a hair from a pig while the swine was sleeping (others say he had the mouse extract the hair) and used it to repair the damage.

HOW LONG THEY WERE INSIDE

Humans and beasts were cooped up in the ark for an entire year. The rains came down for forty days and forty nights. When they stopped, the waters began to slowly recede. The ark came to rest atop Mount Ararat five months after the flood had begun. Three months later, the mountaintops became visible (which is when Noah sent out the raven and the dove), and four months after that, the land was dry enough for the inhabitants to emerge from the ark.

THE RAVEN

Noah, who understood bird language, knew that the raven was the smartest bird and could recognize signs of life from high up. Therefore he decided to send out the raven to see if the waters had subsided. The raven was reluctant to go and argued with Noah: "Of all the birds," he said, "why do you have to send me?"

Noah responded, "What need does the world have of you?"—meaning that ravens are good neither for eating nor for holy sacrifices. "God hates me and you do, too," said the raven. "God told you to take seven of the 'pure' animals into the ark but only two of the 'impure' category, to which I belong. And you hate me, because you don't choose as messenger a bird of one of the kinds that have seven represented here but me, of whom there is but one pair. Suppose I should die of the heat or the cold—the world would be poorer by a whole species of animals!"

In the end the raven flew out, but he merely circled around the ark and returned empty-handed, as it were. Another view claims that he did not fulfill his mission because he came upon a dead man's body and proceeded to devour it, forgetting his mission in the process.

In spite of this, God sent the raven back and told Noah to receive it because it was destined for another mission in the far future: to bring food to Elijah when the prophet was exiled by the tyrant Samarian King Ahab during a severe drought.

THE DOVE

The dove was not sent out on a mission with the expectation that she would return to the ark, but, rather, sent in the hope that she would find a place to settle. On her first trip she returned because the land had not dried up and doves do not like to dwell on mountaintops. The second time, she brought back an olive leaf from the Mount of Olives in the Holy Land, which had not been ravaged by the flood, although hot water vapors had led to destruction there, too.

Another view is that the gates of the Garden of Eden opened for the dove, who found her olive leaf there. She did not bring back something "better," like a cinnamon or balsam leaf, to make a point (some say to God, others to Noah): "Let my food be as bitter as the olive and dependent on God, rather than sweet as honey and dependent on flesh and blood."

When the third time the dove was sent out it did not return, Noah knew that the land had dried.

NEVER AGAIN

A week later, Noah removed the roof of the ark and saw that the waters were gone. God then instructed him to let everyone out of the ark, and after they all emerged, Noah made a sacrifice of every clean animal and bird to thank God. God, for his part, promised never to destroy the earth again, and He made a rainbow in the sky as a sign of this covenant between Him and all the creatures of the earth, that never again would they be wiped out. "Never again shall all flesh be cut off by the waters of a flood, and never again shall there be a flood to destroy the earth." (Gen. 9:11)

—A.C.

A CHAPTER OF SONG: PEREK SHIRA

Introduction

Perek Shira is one of the most unusual pieces of writing in Jewish literature. According to contemporary scholars, *Perek Shira* is one of the oldest texts of Merkabah mysticism, the first flowering of Jewish mysticism in the early centuries of the Common Era. The text was known for hundreds of years, but during the great mystic revival in Safed in the sixteenth century, *Perek Shira* began to be recited as a prayer and to appear in printed prayerbooks.

Perek Shira is a mysterious and compelling vision of the entire world of God's creation, the entire cosmos, engaged in song. Every creature, every living and inanimate thing sings its own special song. And the song each sings is almost invariably a verse from the Bible. The difficulties lie in the relationship between the creature or object mentioned and the verse ascribed as its "song."

Many of the verses are clear. One kind of song chooses a verse in which the subject is mentioned—for examples, see the songs of the earth, the sun, and the sparrow. In other cases an attribute of the subject is mentioned—for example the cat is associated with its hunting instincts and the lion with its fearsome roar. Occasionally the songs depend on Hebrew puns. The elephant, for instance, sings, "How *great* are your works . . ."

The aptness of many verses remains unclear, especially if other, more obvious verses from the Bible come to mind. With Psalm 147 available ("He does not prize the strength of horses"), one wonders why the song for the horse was chosen. Why not the familiar "little foxes" of the Song of Songs? Surprises such as these and choices even more incomprehensible, such as the songs of the wolf and the rooster, lead one to suspect allegorical or mystical meanings associated with *Perek Shira* that have been lost. Such a view is borne out by the stories of King David and the singing frog which were chosen (probably later) to preface the work.

The Israeli scholar Malachi Beit-Arie has done an exhaustive study of this marvelous work complete with a critical edition, lengthy introductions, and scholarly notes. Unfortunately this doctoral dissertation is in Hebrew and is not accessible to the English reader.

The translation of *Perek Shira* that follows is quite possibly the first done in English. Because some may wish to use this translation as an aid to understanding the Hebrew version found in a traditional prayerbook, the Beit-Arie edition has not been followed, but instead a version has been chosen which stays close to a standard prayerbook printing (such as those found in the little *siddurim* published by Eshkol Press in Israel or the large *Otzar ha-Tefilah* published by Hebraica Press in New York). Occasionally Beit-Arie's notes and emendations have been relied upon when there were difficult textual problems, and certain untranslatable puns or major textual confusions have been eliminated. Aside from those few exceptions what follows below is the complete text.

The Preface

> "By the beasts of the earth and the birds of the sky, He makes us wise." (Job 35:11)
>
> "Rabbi Yochanon said: Even if we have not been given the Torah we still would have learned modesty from the cat, honesty from the ant, chastity from the dove, and good manners from the rooster." (Talmud, Eruvin 100b)

Rabbi said: "Anyone who occupies himself with *Perek Shira* in this world will be worthy to teach and to learn, to do and to fulfill God's commandments. His teaching will be realized by the strength of his own hand. He will escape the evil inclination, terrible disasters, punishment after death, the sentence of hell, and the calamitous 'birthpangs' that will precede Messiah. He will be worthy of long life, the messianic days and the World to Come."

Rabbi Eliezar said: "Anyone who says this song in this world will merit the World to Come. How do we know this? Because in Exodus 15:1 where it says, 'And Moses sang' the Hebrew really says 'And Moses *will* sing'—in the future tense. And what else could this mean but in the future of the World to Come!"

Rabbi Eliezar the Great said: "Anyone who occupies himself with *Perek Shira* every day—surely I testify that he will merit the World to Come, will be protected from disasters, the devil, the evil impulse, and all other difficulties and harm.

"Study 'with all your heart and with all your soul' (Deut. 6:5) to know my ways, to guard the gates of my temple and my Torah, and to follow my commandments and precepts. Keep my Torah in your heart and let my awe be before your eyes. Keep your lips away from all sin and I will be with you in every place you go. I will teach you wisdom and understanding in everything.

"Know that all that the Holy One, blessed be He, created, He created for his own glory, as it is written: 'everyone who is called by my name, whom I created for my glory, whom I formed and made' (Isa. 43:7)."

Our rabbis tell the following story: "At the time that King David completed the Book of Psalms, he became full of pride and said to the Holy One, blessed be He, 'Surely there is no creature which you have made that can sing songs and praises greater than mine.'

"At that exact moment a frog appeared before him and said, 'David, do not be so proud, for I can sing songs and praises even greater than yours! And not only that, but in every song that I sing there exist three thousand allegories. For it is said: "He composed three thousand proverbs, and his songs numbered one thousand and five." (1 Kings 5:12)

" 'And not only that, but I also perform a great good deed and this is it: There is in the sea one particular creature whose food can only come from the water. At the time that that creature is hungry, I place myself before him and allow him to devour me. This is indeed a good deed! For it fulfills what is written in the Torah: "If your enemy is hungry, give him bread to eat; and if he is thirsty, give him water to drink." (Prov. 25:21)' "

The Songs

The heavens say: "The heavens declare the glory of God; the sky proclaims his handiwork." (Ps. 19:1–2)

The earth says: "The earth is the Lord's, and the fullness thereof, and they that dwell in it." (Ps. 24:1) And also says: "From the end of the earth we hear singing: glory to the righteous!" (Isa. 24:16)

The Garden of Eden says: "Awake O north wind; and come, thou south; blow upon my garden that the spices thereof may flow out." (Song of Songs 4:16)

Gehenna says: "For he has satisfied the longing soul and filled the hungry soul with goodness." (Ps. 107:9)

The desert says: "The arid desert shall be glad; the wilderness shall rejoice." (Isa. 35:1)

The fields say: "The Lord by wisdom founded the earth: by understanding he established the heavens." (Prov. 3:19)

The waters say: "When he makes his voice heard, there is a rumbling of waters in the skies; he makes vapors rise from the end of the earth." (Jer. 51:16)

The seas say: "The Lord on high is mightier than the noise of many waters, than the mighty waves of the sea." (Ps. 93:4)

The rivers say: "Let the rivers clap their hands; let the mountains sing for joy together." (Ps. 98:8)

The springs say: "And singers and dancers alike shall say: All my springs are in you." (Ps. 87:7)

The day says: "Day to day utters speech, and night to night expresses knowledge." (Ps. 19:3)

The night says: "To relate your steadfast love in the morning, and your faithfulness at night." (Ps. 92:3)

The sun says: "Sun and moon stand still on high as your arrows fly in brightness, your flashing spear in brilliance." (Hab. 3:11)

The moon says: "He appointed the moon for seasons; the sun knows his going down." (Ps. 104:19)

The stars say: "You are the Lord alone; you have made heaven, the heaven of heavens, with all their host, the earth, and all things that are in it, the seas, and all that is therein, and you preserve them all, and the host of heaven worships you." (Neh. 8:6)

The clouds say: "He made darkness his secret place; his pavilion round about him was dark water and thick clouds of the skies." (Ps. 18:12)

The clouds of glory say: "Also he burdens the thick cloud with an overflow; the cloud scatters lightning." (Job 37:11)

The wind says: "I will say to the north: 'Give back!'; and to the south: 'Do not withhold!' Bring my sons from afar, and my daughters from the end of the earth." (Isa. 43:6)

The lightning says: "He makes lightnings for the rain; he brings the wind out of the treasuries." (Ps. 135:7)

The dew says "I will be to Israel like dew; he shall blossom like the lily; he shall strike root like a Lebanon tree." (Hos. 14:6)

The rains say: "You, O God, did send a plentiful rain, whereby you did strengthen your inheritance when it languished." (Ps. 68:10)

The trees in the field say: "Then the trees of the wood shall sing for joy at the presence of the Lord, for he comes to judge the earth." (1 Chron. 16:33)

The vine says: "Thus said the Lord: As when new wine is present in the cluster, one says: 'Don't destroy it: there is good in it,' so I will do for the sake of my servants, and not destroy everything." (Isa. 65:8)

The fig tree says: "He who guards the fig tree shall eat its fruit." (Prov. 27:18)

The pomegranate says: "Your cheek is like a piece of a pomegranate within its locks." (Song of Songs 4:3)

The palm tree says: "The righteous man flourishes like the palm tree: he grows like a cedar in Lebanon." (Ps. 92:13)

The apple tree says: "Like the apple tree among the trees of the wood, so is my beloved among the young men. I sat down under his shadow with great delight, and his fruit was sweet to my taste." (Song of Songs 2:3)

The stalk of wheat says: "A Song of Ascent. Out of the depths I have cried to you, O Lord." (Ps. 130:1)

The stalk of barley says: "A prayer of the afflicted, when he faints and pours out his complaint before the Lord." (Ps. 102:1)

All the rest of the stalks say: "The meadows are clothed with flocks; the valleys also are covered over with corn; they shout for joy, they also sing." (Ps. 65:14)

The vegetables in the field say: "Watering her furrows abundantly, settling her ridges; you make it soft with showers; you bless its growth." (Ps. 65:11)

The grasses say: "May the glory of the Lord endure forever; let the Lord rejoice in his works." (Ps. 104:31)

The rooster says: "At the time that the Holy One, blessed be he, comes among the righteous ones who dwell in the Garden of Eden, all the trees of the Garden pour out fragrant spices and sing and offer praises. Then he too is aroused and offers praises."

The rooster crows in seven voices:

The first voice says: "Lift up your heads, O you gates; and be lifted up you everlasting doors; and the King of glory shall come in. Who is this King of glory? The Lord strong and mighty, the Lord, mighty in battle." (Ps. 24:7)

The second voice says: "Lift up your heads, O you gates; and lift them up, you everlasting doors, that the King of glory may come in. Who is this King of glory? The Lord of hosts, he is the King of glory. Selah." (Ps. 24:9)

The third voice says: "Arise, you righteous ones, and busy yourselves with Torah so that your reward will be doubled in the world to come."

The fourth voice says: "I wait for your salvation, O Lord." (Gen. 49:18)

The fifth voice says: "How long will you sleep, O lazy one?" (Prov. 6:9)

The sixth voice says: "Do not love sleep lest you come to poverty; open your eyes and you shall be satisfied with bread." (Prov. 20:13)

The seventh voice says: "It is time to act for the Lord; they have violated your Torah." (Ps. 119:126)

The chicken says: "He gives food to all flesh. His steadfast love endures forever." (Ps. 136:25)

The dove says: "I piped like a swift or a crane, I moaned like a dove; as my eyes, all worn, looked to heaven: 'My Lord, I am in straits; by my surety.' " (Isa. 38:14) The dove speaks before the Holy One, blessed be he, "Master of the Universe, may my food be as bitter as the olive but entrusted to your hand rather than sweet as honey and dependent on one of flesh and blood." (Talmud, Eruvin 186)

The eagle says: "You, O Lord God of hosts, God of Israel, bestir yourself to bring all nations to account; have no pity on all the treacherous villains." (Ps. 59:6)

The crane says: "Praise the Lord with the lyre; with the ten-stringed harp sing to him." (Ps. 33:2)

The sparrow says: "Even the sparrow has found a home, and the swallow a nest for herself in which to set her young, near your altar, O Lord of hosts, my king and my God." (Ps. 84:4)

The swallow says: "That my whole being might sing hymns to you endlessly; O Lord my God, I will praise you forever." (Ps. 30:13)

The peacock says: "My help is from the Lord who made heaven and earth." (Ps. 121:2)

The desert bird says: "Light is sown for the righteous and gladness for the upright in heart." (Ps. 97:11)

The dove says: "Comfort, O comfort, my people, says your God." (Isa. 40:1)

The stork says: "Speak tenderly to Jerusalem, and declare to her that her term of service is over, that her iniquity is expiated; for she has received at the hand of the Lord double for her sins." (Isa. 40:2)

The raven says: "Who provides for the raven his provision when his young ones cry to God?" (Job 38:41)

The starling says: "Their offspring shall be known among the nations, their descendants in the midst of the peoples. All who see them shall recognize that they are a stock the Lord has blessed." (Isa. 61:9) "Sing forth, O righteous, to the Lord; it is fitting that the upright acclaim him." (Ps. 33:1)

The domestic goose says: "Praise the Lord; call on his name; proclaim his deeds among the nations. Sing praises unto him; speak of all his wondrous acts." (Ps. 105:1–2)

The goose who lives in the desert, when he sees Israel engaged with Torah, says: "A voice rings out: 'Clear in the desert a road for the Lord! Level in the wilderness a highway for our God!' " (Isa. 40:3) And when finding its food in the desert, the goose says, "Cursed is he who trusts in man." (Jer. 17:5) "Blessed is he who trusts in the Lord, whose trust is in the Lord alone." (Jer. 17:7)

The chicken says: "Trust in the Lord forever; for the Lord God is an everlasting rock." (Isa. 26:4)

The vulture says: "I will whistle to them and gather them, for I will redeem them; they shall increase and continue increasing." (Zech. 10:8)

The butterfly says: "I will lift up my eyes to the mountains; from where does my help come?" (Ps. 121:1)

The locust says: "O Lord you are my God; I will extol you, I will praise your name; for you have done wonderful things, counsels of steadfast faithfulness." (Isa. 25:1)

The spider says, "Praise him with resounding cymbals; praise him with clanging cymbals." (Ps. 150:5)

The fly, when Israel is not engaged with Torah, says: "A voice rings out: 'Proclaim!' Another asks: 'What shall I proclaim?' 'All flesh is grass, all its goodness like the flower of the field.' " (Isa. 40:6) " 'Grass withers, flowers fade—but the word of our God is always fulfilled!' " (Isa. 40:8) "I will create a new expression of the lips; peace, peace for the far and the near says the Lord, and I will heal them." (Isa. 57:19)

The sea monsters say: "Praise the Lord, O you who are on earth, all sea monsters and ocean depths." (Ps. 148:7)

Leviathan says: "Praise the Lord for he is good, his steadfast love is eternal." (Ps. 136:1)

The fish say: "The voice of the Lord is on the waters, the God of glory thunders, the Lord is upon the mighty waters." (Ps. 29:3)

The frog says: "Blessed be the name of his glorious majesty forever and ever."

The small cow who is ritually pure says: "Who is like you, O Lord, among the gods? Who is like you, glorious in holiness, fearful in praises, doing wonders?" (Exod. 15:11)

The large cow who is ritually pure says, "Sing joyously to God, our strength; raise a shout for the God of Jacob." (Ps. 81:2)

The small cow who is ritually impure says: "Do good, O Lord, to those who are good, to the upright in heart." (Ps. 125:4)

The large cow who is ritually impure says: "You shall enjoy the fruit of your labors; you shall be happy and you shall prosper." (Ps. 128:2)

The camel says: "The Lord roars from on high, he makes his voice heard from his holy dwelling; he roars aloud over his earthly abode." (Jer. 25:30)

The horse says: "As the eyes of slaves follow their master's hands, as the eyes of a slave-girl follow the hand of her mistress, so our eyes are toward the Lord, our God, awaiting his favor." (Ps. 123:2)

The mule says: "All the kings of the earth shall praise you, O Lord, for they have heard the words you spoke." (Ps. 138:4)

The donkey says: "Yours, O Lord, is the greatness and the power and the glory and the victory and the majesty; for all that is in heaven and on earth is yours, O Lord; yours is the kingdom and you are exalted as head above all." (1 Chron. 29:11)

The bull says: "Then Moses and the Israelites sang this song to the Lord. They said: 'I will sing to the Lord, for he has triumphed gloriously, horse and driver he has hurled into the sea.' " (Exod. 15:1)

The animals of the field say: "Blessed be he who is good and does good."

The deer says: "And I will sing of your strength, extol each morning your faithfulness; for you have been my haven, a refuge in time of trouble." (Ps. 59:17)

The elephant says: "How great are your works, O Lord, how very deep are your thoughts!" (Ps. 92:6)

The lion says: "The Lord goes forth like a warrior, like a fighter he whips up his rage. He yells, he roars aloud, he charges upon his enemies." (Isa. 42:13)

The bear says: "Let the desert and its towns cry aloud, the villages where Kedar dwells; let Sela's inhabitants shout, call out from the peaks of the mountains. Let them do honor to the Lord, and tell his glory in the coastlands." (Isa. 42:11–12)

The wolf says: "In all charges of misappropriation—pertaining to an ox, an ass, a sheep, a garment, or any other loss, whereof one party alleges, 'This is it'—the case of both parties shall come before God; he whom God declares guilty shall pay double to the other." (Exod. 22:8)

The fox says: "Woe to him who builds his house by unrighteousness, and his chambers by injustice; that uses his neighbor's service without pay and does not give him his wages." (Jer. 22:13)

The cat says: "I pursued my enemies and overtook them; I did not turn back till I destroyed them." (Ps. 18:38)

The insects say: "Let Israel rejoice in its maker; let the children of Zion exult in their king." (Ps. 149:2)

The serpent says: "The Lord supports all who stumble, and makes all who are bent down stand straight." (Ps. 145:14)

The scorpion says: "The Lord is good to all, and his mercy is upon all his works." (Ps. 145:9)

The snail says: "Like a snail that melts away as it moves, like a woman's stillbirth, may they never see the sun!" (Ps. 58:9)

The ant says: "Go to the ant, you sluggard; consider her ways and be wise." (Prov. 6:6)

The mouse says: "And you are righteous about all that befalls us, for you act in truth and we have done evil." (Neh. 9:33)

The rat says: "Let everything that has breath praise the Lord. Hallelujah." (Ps. 150:6)

The dogs say: "Come, let us bow down and kneel, bend the knee before the Lord our maker." (Ps. 95:6)

Blessed be the Lord God, God of Israel, who alone does wonders. And blessed be his glorious name for ever—may his glory fill the entire earth. Amen and Amen.

—B.W.H.

AT THE EDGES OF CREATION: ANGELS, DEMONS, AND BEASTS OF FANCY

At the fringes of creation are a number of phenomena that seem to have been hastily planned or made or that appear to be byproducts of the origin of the created universe. They inhabit the world of myth and imagination, but their influence on human events has been considerable, if only because their influence is believed. This is the world of Jewish legend and folklore. It is a strand of human storytelling that is at least as old as Judaism itself. The Bible speaks of mythological wonders only sparsely, and it is very likely that the biblical materials were gleaned from a much larger stock of myth common to the peoples of the ancient Near East. Much of this material resurfaced in the religious literature of a later period—in the Apocrypha, the Apocalypses and sectarian writings, the Greek Jewish writings, the New Testament, the Talmud and Midrash, the Koran and Islamic folklore, and in the Kabbalah.

What follows is a description of some of the more interesting and important motifs. They are generally presented in a composite fashion, with a minimal attempt to show their sources or their history, or to reconcile contradictions. Myth, in fact, often presents facts in a contradictory manner, and it is only by the juxtaposing of many variations on a theme that we can see how myth is a projection of our own desires, fears, and speculations. It is as the latter that myth is most interesting, and the most deserving of study.

Angels

One must understand angels within the framework of the universe as seen by the Jewish mystics. There are, according to the Kabbalah, four worlds. The highest is called the world of Emanation (*Atzilut*), a realm of pure divine light, unmixed with any physical form or substance. Below this is the world of Creation (*Beriah*), also called the Throne or Chariot (*Merkavah*), as the name suggests, God's dwelling-place, insofar as God can be said to dwell anywhere. Below this is the world of Formation (*Yetzirah*), the realm of the angels, and below this the world of Action (*Asiyah*), the physical world in which we dwell. The two lower worlds, *Yetzirah* and *Asiyah*, are thought of as God's "footstool."

There are millions of angels—by one reckoning, 496,000 myriads—and no two are alike. The angels were created on either the second or the fifth day of Creation, and they are appointed as guardians over each and every object in the world, no matter how small (a blade of grass, an insect) or large (nations, continents, seas). Angels are made of a tenuous substance, and are generally invisible. When they do appear they take on a form, usually humanlike, suited to the needs and understanding of a particular perceiver. Some say that the angels become visible by clothing themselves in a clod of dirt. Others say that an angel is an outer manifestation of God Himself. But in general, angels are closely related to the events of human life and are, to some extent, dependent on human action: It is said that angels are created daily by the good deeds of human beings. The angels in heaven must wait each morning for Jewish prayers to begin, before their own songs of praise for God can begin.

Angels belong to the domain of sentience. Each angel embodies a particular emotion or attitude, differing from every other angel both in content and degree. This would seem to make each angel a mere shadow of human impulses, but angels are generally regarded as complete beings, endowed with intelligence, speech, upright posture, and freedom of movement. Each day, angels are dispatched to earth on errands. Their main duties are to sing God's praises in heavenly choruses, to intercede between God and human beings, to carry prayer to God, to announce God's will or plans, to help fight evildoers, and to move the heavenly spheres.

Angels almost always appear in the Bible as anonymous, humanlike messengers. They appear most frequently in the Torah (the Pentateuch) and in the historical narratives (as individual beings) and in the Psalms (as "heavenly hosts" and choruses); they appear least frequently in the Prophets. Only those prophets with a well-developed penchant for the supernatural, such as Isaiah, Ezekiel, and Zechariah, have angelic visions. The most developed angelology in the Hebrew Bible is that of the Book of Daniel, which is generally regarded as the latest in time of composition, reflecting the mythological influences of Babylonian, Persian, and Greek cultures.

Angels are ascribed to some Biblical events where they are not explicitly mentioned. They served as witnesses at the wedding of Adam and Eve, accused them after their transgressions, made Eve pregnant, removed Enoch from the earth, led animals into Noah's ark, rescued Abraham from Nimrod's fiery furnace (an event not found in the Bible, but known by tradition), spoke to Sarah about conceiving a child, argued with God over Isaac's near sacrifice, appeared to Moses in the burning bush, led Israel through the Red Sea to Sinai, mourned the death of Moses and later, the destruction of the Temple.

The language of angels is Hebrew, traditionally believed to be the original language of mankind and of God Himself. Some say that the angels know *only* Hebrew, and thus prayers that are not meant for angels' ears

An etching of "Abraham's Sacrifice" by Rembrandt van Rijn, 1655.

(for fear of inciting their jealousy or wrath) are offered in Aramaic or other languages. Since angels are posted as guardians over each nation of the world, one must imagine that they communicate through interpreters.

The names of angels are almost never mentioned in the Bible, and a tradition maintains that angels' names were not made known to mankind until the Babylonian exile. Certain sects of religious zealots guarded the names of angels as a closely kept secret, but these names became fairly widespread around the beginning of the Christian era. The best-known named angels are the four "Angels of the Presence": Michael (guardian of Israel), Gabriel (guardian of Paradise, and an especially important figure in Islam), Raphael (angel of healing, appointed over individual souls), and Uriel (leader of the angelic hosts, and guardian of the underworld). Other well-known ones are Raguel, Panuel, Suriel, Zagzagel, Sandalfon, and Metatron. Angels' names are usually nouns or verbs compounded with the word "El" (here with the sense of "God's"). Knowledge of these names was particularly important to the mystics: the soul, journeying through the celestial spheres, could slip past an angelic guard by reciting its correct name—a sort of password that made the journeyer invisible to the angel or immune to his authority.

There are also fallen angels, who rebelled against God when man was created, and who invaded the earth (Gen. 6:2–4) to mate with human wives, creating giants and monsters. Some say that these were the first to supply knowledge of civilized arts, such as medicine, astronomy, metallurgy, meteorology, and the manufacture of cosmetics. Some identify Satan and the demons with fallen angels (see "Satan" and "Demons" entries).

There is some debate as to whether angels are superior to human beings. In terms of spiritual substance, abilities, and powers, angels rank higher, but in terms of complexity, free will, and moral potential, human beings rank higher. A repentant evildoer is preferred by God over a thousand angels. It is this distinction between angels and humans that is probably the most instructive about the nature and meaning of angels. Their world is a pale reflection of our own but an exaggerated register of our actions. Each choice, each deed of ours is played out by them as a polyphonic symphony. They are God's bureaucrats, doormen, ushers, messengers, and waiters. They help to make the world a classier place to live in, but it is human beings who make the world (and its continuance) possible. We are the calligraphy; they are the illumination.

Demons

According to one account, God created the demons on the eve of the Sabbath. He had intended to create legitimate creatures whose existence would be beneficial to the world, but because the Sabbath intervened, He had to leave them unfinished, and thus a whole population of beings without souls inadvertently came into being. The demons are innumerable. If the eye had power to see them, no creature could endure the sight. They surround us like the ridge around a field. They are responsible for the crushing of crowds at public meetings, for fatigue in the knees, for the wearing out of clothes. They cause burning noonday heat, wet dreams, bruised feet, the loss of house keys, loss of memory, and loss of mind.

There are demons that look like people or animals and those that are purely spiritual. They live in the interstices of creation, lapping up the fire, water, air, and slime. The males generally have hair; the females are bald. In some respects they are strangely endowed with human moral customs: they won't copulate in the presence of spirits or people; they will not touch alcohol; they will not steal property that is sealed, counted, measured, or tied up; they, in turn, are fiercely jealous of property rights, and strangely respectful of human lawcourt decisions—demons have even been taken to court and sued.

The presence of demons is both perceived and inferred. They inhabit dark or barren places. Like the angels, they have posts and functions. They return to places they have attacked. They consort in nut trees or in damp and dingy locales. Scholars are especially vulnerable to *succubi*, ubiquitous female sprites with long, disheveled hair, who steal into their dreams and beget demon-children by their involuntary issue (see the "Lilith" entry). Some, called *dybbuks*, crawl inside of people's bodies (see the "Dybbuk" entry) and speak through their mouths. If one wants to discover the presence of demons, one should take sifted ashes from the roasted afterbirth of a black cat and sprinkle them around one's bed; the next morning one will see something like the footprints of a chicken. This procedure, unfortunately, does not work very well, especially in good medieval households, where it is often likely that the footprints *are* those of a chicken.

Anger or envy invite demons. Likewise, *courting* anger or envy. Also: loose talk, gossip, and malediction. Speaking of demons frivolously can incite their wrath. Anything that gives the devil a chance to speak, such as hyperbole in criticizing someone, is inadvisable; also, ending one's reading or writing on an ominous phrase, leaving a book lying open, vows and curses—even when reported secondhand, working on Saturday night after the end of the Sabbath, working late any night; Wednesdays are full of trouble from the demons, one should stay indoors. It has been said that the turnings of the life cycle make one vulnerable—thus calling forth precautions around births, circumcisions, weddings, bar mitzvahs, deaths, and burials. Staying in the synagogue alone after the evening prayers carries risk of demons; likewise, hanging out in ruins or abandoned houses.

Demons also have an affinity for letters of the Hebrew alphabet: they suck them dry of vitality for their nourishment. Sacred books should thus be kept in use as long and as much as possible, and not be stored in rooms when worn out, but given a decent burial like human beings, lest they fall into the wrong hands. Demons are associated with the evil eye, winds and storms, thunder and lightning, cold, the north, and northern countries. Demons have an affinity for fixed numbers (census, crowd counting, stating the amount of one's salary or total wealth). They attack food or drink left out overnight, still waters of any kind, pared fingernails, and shorn hair. They go after sleeping people because during that state body and soul are separated.

There are many devices for warding off demons. In general, these fall into three main categories: (1) driving them away by prescribed means, (2) buying them off with gifts and bribes, (3) deceiving them by disguises and switches. More specific weapons against demons include: a good family name; piety; biblical readings, especially Psalm 91; blowing the ram's horn; fasting; charity; posting guards; sprinkling salt; studying sacred writings, especially sitting wrapped in a prayer shawl; donning the prayer phylacteries (*tefillin*); posting *mezuzot*; amulets; incense; onions, garlic, leeks, herbs, and spices; the color blue; contact with metal; keeping a knife on hand; noisemaking, especially with bells and clappers; magical incantations; invocation of divine names, especially the name Shaddai ("Almighty"); exorcism; rinsing with running water; spitting in three directions; flipping the "fig" sign (an obscene gesture); keeping one's house clean and well-swept; the bedtime incantation: "On my right side, Michael; on my left side, Gabriel; before me, Uriel; behind me, Raphael; above me, God's presence."

Because demons are said to travel only in prescribed pathways, one presumably can upset their activity by changing one's habitual movements. Some people, for example, fight bad luck by letting their hair or beards grow long or by changing addresses or phone numbers. It is a frequent custom to change the names of sick people; to avoid naming babies after living relatives; to keep one's eyes on someone departing until the person is out of sight. What might be called dysphemism (the opposite of euphemism) is a means of making demons think that something desirable is not worth attacking: one might say over a handsome baby, "*oy, di sheyne miuskeit*" ("O, what a beautiful ugliness!"). Sometimes, weddings include weeping and wailing, to disguise the festive nature of the occasion.

The following Jewish rituals are believed especially potent weapons against demons: the Yom Kippur ritual, the Passover ritual, the donning of a four-cornered fringed garment, the recitation of *Kaddish*, the *Kiddush* over wine, the partaking of Sabbath bread with salt, the Sabbath prayers and hymns, the bridegroom's breaking of a glass at weddings, the jokes of the wedding jester, the dancing at Simhat Torah, the kissing of a *mezuzah*, the public reading from the Torah (provided those called consecutively for *aliyot* are not from the same family), the performance of any good deed.

The mystics say that the world of demons is the coarser part of the physical world, which imitates the spiritual world with its own hierarchy. Because of events that went awry in the world's creation, this demonic world, called the realm of *kelippot* ("shells"), also contains lost sparks of divinity. In fact, it is only through positive spiritual energy that demons can exist at all: they are drawn to all beings of a higher nature than theirs, which is why they seek their nourishment in the human world. A single evil deed can create a demon. Because demons are often the agents of divine punishment, they play a role in the economy of the universe. If human misdeeds were to disappear, so would the demons. But, in more recent times, because of the evils of the world, they seem to have gained the power to grow and flourish independently. As one expert (A. Steinsaltz) has put it: "Their ontological status is no longer clear." Or, as one of our great-grandparents might put it: ptui, ptui, ptui!

Satan

The word "satan" originally meant simply "adversary" or "obstacle." In Jewish tradition it came to be a proper name, one of several, designating the chief of evil powers. Other common names for the prince of devils include Samael (meaning either "venom-god" or "blind god," or possibly derived from *Shemal*, "left," the name of a Syrian devil), Belial or Beliar ("worthless"), and Ashmodai or Asmodeus ("destroyer"). Sometimes, these names designate separate figures in the army of demons; other times, the names are synonyms for the chief demon. Sometimes, things predicated of one may contradict what is said about another; the Day of Atonement, for example, is the one day of the year on which Satan has no power (because the numerical value of his name in Hebrew is 364), yet it is also said that the "goat for Azazel," the scapegoat bearing the community's sins on Yom Kippur, is sacrificed as a bribe to Samael, who is presumably identified with the demon Azazel, and with Satan.

Most of the lore about Satan in Judaism developed in post-Biblical times, under the influence of Christian, Gnostic, and pagan beliefs. Belief in a devil of some sort is common to most religions, but Satan is surprisingly absent from most of the Hebrew Bible. In fact, the few references that do occur suggest nothing of the Prince of the Underworld known in later times. In the Garden of Eden story the serpent who misled Adam and Eve is not an incarnation of the devil (that idea occurs for the first time in the Greek Apocalypse of Baruch, a Hellenistic work) but a mere "beast of the field whom the Lord God had made" (Gen. 3:1); the suggestion here is of a conflict between man and his own animal nature, not one between God and Satan, as later allegorization of the story stressed. Even when Satan's role in the story came to be believed, he was not always identified directly with the serpent; another source in the Apocalypse of Baruch says that he (here called Sammuel) planted the forbidden tree that led to the downfall of Adam and Eve.

Ṣatan also appears in 1 Chronicles 21:1 as a figure who incited David to take a census of Israel, an act which causes a plague to strike the people. This book is a very late biblical book and not the most representative of biblical thought; in an earlier version of the same story (2 Sam. 24:1), it is God himself who gives the order for the census. It is hard to tell whether the common folkloric belief that fixed numbers are bad luck (see "Demons" entry) caused David's census to be identified with Satan or vice versa, but in any case, the author of Chronicles wanted to avoid ascribing the motivation for the census to God.

The most developed picture of Satan in the rest of the Hebrew Bible (where, in contrast to Chronicles, Satan is always referred to as "the Satan," that is, not as a name but as a common noun, "the Adversary") is in the book of Job's introductory chapters. There he is a *celestial* being (the quasi-"satanic" opposition of angels to human beings is a common motif in Jewish legend), serving in God's employ, and clearly incapable of acting without God's authorization. He "wanders to and fro about the earth," searching out opportunities to challenge the behavior of the righteous. When God boasts of the goodness of his servant Job, the Adversary argues that Job's good behavior is dependent solely on his good fortune, and that if Job were made to suffer, he would curse God—a charge against Job that results in God's allowing the Adversary to afflict Job with grievous injuries to test his faithfulness, thus opening the way to the main body of the work, Job's dialogue with his companions on *God's*—not the Adversary's—justice.

Satan here is a fully lawful being, indeed, a type of intelligence vitally necessary to the law's very existence, that is, the cutting edge of critical thinking. The Adversary seems to be an important advisor of God, yet, since God, as later tradition claimed, "takes counsel with those below Him in rank to teach humility to kings of flesh and blood," the Adversary is but a phase of God's own thinking, a dark mood, a black humor to which God allows others to give voice. In fact, from a literary standpoint *both* God and the Adversary, when appearing engaged in dialogue, are pasteboard figures. God speaks with him as a corporation executive to an advisor over the telephone, spelling out the issue for the record in clear legalese and moralese: "Have you considered my servant Job, who has no equal in the world, whole-hearted and upright, God-fearing and shunning evil?" God does not seem here to invest His whole self in those remarks; as the rabbis would say, He is providing "a mouth opener" to the Adversary—which suggests that He had planned to raise the "satanic" question himself.

The end of Job (chaps. 38–41) shows God as less sedentary and more the awesome divine warrior of Near Eastern mythological poetry. There "the Adversary" is not the heavenly courtier who drops the axe on Job but a panorama of the amoral wonders of nature, whose terrors are painstakingly reined in by God: seas, rains, hailstones, winds, planetary influences, birds and beasts of prey, wild horses and cattle, monsters of land and sea. Here it is God himself, and not a "satan," who is directly responsible for (selectively) orchestrating chaos in the world, for reasons known, if at all, by God alone, who here is clearly, in the words of Isaiah, the one "who makes peace and creates evil."

Still, whether from piety or the need to demonize, popular religion was never comfortable with asserting God's authorship of evil, and "the Adversary" eventually became a proper name, Satan; the sum total of the world's evils came to have a personality of its own. The New Testament stated Satan's proportions in a classic manner that influenced not only Christian belief but Jewish and Islamic, as well: ". . . that old serpent called the devil and Satan, which deceived the whole world. He was cast into earth, and his angels were cast out with him." (Rev. 12:9) Many strands of belief are brought together here, which the Midrash and Kabbalah augmented to a many-faceted demonic being: serpent; member of God's angelic court who rebelled and fell from favor; source of evil impulses in man (the *yetzer ha-ra*); tempter of human beings; accuser (*mekatreg*); author of human suffering; Angel of Death; motivator of all the sins recorded in biblical stories, including, besides the Fall, the golden calf, the Israelite desert rebellions, David's adultery with Bathsheba, etc.; spirit of cynicism behind a Jew's distrust of the "irrational" commandments, such as the prohibition on pork or on garments mixed of wool and flax; guardian angel of Esau and the kingdom of Edom; shadow side of divine emanation (the *sitra ahra*); prince of demons, and the consort of Lilith (see "Lilith" entry). It made little difference in later Jewish belief whether evil was personified in the singular as "Satan" or in the plural as "demons," in a male incarnation as "Samael," or in a female incarnation as "Lilith." The underlying fear was the same. A many-faceted demonic being is still demonic, which is to say, a simplification of reality.

Satan's power is in inverse proportion to our own. For all the service diabolizing has rendered in compelling people to stay on the straight and narrow, it tends to sap our power to confront adversity on our own terms (when it is granted us to do so). The horrors that afflict mankind, whether famine, plague or political terror, do not go away when depicted as "the Adversary." As Pogo used to say, "We have met the enemy, and he is us." The Baal Shem Tov, eighteenth-century founder of Hasidism, recognized that diabolizing is itself a form of diabolical behavior. "The devil," he told his followers, "wants you to be miserable about your sins, to cause you depression, and to make you leave off from serving God. Next time he tries this, say to him: 'I don't worry about small mistakes; my joy is in serving the Creator, and being happy in His presence. Begone!' "

Lilith

This creature is best known in Jewish tradition as the mother of demons. Because the Bible mentions an unnamed female human being with Adam (Gen. 1:27) before recounting the creation of Eve (Gen. 2:18–25), folklore identifies Lilith as the mysterious "first wife" (or "dark lady") in Adam's life. She is popular today with feminists because she vigorously asserted her equality with Adam by virtue of their simultaneous creation, insisting, among other things, on being on top during sexual intercourse. By uttering the divine name, she escaped to the Red Sea, where she begot demon children by the nocturnal emissions of unsuspecting males who were, as we say, thrilled and delighted in the night. God sent three angels—Sanvei, Sansanavei, and Samangalaf—to fetch her back to Adam. She refused to return, but as a result must endure daily the death of one hundred demon children. She takes revenge by injuring infants—boys up to eight days, girls up to twenty, in the actuarial reckoning of an earlier era.

One protects against her attack by posting an amulet bearing the names of the three messenger angels mentioned above, which are also fun to say. Much of what is known about Lilith comes from magical incantation bowls, inscribed in Aramaic, stemming from the milieu of Babylonian Jewry in the same era as that of the Talmud's formation. These ritual objects usually contained bans, excommunications, or "divorce" writs issued in the name of a noted rabbi, declaring Lilith's power over an individual household to be null and void.

In that Lilith, like most angels, imps, and demons, is a part of the world of human emotion and imagination, one must accord her reality and view her in service to no particular ideology. She has been created by the licentiousness of wayward husbands, the priggishness of puritanical preachers, the troubled sleep of virtuous scholars, the despair of barren or under-appreciated housewives, the arrogance of sexists, the anger of feminists, and the prurience of recreational readers. Academically speaking, she is a special category of spiritual blight (or plight) known as the *succubus* (and in Babylonian mythology as a *lilitu*), best personified, perhaps, as a night-travelling water sprite with long, thick, unkempt hair, a sweat shirt, black leotard, black Danskin tights, and red jogging shoes.

And when one reads, according to the Kabbalists, that even the Holy One, blessed be He, has, God forbid, a bit of Lilith in Him (or vice versa), one becomes aware of the gravity of Lilith's existence. The Torah is said to be written in black fire on white fire, and Lilith is a burning smudge of ink. She is as much a state of mind as a demon, indeed, a whole network of states of mind.

She is the alter ego of domesticated woman, of sibling-rival man, even of God's Shekhinah. She helped explain high infant mortality and Wednesday croupe. Freud met the like of her in patients under hypnosis. Generations of Portnoys begot demons by her through self-help. I. B. Singer saw her in the ever-present literary groupie—which reveals one important facet of her chracter: that she is, after all, in the male chauvinist viewpoint at least, a bit of a waif, and therefore in need of some care and kindness, for she, too, is one of God's creatures.

In fact, some of her other analogues in myth and folklore share one important feature: nobility of birth, often leading to exile and disgrace. Helen of Troy, Selene the moon-goddess, the queen of Sheba, the bride of Simon Magus, the fallen divine emanation Sophia, Antony's Cleopatra, and other itinerant or waxing-waning antiheroines, are all, in some sense, variations on Lilith, as well as, perhaps, Mary Magdalene the way the Christian heretics imagined her. A spacy (but authentic) Gnostic book called the Gospel of Philip contends that Jesus adopted Mary Magdalene as one of his close companions. He used to kiss her a lot on the mouth, according to this account, and when his other disciples asked in complaint, "How come you love her more than us?" he replied (one can't help imagining here a Groucho leer), "How come I don't love you as much as I love her?" Perhaps a demonic or disgraced woman is not as much the focus of these myths as the man in thrall to her. The biblical book of Proverbs (5:3ff., 6:24ff., 7:6ff.) warned against the blandishments of the evil woman in the crossroads. A hidden image in this caricature is precisely that of the unfortunate male embarked on his crazed path into the arms of the seductress; a hidden counter-image is that of the hero of virtue who, going beyond Joseph with Potiphar's wife, turns the tables and *saves* his female captor. Here the myth takes on the familiar contours of the man-slaps-semiliberated-woman scenario of many a 1930's movie, minus the romantic dénouement.

But Lilith has helped to highlight more august tragedies in Jewish history. Mystical legend made her into the consort of God himself at one critical juncture: the time of the destruction of the Temple, whose ruins became their marriage bed. Simultaneously, the Shekhinah, God's worldly presence, (see "Feminine Imagery in Judaism") went into exile with Israel. The event is compared to Abraham's going in unto Hagar the handmaiden, to the chagrin (even if at the behest) of his wife Sarah, only reversed in result: it is the wife, not the handmaiden, who is driven out. The Shekhinah in exile was a fundamental theme of the Kabbalah, and eventually her exile gave rise to a new twist in the legend: the Shekhinah, during times of suffering, especially just prior to the End of Days, begins to metamorphose into Lilith. She goes beserk, wreaking destruction and suffering in the world, until she can be brought back to her right mind by a change of heart in the upper worlds. She does this because she has become the captive of demonic forces, who enslave her to their whims. A kind of theosophic Patty Hearst, she enacts the punishments of an evil nation foretold in Deuteronomy, Chapter 28: "Thou shalt beget sons and daughters, but they shall go into captivity. . . . The stranger that is in the midst of thee shall mount up higher and higher, and thou shalt come down lower and lower." But at last she is brought back home and fed milk and cookies. She is changed back into the Shekhinah and like Hosea's wayward wife Gomer (Hos. 1–3), recourted and rebetrothed.

It is clear that Lilith, far more than the other demonic personalities, is a register of complex sexual diplomacy in a long era of at least formal male dominance. Women, it must be said, helped to write out the legend, and are helping now to reshape its meaning. Those who agree that myths are "goods to think with" must recognize that the Queen of Demons has helped to tell very accurately the long, troubled, and now unprecedentedly renegotiated history of the sexual relationship. We've come a long way, baby, from the days that the Sumerian *lilitoos* crouched in the shadows of the Tower of Babel, waiting for a customer.

Dybbuk

A *dybbuk* (from the Hebrew verb *dabbek*, "to cling") is a clinging spirit, a type of demon or misplaced soul that enters a person's body and speaks through his mouth. Although the term "*dybbuk*" is comparatively recent, originating in the spoken language of seventeenth-century German and Polish Jewry, the notion of possession by an evil spirit is very ancient and present in most cultures. It will certainly endure as the most reliable explanation of madness as long as the causes of mental illness continue to elude, as they do, scientific understanding. The earliest example of demonic possession in Jewish tradition is the "evil spirit" that intermittently overtakes the biblical monarch Saul (1 Sam. 16:14ff., 18:10ff.), causing him to fly into a murderous rage with no apparent provocation. When young David, the future king of Israel, is brought in to play his lute and serenade the ailing king with calming music, the remedy seems to take effect for a while, but Saul, his jealousy of David growing malignant, one day explodes in fury at the musician and hurls his spear at him, missing him by a hair.

Sooner or later, the available lore about invading evil spirits was bound to merge with thoughts about the dead—perhaps during a time when the number of dead had increased to the point that concern arose regarding the unburied dead and the claims of the dead upon the living. Saul himself, late in his madness, sought out the spirit of the dead prophet Samuel (1 Sam. 28:3ff.). *Dybbuks* eventually were thought to be those dead not properly laid to rest or (once reincarnation, a Kabbalistic doctrine, came to be widely acknowledged by Jews) souls of sinners or souls with an uncompleted mission in the world, who, denied the possibility of transmigration and shivering from the nudity of disembodiment, sought refuge in a living person.

Not all such *dybbuks* were "evil" spirits in a strict sense. Rabbi Hayyim Vital recounts the spirit-possession of a young woman, in which the (male) voice speaking through her claimed to be the spirit of a God-fearing sage who was sent out from the Garden of Eden to perform a brief "mission" (*tikkun*) in expiation of a minor sin. The mission itself is not minor: to warn Rabbi Vital that the Jews of Damascus are in grave danger unless he can convince them to repent of their sins. Vital himself was both suspicious of the authenticity of this voice and not convinced that his own activity would have any effect on Damascene Jewry, but in the end the virtuousness of the message led him to record it for posterity.

How the spirit came to possess the woman is somewhat comical: descending via the rivers of Paradise, he wound up initially in a fish about to be sold in the marketplace in Damascus to a notorious evildoer named El-Tawil. At the last moment the fish was bought instead by a more pious man named Raphael, who took it home for a Sabbath meal. As the fish was divided up, the spirit took refuge in its head, which finally was eaten by Raphael's daughter, whom the spirit possessed. And we think Jonah had troubles? A fish head seems a terrible place to spend a weekend away from Paradise, let alone on business. Eventually the spirit was coaxed out of the woman, but he continued to converse with her in dreams.

Many folktales were told of *dybbuks*, and eventually these found their way to literary expression. S. Z. Rappaport (S. Ansky) was the author of the most famous *dybbuk* story, his Yiddish play *Der Dybbuk*. Ansky had begun his career as a socialist revolutionary in Russia. After a period of exile in Europe he came to be involved with the East European Jewish poor. In 1911 he became an ethnographer, traveling through the Jewish villages of the Ukraine, collecting folktales and songs. He learned his *dybbuk* story from an innkeeper's wife and wrote out the play initially in Russian, submitting it to the great Russian director Stanislavski. The latter suggested rewriting it into Yiddish and performing it through a Jewish troupe. It was rejected by the Vilna Troupe, and Ansky eventually died penniless and alone. After his death the Vilna Troupe, haunted by Ansky's *dybbuk*, performed the play in belated tribute to him, and its members were surprised to see the play become one of the most popular and successful Yiddish plays of all time. A 1938 film of the play by a Polish Yiddish company, besides being one of the great classics of film, is the last authentic (if stylized) glimpse of Jewish life in Eastern Europe. The film in its own way is a kind of a *dybbuk*—that of a buried culture.

In this story, Chonnun, a young itinerant yeshiva student, falls instantly and passionately in love with Leah, daughter of a wealthy merchant, Reb Sender, who hosts the young man for a Sabbath supper. Chonnun wants to marry her, but her father arranges for her to marry a more affluent candidate. Chonnun, in a desperate and frenzied attempt to become wealthy, turns to Kabbalistic magic, which drives him into madness, blasphemy, and death. Leah, sorrowed and increasingly disoriented, begins to frequent the cemetery, and on the eve of her wedding to the arranged bridegroom, becomes inhabited by the spirit of Chonnun, who refuses to depart from her. Her father consults with the great Miropoler *rebbe*, who then dreams of a meeting with the spirit of Chonnun's father, who informs him that Sender and he were once dear friends who had pledged their yet unborn children in marriage if they turned out to be a boy and a girl. Chonnun's father died, and Sender forgot his vow. Chonnun's father now demands justice from a rabbinical court. The *rebbe* summons a *minyan* of ten judges, who rule that the lives of the unborn cannot be pledged, and that Sender must do penance, but that Chonnun's spirit must leave Leah. When the *dybbuk* refuses, he is excommunicated by the solemn pronouncement of the court and the blast of a ram's horn. Chonnun, unable to withstand the force of the edict, departs from Leah's body. A signal is given for the wedding preparations to resume, but before this can happen Leah's soul likewise departs to join her dead lover in eternal wandering.

According to informants familiar with the

idiom of I. B. Singer, *dybbuks* have been known to invade mechanical objects, such as typewriters and automobiles. Here the procedures of exorcism are neither as clearly prescribed nor as effective as in the preceding example, and the human beings affected by such mishaps have been known to waste a lot of money on fruitless consultations. If such machinery starts to spew out green pea soup, it is definitely beyond help.

***A scene from a production of* The Golem**

Golem

The word "*golem*" means a lump of earth or clay. In Jewish folklore the term came to signify an artificial human being fashioned from clay and activated by a magical formula. A *golem* is capable of movement and, in some accounts, of speech and reason. The most famous *golem* stories are those recounted of Rabbi Judah Loewe (the Maharal) of sixteenth-century Prague and his *golem* servant—stories that began as popular legends in eighteenth-century Prague and metamorphosed into a compelling novel by the Bohemian writer Gustav Meyrink in 1915. Americans are indirectly familiar with the *golem* legend in the form of Mary Shelley's *Frankenstein*, which became Boris Karloff's most famous movie. Both the *golem* and Frankenstein's monster are human-made creatures who run amok and have to be destroyed—a character whose most interesting recent incarnation is the space-station computer "HAL" in Stanley Kubrick's film *2001*.

Curiously enough, this theme of "uncontrollability" was added to the legend only in its latest stages; prior to the eighteenth century a *golem* generally was described as a harmless and largely immobile creature, called into being for the most restricted purposes or even as a by-product of other activity. In some accounts the *golem* is enough of a good sport to instruct his makers about the procedures for his own deactivation. Considered logically, this creature is the exact opposite of a *dybbuk*: a *dybbuk* is a sturdy spirit in a fragile body; a *golem* is a fragile spirit in a sturdy body.

The ultimate source of the legend among Jews is the biblical account of the creation of the first human being: "The Lord God fashioned the human being of dust from the ground, and breathed into his nostrils breath of life, and he became a living being" (Gen. 2:6–7). This simple depiction of the moment of human origin never ceased to fascinate and to invite elaboration. The Aramaic translator Onkelos renders "living being" as "speaking being," so to suggest that the divine breath of life included the gift of speech—speech being the first act of creation ascribed to God (Gen. 1:3) and the essential ingredient of the "divine image" (Gen. 1:26) transferred to Adam.

The human ability to create endlessly new combinations or meanings from a finite number of speech sounds has always seemed—with justification—our most preternatural faculty, and so, next to our moral sense, the most divine. It was natural for us to meditate on the marvellous union of elements involved in Adam's creation: man's kinship with the earth, his upright posture, his power of speech, his "divine image." Given these as the main properties of human nature, is God's power of *creation*, in its most literal sense, also man's? In an obvious sense, yes: the human being can *procreate* in the human image. But is there also a more direct way? Can a human being shape another human being from the ground and give it life? If so, what kind of life? Something more akin to God or to earth?

"*Golem* speculation" has always seen the human (or divine) power of speech as the activating force of a *golem*'s life. The Hebrew Bible, a book crammed with word play, encouraged a people addicted to word play to meditate on the wonder of speech. In late talmudic times (300–600 C.E.) an anonymous treatise appeared called the *Sefer Yetzirah* ("Book of Formation"), a Judeo-Pythagorean mystical work that purported to be Abraham's meditations on the laws of creation, immediately before his first revelation from God (Gen. 12:1–3). This work portrays the origins of the universe in the combinations, reversals, and augmentations of letters and syllables that underlie all human speech. A talmudic story emerged around the same time, stating that "Rava created a man and sent him to Rabbi Zera. The rabbi spoke to him, but he didn't answer. [Zera] said: you must have been made by my colleagues; return to dust." (Sanhedrin 65b) The same source reports that "Rav Haninah and Rav Oshaya occupied themselves each Sabbath eve with the *Sefer Yetzirah*: they made a calf one-third the normal size and ate it." But was it kosher? As food, yes; as learning, no—for this daring feat, the two rabbis were made to forget all that they had learned of "the laws of creation."

The motif of an artificial human being continued to play a role in mystical legends throughout the middle ages, especially among the pietistic Jews of Germany and northern France. Over the years this or that mystical sage was credited with the production of a human figure through meditation on the letters of the alphabet and the recitation of scriptural verses and divine names. In almost every case the creature produced was immobile, devoid of speech or consciousness, and merely a by-product of meditation. The creature would revert to its earthly elements when meditation ceased. Some sources suggest that the whole procedure was a mystical initiation rite, but the legend's main purpose seems to have been to affirm two things: the mystery of man's kinship to God in speech and creativity, and man's inability to equal the marvel of his own creation.

Only gradually did the legend emerge of a *golem* that could walk and perform tasks. In the Prague *golem* legends the creature was made by Rabbi Loewe to help him counter blood-accusations against the Jews: the *golem*, made invisible by a talisman around his neck, would wander the town in search of people who were planning to leave a dead body inside the ghetto walls as the pretext for an accusation; when such a culprit was found, the *golem* would tie him up and deposit him and his stolen corpse at the door of the local authorities. This *golem*, as in previous versions of the legend, was activated by the mystical combinations of letters, and in some accounts had the Hebrew word *emet* ("truth") inscribed on his forehead—when one needed to deactivate him, one would erase the *alef* of that word so that it spelled *met* ("dead"), and the creature would collapse. The *golem*'s large size and superhuman strength provoked a series of legends that dwelt on his potential uncontrollability. Rabbi Loewe's *golem* was a gentlemanly critter, who never did anything he wasn't ordered to do, and the rabbi's reason for destroying him was that he had outlived his usefulness. But other versions portray a creature who would not stop growing or who broke from its prescribed duties and wrought harm. In one example, a rabbi (not Rabbi Loewe), deciding that his giant servant had to be destroyed, ordered the *golem* to tie his master's shoelace: as the creature bent down, the rabbi erased a letter from his forehead, causing the *golem* to collapse—alas—on the rabbi himself, crushing him to death!

The Industrial Revolution, needless to say, has made the *golem* legend into a parable of human technology and with good reason. The *golem* has always united three preoccupations: the (upright) human image, the power of language and speech, and the divine gift of creativity. From the standpoint of functional anatomy these faculties are closely related: our upright posture does, in fact, make us a kind of travelling armature for a compact thinking-speaking apparatus—lungs, windpipe, gullet, vocal cords, mouth, nose, and brain, all borne aloft like a wine cup or a microphone, two other producers of speech. And it may be no accident that the major revolutions of modern science, whether in the godlike fashioning of new machines or in the search for the secrets of life and matter, have been largely linguistic, mathematical, and cybernetic in nature. Machines now imitate human reasoning (a computer at the Weizmann Institute in Israel is called, appropriately enough, "the *Golem*"), and the building blocks of life, DNA molecules, are now shown to behave like the combination of letters and syllables in speech. But the limits of artificiality, as in the traditional legend, still hold: no machine has yet become an unbeatable chess player, an inspired poet, a good lover, an effective comedian, a principled lawbreaker, or an intrinsically moral human being. But then, not many people have either.

Some Fabulous Beasts

A number of God's creatures you won't find in any zoo. A Jewish bestiary would have to take into account a few awesome, miraculous, or curious animals whose existence is known only by hearsay. This would include *Behemoth*, most gigantic of terrestrial dwellers, who, for all his wondrous dimensions, does not have quite the same storied reputation as his aquatic cousin, *Leviathan*, who will be described later. Behemoth was created out of one thousand mountains (Ps. 50:10) and, like Leviathan, was deprived of the power of procreation, so he would not overpopulate the earth. He appears in Paradise daily to give God delight, and drinks from a paradisaic stream called Yuval (a year's flow from the Jordan would supply him with only one gulp), and he eats daily the produce of one thousand mountains. His flesh will be served to the righteous at the end of days, when he and Leviathan are destined to slaughter each other in mortal combat (Ps. 50:11).

The *Ziz*, or Ziz-Saddai, is the ruler of the birds. He is five hundred miles high—with his feet on the ground, his head touches the sky. His name is an abbreviation of *kazeh ve-kazeh* ("like this and that"), which refers to the changeable taste of his flesh. His wings are large enough to darken the sky when spread, and they often serve to shield the earth against the harsh south winds. An egg once dropped by the female Ziz crushed three hundred cedars and flooded sixty cities. This cosmic chicken is a singing bird, who daily chants the praises of God and, like the angel Sandalfon with whom he is sometimes identified, fashions wreaths of prayer on behalf of Israel. During the summer, when the bird kingdom gets noisy and restive, sharp squawks from the Ziz keep them in line. The Ziz was the subject of a learned treatise, Johann Heinrich Wolfin's *Dissertatio de portentosae magnitudinis ave Ziz-Saddai* (Leipzig, 1685).

The *Re'em* is a giant animal whose entire population consists of only one male and one female. Each lives at the opposite end of the earth from the other, and at the end of seventy years, they find their way to one another to mate. The male dies from a bite inflicted by the female during copulation, and the female undergoes a pregnancy of twelve years. During this time she cannot move, but can only roll from side to side; she feeds herself on the produce that grows around her in ground fructified by her spittle. Eventually her belly bursts, and out come twins, one male and one female, who depart to opposite ends of the earth . . . etc.

The *Barnacle-goose* (Branta leucopsis) is a bird that grows on trees, affixed by its bill. This creature has always aroused scientific and literary interest, and is mentioned in sources as diverse as Aristotle, Mas'udi ibn Tufail, Pseudo-Callisthenes, the "Thousand and One Nights," and Shakespeare. Extensive debate exists in Jewish sources as to whether this creature is kosher—by some authorities it is permitted as a fruit, and by some it is banned as a shellfish. Rabbenu Tam, Rabbi Meir of Rothenburg, R. Isaac ben Joseph of Corbeil, R. Jacob ben Asher, R. Joseph Caro, and many others have put in their two cents on this vital issue.

The *Milham* (or Hol, or Phoenix) was the only bird who refused to eat of the Tree of Knowledge along with Adam and Eve. For this steadfastness the bird was rewarded with eternal life. At the end of one thousand years its feathers drop off and its body shrinks down to the size of an egg—from which it hatches and grows anew. Its wings catch the flames of the sun; its food is dew and manna. Its excrement produces a worm whose excrement, in turn, is cinnamon. The bird has the head of a crocodile, the feet and tail of a lion, a purplish rainbow hue, and twelve angelic wings. It was hidden away in the ancient city of Luz, where the Angel of Death could not enter.

The *Shamir* is a worm that was made on the twilight before the first Sabbath. The size of a barleycorn, it has the ability to gnaw through the hardest diamonds or other precious stones and metals without leaving a grain of dust. It was used to cut the stones and engrave the metal for the high priest's breastplate, and because metal tools were prohibited for building the Temple, it was used to hew the Temple stones. The *Shamir* was kept in a woolen cloth inside a lead basket filled with barley bran. Solomon had fetched it from Paradise. No specimen has been seen since the Temple was destroyed.

Adne Sadeh (also called Adam Kadmon and Man of the Mountain) is a quasi-human creature fastened by his umbilical cord to the ground. He feeds himself by whatever grows within range of his tether. He is quite ferocious and demolishes whatever comes within his grasp. If one severs his umbilical cord, however, he will die, but one must be careful to do this from afar. He has been used by human beings for food, with no implication of cannibalism, but he is without question banned by Jewish dietary law, being a creature who manifests neither severed hoofs nor chewing of cud. One time, a wayfarer heard his hosts say they were going to prepare "our man" for supper. Thinking that he himself was going to be eaten, he fled, not realizing that they were referring to Adne Sadah.

Last, but not least, is *Leviathan*—also known as *Tannin*, *Rahab*, and *Yam*. He is the most magnificent of sea creatures, and ruler of the seas. Though sometimes taken for a common whale or crocodile, this water dragon, having strayed into the kingdom of Imagination, burgeoned to proportions that the world was scarcely able to contain. His nearest analogue might be the sea itself—indeed, the ocean mantle of the globe was said by myth to be the briny remnants of Leviathan's primordial female partner—but the Bible and the Midrash speak with more restraint: the fifth day of Creation (Gen. 1:21), God had made a male and female of the species; seeing, however, that their procreation would destroy the world, the Holy One unsexed the male and killed his mate (an early precedent for birth control). The latter's flesh He stored away in brine as food to serve the righteous in the world to come; her partner, tamed and harnessed like a puppy, God installed as guardian of the deep. This creature sits upon the ocean bottom like a giant bathtub plug, stopping the flow into the abyss that drains off the excess waters. He drinks up the river Jordan as it flows into the sea and eats the fish that voluntarily swim through the curtain of his teeth.

In fact, he is a kind of maritime Angel of Death: when each sea creature's designated time is up, he must report in to Leviathan to be devoured. Whales three hundred parasangs in length are gobbled up just like the minnows, plankton, and sardines. This range of diet gives Leviathan, alas, a frightful breath—one belch would cause the forests of the world to wither and the cities to revert to dust. His flesh, nevertheless, is kosher and, one must suspect (given its presence on our Messianic deli menu), a genuine gourmet delight.

Leviathan is wonderfully made: his fins and eyes give forth a light that sometimes beams more brilliantly than the sun, causing the darkest ocean depths to light up like a living room. His iridescent skin gives off a glow, as well; Adam and Eve (Gen. 3:21) received from God "skin clothes"—actually, garments of light made from the skin of the Leviathan female. The male is playful as a house pet, which, in fact, he is: each waking day, the Master of the universe studies the Torah for three hours; then for three more hours He sits in judgment of the world; for three more hours He feeds His creatures; and for the last three hours He sports about the sea with Br'er Leviathan, while water siphons down the abyss.

Jewish vegetarians have raised some justifiable concern about the merits of partaking of a banquet of his flesh, much less his pickled and gefilted Mrs., and they have suggested substituting an enormous cucumber. The way things stand, however, *fleish* is in for the hereafter-Sabbath—meted (meated?) out to each according to his share, with no one jealous of his neighbor's portion. After they have taken out their shares, the rest will be divided up among the markets and the food stands in Jerusalem, and since the monster's fat is good for energy, Israel will wind up running OPEC out of business.

But the mystics tell us that this banquet is to be the last meal of the physical life and the beginning of a life purely of spirit. Even as Leviathan is downed, strange things will happen: his skin, stretched out as a canopy over the walls and buildings of the Holy City, will phosphoresce, casting a golden warmth upon the white and purple prayer shawls of the pilgrims, turning everything to rainbow hues, sparkles dancing in the beards of the old men. Old women, radiant as girls of eighteen, will begin to grow back luxuriant braids. Light will issue from people's eyes and mouths. Children will utter languages they didn't know before. A thousand types of music will come through the windows. Lions and bunny rabbits from the biblical zoo will be let loose to romp peacefully on the grasses of Independence Park. Everyone will get acquainted for the first time—a close encounter of the final kind, in which Leviathan, symbol of reined-in terror, whose name Hobbes gave to human commonwealths (and Melville to the nameless maelstrom of mad Ahab's heart), digests himself like words of Torah, and takes on the contours of the world.

—J.R.

JEWISH FOLK BELIEFS AND SUPERSTITIONS

The notion that Jewish superstition exists separate from or can be isolated from Jewish culture and religious belief runs counter to the holistic approach of contemporary anthropologists and folklorists. Even the term "superstition" is misleading since it implies an irrational component to the belief, as if the irrationality of superstition separates it completely from religion and science. Such a simple dichotomy does not work, however, since superstition has a great deal in common with both science and religion. In traditional, premodern communities religious belief (as defined by a rabbinical elite) and the beliefs of folk religion (which had considerable popular support) coexisted, albeit uneasily. Jewish folk beliefs are neither contrary to religious belief by definition nor are they the exclusive domain of the common folk. Despite the fact that these beliefs seem at first glance to contradict Jewish notions of monotheism, their incorporation of a vast array of demons and other occult figures into a folk pantheon and their successful assimilation into religious ideology is as old as the Bible and, like it, are a vital feature of Jewish belief and practice.

Cultures are not islands. Modern biblical criticism indicates clearly that the Hebrews made extensive use of the myths and legends of neighboring people in shaping their own myths. Nevertheless, the Bible is indisputably an original Jewish contribution. Its originality rests more within the nature of the synthesis of ideas, however, than in the uniqueness of the motifs or myths contained within it. The same is true of Jewish folk beliefs. While the particular elements themselves frequently lack even a semblance of Jewish origin, the general rubric under which they fall has a distinctive Jewish character. The area of demons is a case in point. Christians have viewed them as accomplices of the devil, who, together with witches and wizards, conducted an ongoing campaign against God. Jews, however, believed that all the evil spirits, including "Asmodeus, the king of the devils, and Lilith, their queen, were emissaries of God and subject to His will."

For the Jews even divination could be easily contained within the overall structure of accepted behavior. Solomon Simon indicates in his autobiographical work *My Jewish Roots*: "In order to learn what the future held in store, there was no better guide than a verse from the sacred writings. The statement in the Talmud that: 'If upon awakening, a verse occurs to one, this is a minor form of prophecy,' was believed implicitly. Boys as well as older men therefore tried to penetrate the curtain of future events by means of verses. The boys had their own technique. To know the end of a matter they would open any sacred volume at random. If the first word on the page (or the first word of the first new verse on that page, depending on the 'condition' mentally made in advance) began with a *mem,* it was a good sign, because the word *mazal* (luck) begins with a *mem.* If the first word began with a *nun* the matter was in doubt, because a *nun* could mean either *nes* (miracle) or *nein* (no). If the first word began with a *reish* it was a bad sign, because it signified *ra'* (evil). Sometimes the first attempt was supposed to be conclusive; at other times only three attempts decided the matter. There was considerable cheating. A boy might mentally decide that the first attempt should be conclusive, yet when he opened the book and the first letter proved to be a *reish,* he would announce that he had really intended the third time to be conclusive."

What is evident in this practice is the wish for certainty and order in the universe. The principle at work is probably typical of the way in which folk beliefs are integrated into peoples' lives, that is to say, pragmatically. The beliefs are instruments for control. The efficacy of the instrument is closely related to the medium, in this case the sacred text, which is itself the primary Jewish means of determining the order of the universe. If the sacred text could be used to reduce chance and establish order, then chance would have no real autonomy. In a sense it would be subservient to the sacred text.

The noted cultural anthropologist Theodor Gaster describes, in his *Customs and Folkways of Jewish Life*, how Jews adapted "pagan" customs and gave them a specifically Jewish connotation: "The parade example is, of course, the way in which the letters N G H S on the four sides of the Chanukah *trendl* were converted from the original meaning of Nichts (nothing), Ganz (all), Halb (half) and Stell (put) in a game of chance to the initials of the Hebrew motto, Nes Gadol Hayah Sham, 'a great miracle occurred there'—referring to the victory of the Maccabees and to the legend that, when the temple was rededicated, oil which was really sufficient only for one day miraculously lasted for eight."

Here a game of chance takes on a specifically Jewish connotation because a Jewish theme is imputed to its elements. It was precisely in this way that countless elements of non-Jewish culture were incorporated into the Jewish mainstream without jeopardizing the integrity and seeming autonomy of the culture. In fact, the vast majority of elements found within Jewish folk beliefs and folkways have non-Jewish origins. These elements were never simply mechanically copied from the surrounding non-Jewish cultures, though. For an element to become an integral component of Jewish culture it had to fit or be fitted to the underlying precepts of Jewish belief and practice. Despite considerable borrowing of cultural traits and folk elements, Jewish culture was and is distinct from the culture of its neighbours.

Living dispersed among the nations for two millenia, Jews have had the opportunity to observe, adopt, and assimilate into their own culture a wide variety of customs and folkways. Although the root of their heritage is a common element, each Jewish community has its own unique form. Gaster states the problem of multiplicity as follows: ". . . it is both unsafe and unsound, in speaking of popular usages, to say roundly that 'the Jews' in toto do or believe this or that, and it must be clearly understood that the expression 'Jewish folkways' is but an overall, comprehensive term covering what is in fact a manifold, heterogeneous diversity. Indeed, if there is one thing that the study of these folkways brings home especially, it is that Jewish life is, and always has been, a sea fed by many rivers."

The folk beliefs discussed below are largely Ashkenazic beliefs, which may or may not have correspondence with non-Ashkenazic groups. Also, the variations within Ashkenaz itself are large. Nevertheless, these folk beliefs are rather widespread and should be familiar to most Ashkenazic Jews. The sources used include: Theodor H. Gaster's *Customs and Folkways of Jewish Life*, Joshua Trachtenberg's *Jewish Magic and Superstition*; and Hayyim Schauss's *The Lifetime of a Jew*. These along with Dov Noy's articles on superstition in the *Encyclopaedia Judaica*, and Haim Schwartzbaum's *Jewish and World Folklore* are the best sources to turn to for further information.

PROTECTIVE MEASURES

Light and water are two powerful agents used to dispel the evil intentions of demons. The Talmud mentions the value of carrying a torch at night to ward off evil spirits and light is virtually a universal element in ritual processes. Candles, for example, are carried at wedding processions even when they take place during the day. Water, too, has a protective and ritually cleansing quality. Spittle, the most powerful of waters, has special antidemonic properties. Spitting three times is a common way to protect oneself from demons or from evil thoughts, which are believed to be the work of demons. Spitting three times is also an effective way to ward off the evil eye.

The number three is particularly significant because it is commonly believed that even numbers are both unlucky and dangerous. Three, the first odd number after one, has a rich history as a favored number in magic and religion.

Loud noises are supposed to be able to startle demons and frighten them away. The blowing of the *shofar* (ram's horn), either by itself or in conjunction with specific holidays has this effect, as does the breaking of the glass at the wedding ceremony. In medieval times the glass was sometimes thrown at the north wall of the synagogue—that being the locale favored by demons. Schauss, however, suggests that there was another motive or, more correctly, an earlier form to the breaking of the glass that suggests another interpretation: it seems that the glass was thrown at the northern wall with wine still in it, which suggests that the act was one of propitiation through an offering rather than an attempt to frighten off. Other acts of propitiation include shaving the bride's head and cutting a three-year-old child's hair on Lag b'Omer.

Protection through incorporation is a frequently used device against the machinations of hostile demons. Demons are notorious for their jealousy of bridegrooms and the latter are believed to be in mortal danger until their brides walk three or seven times around them under the *huppah* (bridal canopy). The protective power of the circle is frequently

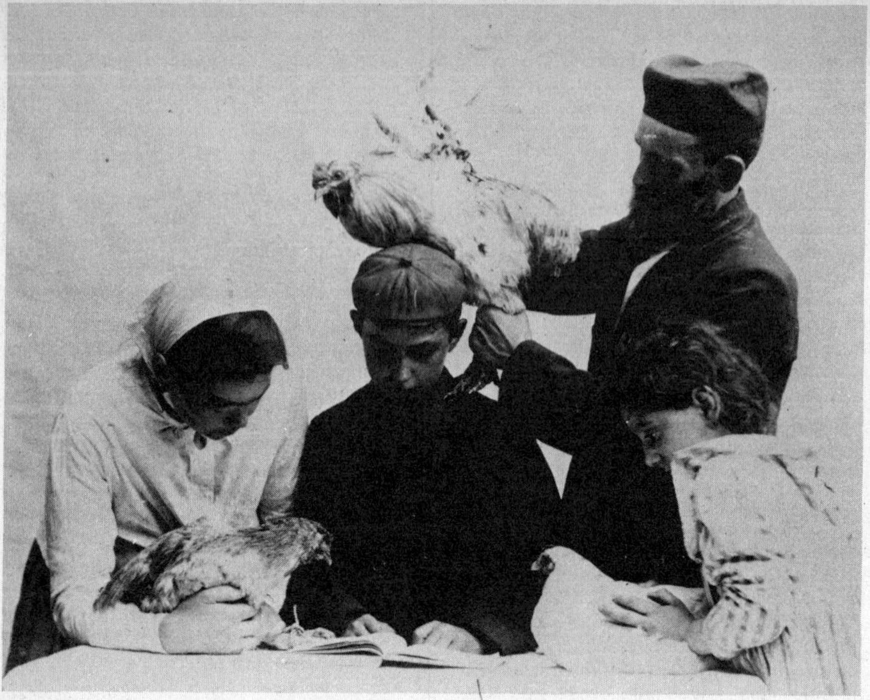

Shlugin kappores, ***a ritual for expiating one's sins prior to Yom Kippur.***

used in magical practice, since it allows the practitioner the safety of a protected space from which he can invoke various spirits to carry out his wishes. Drawing a circle around someone who is believed to be in mortal danger protects them from the demonic attack. Prohibiting a person from leaving the house or going out unaccompanied by friends or relatives also serves as protection by incorporating the person who is thought to be in danger. These proscriptions are associated with life-cycle crises or rites of passage. Indeed, Gaster indicates that the word for bride in Hebrew, *kallah,* means "one who is shut in, secluded."

Deception and concealment are frequent elements in Jewish folk beliefs and ritual practice. Demons may be a thorne in the side, but no one thought that they were particularly bright. Indeed, one might say that deception is a leitmotif of Jewish folk belief. Jewish weddings provide ample evidence of this. Gaster relates that in the fifteenth century bridegrooms in the Rhineland wore mourning garb and covered their hair with ashes. This is an extreme expression of the implicit funereal aspect of the wedding ceremony and is carried out in order to fool evil forces. In traditional Eastern European Jewish weddings both bride and groom wore white shrouds; the groom wore the *kitel* under his *tallit* (prayer shawl) and covered his head with ashes. Prior to the completion of the *huppah* the mood of the ceremony was sombre; weeping rather than laughter prevailed. Among present-day Hasidim, the *badhan's* ("jester") task prior to the *huppah* is to elecit tears and weeping among the women. Both bride and groom fast prior to the *huppah* ceremony to enhance the mood of sobriety and mourning. Among Oriental Jews the act of deception takes the form of painting the faces of the bride and groom to disguise their real identities.

The use of deceptive names to conceal endangered persons is another common practice. A change of name has the effect of confusing the demons and preventing them from locating their intended victim. This practice was apparently extremely common among medieval German Jews in cases of severe illness. The more contemporary procedure was to change the name of a sick person to Hayim (meaning "life"), or Alter (meaning "old man"), or Zeyde (meaning "grandfather"). During the Middle Ages the Bible would be opened at random and the first name that appeared became the new name of the person in question. Since Jews were known by their parents name as well as their own, to avoid detection it was sometimes necessary to "sell" the child to a new set of parents whose own healthy children were proof of divine favor.

Another form of concealment is one that is more closely connected to life-cycle rites. Schauss mentions a custom of not naming the child until the *bris* (circumcision), since it is thought that the days which preceed the *bris* are critical ones for the newborn child. If Lilith, the spirit whose enmity is greatest to the child and its mother, is not presented with a name she cannot pursue her malicious intentions. When parents have experienced the loss of children, they frequently have resorted to a more permanent deception through the use of charm-names or pseudonyms, distinct from the real name of the child. Here again, names such as Alter or Zeyde for a boy and Alte or Babke or Babtche (meaning "little grandmother") for a girl were deemed to be effective ruses aimed at the Angel of Death. Names such as Hayim or Haye, which invoke the word "life," have their own efficacy as protective devices. The name Ben-Zion, however, would totally confuse the Angel of Death, who would become hopelessly lost in attempting to locate the "son of Zion." If the mother believed herself to be the cause for her children's deaths, she might go by her given name, while the grandmother assumed the name-title *mame* (mother).

Life-cycle rites provide protection for members of the community undergoing changes in status. The rites surrounding circumcision, for example, contain various protective measures. The child was closely guarded during the week preceding the circumcision. Protection took the form of studying Torah late into the night. The night before the circumcision is believed to be particularly dangerous for the child, since the demons make a concerted effort to prevent the fulfillment of the commandment. For this reason, the night preceding the circumcision is known as *vakhnakht* (the night of the vigil), during which special precautions are taken to protect the mother and child. These may include lighting candles (light frightens off demons) and placing the *mohel's* (circumcisor) knife under the pillow of the mother. The prophylactic quality of an iron knife is not limited to the *vakhnakht*. It appears in other forms such as the groom carrying a piece of iron in his pocket during the *huppah* ceremony. Iron's efficacy stems from the idea that demons live in caves or mountains "cut by iron."

Other charms that ward off evil spirits are salt, weapons, and plants with strong odors, such as myrtle and garlic. In the category of strong odors, one might include smoke, which also keeps demons at bay. Since water has a protective quality, the ritual bath (*mikveh*) prior to the *huppah* may be seen at one level as a way of warding off the demons.

Amulets provide an important line of defence against evil spirits. These include coral (red wards off demons), aromatic herbs, stones, cauls, pieces from the *afikoman*, gems, and, of course, written amulets. These latter employ the sacred names of God and His angels and biblical quotations to ward off the evil eye, Lilith, and other demons. Sacred symbols adorn the text and add to the efficacy of the charm. Special care must be given to their preparation in order to insure effectiveness. Ritual cleanliness for the writer and the parchment are essential, while appropriate benedictions should precede the writing. And writing at specific hours correlative with particular days of the week is equally as important as the text in assuring the success of the amulet. The *mezuzah* (which is placed on the doorpost) is seen as a particularly effective amulet and must be checked periodically to guard against eradication of key letters or phrases. Without the correct formulation the inhabitants of the house might forfeit the protection they seek.

SYMPATHETIC MAGIC

Sympathetic magic operates on the principle that acting out an event or in some way imitating the quality of the desired event, would induce or facilitate the occurance of the event. Eating honey on Rosh Hashanah as an inducement for a sweet year is one example of this type of magical practice. Throwing raisins, almonds, rice, and the like at the bridal couple is a magical act, a wish that the couple fulfil the commandment to "be fruitful and multiply." Eating eggs, hens, and fish after the marriage ceremony to break the fast are also inducements for fertility.

Births, too, were facilitated through magic. A woman in labor would be led to and from the threshold of her home, and anything that could be opened, such as chests and drawers, was opened. Even the key to the synagogue has its own special power as an opening device useful in facilitating delivery.

Perhaps the custom of the mother's slapping the face of her daughter at her first menstruation can be interpreted as an example of sympathetic magic, which by reddening the cheeks, limits the flow of blood from the body.

Customs associated with death and burial also contain aspects of sympathetic magic. One reason for pouring out household water from the house of mourning was that spirits cannot cross water. The intention in this act, therefore, is to insure that the soul is not trapped inside the home. Graves are not supposed to be left empty overnight, for fear of someone else dying. In the event that a grave was left empty, Russian Jews would fill it in and bury a rooster inside.

Medieval Jewish notions of procreation contain various elements of sympathetic magic. Certain types of food were believed to influence the "seed" and effect the nature of the offspring. Spicy or heavy foods thicken the blood, which increases the flow of semen and produces quick tempered and witty offspring. Salt and salted fish, melons and vegetables were less conducive to sexual desire and would not produce the same quality offspring that spices, strong wines, dairy foods, and so on produced. What a woman sees when she leaves the *mikveh* prior to having sexual relations would also influence the child to be conceived. Seeing a dog is likely to result in an ugly child, whereas an ass will result in a stupid child. Seeing a scholar augered well for the child.

Sympathetic magic has a negative side to it, as well. If simulating an event, causes or facilitates the occurrence of the event, then how does one prevent unwanted events from occurring? The prohibition against leaving the grave unoccupied overnight has already been mentioned. Other examples of prohibitions designed to ward off the effect of a sympathetic occurrence are as follows: Pregnant women should not step over ropes, for fear that the baby will become entangled and die. Floors should not be swept or cleaned after someone leaves the house since this is the customary procedure after someone dies. Nothing should be removed from the house on Saturday night, since a new week should begin full. Babies should not be dressed by more than one person, since this is how dead people are dressed (i. e. by the *hevre kadisha*—burial society). One should not walk backwards, because the devil walks backwards, nor should one whistle, since the devil does this, too, and both might lead to possession by the devil. Knots are considered to be rather potent instruments of a negative variety. Careful attention should be paid to eliminate knots from the hair and clothing of the bride. Even sewing buttons onto a piece of clothing while it is being worn creates the possibility of interfering with a person's ability to reason. However, chewing something or leaving the thread unknotted guards against such interference. Perhaps it is also for this reason that Torah scrolls are not supposed to be bound with a knot when the Torah is rerolled and closed.

THE EVIL EYE

There are two types of supernatural phenomena contained within the notion of the "evil eye." The first is that eyes themselves contain evil properties and that certain unfortunate individuals are born as *jettatori,* causing destruction wherever they look. The second, more characteristic of Jewish folklore, is that one's enemies become incensed at one's successes and more particularly by the open display of success. As a protective device, laudatory remarks need to be accompanied by a phrase such as *kin ayne hore* ("no evil eye"). Since the evil eye and the spirits that cast it are provoked by success or great joy, enumerating people and wealth could lead to ruin. The proper counting of children, therefore, in Eastern Europe is as follows: *nit eyns, nit tsvey, nit dray,* and so on ("not one, not two, not three"). Double weddings in one household were to be avoided. Parents tended to conceal a good looking child from a stranger, and the prophylactic phrase *kin ayne hore* or *umbarufn* or *umbashrien* was a necessary utterance when looking at a handsome child. The term "evil eye" was itself seen as a danger and frequently the euphemism "good eye" was used in its place. Spitting three times was a further protection from the dangers of the evil eye.

The effect of an evil eye on a child can be detected by the presence of fever, emaciation, and excessive yawning. The method of combatting the spell was to place part of the garment of the suspected culprit on glowing coals together with incense and dirt from the four corners of the room. The smoke that resulted was blown into the child's face. Fumigation is a standard procedure for exorcising demons. Dirt is the favored abode of evil spirits and demons. Another remedy was to take a kerchief or baby cap to a specialist, who placed the object close to his or her mouth and whispered a charm into it. The object was then placed on the child's head or wrapped around the neck. This was repeated on three successive days. Other means of combatting the evil eye are through mirrors, which reflect the curse; obscene gestures or *l'havdl* ("opposite") amulets, which frighten it away; and the placing of precious objects, such as gems, in the way, which will divert the glance and protect the intended victim.

These folk beliefs are by no means the entire repertoire of traditional Jewish lore. But even among the limited number mentioned above there is great variety, and they can be classified according to categories. Folklorist Dov Noy divides beliefs regarding demons into three main categories—those that suggest a direct combat, those that seek a compromise, and those that are designed to deceive. The categories employed above distinguished between those that provide protection and those that are instrumental or sympathetic. However, attempts at classification hardly do justice to either the beauty of these beliefs or their function within Jewish culture. Folk beliefs speak to the broadest range of human consciousness. They reach out and incorporate the elements of human emotion that go beyond the pale of accepted reality. They are holistic and multidimensional. Folk beliefs speak to life's ironies and vicissitudes. They introduce pain where there is pleasure, grief where there is joy, death where there is life. At the same time, they serve the human need for a sense of order in the universe. By presenting a set of practices designed to bring about desired changes or prevent undesirable occurrences, they soothe the pain of helplessness and create the illusion of control. Perhaps, the multiplicity of folk beliefs can be seen as a reflection of the value they have for the members of traditional cultures, who are trying to bring to the natural universe a cultural or a man-made component. Folk beliefs are metaphorical explanations of the structure of the universe. Their efficacy rests upon human nature being the basis of the metaphor.

—J.M.K.

JEWS AND DISEASE

ANCIENT CURES AND REMEDIES

Disorder	Remedy	Source
Asthma	For asthma, take three wheat cakes, soak them in honey, eat them, and then drink undiluted wine.	Talmud,Gittin 69b
	Soup made from an old chicken aids in the cough which is called asthma.	Maimonides, Medical Aphorisms 20,83
Bad breath	R. B. Samuel also said in the name of R. Hiyya: After every food eat salt and after every beverage drink water and you will come to no harm. [One who does not do this] by day, he is liable to be troubled with an evil-smelling mouth.	Talmud, Berakhot 40a
Bleeding	The remedy to stop the flow of blood from a wound is unripe dates in vinegar.	Talmud, Avodah Zarah 28a
Bowel problems	Who wishes to be spared disorder of the bowels should accustom himself to dip [his bread in vinegar or wine].	Talmud, Gittin 7a
	Horsebeans are bad for the teeth but good for the bowels.	Talmud, Berakhot 44b
	R. Hiyya b. Ashi said in the name of Rab: One who eats regularly small fish will not suffer with his bowels.	Talmud, Berakhot 40a
Chronic fever	For a chronic fever, take a black hen, cut it open crosswise, shave the crown of the patient, place the hen over his head, and leave it there until it sticks. He then stands in water up to his neck until he feels faint; after that, he immerses his whole body, comes out of the water, and rests.	Talmud, Gittin 67b
	Soup made from an old chicken is of benefit against chronic fever.	Maimonides, Medical Aphorisms 20, 83
Cough	Fish oil is good for cough.	*Divre Hayyim* II, no. 52
Dog bite	Eating the liver of a mad dog is a cure for a man suffering from the dog's bite.	Talmud, Yoma 83a
Earache	Fill the ear canal with oil; then one makes seven wicks out of green blades of wheat stalks. One lights dry garlic leaves and some white thread at one end of the wicks while the other end is placed in the ear, and the latter is placed above the fumes. When one wick is burned through, it is replaced by another. One must protect against drafts in order not to get burned.	Talmuda, Avodah Zarah 28b

Disorder	Remedy	Source
Epilepsy	Cohabitation immediately after defecation produces epileptic children.	Talmud, Gittin 70a
Foot trouble	They were like a man who suffered with his feet and went around to all the doctors and could not find a cure until at last one came and said to him, If you want to be cured, there is a very easy way of doing it: plaster your feet with excrement of cattle.	Song of Songs Rabbah II, 3, 2
Headache	For the treatment of headache, one rubs the head with wine, vinegar, or oil.	Tosefta, Shabbat 12:11
Heart—angina	For pressure of the heart, take mint to the quantity of three eggs, one of cumin, and one of sesame, and eat them.	Talmud, Gittin 69b
Heart—palpitation	For palpitation of the heart, take three barley cakes, soak them in curdled milk which is not forty days old, eat them, and drink diluted wine.	Talmud, Gittin 69b
Heart trouble (General)	Get yourself a new heart . . . why should you die?	Ezekiel 18:31
Heartburn	R. Hama b. Hanina said: One who takes regularly black cumin will not suffer from heartburn.	Talmud, Berakhot 40a
Hemorrhoids	Flesh of fat chickens and broth made therefrom are the most valuable [foods] with which sufferers from [hemorrhoids] should be nourished.	Maimonides, Treatise on Hemorrhoids
Hypochondria	Do not get in the habit of drinking medicine and do not have the teeth extracted.	Talmud, Pesahim 113a
Impotence	Joy, merrymaking, jubilation, rest, and not overly long sleep are very beneficial in this respect; whereas on the contrary, the following are very harmful: worry, grief, sadness, continuous silence, exertion, and waking (staying awake for long periods of time); all this frustrates erection and renders the sperm dry.	Maimonides on Sexual Intercourse, chap. 2
Indigestion	For indigestion, take 300 grains of long pepper, and each day drink 100 of them in wine.	Talmud, Gittin 69b
Jaundice	To remedy jaundice, swallow eight lice taken from your own head.	*Havot Yair*, no. 105 (Germany, 18th century)
Kidney problems	For pains in the right kidney, engrave the image of a tongueless lion on a plate of silver or gold. In case of pains in the left kidney, the image should represent a woman riding a lion, well wrapped up and holding in her hand reins or a stick.	*Minhat Kenaot*, no. 5, p. 33
Madness	To cure madness, eat the flesh of a fowl which has died a natural death.	*Tashbez*, no. 558 (Warsaw, 1902)
Melancholy	One should always attempt to partake of the meat of chickens, one should always drink their soups, because this kind of fowl has the property of improving the harmful humors and particularly the melancholic humor.	Maimonides, Medical Responsa 20b
Nosebleed	For a nosebleed, take a Kohen whose name is Levi and write his name backward.	Talmud, Gittin 69a

Disorder	Remedy	Source
Obesity	Obesity is harmful to the body and makes it sluggish, disturbs its functions, and hinders its movements. Therefore, extremely obese individuals should travel to the seashore, do much walking in the sun, and especially bathe in the sea in order to lose weight, since the sea air causes dissolution of liquids . . . Stay away from hot water . . . except steam baths.	Maimonides, Medical Aphorisms 9, 101
Sciatica	A patient suffering from sciatica should rub fish brine sixty times on each hip.	Talmud, Gittin 69b
Tapeworm	Thirteen things are said concerning bread eaten in the morning... it destroys tapeworms.	Talmud, Baba Metzia 107b
Toothache	Rabbah B. R. Hama says that [the sufferer] should take the top of a garlic with one stalk only and grind it with oil and salt and put it on his thumb nail on the side where the tooth aches and put a rim of dough around it.	Talmud, Gittin 69a
When all else fails	Sell the disease to another person .	*Sefer Hasidim*, no. 1523

—W.N.K.

CHICKEN SOUP REBOUND AND RELAPSE OF PNEUMONIA: REPORT OF A CASE

A case is reported in which a previously healthy individual, having received an inadequate course of chicken soup in treatment of mild pneumococcal pneumonia, experienced a severe relapse, refractory to all medical treatment and eventually requiring thoracotomy. The pharmacology of chicken soup is reviewed and the dangers of abrupt termination of therapy are stressed.

Chicken soup has long been recognized to possess unusual therapeutic potency against a wide variety of viral and bacterial agents. Indeed, as early as the twelfth century, the theologian, philosopher, and physician Moses Maimonides wrote, "Chicken soup . . . is recommended as an excellent food as well as medication."[1] Previous anecdotal reports regarding the therapeutic efficacy of this agent, however, have failed to provide details regarding the appropriate length of therapy. What follows is a case report in which abrupt withdrawal of chicken soup led to severe relapse of pneumonia.

CASE REPORT

The patient is a 47-year-old male physician who had been in excellent health until 8 days prior to admission, when he experienced the sudden onset of rigors followed by fever to 105°F (40.5°C). He was seen by a physician at that time, when physical examination revealed a severely toxic man, unable to raise his head from the bed. Pertinent physical findings were limited to the chest, where rales were heard over the right middle lobe. Chicken soup was immediately begun in doses of 500 ml po q 4 hours. Defervescence occurred in 36 hours and a chest X-ray film taken 5 days prior to admission was entirely normal. Because he felt symptomatically improved, the patient declined further chicken soup after this time. He continued to feel well and remained afebrile until the night prior to admission, when he developed right upper quadrant pain, nausea, and vomiting while on a visit to Vermont. His vomiting persisted through the night, and the following morning he boarded a plane for Cleveland. En route, he became severely dyspneic, and by the time he deplaned in Cleveland, he was cyanotic and in severe respiratory distress.

He was brought immediately to hospital where physical examination revealed an acutely ill man, febrile to 104°F (40.0°C), breathing shallowly 60 times per minute, with a pulse of 140. Physical findings were again chiefly limited to the chest, where bilateral pleural friction rubs, bibasilar rales and egophony over the right middle lobe were heard. Chest X-ray examination showed consolidation of the right middle lobe, infiltrates at both bases and a questionable right pleural effusion. White cell count was 7,700 without a shift to the left. Electrolytes were within normal limits. Arterial blood gases on 6 liters/min of nasal oxygen were pH = 7.51 $PCO_2 = 20$ torr and $PO_2 = 50$ torr. Gram stain of the sputum showed swarming diplococci, and multiple cultures of sputum and blood subsequently grew out type 4 Pneumococcus.

Chicken soup being unavailable, the patient was started on one million units q 6 hours of intravenous penicillin. Failure to respond led to increases of the dose up to 30 million units daily. Nonetheless, the patient remained febrile and his chest X-ray film showed progressive effusion and infiltration. On the twelfth hospital day he was taken to the operating room for a right thoracotomy. He thereafter made an uneventful recovery, maintained on 30 million units of penicillin daily during his postoperative course, and was discharged on the 25th hospital day.

DISCUSSION

The therapeutic efficacy of chicken soup was first discovered several thousand years ago when an epidemic highly fatal to young Egyptian males seemed not to affect an ethnic minority residing in the same area. Contemporary epidemiologic inquiry revealed that the diet of the group not afflicted by the epidemic contained large amounts of a preparation made by boiling chicken with various vegetables and herbs. It is notable in this regard that the dietary injunctions given to Moses on Mount Sinai, while restricting consumption of no less than 19 types of fowl, exempted chicken from prohibition.[2] Some scholars[3] believe that the recipe for chicken soup[4] was transmitted to Moses on the same occasion, but was relegated to the oral tradition when the Scriptures were canonized. Chicken soup was widely used in Europe for many centuries, but disappeared from commercial production after the Inquisition. It remained as a popular therapy among certain Eastern European groups, however, and was introduced into the United States in the early part of this century. While chicken soup is now widely employed against a variety of organic and functional disorders, its manufacture remains largely in the hands of private individuals, and standardization has proved nearly impossible.

Preliminary investigation into the pharmacology of chicken soup (Bohbymycetin®) has shown that it is readily absorbed after oral administration, achieving peak serum levels in two hours and persisting in detectable levels for up to 24 hours. Parenteral administration is not recommended. The metabolic fate of the agent is not well understood, although varying proportions are excreted by the kidneys, and dosage should be appropriately adjusted in patients with renal failure. Chicken soup is distributed widely throughout body tissues and breakdown products having antimicrobial efficacy cross the blood-brain barrier. Untoward side effects are minimal, consisting primarily of mild euphoria which rapidly remits on discontinuation of the agent.

While chicken soup has been employed for thousands of years in the treatment of viral and bacterial illnesses, there have been no systematic investigations into the optimal course of therapy. The present case illustrates a possible hazard of abrupt chicken soup withdrawal: a previously healthy man, having received what proved to be an inadequate course of chicken soup for clinical signs of pneumonia, experienced a virulent relapse into severe bacterial pneumonia. It was not possible in this case to determine whether the relapse was caused by resistant organisms, as chicken soup was unavailable at the time treatment had to be restarted, and a synthetic product of lesser potency was used instead. Further study is needed to determine the most efficacious regimen for chicken soup. Pending such investigation, it would probably be more prudent to give a ten-day course at full dosage, with gradual tapering thereafter and immediate resumption of therapy at the first sign of relapse.

REFERENCES

1. Rosner F: Studies in Judaica: The Medical Aphorisms of Moses Maimonides. New York, Yeshiva University Press. 1971. Treatise 20, aphorism 67
2. Leviticus 11:13–19
3. Caroline, Mrs. Z. (author's mother). Personal communication
4. Bellin, MG: Jewish Cookbook. New York, Garden City Books, 1958, pp. 19–20 (recipe)

—N.L.C. and H.S. rep.

JEWISH GENETIC DISEASES

Disease	Date of Discovery	Mode of Genetic Transmission	Frequency in Jews	Jews as % of cases	Jewish origins	Description	Defect	Course	Comment
Abetalipoproteinemia	1950	Autosomal recessive	Rare	25	Ashkenazi	Appears in infancy; failure to grow, progressing to difficulty walking and progressive weakness	Unknown	Death by mid-thirties	
Ataxiatelangiectasia	1926	Autosomal recessive	1:40,000 (1:8,000 Moroccan)	75	Sephardi	Onset noted when child starts to walk; difficulty walking, recurrent pulmonary infections	Unknown	Majority die by age 20; rarely live to age 40	
Color Blindness	400 B.C.E.	(Not clear)	9:100 (Ashkenazim) 6:100 (Sephardim)	Above average (general population has about 5:100 incidence)	Mixed	Red-green blindness	Unknown	Lifelong	
Cystinuria	1810	Autosomal recessive	1:2,500 Libyan Jews	Incidence in general population is about 1:20,000	Libyan	Onset commonly in twenties; urinary colic and infection	Unknown	Treatment readily available	
Dubin-Johnson Syndrome	1954	Autosomal recessive	1:1,300 Iranian Jews 1:40,000 Sephardim 1:100,000 Ashkenazim	(Not clear)	Iranian, other	Onset commonly in twenties; jaundice without pathologic disease	Unknown	Benign without treatment	Oral contraceptives can aggravate jaundice. The main problem is that the victim may be thought to have a more serious liver problem
Factor XI deficiency	1953	Varies—autosomal recessive in many cases	1:100 (more pronounced form); 1:20 (mild form)	90	Ashkenazi (mostly Poland and Russia)	Excess bleeding following dental extractions, injuries	Deficiency of clotting factor XI	Bleeding stops spontaneously or is readily treated with plasma	Bleeding screening should be done on all Ashkenazi Jews before significant surgery

Familial dysautonomia (Riley-Day)	1945	Autosomal recessive	1:10,000	99	Rumania Ukraine	Appears in infancy; difficulty swallowing, frequent pneumonias, indifference to pain, decreased tearing	Unknown	Can live to adulthood if survives childhood infections	
Familial Mediterranean Fever	1945	Autosomal recessive	1:600 Libyan 1:5,000 Ashkenazim	85	Libya, North Africa, other	Onset commonly before twenty years old; episodic abdominal and joint pains followed by fever	Unknown	Long survival; drug treatment available	Also commonly affects Arabs and Armenians
Gaucher's (type 1)	1882	Autosomal recessive (incomplete penetrance)	1:2,500	80	Ashkenazi mostly	Appears at any age; anemia, easy fractures, enlarged spleen, bleeding disorders	Deficient glucocerebrocidase	The later the onset, the better the outlook. Compatible with long life	Two other forms of Gaucher's disease infrequently affect Jews, have a different course, and should not be confused with this form
Glucose-6-phosphate dehydrogenase deficiency	400 B.C.E.	Sex-linked recessive	1:4 Iraqi 6:10 Kurd 3:20 Iranian 2:100 European Sephardim	(Not clear)	Multiple Mediterranean sources	Backache, dark urine, on exposure to various drugs or fava beans	Deficient G-6-PD	Does well if avoids offending agents	Sex-linked recessive means that only males are affected. 25% of Egyptian and 15% of Saudi Arabian non-Jewish males also have this disorder. A variant is common in American blacks
Lactase deficiency	1881	Autosomal recessive	2:3 Israelis	1:10 in U.S. population	Ashkenazi, Sephardi	Onset commonly in teens; abdominal cramps and diarrhea after ingesting milk	Deficiency of lactase in small bowel	Lifelong	Lactase digests lactose in milk. Most people with lactase deficiency have minimal symptoms of lactose intolerance. Those with significant symptoms should avoid milk products.
Niemann-Pick (type A)	1914	Autosomal recessive	1:40,000	70	Lithuania	Onset in infancy; difficulty feeding, progressive mental and physical deterioration	Deficient sphingomyelinase	Death by age five	Prenatal diagnosis possible
Pentosuria	1892	Autosomal recessive	1:2,000	Greater than 50	Ashkenazi	False positive reading for glucose in the urine due to excess of other sugars such as xylose and ribose	Reduced levels of xylitol dehydrogenase	Lifelong	If blood test not done in addition to urine, person can be falsely labeled diabetic

Disease	Date of Discovery	Mode of Genetic Transmission	Frequency in Jews	Jews as % of cases	Jewish origins	Description	Defect	Course	Comment
Regional enteritis	1932	(Not clear)	1:5,000	70	Ashkenazi	Onset commonly in twenties; chronic diarrhea and abdominal pain	Unknown	Chronic over many years	
Tay-Sachs	1881	Autosomal recessive	1:3,600 births	90	Lithuania Rare Sephardi	Progressive nervous system degeneration beginning in infancy	Deficient hexosaminidase A	Death by age five	Community screening and prenatal diagnosis available
Torsion dystonia	1908	Various forms	1:17,000 (Ashkenazim); less in Sephardim	30	Eastern European Ashkenazi, mostly (some Sephardi)	Onset from preadolescence to young adulthood; involuntary spasms of muscles	Unknown	Compatible with long life	Neurosurgery as well as various medications have been helpful
Ulcerative colitis	1875	(Not clear)	1:2,500	70	80% Ashkenazi	Onset commonly in twenties; chronic bloody diarrhea and abdominal pain	Unknown	Tends to burn out by age 50 to 60. Increased incidence of late colonic cancer	Because of increased late cancer risk, persons with inactive ulcerative colitis should get periodic checkups

Autosomal recessive: Both parents ("carriers") have the gene for the disease. The disease only expresses itself when they have a child who gets a gene for the disease from each parent.

Incomplete penetrance: Some people get the disease in a severe form. Others get it in a mild form.

Sex-linked recessive: The female carries the gene but it only produces the disease in her male children.

The definitive source on this subject is *Genetic Disorders Among the Jewish People* by Richard M. Goodman, M.D. (Baltimore and London: Johns Hopkins Press, 1979).

—W.N.K.

THE JEWISH ALMANAC'S GUIDE TO KOSHER DINING: NEW YORK AND JERUSALEM

Jews who observe the laws of *kashrut* often find themselves in an unpleasant bind. While the social ethos dictates dining out on occasion, whether for business or pleasure, the strictures of "keeping kosher" severely limit the choices available in most restaurants. Small compromises are sometimes made, such as only eating cold dairy foods ("dairy" because there is no need to worry about non-kosher *(treif)* meat or the mixing of milk and meat; "cold" because even if *treif* meat is served, cold utensils do not transmit these qualities to the dairy foods). Occasionally, even greater leniency is taken; fish or vegetarian hot dishes may be ordered. In any case, there is always a point on the menu beyond which one cannot go without forfeiting all semblance of keeping kosher.

The solution to this quandary, of course, lies in kosher restaurants. In such establishments, kitchens are designed with the rigorous laws of *kashrut* in mind, menus are drawn strictly from the lists of ritually correct foods, and the premises are inspected daily by learned rabbinical authorities. Here the kosher diner is free to relax, order indiscriminately, and eat with abandon. Unfortunately, most communities do not have enough Jews concerned with this problem to support more than one (if even that) kosher restaurant. Jerusalem and New York City, the two epicenters of the Jewish world, however, are blessed with a veritable smorgasbord of strictly kosher delights to thrill the parched palate of the adventurous kosher gourmet. Nine of these culinary oases in each city have been visited, digested, and reported upon by *The Jewish Almanac*'s field correspondents.

Jerusalem offers a wondrous variety of ethnic cuisines from which to choose, including Persian, North African, or Hungarian. In New York the cosmopolitan influence is more apparent in gourmet French and Chinese restaurants, while the Eastern European influence is obvious in the remaining establishments. As a tribute to the integration of the Jew into American culture, a kosher fast-food burger stand was included on the itinerary. (The comment? "Good quality food, quickly served.")

Unfortunately, as the reviews indicate, competition has not resolved all the problems with kosher restaurants. Although there is no reason why such establishments cannot serve interesting food, well prepared, in an attractive ambiance, and at reasonable prices, few of the restaurants visited could satisfy more than two of these four conditions. As might be expected, restaurants which stayed within familiar territory, whether Ashkenazi or Sephardi, fared far better than those that sought to introduce new cuisines to the Jewish palate.

As all of the restaurants are under rabbinic supervision, they should have an official certificate of *kashrut (Te'udat Heksher)* on the premises. If one wants to be reassured about the *kashrut* of any establishment, one should simply ask to see the certificate; either it will already be prominently displayed or the proprietors will be happy to produce it. All of the restaurants are closed for the Sabbath and open on Sunday; some open after the Sabbath is over on Saturday night. One should call in advance for times and, in some cases, reservations. All prices cited are as of winter 1979–80.

—The Eds.

NEW YORK CITY

Lou G. Siegel's

209 West 38th Street
Tel. (212) 947-1262

Lou G. Siegel's, founded in 1917, describes itself as "America's foremost kosher restaurant." It stands solidly in New York's garment district and in its crowded rooms at noontime one can imagine the buzz of deals being closed and thousands of racks of outerwear and foundation garments changing hands. In the evening the atmosphere is more relaxed: work done, men are joined by wives, children, and mothers for dinner in town. The high ceilings and well-spaced tables do make it possible to sit back and talk—but one cannot dally for long. Siegel's closes shop in midevening, and although the kitchens are still open at eight o'clock, one eats then at one's peril. Some menu items were exhausted at that hour and others just looked exhausted—they had a rundown geriatric look to them, but might have been enjoyable if we had come to know them in their prime. Get there early. The waiters, themselves no spring chickens, are vigorous enough, and our man was a good example of the classic Jewish waiter who does a credible job of holding back his derision and making you feel that it was is his special efforts and kindness that your food has been rescued from the kitchen and placed before you.

A remarkably good portion of sweet and sour stuffed cabbage, Rumanian style with raisins, was our first appetizer; as a dish that is enhanced by prolonged cooking, it is the kind of dish that Siegel's does best. Goulash and meatballs are also in this category. A somewhat skimpy serving of pickled herring was fresh and delectable though buried in a pointless sweet mock-cream sauce. The idea of *miltz,* calf's spleen stuffed with flavored bread crumbs and fat, exerted an exotic appeal on us, but it turned out to be rather indistinct in flavor. The chopped liver also cried out for seasoning—a bit of salt, some chopped onion, a little *shmaltz*—although the quality of the liver was good.

Most people order from the dinner menu, which includes appetizer, soup, entree, dessert, and beverage for a single price. But beware: you have to *tell* the waiter you want soup or else before you know it the main course is on the table and you are soupless. And that would be a shame, for the one soup we managed to taste—our waiter gladly brought us some after our entrees—was a marvelous chicken soup with a strong golden broth and a light, airy matzah ball.

When it comes to ordering entrees, it took us a few tries to get things right. When our order of roast Long Island duckling arrived it was so burnt, dry, and stringy that we had to send it back. We were relieved to find that the roast brisket of beef ordered in its place was flavorful and toothsome, though the kitchen had made an error in cutting it in thick slices. We ordered the roast prime ribs of beef medium rare only to have placed before us a slab of leaden grayness. When called on it, the waiter sheepishly agreed that the meat was hardly as we had ordered it and took it back. The replacement was a choice piece of meat that was tasty though lacking in fat. While excitement is probably not the quality one looks for when ordering boiled beef, we thought that we had a right to expect a little more from our boiled choice beef flanken than we got. Our surmise is that the flanken had spent the day on a steam table releasing its precious fluids into the water surrounding it. By this hour that water must have become a broth to remember and we would have gladly chosen it over the limp specimen before us. Pan-fried breaded veal cutlet, the special of the day and recommended by the waiter, turned out to be the best choice of the evening. The veal was good quality, coated in a light flour mixture, and cooked to a turn. The frying was light and crisp, without a hint of grease, and the chops were served with a lemon wedge, a slice of stuffed derma, and good french fried potatoes.

For dessert there was a high and fluffy home-made chocolate cream pie which, despite its ersatz ingredients, managed to be quite satisfying in a gooey, adolescent way. The apple strudel featured perfectly cooked apples surrounded by a fairly heavy dough. An eclair with chocolate icing was satisfactory, though we would have preferred a custard filling to the fake whipped cream. We should have taken the waiter's advice and forgotten about the coffee.

The full dinners range from $12.25 to $16.50 according to the price of the entree, which can be ordered separately for about $4 less. With tax and tip the average dinner should run about $17.

—H.L.G. and A.M.

Moshe Peking

40 West 37th Street
Tel. (212) 594-6500

This is an attractive restaurant that faces no inherent obstacles to success. Chinese food is a dream for the kosher cook: there are no dairy products to worry about; pork and seafood dishes can simply be forgotten; and fresh ingredients with few suspect substances are used. What is required is only the will to be good, the will to be authentic, the will to please.

Moshe Peking's has many things going for it. In contrast to Shmulke Bernstein's American chop suey fantasies of Chinese food (see review below), Moshe Peking's serves the real thing and enables the kosher diner to get a sense of what this cuisine is all about. The physical design of the restaurant is quite winning. Rather than giving in to the frenzied spirit of the wholesale districts (clothes, flowers, furs, cigars) at whose center it is located, Moshe Peking's is a quiet oasis of muted lighting and subdued tones where customers can decompress from the pressures of the avenue. The decor is modernist, the colors browns and grays, the hangings pleasingly abstract. The menu is professionally done and the service is efficient and prompt. The one lapse in taste is the room's dramatic centerpiece: a large plastic tree.

The heartbreak comes in the food, however: it's Chinese but it just isn't good. The dishes are underseasoned; the frying is ineptly greasy; the quality of some ingredients is poor; the relationship between what shows up on one's plate to its description on the menu is unreliable. The leaders of the Jewish community should publicly discipline those responsible for this restaurant for having had the ways and means to offer the community a special experience and having failed to do so.

The extensive menu features standard Cantonese dishes with a sprinkling of the spicier Szechuan specialties that have become popular in recent years. But that's not all. There are some Polynesian flourishes à la Trader Vic's, such as expensive cocktails served in hollowed-out coconuts and pineapples. We were tempted to order the Hawaiian cooler ($3.75), described on the menu as a "marvelous mixture of Hawaiian and citrus juices with vodka and creme de menthe served in a pineapple" just so that we could find out what "Hawaiian" juice is. There is no menu purism at Moshe Peking's. At most other Chinese restaurants in New York you can expect to find only ice cream and fruit for dessert; but *mirabile dictu,* here one can choose from an entire tray of French pastries, gooey napoleons, and overstuffed eclairs.

One can sample the six or seven appetizers on the pu pu platter, an iron kettle with a raised center chimney that conceals a sterno flame. Most of the items we tasted were satisfactory if not delectable, with the Polynesian meatballs winning some admirers with sweet tooths. Our least favorite was a thick, heavy egg roll which seemed to encase nothing but Chinese cabbage. The deep fried drumsticks that materialized instead of the promised barbecued chicken wings were leaden and greasy; but the barbecued ribs, beef wontons, and skewers of beef, onion, green pepper, and mushroom caps were fun to eat. The lull before the storm, our last starter, was a pleasant savory hot and sour soup. The soup was served hot and properly thickened and it floated the traditional ingredients of bean sprouts and tofu. With a little more seasoning, it would have been excellent.

With the entrees, our luck gave out. The menu promises much but only builds one up for the fall. Our worst adventure was sizzling duck, hearteningly described as "chopped and boned duck marinated in a tasty sauce and roasted with Chinese mushrooms, snowpeas, and bamboo shoots, served in a sizzling and steaming dish." We got some large chunks of a meat resembling turkey swimming in an offputting sauce of a gray-brown color; we must have done something especially wicked to have deserved the unplucked feathers adhering to the meat.

Our best experience was the prime ribs of beef with garlic sauce, but even that raised a hint of suspicion. Respectably spicy as we had ordered, the dish was a welcome bit of life in a bland meal. The meat had a light garlicky flavor and the accompanying fresh broccoli was perfectly cooked. Our suspicions were aroused by the fact that the meat was so tender, so absolutely amazingly tender, that we could not help speculating on the number of months the meat had been tenderized until it gave up its last hint of graininess.

Other entrees were plain. The lemon chicken was a boneless breast, lightly floured and sauteed, whose lemon sauce was so mild as to almost fade away. The promised slivered almonds were nowhere in evidence. Peking veal with fine noodles, "shredded veal and Chinese vegetables, gently tossed and served in a mild sauce on a bed of vermicelli," similarly lacked character, and rested instead on a bed of Chinese cellophane noodles. The go ba sizzling rice with beef should have been built on rice refried to the point of crispy crunchiness; what came to our table had some beef and vegetables but virtually no rice.

A particular annoyance, and one that can probably be forestalled, is the way in which the food is served. Rather than putting the dishes in the center of the table and letting the guests divide it among themselves, the waiters serve individual portions from a side serving table. The effect is that one ends up with a plate overloaded with samplings of four or five different dishes; everything runs into everything else and oozes together to form an indistinguishable heap. Speak up and protect yourself.

A closing word about prices. The attractiveness of Chinese restaurants, in addition to the fun of eating in them, is their affordability. Although the quality of the food at Moshe Peking's barely approaches that of a mediocre neighborhood Chinese restaurant, its prices rival those of the two or three top luxury East Side Oriental restaurants. Yes, kosher meat is more expensive; yes, ritual supervision costs money. But for between $9 and $14 per entree, Moshe Peking's is a rip-off. For a full dinner and a bottle of wine, plus tax and tip, four people should be prepared to part with at least $100. *Caveat emptor!*

—H.L.G. and A.M.

La Différence

Roosevelt Hotel
Madison Avenue and 45th Street
Tel. (212) 697-7000

In contrast to Chinese food, in which no dairy products are used, preparing French cooking under the conditions of *kashrut* presents a considerable challenge. There are two possible approaches to the problem: refusing to acknowledge the limitations and striving to reduplicate French dishes using ersatz ingredients, or accepting the restrictions and striving to perfect the many recipes that require no compromise or alteration. La Différence, New York's kosher French restaurant, has chosen the first path, and it's a shame, for in trying to be more than it can be, it fails at being much of anything and denies kosher diners what could have been an attractive restaurant offering a reasonable variety of well-prepared, satisfying dishes.

La Différence can be a pleasant place to eat. The decor seems to conform to somebody's idea of what a fancy French restaurant should be like: overstuffed red banquettes, gold and cream moldings, and a fountain in the middle, yet the effect in reality is rather one of turn-of-the-century New Orleans bordello. The ceilings are high, the room is large, and the tables are well separated so that the noise level is low—that is, when the piano and violin duo are not banging out show tunes fortissimo. This can be a nice place to linger, and linger one must because although the staff are well meaning, they are unprofessional and handicapped by a kitchen which, in terms of timing, seems to step to the music of a different drummer.

The best first course we sampled was the tasty paté maison, an interesting combination of duck and chicken livers pounded together and baked in a pastry shell. It was certainly something more than chopped liver. Also credible was the crêpe maison, a thin crêpe with a chicken filling covered with a wine "cream" sauce; this was the only dish made with substitute ingredients that came off well. The honey-glazed pamplemousse was a superior grapefruit; unfortunately it was taken straight from the refrigerator and placed under the broiler so that the rind was charred and the rest cold. The quiche Lorraine, usually a pastry tart with ham and cheese, turned out to be something entirely different: a crustless and not unpleasant moussaka made from ground beef and tomatoes and bound together with egg custard. The boulette à la sauce tomate, a meatball in tomato sauce, was unbearably dry and the sauce was bitter. Our last appetizer, hors d'oeuvres variés, featured a little of everything but mostly a lot of nothing, especially canned string beans and bland pastrami.

The soups for the most part were badly handled. In the thinness of its stock and the mushiness of its vegetables the potage parmentier brought back memories of dining halls in the summer camps of youth. The chemical taste of the vichyssoise, a cold creamed potato soup, was an object lesson in the ill-advised use of nondairy substitutes. We surmised that the onion soup had once been fairly good, but it had been reduced for so long that the beef broth had attained the consistency of a light sauce, which gave the soup a cloying quality. The fact that the one acceptable soup we tasted, the chicken consommé with matzah balls, was distinctly un-French renewed our longtime faith in the capacity of Jews to make their own good soups when they take time off from aspiring to those of other peoples. (Between the soups and the entrees we enjoyed a decent though cheeseless Caesar salad prepared tableside its one fault was reliance on bright yellow Gulden's mustard when there are respectable kosher mustards on the market. The smaller salads that came with the dinner menu were chilled and crisp and the house's creamy Italian dressing was good.)

The two most satisfying entrees were beef dishes. The prime ribs of beef, cooked as ordered, were quite tasty, though the tomate provençale and the pommes dauphines promised on the menu as accompaniments somehow turned into a baked potato and broccoli by the time they reached our table. Steak Diane, a quick sauté of three thin strips of fillet sauced with mushroom and wine and flamed at table, was a good-tasting dish marred by bad timing. Prepared in four minutes, it stood waiting in the chafing dish for twenty-five until the other entrees arrived; then it had to be sent back for reheating. Another flamed dish, canard à l'orange flambé, was disappointingly tough and salty, while the rice that shared the plate was undersalted. Things picked up a bit with the Veal piccata a limone (why an Italian dish in a French restaurant?), sauteed veal in a lemon sauce. The veal was relatively tender and the scallops thin and lightly breaded, but the sauce was tasteless, being neither tart nor sweet. The suprême de poulet, a boneless breast of chicken in champagne sauce, left us indifferent. That the chicken was overcooked was not as much of a surprise as the mound of corned beef stuffing it covered. This unlikely coupling did not make a happy marriage. We also tried a fish dish to see how the kitchen could manage without using butter. The pan-fried brook trout was dry from overcooking, and its texture and fishy taste gave us reason to suspect that it had been frozen for a long time.

The desserts, sad to report, were the most graphic record of yielding to the temptations of fake ingredients. With fresh eggs, quality chocolate, and stiffly beaten egg whites one can make a fine chocolate mousse without dairy products. Here the chocolate mousse was a hard and dry spray-can variety of chocolate chiffon with enough starch, gelatin, and stabilizers to make it stand bolt upright in the glass. We sent it back and consoled ourselves with some refreshing lemon sherbet and a serviceable fresh fruit salad. There was not much left of the pastry tray by the time we got to it. A chocolate éclair was decent but seemed like it had spent a long time improperly covered in the refrigerator absorbing odors. The napoleon had a good custard filling, but was unfortunately surrounded by layers of leaden pastry. Our final dessert adventure was peach melba, whose *parve* (made without milk or milk products) ice cream and imitation whipped cream did not revive our spirits.

With a little wine, tax, and tip, a full dinner averages $25 at La Différence.

—H.L.G. and A.M.

Ratner's Dairy Restaurant
138 Delancey Street
Tel. (212) 677-5588

New York is blessed with many kosher dairy restaurants: Famous on the upper West Side, Farm Foods in the theater district, and a clutch of others in the garment district. They are reliably uniform: you can always get borscht, blintzes, and fish; the baking may be better in one than another, but you know there will always be cheesecake and danish; and also that the waiters will be tired and brusquely familiar and that the decor will be solidly formica with fluorescent lighting. There are many good things to eat in these restaurants, and if you know the few things to avoid and do not expect intimacy and refinement, eating in that singular institution, a New York kosher dairy restaurant, is delectable fun.

Ratner's is on the lower East Side, at the foot of the Williamsburg Bridge. It is the perfect place to go after rummaging for bargains along Orchard Street or shopping for pickles or Jewish books. Ratner's greatest asset, on which the diner can capitalize at once, is the irresistible onion rolls and black bread. There is nothing as basic and as reassuring as those rolls, and although deep into a Ratner's meal one sometimes gets the sense that the best is over, there is much that comes later to keep up flagging spirits.

As in other dairy restaurants, the menu is extensive: various smoked fish and broiled fresh fish, eggs and omelettes in various combinations, vegetables and sour cream, vegetarian simulated dishes, soups and salads. This is the kind of restaurant in which the appetizers should on no account be passed up. On a mixed platter you can sample mounds of excellent sweet chopped herring, a vegetarian chopped liver remarkably close to the real thing, and a pleasant if slightly bland chopped eggplant. An order of whitefish was lovely: a large flavorful piece of fish that was clean tasting and not overly smoky. For herring mavens who take theirs strong, there is a very piquant *shmaltz* herring.

Of the soups, the borscht is a sure bet. It comes in a big bowl with sour cream and can be ordered with potatoes, eggs, and vegetables for an extra charge. It is sweet, flavorful, and light and conveys a true beet taste. The potato soup is based on a decent broth with dill, tomatoes, and celery in evidence, but we found that the main attraction, the potatoes, had been simmered to the point of disintegration and no longer held much interest.

Jewish specialties come off best among the entrees. The blintzes look gorgeous when they are placed on the table: golden-brown and plump with their fillings. The blueberry and pineapple-cheese fillings are quite good, but the cherry was somewhat flat and sticky. Another specialty is pirogen, dumplings filled with mashed potatoes, which can be ordered boiled or fried, and should be properly smothered in sour cream. Now, the very idea of this dish may cause hardening of the arteries but in fact it comes off with a credible lightness, especially if you don't overdo it and if you choose the boiled rather than the fried. The freshness and tanginess of the sour cream are just right for blintzes and pirogen.

Ratner's, like the other dairy restaurants, has a section of vegetarian specialties comprised of the kind of dishes that were considered health food thirty or forty years ago, such as protose steak, vegetarian cutlet, and stuffed cabbage. This vein of cookery tends to get mixed up on occasion with mock-Chinese food in the American chop suey tradition. This can run to the nightmarish; one combination plate we sampled brought together, in one wilting mound, servings of stuffed cabbage, Spanish rice, chop suey, fried noodles, and creamed mushrooms. The vegetarian cutlet, a little starchy though inoffensive, is less satisfactory than the recognizable vegetable dishes: creamed spinach, beets, and kasha varnishkes.

Desserts can be worth leaving room for. Ratner's does its own baking and the pastry is on a high level (it is also sold retail at the counter). The cream cheese rogalach were meltingly sweet and moist. If one likes cheesecake heavy and densely creamy, this is the right place. A baked apple was excellent but another house specialty, hot rice pudding, was a cold, dry, inedible mass.

With either appetizer or soup plus an entree, dessert, and coffee, plus tax and tip, you should expect to pay about $11 for dinner.

A.M.

Yahalom Restaurant
49 West 47th Street
Tel. (212) 575-1699

There are many wholesale districts in New York: the garment district along Seventh Avenue in the Thirties, the restaurant suppliers on the Bowery, cut flowers along Sixth Avenue in the Twenties. But none is planted as close to the heart of midtown as the diamond district, along 47th Street between Fifth and Sixth Avenues. And none is as Jewish. A large part of the diamond trade is in the hands of Orthodox and Hasidic Jews and their busy presence has formed a delightfully incongruous island right in the middle of the metropolis.

If one wants to view jewels in a setting of stylish refinement, one should go to the chandeliered and wainscoted showrooms of Cartier, Tiffany, or Winston a few blocks away. But if one wants to feel the excitement of the jewelry *business*, then the diamond district is the place. Diamonds are traded not at auction or on a trading floor, but informally in conversations in small groups. A kibitz, a sounding out, a little bargaining, a handshake, perhaps a tiny envelope changes hands, and a deal has been struck. There is usually no paper signed. The diamond business is conducted among a fraternity of families who know each other. Verbal agreements are the norm and are protected by honor and familiarity.

Some of the excitement of the diamond district is exuded by the area's kosher restaurant Yahalom, which, appropriately enough, means "diamond" in Hebrew. The location of the restaurant displays something of the wholesaler's confidence that if you have the goods it doesn't matter where you sell them. To get to Yahalom you have to tunnel your way through some commercial lobby space up a back staircase and along a passageway until you are rewarded by murals that depict Moses leading the Children of Israel and welcome diners to the windowless second-floor restaurant. The restaurant has two sections: in front, a cafeteria where one can eat quickly, and in back, a dining room with waitress service, where one can relax a bit and listen to the babble of conversations in English, Yiddish, Hebrew, Hungarian, Rumanian, and German. While the outer room is done in Jewish primitive murals, the inner restaurant is decorated in an oriental motif, with ceiling designs and hanging brass lanterns, though here too relief plaques of old praying Jews and of the Western Wall are not lacking.

The menu is also divided in two. On the one hand, there are the usual offerings of kosher meat restaurants, such as pot roast, veal cutlet, stuffed cabbage, and rib steak, in addition to delicatessen sandwiches and salad platters. Beyond these clichés, however, Yahalom offers a series of Mideast specialties that are a pleasant surprise. Yahalom serves a variety of salads and some entrees of the sort one might expect to eat at an ordinary oriental restaurant in Jerusalem or Tel Aviv, only here it's not so ordinary.

Among the appetizers is one of the best-prepared homous, ground chickpea dip, we have ever eaten. You can order it mixed with a little tehina, a ground sesame seed puree, and enjoy a dish that is properly piquant but still flavorful and mellow. The baba ganoosh, chopped eggplant dip, was mixed with a little too much tehina for our tastes but was still satisfying. We were all impressed with the felafel, ground and deep-fried balls of chick peas and spices. It's not easy to do felafel well: the oil must not be fresh or overused, the temperature and timing have to be right so that the inside of the balls get done while leaving the outside crisp but not hardened. Yahalom's version of felafel scored well: the frying was crisp and fresh and the seasoning mild enough not to leave an unpleasant cumin aftertaste. All the salads are served with pita bread for dipping and sandwich-making and they are garnished with olives and hot peppers. We must admit to having sneaked over to the other side of the menu to try one of the soups from the conventional European entries (it was a cold day), and we are pleased to report that we enjoyed a very good vegetable soup with a split pea base and plenty of carrots and barley.

The Middle Eastern entrees, although limited, are generally good. An order of shish kebab yielded a generous number of large chunks of good quality steak that had been grabbed from the broiler before being overcooked. The skewers could have used a flash of color from the vegetables promised on the menu but not delivered, and the meat, though good in itself, would have taken on a more distinctive flavor if it had had the benefit of a more pungent marinade, or of any at all. The moussaka, layers of eggplant, meat, and vegetables, was also good, though better in its parts than as the whole. The ground meat filling was delightfully seasoned with onion and pine nuts, bound together with eggs and redolent of cumin. What enclosed the meat was not as good: the top and bottom layers of eggplant together with the skin, spread with a veneer of tomato paste, seemed an afterthought.

The desserts are disappointingly common, except for a distinguished baklava that is made on the premises. This confection of phyllo dough, crushed nuts, and honey departs from the gooey sweet overkill encountered at most restaurants and becomes something solidly flavorful in its own right. Finish the meal with Turkish or Yemenite coffee or take tea with mint leaves (nana) or with cardamom seeds (hel).

The salads and dips are $2.75 and the entrees are $7. A full meal with tax and tip comes to about $14.

—A.M.

Bernstein's-on-Essex
135 Essex Street
Tel. (212) 473-3900

This big deli on the lower East Side, also known as Shmulke Bernstein's, has two menus: Chinese specialties and a glatt kosher delicatessen restaurant menu. Bernstein's is funky, crowded, fun, but most important, it has good food.

To this transplanted New Yorker, Bernstein's is *the* spot to visit on the lower East Side. About one-quarter of the waiters are Chinese, wearing *yarmulkes.* The other three-quarters are Jewish, some wearing Chinese coolie caps.

We were seated with an older couple from Queens who had arrived at about the same time. They were surprised and we were surprised, but four chairs means four people, and Bernstein's is that kind of place.

The decor at Bernstein's, if decor is not too strong a word, is Chinese, sort of. Two yellow plastic panels painted to reflect Chinese screens are back-lit so that they cast a warm, golden yellow glow throughout the room. The dining area is panelled in walnut and a kind of yellow plastic formica printed in a metallic pattern. The tables and chairs are standard deli. Since the tables are rarely empty of food, the decor doesn't matter much.

Our new friends from Queens ordered kosher Chinese, as Bernstein's has been making it for twenty years. As you read the menu, you see such famous Chinese specialties as lo mein Bernstein's ($10), "soft noodles tossed with shredded chicken meat, bean sprouts, delicately flavored," and chow mein Bernstein ($10), "a version of a favorite gourmet style, made with fresh chicken livers, sliced chicken, beef steak, and fine Chinese vegetables."

Conventional Chinese dishes include lemon chicken, almond ding, moo goo gai pan, and egg foo young, which costs $9.50 and is touted on the menu as a "celestial omelette."

One curiosity on the Chinese menu: "Bread and pickles, if requested with Chinese food, 50¢ per person, except *motzi.*" If one wants to say *motzi*, the traditional blessing before eating, they will bring the bread free.

One Chinese specialty you might wish to try is barbecued glatt kosher spare ribs with fried rice and duck sauce, a huge oval platter of beef ribs marinated and glazed with a pleasant sauce, meaty, lean, and very tasty. We sampled it with our new friends and enjoyed every bite of the *bissel* they gave us. The chicken egg rolls, two with fried rice, are tasty, good, hot, and fresh. One item we will save for next time is the Rumanian pastrami fried rice for $5.50. Sounds interesting.

So much for Chinese food!

We went to Bernstein's for deli. And the deli is terrific! They make their own corned beef and they make their own pastrami; not just the Rumanian-style pastrami that is popular all around town, but what Bernstein's calls flanken pastrami, made from the piece of beef which kosher eaters know as flanken, but cured in an old-fashioned, very peppery style.

The pastramis are excellent served on crisp rye bread. The Rumanian-style pastrami is piled high; it's firm, moist, not too lean, and not overwhelmingly spicy. A very good pastrami.

Those who love a peppery taste should try the flanken pastrami. The taste explodes in the mouth. It is much firmer than the Rumanian-style, and although it has to be cut into small pieces because of the type of meat used, it's delicious!

Excellent also is the corned beef at Bernstein's. Somewhat mild for my taste, it is cured on the premises, and is tender and delicious. The sandwiches, which cost $3.95, are probably the best values of all.

If you want deli and action, and the old-time excitement of a restaurant that probably hasn't changed much during the forty-nine years it's been open, then Bernstein's is the place to try.

—H.L.G.

Henry's
295 East Houston Street
Tel. (212) 674-2200

Henry's is the smallest of the three delicatessens visited. Around the corner from the more famous Katz's, Henry's seems to us much, much better.

Henry's corned beef and pastrami sandwiches are $3.25. A large plate of crinkle-cut french fries is $0.80. Surprisingly, a kosher hot dog is a dime cheaper at $0.70. A popular item at Henry's is two thick slices of kishka with brown gravy; fully one-quarter of the tables ordered this dish during our visit. This kishka nosh costs $0.90.

We tried corned beef and pastrami, the soup of the day, mushroom barley, cole slaw, kishka, potato salad, french fries, and a hot dog. Everything except the cole slaw and potato salad was excellent; the exceptions being too plain and white. Basically they consisted of cabbage with mayonnaise and potatoes with mayonnaise—some seasoning—but very basic, and dull.

The hot dogs, all-beef and kosher, of course, were seasoned perhaps a bit mildly, but they appeared to suit the taste of the public.

The french fries were cooked in fresh oil and were crisp and hot. The kishka tasted better without the gravy, but was good nevertheless.

The corned beef and the pastrami were lean, generous sandwiches, spicy or properly seasoned and freshly cut while warm and fragrant. The rye bread was well made, with a crisp crust. For $3.25, a good value sandwich!

—H.L.G.

Second Avenue Delicatessen
156 Second Avenue
Tel. (212) 677-0606

Pastrami, pickles, garlic, and chicken soup. You smell them almost a block away and know immediately that you're close to the Second Avenue Deli, one of New York's most authentic kosher Jewish delicatessens. "Pastrami? You can have it extra-lean, no fat; lean, just a little fat; and regular," the waitress explains as she settles us into our seats in the rushed, crowded back "fancier" of the two dining rooms. Fancier in this case means dark wood tables and chairs, dark wall panelling, and soft lighting.

More traditional deli service is available in the larger front room with its brighter furniture and lights; its well-stocked deli counter full of knishes, hot dogs, salami, and other good things; and its picture windows overlooking the street.

Anyone who succumbs to the warm, fresh, succulent (don't get it too lean) pastrami sandwich will find it an unbeatable buy: at $3.40 it's worth every penny, especially with the two types of pickles, plus pickled tomatoes, that are waiting on the table when one is seated.

Said the waitress, who could double for my Aunt Sadie, about a man who blocked our way to a coat hook, "Tell the fat old man to move." It's a little like home at the Second Avenue Deli.

Not much space between the tables and chairs, but no one seems to mind; they've come to eat—not to dine.

We began with chicken soup because it was cold outside. The soup, promptly served, was bubbling in a stainless steel pot; our waitress carefully ladled it into our soup plates. It was a fragrant soup flavored with fresh dill, with a wonderful aroma. We had opted for no noodles, just the massive matzah ball, which was as light as Mom's and, dare I say it, probably lighter, and three times the size. The broth I thought a bit thin, but no one agreed.

What else to have? After reviewing the wide selection on the menu, we turned to our waitress, who read the confusion on our faces. "The more you look the more confused you get," she said. From the Second Avenue Deli's generous menu we finally chose the aforementioned pastrami and corned beef, sliced thin and piled high. The corned beef was not the best, a little dry, but well worth trying again.

The chopped liver was especially good. Fresh, not too processed, it lived up to its billing on the paper placemats. "Before you get into another pickle, order the best chopped liver in town," we were correctly informed.

Side dishes of kasha varnishkes, noodle pudding, and stuffed derma were better than average, but not exceptional. The stuffed derma was a good-sized portion, but very underseasoned. The favored item, without a doubt, was the boiled beef flanken. One pound or more of good flanken, not overcooked, but very tender and full of flavor—this piece definitely had not been soaking in warm water all day. Only a red horseradish sauce that was much too mild kept the flanken from being excellent.

Coffee was hot, strong, and good. The deli is proud of receiving a golden cup award from the Pan American Coffee Brewers Commission. However, we weren't pleased with the fact that they were out of Dr. Brown's cream soda. Deli just doesn't taste the same without it!

Our desserts, a blueberry tart, chocolate devil's food cake, and warm apple strudel, were very good, particularly for a kosher (non-dairy) restaurant. The strudel, warm apples in a thin, crisp crust, is excellent, and two can share an order.

The Second Avenue Deli is on the corner of Second Avenue and Tenth Street. Go, if you haven't been: you'll go back!

—H.L.G.

Kosher Delight

1223 Avenue J and
East 13th Street, Brooklyn
Tel. (212) 377-6873

Suppose you are in New York City on vacation and you have already eaten in America's three most elegant kosher restaurants: Moshe Peking, La Différence, and Lou G. Siegel's. They have fine, rich Jewish food, but if you are from out-of-town, you or your kids now may want to eat something very simple and "American." Then the easiest thing is to grab a D train and head out to Brooklyn's Sixteenth Avenue J stop, walk 2½ blocks and enter the Kosher Delight, "the Family Restaurant." It looks something like a cross between a Hardees and a Burger King, complete with orange formica seats, butcher block formica tables, orange and yellow plastic coated walls, and an abundance of plastic plants. Tacky, but if you are from America's hinterlands, you are used to chain fast food and know that the sum is more than the parts add up to.

Here the food is good and fast, featuring burgers and fried chicken and strictly glatt kosher. There are prayer books available on the side station, among the condiments, as well as the traditional blessings related to the meal in transliteration, framed.

We enjoyed the big burger, a Burger Delight, flame-broiled and juicy for $1.49. It was a quarter-pound burger similar to the Whopper, served on a sesame seed bun: a large, thin patty, with ketchup, onion, lettuce, pickles, and tomato. The lettuce had been chopped a bit early and showed it, but the hamburger had not been held long and tasted fine.

Decent french fries came in a cup, à la Nathan's; the price was $0.65 and the portion generous. They would have been excellent had they been salted while hot. Salting lukewarm or cool french fries does not work as well.

The plain small hamburger is called the Beefburger ($0.75); it is about two ounces or a little less—more than adequate for a child. Of course, cheeseburgers are not available, but there is a full line of other burgers: doubles, Burger Delights, double Beefburgers, and steak sandwiches.

The other featured main course, a very acceptable fried chicken, comes in a snack box (two pieces of chicken and french fries, $2.25); a dinner box (three pieces of chicken, french fries, and a roll, $2.95); and so on up to giant barrels (21 pieces, $12.95). The chicken was moist and, although I prefer fried chicken more heavily seasoned, this seems to suit the marketplace; it is a big seller.

Accompaniments include knishes, corn on the cob, onion rings, soup, and a limited number of pastries. Altogether, Kosher Delight provides an above-average experience for the pit-stop diner. Good quality food, quickly served.

—H.L.G.

JERUSALEM

Taj

(Persian)
27 Jaffa Road
Tel. 241515

The Taj is in a small courtyard, entered from Jaffa Road across from the Jerusalem Municipal Tourist Office in the center of town. This small, quiet restaurant is attractively decorated in stone, wood, wrought-iron, and several photographs of the former Shah in full coronation regalia. Twenty years in Israel have not dimmed the royalist sympathies of the Karamani family, who own the Taj and are personally responsible for the superb Persian cuisine.

We were shown to our table and served by the single waiter, David, who is of Moroccan extraction and seems equally comfortable speaking Hebrew, English, French, or Arabic. From the triptych menu in Hebrew, Persian, and English we selected our first course, which David kindly offered to divide into two half portions for us. Gondi nichohi, described as "hummus balls roasted and meat," turned out to be delectable dumplings of ground meat and chickpeas, spicy hot. Domei barg was vine leaves stuffed with rice and bits of meat, infused with a dark syrupy sauce whose sweetness was cut by the welcome tang of lemon. Fresh, warm pita bread was served immediately. Having perused the menu for something bland, we were warned off the lamb chop ("too much fat this evening") by David, who wisely suggested kabab barg, two skewers of tender marinated beef medallions charcoal grilled and served with a colorful sprinkle of parsley. This came accompanied by polo aviji kashmesh, saffron rice intermingled with shreds of carrot and sweet with the flavor of raisins—described by a member of our party as tasting "rather like tsimis." I chose choresht sabsi, something between a soup and a stew of beef bits, red beans, and herbs, rich with the flavor of cumin. This was served with chello, fluffy steamed white rice, the perfect background for the pungent sauce of the meat dish. Though a choice of fresh fruits was available for dessert, we were too satiated to partake and settled for a demitasse of Turkish coffee.

The bill for two, including one local beer, one grapefruit juice, and tip (no service charge was included in the bill), was $20 (U.S.). The Taj, which does not accept credit cards, is open from 12:00 noon to 3:00 P.M. and from 7:00 P.M. to midnight.

—M.J.B.

M. Cohen's Restaurant and Bar

(North African)
Yishayahu and Sima Blilious
Streets, Tel. 225020

The only evidence of this long established Jerusalem institution is a small hand-lettered sign in a curtained window on Yishayahu Street. The entrance, which is around the corner from the Edison Cinema, is totally unmarked except for the Diners and Visa credit card stickers. Going through this admittedly unpromising doorway, one enters a tiny, high-ceilinged room containing just four tables, red curtains, flocked red wallpaper, and eastern bric-a-brac—a vision of fin de siecle Casablanca.

Michel Cohen, the proprietor, is known primarily for his remarkable stuffed vegetables (memula'im), so we began with a mixed assortment, including eggplant cooked with meat and walnuts, a huge vine leaf stuffed with a different meat mixture, half an onion holding a hemisphere of yet another meat mixture, and a zucchini stuffed with rice. There was also what our waiter described as a stuffed "carrot" and the menu referred to as a "quince," but what empirically turned out to be, believe it or not, a delicious stuffed beet! This sumptuous first course, which could easily have sufficed for a complete dinner, only whetted our appetites for the main course. My companion had the shashlik—tender, juicy bits of lean veal, mildly seasoned in order not to disguise the taste of the meat. I chose veal cooked in the oven; this turned out to be a thick chop served in its own juice, flavored with cloves and fresh black pepper. Both entrees were served à la carte, but side dishes would have been superfluous. Though pleasantly dazed by these delicacies, we could hardly pass up a round of the famous stuffed prunes. These had been cooked with walnuts, sultanas, and a few pine nuts *(pignoli)* and were infused with their own dark amber sauce, heavily laden with cinnamon, which served as an astringent foil to the sweetness of the prunes—delectable!

The bill, including a local beer, grapefruit juice, tea, and Turkish coffee, was $21 (U.S.). Cohen's is open for lunch from 1:00 to 4:00 P.M. and for dinner from 7:00 to 11:00 P.M. It's a good idea to reserve a table in advance.

—M.J.B.

Fish Shlomo

(North African Fish)
27 Salmon Street
Tel. 233631

Fish can be a fishy business in Jerusalem. Fresh seafish are not always available, even in the fishing ports of Ashdod and Jaffa, and locating them in a Jerusalem restaurant is difficult. Moreover, only a few of the Holy City's fish restaurants are kosher; others prefer to attract less observant guests with seafoods lacking the requisite fins and scales. Nevertheless, we decided to take the plunge and paid a nocturnal visit to one of the newer fisheries, which is definitely kosher and offers a French-North African cuisine.

Shlomo's is in the Nachalat Shiva quarter of Jerusalem, noted for its old stone houses and winding alleyways, on the edge of the city center near Independence Park. The restaurant has the de rigueur fishnet decor, complete with bubbling goldfish-filled fish tanks. For a first course we chose bouillabaisse soup, wondering how this seafood specialty could be made to conform to the strictures of Scripture. We were presented with a tomato soup replete with bits of fish fillet— tasty, but a far cry from the soup of the same name we remembered from San Francisco's Fisherman's Wharf, which was a veritable gastronomic tour through Marineland of the Pacific. As for the main course, we were saddened but not surprised to hear that no fresh seafish were available that evening. My companion fell back on her old favorite, trout amandine, which turned out to be deep-fried and accompanied by a few canned mushrooms, blanched almonds, and less than a *minyan* of dispirited chips. I took up the challenge of the specialty of the house: Tunisian couscous, which might be described as a North African kasha. It was properly fluffy, but the topping was essentially an uninspiring melange of the fish fillet previously encountered in the soup and some thoroughly cooked vegetables.

The bill for two was $16.50 (U.S.). Fish Shlomo, which does not accept credit cards, is open from noon to 11:00 P.M. On leaving we were informed by our very kindly waiter, Sammy, that they plan to serve French-North African meat specialties as well. We hope this will improve the cuisine when fresh fish are in short supply, as on the evening of our visit. It is a good idea to call ahead to check what is available that day.

—M.J.B.

Europa

(Hungarian)
42 Jaffa Road
Tel. 228953

Do not be put off by the entranceway, which leads up an untidy flight of stairs into an office building on Zion Square in the middle of busy downtown Jerusalem. The door on the second floor opens into a comfortable little corner of Central Europe, tastefully decorated in dark wood. The Europa is personally supervised by owner Lea Brummer, a totally professional restaurateur who is famous in Jerusalem for superb Hungarian cuisine. At lunchtime the restaurant was packed, mostly with dark-suited businessmen, but Lea and her one waitress, Shulah, managed to wait on everyone with courtesy, efficiency, and a real sense of warmth.

For the first course we picked vegetable soup, which was thick and rich, full of fresh mushrooms and vegetables. We also ordered goulash soup, a paprika-laced concoction with the large chunks of tender beef and little dumplings that are the hallmark of the Europa's Hungarian fare. My companion followed with grilled trout (fresh from the kibbutz fishponds of the Upper Galilee), which Shulah boned for us at the table before serving; it was accompanied by white rice topped with a meat and vegetable sauce. I had roast goose, which was sizzling hot, admirably crisp, and remarkably lean. I also asked for a second round of the delicious dumplings, which had been tossed in a mild paprika sauce. While savoring our main course we were already looking forward to dessert, because we had often eaten at Lea's previous restaurant in the Rehavia neighborhood, and always finished with her justly renowned palachinka, a large crêpe rolled up around a filling of pureed nuts or fruits, topped with chocolate sauce. Our recollections were not disappointed—it was every bit as good as we remembered.

The custom is not to ask for the check, but to march up to the bar and recount to whoever happens to be handling the cash register what you had to eat.

The bill for two, including tea and Turkish coffee, was $14.50 (U.S.). The Europa, which accepts Isracard/Eurocard, Access, and Master Charge, is open from noon to 10:00 P.M.

—M.J.B.

Feferberg's

(Eastern European)
53 Jaffa Road
Tel. 224841, 225788

Feferberg's is conveniently located at the hub of downtown Jerusalem, a few doors down Jaffa Road from King George Street. The front section, offering take-home cut meats and other carry-out specialties, is a superb delicatessen; but farther inside, away from the hubbub of the street, are two attractive wood-panelled dining rooms, each table invitingly set with red napkins and a sparkling white cloth. Feferberg's is renowned for Ashkenazi food at its best.

My companion began with a bowl of barley soup, rich, tasty, and very warming on a wintry Jerusalem afternoon. I sampled the kishke, tender bits of innards deliciously stuffed and served in a rich meat sauce. For a main course, my companion ordered corned beef, a dinner plate thickly covered with thin slices of meat served cold from the delicatessen section. I had roast duck, half a bird cooked crisp with lots of garlic. The main course was accompanied by several side dishes served family style: freshly mashed potatoes, cooked carrots, and a dish of cabbage cooked with raisins in a sweet and sour sauce. Filled by this wholesome, delicious meal, we decided to forego the many appealing desserts listed on the menu.

The bill for two, including tip, was $22 (U.S.). Feferberg's, which does not accept credit cards, is open from noon to 9:30 P.M.

—M.J.B.

Abu-Shaul

(Oriental Grill)
Shuk Machaneh Yehudah
Tel. 246198

As the owner's name suggests, "Oriental" is used here in the Israeli sense of Middle Eastern. Abu-Shaul, in Jerusalem's open air market, is reached from Jaffa Road by walking down Machaneh Yehudah Street and taking the first turn to the right. This takes you into what is known as the Shuk Hakatan (Little Market), which during the day is jammed with stands selling fruits and vegetables. The restaurant may be recognized by the brazier of glowing charcoal in front of the door on which all the meats are grilled. This is also what distinguishes this, the original Abu-Shaul from a less distinguished restaurant of the same name in the center of town at which all the cooking is done on a griddle. Since its recent redecoration the original Abu-Shaul has become a spiffy place, done out in knotty-pine panelling and checkered plastic tablecloths; however, the hand-lettered menu remains writ large on the walls.

We began with a combined plate of humous and techinah (pureed chickpeas and sesame), Turkish salad (a spicy puree of tomatoes), and amba (a uniquely flavored condiment made from mustard and mangoes); all this was served with fresh, warm pita bread. For the main course, my companion—who protested my ordering the udder offered on the menu—had her standard shashlik. This was three skewers of tender beef cubes charcoal grilled to a perfect medium rare. On reflection, this writer opted for the lamb chops. There arrived a veritable stack of chops, also deliciously grilled. We shared an order of freshly prepared, crisp french fries (obviously made from fresh, not frozen potatoes)—the best, I think, I have ever eaten.

The bill, including a local beer and grapefruit juice, was $11.60 (U.S.). Abu-Shaul is open from noon to midnight.

—M.J.B.

Palmachi Restaurant

(Israeli Oriental)
13 Shamai Street
Tel. 234784

The Palmachi is just down the road from the Orion Cinema, near the center of Jerusalem. The one rather large but comfortable room is pleasantly decorated, with each candlelit table sporting a vase of freshly cut flowers. This long established Jerusalem institution serves what seems to be becoming typical Israeli fare—if any cuisine can be so described in this potpourri of culinary cultures after little more than thirty years of statehood.

While perusing the menu, we nibbled at the fresh, warm pita bread which had been served immediately, accompanied by a plate of olives, hot green peppers, and pickled radishes, which we overheard the waiter describe to some other diners as "turnip." Actually, the Hebrew word for the vegetable, *lefet,* also means any vegetable eaten with bread.

For a first course, my companion had techinah and eggplant, a spread prepared with the sesame seed paste typical of Near Eastern cuisine. I had lentil soup, richly spiced with cumin. We asked what fish was available and were pleased to learn that they had fresh *amnon;* this is the Hebrew name for the local freshwater fish from the Kinneret (Sea of Galilee), also called St. Peter's fish or Tiberias fish. The fish, which was deep-fried but not at all greasy, was quite tasty. I had the mixed grill, which included chunks of liver and beef, a kebab of spicy ground meat, and some lamb chops. This also tasted good but would have been better if charcoal grilled. The main course came with salad and chips. We accompanied the meal with large glasses of freshly squeezed orange and grapefruit juice.

Dinner for two, including tip, was $20 (U.S.). The Palmachi, which accepts many credit cards including Diners, is open from 11:00 A.M. to 11:00 P.M.

—M.J.B.

Georgia Restaurant

(Caucasian)
4 King David Street
Tel. 227577

Georgia—not à la Jimmy Carter, but à la Joseph Stalin, *lehavdil!* This elegant restaurant is the culinary representative of one of the most recent waves of immigration to Israel, the Gruzini Jews from the southern

USSR. Israel's Georgia, located just down the street from the King David Hotel and the Hebrew Union College, has an imposing facade of green marble. On going down the stairs, you enter a large, carpeted dining room, comfortably appointed in heavy wood and leather. The silverware and dinner service, also heavy and antique-looking, contribute to the ambiance appropriate to a unique dining experience.

We began by sharing two hors d'oeuvres. Meat blinches were incredibly light, crisp pastry filled with richly flavored meat pâté. Eggplant Georgian style was a cold salad of thick sliced, marinated eggplant with a delicious, slightly vinegary sauce of techinah and nuts. We also tried two of the soups. Harthsou (Georgian soup) was a spicy, kümmel-laced tomato and meat consommé; the Ukrainian borsht was a hot, rich concoction of cabbage and tiny potatoes. All the main courses, served with spiced white rice and green beans, were exciting. Chicken scoor (Tchahabilly) was simmered in a pungent tomato sauce. Salianka picant, a Georgian beef goulash, was true to its name and was also prepared in a tomato sauce. The filet steak was the best this diner has eaten in Israel—lean, tender, and done medium rare to perfection. Shishlik Georgian was marinated bits of beef of truly remarkable tenderness, charcoal grilled with tiny onions. Turkish coffee and tea came served in a filigree holder with great lumps of sugar to be held between the teeth Russian style. From about 7:30 until 10:30 P.M., dinner is accompanied by a live, loud electronic organist.

Dinner for four adults was $60 (U.S.). The Georgia, which accepts American Express, Diners, and Visa credit cards, is open from noon to midnight.

—M.J.B.

Marina Chinese Restaurant

(Thai-Chinese)
3 Ahad Ha'am Street
Tel. 631279

The Jerusalem branch of this establishment (the original Marina Chinese Restaurant is in Tel Aviv), in the President Hotel in the exclusive Talbieh neighborhood, is about two blocks from Terra Sancta. In the off-season only one room, which contains the bar, is in use; but in the summer a larger room looking out onto the swimming pool is also open. Decor is basic hotel dining room done up in standard chinoiserie; but the real ambiance is provided by the staff, most of whom are recent arrivals from Bangkok. Thus "Chinese" restaurant is a misnomer, apparently necessitated by Israeli unfamiliarity with the national nuances of Oriental cuisine. A glance at the menu is confirmed by the palate; this is really a Thai restaurant and a good one.

The menu features an impressive range of meat, poultry, fish, and vegetable dishes, which all seemed to be available on each of our visits. Do not be upset by the various offerings of "shrimps"; these dishes are all prepared from Israeli seafish, and the *kashrut* certificate is proudly displayed upstairs by the reception desk.

For starters, egg roll (served with a gaudily colored plum sauce) and wonton soup chosen by my companion and her mother were pretty much the standard fare available in Oriental eateries around the Western world. But the Thai fish soup was a real delight; it is like a Szechuan hot and sour soup but with a special spiciness and big chunks of seafish fillet. For the main course the writer succeeded in getting two Thai items accepted by our troika of diners. Chicken Thailand style turned out to be a cold salad with chunks of chicken breast and crisp fresh and cooked vegetables; an amazing and unique variety of flavors such as mint, hot pepper, and lemon was somehow separately discernible. Roast beef in red wine was a "red-cooked" sauté of beef shreds and vegetables in a spicy hot sauce which called up vague associations of barbecue; however, the chicken and almonds was standard Oriental restaurant fare. For dessert, the banana toffee was a fried banana in a candy-like coating replete with sesame seeds and flambéed, *noch!* In toto, the standard Chinese offerings are quite passable; but if you have no objection to giving your mouth a bit of a hot foot, stick to the Thai specialties and have a real treat.

Dinner for three, including fried rice, green tea, and tip, was $28 (U.S.). The Marina "Chinese" Restaurant, which accepts American Express, Diners, and Visa credit cards, is open from 7:00 P.M. to 11:00 P.M.

—M.J.B.

KOSHER AND TREIF: THE DIALECTICS OF EATING

A strong strain of dualism permeates Jewish tradition. Categories are defined, often seemingly arbitrarily, and a given object is either in or out. This is perhaps most evident in the laws of *kashrut* (permissible foods). As stated in the Bible and elaborated upon in the Talmud and subsequent legal codes, certain animals are permissible to eat; others are forbidden. None of the rationales which have been suggested is entirely satisfying. The Bible does not give reasons, but simply defines certain species as "clean" and others as "unclean" (cf. Lev. 11 and Deut. 14:3–21), known today as kosher and *treif* respectively.

(Richard Sobol)

The following lists are not comprehensive but do cite animals mentioned in the Bible or commonly known today. Because there are varying traditions and some controversy about some animals, the lists should not be considered to have halakhic (legal) authority. Also, a kosher animal must be slaughtered and prepared in a ritually correct way to remain permissible to eat. Thus chicken (which is kosher) becomes *treif* if not slaughtered properly; beef, even which is slaughtered properly, can be made *treif* by cooking it with dairy products.

10 KOSHER MAMMALS

All these animals have split hooves *and* chew their cuds, the two necessary signs which render them "clean" and fit for consumption.

1. Antelope
2. Buffalo
3. Gazelle
4. Goat
5. Hart
6. Ibex
7. Kine (cattle)
8. Ox
9. Roebuck
10. Sheep

25 *TREIF* MAMMALS

These animals either are not cloven-hoofed or do not chew their cuds.

1. Ape
2. Ass
3. Bat
4. Bear
5. Boar
6. Camel
7. Cat
8. Dog
9. Elephant
10. Fox
11. Hare
12. Hippopotamus
13. Horse
14. Hyena
15. Jackal
16. Leopard
17. Lion
18. Llama
19. Mouse
20. Mule
21. Pig
22. Rat
23. Whale
24. Wolf
25. Zebra

12 KOSHER BIRDS

The Bible does not stipulate identifying characteristics for birds, but the *Mishnah* states that "a bird that seizes food in its claws is unclean; [while] one which has an extra talon, a craw, and the skin of whose stomach [gizzard] can be peeled, is clean." (Hulin 3:6)

1. Domestic Duck
2. Domestic Goose
3. Hen
4. House Sparrow
5. Palm Dove
6. Partridge
7. Peacock
8. Pheasant
9. Pigeon
10. Quail
11. Turkey
12. Turtle Dove

20 *TREIF* BIRDS

All these birds are either expressly prohibited

in the Bible, are birds of prey, do not have the characteristics of a clean bird, or have no tradition of being permitted.

1. Buzzard
2. Cormorant
3. Crane
4. Crow
5. Eagle
6. Falcon
7. Gull
8. Hawk
9. Heron
10. Hoopoe
11. Kite
12. Osprey
13. Ostrich
14. Owl
15. Pelican
16. Raven
17. Stork
18. Swift
19. Vulture
20. Warbler

20 KOSHER FISH

According to the Bible, only fish which have both fins and scales are considered "clean."

1. Anchovy
2. Bass
3. Bluefish
4. Carp
5. Cod
6. Flounder
7. Fluke
8. Haddock
9. Halibut
10. Herring
11. Mackerel
12. Pike
13. Red Snapper
14. Salmon
15. Sardine
16. Shad
17. Sole
18. Trout
19. Tuna
20. Whitefish

5 *TREIF* FISH

These fish do not have both fins and scales.

1. Catfish
2. Eel
3. Porpoise
4. Ray
5. Shark

2 QUESTIONABLE FISH

There is dispute about whether these fish have true fins and scales. The Conservative movement considers them permissible while most Orthodox Jews prohibit them.

1. Sturgeon
2. Swordfish

4 CREATURES IT IS HARD TO BELIEVE ARE KOSHER

The *Mishnah* (Hulin 3:7) stipulates four signs by which you can recognize permitted insects (four legs, four wings, jointed legs, and wings that cover the greater part of the body), because of the difficulty in identifying them accurately today, most communities refrain from eating these disgusting creatures. (In fact, as scientifically defined, only those "insects" with six legs qualify as true insects. Spiders, ticks, and centipedes, for example, are not true insects.)

1. Bald Locust
2. Locust
3. Cricket
4. Grasshopper

20 OTHER ANIMALS WHICH ARE *TREIF*

These animals are either "swarming things of the water and all other living creatures that are in the water" (Lev. 11:10) or "things that swarm upon the earth, anything that crawls on its belly, or anything that walks on fours, or anything that has many legs." (Lev. 11:42)

1. Black Snake
2. Chameleon
3. Clams
4. Crocodile
5. Flatworm
6. Frog
7. Jellyfish
8. Leeches
9. Lizard
10. Lobster
11. Oyster
12. Scallops
13. Shrimp
14. Salamander
15. Snail
16. Sponges
17. Squid
18. Toad
19. Tortoise
20. Viper

—R.A.S.

Animals forbidden as food to the Jews.

KOSHER WINES AND WINERIES

A TASTE OF THINGS TO COME

How sweet? So sweet you have to coax it out of the bottle. How thick? So thick you can cut it with a knife. There is an endless number of jokes about the typical Jewish wine—heavy, syrupy, deep purple in color—tasted as part of the *Kiddush* ceremony at the beginning of Shabbat and festival meals, quaffed in greater quantities at the Passover *seder*.

Though the majority of Jewish wine does fit this description, supersweetness is in fact not what makes a wine kosher. In ancient times Jews were enjoined from consuming wine produced or handled by a gentile, because it was assumed that such wine had been used in the libation offerings that were part of pagan worship. Even though gentiles have long since ceased to be regarded as idol worshippers, Jewish law still requires that wine be produced under Jewish auspices in order for it to be considered kosher. Orthodox Jews abide by this stipulation generally; while Jews from the liberal branches of Judaism tend to use kosher wine mainly in ceremonial settings: weddings, holiday meals, and circumcisions, for example.

The point to emphasize, however, is that the kosher quality of wines (their *kashrut*) is established in a manner different from that of other foods. In the case of meat, fish, and poultry, certain species are forbidden (pork and shellfish, for example), and the meat and poultry that are permitted must be slaughtered in a special way and submitted to certain blood-removing procedures. Wine is an entirely different story. Kosher wine may be made from any variety of grapes whatsoever and processed according to any method as well; there are certainly no geographical restrictions, requiring, for example, that grapes be grown in upstate New York. The only condition is that the wine's manufacture be in the hands of Jews. *Therefore,* theoretically speaking, there is no reason why a kosher wine could not be as dry, crisp, and subtle as the most beguiling French or California wine. In practice, however, it is the consumers of Jewish wines who have historically preferred to drink their wine undisguisedly sweet and heavy.

There are indications, though, that the situation is changing. In recent years there has emerged an interest in drier wines and in a more sophisticated variety of sweet wines. The change seems to have come about because people want wines that can be enjoyed throughout a meal or a festive occasion, as opposed to wines whose sweetness is such that it only allows them to be savored at special moments. Another factor is the development in Israel of a serious wine industry, with plantings from good European varietals, such as the Rothschild grapes, in a climate favorable to viniculture. Also, some American producers, like Kedem, are importing kosher wines from France and Italy.

There now exists a substantial spectrum of kosher wines that offers the consumer much more choice than the traditional conception of *Jewish* wine would lead one to expect. Now one can sample a variety of dry red and dry white table wines, sauternes, rosés, as well as a creation that seems unique to the new Jewish wine market: "creamed" wines.

How good are the new kosher wines?

The Jewish Almanac set out to answer this question by submitting them to a blind tasting in which a panel of amateur wine lovers were asked to rate wines in various categories against each other. The general opinion of the panelists, as shown in the evaluations below, was that in general kosher wines have a long way to go in attaining the quality and reliability of other inexpensive wines; *however,* there are some pleasant, drinkable wines whose arrival on the scene should be cause for gladness.

Before examining the results, keep in mind the following information: All are relatively inexpensive, in most cases ranging between $2.50 and $4.00 a bottle, with none above $5.00. All are produced under such supervised conditions that they are kosher for use on Passover. There are a variety of kosher wines such as sauternes, hock, and rosés that we did not have the opportunity to taste, and others that will be appearing in the near future. The wines represented in this sampling are only those that are commercially available on a national basis in America; if one's wine merchant does not stock them, urge him to do so. These of course are not the only kosher wines produced in the world. In Israel there is a considerably larger selection than what is exported, and there are several quite credible kosher wines available in France.

Rabbi S. Cohn, religious supervisor of Manischewitz winery

Tasting Results

(N.B. All Carmel wines are imported from Israel and all others are domestic, unless otherwise noted.)

DRY WHITES

Good

KEDEM SEYVAL BLANC: pleasantly light-bodied, smooth, fruity.

KEDEM BORDEAUX (Imported from France): crisp, tart with a slight sweet aftertaste, clean and airy in the mouth.

Acceptable

SCHAPIRO CHABLIS: pale, bland, thin, though inoffensive and drinkable.

MANISCHEWITZ CHABLIS: sweet, fruity with a slight effervescence.

Also tasted

CARMEL SAUVIGNON BLANC: weak, characterless, medicinal-tasting.

CARMEL AVDAT: sharp and acidic with a disturbing apple-juice color.

CARMEL CHENIN BLANC: heavy, bitter, medicinal.

DRY REDS

Good

KEDEM BORDEAUX (Imported from France): pleasant bouquet, medium dry, good color and good fruit.

CARMEL ADOM ATIC: light bouquet, pleasantly dry, good flavor that holds up in the mouth. (N.B. This is one of the least expensive of the Carmel wines.)

Acceptable

CARMEL CHATEAU WINDSOR: full, fruity, nutty taste, dark colored, slightly acidic.

SCHAPIRO BURGUNDY: sweetish, heavy.

Also Tasted

CARMEL AVDAT: dull, vinegary, dry.

CARMEL CABERNET SAUVIGNON: grapey, acidic, chemical-tasting.

NATURAL CONCORD

(Natural Concord wines are those sweet wines that are made without the addition of extra sugar. They are the traditional wines for *Kiddush* and other ceremonies.)

Good

CARMEL SACRAMENTAL GRAPE: darkly colored caramel hue, distinctively fruity, smooth, natural sweetness.

SCHAPIRO MEDIUM CONCORD GRAPE: slightly drier, pungent, pleasant strong taste.

Acceptable

MANISCHEWITZ MEDIUM DRY CONCORD: light, weak, pleasant bouquet but not sweet in the tasting.

KEDEM MATUK ROYALE: bittersweet, bland, acidic aftertaste.

MALAGA

(These wines are very heavy and hard to take for more than a few sips. They can be delightful when mixed with seltzer.)

Good

MANISCHEWITZ EXTRA-HEAVY MALAGA: thick, basic, good texture, smooth.

Acceptable

CARMEL ISRAEL MALAGA: honey-flavored, syrupy, smooth, good for making *haroset* at Passover time.

KEDEM MALAGA: tart, medium, slightly acidic.

Also Tasted

SCHAPIRO MALAGA: too heavy, bitter with an acidic afterkick.

CREAM WINES

(There is nothing dairy about cream wines. "Cream" refers to a kind of finish given the wine that lends a smooth, silken texture. The wines have been commercially very successful.)

Good

KEDEM CREAM WHITE CONCORD: pleasing color, light, fruity taste, refreshing, sweet beer aftertaste.

Acceptable

MANISCHEWITZ CREAM WHITE CONCORD: mild and fruity with an occasional acidic twinge.

Also Tasted

SCHAPIRO CREAM WHITE CONCORD: bitter, sharp, syrupy.

—A.M.

The Wineries

The four companies whose wines were selected for *The Jewish Almanac*'s tasting each produce a variety of types and have broad distribution throughout the United States. Their histories, reputations, and specialties, however, are quite distinct. It is interesting to note that while twenty-four wines were tasted, these four wineries produce over one hundred twenty varieties of wines between them.

Carmel Wine Co. Inc.
271 Madison Ave.
Suite 705
New York, N.Y. 10016
212-532-4016

Wine making is an ancient tradition in Israel, where the climate and soil are well suited to grape cultivation. Although the land supports a number of wineries, Carmel is by far the largest and most well known. This winery owes its beginnings to Baron Edmond de Rothschild, known in these wine circles as "the Benefactor." In 1882 he provided the early Jewish settlers with cuttings from his famous French vineyards, brought in his own agronomist and winemaker as consultants, and constructed two large cellars in Rishon le-Zion and Zichron Yaacov. In 1906, with the industry well on its way, he turned the vineyards over to the growers, who formed a unique cooperative called the Societe Cooperative Vigneronne des Grandes Caves, which currently has over eight hundred members/growers. While the original methods were French (and remain so for the champagne), in recent years modern wine making according to California methods has been increasingly adopted, as has the cultivation of some of the California grape varieties.

Israeli kosher wineries in general, and Carmel in particular because of its size, are handicapped in ways that the American kosher wineries are not. First, Jewish law is more exacting regarding produce within the Land of Israel than outside. While all kosher wineries must ensure that every person who works with the wines is strictly observant of the Sabbath and other religious obligations, three other provisions apply only in Israel: (1) the land must be left uncultivated one year out of every seven; (2) the vineyards must be used only for grapes, with nothing else planted between the rows; and (3) a tithe (ten percent) of the produce must be poured out into the ground every year. (This last requirement created a flood of wine in 1978 due to a clogged sewer system in Rishon le-Zion.) In addition, Israel is a signatory of the Madrid Pact (1961), which established that a wine can only be called by a territorial name if it is actually from that region. The United States, on the other hand, was not a signatory, which accounts for the many American Chablis and Burgundies that have nothing to do with these wine regions in France. This advantage, which can attract unwary consumers because of the recognizability of these names, is one that Israel does not share.

In spite of these obstacles, Carmel has established an impressive list of wines that have won international recognition both in the marketplace and in judged competitions. Trying to counter the belief that "kosher equals sweet," they have produced an extensive and ever increasing line of dry wines that are now selling far better than the sweets (125,000 cases of Adom Atik, a dry red, are sold in Sweden alone.) Moderately priced, these wines offer good value, and Carmel seems well along the way towards establishing its international image as a fine imported Israeli wine.

Kedem Royal Wine Corp.
420 Kent Avenue
Brooklyn, N.Y. 11211
212-384-2400

Kedem Royal Winery
Dock Road
Milton, N.Y. 12547
914-795-2240

MADE WITH
IMPORTED CHERRIES
MANISCHEWITZ
CHERRY
ALCOHOL 12% BY VOLUME
MADE AND BOTTLED BY
MANISCHEWITZ WINE CO., NEW YORK, N.Y. - B.W.21
A CHERRY WINE AND NATURAL FLAVOR
SPECIALLY SWEETENED
UNDER STRICT RABBINICAL SUPERVISION
KOSHER
FOR PASSOVER
MANISCHEWITZ
Cream Blackberry
HOLLANDIA
A double blended cream smooth Blackberry wine, specially sweetened made from Europe's finest blackberries.
SERVE CHILLED
UNDER STRICT RABBINICAL SUPERVISION
ALCOHOL 12% BY VOL. — Cont. 750 ml (25.4 fl. oz.)
PRODUCED & BOTTLED BY MANISCHEWITZ WINE CO., NEW YORK, N.Y. - B.W.21
NATURALLY FERMENTED
כשר
לפסח
COLD DUCK
KOSHER
NEW YORK STATE
A BLEND OF NEW YORK STATE SPARKLING WHITE WINE
AND NEW YORK STATE SPARKLING BURGUNDY
KEDEM
PRODUCED & BOTTLED BY ROYAL WINE CORP. NEW YORK, N.Y. BW 600
CONTENTS 4/5 QUART
ALCOHOL 12% BY VOLUME
KOSHER FOR PASSOVER
SERVE CHILLED
כשר
לפסח
KEDEM
ROYAL
NEW YORK STATE
HAUT SAUTERNE
ALCOHOL 12.5% BY VOLUME
PRODUCED AND BOTTLED BY
ROYAL WINE CORP., NEW YORK, N.Y. B.W. 600
CARMEL
IMPORTED
כשר
לפסח
Kadmon
The Rarest Grape Wine
16% ALC./VOL. 750 ML (25.4 floz)
PRODUCED & BOTTLED IN ISRAEL BY
CARMEL WINE GROWERS COOPERATIVE
RICHON LE ZION & ZICHRON JACOB
SOLE IMPORTERS FOR THE U.S.A. CARMEL WINE Co., INC. NEW-YORK
CARMEL
CHATEAU
de la
MONTAGNE
SERVE CHILLED
WHITE
TABLE WINE
PRODUCED & BOTTLED BY
CARMEL WINE GROWERS COOPERATIVE
RICHON LE ZION & ZICHRON JACOB
12% ALC/VOL 750 ML (25.4 floz)

Once known only within the Jewish community, Kedem wines have been developing an increasing degree of respectability among serious wine drinkers both Jewish and non-Jewish over the past few years. The winery has been a family business for seven (going on eight) generations since Philip Herzog began making wines in 1848 in Vrbove, Czechoslovakia. Although counted among the largest wineries in Eastern Europe, the Holocaust and subsequent Communist takeover forced the family to relocate it to New York's Lower East Side in 1948. The company now maintains its own extensive vineyards and million gallon winery along the Hudson River in upstate New York, as well as an additional bottling and shipping plant in Brooklyn.

Because of their careful and comprehensive control of the wine production from cultivation of the grapes through bottling, Kedem has developed a highly respected and trusted reputation in the Orthodox Jewish community. According to their statistics, seventy-five percent of the kosher hotels, restaurants, and catering operations in the United States serve Kedem wines. The Herzog's goal, however, is to educate their clientele in the rewards and pleasures of the drier wines. They also hope to increase their non-Jewish clientele with the appeal of their quality imported and domestic varieties. At present, a surprisingly large forty percent of their sales are to the non-Jewish community, and Kedem reports that, curiously, they encounter more resistance to purchasing kosher wines from the Jewish non-Orthodox community than from the non-Jewish community.

Although Kedem still produces a large variety of sweet wines, it has developed highly credible drys including a French-American hybrid red *de Chaunac*, as well as three imported Bordeaux from France. In the near future, Kedem expects to add an imported white Burgundy from France and a Valpolicella from Italy. With over one million gallons of wine now in production and with an expectation of two million gallons by 1983, Kedem seems committed to and capable of making a positive impact on the wine-drinking habits of the Jewish community and on the image of the kosher wine outside of this community. As their promotional literature relates, "Kedem is proud to be both a pioneer and a vanguard in the recent renaissance in refined Jewish living and gourmet kosher dining."

The winery and vineyards in Milton, New York are open daily except *Shabbat* and other Jewish holidays for tours of the premises and free tastings of their extensive varieties of wines.

Manischewitz Wine Company
Bush Terminal
Brooklyn, N.Y. 11236
212-965-8800

Perhaps the largest and most well-known kosher wine company, Manischewitz has managed to successfully market its wines to a non-Jewish clientele through its highly effective advertising. So common an idiomatic expression is "Man-O-Manischewitz" that Astronaut Captain Eugene A. Cernan even used it to describe his overwhelming surroundings while on his first moon walk.

Although originally owned by the B. Manischewitz Company, manufacturers of kosher food products for three generations, the wine business has been licensed to the Monarch Wine Company, which has now been granted the right to use the brand name "Manischewitz" on its kosher wines and champagnes. The grapes used in their wines are grown and harvested by independents in the upper New York State "Grape Belt" and shipped to the Brooklyn winery, where the wine is processed under the required rabbinical supervision.

Although Manischewitz offers a few token "dry" wines, the house specialty is in the "sweets." In this realm they have been pioneers in an almost revolutionary process that yields "cream finish" wines. This special group of varietal grape wines are double blended for a velvety smooth taste without the foxiness often associated with the Concord and other New York State grapes. Other companies now carry the "creams" but Manischewitz has virtually cornered the market. Originally producers of Jewish ceremonial wines, particularly for Passover, the company now estimates that "today far more Manischewitz Wine is purchased and consumed during the November, December holiday period than during the Passover and Easter holidays."

The winery may be visited during business hours on weekdays for a tour of the facilities and a tasting of their wine varieties.

Schapiro's Wine Company
126 Rivington Street
New York, N.Y. 10002
212-674-4404

Although not a major wine comapny, Schapiro's is somewhat of a landmark in that it is the only winery still in operation in Manhattan. Located on the Lower East Side, it was founded in 1899 by Samuel Schapiro, a Polish immigrant, as a sideline to his restaurant business, and is now headed by his grandson, Norman.

Nine musky, grape-tinged underground cellars that span one square city block house one hundred ten oak and redwood casks and tanks, some over one hundred years old. While each cask can hold five thousand gallons enabling the winery to produce five hundred thousand gallons each season, production levels are maintained at between two hundred fifty thousand to three hundred fifty thousand gallons to assure consistency.

As opposed to Carmel in Israel and Kedem in the United States, Schapiro's does not own or maintain its own vineyards. Rather, their stock comes from grapes that are harvested and pressed in the Finger Lakes region of New York State by independents under rabbinical supervision and then trucked to the Rivington Street winery for processing. This obviously limits the control that the winery can exercise over its product.

Although Shapiro's has recently begun producing a line of drier table wines in order to take advantage of the growing wine consumption among Americans, it specializes in and is most sought after for its sweet sacramental "Passover" wines. Known as "the wine so thick you can almost cut it with a knife," Schapiro's produces an extensive line of sweets from the traditional Extra Heavy Concord to the more contemporary cream finished varieties. Most of these are specially sweetened, i.e. supplemented with a sugar solution. While this may make them favorites for the holidays, they are a bit too heavy for the everyday table.

From Sunday through Thursday, 10:00 a.m. to 6:00 p.m. Schapiro's offers tours of its facilities, followed by a free tasting of its wines—an opportunity to sample their selection and learn about their procedures that should not be passed up.

—R.A.S.

FACTS ABOUT SELTZER

Seltzer Boy, where are you
hiding?
If you don't come now,
I'm goin' to tell your boss
on you.
Oi! Don't bring me water.
I'd rather have seltzer,
'Cause water don't bubble, and
water don't fizz.
Water, I hate it,
'Cause it ain't carbonated
But a glass of seltzer on the
*other hand is.**

The third generation calls it poor man's Perrier, but the first generation still remembers it fondly as the poor man's champagne. Seltzer, the crucial ingredient of every successful egg cream, not to mention the most effervescent wine *shpritzer* or mixed drink, is also chicken soup's only serious contender as a cure-all—its health promoting quality being its ability to inspire a loud *grebst*, otherwise known as a belch.

Seltzer is local water filtered at least three times through charcoal, sand, and different grades of paper, and then infused with carbon dioxide in high-pressure siphon (*shpritzer*) bottles. No minerals, salts, flavorings, or sweeteners are added.

Seltzer was brought to this country in the 1890's by the wave of East European immigrants who could not envision life without a *shpritzer* on the table and a case in the kitchen or on the fire escape. One theory says that the name "seltzer" comes from the name of a village near Wiesbaden called Selters, where the fizzy water was served, but whatever its exact origins, it certainly made a presence in New York wherever there was a heavy concentration of East European Jews.

*(From "Seltzer Boy," a parody by Allan Sherman of "Water Boy," a song by Avery Robinson, copyright 1932 by Boosey & Hawkes, Inc. Renewed 1959. Reprinted by permission of Boosey & Hawkes, Inc.)

Seltzer's heyday in New York was in the first half of the twentieth century when in Brooklyn alone there were over five hundred seltzermen with carefully guarded routes of customers to whom they delivered the bubbly beverage in crates of heavy crystal bottles. During the 1950's the industry began to slow down when disposable bottles and mixed sodas became popular, but then it began to make a comeback in the late 1970's when the call to roots and the health food movement sparked a new wave of young people who have hunted down supplies of the no-longer produced siphon bottles and taken on seltzer routes in the style of their ancestors.

Seltzer in Jewish households is more than just a cold beverage: It has also achieved the status of a symbol of Jewish life.

"Every Jewish home had a supply of seltzer," says William Blanksteen, president of E. & W. Blanksteen Insurance Agency in Manhattan, who grew up on the Lower East Side. "We used to always have a bottle on the dining-room sideboard and a case in the kitchen. We drank it straight, or, especially on the *shabbos*, with wine—we'd pour an inch of wine at the bottom of a glass and then add a fast shot of seltzer. We also drank it with honey."

Outside the home, the seltzer sold at soda fountains was often called the "Two Cents Plain." "For two cents you could get a large glass of plain seltzer," Blanksteen recalls. "For three cents you could have it with syrup, or for four cents you could have an egg cream."

The Two Cents Plain became part of Jewish literary history when it became the title of Harry Golden's book (1959), and it was also put to music in a song by Frank Silver called "Two Cents Plain (An East Side Madrigal)," whose lyrics include: "Around the soda fountain you will hear somebody say, 'I don't care for Scotch or rye and I don't like champagne. So if you'll be so kind, kindly give to me for TWO CENTS PLAIN.' "*

But it was also as a cure-all that seltzer became famous in Jewish households.

"Oh yes, seltzer always came in handy," Blanksteen says. "Any time we had a stomach problem a shot of seltzer always helped." It is said that seltzer alone is the only effective remedy for an overdose of hot pastrami or leaden matzah balls. In fact, in the case of matzah balls, seltzer was used by some Jewish cooks as a preventative medicine since a *shpritz* in the batter is said to help make them fluffy and light.

Another explanation of the healthful properties of seltzer comes from Manhattan's Marty the Seltzerman, one of the new generation of seltzer deliverers in New York. "It's an aid to good digestion because it's pure and doesn't leave deposits in the system," said Marty, who won't divulge his last name because, "I run a quiet business." Marty also subscribes to the belch theory and quotes his mother: "*A grebst herien iz a gezunt in dein pupik*," which means "a belch is a blessing to your belly."

Where To Get Seltzer

Seltzermen still exist, although not in such great quantities as they did forty years ago. The best way to find a deliverer is by checking the telephone book either in the white pages under Seltzer or in the Yellow Pages under Beverages.

Although the drink remains the same, the rules of seltzer delivery have not. The forty- and fifty-year-old hand-blown bottles, which are no longer made, are relatively scarce, as are parts for their repair; so some seltzermen require deposits of from ten dollars to twenty dollars for each case and have rules such as minimum orders.

"There's no deposit if you're a permanent customer or if you live in a house you own and can't run away," said Joseph Popok, the eighty-year-old owner of Tastee Beverages in Neptune, New Jersey. "But if I don't know you from Adam, it's a twenty-dollar deposit."

Mr. Popok, who still delivers the seltzer himself, said that he doesn't have a minimum order requirement of a case a week or a case a month, but that he blacklists those who don't consume their seltzer fast enough. "I call them the S.P.'s—the slowpokes," Mr. Popok said. "They hold on to the bottles too long, and I put them on my black sheet."

*Copyright 1946 Norman Spencer & Son, Music Publishers, 145 West 45th Street, New York, N.Y. 10019.

Rechargeable Seltzer Siphons and Commercial Bottled Seltzer

Seltzer purists tend to scoff at the rechargeable siphons, claiming that the fizz just is not up to par with "real" seltzer. Its chief advantage is one of storage: There is no big crate of bottles to store and no need to worry about deliveries and pickups. The seltzermen say that metal bottles impart a metallic taste to the seltzer, so crystal and glass is preferred.

A classic quart-size seltzer bottle, made of heavy crystal, and covered with silver-tone metal mesh is available for $39.95 from Hammacher Schlemmer, 147 East 57th Street, New York, N.Y. 10022. To order by telephone, call: (212) 937–8181. Charge cartridges are $2.95 for a package of ten.

A similar metal mesh-covered bottle is available from Zabar's & Company at 2245 Broadway, New York, N.Y. 10024. It is imported from Austria and costs $15.95, with cartridges in boxes of ten for $1.59. It is available at the store or by mail with an additional charge for postage.

Some commercial soda companies sell bottled seltzer. Not to be confused with club soda, this drink has no salts or sugars added. It is convenient for the person who wants only one bottle every now and then, but because it is not in a pressurized container once it is open, it loses some of its effervescence.

Seltzer Recipes

Egg Cream:
The seltzer-fizzed egg cream is another landmark of Jewish cultural life. To William Blanksteen, as it was to many youngsters in the early 1900's, the four-cent egg cream was a special treat. "Since my allowance was a nickel a week I only had an egg cream if I was really hungry. I used to buy it from the soda shop's owner, his wife, or his son. Their siphon was at the window and for an egg cream they'd pour the chocolate syrup in the bottom of a tall metal milkshake cup, add some milk, and then shoot it up with seltzer, so that there was a big head of foam on top. Then they'd hand it to you out the window. Where the hell the egg was still beats me."

Recipes for the perfect egg cream abound, and none of them include eggs as far as this writer could find out.

Joseph Popok of Tastee Beverages recommends these proportions: "1½ ounces of chocolate syrup at the bottom of the glass. Add seltzer until the glass is ¾ full. Stir just a bit—not too much or you lose the bubbles. Add ½ ounce of milk and shoot the seltzer to the top. Drink it within 60 seconds because after 60 seconds it will be flat and tasteless."

Steve Drucker of Gimme Seltzer has his own recipe for an egg cream and a variation: "The traditional egg cream is ¼ to ⅓ glass of milk, chocolate syrup, and seltzer shpritzed into it so that you have a frothy brown drink. This is okay, but I have a more aesthetic version. First you pour in the milk, then shoot it with seltzer so that the foam goes to the top of the glass. Then add chocolate syrup to taste. The syrup sinks to the bottom. Stir it up and you have a nice pure white foamy head on top of a chocolate brown."

***A good, old-fashioned seltzer bottle* (Amy Meadow)**

Pete Rothenberg, who once worked at a soda fountain in Brooklyn, says: "You can't get a good egg cream outside of Brooklyn. In Brooklyn an egg cream is a religious experience. My egg creams were delicious—I spent years perfecting it. A guy named Yogi taught me and he was one of the best. The most important thing is to have a good head on the egg cream. A head is not just for decoration. The secret to a good head is what you put in first. First put in the syrup—it must be Fox's U Bet. Then you put in some milk. Then you put in the rest of the milk and the seltzer at the same time."

Another recipe for the ultimate egg cream comes from Gerald Freeman of Upper Montclair, New Jersey, who set forth his tale in a letter to the editor of *The New York Times* Living section. As far as he is concerned the home of the egg cream is not Brooklyn but the Bronx. He wrote: "The Golden Age of the New York egg cream lasted the spring of 1944. The locale of the Golden Age was Bonder's Candy Store on West Kingsbridge Road in the Bronx. Modestly, I would like to mention that, during that period, I created the perfect, noble egg cream. I was chief soda dispenser at Bonder's, a part-time occupation. . . . My egg cream was good, but not great. Then, like an apple falling on Newton's head, an accident occurred that revolutionized the egg cream. I had placed the standard dollop of chocolate syrup in the bottom of the glass. I added milk, but the milk was frozen. Not frozen into a block of ice, mind you. The interior of the milk container was indeed frozen, but there was enough semi-frozen, semi-liquid milk to pour into the egg cream to fill the glass the obligatory one-third.

"I then dispensed the seltzer, carefully and slowly, against the interior side of the glass, giving it a sharp burst of seltzer when it was seven-eighths full. The result was a poem—chocolaty in color, with a head of creamy foam, not a froth of glassy bubbles that exist in poorly constructed egg creams.

"The recipient of the egg cream was a neighborhood youth named Burton Hecht, later to become an Assistant District Attorney of the Bronx, and now a judge in the New York State judicial system. Even then, he possessed the judicial temperament and paused for a full minute before pronouncing the egg cream 'the ultimate egg cream.'

"Word of my wondrous egg cream spread and Bonder's business trebled and then quadrupled. On West Kingsbridge Road, the words 'calorie' and 'cholesterol' were unknown. It was the perfect setting for the perfect egg cream."

Basic *Shpritzer:*

Pour wine—traditionally a heavy sweet wine, such as the sacramental kosher wines—in the bottom of a glass and add seltzer to the top. As a variation on the *shpritzer*, substitute jam, jelly, honey, flavored syrup, or fruit juice.

Other variations on the Basic *Shpritzer*: Steve Drucker of Gimme Seltzer said that, inspired by his neighborhood—Manhattan's Little Italy—he invented the Manhattan Special. "I add to my basic egg cream a shot of espresso coffee-flavored soda that you can buy in six-packs down here. And if you're into White Russians, you can also make a

White Russian Egg Cream. Pour heavy cream into bottom of glass, add vodka, Kahlua, and then seltzer until foam reaches top of glass."

Other Uses

Matzah Balls: Use seltzer instead of water in any standard recipe.

Fluffy Omelet: Add a quick *shpritz* to the beaten eggs, give a quick beat to incorporate it and then make omelet.

Water Fights: A loaded seltzer siphon is far superior to a plastic hand watergun. The aim is surer, and the *shpritz* is more forceful and has a louder, more dramatic sound.

Self-Defense: People have been known to defend themselves from vicious dogs and taxi drivers by keeping a loaded siphon handy at all times.

Animal Training: Ron Roth, of Seltzer Unlimited, one of Manhattan's newer seltzer deliverers, claims that seltzer was very effective in training his cat, who had begun to develop a habit of napping on his stereo speakers. "Every time I saw him on one of my speakers I squirted him. It was very effective."

Stain Removal: Seltzer helps remove juice, soup, wine, and other stains from tablecloths, napkins, carpets, and clothing. Just *shpritz* a little on the stain, wait a few minutes, and rub with a clean sponge.

Cleaning Metal: Seltzer is good for polishing steel and chrome. *Shpritz* it onto the surface and wipe. There will be no streaks and spots as there is with water.

Seltzer Lamps

Seltzer bottles, which come in blue, amber, clear, fluted, and smooth, are beautiful objects to behold and some ambitious New Yorkers figured that if you could turn a gumball machine into a lamp, why not a seltzer bottle? After months of experimentation they devised for the bottles a plastic, mushroom-shaped shade, replete with bubbles, that is meant to simulate a *shpritz* of seltzer. They market their wired lamps with and without the shades. The prices range from $25 to $75, depending on the rarity of the bottle (the plain unfluted bottles are the cheapest), and they are available by mail with an additional charge for postage and handling. The company also makes water pipes from the plain unfluted seltzer bottles ($20 plus postage and handling) and vases and candlesticks from the fluted bottles ($25 plus postage and handling). The lamp company, Effervescence, is located at 444 Broome Street, New York, N.Y. 10013. Telephone number: (212) 966–7771.

—J. B.

A FISH STORY: GEFILTE

A Sabbath or festival meal would hardly seem complete if it didn't begin with *gefilte* fish—balls of ground freshwater fish, poached in a fish stock that has cooled to a thick jelly, served with horseradish sauce. *Gefilte* means "filled" or "stuffed." Originally designated a filling for baked fish, today the term *gefilte* fish usually designates the filling by itself, shaped into oblong balls.

Fish is eaten on special occasions because of its happy symbolic resonances in Jewish tradition. In the account of Creation in Genesis, chapters 1–2, the phrase "and God blessed them" is used in connection with the creation of fish, man, and the Sabbath, thereby establishing a bond between them that goes back, literally, to the beginning. Fish is strongly identified in tradition with procreation and fruitfulness and thus very much in place on the Sabbath day, which is set aside particularly for conjugal intimacy. The fish, *Pisces*, as the zodiac sign for the Hebrew month of Adar (February-March), the month of rejoicing during which falls the festival of Purim, is given even greater symbolic value. Its ultimate destiny, however, will be fulfilled when the messianic era is ushered in, and the faithful, according to tradition, will eat the legendary fish Leviathan. Since the Sabbath is considered a foretaste of the World to Come, eating fish on that day is a longing anticipation of future delights. Fish is the principal dish of the third Sabbath meal, the *seudah shelishit*, the meal specifically associated with messianic longings, consumed on late Saturday afternoon.

Gefilte fish can be made from scratch, bought freshly prepared from a delicatessen or appetizer shop, or in a can or jar. It will come as no surprise that homemade is best. Given the advent of the food processor, it's now fairly simple to make. (A recipe for homemade *gefilte* fish is included below.) Canned *gefilte* fish is, however, cheaper than homemade, if somewhat lacking in flavor.

There are two variables in the making of *gefilte* fish—in addition, of course, to the dexterity of the maker. Opinion is sharply divided regarding the use of sugar. Jews from Eastern Europe tend to like it tart, while Jews from Rumania and Austria favor a sweeter variety. The second variable is the combination of fish in the recipe. The three traditional varieties are carp, pike, and whitefish, which most often are used in roughly equal proportions.

Prepared *Gefilte* Fish: A Tasting

The following are the results of a blind tasting in which a group of amateur but discriminating eaters were asked to rate the *gefilte* fish that is available in cans and jars.

Sweet *Gefilte* Fish
- *Rokeach Old Vienna*—firm texture, light color, very strong taste.
- *Maneschewitz*—medium sweet, somewhat granular, good flavor.
- *Mrs. Adler's*—fishy tasting, oily, with an undistinguished taste.
- *Mother's Old World*—bland, too much matzah meal, sourly sweet.

Regular *Gefilte* Fish
- *Maneschewitz*—fine grained, peppery, with a full flavor.
- *Rokeach*—well blended with a very good taste.
- *Mother's*—granular with an odd, chemical, sweet and sour taste.

NOTE: Maneschewitz produces a *gefilte* fish that is made from whitefish alone and in the tasting, found to be quite good, having a more delicate texture and a more natural sweetness than some of the other fish.

A *Gefilte* Fish Recipe

The advent of the food processor makes it much easier to prepare *gefilte* fish at home. In the absence of a processor, many fish dealers are willing to grind the fish with onion for their customers. In any case, when ordering the fish it is important to keep the fish trimmings after the fish has been filleted. The heads, skin, and bones are boiled to make the stock. For the sake of efficiency, it makes sense to get the stock going first; by the time that the fish balls are ready, the stock will be, too.

Fish Stock
1 onion, cut in half
3 or 4 carrots
5 sprigs parsley
fish trimmings (heads, skin, bones)
1 tablespoon kosher salt
12 peppercorns

Fish Balls
3 pounds filleted fish (whitefish, carp, and pike)
2 eggs
3 medium onions cut into quarters
1 teaspoon salt
½ cup matzah meal
½ teaspoon pepper

Place all the ingredients for the stock in a large saucepan and cover with a quart of water. Bring to a boil and simmer for about 15 minutes.

Cut the fish into chunks and grind them in the food processor. This will probably have to be done in more than one step. Add the other ingredients to the processor and blend until smooth. Combine the mixtures in a large bowl. Fill a second bowl with water and use this for moistening the hands when forming the fish into balls, since the mixture is extremely sticky. Place the balls in the saucepan with the stock and add water, if necessary, to cover. Simmer for about 1½ hours. Remove the fish balls from the stock to a deep platter and then, using a fine strainer, strain the stock over them. Refrigerate and serve thoroughly chilled.

Yield: 12 portions as appetizers, 6 as a main course.

—A.M.

PART FOUR
THE PEOPLE OF THE BOOK (SCREEN AND TELEVISION)

THE VOCABULARY OF JEWISH LIFE

THE ORIGINS OF THE HEBREW LETTERS

Most modern languages that employ alphabetic writing use alphabets that originated in the Near East—in fact, in and around the Holy Land. Ancient Israel was not the inventor of the alphabet; rather, out of the patchwork of peoples in the region between the Red Sea and the north Syrian coast came a number of scripts that eventually crystallized into the northwest Semitic alphabets, of which the Hebrew alphabet is one example.

At first the people of this region used a syllabic writing made with wedges hammered into clay. This is called cuneiform writing: each sign represents a word or a syllable. Try to imagine the word "catastrophe" written out

—as we can see, even bisyllabic words can have a single sign and can serve as the syllables of a larger word, although the total number of signs to memorize (about 800 in the main system actually used) makes this a cumbersome form of writing.

Eventually the number of syllables was reduced to a minimum number of consonantal signs, all ending in the vowel *a*, but with other vowels substituted by the reader, who could recognize a word from the consonants alone. This is not as hard as one may think; see what can be done with this: "Cnsnntl wrtng 's th' frrnnr 'f 'wr 'lfbt." This is easily read as "Consonantal writing is the forerunner of our alphabet."

Some of the earliest surviving examples of alphabetic signs of this type, in forms possibly borrowed from Egyptian hieroglyphs, are those found in the Sinai region just before the Exodus (c. 1300 B.C.E.): they seem to have been used by the laborers in the Egyptian Pharaoh's copper mines, and are used to express a Canaanite dialect not much different from biblical Hebrew. The writing includes invocations to Canaanite goddesses, but these enterprising slaves were close enough relatives to the Israelites to be considered their immediate forerunners. The slavemasters in Egypt and Canaan, meanwhile, used hieroglyphic and wedge writing, respectively, the latter employed especially in diplomatic correspondence (in Akkadian) with Egypt.

The significance of this innovation must be appreciated. While scribes, members of a learned elite, were using cumbersome syllabaries for their communication, common laborers were using a simplified and highly practical consonantal script, enabling rapid communication across tribal lines and perhaps facilitating a coordinated rebellion against the Egyptian and Canaanite kings—events preserved in the Bible as the Exodus and the Conquest (the biblical books of Exodus through Joshua).

It is generally assumed that the first Semitic alphabet letters were derived from picture-writing by the acrophonic ("initial sound") principle: *alef* ("ox") came to stand for the letter *alef* (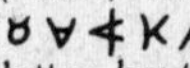); *bayit* or *beyt* ("house"), the letter *beyt* (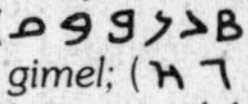); *gimel* ("camel"), the letter *gimel;* (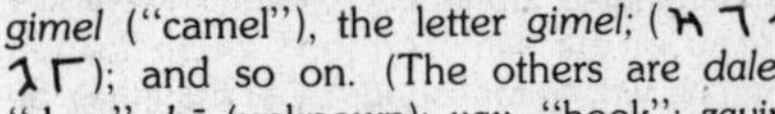); and so on. (The others are *dalet,* "door"; *hē* (unknown); *vav,* "hook"; *zayin,* "weapon" or "phallus"; *het,* "fence"; *tet* (unknown); *yod,* "hand"; *kaf,* "hand-palm"; *lamed,* "ox-goad"; *mem,* "water"; *nun,* "fish"; *samekh,* "prop"; *'ayin,* "eye"; *pe,* "mouth"; *tzade,* "fishhook"; *qof,* "monkey"; *resh,* "head"; *shin,* "tooth"; *tav,* "mark.") But some historians of writing believe that the symbols evolved arbitrarily, and that the names came later. This is suggested by the fact that some alphabetic systems use abstract representations of objects that do not begin with the letters they represent;

also by the fact that the Hebrew letter *zayin* (which now resembles what the word *zayin* means—either "spear" or "phallus": 𐤆) is called in the Greek alphabet *zeta* (from Semitic *zayt,* "olive tree")—the latter developing from a form more like a tree: I, I, Z—suggesting that the letter name evolves to explain the picture rather than the other way around. Also, some similar sounds in the old Semitic alphabets are represented by similar pictures—suggesting that the picture may have something to do with the sound:

𐤄	hē	𐤇	het
𐤍	nun	𐤌	mem
I	zayin	𐤎	samekh
+	tav	⊕	tet

The letters may have represented not objects in the world outside the speaker, but the positions of the mouth that produce the sounds. This is suggested by such symbols as 𐤉 *yod,* which before it came to resemble a hand may have been intended to represent the pursed lips of a *y*-sound. The 𐤄 for *hē* could represent a rush of air from the throat; the 𐤋 for *lamed,* a curled tongue of the *l*-sound; the 𐤌 for *mem,* the closed lips of *m;* the 𐤔 for *shin* ("tooth"), the teeth through which *sh* is pronounced; and so on. Note also that *'ayin,* a throaty sound, was originally represented by a symbol resembling the opening of a gullet O (only later called *'ayin,* "eye"), while the *tet,* originally a throaty *t*-sound, was a *tav* (+) inside of an *'ayin* (O): ⊕ . One could call this system phonography (not to be confused with that of the record industry).

It is impossible, of course, to prove such a theory for the whole Semitic alphabet—many conflicting systems coalesced to produce the alphabet, and there is little or no concrete evidence that ancient people had such a sophisticated grasp of phonology, or that the attempt to adopt such a convention would have been understood by those who disseminated alphabetic writing. (Moreover, many of the same symbols occur in non-Semitic writing for sounds other than their Semitic equivalents, although the pictorial representation of something as elusive as a sound may have been a subjective matter.) But it does serve as an intriguing hypothesis of the system's invention, at least in part.

One can imagine an enterprising young scribe, impatient with the cumbersome conventions of wedge- and picture-writing, who dreamed of a manner of writing that could be easily understood across cultural barriers because it portrayed, not objects or arbitrary designs, but the human speech apparatus.

In any case, in and around the Holy Land, the Semitic alphabet arose roughly in the era of the Exodus, and came to serve the needs of Phoenicians, Canaanites, Syrians (Arameans), Ammonites, Moabites, Edomites, and Israelites. These peoples spoke languages so closely related as to be virtually dialects of the same language. The oldest inscription fully displaying this alphabet is a tombstone legend in Phoenician inscribed by one Itbaal ben Ahiram of Byblos (in southern Lebanon) around 1000 B.C.E.—the time of King David. The beginning of this dedication provides an idea of how close Phoenician was to Hebrew (Hebrew vowels are given here; see bottom of page).

It is clear from the few surviving ancient Hebrew inscriptions that an almost identical alphabet was in general use among Israelites of the First Temple period (c. 950–586 B.C.E.). It is found on a calendar from Gezer (tenth century B.C.E.); in a stone inscription on a wall of the underground water-tunnel of Siloam in Jerusalem (eighth century B.C.E.); on a supply inventory from Arad in the northern Negev (c. 600 B.C.E.); and, in a very developed cursive form, on a military communication from Lachish (c. 587/6 B.C.E.), at the time the First Temple was destroyed. A similar alphabet is also used for the famous Mesha inscription, written for King Mesha of Moab, a ninth-century B.C.E. contemporary of the Bible's King Ahab. Besides being one of the longest and most interesting pieces of writing surviving from biblical days in a Canaanite dialect other than Hebrew, this inscription is one of the few independent corroborations of biblical events—in this case, the events of 2 Kings 3:11ff.: the story of a vassal king who rebelled against the king to whom he paid tribute (Ahab of northern Israel) and established an independent kingdom.

Phoenicians and Jews continued to use this alphabet during the years of the Second Temple (440 B.C.E. onward). A late variant of this script (called misleadingly Paleo-Hebrew) was in use as recently as the sec-

ארן ז פעל [א]תבעל בן אחרם מלך גבל לאחרם אבה

Aron zu pa'al Ithba'al ben Ahiram melek Gubla le-Ahiram abihu
("The ark that Itbaal ben Ahiram, king of Byblos, made for Ahiram, his father")

ond century C.E., when it served for inscriptions on coins minted during the Bar Kokhba rebellion. It gradually came to be replaced by the Aramaic ("square") version of the alphabet, which is the form used by Jews today. This alphabet was easier to write than Paleo-Hebrew, and arose in a milieu that used Aramaic as an international diplomatic language. The first extensive surviving Hebrew texts in this style are the Dead Sea Scrolls.

In late antiquity, the West-Semitic alphabet diverged in two directions. The Phoenicians carried the older script westward to Greece and Rome, where it served as the basis for various European scripts: Runic, Celtic, and Gothic, among others (based on Roman writing), and Slavic-Cyrillic and Armenian (based on Greek writing). The users of Aramaic, meanwhile, helped develop and spread the various alphabets of the Near East and central Asia—among others, Arabic, Syriac, Mandaic, Middle Persian, Mongolian, Manchu, and the Indian Devanagari script used for Sanskrit, Hindi, and Begali. So the Land of Israel can truly be said to have been the cradle of alphabetic writing.

Greek and Roman scribes made some important innovations: *alef, hē* (also *het*), *yod*, *'ayin*, and *waw* went from being primarily consonants to being primarily vowels: *a, e, i, o,* and *u* (or ü), respectively. The letter *g* became a hard *c (k)* in Latin, partly replacing *kaph* (and Greek *kappa*), though keeping its place in the Semitic order of letters. *Waw*, besides becoming the Greek *u (upsilon*, or "Ψ[psi]-shaped u"—Υ), became (via a *v*-sound) the *f* of European alphabets (original *waw:* 𐤅), retaining its position in the Semitic order, and the *zayin* (or Greek *zeta)* metamorphosed (probably via a *zh* sound, as in "pleasure"-) into a soft *g*, keeping its place, but borrowing a variant of the hard *g*-sound for its sign, which came to serve for both sounds. *Z* then got bumped to the end of the alphabet. All of Greek and Roman letters after *t* (the end of the Hebrew alphabet) represent sounds which for one reason or another were moved from their original Semitic positions, or invented anew: Υ , Φ , X , Ψ , Ω , and *u, v, w* (all the same letter), *x* (from Hebrew *samekh* 𐤎 and Greek *xi* Ξ), *y* (see *u*), and *z*. The two Greek *e* letters, *epsilon* ("psi-shaped *e*") and *eta* (H, η), evolved from *hē* and *het* respectively.

Mythological and mystical lore about Hebrew letters evolved in three main ways, apart from numerological interpretations (Gematria): (1) the letters came to be associated with theologically-weighted words whose initials they formed; (2) their sounds became the subject of mystical speculation—especially in works like the Judeo-Pythagorean treatise *Sefer Yetzirah* ("Book of Formation"); (3) their shapes and embellishments came to be the subject of mystical speculation. Some examples follow.

The first type is best represented by the story of how the world came to be created through the letter *bet* (the first letter of the Bible, meaning "in," as in "In the beginning . . ."). Each letter, from *tav* backwards, presents itself before God, pleading to be allowed to serve as the opening letter of the Torah—each claims to represent a positive spiritual value, but each is rebuked with a reminder of some negative quality it also represents: *shin*, for example, pleads that it is the initial of *shalom*, "peace," but it is reminded that it is also the initial of *sheker*, "falsehood." This debate proceeds through each letter in turn, until the letter *bet*, symbol of *berakhah*, "blessing," finally convinces God that it should be the one to begin the Torah (and thus the world). Out of this story came the popular idea that God made the world by means of combining letters. As for what happened to *alef*, see below.

The second type of letter lore is best represented by speculations about the letter *alef*. This letter, correctly speaking, is not a vowel, as its Greek and Roman equivalents have made it, but a consonant, though quite a faint sound: it is the tiny catch in the throat made before each vowel sound. (Say "ate," "eat," "ice," "own," and "urge," and note that the catch in the throat occurs before the vowels *a, e, i, o,* and *u.)* It became natural to think of *alef* as a "silent" or "nonexistent" sound. When the rabbis wished to preserve a sense of mystery about God's giving the Torah to Israel, they said that only the first letter of the first word of the Ten Commandments was actually spoken by God; the rest was divined intuitively by Moses or Israel, and written down in detail. The letter in question is the *alef* of *anokhi* ("I am [the LORD your God] . . ."), and since this is a silent letter, the rabbis seem to suggest that God's "speech" is unlike worldly speech, and that the whole of the Torah is mystically present in one silent letter. Eventually the *alef* came to be associated with the *En-Sof* ("Infinite"), the deepest and most hidden aspect of God's identity.

Another example of the second type of letter lore refers to the so-called *'immot ha-qeriah* (literally, "mothers of reading"), called in Latin *matres lectionis: alef, hē, waw,* and *yod*. These are the four main letters that came to serve partly as vowel indicators before a more precise vowel system was developed. *Alef* and *hē* stood for *a* and *e; yod* for *i* and *é; waw* for *o* and *u*. The *Sefer Yetzirah* and medieval mystics gave these letters mystical connotations—*alef* for reasons already noted, and *hē*, *waw*, and *yod* because they form the sacred Four-Letter Name of God: YHWH. Each of these three letters came to be associated with an emanation of God: the *yod* with the incipient emanation *Hokhmah* ("Wisdom"), the first *hē* with the maternal emanation *Binah* ("Understanding"), the *waw* with the central emanation *Tiferet* ("Beauty"), and the second *hē* with the daughter emanation *Malkhut* or *Shekhinah* ("Kingdom" or "Presence"). There is even a kabbalistic breathing exercise based on this pattern: y = empty lungs, h_1 = filling lungs, w = filled lungs, h_2 = emptying lungs. In non-scriptural and non-liturgical Hebrew texts, the name YHWH is usually indicated by the abbreviation *hē* (ה') or double-*yod* (יי), or less frequently by *dalet* (ד'), meaning "4," or by *yod-vav-yod* (יוי).

The third type of letter lore is represented by a number of important legends. The *bet* (ב) is said to be closed on three sides and open on one side to teach us not to speculate on events before Creation (behind us), or on the heavens (above us), or on the underworld (below us), but only to be focused ahead, on the present and the future, on this world and the World to Come, respectively (represented by the open side of the *bet*, which is "ahead" because Hebrew is read from right to left). One stroke of the *bet*, however, points backward to the *alef*, suggesting that the first letter of the Torah acknowledges its own origin in God.

The *alef*'s raised hand and two legs (א), on the other hand, are said to resemble the form of a human being, the raised hand being interpreted as pointing to God. Some additional teachings of this type:

The *vav* (ו), which resembles a staff, was taken as the weapon to be used against evildoers in the world to come.

The *tet* (ט) has one hand bent down and one hand upright to symbolize the manner of the good person ("good" = *tov*, whose initial letter is *tet*), who performs his good deeds in secret.

The *yod* (י) is the smallest letter, symbolizing the humility of the righteous individual, and the bowing of the congregation of ten (י = 10) in prayer.

The *lamed* (ל) is the tallest letter; its stature was invoked for the negative commandments, which begin with *l* (*lo'* = [do] not . . .).

The *samekh* (ס) is a circular letter to symbolize God's protection and support of the righteous (the letter begins the Hebrew verbs *samakh*, "support," and *sovev*, "surround").

The *ayin* (ע) has two hands pointed upward to symbolize the prayers of those in need.

The *tzadé* (צ) is a bent letter to symbolize the humble posture of the *tzaddik* (the righte-

TABLE OF ALPHABETS

ous), and the manner in which he bends his instincts to the service of God.

The *tav* (ת) has a broken foot to symbolize the labor of the scholars *(talmidei hakhamim)*, who wear out their feet going from town to town, performing their good deeds and learning Torah.

Other qualities are attributed to the sequence of the letters. Each of the first ten letters is correlated with one of the ten divine emanations. Each sequential pair of letters (*alef* and *bet, gimel* and *dalet,* etc.) is regarded as a special pair, each member indispensable to the other, one male and the other female, respectively. Some mystics regard the first and last letters (*alef* and *tav*), the second and penultimate (*bet* and *shin*), the third and antipenultimate (*gimel* and *resh*), and so on, as special pairs, an equation that gave rise to the cryptographic system known as *atbash* (א"ת ב"ש, the word formed by the first two combinations). Some group the letters from *bet* onward into three groups: "Mystery of the Rule of Grace" (ב→ח), "Mystery of the Rule of Mercy" (ט→ס), and "Mystery of the Rule of Justice" (ע→ת).

Seven of the letters, ג, ז, ט, נ, ע, צ, and ש, display crowns of three prongs at their tops in the script of the Torah scroll. These adornments, called *tagin,* are especially associated with Rabbi Akiba, who is reported to have derived legal decisions from their presence in the Torah scroll. It is said that Rabbi Akiba sits in the Heavenly Academy and fashions the *tagin* for each new Torah scroll. The adorned letters are usually learned as a mnemonic: שעטנ"ז ג"ץ *shaatnez getz,* the first word being the name of a garment of mixed wool and flax whose use is prohibited by the Bible, the second word an abbreviation for *ger tzedek,* "righteous proselyte" (Rabbi Akiba, the son of a convert to Judaism, could have taken this as his surname). Some midrashic reasons offered for the three-pronged crowns on these letters:

The *gimel* (numerical value 3) symbolizes the three days that the world made use of the primordial divine light before God made the heavenly luminaries.

The *zayin* (numerical value 7) symbolizes the seventh day of Creation, on which God rested.

The *tet* symbolizes the three "good" families of the Jewish people ("good" = *tov*), Kohanim (priests), Leviim (levites), and Yisraelim (Israelites).

The *nun* symbolizes the Three Crowns that were given *(nittenu)* to Israel: the Crown of Torah, the Crown of Priesthood, and the Crown of Kingship.

The *ayin* symbolizes the peoples of the Land of Israel *(ammei eretz yisrael),* who are beloved of God, of the ministering angels, and of humanity.

The *tzadé* symbolizes (for reasons unclear) the three ancestors of the Jewish people: Abraham, Isaac, and Jacob. An alternative tradition gives the *tzadé* four *tagin* to correspond to the four matriarchs: Sarah, Rebeka, Rachel, and Leah.

The *shin* corresponds to the two sets of prayer phylacteries *(tefillin)* worn by the devout Jew, plus the *mezuzzah.* The *shin* has three prongs, but some say that in the World to Come it will have four.

Five letters of the alphabet, כ, מ, נ, פ, and צ, have special final forms at the end of words: ץף ן ם ך, often heard in the mnemonic *mantzepakh.* (It is worth noting that the final forms are actually more archaic forms of the letters, strongly resembling their equivalents in the Canaanite and Paleo-Hebrew alphabets.) There is a fair amount of lore about how these forms came to be used. According to the Zohar, the letters were hidden away by God along with the primordial light, to be used only by the righteous in the World to Come, although He revealed their forms to Adam. When Adam and Eve transgressed in the Garden, God rescinded knowledge of the final letters, but they were later revealed to Abraham, who passed the knowledge on to Isaac, and Isaac to Jacob. After Joseph's death, when Israel entered servitude in Egypt, knowledge of the final letters was again forgotten, but was revealed to Israel when the people stood at Mount Sinai to receive the Torah. When Israel sinned with the Golden Calf, the knowledge was again forgotten. Only Moses, Joshua, and the seventy elders knew the letters, and they brought them into the land of Israel. When King Solomon wrote the Song of Songs, they were again revealed. According to the Talmud (Shab. 104a), it was the prophets who instituted their general use among the people.

According to the Midrash (Gen. R. 1.11), a new meaning of the final letters was discovered by three small children who wandered into the local house of assembly one rainy day when the scholars had all stayed home. They decided that the doubled forms of the *mantzepakh* letters arose from the giving of the Torah, from speech of God to speech of Moses *(mi-maamar le-maamar),* from faithful God to faithful Moses *(mi-neeman le-neeman),* from righteous God to righteous Moses *(mi-tzaddik le-tzaddik),* from mouth of God to mouth of Moses *(mi-peh le-peh),* and from hand of God to hand of Moses *(mi-kaf le-kaf).* These three children grew up to become Rabbi Eliezer, Rabbi

Joshua, and of course—ever present where letters are concerned—Rabbi Akiba.

The vowels were regarded by the mystics as the soul and spirit of the letters. There have been various attempts to put in vowel markings in the text of the Hebrew Bible, most of them connected with the development of the so-called Masoretic (i.e., Traditional) Text. There are at least three main systems of vocalization: the best known and the one currently in use is that dveloped in Tiberias by the ben-Asher family, a dynasty of Masoretic scholars, during the ninth century C.E. This is the familiar system of dots and dashes known to many a beginning student of Hebrew.

The Masoretes, whose activity goes back to the era of Rabbi Akiba, also compiled useful statistics on the frequency of words in Scripture, on disputed readings of individual words, and on the total number of verses, words, and letters in the Torah and in each Torah book. Certain letters of the Torah are written in an enlarged or minuscule form. The opening letter, for example, a *bet,* is written large (as it is also in Prov. 1:1, Song of Songs 1:1, Eccles. 1:1, and 1 Chron. 1:1). The middle letter of the Torah is written large, as is the middle consonant of the middle verse. Two letters of the Shema passage (Deut. 6:4ff.: "Hear, O Israel: the LORD our God, the LORD is one.") are written large, to draw attention to the passage as a credo to be proclaimed. Ordinarily, these two letters would have been the opening *shin* and the closing *dalet,* but since these spell the word "demon" *(shed),* the *ayin* of the word *"shema"* is enlarged in place of the *shin,* thus spelling the word *'ed,* "witness." Minuscule letters (as in Gen. 23:2 and 27:46) are believed to have been letters inserted at some point in the history of the text. In Judges 18:30, a *nun* is written over the name *Moshe* (Moses) to change it to *Menasseh*—the reference to an idolatrous cult set up in Dan by the grandson of Moses was apparently considered a serious embarrassment to the memory of Israel's greatest leader.

Mystical meanings were read into these peculiarities of printing. From the enlarged *dalet* of the word *ehad* ("one") in the *Shema* passage, the rabbis said that one must prolong the pronunciation of the letter in order to be granted long life. The enlarged *ayin* of the word *Shema* ("Hear") is to indicate that one's ear must be opened wide. The *alef* of the word *vayyiqra'* ("[God] called . . .") at the beginning of the book of Leviticus is written small to indicate that God has two ways of addressing human beings: to Israel, He speaks with a full voice; to other nations, He speaks with only a partial voice (in God's address to Balaam in Num. 23:15, the *alef* is omitted altogether from the word "called").

Some additional lore about letters:

When Moses brought the Ten Commandments to Israel and found the people worshipping the Golden Calf, the letters of the Ten Commandments fled from the Tablets and vanished into the air. The letters had enabled Moses to hold up the enormously heavy stones. When he could no longer hold on he was forced to drop them, and they shattered.

The letters are the garments of the Torah, woven from the various colors of God's light: white, red, green, and black. The words of Scripture draw their nourishment from the letters; the letters, in turn, are replenished by the meanings of the words. The primordial celestial alphabet was engraved by a pen of flaming fire. The Torah is believed to have been written in black fire on white fire.

According to the Sefer Yetzirah, *aleph, mem,* and *shin* reign over the basic elements air, water, and fire. Seven of the letters—*bet, gimel, dalet, kaf, pe, resh,* and *tav*—have a dotted and undotted form (and thus a hard and soft pronunciation). These form a second layer of complexity in Creation, and correspond to the seven principal heavenly bodies in the solar system: Sun, Venus, Mercury, Moon, Saturn, Jupiter, and Mars—as well as to the seven facial apertures of a human being: two eyes, two ears, mouth, and two nostrils. The *bet* reigns over life, the *gimel* over peace, the *dalet* over wisdom, the *kaf* over wealth, the *pe* over gracefulness, the *resh* over seed, and the *tav* over royal dominion.

The twelve remaining letters are simple: *he, waw, zayin, het, tet, yod, lamed, nun, samekh, ayin, tzade, kof.* They are associated with sight, hearing, smell, speech, taste, sexual intercourse, work, movement, wrath, laughter, thinking, and sleep, respectively.

God occasionally gave a letter of His name to a human being. Cain was given the *vav* as a sign of protection engraved on his forehead (see Gen. 4:15), to ward off human avengers of Abel's death (punishment of this crime was reserved for God alone). To both Abraham and Sarah (who were originally called Abram and Sarai), God gave the letter *hē,* indicating that His Presence would travel with them everywhere. A man (*ish* איש) and a woman (*ishah* אשה) share between them the divine Name Yah (the letters *yod* and *hē*), to indicate that no marriage union can last without the divine Presence—if these two letters are removed, both *ish* and *ishah* dwindle into *esh* ("fire").

God created the universe by a combination of letters. This matter is derived from the biblical verse "By the word of God were the heavens made, and by the breath of His lips all their host" (Ps. 33:6). The Talmud and the Sefer Yetzirah suggest that this power of combining letters is sometimes granted to human beings. Enoch, upon his ascent to heaven, was crowned with a crown engraved with the letters by which God made the universe. Bezalel, the architect of the Tabernacle in the desert, likewise knew the secrets of letter-combination *(tzeruf ha-otiyot)*, as did King Solomon. Various rabbis in the Talmud are credited with the same power; in one instance, Rava succeeded in making an artificial human being. This story was the beginning of the famous golem legend (see the "Golem" entry of the "At the Edges of Creation: Angels, Demons, and Beasts of Fancy" article), the most familiar of which is that of the golem made by Rabbi Judah Loewe of Prague, who was activated by the inscription of the word *emet* ("truth") on his forehead, and deactivated by the erasure of the *alef* (thus spelling *met*, "dead"). Various mystics, especially Rabbi Abraham Abulafia, placed special importance on the combination of letters as a vehicle of meditation.

The Hasidim placed special emphasis, beginning in the eighteenth century, on the letters of Torah and prayer. The Baal Shem Tov states that each letter is like a complete living being, and that one who fails to put the proper concentration into each letter of prayer creates a creature with a missing limb. The letters of the Torah and of prayer were believed to shine with a divine light when approached with a spirit of humility and reverence. The person praying could, through his devotion, become a receptive vehicle through whom the letters of prayer and Scripture could take on an independent life. Even if a person is not skilled at reading, his purity of purpose can redeem the divine sparks in the letters. Rabbi Nachman of Bratslav states that as a person prays, each letter of the prayer addresses him and begs for full concentration and devotion, pleading not to be left behind, as it must when the person praying moves on to the next letter.

What, then, are letters? According to French philosopher and critic Jacques Derrida (who himself grew up in a traditional Jewish environment in North Africa, and in his youth imbibed much kabbalistic lore), the fundamental unit of human communication is not the word but the letter. A letter is a discrete unit of "difference," by which is indicated one of two alternative possibilities: vowel or consonant. Each consonant, in turn, comprises other sets of contrasts, coordinately related: voiced/unvoiced, plosive/fluid, labiodental/velar, etc. Each word, then, is not an indivisible atom but a complex "program," analogous to a computer program ("program," "grammar," and "graphic" all come from the same verbal root: "to write"). Every written sign in some sense includes the sign(s) that it is not. Alphabet letters, then, are graphemes in a system of contrasts, a system which operates whether the letters are voiced or not—indeed, perhaps the voicing merely serves the mental "writing," rather than the other way around. Voiced writing, that is, speech, was an important step in the development of writing, which has grown increasingly more complicated and versatile than speech: mathematics, logic, and computer science are further refinements in the human art of writing, as are the subtleties of the humanistic written word.

The alphabet that arose in and around the Holy Land in the era preceding the Exodus came, perhaps, at a major turning-point in the history of this evolution. Its development facilitated reflection *upon* language, which is why it is no accident that the Bible inclines so much to wordplay, and the Bible's interpreters to still more complicated wordplay. The presence or absence of a single letter can determine the meaning of a whole story, or the performance of a whole commandment. The biblical authors and editors knew this as much as the midrashists and kabbalists. Because this book (and the People of the Book) made language (or, better, writing) the most important element of social existence, its letters can with justice be said to have been divine in origin, and an instrument for the creation of a world.

—J.R.

YIDDISH AND HEBREW WORDS USED IN THE AMERICAN LANGUAGE

Most of the words listed appear (sometimes with variant spellings) in at least one of such widely accepted reference books as Eric Partridge's *A Dictionary of Slang and Unconventional English*, Merriam-Webster's *Third New International Dictionary*, and Wentworth and Flexner's *Dictionary of American Slang*. A few words do not appear in the American dictionaries, but ought to. Their listing here is a tug at the sleeve of future lexicographers to include such rich Yiddish terms as *plotz, mentch*, and *kvell*.

Because this is a dictionary of American or English usage only, that is, words that have taken on special meanings in English, the original Yiddish or Hebrew meanings of many words are not always given. To fully explain them would take virtually a full retelling of Jewish history.

English words of Hebrew origin tend to be lofty, idealistic, and spiritual, while words of Yiddish origin are more earthy, domestic, slangy, and less serious. This has more to do with the way the vocabularies of the two languages entered English than with the nature of speakers of the languages. Most Yiddish words entered the American language through Jewish immigrants from Eastern Europe during the latter part of the nineteenth century and the early part of the twentieth. Jewish humorists, peddlers, entertainers, and shopkeepers contributed greatly to the spread of Yiddish terms into the general idiom. Although Yiddish has a rich literature, its literary vocabulary did not capture the American imagination. Its oral vocabulary did.

Hebrew entered English as a dead language, as the language in which an important ancient holy book was written. With the exception of *sabra* and *kibbutz*, no words from modern spoken Hebrew have yet entered American. (*Uzzi*, the Israeli-made machine gun, did not pass an oral recognition exam.) No doubt the ancient Hebrews used slang and had words corresponding to the Yiddish *farblunget* and *yente*, but because the words were not written down, they have been lost forever. Perhaps the list that follows will allow current American speakers readier access to the rich vocabulary of Yiddish and Hebrew words used in English and allow for an expansion of the available verbal repertoire.

Abacus (From the Hebrew word for "dust.") Originally set on a slate, the early adding machine was noted for its chalky, dusty appearance until movable beads were substituted for slash marks.

Abbadon (From the Hebrew word for "destruction.") A bottomless pit. An abyss of hell. Although Milton popularized the word, it was first used in English by Wycliff in 1382—not as a place but as an angel who guards the bottomless pit.

Abigail (From the Hebrew name meaning "my father's joy.") A lady's waiting-maid. From the servant girl by that name in the Beaumont and Fletcher play "The Scornful Lady."

Aleph-null (From the first letter of the Hebrew alphabet + English "null.") Used by Georg Cantor to mean the smallest transfinite cardinal number, the number that counts the integers.

Alphabet (From the first two letters of the Greek alphabet, derived from the Hebrew/Phoenician letters aleph and bet.) A set of letters used to make up words.

Amen (Hebrew, related to the root words for "belief," "right," and "truth.") An interjection used to express affirmation or approval.

Armageddon (From the Hebrew words *har* = "mountain" and Meggido, place name.) The place where all the nations of the world will meet for a final battle, followed by universal peace. Mount Meggido is in the northern Galilee, not far from Lebanon, Syria, Jerusalem, and the West Bank.

Asherah (Hebrew.) A tree or pole found beside the altar in a Canaanite high place of idolatry and considered holy to the local goddess of the same name.

Ashkenazi (Yiddish, from the Hebrew word for "Germany.") A Jew from a Christian country in Europe. The adjective is "Ashkenaz" or "Ashkenazic."

Asphalt (From the Hebrew, via the Greek.) According to Edward Horowitz's *How the Hebrew Language Grew*, this comes from an ancient name for the Dead Sea *(yam shafelet)*, where the Greeks mined a sticky, tough material which they used for road building.

Baal (Hebrew for "master," "proprietor.") One of the main gods of the Canaanite pantheon.

Babel (From the Hebrew word, *Bavel*, for the land of Babylonia: *bab* = "gate"; *el* = "god.") Famous for the ziggurate, whose construction caused so much confusion that to this day a foreigner's words sound like babbling nonsense to a native speaker. To make a Tower of Babel of something means to become so involved in a misguided task as to become impossible to live with.

Babushka (Yiddish, from the Russian word for "grandmother.") A kerchief for the head, folded in triangles.

Bagel (Yiddish, from the German word for "ring.") A doughnut made of bread dough instead of cake dough.

Baitz (Yiddish, from the Hebrew word for "eggs.") An Irishman. Irish Jews referred to the Irish non-Jews in this manner because "*ire*" in Yiddish means "eggs," which the Jews of Ireland transferred to the Hebrew word. The Hebrew plural is *baitzim*. This is not a pejorative and may even be affectionate in tone.

Bedlam (From the Hebrew name of the Judean city Bethlehem: *Bet* = "house" (of); *lehem* = "bread.") Chaos. Not because the biblical town was more chaotic than others, but because of the famous English insane asylum in London, Hospital of St. Mary of Bethlehem.

Beelzebub (Hebrew, from *baal* = "master" + *z'vuv* = "fly.") Lord of the flies. Milton's *Paradise Lost* ranks this fallen angel next to the devil himself.

Behemoth (Hebrew for "cattle.") An awesome yet clumsy animal or power. In the book of Job it may mean a hippopotamus. (See "At the Edges of Creation: Angels, Demons, and Beasts of Fancy.")

Belial (Hebrew, from *beli* = "without"; *el* = "god.") Worthlessness. Milton ranks this fallen angel near Beelzebub.

Bialy (Yiddish, from the Russian word meaning "white.") Like a bagel but made of softer dough, with onions, and an indention instead of a hole.

Blintz (Yiddish, from the Russian.) A Jewish version of a crêpe suzette; the traditional food for the holiday of Shavuot.

Bubeleh (Yiddish.) A term of endearment, from the Yiddish diminutive for a grandmother or midwife, *bubba* or *baube*. Not to be confused with *boobie*, which, though it sounds like Yiddish, is really from the American slang "boob," meaning a dumb person or a breast.

Bubkes (Yiddish, from the Russian word for "beans"; literally means "goat feces" in Yiddish.) 1. Something small, unimportant, and petty, e.g., "This car isn't worth bubkes." 2. That which is picked from the nose, boogies.

Cabal (From the Hebrew, shortened from *Kabbalah*.) A number of persons united in a clandestine way in order to overthrow or usurp; as a verb, "cabal" means to plot. It comes from the word "Kabbalah," which is the body of Jewish mystical literature as well as a genre of Christian esoteric teaching. Although restrictions were placed on who was to study it and how it was to be studied, the Kabbalah has nothing to do with plotting an overthrow.

Cain (From the Hebrew name of the son of Adam and Eve who killed his brother, Abel.) A trouble maker. Also used in combination form, as in "Cain-like" or "raising cain."

Camel (From the Hebrew *gamal* and from Arabic.) The Arabs also use this word for their most important animal as a first name, as in Gamal Abdel Nasser.

Cane (From the Hebrew word for "reed.") A stick for strolling. Also the stick that sugar in its raw form grows in. Other words derived from this Hebrew word are "canister," "canon," "cannon," "canal," and "channel."

Chaldean (From the Hebrew.) A person versed in the occult arts.

Cherub (Hebrew.) An angel of the second rank, depicted in Western literature and arts as a chubby, innocent child. Cupid without romantic interventions. Adjective: "cherubic." Plural: "cherubim."

Chutzpa (Yiddish, from the Hebrew word for "insolence.") Clever audacity. To have chutzpa one must have both bravery and wit; simple courage is not chutzpadic enough. The classic definition of "chutzpa" is a child who kills both parents and pleads for mercy because of being an orphan.

Collah carriage (Yiddish, from the Hebrew.) "A railway carriage filled with women, *collah* being Yiddish for young girls. 1880–1900." (Partridge, *A Dictionary of Slang and Unconventional English*.)

Delilah (From Hebrew name for the Philistine mistress and betrayer of Samson; the name is related to the Hebrew word for "night," just as the name Samson is related to the Hebrew word for "sun.") A woman who seduces and then betrays her lover.

Drek (Yiddish, from German word for "dirt.") Cognate to the English word "dreg," it is used almost as innocently in America. Actually it is the Yiddish word for "feces." Through American slang usage, drek has come to mean simply "crud."

Ebony (From the Hebrew word for "stone.") The wood that today is noted for its black color was in ancient times known for its rock-like hardness.

Eden (From Hebrew for "pleasure," "delight.") The name of the area where Adam and Eve lived. Used in English since 1225 to mean a state of supreme happiness.

Farblunget (Yiddish, from Slavic words meaning "roam" or "travel aimlessly.") Botched up, confused. To be totally mixed up by road signs or assembly kit directions.

Farmisht (Yiddish.) Mixed up. Wentworth and Flexner's *Pocket Dictionary of American Slang* defines it as being ". . . in a state of conflicting emotions; emotionally ambiguous."

Faygeleh (Yiddish for "little bird;" also a common female name.) Pejorative slang for a homosexual.

Fin (From the Yiddish.) A fiver; five dollars. Introduced to America by Jewish gamblers or businessmen. The Yiddish word for "five" is *finif*.

Gauze (Hebrew, from the ancient town of Gaza.) Not a pun on the modern Gaza Strip, this word dates from antiquity, when it referred to a cotton fabric manufactured in or imported from the coastal port of Gaza.

Gefilte fish (Yiddish.) Literally it means "stuffed fish," but rarely is it eaten with the outer part, that is, the fish, showing. It is white in color, made of a variety of fish flesh, pressed into a round loaf, and served with horse-radish. (See "A Fish Story: *Gefilte*.")

Gehenna (From the Hebrew *gai* = "valley"; Hinom, place name.) A valley outside Jerusalem; Gehenna's inhabitants used to conduct human sacrifices to their god Moloch. The word has come to mean "hell."

Gelt (Yiddish, from the German.) Money.

Gemara (Hebrew, from the Aramaic for "completion.") Not to be confused with the sinful city of Gomorrah destroyed with Sodom, this is the rabbinic text which, along with the Mishnah, comprises the Talmud. (See "Ten Jewish Classics at a Glance.")

Ghetto (Yiddish, from the Italian diminutive for *borghetto*, "a little borough.") As early as 1611 the word meant "the place where the whole fraternity of Jews dwelleth together . . ." (Corvat, *Crudities*, as quoted in the *Oxford English Dictionary*.) Today it means a place where Jews (or other minorities) are *forced* to live, either for legal or economic reasons. Force does not seem to have played a part in the original meaning.

Glitch (Yiddish, from the German word for "slip.") A mechanical defect; the "bug" in a new appliance.

Goliath (Hebrew, from the Philistine name.) Something that is so (muscularly) overdeveloped that it cannot defend itself against a small threat. From the biblical story where the frail adolescent David slew the terrible Philistine giant with a simple sling-shot.

Goniff (Yiddish, from the Hebrew.) A thief. Wentworth and Flexner in their *Dictionary of American Slang* make the term more specialized: "One who, though not a professional thief, will take advantage of another when in a position to do so." Some argue that the term "son of a gun" comes from "goniff."

Goy (Yiddish, from the Hebrew.) In Hebrew, the word means "a people who occupy their own land." God promises Abraham to make his seed into a *goy gadol*—"a great nation." Nomads who do not occupy land were called *'am*, not *goy*. To Yiddish-speaking Jews, everybody except the Jews had land of their own, hence the term came to mean any non-Jew. *Goy* is not necessarily a pejorative; it may simply mean a non-Jew. ("Shagetz" and "shikse" are always pejorative.) Plural: "goyim." Feminine: "goya," rarely used.

Greps (Yiddish.) Belch; burp.

Gunsel (Yiddish, from the German word for "gosling.") A young naive boy or one who acts that way to gain another's confidence. Also, a catamite.

Halakhah (Hebrew, related to "to go" or "the way.") The body of Jewish written and oral law.

Hallah (Yiddish, from the Hebrew.) Braided white bread eaten on Sabbath and during festivals. To be "real" hallah, it must be pareve, that is, made with neither dairy nor meat products. As such it can be eaten with either and thereby satisfy the gastronomic needs of any Jewish holiday or household.

Hallel (Hebrew, "praise.") The section of Psalms (chs. 113–118) chanted during the morning service on Jewish festivals.

Halleluja (Hebrew, *hallel* = "praise"; *ya* = "God.") Praise God. An even more enthusiastic affirmation than "amen."

Hazzan (Yiddish, from the Hebrew word for "overseer"; related to the Hebrew word for "visionary.") A cantor. Originally a hazzan was a "shammash" or beadle in a synagogue. When voice became the primary criterion in hiring him, he relinquished his beadle duties such as cleaning up and making sure all the chairs were in place. In slang usage, the word means "prima donna."

Hebrew (From the Hebrew.) The language spoken by the *'Ivrim* in the Bible, by Jews throughout history, and by Israelis today. (see "A Brief History of the Terms for Jew.")

Heder (Yiddish, from the Hebrew.) Hebrew school. The Hebrew word for "room" became the Yiddish word for a room where Hebrew is taught.

Hillelite (Hebrew.) A follower of the liberal talmudic sage Rabbi Hillel; hence, someone of a tolerant inclination.

Hondle (Yiddish.) To wheel and deal; to bargain.

Hoshanna, hosanna (Hebrew, *hosha* = "save" + *na* = "please.") A cry of supplication to God.

Hyssop (From the Hebrew *ezov.*) Blue flowers. In modern Hebrew the word has been mistakenly used to mean "marjoram."

Israel (From the Hebrew.) 1. The name given to Jacob after his dream of wrestling with an angel. His children were called "the children of Israel," and his country, "the Land of Israel." 2. A geographical term, the northern kingdom as opposed to the southern kingdom headed by Judah. In the last few hours before the declaration of the State of Israel there were those who still argued that the state should be called Zion, according to the biblical name for the geographical area around Jerusalem and because of the connotations which the word "Zion" had in Jewish theology and history. (See "A History of the Words for 'Jew.' ")

Jacket (French, from the Hebrew word for "Jacob.") A garment, worn over a shirt but under a coat.

Jaffa orange (From the Hebrew.) After the name of the town from which this orange was exported and where it grew. "Jaffa" is related to the Hebrew word for "pretty" *(yafeh).*

Jasper (From the Hebrew.) A kind of quartz, usually green.

Jehovah (Hebrew; the root is related to the verb "to be" but scholars disagree on its meaning under strict grammatical rules.) One of the most important names of God. Because it was so important, it was to be uttered only once a year, and then only by the High Priest at the Holy Temple on Yom Kippur. To make sure the word was not abused, the correct vowels were never written. *E-o-a* is only a guess English scholars made from the roughly equivalent vowels found in the Hebrew text. To this day many Jews will not write the four Hebrew consonants together, using instead various euphemisms. When the word is seen in a text, it is not sounded by the reader as it is written but rather as *"adonai"* and in certain cases *"elohim"* (more neutral names of God.) So sacred is this Tetragrammaton that even these replacement words are to be said only on special occasions such as in prayer or at public Bible readings. In the Middle Ages it was thought that one who knew the correct vocalization to the four letters would gain magical powers. (See "The Names of God.")

Jereboam (From Hebrew name for a mighty man of valor—1 Kings 11:28—who made Israel sin.) A large bowl or goblet; a very large wine-bottle.

Jeremiad (From the Hebrew.) A sincere complaint. After the lamentations of Jeremiah, a tender Hebrew prophet.

Jerusalem (From the Hebrew for the ancient capital of Judea and Israel.) Any center of religious or scholarly enlightenment, as in "America is the new Jerusalem."

Jew (From the Hebrew.) Short for Judean, that is, a Hebrew from the tribe of Judah. Since by the time of the second exile the only tribe left was Judah, all Hebrews came to be called by that name. (See "A Brief History of the Terms for 'Jew.' ")

Jezebel (From the Hebrew name for the wife of Ahab, king of Israel—1 Kings 26:31.) 1. A wicked, abandoned woman. 2. A woman who puts on a lot of makeup.

Jockey (Scots, from the Hebrew word for "Jacob.") One who rides a horse during races; an operator.

Jonah (From the Hebrew name for the prophet who was swallowed by a big fish after being thrown overboard because his presence caused an evil storm at sea.) A bringer of bad luck. First used in this sense in English in Black's *Sabina Zembra* (1887): "I seem to Jonah everything I touch."

Jot (From the Hebrew little letter *yud.*) The Romans pronounced this letter "jot" after the Greek letter *iota*, which corresponded to *yud.* In English "jot," like *iota*, became the word for "a tiny thing." As a verb, "jot" means to write essential details only; to write briefly and in small letters.

Jubilee (From the Hebrew.) A grand celebration, usually commemorating an anniversary. From the biblical term which referred to the year of freeing Hebrew slaves and to restoring land to its original owners every fifty years. The word is the root of "jubilation," "jubilant," and "jubilate."

Kabbalah (Hebrew, from the word meaing "receive.") The body of Jewish mystical teachings.

Kaddish (From the Hebrew root meaning "holy" or "special.") A prayer of praise to God written in Aramaic and recited several times at each Jewish service where a *minyan* (quorum) is present. It serves as a division between different parts of the service. The most familiar form is the Mourners' *Kaddish*, recited at the end of each service by those who have lost an immediate relative. However, there is nothing in the *kaddish* about death. In American usage the word has become misunderstood to mean a prayer one says before dying. (See "Eight Common Misconceptions Jews Have About Judaism.")

Kibbutz (Hebrew, from the root word meaning "together.") A collective farm in Israel, structured on more or less utopian socialist principles of communal property ownership and democratic decision-making.

Kibitz (Yiddish, from the Hebrew root word meaning "together.") Not to be confused with "kibbutz," this English word of Yiddish extraction means "to offer unsolicited advice" or "to goad someone on." A kibitzer is one who kibitzes.

Kiddush (Hebrew, same root as *"Kaddish."*) A blessing over wine sung at the beginning of the Sabbath and festival meals.

Kishke (Yiddish, from the Russian word for "guts.") 1. Stuffed derma; beef chitlins. 2. Guts, in the slang sense as in English: "She didn't have the kishkes to fire her secretary."

Klezmer (Yiddish, from the Hebrew words for "musical instruments.") In Yiddish it usually means "a wedding band," but *Webster's Third New International Dictionary* defines it in the singular as "a member of the band." Plural: "klezmorim."

Klupper (From the Yiddish.) A slow worker; a slow-thinking, slow-walking person. A little worse and less common than "shlepper."

Klutz (Yiddish, from the German word for "wooden block.") A "shloomp" without an opposable thumb.

Knish (Yiddish.) Dumplings filled with chopped liver, kasha, potatoes, or cheese. In New York knishes are sold and eaten on the streets like hot dogs.

K'nocker (Yiddish.) A big shot, a bragger. Borsht-belt comics introduced this to American slang (without the apostrophe and with a mute *k*) as a term for "breast." Nothing in Yiddish, however, suggests this leap of faith.

Kosher (Yiddish, from the Hebrew word for "proper," "correct," "valid.") The Yiddish word usually refers to food properly slaughtered and prepared, or to anything that requires proper ritual supervision. In American slang, however, the term has returned to its original, more general Hebrew meaning.

Kreplach (Yiddish, from the French *crêpe.*) Jewish wontons or ravioli.

Kvetch (Yiddish, from the German word for "squeeze.") A self-indulgent complaint. As a verb: to whine.

Kvell (Yiddish, from the German word for "to gush" or "to expand.") To feel great satisfaction at the success of a loved one, especially a son or daughter.

Kvutza (Hebrew, from the same root word as "kibbutz.") A Jewish cooperative farm in Israel.

Lechaim (Yiddish, from the Hebrew word meaning "to life.") Used as the Jewish toast word.

Leviathan (Hebrew.) Sea-monster parallel to Behemoth. In registered English it means a vast bureaucratic totalitarian state or anything equally formidable. (See "Angels, Demons, and Beasts of Fancy.")

Levite (Hebrew.) A member of the tribe descended from Levi, Jacob's third son. Hence, any priestly tribe. The book of Leviticus is primarily about Levites and their duties.

Lox (Yiddish, from the German *lahs,* "salmon.") Smoked salmon.

Mammon (Hebrew, from the Aramaic.) In Hebrew it means money; in English it means filthy money.

Mamzer (Yiddish, from the Hebrew word for "a child born from an adulturous married woman.") Used in American slang in a less technical way, that is, a "bastard" in general. The *Oxford English Dictionary,* tracing the word directly from the Bible, reports a first appearance in English print in 1562 C.E.

Manna (Hebrew.) Manna fell from heaven to feed the Israelites during their forty years of wandering in the Sinai desert. The word is used in America to mean "a gift from heaven;" "a gratuitous substance."

Matzah (Hebrew.) Unleavened bread that Jews must eat on Passover. Also known as the "bread of affliction" or "poor man's bread."

Maven (Yiddish, from the Hebrew word "to understand.") A know-it-all. Like "k'nocker," it is usually used in the negative, sarcastically or derogatorily.

Mazel (Yiddish, from the Hebrew, an astrological constellation.) In Yiddish it means "luck." In American slang it means the same, but usually in the negative. "Tough mazel" is common in racing parlance, perhaps because it puns with the Yiddish "Mazeltoff" ("Good luck").

Mazeltoff, mazal tov (Yiddish, from the Hebrew.) Good luck. The greeting to *all* who attend a celebration, whether it's their wedding or not.

Mechia (Yiddish, from the Hebrew.) A real pleasure, like a steam bath. In Hebrew it shares the root with *hai,* "life." God is said to be a *mechiyah metim,* a "bringer of life to the dead." In Yiddish and American slang, however, the word has a more earthy implication.

Megillah (Yiddish, from the Hebrew word for "scroll.") In Jewish circles this refers to the book of Esther, read in its entirety from a scroll on the holiday of Purim. In English the word means "a long task" or "a dreary story."

Melchizedek (Hebrew for "righteous king.") The higher order of the Mormon priesthood. Melchizedek, king of Salem, was a priest who blessed Abram (Abraham) (Gen. 14:18). In the Epistle to the Hebrews in the New Testament, Paul refers to Jesus as a priest "after the order of Melchizedek" (7:11).

Menorah (Hebrew.) A candelabrum used in Jewish worship. Sometimes a reduced facsimile is worn as a charm. (See "10 Jewish Symbols and Their Meanings.")

Mentch (Yiddish, from the German word for "person.") A kind, decent person. The term connotes common sense, flexibility when called for, and compassion; but never at one's own expense. "Manly, sincere, affectionate, and sweet" are some of the adjectives the *Dictionary of American Slang* (Wentworth and Flexner) uses to describe a mentch. Along with "schlemiel" and "kvetch," "mentch" is one of the greatest contributions Yiddish has made to the American idiom.

Meshugaas, meshugah, meshugana (Yiddish, from the Hebrew.) Crazy. Actually "meshugaas" means craziness, "meshugah" means crazy, and "meshugana" means a crazy person, but in American dictionaries they appear interchangeably.

Meshullachim (Hebrew.) A fund raiser for the maintenance of religious institutions in Israel. In English the Hebrew plural became a singular. This tradition of meshullachim predates the nineteenth century when most of the Jewish settlement in Israel was religious. Related to the Hebrew word for "messenger," "sender," "courier."

Meshummad (Yiddish, from the Hebrew.) An apostate from Judaism.

Messiah (From the Hebrew word for "anointed one," later having the connotation of "redeemer.") Shabbatai Zevi, one of the most famous false messiahs in Jewish history, ended his career when, at the hands of the Islamic Turks, he became a meshummad. (See "9 Jewish False Messiahs.")

Metzia (Yiddish, from the Hebrew for "found thing.") A bargain; a really good find; a new item. Usually used sarcastically, as in "It's no metzia."

Mezuzah (Hebrew for "doorpost.") A small box that is affixed to Jewish doorposts. It contains portions of the prayer, the *Shema*. It has been extended to mean an amulet which some Jews wear around their necks.

Mishnah (Hebrew, from Aramaic for "to teach.") Earlier part of the Talmud, compiled in writing about 200 C.E. by Rabbi Judah Ha-Nasi.

Mogen David (From Hebrew for "Shield of David.") The six-pointed "Jewish" star. (See "10 Jewish Symbols and Their Meanings.")

Moloch (Hebrew.) A Semitic but not Hebrew deity worshipped through the sacrifice of first-born sons. Extended in modern poetry to represent all that is wrong with Western materialism. (See Allen Ginsberg's poem "Howl.")

Nachas (Yiddish, from the Hebrew word for "restfulness," "contentment.") Pleasure earned from the success of a loved one. One draws or "sheps" nachas. Or one can kvell, opposite of "tzuris."

Nebich (Yiddish.) Such a pity.

Nebish (Yiddish, from the German.) A drab, pathetic loser.

Nimrod (Hebrew.) One of Noah's grandchildren. A mighty warrior. Used to mean "hunter" in English.

Noodge (Yiddish, from the Russian for "fret.") A pest. As a verb: To pester or coax. One can become noodgie or "antsy" when one is bored.

Nosh (Yiddish.) A snack. Even before the fast-food chain "Bagel Nosh" appeared in New York, there was already a "Nosh Bar" delicatessen in London.

Nu (Yiddish, from the Russian.) So? So what? So come on already. Leo Rosten gives nineteen definitions of the word in *The Joys of Yiddish*. Although it does not yet appear in any conventional usage or slang dictionary, a polling of several Gentiles showed it to be generally understood and used.

Nudnik (Yiddish.) A pest; an obnoxious person; a nagger whose complaints are irritating and whose conversation is boring. Unlike a kvetch, a nudnik can even bore himself. The joke is that if you ask a nudnik how he is feeling he will tell you.

Onanism (From the Hebrew name Onan, a man who performed coitus interruptus to prevent conception with his brother's widow, after he was commanded to take her for a wife.) The term has been used in English for "masturbation" since 1727, and in Jewish circles (in its Hebrew form) for a long time before that. The story is clearly not about masturbation, but even religious scholars have accepted the term. Bucknill and Tuke's

Psychological Medication (1874) is cited by the *Oxford English Dictionary:* "Onanism is a frequent accompaniment of insanity and sometimes causes it."

Ophanim (Hebrew.) An order of angels.

Oy, oy vey, oy veys mier (Yiddish.) Woe! Oh my! Woe is me!

Paatch (Yiddish.) A very small spanking; a slap.

Paatchky (Yiddish.) To dabble in a meddlesome, inefficient manner. This led to the expression "to paatchky around" which has been ignorantly replaced by "to putz around."

Paradise (From Hebrew, from the Persian word for "orchard.") Heaven.

Paschal lamb (From the Hebrew.) The lamb slain and eaten completely at the original *seder* (Passover ritual meal) to commemorate Israelite redemption from Egyptian slavery. Used by the early Christians as an image for Jesus, who they believed was sacrificed for the sake of redemption from sin.

Pasha (Hebrew, from the Persian for "official.") A man of high rank.

Pharisee (Hebrew, from the Aramaic word for "separated.") To the Jews it indicates the normative rabbinic sages who contributed to the Talmud; in standard English, one of its meanings is "hypocrite."

Pilpul (Hebrew, related to the word for "pepper.") To debate hotly. A crafty argument.

Pilpulist (Hebrew, related to the word for "pepper.") The *Oxford English Dictionary* provides this understanding of the Hebrew term: "A subtle or keen disputant, especially in rabbinical argumentation." It cites P. Beaton's 1859 *Jews in East:* "There is not among them a talmudist or pilpulist of any reputation."

Pisgah (Hebrew.) Mountaintop.

Pish (Yiddish.) Urinate; urine. In American slang it also means "drunk."

Pisher (Yiddish.) One who urinates or that with which one urinates. This has come to mean an inconsequential person, a pipsqueak, almost a punk; a squirt, but not a drip. (A drip would be a nebish.)

Plotz (Yiddish, from the German word for the noun "place" or the verb "to burst.") To collapse from overwork or overexcitement.

Pogrom (Yiddish, from the Russian word for "devastation.") An organized raid on a helpless population.

Punim (Yiddish, from the Hebrew.) A face. "What a beautiful punim"—usually accompanied by a pinch on the cheek.

Putz (Yiddish.) Vulgar for penis. In American slang it has been used as a more polite substitute verb for "to crap around," and as a noun, for "fool."

Rabbi (From the Hebrew for "my master.") A Jewish scholar, hence a Jewish religious leader. In American slang the term "rabbi" means a kindly high-ranking bureaucrat who pulls strings to get a deserving, lower-ranking civil service worker (or policeman) a promotion, without seeking a favor in return. A kind of administrative guardian angel.

Raphael (Hebrew for "God heals.") One of the archangels.

Sabaoth (From the Hebrew word for "armies.") Hosts. Exclusively used in referring to God as the Lord of Hosts, that is, armies (of angels). Lifted directly from the Hebrew prayer: *". . . adonai tzvaot."* In some early translations of the Bible, the term was confused with "Sabbath."

Sabbath (From the Hebrew *Shabbat* for "rest"; the Yiddish word is *shabbos.*) The seventh day of the week, which according to Jewish law is a day of ritualized rest beginning at sunset Friday and ending at sunset Saturday. The Christians observe the commanded seventh day of rest on the first day of the week; the Muslims observe the same commandment on Fridays.

Sabbatical (From the Hebrew for "rest.") A recurring period of rest and revitalization. From the biblical prescription that every seventh year one's land is to remain fallow. Tied in with the jubilee year in biblical chronological precepts.

Sabra (Hebrew, after a fruit that grows on cactus.) A native-born Israeli (prickly on the outside; sweet on the inside.)

Sack (Hebrew and other languages.) One of the oldest words in the world, still used in its original vocalization and meaning. Say it the world over and you will be understood.

Sanhedrin (Hebrew, from the Greek meaning "seat of the leaders.") The high council composed of seventy Jewish leaders in pretalmudic times. The word in English usage has taken on negative connotations.

Sapphire (From the Hebrew.) A blue precious stone.

Satan (From the Hebrew, originally meaning "the Accuser.") The Devil. (See "At the Edges of Creation: Angels, Demons, and Beasts of Fancy.")

Scallion (From the Hebrew.) An onion-like plant that grew in the Philistine city-state of Ashkelon.

Selah (Hebrew.) This word was probably used to denote some kind of musical or liturgical direction, either a rest or a clash of cymbals. The word is found almost exclusively in the Psalms. In Middle English there was a speculation that the selah also called for a pause immediately before the signal appeared in a text, giving worshippers a chance to ponder with deep affection on the previous line.

Sephardi (Hebrew, from the word for "Spain.") A Jew from a Muslim country, especially from the once Muslim countries of Spain and Portugal. The adjective is "Sephardi" or "Sephardic."

Seraph, seraphim (Hebrew.) 1. An order of angels. 2. Someone who looks or acts like an angel.

Shadchen (Yiddish.) A marriage broker; a matchmaker.

Shallot (From the Hebrew through the French "echalote.") Shallots, which are like scallions, also grow near or are imported from the ancient port city of Ashkelon.

Shalom (Hebrew for "peace"; related to the Hebrew word for "complete.") In English, "Shalom" is used as a greeting and farewell, literally meaning "Peace."

Shalom Aleichem (Yiddish, from the Hebrew.) Peace be with you. A traditional Ashkenazi Jewish greeting. The reply is "Aleichem shalom." These plural forms are used whether one is addressing an individual or a group.

Shamir (Hebrew.) The hard stone used in building the Holy Temple. Also, since no swords or other implements of war (particularly iron) were permitted in the construction of the Temple, "shamir" came to be the name of the tiny worm which was used to cut the rocks.

Shammaite (Hebrew.) A follower of the strict talmudic sage, Shammai; hence someone of a conservative inclination.

Shammash (Hebrew.) Sexton or beadle in a synagogue. Also, the Hanukkah candle that is used to light the other candles.

Shamus (Yiddish, from the Hebrew.) Policeman; private investigator; detective. (See "Shammash.")

Shekels (From the Hebrew.) Money.

Shekhinah (Hebrew.) The Divine Presence. Since this is a Hebrew feminine noun, kabbalists and some modern Jewish scholars understand it to mean the feminine aspects of God. (See "Feminine Images in Judaism.")

Shema (Hebrew for "hear" or "listen.") A prayer declaring the central creed of Judaism: "Hear, O Israel: the LORD our God, the LORD is one." (Deut. 6:4)

Shemazel, shlemazel (Yiddish.) One who always has bad luck. For some reason the first "*l*" was dropped when the word entered American and English.

Shemittah (Hebrew.) The seventh, sabbatical year.

Shiboleth (Hebrew.) Password; false issue or slogan. From the Hebrew word for either an "ear of corn" (Gen. 41:5) or a "flood of a stream." The English meaning comes directly from its use in Judges, 12:6 where the vocalization of the word was a sign of a soldier's tribal origin.

Shikker (Yiddish, from the Hebrew.) Drunk; a drunk.

Shiksa (Yiddish, from the Hebrew word for "abomination.") Pejorative for a non-Jewish woman. The masculine form is "shagetz"; the plural is "shgutzim."

Shittah (Hebrew.) Probably the acacia tree, whose wood was used for the desert Tabernacle and Temple woodwork.

Shiva (Hebrew, from the word for "seven.") The traditional seven-day Jewish mourning period that follows the death of an immediate relative. One "sits shiva."

Shlemiel (Yiddish, from the son of a leader of the tribe of Simeon—Numbers 2. According to Leo Rosten's *Joys of Yiddish*, the other generals in Zion often won battles, but poor Shlumiel always lost.) A person who always finds the bad luck; a fool. Not unlike "nebbish," "shlemazel," and "putz."

Shlep (Yiddish.) To drag or carry; hence, anything or anyone that is considered a "drag." A shelp is one who gets stuck with a dreary task. (In registered Yiddish a shlepper is a hobo.)

Shlock (Yiddish word for "stroke"; "evil"; "nuisance.") Cheap; poorly made. (The word may come from the Yiddish word "to hit" or "to strike" as in minting a coin.)

Shlong (Yiddish, from the German word for "snake.") Vulgar for "penis." Unlike "putz" and "schmuck," this slang Yiddish term has not entered English as a word for "a fool," but has kept its original Yiddish vulgarity. Evidently only a schmuck would putz around with this German word for "a snake." It has, however, also entered English slang as a word for a crushing defeat. (See "shmise" and "shneider," below.)

Shloomp (Yiddish.) Unkempt; sloppy. A sloppy person. Hence an adjective for casual clothes. (The Yiddish word for "Cinderella" is *Shloomperl.)*

Shmaltz (Yiddish for "chicken fat.") Sentimental music or other art forms; hyperbolic speech.

Shmata (Yiddish, from the Polish word for "rag.") A rag; raggedy clothes.

Shmear (Yiddish, from the German word

for "oil" or "bribe.") 1. To spread generously, as a lot of butter. 2. A bribe. 3. To "cream" as in a fierce football tackle. (The third usage may not be of Yiddish origin.)

Shmeikle (Yiddish for "grin" or "smile.") To flatter insincerely. Defined in *The Pocket Dictionary of American Slang* as "To swindle, to con, to fast talk."

Shmise (Yiddish for "thrash," "lash," "whip.") To crushingly defeat an opponent.

Shmo (Yiddish.) Modified form of "schmuck" ("fool"). Not to be confused with Shmoos, Al Capp's bowling-pin-type creatures who become whatever one wants.

Shmootz (Yiddish.) Filth.

Shmooze (Yiddish, from the Hebrew word for "hearing.") To chat. To verbally putz around. As a noun "schmooze" means unimportant or casual but not gossipy chatter; hearsay.

Shmuck (Yiddish for "ornament," from a number of possible German words meaning "neat," "smart," or "to decorate.") In Yiddish slang the word means a penis, but in American slang it means "a fool." Technically it should be the exact slang equivalent of the American "prick": a stiff, inflexible, rule-following dolt.

Shneider (Yiddish for "tailor" or "cloth cutter.") In American slang the word came to mean a schmising card-shark; then any victor whose opponent is shut out. Used as a verb in the game of gin rummy.

Shnook (Yiddish, from the German for "small sheep.") A fool; a sad sack; one who lets others take advantage of him; a harmless loser. Slang lexicographers Wentworth and Flexner report in their *Pocket Dictionary of American Slang* that "like other derisive words from the Yiddish, this is somewhat affectionate, implying that the person is more to be pitied than scorned and realizing that the person may seem foolish because he is meek, gentle, and idealistic."

Shnorrer (Yiddish.) A Jewish beggar or a person who acts like one. Webster's *Third International Dictionary* defines a shnorrer as "the sound of musical instruments used by beggars." The verb is "to shnor."

Shnozz, shnozzle (From the Yiddish *shnoits* = "nose.") Nose. The late Italian-American comedian Jimmy Durante used to refer to himself as the "old schnozzola."

Shofar (Hebrew.) A hollowed-out ram's horn blown by Jews on the High Holidays. Legend has it that the shofar will be blown by Gabriel when the Messiah is about to arrive.

Shpritz (Yiddish for "spurt," "squirt," or "shower.") 1. A spray. 2. Wine diluted with seltzer.

Shtadlan (Yiddish.) Webster's *Third International Dictionary* explains: "A person appointed by a Jewish community to represent Jewish interests (as before a government or ruler.")

Shtarker (Yiddish for "gangster," from the German word for "strong.") Lenny Bruce made this famous as a word for a brave person who can "take it."

Shtetl (Yiddish; plural *shtetlach.*) A small Jewish town in Eastern Europe.

Shtick (Yiddish, from the German word for "piece.") An act or a routine associated with show-business. (In registered Yiddish it means "pranks," "whims." A *shtickarbeter* is a jobber.)

Shtoonk (Yiddish.) A contemptible and thoughtless person.

Shul (Yiddish, from the Greek *schola*, via the German *Schule.*) A synagogue.

Shvach (Yiddish.) Weak, feeble, mediocre.

Shvitz (Yiddish.) 1. Perspiration. Hence, a steambath. 2. A show-off.

Shwa (Hebrew.) The faint vowel sound used in Hebrew. In the International Phonetic Alphabet the term is used to denote the *e* sound in the word "the"; it is printed as an upside-down *e*.

Sitsfleisch (Yiddish, from the German.) Sitting power, as in chess. Perseverance, particularly of a scholarly nature.

Tallit or **tallis** (Hebrew, Yiddish.) A shawl, with a specified number of fringes and knots, worn during morning prayers.

Talmud (Hebrew, related to the word for "instruction.") This, perhaps the most important book of Jewish tradition, has two parts, the *Mishnah* and the *Gemara*. Technically a commentary on the Pentateuch, it is the text that established rabbinical authority after the destruction of the Temple. (See "10 Jewish Classics at a Glance.") In Russian slang today a *talmud* is a record book filled with bureaucratic minutiae. In American slang a talmudist is one who is preoccupied with petty textual matters to the point of missing the main point. (See "Pilpulist," above.)

Tchatchke (Yiddish, from the Slavic word meaning "to play pranks." Erroneously attributed to the Hebrew word for "toy," *tza'atzuah.*) A toy, a knick-knack, a worthless gizmo.

Teraph (Hebrew.) An image of a Semitic household god; an idol. Plural: "teraphim."

Toreador (From the Spanish *toro* = "bull" via the Latin *taurus,* thanks to the Aramaic *tor* which is the same as the Hebrew *shor.*) A bullfighter. (The word "steer" has a similar history.)

Tsimmes (Yiddish.) 1. A carrot and prune side dish. 2. An unnecessary to-do; a brouhaha.

Tunic (From the Hebrew *kuttonet,* "shirt.") A knee-length robe for street dress, worn by ancient Greeks and Romans.

Tush, tushie (Yiddish, from the Hebrew word *tachat* = "under" or "bottom.") Buttocks. *Tochis* or *tuchus* means the same thing and is closer to the original pronunciation, but probably because of the guttural *ch* these forms are less common in American slang usage.

Tzaddik (Hebrew.) A righteous, saintly person.

Tzedakah (Hebrew, used in Yiddish.) Charity. In the original it has the wider meaning of "righteousness." (See "Tzedakah: The Gift of Giving.")

Tzedek (Hebrew.) Justice. Possibly the slang term "kobetzedek" or "copacetic" (meaning "It's OK") comes from a corruption of the Hebrew *ha-kol be-tzedek,* meaning "Everything is fair and square."

Tzitzit (Hebrew.) "The tassels of entwined threads worn by Jewish males at the four corners of the outer garment on the tallith" *(Webster's Seventh New Collegiate Dictionary).* Actually the tassels are supposed to be worn on *all* four-cornered garments, not just on a tallit. Many Orthodox Jews wear a four-cornered garment under their shirts in order to have a garment on which to place the tzitzit (See Num. 15:37-41.)

Tzuris (Yiddish, from the Hebrew word for "sorrows.") Suffering. In *The Pocket Dictionary of American Slang* the word is defined as a singular noun for "ill fortune, especially chronic ill fortune or bad luck; problems."

Wine (From the Hebrew.) A word as old as "sack." Related to the Hebrew *yayyin* through minor consonant changes.

Yarmulke (Yiddish, from the Ukrainian and Polish.) A skullcap worn for prayer by most Jewish men and at all times by the Orthodox.

Yehuda (Hebrew.) A Jew.

Yente (Yiddish, from the Italian *gentile.*) A gossipy busy-body. Beginning as a nice name, it began to go downhill when associated with the heroine in the Yiddish play *Yentel, the Matchmaker.*

Yentz (Yiddish word for "copulate," from German *jenes.*) In American slang this word has kept only its secondary meaning: to cheat, to screw.

Yeshiva (Yiddish and Hebrew, from the Hebrew word for "to sit.") A Jewish parochial school.

Yeshiva bocher (Yiddish, from Hebrew.) *Webster's Third New International Dictionary* defines the term as a "yeshiva youth."

Yetzer (Hebrew.) Merriam-Webster: "The impulse or inclination with which man is endowed according to Jewish traditional beliefs."

Yetzer ha-ra (Hebrew.) Merriam-Webster: "Evil inclination." Unfortunately the Hebrew term for good inclination, *yetzer ha-tov,* has not yet made its mark in English.

Yid (Yiddish, from the Hebrew *yehudi,* meaning "Judean.") A Jew. Sometimes pejorative. Among Jews, used affectionately.

Yiddish (Yiddish, from the Hebrew *yid* + the Germanic-*ish.*) The Germanic language invented and spoken by Jews in Eastern Europe with a vocabulary derived from Hebrew, Slavic, Latin, Italian, French, Russian, Aramaic, German, and other languages. Written in slightly modified Hebrew characters.

Yiddishkeit (Yiddish, from the Hebrew *yid* + the German-*ish* and -*keit.*) Jewishness; Judaism. The values, customs, and folklore of the Jewish people.

Yizkor (Hebrew, "may He remember.") A memorial prayer for deceased relatives recited by Jews on certain holidays. More generally, a memorial service or ceremony marking the death of a great person.

Yold (Yiddish.) A dupe, according to Wentworth and Flexner's *Pocket Dictionary of American Slang.*

Zaftic, zoftig (Yiddish, from the German word for "juicy.") Plump, almost fat. Used almost exclusively to describe a full-bodied woman.

Zhlob (Yiddish, from the Slavic word for "a coarse person.") A clumsy, sloppy dolt, usually overweight. A shloomp.

Zion (From the Hebrew.) 1. Jerusalem. 2. The center of Judea. In English it has gained the meaning of heaven and utopia. In Hebrew it has expanded to mean all of the Land of Israel.

Zohar (Hebrew for "splendor.") A Jewish mystical commentary on the Bible written down by Moses de Leon of Granada (c. 1300 C.E.), who attributed the book to the second-century talmudic sage Simeon ben Yochai. (See "10 Jewish Classics at a Glance.")

—Z.S.

50 ENGLISH WORDS THAT SOUND LIKE YIDDISH

Many perfectly authentic English words have, for either historical or sonic reasons, come to sound like Yiddish. Some rhyme with or echo familiar Yiddish terms. Some employ distinctive Yiddish prefixes, suffixes, or syllabic sounds. Others do not have an inherent Yiddish sound, but have taken on a particular usage or inflection after a generation of Yiddish speakers.

Determining which English words possess this remarkable characteristic is, obviously, a highly subjective process. In the list that follows, occasional annotations are given to make the connection clearer. Some words may have to be pronounced with a shift in accent to gain the full effect; e.g., bedridden should be beDRIDden.

Bedraggled
Bedridden
Blanching
Box-kite
Cardigan
Coil
Coit
Conniption
Cripple (diminutive -le suffix)
Dealt (but not "delta")
Dental (but not "periodontal")
Dirndl (echoes *trendle*, "a spinning top")
Far-fetched
Far-flung
Fetish
Gargoyle (echoes *moyel*, "circumciser")
High-chair
Ladle
Laser (homonym of a Yiddish name)
Mantle (echoes Yiddish word for "almond," *mandel*)
Mayor (homonym of a Yiddish name)
Melt
Mental (see Mantle)
Mesmerize (echoes *klezmer*, "musicians")
Mish mash
Muffler
Parboil
Peddle
Pelts (echoes *platz*, "fall down")
Ploy
Poised
Puddle (but not "muddle")
Reddish (sounds like an ethnic mispronunciation of *raddish*)
Roosevelt (last syllable sounds like Yiddish word for "world")
Seminal vesicle
Shush
Shyster
Spatula
Svelte
Tendril
Testicle
Toddle
Trickle
Tumult
Tunic
Varnish (echoes the culinary delicacy *kashe varnishkes*)
Ventrical
Verbal
Vestibule
Vile

—Z.S.

ALEPH-BET SOUP

JEWISH ACRONYMS COMMONLY SEEN AND HEARD

From AZA (Aleph Zaddik Aleph) to ZOA (Zionist Organization of America) Jewish life is dotted with acronyms. Originally designed as short-cut devices for cumbersome names, some acronyms have assumed a meaning so distinct that the original words are forgotten; for example Camp Cejwin (Central Jewish Institute) or HIAS (Hebrew Immigrant Aid and Sheltering Society) or YIVO (Yiddisher Vesnshafleker Institut). Acronyms, or the knowledge of their meanings, have also been used to distinguish the inner clique of Jewish cognoscenti from the outsiders.

Acronyms and abbreviations have become so much a part of the American Jewish communal world that, as the saying goes, "You can't tell the players without a program." However, acronyms are by no means a twentieth-century phenomenon: some of the most common ones, such as Tanakh, date back to the talmudic period.

Books

AJYB	*American Jewish Year Book* (published annually by the American Jewish Committee and the Jewish Publication Society since 1909)
EJ	*Encyclopaedia Judaica* (published in 1972, Cecil Roth, ed., Keter Publishing House, Jerusalem)
JE	*Jewish Encyclopedia* (published in 1906, Isidore Singer, ed., New York)
JPS	Jewish Publication Society of America (founded in 1888 in Philadelphia)
Tanakh	Torah, Nevi'im (Prophets), Ketuvim (Writings) (i.e., the Hebrew Bible)

Rabbis

Besht	Rabbi Israel Baal Shem Tov
Ha-Gra	Rabbi Elijah ben Solomon Zalman, known as the Gaon of Vilna
Ralbag	Rabbi Levi ben Gersom—Gersonides
Ramaz	Rabbi Moses Zacuto
Rambam	Rabbi Moses ben Maimon—Maimonides
Ramban	Rabbi Moses ben Nahman—Nachmanides
Rashbam	Rabbi Samuel ben Meir
Rashi	Rabbi Solomon bar Isaac
Rif	Rabbi Isaac bar Jacob haKohen—Alfasi

Give to the Initials of Your Choice

AJC	Allied Jewish Charities
CJA	Combined Jewish Appeal
CJF	Council of Jewish Federations
CJP	Combined Jewish Philanthropies
FJC	Federated Jewish Charities
FJP	Federation of Jewish Philanthropies
JFA	Jewish Federated Appeal
JFC	Jewish Federated Charities
UHC	United Hebrew Charities
UJA	United Jewish Appeal

The Branches of Judaism and Their Many Leaves

Reform

ACC	American Conference of Cantors
CCAR	Central Conference of American Rabbis
HUC/JIR	Hebrew Union College/Jewish Institute of Religion
UAHC	Union of American Hebrew Congregations

Conservative

CA	Cantor's Association
JTS	Jewish Theological Seminary
RA	Rabbinical Assembly
USA	United Synagogues of America

Orthodox

CAA Cantorial Association of America

RAA Rabbinical Association of America

RCA Rabbinical Council of America

UOJCA Union of Orthodox Jewish Congregations of America

UOR Union of Orthodox Rabbis

YU Yeshiva University

Reconstructionist

JRF Jewish Reconstructionist Foundation

RRA Reconstructionist Rabbinical Association

RRC Reconstructionist Rabbinical College

Zionist Organizations

AZF American Zionist Federation

AZYF American Zionist Youth Foundation

J.N.F Jewish National Fund

L.Z.A Labor Zionist Alliance

WZO World Zionist Organization

ZOA Zionist Organization of America

Youth Organizations

BBYO B'nai B'rith Youth Organization; comprised of BBG (B'nai B'rith Girls) and AZA (Aleph Zaddik Aleph)

NCSY National Council of Synagogue Youth

NFTY National Federation of Temple Youth

USY United Synagogue Youth

YI Young Israel Youth

YJ Young Judea

Defense Organizations

A.D.L. Anti-Defamation League of B'nai B'rith

A.J.C. American Jewish Committee

A.J.C. American Jewish Congress

J.D.L. Jewish Defense League

Miscellaneous

BH Baruch Ha-Shem or B'ezrat Ha-Shem (Praise God, or With the Help of God); often inscribed in the right-hand corner of letters or other writings

E.J. Korvettes Eight Jewish Korean Veterans

KBH HaKadosh Baruch Hu (The Holy One, blessed be He)

Habad Hochmah (Wisdom), Binah (Understanding), Da'at (Knowledge); represents Lubavitcher Hasidism

Hazal Hakhamenu, Zikhronam Liverakhah (Our sages, may their memories be for a blessing)

WEVD-FM Call letters of a New York radio station "that speaks your language" (EVD stands for Eugene V. Debs)

YM-YWHA Young Men's and Women's Hebrew Association

Zal Zikrono (ah) Liverakha (May his/her memory be for a blessing); said after mentioning someone who has died

—J.B.S.

THE JEWISH ALMANAC'S LIST OF AMERICAN JEWISH ORGANIZATIONS WITH UNUSUALLY LONG NAMES

1. American Academic Association for Peace in the Middle East (AAAPME)
2. American and European Friends of the Organization for Rehabilitation Through Training (AEFORTT)
3. American Federation of Jewish Fighters, Camp Inmates, and Nazi Victims (AFJFCINV)
4. American Friends of the Jerusalem Mental Health Center-*Ezrath Nashim*, Inc. (AFJMHCEN)
5. American Society for Jewish Farm Settlements in Russia (AMSOJEFS)
6. Commission on Legislation and Civic Action of Agudath Israel of America. (CLCAAIA)
7. Conference of Presidents of Major American Jewish Organizations (CPMAJO)
8. Leadership Conference of National Jewish Women's Organizations (LCNJWO)
9. National Association of Jewish Family, Children's, and Health Services (NAJFCHS)
10. National Federation of Temple Brotherhoods, Sisterhoods, and Youth (NFTBSY)
11. National Jewish Commission on Law and Public Affairs (COLPA)
12. National Jewish Community Relations Advisory Council (NJCRAC)
13. National Jewish Information Service for the Propagation of Judaism, Inc. (NJISPJ)
14. Sons of Jewish War Veterans of the United States of America (SJWVUSA)
15. World Council of International Jewish Lawyers and Jurists Association (WCIJLJA)

—J.B.S.

JEWISH BEST SELLERS

10 JEWISH CLASSICS AT A GLANCE

1. The Torah

It is convenient to think of the Torah as a book—or, more specifically, as the five books of Moses, i.e., the first five books of the Hebrew Bible: Genesis, Exodus, Leviticus, Numbers, Deuteronomy—which pre-modern Jewish and Christian traditions alike have held to have been written by Moses at God's dictation. This collection is also called the Pentateuch (from a Greek term meaning "five volumes") and the *Humash* (Hebrew for "fivefold entity"). The term "Torah" itself means simply "Teaching."

THE DEEPER MEANINGS OF "TORAH"

To religious Jews, however, the Torah is more than a written book, more, even, than a great classic: it is a body of law, the constitution of the nation and people called Israel, the source of Jewish tradition, and still more—the term "Torah" has also variously been applied to the sum-total of the tradition itself, i.e., to the Bible as a whole and the two-thousand-year post-biblical tradition (the "Torah" is thus still being written), to the overall process of Jewish learning, and to the generations of teachers and students who have sustained it. To Jewish mystics, the term has had still more metaphysical meanings: a magical storehouse of divine names, the mysterious "Tree of Life" alluded to in the Garden of Eden story, a blueprint of the universe that antedated Creation, an emanation of God Himself. It is possible to say that "Torah," considered in all of the foregoing senses, is synonymous with "Judaism." It is noteworthy that Jewish tradition speaks only rarely of "the Bible," but endlessly and profusely of "the Torah."

THE ORIGINS OF THE TORAH

This extraordinary status of the concept "Torah" would not be possible were it not for the unique qualities of the written work. "Torah" is justifiably taken as a symbol of the whole Bible, because it represents the decisive stages in the collection of Israelite traditions that led to the growth of biblical literature as a whole. During the days of ancient Israel there were many attempts to collect traditions (the Bible mentions, for example, a "Book of Yashar" and a "Book of the Wars of the Lord"), but these are now lost. Only when an enterprising author or editor (whether Moses or someone else we must consider later) undertook to tell the story of Israel's religion from the earliest days of mankind down to the end of Israel's desert wanderings—and to relate these events in a forceful, simple, graceful, coherent, and continuous manner—were the main lines of earliest Jewish tradition laid down in a way that was memorable and authoritative for later generations of Israel and mankind.

Modern biblical scholarship, of course, finds doubtful the traditional notion that the five books of Moses had a single author, much less that the work's great, humble hero could have been the author, or even the main author. Parts of the Torah, especially some of the legal and poetic material, are indeed very ancient, and may reflect authentic traditions that stem from, or even antedate, the era of Moses (c. thirteenth century B.C.E.). But the present literary form of the five books is believed to have developed in a number of stages, beginning in the most prosperous days of the Israelite monarchy (tenth century B.C.E.) and continuing through the days of the divided kingdom (Israel and Judah, ninth to seventh centuries B.C.E.) into the period of the Babylonian Exile (sixth and fifth centuries B.C.E.). The Torah is a "mosaic" book in more ways than one.

This view of the Torah's origins is called the documentary hypothesis, because it sees a succession of written "documents" making up the layers of its composition: first came the main narratives and the earliest law codes;

then the book of Deuteronomy during a period of religious reform in the late days of the divided kingdom; finally, the book of Leviticus, the priestly legislation, the genealogies and the stately Creation story (Gen. 1) that prefaces the whole collection, these last elements added to the collection during the days of Babylonian exile and the early days of the restoration. Scholars have distinguished sources by studying the variations in vocabulary, style, and religious outlook of the Torah's respective elements. This is mostly guesswork, and firm conclusions are impossible.

WAS THERE AN AUTHOR?

In fact, in recent decades, the concept of the "authorship" of documents has been modified considerably. Some authorities argue that it is more important to study the history of Israel's oral tradition, which may have been fully developed before the materials were ever cast into writing. Others have argued that the most creative phase in the collection of Torah materials may have been not the initial stages of authorship or oral tradition, but rather the final editorial arrangement of stories and traditions, an arrangement that has a distinctive logic and artistic integrity of its own, by virtue of which the Torah must, in the long run, be seen as a unified work.

One way or another, it is probable that the Torah had more or less its present form by the fifth century B.C.E., when Jewish exiles from Babylonia were returning to rebuild the Jewish commonwealth and Temple in the land of Israel. The book of Nehemiah (ch. 8) describes a New Year ceremony in Jerusalem at which the whole Torah was read and explained to the assembled people, who wept and rejoiced to hear their traditions brought together in a definitive collection. 440 B.C.E. is generally taken as the date of this "canonization" of the Torah (the definitive canon of the whole Jewish Bible was not to emerge until 90 C.E.).

THE GROUND-PLAN OF THE TORAH

The contents of the Torah are well-known to all readers of the Bible. Each book has a unique emphasis—Genesis deals with the earliest history of the world, of mankind, and of the first ancestors of Israel; Exodus with the Israelites' sojourn in Egypt, their escape from Egyptian slavery, and their reception of divine commandments at Mount Sinai; Leviticus (and the end of Exodus and parts of Numbers) with the institution of priesthood, including the priestly work of administering sacrifices and ritual purifications; Numbers with the post-Sinai wanderings of the Israelites and their rebellions against Moses; and Deuteronomy with Moses's farewell address to his people—this last book is actually a recapitulation of Israel's laws in the form of a lengthy sermon—just before the people's entry into the land of Canaan, a land Moses himself is forbidden to enter.

At least four main law codes, representing various stages in the history of Israelite law, are present in the Torah: the Covenant Code (Exod. 20-24, including the Ten Commandments) is the earliest; the Deuteronomic Code (Deut. 12-26) is associated with the reforms of the seventh-century B.C.E. Judahite king Josiah, though parts of it are older; the Priestly Code (Exod. 25ff., Leviticus, parts of Numbers) is dated to post-Exilic times; the Holiness Code (Lev. 19-27) is an addendum to the Priestly Code, of separate origin. All of the codes contain strongly archaic elements.

A MASTERPIECE OF EDITING

Signs of careful editorial arrangement of the Torah are clearly evident: the stories follow a steady, chronological pattern, reflecting the Israelite concern for a continuous chain of tradition, going back to the earliest ancestors of mankind; the narrative progresses from mythical and legendary history to progressively more detailed and realistic national history; the various law codes are woven deftly, if not always free of contradictions and duplications, into the main body of narrative; finally, many of the narratives are arranged as parallels, both within narrative cycles (e.g., the Jacob cycle, Gen. 25-35, has a more or less symmetrical structure, centering on the birth of Jacob's children in Gen. 30), and between narratives (each of the Israelite patriarchs—Abraham, Isaac, Jacob, and possibly Joseph—undergoes similar trials and arrives at similar victories and divine blessings), and perhaps between books (the rebellions in Exodus seem to parallel those in Numbers). The whole of the Torah seems preoccupied with a single theme: the unique title and responsibilities of Israel as a people of God and steward of the Holy Land, the tiny land-bridge at the juncture of three continents.

THE TORAH'S DISTINCTIVE LITERARY STYLE

If it is the geographic context and compelling morality of the Torah's laws that give it its religious authority, it is the simplicity and dramatic power of its narratives that give it its place as a classic of world literature. The narrative scenes depend for their effect more on what is left out than on what is present. As Erich Auerbach writes in his book *Mimesis*, these stories present "only so much of the

From a series of engravings of the Book of Job by William Blake

phenomena as is necessary for the purpose of the narrative, all else [is] left in obscurity; the decisive points of the narrative alone are emphasized, what lies between is nonexistent; time and place are undefined and call for interpretation; thoughts and feelings remain unexpressed, are only suggested by the silence and the fragmentary speeches; the whole, permeated with the most unrelieved suspense and directed toward a single goal . . . remains mysterious and fraught with background." Yet, however mysteriously the characters are presented, they are marvellously realistic. They are presented with their faults and foibles; their actions are lucidly submitted to the reader's scrutiny.

THE TORAH AND LATER JUDAISM

It is probable that the Torah evolved together with the historical books Joshua, Judges, Samuel, and Kings, which continue Israelite history down to the beginning of the Exile. The five books of Moses, however, were regarded by Jews as the most sacred and authoritative part of the Bible—one could not render a legal decision on the basis of non-Pentateuchal Biblical sources. The Torah was generally written out separately on a single scroll; to the present day, the Torah scroll remains the most sacred object in a synagogue, and the synagogue ritual is directed to the ark in which it is housed.

The Torah text is divided into fifty-four weekly portions (often overlapped in order to form a yearly cycle of readings) which are read in the synagogue on Mondays, Thursdays, and Sabbaths, together with the *haftarot* ("conclusions"), i.e., Sabbath selections from the prophetic books (including the historical books). While Jews have divided their Bible into Torah, Prophets, and Writings (in Hebrew: *Torah, Nevi'im, Ketuvim*, or, together, *TaNaKh*—the Christian arrangement is in four sections: Law, History, Wisdom, and Prophecy), the ritual of the synagogue and Jewish house of study makes the Torah the core of Jewish consciousness around which the remainder of Scripture, liturgy, and tradition are organized—in this sense, *all* of Israel's sacred literature is only and endlessly Torah.

2. The Book of Job

While numerous non-Pentateuchal books of the Bible rank among the world's greatest literary classics (most notably Samuel, Isaiah, Psalms, and Song of Songs), none has had the power to arouse thought and controversy in quite the same way as the book of Job. Even in its role as a biblical book, Job is a uniquely "literary" product: it is the only one whose characters are held by tradition to be fictional—all others purport to represent historical personages; Jewish tradition maintains that Job was composed by Moses to illustrate the problem of human suffering and divine justice.

THE ORIGINS OF THE BOOK OF JOB

Biblical scholars actually place the book's authorship about 700 or 800 years after Moses—either shortly before or shortly after the beginning of Israel's Babylonian exile. Some even argue that the book is non-Israelite in origin, or at least that an Israelite author borrowed motifs from foreign sources. Controversy exists about the unity of the work, at least with respect to the origins of its elements: the book contains folkloric prose, philosophical poetry, ecstatic prophecy—still, their arrangement seems carefully crafted and thematically unified; only Elihu's speeches (chs. 32-36) seem an intrusion.

Job is a type of book known as Wisdom literature, a genre cultivated by the scribes and teachers of antiquity in many nations. There are three Wisdom books in the Hebrew Bible: Job, Proverbs, and Ecclesiastes, each with its unique style and theme. These books have in common an interest in the meaning of life, in human destiny and the justice of divine providence, and in the nature and purposes of human wisdom. There the similarity ends: Ecclesiastes is a sermon; Proverbs, a collection of aphorisms and short poems; Job, a dramatic dialogue. Of the three, Job is the most ambitious and the most passionately written.

A SYNOPSIS OF THE BOOK

The story of Job has several movements: (1) a prologue in which Job is introduced as a prosperous and godly man, God and Satan debate Job's character, and God, in order to test Job's faith, empowers Satan to strike Job with crime, natural disaster, loss of fortune, family bereavement, and painful disease—which he does; (2) the long central poem in which Job challenges, and his three "comforters," Eliphaz, Bildad, and Zophar, defend, God's justice; (3) the speech of Elihu, a young companion of the comforters, which repeats or underscores their defense of divine providence; (4) God's magnificent speech "out of the whirlwind," in which He catalogues the mysteries of Creation and challenges Job to demonstrate his knowledge of God's ways—at which Job falls silent; (5) an epilogue in which Job's comrades are rebuked and Job is rewarded and restored to his family, possessions, and former glory.

THE ISSUES OF THE BOOK OF JOB

The book's dramatic tension centers on the ideological conflict between Job and his companions. Believing, as orthodox practitioners of religion often do, that all human suffering has its roots in sin, the friends admonish Job repeatedly and in endless variations to acknowledge his mistakes and beg God's forgiveness (Job's wife, by contrast, urges him to "curse God and die"), to recognize that no person can be righteous before God, to see the close connection between sin and punishment, virtue and reward, to understand the efficacy of prayer, to perceive the blasphemy of his complaints, and to rely on the conventional wisdom. But Job repeatedly refuses to accept their mundane sentiments, calls their intimations slanderous, insists on his innocence, laments the shortness of life, and trembles at the august absoluteness of God's power, even as he hopes for God's willingness to allow him to plead his case. As the poem progresses, Job grows stronger in an almost legalistic certainty that God will hear the injustice of his situation, and that his sufferings will be vindicated.

THE VOICE FROM THE WHIRLWIND

God's answer (chs. 38ff.) is one of the most beautiful examples of biblical poetry, reminiscent of the latter chapters (especially 40-55) of the book of Isaiah. God does not answer Job directly, but shifts the whole dialogue from a human to a superhuman perspective—describing the awesome nature of His acts of Creation, the wondrous beauty and precision of His natural phenomena, and His mind-boggling mastery of the earth's most gigantic creatures. Paradoxically, after implicitly rebuking Job for failing to understand the mysteriousness of divine design, God then rewards him for having come closer to the truth than his companions in their conventional beliefs.

TEXTBOOK OR RADICAL THEOLOGY?

Why was this book written? Interestingly enough, it may originally have had a very simple purpose: to serve as a manual of the stock phrases by which people either challenge or defend divine providence. Egyptian and Babylonian parallels suggest that such "topic" books were a common part of the education of scribes, teachers, and counselors in the ancient world. That the editor of this particular theological thesaurus happened to have been gifted with literary genius was a lucky accident for the world, as well as for the Bible, which is one of the few collections of sacred literature to have its own built-in critique of conventional religion.

The timeliness of the book's composition (in the days of the First Temple's destruction and the first exile of Israel from her land) makes it the first in a tradition of writings that sought to plumb the reasons for Israel's misfortunes and human indignities. God's speeches represent the first appearance in Jewish tradition of the motif of "Creation's mysteries," which was to supply Jewish mystics of later eras with material for speculation. Satan appears for the first time in the book of Job as the arch-opponent of the virtuous, though here he is probably a mere heavenly functionary, God's prosecuting attorney.

A FORERUNNER OF KAFKA

The "legal" motifs of the book—the notion of a heavenly trial, a prosecuting attorney, a human defender arguing his own case before an absent tribunal—were to have their greatest impact on modern Jewish literature. The stories of Kafka take up this legalistic obsession, and the events of the Holocaust have given Job's challenges to God a special poignance. (For more about the book of Job, see the "Satan" entry in "At the Edges of Creation: Angels, Demons, and Beasts of Fancy.")

3. The Passover Haggadah

The Passover Haggadah is unique among Jewish classics for one reason: it is the only one that has been read by almost every Jew—young or old, male or female, observant or non-observant, Ashkenazi or Sephardi, rich or poor. It is the only Jewish work that explicitly includes everyone in its intended readership, including the stranger and the wayfarer. It is thus not only a book for converts—it is itself a conversion ritual, and, one could say, a *re*conversion ritual for those born Jewish. It serves this universal function by being short, by being oral, and by being a lively and almost mischievously varied reading experience. It is read from cover to cover, usually word-by-word, in a single evening, and all readers are given an active role. The Haggadah is the oldest and most fundamental curriculum of Jewish education, complete with audio-visual aids.

THE CORE OF THE HAGGADAH

The word *Haggadah* means "telling." The concept of a special category of "telling" of the Passover story derives from the biblical commandment (Exod. 12:26, 13:8, and 14; Deut. 6:20) to tell the story of the Egyptian Exodus to one's children throughout all generations. It is difficult to imagine any other story (there are a few, but not many) which one would consider obligatory for all future generations to tell. To make a story obligatory seems a contradiction, since a story should rarely stray beyond the domain of spontaneous invention. In fact, spontaneity is necessary to the telling of the Haggadah: the Haggadah only gives people a bare outline of the event, and some samples of the way that outline is to be embellished.

The core narrative is almost swallowed up in the embellishment—this core is very old, and very short: "A wandering Aramean was my father, and he went down into Egypt, and he sojourned there, few in number. There, he turned into a nation, great, mighty, and numerous. And the Egyptians dealt ill with us, and afflicted us, and laid upon us hard bondage. And we cried unto the LORD, the God of our fathers, and the LORD heard our voice, and saw our affliction, and our toil, and our oppression, and the LORD brought us forth out of Egypt with a mighty hand, and with an outstretched arm, and with great terrors, and with signs, and with wonders. And He has brought us into this place, and has given us this land, a land flowing with milk and honey." (Deut. 26:5-9)

This simple litany was originally a required ritual not at a Passover meal, but at the dedication of the first-fruits of one's seasonal harvest. A farmer in ancient Israel would take his grains and produce in a basket to the local priest (later, to Jerusalem), and, consecrating them, recite the story of the Exodus, concluding with: "and now, behold, I have brought the first-fruit of the land which Thou, O LORD, hast given me." It was a time of rejoicing, of meeting with strangers and kin, interfused with a deep and solemn sense of memory, equal in stature only to the Creation of the world. And yet the events celebrated are historical, political, human in character. Only the deliverance they represent is told as something divine—here, the verbs crystallize it: "The LORD heard . . . saw . . . brought us forth . . . brought us into . . . and has given . . ."

THE TORAH IN MINIATURE

This bare outline of a story is almost the entire Torah narrative in miniature. Some biblical historians believe it is the oldest stratum of ancestral memory in Israel, the armature on which the collection of the Pentateuch's stories grew. The recitation would seem to describe Abraham, who migrated from his father's house in Haran, Syria (Aram). In fact, it refers to Jacob, whose wanderings duplicate, more or less, those of Abraham—were we to begin Jacob's story at the end of his twenty years in exile, Jacob departing from the house of his Aramean uncle Laban. Like Abraham, Jacob settled for a time in Canaan, after leaving Syria; like Abraham, he is said to have been driven by famine into Egypt; and like Abraham, he (his posterity, that is) emerges from Egypt under divine protection, laden with gifts and tribute. With the Egyptian bondage, the pronouns of the recitation change, and refer to "our" toil in Egypt. The actual events of the deliverance are spoken of only metaphorically: ". . . with a mighty hand . . . an outstretched arm . . . great terrors . . . signs . . . wonders." And the story does not end until it is centered in "a land flowing with milk and honey."

A MODERNISTIC WORK

Around and through this simple core, the Haggadah is woven. And by contrast to the scriptural account, the post-biblical embellishments (free inventions in a spirit of "telling") seem baroque, sophistical, and improvised: rabbinical discussions, riddles, songs, anecdotes, games, condiments, toasts, blessings, and laudings. Truly, we find here a more modern idiom surrounding this most ancient of surviving credos.

The participants in the Haggadah reading are bidden to consider themselves liberated from slavery in Egypt. And so the Haggadah must convey the multiple lenses of later eras through which the memory of liberation is refracted. One hears the voice of the youngest child asking four questions about the commemorative meal (the *seder*); touches and tastes the symbolic foods that help enact the stories; learns of the "four sons," i.e., four types of children to whom the story is to be told (the biblical commandment occurs four times). One recalls the five rabbis who stayed up all night absorbed in their retelling of the story. One blesses over the wine, and drinks a full cup (four times throughout the *seder*, with a single "fifth" cup left for Elijah). One embroiders the narrative with details of slavery in Egypt, of the taskmasters, the bricks and the mortar, and the cruel edicts; multiplies the Egyptian plagues from ten to 250, but one spills thirteen (10 + 3) drops of wine in mourning for the Egyptians. One sings the tongue-twisting jingles, and recites the Hallel (the special psalms of praise sung on the festivals). One holds up the main tokens of the Exodus, the *sine qua non* of the retelling: the Paschal lamb shank (*pesach*) commemorating the first Passover meal; the unleavened bread (matzah) commemorating the flat cakes eaten in haste in going out of Egypt; the bitter herbs (*maror*) commemorating the sorrows of slavery; and (a later embellishment) the fruit-and-nut relish (*haroset*) commemorating the makeshift mortar of the slaves.

THE HAGGADAH GROWS SILENT AND LYRICAL

Finally, one eats: the center of the Haggadah is an empty space—a caesura in which a feast is served, and the most personal and non-textual telling of the story can begin. When the Haggadah resumes, the ceremonies remaining are much more lyrical: psalms, hymns, and numerologies—while, at length, a door is opened, and the future is invited in: Elijah, and the renewed hand of God. The Haggadah closes with the invocation: "Next year in Jerusalem!"

A ROMAN BANQUET?

This experience is textual in the fullest sense: an elaborate cross-weave of discrete and, in some ways, non-comparable moments. Some historians of the Haggadah note that many of the elements of the meal are modelled on the Roman banquet. Parts of the Haggadah resemble Greek and Latin symposium literature. These accounts, such as those of Plato, Plutarch, and Petronius, describe banquets at which nobles and social aspirants exchange discourses and riddles, consume libations, sing hymns, and participate in games. These Hellenistic affectations would seem to imply that the *seder* participants are now "free" persons, and so must adopt the idiom of more affluent civilized life—in truth, this display is partly satirical: the life of Roman nobility is as much a type of bondage as that of Egypt; in exaggerating its colors and flourishes, the Haggadah subtly subverts the cultural assimilation of the *seder* participants themselves, thus permitting one to "convert," as did many Egyptians, to the the tough, lean faith of the Israelite ancestors.

HOW PEOPLE FORM A PAGE

The Haggadah, in its oldest outlines, may be the earliest work of Rabbinic literature (see "The Talmud and Midrash," below)—its main portions evolved probably by the beginning of the Christian era. Part of the impact of the Haggadah on Jewish thought patterns can be seen by looking at the typography of a page of Talmud, Codes, or Bible commentary: the text is in the center, with the commentaries surrounding it—exactly the form of guests around a table. (Indeed, every meal is supposed to include discourse upon the Torah, and thus becomes a kind of text.) That multi-layered sense of text is learned annually by every participant in the reading of the Haggadah.

As for the adornment of the printed Haggadah text, it is not voices but pictures. Here, Judaism makes a curious departure from its normal tendency toward prohibition of imagery. The Haggadah is the most frequently illuminated Jewish book, with a rich history of printing traditions in, among other places, Spain, Italy, and central Europe. Again, this only helps to re-emphasize that the Haggadah pages keep spilling out into the surrounding world, and that its true columns of commentary are its outermost:

the successive generations of live people putting wine stains on its cover, and wrinkling its pages.

4. The Talmud and Midrash

The Talmud is not a single book, but rather dozens of separate treatises, encompassing many volumes and existing in two major versions: the Palestinian and the Babylonian. The latter is the longer of the two, and is accepted by Jews today as the more authoritative—probably because it deals more fully with the problems of Jewish life in the Diaspora.

THE ELEMENTS OF THE TALMUD

At the core of the Talmud is the *Mishnah*, the first major post-biblical Jewish law code (part of a domain called the Oral Law, in contrast to the Written), complied about 200 C.E. by Rabbi Judah the Prince, the leader of the Palestinian Jewish community. The *Mishnah* is also printed separately from the Talmud, and encompasses only one or two volumes. The body of discussion of, and additions to, the *Mishnah* is called *Gemara* ("Completion"), which evolved in both Palestine and Babylonia over the next 400 years (200-600 C.E.). The *Mishnah* and *Gemara*, together with the latter's major medieval commentaries, comprise the Talmud. (The word means "lore" or "teaching.")

The *Mishnah* is the first of several attempts in Jewish history to organize Jewish law topically. The laws occur in the Bible woven together with stories; as theoretical discussion of the laws grew, it was necessary to extract the laws from their narrative settings and to organize them into major categories, of which there are six: *Zera'im* ("Seeds," or agricultural laws), *Mo'ed* ("Festival," or calendrical laws), *Nashim* ("Women," or marital laws), *Nezikin* ("Damages," or civil laws), *Kodashim* ("Holy things," or Temple laws), and *Tohorot* ("Purities," or purification laws). There are sixty-three treatises (called *massekhtot*) in the Babylonian Talmud, distributed across these six major categories, which are called *sedarim*, "orders."

THE THICKET OF TALMUD

The *Mishnah* is written in Hebrew, and the *Gemara* mostly in Aramaic (a Syrian tongue, closely related to Hebrew—at the time of the Talmud's formation, it was the major spoken language of the Jews). The rabbinic discussions in the *Gemara* are lively and colloquial, for they often record transactions of meetings at the scholarly academies and the law courts. These discussions amount to a vast body of case-law, which was necessary to supplement biblical law in situations where the Bible spoke ambiguously or contradictorily. Talmudic discussion, however, is itself often convoluted and confusing. Sometimes it is difficult to know (without consulting later law codes) which stated legal opinion became the actual practice of Jewish communities. Sometimes discussion takes off on digressions and never returns to the main point. Sometimes the digressions have nothing to do with the main point, but are cited merely because it was thought useful to cite other teachings of a sage being quoted on the issue at hand.

PUNCTUATED OR PUNCTURED?

These difficulties are compounded by the manner in which the Talmud is printed—in columns of Hebrew print without punctuation, quotation marks, or paragraph divisions. Each page contains the Talmud text in the center and extensive blocks of commentary crowding the borders. At times the commentary is more difficult than the text it explains. It is said that some of the great geniuses of Talmudic scholarship in Eastern Europe in recent centuries could stick a pin through a word of *Gemara* and tell you what words the pin went through on subsequent pages.

TALMUD TEACHES THINKING

Why do Jews study Talmud? The Talmud is not helpful for knowing normative Jewish practice in any matter of law (the later law codes are better for this), but Talmud has always formed a part of traditional Jewish education because its legal dialectics sharpened the mind and developed skills of inference and analysis. The hair-splitting legalism of talmudic discussion seems to outsiders trivial and nitpicking, but it fostered an approach to reality that was flexible, sophisticated, and articulate. The Talmud's virtues are largely intellectual, but the richness and complexity of its discussions attest to the enormous spiritual commitment of Jews to fulfilling biblical law with care and thoroughness.

HIDDEN SEA-TREASURES

One by-product of the Talmud is perhaps of greatest interest to the untutored reader: *Gemara* often digressed from legal issues to record fascinating bits of folklore and history. This material is called *aggadah* ("story"), in contrast to *halakhah* ("law"), and in some chapters it occupies the bulk of the discussion. *Aggadah* is spread throughout the Talmud, but certain concentrations of it delve into specific subjects—for example, the ninth chapter of the treatise *Berakhot* ("Blessings") deals with dream interpretation; the tenth chapter of *Sanhedrin* ("Parliament"), with beliefs about the Messiah and the World to Come; the second chapter of *Hagigah* ("Festival"), with mysticism. One Mishnah treatise, *Avot* ("Ancestors"), is entirely aggadic, consisting of ethical sayings of the rabbis and litanies about miracles and study of Torah. The Talmud avoided no subject, and for this reason was often called "the Sea of Talmud."

THE MIDRASH

A body of literature closely related to Talmud is Midrash ("Interpretation")—this consists mostly of biblical commentary and other types of *aggadah*. In contrast to the Talmud, which is organized by legal topics, Midrash is usually organized by biblical books, sections, and verses. The Midrash, however, is actually a precursor of Talmud—it began as an endeavor to discuss and interpret biblical law. But as Talmud took over the burdens of legal discussion, the Midrash became devoted more and more to biblical interpretation and commentary, or to sermonic topics for festivals and special occasions. There are hundreds of Midrash collections, and dozens of major ones, of which a dozen or so are translated into English. The Midrash, like the Talmud, is not easy reading, but with some training and practice it is an enjoyable and rewarding experience, especially when pursued slowly and reflectively.

THE RABBIS

Talmud and Midrash are the main products of rabbinic Judaism, which arose early in the Christian era and continues into the present as the main form of Jewish religious life. The main classics of rabbinic literature were produced in late Roman antiquity and the early Middle Ages. Rabbinic literature reflects the Jews' contacts with the three major empires of the Western world before the modern age—the Roman Empire and its competing successors, Christendom, and Islam. The authors of this literature interacted with these empires at all levels of society, and had unique impressions of the ways people and governments wielded power. They were able to maintain a religious faith in the face of enormous obstacles and distractions. They thought clear-headedly about all life topics, and they valued as precious the instrument of human reason. Among themselves they abided by consensus, and they respected the minority opinion by advertising it and preserving it. They frequently imagined themselves and their leaders in a dialogue with the emperor of Rome (whoever he was, and whatever lands he ruled), but they entertained no illusions about his virtues or intentions. And their culture survived: they taught their children, and raised up disciples and teachers. For these accomplishments alone, they and their literature cannot be ignored.

5. The Siddur

If one had to choose a single book that expresses simply, concisely, and fervently the basic ideas and concerns of Judaism, one would have to pick—even over the Bible and the Talmud—the prayer book: the Siddur.

AN UNDERGROUND BOOK

Indeed, the Siddur has occasionally had to serve as an underground means of Jewish education where bans on Jewish study were in effect—a contemporary edition designed for Jews in the Soviet Union contains an encyclopedic compendium of religious laws, biblical and rabbinic passages, calendrical and life-cycle information, illustrations and specifications for ritual objects, and charts of local candle-lighting times. The Siddur has also at times taken prayers themselves underground: during the Spanish Inquisition, when certain prayers or formulas were banned, the Siddur adjusted by burying the forbidden material in passages unlikely to be checked by the censors.

This protean flexibility has always characterized the development of Jewish prayer. The Siddur has no form universal to all Jewish communities. There is an Ashkenazic, a Sephardic, and an Oriental ritual, and within these broad divisions further variations according to era, nationality, local community, and religious ideology. While all the versions are similar in their basic features, each has its unique manner of carrying out the Jewish obligation of prayer.

PRAYER IN JUDAISM

Prayer in Judaism is at least as old as the Bible. In Genesis it is stated that the earliest generations of mankind regularly invoked the name of God (Gen. 4:26). The supplications of the ancestors of Israel are recorded in some detail (e.g., Gen. 15:2ff., 24:12ff., 28:20ff.). Altogether the Bible records some eighty-five instances of prayer, not including the material of the book of Psalms, which is Judaism's oldest public prayer collection. The profusion of terms for prayer in the Bible suggests that the moods of prayer were many: calling, crying out, exclaiming, asking, seeking, imploring, ingratiating oneself, complaining, pouring out one's heart, blessing, thanking, etc. One prayed both for one's personal needs and for the welfare of one's community; for material blessings as well as for spiritual gifts such as wisdom or courage. Prayer was both individual and spontaneous, on the one hand, and public and liturgical on the other. In the days when the Temple and priesthood functioned in Israel, prayer was accompanied by sacrifice.

When the Temple was destroyed for a second time in 70 C.E., and the functions of priesthood were abolished, prayer came to substitute for sacrifice as the main avenue of communication between Israel and God. In the centuries that followed, as rabbinic Judaism developed, the rituals of the synagogue grew in importance. At first, there was a prohibition on writing prayers down—prayers were to be recited by heart—but by the era of the Talmud's completion the ban was ignored, and written prayer collections began to appear. The order of the synagogue service, however, had become more or less fixed several centuries earlier.

THE DAILY PRAYER SERVICE

There are three daily synagogue prayer services: Evening (*Ma'ariv*), Morning (*Shaharit*), and Afternoon (*Minhah*); the longest and most detailed is the *Shaharit*. The *Shaharit* service contains a long preliminary service, which includes miscellaneous blessings, scriptural and talmudic readings, psalms, and hymns. This segment often contained prayers and formulas from the main service that were banned by non-Jewish authorities. The core of the evening and morning services is divided into two main segments: the *Shema* and its blessings (see below), and the "Standing Prayer" (*Amidah*) or "Eighteen Benedictions" (*Shemonah Esreh*). The *Minhah* omits the *Shema*, and begins with the *Amidah*.

The *Shema* is a declaration of God's unity (Deut. 6:4: "Hear, O Israel: the LORD our God, the LORD is one."), and its recitation includes additional biblical passages that command allegiance to God and His ordinances. The *Shema* blessings are four in number, two before the *Shema* and two after: the first celebrates God's rule over the cycles of day and night; the second, God's love for Israel and bestowal of commandments that draw Israel into a close relationship to Him; the third, God's rescue of Israel from slavery in Egypt; the fourth (said only at night), God's nightly protection of the faithful and His watch over the Holy Land and Jerusalem.

The *Amidah* is said silently in a standing posture. It is a more detailed catalogue of God's acts of kindness and protection. Each ends with a formula called a *hatimah* ("seal"): "Blessed are you, O Lord [who does such-and-such] . . ." The whole *Amidah* is then repeated publicly by the prayer leader.

The prayer service concludes with a formula called the *Aleinu* ("[It is incumbent] on us [to praise God] . . .") and the recitation of the mourner's *Kaddish*. The *Kaddish* ("Sanctification") is written in Aramaic. It is not a "prayer for the dead" as such, but a declaration of God's holiness and transcendence that marks all times of transition—it originated in the talmudic academies to mark the end of study sessions. the *Kaddish* is actually recited several times throughout the service in several variations, the most important being the "scholar's *Kaddish*," recited after the study of texts, the "reception *Kaddish*," recited after the *Amidah* prayers, the "half-*Kaddish*," marking minor divisions in the service, and the "mourner's *Kaddish*." Mourners are either those who have recently lost a family member, or those marking the anniversary (*yahrzeit*) of a family member's death.

THE TEXTURE OF PRAYER

The language of Jewish prayer is flowing and repetitive, often accumulating long chains of synonyms for God's attributes and powers. Jesus criticized this type of prayer as wordy and hypocritical (see Matt. 6:7), but this misconstrues its nature. The stream of words is not intended to be a rational exposition of the worshipper's needs, much less a servile flattery of God, but an ecstatic outpouring of devotional fervor, in which each term blends into the next, while awakening half-conscious associations with biblical events and motifs. The Jewish mystics believed different prayers in the service to be addressed to specific aspects of divine being called *sefirot* ("ciphers," or divine potencies), and they mapped out the necessary *kavvanot* ("mystical intentions") with vowel markings and annotations in the text of prayer. Prayer, to them, was a garment of God.

The special texture of Jewish prayer is best perceived in the Orthodox and Hasidic synagogues, where there is an informal interplay of voices all reciting at different speeds and rhythms, alternating with the chants of the prayer leader, who is called the *sheliah tzibbur* ("representative of the congregation"). The non-Orthodox services tend to be more tightly regulated and more formal, with responsive readings in English led by a rabbi, alternating with the polished music of a cantor and choir. In recent years non-Orthodox groups called *havurot* ("fellowships") have sought to return to the traditional prayer service (though, unlike the Orthodox, admitting women to full participation), and many non-Orthodox synagogues have become more traditional (and informal) in style.

PRAYER ON SABBATHS AND FESTIVALS

There are special additions and substitutions to the service for Sabbaths and festivals, and a special prayer book called a *mahzor* ("[annual] cycle") contains the service for the High Holidays—the New Year and the Day of Atonement. These services include long, elaborate hymns called *piyyutim* ("poems"), which are among the most beautiful specimens of medieval Hebrew poetry.

A USER'S WORK

Like the Haggadah, the Siddur is a book that actively engages the reader in its use. Unlike the Haggadah, whose pleasures are at least partly intellectual and analytic, the Siddur is purely devotional in character—even where it presents technical material, such as the talmudic catalogues of Temple sacrifices, or the rabbinical "rules of interpretation of the Torah." The whole tableau of Jewish experience is melted into the steady, rhythmic, forward-moving currents of prayer and hymn. It is a meditative text whose repetition becomes a spiritual practice—not an invocation of vulnerable credos, but a gradually self-enhancing discipline cultivated over a lifetime.

6. Rashi's Commentaries

Rabbi Solomon ben Isaac (abbreviated as "Rashi") is considered the greatest Jewish commentator on Bible and Talmud. He lived in northern France (c. 1030-1105), and raised up a school of illustrious disciples and descendants (including Rabbenu Tam and the Rashbam) who are best known as the Tosafists ("Supplementers"—their talmudic annotations are printed on talmudic pages in columns opposite to Rashi's commentary). So indispensable is Rashi's work to traditional Jewish study of Bible and Talmud that one speaks of "the Rashi" to a given passage, as if it formed a part of the text itself. The typography used for Rashi's commentary came to be known as "Rashi script," even though Rashi did not invent it, and even though it is used for most Hebrew commentaries.

THE FRENCH WINE-MERCHANT

Rashi lived in Troyes, not far from Paris, in France's Champagne district. Jews of his milieu did not differ greatly in language, dress, or custom from their Christian neighbors. They spoke French, interacted freely with non-Jews, and until the Crusades (beginning toward the end of Rashi's life), maintained generally cordial relations with them. Like the rabbis of earlier times, Rashi earned his living not from his scholarship but from a secular trade—he was a wine merchant and owner of vineyards. Details of medieval commerce, technology, law, and social custom color his commentaries.

VINTAGE RASHI

Rashi was a descendant, on his mother's side, of a long line of scholars—according to one genealogy, going back to the talmudic sage Rabbi Yohanan the Sandalmaker. In his early adult years he studied Talmud in nearby Mainz (Mayence), Germany, with the disciples of the great legalist Rabbenu Gershom, whose influence on Franco-German Jewry was gratefully acknowledged by Rashi. Bible commentary of Rashi's time and milieu was dominated by Rabbi Moses the Midrashist of Narbonne, whom Rashi often cites. Rashi's education concentrated on the fundamentals: Bible, Talmud, Midrash, and those works of grammar and lexicography available in Hebrew. Science and philosophy, main preoccupations for Jews of the Islamic world, did not penetrate to northern France. Nor did mysticism, then being developed by the German Hasidim and the Provençal scholars, exercise any great hold on Rashi, though he was probably sympathetic to the mystics' piety and spiritual motives.

Rashi's commentaries are distinguished by their comprehensiveness (he was the first to write a commentary on nearly the whole of Scripture), their extreme conciseness, lucidity, appropriateness, and balanced judgments. He was less of an innovator in his Bible commentaries than in his talmudic. For the latter he meticulously established the correct reading of disputed texts, and often wrote original interpretations of legal issues. Much of our interpretation of the Talmud's punctuation is indebted to Rashi, which is why beginning students of Talmud find him indispensable. For Bible, Rashi generally preferred to base his commentaries on the oldest standard Midrash collections, expecially (for Pentateuch) Genesis Rabbah and the legalistic Midrashim: Mekhilta (on Exodus), Sifra (on Leviticus), and Sifré (on Numbers and Deuteronomy). He did not, however, merely parrot the rabbis: he paraphrased his sources rather than quoting directly, thus giving his work consistency of style; his genius for selection insured that only those midrashim that best suited the sense of the biblical verse would be adduced. The entire rabbinic world, refracted through the lens of Rashi's keen judgment, appears as a unified and informative body of lore on Scripture.

THE SIMPLE MEANING

At the root of Rashi's biblical commentaries was a belief that the biblical text must never become totally divorced from its plain (factual, historical, realistic) sense—the *peshat*. He was not hostile to more symbolic or sermonic interpretations of a text—the *derash*—but he usually indulged in the latter only after he was satisfied that the ordinary meaning had first been adequately explained. He often juxtaposed the two methods (making sure, whenever necessary, that each was properly identified), and only chose sermonic interpretations that best filled out the meaning according to the plain sense: "According to its plain sense, this means . . . and our rabbis of blessed memory have said . . ." is a frequent structure for his observations.

DID MOSES AND KING DAVID READ THE TALMUD?

Rashi's borrowings from the rabbis are especially pertinent where legal matters are at stake, and, in a number of places, he used his knowledge of Jewish law to explain a purely narrative passage: Moses made the Israelites drink the ground-up remnants of the Golden Calf idol (Exod. 32:20) in conformance with the law of a suspected adulteress (Num. 5:12-31); King David sent Uriah the Hittite to be killed in battle, knowing the latter had, as talmudic law prescribes for soldiers, issued Bathsheba a retroactive divorce writ in the event of his death, thus inadvertently (so David hoped) sparing David from suspicion of adultery with her.

A VARIABLE FOCUS

Rashi's commentary on the opening verse of Genesis supplies us with an admirable model of the range and suppleness of his commentator's eye: he begins by citing a Midrash that raises the question of why the Torah, a book of laws, begins with Creation, a question which is answered by the Psalm verse "He declared the power of His deeds to His people in giving them an inheritance from the [seven] nations [of Canaan]"—thus, the stories of Genesis establish Israel's title to the land. Rashi then goes on to cite a homily equating the word "beginning" with "Israel," thus to read "In the beginning . . ." as meaning "For Israel's sake. . . ." But finally he sets aside symbolic meanings, and zeros in on the much-disputed syntax of the verse: because of the vocalization of the first letter, Rashi concludes, the first words are not to be construed as "In the beginning, God created . . ." but rather "When God began to create . . ."—an offbeat interpretation of this famous verse, but one in fact preferred by some modern grammarians and translators.

Rashi saw no contradiction in juxtaposing more than one kind of interpretation, as long as each was well-chosen and a good complement to the rest. In the above example, Rashi moves from the largest literary and theological questions to the minutest and most precise of grammatical questions in the space of a few lines. His exceptional conciseness is best appreciated in his talmudic commentaries, where, adopting the method of a running commentator, he often simply inserts a word or two to fill out the elliptical syntax of a talmudic sentence—always the minimum number of additional words that will enable the reader to understand the sentence.

RASHI THE LINGUIST

Rashi had a sharp sense of linguistic reasoning. He often relied on minute subtleties of the text's traditional vocalization and punctuation, though occasionally differing from these markings where he saw reason to do so. He was, in his own way, a major lexicographer. He glossed obscure terms in Bible and Talmud by a number of means: by reference (for Bible) to biblical parallels, or to the Aramaic translations; by translation of the word into a more familiar Hebrew word; by a simple phrase; or by translation of the word into French. Rashi's French glosses (there are hundreds) are an invaluable guide not only to students of Hebrew and Aramaic, but to scholars of medieval French, who have used them to reconstruct some of the language otherwise lost or underdocumented.

TEACHING HOW TO READ

One's appreciation of Rashi grows with increased exposure to his work. His genius of epitomization, his range of erudition, his stress on the highest ethical and spiritual meanings of the text even as he delved into the most technical matters, his often colorful and dramatic filling-out of narrative nuances, and, above all, his conception of the world of Scripture and Talmud as a unified and timeless treasury of events and insights (Rashi popularized the rabbinic adage: "There is no before or after in Scripture")—all have given Rashi's commentaries their distinctive character and unsurpassed elegance. Merely to note the questions Rashi asks is to gain an invaluable lesson in the art of reading. His fluency and economy convey the misleading impression that his commentaries were easy to write—until one remembers that Rashi himself did not possess (at least, not on the printed page) "the Rashi" on which to rely.

7. The Kuzari

Until the Middle Ages the great works of Jewish literature were not generally written by individuals publishing in their own names.

Jewish "books" were anonymously edited compilations or anonymously written compositions often fictitiously ascribed to famous persons. The *Kuzari* had a known author, Judah Halevi, who in fact was already famous as a Hebrew poet, and while this was not the first Jewish book to be published by an individual, it was one of the first such books to be permanently revered as a popular classic.

RELIGIOUS DIALOGUE OR ORIENTAL ROMANCE?

The *Kuzari* is a gem of a work, a religious dialogue (modelled on Plato's dialogues) charmingly written and impeccable in its grasp of the subject matter it repudiates: philosophy. It also had the advantage of a best-seller setting: based on an event that had happened at the edge of central Asia four hundred years earlier, the dialogue purports to represent the conversations that preceded the remarkable conversion to Judaism of the king of the Khazars, along with many of his courtiers and subjects, members of a Turkic people of the Caucasus region. This event had been made known to the Jewish world in the tenth century by the Spanish Jewish diplomat Hasdai ibn Shaprut, and the notion of an Oriental king embracing Judaism captivated people's imaginations, especially in an era such as Halevi's (about 1140) when Jewish fortunes were declining.

FROM ARAB POET TO ZIONIST

Halevi himself grew up in the relatively tolerant city of Toledo, Spain, where he absorbed some of the best elements of Arab culture—science, medicine, philosophy (including its Greek sources), and poetry, as well as a thorough education in Bible, Talmud, and Midrash. He spoke Spanish and Arabic, wrote Hebrew poetry in Arabic rhythms, and wrote his prose in Arabic. He worked, as did many learned Jews of his time, as a court physician. Visiting Cordova, then under a strict Islamic rule, Halevi was moved to protest the harsh sanctions and levies against the Jewish community. Perhaps out of these discouraging events Halevi became Judaism's first great post-biblical Zionist, a classic formulator of the exilic Jewish yearning for the Holy Land. "My heart is in the East though in the West I live," one of his lyrics read, and in the *Kuzari*, his Jewish sage calls Israel "the heart of nations." Toward the end of his life Halevi set out on a visit to Palestine, getting as far as Damascus before disappearing from the historical record. (A legendary account depicts him slain by an Arab horseman at the gate of Jerusalem.)

"YOUR PRACTICE IS NOT ACCEPTABLE"

The dialogue of the *Kuzari* proceeds as follows: The Khazar king, a faithful practitioner of his ancestral pagan faith, dreams one night that an angel addresses him, who says: "Your intentions are acceptable to God; your practice is not." Troubled by this oracle, he first increases his pagan observances; but when the dream persists, he consults a philosopher, who advises him that God is above all emotion and human sentiment, does not bother with the behavior of individuals but only with the motions of the universe at large and the planetary system. The king need only cultivate a life of philosophic contemplation in order to unite his soul to the so-called Active Intellect, the highest state of illumination attainable by a human being, a domain shared with angels and the great philosophers and seers. His religion, says the philosopher, is a less important matter: he can choose one, invent his own, pick a "philosophical" creed, or profess none—as long as his heart and intentions are pure, his knowledge will suffice.

The king, remembering that the dream oracle had warned him about "practice," is dissatisfied with the philosopher's indifference to practice, and decides to consult a Christian and a Moslem, believing initially that the Jews are too poor and despised to possess the truth. But after hearing both Christian and Moslem acknowledge the source of their doctrines in the Law of Moses and the events of the Hebrew Scriptures, he resolves to consult a Jewish sage.

DEFENSE OF RELIGION OR OF JUDAISM?

The remainder of the dialogue—over 95 percent of the text—Halevi devotes to the answers of the Jewish sage (who is called *haver*, "companion" or "scholar"), who instructs the king fully in the ways of Judaism and eventually wins him as a convert. The bulk of the Jew's defense of his religion is directed against philosophy, although it might seem that the more formidable real-life foes would have been the rival religions. There is a good reason why Halevi prefers this strategy: he frees himself from making any direct attack on the other religions, which could be embarrasssing and dangerous, as well as detrimental to the cause of religion. He also allows Judaism to be the principal (and best qualified) champion of religion as such, for he lays bare a critical danger in the philosophical point of view that (in Halevi's opinion) only Judaism, of the three "revealed" faiths, has confronted most purely and directly: philosophy's failure to recognize that certain ethical principles have their origin in divine commandment, and as such are not merely "preferable" (as the philosopher would maintain) but obligatory in the highest sense—no amount of intellectual attainment can substitute for the reverence, the resoluteness, the personal and communal commitment these commandments must call forth. All classes of the faithful, from the least learned on up, participate in the task of preserving and transmitting that sacred heritage.

JUDAISM IS ITS OWN PROOF

It is no accident, then, that Halevi's scholar proves the existence of God and His commandments not by syllogism and argument, but by pointing to the fact of a religious tradition: so many Jews cooperating across so many generations, enduring so many hardships for so few worldly rewards, cannot have chosen to perpetuate an illusion or deception. A real event must lie at the root of their persistence: God's address at Mount Sinai, the precious memory of which is lovingly handed on, and expounded upon, by the descendants of Jacob.

Halevi's work is unique in medieval religious polemics in justifying Judaism by an appeal to the integrity and fervor of ongoing Jewish life; he thus avoids presenting his case in terms alien to the spirit of Jewish tradition. Not only does he decline the way of the philosophers, but also that of the pseudo-philosophical apologists of religion (called in Arabic the *Mutakallimun,* "spokesmen") who imitate philosophical arguments to provide a cloak of intellectual respectability for their beliefs.

SOLITUDE VS. SOLIDARITY

One should not assume from Halevi's anti-philosophical bias, or from the seeming informality of his dialogue's style and progression, that he was anti-intellectual or unsystematic. The structuring of the *Kuzari* is quite careful, and suggests that Halevi understood philosophy thoroughly, and that, as a former practitioner of its approach, he was not blind to its appeal. He does not simply allow the Jewish scholar to be his spokesman, nor does he present him in direct argument with the philosopher. The two do not confront each other, because it is impossible to weigh the claims of one against the other, and because to do so was a violation of the author's own religious scruples, which militated against raising doubts among fellow Jews. Without retreating into dogma or chauvinism, Halevi gently contrasts the philosophical and the religious way in a manner that compromises neither. The philosophical way must always remain one of solitude and inaction, the religious way one of communal solidarity and responsibility—a way of practice.

8. The Guide of the Perplexed

The author of the *Guide*, Moses Maimonides (1135-1204), is generally considered the greatest legal and philosophical mind of medieval Judaism, and one of the greatest Jewish thinkers of all time. He spent his mature years as a court physician in Cairo, and mixed a busy professional career with extensive communal and diplomatic responsibilities, somehow managing to write his two most important works, the *Mishneh Torah* (a legal compilation) and the *Guide* (a treatise on the esoteric meanings of Scripture), in the small amount of free time that remained. Those who customarily picture Maimonides as a contemplative hermit may be surprised to learn that he actually resisted the opportunity to take up a full-time scholarly life: though deeply shattered by the untimely drowning of his brother David in a sea storm, an event which also left him financially destitute, he resolutely refused to depend on a community stipend, as the Babylonian scholars of his time were accustomed to doing, preferring instead, in mid-life, to pursue his professional career in medicine.

MAIMONIDES MOVES EAST; JUDAISM MOVES WEST— A MEETING IN CAIRO

The *Guide of the Perplexed*, his final work, must be understood in the context of his earlier life and writings. The years before he settled in Cairo gave him vast experience of the Jewish, Christian, and Islamic communities of the Mediterranean: Spain, Provence, Morocco, Palestine, and finally Egypt. During those years he studied not only Jewish law and tradition, but also medicine, astronomy, and Arabic philosophy (as well as Greek philosophy through Arabic sources). In his era Jewish cultural life was beginning to shift westward from Babylonia to the Mediterranean and Europe, and Maimonides himself played a large role in this transition. He attacked the Geonim, the chiefs of the Babylonian Jewish academies, not only for living on scholarly stipends, but also for their piecemeal and pedantic solutions of legal and ritual questions after the fashion of talmudic scholarship, to which they claimed to be the heirs. Maimonides, influenced by the Islamic enlightenment, believed that uneducated Jews faced with any questions of law required a simple, comprehensive, and internally consistent reference work where all topics would be covered clearly and logically—a work that would supplant the Talmud as the chief legal authority for world Jewry.

REORGANIZING JEWISH LAW—AND THE CONTROVERSY IT PROVOKED

That work was the *Mishneh Torah*, a masterpiece of legal scholarship and the first great post-talmudic law code—a lucid and encyclopedic systematization of Jewish law in which lengthy talmudic debates were summarized in a few sentences, and wherever possible, logical and persuasive reasons were offered for the commandments and rabbinic decisions. The work had one flaw, from the perspective of conservative critics, one which the author himself acknowledged, but which brought him a flood of criticism nevertheless (the first wave of a protracted ideological battle that eventually became known as the "Maimonidean controversy")—that flaw was the author's omission from his work of source citations, parenthetic annotations equivalent to our modern device of footnotes. By this omission, Maimonides required readers to rely solely on his individual authority, which, however learned and trustworthy it might have been, was not at that time universally recognized—and Jewish tradition had, at least until then, steadfastly resisted the dominance of individual personalities. The work never achieved the authority Maimonides had hoped it would have, but today no student of Talmud can afford to ignore the cross-references to the *Mishneh Torah* that appear on every printed page of the Talmud. Moreover, Maimonides permanently shifted the center of gravity in legal discussion from the Talmud to post-talmudic codes (see "Shulhan Arukh," below), and the *Mishneh Torah* is generally better written than its more authoritative successors.

ORGANIZING JEWISH LORE—AN EVEN TOUGHER TASK

Maimonides had originally intended to do for biblical narrative and its rabbinic interpretation (*aggadah*) what he had done for Jewish law (*halakhah*), but as he progressed in this task he began to see that he could not address such a work to the lay reader, nor even to Jews whose main interest was the study of the Law. In the work that developed, *The Guide of the Perplexed*, he aimed at nothing less than a thorough attempt to coordinate the world-view of Scripture and tradition with the accepted scientific and philosophical knowledge of his time. Such a project could only be aimed at learned Jews, blameless in character and religious observance, whose reading of Islamic and Greek philosophy (especially that strand of philosophy dominated by Aristotle) had led them into "perplexity" about the truth of the Bible and the *aggadah* which could, in turn, prove damaging to their religious faith. For example, where philosophy spoke of a world that had existed from eternity, the Bible spoke of a universe created in six days; where philosophy saw God as supremely perfect, incorporeal, and abstracted from human qualities, the Bible and the *aggadah* portrayed God frequently with human imagery: eyes, ears, mouth, hand, heart, emotions, even needs and regrets. Such discrepancies had to be accounted for.

DID THE JEWS INVENT SCIENCE?

Maimonides did not attempt a mere "harmonization" of Scripture with philosophy, an activity which in his time was often pursued in an unsystematic and polemical fashion, and which often conveyed the impression that revealed religion had to apologize for its perspective. On the contrary, Maimonides believed that the truths of philosophic wisdom in fact had their own origins in God's revelation to Moses, and that Israel had been the first nation to cultivate science and philosophy—but that conditions of exile caused these teachings to be forgotten, or corrupted, or forced underground to become disguised as a "secret" doctrine passed on by word of mouth only between specially qualified sages. The Talmud had, in fact, spoken cryptically of two bodies of secret lore known as *Ma'aseh Bereshit* ("Work of Creation") and *Ma'aseh ha-Merkavah* ("Work of the Chariot")—oral commentaries on Genesis 1 and Ezekiel 1, respectively—which some have identified as mystical lore, but which Maimonides the rationalist identified as physics and metaphysics, respectively. It was the aim of the *Guide* to show that this secret tradition could be identified with philosophical knowledge, and that the Bible could be interpreted in accordance with its teachings.

DOES THE *GUIDE* MEAN WHAT IT SAYS?

It is here that the uniqueness of the *Guide* becomes apparent. Maimonides recognized that his subject matter was, after all, traditionally regarded as a secret doctrine, and he knew that its secret character had to be respected. He was painfully aware that his book could fall into the wrong hands, and so he contrived to speak esoterically and allusively throughout the work. The book presents itself unassumingly as a "commentary on certain words" occurring in Scripture (especially on corporeal terms describing God), and it seems to meander aimlessly from topic to topic. Only by carefully premeditated digressions and apparent contradictions does the author slowly and painstakingly construct the true subject of his book—which the careful reader must put together for himself from the "chapter headings" (i.e., often imperceptible hints, allusions, and details of format scattered throughout the work).

The amount of secret content to the *Guide* has been much debated, but it is clear that Maimonides sought to write a work whose very precision and intricacy would train a special kind of reader to prepare himself for the immense difficulties inherent in knowledge about God and His universe. A purging of a literal understanding of the Bible's imagery about God was an important cornerstone of this knowledge, but training, as well, in the uniquely delicate art of thinking esoterically (while continuing to teach and counsel the more literal-minded masses) was itself part of the *Guide*'s task. If that is a lifetime task, the *Guide* is, properly speaking, a book that takes a lifetime to read.

The *Guide*, needless to say, aroused an even more bitter phase of the "Maimonidean controversy" than his legal work, and the book was even banned and burned in some communities. But its influence, not only on later Jewish philosophy but on Jewish mysticism (as well as on currents of thought outside Judaism), has been incalculable. Moreover, it is fair to say that Maimonides brought system and order to a badly disorganized tradition plagued by geographical dispersion and sectarian dissension. Some have even argued that without his legal and philosophical genius, Judiasm would have disintegrated into scores of minor sects with no chance of survival. It is hard, in any case, to imagine a Judaism without Maimonides.

9. The Zohar

The Zohar ("Radiance") is the greatest classic of Jewish mysticism. It is a mystical commentary on the Torah, written in Aramaic, purporting to be the teachings of the second-century Palestinian rabbi Shimon bar Yohai. Legend relates that during a time of Roman persecution, Rabbi Shimon hid in a cave for thirteen years studying the Torah with his son. In the Zohar he is represented in somewhat more congenial surroundings, wandering through the Holy Land with his disciples, who commune with the natural beauties of the countryside, routinely encountering miracles and divinely endowed strangers, and pleasantly vying with one another in searching the Torah for ever deeper levels of meaning. The literary charm of this idyllic landscape is partly what endeared the Zohar to the Jewish world, and within a few generations after its first appearance (about 1285), it was revered as a sacred book.

WHO WROTE THE ZOHAR?

The Zohar is traditionally held to be the work of Shimon bar Yohai himself, "discovered" in the late thirteenth century by the Spanish Jew Moshe de Leon. In our own time the historian Gershom Scholem (noting, among other things, the Zohar's frequent errors of Aramaic grammar and its suspicious traces of Spanish words and sentence patterns) has offered persuasive demonstration that Leon himself was most likely the author, a notion still disputed by many Orthodox Jews. One way or the other, the Zohar is a work of genius which profoundly altered Jewish religious life and thought, spread mysticism to the masses, and created a kind of national folklore rooted in mysticism. Many key events in later Jewish history, such as the disastrous "Messiahship" of the seventeenth-century Jewish mystic Shabbatai Zevi, the rise of Hasidism in the eighteenth century, and (in Scholem's opinion) the rise of secular Judaism and Zionism, can be seen as shaped to some extent by the influence of the Zohar and its interpreters.

THE KABBALAH

While mystical speculation in Judaism has existed in one form or another since late antiquity, the particular brand of Jewish mysticism known as "Kabbalah" (literally, "Tradition"), of which the Zohar is the best example, grew up in Spain and southern France in the late twelfth century. The first kabbalists were students of philosophy who were troubled by the differences between the philosophical picture of the world (which stressed the world's existence from eternity, God's abstractness from all human qualities, and the absence of any particular concern on God's part with the behavior of individuals) and the biblical picture (which stressed the creation of the world in six days, the similarity of God to those creatures made "in His image," and God's passionate concern with the affairs of the world and the moral behavior of individuals).

The philosopher Maimonides (see *Guide of the Perplexed* above), a contemporary of the first kabbalists, tried to solve this delimma by showing how the Bible was itself a source of philosophic knowledge disguised as simple stories with two meanings: one for naive readers, one for philosophers. This solution was not satisfactory to the kabbalists, who felt that the "naive" tenets of the popular faith had a deeper meaning than Maimonides was willing to grant. Rather than saying that the Bible "adjusted" itself to human reality by portraying God in physical and human terms, the kabbalists preferred to see all of the human reality portrayed in Scripture as itself a key to the inner life of God. Abraham, Isaac, and Jacob, the people Israel, the laws of the Torah, the Holy Land, the exile of Israel, the yearning for the Messiah, the journey of the human soul through the life of the body—all were "aspects" of God Himself.

THE DIVINE EMANATIONS (*SEFIROT*)

These aspects of God came to be called *sefirot* (literally, "ciphers"), that is, powers of God, or stages of God's unfolding. Though the *sefirot* are only ten (like our ten digits), they have innumerable names and disguises: "lights," "garments," "fountains," "days," "measures," "limbs," "secrets," etc. All the divine names and many of the human names and key words of Scripture could be read as one or another *sefirah*. The kabbalists thus read the entire body of Jewish sacred writings (and all the rituals of Jewish daily life) as a map of God's being—although, bearing in mind Maimonides' warning that God's deepest level of existence is devoid of imagery, they applied the doctrine of *sefirot* only to the "revealed" aspect of divine being; the unrevealed aspect they called the *En-Sof* (the "Boundless" or "Infinite"), a realm where no human thought or language could reach. The hidden and revealed aspects were seen as two sides of the same reality, like a candlewick and flame, or like a white light and a rainbow.

THE EMISSARY IN DISGUISE

The Zohar's genius lay in its ability to convey these difficult and daring ideas in the form of charming stories. A typical Zohar story might proceed as follows: Two sages from the circle of Rabbi Shimon are riding in a donkey cart, and one asks the other for some words of Torah. The other opens his discourse in typical midrashic fashion with a quotation from the prophets, psalms, or wisdom books, gradually unfolding the verse's inner meaning as a particular configuration of divine aspects (*sefirot*), then tying its mystical meaning, sometimes through puns, anagrams, and numerology, to a Torah verse, casting that verse in a novel mystical light. The companion then exclaims in awe at this hitherto undiscovered meaning of the Torah, and the two weep joyously at having uncovered a sublime mystery. Then, unexpectedly, the driver of the donkey cart, who might be the prophet Elijah in disguise, humbly turns to the sages and asks permission to offer his own interpretation—which, in turn, is an even more striking and ingenious revelation, at which the companions, realizing that they are in the presence of an emissary from the upper worlds, fall before him in humility, joyfully weeping, and bless God for permitting such wonders to take place.

THE INNER LIFE OF GOD

But it is the ideas and imagery of their discourse that most rivet one's attention. Behind the surface of biblical narrative (while still at the surface) is shown the swirling play of divine inner life. At Creation, God not only brings light into being, He brings forth *Himself* as light—first, as a dark cloud of primordial will, then as a tiny pinpoint of diamondlike brilliance, in which are embryonically contained all colors and qualities of the created world, then as a full blossoming of the rainbow of attributes; thence the rain of divine life descends upon the lower worlds, balanced between love and justice, speaking out as the God of Sinai, of the sacred name YHWH (the Tetragrammaton); then, concentrated into the power of insemination called *El-Hai* ("Living God") or *El-Shaddai* ("God Almighty"), uniting in love with God's feminine side, the *Shekhina*, prototype of all souls wandering through reincarnations, as she wanders through the nations in the form of the "Assembly of Israel" (*Kenesset Yisrael*). When Sabbath peace prevails (here the liturgy and calendrical cycle enter into this matrix of symbolism), the *Shekhina* and the upper realms of divine life are one—but in times of transgression, she falls prey to demonic powers in the material world, and wreaks havoc in the world, on evildoers and the faithful alike.

RESCUING A DAMSEL IN DISTRESS

But Israel, through prayer, study of Torah, and acts of kindness, can mitigate the bad effects, and so move the upper worlds themselves to compassion toward the exiled Presence, and bring on the light of the long-awaited king of Israel, restoring heaven and earth to harmony. Israel's ritual life, especially by virtue of the divine names and epithets invoked, is a map of the upper (and inner) worlds. The soul itself is a microcosm of the divine emanations. The passion of lovers recorded in the Song of Songs and the union of a married couple on the Sabbath are expressions of the harmony between the masculine and feminine sides of God. Much of the imagery of Kabbalah is influenced by medieval romance and troubador poetry: the *Shekhina* is a damsel in distress, and her partner, called "Beauty" (*Tiferet*), is a knight in shining armor. An almost Franciscan sense of wonder at the marvels of nature and God's creation pervades the discourse of the Zohar.

In this manner, the Zohar encouraged a new adventure in Jewish learning that was to invigorate traditional Jewish life for centuries to come. Jews unlearned in Talmud or philosophy were given, as readers of the Zohar, a sense of participation in the sublime mysteries of Creation and the unfolding of divine life. As the Zohar put it: "For each new meaning found in the Torah, a new heaven is created on high!"

10. The Shulhan Arukh

The importance of the *Shulhan Arukh* ("Prepared Table") in Jewish life may seem at first glance unrelated to its literary merits, since it is, before all else, a law code; indeed, a dry and technical one, occupied with little else than the correct practice, in ritual and daily life, obligatory for the Orthodox Jew. Yet the particular literary form of this guide was the outcome of almost a thousand years of debate over the most appropriate form for a Jewish law code, one that could both teach the law and serve as a reference work in legal cases. While each stage of that debate was shaped by contemporary circumstances, its unfolding was to some extent determined by the stages that had preceded, and the most remarkable feature of this complicated history is that at no point—including the present—has there been a Jewish law code regarded as satisfactory and authoritative in all respects. Each attempt to solve a problem in the existing codes yielded new problems, new disputes, and new attempts to design a more perfect code, although for the past four hundred years, at least, the *Shulhan Arukh* seems to have come closer than any other to being an enduring code. How this came about is an intriguing story that must be told if the *Shulhan Arukh* is to be properly understood.

IS A PERFECT LAW CODE POSSIBLE?

Three main criteria for a good law code are: (1) it must display its rootedness in the oldest legal sources—for Judaism, the Bible and the Talmud; (2) it must reflect the most important legal opinions on a given issue during the intervening centuries, including the most recent authoritative rulings; (3) it must be clear and concise, presented in a format easy to learn and teach. It is easy to see that the first two criteria are likely to conflict with each other, and the third is likely to clash with the first two. The history of Jewish law reflects the continual opposition of these three criteria.

The impulse to reorganize Jewish law into new codes is as old as the Bible itself. Biblical law is not a single code but several overlapping ones (see "The Torah," above), and at least one of them, the code of Deuteronomy (the name means either "copy" or "recapitulation" of the law) is a wholesale revision of earlier codes. The first post-biblical attempt to rearrange biblical law into a topical code reflecting post-biblical legal decisions (the Oral Law) was the *Mishnah* (again, the word means "duplicate"), assembled by Rabbi Judah the Prince about 200 C.E. This code, though phrased in clear and concise language, did not remove all ambiguities from the law, nor could it prevent the normal evolution of law that time and local custom bring about. Thus, additions to the *Mishnah* were necessary, and by 600 C.E. its amplified version, known as the Talmud, was canonized as the definitive code for world Jewry (see "The Talmud and Midrash" above).

CHANGING ATTEMPTS TO PACKAGE JEWISH LAW: RIF, RAMBAM, AND ROSH

Yet, as one might expect, legal evolution continued in two opposed directions: expansion and distillation. The Geonim, leaders of Babylonian Jewry, issued responsa (*teshuvot*) to answer questions about legal practice, and novellae (*hiddushim*), that is, new interpretations and implications, to cover areas left unspoken or implicit in the Talmud. They also made several attempts to issue *pesakim* ("decisions"), digests of talmudic law, following the order of talmudic discussion. The most important of these was the work of the eleventh-century R. Isaac Alfasi (also known by his initials as the "Rif"), and it is still printed at the back of talmudic volumes—serving as a kind of skeletal outline of each treatise that greatly facilitates study of Talmud.

A century after Alfasi, Maimonides (see "The Guide of the Perplexed," above) decided that the time had come for a new codification—one that rearranged talmudic law into a clearer conceptual order, supplying only the outcome of each talmudic discussion, with a brief, pithy explanation of its reason or import, and omitting the names of the teachers of each legal opinion. The result was the *Mishneh Torah* (again: "Recapitulation of the Torah"), which Maimonides hoped would serve as a universal guide to legal practice. Instead, it became the focus of bitter polemics, as Jewish scholars, especially in Europe, attacked its omission of sources and found fault with its formulations even as they admired its brilliant scholarship. One additional defect of the work, in their opinion, was its failure to reflect the practices of Franco-German ("Ashkenazi") Jewry.

A prominent fourteenth-century scholar,

Asher ben Yehiel (known as the "Rosh"), who migrated from Germany to Spain, was one of the few jurists familiar with the practices of both Ashkenazi and Sephardi Jewry. He had absorbed the teachings of Rashi and the Tosafists, the great legal commentators of medieval France, who until his time had been relatively isolated from the cosmopolitan world of Spanish and Oriental Jewry (see "Rashi's Commentaries," above). He too found fault with Maimonides' code, and published an edict that no legal decision could be based on it unless the person deciding first traced its sources in the Talmud and reasoned independently on the basis of his own contact with the sources. The "Rosh" believed that codes such as the *Mishneh Torah* stifled the independence of decision-making necessary to a thorough application of the law to new circumstances.

THE GROUND-PLAN OF THE *SHULHAN ARUKH*

The "Rosh's" son, Jacob ben Asher, undertook to develop a new code that would not have this pitfall. He chose to outline concisely the talmudic discussion of each law, then render a decision, usually based on the authority of Alfasi or (where Maimonides disagreed with Alfasi) his own father, the "Rosh." The work that resulted, the *Arba Turim* ("Four Rows"), rearranged the law into four major categories: *Orah Hayyim* ("Way of Life"), covering prayer and daily life, *Yoreh Deah* ("Teacher of Knowledge"), covering dietary and purification laws, *Eben ha-Ezer* ("Rock of Partnership"), covering marital relations, and *Hoshen Mishpat* ("Breastplate of Judgment"), covering civil law. This format, in contrast to Maimonides' code, dealt only with laws in effect outside the land of Israel, and since the destruction of the Temple. It eventually formed the ground-plan of the *Shulhan Arukh*.

MYSTIC CONVERSATIONS WITH THE LAW

Ironically, the *Shulhan Arukh*'s author, the sixteenth-century Spanish-Palestinian Jew Joseph Karo of Safed, never regarded the *Shulhan Arukh* as his main work, nor did his contemporaries. Karo's masterpiece was the *Bet Yosef* ("House of Joseph"), a detailed commentary on the *Arba Turim*, scrupulously annotating the talmudic sources underlying each legal issue. Only later did Karo recognize the pedagogical value of a simple digest of this work, and so produced the *Shulhan Arukh*. The latter is a restrained and laconic work, presenting no innovations of the law, but modestly resting on the decisions of the "three pillars" of legal authority: Alfasi, Maimonides, and the "Rosh." Karo's removal of personal perspective from his code is all the more striking when one reads his autobiographical writings, where he shows himself to be a fervent mystic, keeping a twenty-five year diary of dream conversations with a preaching voice called a *maggid,* who embodied "the spirit of the *Mishnah*," and who admonished him on his personal ethical and spiritual conduct.

A LEGAL CODE AS POETRY?

English-speaking readers can best avail themselves of the contents of the *Shulhan Arukh* by reading the one-volume translation of Solomon Ganzfried's *Kitzur Shulhan Arukh* ("Abbreviated Shulhan Arukh") by Hyman E. Goldin.* While only an abbreviation of a work that itself had begun as an abbreviation, the *Kitzur* conveys enough of the contents of the original to serve at least as an introduction to Karo's work. It might seem strange to characterize a work as dry and technical as Karo's as a worthwhile reading experience in its own right, but in fact it is. In its laconic reduction of the complicated history of Jewish law to a distillation of concrete practices, the work has a precision that resembles that of poetry. It conveys the nuts-and-bolts of Jewish legal and ritual practice in a manner far more palpable than could be reconstructed by historians. It is intriguing for the way that it segments and synthesizes daily Jewish life into a meaningful pattern, in which each individual legal ruling has a separate life as an image, such as the following: "One must listen carefully to the reciting of the *kaddish* and to make all responses with zeal, especially so when responding *Amen, yehe shemeh rabba* (Amen, let His great name, etc.). It is well to respond *Amen, etc.* in a loud voice, because by doing so one will frustrate all satanic malingers and nullify even a seventy-year-old evil decree. Nevertheless, one should not scream too loud, so as not to cause people to mock him and thereby cause them to commit a sin." (Ganzfried, 1:49)

Or better yet, perhaps: "We must take extreme care not to deceive one another. If anyone deceives his neighbor, whether a seller deceives the buyer, or a buyer deceives the seller, he transgresses. . . . According to our Sages (Shabbat 31a), this is the first question that one is asked when brought before the Heavenly Court: 'Hast thou been dealing honestly?' " (Ganzfried, 2:36)

A CODE FOR TWO COMMUNITIES

The *Shulhan Arukh* would have gone the

*S. Ganzfried, *Code of Jewish Law (Kitzur Shulhan Arukh)—A Compilation of Jewish Laws and Customs*, tr. Hyman E. Goldin (New York: Hebrew Publishing Co., 1961)—four volumes bound as one.

way of earlier law codes were it not for two important factors: (1) increased persecution of Jewry created conditions requiring the spread of learning in compact manuals and digests; (2) a prominent Polish scholar, Rabbi Moses Isserles (the "Ramah"), indirectly lent his prestige to the work by issuing annotations adapting its formulations (which, like those of Maimonides, were criticized as "too Sephardic") to the needs of Ashkenazi Jewry. The conciseness, flexibility, and informativeness of the composite product that emerged have made the *Shulhan Arukh* the normative code today for most of the world's Orthodox Jews. Whether the enormous political, economic, and technological changes of the past century will necessitate a new code remains to be seen.

—J.R.

A LOOK AT THE BIBLE: CHAPTER AND VERSE

There are thirty-nine books in the Bible, separated into three divisions: Torah, Nevi'im (Prophets), and Ketuvim (Writings). The Hebrew acronym of these is *Tanakh*.

Torah:
Genesis
Exodus
Leviticus
Numbers
Deuteronomy

Nevi'im:
Joshua
Judges
1 Samuel
2 Samuel
1 Kings
2 Kings
Isaiah
Jeremiah
Ezekiel
Hosea
Joel
Amos
Obadiah
Jonah
Micah
Nahum
Habakkuk
Zephaniah
Haggai
Zechariah
Malachi

Ketuvim:
Psalms
Proverbs
Job
Song of Songs
Ruth
Lamentations
Ecclesiastes
Esther
Daniel
Ezra
Nehemiah
1 Chronicles
2 Chronicles

The number of letters in the Torah is 304,805, divided as follows:

Genesis	78,064
Exodus	63,529
Leviticus	44,790
Numbers	63,530
Deuteronomy	54,892

The most frequent letter in the Torah is the *yod*, which appears 31,530 times.

The least frequent letter in the Torah is the final *peh*, which appears 834 times.

The middle letter of the Torah is the *vav* in *gahon* ("belly") in Leviticus 11:42 (the "belly button" as it were).

The number of verses in the Torah is 5,845, divided as follows:

Genesis	1,534
Exodus	1,209
Leviticus	859
Numbers	1,288
Deuteronomy	955

The middle verse of the Torah is Leviticus 8:8: "He put the breastplate on him, and put into the breastplate the Urim and Thummim." The middle words of the Torah are *darosh doresh* in Leviticus 10:16.

Of the two versions of the Ten Commandments found in the Torah, the one in Exodus 20 has 172 words while the one in Deuteronomy 5 has 189 words.

All the letters in the Hebrew alphabet are found in Esther 3:13.

The longest verse in the Tanakh is Esther 8:9 (forty-three words).

The shortest verses in the Tanakh are 1 Chronicles 1:1 and 1 Chronicles 1:25, each with only three words and nine letters.

There are fourteen three-word verses in the Torah:

Genesis 25:14, 26:6, 43:1, 46:23 (the shortest, with 10 letters), 49:18
Exodus 1:3, 22:17, 28:13
Leviticus 14:55, 14:56
Numbers 6:24, 26:8
Deuteronomy 28:5, 28:17

The shortest prayer in the Tanakh, consisting of five words and eleven letters, is found in Numbers 12:3, recited by Moses for his sister Miriam, whom God had afflicted with leprosy: *El na refah na lah* ("Please, God, heal her, please").

The shortest chapter in the Tanakh is Psalm 117.

The longest chapter in the Tanakh is Psalm 119.

There are two books in the Tanakh which do not mention God's name: Song of Songs and Esther.

There are 1,299 Hapax Legomena in the Tanakh (words which occur only once). Of these, 411 are absolute, not even traceable to familiar root words. There are none in the books of Joshua, Obadiah, and Haggai. The greatest number occur in Isaiah and Job (sixty each).

—R.A.S.

ORDERS AND TRACTATES OF THE MISHNAH AND TALMUD

	Mishnah	Babylonian Talmud		Jerusalem Talmud	
	No. of Chapters	No. of Folios	Folios Munich Ed.	No. of Folios	Subject matter
Berakhot	9	64	19	14	Benedictions
Pe'ah	8	—	3	7	Gleanings (Lev. 19:9–10)
Demai	7	—	3	6	Doubtfully tithed produce
Kilayim	9	—	4	7	Diverse kinds (Deut. 22:9–11)
Shevi'it	10	—	4	7	The Sabbatical Year (Ex. 23:10–11)
Terumot	11	—	4	9	Heave offering (Lev. 22:10–14)
Ma'aserot	5	—	2	5	Tithes (Num. 18:21)
Ma'aser Sheni	5	—	3	5	Second tithe (Deut. 14:22ff.)
Hallah	4	—	2	4	Dough offering (Num. 15:17–21)
Orlah	3	—	2	4	The fruit of young trees (Lev. 19:23–25)
Bikkurim	3	—	3	3	First fruits (Lev. 26:1–11)
Shabbat	24	157	28	18	The Sabbath
Eruvin	10	105	17	9	The fusion of Sabbath limits
Pesahim	10	121	18	11	Passover
Shekalim	8	—	6	7	The Shekel dues (Ex. 30:11–16)
Yoma	8	88	16	8	The Day of Atonement
Sukkah	5	56	9	5	The Feast of Tabernacles
Bezah	5	40	11	5	Festival laws
Rosh Ha-Shanah	4	35	7	4	Various new years, particularly Rosh Ha-Shanah
Ta'anit	4	31	8	7	Fast days
Megillah	4	32	9	7	Purim
Mo'ed Katan	3	29	7	4	The intermediate days of festivals
Hagigah	3	27	6	5	The Festival offering (Deut. 16:16–17)
Yevamot	16	122	24	16	Levirate marriage (Deut. 25:5–10)
Ketubbot	13	112	20	12	Marriage contracts
Nedarim	11	91	10	7	Vows (Num. 30)
Nazir	9	66	8	8	The Nazirite (Num. 6)
Sotah	9	49	11	9	The suspected adulteress (Num. 5:11ff)
Gittin	9	90	16	7	Divorce
Kiddushin	4	82	14	9	Marriage
Bava Kamma	10	119	22	7	Torts
Bava Mezia	10	119	20	6	Civil Law
Bava Batra	10	176	21	6	Property law
Sanhedrin	11	113	24	14	Judges
Makkot	3	24	5	3	Flagellation (Deut. 25:2)
Shevu'ot	8	49	9	7	Oaths
Eduyyot	8	—	4	—	Traditional testimonies
Avodah Zarah	5	76	13	7	Idolatry
Avot[3]	5	—	2	—	Ethical maxims
Horayot	3	14	4	4	Erroneous ruling of the court (Lev. 4:22ff)

	Mishnah No. of Chapters	Babylonian Talmud No. of Folios	Folios Munich Ed.	Jerusalem Talmud No. of Folios	Subject matter
Zevahim	14	120	21	—	Animal offerings
Menahot	13	110	21	—	Meal offering
Hullin	12	142	25	—	Animals slaughtered for food
Bekhorot	9	61	13	—	Firstlings (Deut. 15:19ff.)
Arakhin	9	34	9	—	Vows of valuation (Lev. 27:1–8)
Temurah	7	39	8	—	The substituted offering (Lev. 27:10)
Keritot	6	28	9	—	Extirpation (Lev. 18:29)
Me'ilah	6	22	4	—	Sacrileges (Lev. 5:15–16)
Tamid[3]	7	9	4	—	The daily sacrifice (Num. 28:3–4)
Middot[3]	5	—	3	—	Measurements of the Temple
Kinnim[3]	3	—	2	—	The Bird offering (Lev. 5:7ff.)
Kelim[3]	30	—	11	—	Uncleanness of articles
Oholot (Ahilot)	18	—	7	—	Uncleanness through overshadowing (No. 19:14–15)
Nega'im	14	—	7	—	Leprosy (Lev. 13,14)
Parah	12	—	5	—	The Red Heifer (Num. 19)
Tohorot	10	—	5	—	Ritual cleanness
Mikva'ot	10	—	5	—	Ritual ablution
Niddah	10	73	14	4	The menstruant
Makhshirin	6	—	3	—	Liquid that predisposes food to become ritually unclean (Lev. 11:37–38)
Zavim	5	—	2	—	Fluxes (Lev. 15)
Tevul Yom	4	—	2	—	Ritual uncleanness between immersion and sunset (Lev. 22:6–7)
Yadayim	4	—	3	—	The ritual uncleanness of the hands
Ukzin[4]	3	—	2	—	"Stalks" parts of plants susceptible to uncleanness

[1] The number given is the last page number. The pagination, however, always begins with page 2; one page should therefore be deducted.
[2] The number of pages is given in accordance with the Krotoschin edition.
[3] There is Tosefta to all the tractates with the exception of *Avot, Tamid, Middot, Kinnim, Kelim*. In the Tosefta, *Kelim* is divided into three sections, respectively called *Bava Kamma, Bava Mezia* and *Bava Batra*.
[4] The tractates are generally arranged in the orders according to the descending numbers of chapters.

20 IMPORTANT JEWISH BOOKS WRITTEN SINCE 1950

The following is a circumscribed list of some of the more significant Jewish books published in America during the past three decades. It does not pretend to be perfectly balanced and representative. For example, it does not include new translations of classic works (like the Jewish Publication Society's translations of various books of the Bible), prayer books, reference works (notably, the monumental *Encyclopaedia Judaica*), anthologies, or new editions of primary source materials.

In addition, the limitations of space make it impossible to list the many important Jewish scholarly works of recent years. Among literary works, it was not possible to single out any one volume by Isaac Bashevis Singer (*Satan in Goray, The Slave*, etc.) or by Bernard Malamud (*The Fixer, The Assistant*, and others), although their works are certainly no less important than those listed here.

The books listed were written chiefly for a popular audience. They are not all great books, and they are not all well-known. But all of them have touched the hearts and minds of American Jewish readers, and for that alone they deserve to be recognized.

The Diary of a Young Girl
by Anne Frank.
Doubleday, 1952.

As soon as it appeared in America (with an introduction by Eleanor Roosevelt), Anne Frank's diary became an instant classic in this country, as it had been in Europe since its publication in 1947. In 1952 American Jews still knew little about the Holocaust, and this book was a fittingly gentle introduction to it; it would be another eight years before Elie Wiesel's *Night* brought to light some of the more terrible aspects of those years.

Anne Frank's diary is the story of an adolescent, fairly assimilated Jewish girl, who was born in Germany in 1929. In 1933 her family fled to Amsterdam, and when, in 1942, the Jews of that city began to be deported, Anne's father took the family into hiding in the rooms behind his business. They remained there for over two years, together with four other Jews. Anne, who hoped to become a writer, kept a diary of this period, which was found by the gentile friends who had hidden the family. Many publishers turned it down before it was finally published in 1947, two years after Anne had died in Bergen-Belsen.

"Anne Frank's diary is too tenderly intimate a book to be frozen with the label 'classic,'" wrote Meyer Levin in a front-page review in *The New York Times Book Review*. "And yet no lesser designation serves." Later Levin wrote what turned out to be a controversial play about Anne Frank, rejecting the 1956 Broadway dramatization because it paid too little attention to the Jewish aspects of the story.

Marjorie Morningstar
by Herman Wouk.
Doubleday, 1955.

Marjorie Morningstar is the story of a "Jewish-American Princess" growing up on New York's Central Park West (although wishing to live on even posher Central Park South). Chronicling her romantic adventures from adolescence to her ultimate destiny as a suburban housewife with four children, this book articulated for the first time what has subsequently become the JAP stereotype, with its emphasis on the superficial—clothes, address, ostentatious wealth, and a high-status professional husband. As the female counterpart to Alexander Portnoy, Marjorie portrays the Jewish woman attracted by the erotic and exotic fantasy of the non-Jewish world.

Little read today, *Marjorie Morningstar* had an enormous following in the 1950's and was one of the earliest of Jewish fiction best-sellers, a novel with specifically Jewish characters and broad popular appeal. At 565 pages, however, many readers found it long and tedious. *The New Republic* called it "a soap opera with psychological and sociological props;" while *The New Yorker* was more direct, terming the book "a damp and endless tale."

There were thousands of readers, however, who found Marjorie an appealing figure and the book a memorable novel; it was praised by one reviewer for being "a Jewish *Vanity Fair*." It is of interest today mostly as a period piece, for by contemporary standards the novel seems unusually dull in its plot and utterly conventional in its values.

God in Search of Man: A Philosophy of Judaism
by Abraham Joshua Heschel.
Farrar, Straus & Giroux, 1955.

More than any of his other works, this book constitutes Heschel's articulation and interpretation of Jewish religion, which he perceives as being grounded not in man's need for cosmic order but rather in God's search for human righteousness and spiritual yearning. Here, as in his other works, Heschel transforms English into a spiritual language, infusing the pages with the revived Presence of the living God of the Bible.

Always presenting a new twist or a radical perspective, Heschel levels a devastating attack on religious behaviorism and "pan-halakhism," the all too prevalent attitudes that define, confine, and reduce Judaism to a set of lifeless rules and perfunctory rituals. By contrast, he serves as a mediator for Hasidic mysticism, translating its spiritual insights for a contemporary consciousness. Heschel speaks about "Wonder," "The sense of Mystery," "Awe," "The Art of Being"—concepts rarely addressed in Jewish literature and never as eloquently or as compellingly as by Heschel. Through his influence an entire generation of Jews was opened up to the riches of "aggadic" Judaism, a Judaism of interpersonal concern and spiritual quest and not just halakhic (legal) obligations: "Man is not for the sake of good deeds; the good deeds are for the sake of man. Judaism asks for more than works, for more than the *opus operatum*. The goal is not that a ceremony be *performed*; the goal is that man be *transformed*; to worship the Holy in order to be holy. The purpose of the mitsvot is *to sanctify* man . . ."

Reviewing *God in Search of Man* in the *Saturday Review*, the Christian theologian Reinhold Niebuhr wrote: "Heschel's volume is genuinely religious in that it seeks to give no rationally compelling arguments for religious faith, but rationally explicates the presuppositions and consequences of such a faith."

Exodus

by Leon Uris.
Doubleday, 1958.

With *Exodus* as its second blockbuster in four years (following *Marjorie Morningstar*), Doubleday seemed to have found the winning combination for Jewish readers. The story of *Exodus* is secondary to its grand theme: the winning of Israel as a refuge for the Jewish people and a home for those who survived the ravages of the Holocaust. Kitty Fremont, a non-Jewish American nurse working with war orphans in the aftermath of World War II in order to forget the deaths of her husband and daughter, falls in love with Ari Ben-Canaan, a Palestine-born Jew deeply involved in smuggling refugees of the Holocaust into Palestine and creating an illegal Jewish defense force in the closing days of the British mandate. Subplots document the harrowing ways in which European and Russian Jews escaped from Nazi-occupied territory and slowly made their way, overland and by sea, to *Eretz Yisrael*, the Land of Israel.

Exodus is really a book about Israel—how the state was created and defended. It served as the most effective propaganda that Israel has ever enjoyed. The book touched many readers, both Jewish and non-Jewish, with its righteous passion and its image of the vigilant Israeli, defender of the oppressed. There was a popular song spin-off and, of course, the movie starring Paul Newman and Eva-Marie Saint. Until *Exodus* Israel was not a commercially viable subject in America. It should be noted, however, that in recent times, its greatest strength has come to be critically reevaluated, as it reinforced a problematic stereotype of the Israeli as superman and morally superior.

Uris sees himself as very different from other American-Jewish writers, as he once told an interviewer from the *New York Post*: "There is a whole school of American Jewish writers who spend their time damning their fathers, hating their mothers, wringing their hands and wondering why they were born. This isn't art or literature. It's psychiatry. These writers are professional apologists. Every year you find one of their works on the best-seller list. Their work is obnoxious and makes me sick to my stomach. I wrote *Exodus* because I was just sick of apologizing—or feeling that it was necessary to apologize."

Night

by Elie Wiesel.
Hill and Wang, 1960.

There have been many books about the Holocaust, but few have had the lasting power of *Night*. Published before Wiesel was known in this country and when he was still calling himself Eliezer, *Night* had an immediate impact on American readers.

This slender volume tells Wiesel's own story, introducing him in his oft-repeated self-image as "witness." At the age of fifteen, along with other Hungarian Jews, he and his father were rounded up and sent to Auschwitz. In understated tones their story is told starkly and unforgettably, as Wiesel created a new kind of literature in which the horrors are drawn not from imagination but from the memory. As Wiesel has elaborated in his other works, in the aftermath of the Holocaust reality can be seen to outstrip the imagination. The role of the artist is, thus, to recreate, to remember, not to imagine.

Focusing on the inadequacy of theology in the face of the Holocaust, Wiesel relates how, at one point, the Jews in the camp are forced to witness the hanging of three saboteurs, including a small child.

> "Where is God now?" a man mutters.
> And I hear a voice within me answer him:
> "Where is He? Here He is—He is hanging here on this gallows . . ."
> That night the soup tasted of corpses.

Night first appeared in French and in a longer Yiddish version entitled *Un di Velt Hot Geshvign*. The English translation played a major role in informing both Jews and other Americans about the Holocaust. "Though this volume is a short one and can be read in a couple of hours," noted a Christian reviewer, "I think I will never forget it."

Herzog

by Saul Bellow.
Viking Press, 1964.

Generally seen as Saul Bellow's greatest literary achievement, *Herzog* is the story of a Jewish-American professor and intellectual and his endless interior monologues. Moses Herzog grew up in Montreal and lived, like Bellow, in both New York and Chicago.

Believing that "brotherhood is what makes a man human," Herzog sees his mission as maintaining "this great bone-breaking burden of selfhood and self-development," despite the failures and terrors of modern life all around him.

During his wanderings, both physical and mental, Herzog is forever writing letters to friends, to famous people, and even to the dead. These letters are never actually sent, but they serve as the key to understanding the man.

Bellow allows the reader great access to Herzog's private thoughts, to his ruminations about matters both profound and trivial; to Herzog they are all related. "Innumerable millions of passengers had polished the wood of the turnstyle with their hips," Herzog thinks while entering the subway. "From this arose a feeling of communion—brotherhood in one of its cheapest forms. This was serious, thought Herzog as he passed through. The more individuals are destroyed (by processes such as I know) the worse their yearning for collectivity." And so on.

This is Bellow's most Jewish book, striking a familiar chord to many readers, especially male Jewish intellectuals of middle age. "*Herzog* should be praised as a marvellously animated performance," wrote Irving Howe in *The New Republic*. "It is a book that makes one greedy for the next page, the next character."

Understanding Genesis

by Nahum Sarna.
McGraw Hill, 1966.

Sarna's book, a commentary on Genesis for the layperson, was originally commissioned by the Melton Research Center of the Jewish Theological Seminary as a source book for teachers. Its purpose was to mediate, through lucid explanations, the fruits of modern biblical scholarship. It also helped to legitimize a critical approach to Bible study in educational environments across the country.

By current standards, the book may seem to place too great an emphasis on ancient Near East parallels to Bible stories and motifs (such as the Gilgamesh Epic and the Flood story); when it was first introduced, these were quite radical and surprising concepts for the general reader. Prior to this the Bible had been taught in a dry, literal manner that limited imaginative responses to the text, and the new approach represented a revolution in Jewish education. *Understanding Genesis*, together with its teacher's guide, was a major influence on a whole generation of children, particularly in the Conservative and Reform movements, who were introduced to the new perspectives of modern biblical scholarship and to an inquisitive approach to biblical text, which was its concomitant. These same elements account for the book's popularity in university and adult education courses, as well.

After Auschwitz

by Richard Rubenstein.
Bobbs-Merrill, 1966.

Rubenstein's book, actually a collection of essays, confronted the Jewish community with an extremely provocative and controversial challenge: to consider the theological implications of "the two decisive events of our time for Jews, the death camps and the birth of Israel." It was the Holocaust that concerned Rubenstein most, however, and in the light of that catastrophe he dared to ask the most difficult question: How can Jews continue to believe in a God who acts in history?

One reason for the popularity of Rubenstein's book is that it appeared during and entered into the "God-is-dead" controversy. While the author maintained that the "death of God" is a Christian phenomenon, which cannot be transfered onto the Jewish concept of God, he asserted that Jews can no longer think of a God who is active and present in history. As an alternative, he poses the revival of a nature paganism based on the return of Jews to the land in Israel.

When first published, *After Auschwitz* was especially appealing to younger Jews and to those of a Freudian persuasion. For a number of years Rubenstein's views were hotly debated within the Jewish community and were opposed by other Jewish thinkers, most notably, Emil Fackenheim, who also views the Holocaust as a theological challenge, but not one that is insurmountable.

The Jews of Silence: A Personal Report on Soviet Jewry

by Elie Wiesel.
Holt, Rinehart & Winston, 1966.

This singular contribution to Jewish travel literature is an eyewitness report on the High Holidays in 1965 and their aftermath among the Jews of the Soviet Union. Wiesel, a Holocaust survivor who began his writing career as a journalist after the war, travelled to Russia to write a series of articles for the Israeli newspaper *Yediot Aharonot*. The book he produced is a moving account of the lives and hopes of the captive Soviet Jews, who are not allowed to practice or teach their religion.

"I went to Russia drawn by the silence of its Jews," he writes. "I brought back their cry." Indeed he did. More than any other factor, perhaps, *The Jews of Silence* was the first step in alerting the American Jewish community to the real plight of Soviet Jews; the book moved many people to direct action.

Wiesel could not have anticipated the significance of his book, which brought the idea of *klal yisrael* (the unity of the Jewish people) to an American Jewish public unaccustomed to thinking in such terms. "I returned from the Soviet Union disheartened and depressed," he wrote. "But what torments me most is not the Jews of silence I met in Russia; but the silence of the Jews I live among today."

The Condition of Jewish Belief

by the editors of Commentary magazine.
Macmillan, 1967.

It was an inspired idea from the editors of *Commentary*: to ask fifty-five rabbis, representing the full spectrum of Jewish thought and practice, to say, in public, what it was they actually believed. Thirty-eight responded (15 Reform, 12 Conservative, and 11 Orthodox), and the result is a unique and important document.

There were five questions: the relevance of Torah, the idea of the chosen people, the distinctive features of Judaism, the political imperatives of being a Jew, and the relevance of the God-is-dead controversy to Judaism.

Of particular interest, as Milton Himmelfarb noted in the introduction, was the influence, not of Martin Buber, as had been expected, but rather of his hitherto less celebrated colleague, Franz Rosenzweig. Of even greater interest, perhaps, was that *Commentary* could make such an inquiry about the state of Jewish belief without mentioning the two major events of modern Jewish life: the Holocaust and the rebirth of the Jewish state.

While Six Million Died: A Chronicle of American Apathy

by Arthur D. Morse.
Random House, 1967.

This is the book that destroyed the mythical image of Franklin D. Roosevelt, the hero of American Jewry for almost four decades. Morse documented what many had long suspected but had not known for sure: The record of the Roosevelt administration in dealing with the fate of European Jews during World War II was disgraceful. Shunning involvement in what it termed "an internal German problem," this administration categorically refused to make any effort to rescue European Jewry from the Nazi Holocaust until 1944, despite the Jewish community's pleas and the evidence that was made available to it by the Red Cross as early as 1937.

Morse was a journalist, not a historian, and it remained for others to properly analyze the documents, hitherto unavailable, which chronicled the apathy. But it was Morse who opened the door, writing of those who, in Telford Taylor's words, "against the backdrop of murder squads and extermination camps in eastern Europe . . . thumb their rulebooks and write the memoranda, ingenious in finding ways of doing nothing."

Making It

by Norman Podhoretz.
Random House, 1967.

Podhoretz's book, a literary biography of Jewish upward mobility in American intellectual life, was greeted with so vicious a response upon its publication, that its author has apparently never recovered. For the most part, the criticisms were unfair; the book's intent was simply to chronicle one aspect of the author's life—his ambition—and in this he succeeded only too well.

Making It is intelligent, enormously revealing, and consistently interesting. It reads like a novel, with richly drawn portraits and thoughtful insights about the publishing world, power, and the Jewish aspects of both. However, as Podhoretz's story dealt not only with his own career but with those of Norman Mailer, Saul Bellow, Lionel Trilling, Irving Howe, and several other New York Jewish intellectuals, its frank detailing of social ambition embarrassed quite a few people.

The book revealed the personal and human side to one of the greatest success stories in American life, the rise of the Jewish intellectuals in the New York literary establishment and their ascendancy as the leading intellectuals in America. In the course of this, however, Podhoretz told "secrets out of school." He exposed the unpleasant sides of the exercise of ambition in these literary circles, an ambition which had previously been considered a "gentlemanly" pursuit.

The Chosen

by Chaim Potok.
Simon and Schuster, 1967.

The Chosen is the story of a friendship between two Jewish boys in Brooklyn during the 1940's. Although they first meet at a baseball game, their friendship is mostly concerned with intellectual and spiritual issues. Both come from Orthodox families, but one boy is the scion of a Hasidic dynasty, while the father of the other is a scientifically minded Orthodox scholar.

That a novel with such serious themes could be appealing to anyone, let alone to young people, is a tribute to the talents of its author. Chaim Potok is clearly not in the category of *shlock* writers, although he has frequently been dismissed as such. On the other hand, neither is he a literary stylist, but, rather, occupies a lonely perch in the middle.

The triumph of *The Chosen* is its serious and thoughtful treatment of certain profound issues of Jewishness. Its failures are that its plot and character portraits are unable to adequately support the themes. As the reviewer from *Time* observed, "In craft and characterization, particularly in the passages dealing with a boy's reaction to World War II, it rings as flat as a shofar blown by a gentile."

Portnoy's Complaint
by Philip Roth.
Random House, 1969.

Portnoy is probably the most outrageously *funny* Jewish book ever published, but that is not the only reason for its importance. Despite its many enemies, the book touched the soul of many readers (especially, but not exclusively, Jewish men) and opened the floodgates for a Freudian approach to the meaning of Jewish life in America.

"This is my life, my only life," Portnoy complains to his analyst, "and I'm living it in the middle of a Jewish joke. I am the son in the Jewish joke—*only it ain't no joke!*" Before writing this book, Roth had been reading Kafka, and, as he later observed, "Not until I had got hold of guilt, you see, as a *comic idea* did I begin to feel myself lifting free and clear of my last book and my old concerns."

Not all readers agree that *Portnoy* is, in the words of one reviewer, "the very novel that every American-Jewish writer has been trying to write . . . since the end of World War II," and the book has been fiercely debated and strongly attacked by those who see Roth as a self-hating Jew inflicting damage on his own people. On the other hand, the book's many defenders point to its liberating effect, and also to its serious side: its probing of various Jewish issues and practices, its examination of the psychic meaning of Jewishness in gentile America, and its concern with the power of individual guilt and collective discomfort, which has been so basic to the American Jewish condition, and which had never before been looked at in so uninhibited a manner.

The Seventh Day: Soldiers Talk About the Six-Day War
by Avraham Shapira, ed.
Scribners, 1968.

This book probably had less than one percent of the readership of *Exodus*, but had those figures been reversed, *The Seventh Day* might have opened the way for a most constructive dialogue between American Jews and Israelis. Whereas *Exodus* popularized the problematic stereotype of the invincible Israeli, this book revealed the truer counter-image of the Israeli soldier as a modern man, confronted with existential doubts and fears and yearnings for peace.

Published in Israel under the title of *Siach Lochamim*, this compendium is the outgrowth of a group of Israeli soldiers talking about the Six-Day War and the personal and religious issues it raised for them. The kibbutzniks who made up the interviews in this book were mostly nonreligious, but the war had forced them to confront, often for the first time, the essential questions of Judaism and the Jewish state: Why are we here, and what are we fighting for?

No one answer emerged from their conversations, but the book is a rare document of introspection, sensitivity, and the existential exploration of Jewishness and Jewish values as reflected through the trauma of a war. The book provides a rare (in English) glimpse of some of the most hidden parts of the Israeli soul—parts even most Israelis weren't aware of until the book appeared.

The Israelis: Founders and Sons
by Amos Elon.
Holt Rinehart & Winston, 1971.

Amos Elon, foreign correspondent for the Israeli newspaper *Ha'Aretz*, set out to produce the first critical analysis of Israeli society written from within, and he succeeded brilliantly. The book describes the struggle between the philosophy and the spirit of the founding Zionist generation, who came to Palestine from Europe, and their offspring, the second and third generation *sabras* (native-born Israelis).

The reviewer for *Book World* noted that Elon "has a novelist's eye and an historian's judgment," qualities which served him well not only in this book but also in his next, a biography of Theodor Herzl. In *Harpers*,

Irving Howe called the book "wildly overpraised" but went on to praise it for its fairness and good spirit. It remains the best general book about Israel and its people published in English.

Sabbtai Sevi: The Mystical Messiah 1626–1676

by Gershom Scholem.
Princeton University Press, 1973.

It is almost impossible to single out any one work by Gershom Scholem as being more important than the others. Through half a dozen major books and countless articles, Scholem has come to "own" the fields of Kaballah and Jewish mysticism. As a result of his work, these areas have become established as major academic disciplines.

Sabbtai Sevi, originally published in Hebrew in 1957, was eagerly awaited in translation by Scholem's readers all over the world. It tells the story of the most famous of the false Messiahs in Jewish history, a man whose life affected Jewish communities all over the world. The English translation, by Professor Werblowsky, was hailed as a masterpiece in its own right, and the English-language version also made use of some new documents, found in 1960, from the archives of a secret group of Sabbatians who had survived in Salonika until the twentieth century.

By the time this book was published, Scholem was widely known all over the world, and *Sabbtai Sevi* drew long and positive articles in *The New York Review of Books* and *The New Yorker*. In *The New York Times* Book Review Cynthia Ozick praised it as one of "certain magisterial works of the mind that alter ordinary comprehension so unpredictably and on so prodigious a scale that culture itself is set awry, and nothing can ever be seen again except in the strange light of that new knowledge."

The Jewish Catalog

by Richard Siegel, Michael Strassfeld, and Sharon Strassfeld.
Jewish Publication Society, 1973.

The Jewish Catalog's success was almost totally unexpected. Assembled by members of Boston's Havurat Shalom Community, with contributions by *havurah* members and fellow-travellers around the country, the book's audience was assumed to be small. It was not. The first volume has now sold more than a quarter of a million copies, and Volume II is over the 100,000 mark. A third volume is being published this year.

Especially successful in smaller Jewish communities, the *Catalog*, without entirely intending to do so, offered a new kind of Judaism, one which combined the traditionalism of Orthodoxy with the flexibility of Reform. More important, the emphasis of the *Catalog* was on a personal, physical Judaism, in sharp contrast to the increasingly plastic, mass-market Judaism that has become so prevalent in this country.

An attractive and humorous book, with delightful drawings by Stuart Copans, the *Catalog* served as a reminder that Judaism need not always be somber and need never be mechanical and impersonal.

World of Our Fathers

by Irving Howe.
Harcourt, Brace, Jovanovich, 1976.

Howe's book is a sociological and cultural study of the lives of Eastern European Jews who migrated to America, and especially to New York's Lower East Side, between 1880 and 1920. Using material from published sources, as well as scholarship, oral histories, memoirs, and newspaper articles, Howe tells the dramatic story of a community's response to an aptly named New World. Coming out at the same time as the wildly popular book and television movie, *Roots, World of Our Fathers* tied in well with the general American search for and interest in their origins.

In an attempt to avoid melodrama and sentimentality, Howe does his best to stick to the facts and brings forward a wealth of detail, especially about the grim poverty of this community and the abhorrent working conditions. He places special emphasis, some say too much, on the labor movement and socialism, and on their influence on intellectual life.

Jacob Neusner, reviewing the book for the *National Review*, called it "a stunning, monumental work—a triumph of sustained and brilliant narrative . . . the finest work of historical literature ever written on American Jews."

And the *Newsweek* reviewer, commenting on the importance of Yiddish culture, writing, and theater on the Lower East Side, remarked that the author's "flavorful quotations from Yiddish poets and from the columns of the *Daily Forward* make one ache to know the language."

Letters to an American Jewish Friend: A Zionist's Polemic

by Hillel Halkin.
Jewish Publication Society, 1977.

After the State of Israel was established in 1948, Zionist thought and ideology suffered a new and strange crisis: It was no longer clear what it meant to be a Zionist. With Halkin's book, the spirit of Zionism was reborn. Here was an American Jew who had made *aliyah* (emigrated to the Land of Israel), espousing the classic Zionist position: that Jews ought to live in Israel. He writes of his experience with such wit, so inventive an analysis, and such exquisite phrasing that it was almost as though these arguments had not previously been made.

Amos Elon, reviewing this book in *The New York Times*, noted that "few books in recent years have brought out so sharply a basic fact . . . that Israel is at base a community of faith."

Halkin's book featured a sensitive and realistic discussion of the Arab problem and a critique of Israeli society as well. His sharpest words, however, were reserved for American Jewish culture, which he all but dismissed. Not all of Halkin's arguments are valid, but if ever a book can make the Jewish case for *aliyah*, this one has the best chance of succeeding. Unfortunately, while the book received prominent and highly favorable reviews, it did not achieve the commercial success it deserves, perhaps the most telling indictment of the current state of Zionist thinking.

—W.A.N.

THE NATIONAL JEWISH BOOK AWARDS

Since 1947 the Jewish Book Council of the National Jewish Welfare Board has presented annual awards for the year's outstanding Jewish books. Books considered must be related to a Jewish theme, dealing with Jewish events or Jewish characters in a Jewish context. Authors need not be Jewish, but must be citizens or residents of the United States or Canada. With the exception of the new Yiddish literature award (to be presented in 1980), the awards are primarily for English-language books. Works published in Hebrew and Yiddish, however, are eligible for the Holocaust Studies and Poetry awards.

The winning authors, chosen by a panel of three distinguished literary judges, receive $500 and a certificate of recognition. There are eight categories: (1) Fiction, (2) Poetry—English, Hebrew, and Yiddish, (3) Juvenile, (4) Nonfiction—Jewish thought, (5) Nazi Holocaust, (6) Jewish history, (7) Israel, and (8) English translation of a Jewish classic.

FICTION

(The William and Janice Epstein Award for Jewish Fiction)

1948 HOWARD FAST, *My Glorious Brothers*. Boston, Little, Brown.

1949 JOHN HERSEY, *The Wall*. New York, Alfred A. Knopf.

1950 SONA MORGENSTERN, *The Testament of the Lost Son*. Philadelphia, Jewish Publication Society.

1951 ZELDA POPKIN, *Quiet Street*. Philadelphia, J. B. Lippincott.

1952 MICHAEL BLANKFORT, *The Juggler*. Boston, Little, Brown.

1953 CHARLES ANGOFF, *In the Morning Light*. New York, Beechhurst Press.

1954 LOUIS ZARA, *Blessed is the Land*. New York, Crown.

1955 JO SINCLAIR, *The Changelings*. New York, McGraw-Hill.

1956 LION FEUCHTWANGER, *Raquel: The Jewess of Toledo*. New York, Julian Messner.

1957 BERNARD MALAMUD, *The Assistant*. New York, Farrar, Straus & Cudahy.

1958 LEON URIS, *Exodus*. New York, Doubleday.

1959 PHILIP ROTH, *Goodbye, Columbus*. Boston, Houghton Mifflin.

1960 EDWARD L. WALLANT, *The Human Season*. New York, Harcourt, Brace.

1961 SAMUEL YELLEN, *Wedding Band*. New York, Atheneum.

1962 ISAAC BASHEVIS SINGER, *The Slave*. New York, Farrar, Straus & Cudahy.

1963 JOANNE GREENBERG, *The King's Persons*. New York, Holt, Rinehart and Winston.

1964 ELIE WIESEL, *The Town Beyond the Wall*. New York, Atheneum.

1965 MEYER LEVIN, *The Stronghold*. New York, Simon and Schuster.

1966 CHAIM GRADE, *The Well*. Philadelphia, Jewish Publication Society of America.

1968 CHARLES ANGOFF, *Memory of Autumn*. South Brunswick. N.J., Thomas Yoseloff.

1969 LEO LITWAK, *Waiting for the News*. New York, Doubleday.

1971 CYNTHIA OZICK, *The Pagan Rabbi and Other Stories*. New York, Alfred A. Knopf.

1972 ROBERT KOTLOWITZ, *Somewhere Else*. New York, Charterhouse.

1974 FRANCINE PROSE, *Judah the Pious*. New York, Atheneum.

1975 JEAN KARSAVINA, *White Eagle, Dark Skies*. New York, Charles Scribner's Sons.

1976 JOHANNA KAPLAN, *Other People's Lives*. New York, Alfred A. Knopf.

1977 CYNTHIA OZICK, *Bloodshed and Three Novellas*. New York, Alfred A. Knopf.

1978 CHAIM GRADE, *The Yeshiva*. Indianapolis, Bobbs-Merrill.

1979 GLORIA GOLDREICH, *Leah's Journey*. New York, Harcourt Brace Jovanovich.

1980 DANIEL FUCHS, *The Apathetic Bookie Joint*. New York, Methuen.

POETRY

(JWB Jewish Book Council Awards for Poetry)

ENGLISH POETRY

1950 JUDAH STAMPFER, *Jerusalem Has Many Faces*. New York, Farrar, Straus.

1951 A. M. KLEIN, cumulative contributions to English-Jewish poetry.

1952 ISIDORE GOLDSTICK, translation of *Poems of Yehoash*. London, Ontario.

1953 HARRY H. FEIN, cumulative contributions to English-Jewish poetry.

1958 GRACE GOLDIN, *Come Under the Wings: A Midrash on Ruth*. Philadelphia, Jewish Publication Society.

1959 AMY K. BLANK, *The Spoken Choice*. Cincinnati, Hebrew College Press.

1961 IRVING FELDMAN, *Work and Days and Other Poems*. Boston, Little, Brown.

1962 CHARLES REZNIKOFF, *By the Waters of Manhattan*. New York, New Directions.

1965 RUTH FINER MINTZ, *The Darkening Green*. Denver, Big Mountain Press.

1968 RUTH WHITMAN, *The Marriage Wig and Other Poems*. New York, Harcourt, Brace & World.

1970 RUTH FINER MINTZ, *Traveler Through Time*. New York, Jonathan David.

1974 HAROLD SCHIMMEL, translation of Yehuda Amichai's *Songs of Jerusalem and Myself*. New York, Harper & Row.

1977 MYRA SKLAREW, *From the Backyard of the Diaspora*. Washington, D.C., Dryad Press.

1980 CHARLES REZNIKOFF, for the "totality of his poetic literary achievement."

HEBREW POETRY

1950 AARON ZEITLIN, *Shirim u'Poemot* (Songs and Poems). Jerusalem, Mossad Bialik.

1951 HILLEL BAVLI, cumulative contributions to Hebrew poetry.

1952 A. S. SCHWARTZ, cumulative contributions to Hebrew poetry.

1953 EPHRAIM E. LISITZKY, *Be-Ohalei Kush* (In Negro Tents). Jerusalem, Mossad Bialik.

1954 GABRIEL PREIL, *Ner Mul Kochavim* (Candle Under the Stars). Jerusalem, Massad Bialik.

1955 HILLEL BAVLI, *Aderet Ha-Shanim* (Mantle of Years). Jerusalem, Mossad Bialik.

1956 MOSHE FEINSTEIN, *Avraham Abulafia*. Jerusalem, Mossad Bialik.

1957 AARON ZEITLIN, *Bein ha-Esh veha-Esha* (Between the Man and the Woman). Tel Aviv, Yevneh.

1958 MOSHE BEN-MEIR, *Tzil va-Tzel* (Sound and Shadow). New York, Ogen.

1959 EISIG SILBERSCHLAG, *Kimron Yamai* (Arch of My Days). Jerusalem, Kiryat Sefer.

1960 EPHRAIM E. LISITZKY, *K'Mo Hayom Rad* (As the Day Wanes). Tel Aviv, Mahbarot Lesifrut.

1961 GABRIEL PREIL, *Mapat Erev*. Tel Aviv, Dvir.

1963 ARNOLD BAND, *Ha-Rei Boer ba-Esh* (The Mirror Burns in Fire). Jerusalem, Ogdan; New York, Ogen.

1965 SIMON HALKIN, *Ma'avar Yabok* (Crossing the Yabok). Tel Aviv, Am Ovcd.

1966 LEONARD D. FRIEDLAND, *Shirim be-Sulam Minor* (Poems in a Minor Key). Tel Aviv, M. Newman.

1968 REUVEN BEN-YOSEF, *Derech Eretz*. Tel Aviv, Hakebutz Hameuchad.

1971 EISIG SILBERSCHLAG, *Igrotai El Dorot Aherim* (Letters to Other Generations). Jerusalem, Kiryat Sofer.

1975 REUVEN BEN-YOSEF, *Metim ve-Ohavim*. Ramat Gan, Massada.

1978 T. CARMI, *El Eretz Aheret* (To Another Land). Tel Aviv, Dvir.

YIDDISH POETRY

1950 BER LAPIN, *Der Fuller Krug* (The Brimming Jug). New York, Ykuf.

1951 MORDECAI JAFFE, editing and translating *Antologia fun Der Hebraishe Poesie* (Anthology of Hebrew Poetry). New York, CYCO. 2 volumes.

1952 MARK SCHWEID, *Collected Poems*. New York.

1953 ELIEZER GREENBERG, *Banachtiger Dialog* (Night Dialogue). New York, Gezelten.

1954 ALTER ESSELIN, *Lider Fun a Midbarnik* (Poems of a Hermit). Milwaukee, Culture Club of the Peretz Hirschbein Folk Theater.

1955 NAFTALI GROSS, cumulative contributions to Yiddish poetry.

1956 JACOB GLATSTEIN, *Fun Mein Gantzer Mei: 1919-1956* (Of All My Labour: Collected Poems, 1919-1956). New York.

1957 I. J. SCHWARTZ, cumulative contributions to Yiddish poetry.

1958 BENJAMIN J. BIALOSTOTZKY, *Lid Tzu Lid* (Poem to Poem). New York, CYCO.

1959 EPHRAIM AUERBACH, *Gildene Shekiah* (Golden Sunset). Buenos Aires, Kium.

1960 JOSEPH RUBINSTEIN, *Megilath Russland* (Scroll of Russia). New York, CYCO.

1961 ISRAEL EMIOT, *In Nigun Eingehert* (In Melody Absorbed). Rochester, N.Y., Culture Council.

1962 CHAIM GRADE, *Der Mentsh Fun Fier* (The Man of Fire). New York, CYCO.

1963 AARON GLANZ-LEYELES, *Amerike un Ich* (America and I). New York, Der Kval.

1964 ALEPH KATZ, *Di Emesse Hasunah* (Some Wedding). New York, CYCO.

1965 KADIA MOLODOWSKY, *Licht fun Dorenboim* (Light from the Thornbush). Buenos Aires, Kium.

1966 JACOB GLATSTEIN, *A Yid fun Lublin* (A Jew from Lublin). New York, CYCO.

1967 AARON ZEITLIN, *Liderfun Hurban un Lider fun Gloiben* (Poems of the Holocaust and Poems of Faith). New York. World Federation of Bergen-Belson Associations.

1969 RACHEL H. KORN, *Di Gnod fun Vort*. (The Game of Words). Tel Aviv, Hemenora.

1969 ELIEZER GREENBERG, *Eibiker Dorsht* (Eternal thirst). New York, Knight Printing Corp.

1971 MEIR STICKER, *Yidishe Landshaft* (Jewish Landscape). Tel Aviv, Peretz Farlag.

1976 M. HUSID, *A Shotn Trogt Main Kroin* (My Crown Wears a Shadow). Montreal.

1979 MOISHE STEINGART, *In Droisen Fun der Velt* (Outside of the World). New York, Shulsinger Brothers.

JUVENILE LITERATURE

(The Charles and Bertie G. Schwartz Award)

1951 SYDNEY TAYLOR, *All-of-a-Kind Family*, New York, Wilcox and Follet.

1952 LILLIAN S. FREEHOF, *Stories of King David*. Philadelphia, Jewish Publication Society; and *Star Light Stories*. New York, Bloch.

1953 DEBORAH PESSIN, *The Jewish People: Book Three*. New York, United Synagogue Commission on Jewish Education.

1954 NORA BENJAMIN KUBIE, *King Solomon's Navy*. New York, Harper & Brothers.

1955 SADIE ROSE WEILERSTEIN, cumulative contributions to Jewish juvenile literature.

1956 ELMA E. LEVINGER, cumulative contributions to Jewish juvenile literature.

1957 NAOMI BEN-ASHER and HAYIM LEAF, *Jewish Junior Encyclopedia*. New York, Shengold.

1958 LLOYD ALEXANDER, *Border Hawk: August Bondi*. New York, Farrar, Straus and Cudahy; Philadelphia, Jewish Publication Society.

1959 SYLVIA ROTHCHILD, *Keys to a Magic Door: Isaac Leib Peretz*. New York, Farrar, Straus and Cudahy; Philadelphia, Jewish Publication Society.

1960 REGINA TOR, *Discovering Israel*. New York, Random House.

1961 SADIE ROSE WEILERSTEIN, *Ten and a Kid*. New York, Doubleday.

1962 JOSEPHINE KAMM, *Return to Freedom*. New York, Abelard-Schuman.

1963 SULAMITH ISH-KISHOR, *A Boy of Old Prague*, New York, Pantheon.

1964 DOV PERETZ ELKINS and AZRIEL EISENBERG, *Worlds Lost and Found*. New York, Abelard-Schuman.

1965 BETTY SCHECHTER, *The Dreyfus Affair*. Boston, Houghton Mifflin.

1966 MEYER LEVIN, *The Story of Israel*. New York, G. P. Putnam's Sons.

1969 CHARLIE MAY SIMON, *Martin Buber: Wisdom in Our Time*. New York, E. P. Dutton.

1969 GERALD GOTTLIEB, *The Story of Masada by Yigael Yadin: Retold for Young Readers*. New York, Random House.

1970 SONIA LEVITIN, *Journey to America.* New York, Atheneum.

1971 SULAMITH ISH-KISHOR, *The Master of Miracle: A New Novel of the Golem.* New York, Harper & Row.

1972 JOHANNA REISS, *The Upstairs Room.* New York, Thomas Y. Crowell.

1974 YURI SUHL, *Uncle Misha's Partisans.* New York, Four Winds Press.

1975 BEA STADTLER, *The Holocaust: A History of Courage and Resistance.* New York, Behrman House.

1976 SHIRLEY MILGRIM, *Haym Salomon: Liberty's Son.* Philadelphia, Jewish Publication Society.

1977 CHAYA BURSTEIN, *Rifka Grows Up.* New York, Bonim Books, Hebrew Publishing Co.

1978 MILTON MELTZER, *Never to Forget: The Jews of the Holocaust.* New York, Harper & Row.

1979 IRENA NARELL, *Joshua: Fighter for Bar Kochba.* Pebble Beach, Calif., Akiba Press.

1980 ARNOST LUSTIG, *Dita Saxova.* New York, Harper and Row.

NONFICTION

(The Frank and Ethel S. Cohen Award for a Book on Jewish Thought)

1947 HARRY A. WOLFSON, *Philo: Foundations of Religious Philosophy in Judaism, Christianity, and Islam.* Cambridge, Mass., Harvard University Press.

1948 GUIDO KISCH, *The Jews in Medieval Germany: A Study of Their Legal and Social Status.* Chicago, University of Chicago Press.

1962 MOSES RISCHIN, *The Promised City: New York's Jews, 1870-1914.* Cambridge, Mass., Harvard University Press.

1963 BEN ZION BOKSER, *Judaism: Profile of a Faith.* New York, Burning Bush Press and Alfred A. Knopf.

1964 ISRAEL EFROS, *Ancient Jewish Philosophy.* Detroit, Wayne State University.

1965 DAVID POLISH, *The Higher Freedom: A New Turning Point in Jewish History.* Chicago, Quadrangle Press.

1966 NAHUM M. SARNA, *Understanding Genesis: The Heritage of Biblical Israel.* New York, Jewish Theological Seminary of America.

1967 MICHAEL A. MEYER, *Origins of the Modern Jew.* Detroit, Wayne State University Press.

1968 EMIL L. FACKENHEIM, *Quest for Past and Future: Essays in Jewish Theology.* Bloomington, Indiana University.

1969 ABRAHAM JOSHUA HESCHEL, *Israel: An Echo of Eternity* (New York, Farrar, Straus & Giroux), and cumulative contributions to Jewish thought.

1970 MORDECAI M. KAPLAN, *The Religion of Ethical Nationhood: Judaism's Contribution to World Peace.* (New York, Macmillan), and cumulative contributions to Jewish thought.

1971 ABRAHAM E. MILLGRAM, *Jewish Worship.* Philadelphia, Jewish Publication Society of America.

1972 SAMUEL SANDMEL, *Two Living Traditions: Essays on Religion and the Bible.* Detroit, Wayne State University Press.

1972 ELIE WIESEL, *Souls on Fire: Portraits and Legends of Hasidic Masters.* New York, Random House.

1974 EUGENE B. BOROWITZ, *The Mask Jews Wear: The Self-Deceptions of American Jewry.* New York, Simon and Schuster.

1975 ELIEZER BERKOVITS, *Major Themes in Modern Philosophies of Judaism.* New York, Ktav.

1976 SOLOMON B. FREEHOF, *Contemporary Reform Responsa.* New York, Hebrew Union College Press.

1977 DAVID HARTMAN, *Maimonides: Torah and Philosophic Quest.* Philadelphia, Jewish Publication Society.

1978 RAPHAEL PATAI, *The Jewish Mind.* New York, Charles Scribner's Sons.

1979 ROBERT GORDIS, *Love and Sex: A Modern Jewish Perspective.* New York, Women's League for Conservative Judaism & Farrar, Straus and Giroux.

1980 DAVID BIALE, *Gershom Scholem: Kabbalah and Counter History.* Cambridge, Harvard University Press.

NAZI HOLOCAUST

(Leon Jolson Award)

1965 ZOSA SZAJKOWSKI, *Analytical Franco-Jewish Gazetteer 1939-1945.* New York (American Academy For Jewish Research), Shulsinger Bros.

1966 ABRAHAM KIN, MORDECAI KOSOVER, and ISAIAH TRUNK, editorship of *Algemeyne Entsiklopedye: Yidn VII* (General Encyclopedia: Jews VII). New York, Dubnow Fund and Encyclopedia Committee.

1967 JACOB ROBINSON, *And the Crooked Shall Be Made Straight: The Eichmann Trial, Jewish Catastrophe, and Han-*

nah Arendt's Narrative. New York, Macmillan.

1968 JUDAH PILCH, *The Jewish Catastrophe in Europe.* New York, American Association for Jewish Education.

1968 NORA LEVIN, *The Holocaust: The Destruction of European Jewry.* New York, Thomas Y. Crowell.

1972 AARON ZEITLIN, *Veiterdike Lider Fun Hurban un Lider Fun Gloiben un Yanish Kortshaks Letzte Gang* (More Poems of the Holocaust and Poems of Faith and Yanish Kortshak's Last Walk). New York, Bergen Belsen Memorial Press.

1975 ISAIAH TRUNK, *Judenrat: The Jewish Councils in Eastern Europe Under Nazi Occupation.* New York, Macmillan.

1976 LEYZER RAN, *Yerushalayim de Lite* (Jerusalem of Lithuania). New York.

1977 RABBI EPHRAIM OSHRY, *Sefer She'elot U-Teshuvot Mi-Maamakim* (Book of Questions and Responses from the Depths), Part 4, New York.

1978 TERRENCE DES PRES, *The Survivor: An Anatomy of Life in the Death Camp.* New York, Oxford University Press.

1979 MICHAEL SELZER, *Deliverance Day: The Last Hours at Dachau.* Philadelphia, J. B. Lippincott.

1980 BENJAMIN B. FERENCZ, *Less Than Slaves: Jewish Forced Labor and the Quest for Compensation.* Cambridge, Harvard University Press.

JEWISH HISTORY

(Gerrard and Ella Berman Award)

1972 ARTHUR J. ZUCKERMAN, *A Jewish Princedom in Feudal France, 768-900.* New York, Columbia University Press.

1974 BERNARD D. WEINRYB, *The Jews of Poland: A Social and Economic History of the Jewish Community in Poland from 1100 to 1800.* Philadelphia, Jewish Publication Society.

1975 SOLOMON ZEITLIN, cumulative contribution to Jewish history.

1976 RAPHAEL PATAI and JENNIFER PATAI WING, *The Myth of the Jewish Race.* New York, Charles Scribner's Sons.

1977 IRVING HOWE, *World of Our Fathers.* New York, Harcourt Brace Jovanovich.

1978 CELIA S. HELLER, *On the Edge of Destruction.* New York, Columbia University Press.

1978 SALO W. BARON, cumulative contribution to Jewish historic research and thought.

1980 TODD M. ENDELMAN, *The Jews of Georgian England.* Philadelphia, Jewish Publication Society.

ISRAEL

(Morris J. Kaplun Memorial Award)

1974 ISAIAH FRIEDMAN, *The Question of Palestine: 1914-1918: British-Jewish-Arab Relations.* New York, Schocken Books.

1975 ARNOLD KRAMMER, *The Forgotten Friendship: Israel and the Soviet Bloc, 1947-1953.* Urbana, University of Illinois Press.

1976 MELVIN I. UROFSKY, *American Zionism from Herzl to the Holocaust.* Garden City, N.Y., Doubleday.

1977 HOWARD M. SACHAR, *A History of Israel.* New York, Alfred A. Knopf.

1978 HILLEL HALKIN, *Letters to an American Jewish Friend.* Philadelphia, Jewish Publication Society.

1979 RUTH GRUBER, *Raquela: A Woman of Israel.* New York, Coward, McCann & Geoghegan.

1980 EMANUEL LEVY, *The Habimah—Israel's National Theater 1917–1977: A Study of Cultural Nationalism.* New York, Columbia University Press.

ENGLISH TRANSLATION OF A JEWISH CLASSIC

(Rabbi Jacob Freedman Award)

1975 JEWISH PUBLICATION SOCIETY COMMITTEE OF TRANSLATORS OF THE PROPHETS (DR. MAX ARZT, DR. BERNARD J. BAMBERGER, DR. HARRY FREEDMAN, DR. H. L. GINSBERG, DR. SOLOMON GRAYZEL, and DR. HARRY M. ORLINSKY), *The Book of Isaiah.* Philadelphia, Jewish Publication Society.

1976 RABBI WILLIAM G. BRAUDE and PROF. ISRAEL J. KAPSTEIN, *Pesikta de-Rab Kahana* (R. Kahana's Compliation of Discourses for Sabbaths and Festal Days). Philadelphia, Jewish Publication Society.

1977 ZVI L. LAMPEL, *Maimonides' Introduction to the Talmud.* New York, Judaica Press.

1979 WILLIAM M. BRINNER, Nissim Ben Jacob ibn Shahin's *An Elegant Composition Concerning Relief After Adversity.* New Haven, Conn., Yale University Press.

—The Eds.

ISAAC BASHEVIS SINGER'S 1978 NOBEL LECTURE

NOBEL PRIZE CITATION

"The Nobel Prize for Literature to
Isaac Bashevis Singer
for his impassioned narrative art
which, with roots in a Polish-Jewish
cultural tradition, brings universal
human conditions to life."

Isaac Bashevis Singer

Mr. Singer read the following in Yiddish, at the start of the lecture:

The high honor bestowed upon me by the Swedish Academy is also a recognition of the Yiddish language—a language of exile, without a land, without frontiers, not supported by any government, a language which possesses no words for weapons, ammunition, military exercises, war tactics; a language that was despised by both gentiles and emancipated Jews. The truth is that what the great religions preached, the Yiddish-speaking people of the ghettos practiced day in and day out. They were the people of the Book in the truest sense of the word. They knew of no greater joy than the study of man and human relations, which they called Torah, Talmud, Musar, Kabbalah. The ghetto was not only a place of refuge for a persecuted minority but a great experiment in peace, in self-discipline, and in humanism. As such, a residue still exists and refuses to give up in spite of all the brutality that surrounds it.

I was brought up among those people. My father's home on Krochmalna Street in Warsaw was a study house, a court of justice, a house of prayer, of storytelling, as well as a place for weddings and Hasidic banquets. As a child I had heard from my older brother and master, I. J. Singer, who later wrote *The Brothers Ashkenazi*, all the arguments that the rationalists from Spinoza to Max Nordau brought out against religion. I have heard from my father and my mother all the answers that faith in God could offer to those who doubt and search for the truth. In our home and in many other homes the eternal questions were more actual than the latest news in the Yiddish newspaper. In spite of all the disenchantments and all my skepticism, I believe that the nations can learn much from those Jews, their way of thinking, their way of bringing up children, their finding happiness where others see nothing but misery and humiliation.

To me the Yiddish language and the conduct of those who spoke it are identical. One can find in the Yiddish tongue and in the Yiddish style expressions of pious joy, lust for life, longing for the Messiah, patience, and deep appreciation of human individuality. There is a quiet humor in Yiddish and a gratitude for every day of life, every crumb of success, each encounter of love. The Yiddish mentality is not haughty. It does not take victory for granted. It does not demand and command but it muddles through, sneaks by, smuggles itself amid the powers of destruction, knowing somewhere that God's plan for Creation is still at the very beginning.

There are some who call Yiddish a dead language, but so was Hebrew called for two thousand years. It has been revised in our time in a most remarkable, almost miraculous way. Aramaic was certainly a dead language for centuries, but then it brought to light the Zohar, a work of mysticism of sublime value. It is a fact that the classics of Yiddish literature are also the classics of modern Hebrew literature. Yiddish has not yet said its last word. It contains treasures that have not been revealed to the eyes of the world. It was the tongue of martyrs and saints, of dreamers and kabbalists—rich in humor and in memories that mankind may never forget. In a figurative way, Yiddish is the wise and humble language of us all, the idiom of frightened and hopeful humanity.

THE ADDRESS:

The storyteller and poet of our time, as in any other time, must be an entertainer of the spirit in the full sense of the word, not just a preacher of social or political ideals. There is no paradise for bored readers and no excuse for tedious literature that does not intrigue the reader, uplift his spirit, give him the joy and the escape that true art always grants. Nevertheless, it is also true that the serious writer of our time must be deeply concerned about the problems of his generation. He cannot but see that the power of religion, especially belief in revelation, is weaker today than it was in any other epoch in human history. More and more children grow up without faith in God, without belief in reward and punishment, in the immortality of the soul, and even in the validity of ethics. The genuine writer cannot ignore the fact that the family is losing its spiritual foundation. All the dismal prophecies of Oswald Spengler have become realities since the Second World War. No technological achievements can mitigate the disappointment of modern man, his loneliness, his feeling of inferiority, and his fear of war, revolution, and terror. Not only has our generation lost faith in Providence, but also in man himself, in his institutions, and often in those who are nearest to him.

In their despair a number of those who no longer have confidence in the leadership of our society look up to the writer, the master of words. They hope against hope that the man of talent and sensitivity can perhaps rescue civilization. Maybe there is a spark of the prophet in the artist after all.

As the son of a people who received the worst blows that human madness can inflict, I have many times resigned myself to never finding a true way out. But a new hope always emerges, telling me that it is not yet too late for all of us to take stock and make a decision. I was brought up to believe in free will. Although I came to doubt all revelation, I can never accept the idea that the universe is a physical or chemical accident, a result of blind evolution. Even though I learned to recognize the lies, the clichés, and the idolatries of the human mind, I still cling to some truths which I think all of us might accept someday. There must be a way for man to attain all possible pleasures, all the powers and knowledge that nature can grant him, and still serve God—a God who speaks in deeds, not in words, and whose vocabulary is the universe.

I am not ashamed to admit that I belong to those who fantasize that literature is capable of bringing new horizons and new perspectives—philosophical, religious, aesthetical, and even social. In the history of old Jewish literature there was never any basic difference between the poet and the prophet. Our ancient poetry often became law and a way of life.

Some of my cronies in the cafeteria near the *Jewish Daily Forward* in New York call me a pessimist and a decadent, but there is always a background of faith behind resignation. I found comfort in such pessimists and decadents as Baudelaire, Verlaine, Edgar Allan Poe, and Strindberg. My interest in psychic research made me find solace in such mystics as your Swedenborg and in our own Rabbi Nachman Bratzlaver, as well as in a great poet of my time, my friend Aaron Zeitlin, who died a few years ago and left a spiritual inheritance of high quality, most of it in Yiddish.

The pessimism of the creative person is not decadence, but a mighty passion for the redemption of man. While the poet entertains he continues to search for eternal truths, for the essence of being. In his own fashion he tries to solve the riddle of time and change, to find an answer to suffering, to reveal love in the very abyss of cruelty and injustice. Strange as these words may sound, I often play with the idea that when all the social theories collapse and wars and revolutions leave humanity in utter gloom, the poet—whom Plato banned from his Republic—may rise up to save us all.

—I.B.S. rep.

THE 10 BEST AND 10 WORST JEWISH FILMS

Amassing a list of the ten best and worst Jewish films raises a number of difficult questions, foremost of which is: "What constitutes a Jewish film?" For the purpose of this listing, a Jewish film is any picture which focuses on Jews and such uniquely Jewish experiences as Israel, anti-Semitism, Kabbalah, the Holocaust, or growing up Jewish in America. Only feature-length pictures which have been shown in theaters in the United States and Canada are listed. They have been chosen on the basis of cinematic as well as Jewish considerations.

The ten best Jewish films had to score high in both Jewish and cinematic areas. Each film has added considerably to contemporary comprehension of the Jewish condition. Some of the films romanticize Jewish life, others are critical of it, but all stimulate reflection and contribute to an understanding of the Jewish experience in modern life. The ten worst Jewish films are listed not only because they failed to meet these criteria, but because they failed to meet broader expectations.

Obviously, selecting the ten best or worst films is subjective. Some well-known films missing from both lists are *Exodus, The Jazz Singer, Cast a Giant Shadow, Gentlemen's Agreement,* and *Hester Street.* Quality has been the key factor of choice.

***A scene from the 1937 Polish production of* The Dybbuk**

THE TEN BEST JEWISH FILMS (in alphabetical order)

1. *The Dreamer* (*Ha-Timhoni*), Israel, 1970. Hebrew with English subtitles. Written and directed by Dan Wolman; produced by Ami Artzi; cinematography by Paul Glicksman; music by Gershon Kingley. Running Time: 86 minutes. With Tuvia Tavi, Leora Rivlin, and Berta Litvina.

The Dreamer is the sensitive story of a young handyman who works at the Safed home for the aged and who develops a special relationship with Rachel, one of the older residents. For a brief period the dreamer has an affair with a beautiful girl his own age and finds himself torn between his feelings for Rachel and his current lover.

This was Israeli director Dan Wolman's first feature film and probably his best (others include *Floch* and *My Michael*). What is so special about this picture is Wolman's tender treatment of old people, especially older women. Vincent Canby, writing in the *New York Times*, praised this film "because although it looks simple, its heart is complex."

2. *The Dybbuk* (*Der Dibuk*), Poland, 1937. Directed by Michal Waszynski; screenplay by Alter Kacyzna and Andrew Marek, with assistance from Anatol Stern, from play by S. Anski; produced by Ludwig Prywes; cinematography by Albert Wywerka, music by Henikh Kahn; dance by Judith Berg. Running time: 125 minutes. With Avrom Marevsky, Isaac Samberg, Lili Liliana, Leon Liebgold, and Dina Halpern.

The story is one of unfulfilled love. Parents make a pledge to have their children marry and the destined couple, Khonon and Leah, meet and fall in love. However, the girl's father, forgetting his vow, keeps them apart. Khonon, despondent, tries to find a remedy through mystical Kabbalah, but dies in the process. Then, just as Leah is about to be married to another, Khonon's persona enters her body and possesses her.

This is the boldest Yiddish film undertaking ever prepared, requiring special sets and unusual lighting. Noted Warsaw historian Meyer Balaban oversaw the accuracy of the presentation. The expressionistic film captures with great success the mystical character of the Anski play.

3. *The Great Dictator*, U.S.A., 1940. Written, produced, and directed by Charles Chaplin; cinematography by Rollie Totheroh; music by Charles Chaplin. Running time: 126 minutes. With Charles Chaplin, Paulette Goddard, Jack Oakie, and Reginald Gardiner.

Released in the United States only thirteen months after Hitler's invasion of Poland, *The Great Dictator* tells the story "in the manner of . . . a children's fairy tale" of a Jewish barber, who suddenly finds himself persecuted by Adenoid Hynkel, Dictator of Tomania. After his shop has been burned to the ground, the Jewish barber is arrested and sent to a concentration camp. He escapes from the camp, is mistaken for Hynkel (his look-alike), and is welcomed as the conqueror of Austerlich. Much to the amazement of Tomania's generals, the Jewish barber, posing as Hynkel, makes a dramatic speech castigating race hatred and praising the brotherhood of man.

***Charlie Chaplin in a scene from* The Great Dictator**

Although the film was attacked by isolationists and the German American Bund when it opened in New York City in 1940, it was generally well received by Americans. The Academy of Motion Picture Arts and Sciences nominated the film for five Oscars, including Best Film, Best Motion Picture Based on an Original Screenplay, and Best Original (Musical) Score. In addition, Chaplin was nominated by the Academy as Best Actor for his portrayal of the Jewish barber and Hynkel. Jack Oakie was nominated for Best Supporting Actor for his portrayal of Il Dig-a-Ditchy, otherwise known as Benito Mussolini.

4. *Jewish Luck* (*Yidishe Glikn*), U.S.S.R., 1925, silent. Directed by Alexei Granovsky; written by G. Gricher-Cherikover, I. Tenerama, and L. Leonidov from stories by Sholom Aleichem; cinematography by Edward Tisse, Vasili Khvatov, and N. S. Strukov; music by Lev Pulver. Running time: 66 minutes. With Solomon Mikhoels, Tamara Adelheim, T. Hazak, and M. Goldblatt.

Menakhem Mendl is always in search of a promising business deal. He first fails as a corset salesman, then tries his hand at being a *shadkhan* (matchmaker). He imagines himself outside Odessa's Grand Palace with Baron de Hirsch preparing to export his brides to America, but one calamity after another befalls him and he is left without money and profession. He goes off in search of better luck.

The picture was the first and only Jewish film endeavor by Yiddish theater director Alexei Granovsky. Granovsky, who created the Moscow Yiddish State Art Theater (*Goset*), used some of the finest Jewish actors and artists in the Soviet Union to create this silent film masterpiece.

5. *The Light Ahead* (*Di Kliatshe—The Mare*), U.S.A., 1939, Yiddish dialogue. Produced and directed by Edgar G. Ulmer (*Green Fields*); screenplay by Chaver-Paver, based on the fictional writings of Mendele Mokher Seforim; cinematography by J. Burgi-Contner and Edward Hyland. Running time: 80 minutes. With Isidore Casher, Helen Beverly, and David Opatashu.

The Light Ahead is about two young lovers: Fishke, a lame man who is the ward of an 1880's Polish Jewish village, and his lover, the blind Hodel, "who according to tradition are wed by decree of the Town Council in the cemetery during a cholera epidemic to appease the evil spirits." Later the two leave the village in search of a better life.

The film was praised by the *New York Times* as being "remarkably honest and forthright in its portrayal of the trials and tribulations of the Jew and is unsparing of those Jews (in this case the Town Council) who would exploit their own people." This film is probably the best example of a film adaptation from a classic Jewish literary work.

6. *Peeping Toms* (*Metsitsim*), Israel, 1972, Hebrew dialogue. Directed by Uri Zohar; screenplay by Zohar and Arik Einstein; cinematography by Adam Greenberg; music by Shalom Chanoch. Running time: 88 minutes. With Uri Zohar, Arik Einstein, Mona Silberstein, and Sima Eliahu.

The story of an aging "hippie" whose entire life centers on one of Tel Aviv's beaches. Dirty, unshaven, half-dressed, and common, he is in charge of a variety of enterprises on the beach. He is also a peeping tom who allows friends to bring women to his beach in exchange for a glimpse through the dressing-room walls. One of his closest friends is a married pop singer who does not lack for companionship. The contrast between the two provides the focus of the film.

The film is a pointed study of Israeli life and society. With all its humor, the film is really a stirring look at pointless existence. The "peeping tom" analogy of someone on the outside, not participating, makes the point of the film that much more apparent.

7. *Sallah* (Sallah Shabati), Israel, 1965, Hebrew with English subtitles. Written and directed by Ephraim Kishon; produced by Menachem Golan; cinematography by Floyd Crosby; music by Yohana Zarai. Running time: 105 minutes. With Haym Topol, Gila Almagor, and Arik Einstein.

An endearing story of a bearded Oriental Jew's arrival in Israel in 1949 with his wife and seven children and his subsequent battle with entrenched Israeli bureaucracy. He is not understood, nor is his way of life, and he resists attempts to be acculturated to a Western way of life.

Although essentially a comedy, the film also touches on a number of extremely thorny Israeli social problems including the lack of adequate housing and the exploitation of new immigrants by Israeli politicians. The first Israeli film to gain critical acceptance outside Israel, *Sallah* was nominated by the American Academy of Motion Picture Arts and Sciences as one of the five Best Foreign Language Films for 1964.

8. *The Shop on Main Street* (*Obshad Na Korze*), Czechoslovakia, 1965, Czech dialogue. Written and directed by Jan Kadar and Elmar Klos with writing assistance by Ladislav Grosman, based on a story by Grosman; cinematography by Vladimir Novotny; music by Zdenek Liska. Running time: 128 minutes. With Josef Kroner, Ida Kaminska, Hana Slivkova, and Frantisek Svarik.

Set in a small provincial town in Nazi-occupied Czechoslovakia in 1942, the film is about a simple carpenter who is appointed "Aryan controller" of a button shop owned by an elderly nearly-deaf Jewish lady. The woman cannot comprehend why he is there and he eventually decides he is her assistant. Later he grows attached to her, becomes her protector, and in gratitude is financially supported by local Jewish merchants. When the deportations are ordered he hides her but then inadvertently kills her.

***Ida Kaminska in a scene from* Shop on Main Street**

The film won an Academy Award for Best Foreign Picture, the first time a Czech film achieved this award. A powerful study of complicity and an entire generation's failure to fight anti-Semitism, the film provides a subtle portrait of the Holocaust.

9. *Les Violons du Bal*, France, 1974, French with English subtitles. Written and directed by Michel Drach; cinematography by Yann le Masson and William Lubtchansky; music by Jean Manuel de Scarano and Jacques Monty. Running time: 110 minutes. With Marie Josée Nat, Jean-Louis Trintignant, Gabrielle Doulcet, Michel Drach, and David Drach.

This film chronicles Michel Drach's childhood in Paris during the Nazi occupation, including the efforts of his family to go into hiding and their eventual successful escape to neutral Switzerland. Critics in the United States found the film to be "so tasteful it makes you feel boorish. . . . The elegant camera angles, the lovely clothes, the comely faces, and the lush colors combine to cancel out the suffering of the French Jews." European critics were more generous. The film was the official French entry at the Twenty-seventh Cannes International Film Festival and Miss Nat, the actress who portrays Drach's mother, won the Cannes award for Best Actress.

10. *Yidl Mitn Fidl (Yiddle with His Fiddle)*, Poland, 1936, Yiddish dialogue. Directed by Joseph Green and Jan Nowina-Przybylski; produced by Edward Hantower, Josef Frankfurt, and Joseh Green; written by Konrad Tom; cinematography by Jacob Janilowicz; music by Abe Ellstein. Running time: 92 minutes. With Molly Picon, Simche Fostel, Max Bozyk, Leon Liebgold, and Samuel Landau.

Cast in her first feature Yiddish musical comedy, Molly Picon, the darling of the Yiddish theater, portrays a young Jewish woman musician who masquerades as a boy in order to be able to play in the Polish countryside alongside her father. The high point of the movie comes when Yiddle, "finally shedding her 'disguise,' is forced onto the stage of a Warsaw theater and takes the place of the near-bride who has been hired on the strength of her sweet voice, but who flees with her original young admirer just as the curtain is going up."

Opening in New York City at the Ambassador Theater in January 1937, the film received much critical praise. The *New York Times* described the film: "Miss Picon puts so much infectious gayety, not forgetting the proper modicum of sadness, into the action that the result is genuine entertainment."

Yidl Mitn Fidl was the first Yiddish-language film that had an adequate budget. Its success set into motion the so-called Golden Age of Yiddish Cinema, a period which lasted from 1936 until the Nazi invasion of Poland in September 1939.

THE TEN WORST JEWISH FILMS (in alphabetical order)

1. *Children of Rage*, U.S.A., 1975. Written and directed by Arthur Allen Seidelman; screenplay by Arthur Seidelman, based on a story by Ana Laura; produced by George R. Rice; cinematography by Ian Wilson; music by Patrick Gowers. Running time: 106 minutes. With Helmut Griem, Olga Georges-Picot, Richard Alfierl, and Simon Ward.

When *Children of Rage* opened in New York City at the Fine Arts Theater in May 1975, Vincent Canby, film critic of the *New York Times*, described it: "If a movie could be made by a computer, it might look like 'Children of Rage,' a fastidiously well-meaning, completely lifeless film that attempts to dramatize the Israeli-Palestinian conflict in what producers call human terms." David Shalmon, an Israeli M.D., sneaks off to Jordan to care for Palestinian refugees, where one of his patients, a Palestinian woman and the sister of a terrorist, falls in love with him. The dialogue is slow and the plot is confusing, leaving the viewer feeling that

Molly Picon in a scene from Yidl Mitn Fidl

Children of Rage is "totally lacking in the kind of idiosyncratic detail that forever separates cinema from mere picture-taking."

2. *Daughters, Daughters*, Israel, 1975, Hebrew with English subtitles. Directed by Moshe Mizrahi; produced by Menahem Golan; written by Shai K. Ophir and Moshe Mizrahi; cinematography by Adam Greenberg. Running time: 88 minutes. With Shai K. Ophir, Zaharira Harifai, and Michal Bat-Adam.

Daughters, Daughters is a failed tragicomedy involving a rich Israeli businessman, the father of eight daughters, who despairs that he has no male heir. He is terrible to his wife, to his daughters, and to his young mistress.

Although this was the official Israeli entry at the 1974 Cannes Film Festival, director Moshe Mizrahi (*I Love You Rosa; The House on Chelouche Street; Madame Rosa*) somehow missed the mark completely with this "bleak" comedy. Focussing on the father's male chauvinist attitudes, the film attempts to provide humor where there is none. Plot is virtually nonexistent and the acting, with the exception of Miss Harifai's is poor.

3. *The Dybbuk* (*HaDibuk*), Israel, 1970, Hebrew dialogue. Directed by Ilan Eldad; produced by Amatzia Hiuni and Adi Cohen; written by Shraga Friedman, based on the play by S. Anski; cinematography by Goetz Neumann; music by Noam Sheriff. Running time: 95 minutes. With David Opatashu, Peter Frye, and Tina Wodetzky.

This is the classic story of two lovers who are betrothed to marry from the time of their childhood. However, at adolescence the young woman is to marry another and her betrothed groom seeks redress through Kabbalah.

The story, although a powerful classic on the Yiddish stage, is butchered here through inept sets, poor transitions, and poor direction. This attempt to make the Dybbuk come alive for the modern Israeli filmgoer misses the mark and wastes potentially fine performances by Opatashu, Frye, and Wodetzky. One cannot even begin to compare this version with the 1937 classic version.

4. *The Jerusalem File,* U.S.A., 1972. Directed by John Flynn; written by Troy Kennedy Martin; cinematography by Raoul Coutard and Brian Probyn; music by John Scott. Running time: 95 minutes. With Bruce Davison, Nicol Williamson, Daria Halprin, Donald Pleasence, and Zev Revach.

A young archeologist from the United States arranges for a meeting between an Arab nationalist and an Israeli student leader, interested in ending the conflict between Palestinians and Israelis. Trailing all three is Donald Pleasence, an Israeli intelligence officer. The plot is simplistic and unreal. Wasting good acting by Donald Pleasence and brilliant color shots of Jerusalem by Raoul Coutard, Troy Martin's script was simply another failed effort in the post-1967 period to attempt to suggest a means to a Mid-East peace.

5. *The Jewish Gauchos*, Argentina, 1975, Spanish with English subtitles. Directed by Juan Jose Jusid; written by Alejandro Saderman, Ana Maria Gerchunoff, Oscar Viale, and Mr. Jusid; cinematography by Juan Carlos Desanzo; music by Gustavo Beytalmann; choreography by Lia Jelin. Running time: 92 minutes. With Pepe Soriano, Dora Baret, Victor Laplace, and Ginamaria Hidalgo.

The Jewish Gauchos is an Argentinian musical about a group of Jewish immigrants who settle on the pampa at the end of the nineteenth century. Immediately, there are conflicts between the newly arrived Jewish cowboys and their Catholic ranch-owning neighbors. The movie, intended to be epic in scope, includes an arranged marriage gone awry, natural and man-made disasters, and poisoned wells. Richard Eder in the *New York Times* described the film as "Fiddler on the Hoof."

6. *Kuni Lemel in Tel Aviv* (*Kuni Lemel B' Tel Aviv*), Israel, 1977, Hebrew dialogue. Written and directed by Yoel Silberg; cinematography by Nissim Leon; lyrics by Amos Ettinger and Michael Burstyn; music by Dor Seltzer. Running time: 90 minutes. With Mike Burstyn and Mandy Rice-Davies.

An elderly American Jew vows to leave all his property to the first grandson who marries a Jewish woman and settles in Israel; his two grandsons, one a student at a New York yeshiva, the other a musician living with a non-Jewish girl friend, proceed to compete with one another for the old man's estate. Unlike the earlier well-made *Two Kuni Lemels* (1970), this film does little but play havoc with the Yiddish classic which provided the plot for a cinematic disaster. The film is weakened still further by cutesy music and unimaginative choreography. Burstyn, in the dual role of the two brothers, is fair but nowhere near as good as he was in the earlier film. Mandy Rice-Davies, better known for her role in England's Profumo scandal, is incredibly dull as the blond shikse.

7. *Lepke*, U.S.A., 1975. Produced and directed by Menahem Golan; written by Wesley Lau and Tomar Hoffs; cinematography by Andrew Davis. Running time: 110 minutes. With Tony Curtis, Anjanette Comer, Milton Berle, and Vaughn Meader.

The story of Jewish gangster Louis (Lepke) Buchalter, who terrorized New York as head of Murder, Inc.; the film follows his life from deliquent childhood to gangster adulthood.

This is Menahem Golan's abortive attempt to show that Jews are part and parcel of every walk of life. A major undertaking with a fine cast, the film falls flat on its face due to a mediocre plot. The film also tends to spend more time exploiting "gore" than telling a story. Special lighting effects, which were incorporated to add to the picture, only detract.

Opening in New York City at the Loew's Cinema in May 1975, the film was panned by critics as a "dour, witless movie."

8. *Magician of Lublin*, U.S.A., 1979. Directed by Menahem Golan; produced by Golan and Yoram Globus; screenplay by Golan and Irving S. White, based on a novel by Isaac Bashevis Singer; cinematography by David Garfinkel; music by Maurice Jarre. Running time: 115 minutes. With Alan Arkin, Louise Fletcher, Vallerie Perrine, Shelley Winters, and Lou Jacobi.

Yasha is a poor Jewish magician who travels the Polish countryside. His sole ambition in life is to perform in Warsaw; to this end he is prepared to sacrifice everything else.

The Magician of Lublin was the first of I. B. Singer's novels to be made into a feature film and for this reason the film's release was eagerly anticipated. Unfortunately, Menahem Golan's adaptation fails to do justice to the novel, and the film lacks all the nuances which made the novel so special. Singer himself disavowed any association with the picture. A fair performance by Alan Arkin was not enough to save this film.

9. *Portnoy's Complaint*, U.S.A., 1972. Directed, produced, and written by Ernest Lehman from a novel by Philip Roth; cinematography by Philip Lathrop; music by Michel Legrand. Running time: 101 minutes. With Richard Benjamin, Lee Grant, Karen Black, and Jill Clayburgh.

Virtually a modern classic as a novel, the story portrays the misadventures of Alexander Portnoy, a middle-class Jewish male, and his experiences with youthful masturbation, a domineering mother, and an active sex life. Where author Roth gave his book a subtle richness, however, screenwriter Lehman failed to translate it onto the "big screen." The comic and piercing portrait that caught the attention of a generation of readers is lost in this poor film adaptation. Lehman did not adequately visualize what is taking place on the screen, leaving most of the plot to our imaginations. The sexual innuendos, so integral a part of the work, are lost. The resulting picture is a bland hundred minutes, lacking in depth or comic relief.

Vincent Canby, writing in the *New York*

Times, summarized the film adaptation this way: " 'Portnoy's Complaint' . . . really is a Jewish joke, but a distressingly poor one. . . . Mr. Lehman has lifted directly from the novel as if he were dismembering it."

10. *Yidishe Keneg Lir (Yiddish King Lear)*, U.S.A., 1935, Yiddish dialogue. Directed by Harry Thomashefsky; screenplay by A. Armband from a play by Jacob Gordin; cinematography by Joe Freeman. Running time: 80 minutes. With Maurice Krohner, Fannie Levenstein, and Morris Zarlovsky.

Based largely on Shakespeare's *King Lear*, this is a story of an aging father in 1892 Vilna who divides his fortune among his three daughters just before he is to leave for Palestine. Because of greed, two of the daughters are cut off from the inheritance and the father, for want of money, is forced to return from the Holy Land as a beggar and wanderer going blind.

Made on a very low budget, this film rendered an injustice to the Gordin play. It is slow paced and monotonous, and the viewer is left with a static film and uninspired performances.

—E.A.G.

Richard Benjamin as Alexander Portnoy

THE JEWISH ALMANAC'S GUIDE TO TV VIEWING

If the Nielson ratings also indicated an ethnic quotient, then Jewish identity would have been canned years ago. From the onset of network television in 1946, programs about Jews and Jewish life have rarely been scheduled during prime time viewing. Jewish characters had been featured in a number of dramatic series, but it was not until the early 1970's that programs, mostly situation comedies, with distinctive Jewish flavor began to appear with any frequency. Even here, a common theme was the jockeying between "modern" or assimilated Jewish offspring and their "old-fashioned," often European-born, possessive parents. Even as late as the 1970's Jewish identity was still being reduced on television to a series of Jewish sounding names and stock ethnic traits.

"*The Jewish Almanac*'s Guide to TV Viewing" features series whose central characters are distinctly "Jewish." We have not included made-for-TV movies or special limited series, such as "Holocaust," Moses the Lawgiver," "Seventh Avenue," or Rob Reiner's 1978 five-part series, "Free Country." The following programs are listed in order of the year they were first broadcast. The format of this article is based on Tim Brooks' and Earle Marsh's prizewinning book, *The Complete Directory to Prime Time Network TV Shows 1946–Present* (New York, 1979).

"The Goldbergs"

Situation Comedy (CBS, NBC, Dumont)
Telecast: 1949–1955
Cast of Jewish Characters:
Molly Goldberg .... Gertrude Berg
Jake Goldberg
(1949–51) .... Philip Loeb
Jake Goldberg
(1952) .... Harold J.Stone
Jake Goldberg
(1953-54) .... Robert H. Harris
Sammy Goldberg
(1949–52) .... Larry Robinson
Sammy Goldberg
(1954) .... Tom Taylor
Rosalie Goldberg .... Arlene McQuade
Uncle David .... Eli Mintz
Mrs.Bloom .... Olga Fabina

One of TV's earliest situation comedies, "The Goldbergs" starred an all-Jewish cast. For almost twenty years prior to its television incarnation, "The Goldbergs" had been an enormously successful radio program, conceived by its star, Gertrude Berg. Both on radio and TV, Berg played Molly Goldberg, mother and full-time problem-solver of a middle-class Jewish family in the Bronx. With her gentle Yiddish accent and persistent malapropisms, Molly brought all crises to resolution with a mixture of kindliness and common sense. The rest of the household consisted of her overly good-hearted husband Jake and their typically American teenage children, Sammy and Rosalie. Next-door neighbor Mrs. Bloom was Molly's favorite gossip-mate, always responsive to the call, "Yoo-hoo, Mrs. Bloom," with its promise of juicy news.

"Like many other New Yorkers, the 'Goldbergs' decided to leave New York City" for good. On September 22, 1955, the program began its twenty-fifth year as a radio and television attraction with the announcement that the family was abandoning its apartment in the Bronx for a "handsome saltbox cottage with a master bedroom and a dining alcove" in suburban Haverville. Just as the move to the suburbs can be seen as a further step in Jewish assimilation, so too did the Goldbergs' move foretell the end of their uniquely Jewish character.

(See "Philip Loeb, the Goldbergs, and the Blacklist".)

"Menasha The Magnificent"

Situation Comedy (NBC)
Telecast: July 1950–September 1950

Cast of Jewish Characters:
Menasha .... Menasha Skulnick

During its brief run, "Menasha the Magnificent" starred Yiddish theater comedian Menasha Skulnick. Skulnick played an ineffectual *schlemiel* who managed a restaurant owned by the intimidating Mrs. Davis (Zanah Cunningham). At the beginning of each day Menasha would fortify his spirits by singing "Oh, What A Beautiful Morning." For the rest of the day, he would fall victim to Mrs. Davis' wrath and his own ineptitude.

"The Gertrude Berg Show"

Situation Comedy (CBS)
Telecast: October 1961–April 1962
Cast of Jewish Characters:
Sarah Green .... Gertrude Berg

Six years after the termination of "The Goldbergs," Gertrude Berg starred again in her own series, this time as Sarah Green, a widow who, in late middle age, had enrolled for a college degree. Berg's new character was essentially an older Molly Goldberg in a different setting. The show's humor relied often on the interaction between the Yiddish-accented Mrs. Green and Professor Crayton (Sir Cedric Hardwicke), her professor of English on exchange from Cambridge University. In pairing Hardwicke and Mrs. Berg, the show's creators hoped to repeat the success that the two performers had achieved together as stars of the hit Broadway comedy, *A Majority of One*. During its first few weeks on the air, the series was entitled "Mrs. G. Goes to College."

"Bridget Loves Bernie"

Situation Comedy (CBS)
Telecast: September 1972–September 1973
Cast of Jewish Characters:
Bernie Steinberg .... David Birney
Sam Steinberg .... Harold J. Stone
Sophie Steinberg................. Bibi Osterwald
Uncle Moe .... Ned Glass

Because it seemed to condone intermarriage, this show caused distress in both the Roman Catholic and Jewish communities. Like the stage and radio hit of the 1920's, *Abie's Irish Rose*, "Bridget Loves Bernie" involved the marriage of a young Jewish writer, Bernie Steinberg, to Bridget Mary Theresa Colleen Fitzgerald, an elementary school teacher and the devoted sister of an Irish-American priest.

Much of the show's ethnic humor depended on the cultural friction between the Steinberg and Fitzgerald families, who differed from each other both in terms of class and religion. Bridget's affluent parents occupied a luxurious townhouse, while the elder Mr. and Mrs. Steinberg made ends meet by running a kosher-style delicatessen together with Bernie's Uncle Moe. The show's satiric, if affectionate, depiction of the two families implied that their opposition to the marriage of their children was narrow-minded and parochial.

Organized Jewish groups saw in "Bridget Loves Bernie" an endorsement of intermarriage and a mockery of particularist Jewish values. Typical was the accusation of Rabbi Abraham Gross, president of the Rabbinical Alliance of America (the body of Orthodox Rabbis), that the program was a "flagrant insult" to Jews. Representatives of the Orthodox, Conservative, and Reform movements launched a successful campaign to force cancellation of the series. After just one season CBS took the show off the air, despite its being the fifth most popular program on television at the time.

"Rhoda"

Situation Comedy (CBS)
Telecast: September 1974–September 1979
Cast of Jewish Characters:
Rhoda Morgenstern............ Valerie Harper
Brenda Morgenstern................ Julie Kavner
Ida Morgenstern .... Nancy Walker
Martin Morgenstern .... Harold J. Gould
Myrna Morgenstern .... Barbara Sharma
Gary Levy .... Ron Silver

As a result of the popularity of Rhoda Morgenstern on "The Mary Tyler Moore Show," Valerie Harper was rewarded in 1974 with her own series. In order not to allow the program "to founder in some ethnic sea," Rhoda's creators had her move out of the home of her possessive Jewish parents and marry non-Jew Joe Gerard (David Groh), owner of a wrecking company. They also diminished her stereotypically Jewish guilt and sexual insecurity. Subsequently in the series, Rhoda divorced Joe and opened a window-dressing shop with a timid friend who, although no relation, was named Myrna Morgenstern.

Rhoda's newly acquired independence, self-esteem, and ease in the non-Jewish world contrasted to the unhappiness of her sister Brenda. Overweight and lonely for a man, Brenda remained under the thumb of her interfering mother (Nancy Walker). Some observers criticized "Rhoda" for implying that Jewish family values lead inevitably to misery and neurosis. They also objected to Rhoda's marriage to Joe as a suggestion that one's Jewish identity, in general, is a burden to be discarded. Allan Burns, chief writer for the show, denied that "Rhoda" was about specifically Jewish issues: "The show is about people—the effect a Jewish mother has on her daughter is universal. It applies to Irish mothers, German mothers right down the line." If laughter can be found in our commonality, then surely Rhoda's ethnicity appealed to all audiences, especially between 1974 and 1976 when the program was among the ten most popular American TV shows on the air.

"Busting Loose"

Situation Comedy (CBS)
Telecast: January 1977–November 1977
Cast of Jewish Characters:
Lenny Markowitz .... Adam Arkin
Sam Markowitz .... Jack Kruschen
Pearl Markowitz .... Pearl Markowitz

Like "Rhoda," this was another situation comedy in which a young adult asserted independence by moving away from parents and setting up house for him/herself. Lenny Markowitz, played by Adam Arkin (Alan Arkin's son), found himself unemployed after graduating from engineering school. But, determined to make his own way, he rented a run-down apartment and went to work as a salesman in a shoe store. Following a pattern familiar from other shows, many of the jokes in the series grew out of the interaction between Lenny and his overly solicitous parents (Pat Carroll and Jack Kruschen). Other parts of the show were taken up with Lenny's hunt for a girl friend, which he finally acquired shortly before the series ended.

"Lanigan's Rabbi"

Mystery Drama (NBC)
Telecast: January 1977–July 1977
Cast of Jewish Characters:
Rabbi David Small .... Bruce Solomon
Miriam Small .... Janet Margolin

This program, which drew its main inspiration from Harry Kemelman's *Rabbi* mystery novels, has been the only prime time series on American television to portray Judaism, not just ethnic Jewish identity, in a positive light. Even so, "Lanigan's Rabbi" shied away from Kemelman's literary characterization of Rabbi David Small as a man preoccupied with talmudic scholarship and reasoning. Small's talmudic skills were, in the novels, the rules by which he was able to find the solution to the crimes that stumped local Police Chief Hugh Lanigan (played in the series by Art Carney). On television, however, his talent for crime detection consisted simply of a knack for the right guess. Neither the novels nor the TV series specified Rabbi Small's denomination by name, but his philosophy in Kemelman's novels was clearly Conservative, while he emerged on television as a Reform rabbi. Although "Lanigan's Rabbi" made its hero less religiously traditional, its positive attitude towards Judaism was unambiguous. The rabbi and his congregants seemed to engage in their Jewish activities with genuine pleasure. "Lanigan's Rabbi" was one of four sub-series that constituted the NBC "Sunday Night Movie." It rotated with "Columbo," "McCloud," and "MacMillan."

"Archie Bunker's Place"

Situation Comedy (CBS)
Telecast: September 1979—
Cast of Jewish Characters:
Murray Klein .... Martin Balsam
Stephanie Mills .... Danielle Brisebois

This series functioned as a sequel after the cancellation of the popular "All in the Family." During the last season of "All in the Family," Archie Bunker went into business for himself as coowner of a bar, which he named "Archie's Place." The same season saw the departure to California of Archie's daughter and son-in-law. They were replaced, however, by a new addition to the Bunker household: Archie and his wife Edith took in their small abandoned niece, Stephanie Mills (Danielle Briseboise), only to discover that the child's late mother had been Jewish and Stephanie had been raised accordingly. Despite Archie's proclaimed distaste for "hebes," he and Edith arranged for Stephanie to continue her Jewish education with a local Queens rabbi.

Stephanie was the first regular Jewish character in eight years of "All in the Family," and she continued to turn up in "Archie Bunker's Place."

In the latter series Archie remained a main character, but the focus shifted from his home to his bar. The series' crucial Jewish figure and second major character was Murray Klein (Martin Balsam), a middle-aged liberal businessman, who became Archie's new partner in commerce and opponent in outlook. In the first episode Murray bought a half-interest in the bar from Archie's ex-partner. Outraged Archie let it be known that there could be no successful cooperation between Christian and Jew. Murray was about to give up hope of an amicable business relationship when he met Stephanie (who was wearing a Jewish star), heard her story, and decided that a heart of gold beat under Archie's bigoted bluster.

—M.N.

THE MEDIA PURGE

10 BLACKLISTED JEWS OF THE 1950s

At its height, the blacklist of the late 1940's and early 1950's affected hundreds of Americans who were dismissed or denied employment because of alleged Communist or pro-Communist sympathies. More often than not, these individuals were either witnesses who had been called before the House Un-American Activities Committee (HUAC) or were persons identified as Communists by desperate HUAC witnesses eager to protect themselves. The list spread from Hollywood to Broadway, from television studios to Madison Avenue advertising firms. Those listed were dismissed from their jobs in film, radio, television, and theater.

Although the number implicated was only one-half of 1 percent of the total number of persons employed in the entertainment industry, the repercussions of the blacklist were pervasive. A chill swept through the entertainment world; the quality of television programming and film content suffered. Liberals shivered at the successful collusion of government and big business to stifle dissent and to discredit the political Left. Film and TV people eyed one another cautiously, never certain who would name names in order to protect a career.

Once named, those blacklisted had to work pseudonymously or at a fraction of their worth. In *Scoundrel Time* Lillian Hellman notes that, after being blacklisted, her yearly earnings plunged from $140,000 to $10,000. When they dropped below that figure she had to take a part-time job in a department store to make ends meet. Other people changed occupations, some emigrated, a few took their own lives.

The following profiles examine the blacklist's impact on the lives and careers of ten Jews in the entertainment industry. A few of these men were Communists; most, however, were not. Some of them stood firm under HUAC pressure and went to jail; others cooperated with HUAC for fear that they would lose their jobs if they resisted.

Albert Maltz, one of the Hollywood Ten, is an example of a man who did have Communist sympathies, who went to prison in defense of his right to adhere to Marxist principles, and who was subsequently blacklisted.

Lewis Milestone, Irving Pichel, and Robert Rossen were members of the so-called Unfriendly Eighteen singled out by HUAC. Having been subpoenaed, they declared that they would not answer questions before the Committee. While none of them were actually called to testify during the 1947 Hollywood hearings, each of them suffered from the association. Milestone's career slowed down dramatically because of the subpoena and its implication. Pichel's career stopped entirely for a time. He was able to find work in Hollywood only after a "clearance specialist" suggested that he repudiate his liberal past. Rossen, called to give testimony both in 1951 and 1953, refused to testify during his first appearance before the Committee. Two years later, having felt the fear generated by the blacklist, he succumbed and supplied names.

Although not part of these groups, actors Howard Da Silva and Zero Mostel, writer Abe Polonsky, and actor/writer/director Jules Dassin also refused to cooperate with HUAC and were blacklisted. Dassin emigrated to Europe; Da Silva tried, often unsuccessfully, to work on Broadway; Polonsky wrote pseudonymously; and Mostel painted.

Actors like Larry Parks and John Garfield who cooperated with HUAC also suffered. While both men tried desperately to maintain their careers, neither succeeded. Those whom HUAC named and whom the blacklist touched were doomed whether or not they had been Communists, whether or not they cooperated.

Albert Maltz (1908—)

Maltz was the son of Lithuanian immigrants. His early years were typical of those of children of poor first generation American Jews. After attending City College of New York, he decided to use his artistic talent to expose political corruption. In 1931 he collaborated on *Merry-Go-Round*, a play which indicted New York City's corrupt Tammany Hall politicians; later he associated with the left-wing Theater Union.

In 1938 Maltz won the O. Henry Memorial Award for "The Happiest Man on Earth," a short story which appeared in *Harper's* magazine. Two years later he moved to Hollywood hoping that screenwriting would subsidize his literary pursuits, and for a while it did. *Moscow Strikes Back* (1942) was named Best War Documentary by the New York Film Critics and won the Academy Award for Best War Documentary.

Often called the most talented (or at least the most literary) of the Hollywood leftists, Maltz was active in the Communist Party for years. He defended artistic freedom in a 1946 tract, "What Shall We Ask of Writers?" Severely attacked by his Hollywood comrades, Maltz confessed two months later that he had been "one sided and nondialectical." During the House Un-American Activities Committee hearings many former leftists testified that Maltz's humiliation had soured them on the Party.

HUAC

Maltz was the third of the so-called Hollywood Ten to testify. For some unknown reason, he was the only one allowed to read a prepared statement to the Committee. When asked if he was a member of the Screen Writers Guild, Maltz replied, "Next you are going to ask me what religious group I belong to."

The House of Representatives found Maltz guilty of contempt of Congress. He was fined $1,000 and sentenced to one year in prison. He was released from Federal prison after serving nine months.

AFTERMATH

Before HUAC subpoenaed him, Maltz was working on a screenplay of his novel *The Journey of Simon McKeever*. Although a studio had bought the property, they dropped it immediately after his sentencing. Unable to find work in Hollywood, Maltz moved to Mexico where he supported himself writing fiction.

A staunch Communist, Maltz continued to support the USSR until 1956 when Khrushchev revealed to the Russian Communist Party the truth about Stalin's excesses during the 1930's. Maltz has since stated that his "boundless idealism" had caused him to turn a deaf ear to those who tried to tell him the truth about Soviet life.

As late as 1960 Maltz was still underemployed. Frank Sinatra had wanted to hire him to write a script for a new motion picture, but public pressure forced Sinatra to reconsider.

By the late 1960's, however, Maltz was back in the United States and writing commercially. Asked about the blacklist in a *New York Times* interview, he commented:

"If we had won our case, the McCarthy era would not have occurred . . . The bludgeon of a blacklist is precisely what the Soviet Union is doing today. A Jew applies to them to go to Israel, he gets fired from his job—like that. No matter what his position. And the purpose of that is to intimidate 10,000 Jews from applying to go to Israel."

PARTIAL CREDITS
(writer)

Merry-Go-Round (collaboration), play, 1931

Peace on Earth, play, 1933

Black Pit, play, 1935

Happiest Man on Earth, novel, 1938

The Underground Stream, novel, 1940

This Gun for Hire; Moscow Strikes Back, films, 1942

Destination Tokyo, film, 1943

The Cross and the Arrow, novel, 1944

The Naked City, film, 1948

The Journey of Simon McKeever, novel, 1949

A Short Day in a Long Life, novel, 1957

Two Mules for Sister Sara, film, 1972

Irving Pichel (1891–1954)

Born in Pittsburgh in 1891, Pichel attended Harvard and made his acting debut in Boston with the Castle Square Theater Company. In 1919, he moved to New York to join the Shubert organization as a director. Hollywood beckoned next and in 1927 he went to MGM as a writer. Three years later he joined Paramount Studios as an actor. For the duration of his career, Pichel acted, directed, and wrote.

HUAC

Although he was one of the so-called Unfriendly Eighteen, a group of witnesses who in 1947 announced that they would not cooperate with HUAC, Pichel was never called to testify. It is doubtful that he was a Communist. His "sins" were having been a member of several Communist front organizations and having directed *A Medal for Benny*, a wartime film which depicted Mexican Americans in a positive light.

AFTERMATH

Once he was cited by the Committee, Pichel had difficulty finding work in Hollywood. He taught for several years at UCLA's Department of Fine Arts.

Anxious to return to his first love, films, Pichel worked with Roy Brewer, a "clearance specialist," to repudiate his leftist ideas and associations. With Brewer's help, Pichel was cleared and reinstated within the industry in early 1953. He died of a heart attack six months later.

PARTIAL CREDITS
(film actor or d = director)

The Road to Reno; An American Tragedy, 1931

Westward Pass; Madame Butterfly, 1932

Oliver Twist; I'm No Angel, 1933

She Was a Lady; Cleopatra, 1934

Hearts in Bondage; Dracula's Daughter, 1936

Jezebel, 1937

Torture Ship; Rio, 1939

The Moon Is Down, d 1943

The Bride Wore Boots, d 1946

Destination Moon, d 1950

Santa Fe Trail, d 1951

Martin Luther, d 1953

Lewis Milestone (1895—)

Born in Chisinau, Russia, in 1895, Milestone immigrated to the United States in 1917 and arrived in Hollywood three years later. He studied under the "greats" as an assistant editor and writer and won an Oscar for Best Comedy Director (*Two Arabian Knights*) in 1927. Three years later, he won the Academy Award for Best Director for *All Quiet on the Western Front*.

Milestone had an eye and ear for good material. Among his credits are *The Front Page*, *Rain*, and *Of Mice and Men*. Many people felt that this last film, with its sympathetic treatment of blacks, caused him to be cited by HUAC.

HUAC

Milestone was one of the "Unfriendly Eighteen" but he was never called to testify before the Committee.

AFTERMATH

Although Milestone was not officially blacklisted, some superpatriots did what they could to ruin his career. When Milestone hired Ring Lardner, Jr. (one of the Hollywood Ten), Hedda Hopper wrote in her column:

". . . let's take a look at Lardner's new boss. He was born in Russia and came to this country years ago . . . He has a beautiful home in which he holds leftish rallies, is married to an American and has a fortune here. But still his heart seems to yearn for Russia. Wonder if Joe [Stalin] would take him back?"

Milestone's later work never fulfilled his early promise. In a 1949 interview he remarked: "As a creative artist it ought to be my business to create. Yet today I must concern myself with more than the aesthetic principles of filmmaking . . . I must have a vital interest in the climate in which I work."

PARTIAL CREDITS
(film director)

Seven Sinners, 1925

The New Klondyke, 1926

Two Arabian Knights, 1927

All Quiet on the Western Front, 1930

The Front Page, 1931

Hallelujah, I'm a Bum, 1933

The General Died at Dawn, 1936

Of Mice and Men, 1939

A Walk in the Sun, 1946

The Red Pony; Halls of Montezuma, 1948

Pork Chop Hill, 1959

Ocean's 11, 1961

Mutiny on the Bounty, 1962

Robert Rossen (1908–1966)

Rossen was born in the poor, Jewish section of Manhattan, on Rivington Street. His mother had been a member of the Russian-Jewish intelligensia, his grandfather was a rabbi, and an uncle wrote Hebrew poetry. Rossen himself worked as a prizefighter on the lower East Side before entering New York University.

At college Rossen enjoyed acting and directing with the Washington Square Players. After the 1935 Broadway debut of his play *The Body Beautiful* he received several Hollywood offers. He moved west in 1939 under contract to MGM.

Rossen was politically active during his early Hollywood years. His films—*The Roaring*

Twenties, They Won't Forget, Dust Be My Destiny—embody his concern, and that of the Communist Party, with social and psychological realism.

As a member of the Party Rossen chaired, in 1943, the Hollywood Writers Mobilization (a "leftist" group which Lillian Hellman notes developed 120 film documentaries and 1,069 radio scripts for the Armed Forces and civilian war agencies). Returning to New York in 1944, Rossen re-evaluated his political commitments and decided to leave the Party.

Back in Hollywood, Rossen directed and produced *Body and Soul*, his first big hit. *All the King's Men* (1949) won an Academy Award for Best Film.

HUAC

An original member of the Unfriendly Eighteen, Rossen was not called to tesitfy until the Hollywood HUAC hearings of 1951. At that time he took what was dubbed "the augmented Fifth." He said that he was not presently a Communist Party member or sympathizer but he refused to answer if he had been in the past.

Two years later, after having lost $100,000 worth of contracts, Rossen reappeared before the Committee. This time he admitted to having belonged to the Party and having contributed $40,000 to Communist Party coffers. Under pressure he broke down and named fifty-seven alleged party members.

AFTERMATH

Despite his cooperation with the Committee, Rossen had difficulty finding work in Hollywood during the 1950's. Not only had he been a Party member but he had become an informer. Later he tried to make movies in Europe, but they lacked the deftness and consistency of his American films.

Twelve years after *All the King's Men*, Rossen won acclaim for *The Hustler*. However, his next and last film, *Lilith*, was not well received.

PARTIAL CREDITS
(film writer or d=director, p=producer; also playwright)

The Body Beautiful, play, 1935

The Roaring Twenties, 1939

The Sea Wolf, 1941

Edge of Darkness, d 1942

A Walk in the Sun, 1945

Body and Soul, d 1947

All the King's Men, dp (also wrote), 1949

The Cool World, play, 1960

The Hustler, dp (also wrote), 1961

Billy Budd, co-writer, 1962

Lilith, dp (also wrote), 1964

Howard Da Silva (1909—)

Née Howard Silverblatt

Born in Cleveland, Ohio, Howard Silverblatt's first real job was as a manual laborer. In the early 1930's he moved to New York City, changed his name, and started to act professionally. In 1934 he joined the Civic Repertory Company.

Five years later Da Silva arrived in Hollywood. He was well paid and worked at every studio. Between 1939 and 1951 he was cast in over forty films. At the 1947 Hollywood HUAC hearings, however, friendly witness Robert Taylor testified that Da Silva "always had something to say at the wrong time" during Screen Actors Guild meetings.

HUAC

Taylor's remark poisoned Da Silva's career. He was forced to switch agents four times between 1947 and 1951, but each agent heard the same answer from producers: "We can't hire him, he's too hot."

Da Silva was called to testify before HUAC in March 1951. When asked about his affiliations with the Civil Rights Committee, the Actors Lab, and the Communist Party, Da Silva invoked the First and Fifth Amendments.

AFTERMATH

Prior to his appearance before the Committee Da Silva had acted in RKO's *Slaughter Trail*. After he testified, RKO announced that it would excise Da Silva's part and re-shoot it with another actor. Later Da Silva moved to New York and found work on radio, but American Legion posts bombarded his sponsors with hostile mail every time he was on the air. Broadway producers were afraid to hire him for fear his presence would trigger boycotts. Between 1950 and 1962 Da Silva was shut out of Hollywood and Broadway. Eventually he worked again. Ironically, one of his recent parts was in *1776*, where he played the part of the American patriot Benjamin Franklin.

PARTIAL CREDITS
(film actor)

Sea Wolf; Sergeant York, 1941

Omaha Trail, 1942

Lost Weekend, 1943

Duffy's Tavern; Two Years Before the Mast; Blue Dahlia, 1946

They Live by Night, 1948

Great Gatsby, 1949

Underworld Story; Three Husbands, 1950

Fourteen Hours, 1957

David and Lisa, 1962

The Outrage, 1964

Nevada Smith, 1966

1776, 1972

The Great Gatsby, 1974

Zero Mostel (1915–1977)
Née Samuel Mostel

Born in the Brownsville section of Brooklyn in 1915, Zero Mostel's childhood was not typical of New York Jewish children. In 1916 his ten-member family moved to Connecticut to farm the land. Returning to New York City during the 1920's, Mostel did miserably at Seward Park High School, graduating near the bottom of his class—the explanation, he would later claim, for the nickname Zero.

Although Mostel's father wanted him to be a rabbi like himself, the younger Mostel yearned to be an artist. His mother offered encouragement and Zero attended City College to study fine arts and English. He enrolled at New York University for a Master of Fine Arts degree, but dropped out in 1936 and spent the next ten years travelling throughout the country, working in factories, on the docks, and in the mines.

During the late 1930's Mostel was employed as a WPA lecturer. His presentations about paintings at the Metropolitan Museum of Art and the Frick were, reputedly, the most informative and hilarious art lectures ever given.

Eager to subsidize his artistic ambitions, Mostel began to work as a comedian. He earned five dollars a night doing stand-up comedy acts at private parties. In 1942 he made his professional debut and within three weeks was signed up for a radio show and vaudeville spots. In one year his salary rose from $40 to $4,000 a week.

Mostel went west in 1942 where he made several forgettable movies before being drafted. After the war he worked in film, television, radio, and theater.

HUAC

Mostel was blacklisted in the early 1950's. Although he denied being a Communist, he had supported groups like the National Negro Congress and the Spanish Refugee Appeal of the Joint Anti-Fascist Refugee Committee. After his name appeared in *Red Channels*, an anti-Communist publication, he lost film and TV contracts.

Back in New York, Mostel rented a small studio on West 28th Street and spent the next few years painting. He and his family lived on West 86th Street in the same apartment building as fellow blacklisted actor Philip Loeb. One month after Loeb's suicide, Mostel was called to testify before HUAC.

AFTERMATH

Years later Mostel said: "Maybe the blacklist was a good thing. If I'd kept on making lousy movies I might be the most hackneyed, tired actor you ever saw today. This way I returned to painting. And I got a chance to do James Joyce and Shalom Aleichem."

Mostel's performance in *Ulysses in Nighttown* (1958) turned heads and in 1961 he won a Tony for his acting in Ionesco's *Rhinoceros*. Each success topped the one before; in 1963 Mostel starred in *A Funny Thing Happened on the Way to the Forum* and in 1964 he played the legendary Tevye in Shalom Aleichem's *Fiddler on the Roof*.

Mostel returned to films and made several light comedies like *Angel Levine* and *The Producers*. In *The Front*, his last film, he played a blacklisted comedian who commits suicide. When his performance was criticized for lacking credibility, writer Walter Bernstein commented that Mostel found it too painful to relive some of his experiences.

Mostel died in September 1977 while rehearsing a new show in Philadelphia. A critic eulogized him as "the actor's actor, the critic's actor, and, perhaps most importantly, the theatergoer's actor."

PARTIAL CREDITS
(*actor in films and plays*)

Du Barry Was a Lady; Mr. Belvedere Rings the Bells, 1942

Panic in the Streets, 1950

The Enforcer, 1951

Ulysses in Nighttown, play, 1958

Rhinoceros, play, 1961

A Funny Thing Happened on the Way to the Forum, play, 1963

Fiddler on the Roof, play, 1964

A Funny Thing . . ., 1966

The Great Bank Robbery, 1967

Great Catherine; The Producers, 1968

Angel Levine, 1969

The Hot Rock, 1972

The Front, 1973

Fiddler . . ., play, 1976

Jules Dassin (1911—)

Born in Middletown, Connecticut, Dassin began his theatrical career as an actor in the New York City Yiddish Theater. From there he went to the Group Theater and then began writing radio plays. In 1940 MGM hired him to direct short subjects. Within ten years he had a long list of detective and gangster films to his credit.

HUAC

As a result of the political climate in Hollywood, Dassin was forced to seek employment abroad.

AFTERMATH

While living in Europe Dassin wrote, acted in, and directed several popular films. Nevertheless, American actors were afraid to work with him. His days on the blacklist ended when Hollywood turned out to see and celebrate his famous *Never on Sunday* (1960). Only eighteen months earlier, Dassin's colleagues had rebuffed him when he brought *He Who Must Die* to the United States. But after the warm reception given him in 1960, Dassin predicted that the blacklist would soon end.

PARTIAL CREDITS

(*film director or a = actor or w = writer*)

Brute Force, 1946

Naked City, 1947

Thieves Highway, 1948

Night and the City, 1949

Rififi, w (also directed) 1955

He Who Must Die, 1956

La Loi, 1958

Never on Sunday, aw (also directed) 1960

Phaedra, 1962

Topkapi, 1964

10:30 PM Summer, 1966

Survival! (cowritten with Irwin Shaw), 1967

Uptight, 1968

Promise At Dawn, 1969

Abraham Polonsky (1910—)

Village Voice critic Andrew Sarris has bemoaned the blacklisting of Abe Polonsky as one of the most tragic wastes (along with Charles Chaplin and Joseph Losey) of the McCarthy era. Indeed, twenty-two years elapsed between Polonsky's first and second directorial attempts.

Born in New York City, Polonsky grew up in a Socialist-Zionist family, attended City College, and went on to study at Columbia Law School. From 1932 on he taught at City College; when the war began he served with the OSS in Europe. In the late 1940's Polonsky went to Hollywood.

His first two films, *Body and Soul* and *Force of Evil*, were produced by Enterprise Productions, an independent company which John Garfield helped set up.

HUAC

During HUAC's hearings in 1951, three witnesses named Polonsky as a Communist. When he was called to testify he invoked the Fifth Amendment. His wartime experience in the OSS made some Committee members worry that he was a double agent. One congressman called Polonsky "the most dangerous man in Hollywood."

AFTERMATH

Polonsky was blacklisted longer than most. It was not until 1968 that he received another Hollywood screen credit. For many years he worked under assumed names, an experience which friend and fellow blacklistee Walter Bernstein wrote about in the 1975 film *The Front*.

The second film Polonsky directed, *Tell Them Willie Boy Is Here*, was released in 1970. *New York Times* critic Roger Greenspun wrote:

"The intervening twenty years apparently without directorial assignments and virtually without screen credits, perhaps the most wasteful injustice of the late 40's, have invested Polonsky with exemplary glamour and saddled him with a reputation no director of a second film should have to justify."

PARTIAL CREDITS

(*film director or w = writer*)

Body and Soul, w 1947

Force of Evil, w (also directed) 1949

I Can Get It for You Wholesale, w 1950

Madigan, w 1968

Tell Them Willie Boy Is Here, 1970

Romance of a Horse Thief, 1971

Larry Parks (1914–1975)

Née Samuel Klausman

Dalton Trumbo, a non-Jewish member of the Hollywood Ten, wrote that during the McCarthy era both the accused and the accusor were "victims." Others, notably

Albert Maltz, have taken issue with Trumbo, claiming that to whatever moral purgatories the accusers were damned, the accused faced the hell of unemployment and social ostracism.

The case of Larry Parks illustrates the wretchedness of those who named their friends and colleagues. Parks was the first Hollywood witness to admit that he had been a Communist and the first to name names.

Parks worked as an actor with the Group Theater in New York during the 1930's. With John Garfield's help he was signed as a contract player by Columbia Pictures. During the 1940's he made more than thirty low budget films before he was "discovered" to play the title role in *The Jolson Story*, which made him an overnight star.

HUAC

Parks testified before the Committee on the day Alger Hiss went to jail. He admitted that he had belonged to a Communist cell from 1941 to 1945. After identifying himself as a former Communist he was told that he would have to name other Communist Party members. Parks was reluctant: "Don't present me with the choice of either being held in contempt of this committee and going to jail or forcing me to really crawl through the mud to be an informer."

By the end of the session, however, Parks supplied names.

AFTERMATH

Although Parks had named others in order to salvage his career, it did little good. As one Hearst newspaper columnist put it: "The hell with Larry Parks and all the late confessors." Parks was equally unpopular with the Left.

Although Parks did do some film and stage work during the 1950's and the 1960's, for the most part he supported himself and his family by selling real estate. His last film role was *Freud* (1963).

PARTIAL CREDITS
(*film actor*)

Mystery Ship, 1941

Blondie Goes to College, 1942

The Deerslayer, 1943

Hey Rookie, 1944

Sergeant Mike; Jealousy, 1945

The Jolson Story, 1946

The Gallant Blade, 1948

Jolson Sings Again, 1949

Love Is Better Than Ever, 1952

***John Garfield* in They Made Me a Criminal**

Tiger by the Tail, 1955

Freud, 1963

John Garfield (1913–1952)
Née Julius Garfinkle

By Hollywood standards John Garfield was a diamond in the rough. A Bronx boy, deeply troubled by his mother's early death, he was in and out of street gangs and always truant from school. A wise counselor steered Garfield toward the theater but he never fully shed his street ways. Garfield was typecast as an outsider, a tough guy, the guy with a chip on his shoulder.

During the 1930's Garfield worked with the Group Theater. In the forties he moved to Hollywood, where he soon became one of America's best-known and popular actors.

HUAC

The Committee subpoenaed Garfield, supposedly because he had been involved with Communist front groups. His behavior before the Committee was hardly heroic; he was scared of losing the fame and fortune he had recently acquired. Garfield insisted that he had never been a Communist and, therefore, had no names to give. He did thank the Committee, however, for protecting innocent citizens from the "Red Menace."

AFTERMATH

Garfield's answers before the Committee had no impact on Hollywood's producers; many still refused to hire him. Out of desperation Garfield accepted jobs on Broadway for less than $100 a week. This was not the end of it, however. HUAC contacted him a second time and intimated that the Committee had in its possession checks made out to the Communist Party which had been issued by Garfield. Frightened of losing whatever respectability he still had, Garfield turned to Arnold Forster, general counsel for B'nai B'rith's Anti-Defamation League. Together Garfield and Forster wrote "I Was a Sucker for a Left Hook" for *Look* magazine, an article designed to clear Garfield. They maintained that Garfield's naivete had been exploited by the Party.

Garfield died of a heart attack before the article appeared. Some said he had been hounded to death by red-baiters. Abe Polonsky commented: "He defended his street boy's honor and they killed him for it."

PARTIAL CREDITS
(*film actor*)

Juarez; Four Wives, 1939

Sea Wolf, 1941

Tortilla Flat, 1942

Air Force, 1943

Destination Tokyo, 1944

Pride of the Marines, 1945

Nobody Lives Forever; The Postman Always Rings Twice, 1946

Body and Soul; Gentlemen's Agreement, 1947

Force of Evil, 1948

We Were Strangers, 1949

Under My Skin, 1950

He Ran All the Way, 1952

—D.H.W.

PHILLIP LOEB, "THE GOLDBERGS," AND THE BLACKLIST

Whenever Molly Goldberg yelled out the window to her neighbor Mrs. Bloom, millions across America heard her. Molly's voice, actually that of her creator and alter ego actress Gertrude Berg, reached them on "The Goldbergs," radio's longest running daytime serial (1929-1948) and one of television's earliest hits (1949–1955). For many of those who watched "The Goldbergs" it was their first taste of authentic Jewish life in America. The Goldberg family's struggles—told with warmth and humor—symbolized the dreams of countless first and second generation American Jews.

For Phillip Loeb, the actor who played Molly's husband Jake on television from 1949 to 1951, "The Goldbergs" represented the peak of his career. By 1950 he was earning close to $30,000 per year. The Boys Clubs of America voted him "Television Father of the Year." But his name appeared on another "honor" roll in 1950. Phillip Loeb was listed seventeen times in *Red Channels*, an index of alleged Communists currently working in the television industry. Published by professional red-hunters, *Red Channels* became a "hit list" for anti-Communist organizations. Phillip Loeb was, in short, blacklisted. "The Goldbergs" and the good parts and the money dried up quickly. But the brand he carried did not—until Loeb tragically found peace from it all five years later.

As Jake in "The Goldbergs," Loeb struggled to move up from skilled worker to proprietor of his own garment shop. Jake was stubborn, moody, yet a devoted husband and father. Jake was too kind to be a good businessman—an easy mark for disreputable partners and customers.

In real life, Phillip Loeb was well-known in New York theater circles for his total dedication to the craft. Born in Philadelphia in 1891, Loeb graduated with honors in English from the University of Pennsylvania in 1913. He gave law school a try, and newspaper reporting, but the lure of the stage drew him to New York's American Academy of Dramatic Arts in 1914.

After a stint in the Army medical corps in France in World War I, Loeb returned to New York to break into the theater. He didn't have any luck as an actor, so he turned to stage management with the Theater Guild. But the acting bug wouldn't go away, so he began making the rounds again in 1927 and this time he made it. He remained little known to the public, but he blossomed into a busy, versatile character comedian "who can dance on moonbeams with skill, charm and frenzy," as critic Brooks Atkinson wrote. Loeb also found work in movies (including the Marx Brothers' *Room Service* in 1938) and in radio.

When he wasn't acting, Loeb could be found teaching what he knew about it. He became known for his brilliance as a teacher at the American Academy of Dramatic Arts, of which he was the director. He also supported Harold Clurman's Group Theater and the ill-fated Federal Theatre Project.

But he was best known among his colleagues for his role in the trade union movement. From 1934 to 1950 Loeb served on the Actors Equity Association (AEA) Council as a rank-and-file leader. He was noted for his "dogged obsessiveness in pursuing the business of trade unionism."

Like many men and women during these years, Phillip Loeb's union participation led him to other politically important issues. He opposed fascism abroad and racial discrimination at home—which placed him, on occasion, on the same side as the radical left. This opened Loeb and his fellow Equity members to attacks by government investigators and by union dissenters who objected to the militancy of their organization and its leadership. When Representative William Lambertson of the Dies Committee charged in 1940 that Communists ran Equity, Loeb responded, "I am not a Communist, Communist sympathizer, or fellow traveler, and I have nothing to fear from an impartial inquiry."

In 1945 Phillip Loeb joined the cast of America's favorite radio family. When "The Goldbergs" went off the air in 1948, Gertrude Berg saw it as an opportunity to move into that dynamic young medium, television. To make it back to the airwaves, she wrote and starred in a Broadway production of *Me and Molly*, and cast Loeb as Jake. The play's success promptly led to a TV offer, and on January 10, 1949, Berg and Loeb premiered "The Goldbergs" on CBS-TV under the sponsorship of the General Foods Corporation.

"The Goldbergs" quickly became one of the most popular and lucrative shows on the air. Critics agreed that it was "far from an artistic tour de force," but they predicted that the "inherent substance of Mrs. Berg's characters" guaranteed that the show "would be on the air for as long as they choose." Vital to the show's success was the interaction between Berg and Loeb. Those who worked on the show have noted that "the spark between them as players was wonderful."

Phillip Loeb was a star. Then his name was put on the hit list, along with other performers and writers. The first ax fell in New York on

Gertrude Berg as "Molly Goldberg"

August 29, 1950. Responding to threats of a product boycott, General Foods fired actress Jean Muir from "The Aldrich Family" for her alleged political activities. The sponsor wanted to ban Loeb as well, but backed down pending the emergence of a clearer set of guidelines to who should be blacklisted. Although the unions passed resolutions against blacklisting, little short of a general strike by actors seemed remotely capable of breaking the blacklist—so long as sponsors and networks controlled final approval of talent.

"The Goldbergs," and Loeb, played out the 1950/51 season unscathed. But in the spring of 1951 General Foods gave in to the pressure and told Gertrude Berg that it would pull out unless Loeb was dropped from the cast. She consulted with her co-star and, convinced of his innocence, decided to resist the pressure from her sponsor. When General Foods did withdraw its support—claiming it was "dissatisfied with the show's ratings"—millions of viewers were aware of the real reason.

CBS dropped the show, but NBC quickly picked it up. Still, no sponsor would touch the show with Loeb in the cast. Berg held firm, but she knew that unless she went back on the air soon, "The Goldbergs" would be doomed. She faced the choice of putting one man out of work or forty. Reluctantly, in December 1951, she offered Loeb an $85,000 cash settlement if he would leave the show. "I certainly have tried," she explained. "I think everybody in the business knows it pretty well."

***Phillip Loeb in* Heavenly Express**

He turned her down. It was not easy—money had become a serious problem. Loeb's only son was a schizophrenic (he suffered from the delusion that "unknown Communists were trying to kill him") and the cost of treatment at a private sanitorium was $12,000 a year.

But he turned Berg down and he fought. He said he was innocent and demanded a fair hearing. He called on the AEA and the Television Authority (TvA) to brand the show as unfair and off-limits to union members. AEA members supported the move, but the Equity Council ruled the matter was actually under TvA jurisdiction, and withdrew "The Goldbergs" from its unfair list. The TvA was incapable of dealing with the situation. It opposed blacklisting in principle, but it had no means—short of a strike—to enforce its resolutions. The TvA refused to place "The Goldbergs" on its unfair list, citing the potential damage to other members, including Berg, and its doubt that the action would genuinely assist Loeb.

The TvA's decision was hailed by the conservative press as "a victory for the anti-left wing group within the entertainment industry." "It is not our problem," agreed columnist Victor Riesel, "to work out a way for [Loeb] to find work." The *New York Times*, however, condemned the decision. Loeb, maintained the *Times*, "has been read out of his profession without a semblance of a hearing or a trial."

Desperate for funds to maintain his son's care—and haunted by the knowledge that he was keeping so many other people out of work—Loeb finally gave in to the inevitable. He surrendered. He accepted Gertrude Berg's offer (although the pay-off was now only $40,000) and praised her behavior throughout the affair. His friend, actor Sam Jaffe, later remarked that Loeb sacrificed his position in the union in order to save his son. The Vitamin Corporation of America stepped in as new sponsor of "The Goldbergs." Loeb's "flat-footed denial that he is a Communist has me on edge," admitted Morton Edell, the company's president. Edell said he felt terrible about Loeb's exclusion if, in fact, he wasn't a Communist. However, Edell added, NBC—not the sponsor—determined the casting. "My contract only says that Gertrude Berg will be the star as Molly," he said.

"The Goldbergs" returned to the air in February 1952, with Harold J. Stone in the role of Jake.

Loeb's troubles had only begun. Subpoenaed by the Senate Internal Security Committee, he expressed his opposition to Communism but defended his political activities as "justifiable enterprises." he attacked the government's invasion of individual political privacy as doing "more harm than I could as a Communist." Criticized by Senate investigators for his willingness to work with leftists in social and political movements, Loeb replied, "If the purpose of the movement seemed to me a laudable one . . . I was free to join it . . . I had no compunction about joining with those that I assumed were good American citizens."

And then there were the financial woes. Although Loeb reportedly settled with Berg for $40,000 spread over two years, his federal income tax returns showed only $8,650 in income for 1952. He also owed $3,000 in legal bills and was under investigation by the Internal Revenue Service. Loeb borrowed money from Sam Jaffe and from another friend, Ezra Stone. He continued to teach acting and to perform on stage—when possible. The theater, while bending, refused to buckle totally to the blacklist. Loeb managed to find work in a few Broadway productions from 1952 to 1955, but he was more often reduced to working summer stock and off-Broadway for extraordinarily low wages.

He had to remove his son from the private

hospital and transfer him to a Veterans Administration mental hospital. Broke and deeply depressed, Loeb moved in with another blacklisted actor and his family—Zero and Kate Mostel. One day he received a desperate plea from his son to be sent back to the private sanitorium. That was when Phillip Loeb began to talk about how badly he needed some "long peace." On September 1, 1955, Loeb registered at the Taft Hotel in New York, site of Equity meetings, under the alias of Fred Lange of Philadelphia. The name, loosely translated from the German, means "long peace." Loeb went up to his room, closed the door, and ended his life by taking an overdose of sedatives.

Three weeks after his death, the Goldberg family moved to surburbia in a futile attempt to salvage the program's ratings. In the age of "I love Lucy" and John Foster Dulles, the show's folksy immigrant humor was wearing thin. Gertrude Berg went on to other artistic triumphs, but that season proved to be the last for "The Goldbergs."

At the time, Phillip Loeb's death served to unite friends and supporters in their continued resistance to the monstrous blacklist. "Phillip Loeb died of a sickness called the blacklist," said one friend. "We must resolve that never shall such things happen again. This is the only adequate memorial we can offer to the real Phillip Loeb, who was unafraid."

Years later Zero Mostel incorporated a number of Phillip Loeb's experiences into his portrayal of Hechy Green in the movie *The Front*, written by Walter Bernstein, who had also been blacklisted.

—M.S.

THE JEWISH HIT PARADE

10 ALL-TIME ISRAELI FAVORITES

Bashana Haba-a (In the Coming Year)
Nurit Hirsh and Ehud Manor
Recording: *Bashana Haba-a,* CBS 64581
Since this song was first heard in 1969, it has become an international favorite. An English version titled "Any Time of the Year" appeared in the United States. Its popularity increased when it became the background for television commercials sponsored by El Al and the Israel Ministry of Tourism.

Erev Shel Shoshanim (Evening of Roses)
Josef Hadar
Recording: *Twenty-five Years of Song from Israel,* CBS P11704
This is the best-known song by Josef Hadar, one of Israel's popular composers. Written in the late 1950's, it marks the beginning of what could be described as modern Israeli music. The melody is so well known that it is mistakenly thought to be a folksong. It is frequently played as the processional at Jewish wedding ceremonies.

Halleluyah
Kobi Oshrat and Shimrit Or
Recording: *Israel Song Festival,* CBS 83258
This 1979 Eurovision Festival winner registered high on the popular music charts in England and West Germany. Steve Lawrence and Edie Gorme recorded it in 1979, but no record company would list it under their names because they were considered too "middle of the road," i.e., out of style. When they used the pseudonym Parker and Penny Morer (*M*iddle *o*f the *r*oad), however, their recording as subsequently released in the United States.

Hamilhama Ha-ahrona (The Last War)
Dov Seltzer and Haim Hefer
Recording: *Songs of the Yom Kippur War,* CBS Israel
The plaintive mood of this song, composed during the Yom Kippur War of 1973, is unlike the ebullient compositions which characterized the Six-Day War. The text expresses the determination that this, the Yom Kippur War, shall be the last conflict Israel will have to endure.

Yerushalayim Shel Zahav (Jerusalem of Gold)
Naomi Shemer
Recording: *Twenty-five Years of Song from Israel,* CBS P11704
Without doubt this was the most popular song in the immediate aftermath of the Six-Day War. It was introduced at the yearly Israel Song Festival, the climax of the Israel Independence Day celebrations. Referring to the reunification of Jerusalem, the song's title is as emotionally laden as its lyrics, which tell of the retaking of the Old City and the return of the Western Wall. Such was its popularity that within a few days after the war the song was recorded by a large number of artists in Israel and abroad.

Kachol V'lavan (Blue and White)
I. Reshel
Recording: *The New Slavery,* SAME-1
The text of this song, dedicated to the Israeli flag as symbol of the Jewish homeland, was set to a Russian melody following the Six-Day War. First appearing among the young Jews of Russia, it became a spirited rallying song for the State of Israel. From Russia it spread quickly to Israel and the United States, symbolizing the aspirations and struggles of Soviet Jews.

Machar (Tomorrow)
Naomi Shemer
Recording: *Twenty-five Years of Song from Israel,* CBS P11704
Written by one of Israel's most beloved composer-singers before the Six-Day War, this is a song of ebullient optimism. It achieved its wide popularity immediately thereafter in that it captured the idealistic sentiment of the times. Peace, it proclaims, is around the corner, and if for some reason it should not arrive tomorrow, then it will

certainly arrive the day after. *Machar* has also become a popular Israeli threesome folk dance.

Oseh Shalom (He Who Makes Peace)
Nurit Hirsh
Recording: *Bashana Haba-a,* CBS 64581
It is interesting that Israel, which has been through so many wars since its founding, has so many songs with the theme of *shalom* ("peace"). This song, with words from the prayer book, was introduced at the first Israel Hasidic Song Festival in the fall of 1969 and has remained one of Israel's most popular songs. "May He who makes peace in the heavens also make peace among us and among all Israel. And let us say, Amen!"

Shir Hu Lo Rak Milim (A Song Is Not Just Words)
G. Becaud and D. Menossi
Recording: *Songs of the Yom Kippur War,* CBS Israel
This is another foreign melody which became popular in Israel after the addition of a Hebrew text. The melody, originally "Chante" by the French composer Gilbert Bécaud, was sung throughout Israel during the Yom Kippur War and its aftermath. The words reflect on the melancholy nature of war with the refrain "A song is not merely words or tones. A song is but the beginning. Sing out a song of great hope."

Shir Baboker Baboker (Song of the Morning)
S. Artzi, G. Koren, and A. Gilboa
Recording: *The Messengers' Greatest Hits,* Hy 106
This song is often referred to by its opening words, *Pitom kam adam* (Suddenly a Man Arises). Originally a rock song, it has become extremely popular, especially as a women's line dance at Orthodox Jewish weddings in the United States. "Suddenly a man arises in the morning and feels that he is a nation. To whomever he meets, he calls out *shalom.*"

—V.P.

10 GREAT YIDDISH SONGS OF THE 20TH CENTURY

A Brivele Der Mamen (A letter to Mother)

My child, you are crossing distant seas. Arrive in good health and do not forget to write your dear mother every week. She will read your letter and be comforted. Remember to ease the pain within her heart and refresh her spirit.

With music and lyrics by Solomon Shmulewitz (1868–1943), this was one of the most beloved songs of the immigration period on both sides of the Atlantic. In a heart-breaking plea of a mother for letters from her only son who has emigrated to America and apparently forgotten her, Shmulevitz tapped a theme of great pathos and all too familiar experience. Its final lines describe the son receiving the news of his mother's death and her final plea that he recite the prayer for the dead for her. The song was so popular that it was developed into a movie produced in 1939, the last Yiddish film made in Poland before the Nazi invasion.

A Chazendl Oif Shabbos (A Cantor for the Sabbath)

A new cantor led the Sabbath services. Three leading townsmen, a blacksmith, a tailor, and a coachman, describe his singing in occupational terms. To the smith his voice was like the strong blow of the hammer, to the tailor it was like beautiful sewing, and to the coachman, it was like the sharp crack of a whip.

This song, long a favorite in the repertoire of many cantors, was published in 1918 by M. Kipnis. Its authorship is unknown but it is evident that the composer was thoroughly versed in the Sabbath *nusach* (chant style), for the melody incorporates the traditional synagogue mode.

Bei Mir Bistu Shein (For Me You Are Beautiful)

For me you are beautiful. For me you have charm. For me you are the only girl in the world. Many a maiden has wanted me but I have chosen only you.

Der Rebbe Elimelech (The Rabbi Elimelech)

When Rabbi Elimelech grew merry he took off his *tefillin* (phylacteries), put on his eyeglasses, and summoned his two fiddlers. When he grew merrier he recited Havdalah (post-Sabbath prayer) with his sexton, Naftali, and sent for his two drummers. When he became ecstatic he took off his coat, put on his cap, and summoned his two cymbal players.

This is still one of the most popular Yiddish songs. Composed by Moshe Nadir (1885–1943), the song is a Yiddish version of the English nursery rhyme ("Old King Cole." Because of its great popularity it is commonly believed to be a folksong.

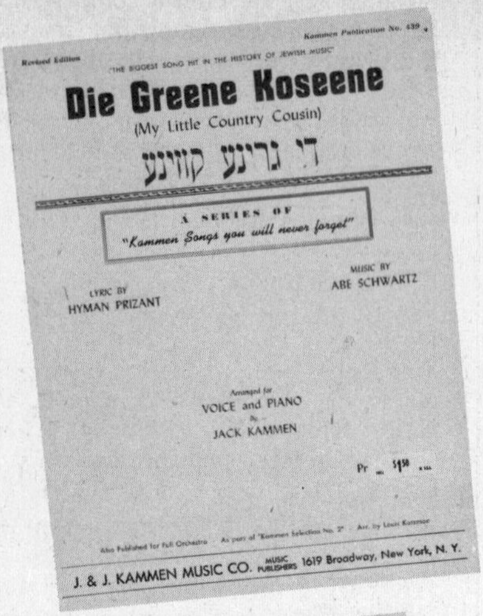
Kammen Publication No. 459
Revised Edition
"THE BIGGEST SONG HIT IN THE HISTORY OF JEWISH MUSIC"
Die Greene Koseene
(My Little Country Cousin)
די גרינע קוזינע
A SERIES OF
"Kammen Songs you will never forget"
LYRIC BY
HYMAN PRIZANT
MUSIC BY
ABE SCHWARTZ
Arranged for
VOICE and PIANO
By
JACK KAMMEN
J. & J. KAMMEN MUSIC CO. MUSIC PUBLISHERS 1619 Broadway, New York, N. Y.

Sensational Song Hit
Rumania, Rumania
רומעניע, רומעניע
As Sung by the
Inimitable Stage and Radio Artist
Melody and Words by
Aaron Lebedeff
Arranged for Voice and Piano
by
Sholom Secunda
featured and recorded by
Aaron Lebedeff
Lee Fuchs
Yaffa Yarkoni
and others...
Aaron Lebedeff
Ethnic Music Publishing Co., Inc.

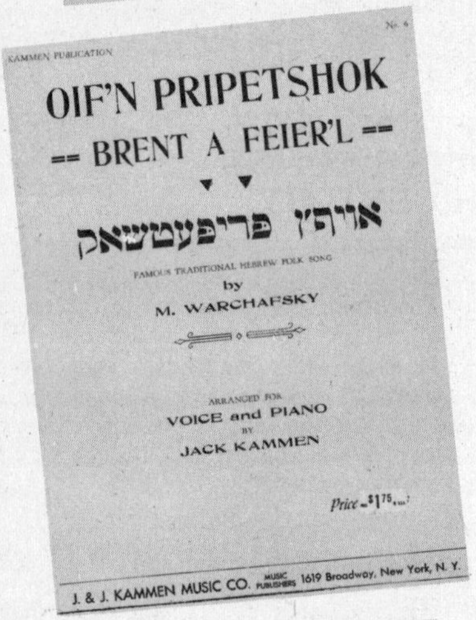
KAMMEN PUBLICATION
No. 6
OIF'N PRIPETSHOK
== BRENT A FEIER'L ==
אויפ'ן פריפעטשאק
FAMOUS TRADITIONAL HEBREW FOLK SONG
by
M. WARCHAFSKY
ARRANGED FOR
VOICE and PIANO
BY
JACK KAMMEN
Price $1.75
J. & J. KAMMEN MUSIC CO. MUSIC PUBLISHERS 1619 Broadway, New York, N. Y.

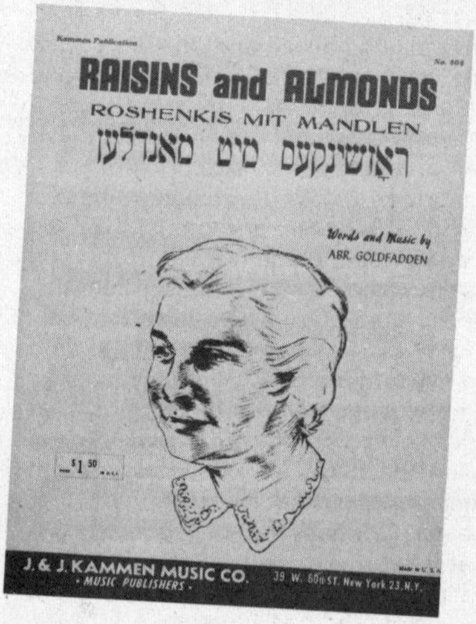
Kammen Publication
RAISINS and ALMONDS
ROSHENKIS MIT MANDLEN
ראזשינקעס מיט מאנדלען
Words and Music by
ABR. GOLDFADDEN
$1.50
J. & J. KAMMEN MUSIC CO.
MUSIC PUBLISHERS
39 W. 60th ST. New York 23, N.Y.

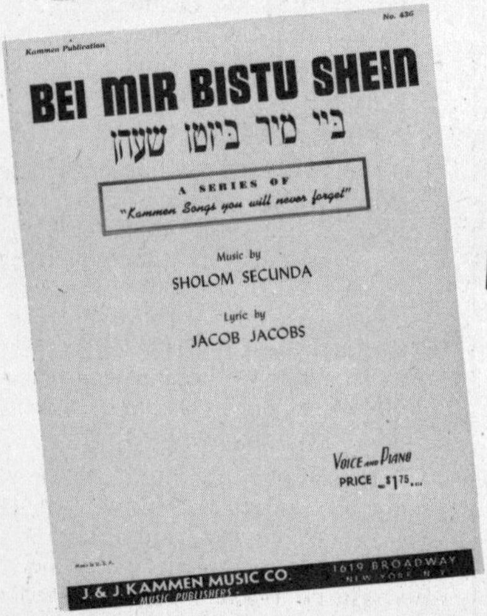
Kammen Publication
No. 430
BEI MIR BISTU SHEIN
בײַ מיר ביזטו שעהן
A SERIES OF
"Kammen Songs you will never forget"
Music by
SHOLOM SECUNDA
Lyric by
JACOB JACOBS
VOICE and PIANO
PRICE $1.75
J. & J. KAMMEN MUSIC CO.
MUSIC PUBLISHERS
1619 BROADWAY
NEW YORK, N.Y.

Die Grine Kuzine (My Greenhorn Cousin)

A pretty greenhorn cousin came to America full of life. Many years passed and she became worn out in this "golden land." Today when I meet her and ask how she is, she answers, "May the blazes take Columbus's land."

This was the most popular song of immigrant life in America. It was featured across the country and throughout the world in cafes and theaters after its debut at the Grand Street Theater in New York City. It was composed by Abe Schwartz to lyrics by Hyman Prizant.

Oifn Pripitchik (At the Fireplace)

A *rebbe* (teacher) sits near the fireplace teaching his young students the mechanics of reading Hebrew.

Originally titled *Der Aleph Beyz* (The Alphabet), it was written by Mark Warshawsky (1840–1907), one of the most successful Yiddish composers and a travelling/performing companion of story-teller Sholom Aleichem. Its popularity has been so widespread that it is commonly thought to be an anonymous folksong. It served as a musical theme in a movie based on the life of George Gershwin. Singable translations have appeared in English and in a variety of other languages. During the Holocaust, a parody version circulated throughout the ghetto, the opening lyrics of which were: "At the ghetto wall a fire burns, the surveillance is keen."

Rozhinkes Mit Mandlen (Raisins and Almonds)

In a corner of the holy Temple, the widowed daughter of Zion sits, rocking her only son Yidele to sleep.

This exquisite lullaby, long a favorite of Yiddish singers, first appeared in the opera *Shulamis* (1880) by Abraham Goldfaden (1840–1908), the founder of the modern Yiddish theater. As in Goldfaden's many other poems and songs, these lyrics blend allegory, history, and folk motifs. The refrain is an adaptation of another well-known Yiddish folksong, *Unter Yankeles Vigele* (Beneath Yankel's Cradle).

Rumania, Rumania

Once there was a beautiful land—Rumania. Life was so good! No cares, just wine, *mamalige* (Rumanian food specialty), beautiful girls, and merriment.

This song, extolling the virtues of the mother country, Rumania, has become one of the great standards of the Yiddish theater and has remained popular to the present day. It was composed over a period of years by Aaron Lebedeff, one of the luminaries of the Yiddish stage. He added and deleted material in response to audiences. Finally set by Sholom Secunda, it was recorded by Lebedeff and many other singers.

Tumbalalaika

"Maiden can you tell me what grows without rain, what yearns without tears, what can burn forever?"

"Silly lad, why do you ask? A stone can grow without rain, a heart can yearn without tears, and love can burn forever."

The authorship of this popular song is unknown. It was published for the first time in the United States in 1940 by A. Bitter. Numerous recordings appeared, including a version by the Barry Sisters. The song is in the form of a riddle; although a number of varying texts have appeared, the questions about the stone, the heart, and love are the most popular ones.

Music by Sholom Secunda (1894–1974), lyrics by Jacob Jacobs. The most financially successful Yiddish song of all time. During the early days of his musical career Secunda sold the copyright for a small amount. The new copyright holders realized huge royalties from the sheet music, numerous recordings, and public performances. Toward the end of his life the copyright reverted back to Secunda and he received royalties until his death.

Zog Nit Keinmol (Never Say)

Never say that you have reached your journey's end; that heavy clouds conceal the light of day. Upon us yet will dawn the day for which we yearn. Our trampling feet will proclaim that we are here.

This song of the Jew's eternal faith was composed by Dmitri Pokrass and set to a poem of Hirsh Glick (1922–1944). It became the hymn of the United Partisan Organization in 1943 and spread to all the concentration camps and later to Jewish Ghettoes and communities the world over. It is known in a number of singable translations, including Hebrew and English. Since the Second World War it has become one of the songs presented at the annual memorial services in remembrance of the Nazi Holocaust and martyred Jews.

—V.P.

THE STORY OF HASIDIC MUSIC

The origin of Hasidic music may be traced to Rabbi Isaac Luria (1534–1572) and the kabbalists (mystics) in Safed who regarded song as a vehicle of inspiration and devotion. Melody stood at the cradle of Kabbalah, surrounding it with the spiritual yearnings of its followers. The Hasidic movement, legitimate heir of the kabbalists, also assigned to music a primary importance.

Beginning in the mid-eighteenth century, the Hasidic movement spread throughout Eastern Europe, its adherents numbering between three and four million by the end of the nineteenth century. The founder of this movement, Rabbi Israel Baal Shem Tov ("Master of the Good Name"), or the Besht as he came to be known, felt that Jewish religious observance had become a joyless and arid habit rather than a daily rejuvenating experience. Giving radical interpretations to such verses as Psalm 100:2, "Worship the Lord with joy, come before Him with song," the Besht preached that the simple man, imbued only with native faith and a sense of joy in his heart, was nearer and dearer to God than the learned but joyless formalists who spent their whole life in the pedantic study of the legal texts. The essence of faith, he taught, lies in the emotions, not the intellect; the more profound the emotions, the nearer a person is to God.

The ecstasy of melody is one of the primary keys that Hasidism used to unlock the gates of heaven. It is, so to speak, the "ladder to the throne of God." Music, the natural concomitant of joy, fills the head with a holy ecstasy of unearthly happiness. Music is not only religious, it is religion. "All melodies," said Rabbi Nachman of Bratslav (1772–1810), "are derived from the source of sanctity, from the Temple of Song. Impurity knows no song, for it is the source of all melancholy."

Traditionally, Hasidic leaders, known as *rebbes* or *tzaddikim,* believed that vocal music is the best medium for approaching God. They felt that the power of *neginah* (melody) was such that it could reach the heavens faster and be more acceptable to God than spoken prayer. Many *rebbes* understood that the realms of Torah, penitence, and song were closely aligned.

Most of the original Hasidic melodies were composed by the *rebbes.* To possess a good and pleasing voice was as great an asset to a *rebbe* as Torah scholarship was to other religious leaders. To many Hasidic *rebbes* music was a native talent, and the art of composition, God-given. If the leaders were not blessed with these gifts, special court composer/singers were hired. It was their duty to study the mood, emotions, and character of the *rebbe* and give them utterance through songs which would be creditied to the *rebbe.*

Much Hasidic music, unfortunately, has been lost. Little attempt was made to copy down these melodies for future generations. In fact, many *rebbes* prohibited it. Once written down and generally accessible, they felt, the melodies might be misused in secular environments and by individuals not dedicated to the proper service of God. So, like most folksongs of the world, the melodies were transmitted orally.

Each major Hasidic dynasty had its own court, as the *rebbe*'s residence was called, at which it was customary for Hasidim to spend the major holidays and special Sabbaths. Devotees would leave their homes and families and often travel great distances in order to spend the festival in the presence of the *rebbe.* At these occasions new melodies were introduced and old ones resung. At the prayer services, the meals, and the festival celebrations, the newly composed melody would be sung over and over. By the time the Hasid returned home, he was equipped to share new songs with his family, friends, and neighbors.

Much Hasidic song is wordless, employing only vocalized syllables, such as "bim bom," "aha aha," "dai dai," and "yam bam." This form is unique to Hasidism, being common to no other people! For the *rebbes,* the melody is of primary importance. It is the melody that brings one to the heights of ecstasy and true religious fervor; the textual material is secondary. Rabbi Shneor Zalman of Liadi (the first Lubavitcher Rebbe, 1747–1813) wrote, "Melody is the outpouring of the soul. Words interrupt the stream of emotions. The songs of the souls, at the time they are swaying in the high regions to drink from the well of the Almighty King, consist of tones only, dismantled of words." A melody with text was, to his mind, limited to time, for with the conclusion of the verbal phrase, the melody would come to an end too; but a tune without words could be repeated endlessly. The texts used were usually passages found in the liturgy, the Bible, or Talmud; rarely were new texts created. Because of the de-emphasis on words, little consideration was given to the proper wedding of melody and text. The Hasidim invariably used poetic license, fitting the texts with the melodies as best they could. While for the most part the syllables used in place of words were arbitrary, specific syllables came to be associated with particular dynasties, and it is possible for the trained listener to identify a group of Hasidim solely on the basis of the syllables they use while singing.

Hasidic *nigunim* have three categories (although latter-day Hasidim have added several other types): the *rikud* (dance), the *tish nigun* (song sung at the *rebbe*'s table), and the *deveykus nigun* (melody of spiritual attachment).

Based on the verse "All my being shall say, 'O Lord, who is like Thee?' " dance was an integral part of Hasidism, and the unique style of the Hasidic dance became known throughout the world. The earliest dances were usually structured in an ABCB form, i.e., a three-part song with the second part repeated. Most dances were in the major mode; even those in the minor had a happy lilt to them. Dances would sometimes last as long as half an hour, until the dancers were spent or a new melody was introduced.

The *tish nigun* is a long, slow meditative melody sung at the *rebbe*'s table, usually not by him but by one of his Hasidim or by a son. The song would have several parts, often in varying moods, with a refrain appearing toward the end. Between sections a *wolloch* would often be inserted, a peasant melody which rises coloratura like the sound of a shepherd playing the flute.

The *deveykus nigun* is a slow, introspective, rapturous, soul-stirring melody, usually long and sung with deep feeling. Hasidim often sang it when they were absorbed at the study-desk just before the *rebbe* began a discourse of Torah. As the song was repeated, the soul would rise above the physical world and be transformed into disembodied spirit in communion with God.

Some historians of Jewish music, detecting in Hasidic song the admixture of foreign elements such as standard folk tempi and forms, have critically labeled it a jargon of East European folksong and dance. However, such adaptation was not unusual or particular to Hasidism. The Jews, as they were shuttled between countries all over the face of the earth, borrowed from the adopted cultures which surrounded them. What was unique in Hasidism, however, was that the Hasid reworked what he took and dedicated it to the service of God. In fact, many *rebbes* considered it to be a sacred duty to take secular melodies from the foreign cultures and incorporate them into the body of Hasidic song. This was known as "*makdish zein a nigun*" (making a song holy). Many examples are found in the songs of Hasidic dynasties, especially in the Habad (Lubavitch) movement, which incorporated into its repertoire a host of Russian and Ukrainian folksongs, often in their original tongue. This also accounts for the many rather incongruous military marches found in Hasidic music. In the mouths of the Hasidim, however, militaristic songs were transformed into melodies of the victorious "heavenly hosts" and the royal ascendancy marches of God, King of the universe.

The Hasidic movement, as it developed, branched out in two directions: the system of the Besht, and Habad. The Beshtians lived mostly in Poland, southern Russia, Rumania, and Hungary; the Habad followers were residents of Lithuania and White Russia. Besht was more emotional, tending toward ecstatic and joyous songs; Habad, more philosophical, tending toward the reflective and mystical. A strong melody luring one to dance is characteristic of the Beshtian group, whose primary teaching is *simhah* (joy). A more subdued, pensive, introspective, rapturous, and yearning tone is the theme of the Habad group, whose primary teaching is *deveykus* (union with God).

Traditional Hasidic music continues to be created today by *rebbes* and disciples of the active dynasties such as Habad, Satmar, Bobov, Ger, Stolin, Belz, Modzitz, and Klausenberg. Today one can find strains of American, Oriental, and Israeli motifs. Through recordings and new creations, the uniqueness of Hasidic music is being preserved and perpetuated for this and future generations.

—V.P.

10 CLASSIC HASIDIC NIGUNIM (MELODIES)

Nye Zuritse Chloptsi

Nye zuritse chloptsi shto s'nami budyet
Mi poyedem na kartshonku tam i vodka budyet

Don't worry, fellows, about what will become of us.
We will travel to an inn. There will surely be vodka to drink.

One of the favorite *nigunim* of Lubavitcher Hasidim, this song was adopted in the original Russian language from the folk repertoire. During the time of the *Mitler* (Middle) Lubavitcher *rebbe,* Dov Baer (1773–1827), it was sung by Hasidim as they journeyed to and from the city of Lubavitch. For the Hasidim it has a deeper meaning than is evident from the literal translation. According to them, the song offers Jews consolation by proclaiming that God will provide for all their material needs.

The reason for using the Russian vernacular was in keeping with historical ploys that Jews in the Diaspora would often employ. Jewish study in Cossack Russia was forbidden and classes were held underground. Upon a prearranged signal a lookout would report that Cossacks were in the immediate area and the teacher would order his students to hide their holy books and to begin a drinking song. The children had already been taught that this song must not be taken literally but must be thought of as a song of faith in God. The inspecting Cossacks exulted in the "knowledge" that the Jewish children were becoming part of the greater Russian culture. The song often ends the *farbrengen* (Hasidic gatherings) held in Lubavitch.

Der Alter Rebbi's Nigun

(Song of the Old Rebbe)

Referring to Rabbi Shneor Zalman of Liadi, (1745–1813, the first Lubavitrcher *rebbe*), and also known as the *nigun* of four sections, this is the chief and fundamental *nigun* of the Lubavitch movement. It is sung on special occasions such as the last days of the three Festivals, the nineteenth day of Kislev, and the twelfth day of Tammuz; and at the wedding ceremony. According to Habad philosophy each of the four sections of this *nigun* represents one of the four *olomot* (worlds): *Beriah*—the creation of the lowest elements of minerals; *Yetzirah*—the creation of living beings; *Asiyah*—the creation of man; and *Atzilut*— emanation, the heavenly region. According to Hasidic record, Rabbi Zalman composed this *nigun* during his imprisonment in Petersburg in 1799.

Szol a Kakas Már

Hasidic legend relates that Rabbi Isaac Taub, the Tzaddik of Kalev (1751–1821), used to travel among the Hungarian shepherds and peasants to learn their songs and preserve them for sacred purposes. During these forays he used to dress in peasant garb so as not to attract undue attention. On one occasion he heard a shepherd sing a melody with these words:

The rooster is already crowing;
The sun will soon rise.
Our Lord, see our affliction.
Why does He not yet come?

The *rebbe* immediately felt that the words contained the prophecy of the coming of the Messiah. According to Hasidic legend, once the *rebbe* learned the melody, he gently snapped the shepherd above the upper lip in the small cleft area and the shepherd forgot the tune.

Napoleon's March

This tune was among those played by the military band which led Napoleon's army on its ill-fated march into Russia. A number of Hasidim learned it and sang it for the first Lubavitcher *rebbe,* Rabbi Shneor Zalman of Liadi (1745–1813). The *rebbe* proclaimed that this was truly a *shir shel nitz ahon* (song of victory) possessing a *nitz otz shel kedushah* (spark of holiness). The *rebbe* ordered his Hasidim to sing the melody in the synagogue at the close of the Yom Kippur Neilah service before the final *shofar* blast which ends the fast. This custom is still adhered to in Lubavitcher synagogues worldwide.

The *nigun* has assumed other levels of importance in that it is used at wedding ceremonies as the groom's processional, during the *brist milah* (circumcision), and at Lubavitcher *farbrengen* (Hasidic gatherings), which have dignitaries in attendance.

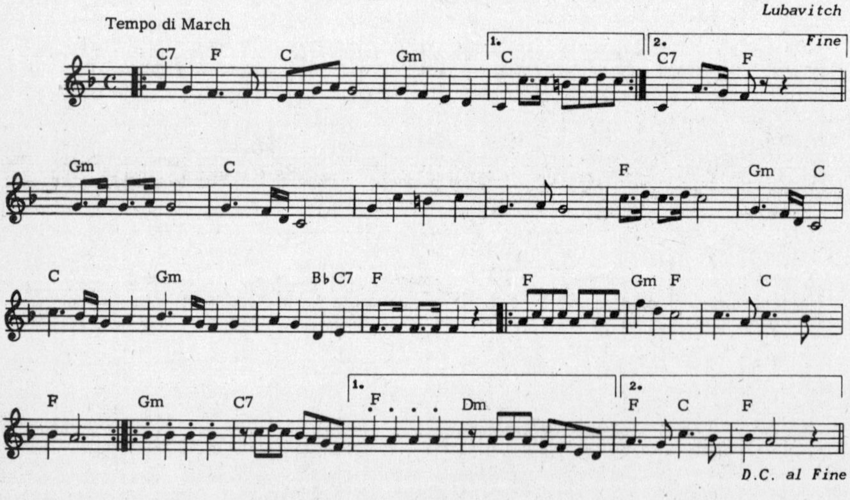

Ezkero Hagodol

When I remember this, O God, I moan;
When I see each town built on its site,
While God's own city is down to the grave.
Notwithstanding this, we look hopefully to the Lord.

This is perhaps the longest Hasidic *nigun* ever composed. In fact it is not a *nigun* but a musical composition containing thirty-two short movements. According to Hasidic record, Rabbi Israel Taub, the first *rebbe* of Modzitz (died 1921) once travelled to Berlin for medical treatment. The surroundings of the hospital, the white stone buildings reminded the *rebbe* of Jerusalem, and the poem *Ezkero Elohim V'emoyo* ("When I remember this, O God, I moan," from the Concluding Service of Yom Kippur), which is dedicated to the holy city, came to his mind. The doctors felt that a leg amputation was the only way to save the *rebbe*'s life. He agreed to the surgery but refused to have anesthesia. While his leg was being removed he composed the entire *nigun*. The composition, which takes approximately a half hour to sing, is performed by the Hasidim of Modzitz on each anniversary of the *rebbe*'s death. The music encompasses contrasting moods and closes with a splendid regal march. A number of musical settings have appeared in Europe and the United States, including a score for piano and cello. Too long to reproduce here, the music can be found in *Music and Hassidism in the House of Kuzmir and Its Affiliations* by M. S. Geshuri (Jerusalem, 1952).

Loel Asher Shovas

To God who rested from all the work of Creation on the seventh day and ascended to sit upon His throne of glory. He vested the day of rest with beauty and called the Sabbath a delight. (From the Sabbath morning liturgy)

Among Hasidim this is known as "The Song of the Angels." According to Hasidic lore, the Hoze (Seer) of Lublin (1745–1815) fell into a trance during a Friday evening *tish* (table gathering). His Hasidim at first thought that their *rebbe* had fallen asleep, but when he emerged from the trance he proclaimed that he had been in heaven. He then proceeded to teach the song, which he claimed the angels had been singing during his visit. The song was immediately accepted by all the followers of the Hoze and is to this day included in the musical repertoire of many groups, among them the Hasidim of Ropshitz, Sanz, and Bobov.

"Choze" of Lublin

Hava Nagila

Come let us be glad and rejoice.
Come sing and be gay.
Awake brothers with a joyful heart.

Without doubt *Hava Nagila* has come to represent Israeli music not only to Jews but people worldwide. It has taken on universal characteristics and has been recorded by many artists in many countries, among them Richard Tucker, Harry Belafonte, and Sammy Davis, Jr. The melody, however, is not Israeli but rather a Hasidic *nigun* created in the court of the *rebbe* of Sadigura at the turn of the century. Soon after, professor Abraham Zvi Idelsohn, the foremost musicologist of the Jewish people, introduced the song as a wordless *nigun* to a Hebrew class of young boys in Jerusalem. Several children complained that it was too hard to learn without words and that it would be more interesting attached to a text. Dr. Idelsohn assigned the composition of a text to the class and at the next music lesson a young lad, Moshe Nathanson, brought in lyrics which he had written. With the addition of these simple words the song achieved instant popularity, later becoming the song most closely associated with Israel and its national dance, the *hora*.

A.Z. Idelsohn — *Sadigura*

A Dudule

O Lord of the world,
I shall sing to You a "dudele."
Where can You be found
and where can You not be found?
Wherever I go You are there.
You, only You, always You!
Prosperity is from You; and suffering,
oh, it too comes from You!
You are, You have been, and You will be!
You did reign, You now reign, and You will reign.
Yours is heaven, Yours is earth.
You fill the high and low regions.
Wherever I turn, You are there!

Secure in the cantorial and Yiddish song repertoire, this song is often thought of as a Yiddish art song, but it is a Hasidic composition, attributed to Rabbi Levi Yitzhak of Berditchev (1740–1810). The tune, partly unrhythmical and partly rhythmical, uses a text of mixed Hebrew and Yiddish. The title refers to playing on the primitive shepherd's bagpipe instrument, known as the dudelsack. *Dudlen* is German for "to tootle."

Here the name is used as a play on the words *du, du* (Thou, Thou). The Tzaddik (holy man) addresses himself to God, adding the endearing German diminutive "le."

Levi Yitschok of Berditchev

Shkhineh

The melody of this song is used with many texts by the Hasidim of Kalev, Sanz, Bobov, and others. It is related that Leib Sarah (1730–1791) and his disciple Rabbi Isaac Taub, the Tzaddik of Kalev, used to stroll through woods and meadows to listen to the songs of the shepherds and to rework their secular songs into religious meditations. Once, upon listening to the love song of a shepherd, the Tzaddik of Kalev immediately copied the text and paraphrased it in Yiddish. Both versions circulated among the people, the secular and the reworked religious.

Secular

Ros, Ros, wie weit bist du!
Wald, Wald, wie gross bist du!
Wolt die Ros' nit aso weit gewe'n
Wolt der Wald nit aso gross gewe'n

Rose, Rose, how far are you!
Woods, woods, how large you are!
The rose would not have been so far,
Were the woods not so large.

Religious

Shekhinah, Shekhinah, wie weit bist du!
Golus, Golus, wie lang bist du!
Wolt die Shekhinah nit aso weit gewe'n

Shekhineh, Shekhineh how far you are!
Exile, Exile, how large you are!
The Shekhineh would not be so far,
was the exile not so large.

Isaac of Kalev

Nigun Hameshulash
(Melody in Three Parts)

This song is of particular interest, not only because it is one of the few which tradition attributes to joint authorship but because its composers were three of the greatest Hasidic masters: the Baal Shem Tov (1700–1760), his disciple the Maggid of Mezeritch (1710–1772), and the Alter *rebbe* of the Lubavitch Hasidim, Shneor Zalman of Liadi (1747–1813). The three parts of this serious *deveykus* (spiritual yearning) melody are musically similar, but with each section the intensity of feeling increases.

—V.P.

"Besht", "Maggid", Shneor Zalman

THE ALL-TIME, ALL-STAR JEWISH JAZZ BAND

As in all other attempts at tracing the influences on a particular way of creating music, certain distinctions must be made at the start to avoid such a confusion of categories as to produce dissonance without meaning. Therefore:

- Certain musicians who are Jewish have contributed to the jazz heritage.
- Only a relatively few of these, however, have brought a distinctively Jewish flavor to their improvising. Of the others, their Jewish background, such as it is, usually cannot be discerned from their playing.
- Jazz always has been, and still is, rooted in black music, so that all the key innovators so far have been black, for example, Louis Armstrong, Coleman Hawkins, Count Basie, Lester Young, Charlie Christian, Charlie Parker, Dizzy Gillespie, Thelonious Monk, Miles Davis, John Coltrane, Ornette Coleman, Cecil Taylor, and the Art Ensemble of Chicago.

Of those whites who have achieved an utterly singular voice on a level just below that of the pervasive innovators—Jack Teagarden, Bix Beiderbecke, Pee Wee Russell, Roswell Rudd, and others—only one has been Jewish: Benny Goodman. This is not to say that there have not been a number of other Jewish jazzmen who have won the respect of their peers and of audiences throughout the world.

Of the few who actually *sound* Jewish from time to time, one of the more obvious was trumpeter Ziggy Elman, who in his work with Benny Goodman sometimes seemed to be playing a Jewish wedding—in terms of the *klezmer*-like (a type of East European Jewish music) phrasing, timbres, and the general *frailak* (joyous, exuberant) flavor of his swinging. Benny Goodman himself has revealed traces, from time to time, of his musical origins in the Chicago synagogue band that he played with, as a child, at bar mitzvahs and weddings.

Ruby Braff, the most lyrical of contemporary jazz trumpeters, was primarily shaped by black sounds (Louis Armstrong, Billie Holiday, Lester Young); but often, in the curve of a phrase and the "cry" of his sound, there are echoes of the Yiddish musical festivities in the Boston neighborhoods of forty years ago, where he was raised.

With regard to the other Jewish jazzmen—and there have probably been more Jews involved in jazz than any other white group—their backgrounds are much harder to discern from their sound and phrasing. Yet, once in a great while, there is the sense that Stan Getz is creating variations on a *nigun*, and the same can be said of another tenor saxophonist, Al Cohn.

In any case, Jewish players have been vigorously audible at all stages of jazz history. Trumpeter Max Kaminsky, for instance, is a stalwart of the Dixieland idiom (among others) who also has had big band experience. And tenor saxophonist Bud Freeman, with a sound like no one else's, was a vital member of the rambunctious school of "Chicago jazz" starting in the 1920's. Benny Goodman, of course, was the most popular leader and instrumentalist of the swing era, and among the modernists, Stan Getz has made a considerable impact, as did, among the cognoscenti, powerful lead trumpeter Irvin "Marky" Markowitz. Red Rodney, another trumpeter, was a sometime associate of Charlie "Bird" Parker; and in the post-bop era, alto saxophonist Lee Konitz and flutist Jeremy Steig were among those players who discovered new dimensions on their instruments.

Also among the notable Jews in jazz is one of the most influential teachers of the music, Sanford "Sandy" Gold, an impressively knowledgeable pianist. The two leading international jazz impressarios, Norman Granz and George Wein, are Jews. Granz, who originated the Jazz at the Philharmonic tours, has recorded more durable jazz through the decades than any other single producer, and he continues this essential stockpiling of history on his Pablo label. Wein, who began as a pianist, created the Newport Jazz Festival, now based in New York, and produces tours and festivals throughout the United States and the rest of the world.

The assembling of an all-time, all-star, all-Jewish jazz band must necessarily be a subjective enterprise, and the fun of it for the reader is in disagreeing with the assembler and making up an all-star band of his/her own.

Trumpet: Ruby Braff had established himself as a highly personal improviser in Boston, where he was born in 1927, before moving

The "King of Swing," Benny Goodman

to New York in the 1950's. He has worked with Tony Bennett, toured with various George Wein jazz troupes, and led groups of his own.

Max Kaminsky, born in Brockton, Massachusetts in 1908, is an alumnus of the Tommy Dorsey and Artie Shaw orchestras, as well as many small combos at the core of the hot jazz scene.

Ziggy Elman, originally from Philadelphia (born 1914), died in 1968 after a career in big bands (with Benny Goodman in particular) and later as a leader.

Trombone: For unknown reasons, there has been a dearth of Jewish jazz trombonists of big-league caliber. One who came close, during the 1950's and 1960's, was **Ephy Resnick,** who played in both traditional and more flexible contexts with zest, wit, and imagination.

Saxophonist Stan Getz

Clarinet: Benny Goodman, of course. Born in Chicago in 1909, he was a professional at twelve, became a highly proficient studio musician in New York, and then, in 1934 formed his own band, which to millions came to exemplify the swing era. Goodman also developed into an eminently skillful classical clarinetist, but he never abandoned jazz and, indeed, continues to improvise on recordings and at occasional concerts with undimmed pleasure in the art of surprise.

Tenor Saxophone: Bud Freeman, born in Chicago in 1906, has always been an individualist—from his work with the "Austin High Gang" (pioneers of Chicago jazz in the 1920's) to his stays with the big bands of Ray Noble, Tommy Dorsey, and Benny Goodman. During the past forty years Freeman has worked both as a leader, with a variety of small groups, and as a single, with local rhythm sections in the United States and Europe. His playing is joyful, resilient, and lyrical without being in the least sentimental.

Al Cohn, born in Brooklyn in 1925, has played in big bands (Woody Herman, Buddy Rich, Artie Shaw) and many small combos, including a long period when he and Zoot Sims were coleaders of an especially swinging group. Cohn is also a skilled arranger.

Stan Getz, born in Philadelphia in 1927, first attained renown with Woody Herman's orchestra in the 1940's and has been leader of his own groups ever since. His playing is marked by a glowing tone, a fluid beat, and an exceptionally fertile melodic imagination. In recent years, without losing his basic romanticism, Getz has been playing with more force, sounding younger as he gets older.

Saxophonist Lee Konitz

Alto saxophone: Lee Konitz, born in 1927 in Chicago, was a student and then close associate of the late Lennie Tristano, a master of advanced jazz improvisation. He worked with Stan Kenton and Gerry Mulligan, among other contexts, and has developed a number of groups of his own. While Konitz was first known for his "cool" sound, he, like Getz, has opened up more in the past decade, playing with increasing fire.

Flute: Herbie Mann, born in Brooklyn in 1930, has been leader of his own group since 1959, evolving into a popularly successful ecumenicist as he fuses Afro-Latin, jazz, blues, soul, Brazilian, and Middle Eastern ingredients into his continually changing textures and forms.

One of the more venturesome flutists in jazz is **Jeremy Steig,** born in New York City in 1942, the son of artist-writer William Steig. He not only has total command of the instrument but also stretches its capacities—sometimes with the aid of electronics—farther than most of his peers have been able to.

Piano: Among the more resourceful and durable jazz pianists are **Dick Katz,** born in Baltimore in 1924 and long part of the New York jazz scene; **Lou Levy,** born in Chicago in 1928 and a superior accompanist for such singers as Peggy Lee and Ella Fitzgerald, while also being a vital component of small combos; and **Barbara Carroll,** born in Worcester, Massachusetts in 1925 and a perennially rewarding leader of her own trios.

Bass: A powerful rhythm section presence during the swing era was **Arthur Bernstein,** born in Brooklyn in 1909, and a member of the Red Nichols, Dorsey Brothers, and Benny Goodman bands. Meanwhile, **Jack Lesberg,** born in Boston in 1920, became a pillar of such traditional combos as those of Muggsy Spanier and Eddie Condon, while also being proficient in swing-style units and in the symphonic field. Among modern bassists, **Chuck Israels,** born in New York in 1936, has been with the Bill Evans trio and founded the National Jazz Ensemble to provide a jazz equivalent of the symphonic repertory orchestra that could program compositions from the whole spectrum of jazz.

Flutist Herbie Mann

Drums: In the front rank of jazz drummers, **Mel Lewis,** born in Buffalo in 1929, played with, among others, Gerry Mulligan and Dizzy Gillespie until forming a big band with trumpeter Thad Jones in 1965. He also continues to work small combo dates. Whatever the framework, Lewis is immediately identifiable by his taste, economy, and rhythmic

Norman "Tiny" Kahn

grace. He is known by musicians as "Mel the Tailor" because everything he plays fits so well.

Other Jewish jazz drummers of substance have been the late **Norman "Tiny" Kahn,** born and died in New York City (1924–1953), a modernist of exceptional subtlety and inventiveness as well as a distinctive arranger; and **Stan Levey,** born in Philadelphia in 1925, one of the first drummers to master bop, and an alumnus of groups led by Dizzy Gillespie, Oscar Pettiford, Charlie Parker, Woody Herman, and Stan Kenton.

This, of course, is a selective list of Jewish jazz players. There have been and still are many more, including those who work outside the big-city jazz centers and so have seldom, if ever, recorded but nonetheless still swing.

—N.H.

YIDL MITN FIDDLE: THE JEWISH VIOLINIST

If one were to visualize the most popular image of a Jewish musician from Eastern Europe, that figure would undoubtedly be a fiddler. The *klezmer* (Hebrew/Yiddish: musician; pl. *klezmorim*, from *klei zemer*, meaning "musical instruments") and his fiddle, the most popular instrument of the time, were the cornerstones of Yiddish music in diasporic Europe for over five hundred years.

Historical references to the *klezmorim* of Europe date back to before the fifteenth century according to A.Z. Idelsohn (1882–1938) in his seminal work *Jewish Music in Its Historical Development*, which documents the existence of organized Jewish bands (which sometimes included women) playing at that time. These bands, much like their later Eastern European counterparts, travelled throughout their native countries playing for both Jewish and gentile parties, festivals, and market-day celebrations. The musicians were almost always poor, and the irregular, unpredictable nature of their work demanded an itinerant way of life. Their lifestyle prompted inevitable comparisons between the Jews and the Gypsies (Romany), who shared a musical repertoire and style, as well as a nomadic life.

Although their music was popular among both their own people and non-Jews, the *klezmorim* encountered many societal obstacles. Opposition from gentile musicians, whose petitions accused them of being incapable of playing "Christian" music correctly, frequently led to their being banned from performing at gentile events. The rabbinate itself, concerned with "erecting a fence against hilarity" in remembrance of the destruction of the Second Temple, further restricted their opportunities to play. Jews were also forbidden to play at times of local or national catastrophe, such as pogroms and the deaths of prominent gentile or Jewish personages.

With the advent of the *Haskalah* movement (Hebrew: Enlightenment) in Western Europe, those aspects of Jewish culture that conflicted with the new trend towards "Westernization" were disparaged. This meant that the *klezmer*, as a repository of traditional music, was fated to disappear. In Eastern Europe, however, where political and social reforms were slower in coming and where many people still staunchly adhered to traditional values, the *klezmer* was able to continue his mode of life until the Holocaust.

The Eastern European *klezmorim* performed a wide range of music for their varied audiences, including such distinctly Jewish dances as the *Mitzvah Tants* (dance), the *Broyges Tants* (Dance of Anger and Reconcilliation) and the *Kosher Tants*, as well as Jewish *shers*, *bulgars*, Rumanian *horas*, and the more modern dances, such as the waltz, quadrille, and polka. For their more educated and affluent gentile hosts, the Jewish musician was expected to play light classical compositions and operatic overtures as well.

The traditional instruments of the *klezmer* included the various members of the *viol* family, the *tsimbl* (hammered dulcimer), and the *baraban* (drum). By the nineteenth century, however, wind instruments, such as the clarinet, had become quite common, as had the brasses over the next fifty years such as the trumpet, trombone, and tuba. Other instruments, such as the accordion, were introduced in the late nineteenth century or early twentieth century. Nonetheless through all these developments, the fiddle continued to reign supreme as the single most important instrument in Yiddish life.

Within a short period of time, however, the traditions changed. Prior to the reign of Tsar Alexander II (r. 1855–1881), musical opportunities were slim for Jews who did not convert. This ruler instituted mild reforms for the Jews, liberalizing their entry into large urban universities and allocating appropriate residency permits. These reforms, augmented by the rise of the *Haskalah* movement in Russia in the mid-nineteenth century, whetted

A band of Jewish klezmorim *in Poland, 1927*

the appetites of the young for greater knowledge, opportunities, and experiences in the outside world.

Back in the *shtetl* (Yiddish: village), the *klezmorim* became increasingly familiar with the classical repertoire by playing for noblemen who requested it. Furthermore, as young Jews migrated to the large cities, they kept in contact with the *klezmorim* in their hometowns and sent back instruction books, musical compositions, and other modern musical materials.

Schools such as the Petersburg Conservatory opened new vistas of professional possibilities for Jews seeking musical careers. Following a classic pattern of cultural assimilation, these ambitions were both a rebellion against the traditional cultural boundaries of the *shtetl* and part of a search for social and economic advancement. The new, modern ideology challenged the limitations of their old environment, which had dictated that music belonged only in the *shtetl* with the Jews. Classical or "art", music gave young Jews a chance to play for the world.

Of all the cities that beckoned youth to their doors, Odessa was the most tempting. The city, a "hotbed of modernity" as Odessa is termed by Lucy Dawidowicz in *The Golden Tradition*, was characterized by the "western" outlook of its cultural and social life, its many schools and political organizations, its burgeoning economic development, and the marked participation by Jews in all aspects of urban activity. The influx and interest of Jews was so great, in fact, that at one point during this period the student body at the Government College for Music and the Arts was comprised of sixty percent Jews.

Unfortunately after the assassination of Alexander II in 1881, his son, Alexander III (r. 1881–1894), returned to a strictly authoritarian social policy. He reinstituted harsh, repressive measures against the Jews, including a severe cutback in educational opportunities. Jewish representation in secondary and higher schools in the larger cities dropped to less than five percent. Despite this, however, the world of music had undergone an irreversible change: Jews had become involved with western art music, and had become a moving force in its development.

With the appearance of the Jewish violin prodigies (see *Elman*, *Kreisler*, and *Heifitz* below), it became evident to all that Jews could now achieve great fame playing music without having to convert to Christianity. Although the *klezmorim* had generally encouraged their children to learn and perpetuate traditional Yiddish music as a matter of family and cultural pride, Jewish parents in other social stratas began to view music as a viable professional option for their children and no longer resisted cultivating the musical talents of their youngsters.

By the time *Peter Stolyarski* (see below) began teaching violin in Odessa in 1920, earlier prodigies had grown up and become successful musicians, paving the way for a new generation of child violinists. These children were fortunate to benefit from the experience and teachings of Stolyarski, a gifted and sensitive instructor, who molded them into the outstanding exponents of the early Soviet school of violin playing.

With the advent of World War II the burgeoning movement of Jews in the violin world was all but destroyed, and what remained was subsequently snuffed out entirely by Stalin's anti-Semitic purges. Today, although Stolyarski's school is still open, there are few Jewish students or faculty members within the institution. Even many of those who studied with Stolyarski have been removed from the staff.

However, links in the chain of Jewish violinists still exist in lands outside the U.S.S.R. In countries such as the United States, England, and Israel, where the dispossessed Jewish violinists ultimately found refuge, their teachings have continued to link new generations of violin students with the rich tradition of the "*Yid'l mitn Fiddle*": the Jew and the violin.

The biographies below are a selected list of twenty great Jewish violinists.

—H.H.S.

20 Jewish Violinists

Licco Amar (1891–1959, b. Budapest) Concertmaster of the Berlin Philharmonic Orchestra from 1915–20; organizer of the Amar Quartet and promoter of contemporary music.

Adolf Brodsky (1851–1929, b. Taganrog, Russia) Founder of the internationally known Brodsky Quartet, leader of the Damrosch Symphony Orchestra, noted soloist, and close friend of Tchaikovsky, who dedicated his Violin Concerto to him.

Mischa Elman (1873–1967, b. Talnove, Russia) A child prodigy, he made his debut at age six in Odessa, and at age eleven he was invited to St. Petersburg to study with the renowned teacher Leopold Auer. His brilliant technique, impeccable style, and virtually flawless tone were so unique as to be labelled "the Elman tone." He immigrated to the United States in 1908, taking up residence in New York City.

Ida Haendel (1924— , b. Chelm, Poland) A child prodigy who studied with Carl Flesch, she launched her international concert career after her debut at age thirteen in London. She is regarded by many as the outstanding soloist of her generation.

Emil Hauser (1893— , b. Budapest) Founder of the Budapest String Quartet in 1917 and the Palestine Music Conservatory in Jerusalem in 1933, he was also director of the chamber music class at the Juilliard School of Music.

Jascha Heifetz (1901— , b. Vilna, Lithuania) A child prodigy who performed publicly at age seven, Heifetz entered the St. Petersburg Conservatory to study with Leopold Auer at the age of ten, and performed with the Berlin Philharmonic at age eleven. His style and tone established new standards for violin mastery. In 1925, he performed in Palestine and donated his concert fees to the promotion of music in Tel Aviv.

Joseph Joachim (1831–1907, b. Budapest) Conductor, concertmaster, soloist, composer, and outstanding teacher (among his students were Leopold Auer and Fivadar Nachez), he was considered the most notable violinist of his generation. He played an influential role in ninteenth-century music by introducing Brahms to Liszt and Schumann to Brahms.

Leonid B. Kogan (1924— , b. Dniepropetrovsk, U.S.S.R.) A master of great technical skill, Kogan has won numerous awards, including first price in the international competitions in Prague in 1947 and the Lenin Prize in 1965.

Fritz Kreisler (1875–1962, b. Vienna) A child prodigy, he performed publicly at age seven and won the Premier Grand Prix de Rome at the Paris Conservatory when he was only twelve! He immigrated to the United States and became an American citizen in 1943.

Rudolf Kolisch (1896— , b. Klamim, Austria) Founder of the Kolisch String Quartet, which disbanded in 1939, and leader of the Pro Arte Quartet after he immigrated to the United States in 1940; he was a student of Schoenberg and a promoter of modern music.

Yehudi Menuhin (1916— , b. New York) A descendant of a long line of Hasidic rabbis, Menuhin was a child prodigy who appeared as a soloist with the San Francisco Orchestra at age eight. By the age of twelve his playing had already captivated Paris, London, and New York. He served as president of the international music council of UNESCO, initiated the Gstaad Music Festival in Switzerland, and was awarded the Jawaharal Nehru Prize for International Understanding in 1970.

Nathan Milstein (1904— , b. Odessa, Russia) A virtuoso performer who toured with Vladimir Horowitz as a youth in Russia, Milstein immigrated to the United States in 1929. Aside from his playing, he was noted for his musical arrangements and his violin cadenzas.

Fivadar Nachez (1859–1930, b. Pest, Hungary) A student of Joachim in Berlin, Nachez performed with Liszt as a child prodigy. An international violin virtuoso, he also was a composer and musical editor.

David Oistrakh (1908–1974, b. Odessa, Russia) Oistrakh made his first public appearance in 1914 at the age of six, won first prize at the Queen Elizabeth competition in Brussels in 1937, and became head of the violin department of the Moscow Conservatory in 1950. Also a conductor, many Soviet composers (Prokofiev, Miaskovsky, Shostakovich, Khachaturian) wrote violin works especially for him.

Itzhak Perlman (1945— , b. Tel Aviv) Although stricken with polio at the age of four, Perlman was a child prodigy, making his first public recital at the age of nine. Coming to the United States at thirteen, he studied at Juilliard, and in 1964 won the Levintritt Competition.

Alexander Schneider (1908— , b. Vilna, Lithuania) Leader of the Frankfort Symphony Orchestra until his immigration to the United States in 1933, Schneider became second violin in the Budapest Quartet and together with cellist Pablo Casals, established the annual music festivals in Prades and Puerto Rico.

Isaac Stern (1920— , b. Kremenetz, U.S.S.R.) An internationally renowned virtuoso, Stern was born in Russia but came to the United States at an early age, performing with the San Francisco Symphony Orchestra at the age of eleven. He was a central figure in the successful effort to save Carnegie Hall from demolition, has served as president of the America-Israel Cultural Foundation, and is the sponsor of many Israeli artists.

Peter Stolyarski (1871–1944, b. Ukraine, Russia) Coming from a family of *klezmorim*, Stolyarski played at Jewish wedding ceremonies as a child, prior to enrolling in the music school in Odessa. A noted teacher, he founded a school for gifted children in 1933 and became a professor of violin at the Odessa Conservatory in 1920.

Joseph Szigeti (1892— , b. Budapest) A child prodigy who performed publicly at the age of seven, he was appointed professor of violin at the Geneva Conservatory in 1917 before immigrating to the United States in 1926. His playing is distinguished by an unusual bow-arm position, as well as by its ease and vigor. He has promoted many modern works, including those of composer Ernest Bloch.

Pinchas Zuckerman (1948— , b. Tel Aviv) Although he began his violin instruction at the age of six in Israel, Zuckerman later came to the United States to study at Juilliard. In 1967 he won the prestigious Leventritt Competition.

—H.H.S., J.B.S.

OF ACADEMIC INTEREST

A JEWISH GUIDE TO MAJOR NORTH AMERICAN COLLEGES AND UNIVERSITIES

	Enrollment[1] (Spring 1979)	Estimated Jewish[2] Enrollment	Jewish Studies[3] Major	Hillel Foundation[2] or other Jewish Campus Worker	Kosher food[2]
American University Washington, D.C.	12,583	1,350	Yes	Full-time	Some available
Antioch College Yellow Springs, Ohio	1,300	325	No	Not Available	Not available
University of Arizona Tucson, Ariz.	29,062	1,250	Yes[a,b]	Full-time	Some available
Arizona State University Tempe, Ariz.	37,122	1,300	No	Full-time	Some available
Bard College Annandale-on-Hudson, N.Y.	700	190	No	No	Not available
Boston University Boston, Mass.	23,528	8,500	Yes[a]	Full-time	Two meals daily
Brandeis University Waltham, Mass.	3,545	2,250	Yes	Full-time	Full board
Brown University Providence, R.I.	6,700	1,300	Yes[a]	Full-time	Dinner only
University of California at Berkeley Berkeley, Calif.	30,001	6,000	Yes[b]	Full-time	Some available
University of California at Los Angeles Los Angeles, Calif.	31,743	8,000	Yes	Full-time	Some available
University of California at Santa Cruz Santa Cruz, Calif.	5,880	1,500	No	Part-time	No
Case Western Reserve University Cleveland, Ohio	8,185	1,200	No	Full-time	Full board
University of Chicago Chicago, Ill.	9,425	2,200	Yes	Full-time	Some available
University of Cincinnati Cincinnati, Ohio	33,479	3,000	Yes	Full-time	Full board
City College of New York New York, N.Y.	12,285	3,500	Yes	Full-time	Some available

	Enrollment[1] (Spring 1979)	Estimated Jewish[2] Enrollment	Jewish Studies[3] Major	Hillel Foundation[2] or other Jewish Campus Worker	Kosher food[2]
University of Colorado Boulder, Colo.	22,400	1,200	No	Full-time	Full board
Columbia University New York, N.Y.	17,900	8,000	Yes[a,b]	Full-time	Full board
University of Connecticut Storrs, Conn.	21,349	2,000	No	Full-time	Dinner only
Cornell University Ithaca, N.Y.	18,000	2,550	Yes[b]	Full-time	Two meals daily
Dartmouth College Hanover, N.H.	4,221	400	Yes[a]	Full-time	Some available
Drake University Des Moines, Iowa	6,568	400	No	Part-time	Full board
Duke University Durham, N.C.	9,900	1,000	Yes[a]	Full-time	Some available
Emory University Atlanta, Ga.	7,812	600	Yes[a]	Full-time	No
University of Florida Gainesville, Fla.	31,133	3,000	No	Full-time	Some available
George Washington University Washington, D.C.	12,296	1,800	Yes	Full-time	Full board
Harvard University Cambridge, Mass.	20,525	3,300	Yes	Full-time	Dinner only
Hofstra University Hempstead, N.Y.	11,000	5,000	Yes	Full-time	Some available
University of Illinois Urbana, Ill.	33,684	3,600	Yes[a]	Full-time	Dinner only
Indiana University Bloomington, Ind.	32,600	1,500	Yes	Full-time	Some available
Univeristy of Iowa Iowa City, Iowa	22,990	1,000	No	Full-time	Lunch and occasional dinners
University of Kansas Lawrence, Kan.	25,480	700	No	Part-time	Some available
Kent State University Kent, Ohio	25,130	1,200	No	Full-time	Some available
University of Maryland College Park, Maryland	35,000	6,000	Yes	Full-time	Full board
University of Massachusetts Amherst, Mass.	23,000	3,000	Yes	Full-time	Some available
Massachusetts Institute of Technology Cambridge, Mass.	7,972	1,400	No	Full-time	Dinner only
University of Miami Coral Gables, Fla.	19,235	5,000	Yes	Full-time	Two meals daily
University of Michigan Ann Arbor, Mich.	46,017	3,500	Yes	Full-time	Dinner only
University of Minnesota Minneapolis, Minn.	46,400	1,400	Yes	Full-time	Full board
University of Missouri Columbia, Mo.	23,474	1,500	No	Full-time	Some available

	Enrollment[1] (Spring 1979)	Estimated Jewish[2] Enrollment	Jewish Studies[3] Major	Hillel Foundation[2] or other Jewish Campus Worker	Kosher food[2]
New York University New York, N.Y.	42,000	17,000	Yes	Full-time	Dinner only
University of North Carolina Chapel Hill, N.C.	20,293	650	No	Full-time	No
Northeastern University Boston, Mass.	42,437	7,000	No	Part-time	Not available
Northwestern University Evanston, Ill.	15,117	1,000	No	Full-time	Some
Oberlin College Oberlin, Ohio	2,750	900	Yes[b]	Full-time	One meal only
Ohio State University Columbus, Ohio	54,579	4,000	Yes	Full-time	Dinner only
University of Pennsylvania Philadelphia, Pa.	18,500	6,000	Yes[b]	Full-time	Dinner only
Princeton University Princeton, N.J.	5,931	1,000	Yes[b]	Full-time	Two meals daily
Queens College (CUNY) Flushing, N.Y.	17,458	11,000	Yes	Full-time	Some
Reed College Portland, Ore.	1,152	300	No	Not available	No
University of Rochester Rochester, N.Y.	7,881	3,600	No	Full-time	Some
Rutgers—The State University New Brunswick, N.J.	16,760	2,000	Yes	Full-time	One meal daily
Smith College Northampton, Mass.	2,518	260	No	Full-time	Some
University of Southern California Los Angeles, Calif.	27,879	2,200	Yes [a]	Full-time	Some
Stanford University Stanford, Calif.	11,727	1,000	No	Full-time	Not available
SUNY Albany Albany, N.Y.	15,216	5,800	Yes	Part-time	Dinner only
SUNY Buffalo Buffalo, N.Y.	21,611	3,200	Yes	Full-time	Some
SUNY Stony Brook Stony Brook, N.Y.	15,900	6,000	No	Full-time	Dinner only
Swarthmore College Swarthmore, Pa.	1,292	200	No	Part-timeNo	
Syracuse University Syracuse, N.Y.	15,000	2,000	No	Full-time	Full board
Temple University Philadelphia, Pa.	35,600	7,000	Yes[a]	Full-time	Two meals daily
University of Texas Austin, Tex.	43,094	3,000	Yes	Full-time	Some
Tufts University Medford, Mass.	6,800	1,800	No	Full-time	Some
Tulane University New Orleans, La.	9,633	1,000	Yes	Full-time	Some; available through University of New Orleans

	Enrollment[1] (Spring 1979)	Estimated Jewish[2] Enrollment	Jewish Studies[3] Major	Hillel Foundation[2] or other Jewish Campus Worker	Kosher food[2]
U.S. Military Academy West Point, N.Y.	4,380	40	No	Part-time	Not available
University of Virginia Charlottesville, Va.	15,900	1,800	No	Full-time	Some
Washington University St. Louis, Mo.	10,723	2,800	Yes	Full-time	Two meals daily
Wesleyan University Middletown, Conn.	2,453	700	Yes	Not available	Not available
University of Wisconsin Madison, Wis.	39,000	4,000	Yes	Full-time	Dinner only
Yale University New Haven, Conn.	9,526	2,500	No	Full-time	Full board
Yeshiva University New York, N.Y.	6,921	Not available	Yes	Full-time	Full board
Canada					
McGill University Montreal, Que.	16,171	4,250	Yes	Full-time	Not available
University of Manitoba Winnipeg, Man.	13,603	1,000	Yes[b]	Full-time	Not available
University of Toronto Toronto, Ont.	31,377	3,000	Yes[b]	Full-time	Some
York University Downsview, Ont.	12,337	5,000	Yes[b]	Part-time	Not available

[a]Jewish Studies major available through the Department of Religion.
[b]Jewish Studies major available through the Department of Near Eastern and Oriental Studies.
[1]Source: *The World Almanac and Book of Facts 1980*.
[2]Source: Norman Feingold and Samuel Fishman (eds.), *College Guide for Jewish Youth, 1978-79* (Washington, D.C., 1978).
[3]Source: Samuel Fishman and Judyth Saypol (eds.), *Jewish Studies at American and Canadian Universities* (Washington, D.C., 1979).

—B.D.G.

YALE'S HEBREW COAT OF ARMS

The official seal of Yale University includes two Hebrew words and three Latin words: *"Urim Ve-thummim"* and *"Lux et Veritas."* In the Yale tradition these words are translated as "Light and Truth." The following may shed some "light" on the matter of the Yale seal.

Yale traces its beginnings to 1701 when the General Court of the Connecticut Colony met in New Haven on October 9 and granted a charter "for the founding, suitably endowing, and ordering a Collegiate School within his Majesty's Colony of Connecticut." Rev. Abraham Pierson was chosen the first rector of the school and it opened its doors in 1702 with class being held in Pierpont's Killingworth parsonage. In return for a cargo of gifts for the budding Collegiate School from Elihu Yale, a Boston boy who made good in London, the trustees assigned the philanthropist's name, in 1718, to the school. It was henceforth Yale College. Four years later, in 1722, the Connecticut Assembly authorized the Trustees of Yale to use a seal; but the first tangible evidence of that insignia appears on a diploma of 1740.

It ought to be no surprise that Hebrew and Latin phrases were included on the seal. Hebrew and Latin, along with Greek, were basic courses at Yale from the outset. (The Hopkins Grammar School of New Haven offered the three classical languages when it opened its doors in 1660.) Rev. Pierson had gotten his grounding in these and other

Columbia University's insignia with the Tetragrammaton (four-letter name of God) above the head and Hebrew words meaning "the light of God" on the right.

Dartmouth University's insignia with the Hebrew words "God Almighty" in the top center.

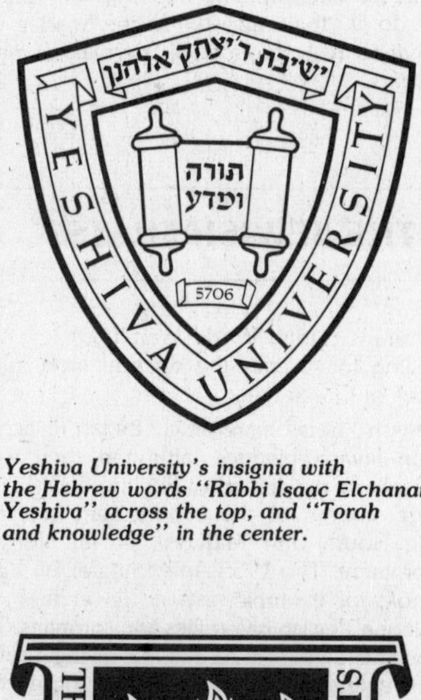

Yeshiva University's insignia with the Hebrew words "Rabbi Isaac Elchanan Yeshiva" across the top, and "Torah and knowledge" in the center.

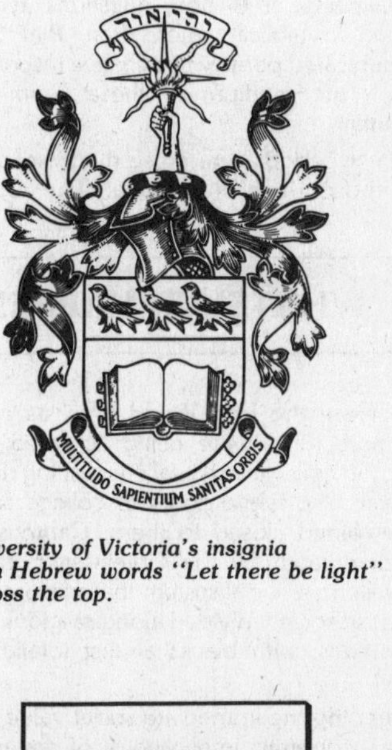

University of Victoria's insignia with Hebrew words "Let there be light" across the top.

Brandeis University's insignia with the Hebrew word "Truth" in the center.

Yale University seal

subjects as a student at Harvard. Regrettably, there is no existing clue to the designer of the seal.

The *Urim* and *Thummim* are mentioned eight times in the Bible. The first reference is to be found in Exodus 28:30: "You shall place the *Urim* and *Thummim* in the breastplate of judgment, that they may be over Aaron's heart, whenever he enters the presence of the Lord." The exact nature of the *Urim* and *Thummim* is uncertain. The best that scholars have offered by way of explanation is that they were objects attached to the breastplate of the High Priest and they were somehow used as a kind of divine oracle. There was a direct question-and-answer type of procedure. One instance, as an example, is to be found in 1 Samuel 23:9–12. David comes to Abiathar the Kohen and asks, "Will Saul come down . . . ?" and "Will the men of Keilah surrender me and my men into the hand of Saul?" David receives an affirmative answer to both questions. It was believed in biblical times, then, that God communicated positive or negative responses through the medium of these *Urim* and *Thummim*.

At a later period there arose much speculation about their etymology. The Greek Septuagint translation of the Bible translates them as "revelation and Truth" and the Talmud as "those whose words give light and whose words are fulfilled."

Rabbi Richard Israel, in a letter to the *Yale Alumni Journal* (February 1967) suggests that the unknown designer of Yale's seal most likely utilized the Geneva Bible (which was popular among the Puritans), in which *Urim* is interpretively translated as "light" and *Thummim* as "truth or perfection." The same designer worked his way, then, into the Latin *Lux et Veritas*. In its early period Yale was basically a theological seminary. The *Urim* and *Thummim* were then looked upon as symbols of the priesthood and Yale graduates were expected to emulate the priestly verities.

In his diary Ezra Stiles makes two references to the *Urim* and *Thummim* (February 26, 1773, and December 1, 1774) but in neither instance does he shed light on the identity of its Yale designer. And if Stiles with his extraordinary curiosity was unable to do it, then apparently the matter will have to rest shrouded in permanent mystery.

—A.A.C. rep.

WHATEVER HAPPENED TO THE JEWISH FRATS?

Just before the First World War, as more and more Jews were being accepted into American colleges, they faced opening doors scholastically, while doors to college social life remained closed to them. Campus life was dominated by the Greek-letter fraternity system: a social system that mirrored an American society divided along religious and ethnic lines, with blacks almost totally excluded.

Recognizing the immediate social value and future economic implications of fraternity membership, Jews built their own parallel Greek-letter societies. In 1898 Jewish men at City College of New York founded Zeta Beta Tau, a Jewish history study group, which later became the largest Jewish collegiate social fraternity in the United States. Although several other Jewish fraternities, including Alpha Epsilon Pi and Tau Epsilon Phi, refused to exclude potential members on the basis of religion or race, ZBT's membership remained almost exclusively Jewish. This pattern of social selection along religious lines was common among all fraternities until the end of World War II, when large numbers of veterans entered college. The democratization process experienced by veterans during World War II left few GI's willing to accept "the discriminatory practices of Greek-letter societies."

Jewish "frats" increasingly began to accept non-Jewish pledges, although they were clearly in the minority. For the Jewish college student of the 1950's, particularly in the South and Midwest, social life was dominant. The 1955 *American Jewish Yearbook*, for example, lists no fewer than ten national Jewish fraternities and sororities. The social change and turbulence of the 1960's, however, almost brought about the demise of the entire fraternity system. With the passage of Federal civil rights legislation, fraternities were forbidden by college administrators to select members on the basis of religion or race, signaling the end of the Jewish Greek. Anti-establishment attitudes further contributed to the unattractiveness of fraternal organizations and severely damaged the entire Greek system. Beta Sigma Rho, an influential Jewish college fraternity for more than fifty years, was absorbed by Pi Lambda Phi in 1972, and Zeta Beta Tau absorbed Phi Epsilon Pi and Phi Sigma Delta. Today, no specifically Jewish Greek-letter societies exist. Almost all of the active national organizations that were once totally Jewish in character report about one-third non-Jewish membership; some chapters are completely non-Jewish.

Fraternity life seems to be enjoying somewhat of a comeback in recent years, albeit of a differing nature than before. A picture of contemporary Greek life has been interestingly reported by the Brothers of XI Chapter of Tau Epsilon Phi at Massachusetts Institute of Technology in the fraternity's official publication, *The Plume* (December 1979). They report the visit of their national executive director George W. Mamo:

"XI Chapter has the honor to be visited again by the redoubtable George W. (We have reliably determined that his middle name is Whitsuntides) Mamo. Last year his arrival was hailed by Operation CLONES (Contrived Lunacy Over the New Executive Secretary). This visitation was celebrated with CLONES II.

"We met Brother Mamo at Logan Airport in a turbocharged '65 Dodge Dart with Mamo flags on each fender. The TEP motorcycle gang provided a six-cycle escort, all with Mamo flags fluttering from their helmets. A sheet-sized portrait of Bro. Mamo's benevolent countenance flew from our flagpole and a framed portrait of him hangs in our dining room. Every room in the house, including the bathrooms, had his picture located somewhere, symbolizing his serene gaze that provides a guiding light to our Chapter.

"A house tour was next on the evening's agenda. The Brothers were all studying in their rooms with their stereos tuned to static. Bro. Mamo's guest room, however, was filled with the Village People dancing to the strains of 'Y.M.C.A.' It was very embarrassing, as they were not expected until the next week.

"Finally, the entire Brotherhood met downstairs for a literary discussion of Sartre's *No Exit* and the moral question: Are you responsible for the actions of your clone? It was very pleasant to see Brother Mamo again and we look forward to his return."

The rich legacy of the Jewish Greek system with its strong ties and capacity for attracting outstanding individuals can be readily seen in the list of distinguished alumni that follows:

Alpha Epsilon Pi
AEΠ

Founded: New York University (1913)
Current campus membership: 2,400
Jewish symbols used in the fraternity crest: Star of David and menorah; Lion of Judah

FAMOUS ALUMNI

Government and Politics:

Major General Robert Bernstein, former Commanding General, Walter Reed Medical Center

Nathaniel L. Goldstein, former New York State Attorney General

Max Rosenn, Justice, U.S. Third Circuit Court of Appeals

Samuel H. Schapiro, former Governor of Illinois

Herman Toll, former U.S. Congressman (D., Pa.)

H. Albert Young, former Delaware Attorney General

Athletics:

Morris Savransky, former Cincinnati Reds pitcher

Steve Stone, Baltimore Orioles pitcher

Business and Finance:

Merrill Hassenfeld, former president, Hasbro Industries

Max Karl, Chairman of the Board of MGIC (Mortgage Guarantee Insurance Corporation)

David Markin, President, Checker Cabs

Arts and Communication:

Benjamin Fine, former *New York Times* education editor

Gerold Frank, author, *The Boston Strangler*

David Horowitz, NBC consumer reporter

Fred Silverman, President, NBC Television

Paul Simon and Art Garfunkel, musicians

Carl Stern, NBC newscaster

Rabbis and Noted Jewish Community Leaders:

Rabbi Eugene Borowitz, professor, HUC-JIR; editor, *Sh'ma* magazine

Samuel Rothstein, former national president of the United Synagogues of America

Louis Stern, former President, Council of Jewish Federations and Welfare Funds; former president, Jewish Welfare Board

Tau Epsilon Phi
TEΦ

Founded: Columbia University School of Pharmacy (1910)
Current campus membership: N/A
Jewish symbols used in the fraternity crest: None

FAMOUS ALUMNI

Government and Politics:

E. J. Evans, former six-term Mayor, Durham, North Carolina

Louis Harris, public opinion analyst

Louis Heller, former U.S. Congressman (D., N.Y.)

Irving Kaufman, Chief Justice, U.S. Second Circuit Court of Appeals
Elliot Levitas, U.S. Congressman (D., Ga.)
Marvin Mandel, former Governor of Maryland
Frederic R. Mann, former U.S. Ambassador to Barbados

Athletics:
Ben Alperstein, former NCAA boxing champion
Arnold "Red" Auerbach, General Manager and former coach, Boston Celtics
Herb Flam, 1951 U.S. Davis Cup Tennis Team

Business and Finance:
Max Abramowitz, noted architect (Lincoln Center, Brandeis University chapel)
Samuel Lefrak, noted builder (Lefrak City)

Arts and Communication:
Bob Evans, CBS news correspondent
Eli Evans, author *(The Provincials)*
Benny Goodman, jazz musician
Lawrence Turman, TV and motion picture producer *(The Graduate)*

Education:
Abraham Feinberg, former Chairman, Board of Trustees, Brandeis University
Maximilian Moss, former President, New York City Board of Education
Dr. Jonas Salk, inventor of Salk polio vaccine

Zeta Beta Tau
ZBT

Founded: City College of New York (1898)
Current campus membership: 4,000
Jewish symbols used in the fraternity crest: Six-Pointed Star

FAMOUS ALUMNI*

Government and Politics:
Walter Annenberg, former U.S. Ambassador to Great Britain
Bernard Baruch, Presidential Advisor
Benjamin Cardozo, former U.S. Supreme Court Justice
Felix Frankfurter, former U.S. Supreme Court Justice
Arthur Goldberg, former U.S. Supreme Court Justice and Ambassador to the United Nations
Philip Klutznick, U.S. Secretary of Commerce
Newton Minow, former Chairman, Federal Communications Commission
Henry Morgenthau, Jr., former U.S. Secretary of the Treasury
Abraham Ribicoff, U.S. Senator (D., Conn.) and former Secretary of HEW

Athletics:
Mel Allen, New York Yankees sportscaster
Mike Epstein, Oakland Athletics
Sid Luckman, Chicago Bears quarterback, member of the Pro Football Hall of Fame
Carroll Rosenbloom, former owner of the Los Angeles Rams, professional football team
Sonny Werblin, sports promoter

Business and Finance:
Burton Baskin, founder, Baskin-Robbins Ice Cream
Bernard Gimbel, Chairman of the Board, Gimbel's Department Store
Andrew Goodman, former President, Bergdorf Goodman
Armand Hammer, President, Occidental Petroleum
Stanley Marcus, President, Neiman-Marcus Department Stores

Arts and Communication:
Jack Benny, entertainer
Leonard Bernstein, composer, conductor
Melvin Douglas, actor
Bruce Jay Friedman, author
Samuel Goldwyn, film producer
Sheldon Leonard, TV producer
Robert Q. Lewis, TV entertainer
Samuel Newhouse, newspaper publisher
William S. Paley, Board Chairman, CBS
Bill Todman, TV game show producer
Jack Warner, President, Warner Brothers
Mike Wallace, CBS news commentator, "60 Minutes"
Peter Yarrow, musician (of Peter, Paul, and Mary)

—B.D.G.

*List also includes honorary members.

MEMOIRS OF A BIG WHEEL ON CAMPUS

When the time came to select a college, my mother urged me to consider Brandeis University, or the universities of Alabama, Georgia, or Florida, where a lot of Southern Jews were. But she couldn't overcome a lifetime of conditioning that drew me inexorably to my father's and my brother's alma mater (and all my uncles, too), the University of North Carolina at Chapel Hill, just eight miles away. . . .

The day before freshmen were due for orientation week, my parents drove me over to Chapel Hill. We had argued mildly two weeks before when my mother insisted that I write down "Jewish" on the housing application in the space calling for roommate preference. She insisted, "You've had no Jewish friends in high school and we want that to change." I complained, saying I didn't want to end up with a "bunch of loud-mouthed Yankees." But my father had intervened, and I complied. I sighed gratefully that afternoon when I checked and found out the housing office had assigned me with two Southerners (Jewish boys from Virginia).

It wasn't too difficult meeting people that first week, we were all so afraid and innocent of college ways, eager to please and be accepted. I ran into Kelly Maness from Greensboro and Ned Meekins from Raleigh, whom I had met at Boys' State a year before when we were all high school student body presidents, and we hung around together because we thought that maybe we would be running as a team for class office. The Farrell twins and Whit Whitfield from Durham High showed up, and I waved hello to the Jewish boys from all around the state I knew from B'nai B'rith conventions and Camp Blue Star.

With fraternity rush coming up in two weeks, the freshman class was already beginning to split off into cliques, as the prep school boys who already wore Bass weejuns and charcoal gray began to chatter a lot among themselves. Kelly and I picked up our envelopes together. He had more than twenty first-night invitations; I had five—the three Jewish fraternities, one non-Jewish that was in so much financial trouble that everybody was invited over, and Sigma Chi, one of the "class" houses. I had been so conditioned to think in terms of Jewish fraternities that, until titillated by the card in that envelope, I had never considered any alternative. I let my imagination soar and toyed with the possibility of pledging Sigma Chi.

That night, Kelly and I strode manfully over to the Sigma Chi house together, hot-shot freshmen with an ice-pack of surface cool over a caldron of apprehension. Once inside we were immediately split off from each other, Kelly ushered through a living-room door to the inner sanctum of the house while I was maneuvered skillfully to a corner of the living room for a short face-off with another brother.

"You Evans?" queried a crew-cut stud, his beer belly hanging over an alligator belt.

"Yes, Kelly and I are friends. . . ."

"Uh, uh—not here. You'll probably want to go TEP or ZBT or Pi Lam, being Jewish and all." He took my arm and guided me toward the front door. "We've cooperated with them through the years by promising not to go after their best guys. So please forgive the mistake." By then we were on the front porch where he could shake my hand and wish me luck.

The TEP house greeted me enthusiastically. I was a "legacy," because my father had helped found the chapter in 1924, and they were wondering where I had been.

"Hey, man, what you been up to?" a grating Yankee accent insisted on knowing.

"Uh, over at Sigma Chi," I replied sheepishly. I told them the story, and they roared so heartily that I felt I had to squeeze out a laugh too.

"Hey, man, don't you know Sigma Chi means Sign of Christ?" Another Yankee slumped his arm around my shoulder in intimate pretense. "I bet you were the first Yid they ever let in that place." I winced. "Yid" was a word a Jewish Southerner would never use to describe himself.

The Jewish fraternities put out a maximum effort to pledge Southerners, because family relationships were so entwined among the Jews in North Carolina that if a fraternity lost a key boy from Fayetteville, say, it might lose out in that city for a decade. The alumni sensed the critical character of rushing much more acutely than we ever did, and they would scrabble for pledges in their home towns, for if Leon Schneider's son Eliot belonged, a vital continuity would be maintained. For years my father and I, along with a lot of other alumni and their sons, had been stopping by the TEP house after football games, and I had sensed the strength in his friendship with Harry Schwartz from Charlotte and Leonard Eisenberg from Winston-Salem. The Jewish fraternity in the South was its own community within a community—close, loyal, and eternal.

There were only fifty Jewish boys going through rush, and the competition was rugged among the Jewish houses; the strategy consisted of mobilizing a core group to commit early, and plotting with them to organize a "snowball" from inside the class.

They urged me to engineer one but all I could do was talk to two or three boys I liked. I parroted clumsily the arguments that I would perfect and use for the years I would be rushing others: that there was no real social life without fraternity because Jewish girls didn't like to visit guys who were "unaffiliated"; that it was better to be with your own kind; that the Jewish houses had higher academic standards—they organized study halls and even kept files of past quizzes in certain courses and old themes that had received "A's"; that you'd make friends for life, not just for college; that alumni could help with jobs and advice; and that you could stay with brothers when you visited New York.

I met the Yankees—Artie and Ritchie and Ira; Maslow, Kushinsky, and Greenblatt—some of them tough types out of Brooklyn and Jersey City who loved big-stakes card games and a violent drunk; some of them flashy and impressive with Thunderbirds and Corvettes from Great Neck and Scarsdale who took to Southern women like Jesse James to the banking business; others from Far Rockaway and the Bronx, who just wanted to make it—through medical school or the business school to the stock market or a big corporation, away from the shops and groceries of their fathers to something on their own. I didn't appreciate the distinctions between Long Island and Brooklyn Heights—it was all Broadway lights and the Empire State Building to me, and they all came from that vast uncharted non-South known as *The North*, products of paved playgrounds and the Dead End kids, of bums in the Bowery, hot dogs in the street, rattling subways, and Mafia shakedowns.

They came South for all the expected reasons: because they heard the business school was good; because they wanted a new experience and new people and had no idea what was in store for them; because they couldn't get accepted at any other school; or because their parents had stopped by once on the way to Florida and had become captivated with the beauty of the place. . . .

The Yankees could be loud and obnoxious—God, how they were loud—embarrassing us with a big wave across the campus and a friendly yell of "How ya doin,' shmuck." "Shmuck" was a Yankee word, and it could be used both as an endearment and a biting epithet. If a rushee wore his national honor society pin during rush week, he was definitely a "shmuck." But if your roommate introduced you to his date and you said, "I love him even though he wets his bed," then your roommate might reply with, "You're a shmuck, you know that?" and his words would ring with the quintessence of friendship.

The pledge master was always the biggest, toughest, meanest, most engaging mixture of father confessor and slave master that the upperclassmen could find. In Brooklyn's own F. F. Kulinsky ("Fat Fred" we called him), they found the ultimate—stocky like a football guard, bellowing and bull-necked, who wallowed in his role like a hippo in a mud bath—but a sweet guy after you waded past his blustering, volatile personality and got to know him.

When "Kulinsk" barked out "Hey pledge" to summon you to some duty, it was like the piercing command of the drill sergeant; he infused those two words with such scorn that fifteen years later, when he called Artie Sobel in New York and began the conversation with "Hey pledge," Artie confessed he was scared all over again.

When the brothers criticized Dickie Shulman for walking too effeminately, Kulinsky gave him swagger drills every day for a month as a corrective. Kulinsk, cigar in his mouth, counting "hut, two, three, four," waddled along the sidewalk beside poor Dickie, his fire-hydrant legs and bulbous rump in perfect rhythm to his personal rhumba-rendition of John Wayne busting into a saloon.

And when Curtis Gans washed a brother's car with steel wool, Kulinsk convened a pledge court at three in the morning, complete with sheets and candles, to pass on the deep and mystical concern for Curtis' fraternal future.

Kulinsk taught us how to drink beer on a memorable night at the annual brother/pledge beerbust. "You gotta learn how to handle beer, and enjoy it. Like there's nothing better than a beer with a steak, or a beer with a pizza. And you gotta know how to sip suds with a friend, or order one for a girl; a beer is elegant, manly, and delicious." He made us all line up straight, and broke open each beer with spurting delight. "Now *guzzle*, you putz-heads." We turned them up and spit up all over the wood paneling and each other and he sat there, a Roman emperor, laughing wildly at his triumph in college indoctrination.

As the years passed, I went home with the Yankees and invited them home with me and we came to know and like each other. Chapel Hill softened them over the years as it sharpened me or maybe I began to see them in less stereotyped terms. They learned how to get along with Southerners and I learned to love the Yankees. . . .

I dated their sisters in New York and invited them down to Carolina for weekends. It was the beginning of a serious "Northern girl" phase, a fascination with the sharp-tongued, matter-of-fact, smart-assed Jewish girl who responded so appreciatively to my courtly ways. They delighted in hearing me say "yes ma'am" to our house mother, never failed to be bowled over when I helped them with a sweater or opened doors for them. I wasn't uptight and their brothers were, and it puzzled them—my inflections and colloquialisms, and carefully honed naïveté, flattering them constantly with easy Southern banter. "Did anybody ever tell you," a girl from Brooklyn once said, "that going out with you is like dating a gentile?"

We lived for TEP house-party weekends, when you piled your dirty socks and underwear in the closet because girls might visit the rooms; the place would be transformed from a zoo into a fantasyland of postcard collegiate cleanliness.

Since Orange County was dry, "Penquin" Lieberman and Malcom Coplon made the liquor run to Durham on Thursday night, "Duck" Saunders assembled the gin, grape juice, lemons, and secret herbs to begin brewing the Purple Jesus.

Buddy Schiff and the social committee would start planning nine months in advance, to beat the other fraternities and reserve motel rooms and boardinghouses for the girls, the ballroom at the Carolina Inn for the Friday night formal, the cabin near East Lake for the Saturday night bash, and the extra football tickets for alumni.

The girls started arriving by bus from Women's College in Greensboro at mid-afternoon on Friday. Gentile girls had to be special to get invited—either beautiful to impress the brothers, or wild (to impress the brothers). The North Carolina Jewish girls had been traipsing to house parties since the tenth grade, and we greeted each other warmly, while we looked over their shoulders at the new crop of freshmen girls who had been fixed up with the gamblers and the losers in our house.

The girls held up well under the more primitive pressures of the system. Seventy Jewish girls were isolated at Women's College, no more than twenty at Duke, and less than five on the Chapel Hill campus, which only accepted girls as juniors and seniors. There were fewer than a hundred and fifty Jewish boys at Carolina, so it was essential to make a good impression at one of the fraternities. If she made a wrong move, she could turn off an entire house, so most girls followed the lead of the N.C. local veteran house-party goers and were nice to everyone, even if they were having a rotten time.

"Reputation," that elusive mother-presence that stalked the girls of the fifties, exaggerated the dilemma. If they were too aloof, the brothers called them "frigid." If they were too warm, they risked a "bad reputation," which could result in a girl's leaving school in disgrace; for that reason, they rarely drank more than a few sips of a drink or ever lost their presence.

Lurking behind the fraternity pressures, behind the good times at college, lay the great prize, the *raison d'être*—to get married before graduation. Part of it was Jewish conditioning from mothers who had done just that, but for Southern Jewish girls, there was a special stress, because the alternatives were so frightening: leaving home ties altogether, finding a job, moving away to Atlanta, or even trying New York. The system made it worse—the "freshman fling" gave way to the "sophomore slump," the "junior jumps," and the "senior shakes," as each new group of girls intrigued the boys more than the girls they already knew. In two years, the girls were intimate with Carolina and had cased Duke and the University of Virginia for prospects; if things weren't going well (and they usually weren't), most transferred south to the universities of Georgia or Florida.

The Friday night formal always included dinner and a speaker, with presentations and awards. My father often spoke at these events since he was a founder of the chapter and had stayed involved as a financial adviser for thirty years, watching mortgage payments, raising money for the new building fund, making his annual presentation on the secrets of rushing, and occasionally intervening when a Yankee blackballed a Southern legacy. He drew my mother into it as well, and she would redecorate the house every few years with the most durable furniture she could find in New York. Once, out of gratitude for designing an additional wing of bedrooms and a new dining area, the fraternity invited her to give a few remarks at a banquet. When she lauded the "outstanding Jewish fraternity in the nation, where Jewish boys and girls come together . . . ," I was told that three Yankees, each dating a surprised gentile schoolteacher who thought this was just another fraternity weekend, slid under the table and out of the room.

The Saturday night cabin party after the football game highlighted the weekend. (We had to rent a cabin to avoid the crotchety old hag who lived across the street and rocked on the porch of her crumbling little house and often called the police to complain about the "Jew noise.") Couples necked in cars parked all around like a drive-in movie, or sweated together inside, where slow dances alternated with the Lindy, and where we'd stand in a circle watching a nervy couple, always a Yankee with a "wild" date, do the dirty bop.

By Sunday, we prayed for the girls to leave, but not before our house mother, "Ma" Cohen, unleashed an all-out Jewish brunch of salami and eggs, homemade strudel, pumpernickel toast, and lox, bagels, and cream cheese from the delicatessen in Raleigh.

Student politics drew me, initially out of high-school habit, but I soon learned that student government at Chapel Hill prided itself on a long tradition of concern for campus issues. The student budget of

$150,000 was appropriated solely by the student legislature, with no university administration control, since in the 1930's the students had voted on a $20-per-student activity fee, which the trustees empowered them to spend independently. Students at the University of North Carolina, I was told over and over again, were privileged to have this unusual power over their own affairs and were often the envy of students elsewhere. . . .

In such an atmosphere, the president of the student body loomed over the campus as the biggest deal around—he inspired the entering freshmen with a fighting speech on student freedom; his picture often appeared in the *Daily Tar Heel*; he could announce with flowery statements the appointments of his friends to committees; and he presented his courageous annual State of the Campus address to the student legislature, text reprinted in full in the paper. I resolved early to try for it, probably because there had never been a Jewish student-body president at Chapel Hill, and as Mister Jew in Durham, I had been running for class offices since junior high school. And I am sure that, subconsciously, I wanted to emulate the first Jewish mayor of Durham, [my father]. . . .

A handful of us in student government anointed ourselves the "new Southerners." We were deeply perturbed that the South was entering an era profoundly different from anything we had grown up with, but determined to listen to the voices of reason and restraint. After the Supreme Court decision every Negro on the street took on a new dimension—we would all be together now, in the same schools, the same neighborhoods, the same offices. Suddenly we were aware of just how little we really knew about him, the black stranger, who was neither meek nor aggressive, suffering nor lustful, pitiable nor irresponsible, as we had been taught. The adjustments to the new relationship would demand more of him than us, as both white and black struggled to overcome the twisted history distorting the hesitant acceptance of the future. Black and white young people were all part of the New South, groping for a way, yet understanding the violence simmering in the soul of the old South we grew up in.

We projected our concern onto student government, because that was the only outlet for action our generation of students perceived. Demonstrations and overt defiance were out of the question, for an arrest or expulsion would be reported on our college records and surely be judged by future employers, graduate schools, and bar examiners. Such were the restraints at the end of the McCarthy era. We treated the smallest risk-taking as a sign of our courage, especially any signal of sympathy for the cause of Negro advance. . . .

The two political parties that battled for control of student government represented the classic college constituencies—the University Party, dominated by the fraternities and sororities, versus the Student Party, dominated by groups with nonfraternity interests—graduate students, dorm rats, and returning veterans. Both parties pursued all the votes with programs and candidates, so the membership in neither was pure. On race, especially, the University Party was more conservative, because the membership in fraternities came out of the elitist Southern tradition of gentlemanly segregation, some of them cultivated in all-white Southern prep schools with no populist influences to leaven their views, most from families new to money, products of the postwar economic boom for whom acceptance in the DKE house represented the ultimate status for their sons and recognition for the family. Many of the fraternities had secret clauses in their charters or initiation ceremonies prohibiting minority groups to membership, and the presence of Negroes on the campus coupled with a national campaign against discriminatory clauses made them uneasy with the prospect, already enforced at some colleges, that someday they might have to prove nondiscrimination by actually pledging a black. Beyond that, the University Party existed primarily as a device to parcel out honors to the Greeks, and they really didn't care much about issues at all.

The Student Party shied away from outspoken pronouncements on race because of the gap between the leadership in the party and the voters in the dorm. The leadership considered itself guardian of the soul of the university, protector of its liberal tradition, custodian of its place in history. It therefore attracted to party meetings all the boys who took themselves terribly seriously—earnest do-gooders, the verbose intellectuals, the consumed activists, the small-town high-school class officers hungry for recognition and struggling to articulate issues they had never thought about before.

To outsiders, there was little ideological difference in the two parties; we exaggerated the differences out of self-importance, a need to believe, no matter how fanciful, that the state and nation were listening, thereby adding importance to our great debates and rationalizing the time student politics soaked up. The Student Party alumni, symbols to us that we mattered, straggled back from time to time to an enthusiastic reception—Allard Lowenstein, former president of the National Students Association, for a speech on the oppression in South Africa and Mississippi; Dick Murphy, former student-body president and then assistant to the chairman of the National Democratic Party, with the latest news on Eisenhower's faltering heart; my brother Bob, former student government attorney general, then CBS correspondent in the South and in Moscow. . . .

On campus, Jimmy Wallace served as elder statesman, a rapier wit whose memory for personalities and events reached back into the thirties. Having run and been defeated three times for editor of the *Daily Tar Heel* during the war years, Jimmy had founded Rho Dammit Rho, his fraternity for the "undaunted"; but his greatest moment, and a Student Party legend we told with relish, was a one-vote victory for delegate to the first international student congress in Prague, in which Al Lowenstein (a New Yorker whose mother came from Birmingham, Alabama) was dragged to the meeting to cast the deciding vote for Wallace, the campus radical, enabling him to edge out a blond, brown-and-white-oxford, fraternity-man great-grandson of a former governor named Junius Scales, later convicted for conspiracy to overthrow the government as chairman of the North Carolina Communist Party.

The Jewish fraternities reacted to campus politics in complicated ways. As was the pattern all over the South, ZBT by and large rushed and pledged the Reform Jews and anxiously sought to project the big "frat-man" image—dating campus queens, wearing coats and ties to class. They joined the University Party and served as legislative leaders and party chairmen, supplying much of the brain power in the party platform and party-sponsored legislation. Invariably, however, in the spring when hundreds of fraternity and sorority members flooded the nominating convention to wheel and deal for high stakes, the big fraternities would shut the ZBT's out of campus-wide nominations.

The wise heads in the TEP house guided me to the Student Party, where a Jewish boy wouldn't have to battle the big fraternities for important nominations. (The annual ZBT–TEP football game was a brutal battle of the Reform Jews against the East Europeans. Of course, we didn't know it was precisely that and it has only struck me in recent years, so naïve was I then, but there was something about being "zeeb'd"—our name for the condescending way the ZBT's treated us.)

Presiding over the S.P. was "Mister Chairman," Joel Fleishman, the latest contribution of the Fleishman clan of eastern North Carolina. The original seven brothers had sired twenty-seven sons, who scattered across the state like locusts, opening, so it seemed, a Fleishman's Clothing Store in every little town in the state. Joel left Fayetteville, N.C., to attend high school at the Yeshiva in Baltimore. His freshman year at the university, he brought his own pots and pans and a hot plate to Chapel Hill so he could cook kosher food in his dorm. He refused out of high principle to join a Jewish fraternity. His laugh—a high-pitched cackle—reflected a hyped-up exuberance that glued the Student Party together in a spirit of joyous warfare. He resolved all disputes by delivering his political judgments with pontifical finality, crisp and unchallengeable.

Joel loved opera and could flip through his mammoth record collection to fill our chasms of cultural ignorance with any aria that crossed his mind. He took voice lessons but none of his friends would let him sing, so he found an outlet acting as cantor in synagogues around the area during the high holy days. To shape up his voice, he would rehearse, mixing Kol Nidre liberally with *La Bohème,* as he dashed around in his convertible, top down and oblivious to the astonished pedestrians recoiling from the warble and blast of his tin-foil tenor.

Joel taught me not to say "sir" to waiters in fancy restaurants ("They like to be treated as waiters; that is why they have chosen a profession of personal service"); he instructed me on the different uses of Burgundy and Chablis; that lobster bisque was a soup requiring a spot of sherry; that sitting in a steam bath was the most civilized way to lose weight; that if you can't go first class, better to stay at home and wait until you can. He bought his suits at Brooks Brothers and smoked Parliament cigarettes while speaking up for the rights of the common dormitory man.

When detractors charged that he was too aloof to win elective office, he merely ran for the legislature and clobbered his opposition with indefatigable handshaking; he became so involved tutoring, finding extra tickets for games, and driving his constituents to the infirmary and to Durham that he became an unbeatable fixture.

He worked incessantly making friends all over the country and kept a cross-referenced file on everyone he met by birthday, county, political party, and potential. His Christmas card list ran to several thousand names. As chairman of the Carolina Forum, he was responsible for bringing speakers to the campus and arranging their schedules, so we were often willingly roped into a lunch with Wayne Morse, a chat with Eleanor Roosevelt, or a seminar with Edward R. Murrow or Adlai Stevenson.

The University Party leaders despised Joel; he outworked them and out-thought them and they viewed him as some sort of eccentric politico who took the game much more seriously than it deserved to be taken; he in return held their life style in total disdain for its philistine emphasis on beer and ball games, hell raising and the gentleman's "C."

Chairman Fleishman took charge of my political career and guided me carefully through three successful elections, grooming me each time for the next step, making certain I didn't run for offices I couldn't win, and building credentials for the final race for student-body president. By my junior year, the numbers were going against the U.P. Although college enrollment was rising, the number of students joining fraternities and sororities remained the same, and thus the base of U.P. support was shrinking. Now that the Student Party was going to nominate me, a fraternity man, the U.P. leaders decided to counter with an unprecedented step: nominate a popular nonfraternity man. They hoped to hold the traditional University Party vote, counting on the loyalty of the big fraternities faced with a nominee from a Jewish fraternity, and cut into the S.P. dorm vote by charging that their candidate was the "true voice" of the dormitory man. It was a brilliant strategy that did credit to the ZBT brain trust running the U.P. (and motivated in part, I always thought, to stop the TEP's from winning a high-prestige office which might be translated into a rushing advantage).

Bill Baum emerged the perfect choice. He was former state-wide president of the North Carolina Conference of the Methodist Youth Fellowship, planned to study for the ministry, and had worked his way through school. He formerly had been an S.P. member and knew the weaknesses of our precinct organization intimately; he had switched parties for political opportunity in the U.P. and had won a student legislature seat in a hardened S.P. dorm district by personal charm and hard work. Baum was a seasoned campaigner, smooth, appealing, articulate. Above all, he was a gifted public speaker who had lost a leg in a childhood accident, and when he hobbled to a microphone and dramatically propped himself up on his crutches, a hush always came over the crowd as it became more attentive. We were in trouble.

Tom Lambeth, my campaign manager as well as the party statistician and historian, scrambled through the records and concluded that I had to win forty percent of the fraternity vote. "You know what this means," counseled Fleishman. "You've got to go up to fraternity court and get votes from guys who don't think you're good enough to belong to their houses."

Walking over to fraternity court, the old aching sense of inferiority sent shudders of apprehension through me. Now I was forced by my own amibtion to return to the scene of that earlier rejection when, as a callow freshman, I swore I would never come back to them again. At the Tri Delt candlelight supper, when a flirtatious girl asked, "And what fraternity are you?" I watched her face sag into indifference, and then imagined her passing it around as I sat there with the eyes of fifty girls fastened on me, taking my measure as I tried to eat spaghetti cleanly. Back at the Sigma Chi house, the president interrupted dinner to introduce me to the impassive brothers hunched over their plates, not even bothering to look up. "Just go on eating your dessert, fellas," he said awkwardly, trying to cover their listless inattention, "I would like to introduce the Student Party [smirk] candidate for president." It all seemed hopeless.

In the fraternities and sororities, Lambeth instructed me to wear an Ivy League suit and a button-down shirt. But in the dorms, I campaigned in shirt sleeves, knocking on doors and brightly drawling to a group of four guys playing poker, "Hey, how're y'all. I'm Sonny Evans, candidate for president of the student body and I'm running on a platform that never interrupts a card game," and they'd invariably chime in, "You've got my vote."

The biggest issues in the campaign broke during a face-to-face debate at the Westminster Fellowship when we were asked our opinions on the university policy of placing all Negro students on the same floor of a selected dorm, regardless of the desires of the students. Baum said he wouldn't "agitate" for change because "the student body is not yet ready to cope with it." I knew my answer would hurt in the fraternities and disenchant part of the Student Party dorm vote, but after visiting the black students isolated up there, I knew the time of reckoning had come. I criticized the university for pursuing a policy of "segregated integration" and said that "the purpose of student government is to see that each student is treated equally. If the dining hall were not open to all students, I would take a stand. I feel the same way about the dorms."

The audience applauded vigorously, but these were the goody-goody religious liberals, and Bill knew it. When the *Tar Heel* bannered the headlines, "Baum, Evans Answer Questions on Racial Issue at Carolina," the Yankees in my fraternity said, "That's telling those rednecks." But two S.P. precinct captains called to tell us, "He blew it."

On election night, I paced the floor upstairs in the student union, fidgety and nervous, glancing from time to time at Lambeth's charts with the bellwether districts marked in red, while the election board counted the ballots downstairs. New York pledge Louis Lefkowitz ran back and forth with the results on a slip of paper copied from the huge blackboard below; Tom would post them to his chart and suggested, "Keep a sharp lookout for Town Men's II, Louie. If we do well there . . ." At midnight, Tom looked up with a big smile and said quietly, "Congratulations, Mister President." It was the closest election in his memory.

A few minutes later, Louie burst through the door and yelled out, "Baum's waiting downstairs and the place is packed," and Tom pulled out a short victory statement he had written that afternoon. "I've got the concession statement in the other pocket," he said with a smile, patting his coat. I walked shakily down the stairs to a steamy crowd of buzzing party workers and flickering flashbulbs to shake Baum's hand, my shoulders stinging from the backslaps of the well-wishers, girls squealing and hugging me; over in the corner studying the returns on the blackboard intently, I saw the mayor of Durham and the "mayoress," as he always called her, joy evident through her tears. Mom squeezed me and murmured how proud they were, and Dad shook my hand tightly, reaching all the way in like he taught me when I was small. He spoke in hard-headed, grudging tones that one political pro reserves for another.

Allard Lowenstein showed up as he usually did for election nights and he offered his crisp appraisal: "Everybody heard they might have a Jewish president so they went out and voted for Sonny Evans to stop Bill Baum." Lambeth pointed out that we had won by carrying the lesser fraternities and sororities, which had members who were once blackballed from the Dekes or the Tri Delts.

The next day I floated to class with a phalanx of the Yankees behind me, all of them for the first time decked out in fraternity pins, like a flying wedge of strutting ducks chasing a canary. Chapel Hill glittered in a shimmering spring day and the apple-blossomed branches covered the walkway to class in a canopy of pink and white fragrance. The coeds from the Tri Delt House now smiled eagerly and I smiled back. A star-struck freshman asked me to autograph a poster and when I stopped to accommodate my new fan, Artie Sobel from Far Rockaway sidled up behind me and leaned in close for a quick word: "You're a shmuck, Evans . . . you know that?"

—E.N.E. rep.

DOCTORAL DISSERTATIONS OF 15 FAMOUS JEWS

• **Theodor W. Adorno** (1903–1969), German sociologist, coauthor of *The Authoritarian Personality*.
Thesis: "The Concept of the Unconscious in the Transcendental Theory of Mind"
Where: The University of Frankfurt, 1927 (Philosophy).
Comment: This was a ground-breaking attempt to blend Kantian philosophy with Freudian psychology.

• **Hannah Arendt** (1906–1975), German political and social philosopher, author of *Eichmann in Jerusalem* and *The Origins of Totalitarianism*.
Thesis: "The Concept of Love in St. Augustine."
Where: The University of Heidelberg, 1929 (Philosophy).
Comment: This work, written under the direction of Martin Heidegger, was an exploration of existentialist elements in the Christian concept of love and set the stage for Arendt's later writings on human freedom and politics.

• **Isaac Asimov** (1920—), well-known U.S. author and biochemist, author of *I, Robot* and *Biochemistry and Human Metabolism*.
Thesis: "The Kinetics of the Reaction Inactivation of Tyrosinose during the Catalysis of the Aerobic Oxidation of Catechol"
Where: Columbia University, 1948 (Biochemistry).
Comment: Asimov recounts that the title of his thesis sounded like a satire that he had written earlier.

• **Salo Wittmayer Baron** (1895—), professor emeritus of history at Columbia University, "dean" of modern Jewish historiography, author of *A Social and Religious History of the Jews* (16 volumes).
Thesis: "The Jewish Question at the Congress of Vienna (based on some previously unpublished sources)"
Where: The University of Vienna, 1917 (Philosophy).
Comment: This was the first major study by Baron of the interrelationship between eman-

cipation, international diplomacy, and the cultural-religious history of the Jewish people. It proved to be a model upon which many of his later works were based.

• **Walter Benjamin** (1892–1940), German philosopher and literary critic.
Thesis: "The Origin of German Tragic Drama"
Where: The University of Frankfurt, 1925 (Aesthetics).
Comment: This famous and abstruse work, presented as a *Habilitationsschrift* (advanced doctoral dissertation), was rejected by the Aesthetics Department because the examining professor "could not understand a word of it." Benjamin's failure to be "habilitated" (employed as a professor) was later cynically explained with the comment that *"Geist kann man nicht habilitieren"* (One cannot inaugurate spirit).

• **Niels Bohr** (1885–1962), Danish physicist, director of Copenhagen's Institute of Theoretical Physics, Nobel laureate in Physics (1922).
Thesis: "The Investigation of Metals"
Where: The University of Copenhagen, 1911 (Physics).
Comment: This briefly titled thesis was a major breakthrough in theoretical physics and laid the groundwork for Bohr's discoveries in the realm of molecular structure.

• **Martin Buber** (1878–1965), German philosopher, theologian, and Zionist leader, author of *I and Thou.*
Thesis: "Towards a History of the Problem of Individuation—Nicholas of Cusa and Jacob Boehme"
Where: The University of Vienna, 1904 (Philosophy).
Comment: From his study of Jacob Boehme's pantheistic mysticism Buber developed his doctrine of "realization," which he later found manifested in Hasidism.

• **Noam Avram Chomsky** (1928—), professor of linguistics at the Massachusetts Institute of Technology, seminal linguisitic theoretician, outspoken critic of both American and Israeli political policy.
Thesis: "Syntactic Structures of Grammar"
Where: Univeristy of Pennsylvania, 1955 (Linguistics).
Comment: This was the first major work of Chomsky to explain in detail his theory of "deep structures" or common grammatical structures in all human languages.

• **Emile Durkheim** (1858–1917), distinguished French sociologist, author of *Elementary Forms of Religious Life.*
Thesis: "The Division of Labor"
Where: The University of Bordeaux, 1893 (Philosophy).
Comment: Durkheim's famous and spirited defense of this dissertation against the skepticism of his professors helped establish sociology as a legitimate discipline and removed from it the stigma of "socialist subversion."

• **Henry Alfred Kissinger** (1923—), political scientist, U.S. Secretary of State under Presidents Nixon and Ford.
Thesis: "A World Restored: Metternich, Castlereagh, and the Problems of Peace, 1812–1822"
Where: Harvard University, 1954 (Political Science).
Comment: Many have seen in Kissinger's admiring study of Metternich, Kissinger's own basic principles of conservative statesmanship.

• **Rosa Luxemburg** (1871–1919), Polish-born revolutionary, founder of the German Communist party.
Thesis: "The Industrial Development of Poland"
Where: The University of Zurich, 1898 (Economics).
Comment: This work, used currently by Polish Communist economists, was originally supposed to demonstrate economically the infeasibility of an independent Poland and, hence, the futility of Polish nationalism.

• **Herbert Marcuse** (1898–1979), German-born U.S. philosopher, greatly influenced the American New Left, author of *One-Dimensional Man.*
Thesis: "Hegel's Ontology and the Foundations of a Theory of Historicity"
Where: The University of Freiburg, 1929 (Philosophy).
Comment: This thesis, written under the direction of Martin Heidegger, was Marcuse's first formulation of his brand of radical Critical Theory from a phenomenological and Hegelian point of view.

• **Karl Heinrich Marx** (1818–1883), German philosopher, chief theoretician of modern socialism, author of *The Communist Manifesto.*
Thesis: "The Difference Between Democratic and Epicurean Natural Philosophy"
Where: The University of Jena, 1841 (Philosophy).
Comment: Many of the humanistic and existentialist strands of the early Marx can be seen in this work. However, because of his revolutionary political views this work did not gain Marx an academic post.

• **Franz Rosenzweig** (1886–1929), German philosopher, influential Jewish theologian, author of *The Star of Redemption.*
Thesis: "Hegel and the State"
Where: University of Freiburg, 1912 (Philosophy).

Comment: This highly acclaimed attack against Hegelian idealism from an existential point of view was developed at greater length in Rosenzweig's most famous book, *The Star of Redemption.*

• **Gershom Gerhard Scholem** (1897—), German-born Israeli historian, leading authority in the field of Jewish mysticism, author of *Major Trends in Jewish Mysticism.*

Thesis: "The *Sefer ha-Bahir*"
Where: The University of Munich, 1920 (Semitics).
Comment: This was the first of Scholem's many penetrating studies into the world of kabbalistic mysticism. The field was so unknown that he wrote his dissertation with virtually no assistance.

—H.N.K.

JEWISH NOBEL PRIZEWINNERS

Peace
1911 Tobias Michael Carel Asser (Holland)
1911 Alfred H. Fried (Austria)
1968 René Cassin (France)
1973 Henry Kissinger (U.S.A.)
1978 Menachem Begin (Israel)

Literature
1910 Paul Heyse (Germany)
1927 Henri Bergson (France)
1958 Boris Pasternak (USSR)
1966 Shmuel Yosef Agnon (Israel)
1966 Nelly Sachs (Sweden)
1976 Saul Bellow (U.S.A.)
1978 Isaac Bashevis Singer (U.S.A.)

Physics
1907 Albert A. Michelson (U.S.A.)
1908 Gabriel Lippmann (France)
1921 Albert Einstein (Germany)
1922 Niels Bohr (Denmark)
1925 James Franck (Germany)
1943 Otto Stern (U.S.A.)
1944 Isidor I. Rabi (U.S.A.)
1952 Felix Bloch (U.S.A.)
1954 Max Born (U.K.-Germany)
1959 Emilio Segre (Italy)
1960 Donald Glaser (U.S.A.)
1961 Robert Hofstadter (U.S.A.)
1962 Lev Davidovich Landau (USSR)
1965 Richard Phillips Feynman (U.S.A.)
1965 Julian Seymour Schwinger (U.S.A.)
1967 Hans Albrecht Bethe (U.S.A.)
1969 Murray Gell-Mann (U.S.A.)
1971 Dennis Gabor (U.K.)
1971 Gerhard Herzberg (Canada)
1973 Brian D. Josephson (U.K.)
1975 Benjamin R. Mottelson (Denmark)
1975 Aage Bohr (Denmark)
1976 Burton Richter (U.S.A.)
1978 Pyotr Kapitsa (USSR)
1978 Arno Penzias (U.S.A.)
1979 Sheldon Glashow (U.S.A.)
1979 Steven Weinberg (U.S.A.)

Writer Shmuel Yosef Agnon

Chemistry
1905 Adolph von Baeyer (Germany)
1906 Henri Moissan (France)
1910 Otto Wallach (Germany)
1915 Richard Willstatter (Germany)
1918 Fritz Haber (Germany)
1943 George de Hevesy (Hungary/Denmark)
1961 Melvin Calvin (U.S.A.)
1962 Max Perutz (U.K.)
1972 William H. Stein (U.S.A.)
1979 Herbert C. Brown (U.S.A.)

Medicine and Physiology
1908 Paul Ehrlich (Germany)

1908 Elie Metchnikoff (Russia)
1914 Robert Barany (Austria)
1923 Otto Meyerhoff (Germany)
1930 Karl Landsteiner (Austria/U.S.A.)
1936 Otto Loewi (Austria)
1944 Joseph Erlanger (U.S.A.)
1944 Herbert Gasser (U.S.A.)
1945 Sir Ernst Boris Chain (U.K.)
1946 Herman Joseph Muller (U.S.A.)
1950 Tadeus Reichstein (Switzerland)
1952 Selman Waksman (U.S.A.)
1953 Sir Hans Krebs (U.K.)
1953 Fritz Albert Lipmann (U.S.A.)
1958 Joshua Lederberg (U.S.A.)
1959 Arthur Kornberg (U.S.A.)
1964 Konrad Bloch (U.S.A.)
1965 François Jacob (France)
1965 André Lwoff (France)
1967 George Wald (U.S.A.)
1968 Marshall Nirenberg (U.S.A.)
1969 Salvador Luria (U.S.A.)
1970 Julius Axelrod (U.S.A.)
1970 Sir Bernard Katz (U.K.)
1972 Gerald Edelman (U.S.A.)
1975 David Baltimore (U.S.A.)
1975 Howard Temin (U.S.A.)
1976 Baruch Blumberg (U.S.A.)
1977 Rosalyn Yalow (U.S.A.)
1978 Daniel Nathans (U.S.A.)

Economics

1970 Paul A. Samuelson (U.S.A.)
1971 Simon Kuznets (U.S.A.)
1972 Kenneth J. Arrow (U.S.A.)
1975 Leonid Vitalyevich Kantorovich (USSR)
1976 Milton Friedman (U.S.A.)
1978 Herbert A. Simon (U.S.A.)

—The Eds.

PART FIVE
THE RELIGIOUS CONNECTION

THE NAMES OF GOD

THE 7 NAMES THAT CANNOT BE ERASED

> Moses said to God, "When I come to the Israelites and say to them 'The God of your fathers has sent me to you,' and they ask me, 'What is His name?' what shall I say to them?" And God said to Moses, "Ehyeh Asher Ehyeh (I Am That I Am or I Will Be What I Will Be)." He continued, "Thus shall you say to the Israelites, 'Ehyeh (I Am or I Will Be) sent me to you.' "
>
> Exodus 4:13–14

Names objectify. Since God is neither an object nor objectifiable, however, God's name cannot be a name in the normal sense. In the Jewish tradition the name actually partakes of the essence of God. Thus, knowledge of the name is a vehicle to God, a conveyor of divine energy, an interface between the Infinite and the finite. Misapplication of the name, on the other hand, can have unfortunate consequences for the casual user.

Fearing more its falling into bad mouths than its being uttered by the clean lipped, the tradition has proscribed both the pronunciation and the writing of God's name. If written, the name cannot be erased and must be taken to a synagogue where it will be buried along with other sacred texts and ritual objects. The prohibition against pronouncing the name has led to various euphemisms being employed, some of which have become so identified as a name of God that they, too, require yet another euphemism. The strictures against writing the name, although applicable only to the Hebrew names, have been extended by particularly meticulous Jews to include the name even in the vernacular. Thus, they would write God as G-d.

It is curious that a tradition that places such a strong emphasis on the One God, possesses such a large number of names for the divine. Each name, however, actually represents a different quality or aspect of God. Unable to grasp the transcendent nature of God, the human addresses a particular "face," using the name as a vehicle for the particular energy. At the end of days, however, "the Lord will be One and His name one." (Zech. 14:9)

El

Although its precise meaning and origin are obscure, El appears as the chief god of the Canaanite pantheon in ancient Ugaritic myths.

In the Bible, used most frequently in combinations such as El Elyon (the Most High) or El Olam (the Eternal), El has come to represent the quality of *hesed* (compassion or lovingkindness) or *gedulah* (largesse). As such, El is symbolized by the Patriarch Abraham, who expressed compassion towards the people of Sodom and loving hospitality towards the three guests who visited him in his desert tent. The festival of Passover falls under this aspect of God, as it is the celebration of the release of the people from the constriction of slavery into the open expanse of freedom.

Elohim

Although Elohim is technically a plural form, it is generally used as a singular. This oddity may be ascribed either to its origin as a pagan deity or to its being a type of superlative meaning "Divinity."

Elohim has come to represent the quality of *din* (stern judgment) or *gevurah* (power) and serves as a balance to El's free-flowing love. Whereas the impulse to create the world was attributed to the benevolence of El, the critical ability to form limits, to suspend creation, and therefore, to define the world is attributed to the critical judgment of Elohim. The Patriarch Isaac symbolizes this aspect in that he voluntarily submitted himself to be bound and offered as a sacrifice by his father Abraham.

The qualities of Elohim are associated with the festival of Shavuot, for it is at this time, when the Torah is given on Mt. Sinai, that the freedom of the people gained at the Exodus becomes channeled by divine legislation. Just as God's limiting the creation defined the world, so too His limiting of tribal excesses ultimately defined the people.

(Richard Sobol)

YHWH

Derived from the root "to be," this name (the Tetragrammaton) speaks of essence, while the other names refer to specific qualities. As the personal name of God, there has been a prohibition against pronouncing it since at least the third century B.C.E. Only the high priest, on Yom Kippur, inside the Temple's Holy of Holies, would be permitted to recite the name and thereby expiate the sins of all Israel. The name Adonai—Lord (see below) has come to be substituted for YHWH wherever the latter appears in the recitation of sacred texts or blessings. To reinforce this tradition, some Hebrew texts even marked the vowel signs for Adonai on the letters of YHWH. (This has led to the interesting but inaccurate English transliteration of the Tetragrammaton as Jehovah.) However, because Adonai has become so closely associated with YHWH, even this substitute is not normally mentioned in ordinary speech but rather a second-level euphemism is employed, i.e. ha-Shem (the Name).

In Jewish mysticism YHWH represents the aspect of *tiferet* (beauty) or *rahamim* (compassion). It is the heart of the system, which receives the flow from above and channels it out to the worlds below. The Patriarch Jacob (Israel) is the personification of this quality as he focused the spiritual legacy received from Abraham and Isaac and transmitted it to his children, the twelve tribes of Israel, the Jewish People. The holiday of Sukkot is associated with this aspect as well, in that it represents the ingathering of the harvest and the time of universal harmony when all nations will serve God as one.

Shaddai

This name is traditionally translated as "the Almighty," derived from the prefix *she* (who) plus *dai* (enough), i.e. He who is enough in and of Himself, self-sufficient. However, its origin could also be from the Akkadian word *sadu* (mountain), in which case it would mean "God of the Mountain" or "God of the Heavens." This latter interpretation would be consistent with its alternative derivation from the Hebrew *shad* (breast). In any case, as recorded in Exodus 6:3, this is the name by which God appeared to the Patriarchs, while YHWH was reserved until His revelation to Moses.

Shaddai is associated with the quality of *netzah* (victory of eternity). Assertive and powerful, this aspect is personified by the figure of Moses the Prophet, who led the People out of Egypt and through the forty years of desert wanderings. As a holiday, it is symbolized by Hanukkah, the celebration of victory through the combination of might and right.

Tzevaot

Although "Lord of Hosts" is the traditional translation of this name, it probably means "He who brings the hosts of heaven into being." In any event, the dominant image is of the entire heavenly array of the universe decked out in all of its splendiferous finery to sing the praises of God.

As a quality, Tzevaot is represented by *hod* (glory or grandeur) and is personified by Aaron the Priest. It was his responsibility and talent to orchestrate the pomp surrounding the service of God in the desert Tabernacle, and as high priest he was the principal actor as well. The drama of these rituals must have been spectacular, accompanied by choruses of Levites, ornate clothing, burning fires, smoking incense, and of course, the elaborate sacrifices themselves. Curiously, it is the feast of Purim that symbolizes this aspect, perhaps more for its regal and dramatic quality than for its humor. Even today Purim is the occasion for dressing up in lavish costumes and for the presentation of elaborate although lighthearted plays.

As Elohim was the balance for El, so too Tzevaot is the balance for Shaddai. Moses commands, while Aaron celebrates. Together they form a complete structure of leadership for the People.

Yah

This is the sturdiest of the names for God in that it is generally used directly without embarrassment and without resorting to euphemism or vocal alterations. For instance, it is the last syllable of the frequently repeated "halleluyah" meaning literally "praise God (Yah)." As the first two letters of the Tetragrammaton, Yah is almost a nickname. The two letters, *yod* and *heh*, are respectively considered male and female. Thus, Yah represents union, harmony, eternity in time.

This name is associated with the quality of *yesod* (foundation), as it is the basic structure upon which anything must be built if it is to be lasting. Joseph the Tzaddik (Righteous One) is the personification of this realm since his rootedness in faith enabled him to overcome innumerable adversities and ultimately rise high to a position second only to Pharoah. The celebration of the New Moon is associated with this quality. This is the moment when the moon, having been dark and hidden for three days, reemerges and begins its new cycle of waxing and waning once again. As Yah represents the union of male and female, so too the moon represents the union of light and darkness, integrating both into its cycle. It is this constancy through change, the expression of nonduality, that typifies the realm of Yah.

Adonai

Derived from the Hebrew *adon* (lord, as of a country or over a slave), Adonai originally meant "my Lords" (the plural form being parallel to the construction of Elohim) but has come to mean simply "the Lord." Although used as a name for God in and of itself, it is perhaps more frequently used as the euphemism for YHWH in liturgical contexts or in the ritual readings of sacred texts.

Adonai, as "Lord over all the earth" (Josh. 3:11), has a regal bearing to it and is, consequently, associated with the quality of *malkhut* (majesty or kingdom). This is the aspect of God which is most attached to the physical world. In its alternative appellation as Shekhinah, it represents the indwelling of God in the world (see "Feminine Imagery in Judaism"). Kabbalistically, the ultimate redemption will occur when the Shekhinah reunites with YHWH, thus bringing the immanent aspect of God and the transcendent aspect of God together.

This realm is personified by David the king, symbol of kingship itself, and scion of the messianic line. The Sabbath is its celebratory corollary as on this day the Queen of the Sabbath (the Shekhinah) merges with the King of the Universe and their union affords a "foretaste of the World to Come."

—R.A.S.

WRITING AND PRONOUNCING THE NAME: SOME LEGAL ISSUES

In any halakhic (legal) study, it is necessary to clarify whether a particular practice is mandated as a halakhic requirement, is to be followed on the basis of *minhag* (custom), or is to be dismissed as being grounded upon superstition and ignorance. Undoubtedly, in the course of Jewish history—particularly in areas having little contact with centers of Torah scholarship—many folk-customs did arise which diverge from the original *halakhah* to so great a degree as to constitute a farcical distortion thereof. On the other side of the coin are the many time-hallowed practices followed by knowledgeable Jews which *are* founded upon authentic halakhic considerations.

A case in point involves practices related to the writing and vocalization of the Names of God. The Tishri-Cheshvan 5730 issue of *Kol Torah* features an article by Rabbi A. Steinsalz in which he examines the widespread tendency to avoid writing the letters of the Divine Name even when such letters occur in a secular context. This practice is most commonly encountered in the writing of proper names in which one of the Divine Names is incorporated as part of the cognitive meaning of the appellation, e.g., Azaryah ("God helped") or Netanel ("God gave"). Many individuals also refrain from employing such letter combinations even in words totally disassociated from reference to the Deity. Thus, for example, when a Hebrew word ends in the letter *he* preceded by a *yod* either the final letter is dropped or the word is written with a dividing mark between the two letters.

The *Gemara, Shevuot* 35a, states that it is forbidden to erase the name of God and for that reason care is taken not to write the

Divine Name upon any document or paper which might be destroyed. *Megillat Ta'anit* 7a and the *Gemara, Rosh Hashanah* 18b, report that during the Hasmonean period promissory notes bore the legend, "In such and such year in the reign of Yochanan, High Priest of the most high God." The Sages, upon hearing of this innovation, exclaimed: "Tomorrow the debtor will repay his debt, with the result that the note will be cast away with the refuse!" Accordingly, they abrogated the practice and declared the day on which they did so to be a holiday. On the basis of this source, Rema, *Yoreh De'ah* 276:13, rules that it is forbidden to write the Divine Name "other than in a book, for it may come to dishonor. Therefore, we take heed not to write the Divine Name in a letter." The prohibition against erasing the Name of God is, however, limited to the specifically enumerated Divine Names which possess intrinsic sanctity. *Mesekhet Sofrim* 4:4 states clearly that even these names may be erased when they do not stand independently but form an integral part of the name of a mortal.

Rabbi Steinsalz notes that examination of early rabbinic manuscripts shows that words combining letter combinations spelling a Divine Name were written out in their entirety. Although it is now universal practice to employ the combination *tet-vav* for the number 15 rather than a *yod* followed by a *he*, this custom is of comparatively recent origin. The usage of *yod* followed by *he* to represent 15 would appear to be particularly objectionable since these two letters standing alone constitute the complete spelling of one of the sanctified names. Yet in earlier times there appears to have been no objection to this practice. One may conclude that since these letters are not intended to stand for a Divine Name their mere juxtaposition does not endow them with sanctity.

The same point is made by Dr. Louis Rabinowitz, former Chief Rabbi of South Africa, in an article entitled "On the Names of God," which appeared in the *London Jewish Chronicle*, April 10, 1970. Rabbi Rabinowitz also discusses the status of the term *shalom*. Rabbi Rabinowitz comments with amazement that he has been told of "one distinguished rabbi who never writes the word *shalom* in full, but writes only the first three letters and an apostrophe—because the Talmud states (*Shabbat* 10b) that *shalom* is one of the names of God." It is indeed true that *Teshuvot ha-Rosh* 3:15 declares, "We have found no one who forbids the erasure of *shalom*." Rabbi Rabinowitz, however, fails to mention the many authorities who insist that *shalom* may not be erased. *Tosafot, Sotah* 10a, comments that the list of seven Divine Names which may not be erased is not exhaustive and that *shalom* is to be included in this category. Writing only the first three letters of this word is a time-honored custom. *Birkei Yosef, Orah Hayyim* 85:8, quotes Rabbenu Yechiel who asserts that, since it is one of the Divine Names, the word *shalom* is not spelled out in a greeting. Rema, *Yoreh De'ah* 276:13, also cites this practice.

Another question requiring clarification is the permissibility of writing the name of God in the vernacular. This question is, of course, relevant only with regard to correspondence or other forms of writing which are likely to be discarded heedlessly. As previously noted, Rema states explicitly that the name of God may be written out in full in printed works which presumably will be treated with respect. The prohibition against obliterating the name of God is limited to the specifically enumerated Divine Names; other cognomens are regarded as adjectival descriptions rather than as names of the Deity and as such are not included in the prohibition against erasure. Both *Shakh, Yoreh De'ah* 179:11, and R. Akiva Eger, *Yoreh De'ah* 276:9, state definitively that the name of God occurring in languages other than Hebrew is regarded as a cognomen and hence the prohibition with reference to erasure does not apply.

Although the prohibition against erasure is not applicable, proper respect must nevertheless be paid to the name of God even when it occurs in languages other than Hebrew. *Nedarim* 7b states: "Every place where the unnecessary mention of the Divine Name is found, there poverty is to be found." This is deduced from the biblical verse ". . . in every place where I cause My name to be mentioned I will come unto thee and bless thee" (Exod. 20:21), indicating that the pronunciation of the Divine Name in a sacred manner is rewarded with blessing and prosperity. From this the converse is also deduced, viz., that the pronunciation of the Divine Name in vain leads to poverty.

Two renowned authorities, R. Yonatan Eibeschutz, *Urim ve-Tumim* 27:2, and R. Ya'akov of Lissa, *Netivot ha-Mishpat* 27:2, maintain that reverence must also be accorded to written occurrences of the Divine Name, whether in Hebrew or in the vernacular. Both scholars decry even the use of the French *adieu* (the root meaning of which is "with God") in written communications because of the dishonor of the Divine Name resulting from careless disposal of such correspondence. These authorities maintain that poverty follows not merely improper vocalization of the Divine Name but also failure to accord proper respect to written occurrences of the Divine Name even in the vernacular.

Rabbi Rabinowitz errs in describing scrupulousness with regard to the writing of the Divine Name in languages other than Hebrew as a recent development and in contending that mention of this prohibition appears for the first time in the comparatively recent *Arukh ha-Shulhan, Hoshen Mishpat* 27.

Another practice questioned by Dr. Rabinowitz is constraint in pronouncing the terms *Shaddai* and *Zeva'ot*. The prohibition against vocalizing the name of God other than in the reading of Scripture, prayer, or recitation of blessings is derived from the positive commandment "The Lord your God shall you fear" (Deut. 6:13). Restraint in not mentioning the name of God in vain is a manifestation of fear and awe. Rav Ahai Ga'on, *She'iltot, Yitro, She'ilta* 53, deems this to be a transgression of the negative prohibition "Thou shalt not take the name of the Lord thy God in vain" (Exodus 20:7). According to numerous authorities, e.g., Rambam *Hilkhot Shavuot* 12:11 (see *Teshuvot R. Akiva Eger*, no. 25), this prohibition embraces all of the seven names of God. Since both *Shaddai* and *Zeva'ot* are enumerated among the seven names of the Deity, common practice is to use the assonant forms *Shakai* and *Zevakot* respectively as substitutes for these names. Dr. Rabinowitz's incredulity at this "strange mispronunciation of Hebrew" is misplaced.

Utterance of the Divine Name in languages other than Hebrew is discussed by *Nimukei Yosef* in his commentary of *Nedarim* 7b. This authority declares that while needless mention of the name of God in secular languages is not encompassed by the biblical prohibition, nonetheless, "*go'arin bo*—the one doing so is to be admonished and chastised." It should be noted that Rabbi Moses Feinstein, *Iggrot Mosheh, Yoreh De'ah*, I, no. 172, states that this statement of *Nemukei Yosef* regarding inappropriate vocalization of the name of God in the vernacular is limited to the proper name of the Deity in such languages (e.g., "God") and not to adjectival cognomens (e.g., "Almighty").

In conclusion, it is quite apparent that regardless of the final adjudication of these questions, the meticulousness with which God-fearing Jews have always conducted themselves in the writing and vocalization of the Divine Name is grounded upon a deeply rooted reverence for *halakhah* in all its ramifications. Improper understanding of the halakhic bases of such practices may at times lead to their being treated with a levity which is unwarranted. To paraphrase a famous dictum, *afilu ketivat hullin shel talmidei hakhamim zerikhah limmud*—even the idle *writing* of Torah scholars bears studious attention.

Religiously motivated forms of conduct practiced by devout Jews over a span of generations are but seldom without a firm basis. Our Sages long ago counseled in this regard, "Even if they are not prophets, they are the sons of prophets." Those who inveigh in caustic tones against the manner in which their coreligionists spell the name of God not only err in their preconceptions but fail to realize that such time-hallowed customs acquire a meaning and significance of their own. The Jew who inserts a dash in spelling the Divine Name is filled with an all-pervasive sense of the immanence of the Almighty. His action demonstrates that he feels no inhibition in expressing his reverence for the divine in all aspects of his daily life. Whether or not one chooses to adopt this practice, whether one regards it as well-grounded or as ill-founded, the usage "G-d" should, at the very minimum, command a dash of respect.

—J.D.B. rep.

JUDAISM IS ONE, DENOMINATIONS ARE MANY

While many individuals refer to "the Jews" as though American Jewry were an indivisible monolithic entity, there are in fact three major denominations of Judaism in this country (Orthodox, Conservative, and Reform) and one minor one (Reconstructionism). What follows is a short description of each: general characteristics, percentage of synagogue-affiliated Jews (it is estimated that 3.5–4.0 million of America's 5.8 million Jews are members of a synagogue), a thumbnail history of the denomination in America until 1960, and developments and trends within the past two decades.

Orthodox Judaism

Orthodox jews are those who adhere most strictly to the *halakhah* (Jewish law) of traditional Judaism, and who are least receptive to the values and practices of modern culture. In general, Orthodox Judaism is characterized by:

• observance of the Sabbath through synagogue attendance and abstention from working, spending money, and travelling outside of walking.

• observance of *kashrut* (Jewish dietary laws) both in and out of the home.

• *mehitzah*, physical separation between men and women during prayer.

• services conducted entirely, or almost entirely, in Hebrew.

• the wearing of a *yarmulke* (skullcap) or other head covering by men and modest clothing by women.

• observance by married couples of the laws of *niddah* (sexual abstinence during and for about twelve days after a woman's period), followed by the woman's immersion in the *mikveh* (ritual bath).

• an emphasis on day school (parochial) education.

• generally earlier marriages and larger families than other Jews. (The overwhelming majority of Orthodox rabbis and religious scholars oppose birth control devices and abortion—except when the mother's life is endangered—on *halakhic* grounds).

Approximately ten to fifteen percent of affiliated Jews belong to Orthodox synagogues. However, many of these individuals must be considered "Orthoprax," i.e. Orthodox in terms of external affiliation but not in terms of personal practice or ideology. On the other hand, because the Orthodox tend to live in relatively close-knit communities in order to adequately provide for their religious needs, synagogue affiliation is not as necessary for providing Jewish social contacts as it is in the other branches of Judaism. Consequently, many observant Jews do not formally "belong" to any synagogue, preferring instead to attend the services and support the operations of a variety of *shuls* (synagogues) in the community. Thus, it is very difficult to determine the true number of Orthodox Jews in America. Depending on the criteria used, estimates range from four hundred thousand to one million.

Beginning with the twenty-three Jews from Holland via Recife, Brazil, who landed in New York City in 1654, the dominant force in American Jewish life until the beginning of the nineteenth century was the Sephardic Jews (those Jews whose ancestors came from the countries bordering the Mediterranean, especially Spain and Portugal), almost all of whom were Orthodox. Primarily merchants, they had built synagogues and established Jewish institutions in five cities (Newport, Rhode Island; New York, New York; Philadelphia, Pennsylvania; Charleston, South Carolina; and Savannah, Georgia) by the time of the American Revolution.

With the successive waves of German Jews, almost all of whom were Reform or unaffiliated, that entered this country between 1820 and 1870, the influence of Orthodoxy in America declined considerably. The first influx of Eastern European Jews (from Rumania and the Russian port of Odessa) arrived in 1871; with the Russian pogroms of 1881, this surge of Jewish immigration into America became a flood and by 1914, a "tidal wave," numbering over two million by the time the first immigration quotas were established in 1921. While many of the immigrant Jews were socialists or otherwise nonreligious, the overwhelming majority of those who were observant were Orthodox. If in 1880 over ninety percent of the nation's two hundred or so synagogues were Reform, by 1890 316 of 533 congregations were Orthodox.

Over half of the Orthodox Jewish immigrants lived in New York City, with most of the remainder in large cities such as Chicago, Boston, Baltimore, and Cleveland. (To this day, Orthodox Jews constitute a far more urban-, and particularly New York-based population than do non-Orthodox Jews.) They established the same kind of support services (*shtieblach*—small storefront or apartment synagogues—kosher butchers, *yeshivot*—religious high schools) that they had known in the "Old Country."

In part because of the sheer number of Orthodox *shuls* (synagogues), the movement resisted efforts at centralization. In 1888 a New York synagogue "imported" from Vilna an outstanding rabbi and scholar named Jacob Joseph and attempted to promote him as the "Chief Rabbi" of the city. The campaign on his behalf got nowhere. However, two years later efforts to create the Union of Orthodox Jewish Congregations (UOJC) as the movement's "umbrella" organization proved successful.

Until well into the twentieth century, the Orthodox movement was nurtured by its Eastern European roots. Because of the traditional decentralization of rabbinical ordination into the jurisdiction of individual rabbis, American Orthodoxy was the last of the three major dominations to create its own rabbinical training institute: the Rabbi Isaac Elkanan Seminary, founded in 1896 and destined to become the core of Yeshiva University (Y.U., which today also has a variety of graduate programs, including schools of medicine, social work, and law).

Among second- and third-generation American Jews in this century, Orthodox affiliation and practice has declined considerably. A 1952 study of a middle-sized eastern city with 5,200 Jews revealed that eighty-one percent of the respondents' *grandparents* were Orthodox but only sixteen percent of the respondents were themselves. This may be explained by sociologist Charles Liebman's observation in 1965 that Orthodox Jews tend to be "older, of more recent immigrant origin, of lower income and occupational status, and with more limited secular education than Conservative, Reform or unaffiliated Jews." In short, as the immigrants, their children, and grandchildren became integrated into American life and moved up the social scale, they tended to move away from Orthodoxy.

In 1912 the Young Israel movement was founded in an attempt to create a "modern" Orthodoxy, i.e. one whose style was more reflective of an American milieu than a European one. While generally as observant as other Orthodox Jews, Young Israel members were often more stylishly dressed (the men eschewed beards) and, like their Conservative and Reform counterparts, more concerned with decorum. Some Young Israel synagogues featured sermons in English; and breaking an Orthodox taboo, a few even permitted mixed dancing at social events.

Reenforcing the Old World image, however, were the half-million or so refugees and Holocaust survivors, many of whom were Orthodox, who entered this country between 1933 and 1951. This new wave of Orthodox immigrants, which included a number of major rabbis and scholars, gave American Orthodoxy a new vitality, as seen most prominently in the growth of *yeshivot* and day schools. In 1915 there were only two day schools in the U.S. with a combined enrollment of several hundred; by 1945 there were 69 such schools with approximately 10,000 students.

The post-World War II years also saw the establishment of a number of ultra-Orthodox groups in New York City, including the Breuer Congregation (from Frankfurt) and the Lubavitch (from Russia) and Satmar (from Rumania) Hasidim. Due largely to their influence, Orthodoxy turned increasingly to the "right" in terms of religious practice and intra-Jewish relations. When Orthodox leaders refused to participate in interdenominational bodies, as in 1955 when eleven yeshiva heads issued an *issur* (prohibition) against joining a body with non-Orthodox rabbis, other Jews complained of the movement's "triumphalism."

Still, many Jews were convinced that with the community's increasing affluence, social and cultural integration into American life, and distance from its immigrant roots Orthodoxy would become a "residual" phenomenon in American Jewish life. The 1960's and 1970's proved them wrong. Although the *number* of Orthodox Jews remained relatively small, it was clear that Orthodoxy had tremendous vitality and adaptability; that it was, in short, "on the ascendency." At least four factors may account for Orthodoxy's recent success story:

• A number of charismatic rabbis, scholars, and teachers, such as Menachem Mendel Schneersohn, the Lubavitcher *rebbe* (spiritual and communal leader); J. B. Soloveitchik, the Rav, generally considered the outstanding Talmudist of this generation; Norman Lamm, the energetic president of Yeshiva University; Shlomo Riskin, rabbi of Manhattan's innovative Lincoln Square Synagogue; and Irving Greenberg, director of the National Jewish Resource Center.

• The continued "boom" in the day school movement, and its emulation by Conservative, Reform, and even some secular Jews. By 1973 the number of day schools had increased about five-hundred percent since 1945 to 401, with approximately 75,000 students.

• What might be called Orthodoxy's "communal integrity." Put simply, Orthodox Judaism was increasingly seen as "authentic" and "wholistic" in an age of disillusionment with secular culture and "compromised" Judaism. Thus, the past twenty years have witnessed the *baalei teshuvah* (literally, "masters of repentence") phenomenon by which previously assimilated Jews have turned to *yeshivot* in Israel and the U.S. and became *frum* (strictly observant).

• Political activism. Although Orthodox Jews traditionally have been less politically active than adherents of the other denominations, they have become more assertive on behalf of Jewish causes during the past two decades. It was largely day school and Orthodox college students who, in 1964, helped create (and still form the core of) the Student Struggle for Soviet Jewry (SSSJ). That same year, predominantly middle- and lower-middle-class Orthodox Jews from New York created the Jewish Defense League (JDL). And since 1967 over half the Americans who have made *aliyah* (immigrated to Israel) have been Orthodox, especially those raised in the Bnai Akiva (religious Zionist) youth movement.

At the beginning of the 1980's Orthodox Judaism appears to be more than holding its own in light of the shattered values, rising intermarriage, and falling birth rates that affect all sectors of the American Jewish community.

Conservative Judaism

Originally called "historical Judaism," the Conservative movement represents the "middle way" between the strict traditionalism of Orthodox and the rationalist modernism of Reform Judaism. It sees itself as rooted in the *halakhah* and Jewish values, while also responding to the life situation of contemporary Jews. Conservative Judaism is characterized by:

• observance of most *halakhah*, with some concessions to modern American life (e.g. no Orthodox, but many Conservative Jews drive to the synagogue on the Sabbath).

• mixed seating in the synagogue and the counting of women in determining a *minyan* (prayer quorum of ten adults).

• limited or nonobservance of *kashrut*. (Only a minority of Conservative Jews keep kosher both in and out of their homes).

It is difficult to generalize about Conservative Judaism, for it is in some ways the most heterogeneous of the three main denominations; it includes both a "right wing," which closely resembles "mainline" Orthodoxy, and a "left wing," which resembles Reform Judaism. Perhaps it is Conservative Judaism's middle position, its "finessing" of Judaism and modernism, which has made it the most popular of the three major denominations: approximately forty percent of affiliated Jews, numbering 1.2–1.5 million, are Conservative.

Conservative Judaism is the only one of the three major denominations that is of American origin. Its founding may be dated to 1886, with the establishment of the Jewish Theological Seminary (JTS) by a group led by Rabbis Sabato Morais and Marcus Jastrow of Philadelphia and Henry Pereira Mendes of New York. This group was responding to what it felt were the rationalist, antihalakhic excesses of the Reform movement (see below). More immediately, the three rabbis were shocked at the now-infamous 1883 banquet honoring the first graduating class of the Hebrew Union College (Reform rabbinical seminary). At this banquet, shrimp and other *treif* (nonkosher) foods were served, precipitating an angry walkout by a number of rabbis present and ultimately, the decision to found an alternative seminary.

For its first fifteen years JTS was a colossal failure. By 1900 it had attracted only three full-time teachers and twenty-one students. In addition, six of the eleven congregations that helped found JTS returned to the Reform fold.

Around the turn of the century, however, JTS was not only saved from a slow death but grew into the influential "flagship" of a major Jewish denomination thanks to the efforts of three remarkable men: the organizational and fund raising acumen of Cyrus Adler, its first president; the generous support of financier Jacob Schiff, one of the leading members of "Our Crowd" (wealthy, Reform, "uptown" German Jews); and the intellectual and personal charisma of the brilliant Solomon Schechter, a scholar in Semitics and rabbinics who, in 1902, was brought from Cambridge University to become JTS's first chancellor. Schechter in turn brought to JTS a number of first-rate teachers and scholars, including the iconoclastic and ever-provocative philosopher Mordecai Kaplan, the Talmudist Louis Ginzburg, and the historian Alexander Marx.

Long before Zionism became popular in America, JTS played a pioneering role in reviving interest in Palestine and Hebrew culture. Unlike both Orthodoxy and Reform Judaism, the new movement was not opposed to Zionist aspirations; indeed, some of its leaders, such as Adler, played key roles in the American Zionist Federation. And in 1912 the faculty of JTS's new Teacher's Institute voted to teach only in Hebrew.

By 1920 a growing number of congregations were calling themselves Conservative and affiliating with the new United Synagogue of America, the "umbrella" organization of Conservative synagogues founded in 1913. The movement drew largely upon first- and especially second-generation American Jews who had grown up Orthodox and were now becoming somewhat less observant and more "American." They were attracted by the "family" (mixed) seating, English sermon, bat mitvah (a girl's equivalent to the bar mitzvah, an innovation introduced by Kaplan), late Friday evening services, and other features of the average Conservative *shul*. While the Conservative movement was once dominated by German Jews, by 1950 the leadership had passed to men such as Louis Finkelstein and Abraham Joshua Heschel, who were Eastern European in origin. At the same time Conservative Judaism also gained recruits from the "right wing" of the Reform movement, individuals who were disenchanted with what they felt was Reform's emphasis on rationalism, Americanism, and social action at the expense of prayer, rituals, and other manifestations of spirituality. By turning to the Conservative movement, such individuals were "coming home again."

The movement was also active on a number of new cultural fronts. In 1929, with the help of a generous grant from Mrs. Felix Warburg, JTS established the Jewish Museum, the first institution in America exhibiting both ritual Judaica and modern Jewish painting and sculpture. Ten years later, the JTS faculty formalized its friendly relationships with two neighboring institutions on Manhattan's Morningside Heights—Columbia University and the (Protestant) Union Theological Seminary—by creating a Conference on Science, Philosophy, and Religion, which organized periodic conferences and consultations involving scholars from all three institutions.

By 1950 the Conservative movement claimed the allegiance of nearly one-half of America's affiliated Jews. For the most part, the movement remained traditional, brooking no changes on such issues as the observance of *kashrut*, the inclusion of *musaf* (the "additional" service that looks to the restoration of the Temple in Jerusalem and of the sacrificial service) in the Sabbath and festival services, and the laws of *gittin* (documents formalizing a divorce; according to *halakhah* a *get* can be issued only by the husband). In practice, however, the Conservative laity tended to be less observant than the "official" Conservative institutional interpretion of *halakhah* would sanction (while Conservative rabbis and scholars are as committed to the laws of *kashrut* as their Orthodox counterparts, many Conservative Jews are not similarly committed). Referring to the Law Committee of the Rabbinical Assembly (R.A.—the professional organization of Conservative rabbis)—the arbiter of Conservative *halakhah*—a JTS faculty member once told sociologist Charles Liebman, "The R.A. deliberates and the laity decides."

In the postwar period the Law Committee voted in favor of two striking reinterpretations of *halakhah*: In 1950 it ruled that it is permissible for an individual to drive to Sabbath services if that is the only reasonable means the worshipper has of attending services, and in 1973 it decreed that women should be counted in determining a *minyan*. Since traditionalist interpretations of the *halakhah* had previously forbidden all mechanized travel on the Sabbath and had counted only men in determining a *minyan*, both these decisions were sharply denounced by Orthodox leaders.

During the 1960's and 1970's the Conservative movement remained the largest American denomination. It also served as the main source of some of the most interesting developments in Jewish life. In the late 1960's a number of JTS graduates and other individuals raised in the Conservative movement played the leading roles in the new *havurah* movement. (*Havurot* are independent or synagogue-based communities with approximately fifteen to thirty members who meet regularly for prayer, study, fellowship, and social action.) Some of these same individuals led the protest at the 1969 General Assembly of the Council of Jewish Federations that successfully appealed for more communal support for Jewish education, and later contributed to the popular *Jewish Catalog*.

The movement could also derive satisfaction from the over five hundred Orthodox and Reform rabbis who had joined the R.A. since 1960, the growth of Solomon Schechter day schools, and the fact that a small, but growing and influential, group of JTS-trained rabbis and educators were settling in Israel and beginning to win a following among both *sabras* and *olim* (respectively, native Israelis and new immigrants).

In recent years, however, some disturbing trends have started to develop. There has been a growing polarization between the movement's "right" and "left" wings. In 1979, for example, a serious split within the JTS faculty over the issue of training women for the rabbinate was barely averted when the faculty voted to postpone consideration of the issue (already pending for over five years) and study it further (there had already been a year's deliberation by a fourteen-person commission appointed by the R.A. and consisting of Conservative rabbis and lay leaders. It had recommended by an eleven to three vote that women be admitted to JTS). Furthermore, many rabbis complained that the movement was *too* broad, that it lacked theological and organizational focus.

In the final analysis, however, the movement's weaknesses also reflect its strengths. Conservative Judaism, by its very nature, appeals to a pluralist constituency. It has not only survived its inner tensions; it often thrives on them.

Reform Judaism

The Reform movement, which represents what in other countries is called "liberal" or "progressive" Judaism, has reinterpreted the tradition, dropping certain traditional laws and practices in response to the conditions and values of modern life. Reform Judaism is generally characterized by:

- a far larger part of the service being in English than is the case among Orthodox and Conservative Jews.
- nonobservance of the second day of the three major Jewish festivals (Passover, Shavuot, and Sukkot).
- nonobservance of the laws of *kashrut*.
- full equality of women in religious life. (There are women Reform rabbis and cantors).
- prominence in social action and ecumenical activities.

Approximately thirty to thirty-five percent of affiliated Jews, numbering 1.2–1.4 million individuals, are Reform.

The roots of the American Reform movement lie in Germany where, between 1810 and 1820, congregations in Seesen, Hamburg, and Berlin instituted fundamental changes in traditional Jewish practices and beliefs. Among the most important: mixed seating, the use of German in services, limiting the observance of festivals and Rosh Hashanah (the Jewish New Year) to one day, the use of a cantor and/or choir during services. Reform Jews also rejected the idea of the messianic restoration of all Jews to Palestine and with it, the reinstitution of the sacrificial cult.

As large numbers of German Jews settled in America in the middle third of the nineteenth century, Reform became the dominant belief system of American Jews. While traditional Jews were concentrated in New York, Reform Judaism was truly a nationwide phenomenon. The first Reform congregation—actually, a "club" which met in members' homes—was a group that seceded in 1824 from Congregation Beth Elohim in Charleston, South Carolina. It only lasted seven years, but in the 1840's and 1850's, major Reform congregations were established in, among other places, Baltimore, New York City, Chicago, Albany, Cincinnati, and San Francisco.

While Orthodox Jews actively battled against Reform tendencies in Germany, the Reform movement in this country benefited from the lack of a central religious authority, the American tradition of religious and denominational pluralism, the mobility of American life as the frontier moved westward—and the concomitant laxness of observance among many American Jews.

The movement also benefited from the prodigious intellectual and organizational energies of one man: Rabbi Isaac Mayer Wise. Wise, who was born in Bohemia (Czechoslovakia) came to the U.S. in 1846. After eight years in Albany, New York, he moved to a new congregation in Cincinnati, then a bustling city along the "Western frontier." In the next thirty-five years Wise almost single-handedly (1) wrote and published in 1857 *Minhag America* ("Religious Practices for America"), the first Jewish prayerbook edited for American worshippers and with an American context in mind; (2) founded in 1873 the Union of American Hebrew Congregations (UAHC) and in 1889 the Central Conference of American Rabbis (CCAR), respectively the Reform synagogal and rabbinical organizations; (3) established in 1875 the Hebrew Union College (HUC) in Cincinnati, the Reform rabbinical seminary. (Today, HUC also has campuses in Los Angeles—as do Yeshiva University and JTS—as well as in New York).

In the pre-Civil War period a number of Reform rabbis were conspicuous for their involvement in abolitionist activities. One of them, in fact, David Einhorn of Baltimore, was driven from the city by mob threats in 1861.

Led by Einhorn and Rabbis Samuel Holdheim, Bernard Felsenthal, and Kaufmann Kohler, the Reform movement also became increasingly radical in its religious orientation. Many rituals and customs were dropped, and a few Reform congregations even held "Sabbath" services on Sunday. The classical articulation of Reform radicalism was the "platform" adopted by a number of prominent Reform rabbis meeting in Pittsburgh in 1885; two of its most striking passages read:

"We recognize in the Mosaic legislation a system of training the Jewish people for its mission during its national life in Palestine, and today we accept as binding only its moral laws, and maintain only such ceremonies as sustain and sanctify our lives, but reject all such as are not adapted to the views and habits of modern civilization.

"We consider ourselves no longer a nation but a religious community, and therefore expect neither a return to Palestine, nor a sacrificial worship under the Sons of Aaron, nor the restoration of any of the laws concerning the Jewish state."

The obverse of the second passage was Reform's unabashed Americanism. As Rabbi Gustave Posnasky of Charleston put it in 1846, "This country is our Palestine, this city our Jerusalem, this house of God our temple."

By 1880 over ninety percent of American synagogues were Reform. While the overwhelming majority of Eastern European Jews who began arriving in the tens of thousands the following year were Orthodox, Reform congregations consisted almost entirely of German Jews. Architecturally resembling Protestant cathedrals, many Reform synagogues were barely distinguishable in terms of the service as well. They too had preachers in robes, pews with mixed seating, services entirely or largely in English, choirs, organs, and hymnals. In 1910 Rabbi Judah Magnes of New York's prestigious Temple Emanu-El (the "Saint Patrick's of American synagogues") informed his congregation that "A prominent Christian lawyer of another city has told me that he entered this building at the beginning of a service on Sunday morning and did not discover that he was in a synagogue until a chance remark of the preacher betrayed it."

Reform Jews established a number of educational and cultural institutions that benefited the entire community. In New York these included the Educational Alliance on the Lower East Side, a center of education and recreation for up to ten thousand (mostly poor) Jews a day, and the Young Men's Hebrew Association (YMHA) movement. Reform leaders also pioneered the two great Jewish "defense" organizations that were remarkably successful in combatting anti-Semitism and promoting Jewish concerns on the national and international scenes: the American Jewish Committee and the Anti-Defamation League of B'nai Brith, founded in 1906 and 1913, respectively.

Religiously, although the Reform movement dropped or substantially modified many traditional prayers and rituals (as in the 1894 *Union Prayer Book*, the successor to Wise's *Minhag America*), there remained a "bottom line." Thus, while an increasing number of Reform Jews married non-Jews, the CCAR formally declared its opposition to intermarriage in 1909. And although it was denounced by some radicals as "archaic" and "barbarian," circumcision remained as central a rite for Reform as for other Jews.

As shown in the Pittsburgh Platform, the Reform movement was traditionally anti-Zionist. Usually the most removed from the immigrant experience, Reform Jews generally felt "at home" in America; they also believed that the Diaspora was necessary, perhaps even beneficial, in allowing Jews to be "a light unto the nations." And during a half-century (1897–1947) of growing popular anti-Semitism, they also feared the charge of "dual loyalty."

Yet, for all the movement's anti-Zionism, a number of Reform rabbis and lay leaders were pioneers in establishing the Zionist movement in America, including Gustav Gottheil and his son Richard Gottheil, Rabbi Stephen S. Wise (who was also a founder of the American Jewish Congress), and Supreme Court Justice Louis D. Brandeis. Following the 1917 Balfour Declaration (which stated British support for a "Jewish homeland in Palestine" and constituted the first great-power recognition of Zionist aspirations), the Reform "mainstream" began to support Jewish settlements in Palestine, as well as such health, educational, and cultural institutions as the Hadassah Hospital, Hebrew University, and Israeli Philharmonic. Finally, meeting in Columbus, Ohio, in 1937, the CCAR effectively reversed the staunch anti-Zionism expressed fifty-two years earlier in Pittsburgh by affirming "the obligation of all Jewry to aid in building a Jewish homeland by endeavoring to make it not only a refuge for the oppressed but also a center of Jewish culture and spiritual life."

Following the Holocaust and the establishment of the State of Israel in 1948, Reform Jews became fully as active as other Jews on behalf of Israel. in 1978 the movement took the last step into full participation in Zionist affairs by establishing the Association of Reform Zionists of America (ARZA) as a party to compete in elections for the World Zionist Congress.

From the Progressive era to the New Deal, and from the Civil Rights movement to the anti-Vietnam War protests of the 1960's and early 1970's, Reform Jews have been particularly prominent in the area of social action. For example, in 1964 and 1965, a number of Reform rabbis and lay leaders participated in "Freedom Summer" activities on behalf of poor and disenfranchised blacks in Mississippi and voter registration drives in Alabama.

The major religious trend in Reform Judaism during the past two decades has been a "return to tradition." Writing of Reform rabbis at the annual convention of the CCAR in a 1973 issue of the quarterly *Judaism*, the pseudononymous Ben Hamon observed: More importantly, Reform rabbis and lay leaders are still struggling to recoup from the modernist excesses of the "classical" period. Then, Reform Judaism seemed far more "modern" than "Jewish"; today, it is trying to strike the right note of "Jewish modernism."

Reconstructionism

Reconstructionism is the small (7,000–9,000 member) "fourth movement" of American Judaism. Founded in this century by the Conservative rabbi and philosopher Mordecai Kaplan, it emphasizes "Judaism as a civilization," i.e. the integration of selected Jewish beliefs with the Jewish people's culture and folkways. To institutionalize this synthesis, Kaplan pioneered the idea of the Jewish center—a building or complex where Jews could pray, learn, express themselves artistically, socialize, and engage in recreational activities.

Kaplan rejected much of the theological "baggage" of traditional Judaism, including the doctrines of revelation and choseness (that God revealed the Torah to the Jewish people at Mount Sinai, where He chose them to be a "holy people" and a "kingdom of priests"). Rather, following Emile Durkheim's philosophy of religion, Kaplan believed that certain Jewish observances and customs reflected the Jewish people's highest values and aspirations; they also served as unifying and sustaining forces throughout the generations. Kaplan called these observances and customs *sancta*.

Kaplan was also a strong proponent of education and programming involving Hebrew and Israel—although he rejected the Zionist beliefs in the "negation of the Diaspora" and the imperative of *aliyah* (emigration to Israel) for all Jews. (Kaplan himself, however, did make *aliyah* in 1963, at the age of eighty-two).

In their services and practices, Reconstructionist Jews are pretty much indistinguishable from most Conservative and Reform Jews, with two exceptions:

- Approximately half of the Reconstructionist congregations either are or contain within them *havurot*.
- Reflecting Kaplan's philosophy, the Reconstructionist liturgy has eliminated most key supernaturalist elements, such as references to divine revelation in history or to the resurrection of the dead. Adherents of Reconstructionism claim that it strikes the right note for the "religious Jewish agnostic"; critics charge that Reconstructionist services are as rationalist and nonspiritual as was the case with classical Reform.

The formal beginning of Reconstructionism as a movement can be traced to 1922, when Kaplan withdrew as the rabbi of the (Orthodox) Jewish Center in Manhattan, which he had helped found, and established a new synagogue for his followers: the Society for the Advancement of Judaism, located a few hundred yards away on 86th Street. During the 1930's, Kaplan's leftist political views appealed to many Conservative and Reform Jews. The 1935 Reconstructionist papers, for example, called for a "cooperative society, elimination of the profit system and public ownership of all natural resources and basic industries." Many Zionists were attracted by Kaplan's clear love of Hebrew culture, while assimilated second- and third-generation American Jews responded to passages such as this (from Kaplan's seminal *Judaism as a Civilization):* "Since the civilization that can satisfy the primary interest of the Jew must necessarily be the civilization of the country he lives in, the Jew in America must be first and foremost an American, and only secondarily a Jew."

In the post-Holocaust period Kaplan's thought fell under increasing criticism. In 1945 he was placed in *herem* (excommunicated) by the *Aggudat ha-Rabbanim* (Association of Orthodox Rabbis, originally from Europe) and his *Sabbath Prayer Book* was denounced by two leading Conservative thinkers, Louis Ginzburg and Alexander Marx. His critics complained that Kaplan viewed *halakhah* in totally nonbinding terms and had "sold out" to contemporary values by arguing that Judaism must be brought "into harmony with the best ethical and social thought of the modern world."

What most hampered the growth of Reconstructionism, however, was not its critics, but Kaplan's failure to establish certain basic institutions to promote his thought. It was not until 1959 that a Federation of Reconstructionist Congregations and Fellowships was established. As Charles Liebman has written in the most comprehensive examination of Reconstructionism to date (a long essay in the 1970 *American Jewish Yearbook*), it has never been clear in the first place whether Reconstructionism is really a religious movement at all, as opposed to an intellectual one. Indeed, argues Liebman, perhaps Kaplan's greatest influence was exercised during the fifty-five years (1909–63) he taught at JTS! His emphasis on the nationalist, folkloric, and cultural aspects of Judaism—what has come to be called "Jewishness"—broadened the horizons of hundreds of Conservative rabbis and educators.

Following Kaplan's retirement, Ira Eisenstein, who had helped found and had edited the widely-read monthly *The Reconstructionist*, assumed the formal leadership of the movement's policy-setting Reconstructionist Foundation. In 1967 the Foundation finally established its own seminary and graduate school—the Reconstructionist Rabbinical College in Philadelphia. From the beginning, "Recon" welcomed women rabbinical students, the first Jewish institution to do so. It was also a Reconstructionist synagogue in Denver which, beginning in 1962, pioneered the creation of congregational *havurot*.

By and large, however, Reconstructionism has never "taken hold" among a critical mass of American Jews. It is difficult to explain why, for according to the influential sociologist, political scientist, and journalist Leonard Fein, "Reconstructionism is probably the dominant belief system of American Jews." Thus, despite the differences among the three major denominations over *halakhah*, the majority of American Jews seem more concerned with Jewish "peoplehood"—concern over Israel's security, the fate of Soviet Jewry, or the "folkways" of Jewish cooking—than they do with questions of observance and faith. Institutionally, as well, the Jewish center movement has had a major impact on Jewish life, influencing and complementing the nature of the American synagogue.

Paradoxically, Reconstructionism as a movement may be a victim of its success as an intellectual current. Perhaps because most American Jews have internalized "Kaplanism" as a secular belief system, they have bypassed Reconstructionism as a denominational option.

A COMPARATIVE LOOK AT FOUR ISSUES

Issue	Orthodox	Conservative	Reform	Reconstructionism
Training and ordaining women rabbis	All subgroups of Orthodox Judaism oppose the training and ordaining of women rabbis. According to the Orthodox interpretation of *Halakhah* (Jewish law), women are exempt from certain time-bound *mitzvot* (commandments), including the three daily services. Therefore, a woman cannot be a *Shlikhat Tzibbur* (leader of the congregation in prayer). Also, according to Orthodox *halakhah*, a woman is prohibited from	At present, the Jewish Theological Seminary does not admit women to its rabbinical program. In December, 1978, a special commission created by the Rabbinical Assembly recommended by an 11–3 majority that women be admitted to this program. However, a year later, the JTS faculty tabled (killed) a motion to this effect by a vote of 25–19. At the same time, two *women rabbis* trained outside the movement—at the Reconstructionist Rabbinical College—*serve Conservative* congregations. The issue will no doubt	The Hebrew Union College has admitted women to its rabbinical program since 1971. Some recently ordained women rabbis have complained of difficulty in finding pulpits, but more often than not, the Reform laity has accepted *women* rabbis.	The Reconstructionist Rabbinical College has admitted women since its founding in 1967. Women rabbis appear to be widely accepted among Reconstructionist laity.

Issue	Orthodox	Conservative	Reform	Reconstructionism
	serving as an *edah* (witness to a legal proceeding or transaction), a role which rabbis are sometimes called upon to play.	come to a head again during the 1980s.		
Kashrut (Jewish dietary laws)	Orthodox Jews are by definition committed to observing the laws of *kashrut*. Most do so both in and out of their homes. (Some Orthodox Jews will eat nonmeat dishes in nonkosher restaurants and many will dine in vegetarian restaurants). Some ultra-Orthodox Jews eat only kosher food that is examined and prepared with particular rigor by other observant Jews; this food is called *Glatt Kosher*.	Officially, the Conservative movement favors a strict observance of *kashrut*. All studies indicate that in practice, however, only a minority of Conservative Jews keep kosher at home, while an even smaller minority (probably less than fifteen percent) keep kosher outside the home as well. However, a larger percentage of Conservative Jews observe some aspect of *kashrut*, e.g. not mixing meat and dairy products at the same meal.	There is no formal commitment to *kashrut* and the overwhelming majority of Reform Jews do not keep kosher either in or out of the home.	Same as Reform. While no formal studies have been made, the impression is that somewhat more Reconstructionist than Reform (but fewer than Conservative) Jews observe *kashrut*. Those that do, base their observance not not on a belief in the divine origin of the laws of *kashrut* as articulated in the Books of Exodus, Leviticus, and Deuteronomy—as is the case among Orthodox Jews—but usually on their affirmation of a "folkway" that has preserved Jewish distinctiveness.
Travelling on the Sabbath	All segments of Orthodox Judaism prohibit travel, other than by foot and then only provided one is not carrying anything, on the Sabbath. This is seen as an extension of the biblical and talmudic prohibitions against kindling a fire on the Sabbath, e.g. igniting the sparkplugs in an automobile.	According to a 1950 ruling of the Rabbinical Assembly's Committee on Law and Standards, a Jew may drive to the synagogue if that is the only way (s)he will be able to attend services. Mechanized travel for other purposes is prohibited. In practice, however, a majority of Conservative Jews drive to the synagogue on the Sabbath, and many drive for other purposes as well.	The movement allows travel on the Sabbath by any means and for any purposes.	Same as Reform
Rabbis officiating or participating in a wedding involving intermarriage	All segments of the Orthodox movement staunchly oppose any sanctioning of intermarriage.	While some Conservative rabbis will counsel couples before and after the wedding, the movement's position on	The (Reform) Central Conference of American Rabbis has twice gone on	The Federation of Reconstructionist Congregations and Fellowships has taken no formal position on rabbis' officiating at

Issue	Orthodox	Conservative	Reform	Reconstructionism
(when the non-Jewish partner does not convert, or agree to convert)	The two major Orthodox rabbinical organizations will expel rabbis performing intermarriages.	rabbis actually participating in the wedding service itself is the same as Orthodoxy's.	record as opposing intermarriage but does not take action against the relatively small number (perhaps twenty in the U.S. and Canada) of Reform rabbis who officiate at an interfaith wedding.	weddings involving intermarriage. In a related decision, however, the Federation resolved in 1968 that it would consider children of mixed marriages Jewish provided (1) boys were circumcised and (2) the children received a Jewish education at least up to, and including, bar or bat mitzvah. —D.M.S.

METAMORPHOSES OF A TREE: 10 JEWISH SYMBOLS AND THEIR MEANINGS

The ten Jewish symbols described in the following pages are perhaps most notable for their lack of comparability: some are objects or beings found in nature; others are mental creations, such as a number or a geometric figure; still others are tools of ritual use. Some are key words or items from a biblical narrative. Some are consumed; others only beheld. All defy pat definitions or unilinear meanings. Each has had a unique life and history, and each has accrued meanings in a unique manner. The symbol's meaning is always the fruit of a collaboration between the symbol and the generations of interpreters who make use of it. The symbol functions on at least two levels: that of visual appearance, and that of verbal and literary association. It has often been erroneously said that Judaism prohibits imagery—it is, however, correct to say that the best way to study a Jewish symbol is to explore, not its outer appearance, but the web of textual, poetic, and narrative associations that surround it.

In one sense, all the symbols explored here are comparable: they allude, however circuitously, to the central symbol of Jewish

existence, the Tree of Life. These symbols are either metamorphoses of the Tree of Life, or a protective ring or flank for such a Tree. While the Paradise story (Gen. 2-3) has rarely been explicitly stressed in Jewish tradition as the core of Jewish myth, the symbolic "center" represented by the Garden of Eden, the Fountain of the Four Rivers, and the Tree of Life returns again and again in a variety of guises: the sacred locales of the Patriarchs, Jacob's ladder, Mount Moriah, Mount Sinai, the Ten Commandments, the "613" commandments, the Sabbath, the Tabernacle, the Ark of the Covenant, the sign of circumcision, the Temple, the sacrament of marriage and sexual union, the ministrations of the High Priest on the Day of Atonement, and above all, in innumerable connotations and layers of meaning: the Torah. "It is a Tree of Life to them that hold fast unto it; its paths are paths of pleasure, and all its byways lead to peace!" (Prov. 3:18). This dictum is proclaimed in song every Sabbath morning as the Torah scroll is replaced in the synagogue Ark after its public reading. During the Torah ceremony the members of the congregation relive some small measure of the Torah's reception at Mount Sinai and enjoy a brief foretaste of the lost pleasure of that human couple who once dwelt in the benign shade of a Tree of Life.

1. Magen David

It is so common today to think of the Magen David ("Shield of David"), the six-pointed star made of two interlocking equilateral triangles, as the symbol of Judaism, that it may surprise the reader to learn that it has been used explicitly in this way only for a few centuries. For most of Jewish history the six-pointed star has gone by other names (or no name), and the term "Magen David" has had other connotations.

The six-pointed star or hexagram is, of course, a product of human geometric imagination particular to no culture. It is a decorative symbol found throughout the ancient world. It appeared for centuries in Jewish art and architecture without symbolic or iconographic meaning. Its earliest attested Jewish use is a seventh-century B.C.E. seal of one Joshua ben Asayahu of Sidon. It is found on a frieze in a second-century C.E. Galilean synagogue, alongside a pentagram, a radial star, and a swastika(!). Throughout the Middle Ages the motif appears mostly in Christian and Muslim settings: on royal seals, notarial signs in Spain, France, Denmark, and Germany; in Byzantine and Spanish church architecture; on church furnishings and sacred objects; and in Bible manuscripts produced in Muslim and Christian countries. Jewish uses of this symbol most likely arose in imitation of its uses in surrounding societies.

The name of the symbol underwent a separate evolution. The Muslims called it the Seal of Solomon, with possible reference to the alleged magical powers of King Solomon's signet ring, alluded to in Hellenistic magical texts such as the *Testament of Solomon*, and in the Talmud (Gittin 68b).

This ring was reputed to give Solomon power over demons, one among many occult skills traditionally attributed to this most worldly of Jewish kings. Jewish legend generally regarded Solomon's ring as engraved with the four-letter divine name (YHVH), but Byzantine Christian amulets, as in Muslim usage, call the six-pointed star the Seal of Solomon.

The term "Magen David," on the other hand, originally had no connection with the hexagram. God Himself is called "Shield of David" in the synagogue *haftarah* blessing (recited after readings from the Prophets), on the model of the term "Shield of Abraham" used in the standing prayer (the *Amidah*). The shield carried by King David on the battlefield was traditionally believed to be engraved either with the name of God, or the Menorah, or Psalm 67. The words of this psalm are a prayer of a general kind, but since it stresses the God of Israel's power over the nations, its presence on the battlefield shield of David is appropriate. The first connection of the hexagram with the name David appears on a tombstone of someone named David in sixth-century C.E. Italy—where a connection with King David may not have been intended.

The uses of the hexagram changed from decorative to magical in the Middle Ages. The oldest magical texts did not make use of the symbol, but it began to appear in Jewish magical texts, and on talismanic *mezuzot* (see "*Mezuzah*," below) in the tenth through fourteenth centuries. More or less simultaneously the "Shield of David" came to be associated magically with divine or angelic names in texts and amulets from Geonic Babylonia and medieval Germany, especially with the names Metatron, Taftafiyyah, and the so-called "seventy-two-letter divine name" (based on the seventy-two letters of Exod. 14:19-21). Because the most popular of these amulets bore a hexagram, the hexagram was identified as "Magen David" in mystical and magical literature with increasing frequency. The first such use is in the mystical work *Sefer ha-Gevul* ("Book of the Boundary"), written about 1300 by the grandson of the Spanish Jewish mystic Nahmanides. Between 1300 and 1700, "Seal of Solomon" and "Shield of David" were used more or less interchangeably in magical texts, but eventually the latter came to be preferred. The symbol also was used by alchemists to symbolize the union of fire △ and water ▽—called "Shield of David" in this context after 1724.

The first known official use of the symbol by a Jewish community occurred in Prague in 1354: Charles IV granted the Jews the right to bear a flag with the hexagram—whence its use spread to synagogues, seals, and books in Moravia, Austria, Germany, and Holland. In 1613 it appeared on the tombstone of the astronomer and historian David Gans, author of a book called *Magen David*. The star was first used as a symbol parallel to the Christian cross on a stone marking the boundary between Jewish and Christian quarters in Vienna in early modern times. It likewise came to be designated as the Shield of the *Son* of David (i.e., of the Messiah) in the seventeenth century, especially in connection with the abortive Messianic movement of the Turkish Jewish mystic Shabbatai Zevi.

After this the hexagram's associations as a national emblem increased dramatically: in the late eighteenth and the nineteenth centuries it accompanied various movements for Jewish emancipation in Europe, its use motivated by the need to find an emblem comparable to the cross. It appeared in similar senses on ritual objects, such as the Passover *seder* plate (1770 onward); on an anti-Semitic engraving (1799); on the Rothschild coat of arms (1822); as a signature by the poet-scholar Heine (himself an involuntary convert to Christianity) in a German newspaper editorial (1840); as an emblem of the Zionist movement in Herzl's paper *Die Welt* (1890's); as a symbol of Judaism in Franz Rosenzweig's monumental philosophical work *The Star of Redemption* (1921), where its six points stood for God/Man/World and Creation//Revelation/Redemption; as the Nazis' badge of shame for Jews (1933–45); as the Palestinian Zionist flag emblem (1930's–40's); and finally, as the symbol on the flag of the State of Israel (1948 onwards).

Does the symbol "mean" anything? One cannot overlook its congruence with six-fold numerical symbolism in Judaism: six days of Creation, six pairs of tribes, 600,000 Israelites at Mount Sinai, reception of the Torah on the sixth of Sivan, six orders of the Mishnah, 613 Commandments, 6 million Jews martyred in the Holocaust. Base-6 numerical reckoning, together with its derived base-12 system, was widespread in the cultures of the ancient Near East because of its conformance to the cycles of lunar motion (its persistence today can be seen in the modern calendar, the recently defunct British monetary system, the clock, and the egg-crate). If the six-pointed star is taken as a simplified model of the astrological cycle (an ancient artistic motif in synagogues), its validity as a national symbol is strengthened, since the twelve-tribe system, according to some historians, may have been founded, at least in theory, on the lunar calendar.

2. Mezuzah

The *Shema* passage in the Torah (Deut. 6:4ff.) commands that the declaration of God's unity ("Hear, O Israel . . .") and the commandment to love God should be present at all times and in all places in the daily life of the Jew: "These words . . . shall be upon your heart; you shall speak them when you sit in your house, when you travel on the road, when you lie down, and when you get up. You shall bind them as a sign on your hand, and they shall serve as pendants between your eyes. You shall write them on the doorposts of your house, and on your gates." From these words are deduced the legal obligations of daily prayer, the wearing of prayer phylacteries (*tefillin*) on hand and forehead, and the posting of a *mezuzah* on one's doorposts and gateposts.

The Hebrew word *mezuzah* originally meant "doorpost" (its derivation, possibly from the Akkadian word *manzāzu*, "standing," is uncertain), but eventually the name was transferred to the encased parchment scroll containing biblical verses (Deut. 6:4-9 and 11:13-21) that enjoin the wearing and posting of the declaration of God's unity. There is a curiously tautological quality to this practice: one posts only the commandment which commands the posting of the commandment.

The *mezuzah* scroll is parchment made from the skin of a kosher animal. The scriptural text is written out in twenty-two lines in square characters on the outer side of the parchment. On the reverse side is usually inscribed the divine name *Shaddai* ("Almighty"), the letters of which also stand for *Shomer Daltot Yisrael* ("Guardian of the Doors of Israel"). These letters normally show through a window in the encasement. The *mezuzah* is affixed to the right-hand doorpost of a room- or house-entrance, and upon a gate-entrance, in the top third of the post, slanting top-inward. The blessing one says in affixing it concludes with the formula ". . . [who] has commanded us to affix a *mezuzah*."

The *mezuzah* is affixed to all doorposts except those of storerooms, bathrooms, or stables—the principal criterion being that the room be used primarily for dwelling-space, though not necessarily for sleeping-space. In Israel, the custom has arisen of affixing *mezuzot* to public buildings and synagogues. They are also placed at gates of apartment buildings and on city-suburb gates, as in Jerusalem's Yemin Moshe. After the Six-Day War in 1967 *mezuzot* were placed on the gates of the Old City. In Israel a *mezuzah* must be attached immediately upon occupation of a dwelling; in the Diaspora, within thirty days of taking up residence. If the house is sold or leased to a Jew, the *mezuzot* must be left in place. Customarily, pious Jews kiss a *mezuzah*, or touch it and kiss their fingers, upon entering or leaving.

Contemporary mezuzah by Ilya Shor

The Talmud stressed the importance of a *mezuzah* as a sign insuring God's protection. One who observes the precept will merit (at least) a beautiful house; one who neglects it places his own life, and those of his children, in danger. An *am ha-aretz* (a non-observant Jew) is known, among other things, by the absence of a *mezuzah* on his door. A doorpost bearing a *mezuzah* requires those entering to engage in respectful gestures toward one another, such as standing aside to let one's companion go first.

Onkelos the Proselyte, translator of the Bible into Aramaic, was arrested three times by the Romans. Each time, by force of the compelling logic of his remarks to the arresting officers, he converted them to Judaism. On the last occasion the officers were instructed not to engage in conversation with him. On their exit from his house, however, Onkelos pointed to the *mezuzah* and commented: "By universal custom, a mortal king dwells inside, and his servants keep watch outside. But in the case of the Holy One, Blessed be He, His servants dwell inside, and He keeps watch outside." Stopped by his remarks, the officers likewise converted, and no further search parties were sent.

The notion of a *mezuzah* as an instrument of divine protection led to a conception of its use as an amulet. In fact, it is probable that a doorpost amulet was a Near Eastern custom in pre-biblical times, and that the biblical ordinance of the *mezuzah* was a means of investing the pagan practice with higher religious significance. In any case, medieval *mezuzot*, especially in Geonic Babylonia, came to be adorned with magical signs such as divine names, angels' names, pentagrams, hexagrams, the Priestly Blessing, runic and numerological symbols, acrostics, and Psalm verses. In some communities these adornments came to have legal status, although the objections of many legal authorities, especially Maimonides, eventually purified the *mezuzah* scroll of its newer encumbrances and returned it to its original specifications. The *mezuzah* worn around the neck, though its scroll is unadorned by magical symbols, is a successor to the amulet-*mezuzah* of medieval times.

A *mezuzah* must be checked twice every seven years to make sure its scroll is legible and free of damage. The Hasidic sects place special emphasis on the importance of this practice, as well as on inspection of *tefillin* scrolls. The Lubavitchers tell of a *hasid* in Israel who suffered a heart attack. He was instructed by the rebbe to have a scribe inspect his *tefillin* scrolls. It turned out that in the verse reading "You shall love the LORD your God with all your heart . . ." a small hole existed in the word "heart." When the scroll was repaired the man recovered.

Tefillin have two additional texts along with those of the *mezuzah*: Exodus 13:1-10 and 13:11-16, a reminder to commemorate the Exodus by dedicating one's first-fruits, culminating in the phrase: "It shall become a sign upon your hand and pendants between your eyes." The four *tefillin* texts, placed together into box-shaped devices, are attached by straps to the left arm and forehead and are worn thus for the morning prayers (some especially pious have worn them all day). So important was the wearing of *tefillin* considered that the rabbis have stated that God Himself wears them. Each verse in God's *tefillin* scrolls corresponds to one in the human-made ones—for example, instead of "Hear, O Israel, the LORD is our God, the LORD is one!" the divine scroll reads: "Who is like your people Israel, a unique nation in the earth?" (2 Sam. 7:23).

And what prayer does God say when He wears His *tefillin?* The following: "May it be My will that My mercy will suppress My anger, that My love will prevail over My other attributes, and that I may deal with My children mercifully, and stop short, for them, of the line of strict justice."

3. Lions

The king of beasts was once more common in the Near East than he is today. There are at least seven names in Hebrew for "lion" (*aryeh* or *ari*, *lavi* [= Leo], *kefir*, *layish*, *shahál*, *shahatz*, and *gur*), at least 150 biblical references to lions, and allegedly over 400 words in Arabic for the shaggy feline. As in other cultures, the lion is proverbial in Judaism as a symbol of courage, strength, and ferocity. The sound of God's voice is compared to a lion's roar (Berakhot 3a). Israel triumphant is likened to a lion (Num. 23:24). Jacob's son Judah is compared to a lion (Gen. 49:9), as are, elsewhere, the tribes of Gad and Dan (Deut. 33:20, 32)—the identification of the lion with Judah is so thorough that the common Hebrew name Yehuda is characteristically followed by the name Aryeh or its Yiddish translation Leib (= Leo). Sometimes all three occur together: Yehuda Aryeh Leib. The famous Italian Renaissance poet and philosopher Judah Abarbanel was called in Italian Leone Ebreo ("Leon the Jew").

The symbol of a lion, according to the Midrash, appeared on the banner of the tribe of Judah. The emperor of Ethiopia in modern times, Haile Selassie, allegedly a descendant of the Judean king Solomon (by the Queen of Sheba), bore as one of his epithets "the Lion of Judah." The Judahite David and the Danite Samson are each reported by Scripture to have killed a lion (Judg. 14:5-6; 1 Sam. 17:34-35). In the book of Daniel, the lion is the symbol of Babylon—first, in the famous story of Daniel in the lions' den (also in the midrashic elaboration of King Nebuchadnezzar's transformation into a beast), and later, in the vision of an eagle-winged lion (griffon) seen by Daniel in his dreams (Dan. 7:1ff.). Lions

Torah ark cover with the two lions flanking the "crown of Torah"

guarded Pharaoh's palace, according to Midrash, and Moses, like Daniel, legendarily had the power to render lions docile.

Besides the poetic, legendary, and metaphorical uses of lions in Judaism, the Bible and Talmud record a fair amount of accurate natural history information about them: delineating their locales, their behavior toward their young, their mode of attacking and devouring (or storing) their prey, and the means used by human beings to fight or to capture them.

Heraldic and architectural use of lions was common in the ancient world. They adorned pagan temples as guard animals, much as they do today at the New York Public Library. Occasionally lions are represented in ancient mythology (and in Ezekiel's "Chariot" vision) as hybrid creatures—part bear, eagle, or even human—known in English as "sphinx" or "griffon." A lion is also universally a sign of the zodiac.

In Jewish ceremonial art, lions are most frequently seen facing one another in symmetrical designs adorning *mezuzot*, *menorot*, Hanukkah lamps, spiceboxes, Ark covers, Torah crowns, breastplates, and pointers, *Mizrah* (eastern-wall) decorations, wall or floor mosaics, bookplates, and amulets. Their symmetrical arrangement (characteristically flanking a divine force, divine words, or a Tree of Life) expresses the ability of divinity (or of its worldly representatives) to tame the forces of nature. Lions similarly adorned Solomon's Temple (1 Kings 7:29) and throne (10:20).

Lions appear frequently in the Midrash. They are known to sing the following hymn of praise to God: "The LORD goes forth like a mighty man; stirs up wrath like a man of war. He cries, yea, He shouts aloud; He acts mightily against His foes." Lions suffered from fever in Noah's ark, and once angrily cuffed Noah for forgetting their daily ration. Noah is said to have slaughtered a lion in an agreement with Satan over the planting of a vineyard—the blood of the lion was poured into the vineyard soil, which is why one who consumes wine in moderation gains the strength of a lion. Jacob saved Laban's sheep from a lion, but later expressed his regrets that he had deprived the beast of his lawful daily share of food. Judah had the facial features of a lion. A lion killed an Ishmaelite who beat Joseph during his Ishmaelite captivity. Solomon had a magical power over lions, and used them as servants. The milk of a lioness is cited by the Talmud as a valuable medicine.

Contemporary Israel has put a lion (or two) into the air: the Kefir ("Young Lion") jet. This particular lion is unique in hoping to have no prey.

4. Tablets of the Law

The Ten Commandments (Exod. 20:1-14; Deut. 5:6-18) are the principal ordinances given by God to Israel at Mount Sinai after Israel's exit from Egyptian bondage. These laws, called "words" or "things" (*devarim*) in Hebrew, serve as a preamble to the so-called "Book of the Covenant," the first major law collection in the Hebrew Bible (both in era of origin and in scriptural sequence), Exodus 21-24. Later Jewish tradition came to maintain that the whole of Pentateuchal law (in the form of the "613 Commandments") was given at Mount Sinai, but Scripture and tradition came to view the Ten Commandments as the quintessence or symbol of the rest. As Exodus 24:12, 31:18, and 32:16 suggest, the Ten (cf. Exod. 34:28) were inscribed by God on the "treaty tablets" carried by Moses back to the encampment of Israelites (cf. Deut. 9:9, 11, 15). When Moses returned and found Israel worshipping a golden calf, he grew enraged and smashed the tablets. He was then required to spend forty more days and nights on the mountain, recopying the tablets which God had made (Exod. 34:1-28).

***Moses receiving the tablets as portrayed in Cecil B. De Mille's* The Ten Commandments**

A second version of the Ten Commandments appears in Deut. 5:6-18, with only minor variations in wording; some later teachers, seeking to uphold the consistency and sanctity of Scripture, identified the second version with the second set of tablets given to Moses, while also claiming that both versions were spoken "simultaneously" to Israel.

Both sets of tablets were said to have been deposited in the Ark of the Covenant, which went forth in battle in front of the Israelite army. Later on the Ark was housed in Solomon's Temple (1 Kings 8:9).

Some controversy exists about which commandments are the Ten. Jewish tradition identifies them as follows: 1. I am the LORD your God who brought you out of the land of Egypt . . . 2. You shall have no other gods before Me; you shall not make for yourself a graven image . . . 3. You shall not take the name of the LORD your God in vain . . . 4. Remember (Deut.: "Keep") the Sabbath day . . . 5. Honor your father and your mother . . . 6. You shall not murder. 7. You shall not commit adultery. 8. You shall not steal. 9. You shall not bear false witness . . . 10. You shall not covet your neighbor's wife, your neighbor's house . . .

The Two Tablets of the Covenant (*Shenei Luhot ha-Brit*, Deut. 9:9, 11, 15) have come to serve as a symbol of Judaism for both Jews and non-Jews. Replicas of the tablets (sometimes containing only the first words of each commandment, or the first letters of each word, or the first ten alphabet letters, or, frequently, no words or letters) appear often in synagogue art and architecture, often seen adorned by a pair of lions (see "Lions," above). They are usually depicted as containing the first five commandments on the right tablet, the second five on the left, although one rabbi (R. Nehemiah) was of the opinion that all ten appeared on both. The Hellenistic Jewish philosopher Philo makes a conceptual division between the first five and the rest, claiming that the former taught "piety" (both religious and filial), the latter "probity" (in dealings with one's fellow human beings).

According to Jewish legend the tablets were among the things created on the eve of the first Sabbath (Avot 5.6). Some say that the remaining 603 commandments (of the "613") were written in between the lines. The tablets were fashioned from sapphire taken from God's throne, although, as one account has it, they were so remarkably thin that they could be rolled up like a scroll. They were still quite heavy, and it was only because of the spiritual nature of the letters, or because of God's supporting hand, that Moses could carry them down the mountain. When the tablets came in range of the Golden Calf, the letters fled into the air. The tablets again became heavy, and Moses was forced to drop them.

The first tablets were the work of God; the second the work of man. Some say that the second tablets contained the Oral Law (*Mishnah*, Talmud, and derived Codes). The tradition that the broken tablets were preserved in the Ark along with their replacements has helped to justify the scribal custom of storing away discarded specimens of writing that contain the name of God. It was because of this practice that historians have been afforded the treasures of manuscript storehouses such as the famous Cairo Genizah, allowing them valuable data about medieval Mediterranean life. The "Broken tablets," perhaps a more arresting image than the surviving tablets themselves, likewise justify respect for the elderly and the handicapped.

The Mosaic Tablets were legendarily stored away by King Josiah before the destruction of the First Temple, and are to be restored to Israel at the End of Days.

5. Crown

In the days of the Israelite monarchy, a king was anointed with olive oil and crowned (1 Sam. 1:10; 2 Kings 11:12) with a *nezer*—the latter perhaps a token of the halo of flames that arises from kindled olive oil, the king thus a symbolic "lamp" to his people, a matter which may likewise underlie the tradition that the future "anointed one" (*Mashiah*, "Messiah") of Israel will arrive by descending the Mount of Olives in Jerusalem. The word *nezer* came to be synonymous with the authority of a king (Prov. 27:24). The biblical word *atarah* ("diadem") designated a ceremonial wreath, usually of branches or flowers, worn on festive occasions such as weddings, festivals, games, and banquets. (Much debate occurs in the Talmud on the permissibility of its use after the Temple was destroyed in 70 C.E.) The word *zer* designated the crowning molding for the Ark, Ark-table, and incense altar (Exod. 25:11, 24-25, 30:3). The least common biblical word for "crown," *keter*, occurring only once, in Esther 2:17 (where it is possibly a Persian loan-word), became the most common and most meaning-laden post-biblical word for "crown."

In rabbinic literature, *nezer, atarah*, and *keter* often occur interchangeably, and "crown" became a metaphorical term of great flexibility. Mishnah Avot 4.5 warns against using one's knowledge of Torah as "a crown to magnify oneself with." Yet the "Crown of Torah" (meaning either the reputation or the spiritual elevation deriving from one's religious learning) was one of the most desirable of human prizes—the others being the Crown of Priesthood and Crown of Kingship—"but the Crown of a Good Name exceeds them all."

God is crowned daily by the archangel Sandalfon, who weaves the crowns and pronounces a divine name over each of them—some say that these crowns are woven from the prayers of Israel; some say, from each new interpretation of the Torah.

The *keter* Torah is a metal ornament, usually of gilded silver adorned with bells, that is placed over the upper stave-handles of a

Torah scroll, or an embroidery that adorns the mantle of the scroll or the Ark-curtain. This ornament is often flanked by figures of lions. In a sense there is something provocatively incongruous about the image: a crown normally adorns a human figure, but in Judaism it adorns, most characteristically, a collection of divine words.

Silver Torah crown, Poland, late eighteenth century

Tagin are the crowns placed on the scribal letters שעטנ״ז ג״ץ in Torah scrolls and other scriptural parchments. It is said that Rabbi Akiba, the second-century C.E. legal genius and mystic, used to derive legal decisions from these *tagin*. In wondrous foreknowledge of this, the Torah mercifully refrained from multiplying these letters excessively lest Jewish law become too distorted from its plain sense through the zeal of a great teacher. The crowned letters are arranged into a mnemonic spelling out the words *shaatnez* (a mixture of wool and flax, prohibited as a garment) and *getz* (abbreviation for *ger tzedek*), a righteous proselyte.

Various terms for "crown" or "royalty" appear in Kabbalah as terms for one or another divine emanation (*sefirah*). *Keter* is the first emanation, a mysterious primordial divine impulse sometimes called "Will." *Atarah* (or *Tiferet*) is the sixth emanation, the normal representation of the transcendent God, the lawgiver and hearer of prayer. *Malkhut* ("Kingdom") is the feminine emanation of God, the Shekhinah, who embodies God's wandering presence in the world.

Rabbi Nachman of Bratslav, interpreting the talmudic dictum that at the End of Days the righteous will sit "with their diadems [*atroteihem*] on their heads" and feast, states that this is not a literal diadem but a halo of light stemming from their higher spiritual natures—Rabbi Nachman thus anticipates the modern theory of the Kirlian aura, a paranormal emanation from the human body visible only to a special technique of photography. While Rabbi Nachman probably took quite literally the notion of a spiritual aura, he did not see this as a property accessible to all persons, but only to those whose words and deeds expressed a higher spiritual nature.

6. Hamza (Hand)

A *hamza* is a hand-shaped amulet. The name is probably a variant or corruption of the Arabic word for "five" (*hams*). This kind of amulet is found mostly in North Africa and is in use among the Arabs as well, who traditionally regard it as the hand of Muhammad's daughter Fatima. The symbol actually goes back to the days of the Carthaginians, who may, as descendants of the Phoenicians, have imported it from further east (the symbol is found on Phoenician tombstones); or perhaps the Carthaginians learned of it from the indigenous Berber peoples of North Africa.

Sometimes the symbol is made into a metal pendant, usually of silver, and sometimes it is inscribed in ink on parchment along with kabbalistic diagrams, cryptographs, and angels' names. In one such figure each of the five fingers is inscribed with a portion of the following verse from Jacob's blessing (of Joseph): "The fingers [literally arms, offshoots] of his hands were kept firm [in the handling of his bow] by the hands of the Mighty One of Jacob—from there, the Shepherd, the Stone of Israel" (Gen. 49:24). The palm bears the Aramaic inscription "I am of the seed of Joseph; I am a *tzaddik* [a righteous one] against whom the evil eye does not prevail." (On the Joseph motif, see also "*Hai*," below.)

The Talmud prohibits making a representation of a hand, probably because the hand is often associated with God in the Bible: "For with a strong hand the LORD brought you out of Egypt" (Exod. 13:9); "Is the hand of the LORD lacking?" (Num. 11:23); ". . . with a mighty hand and with an outstretched arm . . ." (Deut. 5:15, 26:8); "And I myself will fight against you with an outstretched hand and a strong arm" (Jer. 21:5);

Hamza amulet

"The hand of the LORD has done this" (Isa. 41:20); "They remembered not His hand" (Ps. 78:42). The phrase "The hand of the LORD was upon him" (Ezek. 1:3) means that a person was siezed by the spirit of prophecy. The expression "with a high hand" (Exod. 14:8, 15:30) refers to a display of might or power over an enemy, as the Israelites were said to have manifested against the Egyptians during the Exodus—thus implying divine protection and support. "Hand" is a frequent metaphor for possession, affordability, work, means, proximity, protection, war, and violence—and in one instance (Isa. 57:8) possibly a euphemism for "phallus." (The most recent sexual connotation of "hand" in Jewish life is found in Philip Roth's *Portnoy's Complaint.*)

The law of *tefillin* requires one to bind the verses of the *Shema* "as a sign upon [the] hand." Traditional practice invested the action with symbolic weight: the straps are wound in the shape of the Hebrew letters *shin, dalet*, and *yod*, thus placing the divine name Shaddai ("Almighty") on one's hand, and making one's bound hand literally into an amulet analogous to the *hamza*. Some *hamzas* have the name Shaddai on the palm.

The Torah, with its five books, is compared to a hand, with its five fingers. The book of Psalms (traditionally viewed as played on a harp by the skillful hand of King David) is likewise divided into five parts, as is the apocryphal book of Ben Sira (Ecclesiasticus). The law code of Maimonides, the *Mishneh Torah*, is called the *Yad* ("Hand"), because it consists of fourteen books; the numeral 14 (י״ד) is identical with the Hebrew word for "hand."

"Hand" appears as a frequent motif in Jewish legend: Jacob uprooted an oak with one hand; Gabriel caused milk to flow from Abraham's right hand; the right hand of Jacob was supported by Michael, his left by Gabriel; the inhabitants of the earthly layer known as Tebel possess four hands apiece; the serpent originally had hands, but was deprived of them in the Garden of Eden; the hands of the angels seen by Enoch were whiter than snow; Rebekah blessed Jacob with a promise that angels would bear him up in their protective hands; the wicked are suspended in hell by their hands; human hands consisted of one piece until Noah's time.

Even more extensive are the legendary uses of the number "five" (many of them surprisingly negative in connotation): five layers separate each earth from the next; there are five kinds of fire in hell; the soul possesses five powers and five senses; there were five kinds of alphabet allotted to Ham and Japheth; five thrones of Nimrod; five idols given to Abraham to sell; five cities on the Dead Sea plain; five miracles on Jacob's journey to Haran; five brothers of Shechem circumcised by Jacob's sons; five cities subdued by Jacob's sons; five times that Joseph's brothers prostrated themselves before Joseph; five garments of Judah; five changes of clothing given to Benjamin by Joseph; five horses with which Menasseh and Ephraim met Joseph; five sons of Esau; five divisions of the tribe of Benjamin lost in Egypt; five angels who rescued Hagar; five children in each Israelite family leaving Egypt; five sorts of weapons carried by Israelites in the desert; five leaflets on each leaf of Moses' thornbush; five Amorite kings defeated by Jacob; five Angels of Destruction; five names of Bezalel; five sacred vessels concealed by God during the Temple's destruction; five cubits the length and breadth of the altar, and length of the Tabernacle curtains; five daughters of Zelophehad; five sons of Zerah; five shekels required to redeem a first-born; five times that Moses implored God for an answer to his plea for greater knowledge of God; five blessings received by Jacob; five souls to one person; five ells the height of Joshua; five crowns received by Adam; five classes of angels; five sins that caused the Flood; five people called "friends of God"; five voices heard at Sinai; five faces on the idol of Menasseh. Abraham died five years before his time. Five is the age at which children are sent to school. The foregoing is a partial list and does not include references to multiples of 5, such as 50 and 500.

The Hebrew language has a name for each of the five fingers: *bohen* or *agudal* (thumb); *etzba* (index finger); *ammah* (middle finger); *kemitzah* (fourth finger); and *zeret* (pinkie). These terms originally referred to objects or measurements which the fingers helped to measure—eventually the meanings became transferred to the fingers themselves.

The decimal (base-10) number system is said to owe its origins to the handiest and simplest calculator that one takes to the marketplace: one's hands.

The kabbalists cultivated the discipline of chiromancy (palmistry), to determine who was qualified to undertake study of the secret doctrines. They read the biblical verse "*Zeh sefer toldot ha-adam*" ("This is the book of the history of mankind . . ." Gen. 5:1) to imply the gravure of characterological and prophetic markings on the human hand. These included palm lines and fingerprint whorls. In males it was the right hand that was believed to carry these signs; in females, the left. Many mystics correlated the seven palm lines with the seven planets and their influences. The Zohar finds in the palm lines indications of five principal character types, symbolized respectively by the Hebrew letters ז, ס, ת, ה and א (the initials of the words of the verse cited above). The lines were also believed to indicate data of a soul's transmigrations. The most important lines were the life line (*kav ha-hayyim*), the wisdom line (*kav ha-hokhmah*), the table line (*kav ha-shulhan*), and the fate line (*kav ha-mazzal*). Curiously, kabbalistic chiromancy may not have anything to do with the use of the *hamza* as a mystical symbol, although the most skilled chiromancers were reputed in the last century to have been the Moroccan rabbis—dwellers in the region where the *hamza* originated.

Hands are an instrument of speech, especially in the language of deaf-mutes (in recent years much work has been done on a specifically Jewish sign-language), but also in the gestures that punctuate everyday speech. Manual dexterity, along with vision, speech, and thought, evolved together in primates. Because they are a predominantly human prize, they are the attributes most often thought to link humankind with the Divine Image.

7. Hai ("Eighteen")

The word *hai* or *chai* (חי) means "living" or "alive." It is a word weighted with religious and mystical meaning, with many key uses in the Bible and later tradition. Its initial appearance in the Bible is near the end of the Garden of Eden story (Gen. 3:20), where Adam renamed his companion Ishah ("Woman") as Hawwah ("Eve" or "Life-Giver") because "she was the mother of all living" (*em kol-hai*). (The Garden story also plays two meanings of the word *hayyim*, "life," against one another: the transient "breath of life" given by God to all animal life, and the more mythological and elusive "Tree of Life" that appears but twice in the story, and seems to signify eternal life.) When Abraham's exiled handmaiden Hagar and her son Ishmael are rescued in the desert by the miraculous appearance of a well, she names the place *Be'er la-Hai Ro'i*, "Well of the Living One Who Sees Me" (Gen. 16:14). "*Hai-YHWH*" ("As the LORD lives . . .") is a frequent oath throughout the Bible.

The concepts of "life" and "living" have played an important role in Jewish law and symbolism. Unlawful taking of human or animal life was strictly prohibited. The seat of life in an animal was believed to lie in the blood, and for this reason one slaughtering an animal for food was required to drain its blood thoroughly, lest one misappropriate part of the life-force of the animal, which belongs only to God. Similarly, no animal could be exploited for food if it was alive or had had its life taken by any but the most meticulous ritual procedures. "Living waters," that is, fresh or running waters, are an important vehicle of ritual purification in the priestly literature (Lev. 14:5-6, 50, 52; 15:13), and it became natural to use this image metaphorically: Jeremiah refers to God as a "Well of Living Waters." Also, Ezekiel is fond of the image of Israel as a "Land of the Living"; the Torah is called a "Tree of Life"; and the utterances of the righteous, the teachings of the wise, and the fear of God are all called "Fountain of Life" (Prov. 10:11, 13:14, 14:27). God prefers that Israel "should *live* by [His laws], and not die by them."

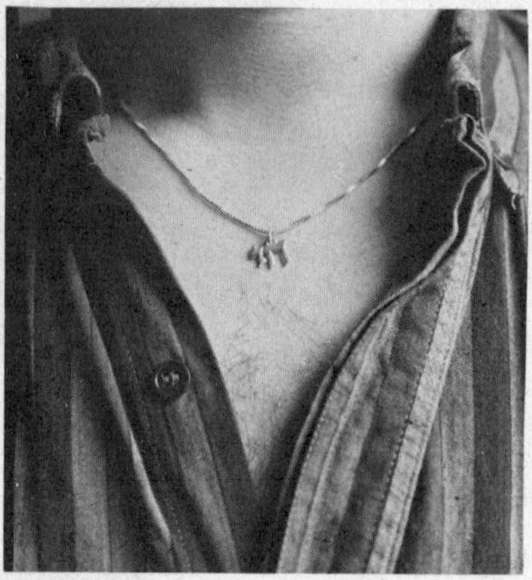

(Amy Meadow)

The word *hai* occurs as a motif throughout the Joseph story, seven times: (1) Joseph's brothers mention to their father that Pharaoh's minister (Joseph) has asked them if their father was still alive (Gen. 43:7—the event is otherwise not reported); (2) Joseph asks them directly if their father is still alive (43:27); (3) the brothers answer that he is still alive (43:28); (4) Joseph reveals his identity, and asks them again, now saying: "I am Joseph; is my father still alive?" (45:3); (5) the brothers tell their father that Joseph is still alive (45:26); (6) the father says to them: "Enough talk! My son Joseph is still alive!" (45:28); and (7) Jacob exclaims to his son Joseph: "Now let me die: I have seen your face, and you're still alive" (46:30). Each of these scenes expresses different aspects of the same event: kin separated by treachery, commerce, and famine, laboriously and tentatively relearning each other's existence. At the center of the series is Joseph, revealing to his long-lost brothers his identity and his disguise in one gesture, and asking: ". . . is *my* father still alive?" At the end of the series is Jacob (Israel) saying "and now let me die" (*you're* still alive!). Generation has tenuously reconnected with generation, and a cycle of human life has been completed.

This use of the motif of "alive" is sweeping in scope, subtle in variation, relentless in poignance. It is the touchstone of faulty relations between parent and child, sibling and sibling. It seems no accident that for the kabbalists the divine emanation (the ninth, Yesod, "Foundation") that is symbolized by Joseph is called by the names *El-Hai* ("The Living God") and *Mekor Mayyim Hayyim* ("Well of Living Waters").

The numerical value of the letters ח״י is 18. This number recurs many times in Jewish legend. Adam and Eve repented for eighteen days after their transgression, before Satan guilefully tried to interrupt their contrition. The primeval giants had thighs measuring eighteen ells. Eighteen newly-circumcised men were killed by Shimeon and Levi. Jacob advanced eighteen miles against the Ninevites in a war with them. Benjamin was eighteen years old when he married his second wife. Samla, an Edomite king in Joseph's time, reigned eighteen years. Anibal (Hannibal?), an Aegean king in Joseph's time, made war against Latinus for eighteen years. Joseph's wife Asenath was eighteen when she first received suitors. Sihon the Amorite had a thigh-bone of eighteen cubits. For eighteen years a heavenly voice resounded in Nebuchadnezzar's palace. The distance between the terrestrial and celestial temples is eighteen miles. Eighteen figures are called "servant of God": Abraham, Jacob, the people Israel, the Messiah, Moses, Joshua, Caleb, David, Isaiah, Eliakim, Job, Daniel, Hananiah, Mishael, Azariah, Nebuchadnezzar, Zerubbabel, and the army of angels. Eighteen years was considered the age of majority. Moses was eighteen when he slew an Egyptian taskmaster; eighteen when he fled Egypt. David engaged in eighteen campaigns; he had eighteen wives. Akiba sits with his disciples in the eighteenth rank of the Heavenly Academy. Eighteen thousand angels destroyed Sodom and Gomorrah. God sails the cosmos in a Chariot of eighteen thousand worlds, a point demonstrated by verse 18 of Psalm 68, which is read to mean: "God's chariots are [two] ten-thousands minus [two] thousands."

There are officially eighteen benedictions in the synagogue standing prayer (the *Amidah*, which is also called the *Shemonah Esreh*, "Eighteen"). Eighteen dollars is most preferred as a small charitable contribution. The word ח״י is a popular amulet and pendant, ideally made of eighteen-carat gold.

Kabbalistic associations with the intertwined motif of Joseph/"*Hai*" include the following motifs: insemination, foundation, upright man (*tzaddik*), oath, memory, sign, circumcision (= Covenant), sexual restraint, sexual fulfillment, fountain, inner chamber of Solomon's Temple, statute (*hoq*—like the sign of circumcision, something "engraved"), commandment (*mitzvah*), mountain, Mount Zion, the divine name *El-Shaddai* ("Almighty"), and the soul's redeeming angel. That is, all of these terms reverberate within the ninth divine emanation portrayed by the kabbalists: the point at which God in the upper worlds meets the feminine divine Presence (Shekhinah) dwelling in the lower world. Their point of union is understood sexually. Nine, the number of months in a pregnancy, is an exact divisor of eighteen, which, in its turn, is an exact divisor of thirty-six, the number of *tzaddikim* in every generation.

8. Grapes and Wine Cup

Wine was believed by the ancients to be the food of the gods, or the blood which coursed through their veins. It has always been used in pagan rituals of libation: many mystery cults, such as those of Orpheus and Dionysus, especially revered the intoxicating beverage. It has always been identified with settled civilization; for this reason, the biblical legend that makes one of Noah's first acts upon reaching dry land the planting of a vineyard, with the drunkenness and sexual indiscretion that followed, is an apt metaphor for the corruptions of agricultural society, which was, to some extent, viewed with distrust in the Bible. In general, nomadic cultures (Israel, of course, was never fully a nomadic culture in the same sense as, say, the Bedouins) have distrusted wine, and abhorred the political and cultural modes of life that grape cultivation normally entails. Even the Egyptians, whose climate and terrain were not suitable for the cultivation of grapes, never warmed up to wine—Joseph is said by legend to have gone without wine for twenty-one years while in Egypt.

Judaism, however, for all of its admonitions against the abuses of wine, has never gone as far as to prohibit its use. The land of Israel has a favorable terrain and climate for vineyards. Not only is wine in moderate amounts permitted by Jewish law and lore, but it is actually encouraged and even ritually obligatory. Wine is used to consecrate the Sabbath (*Kiddush*) and to mark the end of the Sabbath (*Havdalah*). A cup of wine consecrates a wedding ceremony; for seven days after the ceremony, the newlyweds must recite the blessing after meals over a full cup of wine—indeed, such a practice used to be more general after all feasts, especially ones with invited guests. Wine, likewise, is more or less obligatory on Simhat Torah ("Rejoicing of the Torah") and Purim. On the latter holiday one is encouraged to drink enough "so that one cannot tell Mordechai apart from Haman." On Passover every person must drink four cups of wine at the *seder*, and a fifth cup is left "for Elijah."

Contemporary Kiddush cup designed and executed by Ludwig Y. Wolpert
(Frank J. Darmstaedter)

Wine is often associated with Paradise in Jewish legend. The first grapes grew in the Garden of Eden (some even say that it was the forbidden fruit), and a river of the heavenly Paradise flows with wine made from the grapes of the Garden. The beverage is offered to the righteous after death. It is said that at the End of Days, every grape will yield forty kegs of wine, and each grape will beg to be the one through whom the praise of God is offered.

Noah allegedly planted the first ordinary vineyard in a pact with Satan. To close the deal he sacrificed four animals, letting their blood into the soil of the vineyard: a lamb, a lion, a pig, and a monkey—symbolic of the four stages of wine intoxication.

The priests also commanded the use of wine in offering sacrifices in the Tabernacle in the desert, and later, in the days of the Temple. It was forbidden, however, for priests to drink wine themselves when entering the sanctuary—one of the few biblical commandments revealed directly to Aaron. Jewish legend holds that Aaron's sons, Nadab and Abihu, broke this rule, which led to their being struck dead by God for offering "strange fire."

The wine of Gentiles is prohibited by Jewish law, on the grounds that it may have been offered in a libation to idols. According to Midrash it was Phineas (Pinchas), Moses's trusted lieutenant, who first instituted this rule, after Israelites had gone a-whoring with Midianite women at Baal Peor. He invoked the Divine Name and the power of the Tablets of the Law against any transgressors. This rule is observed today by Orthodox Jews, though the dangers of pagan libation are no longer prominent. Wine certified for Jewish use must carry the stamp of a trusted rabbinical inspector. Such wine is usually also designated as kosher for Passover. The wine used sacramentally for the Friday evening meal must be grape-wine; wine for the daytime Sabbath *Kiddush* may be berry-wine, or other beverages or spirits. One can say the blessing ". . . who creates the fruit of the vine" (*bore pri ha-gafen*) only over grape-wine—over other beverages, the proper blessing is "Blessed . . . by whose word everything is made" (. . . *shehakol nihyeh bidvaro*).

Some other legendary associations of wine: a grape-vine symbolizes Israel; the Torah is compared to wine; wine is the color of the flag of the tribe of Naphtali; grapes were prohibited to Samson's mother during her pregnancy (Samson himself was a *nazir*, a member of a monastic order forbidden to cut hair or drink wine); Esau sold his birthright over wine (the Bible simply says "pottage" or "red-stuff," a pun on Esau's other name Edom, "Red"); Jacob gave his aged father Isaac wine fetched from Paradise by the archangel Michael; wine permitted Noah to uncover his nakedness, Lot to sleep with his daughters, Judah to be seduced by his daughter-in-law Tamar, and Israel to sin with the Golden Calf. Pharaoh, it seems, did not share his countrymen's distaste for wine, and one of the reasons his cup-bearer had been thrown in prison (where Joseph met him) is that he had allowed a fly to fall in Pharaoh's wine-cup.

Some proverbs about wine: "Who has wounds without cause? They who tarry late at the wine" (Prov. 23:24). "Wine was created mainly to comfort mourners and reward the wicked for their good deeds" (Erubin 65a). "Wine reddens the face of the wicked in this world, and whitens it in the next" (Sanhedrin 70a). "Wine causes one's voice to be raised, and secrets to be revealed" (Zohar IV, 176b). "No celebration without wine."

Grapes, grape-clusters, grape-vines, and wine-cups are frequent motifs in Jewish art and architecture. They are often found on buildings, monuments, and sarcophagi in and around Israel from Hellenistic times onward. During the Bar Kokhba rebellion (135 C.E.) Jewish coins were minted bearing a grape cluster on one side. *Kiddush* cups have always been objects of beautiful shapes and adornments. They are frequently inscribed with biblical verses or the wine-blessing. The stemless *Kiddush*-cup is a popular variant shape, but the basic form—the goblet shape: cup, stem, and base—is perhaps truest to the meaning of the Friday-evening *Kiddush*. There, wine serves as "a remembrance of Creation . . . a remembrance of the Exodus from Egypt"; the ceremony telescopes the two events through which, for a Jew, life is made possible, and the wine-cup takes on the lineaments of the central fruit-tree of Paradise, the Tree of Life. (See also "Kosher Wines and Wineries")

9. Pomegranates

The pomegranate (*rimmon*) is one of the "seven species" for which, according to Deuteronomy 8:8, the land of Israel is renowned (the others being wheat, barley, grapes, figs, olives, and honey). Grapes, pomegranates, and figs from the land were brought back to the Israelites in the desert by the spies whom Moses had sent as scouts, in order to demonstrate the excellence of the soil. Not all the spies were in favor of bringing back such a demonstration of the land's virtues, for they feared the land's inhabitants (see below), and were reluctant to commit Israel to a conflict with Canaan; but one of their number, Caleb, insisted on bringing back evidence of the land's bounty. The spies had, in fact, entered the land in the first place on the pretext of buying pomegranates and grapes.

The scouts were frightened by the size of the land's inhabitants, and awed by the size of its produce. According to one midrashic tall-tale, the scouts entered what they thought was a cave. They soon discovered that it was a huge pomegranate rind discarded by the daughter of the giant Anak, an inhabitant of Kiriat Arba in Hebron.

Like the grape, the pomegranate is a symbol of life and fertility. It appears frequently as an image in the biblical love-poem the Song of Solomon: "Your cheeks are [red] like the halves of pomegranates" (4:3; 6:7); "Your shoots are an orchard of pomegranates with all choicest fruits" (4:13); "I went down to the nut-orchard to look at the blossoms of the valley, to see whether the vines had budded, whether the pomegranates were in bloom" (6:11); "[Come, my beloved,] . . . let us go out early to the vineyards and see whether . . . the pomegranates are in bloom" (7:13); "I would give you spiced wine to drink, the juice of my pomegranates" (8:2).

Covering for Torah staves called rimmonim, Hebrew for pomegranates

The fruit adorned the robe of the High Priest: ". . . pomegranates of blue and purple and scarlet material" alternating with bells of pure gold (Exod. 28:33-34; 39:24-26). King Solomon's chief Temple architect, Hiram of Tyre, made rows of pomegranates to adorn the Temple's pillars (1 Kings 7:18ff.). A famous pomegranate tree was a landmark in the outskirts of the town of Gibeah (1 Samuel 14:2), and a number of biblical towns had "pomegranate" as part of their names: Rimmon ("Pomegranate"), Rimmon-Peretz ("Pomegranate of the Wellspring"), Sela-Rimmon ("Pomegranate Rock"), Eyn-Rimmon ("Pomegranate Fountain"), and Gath-Rimmon ("Pomegranate Press").

Pomegranates are mentioned frequently in the Talmud as a prized fruit grown in nearly every region of the country. There were sweet and sour varieties. The fruit yielded a red dye, sometimes used as a test for invisible ink. The kernels were eaten fresh or dried, or were pressed into a juice or wine. Because the pomegranate differs from other fruits in having edible seeds and inedible flesh, it lent itself to certain metaphorical uses. Rabbi Meir, who learned Torah from the heretic Elisha ben Abuya, was compared to one who extracts pomegranate seeds to eat, and discards the rest. Schoolchildren sitting in rows in the yeshivas are compared to pomegranate seeds. "Even the most empty of Jews," says the Talmud, "is filled with good deeds [*mitzvot*] like the seeds of a pomegranate" (Berakhot 57a)—the pomegranate was popularly believed to hold 613 seeds, the traditional number of *mitzvot*. Rabbi Yohanan's legendary handsomeness is compared to a silver cup filled with pomegranate seeds, surrounded with a crown of red roses, placed between the sun and the shade.

Pomegranates appear in ancient Jewish art as a Tree of Life, and the bell-laden silver covers for the upper handles of the Torah-scroll staves are called *rimmonim*—perhaps stressing the proverbial conception of the Torah as a Tree of Life (see Prov. 3:18). The pomegranate is engraved on the back of the modern Israeli lira coin as one of several official symbols, on flags, coins, and stamps, for the State of Israel. The pomegranate, being a tough fruit with a tender core, resembles the *sabra* (a species of cactus), another symbol of the native-born Israeli.

10. Menorah

When the Israelites wandered in the wilderness, Moses and his Tabernacle architect Bezalel were commanded (Exod. 25:31-40, 37:17-24) to make a candelabrum consisting of a central shaft and three pairs of branches, seven lamps in all—each branch containing three almond-shaped cups with a floral design, and the central shaft containing four. Knobs adorned each cup, and joined each branch at the central shaft. The whole work was shaped and hammered of a single piece of pure gold, with accompanying lamps, lamp-trays, and snuffers, also of pure gold. The tops of the branches and the central shaft were the same height—according to the Talmud, eighteen handbreadths. The vessel was placed in front of the Ark curtain on

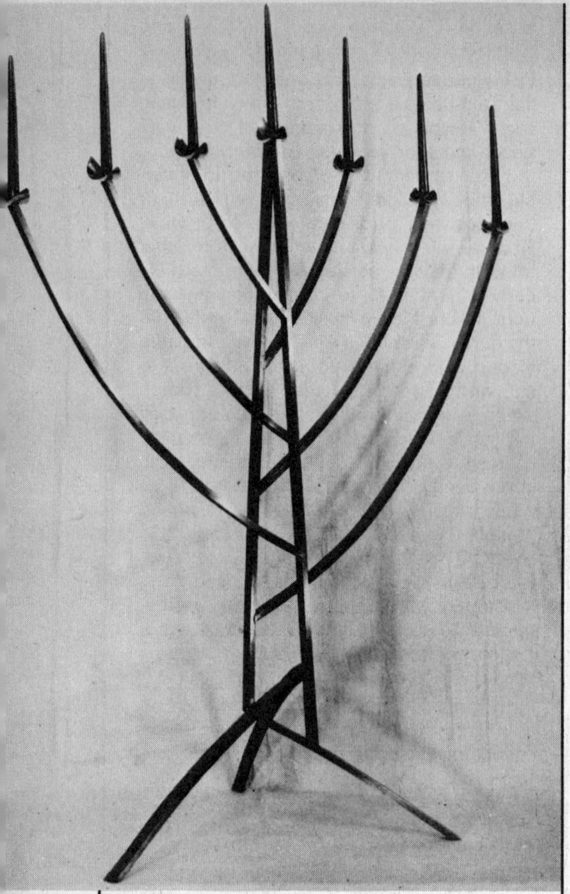

***Contemporary synagogue menorah designed by Ludwig Wolpert.* (Rodeph Shalom)**

the south side of the Tabernacle. It burned from evening to morning—it was lit at dusk, and trimmed by the High Priest at dawn. It stood on a table symbolizing, according to legend, the delights of Paradise, and burned with a light symbolizing the divine Presence.

According to Midrash, Moses was given directions for the Tabernacle menorah several times, a blueprint for its design projected against the cliffs of Mount Sinai with white, red, green, and black fire. God even cast the design against His own palm. Moses repeatedly forgot the design, and there are two versions of how the problem was resolved: in one, God referred Moses to the artisan Bezalel, who carried out the instructions immediately; in another, God bade Moses to cast a talent of gold into a fire—when he did so, the menorah shaped itself. Whichever is the case, it is no surprise that the least idolatrous Israelite should have had trouble remembering imagery. Moses's faculties were most attuned to the spoken word.

The menorah was rebuilt according to the Tabernacle specifications for Solomon's Temple, where it was accompanied by ten other lampstands—five along the northern wall of the Temple, five along the southern. The number ten legendarily corresponded to the Ten Commandments; the seventy lights corresponded to the number of nations in the world. When Nebuchadnezzar, king of Babylon, sought to destroy the Temple, God reputedly concealed the menorah, as one of five sacred objects to be restored to Israel in the rebuilding of the Temple at the End of Days: the Ark, the menorah, the altar fire, the holy spirit of prophecy, and the cherubim. Some say, too, the Tablets of the Law.

A copy of the Temple menorah was made for the Second Temple (minus the accompanying menorot of Solomon's design). Some say that the original menorah was brought back to Zion by the returning exiles. According to tradition, three lamps of this menorah burned by day; the rest were lit in the evening. One of the lamps, probably the central lamp, burned perpetually. In late Hasmonean times the menorah appeared for the first time on Jewish coins.

When the Temple was destroyed a second time in 70 C.E. its menorah was captured by the Romans. A replica of it, shown being carried to Rome in a triumphal procession, appears on the famous Arch of Titus in the Roman Forum—where it symbolizes the subjection of Rome's most rebellious province. Its octagonal base appears there decorated with eagles and sea monsters.

The fate of the Temple menorah is somewhat obscure. After it fell into Roman possession it was deposited along with other Temple treasures in a special "Peace Temple" built by the general (later emperor) Vespasian in Rome. Later these treasures were reputedly removed by the German Vandals to Carthage; still later they were won back by Rome and transferred to Constantinople. There a local official was allegedly warned by a Jew of the bad omens that befell Rome and Carthage when they held the Jewish treasures (compare the stories of the Ark's captivity in the days of Philistine domination in 1 Sam. 5-6); as a result, the vessels were returned to Jerusalem and deposited in a church. Because of Persian and Arab invasions, however, the ultimate fate of these treasures is unknown. Jewish legend still earmarks them for the Messianic Temple at the End of Days.

With the destruction of the Temple, and partly as a result of Roman iconography, the menorah began to be regarded as the national symbol of Judaism—the oldest and most revered of such symbols. Its use in synagogue art and furnishings from Roman times onward is widespread; it appears on ritual vessels, stonework, mosaics, paintings, tombs, sarcophagi, tomb doors, cemetery or mausoleum frescos, ossuaries, bottles, glasses, lamps, amulets, seals, rings, cornelians, and manuscript adornments. It is a common motif in modern synagogue art, and is the symbol of the State of Israel on currency, stamps, and official seals.

Unlike the Star of David which, as a purely geometric design, conforms to the more abstract lineaments of human thought, the menorah is a natural symbol—resembling items in nature and in practical experience: a tree, a hand, the rivulets of rain, a river delta, the rays of sunlight through a cloud, the lines of kinship, the flames of fire. Exegetical imagination has identified the menorah with the seven "eyes of the LORD" perceived by the prophet Zechariah (Zech. 4:10). Philo and others saw the seven branches as corresponding to the seven principal heavenly luminaries: Sun, Venus, Mercury, Moon, Saturn, Jupiter, and Mars. The kabbalists identified them with the seven days of Creation and the seven lower divine emanations (*sefirot*). The four cups of the central shaft have been compared to the four seasons. A less exact midrashic imagination focuses on the light that emerges from the menorah, which has alternatively symbolized Israel, God, Torah, the Crown of Good Deeds, the Shekhinah, and Life.

The wine cup blessed on the Sabbath (see "Grapes and Wine Cup," above) is also in the shape of a tree. The Tree of Life was forbidden to the first human couple after their transgression (Gen. 3:22–24), yet so strong was their yearning for this ultimate wonder of God's Creation that by procreating they made the human family itself into a gigantic Tree of Life extending through time. The Talmud similarly prohibits replication of the seven-branched menorah of the Tabernacle—yet, as if in defiant assertion of the life force, the menorah is found today in many synagogues throughout the world, and is lit in Jewish homes on Friday evenings.

—J.R.

FEMININE IMAGERY IN JUDAISM

It is likely that most, if not all, of the anthropomorphic images in the Jewish religion have been created by men. Since women were traditionally excluded from such public religious enterprises as prayer, Torah study, or discourses on the Law, where such images would tend to arise, it is reasonable to assume that these projections originated with men.

This is not to say that these images only "work" for men. There are aspects of humanity that both men and women share and their projections should be fairly compatible. However, there are bound to be some that are biased, one-sided, and discriminatory, as with the following five feminine images in Judaism. As projections of women by men, they tend to reveal an idealized vision of women or the decidedly mixed feelings men had about women. Nonetheless, some of these images "work" for women, too, although often for different reasons than those originally intended.

—the Eds.

Hokhmah

Hokhmah, Divine Wisdom, is vividly personified as a woman in the Book of Proverbs. At the opening of the book she speaks like a prophetess, admonishing those who ignore her moral teachings (1:20–33). She is also the benefactress who will shower honor, protection, and profit upon her loyal adherents (4:6–9). In a similar context *Hokhmah* is called a tree of life, nourishing those who hold fast to her (3:17– 18). *Hokhmah* is a sister, the good woman who will guard impetuous youths from temptresses (6:4–5). She and Folly figure as rival hostesses inviting men to their respective banquets (9:1–18).

In these images *Hokhmah* is valued as women are valued in patriarchal societies, not for herself but for her usefulness to men. In Chapter 8, however, *Hokhmah* appears as a transcendent value. Goddesslike, she calls men to her discipline and recites her own history. She existed before the universe and worked beside God in its creation. She "makes merry" in God's presence and delights in the world and in human beings. Whether *Hokhmah* was intended as a subordinate but separate divine being is a matter of great scholarly controversy, but the notion is frequently rejected as incompatible both with Israelite monotheism and with the absence of mythological references to her in the wisdom literature of other ancient Near Eastern cultures.

Later wisdom books, such as the Wisdom of Sirach, elaborate on the feminine personifications of *Hokhmah* established in Proverbs. Thus, Sirach praises Wisdom as if she were an especially dutiful *hausfrau*:

> *She will meet him like a*
> *mother*
> *And receive him like a bride,*
> *She will feed him with the*
> *bread of understanding*
> *And give him the water of*
> *wisdom to drink. . . .*
> *She will exalt him above*
> *his neighbors.*
>
> (15:2–5)

But he also recognizes the transcendent and marvelous aspects of Wisdom who "compassed the circuit of heaven" and "walked in the depth of the abyss" (24:4–5), and pictures her as a great and unimaginable tree whose blossoms and fruit, stature and fragrance combine the best features of all earthly trees (24:13–17).

Sabbath

The personification of the Sabbath as bride is one of the most popular and enduring of feminine images in Jewish tradition. An early Midrash makes the Sabbath the mate of Kennesset Yisrael, the Community of Israel. "Rabbi Shim'on ben Yohai said: The Sabbath said before God, 'Master of the universe, each day has its mate but I have none. Why?' The Holy One, blessed is He, answered her, 'The Community of Israel is your mate,' and when Israel stood before Mount Sinai, the Holy One, blessed is He, said to them, 'Remember what I told the Sabbath: the Community of Israel is your mate. Therefore 'Remember the Sabbath day to keep it holy.' " (*Gen. R.* 11:18)

Even in talmudic times there was a developing ritual that extended and elaborated this metaphor, as indicated in the following passage (the sages quoted lived in the third and fourth centuries C.E.): "Rabbi Hanina would say on the eve of the Sabbath, 'Let us go out to meet the bride, the queen.' Rabbi Yanai used to adorn himself and say, 'Come, O bride! Come, O bride!' " (*Shab.* 119a; *B.K.* 32 a,b)

Because the Sabbath day reenacts a cosmic event, the culmination of the creation of the universe, every Sabbath reproduces the first Sabbath. Thus, Sabbath is a bride, always new, always virgin, and the sacred marriage is celebrated anew each week.

WHO IS THE BRIDEGROOM?

In the rabbinic texts it would appear that the Sabbath is queen over the week, preeminent among days. The kabbalists, however, endow her with a royal bridegroom. She becomes identified with the *Shekhinah*, the feminine aspect of the deity, and mated with God the king. The kabbalist Rabbi Isaac Luria and his followers in sixteenth-century Safed dramatized this divine wedding (*hieros gamos*) in the ritual of *Kabbalat Shabbat*, the Reception of the Sabbath. Dressed in white, they would make a wedding procession to the fields singing hymns to welcome the Sabbath. The most famous hymn is *Lekha, Dodi* (Come, My Beloved), written by Solomon Alkabetz. At its climactic last stanza worshippers today still turn toward the door and bow to the entering queen:

> *Come in peace, crown of God,*
> *Come with joy and cheerfulness*
> *Amidst the faithful of the*
> *chosen people,*
> *Come, O bride! Come, O bride!*

Some kabbalists balanced the ritual of welcoming the Sabbath with a celebration at the end of the Sabbath known as *Melaveh Malka*, the Escorting Out of the Queen. Its theme is the hope for the coming of the King Messiah, the final union of the male and female principles, which now unite only on the Sabbath, and the establishment of messianic time "which will be all Sabbath and rest in life everlasting". (*Mishnah, Tamid* 7:4)

The portrayal of *Shabbat* as feminine makes it an effective mediating symbol, allowing men to engage in an intimate relationship with her that is laden with sexual potency (a possibility not afforded with the masculine God under usual circumstances). While she is queen to God's king, she is bride to *Israel's* (i.e. his) groom. Many women, however, do not so much have a *relationship* with *Shabbat* as *identify* with it—their spirituality being a reflection of *Shabbat*'s divinity. Thus, not only is she queen to God's king, but she is also bride to *God*'s groom.

Shekhinah

The *Shekhinah*, literally "the dwelling," is a term used in rabbinic literature to mean God's immanence, the divine Presence that rests upon and participates in this world, as opposed to God's transcendence, His unknowable aspect. While in Talmud and Midrash, the Shekhinah is not personified as female, its imagery stresses radiance and nurturance. In the presence of the Shekhinah the righteous are like a lamp before a torch (*Pes.* 8a). The light that the Shekhinah sheds over the world is like that of the sun (*Hul.* 59b–60a). Converts are said to have been brought "under the wings of the Shekhinah" (*A. Z.* 13b; *Shab.* 31a; *Yev.* 49a). On the wings of the Shekhinah the body of Moses was conveyed to its grave (*Sot.* 13b).

It is in the Kabbalah that the Shekhinah takes female form, a development which the eminent scholar Gershom Scholem calls "one of the most important and lasting innovations of Kabbalism." Thus, in the swiftly changing flow of kabbalistic symbolism, the Shekhinah appears as daughter, queen, and bride, as the archetypal Community of Israel, of which the earthly community of Israel is only a reflection, as Rachel weeping for her children, as Mother of all Israel.

The union of God and the Shekhinah, described in boldly sexual terms, is the prototype of all loving unions between men and women. The exile of the Shekhinah from her consort is the root of all alienation. This cosmic catastrophe was, according to the Zohar, the result of Adam's sin, although in Lurianic Kabbalah Adam's sin is simply the coup de grace following an earlier cosmic accident called "the breaking of the vessels." All sin deepens the break between God and the Shekhinah, while observance of the Torah causes healing and restoration (*tikkun*). For this reason, in some prayerbooks a prefatory "intention" is printed above the blessing for any *mitzvah*: "For the sake of the unification of God and His Shekhinah . . ."

The exile of the Shekhinah mirrors the exile of the Jewish people. Her grief, expressing the full magnitude of theirs, is blinding, and earns her the appellation, "the beauty who no longer has eyes." God the unknowable, the hidden, cannot be seen: "Humankind cannot see Me and live" (Ex. 33:20). But the Shekhinah can be seen embodied in women. Thus, Abraham ha-Levi saw her at the Western Wall in 1571, dressed in black and bewailing the husband of her youth. Hasidic master Levi-Yitzhak saw her in eighteenth-century Berditchev, a distraught mother fearing that her son would not be cleared in divine judgment on Rosh Hashanah.

Among Jewish feminists the feminine personification of the Shekhinah has gained new emphasis, since it enables women to recognize their own kinship with the deity. A major and radical liturgical innovation in some Jewish feminist circles is to address the Shekhinah directly in prayer.

Torah

The Torah's feminine personification stems from her identification with *Hokhmah* (Wisdom). Thus, in rabbinic literature, the claims made by *Hokhmah* in Proverbs 8 are simply transferred to Torah, so that it becomes Torah who preceded the world (*Gen. R.* 1:4) and was instrumental in its creation (*Avot* 3:14). Torah, however, lacks the splendid independence of *Hokhmah* as depicted in Proverbs 8. Her role is much more relationally based; most commonly, she is a daughter and a bride. God figures as father and as father-in-law to the Torah's consort, who is usually identified as Israel but occasionally is said to be Moses! (*Pesikta Rabbati* 20; 95a. *Midrash Ex.* 33:7. *Midrash Shir* 8:11).

The richest symbol that Torah appropriated from *Hokhmah* is that of the Tree of Life. The verses so describing her were incorporated into the liturgy and are sung on Sabbaths and festivals when the Torah is returned to the Ark:

> *She is a tree of life to those*
> *who hold fast to her;*
> *Happy are those who support her.*
> *Her ways are ways of pleasantness,*
> *And all her paths are peace.*
> (Prov. 3:17–18)

The wooden rollers on which the Torah scroll is wound are termed *atzei hayyim*, Trees of Life, and this motif is often embroidered on the Torah's velvet mantle. Midrashic legends identify Torah with the Tree of Life that stood in the Garden of Eden or as a substitute Tree of Life promised to Adam's descendants and delivered on Mount Sinai. The Tree of Life is a symbol found in many widely separated cultures. Among the Celts it is an apple tree, among the Chinese a peach. Ancient Egyptian art portrays a goddess as a date palm nourishing souls. The symbol is a popular one in women's arts. The tree, its branches spread wide and bearing varied fruits, is commonly depicted in embroidery and quilting.

As in the case of *Hokhmah*/Torah, the Tree of Life and the Tree of Knowledge are often the same tree. This tree, rooted in earth but reaching into the sky, is a perfect locus for revelation or enlightenment, as Deborah under her palm tree (Judges 4) and Buddha under his Boddhi tree illustrate. Erich Neumann suggests that the Tree of Life is identified with a feminine principle whose special gifts are ability to nourish, to generate and to transform.

The femininity of the Torah is not simply restricted to concept or allegory. It is dramatically expressed in the rituals and gestures used toward the Torah scroll in the synagogue. Emphasis is placed on ornamenting and bedecking the scroll. It is covered by an embroidered velvet mantle by Ashkenazic congregations or housed in an ornate metal case by Sephardim. Its two wooden "Trees of Life" are often topped by silver ornaments or a silver crown. The processions in which the Torah is carried aloft, kissed, fondled, or, on Simhat Torah, danced with, are reminiscent of bridal processions.

On Simhat Torah, the person called to the Torah for the concluding reading of Deuteronomy is the *hatan Torah*, the bridegroom of the Torah, while the person called for the opening reading of Genesis is the *hatan Bereshit*, the bridegroom of "In the Beginning."

In the Jewish symbol system in which the central dynamic is the romance between God and Israel, Torah, like the Sabbath, functions as a mediating symbol. Since God was traditionally assigned the higher status masculine role, while Israel assumed the subordinate feminine role, another set of symbols arose to fulfil the need of Jewish men to play masculine roles in ritual. In glorifying Torah or entering into the Sabbath or in playing knight to their queen, the Jewish male could draw upon his own gender experience and, thereby reappropriate for himself the power, potency, and dominance that in the God/Israel romance belong exclusively to God.

Many Jewish feminists, consequently, view these mediating symbols as problemmatic because they do not arise out of women's consciousness but instead emphasize those features that patriarchs value in women, such as virginity.

Zion

In the poetry of the prophets, the Jewish people and their land are encompassed in the symbol of a woman known either as Zion, or Jerusalem, or Israel. Her career as virgin, whore, mother, and reclaimed wife serves as a moral commentary on the unfolding of Jewish history in the prophets' time. Zion's femaleness was dictated by ancient conventions in which cities and nations were personified as women. The wise woman of Avel describes her city as "a mother in Israel" (II Sam. 20:19). The book of Lamentations refers to "the maiden [literally, daughter] Edom" (Lam. 4:21–22), Jeremiah to the "maiden Egypt" (Jer. 46:24), and Isaiah and Zechariah to the "virgin Babylon" (Is. 47:1; Zech. 2:11).

The personification of a nation as a virgin is meant to emphasize its "intactness"—that it has not been penetrated by any foreign power—and its purity. Hence, the invaded nation is portrayed as a woman shamed, stripped naked for ravishment or the slave auction (Jer. 46:24; Lam. 4:21; Is. 23:12) or as a menstruant (Lam. 1:17). The erring nation is portrayed as a whore or adulteress (Ez. 16:1–42; Hos. 2:1–14).

Whoring, the act by which women bestow their bodies on someone other than the "rightful owner," is the definitive act of female misbehavior in the Prophets. Not only is it an act of betrayal, it is a rebellion, a throwing off of the yoke of authority in willful autonomy. It is because Zion is personified as female, that whoring is the preferred metaphor for idol worship.

The theme of the nation as adulteress is fashioned by many prophets into a family drama in which God and His wife, Zion, quarrel and reconcile, separate and reunite. In the allegory of Oholah and Oholibah, two promiscuous sisters whose doings are described in vivid detail, Ezekiel indicts idol worship and foreign political alliances in the two nations of Samaria and Judah. Both were wedded to God, but Samaria has already been divorced, while the marriage with Judah teeters on the brink of dissolution (Ez. 23:1–48). In Hosea and Jeremiah, as well, the adulterous wife is divorced by her divine husband (Hos. 2:4; Jer. 3:1–10).

A dire end is promised the adulteress in some prophecies. She will be violated, ruined, destroyed. She will be stoned before an audience of women forced to witness her punishment for their moral edification (Ez. 16:40–41). She will be a mother bereft of children, a homeless exile, a woman alone, unprotected by a male, utterly vulnerable (Is. 49:21). Yet, in an end beyond the end, Zion and God will be reconciled. Hosea, punning on the pagan god Baal, has God promise a more egalitarian relationship: "You shall call Me *Ishi* [my man], and shall no longer call Me *Baali* [my husband/owner—the word for husband in Hebrew means owner]" (Hos. 2:18). Isaiah pledges, "You will be called 'She is my delight' and your land will be called 'Married' " (Is. 62:4). No longer barren and bereaved, Zion will see the homecoming of her lost children in such multitudes that her tent will not hold them, an allusion to barren Sarah who became "a mother of nations" (Is. 49:19–21).

The most unusual metaphor used for the God-Zion relationship, however, is found in Isaiah 49:15, where God and Zion are mother and daughter! When Zion complains of abandonment, God reassures her, "Can a woman forget her baby or disown the child of her womb? Though she might forget, I could never forget you."

Midrashic portrayals of Zion elaborate on themes introduced by the prophets. Zion is the bride of God, one of the seven barren women for whom a miracle was wrought, a mother mourning for her children, an accused adulteress (*sotah*) given the bitter water by her own son. In Kabbalah, Zion's heavenly counterpart is the Shekhinah. In his *Major Trends in Jewish Mysticism*, Gershom Scholem describes a Shavuot custom, dating from the Middle Ages and still observed in some Sephardic congregations, of reading a mystic marriage contract between the Bridegroom God and the Virgin Israel.

—R.A.

8 COMMON MISCONCEPTIONS JEWS HAVE ABOUT JUDAISM

Bar Mitzvah Is a Verb

The term "bar mitzvah" is neither an intransitive verb, as in "Herbie's son got bar mitzvahed last Saturday," nor a transitive verb, as in "The rabbi is going to bar mitzvah him when he's ready." In fact, its use as a noun—"I went to a nice bar mitzvah last week"—is also somewhat suspect. Bar mitzvah is neither an action nor an event. It is, one might say, a state of being.

A boy *becomes* bar mitzvah (literally "a son of the commandment") simply by attaining the age of thirteen years; a girl becomes bat mitzvah by turning twelve. A person who is bar or bat mitzvah is no longer considered a child by the standards of Jewish law and is obligated to fulfill his/her adult religious responsibilities. In traditional communities the boy is obligated to wear *tefillin* (phylacteries) during the morning prayers, can be counted as a member of a *minyan* (quorum for prayer), and can be called up to the Torah for an *aliyah* (honor in the Torah service).

At the time of the child's becoming bar or bat mitzvah the parents are freed from responsibility for the deeds of the child and a blessing denoting this change in status is recited by the parents.

In contemporary usage bar mitzvah often refers to a synagogue ceremony marking the first public occasion of the child's assuming his or her majority. The bar or bat mitzvah ceremony varies depending on the community and the religious orientation of the family. Usually the ceremony consists of an *aliyah* to the Torah and the chanting of the *haftarah* (prophetic portion) on a Sabbath near the child's birthday. In some congregations the child delivers a speech, leads the service, or reads from the Torah scroll.

But even if there is no ceremony, a person becomes bar or bat mitzvah at the age of majority.

Judaism Is a Religion Which Never Sought Converts

Although Judaism is generally thought of as a religion that rejects the seeking of converts, proselytizing, particularly in ancient times, was far from uncommon. The discussions of conversion in the Talmud and later legal codes are extensive, and nontraditional sources (such as Josephus and the New Testament) also indicate that conversion to Judaism was welcomed and at times actively sought. In the Talmud, for example, Rabbi Johanan and Rabbi Eleazar stated that "the Holy One, blessed be He, exiled Israel among the nations only in order to increase their numbers with the addition of proselytes." (*Pesahim* 87b)

The major turning point against proselytizing activity occurred with the ascension of Constantine as emperor of Rome. As a Christian, the emperor enacted various restrictions on Judaism, including a ban on proselytizing, and ordered the death penalty for anyone who converted to Judaism.

Nonetheless, later Jewish history saw a number of important instances of conversion. The most unusual, in this regard, is the story of the Khazars, a Turkish people whose nation Khazaria was located east of the Black Sea. For reasons that are somewhat unclear, the king and the royal house of the Khazars converted to Judaism sometime in the eighth century. Scholars speculate that the conversion was instigated by a desire to find a "neutral" religion between the opposing forces of Christian and Islamic political powers in the region. The story of the Khazars has inspired much legend and speculation. Judah Halevi's medieval philosophical masterpiece, *The Kuzari* (twelfth century), takes its dramatic setting from the story of Khazaria (see "10 Jewish Classics at a Glance").

In 1978 the question of proselytizing arose as an issue after Rabbi Alexander Schindler, president of the Reform movement's Union of American Hebrew Congregations, asserted that he felt it was time "to launch a carefully conceived outreach program aimed at all Americans who are unchurched and who are seeking roots in religion." Schindler's view was based on his sense of crisis in the American Jewish community because of a sharp demographic decline and the growing influence of destructive religious cults. By and large, however, the Jewish community has not advocated a return to active proselytizing.

Mourner's Kaddish Is a Prayer for the Dead

This widely held misconception derives from the fact that during the eleven-month period of bereavement, a form of the *Kaddish* (literally, Sanctification) is recited at the various daily prayer services by the mourner.

However, the prayer itself is not about death nor is its usage limited to the mourner. The "mourner's *Kaddish*" is only one of four similar types of *Kaddish* prayers used during the service. The prayer is an affirmation of God's greatness, stating that God is "glorified and sanctified throughout the world," and that He is "beyond all the blessings and hymns . . . that are ever spoken in the world."

The *Kaddish* is of great antiquity, dating from at least the sixth century C.E., and is written almost entirely in Aramaic, the vernacular tongue of the ancient Babylonian Jewish community.

Originally, the *Kaddish* was not even part of the prayer service itself but was recited as a separate prayer, concluding the public Torah study sessions. This form of the *Kaddish*, now containing an interpolation in behalf of scholars and rabbis and known as the "*Kaddish de-Rabbanan,*" and is recited today after any session of Torah study.

The prayer service contains two other forms of this prayer, in addition to the mourner's *Kaddish* and the *Kaddish de-Rabbanan:* the full *Kaddish* and the half *Kaddish*. These prayers serve the role of "punctuation marks," denoting divisions between different sections of the worship service, and serving as introductions to other sections.

The mourner's *Kaddish* appears several times in the service. The custom of a *Kaddish* for the mourners may have originated during the German persecutions of the thirteenth century. The symbolic significance of the prayer in this context is the assertion by the mourner of God's ultimate justice and power. The mourner, in reciting the *Kaddish*, accepts the divine decision, symbolized by his/her asserting that God is "blessed and praised, glorified and exalted." At no time, however, does the prayer mention the dead or ask for divine intervention on behalf of the departed.

Judaism Does Not Believe in an Afterlife

Jews sometimes like to compare their religion to Christianity and state that while Christianity is "other world" oriented, Judaism is focused on the "here and now." This may be partly true, but it would be incorrect to say that Judaism does not believe in an afterlife.

The Bible has a fairly undefined view of man's fate after death. *Sheol*, a shadowy world of the departed, is alluded to (Num. 16:33), but the details of this existence are unstated. Only in the relatively late book of Daniel is there the first clear statement of a resurrection of the dead; "Many of them that sleep in the dust of the earth shall awake, some to everlasting life, and some to reproaches and everlasting abhorrence." (Dan. 12:2)

Jewish literature, since rabbinic times, however, is filled with statements about "the World to Come," both describing what the afterlife will be like and announcing the ways that one can "attain the World to Come" or be excluded from it! The Talmud, particularly in the tractate *Sanhedrin*, discusses the resurrection of the dead in considerable detail, and the life of the soul after death is a much-discussed topic in many other rabbinic texts, e.g. Exodus Rabbah 52:3, Berakhot 18b–19a. (See "Life in the Hereafter.") Not only can descriptions be found of the heavenly "Garden of Eden," that is Paradise, but also of Gehenna, a hellish abode of wicked souls (Shabbat 152b–153a).

The Jewish mystical tradition also developed a system, known as *gilgul*, describing transmigration of souls. This literature both describes the reincarnation of certain great Jewish figures of the past in the persons of later teachers and delineates the torment of sinners whose souls can wander through various bodies throughout history before achieving rest. (See "Rituals for Jewish Exorcism.")

Judaism Is a Rational Religious System

The idea that Judaism is a *rational* religious system emerges, by and large, as a legacy from the nineteenth-century German Jewish historians and religious theologians such as Heinrich Graetz. In their desire, perhaps, to harmonize the teachings of their religion with post-Enlightenment Western European culture, these historians and theologians denigrated and denied important areas of Jewish experience and consciousness that are only now being placed in their proper perspective. The revitalized interest in mysticism can be seen simply by comparing the few articles on the subject in the 1906 *Jewish Encyclopedia* to the hundreds of pages (more than on any other single subject!) in the recent *Encyclopaedia Judaica.*

The significance of the magical, the mysterious, the superstitious cannot be denied in Jewish thought, particularly in Jewish "folk religion," which prized amulets and demons, *dybbuks* and departed souls. More, important, however, is the realm of serious Jewish spirituality—the world of Kabbalah, Jewish mysticism, and Hasidism. Largely through the pioneering efforts of Gershom Scholem and his students, the richness and importance of the Jewish mystical tradition has begun to be reconstructed. Unlike the historians of a century ago, Scholem has shown that mysticism was not some abnormal divergence from the ongoing path of Jewish rationalism; rather, it was important—in fact, quite possibly *more* important—than what has been called "mainstream Judaism." In many cases, according to Scholem, mysticism *was* mainstream Judaism!

One telling revision in the older view of Jewish history has been the contemporary perception of the importance of Shabbatai Tzvi, the false Messiah of the seventeenth century. For the older Jewish historians Shabbatai Tzvi was an embarrassing but insignificant blemish on the face of Jewish history. Scholem's studies, however, have shown that the messianic movement engendered by Shabbatai Tzvi was startingly widespread and that its later influence on Jewish history has been remarkably profound, particularly its effect on the later growth and development of Hasidism. (See "9 Jewish False Messiahs")

You Need a Rabbi to Have a "Jewish" Marriage Ceremony

Many current perceptions of the role of the rabbi have little to do with traditional Jewish law. According to the tradition, one does not need a rabbi to conduct a marriage ceremony, give a sermon, lead prayers, conduct a "bar mitzvah," officiate at a funeral, or oversee a *brit milah* (ritual circumcision). In short, there is no religious ritual for which a rabbi is required! One possible exception, traditionally, might be in the matter of a *get* (a divorce proceeding) and there only because the law is particularly complex, requiring knowledgeable officials.

From ancient times the primary function of the rabbi was that of teacher and judge. His credentials were his knowledge of law and his acceptance by his peers. His expertise in the law and the commentaries made him the logical choice as preacher, but these public discourses probably resembled teaching more than the preaching of a sermon.

The role of the rabbi began to change in the nineteenth century, when Jews first entered the mainstream of western society. In many places the secular governments refused to accept the jurisdiction of Jewish (rabbinical) courts, and thus the rabbi's role as judge, except in matters of ritual life, began to diminish.

At the same time, Jews, particularly Reform and "Enlightenment" Jews, were influenced by images of the clergy that they saw in the non-Jewish world. In matters of dress, such as in the wearing of robes during prayer services (in England rabbis until recently often wore a clerical collar!), and in matters of function, the rabbi began to resemble his Christian compatriot, particularly in open societies like England, Germany, and the United States. With the rise of Reform Judaism, this change in role and style became quite evident. The rabbi became a cleric—preaching in the synagogue, performing weddings, conducting services, counselling the troubled, and visiting the sick. To some extent all branches of Judaism have been influenced by the new role of the rabbi.

Today in the United States the rabbi, like his Christian counterpart, will sign the marriage license, validating the marriage in the eyes of the secular authorities. Nonetheless, according to *Jewish* law, what counts at the marriage ceremony is the reliability of the witnesses, not the presence of a rabbi.

Yom Kippur Atones for a Person's Sins

This statement is only partially correct. According to the tradition, in most cases Yom Kippur offers a chance for atonement for sins between a person and God, such as descrating the Sabbath or failing to fulfill one's ritual obligations. In certain instances Yom Kippur is not even necessary for atonement. Repentance itself is sufficient. In other cases even Yom Kippur is not adequate—suffering, and in particularly severe situations, death may also be needed for complete atonement.

More noteworthy are the procedures pertaining to sins that occur only between people—such as cheating in business or lying. The Talmud states that in these situations one must first seek forgiveness from the person who has been wronged, then Yom Kippur can complete the process. The tradition asserts that a person must approach the injured party and make an exhaustive effort to gain personal forgiveness. He must make restitution for things that were stolen. If the injured person refuses to forgive him, the sinner must announce in a public forum that he has repeatedly sought forgiveness, but that it has been denied him. Even if the injured party has died, the sinner must assemble a *minyan* at the other's grave and announce his desire for forgiveness before God and the soul of the deceased.

The Talmud undermines a possible loophole in the process by stating that it is a grievious sin to transgress the law while planning to get atonement on Yom Kippur!

All Work Is Forbidden on the Sabbath

Although the statement that work is forbidden on the Sabbath is true, the problem lies in how one defines the concept of work! In what way, for instance, is turning on a light in the present day and age really work? Is carrying a chair work? What about reading or taking a walk or playing chess?

When the Bible states that one "shall not do any manner of work" (Exod. 20:10) on the Sabbath, it does not elucidate its definition of the word "work." Only a few particular deeds are specifically forbidden by the Torah, such as baking, cooking, lighting a fire, and gathering wood.

Later, the rabbis of the Talmud sought to define the concept of work by deducing thirty-nine specific categories of labor forbidden on *Shabbat*. These categories are based on an interpretation of the types of labor mentioned in connection with the building of the Tabernacle in the desert (Exod. 31), which work was suspended for the Sabbath.

A typical example of the problems encountered in thinking of the Sabbath as a time when all "work" is forbidden can be seen in the case of prohibitions about carrying. According to Jewish law, carrying heavy furniture from one part of the house into another is permissible, but carrying even a handkerchief from one's home into the street is forbidden! The important distinction is the public versus the private domain. Carrying from the private domain (the house or enclosed garden) to the public or vice versa is prohibited, as is carrying in the public domain itself for any appreciable distance. Carrying exclusively within the private domain, however, is permitted!

The thirty-nine categories of work leave many issues open for debate. True to its nature, the traditional literature has debated the fine points of these questions throughout the centuries. In the past hundred years many new problem areas, previously unanticipated, have emerged with the growth of "labor-saving" technology, problems such as the permissibility of using totally electric and self-operating devices. If the labor is saved, is the deed still considered "work"?

Jewish theologians have sought to resolve some of these difficulties by attempting to define the underlying *idea* of work that should guide the decision-making process. Some have seen work as connected to effort; some have emphasized the idea that work is a deed that implies man's mastery over the world (on the Sabbath, therefore, work is refrained from in order to reassert God's true dominion over the world); others have argued that work is connected to man's relationship with nature or to the sacredness of time. All definitions agree that "work" is forbidden on the Sabbath. How the distinctions are determined is the challenge and often the bone of contention.

—B.W.H.

SOME LITTLE-KNOWN BUT FASCINATING BLESSINGS

Jewish life is suffused with *brachot*—blessings. Most *brachot* occur during the course of moments of prayer, either in the synagogue or while praying alone. The central weekday prayer, the *Amidah*, contains nineteen such blessings. As it is recited three times daily, the *Amidah* provides the Jew with a frequent avenue of communication with God, and an opportunity to remind himself of certain critical ideas and concepts: the continuity of Jewish history reaching back to Abraham, Isaac, and Jacob; God as reviver of the dead, source of wisdom and sight, forgiver of sins, defender of Israel, healer, provider of food. In it are hopes for the Messiah, the rebuilding of Jerusalem, a desire for the ingathering of the Jews exiled in foreign lands, an awareness of the daily miracles of life, cravings for peace. It is by far the most extensive collection of blessings within the prayerbook, and an excellent place to begin a study of the Jewish understanding of blessings.

Although this particular array of *brakhot* is central to the Jew's daily experience, there are, of course, other blessings to be recited: some in other parts of the prayer-service, and others in the four blessings that constitute the *Birkhat ha-Mazon* (the words of thanks after meals). Jewish literature mentions that a Jew should recite one hundred blessings a day. At first this seems to be an overwhelming figure, but by simple addition the fundamental blessings mentioned above approach this number.

Beyond the blessings encountered in prayer, a variety of *brakhot* focus on the occasions and incidental events in the life of a Jew. Whether it be a unique moment in one's life, or an intense encounter with the sublime in nature, or an articulation of emotions that arise when having contact with the great joys and tragedies of life—the Jewish response has traditionally been a blessing. In addition, blessings are provided for seemingly ordinary events which might otherwise pass unnoticed, considered too common in the flow of daily living to be of any significance. The blessings serve to sensitize the Jew to the particular moment, placing it in a larger context of meaning.

A survey of the *brakhot* can serve two purposes: (1) to help the individual articulate a response to various special events in life, and (2) to arouse his awareness that many events—both great and small—are worthy of attention and reflection. By knowing that there is a *brakhah* for a certain occasion one may seek out opportunities for reciting it, opening himself to a new, more profound sensitivity to numerous life-moments.

Extensive lists of *brakhot* may be found in most complete prayerbooks. The following collection is taken from *Seder Avodat Yisrael* (Tel Aviv, 1957), edited by Rabbi Yitzchak ben Aryeh Yosef Dov Seligman.

Each of the following blessings begins with the standard formula, "Blessed are You, O Lord our God, King of the universe . . ."

on first seeing trees in their springtime blooming:

. . . Who has made the world so full it lacks nothing, and has created in it beautiful creatures and beautiful trees for human beings to enjoy.

on seeing lightning, comets, falling stars, vast deserts, great rivers, high mountains, experiencing a great storm or an earthquake, or seeing a strikingly clear morning after an all-night rainstorm:

. . . Who provides us with moments reminiscent of Creation.

on hearing thunder:

. . . Whose power and might fill the universe.

on seeing the rainbow:

. . . Who remembers the covenant, and keeps the covenant, and is faithful to His promise.

(The reference is to Genesis 9:18–27, which describes the appearance of the rainbow after the Flood. At that time, God promised humanity not to bring such destruction again, the rainbow serving as a sign of this agreement.)

on seeing the ocean:

. . . Who has made the great sea.

(This blessing and the blessing for mountains and deserts—any awesome natural wonder—is recited only at the first sighting of the vista, and thereafter at intervals of thirty days. This time stipulation allows the awestruck observer the opportunity to regain the sense of wonder which might be diminished by everyday contact with these presences.)

on seeing beautifully formed people, animals, or trees:

. . . that such (magnificent) things are found in this world.

on seeing unusual-looking people, such as giants, dwarfs, and albinos:

. . . Who creates a variety of creations.

on seeing a sage distinguished for his knowledge of Torah:

. . . Who has imparted of His wisdom to those who stand in awe of Him.

on seeing a sage distinguished for his secular knowledge:

. . . Who has given of His wisdom to human beings.

on seeing royalty accompanied by an entourage:

. . . Who has given of His majesty to human beings.

on seeing 600,000 Jews in one place:

. . . Who, in His wisdom, knows their innermost thoughts.

(The interpretation of this blessing is that, despite the vast numbers in the crowd, God is aware of each individual's specific dreams, plans, secret wishes, and desires.)

on seeing a place where a miracle has occurred in one's life:

. . . Who has performed a miracle for me in this place.

on seeing a place where a miracle has occurred for one's ancestors:

. . . Who has performed a miracle for my ancestors in this place.

on seeing a place where a miracle has occurred for the Jews:

. . . Who has performed a miracle for our ancestors in this place.

(There are a number of places in Israel where this blessing could be recited.)

on leaving the bathroom:

. . . Who has created human beings in wisdom, and created in them numerous openings and passageways. It is well known by Your Presence that if one of them opens or closes improperly, it would be impossible to continue to exist. Blessed are You, Healer of all bodies, Worker of wonders.

on completion of building a guard-rail around any potentially dangerous place on one's property:

. . . Who has sanctified us by His commandments and commanded us to make a guard-rail.

(This blessing originally applied to a protective rail around the flat roof of one's house, where people often sat. Its application has been expanded to include fences around pits or holes in the ground where one might fall and sustain injury.)

on moving into a house or apartment, at the moment the mezuzah *is attached to the doorpost*:

. . . Who has sanctified us by His commandments and commanded us to attach a *mezuzah*.

(This *brakhah* is accompanied by the *Shehecheyanu*, which is explained below.)

on putting on new clothes:

. . . Who gives clothes to the naked.

(This *brakhah* is also accompanied by the *Sheheheyanu*.)

on smelling fragrant trees or fragrant bark of a tree, such as cinnamon, myrtle, roses, or rosemary:

. . . Who creates fragrant trees.

on smelling fragrant plants, such as mint or rue:

. . . Who creates fragrant plants.

on smelling spices:

. . . Who creates a variety of spices.

(This blessing may also be used for the previous two categories, if one is uncertain of the specific *brakhah*.)

on smelling fragrant fruits:

. . . Who gives a fragrant scent to fruits.

on smelling fragrant oils, such as balsam oil:

. . . Who creates fragrant oils.

on seeing synagogues and Jewish settlements rebuilt from ruins:

. . . Who replaces the widows' boundaries.

(The widow is, of course, the Jewish people, and the boundary is a boundary-mark set up to establish one's domain. The blessing means that, once again, the Jew's right has been reestablished to live or pray in this place. The blessing is based on Proverbs 15:25, "God will bring down the house of the arrogant and restore the boundaries of the widow.")

on hearing bad tidings, or at the moment of tearing one's clothing on the occasion of the death of a family member, or on seeing a synagogue in ruins:

. . . the True Judge.

(Jewish tradition prescribes that even in time of misfortune a blessing should be recited.)

on seeing a Jewish cemetery:

. . . Who created you justly, and fed and sustained you justly, and took your life back justly, and knows the number of all of you for judgment, and who will in the future revive you with justice. Blessed are you, Reviver of the dead.

on emerging from a potentially dangerous situation:

. . . Who gives benefit to people, even beyond their merits; Who has treated me favorably.

(This blessing was originally recited on the following four occasions: on completing a long sea voyage, on having passed through a desert to a settlement, on being released from jail, and on recovering from illness. It has been subsequently broadened to take in all potentially dangerous situations. It is to be recited in the presence of ten people [nowadays, generally at a *minyan*, after receiving an *aliyah*]. The ten people respond: "May He who has treated you favorably continue to do so, Selah.")

on seeing a close friend after a period of twelve months without communication:

. . . Who brings the dead back to life.

on hearing good tidings which are of benefit to oneself and to others:

. . . Who is good and causes good to happen.

(This blessing is also recited by parents on the occasion of the birth of a child.)

on a bar mitzvah having concluded his aliyah (being called up) to the Torah, the blessing is said by the father:

Blessed is He who has freed me from the responsibility for this one.

The final blessing—*Sheheheyanu*—has been mentioned above. Its form is as follows:

"Blessed are You, O Lord our God, King of the universe, Who has kept us alive, preserved us, and allowed us to reach this occasion."

There are many opportunities for the recitation of this *brakhah*, some of which are as follows:

1. As the second *brakhah* when putting on new clothes for the first time.
2. When acquiring and making use of new utensils. This may include a wide array of things, from dishes to an automobile.
3. As the second blessing when attaching a *mezuzah*.
4. When tasting a fruit for the first time as it appears during the new season.
5. On hearing good tidings which are of benefit to oneself alone.
6. On seeing a close friend after a period of a month, if there has been no exchange of letters or phone calls during that time.
7. On inheriting money or property, if one is the sole heir. (If there are other heirs, the *brakhah* ". . . Who is good and causes good to happen" is recited.)
8. On other major life occasions, such as a bar mitzvah, wedding, wedding anniversary, reaching the age of seventy, or arrival in Israel. This expanded application of the blessing is an expression of the Jew's thankfulness for being allowed to live to see that particular moment.

—D.S.

VOICES FROM THE HEART: WOMEN'S DEVOTIONAL PRAYERS

Tehinnot—the petitionary prayers of European Jewish women—are remembered by few and recited by fewer still. And yet, from the late sixteenth century through the nineteenth, so many books of *tehinnot* were published that the great nineteenth-century Jewish bibliographers felt unequal to the task of cataloguing them all.

Personal and intimate, the *tehinnot* were a way of talking to God that arose out of the lives of women and could only have been recited by them. "A prayer for an orphan to say on her wedding day," "A prayer to say when a child is ill, God forbid," "A prayer to say after giving birth"—how different these are from the prayers of the *siddur* (the collection of Hebrew prayers written by and used primarily by Jewish men).

While the men in the synagogue were addressing God as members of the community of Israel, evoking the collective history of the people and praising or beseeching God in the plural voice, each woman in her home or at her labors was asking God's help in her own name, speaking in a private language, direct and emotional. The prayers in the *siddur* are structured around the required daily, Sabbath, and festival services, fixed by clock and calendar. But the *tehinnot* were responses to the special commandments of women—lighting Sabbath candles, separating the *hallah* dough, and ritual immersion—which were carried out privately and not at set times, or to Rosh Hodesh, the celebration of the New Moon each month when women alone were exempted from heavy work. Unlike the *siddur*, written in Hebrew, the sacred tongue then reserved for study and prayer, *tehinnot* were spoken in the Yiddish vernacular, which was easily accessible to any European woman.

Compare the language of asking God to listen in the *Amidah*, the central prayer of the *siddur* services: "Hear our voice, Lord our God, spare us and have pity on us, accept our prayer in mercy and favor, for You are God who hears prayers and supplications; from Your presence, our King, dismiss us not empty-handed, for You hear in mercy the prayer of Your people Israel. Blessed are you, O Lord, who hears prayer," with these lines from a *tehinnah* for a woman to bring up children well: "O great almighty God, who besides You knows the worry of bringing up children which the poor mother must endure. How many illnesses and dangers the poor children are subjected to! And how the poor mother must drain the cup of sorrow and trouble! Merciful Father, hear the prayer of Your handmaid, who comes to pour out her heavy heart before You."

The *Amidah* opens by invoking the God of the Patriarchs, "God of Abraham, God of Isaac, and God of Jacob," while the *tehinnot* refer to the merits of the Matriarchs—Sarah, Rebecca, Rachel, and Leah, as well as other more obscure women out of the Jewish past, such as "the wife of the prophet Obadiah." The *Amidah*, emblematic of the *siddur* as a whole, contains prayers that praise God, prayers of petition and prayers of thanksgiving. But the *tehinnot* were only petitions, reflecting a worshipper who saw herself always engaged in entreaty, beseeching God to protect her domain—home, husband, and children—from harm.

By reading the *tehinnot*, then, it is possible to understand the religious life of European Jewish women, centered around the individual and those closest to her, in contrast to the *siddur*, concerned with the people Israel and its collective relationship to God. The formal and public aspects of religious life were reserved for men, while the domestic and private spheres were for women. The *tehinnot* were part of a devotional literature used by women in those spheres, including the *Tze'nah u-Re'nah*—the Yiddish paraphrase of the Bible—and the *musar* (morality) books.

The most famous woman author of *tehinnot* was Sarah bas Tovim. All that is known about her is that she was born in the late seventeenth century into a respectable and learned family and that for some reason she became impoverished and was forced to wander across the face of Europe. Sarah bas Tovim was the author of two widely-read collections of *tehinnot*: *Sheker ha-Hen* ("Grace is Deceitful," derived from a verse in Proverbs, 31:10–31, known as "The Woman of Valor") contains prayers for Mondays and Thursdays, when the Torah is read in the synagogue, for fast days, and for the High Holidays; *Sheloshah She'arim* ("Three Gates") consists of *tehinnot* for the three women's commandments, for the blessing of the New Moon, and for the High Holidays.

Not all the *tehinnot* attributed to Sarah bas Tovim were actually written by her, however. In the nineteenth century, *tehinnot* as utterances of piety took on a bizarre twist. Starving *maskilim*, supporters of the Enlightenment, began to earn a few pennies by fabricating *tehinnot*, to which they attached the names of well-known women authors. These were then sold to printers on commission and bought by women. Ironically, not only were these *tehinnot* forgeries but they were written in a spirit of cynicism and scorn, for virtually all the *maskilim* despised both the Yiddish language as well as the style and content of the prayers. And yet, the spiritual need was so great that they were accepted by the women as authentic and uttered in the same spirit as the earlier works.

Although the *tehinnot* are too limited a model for women today, addressing themselves to only part of women's lives, they are a way of approaching God that can reverberate for both men and women. The realm of feeling—of love between mother and child, friend and friend, wife and husband—can be offered up for blessing. Once Jewish women called on God to be present in their most intimate daily lives, and that is still the possibility of prayer.

Tehinnot for the New Moon

The Jewish calender is based on the cycles of the moon, and each month begins with the appearance of the new crescent. On the Sabbath before the New Moon a prayer is recited in synagogues announcing the day on which the month will begin and expressing hopes that the new month will bring peace, health, sustenance, and redemption. During the "Blessing the New Moon," women would recite *tehinnot.* Because women biologically have a special affinity with the lunar cycle and until the late Middle Ages celebrated the New Moon as a half holiday, mention of the Matriarchs was common on this occasion. The *tehinnah* of the Matriarchs given below alludes not only to biblical stories but also to the legends of the Midrash, especially those about Rachel and Leah.

From a "*Tehinnah for the blessing of the new moon*":

"Lord of the whole world, You have created no human organ in vain. My eyes have You opened to see Your Kingdom, and my ears to hear the wonder of Your whole world, and my mouth to tell Your greatness. My hands do Your commandments: Dear God, You have commanded us to separate the dough for *hallah*, and to kindle the Sabbath lights, and to inspect ourselves for menstrual impurity, so that our souls may remain pure. And with my feet I go to synagogue to praise You and walk in Your way. My breasts were created to suckle children, so that they may grow strong. Therefore I pray You, dear God, that no evil eye or evil spirits gain power over my children, and that they not meet a violent death. May You strengthen the hearts of my children in the Torah, and may their hearts be open like the doors of the Porch and Sanctuary of the Temple. May we see their children busying themselves with Torah and *mitzvot.* May my eye weep no tear of sadness or worry, and may my ear hear no lament or mourning, not for any of my household. And may our mouths not be fed through the charity of other people. And may we be worthy to see salvation and comfort."

"*The* tehinnah *of the Matriarchs Sarah, Rebecca, Rachel, and Leah*":

"Lord of the world, Almighty God! In Your great mercy, You have created heaven and earth and all their creatures in six days. The seventh day is the holy Sabbath, on which You rested from Your labor. And You have also commanded Your beloved people Israel—in whom You glory, as it says in the verse, 'Israel in whom I glory' (Isaiah 49:3)—them have You commanded to rest on the holy Sabbath from all work and also from unnecessary speech: They should speak only words of Torah, and should learn Torah, each according to his own ability. Women, too, should know how to keep their commandments, which God has commanded them.

"You have also given us New Moons. Just as the Sanhedrin used to consecrate the New Moon, so do we consecrate the New Moon. On the Sabbath before the New Moon we say the blessing, and that time is auspicious for prayer. Therefore we spread out our hands to God, be blessed, and we pray that You bring us back to Jerusalem and renew our days of old. For now we have no Temple, and no altar, and no High Priest who can make atonement for us. We

Girl's heder (Hebrew school) in Poland

have only our prayer in place of the sacrifices.

"Therefore, accept our prayer and may You answer us in this new month, by the merit of our Mother Sarah, for whose sake you said, 'Do not touch for evil my lords, and to my prophets do no harm.' (Ps. 105:15) And by the merit of our Mother Rebecca, who caused our Father Jacob to receive the blessings from his Father Isaac. May those blessings soon be fulfilled for Israel her children! And by the merit of our Mother Rachel, the faithful, about whom you said that for her sake Israel her children would go forth from exile. When Israel was led into the captivity of Nebuzaradan, they passed not far from the grave in which Mother Rachel lay. They pleaded with their captors to let them visit the grave. And when the children of Israel came to the grave of our Mother Rachel and began to weep and cry, 'Our faithful mother, how can you look on while we are being led into captivity?' Rachel stood up to God, be blessed, with a bitter cry, and spoke: 'Lord of the worlds! Your mercy is certainly greater than that of any human being. Moreover, since I had compassion on my sister Leah, when our father switched us and gave her to my husband Jacob in my place, then You, O God, should be completely merciful and compassionate. It is fitting for You to have mercy.' Thus did God answer, 'You have convinced me. I will bring your children out of their troubles.' Therefore we pray You that this may be fulfilled, by her merit. And by the merit of our Mother Leah, who wept day and night for fear she would fall to the lot of Esau, until as a result her eyes became dim. By her merit, may You enlighten our eyes in the darkness.

"We were called the children of our Father Abraham; how is it that today we are so desolate? 'Wash me thoroughly of my sins' (Ps. 51:9) Renew and bring about for us this New Month for joy, and may all be turned around for us for good. You are truly our great King. May You elevate us, and return us to good, by the merit of our holy Fathers, Abraham, Isaac, and Jacob. Amen."

Tehinnot for the "Women's *Mitzvot*"

Since Mishnaic times three commandments were the particular responsibility of women. The first, referred to as "*hallah*" involves the taking out of a small portion of the bread dough, which was then burned in the oven in memory of the portion given to the priests when the Temple was standing. "*Niddah*," the second commandment, requires a woman to separate herself from her husband, physically and sexually, during menstruation. After the completion of her menstrual period she inspects herself daily, counting seven "clean" days on which no blood flows. At the end of this time she bathes and then immerses herself in the ritual bath. She then rejoins her husband as if she were again a bride. "*Hadlakah*," the kindling of the Sabbath lights, is the third commandment. Since Jewish law prohibits lighting fires on the Sabbath, the woman lights the candles just at dusk, before the Sabbath begins. All of these women's observances were naturally popular subjects for *tehinnot*.

"This she says when she throws the piece of dough into the oven":

"Lord of the worlds, You hold all blessing. I come now to honor Your holiness, and I pray You to give Your blessing to what I bake. Send an angel to guard the baking, so that everything will be well baked, pleasing, and not burnt. May this baking, over which we make the holy blessing, honor Your holy Sabbath, which You have chosen, that Your people Israel may rest thereon. God, listen to my voice, for You are the One who hears those who call upon You with the whole heart. May You be praised to eternity!"

"This she says when she goes to immerse herself":

"Lord of all the worlds, You have sanctified Your people Israel more than all peoples, and have commanded them to cleanse themselves of impurity, and to wash their flesh in water and be clean. Almighty God, today, the time for me to purify myself has come. My God, may it be Your will that my cleanness, and washing, and immersion, be accounted before You like all the purity of all the pious women of Israel who purify themselves and immerse themselves at the proper time. God Almighty, listen to my prayer, for You are the One who hears the prayers of Israel Your children. May the words of my mouth and the thoughts of my heart be acceptable before You, God, my creator and redeemer."

"A beautiful tehinnah *to say after lighting candles, with great devotion"*:

"Lord of the world, I praise and thank Your beloved Name that I have been privileged to fulfil the commandment You have given to women. As our sages write in the Talmud (Shabbat 31b), women are obligated to bless the lights on Friday at evening. By Your favor, may I be privileged to perform this *mitzvah* until my hundredth year. And may I take care not to kindle the lights after sunset, by which I would make of this *mitzvah* the greatest of trespasses, the profanation of the Sabbath, which is as bad as violating the entire Torah. And by the merit of this *mitzvah*, I hope and ask of Your Holy Name, that my children will not, God forbid, be profaners of the Sabbath. May the light of the Torah enlighten their eyes, so that they may not, God forbid, stumble in sin. As it is written, 'The righteous walk in the straight, right path, as one who goes in daylight, but the impious walk in darkness.' (Prov. 4:18–19)

"And because I have received the dear holy Sabbath at the proper time, with great honor, and beautified it with lovely lights, I pray You, O Holy One, that I may be privileged to have children who are learned in the Torah, so that I may have joy from them in this world and the next."

Tehinnot for the Cemetery

Going to visit the graves of the dead was an important religious event for both women and men in European Jewish society. In the cemetery, known as the *Bet ha-Hayim*, "House of Life," a woman could talk to the dead, invite them to important family events, tell them her sorrows, and ask them to intercede with God. Standing among the graves of the pious, she also could ask God's help.

The *tehinnah* given here is excerpted from a set of *tehinnot* to be said while visiting the graves of relatives and other pious people. The elaborateness of this cycle shows the importance of the cemetery visit in the religious lives of women: There are *tehinnot* to be said before going to the cemetery, upon entering the cemetery, when prostrating oneself on the graves, when visiting the graves of sainted people, and before leaving. In many collections of *tehinnot*, there are more *tehinnot* for visiting the cemetery than for any other event.

"A tehinnah *to be said at the graves of sainted people"*:

"Happy are you, righteous men and women! Happy are you, pious men and women! Happy are you, O whole ones! Happy are you, completely just ones! Happy are you, O chosen ones! Happy are you, O wise ones! Happy are you, of perfect understanding! Happy are you, O holy ones! Happy are you, who have bestirred yourselves to perform commandments and good works! Happy are you, who have strengthened yourselves to do the will and desire of your Creator, praised be He! Happy are you, who serve the Ground of all being! How much good is laid up for you, and for all those who fear God's holy Name, who take refuge in God's holiness! God of Israel, look upon those who fear You, and call upon You, and trust in Your covenant, these precious ones who lie here at rest. In life and in death, they were not divided from Your holiness, which rests on their pure souls.

"God and Lord, who hears the prayers of Israel Your children, hear me, and may the merit of those buried here illuminate my life. My God, and God of my forebears, fulfill my prayer for good, and give me grace, compassion and mercy, in Your eyes and in the eyes of all Your creatures. Account me, my husband, my children, and all my household among those who join themselves to You, and love You and Your Torah and commandments. Give us long life, blessing and joy, without any cause to blush. Protect us from all evil, shame and slander. May Your name not be profaned through us, and may Your fear and love be with us at every hour. And may we not sin. Nourish us, and give us our food and necessities generously, by Your own holy hand, with peace and blessing, not hardship, and with justice and honor, not disgrace. Protect us from serious illnesses, unfortunate happenings, and torment. Lead us, step by certain step, into the land of eternal life. Remember the piety of our forebears to our credit.

"Call forth Your power to revive the dead, and strengthen Your truth to those who sleep here in the earth, and to all those, buried here and elsewhere, who died in holiness, with great remorse over their misdeeds. You have received their souls and hidden them in Paradise, with all the souls that are pure and worthy of eternal life. Amen."

Tehinnot for Private Occasions

Many *tehinnot* were not connected with any ritual event and were recited on purely private occasions whenever the woman felt the need for them: "A *tehinnah* for a woman when her husband is ill, God forbid," "A *tehinnah* for an unmarried orphan girl," "A *tehinnah* for a woman before the wedding of her son or daughter." The *tehinnah* given here is a prayer for guidance in bringing up children. It expresses the difficulties of child-rearing under the uncertain conditions of Jewish life in Europe.

"*A* tehinnah *for a woman to bring up children well*":

"Lord of all the worlds, Father of all creatures! By Your holy will, You have created human beings, together with all the varied creatures in the world. But while You have endowed human beings with sense and reason to understand Your might, the strong hand with which You guide us in every step of our short life, at the same time, O great Creator, You have set us lower than all other creatures in the world. For all of Your creatures, as soon as they go forth from their mother's flesh, sprout up like grass, and are reared without trouble. But the human, the pride of Your creation, the ornament of Your work, to whom You have given of Your splendor, and whom You have created in Your own image—O, how much suffering and pain, how much trouble and worry does it cost his parents until they stand him on his feet, until they make him into a person! O great almighty God, who besides You knows the worry of bringing up children which the poor mother must endure. How many illnesses and dangers the poor children are subjected to! And how the poor mother must drain the cup of sorrow and trouble! Merciful Father, hear the prayer of Your handmaid, who comes to pour out her heavy heart before You. Hear me, merciful God, and lighten the heavy yoke of bringing up my children. Protect them from the evil eye, and from serious illness. May I be a mother who is worthy to raise her children according to Your will. May I be privileged to see them find favor in Your eyes, and in the eyes of others. May they live as Jews, according to Your holy will, and walk in Your ways, and keep Your Torah. That will be my recompense, the great reward from Your generous hand for the trouble I bear from them now. And I will praise God, and bless Your holy Name throughout my whole life, and I will recall all the great good You have done for me, until I breathe my last. Amen."

—C.W.

DOING WHAT COMES NATURALLY (ALMOST)

THE 613 COMMANDMENTS

(Bill Aron)

According to rabbinic tradition, there are 613 *mitzvot* (commandments) included in the Torah. Although the number (known as *taryag*, a mnemonic formed by translating the numbers into their corresponding Hebrew letters) is in some ways arbitrary, several sources have been cited for deriving it. Noting the biblical passage "The Torah was commanded to us by Moses . . ." (Deut. 33:4), commentators have calculated that the numerical equivalent for the Hebrew word "Torah" is 611; however, since God Himself pronounced the first two of the Ten Commandments directly (not through Moses), the total number of commandments is 613. Another source, noting the division of commandments into positives and negatives (do's and don'ts) and wishing to draw an organic connection between the performance of the *mitzvot* and the life of the individual, comments that the 365 prohibitions correspond to the supposedly 365 veins in the body (or the 365 days of the year) and the 248 positive commandments correspond to the supposedly 248 bones in the body.

Regardless of its derivation, however, the concept of *taryag mitzvot* has long become standard and accepted. Just what these commandments are, where they are found, and how they are to be divided has formed the basis of controversy from early rabbinic times. The list that follows is that enumerated by Maimonides in his *Sefer ha-Mitzvot* (Book of Commandments). These are divided into Mandatory Commandments and Prohibitions with the biblical source (not always obvious) cited in the margins.

—The Eds.

MANDATORY COMMANDMENTS

God.

The Jew is required to [1]believe that God exists and to [2]acknowledge His unity; to [3]love, [4]fear, and [5]serve Him. He is also commanded to [6]cleave to Him (by associating with and imitating the wise) and to [7]swear only by His name. One must [8]imitate God and [9]sanctify His name.

1. Ex. 20:2
2. Deut. 6:4
3. Deut. 6:5
4. Deut. 6:13
5. Ex. 23:25; Deut. 11:13 (Deut. 6:13 and and also 13:5)
6. Deut. 10:20
7. Deut. 10:20
8. Deut. 28:9
9. Lev. 22:32

Torah.

10. Deut. 6:7 The Jew must [10]recite the *Shema* each morning and eve-
11. Deut. 6:7 ning and [11]study the *Torah and teach it to others. He
12. Deut. 6:8 should bind *tefillin* on his [12]head and [13]his arm. He should 13. Deut. 6:8
14. Num. 15:38 make [14]**zizit* for his garments and [15]fix a **mezuzah* on the 15. Deut. 6:9
16. Deut. 31:12 door. The people are to be [16]assembled every seventh year
17. Deut. 17:18 to hear the Torah read and [17]the king must write a special
18. Deut. 31:19 copy of the Torah for himself. [18]Every Jew should have a
19. Deut. 8:10 Torah scroll. One should [19]praise God after eating.

Temple, and the Priests.

20. Ex. 25:8 The Jews should [20]build a *Temple and [21]respect it. It must 21. Lev. 19:30
22. Num. 18:4 be [22]guarded at all times and the [23]*Levites should preform 23. Num. 18:23
their special duties in it. Before entering the Temple or
participating in its service the priests [24]must wash their hands 24. Ex. 30:19
25. Ex. 27:21 and feet; they must also [25]light the candelabrum daily. The
26. Num. 6:23 priests are required to [26]bless Israel and to [27]set the shewbread 27. Ex. 25:30
and frankincense before the Ark. Twice daily they must
28. Ex. 30:7 [28]burn the incense on the golden altar. Fire shall be kept
29. Lev. 6:6 burning on the altar [29]continually and the ashes should be
30. Lev. 6:3 [30]removed daily. Ritually unclean persons must be [31]kept 31. Num. 5:2
32. Lev. 21:8 out of the Temple. Israel [32]should honor its priests, who
33. Ex. 28:2 must be [33]dressed in special priestly raiment. The priests
34. Num. 7:9 should [34]carry the Ark on their shoulders, and the holy
35. Ex. 30:31 anointing oil [35]must be prepared according to its special
formula. The priestly families should officiate in [36]rotation. 36. Deut. 18:6–8
In honor of certain dead close relatives the priests should
37. Lev. 21:2–3 [37]make themselves ritually unclean. The high priest may
38. Lev. 21:13 marry [38]only a virgin.

Sacrifices.

39. Num. 28:3 The [39]*tamid* sacrifice must be offered twice daily and the
40. Lev. 6:13 [40]high priest must also offer a meal-offering twice daily. An
additional sacrifice (*musaf*) should be offered [41]every Sab- 41. Num. 28:9
42. Num. 28:11 bath, [42]on the first of every month, and [43]on each of the 43. Lev. 23:36
seven days of *Passover. On the second day of Passover
44. Lev. 23:10 [44]a meal offering of the first barley must also be brought.
45. Num. 28:26-27 On *Shavuot a [45]*musaf* must be offered and [46]two loaves of 46. Lev. 23:17
bread as a wave offering. The additional sacrifice must also
47. Num. 29:1-2 be made on [47]*Rosh Ha-Shanah and [48]on the Day of 48. Num. 29:7-8
49. Lev. 16 *Atonement when the [49]*Avodah must also be performed.
On every day of the festival of [50]*Sukkot a *musaf* must be 50. Num. 29:13
brought as well as on the [51]eighth day thereof. 51. Num. 29:36

Every male Jew should make [52]pilgrimage to the Temple 52. Ex. 23:14
53. Ex. 34:23 three times a year and [53]appear there during the three
Deut. 16:16 pilgrim Festivals. One should [54]rejoice on the Festivals. 54. Deut. 16:14

On the 14th of Nisan one should [55]slaughter the paschal 55. Ex. 12:6
56. Ex. 12:8 lamb and [56]eat of its roasted flesh on the night of the 15th.
57. Num. 9:11 Those who were ritually impure in Nisan should slaughter
58. Num. 9:11 the paschal lamb on [57]the 14th of Iyyar and eat it with
Ex. 12:8 [58]**mazzah* and bitter herbs.

59. Num. 10:10 Trumpets should be [59]sounded when the festive sacrifices
Num. 10:9 are brought and also in times of tribulation.

Cattle to be sacrificed must be [60]at least eight days old and 60. Lev. 22:27
61. Lev. 22:21 [61]without blemish. All offerings must be [62]salted. It is a 62. Lev. 2:13
63. Lev. 1:2 *mitzvah* to perform the ritual of [63]the burnt offering, [64]the 64. Lev. 6:18
65. Lev. 7:1 sin offering, [65]the guilt offering, [66]the peace offering and 66. Lev. 3:1
67. Lev. 2:1; 6:7 [67]the meal offering.

Should the *Sanhedrin err in a decision its members [68]must 68. Lev. 4:13
bring a sin offering which offering must also be brought [69]by 69. Lev. 4:27
a person who has unwittingly transgressed a **karet* prohibition (i.e., one which, if done deliberately, would incur *karet*).

70. Lev. 5:17-18 When in doubt as to whether one has transgressed such a
prohibition a [70]"suspensive" guilt offering must be brought.

71. Lev. 5:15, 21-25; 19:20-21 For [71]stealing or swearing falsely and for other sins of a like
nature, a guilt offering must be brought. In special circum-
72. Lev. 5:1-11 stances the sin offering [72]can be according to one's means.

73. Num. 5:6-7 One must [73]confess one's sins before God and repent for
74. Lev. 15:13-15 them. A [74]man or [75]a woman who has a seminal issue must 75. Lev. 15:28-29
bring a sacrifice; a woman must also bring a sacrifice [76]after 76. Lev. 12:6
77. Lev. 14:10 childbirth. A leper must [77]bring a sacrifice after he has been
cleansed.

78. Lev. 27:32 One must [78]tithe one's cattle. The [79]*first born of clean 79. Ex. 13:2
(i.e., permitted) cattle are holy and must be sacrificed.
The firstborn of man must be [80]redeemed. The firstling of 80. Ex. 22:28; Num. 18:15
81. Ex. 34:20 the ass must be [81]redeemed; if not [82]its neck has to be 82. Ex. 13:13
broken.

83. Deut. 12:5-5 Animals set aside as offerings [83]must be brought to Jerusalem
84. Deut. 12:14 without delay and [84]may be sacrificed only in the Temple.
Offerings from outside the land of Israel [85]may also be 85. Deut. 12:26
brought to the Temple. Sanctified animals [86]which have 86. Deut. 12:15
become blemished must be redeemed. A beast exchanged
87. Lev. 27:33 for an offering [87] is also holy.

88. Lev. 6:9 The priests should eat [88]the remainder of the meal offering
89. Ex. 29:33 and [89]the flesh of sin and guilt offerings; but consecrated
90. Lev. 7:19 flesh which has become [90]ritually unclean or [91]which was 91. Lev. 7:17
not eaten within its appointed time must be burned.

Vows.

92. Num. 6:5 A *Nazirite must [92]let his hair grow during the period of his
separation. When that period is over he must [93]shave his 93. Num. 6:18
head and bring his sacrifice.

94. Deut. 23:24 A man must [94]honor his vows and his oaths which a judge
95. Num. 30:3 can [95]annul only in accordance with the law.

Ritual Purity.

96. Lev. 11:8, and 24 Anyone who touches [96]a carcass or [97]one of the eight 97. Lev. 11:29-31
species of reptiles becomes ritually unclean; food becomes
98. Lev. 11:34 unclean by [98]coming into contact with a ritually unclean
99. Lev. 15:19 object. Menstruous women [99]and those [100]lying-in after 100. Lev. 12:2
101. Lev. 13:3 childbirth are ritually impure. A [101]leper, [102]a leprous 102. Lev. 13:51
103. Lev. 14:44 garment, and [103]a leprous house are all ritually unclean. A
104. Lev. 15:2 man having [104]a running issue is unclean, as is [105]semen. A 105. Lev. 15:16
106. Lev. 15:19 woman suffering from [106]running issue is also impure.

107. Num. 19:14 A [107]human corpse is ritually unclean. The purification water
108. Num. 19:13, 21 (*mei niddah*) purifies [108]the unclean, but it makes the clean
ritually impure. It is a *mitzvah* to become ritually clean [109]by 109. Lev. 15:16
ritual immersion. To become cleansed of leprosy one [110]must 110. Lev. 14:2
follow the specified procedure and also [111]shave off all of 111. Lev. 14:9
one's hair. Until cleansed the leper [112]must be bareheaded 112. Lev. 13:45
with clothing in disarray so as to be easily distinguishable.

113. Num. 19:2-9 The ashes of [113]the *red heifer are to be used in the
process of ritual purification.

Donations of the Temple.

114. Lev. 27:2-8 If a person [114]undertakes to give his own value to the
Temple he must do so. Should a man declare [115]an unclean 115. Lev. 27:11-12
116. Lev. 27:14 beast, [116]a house, or [117]a field as a donation to the Temple, 117. Lev. 27:16,
he must give their value in money as fixed by the priest. If 22-23
one unwittingly derives benefit from Temple property [118]full 118. Lev. 5:16
resitution plus a fifth must be made.

119. Lev. 19:24 The fruit of [119]the fourth year's growth of trees is holy and
may be eaten only in Jerusalem. When you reap your fields
120. Lev. 19:9 you must leave [120]the corners, [121]the gleanings, [122]the for- 122. Deut. 24:19
121. Lev. 19:9 gotten sheaves, [123]the misformed bunches of grapes and 123. Lev. 19:10
124. Lev. 19:10 [124]the gleanings of the grapes for the poor.

125. Ex. 23:19 The first fruits must be [125]separated and brought to the
126. Deut. 18:4 Temple and you must also [126]separate the great heave
127. Lev. 27:30 offering (*terumah*) and give it to the priests. You must give
Num. 18:24 [127]one tithe of your produce to the Levites and separate
128. Deut. 14:22 [128]a second tithe which is to be eaten only in Jerusalem.
129. Num. 18:26 The Levites [129]must give a tenth of their tithe to the priests.

In the third and sixth years of the seven year cycle you
130. Deut. 14:28 should [130]separate a tithe for the poor instead of the second
131. Deut. 26:13 tithe. A declaration [131]must be recited when separating the
132. Deut. 26:5 various tithes and [132]when bringing the first fruits to the
Temple.

133. Num. 15:20 The first portion of the [133]dough must be given to the priest.

The Sabbatical Year.

In the seventh year (*shemittah*) everything that grows is
134. Ex. 23:11 [134]ownerless and available to all; the fields [135]must lie fallow 135. Ex. 34:21
and you may not till the ground. You must [136]sanctify the 136. Lev. 25:10
Jubilee year (50th) and on the Day of Atonement in that
137. Lev. 25:9 year [137]you must sound the *shofar* and set all Hebrew
slaves free. In the Jubilee year all land is to be [138]returned 138. Lev. 25:24
to its ancestral owners and, generally, in a walled city [139]the 139. Lev. 25:29-30
seller has the right to buy back a house within a year of the
sale.

Starting from entry into the land of Israel, the years of the
140. Lev. 25:8 Jubilee must be [140]counted and announced yearly and
septennially.

141. Deut. 15:3 In the seventh year [141]all debts are annulled but [142]one may 142. Deut. 15:3
exact a debt owned by a foreigner.

Concerning Animals for Consumption.

When you slaughter an animal you must [143]give the priest 143. Deut. 18:3
his share as you must also give him [144]the first of the fleece. 144. Deut. 18:4
When a man makes a *herem* (a special vow) you must
145. Lev. 27:21, 28 [145]distinguish between that which belongs to the Temple
(i.e., when God's name was mentioned in the vow) and
between that which goes to the priests. To be fit for con-
sumption, beast and fowl must be [146]slaughtered according 146. Deut. 12:21
to the law and if they are not of a domesticated species
147. Lev. 17:13 [147]their blood must be covered with earth after slaughter.

148. Deut. 22:7 Set the parent bird [148]free when taking the nest. Examine
149. Lev. 11:2 [149]beast, [150]fowl, [151]locusts and [152]fish to determine whether 151. Lev. 11:21
150. Deut. 14:11 they are permitted for consumption. 152. Lev. 11:9

153. Ex. 12:2 The *Sanhedrin should [153]sanctify the first day of every
Deut. 16:1 month and reckon the years and the seasons.

Festivals.

154. Ex. 23:12 You must [154]rest on the Sabbath day and [155]declare it holy 155. Ex. 20:8
at its onset and termination. On the 14th of Nisan [156]re- 156. Ex. 12:15
move all leaven from your ownership and on the night of
157. Ex. 13:8 the 15th [157]relate the story of the exodus from Egypt; on
158. Ex. 12:18 that night [158]you must also eat *mazzah*. On the [159]first and 159. Ex. 12:16
160. Ex. 12:16 [160]seventh days of Passover you must rest. Starting from the
day of the first sheaf (16th of Nisan) you shall [161]count 49 161. Lev. 23:35
162. Lev. 23 days. You must rest on [162]*Shavuot, and on [163]*Rosh 163. Lev. 23:24
Ha-Shanah; on the Day of *Atonement you must [164]fast 164. Lev. 16:29
165. Lev. 16:29, 31 and [165]rest. You must also rest on [166]the first and [167]the 166. Lev. 23:35
eighth day of *Sukkot during which festival you shall [168]dwell 167. Lev. 23:36
169. Lev. 23:40 in booths and [169]take the *four species. On *Rosh Ha- 168. Lev. 23:42
170. Num. 29:1 Shanah [170]you are to hear the sound of the **shofar*.

Community.

171. Ex. 30:12-13 Every male should [171]give half a shekel to the Temple
annually.

172. Deut. 18:15 You must [172]obey a prophet and [173]appoint a king. You 173. Deut. 17:15
174. Deut. 17:11 must also [174]obey the Sanhedrin; in the case of division,
175. Ex. 23:2 [175]yield to the majority. Judges and officials shall be
176. Deut. 16:18 [176]appointed in every town and they shall judge the people
177. Lev. 19:15 [177]impartially.

Whoever is aware of evidence [178]must come to court to 178. Lev. 5:1
testify. Witnesses shall be [179]examined thoroughly and, if 179. Deut. 13:15
180. Deut. 19:19 found to be false, [180]shall have done to them what they
intended to do to the accused.

When a person is found murdered and the murderer is
181. Deut. 21:4 unknown the ritual of [181]decapitating the heifer must be
performed.

Six cities of refuge should be [182]established. The Levites, 182. Deut. 19:3
who have no ancestral share in the land, shall [183]be given 183. Num. 35:2
cities to live in.

184. Deut. 22:8 You must [184]build a fence around your roof and remove
potential hazards from your home.

Idolatry.

Idolatry and its appurtenances [185]must be destroyed, and a 185. Deut. 12:2;7:5
city which has become perverted must be [186]treated accord- 186. Deut. 13:17
ing to the law. You are commanded to [187]destroy the seven 187. Deut. 20:17
188. Deut. 25:19 Canaanite nations, and [188]to blot out the memory of *Amalek,
189. Deut. 25:17 and [189]to remember what they did to Israel.

War.

The regulations for wars other than those commanded in
190. Deut. 20:11-12 the Torah [190]are to be observed and priest should be
191. Deut. 20:2 [191]appointed for special duties in times of war. The military
192. Deut. 23:14-15 camp must be [192]kept in a sanitary condition. To this end,
193. Deut. 23:14 every soldier must be [193]equipped with the necessary im-
plements.

Social.

194. Lev. 5:23 Stolen property must be [194]restored to its owner. Give
195. Deut. 15:8 [195]charity to the poor. When a Hebrew slave goes free the
Lev. 25:35-36 owner must [196]give him gifts. Lend to [197]the poor without 197. Ex. 22:24
196. Deut. 15:14 interest; to the foreigner you may [198]lend at interest. Re- 198. Deut. 23:21

199. Deut. 24:13; store [199]a pledge to its owner if he needs it. Pay the worker
Ex. 22:25 his wages [200]on time; [201]permit him to eat of the produce 201. Deut. 23:25-26
200. Deut. 24:15 with which he is working. You must [202]help unload an 202. Ex. 23:5
animal when necessary, and also [203]help load man or beast. 203. Deut. 22:4
204. Deut. 22:1 Lost property [204]must be restored to its owner. You are
Ex. 23:4 required [205]to reprove the sinner but you must [206]love your 206. Lev. 19:18
205. Lev. 19:17 fellow as yourself. You are commanded [207]to love the pros- 207. Deut. 10:19
elyte. Your weights and measures [208]must be accurate. 208. Lev. 19:36

Family.

209. Lev. 19:32 Respect the [209]wise; [210]honor and [211]fear your parents. 210. Ex. 20:12
212. Gen. 1:28 You should [212]perpetuate the human race by marrying 211. Lev. 19:3
213. Deut. 24:1 [213]according to the law. A bridegroom is to [214]rejoice with 214. Deut. 24:5
his bride for one year. Male children must [215]be circum- 215. Gen. 17:10
cised. Should a man die childless his brother must either Lev. 12:3
216. Deut. 25:5 [216]marry his widow or [217]release her (*halizah*). He who 217. Deut. 25:9
218. Deut. 22:29 violates a virgin must [218]marry her and may never divorce
her. If a man unjustly accuses his wife of premarital promis-
219. Deut. 22:18-19 cuity [219]he shall be flogged, and may never divorce her.
220. Ex. 22:15-23 The seducer [220]must be punished according to the law.
221. Deut. 21:11 The female captive must be [221]treated in accordance with
her special regulations. Divorce can be executed [222]only 222. Deut. 24:1
by means of a written document. A woman suspected of 223. Num. 5:15-27
adultery [223]has to submit to the required test.

Judicial.

224. Deut. 25:2 When required by the law [224]you must administer the pun- 225. Num. 35:25
ishment of flogging and you must [225]exile the unwitting 226. Ex. 21:20
homicide. Capital punishment shall be by [226]the sword, 229. Deut. 22:24
227. Ex. 21:16 [227]strangulation, [228]fire, or [229]stoning, as specified. In some
228. Lev. 20:14 cases the body of the executed [230]shall be hanged, but it 230. Deut. 21:22
231. Deut. 21:23 [231]must be brought to burial the same day.

Slaves.

232. Ex. 21:2 Hebrew slaves [232]must be treated according to the special
laws for them. The master should [233]marry his Hebrew 233. Ex. 21:8
234. Ex. 21:8 maidservant or [234]redeem her. The alien slave [235]must be 235. Lev. 25:46
treated according to the regulations applying to him.

Torts.

The applicable law must be administered in the case of 237. Ex. 21:28
236. Ex. 21:18 injury caused by [236]a person, [237]an animal or [238]a pit. 238. Ex. 21:33-34
239. Ex. 21:37-22:3 Thieves [239]must be punished. You must render judgment in
240. Ex. 22:4 cases of [240]trespass by cattle, [241]arson, [242]embezzlement by 242. Ex. 22:6-8
241. Ex. 22:5 an unpaid guardian and in claims against [243]a paid guardi- 243. Ex. 22:9-12
244. Ex. 22:13 an, a hirer, or [244] a borrower. Judgment must also be
245. Lev. 25:14 rendered in disputes arising out of [245]sales, [248]inheritance 247. Deut. 25:12
246. Ex. 22:8 and [246]other matters generally. You are required to [247]res- 248. Num. 27:8
cue the persecuted even if it means killing his oppressor.

PROHIBITIONS

Idolatry and Related Practices.

1. Ex. 20:3 It is [1]forbidden to believe in the existence of any but the
One God.

2. Ex. 20:4 You may not make images [2]for yourself or [3]for others to 3. Lev. 19:4
worship or for [4]any other purpose. 4. Ex. 20:20

You must not worship anything but God either in [5]the 5. Ex. 20:5
manner prescribed for His worship or [6]in its own manner of 6. Ex. 20:5
worship.

7. Lev. 18:21 Do not [7]sacrifice children to *Molech.

8. Lev. 19:31 You may not [8]practice necromancy or [9]resort to “familiar 9. Lev. 19:31
spirits” neither should you take idolatry or its mythology
10. Lev. 19:4 [10]seriously. It is forbidden to construct a [11]pillar or [12]dais 11. Deut. 16:22
12. Lev. 20:1 even for the worship of God or to [13]plant trees in the 13 Deut. 16:21
Temple.

14. Ex. 23:13 You may not [14]swear by idols or instigate an idolator to do
so, nor may you encourage or persuade any [15]non-Jew or 15. Ex. 23:13
16. Deut. 13:12 [16]Jew to worship idols.

17. Deut. 13:9 You must not [17]listen to or love anyone who disseminates
18. Deut. 13:9 idolatry nor [18]should you withhold yourself from hating
19. Deut. 13:9 him. Do not [19]pity such a person. If somebody tries to
20. Deut. 13:9 convert you to idolatry [20]do not defend him or [21]conceal 21. Deut. 13:9
the fact.

22. Deut. 7:25 It is forbidden to [22]derive any benefit from the ornaments of
23. Deut. 13:17 idols. You may not [23]rebuild that which has been destroyed
as a punishment for idolatry nor may you [24]have any bene- 24. Deut. 13:18
25. Deut. 7:26 fit from its wealth. Do not [25]use anything connected with
idols or idolatry.

26. Deut. 18:20 It is forbidden [26]to prophecy in the name of idols of proph-
27. Deut. 18:20 ecy [27]falsely in the name of God. Do not [28]listen to the one 28. Deut. 13:3, 4
30. Lev. 20:23 who prophesies for idols and do not [29]fear the false prophet Deut. 13:4
31. Lev. 19:26 or hinder his execution. 29. Deut. 18:22

Deut. 18:10 You must not [30]imitate the ways of idolators or practice 33. Deut. 18:10-11
32. Deut. 18:10 their customs; [31]divination, [32]soothsaying, [33]enchanting, Deut. 10:26
34. Deut. 18:10-11 [34]sorcery, [35]charming, [36]consulting ghosts or [37]familiar spirits 36. Deut. 18:10-11
35. Deut. 18:10-11 and [38]necromancy are forbidden. Women must not [39]wear 37. Deut. 18:10-11
38. Deut. 18:10-11 male clothing nor men [40]that of women. Do not [41]tattoo 39. Deut. 22:5
40. Deut. 22:5 yourself in the manner of the idolators. 41. Lev. 19:28

42. Deut. 22:11 You may not wear [42]garments made of both wool and linen
nor may you shave (with a razor) the sides of [43]your head 43. Lev. 19:27
44. Lev. 19:27 or [44]your beard. Do not [45]lacerate yourself over your dead. 45. Deut. 16:1
Deut. 14:1
also Lev. 19:28

Prohibitions Resulting from Historical Events

It is forbidden to return to Egypt to [46]dwell there permanently 46. Deut. 17:16
47. Num. 15:39 or to [47]indulge in impure thoughts or sights. You may not
48. Ex. 23:32; [48]make a pact with the seven Canaanite nations or [49]save 49. Deut. 20:16
Deut. 7:2 the life of any member of them. Do not [50]show mercy to 50. Deut. 7:2
idolators, [51]permit them to dwell in the land of Israel or 51. Ex. 23:33
52. Deut. 7:3 [52]intermarry with them. A Jewess may not [53]marry an 53. Deut. 23:4
Ammonite or Moabite even if he converts to Judaism but
should not refuse (for reasons of genealogy alone) [54]a de- 54. Deut. 23:8
55. Deut. 23:8 scendant of *Esau or [55]an Egyptian who are proselytes. It is
56. Deut. 23:7 prohibited to [56]make peace with the Ammonite or Moabite
nations.

57. Deut. 20:19 The [57]destruction of fruit trees even in times of war is
forbidden as is wanton waste at any time. Do not [58]fear the 58. Deut. 7:21
59. Deut. 25:19 enemy and do not [59]forget the evil done by *Amalek.

60. Lev. 24:16 Blasphemy.

rather Ex. 22:27 You must not [60]blaspheme the Holy Name, [61]break an oath 61. Lev. 19:12

62. Ex. 20:7 made by It, [62]take It in vain or [63]profane It. Do not [64]try the 64. Deut. 6:16
63. Lev. 22:32 Lord God.

65. Deut. 12:4 You may not [65]erase God's name from the holy texts or
destroy institutions devoted to His worship. Do not [66]allow 66. Deut. 21:23
the body of one hanged to remain so overnight.

Temple.

67. Num. 18:5 Be not [67]lax in guarding the Temple.

The high priest must not enter the Temple [68]indiscriminately; 68. Lev. 16:2
a priest with a physical blemish may not [69]enter there at all 69. Lev. 21:23
70. Lev. 21:17 or [70]serve in the sanctuary and even if the blemish is of a
71. Lev. 21:18 temporary nature he may not [71]participate in the service
there until it has passed.

The Levites and the priests must not [72]interchange in their 72. Num. 18:3
functions. Intoxicated persons may not [73]enter the sanctu- 73. Lev. 10:9-11
ary or teach the Law. It is forbidden for [74]non-priests, 74. Num. 18:4
75. Lev. 22:2 [75]unclean priests or [76]priests who have performed the nec- 76. Lev. 21:6
essary ablution but are still within the time limit of their
uncleanness to serve in the Temple. No unclean person may
77. Num. 5:3 enter [77]the Temple or [78]the Temple Mount. 78. Deut. 23:11

79. Ex. 20:25 The altar must not be made of [79]hewn stones nor may the
80. Ex. 20:26 ascent to it be by [80]steps. The fire on it may not be
81. Lev. 6:6 [81]extinguished nor may any other but the specified incense
82. Ex. 30:9 be [82]burned on the golden altar. You may not [83]manufac- 83. Ex. 30:32
ture oil with the same ingredients and in the same propor-
tions as the annointing oil which itself [84]may not be misused. 84. Ex. 30:32
85. Ex. 30:37 Neither may you [85]compound incense with the same ingre-
dients and in the same proportions as that burnt on the
86. Ex. 25:15 altar. You must not [86]remove the staves from the Ark,
87. Ex. 28:28 [87]remove the breastplate from the *ephod or [88]make any 88. Ex. 28:32
incision in the upper garment of the high priest.

Sacrifices

89. Deut. 12:13 It is forbidden to [89]offer sacrifices or [90]slaughter consecrated 90. Lev. 17:3-4
91. Lev. 22:20 animals outside the Temple. You may not [91]sanctify, [92]slaugh- 92. Lev. 22:22
93. Lev. 22:24 ter, [93]sprinkle the blood of or [94]burn the inner parts of a 94. Lev. 22:22
blemished animal even if the blemish is [95]of a temporary 95. Deut. 17:1
96. Lev. 22;25 nature and even if it is [96]offered by Gentiles. It is forbidden
97. Lev. 22:21 to [97]inflict a blemish on an animal consecrated for sacrifice.

98. Lev. 2:11 Leaven or honey may not [98]be offered on the altar, neither
99. Lev. 2:13 may [99]anything unsalted. An animal received as the hire of
a harlot or as the price of a dog [100]may not be offered. 100. Deut. 23:19

101. Lev. 22:28 Do not [101]kill an animal and its young on the same day.

102. Lev. 5:11 It is forbidden to use [102]olive oil or [103]frankincense in the sin 103. Lev. 5:11
104. Num. 5:15 offering or [104], [105], in the jealousy offering (**sotah*). You 105 Num. 5:15
106. Lev. 27:10 may not [106]substitute sacrifices even [107]from one category 107. Lev. 27:26
108. Num. 18:17 to the other. You may not [108]redeem the *firstborn of
permitted animals. It is forbidden to [109]sell the tithe of the 109. Lev. 27:33
110. Lev. 27:28 herd or [110]sell or [111]redeem a field consecrated by the 111. Lev. 27:28
herem vow.

When you slaughter a bird for a sin offering you may not
112. Lev. 5:8 [112]split its head.

113. Deut. 15:19 It is forbidden to [113]work with or [114]to shear a consecrated 114. Deut. 15:19
animal. You must not slaughter the paschal lamb [115]while 115. Ex. 34:25
there is still leaven about; nor may you leave overnight

116. Ex. 23:10 [116]those parts that are to be offered up or [117]to be eaten. 117. Ex. 12:10

You may not leave any part of the festive offering [118]until 118. Deut. 16:4
the third day or any part of [119]the second paschal lamb or 119. Num. 9:13
120. Lev. 22:30 [120] the thanksgiving offering until the morning.

121. Ex. 12:46 It is forbidden to break a bone of [121]the first or [122]the 122. Num. 9:12
123. Ex. 12:46 second paschal lamb or [123]to carry their flesh out of the
house where it is being eaten. You must not [124]allow the 124. Lev. 6:10
remains of the meal offering to become leaven. It is also
forbidden to eat the paschal lamb [125]raw or sodden or to 125. Ex. 12:9
126. Ex. 12:45 allow [126]an alien resident, [127]an uncircumcised person or an 127. Ex. 12:48
128. Ex. 12:43 [128]apostate to eat of it.

129. Lev. 12:4 A ritually unclean person [129]must not eat of holy things nor
130. Lev. 7:19 may [130]holy things which have become unclean be eaten.
131. Lev. 19:6-8 Sacrificial meat [131] which is left after the time-limit or[132] which 132. Lev. 7:18
was slaughtered with wrong intentions must not be eaten.
The heave offering must not be eaten by [133]a non-priest, 133. Lev. 22:10
134. Lev. 22:10 [134]a priest's sojourner or hired worker, [135]an uncircumcised 135. Lev. 22:10
136. Lev. 22:4 person, or [136]an unclean priest. The daughter of a priest
who is married to a non-priest may not [137]eat of holy things. 137. Lev. 22:12

The meal offering of the priest [138]must not be eaten, neither 138. Lev. 6:16
139. Lev. 6:23 may [139]the flesh of the sin offerings sacrificed within the
140. Deut. 14:3 sanctuary or [140]consecrated animals which have become
blemished.

141. Deut. 12:17 You may not eat the second tithe of [141]corn, [142]wine, or 142. Deut. 12:17
143. Deut. 12:17 [143]oil or [144]unblemished firstlings outside Jerusalem. The 144. Deut. 12:17
145. Deut. 12:17 priests may not eat the [145]sin-offerings of the trespass-
offerings outside the Temple courts or [146]the flesh of the 146. Deut. 12:17
burnt-offering at all. The lighter sacrifices [147]may not be 147. Deut. 12:17
eaten before the blood has been sprinkled. A non-priest
148. Deut. 12:17 may not [148]eat of the holiest sacrifices and a priest [149]may 149. Ex. 29:33
not eat the first-fruits outside the Temple courts.

150. Deut. 26:14 One may not eat [150]the second tithe while in a state of
151. Deut. 26:14 impurity or [151]in mourning; its redemption money [152]may 152. Deut. 26:14
not be used for anything other than food and drink.

153. Lev. 22:15 You must not [153]eat untithed produce or [154]change the 154. Ex. 22:28
order of separating the various tithes.

155. Deut. 23:22 Do not [155]delay payment of offerings—either freewill or
156. Ex. 23:15 obligatory—and do not [156]come to the Temple on the
pilgrim festivals without an offering.

157. Num. 30:3 Do not [157]break your word.

Priests.

158. Lev. 21:7 A priest may not marry [158]a harlot, [159]a woman who has 159. Lev. 21:7
been profaned from the priesthood, or [160]a divorcee; the 160. Lev. 21:7
161. Lev. 21:14 high priest must not [161]marry a widow or [162]take one as a 162. Lev. 21:15
concubine. Priests may not enter the sanctuary with [163]over- 163. Lev. 10:6
164. Lev. 10:6 grown hair of the head or [164]with torn clothing; they must
165. Lev. 10:7 not [165]leave the courtyard during the Temple service. An
ordinary priest may not render himself [166]ritually impure 166. Lev. 21:1
except for those relatives specified, and the high priest
167. Lev. 21:11 should not become impure [167]for anybody in [168]any way. 168. Lev. 21:11
The tribe of Levi shall have no part in [169]the division of the 169. Deut. 18:1
170. Deut. 18:1 land of Israel or [170]in the spoils of war.
171. Deut. 14:1 It is forbidden [171]to make oneself bald as a sign of mourning
for one's dead.

Dietary Laws

172. Deut. 14:7 A Jew may not eat [172]unclean cattle, [173]unclean fish, 173. Lev. 11:11
174. Lev. 11:13 175. Deut. 14:19 [174]unclean fowl, [175]creeping things that fly, [176]creatures that 176. Lev. 11:41
177. Lev. 11:44 creep on the ground, [177]reptiles, [178]worms found in fruit or 178. Lev. 11:42
179. Lev. 11:43 produce or [179]any detestable creature.

An animal that has died naturally [180]is forbidden for con- 180. Deut. 14:21
181. Ex. 22:30 sumption as is [181]a torn or mauled animal. One must not
182. Deut. 12:23 eat [182]any limb taken from a living animal. Also prohibited
183. Gen. 32:33 is [183]the sinew of the high (*gid ha-nasheh*) as is [184]blood 184. Lev. 7:26
185. Lev. 7:23 and [185]certain types of fat (*helev*). It is forbidden [186]to cook 186. Ex. 23:19
187. Ex. 34:26 meat together with milk or [187]eat of such a mixture. It is also
188. Ex. 21:28 forbidden to eat [188]of an ox condemned to stoning (even
should it have been properly slaughtered).

189. Lev. 23:14 One may not eat [189]bread made of new corn or the new
190. Lev. 23:14 corn itself, either [190]roasted or [191]green, before the *omer 191. Lev. 23:14
offering has been brought on the 16th of Nisan. You may
192. Lev. 19:23 not eat [192]**orlah* or [193]the growth of mixed planting in the 193. Deut. 22:9
vineyard (see: *Mixed Species). Any use of [194]wine libations 194. Deut. 32:38
to idols is prohibited, as is [195]gluttony and drunkenness. 195. Lev. 19:26 Deut. 21:20
One may not eat anything on [196]the *Day of Atonement. 196. Lev. 23:29
During *Passover it is forbidden to eat [197]leaven (**hamez*) 197. Ex. 13:3
198. Ex. 13:20 or [198]anything containing an admixture of such. This is also
199. Deut. 16:3 forbidden [199]after the middle of the 14th of Nisan (the day
before Passover). During Passover no leaven may be [200]seen 200. Ex. 13:7
201. Ex. 12:19 or [201]found in your possession.

Nazarites.

202. Num. 6:3 A Nazirite may not drink [202]wine or any beverage made
203. Num. 6:3 from grapes; he may not eat [203]fresh grapes, [204]dried grapes, 204. Num. 6:3
205. Num. 6:4 [205]grape seeds or [206]grape peel. He may not render himself 206. Num. 6:4
207. Num. 6:7 [207]ritually impure for his dead nor may he [208]enter a tent in 208. Lev. 21:11
which there is a corpse. He must not [209]shave his hair. 209. Num. 6:5

Agriculture.

210. Lev. 23:22 It is forbidden [210]to reap the whole of a field without leaving
the corners of the poor; it is also forbidden to [211]gather up 211. Lev. 19:9
the ears of corn that fall during reaping or to harvest [212]the 212. Lev. 19:10
misformed clusters of grapes, or [213]the grapes that fall or to 213. Lev. 19:10
214. Deut. 24:19 [214]return to take a forgotten sheaf.

215. Lev. 19:19 You must not [215]sow different species of seed together or
216. Deut. 22:9 [216]corn in a vineyard; it is also forbidden to [217]crossbreed 217. Lev. 19:19
different species of animals or [218]work with two different 218. Deut. 22:10
species yoked together.

219. Deut. 25:4 You must not [219]muzzle an animal working in a field to
prevent it from eating.

220. Lev. 25:4 It is forbidden to [220]till the earth, [221]to prune trees, [222]to 222. Lev. 25:5
221. Lev. 25:4 reap (in the usual manner) produce or [223]fruit which has 223. Lev. 25:5
grown without cultivation in the seventh year (**shemittah*).
224. Lev. 25:11 One may also not [224]till the earth or prune trees in the
*Jubilee year, when it is also forbidden to harvest (in the
225. Lev. 25:11 usual manner) [225]produce or [226]fruit that has grown without 226. Lev. 25:11
cultivation.

227. Lev. 25:23 One may not [227]sell one's landed inheritance in the land of
228. Lev. 25:33 Israel permanently or [228]change the lands of the Levites or
229. Deut. 12:19 [229]leave the Levites without support.

Loans, Business and the Treatment of Slaves.

230. Deut. 15:2 It is forbidden to [230]demand repayment of a loan after the
seventh year; you may not, however, [231]refuse to lend to 231. Deut. 15:9
the poor because that year is approaching. Do not [232]deny 232. Deut. 15:7
233. Deut. 15:13 charity to the poor or [233]send a Hebrew slave away empty-
handed when he finishes his period of service. Do not
234. Ex. 22:24 [234]dun your debtor when you know that he cannot pay. It is
235. Lev. 25:37 forbidden to [235]lend to or [236]borrow from another Jew at 236. Deut. 23:20
237. Ex. 22:24 interest or [237]participate in an agreement involving interest
either as a guarantor, witness, or writer of the contract. Do
238. Lev. 19:13 not [238]delay payment of wages.

239. Deut. 24:10 You may not [239]take a pledge from a debtor by violence,
240. Deut. 24:12 [240]keep a poor man's pledge when he needs it, [241]take any 241. Deut. 24:17
242. Deut. 24:6 pledge from a widow or [242]from any debtor if he earns his
living with it.

243. Ex. 20:13 Kidnaping [243]a Jew is forbidden.

244. Lev. 19:11 Do not [244]steal or [245]rob by violence. Do not [246]remove a 246. Deut. 19:14
245. Lev. 19:13 landmarker or [247]defraud. 247. Lev. 19:13

248. Lev. 19:11 It is forbidden [248]to deny receipt of a loan or a deposit or
249. Lev. 19:11 [249]to swear falsely regarding another man's property.

250. Lev. 25:14 You must not [250]deceive anybody in business. You may not
251. Lev. 25:17 [251]mislead a man even verbally. It is forbidden to harm the
252. Ex. 22:20 stranger among you [252]verbally or [253]do him injury in trade. 253. Ex. 22:20

254. Deut. 23:16 You may not [254]return or [255]otherwise take advantage of, a 255. Deut. 23:17
slave who has fled to the land of Israel from his master,
even if his master is a Jew.

256. Ex. 22:21 Do not [256]afflict the widow or the orphan. You may not
257. Lev. 25:39 [257]misuse or [258]sell a Hebrew slave; do not [259]treat him 259. Lev. 25:43
258. Lev. 25:42 cruelly or [260]allow a heathen to mistreat him. You must not 260. Lev. 25:53
261. Ex. 21:8 [261]sell your Hebrew maidservant or, if you marry her, [262]with- 262. Ex.21:10
hold food, clothing, and conjugal rights from her. You must
263. Deut. 21:14 not [263]sell a female captive or [264]treat her as a slave. 264. Deut. 21:14

265. Ex. 20:17 Do not [265]covet another man's possessions even if you are
willing to pay for them. Even [266]the desire alone is forbid- 266. Deut. 5:18
den.

267. Deut. 23:26 A worker must not [267]cut down standing corn during his
268. Deut. 23:25 work or [268]take more fruit than he can eat.

269. Deut. 22:3 One must not [269]turn away from a lost article which is to be
returned to its owner nor may you [270]refuse to help a man 270. Ex. 23:5
or an animal which is collapsing under its burden.

271. Lev. 19:35 It is forbidden to [271]defraud with weights and measures or
272. Deut. 25:13 even [272]to possess inaccurate weights.

Justice.

273. Lev. 19:15 A judge must not [273]perpetrate injustice, [274]accept bribes or 274. Ex. 23:8
275. Lev. 19:15 276. Deut. 1:17 be [275]partial or [276]afraid. He may [277]not favor the poor or 277. Lev. 19:15,
278. Ex. 23:6 [278]discriminate against the wicked; he should not [279]pity the rather Ex. 23:3
280. Deut. 24:17 condemned or [280]pervert the judgment of strangers or 279. Deut. 19:13
orphans.

281. Ex. 23:1 It is forbidden to [281]hear one litigant without the other being
present. A capital case cannot be decided by [282]a majority 282. Ex. 23:2
of one.

283. Ex. 23:2 A judge should not [283]accept a colleague's opinion unless
he is convinced of its correctness; it is forbidden to [284]ap- 284. Deut. 1:17
point as a judge someone who is ignorant of the law.

285. Ex. 20:16 Do not [285]give false testimony or accept [286]testimony from a 286. Ex. 23:1
287. Deut. 24:16 wicked person or from [287]relatives of a person involved in
the case. It is forbidden to pronounce judgment [288]on the 288. Deut. 19:15
basis of the testimony of one witness.

289. Ex. 20:13 Do not [289]murder.

290. Ex. 23:7 You must not convict on [290]circumstantial evidence alone.

291. Num. 35:30 A witness [291]must not sit as a judge in capital cases.

292. Num. 35:12 You must not [292]execute anybody without due proper trial
and conviction.

293. Deut. 25:12 Do not [293]pity or spare the pursuer.

Punishment is not to be inflicted for [294]an act committed 294. Deut. 22:26
under duress.

295. Num. 35:31 Do not accept ransom [295]for a murderer or [296]a manslayer. 296. Num. 35:32

297. Lev. 19:16 Do not [297]hesitate to save another person from danger and
298. Deut. 22:8 do not [298]leave a stumbling block in the way or [299]mislead 299. Lev. 19:14
another person by giving wrong advice.

300. Deut. 25:2-3 It is forbidden [300]to administer more than the assigned
number of lashes to the guilty.

301. Lev. 19:16 Do not [301]tell tales or [302]bear hatred in your heart. It is 302. Lev. 19:17
303. Lev. 19:17 forbidden to [303]shame a Jew, [304]to bear a grudge or [305]to 305. Lev. 19:18
304. Lev. 19:18 take revenge.

306. Deut. 22:6 Do not [306]take the dam when you take the young birds.

307. Lev. 13:33 It is forbidden to [307]shave a leprous scall or [308]remove other 308. Deut. 24:8
signs of that affliction. It is forbidden [309]to cultivate a valley 309. Deut. 21:4
in which a slain body was found and in which subsequently
the ritual of breaking the heifer's neck (**eglah arufah*) was
performed.

310. Ex. 22:17 Do not [310]suffer a witch to live.

311. Deut. 24:5 Do not [311]force a bridegroom to perform military service
during the first year of his marriage. It is forbidden to
312. Deut. 17:11 [312]rebel against the transmitters of the tradition or to [313]add 313. Deut. 13:1
314. Deut. 13:1 or [314]detract from the precepts of the law.

315. Ex. 22:27 Do not curse [315]a judge, [316]a ruler or [317]any Jew. 317. Lev. 19:14
316. Ex. 22:27
318. Ex. 21:17 Do not [318]curse or [319]strike a parent. 319. Ex. 21:15

320. Ex. 20:10 It is forbidden to [320]work on the Sabbath or [321]walk further 321. Ex. 16:29
than the permitted limits (**eruv*). You may not [322]inflict 322. Ex. 35:3
punishment on the Sabbath.

323. Ex. 12:16 It is forbidden to work on [323]the first or [324]the seventh day 324. Ex. 12:16
325. Lev. 23:21 of *Passover, on [325]*Shavuot, on [326]*Rosh Ha-Shanah, on 326. Lev. 23:25
327. Lev. 23:35 the [327]first and [328]eighth (**Shemini Azeret*) days of *Sukkot 328. Lev. 23:36
329. Lev. 23:28 and [329]on the Day of *Atonement.

Incest and Other Forbidden Relationships.

330. Lev. 18:7 It is forbidden to enter into an incestuous relationship with 332. Lev. 18:9
331. Lev. 18:8 one's [330]mother, [331]step-mother, [332]sister, [333]half-sister, 333. Lev. 18:11
334. Lev. 18:10 [334]son's daughter, [335]daughter's daughter, [336]daughter, [337]any 336. Lev. 18:10
335. Lev. 18:10 woman and her daughter, [338]any woman and her son's 337. Lev. 18:17
338. Lev. 18:17 daughter, [339]any woman and her daugther's daughter, 341. Lev. 18:13
339. Lev. 18:17 [340]father's sister, [341]mother's sister, [342]paternal uncle's wife, 342. Lev. 18:14
340. Lev. 18:12 [343]daughter-in-law, [344]brother's wife and [345]wife's sister. 345. Lev. 18:18

343. Lev. 18:15 It is also forbidden to [346]have sexual relations with a 346. Lev. 18:19
344. Lev. 18:16 menstruous woman (see **Niddah*).

Do not [347]commit adultery. 347. Lev. 18:20

348. Lev. 18:23 It is forbidden for [348]a man or [349]a woman to have sexual 349. Lev. 18:23
intercourse with an animal.

350. Lev. 18:22 Homosexuality [350]is forbidden, particularly with [351]one's father 351. Lev. 18:7
352. Lev. 18:14 or [352]uncle.

353. Lev. 18:6 It is forbidden to have [353]intimate physical contact (even
without actual intercourse) with any of the women with
whom intercourse is forbidden.

354. Deut. 23:3 A *mamzer may not [354]marry a Jewess.

355. Deut. 23:18 Harlotry [355]is forbidden.

356. Deut. 24:4 A divorcee may not be [356]remarried to her first husband if,
in the meanwhile, she had married another.

357. Deut. 25:5 A childless widow may not [357]marry anybody other than
her late husband's brother (See *Levirate Marriage).

358. Deut. 22:29 A man may not [358]divorce a wife whom he married after
359. Deut. 22:19 having raped her or [359]after having slandered her.

360. Deut. 23:2 An eunuch may not [360]marry a Jewess.

361. Lev. 22:24 Castration [361]is forbidden.

The Monarchy.

362. Deut. 17:15 You may not [362]elect as king anybody who is not of the
seed of Israel.

363. Deut. 17:16 The king must not accumulate an excessive number of
364. Deut. 17:17 [363]horses, [364]wives, or [365]wealth. 365. Deut. 17:17

Reprinted from: *The Encyclopedia Judaica* (Jerusalem: Keter Publishing House), Vol. 5, pp. 763-782.

DEEDS OF RIGHTEOUSNESS AND LOVINGKINDNESS: GEMILUT HASADIM

In Jewish tradition, *gemilut hasadim* are a category of *mitzvot* that obligate the individual to act in certain ways on certain occasions as a mark of basic human decency and respect towards others, living or dead, rich or poor, using one's time, effort, and money whenever necessary. *Gemilut hasadim* are deeds of lovingkindness, but the term has broader connotations: some of these deeds demand a degree of gentleness, extreme care, affection, tenderness—a summoning of all the human resources of sympathy for the benefit of others.

Some sages and commentators derive the obligation of *gemilut hasadim* from the well-known verse "Love your neighbor as yourself." (Lev. 19:18) Others base their understanding on other verses that describe God's love for His creatures. Noticing the words *hen, hesed,* and *rahamim* applied to God, they conclude that it is only right and proper for people, created in His image, to imitate His ways . . . to be kind, merciful, caring. Indeed, the Talmud notes that one of the three traditionally prominent characteristics of the Jews is that they are *gomlei hasadim*, performers of deeds of lovingkindness, concerned to provide for the welfare of others. (*Yevamot* 79a)

Some sages would include a vast array of good deeds under the heading of *gemilut hasadim*, if they are performed with the appropriate sense of lovingkindness. Generally, however, the Talmud and codes of Jewish law speak of six specific *mitzvot*: providing for brides, providing clothes for those in need of them, hospitality, visiting the sick, accompanying the dead, and comforting the mourners. Each of these *mitzvot* is discussed at length in the traditional literature, which sets out rules and guidelines and reveals many insights into human nature.

Providing for Brides—*Hakhnassat Kallah*

The Talmud makes the curious remark that God Himself prepared Eve's hair in an attractive fashion, so that for the First Wedding in the World, the bride and groom would feel greater affection for each other. (*Eruvin*

18a) Thus it is an act of walking in God's ways to make sure that weddings will be held in an appropriately joyous fashion. Everything is to be done to contribute to the *simhah* (basic happiness) of the bride and groom. The bride is a queen on that day, the groom, a king; and all efforts turn to giving the couple a sense of royalty—the majesty of marriage. Singing and dancing are no small part of this *mitzvah*, and the Talmud records how Rabbi Zeira would dance enthusiastically, juggling various twigs for the entertainment of the couple. (*Ketubot* 17a) The greatness of the *simhah* is measured not by the style and plenty of the food, but by the willingness of the guests to express their affection and love for the bride and groom by sweeping them away with music, dance, and laughter. Many weddings employ professional *badhanim*—jokers or clowns, who raise the level of joy with their rhymes and verses and Holy Humor for the sake of the *mitzvah*.

The Talmud goes so far as to prescribe a formula to recite to the bride: "O pleasant and gracious bride!" (or, as we know it, "All brides are beautiful"). Nothing is to be done during the event that will interfere with the *simhah*, no words or deeds dissonant with the music and dance. The importance of physical appearances fades, and there is a reaffirmation of basic human grandeur.

So important is this *mitzvah*, this affirmation, that if there are not enough people available to provide the appropriate joy, Torah study may be suspended and the schools emptied of their Jewish students for additional people to join in the festivities. (*Ketubot* 17a) Often in Eastern Europe portions of the sumptuous meal were provided for the poor so that they too might share the *simhah*. A striking matter of law confirms this affirmation of life: If a wedding entourage and a funeral procession meet by chance at a crossroads, the wedding takes precedence and continues on its way while the funeral waits.

Adjuncts to this *mitzvah* include providing financial assistance for a poor bride to purchase a wedding dress, funding to make the wedding appropriately provided with food, and helping the couple establish themselves financially. Household gifts and loans to provide security for the home are certainly a major part of the *mitzvah*.

To the end that brides and grooms should begin married life with all the necessities, a number of *Hakhnassat Kallah* societies have been established. They exist in local communities everywhere; and it is not unusual to see their signs posted on buildings in Jerusalem.

Providing Clothes for the Needy: *Halbashat Arumim*

God clothed the naked, as it says: "And the Lord God made garments of skins for Adam and his wife, and clothed them." (Gen. 3:21) The Talmud, referring to this verse, relates: "As He clothed the naked, so too should we." (*Sotah* 14a) This *mitzvah* too is a religious act, a following in God's way.

The Talmud and Midrash speak frequently of the importance of clothes and how they effect the personality of people:

1. "Clothes lend dignity to a person." (*Exodus Rabbah* 18:5)
2. "Rabbi Yochanan used to call his clothes 'My dignifiers.' " (*Shabbat* 113b)
3. "Three things ease a person's mind: a pleasant place to live, a pleasant spouse, and pleasant clothes." (*Berakhot* 57b)
4. Among those whose lives are considered deeply miserable are those "who only own one set of clothes." (*Betzah* 32b)

Everyone is acquainted with projects devoted to recirculating used but usable clothes. Goodwill Industries and the Salvation Army are best known for this work; their trucks and collection boxes are prominently displayed in communities throughout America. Jewish communities everywhere are also engaged in this work, and a call to a local Jewish communal agency can obtain necessary information for those wishing to donate.

Halbashat Arumim also implies the purchase of new clothes for the needy. A new hat, suit, bathrobe, or shoes serve well to raise depressed spirits and restore hope. Many agencies in the local communities seek out individuals in need of such clothing. They are, as it were, in the dignity business.

Hospitality—*Hahnassat Orhim*

Jewish history begins with wandering: Abraham, following God's instructions, leaves his home in Ur Kasdim and journeys to the Land of Israel to find a new wife and to found a new faith. (Gen. 12) Since then, history has chronicled many places in which Jews have sojourned: Egypt, Babylonia, Assyria, Rome, and Eastern and Western Europe, to name a few. Jews have been strangers, guests in the homes of many peoples. Perhaps because of their experience, the *mitzvah* of hospitality has been given a high priority, a supreme *gemilut hesed*. Everywhere homes can be found which are opened for meals, for Shabbat and holidays

—particularly Passover and the High Holidays. Soldiers at nearby bases, students in local colleges, travellers passing through are sought out and brought into the atmosphere of a home.

Many are the stories children tell of strangers their parents brought home from the synagogue for a Friday night. Many houses had a spare room filled again and again by the wayfarer, and extra places set in the anticipation of yet another guest. Free shelter is offered in homes in Kansas City, Missouri; Portland, Oregon; Newport News, Virginia; and other cities, though many are unaware that they exist. (A list of such homes is appended to this article.)

Abraham and Sarah, builders of the first Jewish home, have come to represent the archetypical hosts. The Jewish response to wandering is clearly understood from their example: their tent was open to all four directions, so that they might see strangers approaching anywhere in the distance. Jewish hospitality has come to mean food, drink, and a place for the night; even, according to some commentators, accompanying the stranger on his way. (*Rashi, Sotah* 10a)

Additional statements from Jewish literature on *Hahnassat Orhim*:

1. "Rabbi Chana bar Chanila'i's home was open to all directions." (*Berakhot* 58b)

2. "Let all who are hungry come in and eat." (Passover Haggadah)

3. "When Rav Huna would have a meal, he would open his door wide and say, 'Whoever is in need may come in and eat.' " (*Ta'anit* 20b)

4. "It was a prominent custom in Jerusalem that, at the beginning of a meal, a cloth would be hung on the door. As long as the cloth was on the door, guests might enter." (*Baba Batra* 93b)

5. "Yossi ben Yochanan of Jerusalem said, 'Let your home be open wide, and let the poor become members of your household.' " (*Pirkei Avot* 1:5)

Visiting the Sick—*Bikkur Holim*

This act of *gemilut hasadim* is also considered an imitation of God's ways. The Talmud teaches (*Sotah* 14a) that God Himself visited Abraham after his circumcision, while he was still in pain. The worthiness of this *mitzvah* is self-evident, though it is understood that besides physical sickness, heartsickness, depression, and sadness should be attended to with the same care and concern. Particularly nowadays, with the emergence of gigantic medical centers, physical sickness is often complicated by a sense of loneliness and estrangement. The surroundings are unfamiliar and sterile; the terminology is exotic and often incomprehensible to the layperson; there are rules and regulations and pieces of machinery that often confuse and dishearten the patient, slowing the process of recovery.

In recent years the local Jewish community has often relegated this *mitzvah* to the rabbi, giving him a near-impossible task in many instances. The need to restore the *mitzvah* to the purview of all Jews is evident, and to that purpose, many *Bikkur Holim* societies have been established in local communities. The joint efforts of the society's members provide comfort, assistance, and simply conversation when needed—a sense of human caring. Contacting the local Jewish communal agencies is the easiest method of locating local *Bikkur Holim* society.

Additional texts:

1. "It once happened that one of Rabbi Akiva's students fell ill, and no one went to visit. Rabbi Akiva himself went, and because they had swept and mopped the floor in anticipation of his visit, the man recovered. The man said, 'Rabbi, you have given me back my life!' Rabbi Akiva then went and taught the following lesson, 'He who does not visit the sick is like a killer.' " (*Nedarim* 40a) Often the therapeutic process is hastened by friends offering to clean the house, answer calls and mail, shop, and do the day-to-day errands which will free the patient's mind from worry.

2. "Rabbi Hiyya bar Abba became ill and Rabbi Yochanan went to visit him. Rabbi Yochanan said, 'Do you appreciate your suffering?' He replied, 'Neither the suffering nor any reward I might gain from the suffering.' Rabbi Yochanan said, 'Give me your hand.' He gave him his hand, and Rabbi Yochanan raised him from his sickbed." (*Berakhot* 5b) This is an eloquent account, with others mentioned on the same page, of how the human touch is often the greatest curative.

3. "Rabbi Acha bar Hanina said, 'One who visits the sick takes away from him one sixtieth of his pain.' " (*Nedarim* 39b) Sixty is a commonly used number in the Talmud. The intent of this statement is clear: that the lovingkindness and support of those who visit are an essential aid to recovery.

4. "Even a prominent person should visit someone of lesser status, even many times in one day . . . and the more he visits, the better, except in the case where this would be a burden to the patient." (*Shulkhan Arukh, Yoreh De'ah* 335:2)

5. "When one prays for the recovery of

another, in his presence he may pray in any language he wishes." (*Shulkhan Arukh, Yoreh De'ah* 335:5) One of the requirements of this *mitzvah* is to pray for the welfare of the patient, the prayer for God's aid being considered important to the recovery of the patient. Praying in a language the patient understands will certainly help to raise his spirits.

6. "When praying for the patient, he should include the patient among all the sick of Israel, saying, 'May the Almighty be merciful to you among the other Jews who are sick.'" (*Shulkhan Arukh, Yoreh De'ah* 335:6) This is a typical pattern of Jewish practice: joys and misfortunes are not to be viewed as individual events, but rather as part of a wider experience of the entire people of Israel. Plurals are more frequent than singulars in Jewish prayer; the reminder to transcend egocentricity, even in pain, can give strength to the patient. By being a part of a larger community the person's sense of identity is broadened and heightened, his purpose for recovery more meaningful.

7. "Rabbi Eliezer would say, 'May the Almighty remember you in peace.'" (*Shabbat* 12b) Rabbi Eliezer would sometimes say this in Hebrew, and at other times in Aramaic, the spoken language of the Jews in talmudic times. This lends support to the concept that visitors should attempt to speak on behalf of the patient, and *to* the patient, in the language best understood by that particular individual.

8. Finally, a quote from a certain Rabbi Eliezer, an eleventh-century sage: "Be enthusiastic, careful, and quick to visit the sick, because one who visits alleviates the illness. . . . Pray for him, and then depart. Do not fatigue the patient by staying too long, for his illness is a heavy enough burden as it is. When you go to visit, enter with joy, for the patient's eyes and heart are on those who are coming to visit."

Accompanying the Dead— *Levayat* or *Halvayat ha-Met*

The terms *levayat* or *halvayat ha-met* mean following the body to the grave. Jewish law indicates that if one sees a funeral procession, he is required to walk at least four paces alongside—even a funeral for someone unknown to him. For friends and relatives, the *mitzvah* involves attending the funeral services and proceeding with the funeral to the cemetery. Also known as *kevurat ha-met*, the burial of the dead, this *mitzvah* requires that participants in the funeral should take part in the burial, each participant adding a shovelful of dirt to the grave.

As with some of the other *mitzvot* of *gemilut hasadim*, this is considered to be an imitation of God's acts, in that God Himself buried Moses. (Deut. 34, *Sotah* 14a)

Many steps are involved in preparing the body and the funeral, including washing and purifying the body, dressing the body in a white linen shroud, providing a suitable plain wooden coffin, tearing the mourners' garments as a sign of grief, guarding the body from the time of death until burial, reciting *Kaddish*, and delivering a eulogy. The *mitzvah* is considered so important that it is often referred to as *hesed shel emet*, the purest act of lovingkindness, since those who honor the dead cannot expect any repayment from the beneficiary of their work.

In many communities a *Hevra Kaddisha* (burial society) has the responsibility for carrying out this *mitzvah*. Some synagogues are beginning to establish their own *Hevra Kaddishaei*. The Adath Jeshurun Congregation in Minneapolis is willing to assist any group interested in this venture. Their society, called the *Hevra Kevod ha-Met* (The Society for the Honoring of the Dead) includes over 150 congregants. They provide all services including building the coffins, sewing the shrouds, preparing and guarding the body, and setting up an appropriate house of mourning (*shiva*). They have much printed matter on the subject; a film (produced by ABC Media Productions), *A Plain Pine Box*, is available. (For further information write to: *Hevra Kevod ha-Met*, Adath Jeshurun Congregation, 3400 Dupont Ave. S., Minneapolis, Minn. 55408.)

The following is a brief sample of traditional material on *levayat ha-met*:

1. "Upon hearing of the death of someone, one recites, 'Blessed be the True Judge.'" (Prayerbook)

2. "At first, funerals were so expensive, the funeral expenses were harder on the relatives than the death itself. It reached a point that relatives would simply leave the body and run away. Then Rabban Gamliel [the leader of the Jewish community in first-century Israel] insisted that he be buried in plain shrouds. The custom was then accepted to bury people in linen shrouds." (*Ketubot* 8b)

3. "A dying person should not be left alone, so that he or she might not feel abandoned during the last moments of life. And it is a *mitzvah* to be present at the moment of death." (*Shulkhan Arukh, Yoreh De'ah* 339:4) The rules of intensive care units often complicate this matter. Often close relatives are not allowed near the patient at what turn out to be the patient's dying moments. As a reaction to this—and for

other reasons—some relatives are deciding nowadays to bring their dying family members home from the hospital so that the last moments of life may be spent in familiar surroundings, in the presence of family and friends.

4. "And God came and slew the Angel of Death." (Passover Haggadah)

(Many books are available on accompanying the dead, including *A Time To Be Born, a Time To Die* by Rabbi Isaac Klein, United Synagogue Youth Sourcebook, 155 5th Ave., New York, N.Y. 10010; *The Jewish Way in Death and Mourning* by Maurice Lamm, Jonathan David Publishers, New York; and *Jewish Reflections on Death* by Rabbi Jack Riemer, Schocken Books, New York.)

Comforting the Mourners—*Nihum Availim*

Comforting someone who has suffered a loss is an awesome and difficult responsibility, which calls upon all the comforter's resources to bring to the surface the appropriate words and gestures of consolation. The books just mentioned provide many details about this *mitzvah*; as the gravity of the situation is so great, the need for guidance is equally great. It is interesting to note that many psychologists and grief counsellors are turning to traditional Jewish sources for insight and understanding of the mourning process. Only a few sources can be cited here, as an introduction to the larger body of material that is available:

1. "God comforted Isaac after the death of his father Abraham." (*Sotah* 14a)

2. "Rabbi Shimon the son of Elazar said, '. . . do not try to comfort another when his dead lies before him.' " (*Pirke Avot* 4:23) Before the burial a relative is considered in a special category—an *onain*. The regulations concerning relations with an *onain* are different from those concerning an *avail*, a mourner after the funeral. Grief is so deep at this time that words of comfort from "outsiders" would be of no avail. The relatives should be left to express their feelings of bereavement among themselves.

3. "The comforters are not permitted to begin speaking until the mourner begins." (*Shulkhan Arukh, Yoreh De'ah* 376:1) During *shiva* (the seven days of mourning following the funeral) the mourner is the one who controls the situation. If he or she does not wish to speak with the comforters, that is his or her prerogative. As the *Shulkhan Arukh* continues to explain the regulations: The mourner sits in a prominent place, and once the mourner shakes his head indicating that the comforters should leave, the comforters are no longer permitted to remain. A mourner need not rise, even to greet the Nassi (the leader of the community).

4. "May God comfort you among all the other mourners of Zion and Jerusalem." (Prayerbook) This is the traditional statement of comfort offered to the mourners, recited after the burial, at *shiva*, and at services on Friday night when the mourners come to synagogue.

5. "A mourner is forbidden to exchange greetings. How is this to be understood? The first three days of *shiva* he does not greet anyone, and if others do not know he is a mourner, and they greet him, he should not reply, but rather should notify them that he is a mourner. From the third to the seventh day he does not greet others, and if others do not know he is a mourner, he may return their greeting." (*Shulkhan Arukh, Yoreh De'ah* 385:1) The comforters should be aware of this regulation when entering a *shiva* house.

6. "And since it is forbidden to exchange greetings, so much the more is it forbidden to speak too much. If he [the mourner] does it in honor of many, that is to say, many have come to comfort him, he is permitted to say to them, 'Return to your homes in peace.' " (*Shulkhan Arukh, Yoreh De'ah* 385:1) Many mourners regret that comforters, in their well-intentioned desire to offer consolation, become a burden by speaking too much. Frequently—as a defense mechanism in the presence of death—the conversation concerns trivial matters, light banter, or jokes. Good practice would indicate that visits to a *shiva* house for morning and evening services would suffice, with a minimum of additional visiting time, except when the mourners indicate their wish to have others remain.

7. A mourner is forbidden to eat of his own prepared food for the first meal after the funeral . . . and it is a *mitzvah* for the neighbors to prepare their own food for the mourner. (*Shulkhan Arukh, Yoreh De'ah* 378:1) The fear was that the mourner, in his grief, would not eat properly after the funeral. The responsibility was shifted, therefore, to friends and neighbors. This first meal is called *Seudat ha-Havra'ah* ("the Meal of Recovery").

8. "One should not mourn too much for the deceased, and anyone who mourns too much weeps [or: "shall weep"] for another. Rather, there should be three days for tears, seven days for lamenting, and thirty to refrain from cutting the hair and wearing pressed clothes." (*Shulkhan Arukh, Yoreh De'ah* 394:1) Jewish tradition sets bounds to the mourning process. The texts speak

frequently of remarriage and other readjustments to normal life, by degree, after *shiva*, the thirty days, and the first eleven months of mourning are over.

Two Further Notes

1. *Peace*: Some authorities consider one more *mitzvah* under the category of *gemilut hasadim*—bringing peace between individuals who have become estranged. Aaron the High Priest is considered the paradigm of this virtuous behavior, and he is often referred to as a "lover and pursuer of peace." (*Pirkei Avot* 1:12) The Talmud tells a story of two brothers, professional clowns or jokers, who spent their days making saddened people laugh and who declared, "When we see two people alienated from one another, we do everything we can to make peace between them." (*Ta'anit* 22a) This is one of the most difficult *mitzvot* to perform, calling upon rare skills and talents—including humor—to bring about reconciliations between people who have parted ways. (An inspirational book dealing with one such person, a lover and pursuer of peace, is *A Tzaddik in Our Time*, Simcha Raz, Feldheim Publishers.)

2. *Free Loans*: Over the years, *gemilut hesed* has taken on a specific meaning beyond the *mitzvot* described above: an interest-free loan society. Jews in need of money to start out in business, pay tuition for schooling, or purchase household furnishings—whatever the need might be—could come to a *gemilut hesed* society and obtain the money, to be paid back with no interest. These societies (often called *GeMach*) function in many communities. (A partial list of local *GeMach*s is appended below.) This aspect of loving-kindness is a pure expression of the Jew's concern for others, a fulfillment of the obligation to "love your neighbor as yourself."

D.S.

Free Clothes
Jewish Free Store—Malbish Arumin
306 W. 37th St., New York, NY 10018

Free Loans
Arizona
Jewish Free Loan Association
1718 W. Maryland, Phoenix 85712

Hebrew Free Loan Association
4032 E. Whittier, Tucson 85712

California
Federation Free Loan Association
2601 Grand Ave., Long Beach 90815

Jewish Free Loan Association
6505 Wilshire Blvd., Los Angeles 90048

Jewish Family Service
3245 Sheffield Ave., Oakland 94602

Hebrew Free Loan Association of San Francisco
703 Market St., San Francisco 94103

Max Gordon Memorial Loan Fund of the Jewish Community Council
1024 Emory St., San Jose 95126

Connecticut
Hebrew Free Loan Association
187 Eaton St., Bridgeport 06604

Hebrew Free Loan Association
34 Gilbert Ave., New Haven 06511

Hebrew Free Loan
19 Avalon Circle, Waterbury 06710

Delaware
Jewish Family Service
2105 Washington St., Wilmington 19802

Florida
Hebrew Free Loan
500 S.W. 17th Ave., Miami 33160

Georgia
Hebrew Gemilut Hesed Society
P.O. Box 6546, Savannah 31408

Illinois
Gemilut Hesed—Free Loan Fund
3453 W. Foster, Chicago 60625

Iowa
Free Loan Fund
525 14th St., Sioux City 51105

Louisiana
Jewish Family and Children's Service
211 Camp St., New Orleans 70130

Maine
Hebrew Free Loan
341 Cumberland Rd., Portland 04101

Maryland
Hebrew Free Loan Association
5762 Park Heights Ave., Baltimore 21216

Massachusetts
Hebrew Free Loan Association
252 Washington St., Boston 02108

Hebrew Free Loan Society
2 Atwater St., Worcester 01602

Michigan
Hebrew Free Loan Association
18100 Meyers Rd., Detroit 48235

New Jersey
Hebrew Free Loan Association
℅ YM-YWHA, 152 Van Houten St., Paterson 07501

Hebrew Free Loan Association
457 Center, South Orange 07079

Hebrew Free Loan Association
1418 W. State St., Trenton 08618

New York
Hebrew Benevolent Loan Association
787 Delaware Ave., Buffalo 14209

Hebrew Free Loan Society
205 E. 42nd St., New York 10017

Ohio
Hebrew Free Loan Association
338 The Arcade, Cleveland 44114

Jewish Family Service
184 Salem Ave., Dayton 45406

Jewish Family Service
2247 Collingwood Blvd., Toledo 43620

Oklahoma
Free Loan Committee
Jewish Community Council,
200 McBurney Bldg., Tulsa 74103

Pennsylvania
Hebrew Free Loan Association
234 McKee Pl., Pittsburgh 15213

A. B. Cohen Hebrew Free Loan Society
601 Jefferson Ave., Scranton 18510

Rhode Island
Hebrew Free Loan Association
128 N. Main St., Providence 02906

South Providence Hebrew Free Loan
1027 Broad St., Providence 02905

South Carolina
Hebrew Benevolent Society
105 Broad St., Charleston 29402

Texas
Hebrew Free Loan
701 N. Chaparral, Corpus Christi 78401

Hebrew Free Loan Association
2821 Canal, Houston 77003

Hebrew Free Loan Association
107 S. Pecos St., San Antonio 78207

Virginia
Free Loan Society
113 Longwood Dr., Newport News 23606

Hebrew Ladies Charity Society
1416 W. Princess Anne Rd., Norfolk 23507

Washington
Hebrew Ladies Free Loan Society
1110 Harvard St., Seattle 98115

Seattle Hebrew Free Loan
1501 17th Ave., Seattle 98104

Canada
Hebrew Free Loan Association
5775 Victoria Ave., Montreal, Que.

Hebrew Re-Establishment Services
152 Beverly St., Toronto, Ont.

Free Shelter

Hebrew Sheltering Home
699 W. Jackson Ave., Bridgeport, CT 06605

Hebrew Ladies Sheltering Home—Independent Transient Service
992 Albany Ave., Hartford, CT 06114

Kansas City Kansas Relief—Independent Transient Service
826 Minnesota Ave., Kansas City, KS 66101

Hebrew Sheltering Home
53 Wheeler St., Lynn, MA 01908

Jewish Sheltering Home
1231 North and South Rd., St. Louis, MO 63123

Hebrew Free Sheltering Home
65 Quincy, Passaic, NJ 07055

Hebrew Sheltering Home—Independent Transient Service
138 N. Park Ave., Buffalo, NY 14216

Hebrew Shelter Home
1775 S. Taylor Rd., Cleveland, OH 44105

Jewish Relief and Benevolent Society—Independent Transient Service
6651 S.W. Capitol Highway, Portland, OR 97218

Hebrew Sheltering Ladies Aid Society—Independent Transient Service
℅ 540 Westmoreland Ave., Kingston, PA 18704

Hebrew Friendly Inn—Independent Transient Service
2125 Oak Ave., Newport News, VA 23607

Source: Sharon and Michael Strassfeld, *The Second Jewish Catalog.*

TZEDAKAH: THE GIFT OF GIVING

Tzedakah is the specific Jewish method of giving away a portion of one's income for the benefit of others. The Hebrew root means "justice" or "right," and from this etymology it is clear that the Jewish understanding of this *mitzvah* is that it is only right and proper to distribute part of one's own possessions to others. It is part of the "Scheme of Things" as outlined in the Torah and later Jewish texts.

The prescribed range of giving is ten to twenty percent of one's earnings (including gifts), based on a figure after income taxes have been paid. But Jewish tradition does not consider *tzedakah* only a *mitzvah* (an obligation to be fulfilled) but, rather, as a privilege for every Jew. It is appropriate, therefore, to approach this *mitzvah* aggressively by being regularly and constantly on the lookout for occasions and places to give. Among the appropriate times when one might contribute are the following:

1. In honor of the birth of a child (one's own or others' children),
2. In honor of a male circumcision or the naming of a baby.
3. On the occasion of a bar or bat mitzvah. (The bar or bat mitzvah child should also be encouraged to give, since the ceremony is a declaration of the child's attaining Jewish adulthood and full Jewish responsibility towards others in the community.)
4. For a wedding.
5. For a wedding anniversary.
6. At the time of reaching a certain birthday, such as sixty, seventy, or eighty, or in honor of a friend or relative who has reached that age.
7. In memory of someone who has died, and thereafter, each year on the *yahrzeit*.
8. At other significant life-moments, such as graduation from high school, college, or graduate school; moving into a new house or apartment; receiving a gift or foundation grant; inheriting money (even though one might be certain that the one who provided the inheritance has already given generously to *tzedakah*); recovery from an illness; arriving safely in *Eretz Yisrael*, or completing some long or dangerous journey.
9. Before Jewish holidays, contributing to the Jewish poor. This allows the poor the benefit of an appropriately joyous holiday of their own. Before Purim this *mitzvah* is specifically called *Matanot la-Evyonim*, and before Passover, *Me'ot Hittim* or *Kimha de-Pischa*. Subcategories are contributing to Israel on Yom ha-Atzma'ut—Israel Independence Day—and contributing to some foundation for Holocaust research on Yom ha-Shoah ve-Hagevurah—Holocaust and Resistance Day.
10. At a week-day *minyan*, before services begin.
11. Friday afternoon before candlelighting (putting loose change in a *pushka*—a *tzedakah* box).
12. At any time—putting loose change in a *pushka*, and later, when the money has accumulated, deciding where to give it.

THE SOURCES

The Jewish sources on *tzedakah* are many and varied. Even a partial overview of some of these texts should help provide a perspective on the traditional Jewish understanding of this *mitzvah*:

1. "One should not give away more than a fifth of one's income, for fear that he may, thereby, then become in need of assistance." (*Ketubot* 50a)
2. "One should give up to a fifth of one's possessions—that is the *mitzvah* to its fullest extent. One tenth is an average percentage, and less is considered miserly." (*Shulkhan Arukh, Yoreh De'ah* 249:1) Twenty percent is the outer limit, with few exceptions. Maimonides states (*Hilkhot Arachin V'haramin* 8:13) that self-imposed poverty is not a Jewish ideal. He refers to it as *shtut*—foolishness, rather than *hasidut*—saintliness.
3. "*Tzedakah* is a tree of life." (Zohar, Leviticus 111)
4. "Give away a tenth, so that you may become wealthy." (*Shabbat* 119a)
5. "A person never becomes poor from giving *tzedakah*, nor does any harm come from it, as the verse states, 'And the result of *tzedakah* will be shalom—peace.' [Isa. 32:17]" (Maimonides, *Hilkhot Mat'not Ani'im* 10:2)
6. "If a person sees that his resources are limited, let him use them for *tzedakah*, and so much the more so if he has extensive resources." (*Gittin* 7a)
7. "Even a poor person who receives *tzedakah* must give from what he receives." (*Shulkhan Arukh, Yoreh De'ah* 248:1) This clearly indicates that giving is a basic human privilege, a sign of one's *kavod* (dignity). Not allowing someone to give is considered a *bushah* (humiliation).
8. "One who gives even a *perutah* [the smallest coin] to the poor is privileged to sense God's Intimate Presence." (*Baba Batra* 10a)
9. "The three most prominent characteristics of the Jews are that they are *rahmanim*, *byshanim*, and *gomelay hasadim* (filled with basic human lovingkindness, non-arrogant, and doers of acts of extreme lovingkindness." (*Yevamot* 79a)
10. Anyone who runs to do *tzedakah* will find the necessary funds . . . and the proper recipients for his *tzedakah* work." (*Baba Batra* 9b)
11. *Gadol k'vod ha-briot*: "The dignity of God's creatures is very great" or "The respect due to God's creatures is very great." (*Berakhot* 19a)
12. "One should give pleasantly, joyously, with a good heart, showing sympathy for the poor, sharing in their sense of pain and sorrow." (*Shulkhan Arukh, Yoreh De'ah* 249:3) A statement in ancient Jewish literature (*Leviticus Rabbah* 34:5) indicates that as much as the beneficiary receives benefit, so, too, does the benefactor—from an act of *tzedakah*.
13. "One should not be arrogant when giving." (*Shulkhan Arukh, Yoreh De'ah* 249:13, note by Isserles)

14. "If a person convinces others to give, his reward is even greater than when simply giving himself." (*Shulkhan Arukh, Yoreh De'ah* 249:5)

Certainly the best known analysis of the range and variety of giving *tzedakah* is Maimonides's "Eight Degrees of *Tzedakah*," which are enumerated in his classic law code, the *Mishnah Torah* (*Hilkhot Mat'not Ani'im* 10:7–14):

1. "The highest degree is to aid a Jew . . . to become self-supporting, so that he will not have to ask others for anything. . . .
2. "The next . . . degree is when the one who gives *tzedakah* is unaware of the recipient, who, in turn, is unaware of the giver. This is indeed a *mitzvah* performed for its own sake. Of a similar character is one who contributes to a *tzedakah* fund. One should not contribute to a *tzedakah* fund unless he knows that the man in charge of the collections is trustworthy and intelligent and knows how to manage properly. . . .
3. "The third, lesser degree is when the giver knows the recipient, but the recipient does not know the giver. The great sages used to go secretly and cast the money into the doorway of the poor. Something like this should be done, it being a noble virtue, if the *tzedakah* administrators are acting improperly.
4. "The fourth, still lower, degree is when the recipient knows the giver, but the giver does not know the recipient. The great sages used to tie money in sheets, which they would throw behind their backs, and the poor would come and take it without being embarrassed.
5. "The fifth degree is when the giver puts the *tzedakah* money into the hands of the poor without being solicited.
6. "The sixth degree is when he puts the money into the hands of the poor after being solicited.
7. "The seventh degree is when he gives him less than he should, but does so cheerfully.
8. "The eighth degree is when he gives him grudgingly." (This last statement makes clear that (a) no matter what the personal mood of the individual Jew at a particular moment, the obligation to give remains—recalling that it would be a surrendering of one's self-dignity not to give—and (b) *tzedakah* must be an act, not a thought. Though the eighth degree is lowest on the list, it is still considered *tzedakah*, because the act of giving has been carried out.)"

FROM THE LIVES OF THE SAGES

To illustrate the specific laws and guidelines of *tzedakah* there are a number of tales concerning the lives of individuals and the practices of the ancient Jewish community:

1. "Rabbi Yannai once saw a man give *tzedakah* to a poor man in public. He said to him, 'It would have been better not to give than giving as you did, causing him shame.' " (*Hagiga* 5a) *Bushah* (humiliation of the recipient) is to be avoided at all costs, as is clear from Maimonides's Eight Degrees, and the following selection of stories.
2. "There was a Secret Chamber in the Temple where pious people would leave money in secret, and those who had become poor would come and take in secret." (*Mishna Shekalim* 5:6) Another text (*Tosefta Shekalim* 2:16) adds that there were similar Secret Chambers in all major settlements in Israel.
3. "They said of Hillel that he once personally ran before the horse of a man who had recently become impoverished, because they could not find another person to do it." (*Ketubot* 67b) In talmudic times, a sign of wealth and honor was the practice of leading the wealthy person through the street on a horse, a servant holding the reins and walking ahead. This is similar to modern motorcades.
4. "Abba bar Ba gave money to his son Shmuel to distribute to the poor. He went out and found a poor person eating meat and drinking wine. When he told his father what he had seen, his father said, 'Give him more, for his soul is bitter.' " (*Yerushalmi Peah* 8:8) Not only financial need but "bitterness of soul" is a factor in *tzedakah*.
5. "Rabbi Chana bar Chanila'i had sixty bakers in his house day and night, baking for anyone who needed bread. He would leave his hand in his pocket, so that [by the immediacy and naturalness of handing him the money] a poor person who came to ask would not be humiliated. His doors were open to the four directions, and anyone who came in hungry would leave satisfied. Furthermore, in times when food was scarce, he would leave wheat and barley outside the door, so that anyone who was too embarrassed to come and take in the daytime could come unnoticed and take at night." (*Berakhot* 58b)
6. "Rabbi Tanhum, though he needed only one portion of meat, would buy two; one bunch of vegetables, he would buy two—one for himself and one for the poor." (*Ecclesiastes Rabbah* 7:30) This is a prime example of patterning *tzedakah* into one's daily mode of living.
7. "Rabbi Zecharia, the son-in-law of Rabbi Levi, used to accept *tzedakah* money. His colleagues would deride him, thinking he

did not need it. When he died, they discovered that he had been giving it to others." (*Yerushalmi Shekalim* 5:4).

8. "Rabbi Chama bar Chanina and Rabbi Hoshaya were touring the synagogues of Lod. Rabbi Chama bar Chanina said to Rabbi Hoshaya, 'See how much money my fathers have invested here!' He replied, 'How many souls your ancestors have sunk here! Was there no one here who wanted to study Torah [and who would have needed the money for support]?' " (*Yerushalmi Shekalim* 5:4) Rabbi Hoshaya, in his impassioned reply, informs his friend that people take precedence over buildings when funds are limited.

—D.S.

RITUALS FOR JEWISH EXORCISM

The notion of a foreign spirit or demon entering, possessing, or afflicting the body of an innocent person is found in both Jewish and Christian texts of the early talmudic period. The Talmud relates that to help Rav Simon bar Yohai have anti-Jewish decrees annulled, a demon entered the body of the Emperor's daughter. Upon Rabbi Simon's command, the demon left. Thus was Rabbi Simon ingratiated to the Emperor, who then rescinded the edict. Josephus reports that in his own time a certain Eleazer drove a demon out of a possessed man in the presence of Vespasian, by means of putting a certain root to his nostrils and reciting ancient incantations ascribed to Solomon.

Such possession was always regarded as a possibility; however, it was not held to be a serious problem. Although medieval literature, especially the works of Hasidei Ashkenaz, is rife with practical advice on avoiding and appeasing *shedim* (demons) and *mazikim*, (spirits), it seems that they were not troubled by actual possessions. It is only in mid sixteenth-century Italy and Israel that a proliferation of accounts of possessions and exorcisms is found.

The terminology popularly used is, understandably ambiguous and requires some clarification. The term *dybbuk*, used as a noun, is of late development, according to Gershom Scholem, the foremost expert on Jewish mysticism. The term never appears in any rabbinic or kabbalistic literature and is still not used by Sephardim. The original term is "evil spirit" (*ruach ra'ah*) or, in the New Testament, an "unclean spirit." This spirit is spoken of as "clinging" or "cleaving" (*mitdabake*) to the body of the host. However, the root "*dabake*" was not used as a noun until 1752 when the kabbalist and scholar, Jacob Emden, spoke of a certain man being inhabited by a *dybbuk*. From this point, the term *dybbuk* slipped into popular jargon.

The Sephardic kabbalists differentiated between possession by a wandering soul of some deceased Jew (the evil spirit) and possession by a demon (shade). Hayyim Vital gives separate formulae for exorcising each and even states that the formula for exorcising a demon will have no effect upon a spirit. Demons may be distinguished, he says, by the following criteria: "A demon will coerce a man, and make him twitch his hands and feet, and will spit up a white foam, as the foam from the mouths of horses; but a spirit will cause him to feel pain and constriction in his heart, so much so that he occasionally faints. But the matter can be definitively cleared up when it speaks, for if you have adjured it with oaths, it must tell you what it is."

Eyewitness accounts of exorcisms are plentiful from as early as 1571 and became much more popular in the succeeding two decades. The question thus arises as to where this procedure came from? While Jewish sources may indicate, at least partially, the willingness to accept the reality of possession, it is non-Jewish sources which account for both the standardization and the widespread use of the exorcism rite.

In 1626, Menashe ben Israel wrote: "The matter of spirits entering bodies of the living is so widely accepted that it requires no proof. For do not all the books of adjurations, found in the Christian language, called exorcisms, attest this, and give accounts, as you will find in Martin Delrio, Bodin, and Vayeri and many modern and ancient writers." Furthermore, when someone was known to be possessed, Jewish and non-Jewish spectators would come to participate in the questioning of the spirit.

If Menashe ben Israel is to be believed—and there is no reason not to—it appears quite likely that the sudden preoccupation in the sixteenth century with demons, possessions, and exorcisms was a pan-cultural phenomenon, shared by Jews and Christians, and that Jewish authorities borrowed liberally from Christian sources, both live and literary.

The intensity of demonological concern in

the Christian world was as much a sign of the growing thirst for scientific experimentation and medical knowledge as it was of occultism. Demons were generally cited as only one in a number of possible causes for human illness and tragedy. Hence, cures for these illnesses—including frustrating or expelling the demon—were medical questions discussed by humanists, scientists, and theologians alike.

From the last quarter of the sixteenth century and into the seventeenth, several popular manuals for exorcists were printed in Italy in both Latin and Italian. The popularity of these books can be seen from one example: Hieronymus Mengus, who wrote at least six compendia on exorcisms beginning in 1573, had his works published no less than thirteen times before 1601. A *Practica of Exorcists,* by the Franciscan Valerio Polidoro. was published in Padua in 1587. This work, possibly referred to by Menashe, gives step by step instructions for Catholic exorcists: "Among things to be learned from the exorcized spirit are his name, in order that it may be written down and put above an image of the demon on paper to be burned; the names of his associates and satellites and their number; the cause of his entering the body of the possessed in order that a contrary remedy may be applied or, if it be by witchcraft, that the appropriate exorcisms may be read; . . . what holy words he especially abhors in order that these may be repeated; . . . by what exorcist he should be expelled . . . The exorcist is warned, however, to beware of curious digressions and not to repose too much trust in the demon's replies, in fact to shut him off if he volunteers too much information and seems fraudulent."

Other works discuss with great detail the place of repose of the demon in the host's body; usually it is the heart. Furthermore, signs by which demonic possession may be confirmed are listed: "Demons torment the body in five ways: by fascination of the mind and senses (i.e. hallucinations), infirmity of corporal forces, corruption of the organs, contraction and distraction of the limbs, and violent movement in the entire body."

Another influential Christian work was written by the Italian biologist-humanist Andrea Cesalpino (1519–1603). Summoned by the archbishop of Pisa to a conference of theologians and scientists to determine the authenticity of a case of demonic possession, he composed his *Peripatetic Investigation of Demons,* published in 1580. In this work Cesalpino strongly argues for the reality of such phenomena and lists the unmistakable signs of such a possession. Among these are: "speaking of unknown tongues, a movement under the skin to another part of the body, and abstention from divine worship." Other rites described are the soundings of bells, suffumigations, and the repetition of the name of Jesus.

Five Accounts of Jewish Exorcisms

[It should be kept in mind that while all of the incantations and word formulas are transliterated, they are only effective when recited in Hebrew due to the subtleties of vocalization.]

A Formula for Exorcizing an Evil Spirit— R. Hayyim Vital, (1571).

[Note—Isaac Luria, the major kabbalist of this time and Vital's teacher, himself disapproved of "practical" Kabbalah, including the writing of amulets against demons. He did, however, often construct "meditations" (*kavanot*) based on permutations of biblical verses to expel a spirit from its host. This was considered a legitimate usage of the divine names hidden in the verses and did not constitute a magical or theurgic act. Vital seems to have accepted this limitation as long as he was in the land of Israel. However, when he moved to Damascus from Safed in 1594, he began to associate himself with a small group of kabbalists favoring resort to alchemy, chants, and magical incantations borrowed from Christian sources. Unlike the more "Jewish" ceremonies of Luria, this type involved amulets, burning sulphur, and Latin invocations.]

Here is a *yihud* (combination) which my teacher [Luria] taught me, to exorcize an evil spirit (God forbid!); for there are times when the spirit of some evil man, which can not enter paradise because of its sins, wanders about the world and sometimes enters the body of some man or woman (and makes him fall down and this is called epilepsy). By means of this *yihud,* his [i.e. the sinner's] soul is lifted a bit, and it can leave the man's body. These are the details, which I myself have tried: I would take the arm of the man, and put my hand on the pulse of the right or left hand (for that is the garment of the spirit, and it is clothed therein). I direct my mind to the spirit clothed in the pulse, that by the power of the *yihud* it should leave.

While I am still holding the man's arm at the pulse, I say this verse forwards and backwards. I concentrate on the holy names which come from it [e.g. those from the numerical equivalent of each word, and from the initial letters of each word, and from the last letter of each word, as it is known]. During this [i.e. the concentration on the names] I direct my mind that the spirits should exit the body. Then the spirit speaks to you from the body, and tells you anything you might ask, and you should command him to exit.

Sometimes one must blow the shofar near his ear and meditate on the name (*Kra Satan*) [Tear Satan], and also on its reverse, in "At-bash" (*Dezeg Bant*).

Know that this spirit never comes alone, but a devil (*shade*) supports it and leads him wandering to complete the recompense for its sins. And he can do nothing without the permission of this devil, for God has appointed him guard over it, as it is written in the Zohar (Bo, 41b) "The evil inclination rules the wicked."

Sometimes the spirit leaves the body, and the devil remains alone to guard the place. Therefore, the roaming spirit does not constantly inhabit the afflicted body, for it sometimes must leave at appointed times to receive its punishment. Nonetheless, the appointed devil remains to guard the place, and the afflicted person is never healed from his illness, until both of them exit.

And I shall now copy the text of the Meditation:

Hafkaid alov rasha v'satan
ya'amid al yemino.
Yemino al ya'amid v'satan
rasha alov hafkaid.
Onimey la dima'ay natas'v
ahsar vola diakfah.

The order of these vowels follows the order of the vowels of the *sephirot* as it is recorded in the *Tikkune Zohar* (TZ, 70, p. 129). Know, that these seven words, when inverted in the above order, are divine names. I am doubtful whether one should meditate on these names when one recites the verse backwards, or perhaps one should read it forwards and backwards and then meditate on these names. This latter seems more correct.

You should concentrate, that it should leave by the power of all these names. And if it does not exit, repeat the verse, and meditate on all the above names, and after each time say: "Leave! Leave!" quickly. Know, that the most important thing is that you should be strong of heart, without any fear; do not have a soft heart for if you do, he will be strengthened and will not listen to you.

You must also command him not to leave the body from any place except the spot between the nail and flesh of the big toe so as not to injure the body. (In Vital's other writings, it is explained that the place where the spirit exits whithers up.)

Also, command him by the force of these names upon which you have meditated and with excommunication that he may not injure or enter the body of any other Jew.

Know, that when it speaks, the man's body remains mute as a stone, and the spirit's voice comes from the mouth, without any moving of the lips, as a small, child-like voice. Also, when the voice comes up from the body to the mouth to speak, the form of some round gland ascends through the neck to the skin of the neck, and again when it descends to the big toe.

Know, furthermore, that when you ask it who it is and what is its name, it will lie and give another name, either to mock you or so that your command would not take effect [i.e. when you adjure it by name]. Therefore, you must adjure him with threats of excommunication and the power of the names, not to lie at all, but to tell you who he is with all truth. It is necessary to perform this deed with ritual purity and ritual immersions and with holiness and excessive concentration.

To force a demon to leave:
Say the following incantation thirty times in his left ear and thirty times in his right ear, and do not pause between them, and he will leave. Also, if you write it on parchment and hang it around his neck, the demon will leave, or at least it will descend to the foot and will not be able to rise. Seeing that it can no longer ascend, it will leave by itself after a few days. And here is the incantation: Altinum, Sabtinum, Tanrikum, Sabtinotis, Kintiel, Yah, Hai-Hu, Amen, Amen; Kirkorah, Akhsah, Kalba, Da, v'Reshith, Amen, Amen, Tar.

From Eliezer b. Eliyahu ha-Rofeh, c. 1577.
Because, in the matter of demons, whether one believes in them or not will not affect him one way or the other, I will not divulge my opinion regarding them. But this I shall say to you, if your only reason for disbelieving in the existence of demons is that they cannot be perceived by the senses or because their creation is not mentioned in the Torah, you should know that for these reasons alone logic does not compel one to disbelieve in them . . .

We have already heard, in our own time, from those who tell the truth, well-known accounts of people who have fallen down, unconscious and senseless, who are able to speak and answer questions without moving their lips [the voice comes from their throats] and who ask and answer questions appropriately. I have seen a letter coming from Safed this year [1600] about a woman who had taken ill in this way.

Also in the year 1577 came an account told by men, women, and children, and the details from each one were exactly the same, which demonstrated the veracity of the story. The story was that in Ferrara, a Jewish woman fell unconscious, and a voice issued from her throat, her lips not moving. When people asked it who it was, it answered, "I am so-and-so, from the city of so-and-so," and he gave an accurate description.

It is a popular belief that those who fall in such a manner have had an evil spirit enter them, for they [i.e. Gentiles] also call this thing a spirit.

[He proceeds to give a naturalistic explanation of how this is possible. The voice of the spirit cannot normally be heard because the matter of which it is composed is too diffuse and light. However, when the spirit enters a living body, its voice is amplified by the vocal chords of the host just as a trumpet amplifies the "voice" of the musician.]

From Gedaliah ibn Yahye, 1575.
May I have the strength to write you an answer to your question about foreign spirits who enter men's bodies; who, by the power of adjurations, reveal their names and tell us that they were human beings who died different deaths.

It is difficult for us to grasp how such a spirit of some deceased person can act in another's living body and use his limbs and senses accurately; it seems that this is one of the wonders of our time and is very strange.

I myself have experienced such a case, for in the month of Tevet, 1575, when I was in Ferara, I went to visit a young girl, twenty-five years old, the wife of an important man in the community. I found her lying supine on her bed; she was like a body without a soul, her eyes shut, her mouth open, and her tongue very thick. The people attending her told me that the spirit was then in her tongue. I then thought, "This is the day I've waited for, to find out about what happens to the soul at death." After I pleaded with the spirit to answer my questions, he answered in Italian . . . that his name was Betshe De Medina, who was hung as punishment for robbery. Then he began to cry and sigh, but I consoled him and he was calmed. I began to ask him about the soul, to find out its nature, the manner of its leaving the body at death, its whereabouts after that, and about Hell. But I did not ask about Paradise, because I realized he had not been there. I asked other similar questions, and to all of them he answered . . . He said he had been a shepherd and a farmer, and in truth, I saw that he was very much like cattle himself.

He had the power to force the girl to behave as he willed; for example, she would not eat meat on Friday or Saturday; and at evening, when the [vesper] bells rang, she would begin to pray, as is the custom among Gentiles. I asked him, "What does it matter to you if this body eats meat on Friday?" He answered that it would be considered a sin for him, since he too derives enjoyment from her eating. I asked him about the nature of *his* body, but he said he did not know . . . I asked where he is located in the woman's body, and he said, between the ribs and the hip on the right side. I asked who put him there, but he did not know. I asked him to leave, but he said, "I cannot." I asked why he entered the body of a Jewish girl; he answered, he was in pain and did not recognize that she was Jewish; if it had been in his power, he would not have entered . . . I pleaded with him to allow the girl to speak to me and he conceded. As he went to wherever his place was, we saw the throat of the girl becoming very thick. Now, the woman was in great pain, and all her limbs, particularly her right side, were shaking and rattling, as in the fever before malaria.

Suddenly she opened her eyes and looked at me, and I asked how this came about. She responded that on her way back from the *mikveh* (ritual bath) one night, she went down to the community square at two hours after dark to draw water from the well to fix dinner. She left her candle in a hole near the well, and her husband, who was with her, left. As she took the bucket, the candle suddenly went out and the spirit carried her halfway down the well. He then raised her in the air. She, not knowing the cause for all of this, fainted, and her family carried her back to her bed. She then asked what remedy I knew for her affliction, but then, suddenly, the spirit reappeared in her throat, causing great pain to the girl and not allowing her to speak. Such was the event.

Hayyim Vital, c. 1571.
An account from Safed: One day, when we were in the House of Study of my teacher [Luria], they brought a woman before him to ascertain if she was sick or if a spirit had entered her. They told my teacher that she had not been at all afflicted, and then this suddenly came upon her and her whole body trembled. My teacher examined her pulse, and said that a spirit was "clothed" in her body (God forbid!), and he sent her to her home.

At dusk, my teacher commanded me to go to the woman and exorcize the spirit from her body. He said to me, "See that you deal wisely with this spirit, for he is a liar and a deceiver, and when you ask his name he will lie three times." He then gave me the meditations needed to exorcize it, for it was my teacher's custom to send me on such jobs because I am descended from Cain, the left side of the First Man, which is the root of evil [the powers of evil can only be overcome at their roots], and, therefore, I have this power.

Now, I did not go until nightfall. Before I entered the house of that woman, the spirit said to those men standing there, "You will see, that Rabbi Hayyim Vital is about to come to remove me from here. We will see his strength and ability! I am not afraid of him!" And he boasted about my lack of power to remove him.

But when I entered and the spirit saw my face, he bowed to honor me with half his body and began to tremble. Then I asked him his name, and he answered, "So and so." I answered, "You lie! This is not your name!" Thus he lied three times, and the fourth time he gave his true name, as my teacher had said.

I then approached his ear and recited some of the meditations of my teacher, and the spirit shook and spoke harshly and began to leave. But I rebuked it until it gave me a sign that it wanted to leave via the small toe. But this was a lie, for I saw that it was ready to leave by way of the throat, and then extinguish the lights and harm the people there. When I saw this, I proclaimed a ban on him from leaving at all. Thus I left the matter and went to pray *Ma'ariv* [the evening prayers] in my teacher's house.

[He then tells that his teacher rebuked him for not going at evening-time, but rather at night when these forces have power. He warned Vital that the spirit is angry with him and will attempt to harm him, but that he will escape. That night, on the way home, Vital encountered a huge black dog, who pursued him; Vital narrowly escaped.]

The next day, my teacher gave me more meditations, which I have written elsewhere. I whispered them in the ears of the woman, and the spirit began to shake. I asked the spirit how it had entered the house, and it responded that it had come in through a small hole in the wall. It had been unable to enter through the door because there was a proper *mezuzah* affixed there.

I also asked in what manner it had entered this woman. It answered that it had waited in the house three days, looking for an opportunity to enter. On the third day, she had tried to light the fire by striking iron against the hearth stone. It would not ignite, however, because it had been sitting on the stone. She had thrown the iron down in anger, and the spirit seized this opening to enter . . . I then released him from the ban I had placed on him, and he left her body through her toe, after I had said my teacher's meditations.

From Menashe ben Israel, 1571.

After this, he wanted to test the spirit's ability to speak, and it spoke to him in Hebrew, Arabic, and Turkish; and in every language it answered clearly, as it knew them when it was alive. But the woman did not know any of these. And when he spoke to it in German, it did not answer, but said it did not know that language . . .

The spirit asked that we should plead for [Divine] mercy for it, and that we should blow the shofar . . . and we asked it who should blow the shofar, and it responded Rabbi Shlomo Alkabetz . . . and they asked it who should pray for it, and it responded Rabbi Elijah Falkon . . .

And all the spectators decided to hush up the story because of the danger of the Gentiles, who would want to burn the woman [i.e. for witchcraft] . . .

And we put smoke, fire, and sulfur to her nostrils . . .

It should leave by means of her big toe . . .

—D.R.S.

SPACE AGE JUDAISM: MITZVOT ON THE MOON

The Jew tends to examine every phenomenon, whether natural, social, political, or scientific, in the light of his particular interest. Little wonder, then, that the contemporary preoccupation with the conquest of space should be reflected in halakhic writings. One of the more intriguing topics in the current literature is the question of the extent to which *mitzvot* are binding upon Jews who may happen to find themselves in the vast regions of outer space. There has now appeared, for the first time, a serious discussion of man's religious obligations on the moon. Undoubtedly, the subject will become a recurrent one and rabbinic literature dealing with this topic will be considerably enriched in the months and years to come.

Among the opinions published thus far, the most extreme position is advanced by Rabbi Ben-Zion Firrer in the 5730 issue of *No'am*. Rabbi Firrer maintains that *mitzvot* are incumbent upon man only in his terrestrial habitat. The sole supporting evidence for this radical point of view, which is described by its proponent as being "only in the nature of first thoughts; a modest beginning in investigation of this question," is an argument based upon a statement in *Kiddushin* 37a. Asserting that commandments which are personal in character are binding not only in *Eretz Yisrael* but in the Diaspora as well, the Gemara quotes the verse ". . . all the days which you are alive on the earth" (Deut. 12:1) Rabbi Firrer argues that since a pleonasm, "on the earth," is required to establish this obligation, such obligation must be limited to what is specified in this verse. Therefore, man is exempt from performance of *mitzvot* in places other than those which are "on the earth."

In a report of an interview granted by Rabbi Shlomoh Goren, published in *Ha-Zofeh*, 10 Av, 5729 (and cited by Rabbi Firrer in *No'am*), Rabbi Goren is quoted as asserting that theoretically *mitzvot* contingent upon "time" cannot be performed on the moon,

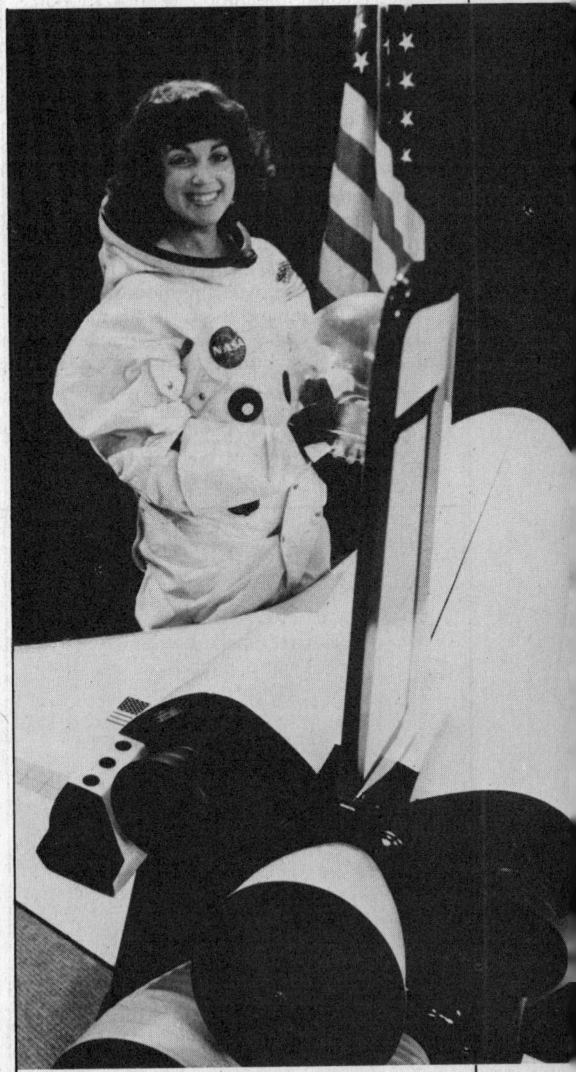

Judith A. Resnik, Mission Specialist, Astronaut Candidate

since "time" as measured by twenty-four-hour day-night sequences does not exist on this celestial body. *Keri'at shema*, (the recitation of the *Shema*) for example, is obligatory only during certain time periods. Since these periods are defined in terms of terrestrial cycles of light and darkness, it is not clear when *keri'at shema* should be recited on the moon where the lunar "day" is equal to a month (which, on the average, is 29 days, 12 hours, 44 minutes, and 2.78 seconds in length). The same question arises with regard to determining the occurrence of the seventh day which is to be hallowed as the Sabbath. However, argues Rabbi Goren, in practice man is obligated to perform such *mitzvot*. Since natural atmospheric conditions on the moon cannot support human life, man will be able to exist only by creating an artificial atmosphere composed of elements transported from earth. In light of his continual dependence upon Mother Earth, man living on the moon will continue to be governed by the laws operating on earth.

Rabbi Firrer contests the assumption that dependence upon terrestrial materials renders such dependents subject to "earth *halakhah*," arguing that once such materials come into contact with the moon they are accorded the same status as lunar material. The Gemara, *Gittin* 7b, declares that bodies of water in *Eretz Yisrael* are not part of the Land of Israel and that a ship plying the lakes and rivers of *Eretz Yisrael*, as long as it does not scrape bottom, is considered to be outside the borders of the Land of Israel. When the vessel does touch bottom, its passengers and cargo, even while submerged, are considered to be within the confines of *Eretz Yisrael*. Rabbi Firrer observes that the ship acquires the halakhic status of the underlying riverbed simply by coming into physical contact with it. Similarly, argues Rabbi Firrer, earth material coming into contact with lunar substance acquires the halakhic status of the moon itself.

Another article in the same issue of *No'am* takes sharp issue with Rabbi Firrer's thesis. In direct contradiction to the opinion of Rabbi Firrer, Rabbi Menachem Kasher declares that halakhic obligations are personal ones and are incumbent upon Jews in any and all places where they may find themselves. Hence, the contention that the observance of *mitzvot* is abrogated in the celestial spheres cannot be entertained. Rabbi Kasher adds that since Rabbi Firrer has described his words as "first thoughts," he is certain that the latter's "second thoughts" will reflect a change of heart. Insofar as the reckoning of time is concerned, Rabbi Kasher opines that this situation is no different from the situation which prevails in the earth's polar regions, which have days and nights of many months' duration. Rabbi Kasher has long been of the opinion that under such circumstances the day must be reckoned on a twenty-four-hour basis with alternating twelve-hour periods of "day" and "night" regardless of the presence or absence of solar illumination. The same practice, contends Rabbi Kasher, should be followed by man on the moon.

—J.D.B. rep.

WAITING FOR THE MESSIAH

SIGNS OF THE MESSIANIC AGE

One would expect that a religion that can identify with staggering precision the signs of a nonkosher chicken ought to have done better than it has in identifying the signs of the coming of the Messiah. In fact, what has been preserved in the classical texts of Judaism is a morass of conflicting opinions and endlessly varied speculations. It has even been seriously suggested that the only reason the Messiah was mentioned at all in Jewish traditional literature was to create so many requirements for validating the Messiah that no one could ever possibly fulfill them. Put in other words, "We Jews will allow just about anybody to be our teacher but nobody can be our Messiah!"

One can readily understand the basic historical reasons for this. During the political chaos that reigned in the Middle East from the time of the conquests of Alexander in 332 B.C.E. through the Moslem conquests of the seventh century C.E., myriads of messianic speculations and messianic claimants competed for popular support. The rabbis could not suppress the hugely popular mass belief that a new heaven and a new earth were just around the temporal corner.

The following is a topical listing of some of the most widely accepted signs of the messianic age that appear in the classic Jewish texts of Bible and Talmud. Even the messianic furor of the sixteenth and seventeenth centuries only built upon the ideology already set down in this formative period of Judaism.

SIGN #1: THE FIGURE OF THE MESSIAH

The appearance of a bona fide Messiah certainly would seem to be a necessary sign of the arrival of a Messianic Age, but even on this point there is dispute within the tradition. Rav Hillel was said to have remarked, "Israel will have no Messiah, for he has already been vouchsafed to them in the days of Hezekiah." (*Sanhedrin* 99a). Hillel's colleagues, like Rav Joseph, apologized for his minority opinion, but in good rabbinic tradition, the opinion was preserved. Hillel's comment actually reflects a long-standing tendency in Judaism—beginning with the biblical references to the Messiah—which emphasizes the human, earthly, noncosmic, political function of the Messiah and limits his role to restoring political sovereignty under the kingship of a "scion of the house of David." (Jer. 23:5; Amos 9:7–9; Hos. 3:5; and especially Jer. 30:9, "But they shall serve the Lord their God, And David their king, Whom I will raise up unto them."). This theme is carried into the rabbinic period with the teaching of Rav Samuel that, "The present world differs from the Messianic age only in respect to the servitude of [Israel to the] kingdoms." (*Sanhedrin* 99a, also *Shabbat* 63a).

The reason for minimizing the importance of the person of the Messiah seems to have been to magnify God's direct involvement in the messianic drama. This perspective can be seen in the *Midrash* to Psalms (31:2): "Israel said to the Holy One, blessed be He: 'Hast Thou not already redeemed us by the hand of Moses and of judges and kings? And now we are enslaved again and put to shame, as though we had never been redeemed!' Said the Holy One, blessed be He, to them: 'Because your redemption was by human agency, and your leaders were mortals who are here one day and in the grave the next, therefore your redemption was of a temporary nature. But in the future I, who live forever, shall redeem you Myself; I shall redeem you with an everlasting redemption.' " Despite this well-meant tendency to teach nothing that would in any way diminish God's direct role as the central actor in the messianic drama, the increasing despair brought on by the brutal Roman occupation added fuel to popular speculation about the name and personality of God's chosen agent who would announce the impending end of the world.

By the second century C.E. the figure of the messianic king had become almost totally mythological. The name of the Messiah, for example, was thought to be one of the seven things that God created before the creation of the world (*Pesahim* 54a). Rav Johanan even went so far as to maintain that the world was only created for the sake of the Messiah (*Sanhedrin* 98b). The highly respected sage Rabbi Akiva, whose hasty choice of Bar Kochba (a military fanatic who led an abortive revolt in 132–135 C.E. against Roman occupation) as the Messiah does not seem to have been an isolated element in his messianic fervor, taught that there are two thrones in Heaven (following Dan. 7:9), one is for God and one is for the Messiah (*Hagigah* 14a).

These rabbinic speculations are modest compared to the virtually unrestrained mythological elements found in intertestamental apocalyptic writings like IV Esdras, where the Messiah is envisioned as a human-like being who is blown up from the depths of the sea, flies through the air, strikes terror into all who hear or behold his presence, defeats the wicked who assemble to war against him by consuming them with the fire of his breath, and only then begins the ingathering of the exiles and the restoration of political sovereignty that was the mark of the Messiah at an earlier time (IV Esdras, chap. 13:1ff.). This represents quite a change from the impressive, but thoroughly human, picture of the Messiah given by Isaiah (11:2), "The Spirit of the Lord shall rest upon him, the spirit of wisdom and insight, the spirit of counsel and heroism, the spirit of knowledge and godliness."

Further complicating any attempt to identify the figure of the Messiah is a little-known but influential rabbinic belief in a *second* Messiah, called the Messiah ben Joseph. The Messiah ben Joseph was supposed to arrive prior to the Messiah ben David and was to die in battle against the forces of evil, and only then would God send the Messiah ben David, who would defeat the enemies of God, gather the exiles, and inaugurate the Messianic Age (*Sukkah* 52a and *Baba Batra* 123b). The suffering of the Messiah ben Joseph is not seen as atonement for the sins of the people but merely as a part of the general violence and moral collapse, which is also a sign of the Messianic Age.

The actual name of the Messiah was also the subject of speculation by the rabbis, who quite often used some version of their teacher's name. Some possibilities were: Menachem, Shilo, Yinon, Hanina, Hezekiah, Tzemach, Hulya, but by far the most popular choice was of course simply David. The most beautiful choice for the name of the Messiah is Rabbi Jose the Galilean's: "Also the Messiah's name is called Peace, for it is written (Isa. 9:5) 'Everlasting Father, Prince of Peace.' "

SIGN #2.
THE APPEARANCE OF ELIJAH THE PROPHET

The basis of the belief that Elijah's appearance on Earth is a necessary prerequisite for the Messianic Age is the prophecy found at the end of the book of Malachi (3:23–24): "Behold, I will send you Elijah the prophet before the coming of the great and dreadful day of the Lord. And he shall turn the heart of the fathers to the children, and the heart of the children to their fathers, lest I come and smite the earth with a curse."

The rabbis added to Elijah's moralistic, conciliatory function, a legalistic one in which Elijah will also be responsible for arbitrating legal disputes that could not previously be settled, the questions called in Aramaic *teku* (*Mishnah Baba Metzia* 1:8, 2:8, 3:4 and also *Menahot* 45a). There is no doubt, though, that this legal function is secondary to Elijah's task of ushering in the peace of the Messianic Age (*Eduyot* 8:7). To prevent Elijah's legal rulings from interrupting observances of *Shabbat* and the festivals, in fact, a tradition emerged that he would not appear on a *Shabbat* or a festival or even on the eve of one (*Eruvin* 43b).

Elijah is identified not only as a prophet but also as a priest in the lineage ot Aaron, Eleazar, and Phinehas. In connection with that priestly role a beautiful teaching is preserved that Elijah will bring with him three things for the Messianic Age. First, the manna that fed the Israelites during their wanderings in the desert; second, the flask of water and the flask of oil that were used to purify and anoint the Tabernacle; and the third, the flowering staff of Aaron (*Mekhilta*). The manna would feed the people during the time of tribulations in the Messianic Age. The word Messiah (Heb.: *mashiah*) means "the anointed one," and so the holy oil would be used to anoint the Messiah, who would then take as his scepter the rod of Aaron with its ripe almonds and flowering blossoms.

SIGN #3.
WARS, MORAL COLLAPSE, BEASTS: THE BIRTH PANGS OF THE MESSIAH

The phrase, "birth pangs of the Messiah," is so picturesque and powerful that it is misleading. Connoting the travail that precedes the joy of birth, it does not refer to sufferings of the Messiah, but rather the general state of anarchy and social chaos that *all must endure* as a sign of the coming of the Messianic Age. This rabbinic concept has its antecedent in the prophetic teaching of a catastrophic "Day of the Lord" that would precede the final judgment,

Woe unto you that desire the
day of the Lord!
Why would you have the day of
the Lord?
It is darkness, and not light.
As if a man did flee from a lion,
And a bear met him;
And went into a house and leaned
his hand on a wall,
And a serpent bit him.
Shall not the day of the Lord
be darkness, and not light?
Even very dark, and no brightness
in it?
(Amos 5:18–20; also, Isa. 2:11)

Also biblical in origin is the belief that this chaos will engulf both man and nature in a truly all encompassing cataclysm (Isa. 2:12–16). The cause of all this is a pervasive moral collapse in society, which leads to a forgetting of the words of God, the Law of life,

Behold, the days come, saith the
Lord God,
That I will send a famine in the
land,
Not a famine of bread, nor a thirst
for water,
But of hearing the words of the Lord.
(Amos 8:11)

Suffering the brutal Hadrianic persecutions, the rabbis had ample reason to continue on this biblical theme of impending doom as a necessary prerequisite to final redemption. The most powerful statement of their views is found in *Sanhedrin* 97a: "With the footprints of the Messiah, insolence will increase and dearth reach its height; the vine will yield its fruit but the wine will be costly. There will be none to offer reproof, and the whole empire will be converted to heresy. The meeting place of the scholars will be laid waste and Golan will be made desolate and the people of the frontier will go about from city to city with none to take pity on them. The wisdom of the scribes will become foolish, and they that shun sin will be despised. The young will insult their elders, and the great will wait upon the insignificant. . . . The face of this generation is as the face of a dog; and a son does not feel ashamed before his father. On whom then can we rely? On our Father who is in heaven." (Quoted from *The Messianic Idea in Israel,* J. Klausner)

Similarly Rav Johanan taught, "If you see a generation continually declining, wait for him [the Messiah]." He also taught, "The son of David will come only in a generation which is wholly wicked." (*Sanhedrin* 98a) Rav Hiyya bar Abba left no doubt that all this pestilence and war was meant to destroy the wicked in preparation for the coming of the Messianic Age.

The sorrows of the period of birth pangs were depicted with such graphic detail that Rabba was said to have exclaimed, "Let him [the Messiah] come but may I not see him!" To which the more ardent Rav Joseph, remembering Zechariah's prophecy that the Messiah would arrive riding an ass, remarked, "Let him come and may I be privileged to sit in the shadow of the dung of his ass!" (*Sanhedrin* 98b)

The wars specified as an element of the travail of the Messiah are sometimes referred to as wars of dragons or wars against Gog and Magog. Rav Hanan bar Tahlifa transmits the contents of a mysterious scroll found by a mercenary in the Roman army: "Four thousand two hundred and ninety one years after its creation, the world will be orphaned. As to the years which follow, some of them will witness the wars of the dragons, some the wars of Gog and Magog, and the rest will be the Messianic Age; and the Holy One, blessed be He, will not renew His world until after seven thousand years." (*Sanhedrin* 97b)

The "dragons" may be a reference to the legendary land and sea monsters, Behemoth and Leviathan, or perhaps to the four beasts prophesied by Daniel (chap. 7), the lion, bear, leopard, and ten-horned beast. Gog and Magog are only slightly more defined. Klausner (*The Messianic Idea in Israel*) believes that the first reference to the wars of Gog and Magog (sometimes Gog from the land of Magog) in Ezekiel, chapters 38 and 39, are really an echo of the prophecy of Jeremiah and Zephaniah concerning the onslaught of the Scythians from the north in the time of Josiah. Over time, however, Gog and Magog became the symbolic exemplars of the enemies of Israel and the foes of the Messiah. The Messiah ben Joseph will fall in battle against these mighty kings from the north, only to be succeeded by the victorious Messiah ben David. Some rabbis thought this apocalyptic battle would endure for one year (*Mishnah Eduyot* 2:10). Others thought that the terror of the battle would be so great that all those who had converted to Judaism only for the gain of the messianic blessings would be scared away (*Avodah Zarah* 3b).

The most inspiring interpretation of the wars that will mark the birth pangs of the Messiah comes from the Jerusalem Talmud: "As Rav Judah ben Ile'ai expounded: 'In the time to come the Holy One, blessed be He, will bring the Evil Inclination and slaughter him in the presence of the righteous and the wicked. To the righteous he will appear as a towering mountain, while to the wicked he will seem like a [mere] strand of hair. Both groups will weep. The righteous will weep and say: How were we able to conquer this towering mountain! And the wicked will weep, saying: How was it possible for us not to vanquish this strand of hair!' " (*Ta'anit* 1:1, quoted from *The Sages: Their Concepts and Beliefs*, E. Urbach) No dragon or army, but the tendency of all people to stray from the way of life ordained by God—this is the true enemy to be overcome in that time.

SIGN #4. THE ARRIVAL OF THE APPOINTED TIME: CALCULATING THE END

The speculations about the signs of the Messianic Age in Judaism did not end with the descriptions of its principal figures. Hope mixed with suffering stimulated ample predictions as to the actual time when the new age would begin. Indeed, Silver (*A History of Messianic Speculation in Israel*) identifies five distinct methods used by the calculators of the Messianic Age:

1) Application of the various cryptic messianic dates given in the book of Daniel. At least six periods of time are mentioned in Daniel: a) time, times and half a time, b) 2300, c) 70 weeks (also 7 weeks, 62 weeks, and 1 week), d) season, seasons and half a season, e) 1290 days, f) 1335 days.

2) Use of other biblical texts that refer to the future or that had become associated with messianic predictions (for example, Gen. 14).

3) Calculations based upon the duration of the Egyptian exile (400 years) and the Babylonian Exile (70 years).

4) Since all Hebrew letters have a numerical equivalent, a technique known as *gematria* developed in which certain messianic passages were reduced to numbers, which were then subtracted or added to the then current year in the Jewish calendar. The widespread acceptance of the use of *gematria* accounts in large measure for the appeal of the seventeenth-century false Messiah Shabbatai Zevi and his calculation of 1648 as a messianic year. Related to *gematria* are the techniques of *notarikon* (acrostics), *ziruf* or *hiluf* (anagrams), and *temurah* (substitution of one letter in a word for another).

5) Despite the biblical prohibition against the use of astrology, it was also one of the techniques used by the calculators. (Deut. 1:19; 17:13 also *Shabbat* 156a). Of particular significance seemed to be the conjunction of Jupiter and Saturn.

Based upon these techniques the following timetables for the Messianic Age were proposed in the classical period of rabbinic literature:

1) Rabbi Simeon ben Yohai taught that there would be a "week" of seven years of wars, famine, and suffering—the birth pangs of the Messiah—followed in the seventh year by the appearance of the Messiah ben David. (*Derekh Eretz Zuta*, chap. 10; *Sanhedrin* 97a)

2) In *Sanhedrin* 99a various rabbis contribute their own personal choices as to the duration (not the starting time) of the Messianic Age:

R. Eliezer ben Hyrcanus .... 40 years.
R. Eleazar ben Azariah .... 70 years.
R. Dosa .... 400 years.
R. Jose the Galilean .... 3 generations.
(also 365 years)

Other rabbis had the duration pegged at a much longer time. Rav Samuel had it as the length of time between the creation and his time in the third century. Other figures: 2,000, 7,000, 365,000 years (*Pesikta Rabbati* 4b). Another influential *baraita* (an anonymous rabbinic teaching before 200 C.E.) states, "The world will endure six thousand years: two thousand in chaos, two thousand under the law, and two thousand during the Messianic Age." (*Sanhedrin* 97ab)

The following *baraita* actually takes a stab at predicting the beginning of the Messianic Age: "If, four thousand two hundred and thirty-one years after the Creation of the World, a man should say to you, 'Take this field, worth a thousand denars, for one denar,' do not take it. [To which Rashi adds the explanation] For in that year the Messiah will come and all fields will be redistributed without price." (*Avodah Zarah* 9b)

Similarly the start of the new age was reckoned by a revelation of Elijah to Rav Judah, the brother of Rav Sallah the Pious, "The world shall endure not less than eighty-five jubilees, and the son of David shall come in the last jubilee." (*Sanhedrin* 97b)

Rabbi Eliezer and Rabbi Joshua even disputed the month in which the Messianic Age would begin. According to Rabbi Eliezer,

"In the month of Nisan they were redeemed [from Egypt], and in Tishri they will be redeemed in time to come," but Rabbi Joshua differed and said, "They were redeemed in Nisan, and in Nisan they will be redeemed in time to come." (*Rosh Ha-Shanah* 11b)

Needless to say, the calculation of messianic dates represented an immense theological and emotional risk because the expected date might pass without the arrival of Elijah or the Messiah. So Rav Samuel ben Rav Nachmani taught in the name of Rav Jonathan, "Blasted be the bones of those who calculate the End, for they used to say: 'Since the [time of the] End has arrived, but he has not come, he will never come.' " (*Sanhedrin* 97b)

One way to protect against this despair was to simply teach that the appointed day was unknowable: "Seven things are hidden from men. These are the day of death, the day of consolation, the depth of judgement; no man knows what is in the mind of his friend; no man knows which of his business ventures will be profitable, or when the kingdom of the house of David will be restored, or when the sinful kingdom will fall." (*Pesahim* 54b) Like the finding of a treasure or the sting of a scorpion, the coming of the Messiah was to be an unexpected event.

Another way to guard against the sin of "forcing the End" was to set an appointed time that was indefinite. Rav Jose ben Halafta taught that whoever knows how many years the Israelites worshiped foreign gods knows when the son of David will come. In another place it is recorded that the son of David will not come into the world until all the souls in the storehouse of souls in Heaven have been dispensed to bodies. (*Niddah* 13b)

The desire to avoid the foredoomed intensity of messianic fervor (such as that which prompted Rabbi Akiba to identify the zealot Bar Kochba as the Messiah) is beautifully expressed in this tender rabbinic saying, "If there was a plant in your hand, and you are told: 'Behold, the Messiah is here,' go and plant the plant, and then go forth to welcome him." (*Avot de-Rabbi Natan* 31:33b–34a) Rabbi Nathan, living after the Hadrianic persecutions, was steadfast in his belief that hope need not be lost just because the exact date of the Messianic Age could not be calculated with precision. He quoted The Book of Habakkuk 2:3 to a weary generation, "For the vision is yet for the appointed time, and it speaks concerning the end, and does not lie; though it tarry, wait for it; because it will surely come, it will not delay."

SIGN #5. ACTS OF HUMAN REPENTANCE AND CHARITY

The most profound way the rabbis found to diffuse the antinomian and anarchistic elements in the messianic expectations of the people was to reinforce the ancient biblical view that redemption only follows repentance. Only Ezekiel in the biblical period and only minor figures like Rav Joshua ben Hananiah and Rav Joshua ben Levi in the rabbinic period seem to have seriously believed that the Messianic Age would arrive whether or not the people repented (Ezek. 36:22–23 and *Yerushalmi Ta'anit* 63d). More normative are the teachings of Amos, Hosea, Isaiah, and Jeremiah, which, succinctly expressed by Rabbi Eliezer, are that, "If they do not repent, they will not be redeemed." Or in the words of Rav, "All the calculated dates of redemption have passed, and now the matter depends upon repentance and good deeds." (*Exodus Rabbah* 5:18)

These rabbinic teachings were meant to blunt the increasing superstitions of the people regarding the signs of the Messianic Age. Traditions of oneiromancy (divination by means of dreams) developed in which dreaming of an ass or a vine meant the coming of the Messiah was not far off. Another ancient superstition held that a certain bird, called the *racham*, would settle on the ground and hiss, thus foretelling the Messiah's speedy arrival.

Charity and repentance are singled out as the most effective qualities in bringing the Messiah: "Rabbi Jose the Galilean said: 'Great is repentance [in another passage 'great is charity'] because it brings near redemption. . . . Why will a redeemer come to Zion? Because of those that turn from transgression in Jacob.' " (*Yoma* 86b)

Even one day of repentance was considered sufficient by the rabbis to bring the Messiah ben David immediately. (*Genesis Rabbah* 49:6) Indeed the horrors of the birth pangs of the Messiah can be eased or eliminated, "by the study of Torah and acts of benevolence." (*Mekhilta*) Further, the observance by all Israel of only one (in an older source, two) *Shabbat* would be enough to bring the Messiah. (*Shabbat* 118b and *Yerushalmi Ta'anit* 64a) This rabbinic emphasis on the messianic importance of the moral and ritual law, which also supported the rhythms of daily Jewish life, was not a mere neutralization of the messianic spirit but rather a reinterpretation of ordinary acts "under the aspects of eternity." In the medieval Jewish mystical literature the role of every mundane righteous act as a part of the reunification of the world was particularly evident in doctrines such as *tikkun olam* (fixing the world) and *yichud kusha brich hu u'shechinteh* (the unification of God and His Shekhinah).

POSTSCRIPT: THE MESSIANIC AGE VS. THE WORLD TO COME

However confused and contradictory rabbinic opinions may have been about the signs of the Messianic Age, there was little disagreement over the belief that this was not the end of the ball game—that was called "the World to Come" (*olam ha-ba*) or "the End" (*ha-ketz*). For example, Rav Hiyya bar Abba teaches in the name of Rav Johanan, "All the prophets prophesied only about the Days of the Messiah, but [as for] of the World to Come, 'The eye has not seen, O Lord, beside Thee.' " (*Sanhedrin* 99a) (See also IV Ezra 7:26–44)

The purest vision of the World to Come is from Rav, a third-century Babylonian sage: "The World to Come is not like this world. In the World to Come there is no eating and drinking, no begetting of children; no bargaining, no jealousy and hatred, and no strife; but the righteous sit with their crowns on their heads enjoying the fullness of the presence of God." (*Berakhot* 17a)

In the light of Rav's teaching, all the various rabbinic references to the great natural abundance and wondrous events that are to come in the *olam ha-ba* should really be seen as visions of a latter part of the Messianic Age. Since they are so marvellous and well known (beginning with Isaiah's "and the wolf shall dwell with the lamb"), some of these rewards are included here as part of the "late" Messianic Age.

Most wonderful are the rabbinic descriptions of the fertility of nature in that time. The kernels of wheat will be as large as two bull's kidneys. Grapes will be so large that each one will yield not less than thirty jars of wine. Wheat stalks will rise higher than palm trees, and both fruit trees and people will bear constantly. (*Sifrei* on Deuteronomy 32:13ff.)

Not only all Jewish exiles, but all the nations shall be gathered to Jerusalem to acknowledge the sovereignty of the Lord. To accommodate them, the boundaries of the Land of Israel will be magically enlarged and "spread out like a fig tree." (*Sifre* on Deuteronomy)

A rabbinic legend has it that when Adam sinned he shrank in stature, so the prediction is found that in the Messianic Age people will grow to the height of twice Adam's original height, two hundred cubits (*Baba Batra* 75a).

The rabbis engaged in a fascinating dispute about the role of animals in the late Messianic Age: " 'And I will cause evil beasts to cease out of the land.' (Lev. 26:6) R. Judah said, 'He will remove them from the world.' R. Simeon said, 'He will cause them to cease from doing harm.' R. Simeon said, 'When does it redound more to the praise of God—when there are no harmful beasts or when there are harmful beasts yet they do no harm? When there are harmful beasts but they do no harm, of course . . .' For it is written, 'And the wolf shall dwell with the lamb, and the leopard shall lie down with the kid; and the calf and the young lion and the fatling together, and a little child shall lead them. And the cow and the bear shall feed, their young ones shall lie down together, and the lion shall eat straw like the ox. And the suckling child shall play on the hole of the asp, and the weaned child shall put his hand on the basilis's den.' (Isa. 11:6–8)" (*Sifra, be-Hukkotai*, chap. 2)

Although the normal harmful beasts will be simply made docile, the great monsters of land, sea, and air that have their place in Jewish folklore will not have so pleasant a fate. (See Louis Ginzberg, *Legends of the Jews*, Vol. I, pp. 27–29.) The great sea monster whose creation, though not its name, is recorded on the fifth day of Creation is called Leviathan. This beast, called the plaything of God and referred to in Job chaps. 40–41, was immense and splendiferous. Leviathan sucks up all the water discharged by the Jordan River in one day, illuminates the sea with the radiance of its fins and eyes, boils the sea with its fiery breath, and apparently smells awful.

Originally there were two Leviathans, but fearing the destructive power of two such creatures, God pickled the female in brine and is saving her for a banquet feast to be served to all the righteous some time in the late Messianic Age. The pickled female Leviathan will be served with the fresh-cooked male Leviathan, who will be killed that day as the result of a battle with the great monster of the land, Behemoth. According to Rav Simeon bar Judan, "Behemoth strikes Leviathan with its horns and slaughters him by piercing, and Leviathan hits Behemoth with his fins and tears him." (*Leviticus Rabbah* 13:3) More miraculous still is the fact that God will make kosher the monster's meat even though it was killed in a ritually impure manner! The amount of meat assigned to each guest at this banquet of beasties will be in direct proportion to their righteousness, and what is left over will be distributed among all peoples. What is left from Leviathan's skin will be stretched over the city of Jerusalem and its light will illumine the world.

Also on the menu at this banquet will be the bird monster called Ziz, a bird so big its ankles rest on earth while its head reaches to heaven. Once, the story is told, one of the Ziz's eggs broke and flooded sixty cities with its yolk. His wings are so huge that they darken the sky when they are spread, and they protect the earth against the vicious storms that blow up from the south. The roast Ziz will also be made kosher by God as a reward to the righteous for abstaining from nonkosher food in their premessianic life.

The rewards of the late Messianic Age are not, however, merely culinary. The unjust distribution of land in this world will be rectified in the World to Come (the reference in the following passage should really be to the Messianic Age and not to the World to Come, where the only activity is receiving divine resplendence): "And the division [of land] in the World to Come will not be like the division in this world. In this world, should a man possess a cornfield he does not possess an orchard; should he possess an orchard he does not possess a cornfield. But in the World to Come, there will be no single individual who will not possess land in mountain, lowland, and valley (that is, every man will have different kinds of land, on which he can grow cereals, grapes, or fruit trees, as he likes.)" (*Baba Batra* 122a)

Learning, which was to languish during the early messianic times, would be revived so that the great academies of Sura and Pumbedita in Babylonia would be transported to the Holy Land. Some rabbis imagined that God would be the chief of the academy and teach the true order of the verses of the Hebrew Bible, which He alone knows. (*Genesis Rabbah* 95:3)

Surely the most important belief about the late Messianic Age was that at that time all the dead would be reunited with their souls in a general resurrection and day of judgment in which final verdicts would be pronounced upon all persons. Since a certain rabbinic tradition believed that this resurrection would only take place in the Land of Israel, a clever doctrine was developed teaching that there is a vast network all over the world of underground tunnels that act as conduits for those souls who died outside the Land. (*Ketuvot* 111a based on Ezek. 37:14)

Perhaps the most moving of all the rabbinic fantasies about the rewards of the Messianic Age concern the ingathering of the exiles to the Land of Israel. The rabbis believed that God's Shekhinah—a term for God's indwelling presence, which later assumed deeper mystical connotations after the rise of Jewish mysticism in the thirteenth century—actually went into exile with the people and would return with them. R. Simeon ben Yohai says: "Come and see how beloved is Israel before the Holy One, blessed be He; for wherever they went into exile the Shekhinah was with them. . . . Likewise, when they shall be redeemed in the future, the Shekhinah will be with them, as it is written [Deut. 30:3], 'Then the Lord thy God will return with thy captivity.' It does not say, 'will bring back thy captivity' but 'will return with thy captivity'—teaching that the Holy One Blessed be He, returns with them from the places of exile." (*Megillah* 29a)

Even before the medieval mystical turn of Judaism, the profound hope took root that the peace and wholeness of the Messianic Age would encompass both God and the people who had wandered and suffered for so long all in the belief that, "Though he tarries, yet will I await him."

Contemporary Reflections on the Messianic Age

What follows is a random reflection on the meaning for our time of all these messianic signs and portents. The preceding only asked of Judaism's messianic vision, "What are its elements?" The question now is, "What are its meanings?"

In the unique rhythms of Jewish messianism, suffering, the surest refutation of God's presence, is transformed into the surest sign of impending redemption. Judaism did not form its messianic vision on a confidence in reason and the inexorable march of progress in human history: that kind of vision makes the Messianic Age nothing but a cashing in of accumulated merits. The "birth pangs of the Messiah" (Sign #3) describe an arc that heads down before heading up—a truth about redemption that later Jewish mystics would formalize in the teaching of ascent within descent (*aliyah b'toch yiredah*). Wars and general moral collapse were signs, not refutations, of the new age aborning. Lest this Jewish messianic rhythm seem too eccentric, it should be remembered that in Marx's notion of the increasing "emiseration" (impoverishment) of the working class as a precondition for revolutionary change, is found exactly the same redemptive rhythm of going down before going up. The doctrine of birth pangs also brings a closer understanding of the intimate relationship between hope and despair. Sufferings that wound but do not crush force one to refocus on a better day and to do something to bring that day about. The rabbis called these kind of sufferings, "the afflictions of love" (*esurin shel ahavah*).

The downward and then upward movement of Jewish messianism gives a hopeful context to the otherwise confusing and seemingly fatalistic notion of an "appointed time" for the Messianic Age. In a religion that stresses human free will with such obdurant tenacity, a doctrine that the "set days must be fulfilled" seems sour. What is present here, however, is rather a sublime awareness that at some point in the descent of man the ascent must begin, and since the turning point is shrouded in the depths of human misery and sin, one must be hesitant to say that human effort alone accomplished it. Just as the physical universe was brought out of physical chaos (*tohu va'vohu*) by God's word; so too the creation of a morally new universe must make room for God's abiding mercy and grace (*hesed* and *rahamim*). In that nodal moment the human will to moral perfection finds a holy ground. That is the "appointed time," a moment of lived time (*kairos*) not merely elapsed time (*chronos*). The two-millennia-old battle between Judaism and Christianity has, unfortunately, distorted them both. Judaism has forgotten the meaning of grace and Christianity has forgotten the meaning of works. The appointed time is a time of grace, and the ascent that follows is a time of works. There is a thin line between patience and acquiescence. The belief in an appointed time allows both for waiting and action, which will make the waiting a true preparation.

Balancing expectation and constancy is far from easy. When one anticipates a banquet of "beasties" like Leviathan, Behemoth, and the Ziz, a chicken on *Shabbat* is bound to pale by comparison. Therefore it is not surprising that the rabbis spent so much time discouraging messianic speculations. Examples of this can be seen in the above list of signs: the teaching that only observance of the law can protect one against the travails of the Messianic Age; the necessity for charity and repentance as prerequisites for the new age; the requirement that all Israel observe at least one *Shabbat* before the Messiah would come; and rabbinic statements that they do not believe in a Messiah or if they do, that they would be just as happy not to witness his coming. The fantastic always has an excitement missing in the mundane, but the genius of the Jewish messianic vision is to give both their due place in the eschatological drama.

What is found here is a remarkable parallel to Soren Kierkegaard's stages along life's way. First, an aesthetic stage in which false absolutes are embraced, the law is abandoned, and a collective ennui sets in. Then, an embracing of the true absolute of the moral law, which raises man, but not to the level of God. The third and final stage is accomplished by an act of human passion for the divine, which encounters the mystery of a divine passion for the human. This is not the Messianic Age, but the true World to Come, the stage where the righteous sit in orgiastic delight, crowns on their heads, clinging to the ultimate divine splendor. The divine-human difference is never bridged; it is made irrelevant. This vision is perhaps the greatest synthesis of law and passion ever encountered, a sublime yet real creation of faith and hope.

A Story: Rav Joshua ben Levi met Elijah at the entrance of Rav Simeon bar Yohai's burial cave and asked him: "When will the Messiah come?" He answered him: "Go and ask him yourself." "Where does he live?" "At the entrance of Rome." "How is he to be recognized?" "He sits among the sick; now all of them untie and tie up [their bandages] at one and the same time, while he unties and reties [his bandages] one at a time, saying [to himself]: 'In case I am needed, I shall not be delayed.'" So he [Rav Joshua ben Levi] went to him [and] said to him, "Peace be upon you, O my master and teacher!" He replied: "Peace be upon you, O son of Levi!" He then said to him: "When will the master come?" His reply was: "Today." He [Rav Joshua ben Levi] then returned to Elijah, who asked him: "What did he tell you?" He answered him: "Peace be upon thee, O son of Levi!" Said [Elijah] to him: "He assured you and your father of a place in the World to Come." [Rav Joshua ben Levi] rejoined "But he lied to me; for he told me 'I shall come today,' yet he did not come." Said [Elijah] to him, "This is what he meant: 'Today, if ye will hearken to His voice.'" (Sanhedrin 98b)

—M.A.G.

9 JEWISH FALSE MESSIAHS

Messianism—the belief in the coming of an age of world peace and personal redemption—is a widespread phenomenon found not only in Judaism. Within Jewish thought, however, messianism is a central concept. Maimonidies, in his usual clear and succinct style, summed up the Jewish belief in a Messiah and in the expectation of his momentary arrival. In the twelfth of his Thirteen Principles of Faith, he states: *"Ani ma'amim be'emunah she'lemah be'viath ha'moshiah. Ve'af al pi she'yith'-ma'meah, im kol zeh ahake lo be'kol yom she'yavo"* ("I believe with perfect faith in the coming of the Messiah, and though he tarry, yet I await daily his coming"). The inspirational value of these words is dramatically evidenced by reports from concentration camps where millions went to the gas chambers chanting these very words.

The basic search for "the birth pangs of the Messiah" has led to intense speculation at every moment of turbulence in Jewish history (see "Signs of the Coming of the Messiah"). Hence, the periods in which terrible massacres of Jews have occured have seen fervent messianic expectations and movements.

The idea of a charismatic individual who would act as the leader of the movement is a postbiblical variation that evolved around the time of the Second Temple (circa 70 C.E.). He was expected to be wise and understanding; he was to bring peace and justice to Israel and mankind; but he was never more than a being of flesh and blood.

The concept of messianism is as old as the existence of pretenders to that role. Their audiences have ranged from the few to the many, and the reaction to their claims has ranged from mockery and derision to complete acceptance. Regardless of their beginnings, their final end has usually been violent death or imprisonment. But along the way they have somehow managed to fire imaginations and raise fervent expectations, if not to produce the desired results.

To dismiss these Messiahs as heretics or agents of the devil explains little. Whatever their intentions, they appealed to a people who needed renewed spiritual energy to resist an external world filled with animosity toward them. The Messiah and his followers existed for each other.

Bar Kokhba (Second Century C.E.)

The saga of false Messiahs must begin with—if not the first messianic pretender in Jewish history—certainly the most important early figure of this genre. Simon Bar Kokhba was the military leader of a rebellion in the second century C.E. of the Jews of Palestine, who had been suffering under a brutal

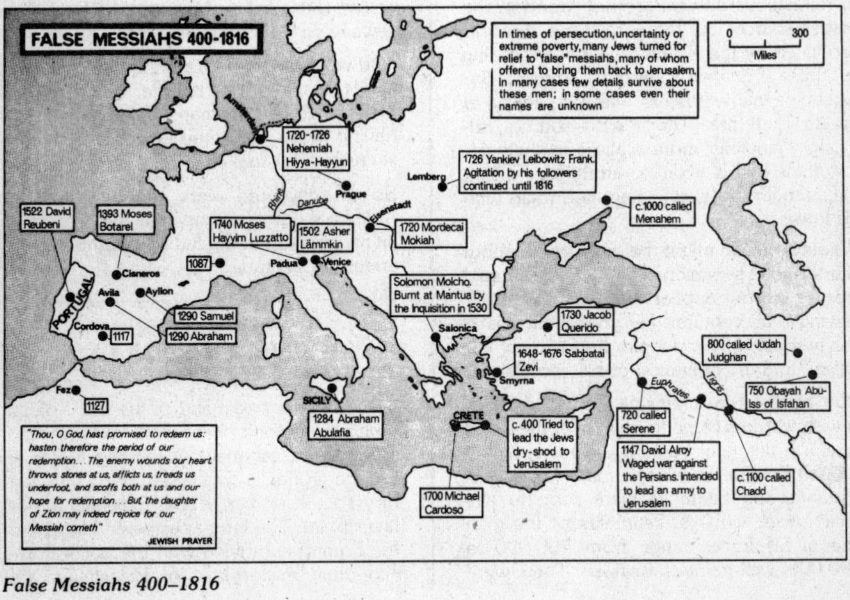

False Messiahs 400–1816

Roman government for close to one hundred years. Such unjust suffering was interpreted by many to mean only one thing, that the Day of Judgment was close at hand and deliverance was near. In this context and for the first time in history, the messianic belief became a political factor of great importance.

When the people were told that the Emperor Hadrian had decided to turn the Holy City into a Roman colony, most of the nation rose up in arms. While the celebrated Rabbi Akiba was recognized as the spiritual leader of the generation, there remained to be found a commander for the ultimate battle. Suddenly, as if from nowhere, such a savior appeared in the person of Bar Kokhba.

Rabbi Akiba, generally accepted as the foremost rabbinic authority of all time, proclaimed upon first seeing Bar Kokhba: "That is a messianic King!" Clearly this was not a Messiah to be taken lightly. So intrigued was Rabbi Akiba that he applied to him the verse: "a star (kokhab) has arisen out of Jacob" (Num. 24:17); thus, at once, presenting Bar Kokhba with both a name and a mission.

Not all were quite so accepting of Bar Kokhba's divine calling however. One rabbi dubiously stated that "sooner shall grass grow from thy chin, Akiba, than the Messiah will appear." But for a people starved for any glimmering of hope, the approval of Akiba was more than enough proof of Bar Kokhba's authenticity.

One might rightly expect that all sorts of divine powers would be attributed to a messianic figure such as Bar Kokhba. Interestingly enough, however, such descriptions of miraculous powers are not found in the Jewish sources but rather in those accounts produced by the Roman writers. According to these "enemy" sources, among Bar Kokhba's many talents was the ability to breath forth fire. The Jewish sources, although generally more realistic in their descriptions of his abilities, attributed to him the strength to deflect catapulted rocks with his knees.

Whatever else might be construed about Bar Kokhba's personality, it must be said that he did not appear to be selfish or self-serving in his ventures. His goals were clearly the freedom of his people, the glory of Judaism, and the liberation of his homeland.

Due to his great charisma and leadership, Jewish warriors came from all over the world to aid in this final battle against the mighty Roman Empire. Even the usually hostile Samaritans and heathens were soon to ally their forces with his. Estimates of the total size of his forces range from 400,000 to 580,000 well-trained warriors. They were ruled by Bar Kokhba's iron hand. To remain in his army a man had to be able to uproot a cedar tree or else lose a finger.

When Bar Kokhba's forces recaptured Jerusalem, the hope arose that the Temple, which had lain in ruins for sixty-two years, might be rebuilt by this new Messiah who had overwhelmed the might of the Romans. The preoccupation of carrying on the warfare, however, precluded the possibility of such an undertaking. Interestingly, Jewish sovereignty did allow for the minting of coins that appeared with Bar Kokhba's likeness bearing a pot of manna and the rod of Aaron, unmistakable symbols of the Messiah.

During the years 132–134 C.E., the kingdom of Bar Kokhba defeated every force sent by Hadrian. In relatively short order, over fifty forts, 985 cities, and all of Judea, Samaria, and Galilee fell to Bar Kokhba. When the potentially disastrous consequences of this uprising were finally realized by the Emperor, he placed the military operations in the hands of Julius Severus, the most successful Roman commander.

Severus understood the problems associated with fighting an essentially guerrilla army in the classical tradition. Therefore, his strategy was to surround and besiege the rebels in their strongholds, forcing them into starvation. By this tactic, one-by-one, the Jewish citadels fell.

The retreating remnants of Bar Kokhba's forces took refuge in the fortress of Betar, southwest of Jerusalem. A final brave stand took place at this site. After almost an entire year under the onslaught of the mighty Roman Army, on the ninth day of the month of Av, Betar fell and close to half a million Jews were bloodily massacred.

And what of the Messiah, the great potential savior of the Jewish people? His head was brought to the Roman general, his body having been—for some inexplicable reason—crushed by snakes.

So disappointed were the Jews in Bar Kokhba's dismal failure that messianism as an anticipation of the future redemption was ended for centuries.

Moses of Crete
(Fifth Century C.E.)

Following the tragic end of the Bar Kokhba rebellion, it took some time for messianic aspirations to stir anew. As the mighty Roman Empire gradually declined into the fifth century C.E., however, hopes reached a new fever point. The long-anticipated collapse of the Empire combined with the political and economic misfortunes of Palestinian and

Babylonian Jewry touched off renewed speculations.

There existed a popular interpretation of a rabbinic passage which fuelled these emotions. Attributed to Elijah the Prophet, it was construed to mean that "The world will endure no less than 85 jubilees (4250 years) and in the last jubilee the son of David will come [i.e. between 440 and 490 C.E.]." In fact, this was but one of a number of passages in various rabbinical sources that pointed to the advent of a messianic era in the fifth century. For a downtrodden people these were more than sufficient signs.

To feed the hungry appetite of the oppressed in the mid fifth century, a pseudo-Messiah named Moses appeared in the Greek island of Crete. Moses of Crete travelled the length and breadth of the island attracting communities to his calling wherever he ventured. As the Messiah, this new Moses would "lead dry-footed the Children of Israel to the Promised Land of Israel." As incredible as his claim might have been, he managed to convince just about the entire Jewish population of Crete of his authenticity.

The power of his persuasion is evidenced by the actions of the population who embraced his words. Everywhere, Jews began neglecting their businesses, abandoning their properties, and awaiting the day when this Moses would lead them to Israel. Never again would they have to live under oppression, for the moment of redemption was at hand.

On the appointed day Moses led a huge procession to a promontory over the sea. The entire Jewish population of Crete followed in his footsteps. Hundreds upon hundreds of men, women, and children bearing all of their goods, solemnly marched behind their possessed leader.

At the cliff, overlooking the sea, Moses raised his arms. As his biblical namesake had done, he ordered the sea to part and for the people to march forth with faith. The people obeyed but the sea did not.

Many were drowned in the cold, unfriendly waters. Others were saved by local fishermen and sailors. Those who survived the ordeal looked to avenge themselves on their leader, but he had vanished, never to be heard from again.

As a result of this unfortunate incident, the great Rabenu Ashi (compiler of the Talmud), who had previously tried to subdue the messianic fervor, reinterpreted the previously mentioned statement of Elijah to mean "Before the 85th jubilee you need not expect him at all, After the 85th jubilee you *may* expect him".

David Alroy (Twelfth Century C.E.)

As a result of the dismal circumstances of the Jews during the Crusades, the last quarter of the eleventh century and the whole of the twelfth century abound in abortive messianic movements. None was more spectacular than that led by David Alroy, who appeared about 1147, during the Second Crusade.

Born in Amadiya, Kurdistan, Alroy was regarded by all who came into contact with him as strikingly handsome and of great personal charm. In his studies at the Baghdad Academy he became a top biblical and talmudic scholar, as well as an expert in everything from Arabic literature to magic.

The Jews in Babylon were not the most learned of Jews in those days (as one commentator puts it "they are not even conversant with Talmud"). Some of the communities were under the oppressive rule of the Sultans of Persia, while others roamed free in the mountains of Chaftan. Yet all, even the nomadic tribes of Jews, accepted the rulings of the rabbis that were sent to them.

Alroy declared himself the Messiah and set out to convince the Jews to revolt against the Sultan of Persia. A letter was sent to Jewish communities throughout the Middle East, announcing his claim and telling people to prepare for the return to Jerusalem with fasting and praying. With his knowledge of magic he was able to perform "miracles" to convince others of his messianic mission. Benjamin of Tudela, a contemporary, in his diary thus sums up Alroy's ventures: "He took it into his head to revolt against the king of Persia, and to gather around him the Jews who lived in the mountains of Chaftan, in order to war against the Gentiles and to capture Jerusalem and to lead them forth from amongst the nations, and the people believed in him and proclaimed him the Messiah."

The Sultan summoned Alroy to demonstrate his magical powers and miracles. Upon Alroy's appearance, he was seized and thrown into prison. But what are the bars of a prison to a Messiah? According to legend, Alroy, using his miraculous powers, escaped the Sultan's prison and fled.

The king, none too pleased to learn of the escape of this Jewish rebel, quickly dispatched some troops to recapture Alroy. One can imagine the king's impatience when his troops returned to tell of hearing Alroy's voice yet not being able to see the man.

As legend would have it, the king gathered up his army and personally went after the elusive Alroy, chasing him to the banks of the mystical River Gosan. Alroy somehow "vanished," but his voice issued forth calling the king and his army "fools." Suddenly Alroy reappeared out of nowhere, and they witnessed him dividing the waters and crossing.

By this time the king began to believe that Alroy might indeed have certain unusual abilities. The officers, on the other hand, insisted that the whole thing was a fraudulent illusion. Their levelheadedness won out, and the king demanded that the Jews hand over Alroy or suffer a massacre.

There exist two endings to this strange tale. One version has Alroy returning to his native Amadiya, where he initiated a revolt against the Persian ruler. In an attempt to storm the citadel he was defeated and probably killed.

According to Benjamin of Tudela, however, Alroy was urged by the Jewish leaders of Baghdad and Mosul to desist from his messianic pretentions for the safety of their communities. When this failed to deter the ambitious Alroy, the governor of Amadiya bribed Alroy's father-in-law with 10,000 crowns to dispose of the troublemaker. At the end of a banquet at which he was the special guest, Alroy had his head cut off by his father-in-law.

Such was Alroy's impact that followers persisted even after his demise, many using his name in all oaths. Benjamin Disraeli, the British Prime Minister, who converted to Christianity, was so intrigued by the Alroy legend that he wrote an unremarkable romantic novel based on it called *Wondrous Tale of Alroy* (1839).

Abraham Ben Samuel Abulafia (1240–1291)

With the last five Crusades and the continued persecutions under the Church, the thirteenth century saw no abatement in messianic speculation. Of all the pseudo-Messiahs of that time, and perhaps of all time, Abraham Abulafia was unique in his extensive scholarship and his quest for spiritual truth.

Born in Saragossa, Spain, Abulafia was always a bit of an eccentric, full of whimsy, and quite adventurous. He gained a thorough grounding in Bible and Talmud from his father, who died when Abulafia was eighteen years old. He then attempted a journey to the Holy Land but could get no further than Acre due to the Crusades.

"Then the spirit of the Lord roused me and I took my wife with me and set my face to reach my people," he wrote in his log. His travels were extensive. He sought the mythical River Sambatyon and the Lost Tribes of Israel dwelling on its banks.

Abulafia's mind was forever searching for higher truths. During his travels he would study the sciences, philosophy, logic, medicine, or any other subject he could obtain material on. But it seemed that none of these disciplines could satisfy his tumultuous mind. They gave him knowledge but not the gift of prophecy that he felt destined to receive.

Travelling between Spain and Italy, Abulafia came into contact with the spreading influence of Kabbalah, Jewish mysticism. His early reading of kabbalistic works led him to proclaim, "The spirit of the Lord reached my mouth and worked through me so that I manifested many dread and awful sights with signs and wonders."

Even the existing works of Kabbalah, however, did not fully satisfy the searching Abulafia. In his search for an even higher truth he began composing a *new* Kabbalah that would be closer to the "real truth." This new system involved the manipulation of the letters of the Tetragrammaton (the four-letter holy name of God) in various combinations and permutations and numeric values. In addition, this new Kabbalah promised the ability to reach meditative states and even prophetic states through ascetic living and various mystical techniques. At the heights of revelation he wrote: "When I reached to the Names and untied the seal bands, the Lord of all revealed Himself to me and made known to me His secret, and informed me concerning the end of the exile and the beginning of the Redemption."

Lecturing on his new Kabbalah, he gained a small following among the less educated Jews of Spain. Mounting opposition to his strange pronouncements forced him to leave for Italy. It was in Sicily, in 1284, that Abulafia alleged that in a personal interview with God he had been appointed the Messiah.

While in Italy, Abulafia hit upon what has to be his most incredible plan of all. On the day before Rosh Hashanah, Abulafia set out for Rome to convert Pope Nicholas III to Judaism. On hearing of his impending arrival, the Pope arranged for a stake to be erected so as to be spared the inconvenience of an audience with him. When he heard of these preparations on his behalf, Abulafia delayed his arrival for a couple of days. But undeterred, he pressed on to Rome and was thrown in prison by some Franciscan monks. For twenty-eight days he sat incarcerated until, according to his account, the Lord gave him "double mouth," which miraculously allowed him to escape. It seems, though, that the Pope's sudden death was the more likely cause of his release.

Following this abortive mission, Abulafia returned to the relatively safer occupation of mysticism and messianism. He immersed himself deeper and deeper into his meditative trances and after each would emerge with ever more extraordinary images.

Once, while meditating on the combinations of letters in the seventy-two-letter name of God, a trembling overcame him and he fell on the floor overcome by terror. The following day he asked his instructor, an old kabbalist, about the incident. The kabbalist assured him that he was on the path to an even higher stage of prophecy and he warned, "Only God can give you the power to control that force."

Continuing his studies and meditations, Abulafia prayed for guidance. As he was praying he felt "oil of anointment" cover him. For him, this was the final sign. Abulafia was the Messiah!

As the Messiah, however, Abulafia received a cold reception from most of his fellow Jews. The rabbis in particular rejected his criticism of their studying traditional scriptures and their ignoring Kabbalah. They particularly objected to being called "apes" by him in contrast to the kabbalists who, he said, were real "men." In turn, the rabbis prohibited his teachings, scorned his ideas, criticized his spiritual exercises, and branded him an "illiterate, dangerous charlatan."

Rejected by his own community, Abulafia found favor with the Christians who accepted his messianic claims. He bitingly commented "whilst the Christians believe in my words, the Jews eschew them, and absolutely refuse to know anything of the calculations of God's name, but prefer the calculation of their money."

A prolific writer, Abulafia wrote twenty-eight books on nonprophetic themes, including some extremely important kabbalistic works and a commentary on the Torah. He is regarded to this day as the most important kabbalist until Isaac Luria. Some of his books realized a wide circulation and were highly influential on later kabbalists, particularly in sixteenth-century Safed.

At the end of his days he was living on the small island of Comino, off Malta, forced out of Sicily by his own community. It was there that he wrote *Sefer ha-Ot*, his only surviving prophetic work of the twenty-two he produced. In it he proclaims: "And the time of salvation and the day of Redemption is come, and no man today pays any regard to this fact."

David Reuveni (1490–1535)

Following the catastrophic expulsions from Spain (1492) and Portugal (1498), expulsions from Germanic provinces, the establishment of the first ghetto in Venice, and generally terrible economic conditions of the Jews, the sixteenth century was not surprisingly, full of messianic interest. One of the most important consequences of the time was the development of the Marrano Community—the estimated three million Jews of Spain and Portugal who had been forced to convert to Christianity but secretly practiced a watered-down version of Judaism. Central to their belief was a strong messianic aspiration. The Messiah would come and relieve them of their misery and guilt, returning them to the Holy Land, where they could live as true Jews.

It did not take much to ignite the imagination of the Marranos. Thus, upon hearing of a Jew named David Reuveni who rode on a white horse to an audience with the Pope, their messianic expectations flourished. For them the long-awaited Messiah had arrived.

Reuveni lacked the striking physical appearance that was the mainstay of many of his predecessors. He was a short, skeleton-thin man, very dark in complexion. He was courageous and intrepid, harsh and cold.

One morning in 1524 he mysteriously appeared in Rome riding to the Pope's palace. This strange visitor claimed that he was the ambassador of his brother, King Joseph, ruler of the ancient tribe of Reuben.

Not quite knowing what to make of this exotic visitor, the Pope, Clement VII, a man of esoteric interests himself, granted Reuveni an audience. On a Sunday morning, Reuveni, with twelve respected Jews and over two hundred Christians, ceremoniously arrived at the palace.

Reuveni presented an extraordinary proposal to the Pope. He wanted aid in arming an army to wrest control of the Holy Land from the Turks. Preposterous as the idea may have sounded, it was not impossible. A successful overthrow of the Turks, even if by the Jews, would have helped restore confidence in the faltering Church. The Pope offered to do what he could to help and made Reuveni an honored guest in Rome.

For the next year Reuveni was treated with the greatest of dignity and honor. When he became ill after one of his many fasts—he was an ascetic who prayed and fasted often—he was attended by the finest physicians. Nevertheless he grew worse, and it looked as though he would not recover. He told his concerned doctor, however, "I will not die until I have brought Israel to Jerusalem, built the altar, and offered sacrifice there." To everyone's astonishment, he soon recovered totally. With this remarkable event, the rumors of his messiahship began to fly.

To the Christians, Reuveni denied the rumors, but with the Jews, he was ambivalent. He talked to them of his descent from the House of David and of bringing the Jews back to the Promised Land. He even went about performing miracles associated with the Messiah, such as curing a young girl of an illness with his prayers.

Not surprisingly, the Jews, particularly the Marranos, were astonished by Reuveni. News of this extraordinary man, this courageous Jew, spread throughout Europe to Italy, England, France, Holland, Turkey, and especially Spain and Portugal (where most Marranos resided).

By the time the Pope gave Reuveni a letter of safe conduct to see the King of Portugal with his request, the Marranos there were already eagerly awaiting his arrival. With the Pope's blessing Reuveni set sail to the land that had expelled all of his coreligionists.

One can imagine the impact that he had, arriving in a ship boldly flying the Star of David, with a retinue of armed Jews, to negotiate an arms deal as a head of state. It is little wonder that the Marranos were ecstatic about his presence, proclaiming him the Messiah. When the king announced a cessation of the persecution of Marranos, the excitement only multiplied. Reuveni, realizing that unbridled enthusiasm might hinder his cause, tried to remain aloof. But nothing he said or did not say could cool the mounting expectations of the oppressed Jews.

An auspicious meeting with John III took place. With his armed Jewish guard Reuveni arrived at the palace with much ceremony and was greeted with great honor. The king promised military aid for the proposed battle and Reuveni left satisfied.

No further proof was needed that the Messiah had arrived in the person of David Reuveni. Everywhere Marranos began making daring preparations for the final return. Unfortunately the ramifications of these actions were being noticed by the authorities and causing much concern. The event that was to stymie Reuveni's plans centered on a young, noble, talented, and handsome Marrano named Diego Pires. It was the conversion, back to Judaism, of this court favorite, inspired by the recent events, that spelled the eventual downfall of Reuveni. Not too long after this event Reuveni was forced to leave Portugal.

Reuveni's departure from Portugal was a sad turn for the Marranos. He left promising that he would soon return for them after he had waged the battle for the Holy City.

The brilliant young nobleman, Diego Pires, now known as Solomon Molcho the Jew, soon became one of the greatest talmudic and kabbalistic scholars of the time. Ever faithful, he followed his master Reuveni in his travels, proclaiming the advent of the messianic era. Molcho, using astrology, even managed to predict a number of major catastrophies and thereby won for himself a large following.

The tandem of Reuveni and Molcho set off on a series of joint messianic ventures ranging from declaring war on the Turks to calling on the Emperor Charles IV, the latter responding by turning them over to the Italian Inquisition. Pope Clement, who had previously saved Molcho from the stake by hiding him in the Vatican, was now on his deathbed and unable to help.

Given a last chance to recant, Molcho defiantly declared: "I am distressed at the thought that in my childhood I clung to your faith. Now you can do with me whatever you please." Before a huge crowd, the gentle Molcho was flung into the flames.

Reuveni's end was much less dramatic. As a born Jew he was not subjected to the death sentence but instead spent the remaining two years of his life languishing in prison.

Isaac Luria (1534–1572)

Following the expulsion of Jews from Spain in 1492, the chief center for mystical studies shifted to Safed in Palestine. The undisputed leader of this community was Isaac Luria. His many followers viewed him as one with almost supernatural powers, calling him the *Ari*, the "Lion."

Luria's father had moved from Germany to Jerusalem, where Luria was born. It is said that at his birth the prophet Elijah appeared to his father and proclaimed to him, "Take heed, now, on the day of the circumcision, not to circumcise this child until you see me standing beside you in the synagogue." According to this account, written by a disciple in Safed in 1606, the father could not find Elijah at first and thus had to find some sort of pretext to delay the ritual. The congregation, unaware of the reason for the wait, became quite agitated and demanded that the ceremony be continued. Unperturbed, the father continued to wait until Elijah finally showed up.

The father was not able to care for the child for very long; he died while the boy was still quite young. The young Luria was taken by his mother to the home of her brother in

Egypt, a wealthy tax collector. A brilliant student, noted for his intelligence, logic, and reasoning, Luria, by the age of fifteen, was superior to all the sages in Egypt in his understanding of talmudic law. After marrying his cousin, he went to study alone with the chief rabbi of Egypt for about seven years. The study of Talmud did not satisfy the inquisitive mind and spirit of the brilliant pupil. In an attempt to quench this thirst, he began to delve into the secrets of the Zohar and Kabbalah. Yet not even the existing kabbalistic literature could answer all of his questions.

For the next seven years, Luria retreated into almost complete solitude on the banks of the Nile River. He maintained contact with almost no one, seeing his wife only during Sabbath and even then only conversing with her when absolutely necessary.

During this time he would experience many strange voices and ecstatic visions. He led the life of an ascetic, living on very little and going through long periods of fasting. This only served to increase the wild images that would possess his inventive mind. At times Elijah the prophet would reveal himself to him and teach the kabbalistic secrets of the Torah.

After two years of extreme asceticism on the Nile, Elijah appeared to him and announced, "The time of your death is approaching. And now go up to Safed. I assure you that I shall reveal myself to you whenever you need me; I will lay bare before you the secrets of the upper and the nether worlds, and God too, will pour upon you his Holy Spirit a thousand more times than you are able to acquire here in Egypt."

Answering the call of his mission, in 1569, Luria moved his family to Palestine, eventually settling in Safed. The circle of mystics already there quickly recognized his talents and made him the spiritual master of the entire mystical community in Safed.

Luria immersed himself in the development of a new kind of Kabbalah whereby the divine order of the world could be brought about. His system was so complicated, though, that he later complained that no one could really understand it. In fact, its complexity is evidenced by his own inability to ever commit the system to written form. All the information available today about Luria's system of so-called "practical Kabbalah" is based mostly on the notes of his disciple Hayyim Vital.

Luria taught that the good souls in heaven could be brought down to inhabit the bodies of men. He saw spirits everywhere. He heard them whispering in the rushing water of rivers, in the movement of trees, in the wind, and in the songs of birds. He was able to see the soul of a man rise out of the body at death. Intimate talks were frequently held with the souls of past figures of the Bible, the talmudic sages, and various respected rabbis. His disciples would often follow him on his walks to the fields and cemeteries where these mystical communions were held.

Every Friday, he and his followers would don special white garments to welcome the Sabbath Queen (a metaphorical representation of the Sabbath) in the streets. They would proceed to the grave of the great Rabbi Simon b. Yohai and there perform mystical rituals and sing secret hymns. All of these procedures were in preparation for the coming of the Messiah.

Although he never actually proclaimed himself the Messiah, this status was abundantly clear to all his disciples because of all that he had told them. His disciples attributed to him the powers of performing exorcisms and miracles, and of speaking the language of the animals. They believed there was little that Luria could not do if he so wished. They wrote: "Luria could read faces, look into the souls of men, recognize souls that migrated from body to body. He could tell you what commandment a man had fulfilled and what sins he had committed since youth."

One may wonder, how things might have turned out if on that fateful day just before his death, his disciples had had stronger faith? On that day Luria had summoned his disciples and asked them to go immediately to Jerusalem with him. The disciples, surprised by the suddeness of the request, hesitated, saying that they would first have to check it out with their wives. Luria cried out, "Woe to us who are unworthy! I saw that the Messiah was about to appear in Jerusalem, and if we had come, all the world would have been redeemed."

A few days later, Luria died, the victim of an epidemic, at the age of thirty-eight.

After his death the veneration of Luria increased. Many began to refer to him as the "Holy and Divine" and stated that if he had only lived another few years, the messianic period would have begun. Whereas Abulafia, the kabbalistic interpreter before him, had been branded a heretic, Luria was almost deified. His works paved the way for all the messianic movements to follow.

Hayyim Vital (1542–1620)

The sudden death of Luria left his disciples in disarray. To whom might they turn as the successor of their revered leader? One ambitious sort—Hayim Vital—had the answer for the confused disciples. Pretending that on his deathbed the master had selected him the successor, Vital usurped authority over most of his fellow disciples. He convinced them to relinquish all the notes that any of them might have had from Luria. Vital was on his way to becoming the "new Messiah."

The son of a scribe who had moved from Italy to Palestine, Vital had been educated in Torah and mysticism. His education, however, had not been intensive, with a smattering in many areas and nothing studied in any great depth. He was possessed with a wild and extravagant imagination, and had an inclination for adventure and sensation.

For two years, from 1563 to 1565, Vital had immersed himself in the study of alchemy. His major interest at that point was finding ways to make gold. Frustrated in his attempts, he eventually abandoned the search and then discovered Luria's Kabbalah, which marked the turning point in his life.

He quickly became Luria's principal disciple. Vital accompanied Luria on all of his wanderings around Safed, journeying with the master to the graves and joining him in his various mystical cantillations. Luria would often send Vital to conjure up spirits from other worlds. Vital became Luria's prime public relations man, circulating reports of all of Luria's latest deeds and powers.

One account from that era reports that a heavenly voice came down to Luria and declared, "You will find a certain scholar whose name is Rabbi Hayyim Vital—may God guard and deliver him. Anoint him in your stead. Lay your hands upon him and teach him all your lore for he will take your place. The sole purpose of your coming into the world has been to improve the soul of Rabbi Hayyim, for it is a precious one. Through you he will merit wisdom, and a great light shall shine forth from him upon all Israel." The influence here of Vital is rather obvious.

After Luria's death Vital ruled with an iron hand. He had twelve of his best disciples sign a pledge to the effect that they would only study Luria's theory from Vital. He further demanded that they promise not to induce him to reveal more of the hidden secrets than he chose to and that anything that he did indeed reveal to them would be kept in strictest confidence. By rulings such as these, Vital managed to maintain almost sole inheritance of Luria's legacy, although it should be noted that there were some dissenters who managed to operate outside of his control, to his unending dismay.

The group around Vital dissolved when he moved to Jerusalem to become the head of the yeshiva there (1577–1585). It was during this time that Vital wrote his last version of his own presentation of Luria's system.

Vital spent the years 1586 to 1592 back in Safed, where he fell ill. During a long period of unconsciousness scholars bribed his younger brother to allow them to copy 600 pages of Vital's writings that had been restricted.

He recovered from his illness and continued travelling and spreading his legacy, finally settling in Damascus in 1598, where he remained until his death. It was in these final years that he became obsessed with his messiahship. A Kabbalah group grew around him, and he began gathering material for his autobiography and testimonies to his greatness. In the year 1609 Vital wrote, with his characteristic conceit, that a certain rabbi visited a seer to inquire about the redemption. The inquirer was told that it was Israel's lack of repentance that delayed the advent of the Messiah, but if they would listen to the great and heaven-esteemed Hayyim Vital, much good would come to they; much suffering would befall them for their failure to listen to him; and if ten great and perfect men joined Vital, he could bring the final redemption.

Vital presented the Lurianic Kabbalah in its extreme and most fantastic form. While he is considered an important figure in the development of Kabbalah, his self-declaration as the Messiah had little, if any, lasting effect on any but his most devout followers.

Shabbatai Zevi (1626–1676)

The ever-turbulent world of the Jews was rarely as topsy-turvy as in the seventeenth century. Eastern European Jewry had been literally decimated by a series of pogroms beginning in 1648, the few fortunate survivors having fled to the Turkish Empire.

The Kabbalah of Luria had spread rapidly and found special favor amongst the downtrodden masses. In it they found hope of redemption, both personal and universal, in the teaching about the Messiah whose coming would mark the beginning of a new world order. These widely held beliefs, combined with the unstable political and economic climate at the time, paved the road for the largest, most momentous, and most catastrophic messianic movement in Jewish history.

Shabbatai Zevi was the son of a wealthy Smyrna merchant, who gave the young lad the best Jewish education possible. He had an attractive and captivating personality but exhibited a soft, malleable character. As he grew older, he came to believe that his destiny was different from that of everyone else;

that in some way he had been marked out by God to perform great deeds.

Following the precepts of Lurianic Kabbalah to the extreme, Shabbatai, during his adolescence, began a life of strict asceticism, fasting frequently and living in solitude for six years. Even his greatest critics were never to accuse him of being an ignoramus. Shabbatai was a prize pupil of the Talmud and became a rabbi by eighteen.

Shabbatai, however, had sexual problems that strongly influenced his messianism. He was very emotionally attached to his mother and despite his ascetic lifestyle was beset with sexual temptations. Between 1646 and 1650 he was married and divorced twice but never consumated either union. His third wife had led a highly publicized life of sexual abandon throughout Europe. One of the major areas of talmudic law that his radical doctrine was to reverse was the laws governing sexual morality, nudity, and forbidden relations.

His personality displayed a textbook case of manic-depressive psychosis. He shifted back and forth between periods of profound depression and spasms of maniacal elation, with long normal periods in between. It was during one of his fits of elation that he first proclaimed himself, to everyone's amazement, the Messiah. The reactions to this outburst ranged from outrage to intense curiosity. Some were impressed by his pleasant appearance, musical voice, and strange actions. But the majority were displeased by his erratic behavior and heretical pronouncements, which led to his expulsion from his hometown in 1651.

For the next few years Shabbatai travelled through Greece spreading his word and finally settling in Salonika. It did not take long for him to be banished from that city, too. While the local rabbis could put up with most of his outbursts, they were outraged by his marriage—in public—to a Torah Scroll!

On the road again, Shabbatai settled in Constantinople for nine months. According to Gershom Scholem, whose biography of Shabbatai Zevi is one of the most comprehensive spiritual profiles written, it was in 1658 in Constantinople that the "essence of the new law is to be found in the santification of transgressions and their elevation to the level of positive religious precepts requiring a formal ritual blessing. Until now Shabbatai's actions had been blind and haphazard; now they acquired the paradoxical character of holy deeds through sinning."

His stay in Constantinople was aborted when, during one particularly ecstatic period, he publicly dismissed the Ten Commandments and tried celebrating Passover, Shavuot, and Sukkot, all in the same week.

For the next few years Shabbatai passed through a much more settled phase. Attempting to control his outbursts, he searched for someone to help him find peace. His travels finally took him to Jerusalem where he married the girl with the dubious reputation. It was his trip the following year to Gaza, however, that was to mark the turning point in his life.

Hearing of a miraculous young man who through the Kabbalah had found the way to restore the soul to a state of peace, Shabbatai set off to meet Nathan of Gaza. Nathan had coincidentally heard many reports of Shabbatai and had already formed his impression of the latter's periods of illusion. Rather than "cure" him, Nathan convinced Shabbatai that he was indeed the Messiah.

Shabbatai Zevi enthroned (from the title page of "Tikkun," Amsterdam, 1666)

At first, the reform-seeking Shabbatai refused to accept Nathan's declaration. The two travelled the Holy Land together, deep in discussion of the Kabbalah and its messianic message. One night Nathan fell into a trance and announced before a large assembly that his new friend and master was the Messiah.

Shabbatai was, by then, convinced. He returned to Gaza and announced his mission. There followed weeks of frenzied excitement as the news of Shabbatai's arrival spread like wildfire. He rode to Jerusalem on a white horse, majestically circled the city seven times, and thereby won over most of the people including many of the rabbis there.

Nathan, meanwhile, actively spread the word, acting as Shabbatai's public relations manager, coach, and prophet. His wild success would be the envy of Madison Avenue. Everywhere people began repenting, fasting, and leading lives of asceticism. The word spread throughout the Mideast and on to the masses of Jewry in Holland, Germany, and England!

Nathan drafted a letter telling of Shabbatai's powers to redeem all, "even Jesus," and "whoever doubts, even the most righteous man in the world, Shabbatai may punish him." The letter—including Shabbatai's plan to capture Turkey without a battle and gather up the Ten Lost Tribes—was circulated throughout Europe in 1665. It had its intended effect. From the poorest soul to the wealthiest merchant, from the most illiterate to the greatest scholar, from the ghetto of Italy to the free city of Amsterdam, virtually everybody became swept up by messianic fervor.

Some rabbis in Smyrna attempted to put a stop to this frenzy, but their actions were too little too late. They faced an uncontrollable uproar of such intensity that they decided it was better to keep quiet than to risk the wrath of the overwhelming majority.

Shabbatai took full advantage of this situation. He stormed the headquarters of the Smyrna rabbinate with a huge mob, grabbed the Torah, and pronounced his divine mission. Even the one rabbi who bravely defied Shabbatai and demanded he prove himself, soon succumbed to his charisma and was swiftly appointed his chief rabbi.

People began flooding in from all over to kiss the hand of the Messiah. The Jewish world turned into one long festival, with all trade and commerce coming to a complete halt. In the mass hysteria, people everywhere were receiving visions and claiming prophecy.

To fulfill his mission, the brave, but foolhardy, Messiah set out to capture Turkey with his appointed "kings." The Jews there were awaiting his arrival with tremendous pride, while the gentiles were making fun of the whole absurdity. Upon his arrival he was, of course, immediately arrested but somehow spared death. "His Extreme Holiness" appealed to the Turks, who treated him very well helped by huge bribes from his disciples.

This treatment by the Turks only helped fan the flame of enthusiasm everywhere. People sold all their property in preparation for the Return; they lay naked in the snow and starved in penance; and they indulged themselves in an orgy of sexuality to fulfill Shabbatai's commandments. Jewish communities all over the world sent emmissaries with proclamations of Shabbatai's messiahship.

The furor ended almost as suddenly as it had started. One day a Polish kabbalist came to visit Shabbatai and argue with him. The kabbalist suddenly declared his intention to convert to Islam and denounced Shabbatai for fomenting sedition. Shabbatai was taken to the Sultan, where he denied any messianic pretentions. He was given the choice of death or apostasy. On September 15, 1666 Shabbatai the Messiah picked up a turban and became a Moslem.

The profound shock took awhile to hit the Jewish world. Some would face up to their gross mistake, others would cling to their Messiah, seeing the conversion as part of his messianic mission. Mostly, they would swiftly hush up the entire affair, destroy all the records, and quietly, if embarrassedly, attempt to reconstruct lives and visions shattered by bitter disillusionment, abandonment, and betrayal.

And what became of the two perpertrators of this notorious chapter of Jewish history? Nathan spent the rest of his life in the Balkans, keeping up communications with Shabbatai and staying true to the master until the very end. Shabbatai himself married yet a fourth time but was exiled to Albania after being caught in sexual extravaganzas.

By the time of his death, on Yom Kippur 1676, most Jews had forgotten about him. Most, but not all. For over one hundred years to follow, secret cells of Sabbateans continued to thrive throughout Europe.

Jacob Frank (1726–1791)

Following the disaster of Shabbatai Tzvi, it would hardly seem possible that anything quite that bad could ever happen again. Unfortunately, not only did it happen again, it happened with a vengeance that is still surprising in its tragic intensity.

The residual Sabbateans were still clinging to their faith in the early eighteenth century, although they were forced to disguise themselves to avoid the wrath of the majority. The times, however, were changing, and it seemed an opportune moment for an attempt to go public. All that was needed was a spirited leader to gather the scattered band, give it cohesion, and mark out a line of action. Just such a leader presented himself, and with his appearance a new movement began that was to throw the entire Jewish world of Poland into intense agitation and despair. This leader was the notorious adventurer, Jacob Frank.

Born Jacob Judah Leib in Koroleno, Poland of middle-class observant parents, the young Frank studied in *heder* but gained no real knowledge, later boasting of his complete ignorance in Jewish matters. Most of his youth was spent playing practical jokes and pranks, even on his unsuspecting father. He became involved with youth gangs and eventually arose as a leader of one of them.

For a while Frank worked as a dealer in cloth and gems, trading in the Balkans. He continued his studies under a teacher who belonged to the Sabbateans and became quite involved in the Zohar. His teacher promised to initiate the young Frank into the secret Sabbatean sect after he became married.

In short order, Frank married the daughter of a respected merchant, while two Sabbateans attended the wedding. All going well, he was initiated into the mysteries of "the faith" and went with the Sabbateans to Salonika where a large group lived.

After marriage Frank all but gave up on his trade, exerting most of his energies into his new role of "prophet." His teachers began spreading the word of Frank's leadership, which served his ambitions all too well. In a short while, Frank began touting himself as the divine reincarnation of the soul of Shabbatai Tzvi.

In this new divine role Frank began travelling to many towns, visiting Sabbatean cells, which fell, so to speak, in his arms. Frank needed followers and they were seeking a leader. He gathered around him many adherents, proclaimed his messiahship, and taught his disciples to acquire wealth and riches for themselves, even by the most fraudulent means.

One day in 1756 he and twenty of his followers were discovered conducting a heretical religious orgy behind locked doors. Opponents claimed that the Frankists were performing an indecent dance around a naked woman and kissing her. Later Frank claimed that he had purposely opened the windows to compel his believers to go public after decades of hiding. The police broke down the doors and arrested the disciples. Frank, mistaken for a Turkish foreigner, was expelled from the country.

The incident caused a sensation; the news spread like wildfire. Everywhere, Frank and his followers were excommunicated by rabbinical courts. The Frankists were denounced to the authorities and eventually Frank was again arrested.

To gain freedom, Frank agreed to convert to Islam and thereby gained great honor from the Turks. Even after this conversion, however, Frank persisted in making secret visits to Poland to confer with his disciples. He remained the leader of the majority of Sabbateans all over Galicia, the Ukraine, and Hungary. These "believers" were outwardly Jewish but secretly transgressed all the Torah prohibitions, especially those concerning fornication, adultery, and incest.

The excommunications provoked a wave of persecution against the Frankists. Never one to miss an opportunity, Frank and his followers put themselves under the protection of the bishop of Poland by exaggerating their common beliefs with Christianity such as the Trinity and rejection of the Talmud.

The Church saw the potential of a mass conversion arising out of the Frankists and began forcing anti-Jewish propaganda out of them. The Frankists, while not fully embracing Christianity, declared themselves "almost" Christians, issued a declaration of faith that would nicely meet the Church's demands, and asked for a public debate against the rabbis. The bishop was only too pleased to protect the Frankists from persecution and foster their hatred of the mass of Jewry.

The resulting public debate was a decidedly one-sided affair with the bishop sitting as judge and jury. It resulted in burnings of the Talmud in public, which were only halted by the sudden death of the bishop. This was taken as a sign from above, and the persecutions of Frankists started anew. Many, including Frank himself, fled Poland altogether.

Never one to give up, Frank sought and gained the protection of the king of Poland, citing his past relationship with the archbishop. Returning to Poland, Frank proclaimed himself as the living embodiment of God, no less. Brazenly rejecting even Sabbatean theology, Frank introduced new rituals with no kabbalistic terminology and highly reminiscent of Christianity, going so far as to appoint twelve "apostles" and twelve female concubines to serve him.

To gain favor with the new bishop, Frank asked for yet another public debate, this time to "prove" Christianity and to demonstrate the blood libel (the supposed requirement of Christian blood to make matzah)! No doubt this was a factor in the commonly held image of Frank amongst Jewry as a "sorcerer and a demon."

The public debates between the Frankists and the rabbis lasted for the entire summer of 1759. Frank himself only took part in the last debate, the one concerning the blood libel, in which he procured misquoted statements and altered documents. External pressure finally halted the debates.

Frank and many of his followers, perhaps thousands of them, were baptized. The ranks of the Frankists included the highly educated, community leaders, wealthy merchants, and even some former rabbis. Frank arrived in Warsaw with much pomp and was baptized a second time under the patronage of the king.

The charade could not last forever, however, and the confessions of some of the Frankists that they saw Frank as God spelled his doom. Frank was arrested, tried, and exiled to a fortress, where he was kept in custody for the next thirteen years.

As the blood libel spread, many Jews were slaughtered. This, in turn, resulted in backlash against the Frankists, who went further underground. Frank maintained contacts with his disciples on the outside, some of whom settled near the fortress, and even held secret sex orgies in the compound.

To the end, Frank, more-or-less successfully, led a double life. His final years were spent in princely style in a luxurious mansion near Frankfort, supported by huge gifts from adherents around the world. He died suddenly in 1791 of an apoplectic stroke. His children tried to take up the leadership, but lacking his charisma and leadership abilities, ended their lives in poverty.

Frank's followers continued to uphold their faith in private for years. Copies of Frank's "Words of the Master" were still being published in the 1820's. The greatest Polish poet, Adam Mickiewicz was a Frankist as were many in the Polish nobility into the nineteenth century. Communities of Frankists are still believed to exist to this day, but knowledge of them is understandably slight.

—M.S.R.

LIFE IN THE HEREAFTER: A TOUR OF WHAT'S TO COME

Death did not frighten the pious Jew of old. He had faith in the talmudic contention that death is simply a transition from one life into another, likened to the ease of taking a hair out of milk. What the Jew wanted above all was to die fully conscious, to be in full possession of his mental faculties at the time that his soul left his body. For the *hasid* (righteous) it was a matter of absolute faith and conviction that the same One God who was worshipped in this world could be served in the worlds to come, as well.

For the not-so-pure, however, the process of extricating from bodily life was a bit more problematic. The soul that had become too fully identified with the body through sensual indulgence would find it difficult to separate from it. To accompany the body to its final resting place and to behold the putrefaction and the decay was understandably painful for such souls. This state of being is known as *hibbut ha-kever*, the pain and anguish of the grave. In order to destroy the illusory identification of soul with body and avert the consequent pain in death, *hasidim* would often engage in ascetic practices while still in this life. Particularly exalted souls would be able to achieve this level of consciousness through prayer and meditation, becoming oblivious to their physical body and surroundings.

REMEMBERING ONE'S NAME:

The earthbound disembodied soul can encounter a number of dangers. If it is unable to separate itself from the body even through pain, it can experience a decay of consciousness and a turning into nothingness. An angel, Dumah (Silence), is the guardian of the dead, and wanting to prevent this decay, asks each soul for its Hebrew name. The rabbis say that some people suffer amnesia due to the shock of dying and are, consequently, unable to remember their identity. In order to dispel this amnesia, the learning of a mnemonic device while one is alive is recommended: At the conclusion of every *Amidah* (the central prayer of the service), the worshipper is instructed to "sign off" by reciting a biblical verse that begins with the first initial of his name and ends with the last letter of his name. Among Sephardic Jews, the child is initiated into his/her own sentence at the bar or bat mitzvah. In this way, the worshipper reinforces the memory of his Jewish name at the end of every prayer service. Thus, in death, even if he is unable to remember his name, he will be able to remember the Torah verse, because Torah is eternal and cannot decay. The soul will therefore be able to follow the angels who summon it before the heavenly court.

THE CATAPULT:

Besides the problem of the soul maintaining its identity, there is another difficulty. All the sounds that a person has heard during his life continue to vibrate within his soul following his death, like clanging coins in a gourd. He is, thus, unable to achieve the subtle stillness necessary to receive the angelic or heavenly voices. The nature of this "static" can be compared to the inner disturbances experienced by someone trying to meditate in silence. In order to rid the soul of this "dust," it is shaken in the *Kaf ha-Kela*, the Catapult. The sages say that "two angels stand at each end of the world and toss the soul from one to the other." It is almost as if the angels try to rid the soul of its accumulated psychic dust by putting it through a cosmic centrifuge until only pure soul remains. Were this treatment not administered to the soul, however, it would be unable to silence all the sense images and noises that were carried with it from this world and would have to wander in the world of *Tohu* (Confusion and Emptiness) for ages. In one Hasidic tale, a lost soul who has already roamed for hundreds of years in such a void cries out, "Would that I already had reached Gehenna!"

GEHENNA:

The Jewish idea of Gehenna (*Gehinnom*) is not hell, but rather a purgatory where the soul is purged from all defilement that has accumulated on it during its life on earth. Although there are worse places to be, there are certainly better. This purgatory is often described in lurid physical details of fire and cold, yet the rabbis warn against seeing Gehenna as a material entity. It is rather lke the pain of anxiety intensified by silence and a deep awareness of the evil committed. Curiously, according to tradition, Gehenna is emptied on the Sabbath. Some claim that this respite is only granted to those who had kept the Sabbath in their lives. Others disagree, claiming that Gehenna is emptied for all; were it not for the weekly bliss and light which the Sabbath provides, the soul would be unable to endure the anguish of Gehenna.

THE GARDENS OF PLEASURE:

When a soul is ready to enter *Gan Eden* (Paradise, literally the Garden of Eden), it must first be immersed in the River of Light, created from the perspiration that flows from the heavenly hosts as they fervently sing glory to the Highest. This immersion is to empty the soul of any lingering earth images so that it may, without further illusion, see heaven for what it really is.

First the soul enters the lower *Gan Eden*, which is a paradise of emotional bliss. While on earth most persons are unable to experience more than one dominant emotion at a time. However, the bliss of the souls in the lower *Gan Eden* is likened to a majestic chord of benign emotions, which the soul feels towards God and towards other souls.

In the Hasidic view heaven is organized into societies. Those souls who share mutual interests are drawn together so they can serve His Blessed Name according to their own specialty and individuality. Each heavenly society is taught by its own rabbi and led to further celestial attainments. Thus, the lower *Gan Eden* is the heaven of emotional fervor.

Before a soul is raised from the lower to the higher *Gan Eden*, it must again immerse itself in the River of Light so that it will forget and forsake the furor of the emotions, for the even greater delights of knowing God through understanding. The serving of God with insight through the study of Torah is itself a reward. The societies of the upper *Gan Eden* are organized into yeshivot (schools) in which a blissful understanding of the divine mind is attained. Each midnight, the Holy One, blessed be He, Himself appears and enters *Gan Eden* to delight in the sharing of His blessed wisdom with the righteous who have gained the upper *Gan Eden*.

MOURNING FOR THE DEAD:

Many of the customs of mourning have developed in order to assist the soul through its many trials in the afterlife. In order to help the soul avoid the amnesia described above, it is customary for the mourners to remind the soul "your name is so-and-so, and do not forget it." The reciting of the mourner's *Kaddish* (see "8 Common Misconceptions Jews Have About Judaism") helps to "cool the fires of Gehenna." The maximum sentence for this purgatory is twelve months; however, the mourner's *Kaddish* is only recited for eleven months, so as not to insult the dead by implying that he/she would have to serve the full term.

Each year on the *yahrzeit* (anniversary of death) a higher rung of *Gan Eden* is achieved by the soul. While the soul celebrates its birthday into heaven with its celestial friends, the living traditionally celebrate the *aliyat ha-neshamah* (ascendancy of the soul) by praying for a more exalted position in heaven for that soul.

Since souls are incapable of acquiring new merit after death, the living can transfer credit to the account of a loved one, thus enabling it to achieve higher levels. One of the most potent means is by offering *tzedakah* (charity) in the name of the deceased. Another is soul. Particularly potent in this regard is the study of Mishnah because it has the same Hebrew letters as the word *neshamah* (soul). In these ways, incarnate souls can help discarnate souls that have gone beyond.

IBBUR AND *DYBBUK*—ON BEING POSSESSED:

Not only can the souls of the deceased be helped by those here below, but the dead can return the favor. At moments of great danger they can come to forewarn their loved ones through dreams and visions, helping them through trials and temptations. A soul is said to have come into *ibbur* (literally, pregnancy) when it enters, in a benign fashion, the body and soul of a person living here on earth. Often such an *ibbur* can raise a person to great temporary heights. *Ibbur*, however, can also help the discarnate soul who is in need of only one *mitzvah* (deed carried out to fulfill God's commandments) in order to round out a particular incarnation. Instead of risking the danger of another incarnate existence, it can receive the needed merit from the living by helping someone as an *ibbur*. The custom of naming children after the deceased is a means of affording the departed another return to life or of creating affinities so that it, as an *ibbur*, may help their offspring and receive help in return.

While the case of *ibbur* is an instance of benign possession, tradition has recorded many accounts of evil possession, known as *dybbuk* (literally, sticking). If a person was wronged by another and this wrong was responsible for its suffering, whether in life or in death, it can seek revenge by possessing someone (not necessarily the wrongdoer) as a *dybbuk*. A *dybbuk* can be educated in how to find spiritual guidance without harming the living or it can be negotiated with by offering the performance of *mitzvot* on its behalf in return for its leaving the possessed body. When it is recalcitrant, however, coercive devices must be resorted to (see "Rituals for Jewish Exorcism").

REINCARNATION:

Nothing new can be gained in heaven. The quantity of *mitzvot* (deeds or blessings) and Torah acquired by the time of death is what remains with a person after death. In heaven one can gain only a deeper and richer understanding of his life on earth. It is for this reason that souls, once they have absorbed all that heaven has to offer, apply for reincarnation, i.e. in order to attain further perfection. Reincarnation is also granted to allow the soul to bring about a restitution of the wrongs it has committed.

Some souls are so filled with the light of knowledge and the warmth of compassion, however, that the heavenly court, the "supernal familia," will engage in all kinds of ruses in order to reinvolve it in the work of saving and helping other souls still on the earthly plane. Reincarnation is an option at any point—after Gehenna, after the lower paradise, or even after the upper paradise. The process repeats until a soul has built its spiritual body.

RESURRECTION AND BEYOND:

After the coming of the Messiah, the resurrection of the dead is to take place. While the majority of commentators understand this to involve a reassemblage of the physical body previously inhabited, a minority opinion maintains that this will be a materialization of the level of spiritual body that the soul has built through its many incarnations. Those souls that have not completed their spiritual body will, at the resurrection, materialize here on earth in order to perform the remaining *mitzvot* required of them in an environment free of death and evil.

The Talmud relates that Rabbi Judah the Prince, the compiler of the Mishnah, used to return in a spiritual body every Sabbath eve to sanctify the Sabbath by celebrating the *Kiddush* (sanctification over the wine) for his family. He did this for an entire year. Only after one of the servants of the family revealed these visits to neighbors did Judah the Prince take final leave of his family, never to return again, on the grounds that his coming would put other saints to shame. Thus, Judah the Prince had attained the fullness of the spiritual body during his last incarnation on earth.

Yet even the completion of the spiritual body is not the ultimate state of being. Having attained such fullness, a soul can be "absorbed into the very Body of the King," the ultimate aim of its yearning and longing. Thus the soul merges finally in God, as a drop in the ocean.

—Z.M.S.

BIOGRAPHIES OF CONTRIBUTORS OF ORIGINAL MATERIAL

Rachel Adler is a Jewish feminist writer and a social worker, living in Minneapolis, Minnesota.

Arlene Agus is director of special projects and broadcasting for the Greater New York Conference on Soviet Jewry and has participated in the founding of many Jewish community action, feminist, and educational projects.

Donald Altschiller, a free-lance writer, is a librarian at Tufts University Fletcher School of Law and Diplomacy.

Misha G. Avramoff is on the staff and Board of Directors of Project Ezra, New York City. He has traveled extensively with his wife and co-contributor, Jacqueline Gutwirth.

Stephen Birmingham is the author of *Our Crowd, The Grandees*, and other books.

Jane Blanksteen is a free-lance writer and is the author of *Nothing Beets Borscht: Jane's Russian Cookbook.*

Marc Joel Bregman is lecturer in rabbinical literature and thought at the Hebrew Union College, Jerusalem and Ben-Gurion University of the Negev. He is completing his doctoral dissertation in Jewish literature at the Hebrew University of Jerusalem.

Aviva Cantor, journalist and lecturer, is a founding editor of *Lilith*, the Jewish feminist magazine. She is currently writing several works about animals.

Mitchell Cohen, editor of the Labor Zionist journal *Jewish Frontier*, is a doctoral candidate and preceptor in the Department of Political Science at Columbia University.

Paul Cowan, a New York writer, is author of *Tribes in America* and is a frequent contributor to the *Village Voice*.

Morris M. Faierstein is a doctoral candidate in the Department of Religion, Temple University, specializing in Hasidism and Jewish mysticism.

Marc A. Gellman, rabbi of Congregation Beth Am in Teaneck, New Jersey, contributing editor of *Moment Magazine*, writes frequently on modern *Midrash*, medical ethics, and Jewish theology.

Everett E. Gendler is rabbi of Temple Emanuel, Lowell, Massachusetts, and is Jewish chaplain and instructor in religion and philosophy, Phillips Academy, Andover, Massachusetts.

Brenda Dale Gevertz, associate for special grants of the Federation of Jewish Philanthropies of New York, is a former Hillel Foundation director and supervisor of Jewish campus professionals.

Howard L. Gevertz is president of Restaurant Planning Inc., a New York City based foodservice consulting firm, associated with the George Lang Corporation.

Leonard B. Glick is a member of the faculty of Hampshire College, Amherst, Massachusetts, where he teaches cultural anthropology and European Jewish history.

J.J. Goldberg is a free-lance writer and editor and a longtime Labor Zionist activist.

Arnold J. Goldman is a member of the Rochester, New York law firm of Goldman and Goldman and is the coauthor of a forthcoming text in the field of business law.

Eric A. Goldman is director of the Jewish Media Service/Jewish Welfare Board and holds a Ph.D. in Cinema Studies from New York University.

Jacqueline A. Gutwirth teaches history at the City University of New York and has travelled extensively with her husband, Misha, visiting Jewish communities throughout the world.

Nat Hentoff is a staff writer for the *Village Voice* and *New Yorker* magazine and is the author of a number of books on Jazz. The most recent is *Jazz Is*.

Barry W. Holtz is chairman of publications of the Melton Research Center of the Jewish Theological Seminary; he is coeditor and cotranslator of *Your Word is Fire: The Hasidic Masters on Contemplative Prayer.*

William N. Kavesh is an internist and a member of the Urban Medical Group, Boston. He is the author of "Jewish Genetic Diseases" and "Medicine," which appeared in the *Second Jewish Catalog.*

Howard N. Katz is a doctoral candidate in European Intellectual History at SUNY-Stony Brook and teaches history at the New York Institute of Technology.

Jack M. Kugelmass is an anthropologist specializing in Eastern European Jewish culture. He teaches at the Max Weinreich Center for Advanced Jewish Study, New York.

Arthur Kurzweil is the author of *From Generation to Generation: How to Trace Your Jewish Genealogy and Personal History* and is coeditor of *Toledot: The Journal of Jewish Genealogy.*

Allan Mintz is a university teacher of Hebrew literature and is the editor of the new edition of Nathan Ausubel's *A Treasury of Jewish Folklore* (Bantam Books). He is known among his friends as a serious eater, and wrote a short-lived food column for *Moment Magazine*.

Mordecai Newman is film critic for *Jewish Frontier* and has written extensively on film and drama.

William A. Novak, former editor of *Response* and executive editor of *MOMENT* magazine, is the author of *High Culture: Marijuana in the Lives of Americans.*

Velvel Pasternak is editor of Tara Publications and is associate professor of Jewish music at Touro College, New York City.

Jonathan D. Porath is rabbi of Temple Beth O'r in Clark, New Jersey and has visited Eastern European and Soviet Jewish communities on eight occasions.

Bernard Postal is the editor of *Jewish Digest* magazine and associate editor of *Jewish Week*. He has coauthored fifteen books on Jewish history.

Carl J. Rheins is coeditor of the *Jewish Almanac.*

Robert A. Rockaway is a senior lecturer in the Department of Jewish History at Tel-Aviv University and specializes in American Jewish history.

Martin S. Rosen is a doctoral candidate in environmental psychology at the City University of New York and is the coauthor of *Not the Jewish Press.*

Joel Rosenberg lives in the Boston area and teaches Hebrew literature and language at Tufts University. He has recently completed a book of poetry and is currently working on a readers guide to the Hebrew Bible.

Gita Segal Rotenberg lives in Montreal, Canada where she does free-lance writing on Jewish and general themes.

Henry H. Sapoznik is a musician and a project director with the National Council for Traditional Arts (Yiddish Division).

Zalman M. Schachter is a rabbi, and professor of religion at Temple University; he is the author of several books and articles on contemporary Jewish spirituality and is the founder of *B'nai Or* religious fellowship in Philadelphia.

Ida Cohen Selavan is founder and director of the Nonformal Academy of Jewish Studies of Pittsburgh, Pennsylvania.

Zev Shanken teaches poetry writing through the New York Poets in the Schools program. He is a former editor of *Response, A Contemporary Jewish Review.*

Daniel R. Shevitz is a rabbi and director of the Hillel Foundation at the Massachusetts Institute of Technology.

Danny Siegel is a poet and free-lance writer who has published four volumes of poetry and prose: *Soulstoned, And God Braided Eve's Hair, Between Dust and Dance,* and *Nine Entered Paradise Alive.*

Jeanne B. Siegel is a planning associate with the Community Centers and Education Department of the Federation of Jewish Philanthropies of New York.

Richard A. Siegel is coeditor of the *Jewish Almanac.*

Jesse H. Silver is coauthor of *Encyclopedia of Jews in Sports*, sports editor of the *Encyclopaedia Judaica* and served between 1964 and 1971 as sports editor of the *Jewish Telegraphic Agency* (JTA).

Roy J. Silver is a writer and producer for NBC TV Network sports and is coauthor of the *Encylcopedia of Jews in Sports.* He has served as international press officer for four U.S.A. Maccabiah teams.

Mark Stern is a museum consultant and doctoral candidate in American labor history at the State University of New York at Stony Brook.

David M. Szonyi is assistant director, *ZACHOR* Division, National Jewish Resource Center, as well as a contributing editor to the *Baltimore Jewish Times.*

Chava Weissler is a doctoral candidate in the Department of Folklore and Folklife at the University of Pennsylvania, and a member of the Germantown *Minyan.*

Diane H. Winston is coeditor of the *Woman's Action Almanac* and coproducer of a documentary, *In Her Hands: Women and Ritual.*

INDEX

B

C

D

E

F

G

H

I

K

L

M

R

S

V

W

Y

PHOTO CREDITS

American Jewish Archives—43 bottom, 53, 175, 176, 245, 435

Alexander Archer—134, 192

Bill Aron—51, 243, 244 right, 546

Austrian Embassy—204

Courtesy of the Leo Baeck Institute (Eric Pollitzer)—518

Isaac Berez—225

From the Collection of Glen Boyer—55

Brandeis University—483 bottom left

British Museum—405

California Historical Society—18

CBS—455

Columbia University—483 top left

Consulate General of Israel—246, 317

Council of the Jewish Communities in Czechoslovakia—142

Frank J. Darmstaedter—525

Dartmouth University—483 top right

Claudio Edinger—29

French Embassy Press and Information Division—201

William P. Gottlieb—474

The Israel Museum—329

The Jewish Daily Forward—210

The Jewish Museum—517, 521, 522, 527

Jewish Theological Seminary—367

Jewish Tribune, September 26, 1924—40

Library of Congress—28, 240, 308, 342, 369, 389

Macmillan, Inc. (*The Jewish History Atlas*, Martin Gilbert, 1976)—127, 162, 583

Macy's—107, 108

Manischewitz, Carmel Wine Company and Royal Wine Corporation—371

Amy Meadow—376, 524

Movie Star News—441

Museum of the City of New York (Byron Collection)—129

Museum of Modern Art Film Still Collection—336, 438, 440, 443, 519

NASA—573

National Conference on Soviet Jewry—224 right

National Press Bureau, Amsterdam—147

New York City Parks and Recreation—42 top

New York Public Library—312, 321, 591

New York Public Library at Lincoln Center—14, 15, 16, 132, 453, 456, 472, 473

Oxford University Press—386

Photo Trends—218

Religious News Service—135, 136, 224 left, 226-27

Rutenberg and Everett Yiddish Film Library—437

Marilyn L. Schrut—242

Rodeph Shalom—528

Richard Sobol—150, 157, 160, 230, 366, 500

State Historical Society of Missouri—45

State Historical Society of Wisconsin—187 right

University of Victoria—483 middle right

UPI—59, 60, 61, 63, 65, 67, 68, 69, 71, 72, 77, 75, 514

U.S. Committee Sports for Israel—90

Roman Vishniac—309

Yad Vashem (*The Borders of Warsaw Ghetto*, Z. Zeiman, 1971)—148

Yale University, 483 bottom right

ABOUT THE AUTHORS

RICHARD SIEGEL has been involved in exploring contemporary forms of Jewish experience for more than a decade. Raised in Pittsburgh and given a solid Conservative Jewish religious training, which was supplemented with Jewish summer camps, Jewish youth groups, and a trip to Israel, Richard was only tangentially Jewish during his undergraduate years at Brandeis University. However, he was challenged by and attracted to the forms of Eastern spirituality that he encountered in various psychology of religion courses and sought to find the same spiritual impulses in his own tradition. Giving up his ambitions for law school and international politics, Siegel entered the recently founded Havurat Shalom Community Seminary in Somerville, Massachusetts in 1969.

The Havurah, as it was referred to, was the first and most intense of a number of Jewish alternative communities that emerged in the late 1960s and early 1970s. Dedicated to revitalizing Judaism for contemporary Jews, the Havurah explored a varied array of teachings, both Jewish and non-Jewish, on the nature of community, spiritual development, and human growth—from the classic rabbinic literature to the most esoteric mystical texts, from Mircea Eliade to Abraham Heschel, from the poetry of the Psalms to the poetry of a new generation of Jews. And it experimented with new or renewed forms of religious and interpersonal expressions—from silent meditation to intense Torah discussions, from communal meals to encounter groups.

Based on his experiences and new orientation to Judaism gained through the Havurah, Siegel began working on his first book, *The Jewish Catalog* (JPS, Philadelphia, 1973). Originally intended as a Jewish *Whole Earth Catalog* with reviews and access to Jewish tools and resources, the *Catalog*, which Siegel coedited, developed into a primary Jewish resource in itself. Subtitled *A Do-It Yourself Kit*, the *Catalog* presented the how's and what's of Jewish religious life from the perspective of the contemporary generation. The book touched a deeper need and exposed a more searching Jewish population than had been anticipated. To date, over 250,000 copies of *The Jewish Catalog* have been sold.

Aside from the *Catalog*, Siegel has published several magazine articles, and since 1975 he has served as coeditor of the annual *Jewish Calendar* (Universe Books, N.Y.).

Wanting to take a more direct role in the development of the new Jewish consciousness, he accepted a position as Hillel director at the State University of New York at Stony Brook in 1974, remaining there until 1978. It was at Stony Brook that Siegel met Rheins and *The Jewish Almanac* was born. Originally, the idea was a division of "God-Box Enterprises," a fictional repository of good ideas that the "New Age" Jewish community could not live without—such as T-shirts with the cover of the Rambam Hebrew school notebook printed on it, or a light-box that flashed different configurations of God's name. However, the idea of compiling a contemporary book of Jewish information became increasingly enticing, and the *Almanac* moved from the realm of fantasy to passion.

Since 1978 Siegel has held an executive position at the National Foundation for Jewish Culture as the director of the Yuval Project, an arts service organization. Viewing the arts as the most undervalued but potentially most revivifying element of Jewish life and culture, he is trying to both establish standards in the fields and develop greater community appreciation for the artistic experimentation currently being undertaken.

Richard married Jeanne Bakst Maman and her son Andrew in July 1979. They now live with their cat, Vashti, on New York's Upper West Side, where they are active in the alternative Jewish community developing in that area.

CARL RHEINS, born in Cincinnati, Ohio, on Yom Kippur 1945, was nurtured on an interesting blend of midwestern Republicanism and Jewish tradition. Carl's father, Joseph M. Rheins, before his retirement, was an attorney, a Republican party office holder, and an opponent of the multinational oil companies. A key midwestern leader of B'nai B'rith during World War II, Joseph Rheins participated in unsuccessful negotiations with U.S. State Department officials to secure immigration visas for Jews trapped in Nazi-occupied Europe. Carl, who believes his Jewish identity is an overwhelmingly positive force in his daily life, also owes much of his positive feelings to his mother, Gertrude Mandell Rheins. Active in the synagogue sisterhood, Gertrude encouraged both of her sons, Carl and Larry, to read widely in the fields of Jewish and Zionist history. Carl's grandmother Yetta Mandell (may her memory be a blessing) was an ardent Labor Zionist and a founder of Pioneer Women in Cincinnati.

Rheins is an honors graduate of the University of Wisconsin, received an M.A. in history from SUNY-Albany, and earned a Ph.D. in modern European history at the State University of New York at Stony Brook. He also attended the University of Pennsylvania Law School and was a visiting student at the University of Vienna, Austria. A political activist and veteran of the 1960s student movement, Rheins participated in several civil rights and antiwar sit-ins and served briefly in 1968 as press secretary of the Eugene McCarthy for President Campaign in southwestern Ohio.

Although as an undergraduate, Rheins was only minimally involved in Jewish activities, his Jewish identity evolved more fully while he was pursuing his graduate studies. The Six-Day War in 1967 and the subsequent abandonment of Jewish interests by elements in the student movement lead Rheins to break with many of his former political associates and to explore his commitments to the Jewish community with renewed vigor. His doctoral dissertation, "German Jewish Patriotism 1918–1935," has formed the basis for a series of scholarly articles on the attitudes and actions of anti-Zionist Jewish organizations in pre-Nazi Germany, articles that have appeared in the *Yearbook of the Leo Baeck Institute*. Rheins has frequently lectured on the Holocaust to college and high school audiences and is a member of the faculty seminar of the Leo Baeck Institute/New York City.

Between 1974 and 1978, Rheins taught courses in modern Jewish history at SUNY-Stony Brook. It was there that he met Richard Siegel. As two of the most eligible (and lonely) Jewish bachelors on campus Siegel and Rheins spent many nights talking about the *Jewish Almanac*, a project that was officially launched in 1977.

Assistant to the academic vice president at SUNY-Stony Brook since 1978, Rheins maintains an active interest in Jewish communal affairs. He is a member of the American Jewish Committee's Long Island chapter and is currently serving out his third term as a member of the advisory board of the B'nai B'rith Hillel Foundation at SUNY-Stony Brook. Rheins and his wife, Brenda Dale Gevertz, reside in suburban Woodbury, L.I., New York.